Contemporary Authors®

NEW REVISION SERIES

ISSN 0275-7176

Contemporary Authors

**A Bio-Bibliographical Guide to
Current Writers in Fiction, General Nonfiction,
Poetry, Journalism, Drama, Motion Pictures,
Television, and Other Fields**

LINDA METZGER
DEBORAH A. STRAUB
Editors

**JAMES G. LESNIAK
DONNA OLENDORF**
Associate Editors

THOMAS WILOCH
Senior Writer

NEW REVISION SERIES
volume 17

 Gale Research Inc. · DETROIT · LONDON

STAFF

Linda Metzger and Deborah A. Straub, *Editors, New Revision Series*

James G. Lesniak and Donna Olendorf, *Associate Editors*

Thomas Wiloch, *Senior Writer*

Candace Cloutier and Margaret Mazurkiewicz, *Senior Assistant Editors*

Joan E. Marecki, Bryan Ryan, and Susan Salter, *Assistant Editors and Writers*

Melissa J. Gaiownik, Anne Janette Johnson, Timothy Marshall,
Nancy E. Rampson, and Michaela Swart Wilson, *Assistant Editors*

Jean W. Ross and Walter W. Ross, *Interviewers*

Debra G. Hunter, *Research Supervisor*
Marian Gonsior, *Research Coordinator*
Mary Rose Bonk, *Assistant Research Coordinator*
Betty Joan Best, Reginald A. Carlton, Clare D. Kinsman, Ellen Koral, Sara A. Lederer, Timothy P. Loszewski,
Christine Joan May, Sharon McGilvray, Kathleen Partykula, Norma Sawaya, Shirley Seip,
Aida M. Smith, Tracey Head Turbett, and Peter Wehrli, *Research Assistants*

Frederick G. Ruffner, *Publisher*
Dedria Bryfonski, *Editorial Director*
Christine Nasso, *Director, Literature Division*
Ann Evory, *Senior Editor, Contemporary Authors*

The paper used in this publication meets the minimum requirements
of American National Standard for Information Sciences—Permanence
Paper for Printed Library Materials, ANSI Z39.48-1984. ∞™

Copyright © 1986
Gale Research Inc.
835 Penobscot Bldg.
Detroit, MI 48226-4094

Library of Congress Catalog Card Number 81-640179
ISBN 0-8103-1946-2
ISSN 0275-7176

Printed in the United States of America.
Published simultaneously in the United Kingdom
by Gale Research International Limited
(An affiliated company of Gale Research Inc.)

Contents

Authors and Media People
Featured in This Volume 7

Preface 9

Volume Update Chart 13

Author Listings 15

Authors and Media People
Featured in This Volume

Raymond Carver—American short story writer and poet; credited with helping to renew critical interest in the short story, Carver writes of working-class people living on the edge of loneliness, desperation, and poverty; his collected works include *Will You Please Be Quiet, Please?*, which was nominated for a 1977 National Book Award, and *Cathedral,* a 1984 nominee for both a National Book Critics Circle Award and Pulitzer Prize.

Janet Dailey—Prolific American romance writer who is currently the fifth best-selling author in the world; Dailey credits her success to both the stories she tells and the traditional values she emphasizes; among her popular works are the four-volume saga about the fictional Calder family and *Silver Wings, Santiago Blue.* (Sketch includes interview.)

Robertson Davies—Canadian novelist, playwright, and author of nonfiction; his international acclaim as one of Canada's leading men of letters stems primarily from his novels, particularly those comprising the "Deptford" trilogy: *Fifth Business, The Manticore,* which won the 1973 Governor General's Award for fiction, and *World of Wonders.* (Sketch includes interview.)

Thomas M. Disch—American author of science fiction, poetry, historical novels, and opera librettos; according to Charles Platt in *Dream Makers,* Disch "has traveled widely, through almost every genre and technique, ...never ill-at-ease or out-of-place, writing with the same implacable control and elegant manners"; he received two O. Henry Awards and a British Science Fiction Award for his short stories and the John W. Campbell Memorial Award for his novel *On Wings of Song.*

Stephen Dixon—American short story writer and novelist; according to *Time* magazine, Dixon is "one of the short story's most accomplished if quirky practitioners"; his stories, which focus on the plight of ordinary urban residents, have received two O. Henry Awards and a Pushcart Prize and are collected in *No Relief, Quite Contrary, 14 Stories, Movies,* and *Time to Go.*

Andre Dubus—American novelist and short story writer; in such short story collections as *Separate Flights, Adultery and Other Choices,* and *Finding a Girl in America,* Dubus describes the loneliness and isolation experienced by people in modern society, focusing especially on the relationships between men and women. (Sketch includes interview.)

Katherine Dunham—American dancer, anthropologist, and writer; known for her fascination with the dances and cultures of displaced Africans in the West Indies, Dunham has developed a style of dance that combines classical ballet with Caribbean-African dance and jazz rhythms; among her books are *A Touch of Innocence, Island Possessed,* and *Dances of Haiti.*

Freeman J. Dyson—British-born American scientist and author of nonfiction; in *Weapons and Hope,* which was nominated for a *Los Angeles Times* Book Prize and garnered the 1984 National Book Critics Circle Award for general nonfiction, he urges both scientists and the general public to take steps that would reduce the threat of nuclear war; another of Dyson's books, *Disturbing the Universe,* was nominated for a 1982 American Book Award.

Georgie Anne Geyer—American journalist whose autobiography, *Buying the Night Flight,* recounts her experiences as one of the first female foreign correspondents; also author of several books on international politics and society. (Sketch includes interview.)

Herbert Gold—American novelist who is considered one of the foremost chroniclers of life in modern America; three of his novels—*Fathers, My Last Two Thousand Years,* and *Family*—are primarily autobiographical and are among his most critically acclaimed works.

Barbara Gordon—American documentary filmmaker, autobiographer, and novelist; in her best-selling work, *I'm Dancing as Fast as I Can,* Gordon describes her former addiction to the prescription drug Valium and her subsequent breakdown when she attempted to quit without professional help; also author of a novel, *Defects of the Heart.* (Sketch includes interview.)

Bill Gulick—American western novelist and screenwriter; the recipient of the Levi's Saddleman Award for the body of his work, Gulick is noted for westerns that emphasize character development rather than action or violence; among his novels are *Bend of the Snake* and *The Hallelujah Trail.* (Sketch includes interview.)

George V. Higgins—American attorney, *Wall Street Journal* columnist, novelist, and author of nonfiction; in such books as *The Friends of Eddie Coyle, Cogan's Trade, Kennedy for the Defense,* and *A City on a Hill,* Higgins draws upon his experience as a former prosecutor and defense attorney to write crime novels "with an authenticity that is unmatched," according to Jonathan Yardley. (Sketch includes interview.)

P. D. James—Professional name of British mystery novelist Phyllis Dorothy James White; she has been critically acclaimed for her ability to combine complex and puzzling plots with psychologically believable characters, particularly in her novels featuring Commander Adam Dalgleish of Scotland Yard; her works include *Cover Her Face* and *Innocent Blood.*

Diane Johnson—American essayist, biographer, novelist, and screenwriter; among her biographies are *Lesser Lives,* which was nominated for a 1973 National Book Award, and *Dashiell Hammett,* a 1984 *Los Angeles Times* Book Prize nominee; also author of the essay collection *Terrorists and Novelists,* which was nominated for a 1983 Pulitzer Prize, and co-author of the screenplay "The Shining." (Sketch includes interview.)

E. L. Konigsburg—American author and illustrator of award-winning children's books; Konigsburg has been praised for conveying serious ideas in a comedic fashion, notably in *From the Mixed-Up Files of Mrs. Basil E. Frankweiler, A Proud*

Taste for Scarlet and Miniver, and *Throwing Shadows.* (Sketch includes interview.)

Ira Levin—American novelist and playwright; in such riveting best sellers as *A Kiss before Dying, Rosemary's Baby,* and *The Boys from Brazil,* Levin displays a preoccupation with evil, murder, horror, and the supernatural; he is also well known for his highly successful stage adaptation "No Time for Sergeants" and his popular comedy-mystery "Deathtrap," the fourth longest running production in Broadway history.

Alison Lurie—American novelist, author of nonfiction and children's fiction, and professor; her craftsmanship has established her as "one of this country's most able and witty novelists," according to Christopher Lehmann-Haupt; among her works are *The War between the Tates, Imaginary Friends,* and *Foreign Affairs,* which was nominated for an American Book Award and National Book Critics Circle Award in 1984 and garnered the 1985 Pulitzer Prize in fiction.

Michael McClure—American poet, playwright, essayist, and novelist who was a member of the Beat generation of writers in the 1950s; his poetic goal is personal expression rather than communication with his readers; author of numerous poetry collections and of such plays as "The Beard" and the Obie Award-winning "Josephine, the Mouse Singer."

Mark H. McCormack—American attorney and management company executive; founder of International Management Group, Inc., a highly successful sports and entertainment marketing firm; his best-selling book *What They Don't Teach You at Harvard Business School* outlines his unorthodox business techniques.

Thomas K. McCraw—American historian; his work *Prophets of Regulation,* which won the 1985 Pulitzer Prize in history, profiles four men who shaped the modern regulatory policies of the American marketplace: Charles Francis Adams, Louis D. Brandeis, James M. Landis, and Alfred E. Kahn.

Colleen McCullough—Australian novelist; author of the best-selling novel *The Thorn Birds,* a multigenerational saga of an Australian family and their life on a remote sheep ranch; the book sold over a half million hardcover copies and more than seven million paperback copies and was successfully adapted as a television miniseries; among her other popular works are *An Indecent Obsession* and *A Creed for the Third Millenium.*

Vonda N. McIntyre—American science fiction writer whose short stories, novelettes, and novels have been favorably compared to the work of Ursula K. LeGuin; her books include *Dreamsnake,* which in 1979 won a Hugo Award and a Nebula Award and in 1980 was nominated for an American Book Award, *The Entropy Effect,* and *Superluminal.*

Michael Moorcock—British magazine publisher and editor, novelist, short story writer, and author of film scripts and songs; in his role as editor of the magazine *New Worlds,* he was associated with the New Wave science fiction of the 1960s, which introduced avante garde literary techniques and a wider range of subject matter to the science fiction field; a prolific writer, he has garnered numerous awards for his work, notably a Nebula Award, five August Derleth Awards, and a John W. Campbell Memorial Award.

Robert A. Nisbet—Controversial American sociologist and social historian; one of his chief concerns, expressed in such works as *The Quest for Community, Twilight of Authority,* and

Prejudices, is the growth of bureaucratic state power at the expense of individual liberty and the more traditional forms of authority. (Sketch includes interview.)

Thomas Powers—American journalist and author of nonfiction; among his works, which address contemporary issues and reveal how people react to them, are *Diana: The Making of a Terrorist* and *The Man Who Kept the Secrets: Richard Helms and the CIA.* (Sketch includes interview.)

Richard L. Rubenstein—American rabbi, professor, and author of nonfiction; one of his most acclaimed works—*The Cunning of History*—came to critical attention only after William Styron discussed the book in his best-selling novel *Sophie's Choice;* also author of *After Auschwitz, The Religious Imagination,* and *The Age of Triage.* (Sketch includes interview.)

Kenneth Silverman—American professor and author of nonfiction; his work *The Life and Times of Cotton Mather,* which in 1985 won both the Bancroft Prize and a Pulitzer Prize, "can well stand as a model for biographers and historians in general," according to John Demos; Silverman also wrote the widely reviewed book *A Cultural History of the American Revolution.*

D. M. Thomas—British poet, novelist, and translator; his 1980 novel *The White Hotel* initially encountered a lukewarm response in England but was met with phenomenal sales and high critical acclaim in the United States; the work won a *Los Angeles Times* Book Prize and was nominated for the Booker McConnell Prize; among his other books are *Selected Poems* and the novels *Ararat* and *Swallow.* (Sketch includes interview.)

James Thurber—American humorist, short story writer, essayist, and cartoonist who died in 1961; Thurber was best known for his work at the *New Yorker,* where he was a mainstay for over thirty years, and for his stories concerned with middle-class domestic situations, which he often based on his own life; his best-loved books include *Is Sex Neccessary?; or, Why You Feel the Way You Do, The Owl in the Attic and Other Perplexities,* and *My Life and Hard Times.*

Jack Vance—Prolific American science fiction novelist and mystery writer who is admired for his craftsmanship; among his numerous works are *The Dragon Masters,* which garnered a Hugo Award, and *The Man in the Cage,* which won an Edgar Award; Vance was granted the World Fantasy Life Achievement Award in 1984.

Kate Wilhelm—American science fiction novelist; Wilhelm has been praised for her strong characterizations and plots, notably in the Hugo and Jupiter Award-winning *Where Late the Sweet Birds Sang,* an examination of cloning and its consequences for humanity, and American Book Award nominee *Juniper Time,* which focuses on environmental disaster and contact with alien beings. (Sketch includes interview.)

C. Vann Woodward—American historian who is considered one of the preeminent scholars of the American South; in *Tom Watson: Agrarian Rebel* and *Origins of the New South: 1877-1913,* Woodward departs from prevailing interpretations of the post-Reconstruction era to argue that internal conflicts, rather than clashes between agrarian Southerners and Northern carpetbaggers, caused postwar political struggles in the South; Woodward received a 1982 Pulitzer Prize for his editing of *Mary Chestnut's Civil War.*

Preface

The *Contemporary Authors New Revision Series* provides completely updated information on authors listed in earlier volumes of *Contemporary Authors* (*CA*). Entries for active individual authors from *any* volume of *CA* may be included in a volume of the *New Revision Series*. The sketches appearing in *New Revision Series* Volume 17, for example, were selected from more than twenty previously published *CA* volumes.

As always, the most recent *Contemporary Authors* cumulative index continues to be the user's guide to the location of an individual author's listing.

Compilation Methods

The editors make every effort to secure information directly from the authors. Copies of all sketches in selected *CA* volumes published several years ago are routinely sent to the listees at their last-known addresses. Authors mark material to be deleted or changed and insert any new personal data, new affiliations, new writings, new work in progress, new sidelights, and new biographical/critical sources. All returns are assessed, more comprehensive research is done, if necessary, and those sketches requiring significant change are completely updated and published in the *New Revision Series*.

If, however, authors fail to reply or are now deceased, biographical dictionaries are checked for new information (a task made easier through the use of Gale's *Biography and Genealogy Master Index* and other volumes in the "Gale Biographical Index Series"), as are bibliographical sources such as *Cumulative Book Index* and *The National Union Catalog*. Using data from such sources, revision editors select and revise nonrespondents' entries that need substantial updating. Sketches not personally reviewed by the biographees are marked with a dagger (†) to indicate that these listings have been revised from secondary sources believed to be reliable, but they have not been personally reviewed for this edition by the authors sketched.

In addition, reviews and articles in major periodicals, lists of prestigious awards, and, particularly, requests from *CA* users are monitored so that writers on whom new information is in demand can be identified and revised listings prepared promptly.

Format

CA entries provide biographical and bibliographical information in an easy-to-use format. In recent volumes, the editors have introduced a number of format changes so that a reader needing specific information can quickly focus on the pertinent portion of an entry. Beginning with *New Revision Series* Volume 15, for example, sketches contain individual paragraphs with rubrics identifying address, membership, and awards and honors information, permitting *CA* users to locate more quickly the facts they need.

As part of the editors' continuing efforts to make the information in entries as accessible as possible, *New Revision Series* volumes now employ a new format for title listings. In sketch sections headed "Writings," the title of each book, play, and other published or unpublished work appears on a separate line, clearly distinguishing one title from another. Now *CA* readers can quickly scan an author's bibliography to find the titles they need. This same convenient bibliographical presentation is also featured in the "Biographical/Critical Sources" sections of sketches where individual book and periodical titles are listed on separate lines.

Comprehensive Revision

All listings in this volume have been revised and/or augmented in various ways, though the amount and type of change vary with the author. In many instances, sketches are totally rewritten, and the resulting *New Revision Series* entries are often considerably longer than the authors' previous listings. Revised entries include additions of or changes in such information as degrees, mailing addresses, literary agents, career items, career-related and civic activities, memberships, work in progress, and biographical/critical sources. They may also include the following:

1) Major new awards—Scientist Freeman J. Dyson, novelist Alison Lurie, historian Thomas K. McCraw, and biographer Kenneth Silverman are only four of the numerous award-winning authors with sketches in this volume. The updated entry for Freeman J. Dyson notes the *Los Angeles Times* Book Prize nomination and the National Book Critics Circle Award his book *Weapons of Hope* garnered in 1984. Alison Lurie's revised sketch records that her novel *Foreign Affairs* was nominated for an American Book Award and a National Book Critics Circle Award in 1984 and was granted a Pulitzer Prize in 1985. Thomas K. McCraw and Kenneth Silverman were also recipients of 1985 Pulitzer Prizes; as their updated listings indicate, McCraw won the award for his work *Prophets of Regulation* and Silverman received the Pulitzer for his biography *The Life and Times of Cotton Mather*, which also garnered the 1985 Bancroft Prize.

2) Extensive bibliographical additions—Among the prolific authors with updated entries in this volume are free-lance writers Lawrence J. Cerri, Mary Blount Christian, and Robert M. Quackenbush. Lawrence J. Cerri, who writes all of his work under the pseudonym Lawrence Cortesi, has written twenty-seven books since his entry last appeared in *CA*, thirteen of which comprise his "World at War" series. The revised sketch for Mary Blount Christian notes twenty-six juvenile books not in her previous *CA* entry. And Robert M. Quackenbush's already lengthy bibliography has been augmented with the addition of forty-seven new titles, including forty-one self-illustrated works for children.

3) Informative new sidelights—Numerous *CA* sketches contain sidelights, which provide personal dimensions to the listings, supply information about the critical reception the authors' works have received, or both. For example, in sidelights for short story writer Andre Dubus, assistant editor and writer Joan E. Marecki comments that Dubus "describes the loneliness and isolation that stretch between people in modern society, focusing especially on the relationships between men and women." Dubus's characters follow all the "rules" of modern life—working, marrying, raising children—without finding fulfillment, prompting *Washington Post Book World* contributor Michael Harris to credit the writer with giving voice to a new mood in America: "a painful awareness, by people who once expected better, that horizons are shrinking."

The work of award-winning novelist and short story writer Vonda N. McIntyre is often compared to that of Ursula K. Le Guin; like Le Guin, McIntyre takes as her major theme the unlimited development of her mostly female characters. In a letter to *CA*, quoted in sidelights by assistant editor Melissa J. Gaiownik, McIntyre explains why she employs the science fiction genre to state her theme: "I write science fiction because its boundaries are the only ones wide enough for me to explore experiences people have not had—*yet;* and because it allows my characters to develop as far as their abilities will take them, unlimited by the crippling demands and unambitious expectations our society puts on us."

James Thurber's considerable reputation is largely based on his shorter pieces about domestic life. Often inspired by his own experiences, these pieces focus on "the conflict between the sexes" and "the dangerously precarious nature of everyday life," senior writer Thomas Wiloch explains in sidelights. Thurber objected to the label "humorist" being attached to himself or other writers of "light pieces," commenting in the foreword to his book *My Life and Hard Times:* "To call such persons 'humorists,' a loose-fitting and ugly word, is to miss the nature of their dilemma and the dilemma of their nature. The little wheels of their invention are set in motion by the damp hand of melancholy." "Thurber's genius," John Updike writes in the essay collection *Thurber,* "was to make of our despair a humorous fable."

These sketches, as well as others with sidelights compiled by *CA*'s editors, provide informative and enjoyable reading.

Writers of Special Interest

CA's editors make every effort to include in each *New Revision Series* volume a substantial number of revised entries on active authors and media people of special interest to *CA*'s readers. Since the *New Revision Series* also includes sketches on noteworthy deceased writers, a significant amount of work on the part of *CA*'s editors goes into the revision of entries on important deceased authors. Some of the prominent writers, both living and deceased, whose sketches are contained in this volume are noted in the list on pages 7-8 headed "Authors and Media People Featured in This Volume."

Exclusive Interviews

CA provides exclusive, primary information on certain authors in the form of interviews. Prepared specifically for *CA*, the never-before-published conversations presented in the section of the sketch headed "*CA* Interview" give users the opportunity to learn the authors' thoughts, in depth, about their craft. Subjects chosen for interviews are, the editors feel, authors who hold special interest for *CA*'s readers.

Authors and journalists in this volume whose sketches include interviews are Janet Dailey, Robertson Davies, Andre Dubus, Georgie Anne Geyer, Barbara Gordon, Bill Gulick, George V. Higgins, Diane

Johnson, E. L. Konigsburg, Robert A. Nisbet, Thomas Powers, Richard L. Rubenstein, D. M. Thomas, and Kate Wilhelm.

Contemporary Authors Autobiography Series

Designed to complement the information in *CA* original and revision volumes, the new *Contemporary Authors Autobiography Series* provides autobiographical essays written by important current authors. Each volume contains from twenty to thirty specially commissioned autobiographies and is illustrated with numerous personal photographs supplied by the authors. The range of contemporary writers who will be describing their lives and interests in the new *Autobiography Series* is indicated by the variety of authors who contributed to Volumes 1 and 2—writers such as Dannie Abse, Vance Bourjaily, Erskine Caldwell, John Ciardi, Doris Grumbach, Elizabeth Forsythe Hailey, Marge Piercy, Frederik Pohl, Alan Sillitoe, and Diane Wakoski. Though the information presented in the autobiographies is as varied and unique as the authors, common topics of discussion include their motivations for writing, the people and experiences that shaped their careers, the rewards they derive from their work, and their impressions of the current literary scene.

Autobiographies included in the *Contemporary Authors Autobiography Series* can be located through both the *CA* cumulative index and the *Contemporary Authors Autobiography Series* index, which lists not only personal names but also titles of works, geographical names, subjects, and schools of writing.

CA Numbering System

Occasionally questions arise about the *CA* numbering system. Despite numbers like "97-100" and "116," the entire *CA* series consists of only 62 physical volumes with the publication of *CA New Revision Series* Volume 17. The following information notes changes in the numbering system, as well as in cover design, to help users better understand the organization of the entire *CA* series.

CA First Revisions	• 1-4R through 41-44R (11 books) *Cover:* Brown with black and gold trim. There will be no further *First Revisions* because revised entries are now being handled exclusively through the more efficient *New Revision Series* mentioned below.
CA Original Volumes	• 45-48 through 97-100 (14 books) *Cover:* Brown with black and gold trim. • 101 through 116 (16 books) *Cover:* Blue and black with orange bands. The same as previous *CA* original volumes but with a new, simplified numbering system and new cover design.
CA New Revision Series	• *CANR*-1 through *CANR*-17 (17 books) *Cover:* Blue and black with green bands. Includes only sketches requiring extensive change; **sketches are taken from any previously published CA volume.**
CA Permanent Series	• *CAP*-1 and *CAP*-2 (2 books) *Cover:* Brown with red and gold trim. There will be no further *Permanent Series* volumes because revised entries are now being handled exclusively through the more efficient *New Revision Series* mentioned above.
CA Autobiography Series	• *CAA*-1 and *CAA*-2 (2 books) *Cover:* Blue and black with pink and purple bands. Presents specially commissioned autobiographies by leading contemporary writers to complement the information in *CA* original and revision volumes.

Retaining *CA* Volumes

As new volumes in the series are published, users often ask which *CA* volumes, if any, can be discarded. The Volume Update Chart on page 13 is designed to assist users in keeping their collections as complete as possible. All volumes in the left column of the chart should be retained to have the most complete, up-to-date coverage possible; volumes in the right column can be discarded if the appropriate replacements are held.

Cumulative Index Should Always Be Consulted

The key to locating an individual author's listing is the *CA* cumulative index, which is published separately and distributed with even-numbered original volumes and odd-numbered revision volumes. Since the *CA* cumulative index provides access to *all* entries in the *CA* series, the latest cumulative index should always be consulted to find the specific volume containing an author's original or most recently revised sketch.

Those authors whose entries appear in the *New Revision Series* are listed in the *CA* cumulative index with the designation **CANR-** in front of the specific volume number. For the convenience of those who do not have *New Revision Series* volumes, the cumulative index also notes the specific earlier volumes of *CA* in which the sketch appeared. Below is a sample index citation for an author whose revised entry appears in a *New Revision Series* volume.

Sagan, Carl (Edward) 1934- CANR-11
Earlier sketch in CA 25-28R

For the most recent information on Sagan, users should refer to Volume 11 of the *New Revision Series,* as designated by "CANR-11"; if that volume is unavailable, refer to *CA* 25-28 First Revision, as indicated by "Earlier sketch in CA 25-28R," for his 1977 listing. (And if *CA* 25-28 First Revision is unavailable, refer to *CA* 25-28, published in 1971, for Sagan's original listing.)

Sketches not eligible for inclusion in a *New Revision Series* volume because the biographee or a revision editor has verified that no significant change is required will, of course, be available in previously published *CA* volumes. Users should always consult the most recent *CA* cumulative index to determine the location of these authors' entries.

For the convenience of *CA* users, the *CA* cumulative index also includes references to all entries in these related Gale literary series: *Authors in the News, Children's Literature Review, Contemporary Literary Criticism, Dictionary of Literary Biography, Something About the Author,* and *Twentieth-Century Literary Criticism.*

Suggestions Are Welcome

The editors welcome comments and suggestions from users on any aspect of the *CA* series. If readers would like to suggest authors whose *CA* entries should appear in future volumes of the *New Revision Series,* they are cordially invited to write the editors.

Volume Update Chart

IF YOU HAVE:	YOU MAY DISCARD:
1-4 First Revision (1967)	1 (1962) 2 (1963) 3 (1963) 4 (1963)
5-8 First Revision (1969)	5-6 (1963) 7-8 (1963)
Both 9-12 First Revision (1974) AND *Contemporary Authors Permanent Series,* Volume 1 (1975)	9-10 (1964) 11-12 (1965)
Both 13-16 First Revision (1975) AND *Contemporary Authors Permanent Series,* Volumes 1 and 2 (1975, 1978)	13-14 (1965) 15-16 (1966)
Both 17-20 First Revision (1976) AND *Contemporary Authors Permanent Series,* Volumes 1 and 2 (1975, 1978)	17-18 (1967) 19-20 (1968)
Both 21-24 First Revision (1977) AND *Contemporary Authors Permanent Series,* Volumes 1 and 2 (1975, 1978)	21-22 (1969) 23-24 (1970)
Both 25-28 First Revision (1977) AND *Contemporary Authors Permanent Series,* Volume 2 (1978)	25-28 (1971)
Both 29-32 First Revision (1978) AND *Contemporary Authors Permanent Series,* Volume 2 (1978)	29-32 (1972)
Both 33-36 First Revision (1978) AND *Contemporary Authors Permanent Series,* Volume 2 (1978)	33-36 (1973)
37-40 First Revision (1979)	37-40 (1973)
41-44 First Revision (1979)	41-44 (1974)
45-48 (1974) 49-52 (1975) ↓ ↓ 116 (1986)	NONE: These volumes will not be superseded by corresponding revised volumes. Individual entries from these and all other volumes appearing in the left column of this chart will be revised and included in the *New Revision Series.*
Volumes in the *Contemporary Authors New Revision Series*	NONE: The *New Revision Series* does not replace any single volume of *CA.* All volumes appearing in the left column of this chart must be retained to have information on all authors in the series.

Contemporary Authors

NEW REVISION SERIES

† Indicates that a listing has been revised from secondary sources believed to be reliable, but has not been personally reviewed for this edition by the author sketched.

ADAMS, Christopher
    See HOPKINS, Kenneth

*   *   *

ADAMS, Cindy

PERSONAL: Born in New York, N.Y.; daughter of Harry (an insurance agent) and Jessica (Sugar) Heller; married Joey Adams (a comedian and writer), February 14, 1952.

ADDRESSES: Office—New York Post, 210 South St., New York, N.Y. 10002. *Agent*—Mrs. Carleton Cole, Waldorf Astoria Hotel, New York, N.Y.

CAREER: Former model and cover girl; former war correspondent in Vietnam; WABC-TV, New York City, newscaster, 1966-68. Correspondent for North American Newspaper Alliance and Womens News Service; professional lecturer and fashion show commentator; conductor with husband of tours to the Orient for Northwest Orient Airlines, beginning 1969; currently writer of column on international affairs for the *New York Post,* New York City.

MEMBER: American Federation of Television and Radio Artists, American Guild of Variety Artists, Screen Actors Guild, Actors' Equity Association.

AWARDS, HONORS: Named professional woman of the year by Yeshiva University and woman of the year by Troupers (theatrical organization), both 1967.

WRITINGS:

Sukarno: An Autobiography as Told to Cindy Adams, Bobbs-Merrill, 1965.
My Friend, the Dictator, Bobbs-Merrill, 1968.
Jolie Gaber: An Autobiography as Told to Cindy Adams, Mason/Charter, 1975.
Lee Strasberg: The Imperfect Genius of the Actors Studio, Doubleday, 1980.

Author of syndicated column "Cindy Says." Regular contributor to popular magazines and contributor of feature articles to *Christian Science Monitor.*

WORK IN PROGRESS: The Quintessential Round-Up Book, for Doubleday.

SIDELIGHTS: Cindy Adams's book *Lee Strasberg: The Imperfect Genius of the Actors Studio* chronicles the life of the man who is considered to be one of the best teachers of acting in recent times. Strasberg was the inventor of the "method" school of acting, which relies on triggering genuine, buried emotions for dramatic motivation. Dale Pollock takes exception to the "chatty" tone of the biography in the *Los Angeles Times Book Review,* remarking that Adams's book is a "textbook example of how *not* to write a popular biography." However, Patricia Bosworth observes in the *New York Times Book Review* that by focusing primarily on the story of Strasberg's life, Adams presents readers with a "gossipy and readable account, full of anecdote and passion." Although Bosworth comments that this biography "consolidates rather than extends our understanding of Lee Strasberg," she admits that the book "provides a fascinating portrait of an elusive and contradictory man."

AVOCATIONAL INTERESTS: Collecting Ming, Sung, and other Oriental objects of art.

BIOGRAPHICAL/CRITICAL SOURCES:

PERIODICALS

Los Angeles Times Book Review, May 18, 1980.
New York Times Book Review, March 16, 1980.
Washington Post Book World, June 15, 1980.

*   *   *

ALLCHIN, A(rthur) M(acdonald)   1930-

PERSONAL: Born April 20, 1930, in England; son of Frank Macdonald (a physician) and Louise (Wright) Allchin. *Education:* Christ Church, Oxford, B.A., 1951, B.Litt. and M.A., 1955; Cuddesdon College, theology study, 1954-56. *Politics:* Socialist.

ADDRESSES: Home—12 The Precincts, Canterbury CT1 2EH, England.

CAREER: Priest of Church of England; St. Mary Abbots, Kensington, London, England, curate, 1956-60; Pusey House, Oxford, England, librarian, 1960-69; Canterbury Cathedral, Canterbury, England, residentiary canon, 1973—. Visiting lecturer in church history, Cuddesdon College, Oxford, 1962—; visiting lecturer in theology, General Theological Seminary,

New York, N.Y., 1967, 1968; visiting lecturer in theology, Catholic Theological Faculty, Lyons, France, 1980; visiting professor at Nashotah House, Wisconsin, 1984-85, and at University of Dallas, Dallas, Tex., 1985. Warden of community, Sisters of the Love of God, Oxford, 1967—. Church of England, member of the Archbishops' Commission on Christian Doctrine, the Anglican Commission for Theological Dialogue with the Orthodox Churches, and the Council on Foreign Relations.

AWARDS, HONORS: Honorary Doctorate of Divinity from Bucharest Theological Institute, 1977, and Nashotah House, Wisconsin, 1985.

WRITINGS:

The Silent Rebellion, S.C.M. Press, 1958.
Abbe Paul Couturier, Faith Press, 1960.
(Editor) *Dialogue: East and West,* Faith Press, 1963.
The Spirit and the Word: Two Studies in Nineteenth-Century Anglican Theology, Faith Press, 1963.
(With John Coulson and Meriol Trevor) *Newman, A Portrait Restored: An Ecumenical Revaluation,* Sheed (London), 1965.
(With H. A. Hodges) *A Rapture of Praise,* Hodder & Stoughton, 1966.
(Editor with Coulson) *The Rediscovery of Newman: An Oxford Symposium,* Sheed (London), 1967.
(Editor) *Sacrament and Image: Essays in the Christian Understanding of Man,* Fellowship of St. Alban and St. Sergius, 1967.
(Editor) *The Tradition of Life: Romanian Essays in Spirituality and Theology,* Fellowship of St. Alban and St. Sergius, 1971.
(Editor) *Orthodoxy and the Death of God: Essays in Contemporary Theology,* Fellowship of St. Alban and St. Sergius, 1971.
(With A. M. Ramsey and Robert E. Terwilliger) *The Charismatic Christ,* Morehouse, 1973.
The Theology of the Religious Life: An Anglican Approach, S.L.G. Press, 1974.
Eucharist and Unity: Thoughts on the Anglican-Roman Catholic International Commissions Agreed Statement on Eucharistic Doctrine, Together with Full Text of That Statement, S.L.G. Press, 1974.
(Editor) *Theology and Prayer: Essays on Monastic Themes Presented at the Orthodox-Cistercian Conference, Oxford, 1973,* Fellowship of St. Alban and St. Sergius, 1975.
Wholeness and Transfiguration: Illustrated in the Lives of St. Francis of Assisi and St. Seraphim of Sarov, S.L.G. Press, 1975.
Ann Griffiths, University of Wales Press, 1976.
(Editor) *Solitude and Communion: Papers on the Hermit Life Given at St. David's, Wales in the Autumn of 1975,* S.L.G. Press, 1977.
The World Is a Wedding: Explorations in Christian Spirituality, Oxford University Press, 1978.
The Kingdom of Love and Knowledge: The Encounter between Orthodoxy and the West, Darton, Longman, & Todd, 1979, Seabury, 1982.
The Living Presence of the Past: The Dynamic of Christian Tradition, Seabury, 1981 (published in England as *The Dynamic of Tradition,* Darton, Longman, & Todd, 1981).
A Taste of Liberty, S.L.G. Press, 1983.
The Joy of All Creation, Darton, Longman & Todd, 1984.

Also author of numerous pamphlets, published lectures, and addresses on theological subjects. Contributor to symposia and to theological journals, including *Studia Liturgica, Irenikon, Theology,* and *Eastern Churches Review.*

WORK IN PROGRESS: A book on the theology of prayer; research on the Danish theologian N. F. S. Grundtvig for an introductory study in English.

*   *   *

ALLEN, James L(ovic), Jr. 1929-
(Jim Allen; Allen James, a pseudonym)

PERSONAL: Born January 2, 1929, in Atlanta, Ga.; son of James Lovic (a civil servant) and Effie (Schell) Allen; married Barbara Foster, June 13, 1953 (divorced September, 1976); children: Melinda Sue, Algernon Foster. *Education:* Tulane University, B.A., 1953, M.A., 1954; University of Florida, Ph.D., 1959. *Politics:* Democrat. *Religion:* Unitarian.

ADDRESSES: Home—2405 Kalanianaole Ave., Apt. 304, Hilo, Hawaii 96720. *Office*—Department of English, University of Hawaii at Hilo, Hilo, Hawaii 96720.

CAREER: University of Tennessee, Knoxville, instructor in English, 1954-56; Stephen F. Austin State College (now University), Nacogdoches, Tex., assistant professor of English, 1959-60; University of Southern Mississippi, Hattiesburg, associate professor of English, 1960-63; University of Hawaii at Hilo, professor of English, 1963—. Visiting professor at Western Washington State College (now Western Washington University), summer, 1968, Hartwick College, summer, 1969, Stephen F. Austin State University, 1970-71, University of Tennessee, Knoxville, 1976-77, and University of Oklahoma, spring, 1986. Member of American Committee for Irish Studies. *Military service:* U.S. Navy, 1946-49.

MEMBER: Modern Language Association of America, American Association of University Professors, Phi Beta Kappa.

WRITINGS:

(Under name Jim Allen) *Locked In: Surfing for Life,* A. S. Barnes, 1970.
Yeats's Epitaph: A Key to Symbolic Unity in His Life and Work, University Press of America, 1982.
(Contributor) Frank N. Magill, editor, *Critical Survey of Poetry,* Salem Press, 1982.
(Contributor) Mary Lynn Johnson and Lydia Seraphia, editors, *Reconciliations: Studies in Honor of Richard Harter Fogle,* University of Salzburg Press, 1983.

Also author of poems under pseudonym Allen James. Also contributor to *Yeats Annual* and *The Yearbook of Research in English and American Literature.* Contributor of scholarly articles, largely about W. B. Yeats, to numerous periodicals, including *Studies in the Literary Imagination, Studies: An Irish Quarterly Review, English Studies, Journal of Aesthetics and Art Criticism, Journal of Modern Literature, Sewanee Review,* and *Twentieth-Century Literature.* First managing editor, *Southern Quarterly,* 1962-63; member of editorial board, *Twentieth-Century Literature.*

WORK IN PROGRESS: Applied Psi: The ESP Revolution and Your Future; Yeats and ESP: Paranormal Phenomena in the Life, Work and Study of W. B. Yeats; How to Have Fun in Hawaii.

SIDELIGHTS: James L. Allen, Jr., told *CA:* "My entire career as a Yeats scholar has been and will continue to be [a] commitment to the proposition that historical and biographical criticism, rather than 'the new criticism,' are fundamental to an understanding of this poet's work and that such a critical approach leads to the inescapable conclusion that Yeats literally and fervently believed in the basic tenets of his personal cosmology and 'religion.' I believe that the extensive publication of previously unpublished materials by the poet has validated beyond question this position in the late 1970s and the 1980s.''

AVOCATIONAL INTERESTS: Surfing, jazz and folk music, playing mandolin, banjo, and saxophone.

* * *

ALLEN, Jim
See ALLEN, James L(ovic), Jr.

* * *

ALLEN, Judson B(oyce) 1932-

PERSONAL: Born March 15, 1932, in Louisville, Ky.; son of Clifton Judson (a clergyman and editor) and Hattie Belle (a speech therapist and children's writer; maiden name, McCracken) Allen; married Jacqueline Johnson Hewitt (an elementary school teacher); children: Wade Cox, Rosalind Toy. *Education:* Baylor University, B.A., 1953; Vanderbilt University, M.A., 1954; additional study at Oxford University, 1960-62; Johns Hopkins University, Ph.D., 1963. *Politics:* Democrat. *Religion:* Baptist.

ADDRESSES: Home—Gainesville, Fla. *Office*—Department of English, University of Florida, Gainesville, Fla.

CAREER: Southern Baptist Historical Commission, Nashville, Tenn., research assistant and editor, 1953-57; Southern Baptist Education Commission, Nashville, research assistant and staff writer, 1957; Johns Hopkins University, Baltimore, Md., junior instructor in English, 1957-60; Wake Forest University, Winston-Salem, N.C., instructor, 1962-63, assistant professor of English, 1964-69; Marquette University, Milwaukee, Wis., associate professor, 1969-79, professor of English, 1980-82; University of Florida, Gainesville, professor of English, 1982—. Visiting professor at University of Chicago, 1978. Member of advisory committee of Centre for Medieval and Renaissance Studies (Oxford, England), 1978—. Member of Baptist World Alliance Commission on Cooperative Christianity, 1969-80.

MEMBER: Modern Language Association of America, Medieval Academy of America, South Atlantic Modern Language Association (section head, 1984).

AWARDS, HONORS: Fellowships from Medieval-Renaissance Institute, summer, 1965, University of North Carolina, 1965-66, and National Endowment for the Humanities, 1969-70, in Italy, 1975-76, in France, and 1982-83, in England; American Philosophical Society grant, 1969; Guggenheim fellow, 1984-85.

WRITINGS:

The Friar as Critic: Literary Attitudes in the Later Middle Ages, Vanderbilt University Press, 1971.
(With Theresa Anne Moritz) *A Distinction of Stories: The Medieval Unity of Chaucer's Fair Chain of Narratives for Canterbury,* Ohio State University Press, 1981.
The Ethical Poetic of the Later Middle Ages: A Decorum of Convenient Distinction, University of Toronto Press, 1982.

Contributor of twenty-nine articles and reviews to scholarly journals. Member of editorial board of "Medieval Academy Reprints for Teaching."

WORK IN PROGRESS: The Process of Piers Plowman, a study that identifies the five books in William Langland's early library and relates their use to his composition of the Z-text and the A-text; a study of the medieval self based on medieval first person discourses and using the psychoanalysis of Jacques Lacan as a conceptual catalyst; research on the city as a rhetorical system, drawing upon medieval theory as a matrix for solving problems of design, positional competition, hierarchy, and limited resources.

SIDELIGHTS: Judson B. Allen writes *CA:* "My work exists in the interface between fact and fiction, which the Middle Ages practiced as rhetoric, and which now may be dominated by anthropologists, since many literary critics cultivate the solipsism. Since I have lived in England, France, and Italy, as well as in the American South and Midwest, I have a lively awareness of the radical differences in sensibility which distinguish (and even alienate) people from one another. As a scholar, I am interested in understanding how a distinctive sensibility comes to be, and what various ones are (and may be) good for; I find literary processes powerful tools of explanation, and literary texts excellent moral and cultural evidence. My work so far has been the technical scholarship of the medievalist, but I achieved through it some positions and methods of more general significance, and I expect to begin now to work on more generally ethical problems, such as the study of the medieval self presently funded by the Guggenheim Foundation, and the urban studies book which seems, paradoxically, to profit from every delay it suffers while I write something else."

* * *

ALLEN, Richard C. 1926-

PERSONAL: Born January 24, 1926, in Swampscott, Mass.; son of Chester G. and Edith (Hickford) Allen; married Elsie Anderson Birrell; children: Steven Richard, Craig Ethan, Scott David. *Education:* Washington University, St. Louis, Mo., A.B., 1948, J.D., 1950; University of Michigan, LL.M., 1963.

CAREER: Attorney in both private and corporate practice, St. Louis, Mo., and Topeka, Kan., 1950-59; with Karl Menninger and Joseph Satten, organized Menninger Foundation programs in law and psychiatry at Menninger School of Psychiatry and Washburn University School of Law, Topeka, Kan., 1959-63; George Washington University, School of Law, Washington, D.C., professor of law and director of Institute of Law, Psychiatry and Criminology, beginning 1963, professor of forensic sciences and chairman of department, beginning 1973; professor of law and dean, Hamline University. Member of the board of Forensic Sciences Foundation and Center for the Study of Psychiatry; member of the board and vice-president, Forsite, Inc.; member of National Advisory Council on Correctional Manpower and Training, 1968-71; chairman of Supreme Court Commission on the Mentally Disabled and the Courts. Director of two three-year studies funded by the National Institute of Mental Health. Consultant, President's Committee on Mental Retardation, 1967-74.

MEMBER: American Academy of Forensic Sciences (fellow), American Bar Association, Missouri Bar Association (member of board of directors), Mental Health Association of Minnesota (member of board of directors), Minnesota Civil Liberties Union, Kansas Bar Association.

WRITINGS:

(With Elyce Z. Ferster and Henry Weihofen) *Mental Impairment and Legal Incompetency,* Prentice-Hall, 1968.

(Editor with Ferster and Jesse G. Rubin) *Readings in Law and Psychiatry,* Johns Hopkins Press, 1968, revised edition, 1975.

(Contributor) R. Wittenborn and others, editors, *Drugs and Youth,* C. C Thomas, 1969.

Legal Rights of the Disabled and Disadvantaged, U.S. Department of Health, Education, and Welfare, 1970.

(Contributor) F. Menolascino, editor, *Psychiatric Approaches to Mental Retardation,* Basic Books, 1970.

(With Ferster and Thomas F. Courtless) *Equal Justice for the Unequal: The Mentally Retarded and the Law,* Institute of Law, Psychiatry and Criminology, George Washington University, 1979.

(Editor) *Mental Health in America: The Years of Crisis,* Marquis Academic Media, 1979.

Editor-in-chief, *MH* (journal of National Association for Mental Health).†

*   *   *

ALLEN, Robert
See GARFINKEL, Bernard Max

*   *   *

ALLMAN, T. D. 1944-

PERSONAL: Born October 16, 1944, in Florida; son of Paul Joseph (a naval officer and ship captain) and Ada Felicia (a businesswoman; maiden name, Edmonds) Allman. *Education:* Harvard University, B.A. (cum laude), 1966; graduate study at St. Antony's College, Oxford, 1971-75.

ADDRESSES: Office—*Harper's* Magazine, 2 Park Ave., New York, N.Y. 10016. *Agent*—Peter Skolnik, Sanford J. Greenburger Associates, 55 Fifth Ave., New York, N.Y. 10022.

CAREER: Journalist. Associated with *Anchorage Daily News,* Anchorage, Alaska, 1964; *Philadelphia Bulletin,* Philadelphia, Pa., reporter on police beat, 1965; Peace Corps volunteer, Nepal, 1966-68; free-lance foreign correspondent in Southeast Asia, for the *New York Times, Washington Post, Time,* and other publications, 1968-71; *Guardian,* London, England, foreign correspondent, 1971-75; Third Century America Project, Berkeley, Calif., director of urban research, 1976—; Pacific News Service, San Francisco, Calif., senior editor, 1977-82; *Harper's* magazine, New York, N.Y., contributing editor, 1977—. Notable assignments include investigative reporting on the war in Indochina and the outbreak of the Cambodian war, cover stories on the urban crisis, the war in El Salvador, the crisis in the Philippines and on the emergence of Miami, Florida, as a major world metropolis.

AWARDS, HONORS: Edward R. Murrow fellowship from Council on Foreign Relations, 1975-76; press awards for reports from Tibet and Turkey.

WRITINGS:

Unmanifest Destiny: Mayhem and Illusion in U.S. Foreign Policy—From the Monroe Doctrine to Reagan's War in El Salvador, Dial, 1984.

Contributor to periodicals, including *Economist, Gentlemen's Quarterly, Penthouse, Esquire, New Republic, Far Eastern Economic Review, New Statesman,* and *New Times,* and to newspapers, including *Washington Post, New York Times, Los Angeles Times, Le Monde diplomatique,* and *Bangkok Post.*

WORK IN PROGRESS: A book on Miami, Florida, for Atlantic Monthly Press; reporting trips to Ethiopia, Cuba, and the Far East.

SIDELIGHTS: T. D. Allman's journalistic assignments have ranged from an analysis of the urban crisis to a critique of the sociology of the nouvelle cuisine, and from a study of the murders of U.S. churchwomen in El Salvador to an account of a harrowing overland journey through a devastated Cambodia to the ruins of Angkor Wat.

Allman told *CA:* "Free-lance journalists are probably the most underpaid and overcompensated people in the world. It's a wonderful career if you love work, new challenges, human beings, and the English language. But it's an absolute disaster if what you want is either security or a life-style. Writing is a vocation, something that chooses you, not the other way around. Now that I am no longer a child in the profession, I tell newcomers: 'Forget Lou Grant and the Woodstein Twins. If you don't have something original to say, in an original way, go to law school.'"

Allman's *Unmanifest Destiny: Mayhem and Illusion in U.S. Foreign Policy—From the Monroe Doctrine to Reagan's War in El Salvador* is described by George Black in the *Nation* as "a bold survey of the recurring traumas of U.S. foreign policy. It muses on the first colonial adventures of the early nineteenth century, treks though the disasters of Southeast Asia and finally arrives, somewhat exhausted, at the present crisis in Central America." According to Black, "it is heartening to see a journalist—particularly one as well versed as Allman in the minutiae of U.S. history—make an unusual foray into the psychological and ideological mysteries of this country's drive beyond its own shores and try to tease out the historical reasons for its excesses, failures and deceptions."

However, "one reason for the rarity of the psychological approach to history may be the problems of method it presents," states Black. "The difficulties are formidable, and Allman, sadly, is only intermittently able to overcome them." Timothy Garton Ash concludes in the *New York Times Book Review* that "inside this fat book there is a thin one trying to get out. The story of the murder of American nuns in El Salvador and the subsequent cover-up, lies and callous evasions is a shocking one, well told by Mr. Allman. Without preaching and hyperbole, it speaks for itself."

BIOGRAPHICAL/CRITICAL SOURCES:

PERIODICALS

Nation, October 20, 1984.
New York Times Book Review, October 7, 1984.

*   *   *

ALROY, Gil Carl 1924-1985

PERSONAL: Born November 7, 1924, in Cernauti, Romania; died May 18, 1985, in New York, N.Y.; son of Samuel and Esther (Bley) AlRoy; married Phyllis Delson, December 26, 1954; children: Carolyn Simone, Iris Jeanne, Aileen Bley. *Education:* College of the City of New York (now City College of the City University of New York), B.A., 1959; Princeton University, Ph.D., 1963.

ADDRESSES: Home—Guttenberg, N.J. *Office*—Department of Political Science, Hunter College of the City University of New York, 695 Park Ave., New York, N.Y. 10021.

CAREER: Hunter College of the City University of New York, New York, N.Y., instructor, 1964-65, assistant professor, 1966-67, associate professor, 1968-71, professor of political science, 1972-85. Senior information assistant, U.S. Diplomatic Mission in Israel, 1950-54; research associate, Center of International Studies, Princeton, N.J., 1963-68.

MEMBER: Middle East Studies Association (fellow), National Honor Society in Economics (president, 1960-61).

AWARDS, HONORS: Pell medal, 1959; Ward medal, 1959; Woodrow Wilson National fellow, 1959-60.

WRITINGS:

The Involvement of Peasants in Internal Wars (monograph), Princeton University, 1966.
(Editor) *Attitudes toward Jewish Statehood in the Arab World,* American Academic Association for Peace in the Middle East, 1971.
The Kissinger Experience: American Policy in the Middle East, Horizon Press, 1975.
Behind the Middle East Conflict: The Real Impasse between Arab and Jew, Putnam, 1975.
The Middle East Uncovered: The Way It Really Is, Princeton Publications, 1979.

WORK IN PROGRESS: Middle East War and Military Science.

OBITUARIES:

PERIODICALS

New York Times, May 21, 1985.
Record (Hackensack, N.J.), May 20, 1985.†

*   *   *

ALTH, Max O(ctavious)   1927-

PERSONAL: Original surname Becker; name legally changed in 1937; born June 17, 1927, in Paterson, N.J.; son of Jake and Anna (Klupavouch) Becker; married Charlotte Annete Liberman (sales manager at Saks Fifth Avenue and writer); children: Simon, Michel, Arabella, Archie. *Education:* Columbia University, B.A., 1950. *Politics:* "Freedom Party." *Religion:* Jewish.

ADDRESSES: Home—6 Tamarack Rd., Rye Brook, N.Y. *Agent*—Richard Curtis Literary Agency, 156 East 52nd St., New York, N.Y. 10022.

CAREER: Free-lance writer, editor, and publicist, 1950-58; *Electronics World,* New York City, associate editor, 1958-60; Kollsman Instrument Corp., Elmhurst, N.Y., proposal writer in Research and Development Division, 1960-63; associate editor, *Fleet International* and *Auto International,* 1963-67; *Diesel Equipment Superintendent,* Stamford, Conn., acting managing editor, 1967-68; Aluminum Association, New York City, writer and editor of technical and popular books, brochures, articles, and pamphlets, 1968—. Instructor at Westchester Community College; host of WMCA home show. Wa-

ter works inspector in Port Chester, N.Y.; technical communications consultant. *Military service:* U.S. Army Air Forces, 1943-46; served in European theater of operations; became staff sergeant; received twelve battle stars.

MEMBER: Society of Automotive Engineers, American Society of Authors and Journalists, Literary Club of America (vice-president), Eastern Writers Union (president, 1960-67).

AWARDS, HONORS: First prize for nonfiction from New York chapter of Technical Writer's Association, 1959.

WRITINGS:

The Wicked and the Warped, Woodford, 1951.
Fur Lined G-String, Midnite, 1952.
Burlesque Doll, Midnite, 1953.
Soldering Aluminum, Aluminum Association, 1969.
Brazing Aluminum, Aluminum Association, 1969.
Aluminum Cryogenic Engineering, Aluminum Association, 1972.
All about Bikes and Bicycling: Care, Repair, and Safety, Hawthorn, 1972, revised edition, 1981.
All about Locks and Locksmithing, Hawthorn, 1972.
Bicycling and Hiking, Award Books, 1973.
Making Your Own Cheese and Yogurt, Crowell, 1973.
Do-It-Yourself Plumbing, Harper, 1975.
All about Motorcycles, Hawthorn, 1975.
All about Keeping Your Car Alive, Hawthorn, 1975.
Collecting Old Radios and Crystal Sets, Wallace-Homested, 1976.
How to Farm Your Backyard the Mulch-Organic Way, McGraw, 1977.
(With son, Simon Alth) *The Stain Removal Handbook,* Hawthorn, 1977.
Do-It-Yourself Roofing and Siding, Hawthorn, 1977.
All about Mopeds, F. Watts, 1978.
Masonry and Concrete Work, Popular Science, 1978.
Homeowner's Quick-Repair and Emergency Guide, Popular Science, 1978.
Wood Stoves and Fireplaces, Grosset, 1979.
Rattan Furniture: A Home Craftsman's Guide, Hawthorn, 1979.
Motorcycles and Motorcycling, F. Watts, 1979.
(With wife, Charlotte Alth) *The Furniture Buyer's Handbook: How to Buy, Arrange, Maintain, and Repair Furniture,* Walker & Co., 1980.
(With C. Alth) *Disastrous Hurricanes and Tornadoes,* F. Watts, 1981.
(With C. Alth) *Making Plastic Pipe Furniture,* Everest House, 1981.
Masonry, Doubleday, 1982.
The Handbook of Do-It-Yourself Materials, Crown, 1983.
(With C. Alth) *Be Your Own Contractor: The Affordable Way to Home Ownership,* TAB Books, 1984.
(With C. Alth) *Constructing and Maintaining Your Well and Septic System,* TAB Books, 1984.

Contributor to a variety of popular magazines and newspapers, including *Woman's Day, Popular Science, American Home, American Photography, Radio-Electronics, Everywoman, Popular Mechanics, Radio News,* and the *New York Times.*

WORK IN PROGRESS: The Life and Times of Boris Tomasheffsky; Rags to Riches; Thirteen Men and a Boy; or, How We Almost Lost World War II.

AVOCATIONAL INTERESTS: Science and invention (holds ten patents).

ALVAREZ, John
  See del REY, Lester

*   *   *

ALVAREZ, Joseph A.   1930-

PERSONAL: Born October 2, 1930, in New York, N.Y.; son of Raul (a utility company supervisor) and Helen (Woehl) Alvarez; married Marianne Besser, December 17, 1955 (died November 14, 1971); married Margaret Hoehn, June 20, 1977 (divorced October 12, 1978); children: (first marriage) Krista. *Education:* City College (now City College of the City University of New York), B.A., 1955; Sonoma State College (now University), M.A. (English), 1975, M.A. (psychology), 1979.

ADDRESSES: Home—Santa Rosa, Calif. *Agent*—Curtis Brown Ltd., 10 Astor Pl., New York, N.Y. 10022.

CAREER: Writer's Digest, Cincinnati, Ohio, circulation director, 1955-58; Book-of-the-Month Club, New York, N.Y., advertising executive, 1958-61; professional writer, 1961—; Santa Rosa Junior College, Santa Rosa, Calif., instructor in English, 1973—.

MEMBER: Authors Guild, Society for Technical Communications.

WRITINGS:

(With C. W. Mattison) *Man and His Resources in Today's World,* Creative Education Press, 1967.
Vice Presidents of Destiny, Putnam, 1969.
Politics in America, Creative Education Press, 1971.
From Reconstruction to Revolution: The Black Struggle for Equality, Atheneum, 1971.
The Elements of Technical Writing, Harcourt, 1980.
The Elements of Composition, Harcourt, 1985.

Also author of educational film strips, ''Streets, Prairies and Valleys: The Life of Carl Sandburg,'' ''The World of Mark Twain,'' ''The Regulatory Agencies,'' ''Mass Media,'' ''The Puritan Legacy,'' ''From Colony to Country: Early American Literature,'' ''We Are Indians: American Indian Literature,'' and ''Do We Really Have Freedom of the Press?''

WORK IN PROGRESS: A biography of Shakespeare.

SIDELIGHTS: Joseph A. Alvarez told *CA:* ''I write to explore those subjects that interest me and to share with others the wonder, mystery, or terror of what I find—and because in doing so I learn about both myself and the world.''

AVOCATIONAL INTERESTS: Tennis, guitar, running.

*   *   *

AMANUDDIN, Syed   1934-

PERSONAL: Born February 4, 1934, in Mysore, India; son of Syed (a businessman) and Shahzadi (Begum) Jamaluddin; married Ashraf Basith (a social worker), February 18, 1960; children: Irfan, Rizwan. *Education:* University of Mysore, B.A. (with honors), 1956, M.A., 1957; Bowling Green State University, Ph.D., 1970; postdoctoral study at University of London, summer, 1973, and New York University, summer, 1974.

ADDRESSES: Home—P.O. Box 391, Sumter, S.C. 29151. *Office*—Department of English, Morris College, Sumter, S.C. 29150.

CAREER: College of Arts, Karimnagar, India, lecturer in English, 1958-61; Osmania University, Hyderabad, India, lecturer in English, 1961-67; Morris College, Sumter, S.C., associate professor, 1970-73, professor of English, 1976—, chairman of Division of Humanities, 1973—. Lilly Scholar in the Humanities, Duke University, 1976-77. Producer of several series on human creativity and world cultures for South Carolina Educational Television in Sumter.

MEMBER: Modern Language Association of America, South Asian Literary Association (co-founder; secretary, 1976-79), Sumter Poetry Club (founder; chairman, 1974-77).

WRITINGS:

Hart Crane's Mystical Quest and Other Essays, Kavyalaya (Mysore, India), 1967.
The Forbidden Fruit (poems), Kavyalaya, 1967.
Tiffin State Hospital (poems), Poetry Eastward, 1970.
Shoes of Tradition, Poetry Eastward, 1970.
The Children of Hiroshima (poems), Poetry Eastward, 1970.
Poems of Protest, Poetry Eastward, 1972.
System Shaker (plays), Poetry Eastward, 1972.
(Editor with Margaret Diesendorf) *New Poetry from Australia,* Poetry Eastward, 1973.
Lightning and Love (poems), Poetry Eastward, 1973.
The Age of the Female Eunuchs (poems), Poetry Eastward, 1974.
Adventures of Atman: An Epic of the Soul, Poetry Eastward, 1977.
The King Who Sold His Wife (play), Prayer Books (Calcutta), 1978.
Gems and Germs, Poetry Eastward, 1978.
(Contributor) C. D. Narasimhaiah, editor, *Awakened Conscience: Studies in Commonwealth Literature,* Sterling Publishers (New Delhi), 1978.
Passage to the Himalayas (novel), Prayer Books, 1979.
World Poetry in English: Essays and Interviews, Sterling Publishers, 1981.
Make Me Your Dream (poems), Skylark, 1984.
Poems, Sterling Publishers, 1984.

Contributor of reviews, short stories, articles, and poems to periodicals, including *Indian Verse, Poetry Australia, Descant, World Literature Today, Indian Literature, Journal of South Asian Literature,* and *Journal of Indian Writing in English.* Editor of *Poetry Eastward,* 1967-75, and of *Creative Moment: World Poetry and Criticism,* 1972-81; guest editor of special issue on Indian writers abroad, *Journal of Indian Writing in English,* 1985.

WORK IN PROGRESS: A novel, *Between Two Worlds; Transnational Sensibility: Essays on Art and Culture; The Doctor's Wife and Other Stories; The Master Last Epic; The City That Woke up to Die: A Poem Sequence on the Union Carbide Incident in Bhopal.*

SIDELIGHTS: Syed Amanuddin wrote to *CA:* ''Creativity is, I think, a characteristic of our being human. Without creativity the caveman could not have come out of his cave and the astronaut could not have reached the moon. Cultures that block creativity are doomed, for creativity means freedom to think, imagine, and create what one wants to and the way one wants to.

''I feel alive only when I am engaged in a creative act. Experiences rush to me as visual and audial experiences. Sometimes I try to express these experiences with the help of the canvas or camera; however, I consider myself primarily a poet or artist in words. I care for the freshness of image and phrase. At the same time, I try to establish a dialogue with my readers. I am fascinated by Sir Philip Sidney's definition of poetry as a speaking picture. Some of my poems are dramatic monologues where I imagine the reader himself playing the role of the mute but involved listener.

"While in my poetry I try to explore three contexts of human experiences—personal, social, and cosmic—my plays and fiction are mostly about men and women whose lives are involved in the clashes of values and cultures."

* * *

AMBROSE, Alice
    See LAZEROWITZ, Alice Ambrose

* * *

ANASTASI, Anne   1908-

PERSONAL: Born December 19, 1908, in New York, N.Y.; daughter of Anthony and Theresa (Gaudiosi) Anastasi; married John Porter Foley, Jr. (a consulting psychologist), July 26, 1933. *Education:* Barnard College, A.B., 1928; Columbia University, Ph.D., 1931.

ADDRESSES: Office—Department of Psychology, Fordham University, New York, N.Y. 10458.

CAREER: Barnard College, New York City, instructor in psychology, 1930-39; Queens College (now Queens College of the City University of New York), New York City, assistant professor and chairman of department of psychology, 1939-46; Fordham University, Graduate School, New York City, associate professor, 1947-51, professor of psychology, 1951-79, professor emeritus, 1979—, chairman of department, 1968-74. Research consultant, College Entrance Examination Board, 1954-56; visiting summer professor at University of Wisconsin, 1951, and University of Minnesota, 1958.

MEMBER: American Psychological Association (recording secretary, 1952-55; member of board of directors, 1956-59, 1968-70; president, division of general psychology, 1956-57, division of evaluation and measurement, 1965-66; president of national association, 1971), American Psychological Foundation (president, 1965-67), Psychometric Society (member of board of directors, 1941), Psychonomic Society, Eastern Psychological Association (member of board of directors, 1944-46, 1948-51; president, 1946-47), New York State Psychological Association (president, division of general psychology, 1952-53; member of board of directors, 1953-54, 1958-61, 1962-64), Phi Beta Kappa, Sigma Xi.

AWARDS, HONORS: Litt.D., University of Windsor, 1967; Sc.D., Cedar Crest College, 1971, Fordham University, 1979, and La Salle College, 1979; Paed.D., Villanova University, 1979; Educational Testing Service annual award for distinguished service to measurement, 1977; American Psychological Association distinguishd service award for the applications of psychology, 1981; American Educational Research Association Award for distinguished contributions to research in education, 1983; E. L. Thorndike Medal, Division of Educational Psychology, American Psychological Association, 1984, for distinguished contributions to education; American Psychological Foundation Gold Medal, 1984.

WRITINGS:

Differential Psychology: Individual and Group Differences in Behavior, Macmillan, 1937, 3rd edition, 1958.
(With husband, J. P. Foley, Jr.) *Human Relations and the Foreman,* National Foreman's Institute, 1951.
Psychological Testing, Macmillan, 1954, 5th edition, 1982.
Fields of Applied Psychology, McGraw, 1964, 2nd edition, 1979.
Individual Differences, Wiley, 1965.
Testing Problems in Perspective, American Council on Education, 1966.
Contributions to Differential Psychology, Praeger, 1982.

MONOGRAPHS

A Group Factor in Immediate Memory, [New York], 1930.
Further Studies on the Memory Factor, [New York], 1932.
The Influence of Specific Experience upon Mental Organization, Clark University, 1936.

Also author or co-author of two monographs on selection of flying personnel for USAF School of Aviation Medicine, and others in *Annals of New York Academy of Science* and *Psychological Monographs.*

CONTRIBUTOR

Fields of Psychology, Van Nostrand, 1940, 3rd edition, 1966.
Foundations of Psychology, Wiley, 1948.
Group Relations at the Crossroads, Harper, 1953.
Handbook of Research Methods in Child Development, Wiley, 1960.
Comprehensive Textbook of Psychiatry, Williams & Wilkins, 1967, 2nd edition, 1975.
T. S. Krawiec, editor, *The Psychologists,* Oxford University Press, 1972.
G. Lindzey, editor, *History of Psychology in Autobiography,* Volume VII, Freeman, 1980.
Measuring Achievement: Progress over a Decade, Jossey-Bass, 1980.
Privacy: A Vanishing Value?, Fordham University Press, 1980.
Issues in Testing: Coaching, Disclosure, and Ethnic Bias, Jossey-Bass, 1981.
Handbook of Clinical Psychology, Dow Jones-Irwin, 1983.
Principals of Modern Psychological Measurement, Lawrence Erlbaum, 1983.
Social and Technical Issues in Testing, Lawrence Erlbaum, 1984.
Foundations of Psychology: Some Personal Views, Praeger, 1984.
Psychology and Gender, University of Nebraska Press, 1985.

Contributor to *Encyclopaedia Britannica, Collier's Encyclopedia, International Encyclopedia of the Social Sciences, Lexicon der Psychologie, Encyclopedia of Education, Encyclopedia of Educational Research,* and *Encyclopedia of Psychology.*

OTHER

Contributor of more than 130 articles to scientific and professional journals.

SIDELIGHTS: Differential Psychology: Individual and Group Differences in Behavior has been translated into German, Italian, Portuguese, and Spanish; there have been Italian, Portuguese, Spanish, Russian, and Thai translations of *Psychological Testing;* and *Fields of Applied Psychology* has been translated into German, Chinese, Dutch, Italian, Japanese, Portuguese, and Spanish.

ARNETT, Ross H(arold), Jr. 1919-

PERSONAL: Born April 13, 1919, in Medina, N.Y.; son of Ross Harold (a veterinarian) and Hazel Dell (a musician; maiden name, Oderkirk) Arnett; married Mary Catherine Ennis (an editor's assistant), February 16, 1942; children: Ross III, Michael J., Mary Anne Arnett Held, Barbara Ellen, Francis Xavier Armestrong, Joseph Anthony, Bernadette Teresa D'Alessandro, Matthew Christopher. *Education:* Cornell University, B.S., 1942, M.S., 1946, Ph.D., 1948. *Politics:* Independent. *Religion:* Roman Catholic.

ADDRESSES: Home—2406 N.W. 47th Ter., Gainesville, Fla. 32606. *Office*—American Entomological Institute, 3005 S.W. 56th Ave., Gainesville, Fla. 32608.

CAREER: Cornell University, Ithaca, N.Y., instructor in biology, 1946-48; U.S. Department of Agriculture, Washington, D.C., beetle taxonomist, 1948-54; Saint John Fisher College, Rochester, N.Y., associate professor of biology, 1954-58; Catholic University of America, Washington, D.C., associate professor, 1958-61, professor of biology, 1961-66, chairman of department, 1962-66, founder and director of Institute for the Study of Natural Species, 1961-66; Purdue University, Lafayette, Ind., professor of entomology, 1966-70; Florida State University, Tallahassee, adjunct professor of biology, 1971-73; Siena College, Loudonville, N.Y., professor of biology, 1973-79; University of Florida, Gainesville, professor of entomology, 1982—.

Visiting professor, University of Oklahoma, 1969. Collaborator, U.S. Department of Agriculture, 1954—; research associate, Florida State Collection of Arthropods, 1964—; vice-president and member of board of directors, Bio-Rand Foundation, Inc., 1968-73; managing director, North American Beetle Fauna Project, 1971—; co-founder and member of board of directors, Biological Research Institute of America, 1973-80; president, World Digests, Inc., 1973-74. *Military service:* U.S. Army, 1942-45; became technical sergeant.

MEMBER: International Congress of Entomology, International Congress of Systematic and Evolutionary Biology, Botanical Society of America, American Society of Information Science, Entomological Society of America, (vice-president, 1967), American Society of Plant Taxonomists, American Ornithological Society, American Institute of Biological Sciences, American Association for the Advancement of Science (fellow), American Institute of Biological Science, American Entomological Institute (vice-president), Coleopterists Society (president, 1971), Society of Systematic Zoology (member of council, 1960-63), Royal Entomological Society of London (fellow), Entomological Society of Washington (president, 1964), Sigma Xi, Phi Kappa Phi, Cosmos Club (Washington), Explorers Club (New York).

AWARDS, HONORS: American Philosophical Society grants, 1957, 1959, 1968; National Science Foundation grant, 1958-65; McDonald Foundation grant, 1964-66; U.S. Army grant, 1966-67; Henry L. Beadel fellowship from Tall Timbers Research, Inc., 1971-73; Rockefeller grant, 1973.

WRITINGS:

(With D. C. Braungart) *Introduction to Plant Biology*, Mosby, 1962, 4th edition published as *Plant Biology: A Concise Introduction*, 1977.

The Beetles of the United States, Catholic University of America, 1963.

(With G. Allan Samuelson) *Directory of Coleoptera Collections of North America*, Purdue University Press, 1969.

Entomological Information Storage and Retrieval, Bio-Rand Foundation, 1970.

(With N. M. Downie) *How to Know the Beetles*, W. C. Brown, 1980.

(With R. L. Jacques, Jr.) *Simon & Schuster's Guide to American Insects*, Simon & Schuster, 1980.

American Insect: A Handbook of the Insects of America North of Mexico, Van Nostrand, 1985.

(With Jacques) *Insect Life: A Field Entomology Manual for the Amateur Naturalist*, Prentice-Hall, 1985.

Also author of *The Naturalists Directory and Almanac*, 43rd edition, 1978, and *Checklist of the Beetles of North and Central America and West Indies*, ten volumes, 1983.

Contributor to proceedings and to journals in his field. *Coleopterists' Bulletin*, founder and editor, 1947-61, member of editorial board, 1962—; editor of *Studies on Speciation*, 1962—, *Entomological News*, 1967-72, and *Bulletin of Tall Timbers Research Station*, 1971-73; editor and publisher, *Insect World Digest*, 1973—.

WORK IN PROGRESS: American Beetles: A Handbook of the Coleoptera of America North of Mexico, for Flora & Fauna Publications.

SIDELIGHTS: Ross H. Arnett, Jr., told *CA:* "I have two major concerns: 1) teaching people to love the earth on which we live so they will treat it as if it were their own; 2) providing people with the necessary tools to help them learn about the plants and animals of the world. After years of teaching, moving, and traveling throughout much of the world during summers, I have settled in Gainesville, Florida, to write those books that are relevant to these interests."

*   *   *

ATHANASSIADIS, Nikos 1904-

PERSONAL: Born July 14, 1904, in Mytilene, Island of Lesbos, Greece; son of Apostolos (an industrial worker) and Irena (Michailidi) Athanassiadis; married Vanna Lambropoulou, June 6, 1944; children: Apostolos. *Education:* Educated at Lyceum of Mytilene of the Island of Lesbos, Greece.

ADDRESSES: Home—Spefsippou No. 39, Athens, Greece.

CAREER: Agricultural Bank of Greece, Athens, Greece, director, 1935-58; writer, 1958—. Member of Greek International Council on Social Welfare. *Military service:* Greek Navy, 1925-27.

MEMBER: Greek National Authors Society (member of administrative board).

AWARDS, HONORS: "Ourani" literary award (Greece), 1957, for *Pera apo to anthropino;* first government prize, 1972, for *Theos archaios.*

WRITINGS:

NOVELS

To vivlio tou nissiou mou (title means "The Book of My Island"), Xenos (Athens), 1950.
Pera apo to anthropino (title means "Beyond the Human"), Stegi tou Vivliou (Athens), 1956, 3rd edition, Dorikos (Athens), 1972.

Stavrossi choris anastassi (title means "Crucifixion without Resurrection"), Fexis (Athens), 1963, 2nd edition, Dorikos, 1972.

To gymno koritsi, Alvin Redman-Hellas (Athens), 1964, 2nd edition, Dorikos, 1968, translation by Stefanos Zotos published as *A Naked Girl,* Orion Press, 1968.

Psilafitos kosmos (title means "The Vague World"), Dorikos, 1970.

Thyella ke Galini, Dorikos, 1975.

Aetiotou Delfon, Dorikos, 1978.

Anonymoi, Dorikos, 1978.

Symbal, the Delphin of the Ocean, Dorikos, 1979.

PLAYS

"Protomi" (title means "The Bust"), first produced in 1933.

"Triti praxi" (title means "The Third Act"), first produced in 1934.

OTHER

(Contributor of translation) *Der Tod des grossen Ochsen* (anthology), Paul Neff Verlag (Vienna), 1962.

Theos archaios (title means "Ancient God"; collection of fourteen short stories), Sideris (Athens), 1971.

Contributor of articles, critiques, and short novels to literary journals and periodicals in various countries.

WORK IN PROGRESS: Two novels, *To karo me ta scoupidia* (title means "The Rublish Card"), and *Den tha xanagyrisso spiti* (title means "I Won't Come Back Home").

SIDELIGHTS: Nikos Athanassiadis's novels have been translated into several languages, including French, German, Spanish, Danish, and Japanese.

BIOGRAPHICAL/CRITICAL SOURCES:

BOOKS

Sachinis, Apostolos, *Nei pezographi,* J. D. Kollaros, 1965.

Valetas, G., *Epitomi istoria tis neoellinikis logotechnias,* Petros K. Ranos, 1966.

PERIODICALS

Best Sellers, November 1, 1968.

Le Figaro, June 20, 1966.

Le Monde, August 20, 1966.

Les Nouvelles Litteraires, March 4, 1965, August 18, 1966.

National Herald, November 20, 1966.

New York Times, October 9, 1966.

New York Times Book Review, November 17, 1968.

Sunday Advocate, January 26, 1969.

*   *   *

ATKINS, G(eorge) Pope 1934-

PERSONAL: Born March 4, 1934, in Austin, Tex.; son of George Taylor (in advertising, printing, and publishing business) and Louise (Long) Atkins; married Joan Jorns, August 27, 1960; children: Forrest Taylor, Virginia Louise, Kristen Audra. *Education:* University of Texas, Main University (now University of Texas at Austin), B.A., 1955, graduate study, 1959-60; American University, Washington, D.C., M.A., 1962, Ph.D., 1966.

ADDRESSES: Home—34 Decatur Ave., Annapolis, Md. 21403. *Office*—Department of Political Science, U.S. Naval Academy, Annapolis, Md. 21401.

CAREER: First National City Bank (now Citibank of New York), New York, N.Y., Cordoba and Buenos Aires, Argentina, and Guayaquil, Ecuador, bank officer in Overseas Division, 1962-66; U.S. Naval Academy, Annapolis, Md., assistant professor, 1966-70, associate professor, 1970-77, professor of political science, 1977—, chairman of department, 1979-83. Taught course at Universidad de Guayaquil; faculty advisor, World Academy, 1969; visiting assistant professor, American University, summer, 1970; guest scholar, Brookings Institution, 1972; visiting associate professor, University of Texas at Austin, summers, 1973, 1974, and 1976; University of Maryland, adjunct associate professor, 1974—, professor, 1977-78; visiting professor, Institute of Latin American Studies, University of London, 1977; research associate, Santo Domingo, summer, 1978; visiting professor, London School of Economics and Political Science, 1983-84; visiting research associate, Ebenhausen, Germany; adjunct fellow, Georgetown University, 1985—. *Military service:* U.S. Navy, 1955-59; served as aviator.

MEMBER: International Studies Association, American Political Science Association, American Association of University Professors (president of Naval Academy chapter, 1976-78), Latin American Studies Association, British Society of Latin American Studies, Middle Atlantic Council of Latin American Studies (member of organizing executive committee, 1978-80; program chair of annual conference, 1981; president, 1982-83), Inter-American Council of Washington, D.C. (president, 1970-71).

AWARDS, HONORS: Distinguished Alumnus, American University, School of International Service, 1985.

WRITINGS:

(Contributor) Paolo E. Coletta, editor, *Threshold to American Internationalism,* Exposition Press, 1970.

(With Larman C. Wilson) *The United States and the Trujillo Regime,* Rutgers University Press, 1972.

(Contributor) Charles Cochran, editor, *Civil-Military Relations,* Free Press, 1974.

(Contributor) Harold E. Davis, Wilson, and others, editors, *Latin American Foreign Policies,* Johns Hopkins University Press, 1975.

Latin America in the International Political System, Free Press, 1977.

Arms and Politics in the Dominican Republic, Westview, 1981.

(Contributor) J. W. Hopkins, editor, *Latin America and Caribbean Contemporary Record,* Holmes & Meier, Volume I, 1983, Volume II, 1984, Volume IV, 1986.

(Contributor) Howard J. Wiarda, editor, *Iberia and Latin America,* American Enterprise Institute for Public Policy Research, 1985.

Contributor of articles and reviews to periodicals, including *Social Science Quarterly, Journal of Latin American Studies, American Political Science Review, Hispanic American Historical Review,* and *Chronicle.* Member of editorial advisory board, *Journal of Political and Military Sociology,* 1972—; member of editorial board, *Millennium: Journal of International Studies,* 1983-84.

*   *   *

AVRAMOVIC, Dragoslav 1919-

PERSONAL: Born October 14, 1919, in Skoplje, Yugoslavia; son of Nikoa and Jelena (Sahovic) Avramovic; married Marija

Jovanovic, May 23, 1943; children: Zoran, Mila, Dora. *Education:* University of Belgrade, Ph.D., 1956.

ADDRESSES: Home—13200 Cleveland Dr., Rockville, Md. 20850. *Office*—Bank of Credit and Commerce International, S.A., Washington, D.C. Representative Officer, 1667 K St. N.W., Washington, D.C. 20006.

CAREER: Yugoslav Monetary Reform Commission, Belgrade, Yugoslavia, secretary, 1945-46; National Bank of Yugoslavia, Belgrade, deputy secretary, 1946-47, secretary, 1948-50; University of Belgrade, Belgrade, lecturer in economics, 1947-53; International Bank for Reconstruction and Development, Washington, D.C., staff member, 1953-77, General Studies Division, chief of economic staff, 1959-63, assistant director of economics department, 1964, director of special economic studies, 1965-67, director of commodity stabilization studies, 1968, director of industrialization studies in South Asia, 1969, Latin American Department, economic advisor, 1970-72, Latin American and the Caribbean Regional Office, chief economist, 1973-74, senior advisor to development policy staff, 1975-76, director of development economics department, 1976-77; Independent Commission on International Development Issues, Geneva, Switzerland, director of the secretariat, 1978-79; senior adviser, Office of the Secretary General, United Nations Conference on Trade and Development, 1980-84; Bank of Credit and Commerce International, S.A., Washington, D.C., special adviser on international commodity stabilization, 1984—.

Headed economic mission to Philippines, 1961-62, Nigeria, 1965-66, Algeria, 1966, Brazil, 1967, Iran, 1969, Pakistan, 1969, and Colombia, 1970. Advisor, Yugoslav Ministry of Finance and National Bank of Yugoslavia, 1950-53; special advisor on international commodity stabilization, United Nations Conference on Trade and Development, 1974-75.

WRITINGS:

Postwar Economic Growth in Southeast Asia, International Bank for Reconstruction and Development, 1955.
Debt Servicing Capacity and Postwar Growth in International Indebtedness, Johns Hopkins Press, 1958.
The Coffee Problem, International Bank for Reconstruction and Development, 1958, 2nd edition, 1960.
Debt Servicing Problems of Low-Income Countries, Johns Hopkins Press, 1960.
The Commodity Problem, International Bank for Reconstruction and Development, 1964.
Economic Growth and External Debt, Johns Hopkins Press, 1965.

International Trade, Industrialization, and Growth, International Bank for Reconstruction and Development, 1968.
(Editor and coordinating author) *Economic Growth of Colombia: Problems and Prospects,* Johns Hopkins Press, 1972. .
Stabilization, Adjustment, and Diversification: A Study of the Weakest Commodities Produced by the Poorest Regions, International Bank for Reconstruction and Development, 1976.
The Common Fund: Why and What Kind?, International Bank for Reconstruction and Development, 1978.
(Editor) *The Brandt Commission Papers,* Brandt Commission, 1981.
The Developing Countries after Cancun: The Financial Problem and Related Issues, International Bank for Reconstruction and Development, 1982.
(Editor) *South-South Financial Cooperation: Approaches to the Current Crisis,* Pinter, 1983.
The Debt Problem of Developing Countries at End-1982, [St. Gallen], 1983.
(Editor) *Third World Alternative to the Present International Financial Institutions,* Pinter, 1983.

Also author of papers and monographs on international banking issues.

SIDELIGHTS: Dragoslav Avramovic is an expert on international finance and development. In 1974 he and three other members of the International Bank for Reconstruction and Development took part in a *New York Times* discussion concerning food production problems in the developing countries. Avramovic asserted that "despite a continuance of enormous problems, there have been substantial advances in a large part of the developing world in the building of skills, technical capacity and capabilities for using resources." Speaking of South America's more developed regions, Avramovic said that "the situation is likely to be considerably better than in the past. Prospects are that [the production of] both foodgrains and livestock will expand. . . ." His optimism was tempered, however, by the anticipation of rising fuel costs. "Developing countries that import oil . . . will not have an easy situation." He explained that those countries with a growing export trade will be able to meet rising fuel costs whereas those with little trade will be able to purchase even less as prices rise.

Some of Dragoslav Avramovic's writings have been translated into Spanish.

BIOGRAPHICAL/CRITICAL SOURCES:

PERIODICALS

New York Times, January 27, 1974.

B

BAILEY, George 1919-

PERSONAL: Born November 28, 1919, in Chicago, Ill.; son of George Theodore (a steward) and Ila Ruth (Jacobson) Bailey; married Beate Ross, September 27, 1949; children: Ariane Eliza. *Education:* Columbia University, B.A., 1943; Magdalen College, Oxford, B.A. and M.A., 1949.

ADDRESSES: Agent—Carl Brandt, Brandt & Brandt Literary Agents, Inc., 1501 Broadway, New York, N.Y. 10036.

CAREER: U.S. Army, civilian employee in Germany, 1950-55, as resettlement officer, 1950-51, and Russian liaison officer at Supreme Headquarters, Berlin, 1951-55; *Reporter,* New York City, foreign correspondent, 1956-67, executive editor, 1967-68; *Harper's,* New York City, foreign correspondent, 1968-70; currently editor of international magazine, *Kontinent,* based in Berlin. Commentator on television and radio. *Military service:* U.S. Army, 1943-46; became first lieutenant; received Bronze Star.

AWARDS, HONORS: Award of Oveseas Press Club for best magazine reporting of foreign affairs, 1960.

WRITINGS:

(With Seymour Freidin) *The Experts,* Macmillan, 1968.
Germans: The Biography of an Obsession, World Publishing, 1972.
The Strauss Family: The Era of the Great Waltz, Pan Books, 1972.
(With others) *Munich,* Time-Life, 1981.
(Editor) *Kontinent Four: Contemporary Russian Writers,* Avon, 1982.

Contributor to *C. S. Lewis Speaks.* Contributor of about eighty articles and short stories to magazines.

WORK IN PROGRESS: "Class Reunion," a play.

SIDELIGHTS: George Bailey has spent thirty-one years abroad, mainly in eastern Europe, but also as a resident in the Middle and Far East. Besides Russian, he speaks German, French, Hungarian, Greek, Czech, Italian, Serbo-Croat, and Spanish.

BIOGRAPHICAL/CRITICAL SOURCES:

PERIODICALS

Christian Science Monitor, June 20, 1968.
New York Times, June 29, 1968.
Washington Post, July 18, 1968.†

*   *   *

BAKER, Augusta 1911-

PERSONAL: Born April 1, 1911, in Baltimore, Md.; daughter of Winfort J. and Mabel (Gough) Braxston; married second husband, Gordon Alexander, November 23, 1944; children: (first marriage) James Henry Baker III. *Education:* New York College for Teachers (now State University of New York at Albany), A.B., 1933, B.S. in Library Science, 1934. *Religion:* Presbyterian.

ADDRESSES: Home—830 Armour St., Columbia, S.C. 29203.

CAREER: New York Public Library, New York, N.Y., children's librarian, 1937-53, assistant coordinator and storytelling specialist, 1953-61, coordinator of children's services, 1961-74; University of South Carolina, College of Library and Information Sciences, storyteller-in-residence, 1980—. Visting lecturer, Columbia University, 1955-79. Organized children's library service for Trinidad Public Library, Port of Spain, Trinidad, 1953. Founded James Weldon Johnson Memorial Collection at the Countee Cullen Regional Branch of the New York Public Library. Broadcaster of weekly series, "The World of Children's Literature," for WNYC-Radio, beginning 1971. Has served as consultant to various organizations.

MEMBER: International Reading Association, American Library Association (councillor, 1965-72; president of child services division, 1967-68; member of board of directors, 1958-61, 1966-69; member of executive board, 1968-72), Newbery-Caldecott Committee (chairman, 1966), Association of Early Childhood Education, Private Libraries Association, Southeastern Library Association, New York Library Association (member of executive board, 1960), South Carolina Library Association, Friends of Children's Services of the New York Public Library.

AWARDS, HONORS: Dutton-Macrae Award, 1953, for advanced study in field of library work with children; *Parents' Magazine* Medal Award, 1966, for "outstanding service to the nation's children"; Grolier Award from American Library Association, 1968, for "outstanding achievement in guiding and stimulating the reading of children and young people"; Constance Lindsay Skinner Award from Women's National Book Association, 1971; Distinguished Alumni Award from State University of New York at Albany, 1974; Harold Jackson Memorial Award, 1974; honorary doctorate of letters, St. John's University, Jamaica, N.Y., 1978; Regina Medal from Catholic Library Association, 1981.

WRITINGS:

(Editor) *Talking Tree,* Lippincott, 1955.
(Editor) *Golden Lynx,* Lippincott, 1960.
(Editor with Eugenia Garson) *Young Years: Best Loved Stories and Poems for Little Children,* Parents' Magazine Press, 1960.
(Editor) *Once Upon a Time,* 2nd edition, New York Library Association, 1964.
(Contributor) *Come Hither! Papers on Children's Literature and Librarianship,* Yeasayers Press, 1966.
(Editor) *The Black Experience in Children's Books,* New York Public Library, 1971.
Storytelling (sound recording), Children's Book Council, 1975.
(With Ellin Greene) *Storytelling: Art and Technique,* Bowker, 1977.

Contributor of introductions to books. Compiler of numerous reading lists and pamphlets.

AVOCATIONAL INTERESTS: Gardening, civic work.

BIOGRAPHICAL/CRITICAL SOURCES:

BOOKS

Flynn, James J., *Negroes' Achievement in Modern America,* Dodd, 1970.
Josey, E. J., editor, *The Black Librarian in America,* Scarecrow, 1970.

PERIODICALS

Bookwoman, November, 1971.
Horn Book, August, 1971.

*   *   *

BALDRIGE, Letitia (Katherine)

PERSONAL: Born in Miami Beach, Fla.; daughter of H. Malcolm and Regina (Connell) Baldrige; married Robert Hollensteiner (a real estate executive), December 27, 1963; children: Clare Louise, Malcolm Baldrige. *Education:* Vassar College, B.A.; University of Geneva, graduate study. *Politics:* Republican. *Religion:* Catholic.

ADDRESSES: Office—151 East 80th St., New York, N.Y. 10021.

CAREER: Social secretary to Ambassador and Mrs. David Bruce, American Embassy, Paris, France, 1948-51; intelligence officer in Washington, D.C., 1951-53; social secretary to Ambassador Clare Boothe Luce, American Embassy, Rome, Italy, 1953-56; Tiffany & Co., New York City, public relations director, 1956-60; social secretary to Mrs. John F. Kennedy, the White House, Washington, D.C., 1961-63; Letitia Baldrige Enterprises (public relations), Chicago, Ill., president, 1964-69; director of consumer affairs, Burlington Industries, 1969-71; Letitia Baldrige Enterprises, Inc., New York City, president, 1971—. Lecturer and television hostess.

MEMBER: American Institute of Interior Designers (public relations associate member), Institute of International Education (director), National Home Fashions League of New York, Fashion Group of New York, Women's Forum, Woodrow Wilson National Foundation (director), Committee of 200.

WRITINGS:

Roman Candle, Houghton, 1956.
Tiffany Table Settings, Crowell, 1959.
Of Diamonds and Diplomats: An Autobiography of a Happy Life, Houghton, 1968.
Home, Viking, 1970.
Juggling: The Art of Balancing Marriage, Motherhood, and Career, Viking, 1976.
(Reviser) *Amy Vanderbilt's Book of Etiquette,* Doubleday, 1978, published as *Amy Vanderbilt's Everyday Etiquette,* Bantam, 1981.
The Entertainers, Bantam, 1981.

Author of syndicated column, *Los Angeles Times.* Contributor to magazines and newspapers.

SIDELIGHTS: Letitia ("Tish") Baldrige, who was the White House social secretary during the Kennedy administration, writes in her book *Amy Vanderbilt's Everyday Etiquette* that good manners are "nothing more than a combination of kindness and efficiency." In revising Vanderbilt's classic work on the social graces, Baldrige, according to Clarence Petersen in the *Chicago Tribune Book World,* addresses many forms of modern behavior, including "how to fight teen drug problems (talk openly and honestly) and . . . 16 ways to combat loneliness if you're suddenly single."

BIOGRAPHICAL/CRITICAL SOURCES:

BOOKS

Baldrige, Letitia, *Amy Vanderbilt's Everyday Etiquette,* Bantam, 1981.

PERIODICALS

Chicago Tribune Book World, April 26, 1981.

*   *   *

BALDWIN, Stan(ley C.) 1929-

PERSONAL: Born December 17, 1929, in Bend, Ore.; son of Leonard Rite (a cowboy) and Irma Mae (Brown) Baldwin; married Marjorie Antoinette Iverson, December 17, 1948; children: Kathleen (Mrs. Morton Holland), Krystal (Mrs. Arthur W. Brown), Steven, Karen (Mrs. David Kraus), Gregory Laverne Todd. *Education:* Attended Powellhurst College, Prairie Bible Institute, and Oregon State University.

ADDRESSES: Home—17901 South Canter Lane, Oregon City, Ore. 97045.

CAREER: Pastor of community church in Albany, Ore., 1955-62, and of Baptist churches in Corvallis, Ore., 1962-65, and Burns, Ore., 1965-69; Scripture Press, Wheaton, Ill., editor of Victor Books and consulting editor for *Power for Living,* 1970-75; free-lance writer and lecturer, 1975—. Pastor of Village Church in Carol Stream, Ill., 1970-75.

WRITINGS:

Will the Real Good Guys Please Stand?, Victor Books, 1971.
Games Satan Plays, Victor Books, 1971.
(With wife, Marjorie Baldwin) *Tough Questions Boys Ask,* Victor Books, 1972.
(With M. Baldwin) *Tough Questions Girls Ask,* Victor Books, 1972.

(With James D. Mallory) *The Kink and I,* Victor Books, 1973.
(With Hank Aaron and Jerry Jenkins) *Bad Henry,* Chilton, 1974.
What Did Jesus Say about That?, Victor Books, 1975.
What Makes You So Special?, Baker Book, 1977.
(With Malcolm MacGregor) *Your Money Matters,* Bethany House, 1977.
(With Jerry Cook) *Love, Acceptance and Forgiveness,* Regal Books, 1979.
A True View of You, Regal Books, 1982.
How to Build Your Christian Character, Victor Books, 1982.
Bruised But Not Broken, Multnomah, 1985.

Contributor of articles and stories to periodicals, including *Christianity Today, Eternity, Moody Monthly,* and *Guideposts.*

WORK IN PROGRESS: A book, tentatively entitled *At Cross Purposes,* for Multnomah; a book on Christian attitudes toward the secular workplace; an update and total revision of *Your Money Matters,* with Malcolm MacGregor; and a second book with Jerry Cook.

SIDELIGHTS: Stan Baldwin told *CA:* "I write as a ministry: to influence people, teach them, communicate truth to them. I suppose I'm nothing but a preacher at heart, only I've found a bigger pulpit—the printed page.

"It was an awesome experience for me, early in my career, to attend a Billy Graham crusade in Chicago and see 25,000 people gathered to hear the evangelist. I realized then that almost everything I write reaches an audience that large and maybe ten times larger.

"So I must write, I suspect, for the same reason Graham must preach. It's the most effective use I can make of my talents and represents an opportunity I cannot neglect. How else could I reach such multitudes, including people who read only German, Spanish, French, Japanese, or Indonesian, into all of which at least some of my works have been translated?

"As a co-author, I am able also to provide an important service by teaming with people who have something vitally important to say but lack the skill or time to say it in writing. The large success of my books of this type has brought many people to seek my services as a co-author. I try to limit my involvement to those people with whom I feel a strong kinship.

"I find writing hard work. I'm an active person, and it's difficult to sit inside at a typewriter when the whole world beckons outside. Often I spend the earliest hours of my day writing and then give in to the call of other things. But I keep at the writing relentlessly, slow as the progress seems, because I know something worthwhile will eventually emerge."

AVOCATIONAL INTERESTS: Sports, fishing, property development, automobile mechanics, home and yard work, boating, water skiing, travel (has visited Mexico, Israel, Asia, Africa, and Europe).

*   *   *

BALL, Howard   1937-

PERSONAL: Born August 13, 1937, in New York, N.Y.; son of Abe (a businessman) and Fay (Kintish) Ball; married Carol Neidell, July 7, 1963; children: Susan Gabrielle, Sheryl Lisa, Melissa Paige. *Education:* Hunter College (now Hunter College of the City University of New York), B.A., 1960; Rutgers University, M.A., 1963, Ph.D., 1970.

ADDRESSES: Office—Office of the Dean, College of Social and Behavioral Science, University of Utah, Salt Lake City, Utah 84112.

CAREER: Rutgers University, New Brunswick, N.J., instructor in political science, 1960-65; Hofstra University, Hempstead, N.Y., assistant professor of political science, beginning 1965; Mississippi State University, Starkville, professor of political science, 1976-82; University of Utah, Salt Lake City, professor, 1982—, chairman, 1982-83, dean of the College of Social and Behavioral Science, 1983—. *Military service:* U.S. Air Force National Guard, 1958-66; became staff sergeant.

MEMBER: National Association of Schools of Public Affairs and Administrators, American Political Science Association, Pi Sigma Alpha.

WRITINGS:

(Editor with Thomas P. Lauth, Jr.) *Changing Perspectives in Contemporary Political Analysis,* Prentice-Hall, 1971.
The Warren Court's Conceptions of Democracy: An Evaluation of the Supreme Court's Apportionment Opinions, Fairleigh Dickenson University Press, 1971.
The Vision and the Dream of Justice Hugo L. Black: An Examination of a Judicial Philosophy, University of Alabama Press, 1975.
No Pledge of Privacy: The Watergate Tapes Litigation, 1973-1974, Kennikat, 1977.
Judicial Craftsmanship or Fiat?: Direct Overturn by the United States Supreme Court, Greenwood Press, 1978.
Courts and Politics: The Federal Judicial System, Prentice-Hall, 1980.
Constitutional Powers: Cases on the Separation of Powers and Federalism, West Publishing, 1980.
Compromised Compliance: The 1965 Voting Rights Act, Greenwood Press, 1982.
Federal Regulatory Agencies, Prentice-Hall, 1984.
Controlling Regulatory Sprawl: Presidential Strategies from Nixon to Reagan, Greenwood Press, 1984.
Justice Downwind, Oxford University Press, 1986.

Contributor to periodicals, including *Hofstra Review* and *Annals.*

WORK IN PROGRESS: Civil Rights Groups in America; Justices Black and Douglas.

*   *   *

BARCLAY, Bill
See MOORCOCK, Michael (John)

*   *   *

BARCLAY, William Ewert
See MOORCOCK, Michael (John)

*   *   *

BARKER, Larry L(ee)   1941-

PERSONAL: Born November 22, 1941, in Wilmington, Ohio; son of Milford (a teacher) and Ruth Maxine (a teacher) Barker; children: Theodore Allen, Robert Milford. *Education:* Ohio University, A.B., 1962, M.A., 1963, Ph.D., 1965.

ADDRESSES: Home—540 North College, Auburn, Ala. 36830. *Office*—Department of Speech Communication, Auburn University, Auburn, Ala. 36849.

CAREER: Southern Illinois University at Carbondale, assistant professor of speech, 1965-66; Purdue University, West Lafayette, Ind., assistant professor of speech, 1966-69; Florida State University, Tallahassee, associate professor, 1969-71, professor of communications, 1971-75; Auburn University, Auburn, Ala., alumni professor, 1975—.

MEMBER: International Communication Association, Speech Communication Association of America, American Educational Research Association, American Psychological Association, Southern Speech Association, Tau Kappa Alpha, Phi Mu Alpha, Kappa Kappa Psi, Phi Delta Kappa.

WRITINGS:

Speech: Interpersonal Communication, Chandler Publishing, 1967, revised edition, 1974.
Behavioral Objectives and Instruction, Allyn & Bacon, 1970.
Listening Behavior, Prentice-Hall, 1971.
Speech Communication Behavior: Perspectives and Principles, Prentice-Hall, 1971.
Communication, Prentice-Hall, 1978.
Groups in Process, Prentice-Hall, 1978.
Communication in the Classroom, Prentice-Hall, 1982.
Effective Listening, Addison-Wesley, 1983.
Nonverbal Communication, Addison-Wesley, 1983.
Groups in Process, Prentice-Hall, 1983.

Contributor to academic journals.

WORK IN PROGRESS: Research on interpersonal communication and professional opportunities in the field of speech communication.

*   *   *

BARMASH, Isadore 1921-

PERSONAL: Born November 16, 1921, in Philadelphia, Pa.; son of Samuel (a tailor) and Sarah (Griff) Barmash; married Sarah Jasnoff; children: Elaine (Mrs. Morris Charnow), Stanley, Marilyn (Mrs. Michael Weinberger), Pamela. *Education:* Charles Morris Price School, diploma in journalism, 1941.

ADDRESSES: Home—85-33 215th St., Hollis Hills, New York, N.Y. 11427. *Office—New York Times,* 229 West 43rd St., New York, N.Y. 10036. *Agent*—International Creative Management, 40 West 57th St., New York, N.Y. 10019.

CAREER: Fairchild Publications, New York City, bureau chief, copy chief, managing editor, and editor-in-chief, 1946-62; *New York Herald Tribune,* New York City, feature writer, 1962-65; *New York Times,* New York City, assistant to financial editor, 1965—. Lecturer at School of Journalism, University of Missouri, 1979. *Military service:* U.S. Army, 1942-45; became staff sergeant.

MEMBER: Authors Guild, Authors League of America, American Newspaper Guild, Actor's Studio (member of playwriting unit).

AWARDS, HONORS: Certificate of distinction, Charles Morris Price School, 1975.

WRITINGS:

The Self-Made Man, Macmillan, 1969.
Welcome to Our Conglomerate: You're Fired (Book-of-the-Month Club selection), Delacorte, 1971.
Net Net (novel), Macmillan, 1972.
(Editor) *Great Business Disasters,* Playboy Press, 1973.

The World Is Full of It, Delacorte, 1974.
For the Good of the Company, Grossett, 1976.
The Chief Executives, Lippincott, 1978.
More Than They Bargained for: The Rise and Fall of Korvettes, Lebhar-Friedman, 1981.
"Always Live Better Than Your Clients," Dodd, 1983.

Also author of two plays. Columnist for *Harper's Bazaar,* 1971-72. Contributor to *New York Times Magazine.*

SIDELIGHTS: Isadore Barmash's *More Than They Bargained for: The Rise and Fall of Korvettes* chronicles the fortunes of Korvettes, the first discount chain store. Established in New York City by Gene Ferkauf in the years following World War II, Korvettes eventually inspired dozens of imitators, including K-Mart. When Korvettes began nationwide expansion in the 1950s, Ferkauf found himself unable to handle the management of his operation, and so decided to merge his business with Charles Bassine's Spartans Industries. Bassine raised prices while filling Korvettes with low-grade products, thus ruining the reputation for quality that Ferkauf had so carefully established. The store fell on hard times and closed in 1981.

Barmash, a longtime business reporter, has observed the fortunes of Korvettes from its earliest days; he estimates that he has written one hundred articles about the company since the 1950s. Robert Sobel declares in the *New York Times* that *More Than They Bargained for* is a "penetrating and lively history" of the discount chain. Barmash "clearly considers Mr. Ferkauf the 'hero' of this saga, a man who built well but expanded beyond his capabilities and couldn't make the necessary adjustments. . . . Mr. Barmash shows why this happened, and in the process offers the reader a short course in store management and marketing techniques. These are his strong suits; he is weakened . . . when it comes to financial analysis. . . . In the end, however, this is a most satisfying and enjoyable book," concludes Sobel.

BIOGRAPHICAL/CRITICAL SOURCES:

PERIODICALS

New York Times, December 30, 1981, November 14, 1983.
New York Times Book Review, December 26, 1976.
Saturday Review, September 10, 1971.

*   *   *

BARRATT-BROWN, Michael 1918-

PERSONAL: Born March 15, 1918, in Birmingham, England; son of Alfred (a college principal) and Doris Eileen (Cockshott) Barratt-Brown; married Frances Mary Lloyd, August 8, 1940 (divorced, June, 1946); married Eleanor Mary Singer (a medical practitioner), July 15, 1946; children: Christopher John, Richard Rollo, Daniel, Deborah. *Education:* Corpus Christi College, Oxford, B.A., 1940, M.A., 1945. *Politics:* Labour. *Religion:* None.

ADDRESSES: Home—Robin Hood Farm, Baslow, near Bakewell, Derbyshire, England.

CAREER: Special assistant to chief of Balkan and Yugoslavian missions, United Nations Relief and Rehabilitation Administration, 1944-47; Cambridge University, Cambridge, England, part-time tutor, 1947-61; University of Sheffield, Sheffield, England, lecturer, 1961-66, senior lecturer in extra-mural studies, 1966-77; Northern College, Barnsley, England, principal, 1977-83. Member of council of Institute for Workers' Control; member of board of directors of Bertrand Russell

Peace Foundation; chairman of Third World Information Network Ltd. and Twin Trading Ltd. Member of editorial board, Spokesman Books.

MEMBER: Royal Statistical Society (fellow), Society of Industrial Tutors (chairman, 1965-77; president, 1978—).

AWARDS, HONORS: Associate fellow of Institute for Developmental Studies, University of Sussex, 1976; fellow of Sheffield City Polytechnic, 1984; honorary doctorate, Open University, 1985.

WRITINGS:

(With John Hughes) *Britain's Crisis and the Common Market*, New Left, 1962.
After Imperialism, Heinemann, 1963, 3rd edition, 1970.
Adult Education for Industrial Workers, National Institute of Adult Education, 1969.
What Economics Is About, Weidenfeld & Nicolson, 1970.
Trade Unions and Rising Prices, Institute for Workers' Control, 1971.
Essays on Imperialism, Spokesman Books, 1972.
From Labourism to Socialism: The Political Economy of Labour in the 1970s, Spokesman Books, 1972.
The Economics of Imperialism, Penguin, 1974.
(With Ken Coates) *Accountability and Industrial Democracy: Evidence to the Bullock Committee*, Institute for Workers' Control, 1976.
Resources and the Environment: A Socialist Perspective, Spokesman Books, 1976.
Full Employment: Priority, Spokesman Books, 1978.
Information at Work, Arrow Books, 1978.
(With Coates) *What Went Wrong*, Spokesman Books, 1979.
(With Coates) *The Right to Useful Work*, Spokesman Books, 1979.
(With Su Shaozhi and others) *Democracy and Socialism in China*, Spokesman Books, 1982.
(With John Eaton and Coates) *An Alternative Economic Strategy for the Labour Movement*, Spokesman Books, 1982.
Models in Political Economy, Penguin Books, 1984.

EDITOR

Red Paper: A Response to the Labour Party's Green Paper, Institute for Workers' Control, 1972.
Europe: Time to Leave—and How to Go, Spokesman Books, 1973.
Anatomy of Underdevelopment: Documents on Economic Policy in the Third World, Spokesman Books, 1974.
(With Coates) *Trade Union Register*, Spokesman Books, 1973 edition, 1975, 1974 edition, 1976.
Social and Economic Study Packs, Greater London Council, 1984-85.

CONTRIBUTOR

Teodor Shanin, editor, *Introduction to the Sociology of Developing Societies*, Macmillan, 1980.
Coates, editor, *How to Win? Democratic Planning and the Abolition of Unemployment: Some Agreed Principles and Some Problems to Be Resolved*, Spokesman Books, 1981.
Anthony Topham, editor, *Planning the Planners: How to Control the Recovery—An Examination of the 1982 TUC-Labour Party Report on Economic Planning and Industrial Democracy*, Spokesman Books, 1983.

Contributor to *Socialist Encyclopaedia*.

OTHER

Member of editorial boards of *Universities, Left Review, New Reasoner, New Left Review, May Day Manifesto*, and *New Socialist*.

WORK IN PROGRESS: The Economics of Resources and Basic Needs; revisions of *What Economics Is About* and *From Labourism to Socialism;* editing more volumes of *Social and Economic Study Packs*.

SIDELIGHTS: Michael Barratt-Brown told *CA:* "I write because I am driven to try to explain to others in simple terms what I believe to be the right way of understanding the complex society we live in. Writing is an extension of my role as a teacher."

*   *   *

BARRINGTON, Michael
See MOORCOCK, Michael (John)

*   *   *

BAUGHN, William Hubert   1918-

PERSONAL: Born August 27, 1918, in Marshall County, Ala.; son of J. W. and Beatrice (Jackson) Baughn; married Mary Morris, February 20, 1945; children: Charles Madiera, William Marsteller. *Education:* University of Alabama, B.S., 1940; University of Virginia, M.A., 1941, Ph.D., 1948.

ADDRESSES: Home—555 Baseline Rd., Boulder, Colo. 80309. *Office*—College of Business and Administration, University of Colorado, Boulder, Colo. 80309.

CAREER: University of Virginia, Charlottesville, instructor, 1941-42, assistant professor, 1946-48; Louisiana State University, Baton Rouge, associate professor, 1948-53, professor, 1953-56; University of Texas, Main University (now University of Texas at Austin), professor of finance, 1956-62, chairman of department, 1958-60, associate dean of College of Business Administration, 1959-62; University of Missouri—Columbia, dean of School of Business and Public Administration, 1962-64; University of Colorado at Boulder, dean of College of Business and Administration, 1964-84, president of university, 1985, acting chancellor, 1985—. Associate director, School of Banking of the South, Louisiana State University, 1952-66; director, Stonier Graduate School of Banking, Rutgers University, 1966—. President, American Assembly of Collegiate Schools of Business, 1973-74. Consultant to American Bankers Association and other business groups. Chairman, Big Eight Athletic Conference, 1970-71, 1978-79. *Military service:* U.S. Army Air Forces, three and one-half years; became lieutenant; currently lieutenant-colonel in U.S. Air Force Reserve.

WRITINGS:

(Co-author) *Financial Planning and Policy*, Harper, 1961.
(Editor with C. E. Walker) *The Bankers Handbook*, Dow Jones-Irwin, 1966, revised edition, 1978.
(Editor) *Advanced Bank Holding Company Management Problems*, Southern Methodist University Press, 1975.
(Editor with Donald R. Mandich) *International Banking Handbook*, Dow Jones-Irwin, 1983.

Also author of several monographs in economics and business.

WORK IN PROGRESS: Research for publication in money and capital market fields.

BAUM, Robert J(ames) 1941-

PERSONAL: Born October 19, 1941, in Chicago, Ill.; son of Adam (a clergyman) and Jean (TerMeer) Baum. *Education:* Northwestern University, B.A. (with honors), 1963; Ohio State University, Ph.D., 1969.

ADDRESSES: Office—Department of Philosophy, University of Florida, Gainesville, Fla. 32611.

CAREER: U.S. Peace Corps, Washington, D.C., visiting lecturer in mathematics at Middle East Technical University, Ankara, Turkey, 1965-67; Rensselaer Polytechnic Institute, Troy, N.Y., assistant professor, 1969-73, associate professor, 1973-79, professor of philosophy, 1979-81, director of Center for the Study of the Human Dimensions of Science and Technology, 1976-81; University of Florida, Gainesville, professor of philosophy, chairman of department, and director of Center for Applied Philosophy and Ethics in the Professions, 1981—. Program director for National Science Foundation, 1974-76.

MEMBER: American Philosophical Association, American Association for the Advancement of Science, Philosophy of Science Association, American Society for Engineering Education, American Association of University Professors, American Civil Liberties Union.

WRITINGS:

(Editor with James Randell) *Ethical Arguments for Analysis,* Holt, 1973, 2nd edition, 1977.
Philosophy and Mathematics, Freeman, Cooper, 1974.
Logic, with workbook, Holt, 1975, revised edition, 1980.
(Editor with Albert Flores) *Ethical Problems in Engineering,* Rensselaer Polytechnic Institute, 1978, revised edition, 1980.
Ethics and Engineering Curricula (monograph), Hastings Center, 1980.

Contributor to philosophy and science journals. Editor of *Business and Professional Ethics Journal.*

*   *   *

BEATTIE, Jessie Louise 1896-

PERSONAL: Born October 2, 1896, in Blair, Ontario, Canada; daughter of Francis Walker and Janet (Fleming) Beattie. *Education:* Attended Galt Collegiate Institute; special courses at University of Buffalo (now State University of New York at Buffalo), 1925-26, and University of Toronto, 1943-44. *Religion:* Protestant.

ADDRESSES: Home—St. Joseph's Villa, 56 Governor's Rd., Dundas, Ontario, Canada L9H 5G7.

CAREER: Librarian in Kitchener, Ontario, Buffalo, N.Y., Preston, Ontario, and Atlantic City, N.J., 1929-30; operator of private school, Blair, Ontario, 1930-34; Community Welfare Council, Toronto, Ontario, director of cultural activities and lecturer on dramatics, 1934-36; Ontario Training School, Galt, house mother, 1937-40; Big Sister Association, Toronto, social worker, 1941-44; free-lance writer, 1944—, earlier as journalist, more recently as author of books.

MEMBER: Canadian Women's Press Club (Hamilton), Canadian Authors Association (Toronto), Tower Poetry Society (Hamilton).

AWARDS, HONORS: Hamilton Arts Council Award for Literary Excellence, for *A Walk through Yesterday;* William Arthur Deacon Arts Council Award, for *A Skylark's Empty Nest;* Canada Council grant.

WRITINGS:

Blown Leaves (poetry), Ryerson, 1929.
Shifting Sails (poetry), Ryerson, 1931.
Hill-Top (novel), Macmillan (Canada), 1935.
Three Measures (novel), Macmillan (Canada), 1939.
(With Donald Green) *White Wings around the World* (travel), Ryerson, 1953.
Along the Road (autobiographical stories), Ryerson, 1954.
John Christie Holland, Ryerson, 1956.
Black Moses (biography), Ryerson, 1958.
The Split in the Sky, Ryerson, 1960.
Hasten the Day (short stories), United Church of Canada, 1961.
Strength for the Bridge: A Chronicle of Japanese Immigration, McClelland & Stewart, 1966.
A Season Past (biography), McClelland & Stewart, 1968.
The Log-Line (biography), McClelland & Stewart, 1972.
Winter Night and Other Poems, D. G. Seldon, 1975.
A Rope in the Hand (biography), D. G. Seldon, 1975.
A Walk through Yesterday (autobiography; Literary Guild selection), McClelland & Stewart, 1976.
William Arthur Deacon: Memoirs of a Literary Friendship (biography), Fleming Press, 1978.
A Skylark's Empty Nest (novel; Literary Guild selection), Fleming Press, 1979.
Black Sheep Folklore of Canada, Fleming Press, 1981.
Goofy Willie Nye (novel), Fleming Press, 1983.

Also author of play "Four-Leafed Clover," 1930, and operetta "Call of the Caravan." Contributor of articles to *Canadian Home Journal, Chatelaine, Liberty,* and to church publications and library and school magazines.

SIDELIGHTS: Plagued by ill health as a child, Jessie Louise Beattie began to write at age nine and published poetry at thirteen and short stories and a serial at eighteen. *Black Moses* and *The Split in the Sky* were chosen for reading courses by the Baptist Church and the United Church of Canada; *The Split in the Sky* was also read in full on Canadian Broadcasting Corp.'s "Trans-Canada Matinee." *A Skylark's Empty Nest* was dedicated by Macmillan to the International Year of the Child.†

*   *   *

BELL, David Victor John 1944-

PERSONAL: Born in 1944 in Toronto, Ontario, Canada; son of Herbert McLean and Violet (Bryan) Bell; married Kaaren Cambelle Macdonald, 1966; children: Kristin Cassandra, Jason David. *Education:* Attended York University, 1962-65; University of Toronto, B.A. (first class honors), 1965; Harvard University, A.M., 1967, Ph.D., 1969.

ADDRESSES: Home—5 Shaindell St., Thornhill, Ontario, Canada L3T 3X5. *Office*—Department of Political Science, York University, 4700 Keele St., Downsview, Ontario, Canada M3J 1P3.

CAREER: Michigan State University, East Lansing, assistant professor of political science, 1969-71; York University, Downsview, Ontario, assistant professor, 1971-73, associate professor, 1973-81, professor of political science, 1981—, dean of graduate studies, 1981—. Visiting professor of peace studies, Juniata College, spring, 1978. Co-founder and president, Grindstone Cooperative Ltd., 1976-81; chairman, Leave Fellowship Selection Committee, Social Science and Humanities Research Council, 1978. Lecturer; has appeared on television and radio programs.

MEMBER: International Studies Association, Canadian Political Science Association, Canadian Association for American Studies (vice-president, 1972-74; president, 1974-76; past president, 1976-79), Canadian Peace Research and Education Association, Association of Canadian Television and Radio Artists.

AWARDS, HONORS: Woodrow Wilson fellowships, 1965, 1967; Canada Council leave fellowship, 1976-77; grants from Canadian Department of Transport, 1977-78, Transport Canada, 1978-79, Social Science and Humanities Research Council, 1979-80, 1984, and Canadian Department of Labour, 1980-81.

WRITINGS:

(With Karl W. Deutsch) *Instructor's Manual to Accompany "Politics and Government"*, Houghton, 1970, 2nd edition (with wife, Kaaren C. M. Bell), 1974.
(Editor with Deutsch and Seymour Martin Lipset) *Issues in Politics and Government*, Houghton, 1970.
(Contributor) Jack Bumsted, editor, *Canadian History before Confederation*, Irwin, 1972.
Resistance and Revolution, Houghton, 1973.
Power, Influence, and Authority, Oxford University Press, 1975.
(Contributor) Paul Fox, editor, *Politics Canada*, 4th edition, McGraw, 1977.
(Contributor) Joseph S. Tulchin, editor, *Hemispheric Perspectives on the United States*, Greenwood Press, 1978.
(With Lorne J. Tepperman) *The Roots of Disunity: A Study of Canadian Political Culture*, McClelland & Stewart, 1979.
(Author of foreword) H. Darling, *The Politics of Freight Rates*, McClelland & Stewart, 1980.
(With M. Goodstadt and others) *Alcohol: Public Education and Social Policy*, Addiction Research Foundation, 1981.
(Author of foreword) David Brooks, *Zero Energy Growth*, McClelland & Stewart, 1981.
(Contributor) Michael Whittington and Glen Williams, editors, *Canadian Politics in the 1980s*, Methuen, 1981.
(Contributor) G. Dlugos and others, editors, *Management under Differing Value Systems*, De Gruyter, 1981.
(Contributor) M. M. Rosenberg, W. B. Shaffir, A. Turowetz, and M. Weinfeld, editors, *An Introduction to Sociology*, Methuen, 1983.
(Author of foreword) Glen Williams, *Not for Export: Toward a Political Economy of Canada's Arrested Industrialization*, McClelland & Stewart, 1983.

Co-editor of a series of monographs, "Canada in Transition: Crises in Development," McClelland & Stewart, 1975—. Contributor of articles and reviews to periodicals, including *Issues in Politics and Government, Journal of Canadian Studies, Yale Review, Newsletter* of Association for Canadian Studies in American Universities, *Windsor Review, Harvard Alumni Bulletin*, and *Canadian Journal of Political Science*. Member of editorial board, *Teaching Political Science* and *International Interactions*, both 1972—; guest editor of a special issue of *International Interactions*, 1979.

AVOCATIONAL INTERESTS: Tennis, squash, touch football, music (has been a professional chorister and jazz bassist).

BENNETT, Dwight
See NEWTON, D(wight) B(ennett)

* * *

BENSON, Mary 1919-

PERSONAL: Born December 9, 1919, in Pretoria, South Africa; daughter of Cyril (an administrator) and Lucy (Stubbs) Benson. *Education:* Attended schools in Australia.

ADDRESSES: Home—34 Langford Ct., Abbey Rd., London N.W.8, England.

CAREER: Secretary with British High Commission, Pretoria, South Africa, 1940-41, and David Lean (film director), London, England, 1947-49; Africa Bureau, London, co-founder and secretary, 1950-57 (lobbied in England and at United Nations on South African issues during that period and later); writer. Active in African Development Trust and National Campaign for the Abolition of Capital Punishment. *Military service:* South African Women's Army, 1941-45; served in Cairo, Algiers, Italy, Greece, and Austria; became captain.

WRITINGS:

Tshekedi Khama, Faber, 1960.
Chief Albert Lutuli of South Africa, Oxford University Press, 1963.
The African Patriots: The Story of the African National Congress of South Africa, Faber, 1963, Encyclopaedia Britannica (Chicago), 1964, revised and enlarged edition published as *South Africa: The Struggle for a Birthright*, Penguin (London), 1966, Funk, 1969.
(Contributor) Nadine Gordimer, editor, *South African Writing Today*, Penguin, 1967.
At the Still Point (novel; also see below), Gambit, 1970.
(Contributor) R. L. Markovitz, editor, *African Politics and Society*, Free Press, 1970.
(Editor) *The Sun Will Rise: Statements from the Dock by Southern African Political Prisoners*, International Defence and Aid Fund, 1974.
Nelson Mandela, Panaf Books, 1980.
(Editor) *Athol Fugard's Notebooks*, Knopf, 1983.

RADIO PLAYS; PRODUCED BY BRITISH BROADCASTING CORP.

"At the Still Point" (based on novel of same title), 1972.
"Nelson Mandela and the Rivonia Trial," 1972.
"The Hour Is Getting Late," 1973.
(Adaptor) Sheila Fugard, "The Castaways," 1974.
"Robben Island," 1976.
"Rainer Maria Rilke: Four Documentaries," 1979-80.
(Adaptor) Ngugiwa Thiong'o, "Petals of Blood," 1980.
"Mr. Wolfe, Mr. Perkins, Dear Max, Dear Tom," 1984.
"The Diffident Rebel," 1985.

OTHER

Contributor to periodicals, including *London Magazine, Times, Guardian, Observer, New Statesman, Spectator*, and *New York Times*.

WORK IN PROGRESS: Her memoirs.

SIDELIGHTS: An outspoken activist against and critic of South Africa's policy of apartheid, Mary Benson notes that she had the "normal prejudiced attitude of white South Africans" until she read Paton's *Cry the Beloved Country* in 1948. She has since studied, lobbied, written, and lectured about her country, testifying before United Nations committees on apartheid and human rights between 1963 and 1985, and before the United States Congressional Committee on South Africa in 1966. While reporting on political trials in South Africa she was put under house arrest and banned from all writing. Finally, in March of 1966, Benson left South Africa and became a political exile.

Since moving to London, England, she has written several books that focus on South African problems. According to Thomas Lask in the *New York Times,* "the slow, inexorable movement to a racist dictatorship is documented" in Benson's *South Africa: The Struggle for a Birthright,* "an impassive chronicle that tries to mask the author's outrage." *At the Still Point* is a novel about a South African journalist who, after having spent several years in London and New York, returns to her native land and covers the trial of several blacks charged with sabotage. She then falls in love with an Afrikaans lawyer and becomes an activist. Though some critics find the subject matter not entirely suited to a novelistic treatment, a *New York Times Book Review* critic indicates that "there is enough action in the book to speak louder than some of its words."

BIOGRAPHICAL/CRITICAL SOURCES:

PERIODICALS

New Republic, February 7, 1970.
New York Times, December 23, 1969.
New York Times Book Review, January 4, 1970.
Observer, May 30, 1971.
Times Literary Supplement, January 12, 1967, July 16, 1971, February 10, 1984.

*   *   *

BERGER, Ivan (Bennett)   1939-
(Bennett Evans, I. L. Grozny, Martin Leynard)

PERSONAL: Born July 9, 1939, in Brooklyn, N.Y.; son of Leynard and Cecelia (Berlin) Berger. *Education:* Attended Yale University, 1957-61.

ADDRESSES: Home and office—161 West 75th St., New York, N.Y. 10023.

CAREER: Broadcast Music, Inc., New York City, writer for "BMI: The Many Worlds of Music," 1964-66; Kameny Associates, New York City, copywriter, 1966-69; free-lance writer, 1969-72; *Popular Mechanics,* New York City, electronics and photography editor, 1972-76; *Popular Electronics,* New York City, senior editor, 1977-78; free-lance writer, 1978-82; *Audio,* New York City, technical editor, 1982—.

MEMBER: Audio Engineering Society.

WRITINGS:

(With Hans Fantel) *The True Sound of Music,* Dutton, 1973.
The New Sound of Stereo, Plume Books, 1985.

Also author, sometimes under pseudonyms, of numerous columns, including "Crosstalk" in *HFD,* 1979-83, "Computer Ease" in *Video,* 1982-84, "Spectrum" and "Roadsigns" in *Audio,* 1983—, *Los Angeles Times* column, 1978-82, and a car stereo column in *Stereo Review,* 1980-82.

WORK IN PROGRESS: Literary Sites in London.

SIDELIGHTS: Ivan Berger told *CA:* "I got into writing because no one had written the book on audio that I needed to read. (I finally have.) I find writing a learning tool: if I need or want to learn something, I get assigned to write about it, so I can't shirk the research. Lately, I've learned to do it on

my own. I try to be accurate, clear, entertaining, and comprehensive, in that order; I sometimes succeed. For me, writing is more a craft than an art, but I'm not ashamed of being a craftsman—they're as rare as artists nowadays."

*   *   *

BERGMAN, Floyd L(awrence)   1927-

PERSONAL: Born June 20, 1927, in Duluth, Minn.; son of Carl August (a laborer) and Anna J. (Larson) Bergman; married Virginia Bort, July 3, 1959; children: Sandra (Mrs. Gary Tallenger), Carol (Mrs. Robert C. Kime III), Elizabeth Ann. *Education:* Attended University of Idaho, 1945-46; University of Minnesota, B.S., 1951, M.A., 1961; Wayne State University, Ed. D., 1966; Florida Atlantic University, post doctoral study, 1976-77.

ADDRESSES: Home and office—37 Deerfield Rd., Hilton Head Island, S.C. 29928.

CAREER: English and social studies teacher in Floodwood, Minn., 1951-55, and Duluth, Minn., 1956-62; Wayne State Univeristy, Detroit, Mich., instructor in education, 1962-66; University of Michigan, Ann Arbor, instructor in education, 1966-76; Westminister Academy, Ft. Lauderdale, Fla., elementary school principal, 1975-84; Hilton Head Christian Academy, Hilton Head Island, S.C., headmaster, 1985-86; The Write People: Writers, Teachers, Consultants, Inc., Hilton Head Island, president, 1985—. *Military service:* U.S. Naval Reserve, 1945-46.

WRITINGS:

(With William Hoth and Ray Budde) *Basic Composition Laboratory: Series III,* Science Research Associates, 1965.
(With Paul O'Dea and Robert Lumsden) *Developing Ideas: An Individualized Writing Sequence,* Science Research Associates, 1966.
Reading: Who, What, When, Where, Why and How, Campus Publishers, 1969.
Occupation: English Teacher—A Methods Laboratory Manual, Campus Publishers, 1969.
(With Glenn Knudsvig) *The Voluntutor's Handbook,* School of Education, University of Michigan, 1971.
Manuscript Diagnosis: The Text-Ray, Campus Publishers, 1974.
(With Mary Bradford, Harold Fine, and Hoth) *From Auditing to Editing* (writing manual), U.S. Government Printing Office, 1974.
The English Teacher's Activities Handbook, Allyn & Bacon, 1976, 2nd editon, 1982.
Duplicating Masters for Improving Composition and Grammar, Allyn & Bacon, 1979.
(With wife, Virginia Bergman) *A Guidebook for Teaching Grammar,* Allyn & Bacon, 1985.

Contributor of articles and cartoons to academic journals, including *English Journal, English Education, College Composition and Communication,* and *Journal of Reading.* Editor of *Michigan English Teacher,* 1968-69.

WORK IN PROGRESS: A K-12 grammar composition program.

SIDELIGHTS: Floyd L. Bergman told *CA:* "My current literary thrust is to provide some practical books for teaching English, reading, and composition. I am particularly interested in expanding and refining an objective manuscript evaluation approach called Sentence Emphasis Editing (or SEE). Most writers in education, government, and industry could improve their messages by recalling a few rhetorical principles and by checking their work using a 'text-ray.' My approach forces writers to place key words in simple subject, verb, and complement positions, rather than in modifying phrases and clauses—a common 'doublespeak' approach. I hope to speed up that process by forming my own writing/training corporation.''

AVOCATIONAL INTERESTS: Reading, cartooning, writing, trailer camping.

*   *   *

BERMAN, Susan 1945-

PERSONAL: Born May 18, 1945, in Minneapolis, Minn.; daughter of Dave (a hotel owner) and Lynell (a dancer; maiden name, Ewald) Berman. *Education:* University of California, Los Angeles, B.A., 1967; University of California, Berkeley, M.A., 1969. *Politics:* Democrat. *Religion:* Jewish.

ADDRESSES: Agent—Rhoda Weyr, William Morris Agency, 1350 Avenue of the Americas, New York, N.Y. 10019.

CAREER: Free-lance journalist. Reporter, *San Francisco Examiner*, San Francisco, Calif., 1971-74; associate editor, *City*, San Francisco, 1975; writer for ''Evening Show,'' KPIX-Television, San Francisco, beginning 1976.

WRITINGS:

Underground Guide to the College of Your Choice, Signet, 1971.
Driver, Give a Soldier a Lift (novel), Putnam, 1976.
Easy Street, Doubleday, 1981.

EDITOR

Clifford T. Fay, Jr., *Basic Financial Accounting for the Hospitality Industry*, Educational Institute of the American Hotel and Motel Association, 1981.
Jack P. Jefferies, *Understanding Hotel-Motel Law*, Educational Institute of the American Hotel and Motel Association, 1982.
Jack D. Ninemeir, *Food and Beverage Security: A Systems Manual for Restaurants, Hotels and Clubs*, CBI Publishing, 1982.

SIDELIGHTS: Susan Berman once told *CA:* ''Although the word at this point is a cliche, interactions are what I write about. I include much about my feelings and perceptions to help the reader identify with my pieces. I was born to write. I grew up in Las Vegas and I handicapped the Academy Awards for my block when I was nine.''

In *Easy Street*, Berman describes growing up in Las Vegas as the daughter of Dave Berman, the owner of several of city's major hotels and reportedly a powerful member of organized crime. Neal Johnston writes in the *New York Times Book Review* that ''Berman grew up as a fairy-tale princess in the world of Vegas gambling. . . . She had the run of her father's Riviera Hotel casino counting room. He was a sometime hoodlum who was not only responsible for an appalling amount of crime but also for helping make Las Vegas what it is today.''

''Susan Berman grew up in an emotional fog about her parents, her origins,'' explains Carolyn See in the *Los Angeles Times*. ''She had been taught—somehow—to be both proud and ashamed of what she came from. . . . [*Easy Street*] is an awesome story, a work of desperate love. Susan Berman fought

her own depression to write it and she won: 'I felt that my father belonged more to Mob mythology than he did to me: now both of my parents are mine. I have reclaimed them forever.' ''

BIOGRAPHICAL/CRITICAL SOURCES:

PERIODICALS

Los Angeles Times, November 9, 1981.
New Yorker, January 4, 1982.
New York Times Book Review, October 24, 1976, November 15, 1981.†

*   *   *

BERTOLINO, James 1942-

PERSONAL: Born October 4, 1942, in Pence, Wis.; son of James A. (a sales manager) and Doris (a teacher; maiden name, Robbins) Bertolino; married Lois Behling, November 29, 1966. *Education:* University of Wisconsin—Oshkosh, B.S., 1970; Washington State University, graduate study, 1970-71; Cornell University, M.F.A., 1973.

ADDRESSES: Home—P.O. Box 1157, Anacortes, Wash. 98221.

CAREER: Cornell University, Ithaca, N.Y., lecturer in English, 1973-74; University of Cincinnati, Cincinnati, Ohio, assistant professor, 1974-77, associate professor of English, 1977-84; Skagit Valley College, Mt. Vernon, Wash., instructor in English, 1984-85. Has conducted creative writing workshops and given poetry readings at high schools, colleges, and writing centers throughout the United States; has taught high school poetry. Member of board of directors, Print Center, Inc., 1972-74; member of editorial board, Ithaca House, 1972-74; member of literature panel, Ohio Arts Council, 1979-80. Founder, Elliston Book Award for small press poetry books, 1975, and Cincinnati Area Poetry Project, 1977. Member of board of consultants, Coordinating Council of Literary Magazines, 1975—.

AWARDS, HONORS: Hart Crane Memorial Foundation award, 1969, for poems appearing in *Foxfire;* Book-of-the-Month Club award for poetry, 1970; winner of Discovery-72 poetry competition sponsored by the New York City YM-YWHA Poetry Center, 1972; National Endowment for the Arts creative writing grant, 1974-75; William Howard Taft summer research fellowship, 1976, 1980; Charles Phelps Taft Memorial Fund grant, 1977, 1981; Ohio Arts Council individual artist grant, 1979; Betty Colladay Book Award, Quarterly Review of Literature Poetry Series, 1985, for *First Credo*.

WRITINGS:

POETRY

(Editor) *Northwest Poets Anthology*, Quixote Press, 1968.
Day of Change, Gunrunner Press, 1968.
Drool, Quixote Press, 1968.
Ceremony, Morgan Press, 1969.
Mr. Nobody, Ox Head Press, 1969.
Stone-Marrow, Anachoreta Press, 1969.
Becoming Human, Road Runner Press, 1970.
Employed, Ithaca House, 1972.
Edging Through, Stone-Marrow Press, 1972.
Soft Rock, Charas Press, 1973.
Making Space for Our Living, Copper Canyon Press, 1975.
Terminal Placebos, New Rivers Press, 1975.

The Gestures, Bonewhistle Press, 1975.

The Alleged Conception, Granite Publications, 1976.

New and Selected Poems, Carnegie-Mellon University Press, 1978.

Are You Tough Enough for the Eighties?, New Rivers Press, 1979.

Precinct Kali and the Gertrude Spicer Story, New Rivers Press, 1982.

First Credo, Quarterly Review of Literature Poetry Series, 1985.

CONTRIBUTOR TO ANTHOLOGIES

New Poetry Out of Wisconsin, edited by August Derleth, Stanton & Lee, 1969.

Stoney Lonesome, edited by Roger Pfingston, Stoney Lonesome Press, 1970.

I Love You All Days/It Is That Simple, edited by Phillip Dacey, Abbey Press, 1970.

Poems One Line and Longer, edited by William Cole, Grossman, 1973.

Heartland II: Poets of the Midwest, edited by Lucien Stryk, Northern Illinois University Press, 1975.

OTHER

Editor of pamphlets for Abraxas Press, 1969-71, and Stone-Marrow Press, 1970-76. Contributor of poems and articles to magazines and newspapers, including *Poetry, Partisan Review, Foxfire, Minnesota Review, Greenfield Review, Sou'wester,* and *Choice.* Editor, *Abraxas,* 1968-71; *Epoch,* assistant editor, 1971-73, poetry editor, spring, 1973; guest poetry editor, *Rapport,* 1974; *Cincinnati Poetry Review,* founder, 1975, co-editor, 1975-81; poetry editor, *Eureka Review,* 1976-81; co-editor, *Cornfield Review,* 1984.

SIDELIGHTS: "An incurable optimism, or perhaps a yearning for lost metaphysical anchors, has given [James Bertolino] an Emersonian vision of this country's creative processes," writes Edward Butscher in *Poet Lore.* As Bertolino told *CA:* "The phenomenon of little magazines and small presses in America over the last [twenty-five] years, explosive in nature, has brought on a kind of renaissance in American poetry, and to a lesser extent, fiction. The energy and health of the wildly proliferate accomplishments in this field have sustained my hopes for the future of American literature."

Employed reveals, according to Butscher, the characteristics of Bertolino's early poetry. "Playful and surreal, often revealing a fondness for scientific and technological references, the poems betray what can only be described as an old-fashioned romanticism in their struggles to fuse modernist consciousness with traditional love and death themes." Bertolino's poetry has evolved a great deal since *Employed,* showing, according to Butscher, the poet's ability to recharge his "emotive batteries." As a result, concludes Butscher, "Bertolino is patently an important factor in the current poetry scene, a poet who has . . . pioneered verse assimilations of the vocabulary and noetic dilations supplied by revolutionary advances in the physical sciences."

BIOGRAPHICAL/CRITICAL SOURCES:

PERIODICALS

Poet Lore, fall, 1984.

BIRD, Lewis P(enhall) 1933-

PERSONAL: Born November 12, 1933, in Dover, N.J.; son of Floyd Bennett and Hettie (Penhall) Bird; married Carole Ann Fiscus (a teacher), June 18, 1960; children: Susan Carole, Kenneth Penhall. *Education:* Nyack College, B.S., 1956; Gordon Divinity School, B.D., 1959; Lutheran School of Theology, Chicago, Ill., S.T.M., 1968; New York University, Ph.D., 1976. *Politics:* Independent.

ADDRESSES: Office—Medical Center of Havertown, 2050 West Chester Pike, Havertown, Pa. 19083.

CAREER: Ordained minister, 1961; assistant minister of church in Elmhurst, Ill., 1959-64; Christian Medical Society, Oak Park, Ill., eastern regional director in Havertown, Pa., 1964—, co-chairman of Medical Ethics Commission. Co-director of Medical and Family Counseling Service of Medical Center of Havertown, 1970—. Associate member of faculty of Kellogg Centre for Advanced Studies in Primary Care at Montreal General Hospital and McGill University, 1978-80. Guest lecturer at colleges and universities, including Barrington College, Eastern Baptist Theological Seminary, West Virginia University, University of North Carolina, and Syracuse University. Delivered testimony to U.S. Senate Subcommittee on Family and Human Services hearing, 1984. Guest on television programs. Consultant, Joseph P. Kennedy, Jr., Foundation, 1977-78, and U.S. Department of Health and Human Services.

MEMBER: American Association of Marriage and Family Therapists (associate member), American Association of Sex Educators, Counselors, and Therapists, Christian Association for Psychological Studies (member of board of directors, 1976-82), Phi Delta Kappa.

WRITINGS:

The Ten Commandments in Modern Medicine, Christian Medical Society, 1965.

(Contributor) Walter O. Spitzer and Carlyle L. Saylor, editors, *Birth Control and the Christian,* Tyndale, 1969.

(With Christopher T. Reilly) *Learning to Love: A Guide to Family Life Education through the Church,* Word, Inc., 1971.

(Contributor) Claude S. Frazier, editor, *Is It Moral to Modify Man?,* C. C Thomas, 1973.

(Contributor) Carl F. H. Henry, editor, *Dictionary of Christian Ethics,* Baker Book, 1973.

(Contributor) Henry, editor, *Horizons of Science: Christian Scholars Speak Out,* Harper, 1978.

You Can Reduce Tension in Your Family, Baker Book, 1980.

(With Fred D. Bergamo) *A Personal Probe: Ethical Problems in Dental Practice,* Christian Medical Society, 1980.

(With others) *A Community of Caring: Helping the Pregnant Adolescent Have a Successful Pregnancy,* Joseph P. Kennedy, Jr., Foundation, 1980.

(Editor with David E. Allen and Robert L. Herrmann and contributor) *Whole-Person Medicine: An International Symposium,* Inter-Varsity Press, 1980.

(Contributor) Hermann, editor, *Whole-Person Medicine in Evangelical Perspective,* Inter-Varsity Press, 1980.

The Mid-Life Syndrome and Maturity, Word, Inc., 1981.

(Contributor) Janet Christie-Seely, *Working with the Family in Primary Care: A Systems Approach to Health and Illness,* Praeger, 1984.

Also author of *Please Treat Me Right: Whole-Person Medicine in Clinical Perspective,* in press; also contributor to Austin H. Kutscher, editor, *Pastoral Care Issues in Experiences of Loss,*

Death, and Bereavement, in press, and to Kutscher, editor, *Suffering and Thanatology: The Patient, Family, Staff, and Community,* in press.

Contributor of about forty articles and reviews to magazines, including *Eternity.* Contributing editor of *Bulletin* of Christian Association for Psychological Studies, 1979—.

WORK IN PROGRESS: Four Models for Modern Marriage.

SIDELIGHTS: Lewis P. Bird told *CA:* "Of considerable interest to me is the creative, valid integration of research studies in marriage, family, and human sexuality with the Biblical tradition. Many of us are aware of areas of conflict, transition, or puzzling problems. To seek a synthesis of truth which permits new and compelling insights to emerge, though not an easy task, nonetheless provides fascinating new blends of reason and revelation. Both the scholar and the father in me rejoice for fresh perspectives. Issues in biomedical ethics furnish areas for continuing research as well, since my association with the Christian Medical Society continues to trigger occasions for study, lecturing, and writing.

"Having roots both in the lake district of northern New Jersey and, on my mother's side, in the Cornish village of Tregrehan Mills has given me an abiding love for hills whose banks slope ultimately waterward. Sunset over the sea has to be one of God's choicest artistic achievements. And, since I turned forty, each day becomes a fresh opportunity to find refreshment from the diverse patterns the going down of the sun can emblazon across the western skies.

"Having sunk further roots in the providence and presence of God, I find both a vigor and a humility for dealing with the ethical issues that marriage, family, and human sexuality studies provide. Personal family experiences, research data, and Judaeo-Christian values seek a blend that offers both fresh insight and creative integration. Then the roles of husband and father are as gratifying as the lecturing and counseling aspects of my career.

"When one is aware of his roots and his destiny, then life has meaning, and writing becomes a vehicle to express a synthesis between twentieth-century problems and eternal values. Such a venture can be rather stress-inducing, since modern dilemmas have a way of vexing the best of minds, and eternal values are not always clear in their application to many of our current questions. Out of such reflection, however, can come creative spurts which move difficult ambiguities at least one step closer to resolution. And out of such work can come a deeper sense of God's involvement with our daily tasks."

AVOCATIONAL INTERESTS: Sailing, antiques, family genealogy, travel, tennis, history, reading, woodworking, his Model-A roadster pickup truck.

*   *   *

BLUM, Carol (Kathlyn) O'Brien   1934-

PERSONAL: Born May 22, 1934, in St. Louis, Mo.; married Martin Blum (a psychoanalyst), 1964; children: Asher, Agnes. *Education:* Washington University, St. Louis, Mo., B.A., 1956; Columbia University, M.A., 1960, Ph.D., 1966.

ADDRESSES: Office—Department of French and Italian, State University of New York at Stony Brook, Stony Brook, N.Y. 11794-3359.

CAREER: Columbia University, New York, N.Y., lecturer in French, 1961-62; State University of New York at Stony Brook,

1962—, began as instructor, became associate professor of French.

MEMBER: American Society for Eighteenth Century Studies, Modern Language Association of America.

AWARDS, HONORS: National Endowment for the Humanities fellow, 1973; Guggenheim fellow, 1975-76.

WRITINGS:

Diderot: The Virtue of a Philosopher, Viking, 1974.
Anne's Head (novel), Dial, 1982.
Rousseau and the Republic of Virtue: Radical Discourse in the French Revolution, Cornell University Press, 1986.

Contributor to periodicals.

SIDELIGHTS: Carol O'Brien Blum's novel *Anne's Head* is based on a tragedy in her father's family during the early part of this century. In this novel, James and Catherine O'Brien are Irish-Catholic immigrants who have successfully raised ten children in turn-of-the-century St. Louis. Trouble begins when the eldest daughter, Anne, becomes involved with a suave lawyer named Chris Schneider. James and Catherine are first upset because Schneider is Protestant; they become even more alarmed upon hearing rumors that he is involved in white slave trade. Their attempts to separate their willful daughter from her lover only cause her to run away to Chicago with him. Before the O'Briens can even attempt to contact Anne, they receive word from Schneider that she is dead and buried. Catherine, believing that her daughter has really been sold into white slavery, sends two of her sons to unearth the coffin and confirm Anne's death.

Blum's evocation of turn-of-the-century St. Louis is highly praised by many reviewers, including Valerie Miner, who writes in the *Los Angeles Times Book Review:* "Blum has created a harrowing set of family tensions. The dialog—a credible mixture of Irish and working-class American—is rich and lively. And St. Louis, from August 1902 to February 1909, is drawn with sharp, engaging detail."

Both Miner and *Washington Post Book World* contributor Joseph McLellan praise *Anne's Head* as much more than a suspense novel. "Her real subject," writes McLellan, "is America's loss of innocence (or, if you prefer, its coming of age). . . . [The O'Brien] family embodies a variety of ways to approach the transition from the Old World to the 20th century—represented on many levels by the St. Louis World's Fair, which looms constantly in the background." Miner agrees that the World's Fair "is an apt metaphor for a story that distinguishes between the promises and realities of the new century."

Concludes McLellan: "Blum's novel works not only as a story of ultimately tragic intensity, but as an evocation of a vanished past in a thousand small details and as a symbolic drama, in which various elements of an adolescent nation encounter one another with painful misunderstanding. . . . And above all [it is] about the simple and terribly complicated plight of being human."

BIOGRAPHICAL/CRITICAL SOURCES:

PERIODICALS

Los Angeles Times Book Review, January 10, 1982.
Washington Post Book World, January 23, 1982.

BODDEWYN, J(ean) J.   1929-

PERSONAL: Surname is pronounced *Bod*-win; born February 3, 1929, in Brussels, Belgium; naturalized U.S. citizen; son of Joseph D. and Gilberte (Toitgans) Boddewyn; married Luella Adams, June 18, 1955 (divorced); married Marilyn Stiefel, December 27, 1979; children: (first marriage) Michele, Noelle, Marc. *Education:* University of Louvain, Commercial Engineer, 1951; University of Oregon, M.B.A., 1952; University of Washington, Seattle, Ph.D., 1964. *Religion:* Roman Catholic.

ADDRESSES: Home—372 Fifth Ave., Apt. 9K, New York, N.Y. 10018. *Office*—Bernard M. Baruch College of the City University of New York, 17 Lexington Ave., New York, N.Y. 10010.

CAREER: Galeries Anspach, Brussels, Belgium, systems and market analyst, 1952-55; Jantzen, Inc., Portland, Ore., time and motion analyst, 1955-57; University of Portland, Portland, instructor, 1957-60, assistant professor of business administration, 1960-64; New York University, Graduate School of Business Administration, New York City, assistant professor, 1964-66, associate professor, 1966-71, professor of international business, 1971-73; Bernard M. Baruch College of the City University of New York, New York City, professor of international business and coordinator of international business programs, 1973—. Lecturer at Portland State College (now University), 1956; visiting professor of international business at Columbia University, summer, 1979. Co-leader at International Executive Training Center, Cahors, France, spring, 1968. Director and organizer of Comparative-Management Workshop at New York University, 1970. Manager of International Business Services (consulting). Member of the marketing, advertising, and distribution committee of the U.S. Council for International Business, 1980—. Consulting editor to various publishers, including McGraw-Hill Book Co., Holt, Rinehart & Winston, Inc., and Prentice-Hall, Inc.

MEMBER: International Academy of Management (fellow), International Studies Association, Academy of International Business (fellow; director of Eastern area, 1969-70, 1973-74; vice-president, 1974-76), Academy of Management (fellow; chairman of International Management Division, 1975-76), European Academy of Marketing, European International Business Academy, Beta Gamma Sigma.

AWARDS, HONORS: Fulbright exchange scholar, 1951-52; Ford Foundation research grants, 1965, 1966, 1967-68, 1969; Research Foundation grants from the City University of New York, 1978—; additional grants from New York University, American Management Association, Scaife Foundation, and U.S. Department of State.

WRITINGS:

(With John Fayerweather and Holger Engberg) *International Business Education: Curriculum Planning,* Graduate School of Business Administration, New York University, 1966.
Comparative Management and Marketing: Text and Readings, Scott, Foresman, 1969.
(Editor) *Comparative Management Teaching, Training, and Research,* New York University, 1970.
Belgian Public Policy towards Retailing since 1789, Division of Business Research, Michigan State University, 1972.
(Editor) *World Business Systems and Environments,* Intext Press, 1972.

(Editor with Stanley C. Hollander) *Public Policy toward Retailing: An International Symposium,* Lexington Books, 1972.
(With Ashok Kapoor) *International Business-Government Relations: U.S. Corporate Experience in Asia and Western Europe,* AMACOM, 1973.
Western European Policies toward U.S. Investors, Institute of Finance, Graduate School of Business Administration, New York University, 1974.
(With Kapoor and Jack N. Behrman) *International Business-Government Communications: U.S. Structures, Actors, and Issues,* Lexington Books, 1975.
Corporate External Affairs, Business International, 1975.
(Editor and author of introduction) *European Industrial Managers: West and East,* International Arts and Sciences Press, 1976.
(With others) *International Divestment: A Survey of Corporate Experience,* Business International, 1976.
Multinational Government Relations: An Action Guide for Corporate Management, International Business-Government Counsellors, 1977.
Premiums, Gifts and Competitions: An International Survey, International Advertising Association, 1978.
(With Katherin Marton) *Comparison Advertising: A Worldwide Study,* Hastings House, 1978.
(With others) *Investment and Divestment Policies of Multinational Corporations in Europe,* Saxon House, 1979.
(With Samuel Watson Dunn and Martin F. Cahill) *How Fifteen Transnational Corporations Manage Public Affairs,* Crain Books, 1979.
(Translator and editor) Marcel Bleustein-Blanchet, *The Rage to Persuade: Confessions of a French Advertising Man,* Chelsea House, 1982.
Comparison Advertising Update, International Advertising Association, 1983.
Medicine Advertising: Regulation and Self-Regulation in Fifty-four Countries (monograph), International Advertising Association, 1985.

CONTRIBUTOR

P. M. Dauten, editor, *Current Issues and Emerging Concepts in Management,* Houghton, 1962.
Joseph W. McGuire, editor, *Interdisciplinary Studies in Business Behavior,* South-Western, 1962.
S. B. Prasad, editor, *Management in International Perspective,* Appleton-Century-Crofts, 1967.
M. S. Sommers and J. B. Kernan, editors, *Comparative Marketing Systems,* Appleton-Century-Crofts, 1968.
M. J. Thomas, editor, *International Marketing Management,* Houghton, 1969.
R. J. Lavidge and R. J. Holloway, editors, *Marketing and Society: The Challenge,* Irwin, 1969.
George Fisk, editor, *Essays in Marketing Theory,* Allyn & Bacon, 1970.
R. I. Hartman and J. T. Wholihan, editors, *The Environment of Business,* Dickenson Publishing, 1971.
Fisk, editor, *New Essays in Marketing Theory,* Allyn & Bacon, 1971.
L. K. Sharpe and W. T. Anderson, editors, *Perspectives on Marketing Management: Functional, Societal, Philosophical,* Allyn & Bacon, 1972.
Kapoor and P. D. Grub, editors, *The Multinational Enterprise in Transition,* Darwin Press, 1972.
H. Koontz and C. O'Donnell, editors, *Management: A Book of Readings,* 3rd edition, McGraw, 1972.

G. A. Steiner, editor, *Business and Society: References and Cases,* Random House, 1972.
George Modelski, editor, *Multinational Corporations and World Order,* Sage Publications, 1972.
C. G. Alexandrides, editor, *International Business Systems Perspectives,* Georgia State University, 1973.
P. E. Toma and A. Gyorgy, editors, *Basic Issues in International Relations,* Allyn & Bacon, 1973.
Fayerweather, editor, *International Business-Government Affairs,* Ballinger, 1973.
McGuire, editor, *Contemporary Management: Issues and Viewpoints,* Prentice-Hall, 1974.
S. P. Sethi and R. H. Holton, editors, *Management of the Multinationals,* Free Press, 1974.
A. R. Negandhi, editor, *Organization Theory and Interorganizational Analysis,* Center for Business and Economic Research, Kent State University, 1974.
R. L. Gamble and R. T. Shaw, editors, *Controversy and Dialogue in Marketing,* Prentice-Hall, 1975.
J. C. Baker and J. K. Ryans, editors, *Multinational Marketing,* Grid Publishing, 1975.
S. J. Warnecke and E. N. Suleiman, editors, *Industrial Policies in Western Europe,* Praeger, 1975.
The Earth as Community, Manhattan College, 1975.
P. M. Boarman and Hans Schollhammer, editors, *Multinational Corporations and Governments,* Praeger, 1975.
L. E. Boone and J. C. Johnson, editors, *Marketing Channels,* Petroleum Publishing, 1977.
Fisk and others, editors, *Future Directions for Marketing,* Marketing Science Institute, 1978.
Walter B. Wentz, *Marketing,* West Publishing, 1979.
Ingo Walter and Tracy Murray, editors, *Handbook of International Business,* Wiley, 1982.
G. M. Hampton and A. P. van Gent, editors, *Marketing Aspects of International Business,* Kluwer-Nijhoff, 1984.
Wolfgang Streeck and P. C. Schmitter, editors, *Private Interest Government and Public Policy,* Sage Publications, 1985.

OTHER

Contributor to proceedings of professional organizations, including the Academy of Management. Contributor of more than 100 articles to marketing, management, and business journals, including *Management International Review, Business Horizons, Journal of Marketing, International Studies of Management and Organizations,* and *Journal of Advertising Research.* Editor, *International Studies of Management and Organization,* 1971—; member of editorial board, *Academy of Management Journal,* 1966-74, *Journal of International Business Studies,* 1977—, *Journal of Business Research,* 1978—, *International Marketing Review,* 1979—, *Journal of Macromarketing,* 1982—, and *Academy of Management Review,* 1984—; member of editorial review board, *South Carolina Essays in International Business,* 1977—.

*   *   *

BOKENKOTTER, Thomas   1924-

PERSONAL: Born August 19, 1924, in Cincinnati, Ohio; son of Anthony J. and Gertrude P. (Wessel) Bokenkotter. *Education:* St. Gregory Seminary, A.B., 1947; graduate study at Mount St. Mary Seminary, 1947-50; Angelicum, Rome, Italy, lic.theol., 1951; University of Louvain, Ph.D., 1954.

ADDRESSES: Home and office—2622 Gilbert Ave., Cincinnati, Ohio 45206.

CAREER: Ordained Roman Catholic priest; Assumption Church, Cincinnati, Ohio, currently pastor. Former professor of history at St. Gregory Seminary; currently adjunct professor of theology, Xavier University, Cincinnati. Director of Over the Rhine Kitchen.

MEMBER: American Historical Association, American Association of University Professors, Catholic Historical Association.

WRITINGS:

Cardinal Newman as an Historian, Duculot, 1959.
A Concise History of the Catholic Church, Doubleday, 1977.
Essential Catholicism, Doubleday, 1985.

Contributor to *New Catholic Encyclopedia.* Contributor of articles and reviews to history and theology journals.

WORK IN PROGRESS: Research on social history.

SIDELIGHTS: Thomas Bokenkotter writes: "I have a strong interest in prison reform and serve on a number of church commissions dedicated to reform of prisons. Major influences on my concept of history have been Cardinal Newman and Lord Acton."

AVOCATIONAL INTERESTS: Photography, European travel.

*   *   *

BOLLE, Kees W.   1927-

PERSONAL: Sometimes uses Cornelius, the English version of his given name; born December 2, 1927, in Dordrecht, Netherlands; married, 1956; children: two. *Education:* University of Leiden, Cand. Theol., 1955; University of Madras, additional study, 1959, 1960; University of Chicago, Ph.D., 1961.

ADDRESSES: Office—Department of History, University of California, Los Angeles, Calif.

CAREER: University of Chicago, Chicago, Ill., instructor in history of religions, 1962; Northern Illinois University, De Kalb, associate professor of history, 1962; Brown University, Providence, R.I., assistant professor of history of religions and Sanskrit, 1962-66; University of California, Los Angeles, associate professor, 1966-72, professor of history, 1972—, chairman of program in study of religion, 1973—.

MEMBER: American Society for the Study of Religion (member of executive council, 1968-69), Forschungskreis fuer Symbolik (Heidelberg).

WRITINGS:

The Persistence of Religion: An Essay on Tantrism and Sri Aurobindo's Philosophy, E. J. Brill, 1965.
(Translator and author of introduction) Jan de Vries, *The Study of Religion: A Historical Approach,* Harcourt, 1967.
(Contributor) Joseph Kitagawa, editor, *The History of Religions: Essays on Understanding,* University of Chicago Press, 1967.
The Freedom of Man in Myth, Vanderbilt University Press, 1968.
(Translator and author of introduction) de Vries, *Perspectives in the History of Religions,* University of California, 1977.
(Editor) *Reading in Mythology* (reprint series), forty-five volumes, Ayer Co., 1978.
(Translator) *The Bhagavadgita,* University of California Press, 1979.

General editor, "Hermeneutics: Studies in the History of Religions" series, University of California Press, and "Mythology" series, Ayer Co., 1978. Contributor to *Encyclopaedia Britannica* and *New Catholic Encyclopedia* and to *Bibliographie zur Symbolik, Ikonographie und Mythologie,* and *Studies of Esoteric Buddhism and Tantrism;* also contributor of articles and reviews to professional journals.

WORK IN PROGRESS: Goddesses in South Asia.

SIDELIGHTS: Besides his native language, Kees W. Bolle has competence in German, French, Sanskrit, Latin, Greek, Italian, Swedish, Hebrew (listed in descending order of competency).

AVOCATIONAL INTERESTS: Playing the piano and clarinet ("fond of Bach, Chopin, and Bartok").

*　　*　　*

BOOTY, John Everitt 1925-

PERSONAL: Born May 2, 1925, in Detroit, Mich.; son of George Thomas and Alma (Gamauf) Booty; married Catherine Louise Smith, June 10, 1950; children: Carol Holland, Geoffrey Rollen, Peter Thomas, Catherine Jane. *Education:* Wayne State University, B.A., 1952; Virginia Theological Seminary, B.D., 1953; Princeton University, M.A., 1957, Ph.D., 1960. *Politics:* Democrat.

ADDRESSES: Home—Clara's Point Rd., Sewanee, Tenn. 37375. *Office*—Hamilton Hall, School of Theology, University of the South, Sewanee, Tenn. 37375.

CAREER: Ordained Episcopal minister, 1953; curate of Christ Episcopal church in Dearborn, Mich., 1953-55; Virginia Theological Seminary, Alexandria, Va., assistant professor, 1958-64, associate professor of church history, 1964-67; Episcopal Divinity School, Cambridge, Mass., professor of church history, 1967-81; University of the South, School of Theology, Sewanee, Tenn., dean, 1982-85, professor of Anglican studies, 1984—. Visiting professor and research scholar at Yale Divinity School, 1985-86. Acting director of Institute for Theological Research, 1974-76.

MEMBER: American Historical Association, American Society of Church History, Renaissance Society of America, Modern Language Association of America.

AWARDS, HONORS: Fulbright scholar at University of London, 1957-58; award from American Philosophical Society, 1964; fellow of Folger Shakespeare Library, 1964, and National Endowment for the Humanities, 1978-79.

WRITINGS:

John Jewel as Apologist of the Church of England, S.P.C.K., 1963.
(Editor) John Jewel, *An Apology of the Church of England,* Cornell University Press, 1963.
Yearning to Be Free, Greeno, Hadden, 1974.
(Editor) *The Book of Common Prayer, 1559: The Elizabethan Prayer Book,* University Press of Virginia, 1976.
Three Anglican Divines on Prayer: Jewel, Andrewes, and Hooker (booklet), Cowley Fathers, 1978.
The Church in History, Seabury, 1979.
The Spirit of Anglicanism, edited by William J. Wolf, Morehouse, 1979.
(Editor) Richard Hooker, *Works,* Harvard University Press, Volume IV: *Of the Laws of Ecclesiastical Polity: Attack*

and Response, 1981, Volume VI (with Speed Hill), in press.
The Godly Kingdom of Tudor England: Great Books of the English Reformation, Morehouse, 1980.
Anglican Spirituality, edited by Wolf, Morehouse, 1981.
The Faithful Church, edited by O. C. Edwards and John Westerhof, Morehouse, 1981.
The Servant Church: Diaconal Ministry and the Episcopal Church, Morehouse, 1982.
What Makes Us Episcopalians? (booklet), Morehouse, 1982.
Meditating on Four Quartets, Cowley, 1983.
Anglican Moral Choice, edited by Paul Elmen, Morehouse, 1983.
The Divine Drama in History and Liturgy: Essays Presented to Horton Davies on His Retirement from Princeton University (monograph), Pickwick, 1984.
Health and Medicine in Faith Traditions, edited by Ronald L. Numbers, McMillan, 1985.
Authority in Anglicanism, edited by Stephen Sykes, S.P.C.K., 1986.
Spirituality as Communion, Cowley, 1986.
(Editor with Sykes) *The Study of Anglicanism,* S.P.C.K./Fortress, 1986.
The History of the Episcopal Church, Morehouse, in press.

Contributor to *Encyclopaedia Britannica, World Book Encyclopedia,* and *Westminster Dictionary of Church History.* Contributor to theology and history journals and to newspapers. Member of advisory board of *Classics of Western Spirituality,* Paulist Press, 1976—; member of editorial committee of Richard Hooker's *Works,* Harvard University Press, 1977—.

WORK IN PROGRESS: Biography of Stephen F. Bayne, Jr.; Five Short Stories in Sixteenth-Century Settings; editing *Sermons of John Jewel.*

SIDELIGHTS: John Everitt Booty comments: "My scholarly efforts (and writing) seem to be concentrated on sixteenth-century Anglican liturgy and piety. But my interests are broader, encompassing work on the seventeenth-century metaphysical poets and the Christian understanding of history. To further that understanding, I have recently written five short stories in sixteenth-century settings."

*　　*　　*

BRACHER, Karl Dietrich 1922-

PERSONAL: Born March 13, 1922, in Stuttgart, Germany (now West Germany); son of Theodor (an educator) and Gertrud (Zimmermann) Bracher; married Dorothee Schleicher, May 13, 1951; children: Christian, Susanne. *Education:* University of Tuebingen, Ph.D., 1948; Harvard University, postdoctoral study, 1949-50. *Religion:* Protestant.

ADDRESSES: Home—Stationsweg 17, Bonn, West Germany. *Office*—University of Bonn, Am Hofgarten 15, Bonn, West Germany.

CAREER: Free University, Berlin, Germany, assistant, 1950-53; lecturer, 1954-55; professor of modern history and political science, 1955-58; University of Bonn, Bonn, West Germany, professor of political science and contemporary history, 1959—. Guest professor, Sweden, 1962, Athens, Greece, 1966 and 1978, London, England, 1967, Oxford University, 1971, Tel Aviv University, 1974, Jerusalem, Israel, 1974, Japan, 1975, Florence, Italy, 1976, Madrid, Spain, 1976, and Rome, Italy, 1979. Fellow, Center for Advanced Study in the Behavioral Sciences, 1963-64; member, Institute for Advanced Study, 1967-68 and 1974-75. Consultant to and member of science and government committees of the Federal Republic of Germany.

MEMBER: German Association of Political Science (chairman, 1965-67), Association of German Scientists, German Association of Foreign Policy, Historical Association, Commission on History of Parliamentarism and Political Parties (chairman, 1962-68), Institute for Contemporary History (chairman of board), German P.E.N. Center, German Academy of Language and Poetry, Austrian Academy of Sciences (corresponding fellow), British Academy (corresponding fellow), American Philosophical Society, American Academy of Arts and Sciences (honorary member).

AWARDS, HONORS: Doctor of Humane Letters from Florida State University; Doctor of Law from University of Graz; Premio Acqui Storia, 1973, for *The German Dictatorship: The Origins, Structure, and Effects of National Socialism;* Prix Adolphe Bentinck, 1981, for *Europa in der Krise: Innengeschichte und Weltpolitik seit 1917.*

WRITINGS:

(Compiler with Annedore Leber and Willy Brandt) *Das Gewissen steht auf: Vierundsechzig Lebensbilder aus dem deutschen Widerstand, 1933-1945,* Mosaik Verlag, 1954, translation by Rosemary O'Neill published as *Conscience in Revolt: Sixty-four Stories of Resistance in Germany, 1933-45,* Associated Booksellers, 1957.

Die Aufloesung der Weimarer Republik: Eine Studie zum Problem des Machtverfalls in der Demokratie (title means "The Dissolution of the Weimer Republic"), Ring-Verlag, 1955, 16th edition, 1978.

Nationalsozialistische Machtergreifung und Reichskonkordat (title means "Nazi Seizure of Power and the Concordat"), C. Ritter, 1956.

(Editor with Ernst Fraenkel) *Staat und Politik* (title means "State and Politics"), Fischer Buecherei, 1957.

(Compiler with Leber and Brandt) *Das Gewissen entscheidet: Bereiche des deutschen Widerstandes von 1933-45 in Lebensbildern* (sequel to *Das Gewissen steht auf;* title means "Conscience Decides"), Mosaik Verlag, 1957.

Die Nationalsozialistische Machtergreifung (title means "The National Socialist Seizure of Power"), Westdeutscher Verlag, 1960, 3rd edition, 1974.

Ueber das Verhaeltnis von Politik und Geschichte (title means "On the Relation of Politics and History"), Peter Hanstein, 1961.

Die Entstehung der Weimarer Verfassung (title means "The Genesis of the Weimar Constitution"), [Hannover], 1963.

Adolf Hitler, Scherz Verlag, 1964.

Deutschland zwischen Demokratie und Diktatur (title means "Germany between Democracy and Dictatorship"), Scherz, 1964.

Theodor Heuss und die Wiederbegruendung der Demokratie in Deutschland (title means "Theodor Heuss and the Refounding of Democracy in Germany"), R. Wunderlich Verlag, 1965.

(Editor with others) *Modern Constitutionalism and Democracy,* two volumes, J. C. B. Mohr (Tuebingen), 1966.

(Editor with Fraenkel) *Internationale Beziehungen,* Fischer-Buecherei, 1969.

Die deutsche Diktatur: Entstehung, Struktur, Folgen des Nationalsozialismus, Koeln, Kiepenheuer & Witsch, 1969, 6th edition, 1979, translation by Jean Steinberg published

as *The German Dictatorship: The Origins, Structure, and Effects of National Socialism,* Praeger, 1970.

(Editor) *Nach fuenfundzwanzig Jahren* (title means "After Twenty-five Years"), Kindler, 1970.

(Editor with others) *Bibliographie zur Politik,* Droste, 1970.

Das deutsche Dilemma: Leidenswege der politischen Emanzipation, R. Piper, 1971, translation published as *The German Dilemma: The Throes of Political Emancipation,* Weidenfeld & Nicolson, 1974.

Zeitgeschichtliche Kontroversen (title means "Controversies in Contemporary History"), Piper, 1976, 5th edition, 1984.

Die Krise Europas, 1917-1975 (title means "The Crisis of Europe, 1917-1975"), Propylaen, 1976, new edition published as *Europa in der Krise: Innengeschichte und Weltpolitik seit 1917,* 1979.

Schluesselwoerter in der Geschichte (title means "Key Words in History"), Droste, 1978.

Geschichte und Gewalt (title means "History and Violence"), Severin & Siedler, 1981.

Zeit der Ideologien: Eine Geschichte politischen Denkens im zwanzig Jahrhundert, Deutsche Verlags Anstalt, 1982, translation by Ewald Osers published as *The Age of Ideologies,* Weidenfeld & Nicolson, 1984.

CONTRIBUTOR

Max Beloff, editor, *On the Track of Tyranny,* Valentine, Mitchell, 1960.

J. E. Black and K. W. Thompson, editors, *Foreign Policies in a World of Change,* Harper, 1963.

H. W. Ehrmann, editor, *Democracy in a Changing Society,* Praeger, 1964.

Stephen R. Graubard, editor, *A New Europe?,* Houghton, 1964.

The Times History of Our Times, [London], 1971.

R. Mayne, editor, *Europe Tomorrow,* Fontana, 1972.

Hajo Holborn, editor, *Republic to Reich,* Pantheon, 1972.

Walter Laqueur, editor, *Fascism: A Reader's Guide,* University of California Press, 1976.

OTHER

Contributor to *International Encyclopedia of the Social Sciences* and *Dictionary of the History of Ideas.* Editor, *Vierteljahrshefte fuer Zeitgeschichte;* member of editorial boards, *Politische Vierteljahresschrift, Neue Politische Literatur, Bonner Historische Forschungen, Journal of Contemporary History, Government and Opposition, Societas, History of the Twentieth Century,* and *Bonner Schriften zur Politik und Zeitgeschichte.*

WORK IN PROGRESS: Analysis of the Federal Republic of Germany; History of the Twentieth Century; History of Political Ideas.

AVOCATIONAL INTERESTS: Playing the piano, mountain hiking.

BIOGRAPHICAL/CRITICAL SOURCES:

PERIODICALS

Times Literary Supplement, March 25, 1983.

* * *

BRADBURY, Edward P.
See MOORCOCK, Michael (John)

BRAND, Garrison
    See BRANDNER, Gary

*   *   *

BRANDNER, Gary   1933-
    (Garrison Brand, Phil Garrison, Barnaby Quill;
    joint pseudonyms: Clayton Moore, Lee Davis
    Willoughby)

PERSONAL: Born May 31, 1933, in Sault Sainte Marie, Mich.; son of Henry Phil and Beada (Gehrman) Brandner; married Barbara Grant Nutting, 1979 (divorced, 1983). *Education:* University of Washington, B.A., 1955.

ADDRESSES: Home—3614A Valihi Way, Glendale, Calif. 91208. *Agent*—Jay Garon, 415 Central Park W., 17-D, New York, N.Y. 10025.

CAREER: Dan B. Miner (advertising agency), Los Angeles, Calif., copywriter, 1955-57; Douglas Aircraft, Santa Monica, Calif., technical writer, 1957-59; North American Rockwell, Downey, Calif., technical writer, 1959-67; full-time free-lance writer, 1969—.

MEMBER: Private Eye Writers of America, Mystery Writers of America, Writers Guild of America West.

WRITINGS:

Vitamin E: Key to Sexual Satisfaction, Nash Publishing, 1971, revised edition, Paperback Library, 1972.
(Contributor) Richard Davis, editor, *Year's Best Horror Stories,* Sphere Books, 1971.
Living off the Land, Nash Publishing, 1971.
Off the Beaten Track in London, Nash Publishing, 1972.
(With Clayton Matthews) *Saturday Night in Milwaukee,* Curtis Books, 1973.
(Under pseudonym Clayton Moore) *Wesley Sheridan,* Berkley Publishing, 1974.
The Aardvark Affair, Zebra Publications, 1975.
The Beelzebub Business, Zebra Publications, 1975.
The Players, Pyramid Publications, 1975.
London, Pocket Books, 1976.
Billy Lives!, Manor, 1976.
The Howling, Fawcett, 1977.
The Howling II, Fawcett, 1978.
Offshore, Pinnacle Books, 1978.
Walkers, Fawcett, 1980.
The Sterling Standard, Fawcett/Popular Library, 1980.
Hellborn, Gold Medal, 1981.
A Rage in Paradise, Playboy Paperbacks, 1981.
Cat People, Gold Medal, 1982.
(Under pseudonym Lee Davis Willoughby) *The Express Riders,* Bryans, 1982.
Quintana Roo, Ballantine/Fawcett, 1984.
The Brain Eaters, Ballantine/Fawcett, 1985.
The Howling III, Ballantine/Fawcett, 1985.

Contributor of over fifty short stories, sometimes under pseudonyms, to *Ellery Queen's Mystery Magazine, Alfred Hitchcock's Mystery Magazine, Mike Shayne Mystery Magazine, Zane Grey, Cavalier, Gem,* and *Twilight Zone.*

WORK IN PROGRESS: Two novels, *Carrion,* for Ballantine/Fawcett, and *Bedfellows.*

SIDELIGHTS: Gary Brandner told *CA:* "It is, in a way, lucky for those of us who write for a living that it is so difficult.

Otherwise, everyone would be doing it, because it is a fine way to live, and there would be no one left to read.

"The best things about writing are that you can wear whatever you want to work, and you can set your own schedule, and you get to hang around with other writers. The worst thing is that your family never believes you have a real job.

"My advice to aspiring writers is (a) never identify yourself as an aspiring writer, and (b) don't read your stuff to friends."

MEDIA ADAPTATIONS: A movie based on *The Howling* was filmed by Avco Embassy Pictures Corp. in 1981.

*   *   *

BRETT, Bernard   1925-

PERSONAL: Born July 18, 1925, in Birmingham, England; son of Francis Bernard and Annie (Ezra) Brett; married Daphne Joan Goodchild (a researcher), December 21, 1946; children: Bernard Anthony, Nigel Colin, Carolyn Joan, Adrian Francis. *Education:* Brighton College of Art and Design, art teacher's diploma and National Diploma of Design, 1951. *Politics:* "Apolitical." *Religion:* Church of England.

ADDRESSES: Home and office—Marlipins, Scotlands Close, Haslemere, Surrey, England.

CAREER: Wolverhampton College of Art, Wolverhampton, England, head of department of graphic design, 1948-67; West Surrey College of Art and Design, Farnham, England, vice-principal, 1967-76; editorial consultant in London, England, 1976—; free-lance writer, illustrator, and designer. Work has been exhibited at the Royal Academy, London, 1950-68, and at the Best 200 Children's Book of the Year exhibition. Town councillor in Haslemere, 1976—. *Military service:* Royal Navy, 1943-46.

MEMBER: Royal Society of Industrial Artists and Designers (fellow).

AWARDS, HONORS: First prize at Bologna Book Fair, 1973, for *Marco Polo.*

WRITINGS:

JUVENILES

(With Nicholas Ingman) *The Story of Music,* Ward, Lock, 1972, Taplinger, 1976.
(With Ingman) *What Instrument Do You Want to Play?,* Ward, Lock, 1975, published as *What Instrument Shall I Play?,* Taplinger, 1976.
(With Victor Sidney Griffiths) *Take-Off,* Collins, 1975.
(With Ingman) *Gifted Children of Music,* Ward, Lock, 1978.

SELF-ILLUSTRATED JUVENILES

Captain Cook, Collins, 1970.
Marco Polo, Collins, 1971.
Mohammed, Collins, 1972.
Bernard Brett's Book of Explorers and Exploring, Longman, 1973.
Stream of Culture, Angus & Robertson, 1973.
Community and Leadership, Angus & Robertson, 1974.
On the Move, New Educational Press, 1975.
(With Lewis Jones) *Race to the South Pole,* Longman, 1976.
Monsters, Firefly Press, 1977.
Submarine Disaster, Longman, 1978.
True Adventures, Hamlyn, 1978.
A Book of Ships, Hamlyn, 1979.

Jumbo Jet, Longman, 1979.
A Book of Ghosts, Granada, 1980.
A Book of Witches, Granada, 1980.
Hamlyn Book of Mysteries, Hamlyn, 1981.
Vampires and Werewolves, Marshall Cavendish, 1982.
The Fighting Ship, Oxford University Press, 1985.

ADULT NONFICTION

A History of Watercolour, Optimum, 1984.
A History of Sea Power, Optimum, 1985.

ILLUSTRATOR

Ada Williams, *Between the Lights,* Dent, 1952.
Julia Clark, *Crab Village,* Dent, 1954.
Edward Thomas, *The Green Roads,* Bodley Head, 1965.
Alan Taylor Dale, *The Message,* Oxford University Press, 1966.
Dale, *Paul the Explorer,* Oxford University Press, 1966.
Dale, *The Beginning,* Oxford University Press, 1966.
Dale, *From Galilee to Rome,* Oxford University Press, 1966.
Dale, *The Poetry Makers,* Bodley Head, 1968.
Eric Baxter, *Safety at Sea,* Bodley Head, 1969.
Benjamin Wigley, *From Fear to Faith,* Longmans, Green, 1969.
Child's Play, Dent, 1969.
Rowland Purton, *The Fire Service,* Bodley Head, 1969.
Arthur Catherall, *Keepers of the Cattle,* Dent, 1970.
The Crusades, Hulton Press, 1970.
Louise Foley, *A Job for Joey,* Western Publishing, 1970.
Samuel Frederick Wooley, *The Romans,* University of London Press, 1972.
Raymond Ward, *Tales of Lone Sailors,* Blackie & Son, 1973.
Anthony Gascoigne Eyre, *The City of Gold and Lead,* Longman, 1974.
Jenny Seed, *The Bushman's Dream: African Tales of the Creation,* Hamish Hamilton, 1974, Bradbury, 1975.
Eyre, *The White Mountains,* Longman, 1974.
Eyre, *The Pool of Fire,* Longman, 1974.
Frances Wilkins, *Magna Carta, June 15, 1215,* Lutterworth, 1975.
Kathleen Fidler, *Pirate and Admiral: The Story of John Paul Jones,* Lutterworth, 1975.
Eilis Dillon, editor, *The Hamish Hamilton Book of Wise Animals,* Hamish Hamilton, 1975.
Eve Sutton, *The Moa Hunters,* Hamish Hamilton, 1978.
Desmond Dunkerley, *Robin Hood and the Silver Arrow,* Ladybird Books, 1978.
Dunkerley, *Robin Hood Outlawed,* Ladybird Books, 1978.
Dunkerley, *Robin Hood to the Rescue,* Ladybird Books, 1978.
Dunkerley, *Robin Hood and the King's Ransom,* Ladybird Books, 1978.

SIDELIGHTS: Bernard Brett told *CA:* "I have always been fascinated by books—books per se, the feel of them, their design, typography and illustration, their paper and binding.

"Having joined the Royal Navy virtually straight from school, at the end of the war I found myself having to choose a career to follow. Torn between a degree in letters and one in the visual arts, I eventually plumped for the latter. Being a student in Brighton was really some experience. The town, an odd mixture of Regency charm, 'Prinney's' phantasies, vulgar cafes, tourist traps, offshore fishing fleets, and incredible Victoriana, completely captivated me. In a very short time I realized that my bent lay in the direction of illustration and typography, but toward the end of my course I became involved in teaching, having a natural inclination towards lecturing.

"So I changed direction and became a lecturer in graphics at a Midland college of art; eventually I became head of the graphics department. It was a very happy and rewarding time—I like people. At the same time I began illustrating books and commercial brochures. Industrial scenes of the Midlands held a fascination for me. Bessemer converters belching out fierce flame and thick, acrid smoke inspired me to produce a number of lithographs based on this theme that were exhibited in many national and international exhibitions, including the Royal Academy. In fact, my work was regularly accepted at the Royal Academy for ten consecutive years, until once again I changed direction. It was during this period that I produced a number of murals—several of which were in glass applique—building up sheets of colored glass, sometimes to a depth of from six to nine inches.

"Around 1958 I moved into publicity design, becoming a partner in a design consultancy. My role in the company, apart from graphic design and illustration, was to handle the public relations aspect of the company's business. This is when I began to formulate ideas, interview people, and write. However, some time later, I was offered the post of vice-principal in the south of England, and I once again found myself in teaching, but as an administrator, and when the novelty had worn off, the endless round of protracted meetings became irksome. I began to get 'itchy feet'—better to be a doer than a talker! It was about this time that a filmstrip on Captain Cook, which I was doing for the BBC, triggered a long suppressed desire to research and write nonfiction books for children, and educational material, the latter aimed to extend the pupil's knowledge and introduce multidiscipline teaching—something in which I believe very strongly—and in which I have collaborated with a number of well-known educationalists. So, what else could I do but give up teaching and became a free-lance author, illustrator, designer, and editor? I have done this ever since, and I love it!

"I now edit and design a national house journal and also act as an editor to a number of publishers. This enables me to devote most of my time to the things I love the most: research, writing, illustrating, and painting."

Asked about his art work, Brett commented: "I work very much in mixed media: acrylic color, colored inks, oil crayons, pen. I adore bright color—all mixed up with color rejection techniques—everything but the kitchen sink, and sometimes that! Basically an English Romantic, I was, and for that matter still am, very influenced by Samuel Palmer, and to a lesser degree William Blake."

*   *   *

BRIAN, Alan B.
  See PARULSKI, George R(ichard), Jr.

*   *   *

BRICKMAN, William Wolfgang   1913-

PERSONAL: Born June 30, 1913, in New York, N.Y.; son of David Shalom and Sarah (Shaber) Brickman; married Sylvia Schnitzer, February 26, 1958; children: Joy, Chaim, Sara. *Education:* City College (now City College of the City University of New York), B.A., 1934, M.S. in Education, 1935; New York University, Ph.D., 1938.

ADDRESSES: Home—15 Jade Lane, Cherry Hill, N.J. 08002. *Office*—Graduate School of Education, University of Pennsylvania, Philadelphia, Pa. 19104.

CAREER: City College (now City College of the City University of New York), New York City, tutor in German, 1937; New York University, New York City, instructor, 1940-42, 1946-48, lecturer, 1948-50, assistant professor, 1950-51, associate professor, 1951-57, professor of education, 1957-62; University of Pennsylvania, Philadelphia, professor of educational history and comparative education, 1962-81, professor emeritus, 1981—. Dean, Touro College, New York City, 1977-79. Visiting professor, University of California, Los Angeles, 1953 and 1954, Yeshiva University, 1953-57, 1959, and 1964, University of Hamburg, 1957, University of Illinois, 1958, University of Toledo, 1959, Teachers College, Columbia University, 1964, University of Pittsburgh, 1965, University of Wyoming, 1968, Bar Ilan University, Ramat Gan, Israel, 1970 and 1979, and University of Cape Town, South Africa, 1981. President's research fellow, Brown University, 1950-51. Member of committee on international education, College Entrance Examination Board, 1969-70; member of National Fulbright Selection Committee; member of committee of religion and education, University of Notre Dame. Member of academic advisory board, Yeshiva University; educational consultant, Emeritus, Inc., 1981—. *Military service:* U.S. Army, 1943-46; became staff sergeant.

MEMBER: International Association for the Advancement of Educational Research (member of council), Comparative Education Society (president, 1956-59 and 1967-68), American Historical Association, National Society for the Study of Education, History of Education Society.

AWARDS, HONORS: M.A., University of Pennsylvania, 1972.

WRITINGS:

Guide to Research in Educational History, New York University Bookstore, 1949, published as *Research in Educational History,* Norwood, 1976.

(Co-author) *The Changing Soviet School,* Houghton, 1960.

Educational Systems in the United States, Center for Applied Research in Education, 1964.

Foreign Students in American Elementary and Secondary Schools, International House, 1967.

Bibliographical Essays on Curriculum and Instruction, Norwood, 1974.

Bibliographical Essays on Comparative and International Education, Norwood, 1975.

Bibliographical Essays on Educational Psychology and Sociology of Education, Norwood, 1975.

Bibliographical Essays on the History and Philosophy of Education, Norwood, 1975.

Bibliographical Essays on the System of Education, Norwood, 1975.

Two Millenia of International Relations in Higher Education, Norwood, 1976.

The Jewish Community in America: An Annotated and Classified Bibliographical Guide, Burt Franklin, 1977.

(Co-author) *Ideas and Issues in Educational Thought: Past and Recent,* Norwood, 1978.

Educational Historiography: Tradition, Theory, and Technique, Emeritus, 1982.

Educational Roots and Routes in Western Europe, Emeritus, 1985.

Pedagogy, Professionalism, and Public Policy: History of the Graduate School of the University of Pennsylvania, University of Pennsylvania, 1985.

EDITOR

(With Stanley Lehrer) *John Dewey: Master Educator,* Society for the Advancement of Education, 1959, 2nd edition, 1961.

(With Lehrer) *The Countdown on Segregated Education,* Society for the Advancement of Education, 1960.

(With Lehrer) *Religion, Government, and Education,* Society for the Advancement of Education, 1961.

(With Lehrer) *A Century of Higher Education,* Society for the Advancement of Education, 1962.

John Dewey, *Impressions of Soviet Russia and the Revolutionary World,* Columbia University, 1964.

(With Lehrer) *Automation, Education, and Human Values,* School & Society Books, 1966.

Educational Imperatives in Changing Culture, University of Pennsylvania Press, 1967.

(With Stewart E. Fraser) *A History of International and Comparative Education,* Scott, Foresman, 1968.

(With Lehrer) *Conflict and Change on the Campus: The Response to Student Hyperactivism,* School & Society Books, 1970.

(With Lehrer) *Education and the Many Faces of the Disadvantaged: Cultural and Historical Perspectives,* Wiley, 1972.

Comparative Education: Concept, Research, and Application, Norwood, 1973.

(With Francesco Cordasco) *A Bibliography of American Educational History: An Annotated and Classified Guide,* AMS Press, 1975.

OTHER

Contributor to *Encyclopaedia Britannica, Encyclopedia of Educational Research, Encyclopedia of Education, International Encyclopedia of Higher Education, Encyclopedia Judaica, International Encyclopedia of Education: Research and Studies, Lexikon der Paedagogik, Antziklopediah Hinuchet,* and *Encyclopedia Americana.* Contributor of numerous articles and reviews to professional journals, literary periodicals, and newspapers. Editor, *School and Society,* 1953-76, and *Western European Education,* 1979—; assistant managing editor, *Modern Language Journal;* member of editorial board, *Paedagogica Historica.*

WORK IN PROGRESS: Anna Marie van Schurman: Learned Lady; Bengt Skytte's Plan for an International University; History of Educational Historiography; Multilingual Education in Historical and International Perspectives.

SIDELIGHTS: William Wolfgang Brickman has a reading knowledge of most European and several Asian and African languages.

AVOCATIONAL INTERESTS: Music history and appreciation.

*   *   *

BRO, Bernard (Gerard Marie) 1925-

PERSONAL: Born May 22, 1925, in Paris, France; son of Louis (an administrator) and Suzanne (Courtois) Bro. *Education:* Attended Sorbonne, University of Paris; received Licence de philosophie and Doctorat de theologie from University of Fribourg.

ADDRESSES: Home and office—29 Boulevard de la Tour-Maubourg, 75007 Paris, France.

CAREER: Roman Catholic Dominican monk, 1944—; professor of dogmatic theology at Saulchoir, 1953—; Editions du Cerf, Paris, France, director of *La Vie Spirituelle,* 1958-63, company literary director, 1962, general director, 1964-71, administrator, 1971—; Notre Dame de Paris, Paris, teacher, 1975—.

WRITINGS:

IN ENGLISH TRANSLATION

Apprendre a prier, Aux Equipes Enseignantes, 1962, translation by John Morris published as *Learning to Pray,* Alba House, 1966, published as *The Rediscovery of Prayer,* Alba Books, 1966.
Le Temoignage des cloitrees: Benedictines, carmelites, clarisses, dominicaines, trappistines, visitandines; Dieu leur suffit, Cerf, 1962, translation by Isabel McHugh and Florence McHugh published as *Contemplative Nuns Speak: Benedictine, Carmelite, Poor Clare, Dominican, Trappistine, and Visitation Nuns Reply to a Questionnaire,* Helicon, 1964.
Faut-il encore pratiquer? L'Homme et les sacrements, Cerf, 1967, translation by Theodore Du Bois published as *The Spirituality of the Sacrament: Doctrine and Practice for Today,* Sheed & Ward, 1968.
Heureux de croire, Cerf, 1968, translation by John M. Morriss published as *Happy Those Who Believe,* Alba House, 1970.
La Gloire et la mendiant, Cerf, 1974, translation by Alan Neame published as *The Little Way,* Darton, 1979.

OTHER

On demande des pecheurs: Le Livre du pardon, Cerf, 1969.
Dieu seul est humain, Cerf, 1973.
Contre toute esperance, Cerf, 1975.
Le Pouvoir du mal, Cerf, 1976.
Jesus-Crist ou rien, Cerf, 1977.
Devenir Dieu, Cerf, 1978.
Surpris par la certitude, four volumes, Cerf, 1980.
La Meule et la cithare, Cerf, 1982.
Le Secret de la confession, Cerf, 1983.
Les Portiers de l'aube, Cerf, 1984.
La Stupeur d'etre, Cerf, 1985.

SIDELIGHTS: The first of Bernard Bro's books to appear in English translation was *Contemplative Nuns Speak: Benedictine, Carmelite, Poor Clare, Dominican, Trappistine, and Visitation Nuns Reply to a Questionnaire.* It is the result of Bro's questionnaire to French contemplatives on the genesis of their vocations, prayer, the use of time, and what he has called "the mystery of God." The nuns were of varying age and background as well as intellect and temperament, but out of their various responses, a *Times Literary Supplement* reviewer observed, the reader must realize two facts: "First, something other than their own selves, individual, collective conscious and unconscious, is expressed through these hundreds of human voices speaking of God. Second, here is theology illuminated from within, seen not only as a succession of logically integrated formulas, but as an attempt to state direct experience."

Another volume, *The Spirituality of the Sacrament: Doctrine and Practice For Today,* examines the implications of the rites of baptism, confirmation, penance, eucharist, holy orders, matrimony, and extreme unction. J. J. McDonald observed that Bro "succeeded in establishing the underlying agreement between the modern Christian's need and God's loving, transforming action embodied in the sacraments."

BIOGRAPHICAL/CRITICAL SOURCES:

PERIODICALS

America, February 15, 1969.
Commonweal, May 8, 1964.
Times Literary Supplement, May 21, 1964.

* * *

BROOKS, Polly Schoyer   1912-

PERSONAL: Born August 11, 1912, in South Orleans, Mass.; daughter of William Edgar and Lucy (Turner) Schoyer; married Ernest Brooks (a foundation president), June 23, 1934 (died, 1984); children: Joan B. (Mrs. J. R. McLane III), Peter, Turner, Ernest III. *Education:* Radcliffe College, B.A., 1933.

ADDRESSES: Home—152 Marvin Ridge Rd., New Canaan, Conn. 06840.

WRITINGS:

(With Nancy Zinsser Walworth) *The World Awakes: The Renaissance in Western Europe,* Lippincott, 1962.
World of Walls: The Middle Ages in Western Europe, Lippincott, 1966.
(With Walworth) *When the World Was Rome,* Lippincott, 1972.
Queen Eleanor, Independent Spirit of the Medieval World: A Biography of Eleanor of Aquitaine, Harper, 1983.

Also contributor to *Junior Encyclopaedia Britannica,* 1968.

WORK IN PROGRESS: A biography.

BIOGRAPHICAL/CRITICAL SOURCES:

PERIODICALS

New York Times, December 3, 1962.

* * *

BROWN, Fern G.   1918-

PERSONAL: Born December 23, 1918, in Chicago, Ill.; daughter of Samuel M. (in business) and Miriam (Portnoy) Goldberg; married Leonard J. Brown (a plumbing contractor), November 21, 1940; children: Hal Murray, Marilyn Bette Brown Barnett. *Education:* Chicago Teachers College, B.A., 1940; Northwestern University, M.A., 1956. *Politics:* Independent. *Religion:* Jewish.

ADDRESSES: Home and office—2929 Orange Brace Rd., Riverwoods, Deerfield, Ill. 60015.

CAREER: Teacher in Chicago, Ill., 1940-49; writer, 1958—. Conducts creative writing workshops; public speaker in the Chicago area; lecturer at University of Illinois.

MEMBER: Society of Children's Book Writers, Children's Reading Round Table, Midwest Writers, Society of Midland Authors, Off Campus Writer's Workshop (chairman, 1960-61).

AWARDS, HONORS: Carl Sandburg Award for best children's book of 1982-83, Chicago Public Library Friends, for *Behind the Scenes at the Horse Hospital.*

WRITINGS:

JUVENILES

(With Andree V. Grabe) *When Grandpa Wore Knickers,* Albert Whitman, 1966.

Hard Luck Horse, Albert Whitman, 1975.
Racing against the Odds: Jockey Robyn Smith, Raintree, 1976.
Scooby Doo and the Headless Horseman, Rand McNally, 1976.
Scooby Doo and the Counterfeit Money, Rand McNally, 1976.
Scooby Doo and the Santa Claus Mystery, Rand McNally, 1977.
Clue Club and the Case of the Missing Race Horse, Rand McNally, 1977.
Dynomutt and the Pie in the Sky Caper, Rand McNally, 1977.
Bugs Bunny, Pioneer, Western Publishing, 1977.
You're Somebody Special on a Horse, Albert Whitman, 1977.
Jockey, or Else!, Albert Whitman, 1978.
The Great Money Machine, Messner, 1981.
Behind the Scenes at the Horse Hospital, Albert Whitman, 1981.
Valentine's Day, F. Watts, 1983.
Etiquette, F. Watts, 1985.
Amelia Earhart Takes Off, Albert Whitman, 1985.

Also author of coloring books. Contributor of more than fifty articles and stories to periodicals, including *American Girl, Outdoor World, Instructor, Modern Maturity, Catholic Sign,* and *Teen Time.* Contributing editor of *American Horseman,* 1977.

WORK IN PROGRESS: Our Love, for Juniper; *Horses and Foals,* for F. Watts; *News at the Zoo,* for World Book.

SIDELIGHTS: Fern G. Brown told *CA:* "I am interested in children and in getting them to read because I think reading is very important for each child's future."

AVOCATIONAL INTERESTS: Reading, horse riding, playing golf, swimming, bowling, playing the piano, all kinds of music, ballet and modern dance, travel (Mexico, Dominican Republic, Puerto Rico, Virgin Islands, Jamaica).

BIOGRAPHICAL/CRITICAL SOURCES:

PERIODICALS

Chicago, winter, 1969.
Highland Park News, December 11, 1975.
Highland Park Star, December, 1964.
North Shore, April-May, 1978.
Wheeling Herald, December 27, 1974.

*   *   *

BROWN, Raymond E(dward)   1928-

PERSONAL: Born May 22, 1928, in New York, N.Y.; son of Robert H. and Loretta Brown. *Education:* Attended St. Charles College, 1945-46; Catholic University of America, B.A., 1948, M.A., 1949; attended Gregorian University, 1949-50; St. Mary's Seminary, Baltimore, Md., S.T.B., 1951, S.T.L., 1953, S.T.D., 1955; Johns Hopkins University, Ph.D., 1958; Pontifical Biblical Commission, S.S.B., 1959, S.S.L., 1963.

ADDRESSES: Home—3041 Broadway, New York, N.Y. 10027. *Office*—Department of Biblical Studies, Union Theological Seminary, 3041 Broadway, New York, N.Y. 10027.

CAREER: Entered Society of St. Sulpice (S.S.), 1951, ordained Roman Catholic priest, 1953; St. Mary's Seminary, Baltimore, Md., professor of sacred scripture, 1959-71; Union Theological Seminary, New York, N.Y., Auburn Professor of Biblical Studies, 1971—. Adjunct professor of religion at Columbia University, 1979—. Endowed lecturer at numerous schools, colleges, and universities of theology, including La-

grange Lecturer at Aquinas Institute of Theology, 1963, Thomas More Lecturer, 1966, and Shaffer Lecturer, 1978, both at Yale University, Kearnes Seminar Lecturer at Duke University, 1967, Charles McDonald Lecturer at University of Sydney, 1969, Boylan Lecturer at National University of Ireland, University College, Dublin, 1971, Welch Lecturer at Brigham Young University, 1974, W. H. Hoover Lecturer at University of Chicago, 1975, Paul Wattson Lecturer at Catholic University of America, 1977, Cole Lecturer at Vanderbilt University, 1980, Bellarmine Lecturer at St. Louis University, 1980, Armstrong Lecturer at Kalamazoo College, 1981, McMartin Lecturer at Carleton University, 1982, William F. Albright Lecturer at Johns Hopkins University, 1983, and Wickenden Lecturer at Miami University, 1985; visiting professor at Pontifical Biblical Institute, 1973; annual professor at Albright School, Jerusalem, Israel, 1978.

American Schools of Oriental Research, Jerusalem, Jordan fellow, 1958-59, member of board of trustees, 1962-63, 1974-75. Co-president of Journees Bibliques de Louvain, 1966. Named consultor of Vatican Secretariat for Christian Unity, 1968-73. Member of National Commission of Lutheran Churches of the United States and the Roman Catholic Church, 1965-74, Joint Theological Commission of World Council of Churches and the Roman Catholic Church, 1967-68, Faith and Order Commission of World Council of Churches, 1968—, and Roman Pontifical Biblical Commission, 1972-78.

MEMBER: American Schools of Oriental Research, Catholic Biblical Association (president, 1971-72), Society of Biblical Literature (president, 1976-77), Biblical Theologians, American Theological Society, American Academy of Arts and Sciences, Society of New Testament Studies (president elect, 1986), Phi Beta Kappa.

AWARDS, HONORS: National Catholic Book Award, 1969, for *The Jerome Biblical Commentary,* 1971, for *The Gospel according to John,* Volume II, and 1973, for *The Virginal Conception and Bodily Resurrection of Jesus;* Christopher Award from the Christophers, 1971, for *The Gospel according to John,* Volume II; Cardinal Spellman Award from Catholic Theological Society of America, 1971; National Religious Book Award, 1977, for *The Birth of the Messiah,* and 1978, for *Mary in the New Testament;* Edgar J. Goodspeed Award, 1980; Edmund Campion Award from Catholic Book Club, 1984; Catholic Book Award from the Catholic Press Association, 1984, for *Antioch and Rome;* Biblical Archaeology Society Award from *Biblical Archaeology Review,* 1984, for *The Epistles of John;* honorary degrees include D.D. from University of Edinburgh, 1972, and University of Glasgow, 1978, Th.D. from University of Uppsala, 1974, University of Louvain, 1976, St. Anselm's College, 1977, Dominican School of Theology, 1979, and Immaculate Conception Seminary, 1980, L.H.D. from DePaul University, 1974, Loyola College, Baltimore, Md., 1980, and Hofstra University, 1985, and Litt.D. from Villanova University, 1975, Boston College, 1977, and Fordham University, 1977.

WRITINGS:

The Gospel and Epistles of John, Liturgical Press, 1960, new edition, 1965.
Daniel, Paulist Press, 1962.
The Parables of the Gospels, Paulist Press, 1963.
New Testament Essays, Bruce, 1965.
Deuteronomy, Liturgical Press, 1965.
The Gospel according to John, Doubleday, Volume I, 1966, Volume II, 1970.

Jesus, God, and Man, Bruce, 1967.
(Co-editor) *The Jerome Biblical Commentary*, Prentice-Hall, 1968.
The Semitic Background of the Term "Mystery" in the New Testament, Fortress, 1968.
(With P. J. Cahill) *Biblical Tendencies Today: An Introduction to the Post-Bultmanians*, Corpus, 1969.
Priest and Bishop: Biblical Reflections, Paulist/Newman, 1970.
The Virginal Conception and Bodily Resurrection of Jesus, Paulist/Newman, 1973.
(Editor) *Peter in the New Testament*, Paulist/Augsbury, 1973.
Biblical Reflections on Crises Facing the Church, Paulist/Newman, 1975.
The Birth of the Messiah: A Commentary on the Infancy Narratives in Matthew and Luke, Doubleday, 1977.
(Editor) *Mary in the New Testament*, Paulist/Newman, 1978.
An Adult Christ at Christmas, Liturgical Press, 1978.
The Community of the Beloved Disciple, Paulist/Newman, 1979.
The Critical Meaning of the Bible, Paulist Press, 1981.
The Epistles of John, Doubleday, 1982.
Antioch and Rome, Paulist Press, 1983.
Recent Discoveries and the Biblical World, Michael Glazier, 1983.
The Churches the Apostles Left Behind, Paulist Press, 1984.
Biblical Exegesis and Church Doctrine, Paulist Press, 1985.

Member of editorial board of *The Anchor Bible*. Contributor to dictionaries and encyclopedias, including *Encyclopedia Americana, The New Catholic Encyclopedia, Interpreters Dictionary of the Bible*, and *Dictionary of Theology*. Contributor to theology journals and popular magazines, including *America, Catholic Biblical Quarterly, Journal of Biblical Literature, Biblica, Theological Studies, Interpretation*, and *Theology Digest*. Member of editorial board of *Catholic Biblical Quarterly, Journal of Biblical Literature, New Testament Studies*, and *Theological Studies*.

*   *   *

BROWN, Richard C(arl) 1917-

PERSONAL: Born April 9, 1917, in Logan, Ohio; son of Carl M. (a postal worker) and Jessie (Bowen) Brown; married Genevieve Canty, June 8, 1946. *Education:* Ohio State University, B.S. (cum laude), 1947; Colgate University, M.A., 1948; University of Wisconsin, Ph.D., 1951.

ADDRESSES: Home—521 Boone Trail, Danville, Ky. 40422.

CAREER: Colgate University, Hamilton, N.Y., instructor in public affairs, 1947-48; U.S. Armed Forces Institute, Madison, Wis., assistant director, 1951-52; State University of New York College at Buffalo, professor of history, 1952-79. *Military service:* U.S. Army, 1942-46; became captain; received Presidential Unit Citation, three battle stars.

MEMBER: Organization of American Historians.

AWARDS, HONORS: Social Science Research Council fellowship; New York State University research fellowship; named distinguished service professor, 1977; Augsburger Award for excellence in local history, 1979.

WRITINGS:

Teaching of Military History in American Colleges and Universities, Air University, 1957.
(Editor) *The Human Side of American History*, Ginn, 1961.
(With Arlan Helgeson and George Lobdell) *The United States of America*, Silver Burdett, 1962.

They Were There: A Guide to First-hand Literature for Use in Teaching American History, Service Center for Teachers of History, 1962.
(With others) *The American Achievement*, Time-Life, 1966.
Man in America, Silver Burdett, 1975.
Let Freedom Ring, Silver Burdett, 1977.
Social Attitudes of American Generals, Arno, 1979.
Buffalo: Lake City Niagara Land, Windsor, 1981.
The Presbyterians: 200 Years in Danville, Kingston, 1983.
One Flag, One Land, Silver Burdett, 1985.

SIDELIGHTS: Richard C. Brown told *CA:* "All my writing has been historical nonfiction. Since retiring as a university professor in 1979, I have moved to central Kentucky, a land with a long and colorful history. Here, I have pursued my interest in local history, as I did while living and teaching in western New York. My advice to beginning writers eager to supplement their incomes is this: write nonfiction—there's ten times more nonfiction published than fiction."

AVOCATIONAL INTERESTS: Writing.

*   *   *

BROWN, Seyom 1933-

PERSONAL: Born May 28, 1933, in Hightstown, N.J.; son of Benjamin (a community planner) and Sarah (Sokolow) Brown; married Rose Samuels, February, 1963 (died August, 1974); married Martha Morelock (a folksinger), January 16, 1976; children: (first marriage) Lisa, Steven, Elliot, Nell, Christina, Benjamin. *Education:* University of Southern California, B.A., 1955, M.A., 1957; University of Chicago, Ph.D., 1963.

ADDRESSES: Office—Foreign Policy Studies Program, Brookings Institution, 1775 Massachusetts Ave. N.W., Washington, D.C. 20036.

CAREER: University of Southern California, Los Angeles, lecturer, 1958-59; University of Chicago, Chicago, Ill., instructor, 1960-61; RAND Corp., Santa Monica, Calif., social scientist, 1962-69; Brookings Institution, Washington, D.C., senior fellow in foreign policy studies, 1969—. Visiting lecturer at University of California, Los Angeles, 1963-65, and Johns Hopkins School of Advanced International Studies, 1966-69; visiting professor at University of Southern California, summer, 1970; adjunct professor at Johns Hopkins School of Advanced International Studies, 1970—. Research at Johns Hopkins University's Washington Center of Foreign Policy Research, 1965-66. Speaker for Educational Resource Network of the Institute for World Order. Consultant to U.S. Department of State, U.S. Department of Defense, and U.S. Navy.

MEMBER: International Political Science Association, Amnesty International, International Studies Association, American Political Science Association, Council on Foreign Relations, Council on Religion and International Affairs, United Nations Association, Phi Beta Kappa.

AWARDS, HONORS: Fulbright scholarship to India, 1957-58.

WRITINGS:

(With Bernard L. Hyink and Ernest W. Thacker) *Politics and Government in California*, Crowell, 1959, 10th edition, 1979.
(Contributor) E. S. Quade and W. I. Boucher, editors, *Systems Analysis and Policy Planning*, Elsevier, 1968.

The Faces of Power: Constancy and Change in United States Foreign Policy from Truman to Johnson, Columbia University Press, 1968, 2nd edition, 1983.

(With P. Hammond, W. Jones, and R. Patrick) *An Information System for the National Security Community,* RAND Corp., 1969.

(Contributor) Sam Brown and Len Ackland, editors, *Why Are We Still in Vietnam?,* Random House, 1970.

(Contributor) Henry Owen, editor, *The Next Phase in Foreign Policy,* Brookings Institution, 1973.

The Changing Essence of Power, Brookings Institution, 1973.

New Forces in World Politics, Brookings Institution, 1974.

(With Larry L. Fabian) *Diplomats at Sea,* Brookings Institution, 1974.

(Contributor) James Chace and Earl Ravenal, editors, *Atlantis Lost: The U.S./European Relationship,* New York University Press, 1976.

(With others) *Regimes for the Ocean: Outer Space and Weather,* Brookings Institution, 1977.

The Crises of Power: An Interpretation of United States Foreign Policy during the Kissinger Years, Columbia University Press, 1979.

(With others) *Foreign Policy Priorities for the President: Toward a Future Agenda,* American Enterprise Institute for Public Policy Research, 1980.

On the Front Burner: Issues in U.S. Foreign Policy, Little, Brown, 1984.

Contributor to *Saturday Review, Reporter,* international studies journals, and newspapers.

SIDELIGHTS: Seyom Brown's *New Forces in World Politics* is, according to a *Choice* reviewer, "an excellent, factually based analysis of diverse forces which challenge and change the present international systems. . . . This book provides a fine overview both of the existing system and prospects for change." And J. H. E. Fried writes in *Annals of the American Academy of Political and Social Science* that *New Forces in World Politics* is "a brilliant addition to the still sparse 'committed' literature in the world's worsening disarray. Brown soberly warns that the clock is ticking, and the old ways will not do. . . . He makes . . . proposals for a U.S. 'constructive statesmanship'; 'the playing down of force as a sanction behind diplomacy'; 'dismantling of permanent military coalitions'; [and] fostering 'a more open global market' with due concessions to the poor countries 'on grounds other' than U.S. economic or military advantages."

BIOGRAPHICAL/CRITICAL SOURCES:

PERIODICALS

Annals of the American Academy of Political and Social Science, March, 1975.
Choice, December, 1974.
Saturday Review, September 14, 1968.

*   *   *

BROWNE, Robert
    See KARLINS, Marvin

*   *   *

BURCH, Robert J(oseph)   1925-

PERSONAL: Born June 26, 1925, in Inman, Ga.; son of John Ambrose (a bookkeeper) and Nell (Graham) Burch. *Education:* Attended Hunter College (now Hunter College of the City University of New York). *Politics:* Democrat. *Religion:* Methodist.

ADDRESSES: P.O. Box 243, Fayetteville, Ga. 30214.

CAREER: Civil service employee with Atlanta Ordnance Depot, Atlanta, Ga., 1951-53, and with U.S. Army, Yokohama and Tokyo, Japan, 1953-55; Muir & Co. (advertising agency), New York City, clerical worker, 1956-59; Walter E. Heller & Co. (industrial finance company), New York City, clerical worker, 1959-62. *Military service:* U.S. Army, 1943-46; served in New Guinea and Australia.

MEMBER: Authors Guild, Authors League of America, Juvenile Writers' Forum.

AWARDS, HONORS: Fellowship in juvenile literature, Bread Loaf Writers' Conference, 1960; children's book award from Child Study Association of America and Jane Addams Children's Book Award, both 1967, for *Queenie Peavy.*

WRITINGS:

JUVENILE FICTION

The Traveling Bird, Helene Obolensky, 1959.
(Translator) *A Jungle in the Wheat Field* (Danish picture book), Helene Obolensky, 1960.
A Funny Place to Live (Junior Literary Guild selection), Viking, 1962.
Tyler, Wilkin, and Skee, Viking, 1963.
Skinny (Weekly Reader Book Club selection), Viking, 1964.
D. J.'s Worst Enemy, Viking, 1965.
Queenie Peavy, Viking, 1966.
Renfroe's Christmas, Viking, 1968.
Joey's Cat, Viking, 1969.
Simon and the Game of Chance, Viking, 1970.
The Hunting Trip, Scribner, 1971.
Doodle and the Go Cart, Viking, 1972.
Hut School and the Wartime Home-Front Heroes, Viking, 1974.
The Jolly Witch, Dutton, 1975.
Two That Were Tough, Viking, 1976.
The Whitman Kick, Dutton, 1977.
Wilkin's Ghost, Viking, 1978.
Ida Early Comes over the Mountain (Junior Literary Guild selection), Viking, 1980.
Christmas with Ida Early, Viking, 1983.

WORK IN PROGRESS: A story about a girl who is elected poet laureate of her sixth grade class; a third book in the "Ida Early" series.

SIDELIGHTS: Robert J. Burch wrote *CA:* "When I first started writing, more than thirty years ago, much of the realistic fiction for children was not realistic at all. Home situations were often perfect, and endings—almost always happy—were too pat. It was interesting to be one of the 'pioneers' in the so-called new realism; yet I'm not sure but what we've moved too far in the opposite direction by now. Too often *new-realism* has given way to *grim-realism.* Perhaps eventually we'll arrive at an appropriate balance."

AVOCATIONAL INTERESTS: Travel (has lived in Europe and made a tour of the world), water gardening, raising Japanese carp and waterfowl.

BIOGRAPHICAL/CRITICAL SOURCES:

PERIODICALS

New York Times Book Review, May 5, 1974, January 18, 1981.

BURKE, Leda
  See GARNETT, David

*   *   *

BURN, A(ndrew) R(obert)   1902-

PERSONAL: Born September 25, 1902, in Kynnersley, Shropshire, England; son of Andrew Ewbank (a clergyman) and Celia Mary (Richardson) Burn; married Mary Wynn Thomas, December 31, 1938. *Education:* Christ Church, Oxford, B.A., 1925, M.A., 1928. *Politics:* Social Democrat. *Religion:* Anglican (''skeptical'').

ADDRESSES: Home—23 Ritchie Ct., Oxford OX2 7PW, England.

CAREER: Uppingham School, Uppingham, England, senior classical master, 1927-40; British Embassy, Athens, Greece, second secretary, 1944-46; University of Glasgow, Glasgow, Scotland, senior lecturer, 1946-65, reader in ancient history, 1965-69. Gillespie Professor, College of Wooster, Wooster, Ohio, 1958-59; member of Institute for Advanced Study, Princeton, N.J., 1961-62; professor, A College Year in Athens, Inc., 1969-72. *Military service:* Intelligence Corps, 1941-43; became captain.

MEMBER: Society for the Promotion of Hellenic Studies (member of council, 1959-62), Society for the Promotion of Roman Studies, Glasgow Archaelogical Society (president, 1969-72).

AWARDS, HONORS: Silver Cross, Order of the Phoenix (Greece), 1975; D. Litt., Oxford University, 1982.

WRITINGS:

Minoans, Philistines, and Greeks, Knopf, 1930, reprinted, Greenwood Press, 1975.
The Romans in Britain: An Anthology of Inscriptions, Basil Blackwell, 1932, 2nd edition, University of South Carolina, 1968.
The World of Hesiod, Knopf, 1936, reprinted, Blom, 1968.
This Scepter'd Isle: An Anthology of English Poetry, Pyros (Athens), 1940.
Philoi toi Vivliou, [Alexandria], 1942, translation published as *The Modern Greeks,* Thomas Nelson, 1944.
Alexander the Great and the Hellenistic Empire, Hodder & Stoughton, 1947, Macmillan (New York), 1948, enlarged edition published as *Alexander the Great and the Hellenistic World,* Collier, 1962.
Pericles and Athens, English Universities Press, 1948, Collier, 1962.
Agricola and Roman Britain, English Universities Press, 1953, revised edition, Collier, 1962.
(Contributor) John Bowle, editor, *An Encyclopedia of World History,* Hutchinson, 1958.
The Lyric Age of Greece, Edward Arnold, 1960.
Persia and the Greeks, St. Martin's, 1962, revised edition (with D. M. Lewis), Duckworth, 1985.
(Contributor) Michael Grant, editor, *The Birth of Western Civilization,* Thames & Hudson, 1964.
A Traveller's History of Greece, Hodder & Stoughton, 1965, published as *The Pelican History of Greece,* Pelican, 1966.
The Warring States of Greece, Thames & Hudson, 1969.
Greece and Rome, Scott, Foresman, 1971.

(With Mary Burn) *The Living Past of Greece,* Little, Brown, 1980.
(Contributor) *The Cambridge History of Iran,* Volume II, Cambridge University Press, 1985.
(Contributor) M. Grant and Rachel Kitzinger, editors, *Civilizations of the Ancient Mediterranean,* Scribner, in press.

Contributor to encyclopedias and professional journals.

WORK IN PROGRESS: A one-volume history of civilization, tentatively entitled *Man: A Brief History,* for Hodder & Stoughton; *Greece Has Four Dimensions,* an autobiography.

SIDELIGHTS: A. R. Burn told *CA:* ''Why do I write? Believe it or not, to try to make the world better, even if by an amount not visible to the naked eye. It is a matter of earliest influences—I was born in Shropshire rectory, brought up by very good and fairly enlightened, Victorian-educated parents, and destined for the Church—but I could not accept the theology. So I kept the ethics and chucked the dogma.

''*Man: A Brief History* contains much thought on Marx, whose works are of major importance to the understanding of modern human society. I conclude that while we cannot do much about changing our genetically-conditioned natures, *social* conditions can do much, for good or ill, about how we channel those natures—producing, for instance, Athenians or Spartans. The book will end, if I live to finish it, with a severe criticism of what Marxist-Leninist parties have done in practice, for they have evolved all the worst characteristics of intolerant churches.''

A reviewer for *Times Literary Supplement* describes Burn as ''a scholar whose detailed grasp of the minutiae of ancient history is reinforced by wide personal and topographical knowledge, great imaginative insight, and a pleasantly warm style.'' This observation is seconded in a *Times Literary Supplement* review of Andrew and Mary Burn's handbook for travelers, *The Living Past of Greece:* ''For a book of this kind and size, the topographical description of Athens is masterly, being detailed enough without risking confusion, and by the end of it, the reader has been conducted with affectionate facility through a history of Athenian political institutions.''

AVOCATIONAL INTERESTS: Formerly mountaineering and gliding; now travel.

BIOGRAPHICAL/CRITICAL SOURCES:

PERIODICALS

Times Educational Supplement, October 24, 1980.
Times Literary Supplement, April 21, 1961, March 6, 1969, May 9, 1980.

*   *   *

BURN, Barbara   1940-

PERSONAL: Born January 24, 1940, in Boston, Mass.; daughter of Henry J. and Louise Marie (Buff) Burn; married John C. Kohr, July 11, 1964 (divorced January 31, 1967); married Emil P. Dolensek (a veterinarian), May 15, 1976; children: Philip Henry. *Education:* Smith College, B.A., 1961; additional study at New York University, 1961-65.

ADDRESSES: Home—21 Tier St., City Island, N.Y. 10464. *Office*—Metropolitan Museum of Art, Fifth Ave. at 82nd St., New York, N.Y. 10028.

CAREER: Solomon R. Guggenheim Museum, New York City, administrative assistant, 1961-65; Viking Press, New York

City, editor, 1965-82, editorial director of studio books, 1978-82; Metropolitan Museum of Art, New York City, executive editor of museum publications, 1982—. Member of Tastemaker Award nomination committee.

MEMBER: American Society for the Prevention of Cruelty to Animals (member of board of directors), New York Zoological Society.

WRITINGS:

(With husband, Emil P. Dolensek) *A Practical Guide to Impractical Pets*, Viking, 1976, published as *The Penguin Book of Pets*, Penguin, 1978.
(With Steven Price, Gail Rentsch, and David Spector) *Whole Horse Catalog*, Simon & Schuster, 1977.
(With Nancy Dolensek) *Mutt*, C. N. Potter, 1978.
The Horseless Rider: A Complete Guide to the Art of Riding, Showing, and Enjoying Other People's Horses, St. Martin's, 1979.
The Morris Approach (on cat care), Morrow, 1979.
(Editor) *Utamaro: Song of the Garden*, Metropolitan Museum of Art, 1984.
Metropolitan Children, Abrams, 1984.

Also author of four books on North American natural history, 1984. Author, with E. P. Dolensek, of column for *Animal Kingdom*. Contributor to *Better Homes and Gardens* and *American Home*.

SIDELIGHTS: Barbara Burn told *CA:* "My experience as an editor of other writers' books, combined with my marriage to a veterinarian and renewed interest in owning pets and horseback riding, managed to result in a group of books in which I could focus on my favorite subjects, popularize serious information, and share some of my personal experiences."

*   *   *

BURNEY, Anton
    See HOPKINS, Kenneth

*   *   *

BURTON, Robert (Wellesley)   1941-

PERSONAL: Born June 18, 1941, in Sherbourne, Dorsetshire, England; son of Maurice (a zoologist) and Margaret (Maclean) Burton. *Education:* Attended Downing College, Cambridge, 1960-63.

ADDRESSES: Home and office—Manor Cottage, 46 West St., Great Gransden, Sandy, Bedfordshire SG19 3AU, England. *Agent*—Murray Pollinger, 4 Garrick St., London WC2E 9BH, England.

CAREER: Writer, 1967—. Meteorologist and biologist for British Antarctic Survey, 1963-66; biologist, 1971-72.

MEMBER: Society of Authors, Institute of Biology, Zoological Society of London.

WRITINGS:

Animals of the Antarctic, Abelard Schuman, 1970.
Animal Senses, David & Charles, 1970.
The Life and Death of Whales, Deutsch, 1973, 2nd edition, revised and enlarged, Universe Books, 1980.
How Birds Live, Elsevier Phaidon, 1975.
The Mating Game, Elsevier Phaidon, 1976.
Ponds: Their Wildlife and Upkeep, David & Charles, 1976.

The Cat Family, illustrated by Richard Hook, Silver Burdett, 1976.
The Language of Smell, Routledge & Kegan Paul, 1976.
The Love of Baby Animals, Octopus Books, 1976.
Exploring Hills and Moors, Elsevier Phaidon, 1976.
(With Carole Devaney and Tony Long) *The Living Sea: An Illustrated Encyclopedia of Marine Life*, Putnam, 1976.
Nature by the Roadside, Elsevier Phaidon, 1977.
The Seashore and Its Wildlife, Putnam, 1977.
First Nature Book, St. Michael, 1977.
Seals, Bodley Head, 1978.
Carnivores of Europe, Batsford, 1979.
Horses and Ponies, Macmillan, 1979.
Nature's Night Life, Blandford, 1982.
Bird Behavior, Grenada/Knopf, 1985.

WITH FATHER, MAURICE BURTON

The Life of Meat Eaters, Golden Press, 1974.
World of Nature, Purnell, 1974.
(Editor) *Encyclopedia of Reptiles, Amphibians, and Other Cold-blooded Animals*, introduction by M. Burton, Octopus Books/Phoebus, 1975.
Encyclopedia of Fish, introduction by Gareth Nelson, Octopus Books, 1975.
Encyclopedia of Insects and Arachnids, introduction by Michael Tweedie, Octopus Books, 1975.
Encyclopedia of Mammals, introduction by L. Harrison Matthews, Octopus Books, 1975.
Encyclopedia of the Animal Kingdom, Octopus Books/Phoebus, 1976.
Inside the Animal World: An Encyclopedia of Animal Behavior, Quandrangle/New York Times, 1977.
The World's Disappearing Wildlife, Marshall Cavendish, 1978.

Also editor of *Purnell's Encyclopedia of Animal Life*, BPC Publishing, 1968-70, published in the United States as *The International Wildlife Encyclopedia*, 1970, four-volume edition, Octopus, 1974.

OTHER

Contributor to *BBC Wildlife, Guardian, Natural World, World Wildlife News*, and *Sea Frontier*.

AVOCATIONAL INTERESTS: Whaling, history of polar expeditions, and restoring his thatched cottage.

BIOGRAPHICAL/CRITICAL SOURCES:

PERIODICALS

New York Times Book Review, August 18, 1985.

*   *   *

BUZO, Alexander (John)   1944-

PERSONAL: Born July 23, 1944, in Sydney, Australia; son of Zihni Jusef (a civil engineer) and Elaine (a teacher; maiden name, Johnson) Buzo; married Merelyn Johnson (a teacher), December 21, 1968; children: Emma Jane, Laura Clare. *Education:* University of New South Wales, B.A., 1965.

ADDRESSES: Home—14 Rawson Ave., Bondi Junction, Sydney, New South Wales 2022, Australia. *Agent*—June Cann, P.O. Box 1577, North Sydney, New South Wales 2060, Australia.

CAREER: David Jones Ltd. (retail store), Sydney, Australia, salesman, 1960; E. L. Davis & Co. (stockbroker), Sydney, clerk, 1961; actor and waiter, 1966-67; New South Wales Public Service, Sydney, clerk, 1967-68; playwright, 1968—. Resident playwright at Melbourne Theatre Company, 1972-73.

MEMBER: Australian Writers Guild.

AWARDS, HONORS: Gold medal from Australian Literature Society, 1972, for plays "Macquarie" and "Tom"; fellow of Literary Board, 1974 and 1979.

WRITINGS:

PLAYS

The Front Room Boys (first produced in Perth, Australia, at Perth Festival, 1970; produced in London at Royal Court Theatre, 1971), Penguin, 1970.

Macquarie (first produced in Melbourne, Australia, at Melbourne Theatre Company, 1972), Currency Press, 1972.

Norm and Ahmed, Rooted, [and] *The Roy Murphy Show: Three Plays* (contains "Norm and Ahmed," first produced in Sydney, Australia, at Old Tote Theatre, 1968, produced in London, 1974; "Rooted," first produced in Sydney at Jane Street Theatre, 1969, produced in Hartford, Conn., at Hartford Stage Company, 1972; and "The Roy Murphy Show," first produced in Sydney at Nimrod Theatre, 1971), Currency Press, 1973.

Coralie Lansdowne Says No (first produced in Adelaide, Australia, by Nimrod Theatre, 1974), Currency Press, 1974.

Tom (first produced in Melbourne at Melbourne Theatre Company, 1972; produced in Washington, D.C., at Arena Stage, 1973), Angus & Robertson, 1975.

Martello Towers (first produced in Sydney at Nimrod Theatre, 1976), Currency Press, 1976.

Makassar Reef (first produced in Melbourne at Melbourne Theatre Company, 1978; produced in Seattle, Wash., at ACT Theater, 1978), Currency Press, 1978.

The Marginal Farm [and] *Big River* (contains "The Marginal Farm," first produced in Melbourne at the Melbourne Theatre Company, 1983; and "Big River," first produced in Adelaide, Australia, at Adelaide Festival, 1980), Currency Press, 1985.

RADIO PLAYS

"Duff," Australian Broadcasting Corporation, 1981.

"East of Singapore," Australian Broadcasting Corporation, 1985.

OTHER

Tautology (nonfiction), Penguin, 1981.

Meet the New Class (nonfiction), Angus & Robertson, 1981.

The Search for Harry Allway (novel), Angus & Robertson, 1985.

Also author of screenplay, "Rod," 1972. Author of television scripts "King Arthur" and "Legend of Robin Hood"; author of animated telefeatures "A Christmas Carol," "Great Expectations," "David Copperfield," and "The Old Curiosity Shop," all adapted from works by Charles Dickens, Burbank Films, 1981-82. Contributor to anthologies, including *Buzo/Hibberd/Romeril: Four Australian Plays,* Penguin, 1970. Contributor of articles to the *National Times, Financial Review, Sidney Morning Herald, Age, Pol Magazine,* and *Reader's Digest.*

SIDELIGHTS: Alexander Buzo wrote *CA:* "My early plays [were] influenced by surrealism in their style. In the 1960s I admired the work of Beckett, Pinter and Albee. My plays were sardonic comedies concerned with individuals who ran up against the forces of reality, and the themes were concerned with morality and the issues of this conflict. For example, in 'Rooted,' an innocent urban man called Bentley does everything he is supposed to in an affluent western society—he acquires a wife, a smart house, a good job, a new stereo, and lots of friends. An unseen power broker called Simmo challenges Bentley for all these possessions and the unequal battle is joined." Reviewing the play in the Boston *Record American,* Elliot Norton commented that "Rooted" is "a lovely play, . . . a strange free-form farce about a man doomed to lose, deliriously funny and, at the same time, deadly serious." And *Time* critic T. E. Kolem indicated that "rarely has black comedy been more lavish in its laughter."

A similar conflict is at the center of "Norm and Ahmed," a play in which "a Pakistani student runs smack into a middle-aged Australian," Buzo told *CA.* "Norm is the antithesis of the unworldly Ahmed and finally his nemesis." According to Buzo, in his later plays "the conflict remains similar, but less stark. The central characters are less rigid, less idealistic, more fully defined. Nevertheless, these later protagonists such as Adela Learmonth in 'Big River,' and Weeks Brown in 'Makassar Reef' are still struggling to avoid the submerging of their individual values. The style of the later work aims at a more dramatic and romantic effect rather than the satire of the early pieces and the surrealism has been replaced by a more realistic style of writing."

MEDIA ADAPTATIONS: A radio version of "The Front Room Boys" was broadcast by the British Broadcasting Corp. in 1975; a television version of "Coralie Lansdowne Says No" was broadcast by the Australian Broadcasting Company in 1980.

AVOCATIONAL INTERESTS: Playing cricket and tennis, watching rugby and football, travel, wine.

BIOGRAPHICAL/CRITICAL SOURCES:

BOOKS

Fitzpatrick, Peter, *After the Doll,* Edward Arnold, 1979.

Holloway, Peter, editor, *Contemporary Australian Drama,* Angus & Robertson, 1978.

Palmer, Jennifer, editor, *Contemporary Australian Playwrights,* University Union Press, 1979.

Rees, Leslie, *The Making of Australian Drama,* Currency Press, 1981.

PERIODICALS

Meanjini, 1980.

Record American (Boston), January 26, 1972.

Southerly 4, December, 1975.

Time, February 14, 1972.

Westerly 4, December, 1975.

*   *   *

BYHAM, William C(larence) 1936-

PERSONAL: Born September 14, 1936, in Parkersburg, W. Va.; son of Edgar William and Brice Irene (Michael) Byham; married Carolyn Ann Mentzer, February 11, 1967; children: Jennifer Tacy, William Carter. *Education:* Ohio University, B.S., 1958, M.S., 1959; Purdue University, Ph.D., 1962.

ADDRESSES: Home—1440 Pueblo Dr., Pittsburgh, Pa. 15228. *Office*—Development Dimensions, Inc., 250 Mount Lebanon Blvd., Pittsburgh, Pa. 15234.

CAREER: Certified pscyhologist in the states of New York and Pennsylvania; Kenyon & Eckhardt, Inc. (advertising agency), New York City, administrative assistant to executive vice-president, 1962-64; J. C. Penny Co., New York City, general management training specialist, 1964-70; University of Pittsburgh, Graduate School of Business, Pittsburgh, Pa., director of executive development and continuing education, 1970-73; Development Dimensions, Inc., Pittsburgh, president, 1973—. Lecturer at Bernard M. Baruch College of the City University of New York, 1965-69, and Cornell University, 1969. Member of national personnel advisory board, Junior Achievement, 1967-70. Diplomate of American Board of Professional Psychology.

MEMBER: American Psychological Association, Sigma Xi.

WRITINGS:

(Contributor) *The School of Tomorrow,* Macfadden, 1964.
(Contributor) *The Personality and Labor,* Bureau of Applied Social Research, Columbia University, 1966.

The Uses of Personnel Research, American Management Assocation, 1968.
(With Moit Spitzer) *The Law and Personnel Testing,* American Management Association, 1971.
(Editor with Dennis P. Slevin) *Women: Action Not Reaction,* [Pittsburgh], 1971.
(Editor with Mildred Katzell) *Women in the Work Force,* Behavioral Publications, 1972.
(Editor with Donna Bobin) *Alternatives to Paper and Pencil Testing,* Graduate School of Business, University of Pittsburgh, 1973.
(Editor with Bobin) *Changing Employee Behavior,* University of Pittsburgh, 1973.
(Editor with Joseph L. Moses) *Applying the Assessment Center Method,* Pergamon, 1977.
(With George C. Thornton) *Assessment Centers and Managerial Performance,* Academic Press, 1982.

Contributor to *AMA Management Handbook* and to journals.†

C

CADWALLADER, Sharon 1936-

PERSONAL: Born January 12, 1936, in Jamestown, N.D.; daughter of Herman Julius (an insurance agent) and Mildred A. (Hull) Wulfsberg; married Mervyn Leland Cadwallader, July 4, 1959 (divorced, 1966); children: Leland Hull. *Education:* San Jose State College (now University), A.B., 1958. *Politics:* Democrat. *Religion:* None.

ADDRESSES: Home and office—174 12th Ave., Santa Cruz, Calif. 95062.

CAREER: Former teacher of mentally retarded children and of English to speakers of foreign languages; medical social worker in public clinic in Santa Cruz County, Calif.; organized and operated Whole Earth Restaurant at University of California, Santa Cruz; writer, 1972—.

WRITINGS:

(With Judi Ohr) *Whole Earth Cookbook,* Houghton, 1972.
In Celebration of Small Things, Houghton, 1975.
Cooking Adventures for Kids, Houghton, 1975.
Whole Earth Cookbook 2, Houghton, 1975.
Sharon Cadwallader's Complete Cookbook, San Francisco Book Co., 1977.
Sharing in the Kitchen: A Cookbook for Single Parents and Children, McGraw, 1979.
Savoring Mexico: A Travel Cookbook, McGraw, 1980.
Whole Earth Cooking for the 80s, St. Martin's, 1981.
The Living Kitchen, Sierra Books, 1983.
Surf's Up for Laney (young adult novel), Silhouette Books, 1984.

Syndicated newspaper food columnist.

SIDELIGHTS: Sharon Cadwallader told *CA:* ''People ask me quite frequently how I created a career such as mine—a food writer with a healthy emphasis. I always respond that I like to write, I like to cook, I like to eat, and I like to eat well. What else can I do but what I am doing? I am, however, doing some writing for children now. It's also writing of a nurturing nature, I think.''

*   *   *

CALAFERTE, Louis 1928-

PERSONAL: Born July 14, 1928, in Turin, Italy; son of Ugo (a mason) and Marguerite (Crepet) Calaferte; married Guillemette Maurice, January 10, 1956. *Education:* Attended primary school in Lyon, France. *Religion:* Christian.

ADDRESSES: Home—9 bis, rue Roux-Soignat, Lyon 3, France.

CAREER: Held various jobs from age of fourteen, in factories, as movie extra, and as newspaper vendor; Office de Radio Television Francais, Lyon and Paris, France, radio and television producer, 1956—.

AWARDS, HONORS: Laureat de la Bourse Del Duca, 1953; Bourse Nationale des Lettres, 1956; Prix Ponceton de la Societe des Gens de Lettres, 1976; Prix Ibsen, 1979; Prix Lugne-Poe, 1979; Prix Michel Dard, 1983, for *Ebauche d'un autoportrait.*

WRITINGS:

Requiem des innocents, Julliard, 1952.
Partage des vivants (novel), Julliard, 1953.
''Clotilde du Nord'' (one-act play), first produced in Paris, France, at Comedie de Paris, March, 1955.
Septentrion (novel), Cercle du Livre Precieux, 1963, reprinted, Denoel, 1984.
No Man's Land, Julliard, 1963.
Satori, Denoel, 1968.
Rosa mystica (novel), Denoel, 1968.
Portrait de l'Enfant, Denoel, 1969.
Hinterland, Denoel, 1971.
Limitrophe: Recit, Denoel, 1972.
Megaphonie (full-length play), Stock, 1972.
Rag-Time (poems), Denoel, 1972.
''Chez les Titch'' (also see below; one-act play), first produced in Paris at Theatre National du Petit Odeon, 1973.
Paraphe, Denoel, 1974.
La Vie parallele, Denoel, 1974.
Episodes de la vie des mantes religieuses, Denoel, 1976.
Mo (one-act play; first produced in Paris at Theatre National du Petit Odeon, 1976), Stock, 1976.
Les Mandibules (full-length play; first produced in Paris at Centre National Beaubourg, 1977), Stock, 1976.
Campagnes, Denoel, 1979.
L'Amour des mots (one-act play), Revue de Centre Dramatique National de Reims, 1979.
Trafic (also see below; one-act play; first produced in Paris at Theatre National du Petit Odeon, 1976), Stock, 1980.

Les Miettes (also see below; one-act play; first produced in Paris at Theatre Essaion, 1978), Stock, 1980.

Theatre intimiste (contains "Chez les Titch," "Trafic," "Les Miettes," and "Tu as bien fait de venir, Paul"), Stock, 1980.

Le Chemin de Sion (memoirs), Denoel, 1980.

"Les Beaux Dimanches" (screenplay), produced by French television, 1980.

L'Or et le plomb (memoirs), Denoel, 1981.

Ebauche d'un autoportrait, Denoel, 1983.

Les Derniers Devoirs (play; first produced at L'Avant-Scene, 1983), Revue du Centre Dramatique National de Reims, 1983.

Lignes interieures (memoirs), Denoel, 1985.

Londoniennes (poems), illustrations by Jacques Truphemus, Le Tout sur le Tout (Paris), 1985.

Contributor to newspapers.

WORK IN PROGRESS: Langages, poems and paintings; "Opera Bleu," a full-length play.

SIDELIGHTS: Louis Calaferte told *CA* that drawing and painting have become as important to him as writing. His gouaches and tint-drawings were exhibited in 1973 in Lyon-Miribel, France, at Gallery Corine Martin.

*   *   *

CALDWELL, (James Alexander) Malcolm 1931-1978

PERSONAL: Born September 27, 1931, in Stirling, Scotland; died December 23, 1978, in Southeast Asia; son of Archibald Thomson and Violet (Sutherland) Caldwell; married Ann Rosemary Bee (a superintendent of play parks), May 14, 1954 (divorced, 1972); married Lyn Mary Gilmore, 1972; children: (first marriage) Fiona, Richard, Jeremy, Louise. *Education:* University of Edinburgh, M.A. (first class honors in economics), 1953; University of Nottingham, Ph.D., 1956. *Politics:* Socialist.

ADDRESSES: Home—110 Bexley High St., Bexley, Kent, England. *Agent*—Frances Kelly, Curtis Brown Group Ltd., 162-168 Regent St., London W1R 5TA, England. *Office*—School of Oriental and African Studies, University of London, London W.C.1, England.

CAREER: University of London, School of Oriental and African Studies, London, England, lecturer in economic history of Southeast Asia. *Military service:* British Army, Royal Army Educational Corps, 1956-58; became sergeant.

WRITINGS:

(With J. D. Henderson) *The Chainless Mind,* Hamish Hamilton, 1968.

The Modern World: Indonesia, Oxford University Press, 1968.

Oil and Imperialism in East Asia, Spokesman Books, 1971.

(With Lek Tan) *Cambodia in the South East Asian War,* Monthly Review Press, 1973.

(Editor) *Ten Years' Military Terror in Indonesia,* Spokesman Books, 1975.

The Wealth of Some Nations, Zed Press, 1977.

(Editor) *Marx and the Third World,* Macmillan, 1977.

(Editor with Mohamed Amin) *Malaya: The Making of a Neo-Colony,* Spokesman Books, 1977.

(Editor with Nick Jeffrey) *Planning and Urbanism in China,* Pergamon, 1977.

(Editor with Andrew Turton and Jonathan Fast) *Thailand: Roots of Conflict,* Spokesman Books, 1978.

CONTRIBUTOR

C. D. Cowan, editor, *Economic Development of South East Asia,* Allen & Unwin, 1964.

J. W. Burton, editor, *Nonalignment,* Deutsch, 1966.

C. R. Hill, editor, *Rights and Wrongs,* Penguin, 1969.

Tariq Ali, editor, *New Revolutionaries,* P. Owen, 1969.

K. Boates, editor, *Socialism and the Environment,* Spokesman Books, 1972.

M. Seldon, editor, *Re-Making Asia,* Pantheon, 1974.

OTHER

Contributor to academic journals, magazines, and newspapers. Editor, *Journal of Contemporary Asia,* beginning 1970.

AVOCATIONAL INTERESTS: Cricket, music, literature, beer.†

*   *   *

CAREY, M. V.
See CAREY, Mary (Virginia)

*   *   *

CAREY, Mary (Virginia) 1925- (M. V. Carey)

PERSONAL: Born May 19, 1925, in New Brighton, England; brought to the United States in 1925, naturalized citizen in 1955; daughter of John Cornelius (an engineer) and Mary (Hughes) Carey. *Education:* College of Mount St. Vincent, B.S., 1946. *Religion:* Roman Catholic.

ADDRESSES: Home—645 Westlake Rd., No. 137, Westlake Village, Calif. 91361.

CAREER: Coronet, New York, N.Y., editorial associate, 1948-55; Walt Disney Productions, Burbank, Calif., assistant editor of publications, 1955-69; free-lance writer, 1969—. Editorial consultant to Oak Tree Publications.

MEMBER: Women in Communications.

WRITINGS:

NOVELIZATIONS OF WALT DISNEY MOTION PICTURES

(With George Sherman) *Walt Disney's "Babes in Toyland,"* Golden Press, 1961.

Walt Disney's "The Sword in the Stone," Whitman Publishing, 1963.

The Story of Walt Disney's Motion Picture "Mary Poppins," Whitman Publishing, 1964.

Walt Disney's "The Misadventures of Merlin Jones," Whitman Publishing, 1964.

Walt Disney's "Donald Duck and the Lost Mesa Ranch," Whitman Publishing, 1966.

The Story of Walt Disney's Motion Picture "Jungle Book," Whitman Publishing, 1967.

The Story of Walt Disney's Motion Picture "Blackbeard's Ghost," Whitman Publishing, 1968.

Mrs. Brisby's Important Package (adapted from film "The Secret of NIMH"), Golden Press, 1982.

JUVENILES

Raggedy Ann and the Glad and Sad Day, Golden Press, 1972.

Little Lulu and the Birthday Surprise, Whitman Publishing, 1973.

The Tawny, Scrawny Lion and the Clever Monkey, Golden Press, 1974.
Alonzo Purr, the Seagoing Cat, Western Publishing, 1974.
The Owl Who Loved Sunshine, Golden Press, 1977.
The Gremlins Storybook, Golden Press, 1984.

UNDER NAME M. V. CAREY; "THE THREE INVESTIGATORS" JU-
VENILE MYSTERY SERIES

The Mystery of the Flaming Footprints, Random House, 1971.
The Mystery of the Singing Serpent, Random House, 1972.
The Mystery of Monster Mountain, Random House, 1973.
The Secret of the Haunted Mirror, Random House, 1974.
The Mystery of the Invisible Dog, Random House, 1975.
The Mystery of Death Trap Mine, Random House, 1976.
The Mystery of the Magic Circle, Random House, 1978.
The Mystery of the Sinister Scarecrow, Random House, 1979.
The Mystery of the Scar-Faced Beggar, Random House, 1981.
The Mystery of the Blazing Cliffs, Random House, 1981.
The Mystery of the Wandering Cave Man, Random House, 1982.
The Mystery of the Missing Mermaid, Random House, 1984.

OTHER

(Editor) Jane Black, *The Indispensables*, Hewitt House, 1971.
Step-by-Step Candlemaking, Golden Press, 1972.
Step-by-Step Winemaking, Golden Press, 1973.
Love Is Forever (collection of prose and poetry), C. R. Gibson, 1975.
(With George Sherman) *A Compendium of Bunk*, C. C Thomas, 1976.
(Editor) *Grandmothers Are Very Special People*, C. R. Gibson, 1977.
A Place for Allie (young adult novel), Dodd, 1985.

SIDELIGHTS: Mary Carey told *CA:* "I began writing late; my first articles and stories were published after I was thirty, and I was motivated by money. Money is not a bad motivation. The need to eat keeps us from laziness, and the fact that someone is willing to pay to read what we write assures us that we have indeed written.

"I think that writing should be honest and simple, and it should say something about what it means to be a person. When God is good to us, we write in such a way that the act of reading becomes a pleasure to those who buy our books. This experience doesn't happen all the time, but when it does it is at least as heady as winning the Irish sweepstakes. It makes mere competence seem dull. It is probably also what makes writing a compulsive occupation; some of us are uncomfortable when we are away from our typewriters for any length of time.

"My lifelong ambition, aside from writing, is to finish exploring the American West. This should keep me busy for at least another thirty years, since there is a great deal of space here and we have always attracted great individualists."

She added: "More and more I don't have any philosophy about writing, except that it is something we can do if God is good to us.

"A couple of years ago an old friend came visiting and reminded me of how it was when were were children. She told how we used to sit on my front porch and every day we read, and since we tackled some great long books, we couldn't finish them at a sitting. So each day I would tell her what had happened the day before, condensing the story and leaving out the parts that weren't really important. 'And then sometimes you told your own stories,' she said. So I am lucky. I have gotten back to where I was when I was nine. The long detour I took on the way enabled me to learn how to spell—I don't think I spelled that well at nine.''

*   *   *

CARLISLE, Regis   1955-

PERSONAL: Born November 9, 1955, in Pontiac, Colo.; son of Pedro Guido (a fisherman) and Cloris (a plastic tester; maiden name, King) Carlisle; married Bonnie Lindahll (a poet and marketing analyst), June 12, 1973; children: Calen Jeremy, David Brandon, Duncan Guido, Lindon Lindahll. *Education:* Bueshwaugh State University, B.A., 1978, M.B.A., 1980. *Politics:* "I vote for the party—not the man." *Religion:* "None right now—perhaps if the tithe percentage was lowered. . . .''

ADDRESSES: Home—221 Lewiston Rd., Grosse Pointe Farms, Mich. 48236.

CAREER: Writer. Worked as gardener in Sands, Mich,. 1974-75; pole vault instructor in Everglades Edge, Fla., 1975-77; newspaper deliverer, 1977-80; Compintex E.M.D. World International, Upper Mobile, Mich., trainee, 1980-81, assistant to the vice-president, 1981-82, vice-president, 1982-83, president, 1983-84, chairman of the board, 1984—.

AWARDS, HONORS: Golden Seat Award from Thinkers Society, 1969, for *The Philosopher of Paris;* New Star on Horizon Trophy from Discoverers of Unknown Learners (DUL), 1978, for *Anarchists Unite!;* Social Climbers Award, 1980, for *Y.U.P.P.I.E. Spells Success!.*

WRITINGS:

The Philosopher of Paris (novel), Dis Counte Press, 1969.
Eiffel Eyefull (travelogue), Tourer's Guidebooks, 1969.
Europe on $1.00 a Day (travelogue), Tourer's Guidebooks, 1970.
The Essential Relevance of Disbelief and Other Essays, Dis Counte Press, 1971.
The Sheer Hopelessness of Life, Existence, and Social Participation (novel), Loathers Society Press, 1973.
Pity the Thinker (novel), Dis Counte Press, 1975.
Life Has Nothing to Do with What Happens, Loathers Society, 1977.
Anarchists Unite!, Organizations Ltd., 1978.
Y.U.P.P.I.E. Spells Success!, Uppenkomin Press, 1980.
How to Be a Success without Sacrificing Anything, Trendy Ltd., 1980.
What's New and Exciting: A Primer of Social Dos and Don'ts, Yupbooks, 1982.
Raising Your Children to Be Upwardly Mobile, Yupbooks, 1983.
(With wife, Bonnie Carlisle) *Bonnie and Regis Carlisle's Fifty Ways with Tofu* (cookbook), Gastronomica, 1985.
(With B. Carlisle) *Bonnie and Regis Carlisle's Imported Car Notebook*, Yupbooks, 1985.

WORK IN PROGRESS: *Compintex: One Man's Personal Rise to the Top;* a screenplay adaptation of *Raising Your Children to Be Upwardly Mobile*, entitled "Johnny Gets His M.B.A."

SIDELIGHTS: Regis Carlisle told *CA:* "It's true! You *can* have it all. I am a personal monument to this ideal. My lovely wife and I both work at a multi-million dollar company, have four gifted children and an imported car, manage to write books in our spare time, eat well yet exercise our bodies to perfection, and make an income well over the national average.

"Achieving this lifestyle took a change of viewpoint for me personally. At one point in my life, I was overwhelmed by *ennui.* So I scrapped my silly infatuation with philosophy, got an M.B.A. and a job, and started my rise up the corporate ladder. I came to realize that money and material goods were the only answer to my personal *angst.* My writing career also reflects this notion. As Samuel Johnson once quipped: 'Nobody but a blockhead ever wrote for anything but money.'

"Friends sometimes lambaste me for my excessive lifestyle. Even my wife whines about our neglect of, as she puts it, 'the simpler things in life.' Horsefeathers! I reply. There's nothing worth having that can't be attained by enough of the cold, green stuff!"

*　　*　　*

CARNEY, T(homas) F(rancis)   1931-

PERSONAL: Born February 7, 1931, in Brooklyn, N.Y.; son of Felix Francis (a civil servant) and Cecelia (Burke) Carney; married Barbara Parr (a teacher), August 17, 1954; children: Michael, Judith. *Education:* University of London, B.A. (honors), 1952, Ph.D., 1957; University of South Africa, D.Litt. et Phil., 1959.

ADDRESSES: Home—Windsor, Ontario, Canada. *Office*—Department of Communication Studies, University of Windsor, Windsor, Ontario, Canada N9B 3P4.

CAREER: Victoria University, Wellington, New Zealand, lecturer in classics, 1953-57; University College of Rhodesia and Nyasaland, Salisbury, South Rhodesia, professor of classics and head of department, 1957-62; University of Sydney, Sydney, Australia, associate professor of history, 1962-66; University of Manitoba, Winnipeg, associate professor, 1966-67, professor of history, 1967-77, professor of resource management in Natural Resource Institute, 1974-77, head of department of history, 1968-69; University of Windsor, Windsor, Ontario, professor of communication studies, 1977—. Visiting research scholar at University of Vienna, 1957-58, University of Pisa, 1959-60, University of Athens and University of Thessaloniki, 1961-62, Birkbeck College, University of London, 1969-70, Princeton University, 1972-73, and University of Western Ontario, 1981-82.

AWARDS, HONORS: Senior Fulbright scholar, Center for International Studies, Massachusettts Institute of Technology, 1965-66; Killam Award, 1969; Canada Council fellowship, 1972-73; Rh Institute Award, 1974, and Zubek Award, 1975, both from University of Manitoba; Ontario Confederation of University Faculty Associations Award for excellence in teaching, 1979; Canadian Association for University Continuing Education Award of Program Distinction.

WRITINGS:

A Biography of Caius Marius (monograph), Classical Association of Rhodesia and Nyasaland, 1961.
(Translator) A. P. Vacalopoulos, *History of Thessaloniki,* Institute of Balkan Studies, 1963.
(Editor) Terence, *Hecyra,* Classical Association of Rhodesia and Nyasaland, 1964.
(Translator) John the Lydian, *On the Magistracies of the Roman Constitution,* Wentworth Press, 1965.
(Editor and translator) John the Lydian, *De Magistratibus,* Coronado Press, 1971.
Bureaucracy in Traditional Society, Coronado Press, 1971.

Content Analysis: A Technique for Systematic Inference from Communications, University of Manitoba Press, 1972.
The Economies of Antiquity, Coronado Press, 1973.
Time-Budgeting a Thesis: The Critical Path Method, Faculty of Graduate Studies, University of Manitoba, 1973.
Constructing Instructional Simulations Games, Natural Resource Institute, University of Manitoba, 1974, revised edition, 1975.
The Shape of the Past: Models and Antiquity, Coronado Press, 1975.
Communications and Society: A Social History of Communications, Natural Resource Institute, University of Manitoba, 1975.
Historical Methods: A Reader, University of Manitoba Bookstore, 1976.
No Limits to Growth: Mind-Expanding Techniques, Harbeck & Associates (Winnipeg), 1976.
Career Karate: A Career Management Strategy, Methuen, 1983.
Job Smarts: How to Play the Career Game—and Win, Methuen, 1984.

Contributor of over 100 articles and reviews, mostly to academic journals in North America and Europe.

WORK IN PROGRESS: Collaborative Inquiry: A New Paradigm Research Approach, for Ablex.

SIDELIGHTS: T. F. Carney wrote *CA:* "I'm trying to help others not to make the same mistakes that I've made in my career. *Career Karate* is about how to build and document a track record; it puts the subordinate in control of the performance assessment review and so of his/her career. I wrote the script for, and narrated parts of, videotapes on this topic and on self-directed job hunting. The TV units weren't great, but the back-up manuals were well regarded. I'm trying to develop interactive computer disks, to go with the manuals in a self-directed learning package (there's too much demand for workshops on these topics for me to be able to cope with).

"Learning word processing has been an ego-bruising but eventually rewarding experience; and, thanks to an understanding wife, I still have a marriage. The new research techniques which allow one's interviewees to be collaborators instead of subjects seem very promising for new directions in social science; they fascinate me."

*　　*　　*

CARRICK, Carol   1935-

PERSONAL: Born May 20, 1935, in Queens, N.Y.; daughter of Chauncey L. (a salesman) and Elsa (Schweizer) Hatfield; married Donald Carrick (an artist), March 26, 1965; children: Christopher, Paul. *Education:* Hofstra University, B.A., 1957.

ADDRESSES: Home—High St., Edgartown, Mass. 01539.

CAREER: Writer for children.

AWARDS, HONORS: Award from New York Society of Illustrators, 1970, for *The Pond;* Children's Book of the Year award from Library of Congress, and Children's Book Showcase listing from Children's Book Council, both 1974, for *Lost in the Storm;* Children's Books of the Year award from Child Study Association, named to *Saturday Review*'s Best Children's Books of the Season list, Children's Book Showcase award from International Reading Association, and Outstanding Books for Children award from National Science Teachers Association, all 1975, all for *The Blue Lobster;* Children's

Book Showcase award from Children's Book Council and science book award from New York Academy of Science, both 1976, both for *The Blue Lobster;* Children's Book Showcase award from Child Study Association, 1978, for *The Washout;* Children's Books of the Year award from Child Study Association, 1979, for *Some Friend!;* 100 Best Books of the Year listing from New York Public Library, Outstanding Science Trade Book for Children award from Children's Book Council, and National Science Teacher's Association award, all 1980, all for *The Crocodiles Still Wait;* Ambassador of Honor Book award from New York English Speaking Union and Children's Books of the Year award from Child Study Association, both 1981, both for *Ben and the Porcupine;* Children's Books of the Year award from Child Study Association, 1981, for *The Accident;* Children's Choice awards from International Reading Association and Children's Book Council, 1982, for *The Empty Squirrel;* Children's Books of the Year award from Child Study Association, 1983, for *What a Wimp!*

WRITINGS:

JUVENILES; ILLUSTRATED BY HUSBAND, DONALD CARRICK

The Old Barn, Bobbs-Merrill, 1966.
The Brook, Macmillan, 1967.
Swamp Spring, Macmillan, 1969.
The Pond, Macmillan, 1970.
The Dirt Road, Macmillan, 1970.
The Clearing in the Forest, Dial, 1970.
The Dragon of Santa Lalia, Bobbs-Merrill, 1971.
The Sleep Out, Seabury, 1973.
Beach Bird, Dial, 1973.
Lost in the Storm, Seabury, 1974.
Old Mother Witch, Seabury, 1975.
The Blue Lobster, Dial, 1975.
The Accident, Seabury, 1976.
The Sand Tiger, Seabury, 1977.
The Highest Balloon on the Common, Greenwillow, 1977.
The Foundling, Seabury, 1977.
The Octopus, Seabury, 1978.
The Washout, Seabury, 1978.
Paul's Christmas Birthday, Greenwillow, 1978.
A Rabbit for Easter, Greenwillow, 1979.
Some Friend!, Houghton, 1979.
The Crocodiles Still Wait, Houghton, 1980.
The Climb, Clarion Press, 1980.
Ben and the Porcupine, Clarion Press, 1981.
The Empty Squirrel, Greenwillow, 1981.
The Longest Float in the Parade, Greenwillow, 1982.
Two Coyotes, Clarion Press, 1982.
Patrick's Dinosaurs, Clarion Press, 1983.
What a Wimp!, Clarion Press, 1983.
Stay Away from Simon, Clarion Press, 1985.

SIDELIGHTS: Carol Carrick's books have been published in Swedish, Danish, German, and Japanese.

*   *   *

CARRINGER, Robert L. 1941-

PERSONAL: Born May 12, 1941, in Knoxville, Tenn.; son of Lloyd T. and Marie (Simpson) Carringer; married Sonia Raysor (an academic administrator), September 7, 1968. *Education:* University of Tennessee, A.B., 1962; Johns Hopkins University, M.A., 1964; Indiana University, Ph.D., 1970.

ADDRESSES: Home—R.R. 1, Box 59, Seymour, Ill. 61875. *Office*—Department of English, University of Illinois, 608 South Wright St., Urbana, Ill. 61801.

CAREER: University of Illinois at Urbana-Champaign, assistant professor, 1970-76, associate professor of English and cinema studies, 1977—.

MEMBER: Modern Language Association of America (chairperson of Film Division, 1980), Society for Cinema Studies, University Film Association, Midwest Modern Language Association (chairperson of film study section, 1978).

AWARDS, HONORS: Undergraduate Instructional Award, 1979; Amoco Curriculum Development Award, 1980; Center for Advanced Study award, 1983-84; Distinguished Professorship Award, 1985.

WRITINGS:

(Co-author) *Film Study Guides,* Stipes, 1977.
(With Barry Sabath) *Ernst Lubitsch,* G. K. Hall, 1978.
(Editor) *The Jazz Singer,* University of Wisconsin Press, 1979.
(With Nancy Allen) *Annotated Catalog of Unpublished Film and Television Scripts,* University of Illinois Library, 1983.
(Editor) *Citizen Kane,* Laser Videodisc Critical Edition, Criterion Press, 1984.
The Making of Citizen Kane, University of California Press, 1985.

Contributor to journals, including *Critical Inquiry* and *Publications of the Modern Language Association.*

WORK IN PROGRESS: Hitchcock: The Major Phase.

SIDELIGHTS: In *The Making of Citizen Kane,* Robert L. Carringer goes behind the scenes of the late Orson Welles' acclaimed film to reveal the processes that created it. His account of the film's production is unique because, after lengthy negotiations with RKO—the studio where "Citizen Kane" was filmed—Carringer was allowed access to the studio's archives. This enabled him to consult the original storybooks, production stills, shooting schedules, and other records. Carringer also spoke with Welles and with others who had worked on the film.

In his book, Carringer attempts to answer two long-standing questions about the classic film. John Blades states these questions in the *Chicago Tribune Book World* as, "Was Welles the film's sole creator . . . or was he simply the master showman, the gifted packager and self-promoter, who grabbed most of the credit for himself?" and "Why did Welles' career as a director peak with his first Hollywood film?" Carringer answers these questions by emphasizing the collaborative nature of filmmaking. On "Citizen Kane," Carringer argues, Welles worked with a highly-talented co-author, cinematographer, and art director whose efforts, combined with his own, resulted in the success of the film. In later work, Welles did not have these same collaborators and many of his films were failures. Carringer's judgement is not meant to detract from Welles' talents but to suggest that the film hailed as one of the best in cinematic history was, Blades states, "a serendipitous accident, an inspired collaboration." Gary Houston of the *Chicago Tribune Book World* calls *The Making of Citizen Kane* "a fascinating look at how the movie's myriad illusions were accomplished [and] a good primer on filmmaking procedure, even today's." Writing in the *New York Times,* John Gross judges the book "a comprehensive study, packed with fascinating detail about every step of the production process."

BIOGRAPHICAL/CRITICAL SOURCES:

PERIODICALS

Chicago Tribune Book World, September 8, 1985.
New York Times, September 6, 1985.
New York Times Book Review, September 15, 1985.
Washington Post Book World, September 15, 1985.

*   *   *

CARVER, Raymond   1938-

PERSONAL: Born May 25, 1938, in Clatskanie, Ore.; son of Clevie Raymond (a laborer) and Ella (Casey) Carver; married Maryann Burk (a teacher), June 7, 1957 (divorced October, 1982); children: Christine L., Vance L. *Education:* Humboldt State College (now California State University, Humboldt), A.B., 1963; University of Iowa, further study, 1963-64. *Politics:* Democrat.

ADDRESSES: Home—832 Maryland Ave., Syracuse, N.Y. 13210. *Agent*—Amanda Urban, International Creative Management, 40 West 57th St., New York, N.Y. 10019.

CAREER: Science Research Associates, Inc., Palo Alto, Calif., editor, 1967-70; University of California, Santa Cruz, lecturer in creative writing, 1971-72; University of California, Berkeley, lecturer in fiction writing, 1972-73; Syracuse, N.Y., professor of English, 1980-83; writer. Visiting lecturer, Writers Workshop, University of Iowa, 1973-74; visiting distinguished writer, University of Texas at El Paso, 1978-79.

AWARDS, HONORS: National Endowment for the Arts Discovery Award for poetry, 1970; Joseph Henry Jackson Award for fiction, 1971; Wallace Stegner Creative Writing Fellowship, Stanford University, 1972-73; National Book Award nomination in fiction, 1977, for *Will You Please Be Quiet, Please?;* Guggenheim fellowship, 1977-78; National Endowment for the Arts Award in fiction, 1979; Carlos Fuentes Fiction Award, for short story "The Bath"; Mildred and Harold Strauss Living Award, American Academy and Institute of Arts and Letters, 1983; National Book Critics Circle Award nomination in fiction, 1984, and Pulitzer Prize nomination in fiction, both for *Cathedral.*

WRITINGS:

Near Klamath (poems), Sacramento State College, 1968.
Winter Insomnia (poems), Kayak, 1970.
Put Yourself in My Shoes, Capra, 1974.
Will You Please Be Quiet, Please? (short stories), McGraw, 1976.
At Night the Salmon Move (poems), Capra, 1976.
Furious Seasons (short stories), Capra, 1977.
What We Talk about When We Talk about Love (short stories), Knopf, 1981.
Two Poems, Scarab Press, 1982.
The Pheasant, Metacom, 1982.
Fires: Essays, Poems, Stories, 1966-1982, Capra, 1983.
(Author of foreword) John Gardner, *On Becoming a Novelist,* Harper, 1983.
(Author of introduction) William Kittredge, *We Are Not in This Together,* Greywolf Press, 1984.
Cathedral (short stories), Knopf, 1984.
If It Please You, Lord John, 1984.
Dostoevsky: The Screenplay, Capra, 1985.
The Stories of Raymond Carver, Picador, 1985.
Where Water Comes Together with Other Water (poems), Random House, 1985.

This Water, Ewert, 1985.
Ultramarine (poems), Random House, 1986.

Also author, with Michael Cimino, of script "Purple Lake." Guest editor, *The Best American Short Stories,* 1986. Contributor to anthologies, including *The Best American Short Stories,* 1967, 1982, and 1983, *Short Stories from the Literary Magazines, Best Little Magazine Fiction,* 1970, and 1971, *Prize Stories: The O. Henry Awards,* 1973, 1974, 1975, and 1983, *Pushcart Prize Anthology,* 1976, 1981, 1982, and 1983, *New Voices in American Poetry,* and *The Generation of 2000: Contemporary American Poets.*

Contributor of poems and stories to national periodicals, including *Esquire, New Yorker, Atlantic,* and *Harper's,* and to literary journals, including *Paris Review, Antaeus, Georgia Review, Ohio Review,* and *Poetry.* Editor, *Quarry* (magazine), 1971-72; editor, *Ploughshares,* Volume IX, number 4, 1983.

WORK IN PROGRESS: Stories, poems, and a novel.

SIDELIGHTS: Raymond Carver is one of a handful of contemporary short-story writers who are credited with reviving what was once thought of as a dying literary form. His stories mainly take place in his native Pacific Northwest region; they are peopled with the type of lower-middle-class characters the author was familiar with while he was growing up. In a *New York Review of Books* article, Thomas R. Edwards describes Carver's fictional world as a place where "people worry about whether their old cars will start, where unemployment or personal bankruptcy are present dangers, where a good time consists of smoking pot with the neighbors, with a little cream soda and M&M's on the side. . . . Carver's characters are waitresses, mechanics, postmen, high school teachers, factory workers, door-to-door salesmen. [Their surroundings are] not for them a still unspoiled scenic wonderland, but a place where making a living is as hard, and the texture of life as drab, for those without money, as anywhere else."

Carver's own life would seem to parallel that of one of his characters. Born in an Oregon logging town, the author was married and the father of two before he was twenty years old. Also like his characters, Carver worked at a series of low-paying jobs: he "picked tulips, pumped gas, swept hospital corridors, swabbed toilets, managed an apartment complex," according to Bruce Weber in a *New York Times Magazine* profile of the author. Carver's then wife, continues Weber, "worked for the phone company, waited tables, sold a series of book digests door-to-door." Not coincidentally, "of all the writers at work today, Carver may have the most distinct vision of the working class," as Ray Anello observes in a *Newsweek* article. Carver taught creative writing in California and produced two books of poetry before his first book of short stories, *Will You Please Be Quiet, Please?,* was published in 1976.

In introducing readers to his world of the desperation of ordinary people, Carver created tales that are "brief . . . but by no means stark," notes Geoffrey Wolff in his *New York Times Book Review* piece on *Will You Please Be Quiet, Please?* Continues the critic: "They imply complexities of action and motive and they are especially artful in their suggestion of repressed violence. No human blood is shed in any of these stories, yet almost all of them hold a promise of mayhem of some final, awful breaking from confines, and breaking through to liberty." The theme of breaking from confines is central to one of the stories, "Neighbors," in which Bill and Arlene Miller agree to feed their neighbors' cat while the neighbors, the Stones, are on vacation. With access to the Stones' home, the Millers find themselves increasingly taken with their friends' clothes, furniture, and other belongings. Bill and Arlene, in fact, begin to assume the identities of the Stones; "each finds this strangely stimulating, and their sex life prospers, though neither can find anything much to *say* about it at all," reports Edwards. The end of the story finds the Millers clinging to the Stones' door as their neighbors return, knowing that their rich fantasy life will soon end.

The author's "first book of stories explored a common plight rather than a common subject," notes *New York Times Book Review* critic Michael Wood. "His characters were lost or diminished in their own different ways. The 17 stories in [Carver's third collection, *What We Talk about When We Talk about Love*,] make up a more concentrated volume, less a collection than a set of variations on the themes of marriage, infidelity and the disquieting tricks of human affection." "The first few pieces seem thin and perfunctory," Adam Mars-Jones writes in the *Times Literary Supplement,* "and there is a recurring pattern . . . of endings which lurch suddenly sideways, moving off in a direction that seems almost random." Anatole Broyard finds such endings frustrating. In his *New York Times* review of *What We Talk about When We Talk about Love,* Broyard criticizes what he calls "the most flagrant and common imposition in current fiction, to end a story with a sententious ambiguity that leaves the reader holding the bag."

"Perhaps there is a reason for this," says Mars-Jones. "Endings and titles are bound to be a problem for a writer like Carver, since readers and reviewers so habitually use them as keys to interpret everything else in a story. So he must make his endings enigmatic and even mildly surrealist, and his titles for the most part oblique. Sometimes he over-compensates." And *Newsweek*'s Peter S. Prescott feels that all seventeen stories in Carver's third collection "are excellent, and each gives the impression that it could not have been written more forcefully, or in fewer words."

Prescott also notes that the author is concerned "with the collapse of human relationships. Some of his stories take place at the moment things fall apart; others, after the damage has been done, while the shock waves still reverberate. Alcohol and violence are rarely far removed from what happens, but sometimes, in another characteristic maneuver, Carver will nudge the drama that triggers a crisis aside to show that his story has really been about something else all along." "Carver's is not a particularly lyrical prose," says Weber in his *New York Times Magazine* article. "A typical sentence is blunt and uncomplicated, eschewing the ornaments of descriptive adverbs and parenthetical phrases. His rhythms are often repetitive or brusque, as if to suggest the strain of people learning to express newly felt things, fresh emotions. Time passes in agonizingly linear fashion, the chronology of a given scene marked by one fraught and simple gesture after another. Dialogue is usually clipped, and it is studded with commonplace observations of the concrete objects on the table or on the wall—rather than the elusive, important issues in the air."

In Carver's fourth collection, *Cathedral,* "it would be hard to imagine a more dispirited assortment of figures," declares David Lehman in a *Newsweek* review. A "note of transcendent indifference, beyond resignation or fatigue, is sounded" in each story, adds Lehman, cautioning, "fun to read they're not." But, the critic stresses, "it's impossible to ignore Carver's immense talent." In *Cathedral,* Carver rewrites the end-

ing of one of his most acclaimed stories from *What We Talk about When We Talk about Love.* The original story, "The Bath," is about a mother who orders a special cake for her eight-year-old son's birthday—but the boy is hit by a car on that day and is rushed to the hosptial, where he lingers in a coma. The baker, aware only that the parents haven't picked up their expensive cake, badgers them with endless calls demanding his money. As the story ends, the boy's fate is still unknown, and the desperate parents hear the phone ring yet again. In *Cathedral,* the author retells this story (now entitled "A Small, Good Thing") up to the final phone ring. At this point, ambiguity vanishes; Carver reveals that the boy has died, and the call is from the irate baker. But this time the parents confront the baker with the circumstances, and the apologetic man invites them over to his bakery. There he tells the parents his own sad story of loneliness and despair and feeds them fresh coffee and warm rolls, because "eating is a small, good thing in a time like this."

"In revising 'The Bath' into 'A Small, Good Thing,' Carver has indeed gone into [what he describes as] 'the heart of what the story is *about*,' and in the process has written an entirely new story—has created, if you will, a completely new world," declares Jonathan Yardley in the *Washington Post Book World.* "The first version is beautifully crafted and admirably concise, but lacking in genuine compassion; the mysterious caller is not so much a human being as a mere voice, malign and characterless. But in the second version that voice becomes a person, one whose own losses are, in different ways, as crippling and heartbreaking as the one suffered by the grieving parents." As Broyard writes in a *New York Times* review of *Cathedral,* "it is typical of Mr. Carver's stories that comfort against adversity is found in incongruous places, that people find improbable solace. The improbable and the homely are [the author's] territory. He works in the bargain basement of the soul." Yardley maintains that "'The Bath' is a good short story," while "'A Small, Good Thing' comes breathtakingly close to perfection."

New Republic reviewer Dorothy Wickenden agrees that "A Small, Good Thing" and the story "Cathedral" "are astute, even complex, psychological dramas," but remarks that "a touch of sentimentality, an element previously foreign to Carver's work, has crept into these stories. Perhaps because he doesn't quite trust the sense of hope with which he leaves his characters, the writing at the end becomes self-consciously simple and the scenes of resolution contrived." Yet "compared with his previous two collections of stories," Broyard concludes, "[*Cathedral*] shows an increase in vitality. Like a missionary, Mr. Carver seems to be gradually reclaiming or redeeming his characters."

According to *New York Times Book Review* critic Irving Howe, Carver's stories evoke "strong American literary traditions. Formally, they summon remembrances of Hemingway and perhaps Stephen Crane, masters of tightly packed fiction. In subject matter they draw upon the American voice of loneliness and stoicism, the native soul locked in this continent's space. [The author's] characters, like those of many earlier American writers, lack a vocabulary that can release their feelings, so they must express themselves mainly through obscure gesture and berserk display." And Paul Gray, writing about *Cathedral* in *Time,* says that "Carver's art masquerades as accident, scraps of information that might have been overheard at the supermarket check-out or local beer joint. His most memorable people live on the edge: of poverty, alcoholic self-destruction, loneliness. Something in their lives denies them a sense of community. They feel this lack intensely, yet are too wary of intimacy to touch other people, even with language.''

Such appraisals of his writing leaves Carver himself a little wary. He tells Weber: ''Until I started reading these reviews of my work, praising me, I never felt the people I was writing about were so bad off. . . . The waitress, the bus driver, the mechanic, the hotel keeper. God, the country is filled with these people. They're good people. People doing the best they could.''

Carver's work has been translated into some twenty foreign languages, including Dutch, Arabic, and Japanese.

AVOCATIONAL INTERESTS: Travel.

BIOGRAPHICAL/CRITICAL SOURCES:

BOOKS

Carver, Raymond, *Cathedral*, Knopf, 1984.
Contemporary Literary Criticism, Volume XXII, Gale, 1982.
Dictionary of Literary Biography Yearbook: 1984, Gale, 1985.
Lohafer, Susan, *Coming to Terms with the Short Story*, Louisiana State University Press, 1983.
Weaver, Gordon, editor, *The American Short Story, 1945-1980*, Twayne, 1983.

PERIODICALS

Akros Review, spring, 1984.
Antioch Review, spring, 1984.
Atlantic, June, 1981.
Boston Globe, July 17, 1983.
Canto, Volume II, number 2, 1978.
Chariton Review, spring, 1984.
Chicago Tribune Book World, October 2, 1983.
Contemporary Literature, winter, 1982.
Detroit News, October 2, 1983.
Eureka Times-Standard (Eureka, Calif.), June 24, 1977.
Georgia Review, fall, 1982.
Globe and Mail (Toronto), November 24, 1984.
Harper's Bookletter, April 26, 1976.
Hudson Review, summer, 1976, autumn, 1981, spring, 1984.
Iowa Review, summer, 1979.
London Review of Books, February 2-15, 1984.
Los Angeles Times Book Review, May 24, 1981, October 2, 1983.
Nation, July, 1981.
New Republic, April 25, 1981, November 14, 1983.
Newsweek, April 27, 1981, September 5, 1983.
New York, April 20, 1981.
New York Review of Books, November 24, 1983.
New York Times, April 15, 1981, September 5, 1983.
New York Times Book Review, March 7, 1976, April 26, 1981, September 11, 1983.
New York Times Magazine, June 24, 1984.
Paris Review, summer, 1983.
Philological Quarterly, winter, 1985.
Saturday Review, April, 1981, October, 1983.
Studies in Short Fiction, winter, 1984.
Time, April 6, 1981, September 19, 1983.
Times (London), January 21, 1982, April 17, 1985, May 16, 1985.
Times Literary Supplement, January 22, 1982, February 17, 1984, May 24, 1985.

Village Voice, September 18, 1978.
Washington Post Book World, May 3, 1981, September 4, 1983.

—*Sketch by Susan Salter*

* * *

CASTLES, Francis G(eoffrey) 1943-

PERSONAL: Born September 16, 1943, in Melbourne, Australia; son of Henry (an engineer) and Fay (Stackson) Castles; married Margaret Norton, August 24, 1963; children: Penelope Ann. *Education:* University of Leeds, B.A., 1964. *Politics:* ''Of cynicism.'' *Religion:* None.

ADDRESSES: Home—33 Goulburn Pl., Macquarie, Australian Capital Territory, Australia.

CAREER: Former faculty member at Australian National University, Canberra.

MEMBER: Political Studies Association (United Kingdom), Australian Political Science Association, Sociological Association of Australia and New Zealand.

WRITINGS:

Pressure Groups and Political Culture, Humanities, 1967.
Politics and Social Insight, Routledge & Kegan Paul, 1971.
(Editor) *Decisions, Organizations and Society*, Penguin, 1971, 2nd edition, 1976.
Political Stability, Open University Press, 1974.
(With Paul Lewis and Susan Saunders) *Questions in Soviet Government and Politics*, Open University Press, 1976.
Power, Coercion and Authority, Open University Press, 1976.
The Social Democratic Image of Society: A Study of the Achievements and Origins of Scandinavian Social Democracy in Comparative Perspective, Routledge & Kegan Paul, 1978.
(Editor) *The Practice of Comparative Politics*, 2nd edition (Castles was not associated with previous edition), Longman, 1978.
Democratic Politics and Policy Outcomes, Open University Press, 1980.
(Editor) *The Impact of Parties: Politics and Policies in Democratic Capitalist States*, Sage Publications, 1982.

BIOGRAPHICAL/CRITICAL SOURCES:

PERIODICALS

Times Literary Supplement, January 18, 1968.†

* * *

CERRI, Lawrence J. 1923-
(Lawrence Cortesi)

PERSONAL: Born August 6, 1923, in Troy, N.Y.; son of Vincent (a locomotive engineer) and Assunta (Cortesi) Cerri; married Frances Barringer (a registered nurse), January 17, 1953; children: David, Diane, Richard, Catherine, Elizabeth. *Education:* Siena College, B.A., 1950; Albany State Teachers College (now State University of New York at Albany), M.A., 1951. *Politics:* Independent. *Religion:* Roman Catholic.

ADDRESSES: Home—79 Boght Rd., Watervliet, N.Y. 12189.

CAREER: Equifax, Inc., Atlanta, Ga., claim director and investigator, 1942-43, 1950-57; *Albany Times Union*, Albany, N.Y., reporter, 1957-58; Waterford-Halfmoon High School,

Waterford, N.Y., teacher of English, 1958-76; free-lance writer, 1976—. Maplewood School Board, Watervliet, N.Y., member, president, beginning 1975. *Military service:* U.S. Army Air Forces, aerial gunner, 1943-45; served in Pacific theatre; received Air Medal.

MEMBER: Watervliet Historical Society (past president), Waterford Teachers Association (president, 1965-70), Siena College Alumni Association.

AWARDS, HONORS: Children's Books of the Year award, Child Study Association, 1973, for *Jim Beckwourth: Explorer Patriot of the Rockies.*

WRITINGS—Under pseudonym Lawrence Cortesi:

Mission Incredible (fiction), Tower Publications, 1967.
Battle of the Bismarck Sea (fiction), Tower Publications, 1968.
The Magnificent Bastards (fiction), Tower Publications, 1969.
Jim Beckwourth: Explorer Patriot of the Rockies (juvenile nonfiction), Criterion, 1973.
Jean du Sable: Father of Chicago (juvenile nonfiction), Chilton, 1974.
Operation Bismarck Sea (nonfiction), Major Books, 1977.
Escape from Mindanao (fiction), Tower Publications, 1978.
Rogue Sergeant (fiction), Tower Publications, 1979.
Target: Daimler-Benz (nonfiction), Tower Publications, 1979.
Forty Fathoms Down, Tower Publications, 1979.
Operation Friday the Thirteenth (nonfiction), Major Books, 1980.
The Last Outlaw (fiction), Tower Publications, 1980.
Bloody Friday off Guadalcanal, Zebra Books, 1981.
Operation Bodenplatte, Zebra Books, 1981.
Pacific Breakthrough, Zebra Books, 1981.
Valor at Okinawa, Zebra Books, 1981.
Justice at Iritara, Tower Publications, 1982.
Operation Cannibal, Leisure Books, 1982.
Target: Tokyo, Zebra Books, 1983.
The Deadly Skies, Zebra Books, 1983.
Valor at Leyte, Zebra Books, 1983.
Gunfight at Powder River (fiction), Dorchester Publishing, 1984.
Take the 505 Alive (nonfiction), Zebra Books, 1986.
The Bastards of Chu Lai, Zebra Books, 1986.

"WORLD AT WAR" SERIES; PUBLISHED BY ZEBRA BOOKS

Valor at Samar, 1981.
Hitler's Final Siege, 1982.
Pacific Strike, 1982.
Operation Cartwheel: The Final Countdown to V-J Day, 1982.
Pacific Hellfire, 1983.
Rommel's Last Stand, 1984.
D-Day Minus One, 1984.
Battle for Manila, 1984.
Last Bridge to Victory, 1984.
Gateway to Victory, 1984.
Valor in the Sky, 1985.
Objective Paris, 1985.
Operation Rome, 1985.

Also author of *Pacific Siege* and *Wipe Out at Wewak.*

PLAYS

Adorable Imp (three-act juvenile; first produced in Trafalgar, Ind., at Indian Creek High School, 1970), Arts Craft Publishers, c. 1970.
For Services Due (three-act juvenile; first produced in Claremont, S.D., at Claremont High School, 1972), Arts Craft Publishers, c. 1972.

OTHER

Author of educational filmscripts. Contributor of stories to magazines, including *True Detective, Fate, Wild West,* and *American History Illustrated.*

WORK IN PROGRESS: Research for a series of educational mystery story controlled reading filmstrips for A/V Concepts; research for nonfiction western, *Bill Doolin: Last of Horseback Outlaws,* for Tower Publications; *Valor in the Bulge,* a World War II story; *Tragic Jane McCrea,* based on a Revolutionary War incident.

SIDELIGHTS: Lawrence J. Cerri writes: "I have had a love for storytelling since I was seven or eight years old. My motivation is generally an interest in a subject that starts me researching. I have often taken one of my magazine stories and researched the story further for a book. I do not consider myself a social mover, but merely a writer who likes to entertain and who likes to write about people and events that have had little coverage in books or other media."

AVOCATIONAL INTERESTS: Travel, fishing, bowling, model railroading.

*   *   *

CHADWIN, Mark Lincoln 1939-

PERSONAL: Born August 18, 1939, in New York, N.Y.; son of Louis (a business executive) and Vivian (Goodman) Chadwin; married Adrienne Lee Deutsch, June 25, 1961; children: Dean Kennedy, Rebecca Elizabeth. *Education:* Yale University, B.A., 1961; Columbia University, M.A., 1962, Ph.D., 1965.

ADDRESSES: Home—1146 Jamestown Crescent, Norfolk, Va. 23508. *Office*—School of Business Administration, Old Dominion University, Norfolk, Va. 23508.

CAREER: Personal assistant to Ambassador W. Averill Harriman, Washington, D.C., 1965-68; assistant to the president of Brandeis University, Waltham, Mass., 1968-69; assistant to Governor W. Averill Harriman, 1969-71; director of Illinois Economic and Fiscal Commission, 1972-75; senior research associate, Urban Institute, 1976-80; Old Dominion University, School of Business Administration, Norfolk, Va., associate professor of management and director of maritime research program, 1980—. Member of Norfolk Enterprise Zone Coordinating Committee, Norfolk Chamber of Commerce, 1982-84; member of board of directors, World Affairs Council of Greater Hampton Roads, 1984-86. Consultant to Chesapeake Research Consortium, Virginia National Bank, City of Norfolk, Urban Institute, Technology Resources, Inc., U.S. General Accounting Office, and Joint Legislative Audit and Review Commission, Virginia Legislature.

MEMBER: International Studies Association, Society for International Development, Academy of Political Science, American Historical Association, Organization of American Historians, Urban League of Tidewater (member of board of directors, 1982-86).

AWARDS, HONORS: Virginia Foundation for Excellence summer travel grant for international business, 1983.

WRITINGS:

The Hawks of World War II, University of North Carolina Press, 1968, revised edition published as *The Warhawks:*

American Interventionists before Pearl Harbor, Norton, 1970.
Legislative Program Evaluation in the States, Eagleton Institute of Politics, Rutgers University, 1974.
(With others) *The Employment Service: An Institutional Analysis,* Employment and Training Administration, U.S. Department of Labor, 1977.
(With others) *Implementing Welfare-Employment Programs: An Institutional Analysis of the Work Incentive Program,* Employment and Training Administration, U.S. Department of Labor, 1980.

WORK IN PROGRESS: Studies concerning United States political and economic relations with eastern and western Europe and with Latin America.

*　　*　　*

CHARLTON, Donald Geoffrey　1925-

PERSONAL: Born April 8, 1925, in Bolton, Lancashire, England; son of Harry and Hilda (Whittle) Charlton; married Thelma D. E. Masters, 1952; children: Katharine Penelope, Nicholas John, Jane Victoria. *Education:* Attended St. Edmund Hall, Oxford, 1943-44; Emmanuel College, Cambridge, B.A., 1948, M.A., 1953, Ph.D. (London), 1955.

ADDRESSES: Home—Loxley Hall, University of Warwick, Coventry, England. *Office*—Department of French Studies, University of Warwick, Coventry, England.

CAREER: University of Hull, Hull, England, lecturer, 1949-60, senior lecturer in French, 1960-64; University of Warwick, Coventry, England, professor of French, 1964—. Visiting professor of French, Trinity College, University of Toronto, Toronto, Ontario, 1961-62, and University of California, Berkeley, 1966. Gifford lecturer at University of St. Andrews, Scotland, 1982-83. *Military service:* Royal Navy, 1944-46; became petty officer.

MEMBER: Society for French Studies (secretary, 1961-62), Association of University Professors of French.

WRITINGS:

Positivist Thought in France during the Second Empire, 1852-1870, Clarendon Press, 1959, reprinted, Greenwood Press, 1976.
Secular Religions in France, 1815-1870, Oxford University Press, 1963.
France: A Companion to French Studies, Methuen, 1972, 2nd edition, 1979.
(Editor with others) *Balzac and the Nineteenth Century: Studies in French Literature Presented to Herbert J. Hunt by Pupils, Colleagues and Friends,* Humanities Press, 1972.
(With D. C. Potts) *French Thought since 1600,* Methuen, 1974.
(Editor and contributor) *The French Romantics,* two volumes, Cambridge University Press, 1984.
New Images of the Natural in France, 1750-1800, Cambridge University Press, 1984.

Contributor to professional journals in England and the United States.

WORK IN PROGRESS: Writing on Romanticism and on French intellectual and cultural history of the eighteenth and nineteenth centuries.

BIOGRAPHICAL/CRITICAL SOURCES:

PERIODICALS

Times Literary Supplement, January 4, 1985, February 1, 1985.

*　　*　　*

CHEN, Theodore Hsi-En　1902-

PERSONAL: Born July 14, 1902, in China; married Wen-Hui Chung, June 6, 1932; children: Helen Cheng. *Education:* Fukien Christian University, A.B., 1922; Columbia University, A.M., 1929; University of Southern California, Ph.D., 1939.

ADDRESSES: Home—5564 Village Green, Los Angeles, Calif. 90016. *Office*—701 WPH, University of Southern California, Los Angeles, Calif. 90007.

CAREER: Fukien Christian University, Foochow, China, dean of faculty, 1929-37, president, 1946-47; University of Southern California, Los Angeles, professor of education and Asian studies, 1938-74, professor emeritus, 1974—.

MEMBER: Phi Beta Kappa, Phi Kappa Phi, Phi Delta Kappa.

AWARDS, HONORS: LL.D., University of Southern California, 1967.

WRITINGS:

Developing Patterns of the College Curriculum in the United States, University of Southern California Press, 1940.
Elementary Chinese Reader and Grammar, Perkins Oriental Books, 1945.
Chinese Communism and the Proletarian-Socialist Revolution, University of Southern California Press, 1955.
Thought Reform of the Chinese Intellectuals, Oxford University Press, 1960.
Teacher Training in Communist China, U.S. Office of Education, 1960.
The Chinese Communist Regime: Documents and Commentary, Praeger, 1967.
Maoist Educational Revolution, Praeger, 1974.
Chinese Education since 1949, Pergamon, 1981.

CONTRIBUTOR

J. S. Roucek and Moehlman, editors, *Comparative Education,* Dryden, 1952.
Roucek, editor, *Contemporary Political Ideologies,* Philosophical Library, 1961.
S. H. Gould, editor, *Sciences in Communist China,* American Association for the Advancement of Science, 1961.
Roucek and K. V. Lottich, editors, *Behind the Iron Curtain,* Caxton, 1964.
Stewart Fraser, editor, *Governmental Encouragement and the Control of International Education in Communist China,* Wiley, 1965.
Ruth Adams, editor, *Contemporary China,* Pantheon, 1966.
George P. Jan, editor, *Government of Communist China,* Chandler Publishing, 1966.
The China Giant: Perspective on Communist China, Scott, Foresman, 1967.
Paul K. T. Sih, editor, *The Strenuous Decade: China's Nation-Building Efforts, 1927-1937,* St. John's University Press, 1970.
Frank Traeger and William Henderson, editors, *Communist China: 1949-1969,* New York University, 1970.
Yuan-li Wu, editor, *China, a Handbook,* Praeger, 1973.

James C. Hsiung, editor, *Contemporary Republic of China, 1950-1980*, Praeger, 1981.

Hungdah Chiu, editor, *China: Seventy Years after the 1911 Hsin-Hai Revolution*, University Press of Virginia, 1984.

Also contributor to *Encyclopaedia Britannica, Encyclopedia Americana, World Book Encyclopedia, Encyclopedia of Modern Education*, and *Encyclopedia of Vocational Guidance*.

OTHER

Contributor of numerous articles to newspapers and professional journals, including the *Los Angeles Times, Christian Science Monitor, School and Society, Current History, Far Eastern Survey*, and *Sociology and Social Research*.

BIOGRAPHICAL/CRITICAL SOURCES:

PERIODICALS

Chicago Tribune Book World, March 17, 1968.

* * *

CHILVER, Peter 1933-

PERSONAL: Born November 18, 1933, in Southend, Essex, England; son of A. H. and A. E. (Mack) Chilver. *Education:* St. Edmund Hall, Oxford, B.A. (with honors), 1956, M.A., 1964; Royal Academy of Dramatic Art, London, England, Diploma in Speech and Drama (with honors), 1963; University of London, Postgraduate Certificate of Education (with distinction), 1965, Academic Diploma in Education (with distinction), 1969, M.Phil., 1973, Institute of Education, Ph.D., 1976.

ADDRESSES: Home—27 Cavendish Gardens, Barking, Essex, England. *Office*—Department of English, Langdon School, London, England.

CAREER: Southend Education Authority, Southend, England, teacher, 1957-60; Inner London Education Authority, London, England, teacher, 1964-68; Acton College of Education, London, lecturer in English and drama, 1968-70; Thomas Huxley College, London, senior lecturer in drama, 1970-77; University of London, London, member of faculty of education, 1974-77; Langdon School, London, head of department of English, 1977—. Visiting lecturer, Ontario Conference of Teachers of English, 1980, 1981, 1982, and 1985.

AWARDS, HONORS: W. H. Page scholarship, English-Speaking Union, 1974; British Council travel award, 1985.

WRITINGS:

Staging a School Play, Batsford, 1967, Harper, 1968.
Improvised Drama, Batsford, 1967.
Dirty Bertie (musical play), Evans Brothers, 1968.
The Nine Scandalous Lives of Dick Turpin, Highwayman (musical play), Evans Brothers, 1968.
Talking: Discussion, Improvisation, and Debate in Schools, Batsford, 1968.
(With Eric Jones) *Designing a School Play*, Batsford, 1968, Taplinger, 1970.
Stories for Improvisation in Primary and Secondary Schools, Batsford, 1969.
Producing a Play, Batsford, 1974.
Teaching Improvised Drama: A Handbook for Secondary Schools, Batsford, 1978.
(With Gerard Gould) *Learning and Language in the Classroom: Discursive Talking and Writing across the Curriculum*, Pergamon, 1982.

(Contributor) Jon Nixon, editor, *Drama and the Whole Curriculum*, Hutchinson, 1982.
"In the Picture" series (English and drama textbooks), Thornes, 1985.

Regular reviewer for *Technical Education*.

WORK IN PROGRESS: The Role of Drama in Education.

* * *

CHOUDHURY, G(olam) W(ahed) 1926-

PERSONAL: Born January 1, 1926, in Habigunj, East Pakistan (now Bangladesh); son of Golam Mawla and Fatema Choudhury; married November 3, 1960; wife's name, Dilara; children: G. Mabud, G. Sayeed. *Education:* Calcutta University, B.A. (with honors), 1944, M.A., 1946; Columbia University, Ph.D., 1956. *Politics:* None. *Religion:* Islam.

ADDRESSES: Home—21 Central Rd., Dacca, Bangladesh.

CAREER: Dacca University, Dacca, East Pakistan (now Bangladesh), lecturer, 1949-56, reader, 1956-63, professor, 1964-67; Government of Pakistan, Islamabad, director general of Ministry of Foreign Affairs, 1967-69, cabinet-minister in Pakistan (now Bangladesh), 1969-71; professor of political science and director of Center for International Studies, North Carolina Central University, Durham. Research associate, School of Oriental and African Studies, University of London, 1961; visiting fellow, Cambridge University, 1965-66, Royal Institute of International Affairs, London, 1973-74; visiting professor at Columbia University and University of Pennsylvania, 1973-74; adjunct professor of political science, Duke University. Honorary adviser to Pakistan Constitution Commission, 1960; member of Pakistan delegation to UNESCO, 1960, and United Nations, 1961-64.

WRITINGS:

Constitutional Development in Pakistan, Longmans, Green, 1959, 2nd edition, 1969.
Democracy in Pakistan, University of British Columbia Press, 1963.
Documents and Speeches on the Constitution of Pakistan, University of British Columbia Press, 1967.
Pakistan's Relations with India, 1947-1966, Praeger, 1968.
The Last Days of United Pakistan, Indiana University Press, 1974.
India, Pakistan, Bangladesh and Major Powers: Politics of a Divided Subcontinent, Free Press, 1975.
The Soviet Asian Collective Security Plan, Center for Strategic and International Studies, Georgetown University, 1976.
Brezhnev's Collective Security Plan for Asia (monograph), Center for Strategic and International Studies, Georgetown University, 1976.
Chinese Perception of the New World, University Press of America, 1978.
China in World Affairs: The Foreign Policy of the People's Republic of China since 1970, Westview, 1982.

Contributor to history and political science journals.

WORK IN PROGRESS: Bangladesh: Problems and Challenges.

SIDELIGHTS: G. W. Choudhury has traveled extensively in Europe, the United States, the Soviet Union, and the Far East.†

CHRISTIAN, Mary Blount 1933-

PERSONAL: Born February 20, 1933, in Houston, Tex.; daughter of George D. and Anna (Dill) Blount; married George L. Christian, Jr. (a book review editor), September 22, 1956; children: Scott, Karen, Devin. *Education:* University of Houston, B.S., 1954.

ADDRESSES: Home—1108 Danbury Rd., Houston, Tex. 77055.

CAREER: Houston Post, Houston, Tex., reporter and columnist, 1953-57; free-lance writer in Houston, Tex., 1959—. Has taught writing for children at university workshops and adult education programs. Instructor in creative writing, Houston Community College, 1973-78, and Rice University, 1980—; instructor, Institute of Children's Literature, 1979—. Creator and moderator for ''Children's Bookshelf,'' PBS-TV, syndicated through Eastern Educational Television.

MEMBER: Society of Children's Book Writers (charter member; member of board of advisors, 1975-76), Mystery Writers of America (secretary of Southwest chapter, 1982—), Authors Guild, Authors League of America.

AWARDS, HONORS: Special Scroll, Mystery Writers of America, 1981, for *The Doggone Mystery;* Ann Martin Bookmark Award, Gulf Coast Catholic Libraries Association, for consistent work of moral standard.

WRITINGS:

JUVENILES

Scarabee: The Witch's Cat, Steck, 1973.
The First Sign of Winter, Parents' Magazine Press, 1973.
Nothing Much Happened Today (also see below), Addison-Wesley, 1973.
Sebastian: Super Sleuth, J. Philip O'Hara, 1974.
Devin and Goliath, Addison-Wesley, 1974.
No Dogs Allowed, Jonathan! (also see below), Addison-Wesley, 1975.
Hats Are for Watering Horses, Rand McNally, 1976.
When Time Began, Concordia, 1976.
Jonah, Go to Nineveh!, Concordia, 1976.
Il a du Flair, Babylas! (two novellas in French), Hachette, 1976.
Daniel Who Dared, Concordia, 1977.
The Goosehill Gang Cookbook, Concordia, 1978.
The Goosehill Gang Craft Book, Concordia, 1978.
The Sand Lot, Harvey House, 1978.
Felina, Scholastic Action, 1978.
His Brother's Keeper, Concordia, 1978.
J. J. Leggett, Secret Agent, Lothrop, 1978.
The Lucky Man, Macmillan, 1979.
The Devil Take You, Barnabas Beane!, Crowell, 1979.
Anah and the Strangers, Abingdon, 1980.
Christmas Reflections, Concordia, 1980.
The Doggone Mystery, Albert Whitman, 1980.
The Two Ton Secret, Albert Whitman, 1981.
The Ventriloquist (Junior Literary Guild selection), Coward, 1982.
April Fool, Macmillan, 1982.
The Green Thumb Thief, Albert Whitman, 1982.
The Firebug Mystery, Albert Whitman, 1982.
Just Once (novella), New Readers Press, 1982.
Grandmothers: God's Gift to Children, Concordia, 1982.
Grandfathers: God's Gift to Children, Concordia, 1982.

Sebastian (Super Sleuth) and the Hair of the Dog Mystery, Macmillan, 1982.
The Museum Mystery, Albert Whitman, 1983.
Swamp Monsters, Dial, 1983.
Sebastian (Super Sleuth) and the Crummy Yummies Caper, Macmillan, 1983.
Sebastian (Super Sleuth) and the Bone to Pick Mystery, Macmillan, 1983.
Microcomputers (nonfiction), Crestwood House, 1983.
Sebastian (Super Sleuth) and the Santa Claus Caper, Macmillan, 1984.
Sebastian (Super Sleuth) and the Secret of the Skewered Skier, Macmillan, 1984.
The Mysterious Case Case, Dutton, 1985.
Sebastian (Super Sleuth) and the Clumsy Cowboy, Macmillan, 1985.
Mystery at Camp Triumph (novel), Albert Whitman, 1985.
Go West, Swamp Monsters!, Dial, 1985.
Growin' Pains, Macmillan, 1985.
Deadman in Catfish Bay, Albert Whitman, 1985.
Everybody Else Is, Concordia, 1985.
The Toady and Dr. Miracle, Macmillan, 1985.
Sebastian (Super Sleuth) and the Purloined Surloin, Macmillan, 1986.
Penrod's Pants, Macmillan, 1986.

Also author of *Thinking of You,* Dutton, and co-author of *Bible Heroes, Kings and Prophets.*

''THE GOOSEHILL GANG'' SERIES I

The Vanishing Sandwich, Concordia, 1976.
The Test Paper Thief, Concordia, 1976.
The Disappearing Dues, Concordia, 1976.
The Chocolate Cake Caper, Concordia, 1976.

''THE GOOSEHILL GANG'' SERIES II

The C.B. Convoy Caper, Concordia, 1977.
The Pocket Park Problem, Concordia, 1977.
The Runaway House Mystery, Concordia, 1977.
The May Basket Mystery, Concordia, 1977.

''THE GOOSEHILL GANG'' SERIES III

The Stitch in Time Solution, Concordia, 1978.
The Ghost in the Garage, Concordia, 1978.
The Shadow on the Shade, Concordia, 1978.
The Christmas Shoe Thief, Concordia, 1978.

FILMSTRIPS

''No Dogs Allowed, Jonathan!'' (based on her book of the same title), Taylor Associates, 1976.
''Nothing Much Happened Today'' (based on her book of the same title), Taylor Associates, 1976.

OTHER

Work represented in anthologies, including *Hootnanny,* Scott, Foresman, *The Very Last First,* Ginn, and *Something Special,* Scott, Foresman. Juvenile book critic, *Houston Chronicle.*

WORK IN PROGRESS: A novel, *Singin' Somebody Else's Song,* for Macmillan; *Merger on the Orient Expressway,* for Dutton; a third book in the ''Swamp Monsters'' series, for Dial.

SIDELIGHTS: Mary Blount Christian told *CA:* ''Everything I write comes both from a deep inner feeling and an experience (my own or someone else's), but they are so evolved by the time they are written that the original stimuli are invisible. I feel a deep responsiblity for the reader. While I start out to entertain, I never send anything out without being very sure that it contains nothing that will mislead or misinform a child about the world as I know it. I try to tell myself in one sentence just what theme, what universal message, each story conveys. After all, we can't follow the book around and add footnotes to the reader. It leads its own life apart from us, and nothing we could say later can erase a misconception we may have caused. Children look much deeper into stories than adults—perhaps not consciously, but they decode everything into validity to life.''

Her *Sebastian (Super Sleuth)* books have been translated into Japanese.

MEDIA ADAPTATIONS: The "Goosehill Gang" mysteries were adapted for a live action film series by Family Films, 1982, as "The Mystery of the Vanishing Schoolmate," "The Mystery of the Disappearing Necklace," "The Mystery of the Gold Rush Map," "The Mystery of the Howling Woods," and "Treehouse Ghost."

BIOGRAPHICAL/CRITICAL SOURCES:

PERIODICALS

Houston Chronicle, December 24, 1972.
Westside Reporter (Houston), June 1, 1979.

*　　*　　*

CLARDY, Andrea Fleck   1943-

PERSONAL: Born November 3, 1943, in New York; daughter of G. Peter (in business) and Ruth (a social worker; maiden name, Melchior) Fleck; married Jon Christel Clardy (a professor of chemistry), December 30, 1966; children: Peter Fleck, Benjamin Christopher. *Education:* Swarthmore College, B.A., 1965; Harvard University, M.A.T., 1966. *Politics:* Democrat. *Religion:* Unitarian-Universalist.

ADDRESSES: Home—616 Cayuga Heights Rd., Ithaca, N.Y. 14850. *Office*—ILR Press, Cornell University, Ithaca, N.Y. 14853.

CAREER: English teacher in Weston, Mass., 1966-68; community organizer in Ames, Iowa, 1970-76; *Ames Daily Tribune*, Ames, author of editorial column, 1976-78; City of Ithaca, N.Y., Ithaca Commons coordinator, 1978-81, publicity director of Ithaca Festival, 1978, general coordinator of festival, 1979; Crossing Press, Trumansburg, N.Y., director of promotion, 1982-84; ILR Press, Ithaca, promotions associate, 1984—. President, Story County Housing, Inc., 1969-72; cofounder, Story County Health Center, 1976-77. Member of board of education, Ithaca City School District, 1981-84; affiliated with New York State Department of Education Project Equity and Excellence, 1983—.

MEMBER: National Organization for Women, Phi Beta Kappa.

WRITINGS:

(Editor) *Gordon Gammack: Columns from Three Wars*, Iowa State University Press, 1979.
(Editor) *Ithaca: A Book of Photographs*, McBooks, 1981.
(Editor) *A Sense of Place: Small Communities near Ithaca, New York*, McBooks, 1983.
Dusty Was My Friend, Human Sciences, 1984.

Also author of biographical material for the wall calendars *Heroines 1983*, *Heroines 1984*, and *Heroines 1985*, Crossing Press.

WORK IN PROGRESS: A children's book on learning disabilities; a collection of biographical and photographic sketches of remarkable American women.

SIDELIGHTS: Andrea Fleck Clardy comments: "The collection of Gordon Gammack's columns is really a commentary on changes in the American soldier's attitudes toward war in the past thirty-five years. I found the material fascinating, but I am ready now to work on my own material in nonfiction and children's literature."

*　　*　　*

CLARK, Frank J(ames)   1922-

PERSONAL: Born August 4, 1922, in Brooklyn, N.Y.; son of J. Franklin and Anna (Koch) Clark; married Betty Schulte, November 8, 1946 (divorced, 1963); children: John, Donald. *Education:* New York University, B.A., 1953, additional study, 1966-72; Columbia University, M.A., 1961; additional study, Mannes College of Music, 1961-62; Electronic Computer Programming Institute, certificate, 1965; also attended State University of New York at New Paltz, Duchess Community College, and Genessee Community College, 1966-70.

ADDRESSES: Home—22 William St., Highlands, N.J. 07732. *Office*—AT&T Information Systems, Lincroft, N.J.

CAREER: Trumpeter with Boston Pops Orchestra, Boston, Mass., 1953, Band of America, New York, N.Y., 1964-65, and Gershwin Orchestra, American Album of Famous Music Orchestra, and others; music teacher in public schools, Plainview, Long Island, N.Y., 1958-64; teacher of mathematics in other schools; Dutchess Community College, Poughkeepsie, N.Y., assistant professor of data processing, 1965-68; Genessee Community College, Batavia, N.Y., director of data processing and associate professor of data processing, 1968-78; Rochester Institute of Technology, Rochester, N.Y., associate professor of computer science, 1978-80; Radio Shack-Tandy Corp., Fort Worth, Tex., manager of technical publications, 1980-81; consultant on Fortran to Perkin-Elmer, 1982; consultant to Peat, Marwick, Mitchell (accounting firm), New York City, and Chase Manhattan Bank, New York City, 1982-83; AT&T Information Systems, Lincroft, N.J., documentation consultant, 1983—. Programmer, International City Manager's Association, spring, 1967; designer of several city and county data processing systems. *Military service:* U.S. Navy, 1942-45; musician on U.S.S. "Iowa"; received twelve battle stars, Presidential Unit Citation.

WRITINGS:

(With Melvin Berger) *Science and Music: From Tom-tom to Hi-fi*, McGraw, 1961.
(With Alan Vorwald) *Computers: From Sand Table to Electronic Brain*, McGraw, 1961, 3rd edition, 1970.
(With Berger) *Music in Perspective*, S. Fox, 1962.
Contemporary Studies for the Trumpet, Adler, 1963.
Contemporary Math, F. Watts, 1963.
Contemporary Math for Parents, F. Watts, 1965.
Speed Math, F. Watts, 1966.
Information Processing, Goodyear Publishing, 1970.
Introduction to PL/I Programming, Allyn & Bacon, 1970, new edition, 1971.
(With Robert L. Gray) *Accounting Programs and Business Systems: Case Studies*, Goodyear Publishing, 1971.
Business Systems and Data Processing Procedures, Prentice-Hall, 1972.

(With Joseph M. Whalen) *RPG I and RPG II Programming*, Addison-Wesley, 1974.
Mathematics for Data Processing, Reston, 1974.
Data Recorder, Reston, 1974.
The Accountant and the Personal Computer, Prentice-Hall, 1986.

Also author of television scripts.

SIDELIGHTS: There is a collection of Frank J. Clark's writings at the University of Mississippi.

* * *

CLARK, Gordon H(addon) 1902-1985

PERSONAL: Born August 31, 1902, in Philadelphia, Pa.; died April 9, 1985; son of David Scott and Elizabeth (Haddon) Clark; married Ruth Schmidt, March 27, 1929; children: Lois A. Zeller, Nancy Elizabeth George. *Education:* University of Pennsylvania, A.B., 1924, Ph.D., 1929; attended Sorbonne, University of Paris, 1931; Reformed Episcopal Seminary, D.D., 1966.

CAREER: University of Pennsylvania, Philadelphia, instructor, 1924-36; Reformed Episcopal Seminary, Philadelphia, lecturer, 1932-36; Wheaton College, Wheaton, Ill., associate professor of philosophy, 1936-43; ordained minister of Orthodox Presbyterian Church, 1944; Butler University, Indianapolis, Ind., professor of philosophy and chairman of department, 1945-73; Covenant College, Lookout Mountain, Tenn., professor of philosophy, 1974-85. Moderator of General Synod, Reformed Presbyterian Church, 1961.

MEMBER: American Philosophical Association, Evangelical Theological Society, Indiana Philosophical Society, Phi Beta Kappa.

WRITINGS:

(Editor with Thomas V. Smith) *Readings in Ethics*, Appleton, 1931, 2nd edition, 1935.
(Editor) *Selections from Hellenistic Philosophy*, Appleton, 1940, reprinted, 1964.
(With others) *A History of Philosophy*, F. S. Crofts, 1941.
A Christian Philosophy of Education, Eerdmans, 1946.
(Contributor) Vergilius Ferm, editor, *History of Philosophical Systems*, Philosophic Library, 1950.
A Christian View of Men and Things, Eerdmans, 1952.
What Presbyterians Believe, Presbyterian & Reformed, 1956, 2nd edition published as *What Do Presbyterians Believe?*, 1965.
Thales to Dewey, Houghton, 1956.
(Contributor) Carl F. H. Henry, editor, *Contemporary Evangelical Thought*, Channel, 1957.
(Contributor) Henry, editor, *Revelation and the Bible*, Baker Book, 1958.
Dewey, Presbyterian & Reformed, 1960.
Religion, Reason, and Revelation, Presbyterian & Reformed, 1961.
James, Presbyterian & Reformed, 1963.
Karl Barth's Theological Method, Presbyterian & Reformed, 1963.
(Contributor) *Can I Trust My Bible?*, Moody, 1963.
(Contributor) Henry, editor, *Christian Faith and Modern Theology*, Channel, 1964.
The Philosophy of Science and Belief in God, Craig, 1964.
(Contributor) Henry, editor, *Jesus of Nazareth: Savior and Lord*, Eerdmans, 1966.

Peter Speaks Today, Presbyterian & Reformed, 1967.
(Contributor) Henry, editor, *Fumdamentals of the Faith*, Zondervan, 1969.
Biblical Predestination, Presbyterian & Reformed, 1969.
Historiography: Secular and Religious, Craig, 1971.
Three Types of Religious Philosophy, Presbyterian & Reformed, 1974.
First Corinthians: A Contemporary Commentary, Presbyterian & Reformed, 1975.
Colossians, Presbyterian & Reformed, 1979.
Concept of Biblical Authority, Presbyterian & Reformed, 1979.
Language and Theology, Presbyterian & Reformed, 1980.
First and Second Peter, Presbyterian & Reformed, 1980.
First John: A Commentary, Presbyterian & Reformed, 1980.

Contributor to *Dictionary of Theology, Dictionary of Christian Ethics, American People's Encyclopedia, Collier's Encyclopedia,* and *Encyclopedia of Christianity*. Contributor to professional journals.

WORK IN PROGRESS: The Pastoral Epistles; Behaviorism and Christianity.

AVOCATIONAL INTERESTS: Chess, oil painting.

BIOGRAPHICAL/CRITICAL SOURCES:

BOOKS

The Philosophy of Gordon H. Clark: A Festschrift, Presbyterian & Reformed, 1968.†

* * *

CLARKSON, Ewan 1929-

PERSONAL: Given name is pronounced *You*-an; born January 23, 1929, in England; son of Frank (a pharmacist) and Jenny (Johnston) Clarkson; married Jenny Maton, September 8, 1951; children: Bruce Andrew, Sheila Jane. *Education:* University of Exeter, M.A., 1984.

ADDRESSES: Home—Moss Rose Cottage, Preston Kingsteignton, Newton Abbot, Devon, England.

CAREER: Has worked as a scientist, veterinarian, zookeeper, mink farmer, rabbit farmer, beach photographer, and truck driver; currently broadcasting short talks on local radio. Freelance writer. *Military service:* British Army, national service, two years.

WRITINGS:

Break for Freedom, George Newnes, 1967, published as *Syla the Mink*, Dutton, 1968.
Halic: The Story of a Grey Seal, Dutton, 1970.
The Running of the Deer (novel), Dutton, 1972.
In the Shadow of the Falcon (novel), Dutton, 1973.
Wolf Country: A Wilderness Pilgrimage (nonfiction), Dutton, 1975.
The Badgers of Summercombe, Hutchinson, 1977.
The Many-Forked Branch (novel), Dutton, 1980.
Wolves, Raintree Publishers, 1980.
Reindeer, Wayland, 1981.
Eagles, Wayland, 1981.
Beavers, Wayland, 1981.
The Wake of the Storm, illustrated by Edward Mortelmans, M. Joseph, 1983, St. Martin's, 1984.

Former author of column "Clarkson's Commentary" for *Fishing* (monthly magazine published by Angling Times Co., now defunct).

WORK IN PROGRESS: A novel on the Alaskan wilderness.

SIDELIGHTS: Ewan Clarkson's animal stories are motivated by his belief that "man is a part of nature and it is only possible for man to survive as a species if he is prepared to co-exist in harmony with other species of life. If he destroys his environment he will destroy himself."

BIOGRAPHICAL/CRITICAL SOURCES:

PERIODICALS

Best Sellers, August 15, 1968.
New York Times Book Review, August 4, 1968.
Washington Post, March 27, 1970.

*   *   *

CLEGG, Charles (Myron, Jr.)   1916-

PERSONAL: Born June 29, 1916, in Youngstown, Ohio; son of Charles Myron and Ruth (Standish) Clegg. *Education:* "Informal. Special student of G. Ghrislain Lootens in photography and darkroom techniques; special student in high frequency electronics; special student in French and Spanish." *Politics:* Republican. *Religion:* Protestant.

ADDRESSES: Home—2 South A St., P.O. Box 429, Virginia City, Nev. 89440.

CAREER: Junior executive with Julius Garfinckle Co., Washington, D.C., 1937-40, and Arnold Constable, New York City, 1941-42; Gotham DeLuxe (luxury information service), New York City, president, 1945-46; *Territorial Enterprise* (newspaper), Virginia City, Nev., editor and president, 1952-60; Nevada Alvarado Corp., Reno, president, 1965—. Collaborator with Lucius Beebe in fields of public relations, western Americana, and railroadiana; president of Lucius M. Beebe Memorial Foundation (animal charities), Reno, 1966-74.

MEMBER: Railway and Locomotive Historical Society, National Railway Historical Society, American Wine and Food Society (honorary member).

WRITINGS:

WITH LUCIUS BEEBE

(Contributor) *Highball: A Pageant of Trains,* Appleton-Century, 1945.
Mixed Train Daily: A Book of Short Line Railroads, Dutton, 1947, 2nd edition, 1975.
(Editor and author of foreword) H. Helper, *Dreadful California,* Bobbs-Merrill, 1948.
U.S. West: The Saga of Wells Fargo, Dutton, 1949, reprinted, Bonanza Books, 1975.
Virginia and Truckee: A Story of Virginia City and the Comstock Times, G. Hardy, 1949, reprinted, Howell-North Books, 1980.
Legends of the Comstock Lode, G. Hardy, 1951, 4th edition, Stanford University Press, 1956.
Cable Car Carnival, G. Hardy, 1951.
Hear the Train Blow: A Pictorial Epic of America, Dutton, 1952.
The American West: The Pictorial Epic of a Continent, Dutton, 1955.
Steamcars to the Comstock, Howell-North Books, 1957, 3rd edition, 1960.
The Age of Steam: A Classic Album of American Railroading, Holt, 1957, 2nd edition, Howell-North Books, 1972.
Narrow Gauge in the Rockies, Howell-North Books, 1958.

San Francisco's Golden Era, Howell-North Books, 1960, 2nd edition, 1975.
When Beauty Rode the Rails, Doubleday, 1962.
Rio Grande: Mainline of the Rockies, Howell-North Books, 1962.
Great Railroad Photographs, USA, Howell-North Books, 1964.
The Trains We Rode, Howell-North Books, Volume I, 1965, Volume II, 1966.

OTHER

(Editor with Duncan Emrich) *The Lucius Beebe Reader,* Doubleday, 1967.
(With Jean Stephens) *Lucius M. Beebe: Seeing the Elephant,* 1972.

Contributor to periodicals.

WORK IN PROGRESS: A book composed of hitherto unpublished railroad photographs with text; a special low calorie, low cholesterol cookbook.

SIDELIGHTS: Charles Clegg was once the youngest government-licensed radio operator in the United States.†

*   *   *

COCAGNAC, Augustin Maurice(-Jean)   1924-
(J. M. Warbler)

PERSONAL: Born June 20, 1924, in Tarbes, Haut Pyrenees, France; son of Joseph and Clemence (Rebeille) Cocagnac. *Education:* Received license in theology from the Dominican Fathers; attended Institut de Civilisations Indiennes.

ADDRESSES: Home—Couvent St. Jacques, 20 rue des Tanneries, 75013 Paris, France. *Office*—Le Periscope, 33 rue du Rocher, Paris 8e, France.

CAREER: Roman Catholic priest; Editions du Cerf, Paris, France, director of *Art Sacre* (periodical), 1954-70, and director of children's bible series, 1970; Le Periscope, Paris, director, 1970—. Theatrical chaplain.

MEMBER: Societe des Auteurs, Compositeurs et Editeurs de Musique.

WRITINGS:

Le Jugement dernier dans l'art, Editions du Cerf, 1958.
Pour comprendre ma messe (youth book), Editions du Cerf, 1965, translation by William Barrow published as *When I Go to Mass,* Macmillan, 1965.
Natale, Salani, 1965.
Ce que Jesus a fait pour moi, Editions du Cerf, 1966.
La Bible pour les jeunes, Editions du Cerf, Volume I: *L'Ancienne Alliance,* 1966, Volume II: *La Nouvelle Alliance,* 1967.
(With Rosemary Haughton) *Bible for Young Christians,* Volume I: *The Old Testament,* Geoffrey Chapman, 1966, Macmillan, 1967, Volume II: *The New Testament,* Macmillan, 1967.
Jesus ressuscite Lazare, Editions du Cerf, 1967.
La Creation du monde, Editions du Cerf, 1967.
Pierre, pecheur du Christ, Editions du Cerf, 1968.
Pour comprendre mon bapteme, Editions du Cerf, 1968.
L'Esprit de Pentecote, Editions Fides, 1968.
Les Mots de la Bible, Editions du Cerf, 1968.
Si Dieu etait mort il ne parlerait si fort, Editions du Cerf, 1969.

(Adaptor from the Japanese) *Les Trois Arbres du samourai*, Editions du Cerf, 1969, translation published as *The Three Trees of the Samurai*, Quist, 1969.
Pouf, pouf, le petit train dans les nuages, Editions du Cerf, 1969.
Les Hommes regardent la lune, Editions du Cerf, 1969.
L'Opera de Jonas, Le Periscope, 1970.
A la table du Seigneur, Maison Mame, 1973.
Chantons les fetes, Maison Mame, 1974.
Histoire d'un chat peau-de-laine, Parents' Magazine Press, 1975.
Aujourd'hui l'Inde spirituelle, CELT, 1976.

Editor of collection "Les Albums de l'arc-en-ciel," Editions du Cerf, published in England under pseudonym J. M. Warbler, Geoffrey Chapman. Has done recordings of Bible songs in French.†

* * *

COHEN, Arthur A(llen) 1928-

PERSONAL: Born June 25, 1928, in New York, N.Y.; son of Isidore M(eyer) and Bess (Junger) Cohen; married Elaine Firstenberg Lustig (a painter), October 14, 1956; children: Tamar Judith. *Education:* Attended Friends Seminary, New York, N.Y., 1941-44; University of Chicago, B.A., 1946, M.A., 1949, graduate study, 1949-51; additional studies at Union Theological Seminary, 1950, New School for Social Research, 1950, Columbia University, 1950, and Jewish Theological Seminary of America, 1950-52. *Politics:* "Liberal, if not left, Democrat." *Religion:* Jewish.

ADDRESSES: Home—160 East 70th St., New York, N.Y. 10021. *Office*—160A East 70th St., New York, N.Y. 10021. *Agent*—Wallace & Sheil Agency, 177 East 70th St., New York, N.Y. 10021.

CAREER: Noonday Press, New York City, co-founder and managing director, 1951-55; Meridian Books, Inc., New York City, founder and president, 1955-60; World Publishing Co., New York City, vice-president, 1960-61; Holt, Rinehart & Winston, Inc., New York City, director of religion department, 1961-64, editor-in-chief and vice-president of General Books Division, 1964-68; Viking Press, Inc., New York City, managing editor, 1968-75; Ex Libris (rare book dealer), New York City, founder and president, 1974—. Visiting lecturer, Brown University, 1972, and Jewish Institute of Religion, 1977; Tisch Lecturer in Judaic Theology, Brown University, 1979. Consultant, Fund for the Republic "Religion and the Free Society" project, 1956-59; member of advisory board, Institute for Advanced Judaic Studies, Brandeis University.

AWARDS, HONORS: Edward Lewis Wallant Prize, 1973, for *In the Days of Simon Stern;* National Jewish Book Award in fiction, Jewish Book Council, 1984, for *An Admirable Woman.*

WRITINGS:

Martin Buber, Hillary House, 1958.
The Natural and the Supernatural Jew: An Historical and Theological Introduction, Pantheon, 1963.
The Myth of the Judeo-Christian Tradition, Harper, 1970.
A People Apart: Hasidic Life in America, Dutton, 1970.
If Not Now, When? Conversations between Mordecai M. Kaplan and Arthur A. Cohen, Schocken, 1970.
Osip Emilevich Mandelstam: An Essay in Antiphon, Ardis, 1974.
Sonia Delaunay, Abrams, 1975.

Herbert Bayer: The Complete Works, MIT Press, 1984.

NOVELS

The Carpenter Years, New American Library, 1967.
In the Days of Simon Stern, Random House, 1973.
A Hero in His Time, Random House, 1976.
Acts of Theft, Harcourt, 1980.
An Admirable Woman, David Godine, 1983.

EDITOR

The Anatomy of Faith: Theological Essays of Milton Steinberg, Harcourt, 1960.
Humanistic Education and Western Civilization: Essays in Honor of Robert Maynard Hutchins, Holt, 1964.
Arguments and Doctrines: A Reader of Jewish Thinking in the Aftermath of the Holocaust, Harper, 1970.
The New Art of Color: The Writings of Robert and Sonia Delaunay, Viking, 1978.
The Jew: Essays from Martin Buber's Journal "Der Jude," University of Alabama Press, 1980.
(With P. Mendes-Flohr) *A Handbook of Jewish Religious Thought*, Scribner, 1986.

CONTRIBUTOR

Religion and the Free Society, Fund for the Republic, 1958.
American Catholics: A Protestant-Jewish View, Sheed, 1959.
Religion and Contemporary Society, Macmillan, 1963.
Christianity: Some Non-Christian Appraisals, McGraw, 1964.
What's Ahead for the Churches? Sheed, 1964.
Varieties of Jewish Belief, Reconstructionist Press, 1966.
Confrontations with Judaism, Anthony Blond, 1966.
Negro and Jew, Macmillan, 1967.
McLuhan: Pro and Con, Funk, 1968.
Dada Spectrum, Coda Press, 1979.

OTHER

Contributor of articles and short stories to numerous publications, including *Commonweal, Partisan Review, Commentary, Harper's, Saturday Review,* and the *New York Times Book Review.*

SIDELIGHTS: After spending over twenty successful years as an editor, publisher, and writer of nonfiction, Arthur A. Cohen decided to try his luck as a novelist. "I was terrified of writing fiction," he recalls, "[and] for years put it off and, as a result, have no drawerful of partial manuscripts or shards from broken ideas. My training was in philosophy and theology, and my passion remains philosophy and theology. People, unfortunately, don't read philosophy and theology, certainly not Jewish theology." Despite this awareness of the reading preferences of the general public, Cohen has chosen to draw heavily from philosophy and Jewish theology as a basis for his novels. "Cohen has said that in his novels he seeks to give the reader 'a tale plus something else,'" notes Diane Cole in the *Dictionary of Literary Biography.* "He sees fiction as a 'smuggling device' which will allow him to follow the advice of philosopher Franz Rosenzweig 'to smuggle Jewish ideas into general culture.'"

The Carpenter Years, for example, tells the story of a Jewish man who, perceiving himself as a failure, abandons his faith, his job, and his family and creates a new identity for himself as a successful and respected "WASP." Many reviewers praise this book for its theme while pointing out that Cohen lacks the skill of an accomplished novelist. "Mr. Cohen is not a novelist," observes a *Book World* critic. "Yet *The Carpenter*

Years is a good novel. It is good because the man who made it, though not imaginatively gifted, has known how to take advantage of the possibilities of conventional fiction as a medium of discourse and as a tool of investigation. As philosophers use myth, as novelists have sometimes used theology, so Mr. Cohen, a theologian, uses fiction—for purposes foreign to its ends, but proper to his.''

Describing *The Carpenter Years* as ''a contemporary parable about religion in the United States,'' Leonard Kriegel remarks in the *Nation* that Cohen, if not ''particularly successful, . . . has been daring in his choice of a theme.'' Like several of his fellow reviewers, Kriegel faults the author's characterization. ''Cohen's protagonist exists only on the edges of the reader's perceptions,'' explains Kriegel. Consequently, the story ''leaves one in a kind of spiritual torpor. . . . The failure in this novel is [the author's] inability to make his religious consciousness decisive for the reader.''

Richard Horchler makes a similar observation in *Commonweal*. ''Because Mr. Cohen is not a novelist—at least not yet a novelist—his interests, reflections and ideas are only hung on his characters and events, not embodied in them,'' writes the critic. ''It is hard to believe in any of the characters, in fact, and therefore hard to take very seriously the objectively very serious things that happen in the novel.'' In short, declares Bernard Bergonzi in the *New York Review of Books*, Cohen's ''seriousness exists only on the level of intention, not of imaginative enactment.''

On the other hand, *Christian Century* reviewer Mark Perlberg believes that the novel's characters are ''vividly drawn and . . . observed at close range, as through a zoom lens. Hence the air of claustrophobic tension throughout. [*The Carpenter Years*] holds the reader's attention as it speeds to its climax.'' An *Illustrated London News* critic also takes a favorable view of the novel, pronouncing it to be a ''strong, simple narrative'' that is ''beautifully written, . . . well observed, and full of implicit wisdom.''

Horchler admits that ''the barest outline of Arthur Cohen's first novel is intriguing, exciting, filled with promise. . . . It would have been sure-fire, it would seem, especially if it were by a writer of Arthur Cohen's demonstrated intelligence, cultivation and sensitivity.'' But as the critic ultimately concludes, ''it isn't sure-fire at all. *The Carpenter Years* is not a successful novel, which makes for a particularly keen disappointment because it is—or has—a number of other very good things. . . . I am afraid that what [Cohen] was trying to convey in [his novel] would have been clearer—and better realized—in one of his philosophic essays.''

In the Days of Simon Stern, the story of a post-World War II messiah who uses his vast financial resources to set up a haven for victims of the Holocaust, came under fire for its often obscure and confusing references to personages and concepts of Jewish theology. As a *Book World* critic writes: ''*In the Days of Simon Stern* is hollow. It blunders about in sociology, psychology, philosophy, all gracelessly, but never tells a convincing story. Instead, Arthur Cohen . . . over-explains every moment to prepare us for any surprise the plot holds in store. . . . [His] fiction is not adequate to his sense of history.''

A *Books and Bookmen* reviewer is equally unimpressed. ''Although no human being can be other than harrowed and driven to compassion by the sufferings the Jews have undergone this century, few Gentiles will be able (or willing) to follow Mr. Cohen through this fictional labyrinth, with its theological

meanderings, symbolical cobwebberies, stylistic obfuscations and anecdotal cul-de-sacs,'' declares the reviewer. ''No doubt some discerning critics will discover monumental significance in it. Certainly some Jews will be moved by it. I regret to say that I found [*In the Days of Simon Stern*] not so much 'deeply moving' as profoundly boring.''

Cynthia Ozick is of the opposite opinion, writing in the *New York Times Book Review* that ''for a small mountain of reasons, this book ensnares one of the most extra-ordinarily daring ideas to inhabit an American novel in a number of years. . . . In its teeming particularity every vein of this book runs with a brilliance of Jewish insight and erudition to be found in no other novelist. . . . Arthur Cohen is the first writer of any American generation to compose a profoundly Jewish fiction on a profoundly Western theme.'' M. J. Bandler, a contributor to *Commonweal,* describes *In the Days of Simon Stern* as ''a jewel to be treasured; a majestic work of fiction that should stand world literature's test of time, to be read and reread in a search for new meanings and interpretations.''

A Hero in His Time was greeted with less polarized reactions. It tells the story of an obscure Soviet Jewish poet who is chosen to attend a writers' conference in New York to read a special poem which, unknown to him, is really a coded message intended for a KGB agent. According to Ruth R. Wisse, *A Hero in His Time* is ''politically and artistically a more complex work'' than the plot suggests, and its focus is quite different from the strong religious and philosophical orientation of Cohen's previous novels. ''Well-written and engaging in its ideas, this novel steers an uneven course between comedy and high seriousness,'' explains the critic in her *Commentary* review of *A Hero in His Time*. In an observation reminiscent of those made on Cohen's earlier works, Wisse also notes that ''some of the characters are mere occasions for aspects of social history, and even the hero, though witty and interesting, seems emotionally underdone, too flat for the fictional load he must carry.''

Time's John Skow writes that Cohen's novel is ''a delightful minor-key farce. . . . [The author] uncannily manages to sound like a U.S.S.R. satirist writing riskily for *Samizdat* circulation. The New York section of the book is weaker; perhaps it should have been written by a Soviet. For the satire of the left-wing academic community lacks teeth, and too many plot turns seem to occur in the last third of the novel, simply because something has to happen.'' A *National Observer* reviewer thinks that *A Hero in His Time* ''may well be the most deceptive book of the season. In tone, in 'feel,' Arthur A. Cohen's novel seems at the outset a kind of fable. . . . [It] is indeed an acidly funny fable, but it is a deeply human, moving fable as well. It is the sort of book that a rummager always hopes to find.''

Finally, Valentine Cunningham declares in the *New Statesman:* ''It takes, perhaps, a scholarly Jewish writer such as Arthur Cohen . . . to be able to get inside the imaginative life of Russian Jews. . . . But important though the author's Jewish sympathies and inside knowledge are, they're not by themselves enough to guarantee the amazing *tour de force* that *A Hero in His Time* represents. . . . [It] is solid, believable, and quite astonishing from an American, even a Jewish-American, writer.''

Acts of Theft represents somewhat of a departure from Cohen's previous novels in that it does not deal specifically with American Judaism; instead, it tells the story of a European sculptor residing in Mexico who supplements his income by stealing various pieces of pre-Colombian art from archaeological sites in order to sell them to collectors. The tone of the novel is decidedly philosophical, however, because in the confrontation between the thief and the clever Mexican detective who tracks him down, the author's real concerns come to the forefront. As the *New York Times*'s John Leonard explains, *Acts of Theft* is an exploration of "the artist as God, art as theft, the ransom of the past, the ancient made modern, pride and sacrifice"; Mark Shechner of the *New York Times Book Review* describes it as a study of "the corruptions that attend the worship of graven images."

As a result of these preoccupations, continues Schechner, "those who buy this book expecting a straightforward drama of crime and detection will find Mauger [the main character] sadly easy to catch. He drops clues everywhere. This is because, I guess, Mr. Cohen doesn't want the dramatics of pursuit and evasion to distract us from his ruminations on the morality of art. Hence he short-circuits his plot with flashbacks, asides, interior monologues, lectures, the works, for the sake of depth, weight and moral tone." But as the critic goes on to point out, "rather than challenging the reader, this strategy only exasperates him. . . . Mr. Cohen plies us with vivid and passionate yearnings that overpower his plot and overwhelm his sentences. . . . The trouble with *Acts of Theft* is that Mr. Cohen wants the sublime but can achieve only the breathless, which works in fiction about as well as it does in religion."

The *Washington Post*'s Joseph McLellan, on the other hand, feels that Cohen *has* achieved a successful blend of philosophy and drama in *Acts of Theft*. He explains: "On one level, *Acts of Theft* is a very elaborate story of cops and robbers—but it aspires to much more and its aspirations are largely fulfilled. The parallels that spring to mind are *Crime and Punishment* or *Les Miserables*, and if it does not have quite the depth of the one or the sweeping scope of the other, it is certainly more than a routine novel. Its texture is rich. . . . Its central characters are deeply pondered, and the metaphysical concerns that drive them are rendered not only in occasional dialogues a la Plato but in gestures both concrete and symbolic that add up to a well-engineered plot. . . . Underlying all these is the subject of sculpture—though the intricate weaving of thematic strands makes Arthur Cohen's technique seem more like that of a tapestry."

Cohen continued to broaden his writing scope with his fifth novel, *An Admirable Woman*, by writing in a female voice. The book is a fictional memoir of Erika Margaret Hertz, a character who, reports Anatole Broyard in the *New York Times*, Cohen says was "suggested to me by the remarkable personality and intellectual career of an old friend, Hannah Arendt." Arendt, a philosopher and political scientist, was considered one of the most important political thinkers of her time. Like Hannah Arendt, Erika Hertz came to New York's West Side from Nazi Germany to become part of the community of "exiled German geniuses who transformed America's cultural landscape in the years after World War II," explains Jim Miller in *Newsweek*. "Mr. Cohen has not written a biography of Hannah Arendt, nor has he intended a biography," explains Earl Shorris in the *New York Times Book Review*. "Rather, he has used the novelist's imagination to explore fame in the intellectual world, to reveal life overwhelmed by ethics, to take the reader to a miraculous town [New York's West Side]. All through her memoir, Erika Hertz ponders the quality of admirableness, examines it in relation to each of her attributes. She is a doubter, a critic of herself. A measure of Mr. Cohen's

accomplishment is that the reader wants to argue with her, often to insist that she *is* a 'wholly admirable' woman."

Like Cohen's earlier works, *An Admirable Woman* received some criticism for being too abstract, especially in its portrayal of the main character. For example, Broyard notes that Erika's "career in New York City is more often summarized than dramatized. . . . [Cohen] has not given Erika the style, the intellectual texture, of a great woman." Miller remarks in a similar vein, "Unfortunately, Cohen's creation lacks Arendt's caustic wit and flair for philosophical fireworks; to evoke Erika's quality of mind, he is reduced to describing prodigious feats of reading and inventing walk-on roles for figures like John-Paul Sartre." But Sharon Dirlam maintains in the *Los Angeles Times Book Review* that if Erika "is never more than a conduit for Cohen's philosophies of truth and meaning, this alone may justify her existence as a fictional character. . . . The book is a treasure."

"Arthur A. Cohen has produced work whose erudition, invention, and passion have established him as one of American Judaism's foremost men of letters," summarizes Cole in the *Dictionary of Literary Biography*. "Though ideas attract him, he is not satisfied with ideas in the abstract. His imagination also seizes on the dramas that make up people's lives. There would be no point in discussing faith, after all, if there existed no men and women to believe—or to deny belief. Cohen's purpose as a writer is not to convert readers, but to illuminate the intricate and various pathways of faith and to show the blackness of history. In presenting his vision of the world, Arthur A. Cohen helps clarify our own. His voice arouses his readers to thought, perplexity, the possibility of faith, and finally, the perception of art."

AVOCATIONAL INTERESTS: Horseback riding, traveling, learning languages.

BIOGRAPHICAL/CRITICAL SOURCES:

BOOKS

Contemporary Literary Criticism, Volume VII, Gale, 1977.
Dictionary of Literary Biography, Volume XXVIII: *Twentieth-Century American-Jewish Fiction Writers*, Gale, 1984.

PERIODICALS

Books and Bookmen, July, 1967, March, 1976.
Book World, March 12, 1967, July 29, 1973.
Christian Century, March 1, 1967, March 10, 1971.
Christian Science Monitor, February 23, 1967.
Commentary, April, 1967, November, 1969, November, 1970, October, 1976.
Commonweal, September 8, 1967, September 28, 1973.
Illustrated London News, April 22, 1967.
Library Journal, October 1, 1966.
Los Angeles Times Book Review, November 20, 1983.
Nation, July 3, 1967.
National Observer, April 3, 1976.
Newsweek, January 12, 1976, November 14, 1983.
New Statesman, February 27, 1976.
New York Review of Books, June 1, 1967.
New York Times, January 27, 1968, February 12, 1980, February 22, 1980, November 17, 1983.
New York Times Book Review, June 3, 1973, March 9, 1980, November 20, 1983.
Observer, April 2, 1967.
Publishers Weekly, January 19, 1976.

Time, January 5, 1976.
Times Literary Supplement, April 27, 1967, November 9, 1967.
Washington Post, March 21, 1981.

                —*Sketch by Joan E. Marecki and Deborah A. Straub*

*   *   *

COHEN, Marvin 1931-

PERSONAL: Born July 6, 1931, in Brooklyn, N.Y.; son of Milton (a salesman) and Sarah (Siminow) Cohen. *Education:* Attended Hunter College of the City University of New York, Brooklyn College of the City University of New York, and Cooper Union.

ADDRESSES: Home—P.O. Box 460, Peter Stuyvesant Station, New York, N.Y. 10009. *Agent*—Ronald Hobbs Literary Agency, 516 Fifth Ave., Suite 507, New York, N.Y. 10036.

CAREER: Worked as a market researcher and a free-lance writer and held numerous other positions, 1951-68; *National Camp Directors Guide,* New York City, editor, 1960-61; Monarch Press, New York City, copy editor and proofreader, 1963-65; *New Yorker,* New York City, book reviewer, 1968; City College of the City University of New York, New York City, teacher, 1968-75; Cooper Union, Division of Continuing Education, New York City, teacher, 1978—; Hofstra University, Division of Continuing Education, Hempstead, N.Y., teacher, 1978—.

MEMBER: P.E.N.

AWARDS, HONORS: Yaddo resident fellow, Saratoga Springs, N.Y., 1963; C.A.P.S. grant, 1974-75.

WRITINGS:

The Self-Devoted Friend, Rapp & Carroll, 1967, New Directions, 1968.
Dialogues (limited edition), Turret Books, 1967.
The Monday Rhetoric of the Love Club, and Other Parables, New Directions, 1973.
Baseball the Beautiful: Decoding the Diamond, illustrations by Paul Spina, Links, 1974.
Fables at Life's Expense, Latitudes Press, 1975.
Others, Including Morstive Sternbump (novel), Bobbs-Merrill, 1976.
The Inconvenience of Living, and Other Acts of Folly, Urizen Books, 1977.
The Department Store of Global Confinement, and Other Entireties, Seagull Publications, 1978.
Aesthetics in Life and Art: Existence in Function and Essence and Whatever Else Is Important, Too, Gull Books, 1983.

Author of mini-plays produced in 1968 at Mercury Theatre, London, England, and Boston Arts Festival. Also author of numerous review notes for Educational Research Associates. Contributor to *New Directions Anthology,* Numbers 18 and 19, and *Anthology of Fables,* Random House. Also contributor of stories, dialogues, prose poems, and parables to magazines in America, England, Italy, and Switzerland, including *Harper's Bazaar, Vogue, Ambit, Beat Scene, Hudson Review, Books, Midstream,* and *Fire Exit.*

WORK IN PROGRESS: Dialogues, short stories, and fables.

SIDELIGHTS: Marvin Cohen lists as his influences James Joyce, Franz Kafka, Henry James, Henri Michaux, William Faulkner, and the eighteenth-century English prose style. He also lists "such personal factors as my rather isolated Brooklyn childhood, my semi-deafness from the age of three; my inter-

ests in Major League baseball, art, and music; early abortive love life, poverty, the cosmos of New York City, travelings and tattered abundance of jobs and idlenesses."

AVOCATIONAL INTERESTS: Baseball, football, London.

BIOGRAPHICAL/CRITICAL SOURCES:

PERIODICALS

Hudson Review, autumn, 1968.
Listener, November 26, 1967.
New Statesman, November 17, 1967.
New Yorker, May 11, 1968.†

*   *   *

COHEN, Wilbur J(oseph) 1913-

PERSONAL: Born June 10, 1913, in Milwaukee, Wis.; son of Aaron (operator of a variety store) and Bessie (Rubenstein) Cohen; married Eloise Bittel, April 8, 1938; children: Christopher, Bruce, Stuart. *Education:* University of Wisconsin, Ph.B., 1934. *Politics:* Democrat. *Religion:* Jewish.

ADDRESSES: Home—3700 Stevenson Ave., Austin, Tex. 78703; and 620 Oxford Rd., Ann Arbor, Mich. 48104. *Office*—Lyndon B. Johnson School of Public Affairs, University of Texas, Austin, Tex. 78712.

CAREER: President Roosevelt's Cabinet Committee on Economic Security, Washington, D.C., research assistant, 1934-35; U.S. Social Security Administration, Washington, D.C., technical adviser, 1935-53, director of Division of Research and Statistics, 1953-56; University of Michigan, Ann Arbor, professor of public welfare administration, 1956-61; U.S. Department of Health, Education, and Welfare, Washington, D.C., assistant secretary for legislation, 1961-64, undersecretary, 1965-68, secretary of department, 1968; University of Michigan, professor of education and dean of School of Education, 1969-79; University of Texas at Austin, Lyndon B. Johnson School of Public Affairs, Sid W. Richardson Professor of Public Affairs, 1980-83, professor of public affairs, 1983—.

Visiting professor, University of California, Los Angeles, 1957; lecturer, Catholic University of America, 1961-62. Member of Advisory Council on Public Assistance, 1959, house of delegates, Council on Social Work Education, 1959-62, 1974-76, and National Committee on Social Security, 1978-81; chairman of President's Committee on Mental Retardation, 1968, President's Committee on Population and Family Planning, 1968, and National Committee on Unemployment Compensation, 1978-80. President, National Conference on Social Welfare, 1969-70; has represented U.S. government at international conferences on social security, social work, and labor. Chairman of advisory council of Retirement Advisors, Inc., 1958-60, 1969-70; chairman of Save Our Security, 1977—. Consultant on aging to U.S. Senate Committee on Labor and Public Welfare, 1956-57, 1959, and to United Nations, 1956-57.

MEMBER: American Economic Association, American Public Welfare Association (director, 1962-65; president, 1975-76), American Public Health Association, National Association of Social Workers, Industrial Relations Research Association (member of executive board, 1969-72), Phi Kappa Phi, Artus.

AWARDS, HONORS: Distinguished Service Award, U.S. Department of Health, Education, and Welfare, and Group Health Association Award, both 1956; Florina Lasker Award, National Conference on Social Welfare, and Terry Award, American Public Welfare Association, both 1961; Blanche Ittelson Award, New York Social Work Recruiting Commission, 1962; awards from National Association of Social Workers, National Association for Mentally Retarded Children, and Association of Physical Medicine, all 1965; Bronfman Public Health Prize and Rockefeller Public Service Award, both 1967; Murray-Green Award and Volunteers of America Annual Service Award, both 1968; Forand Award from National Council of Senior Citizens, 1969; Jane Addams-Hull House Award, 1975; Merrill-Palmer Award, 1975; International Association for Social Security Award, 1979.

Holds honorary degrees from Adelphi University, Yeshiva University, Cleveland State University, University of Wisconsin, Central Michigan University, Florida State University, Eastern Michigan University, Northern Michigan University, Brandeis University, Kenyon College, University of Detroit, University of Louisville, Ohio State University, and Michigan State University.

WRITINGS:

Unemployment Insurance and Agricultural Labor in Great Britain, Social Science Research Council, 1940.
(Editor) *War and Post-War Security*, American Council on Public Affairs, 1942.
(Editor with William Haber) *Readings in Social Security*, Prentice-Hall, 1948.
Retirement Policies under Social Security, University of California Press, 1957.
(Editor with Haber) *Social Security: Programs, Problems, and Policies*, Irwin, 1961.
(With Sydney E. Bernard) *The Prevention and Reduction of Dependency*, Washtenaw County Department of Social Welfare, 1961.
(Contributor) *Income and Welfare in the United States*, McGraw, 1962.
The Program against Poverty (Sidney A. Teller lecture), Graduate School of Social Work, University of Pittsburgh, 1964.
(Editor with Sar A. Levitan and Robert J. Lampman) *Towards Freedom from Want*, Industrial Relations Research Association, 1968.
Health in America: The Role of the Federal Government in Bringing High Quality Health Care to All American People, U.S. Department of Health, Education, and Welfare, 1968.
(Author of introduction) *Toward a Social Report*, University of Michigan Press, 1970.
(With others) *Social Security: The First Thirty-five Years*, Institute of Gerontology, University of Michigan, 1971.
(With Milton Friedman) *Social Security: Universal or Selective*, American Enterprise Institute for Public Policy Research, 1972.
(Contributor) *Welfare Reform: Why?*, American Enterprise Institute, 1976.
(With Charles F. Westoff) *Demographic Dynamics in America*, Free Press, 1977.
(With W. Joseph Heffernan) *Welfare Reform: State and Federal Roles*, Lyndon B. Johnson School of Public Affairs, University of Texas at Austin, 1983.

Also author of other survey reports and government publications. Contributor to *Encyclopaedia Britannica* and to social welfare, education, and health journals.

AVOCATIONAL INTERESTS: Stamp-collecting, floral arrangements.

BIOGRAPHICAL/CRITICAL SOURCES:

PERIODICALS

New York Times, March 25, 1968.†

*   *   *

COLVETT, Latayne
    See SCOTT, Latayne Colvett

*   *   *

COLVIN, James
    See MOORCOCK, Michael (John)

*   *   *

COMPERE, Mickie
    See DAVIDSON, Margaret

*   *   *

COMPTON, D(avid) G(uy)   1930-
    (Guy Compton; Frances Lynch, a pseudonym)

PERSONAL: Born August 19, 1930, in London, England; son of George (a stage manager) and Margaret (Symonds) Compton; married Elizabeth Tillotson, February 23, 1952 (divorced, 1967); married Carol Curtis-Brown Savage, 1969; children: (first marriage) Margaret Jane, Hester Josephine, James Samuel. *Education:* Attended Cheltenham College, Gloucester, England, 1941-50. *Politics:* None. *Religion:* "Confused."

ADDRESSES: Agent—Virginia Kidd, Box 278, Milford, Pa. 18837; and Murray Pollinger, 4 Garrick St., London WC2E 9BH, England.

CAREER: Former stage electrician, furniture-maker, salesman, docker, and postman; free-lance writer and editor, 1960—. *Military service:* British Army, National Service, 1950-52.

AWARDS, HONORS: Arts Council play-writing bursary, 1964.

WRITINGS:

SCIENCE FICTION

The Quality of Mercy, Ace Books, 1965, revised edition, 1970.
The Silent Multitude, Ace Books, 1966.
Farewell, Earth's Bliss, Ace Books, 1966.
Synthajoy, Ace Books, 1968, reprinted with a new introduction by Algis Budrys, Gregg, 1977.
The Palace (novel), Norton, 1969.
The Steel Crocodile, Ace Books, 1970 (published in England as *The Electric Crocodile*, Hodder & Stoughton, 1970), reprinted with a new introduction by David G. Hartwell, Gregg, 1976.
Chronocules, Ace Books, 1970 (published in England as *Hot Wireless Sets, Aspirin Tablets, The Sandpaper Sides of Used Matchboxes and Something That Might Have Been Castor Oil*, M. Joseph, 1971).
The Missionaries, Ace Books, 1972.
The Unsleeping Eye, DAW Books, 1974 (published in England as *The Continuous Katherine Mortenhoe: A Novel*, Gollancz, 1974, published as *Death Watch*, Magnum, 1981), published with a new introduction by Susan Wood as *The Continuous Katherine Mortenhoe*, Gregg, 1980.
A Usual Lunacy, Borgo Press, 1978.
Windows, Berkley Publishing, 1979.

Ascendancies, Berkley Publishing, 1980.
Scudder's Spiel (title means "Scudder's Game"), Heyne (West Germany), 1985.
The Masters of Talojz, Heyne, 1986.

UNDER NAME GUY COMPTON; CRIME NOVELS

Too Many Murderers, John Long, 1962.
Medium for Murder, John Long, 1963.
Dead on Cue, John Long, 1964.
Disguise for a Gentleman, John Long, 1964.
High Tide for Hanging, John Long, 1965.
And Murder Came Too, John Long, 1966.

UNDER PSEUDONYM FRANCES LYNCH; ROMANCE NOVELS

Twice Ten Thousand Miles: A Novel, St. Martin's, 1974.
The Fine and Handsome Captain: A Novel, St. Martin's, 1975.
Stranger at the Wedding: A Novel, St. Martin's, 1976, large print edition published as *Stranger at the Wedding*, J. Curley, 1978.
A Dangerous Magic, St. Martin's, 1978.
In the House of Dark Music, Hodder & Stoughton, 1979, Warner Books, 1984.

OTHER

Author of numerous stage plays, television plays, radio scripts, and short stories.

WORK IN PROGRESS: A "world held hostage" adventure novel, *Ragnarok*, in collaboration with scientist/author John Gribbin.

SIDELIGHTS: D. G. Compton says that he "never wanted to do anything but write, but only dared try to support a wife and three children on it when I found that nothing else I could do was marketable. I write books set in the future as a way of gaining perspective on the tendencies of the present. A deep pessimism about mankind wars with a conviction that writing should be inspirational, that writers have a priestly, interpretive function. Formal spirituality seems so irrelevant to the mass of the people I would like to reach. Yet I need a sharper edge than flabby liberalism."

*   *   *

COMPTON, Guy
See COMPTON, D(avid) G(uy)

*   *   *

CONTOSKI, Victor   1936-

PERSONAL: Born May 4, 1936, in St. Paul, Minn.; son of Victor (a plumber) and Josepha (Kowalewski) Contoski; married Wieslawa Babula (a teacher), July 1, 1962. *Education:* University of Minnesota, B.A., 1959, M.A., 1961; Ohio State University, additional study, 1964-65; University of Wisconsin, Ph.D., 1969.

ADDRESSES: Home—Box 230, Route 6, Lawrence, Kan. 66044. *Office*—Department of English, University of Kansas, Lawrence, Kan. 66045.

CAREER: University of Lodz, Lodz, Poland, teacher of American literature, 1961-62, Fulbright professor, 1963-64; currently professor of English, University of Kansas, Lawrence.

AWARDS, HONORS: Edward Gardiner Poetry Award, University of Wisconsin, for "A Tapestry."

WRITINGS:

Four Contemporary Polish Poets (bilingual edition concerning Tadeusz Rozewicz, Stanislaw Grochowiak, Jerzy Harasymowicz, and Roman Sliwonik), Quixote Press, 1967.
(Contributor) *Thirty-one New American Poets*, Hill & Wang, 1969.
Astronomers, Madonnas, and Prophesies, Northeast Books, 1970.
Stroking the Animals, Albatross Press, 1972.
Broken Treaties (poetry), New Rivers Press, 1973.
(Translator) Jerzy Harasymowicz, *Planting Beeches*, New Rivers Press, 1975.
Names, New Rivers Press, 1979.
(Editor) *Blood of Their Blood: An Anthology of Polish-American Poetry*, New Rivers Press, 1980.
(Translator) Tadeusz Rozewicz, *Unease*, New Rivers Press, 1980.
A Kansas Sequence, Tellus/Cottonwood, 1983.

Author of column of fables, "The Fabulist," *North American Review*, 1966-69. Former associate editor, *Minnesota Review;* former contributing editor, *Margins*.

WORK IN PROGRESS: Collected poems.

*   *   *

COOPER, Jane (Marvel)   1924-

PERSONAL: Born October 9, 1924, in Atlantic City, N.J.; daughter of John Cobb (a specialist in air and space law and a writer) and Martha (Marvel) Cooper. *Education:* Attended Vassar College, 1942-44; University of Wisconsin, B.A., 1946; University of Iowa, M.A., 1954. *Religion:* Episcopalian.

ADDRESSES: Home—545 West 111th St., Apt. 8K, New York, N.Y. 10025. *Office*—Sarah Lawrence College, Bronxville, N.Y. 10708.

CAREER: Sarah Lawrence College, Bronxville, N.Y., began as poet in residence, professor of literature and creative writing, 1950—.

AWARDS, HONORS: Guggenheim fellowship in poetry, 1960-61; Lamont award, 1968, for *The Weather of Six Mornings;* Ingram Merrill Foundation grant, 1970-71; Creative Artists Public Service grant in poetry, 1975; Shelley Award, 1978; National Endowment for the Arts fellowship, 1982; Maurice English Poetry Award, 1985, for *Scaffolding.*

WRITINGS:

POETRY

The Weather of Six Mornings, Macmillan, 1969.
Maps and Windows, Macmillan, 1974.
Threads: Rosa Luxemberg from Prison, Flamingo Press, 1979.
Scaffolding: New and Selected Poems, Anvil Press, 1984.

Also contributor to poetry anthologies.

OTHER

(With Malcolm Cooper) *Senior English Reading*, Longman, 1980.
(Co-editor and author of introduction) *Extended Outlooks: The Iowa Review Collection of Contemporary Women Writers*, Macmillan, 1981.

Contributor to *New Yorker, Transatlantic Review, American Poetry Review,* and other periodicals.

BIOGRAPHICAL/CRITICAL SOURCES:

PERIODICALS

Washington Post Book World, June 23, 1985.

*   *   *

CORNELISEN, Ann 1926-

PERSONAL: Born November 12, 1926, in Cleveland, Ohio; daugher of Ralph White and Ydoine (Rose) Cornelisen; divorced. *Education:* Attended Vassar College, 1944-46. *Politics:* Independent. *Religion:* Episcopal.

ADDRESSES: Home—La Torre, Presso, Il Palazzone, Cortona, Arezzo 52044, Italy; 5 Bass Ave., Rome, Ga. 30161. *Agent*—Lois Wallace, Wallace & Sheil, 177 E. 70th St., New York, N.Y. 10021.

CAREER: Social worker and administrator with British Save the Children Fund in Italy, 1954-63.

MEMBER: Authors Guild, Authors League of America.

AWARDS, HONORS: National Institute of Arts and Letters special award and American Academy Award in literature, both 1974; Christopher Award, 1980.

WRITINGS:

Torregreca: Life, Death, Miracles (excerpt originally appeared in *Atlantic*, August, 1968), Little, Brown, 1969.
Vendetta of Silence, Little, Brown, 1971.
Women of the Shadows, Little, Brown, 1976.
Strangers and Pilgrims: The Last Italian Migration, Holt, 1980 (published in England as *Flight from Torregreca*, Macmillan, 1980).
Any Four Women Could Rob the Bank of Italy (novel), Holt, 1983.

Contributor of a story, "Our Friend Pasquale," to *Atlantic*.

WORK IN PROGRESS: A book about her early years in Italy.

SIDELIGHTS: American-born Ann Cornelisen has made Italy her home since 1954, when she began working there for the British Save the Children Fund. Her experiences as a social worker in a poverty-stricken town in the south of Italy have formed the basis for much of her published work, including *Torregreca: Life, Death, Miracles, Women of the Shadows,* and *Strangers and Pilgrims: The Last Italian Migration.* In order to write truthfully about sensitive subjects, Cornelisen uses aliases and the name "Torregreca" to shield the identity of the village in which she lived.

A *Time* magazine writer calls *Torregreca: Life, Death, Miracles,* "an exquisite nonfiction novel of sensibility." Thomas G. Bergin, writing in *Saturday Review,* believes that the book "has rather more humor than most studies of this kind," and that Cornelisen has "a skillful pen for depicting landscape and scenes of activity. She is equally successful in her portraits of the rugged characters she meets in the course of her laudable enterprise [of beginning a day care center for the town's children]." *Harper's* reviewer R. R. Gambee finds that Cornelisen "is not only an accomplished and entertaining writer, but [she] also offers frank, knowledgeable appraisals of the character of the church, of rural Italian mentality, of a cycle of poverty and despair with parallels in American society."

In *Strangers and Pilgrims: The Last Italian Migration,* Cornelisen traces the migration of some of her Torresi friends from Torregreca to the industrialized cities of northern Italy and West Germany, where they have found work as unskilled laborers. Peter Nichols praises the book in the *Times Literary Supplement* as a "deeply human study of southern Italians who have sought their fortunes in emigration." Nichols further notes that Cornelisen "is a great recorder . . . she avoids any resemblance to a sociological report, although she is handling a serious sociological problem." Ronald Blythe, in the *New York Times Book Review,* feels that Cornelisen has managed to continue a genuine relationship with members of the Torregreca community while writing about their deepest personal problems "by ennobling her account of the experience by using some of the literary techniques of a first-class novelist." In a review for the *Detroit News,* Joseph Barbato writes: "Cornelisen succeeds brilliantly in depicting these courageous survivors as people, not the 'docile ergs' of the government statistics. In the end, 'Strangers and Pilgrims' transcends place and time, forming a heart-breaking testament to the spirit of all migrant people."

Cornelisen turns to the novel, and a wealthier area of Italy, for *Any Four Women Could Rob the Bank of Italy.* As the title suggests, the story concerns a group of women who set out to prove that their gender will shield them from any suspicion after a dramatic theft. According to Pico Iyer in *Time,* "Cornelisen is so much at home with the Italian scene and its cosmopolitan settlers that she can at once see through them and like what she perceives." "Miss Cornelisen has produced a novel that is a romp," writes Helen Dudar in the *New York Times Book Review*. "The whole book teems with juicy characters and plot complications." Elaine Kendall calls the work "an airy satire" in the *Los Angeles Times,* and concludes: "Although this proof of Cornelisen's versatility is a pleasant surprise, her heart clearly remains with the unsung forgotten heroines of the Southern provinces, her disdain for the footling problems of the overprivileged . . . obvious despite the good-natured humor."

BIOGRAPHICAL/CRITICAL SOURCES:

PERIODICALS

Detroit News, April 13, 1980.
Harper's, April, 1969.
Los Angeles Times, February 2, 1984.
New York Times, January 24, 1984.
New York Times Book Review, September 13, 1980, February 12, 1984.
Saturday Review, March 8, 1969.
Time, March 8, 1969, February 20, 1984.
Times Literary Supplement, August 15, 1980.
Washington Post Book World, June 22, 1980.

*   *   *

CORTESI, Lawrence
See CERRI, Lawrence J.

*   *   *

COTTLE, Thomas J. 1937-

PERSONAL: Born January 22, 1937, in Chicago, Ill.; son of Maurice H. (a physician) and Gitta (a pianist; maiden name, Gradova) Cottle; married Kay Mikkelsen, June 28, 1964; children: Claudia Mari, Jason Edwin, Sonya Ruth. *Education:* Harvard University, B.A., 1959; University of Chicago, M.A., 1964, Ph.D., 1968. *Religion:* Jewish.

ADDRESSES: Agent—William Morris Agency, 1350 Avenue of the Americas, New York, N.Y. 10019. *Office*—12 Beaconsfield Rd., Brookline, Mass. 02146.

CAREER: Harvard University, Cambridge, Mass., assistant professor of social relations, 1965-70; Massachusetts Institute of Technology, Cambridge, research sociologist in medical department and Education Research Center, 1970-73; Children's Defense Fund, Cambridge, researcher-writer, 1973-75; Tavistock Clinic, London, England, attached staff member, 1975-77; Harvard University, Medical School, Cambridge, lecturer in psychology, 1977-78; also affiliated with University of Illinois and Anna Freud Clinic, London. Visiting distinguished professor of psychology, Amherst College, 1977-78.

MEMBER: American Sociological Association, American Psychological Association.

AWARDS, HONORS: Young psychologist award, American Psychological Association; Guggenheim fellow.

WRITINGS:

Time's Children: Impressions of Youth, Little, Brown, 1971.
The Prospect of Youth, Little, Brown, 1972.
(With Craig Eisendrath and Laurence Fink) *Lighting a Fire in the University,* Schenkman, 1972.
The Abandoners: Portraits of Loss, Separation and Neglect, Little, Brown, 1973.
The Voices of School, Little, Brown, 1973.
(With Stephen L. Klineberg) *The Present of Things Future,* Free Press, 1973.
Black Children, White Dreams, foreword by Walter F. Mondale, Houghton, 1974.
A Family Album: Portraits of Intimacy and Kinship, Harper, 1974.
Perceiving Time: A Psychological Investigation with Men and Women, Wiley, 1976.
Busing, Beacon Press, 1976.
Barred from School: Two Million Children!, New Republic, 1976.
Readings in Adolescent Psychology: Current Perspectives, Harper, 1977.
Children in Jail, Beacon Press, 1977.
College: Reward and Betrayal, University of Chicago Press, 1977.
Private Lives and Public Accounts, University of Massachusetts Press, 1977.
Children's Secrets, Anchor Press, 1980.
Hidden Survivors: Portraits of Poor Jews in America, Prentice-Hall, 1980.

SIDELIGHTS: Thomas J. Cottle is a sociologist and psychologist who specializes in civil rights, especially as they relate to minors. As the author of such books as *Barred from School: Two Million Children!, Children in Jail,* and *Black Children, White Dreams,* Cottle has established himself as "America's most faithful and imaginative observer of the radically changing values and circumstances of young people in our time," according to *New Republic* critic Martin Peretz.

In compiling these works, Cottle often lets his young subjects speak for themselves and then summarizes and analyzes what he has recorded. As a result, he sometimes gets startling responses from the children, many of whom seem to have deeper goals and fears than the reader would expect. To hear such confessions, "and to record [them,] one must be something more than a social scientist," says Neil Postman in a *New York Times Book Review* article about *Time's Children:*

Impressions of Youth. "One must have a touch of the artist. And right there is the most remarkable feature of the book. It reads as if it were written by J. D. Salinger or, even better, James Agee." Postman also finds that "whether he is writing about the attitudes of young people toward authority, toward race, toward education, or toward parents, Cottle seems incapable of making a superficial statement. For every yin, there's a yang. And this is not to suggest that he tries to impose 'balance.' His way of listening and writing just naturally insures that he will probe at levels where, behind every happiness, there's a sadness, behind every strength, a weakness, and behind every boldness, a fear."

When Cottle's subject involves controversy, as does his profile of two ghetto youngsters in *Black Children, White Dreams,* critics sometimes respond with skepticism. Sara Blackburn, for instance, writing about the work in the *New York Times Book Review,* says that "we don't need more studies by experts, no matter how caring, of how bright, sensitive and thus worthy of salvation are the victims of our political and social crimes. Whether Cottle intends it or not, that is the undeniable thrust of this [book]. We do need books that deal with exposing and changing the system that makes the victims."

On the other hand, Theodore Solotaroff, in a *New York Times Book Review* piece on *The Abandoners: Portraits of Loss, Separation and Neglect,* thinks that the author's first-hand involvement with his subjects provides "the main virtue of Cottle's approach." And while Solotaroff agrees that Cottle's "role of witness and advocate rather than analyst tends to make his commentary . . . unduly diffident or admiring about his people, creating soft spots of sentiment along the path of understanding," the critic concludes that this "may be the price Cottle is willing to pay to do the very valuable work he does of listening and reporting, which is grounded in trust and scruple and informed by respect, in his words, for 'the totality of a single emerging soul [which] ultimately defies interpretation and begs, instead, for expression and the right to be heard.'"

BIOGRAPHICAL/CRITICAL SOURCES:

BOOKS

Cottle, Thomas J., *The Abandoners: Portraits of Loss, Separation and Neglect,* Little, Brown, 1973.

PERIODICALS

Nation, January 16, 1977.
New Republic, February 17, 1973, April 19, 1975.
New York Times Book Review, July 25, 1971, March 4, 1973, March 3, 1974, November 21, 1976, May 4, 1980.
Saturday Review, October 16, 1971.
Times Literary Supplement, March 24, 1978.
Washington Post Book World, February 3, 1974, October 24, 1976, March 23, 1980.

*   *   *

COVELL, Jon Carter   1910-

PERSONAL: Born March 3, 1910, in Wisconsin; children: Carole Covell Alexander, Alan Carter. *Education:* Oberlin College, B.A., 1930; Columbia University, Ph.D., 1941. *Religion:* Zen Buddhist.

ADDRESSES: Home—497 Kawaihae St., Honolulu, Hawaii 96825.

CAREER: California State University, Long Beach, professor of Chinese and Japanese art history, 1965-73; University of

Hawaii, Honolulu, professor of Japanese and Korean art history, 1973-77; Ewha Woman's University, Seoul, Korea, professor of Korean art history, 1978-79; writer, 1979—.

MEMBER: Phi Kappa Phi.

AWARDS, HONORS: Fellowships from Carnegie Foundation, Ford Foundation, American Council of Learned Societies, Institute of Pacific Relations, and Kokusai Bunka Shinkokai; Fulbright fellow in Korea, 1978-79.

WRITINGS:

Under the Seal of Sesshu, De Pamphilis Press, 1941, reprinted, Bunker Books, 1975.
Masterpieces of Japanese Screen Printing, Crown, 1962.
Japanese Landscape Painting, Crown, 1963.
Zen at Daitoku-ji, Kodansha, 1974.
Zen's Core: Ikkyu's Freedom, Tohokai, 1979.
Highlights of Korean Art, Royal Asiatic Society, 1979.
(With Abbot S. Yamada) *Unraveling Zen's Red Thread: Ikkyu's Controversial Way,* Hollym International, 1980.
Korea's Cultural Roots, Moth House, 1981, 5th edition, Hollym International, 1983.
(With son, Alan Carter Covell) *Japan's Hidden History: Korea's Impact on Japanese Culture,* Hollym International, 1984.
On Center Stage for Seventy Years, Hollym International, 1984.
Pageant of Korean Art, Hollym International, 1985.
Korea's Heritage, Si-sa-yong-osa, 1985.

Also author of *Zen Aesthetic Intimations: Shibui-ya,* 1968. Former columnist for *Korea Times;* columnist for *Korea Herald;* contributor to eleven international magazines.

SIDELIGHTS: Jon Carter Covell has traveled in fifty countries, including China, Cambodia, Ceylon, India, Burma, Thailand, and Korea. She has spent ten years in Japan and seven years in Korea.

Covell told *CA:* "I write when I get angry at something in print that is wrong, or because something isn't in print that should be. I like to do pioneering work, and let the crowd follow later. Religion and how it motivates art works is my major interest.

"Most of my time the past seven years has been spent in Seoul, absorbing Korea and her culture, and writing about eight million words on the subject. Much of the outside world is still shockingly ignorant or misinformed about Korea."

* * *

CRAIG, Gordon A(lexander) 1913-

PERSONAL: Born November 26, 1913, in Glasgow, Scotland; came to the United States in 1925; U.S. citizen by derivation; son of Frank Mansfield (a compositor) and Jane (Bissell) Craig; married Phyllis Halcomb (director of a school), June 16, 1939; children: Susan, Deborah Gordon, Martha Jane (Mrs. Richard Hackman), Charles Grant. *Education:* Princeton University, B.A., 1936, M.A., 1939, Ph.D., 1941; Balliol College, Oxford, B.Litt., 1938. *Politics:* Democrat. *Religion:* Presbyterian.

ADDRESSES: Home—451 Oak Grove Ave., Menlo Park, Calif. 94025. *Office*—Department of History, Stanford University, Stanford, Calif. 94305.

CAREER: Yale University, New Haven, Conn., instructor in history, 1939-41; Princeton University, Princeton, N.J., in-structor, 1941-43, assistant professor, 1943-46, associate professor, 1946-50, professor of history, 1950-61; Stanford University, Stanford, Calif., professor of history, 1961-69, J. E. Wallace Sterling Professor of Humanities, beginning 1969, currently professor emeritus. Visiting professor, Columbia University, 1947-48, 1949-50; professor of modern history, Free University of Berlin, 1962—. Fellow, Center for Advanced Study in the Behavioral Sciences, 1956-57. Research associate, Office of Strategic Services, 1942; special assistant, U.S. Department of State, 1943. Member of social science advisory board, U.S. Arms Control and Disarmament Agency, 1964-70; member of U.S. Air Force Academy advisory council, 1968-71. *Military service:* U.S. Marine Corps Reserve, 1944—; now captain (retired).

MEMBER: International Committee of Historical Sciences (vice-president, 1975-85), American Historical Association (president, 1981), American Academy of Arts and Sciences, American Philosophical Society, American Academy of Political Science, Berlin Historical Commission (honorary member), Phi Beta Kappa (visiting scholar, 1965, 1972, senator, 1980-85).

AWARDS, HONORS: Rhodes scholar, 1936-38; Henry Baxter Adams Prize of American Historical Association, 1956, for *The Politics of the Prussian Army, 1640-1945;* Guggenheim fellow, 1969-70 and 1982-83; D. Litt, Princeton University, 1970; Gold Medal for Nonfiction, Commonwealth Club of California, 1979, and Historikerpreis of Muenster, West Germany, 1980, both for *Germany, 1866-1945; Los Angeles Times* history prize nomination, 1982, and American Book Award nomination in history, 1983, both for *The Germans;* D. Phil, Free University of Berlin, 1983; D. Hum., Ball State University, 1984; Commander's Cross of the Legion of Merit of the Federal Republic of Germany, 1984.

WRITINGS:

(Editor with Edward Meade Earle and Felix Gilbert) *Makers of Modern Strategy: Military Thought from Machiavelli to Hitler,* Princeton University Press, 1943, reprinted, 1971.
(Editor with Gilbert) *The Diplomats, 1919-1939,* Princeton University Press, 1953, reprinted, Atheneum, 1971.
The Politics of the Prussian Army, 1640-1945, Clarendon Press, 1955.
From Bismarck to Adenauer: Aspects of German Statecraft, Johns Hopkins University Press, 1958, revised edition, Harper, 1965.
Europe since 1815, Holt, 1961, 2nd edition published as *Europe, 1815-1914,* 1968, 3rd edition published as *Europe since 1815,* 1971, alternate edition, 1974.
The Battle of Koeniggraetz: Prussia's Victory over Austria, 1866, Lippincott, 1964.
War, Politics and Diplomacy: Selected Essays, Praeger, 1966.
(Editor and author of introduction) Herbert Rosinski, *The German Army,* Praeger, 1966.
Military Policy and National Security, Kennikat, 1972.
(Editor and author of introduction) Heinrich Gotthard von Treitschke, *History of Germany in the Nineteenth Century: Selections from the Translations of Eden and Cedar Paul,* University of Chicago Press, 1975.
(Editor and author of introduction) *Economic Interest, Militarism and Foreign Policy: Essays by Eckart Kahr,* University of California Press, 1977.
Germany, 1866-1945, Oxford University Press, 1978.
The Germans, Putnam, 1982.

(With Alexander L. George) *Force and Statecraft: Diplomatic Problems of Our Times*, Oxford University Press, 1983.
The End of Prussia: The Corti Lectures, 1982, University of Wisconsin Press, 1984.

Also contributor to *The Second Chance: America and the Peace*, edited by John B. Whitton, 1944, reprinted, Books for Libraries Press, 1971, and *The Quest for a Principle of Authority in Europe, 1715-Present*, 1948.

SIDELIGHTS: Few American historians are as well versed in the history, politics, and modern culture of Germany as Gordon A. Craig. As Fritz Stern relates in a *New York Times Book Review* article, Craig "first visited Germany as a student in 1935, attracted by the country's cultural richness, appalled by 'the many examples that I encountered of abuse of culture and, indeed, of inhumanity and barbarism.' In the ensuing decades he became an authoritative interpreter of German political history, known especially for his study of the Prussian army" and for *Germany, 1866-1945*.

In *Germany, 1866-1945*, Craig examines a most important period of that country's history: the establishment, rise, and fall of the *Reich*, beginning with the Bismarckian empire and ending with Germany's surrender in World War II. The period was characterized by a devotion to the militia and authority in general; it was also during that time that some of Germany's most distinguished literature was published. While *New York Times Book Review* contributor H. R. Trevor-Roper describes Craig's book as "somewhat austere," he also cites "excellent chapters on the Weimar experiment; [the author] is particularly good on Gustav Stresemann, whose patient and successful foreign policy was frustrated by the economic and political weakness of the Republic; and he recognizes and illustrates the real political genius that enabled Hitler to re-create, out of that weakness, a new structure of authoritarian power even more formidable, because it was less conservative than the old."

New Republic reviewer Charles Maier finds "individual judgements sensible and sound" in *Germany, 1866-1945*, adding, "Without being strident or anti-German as such, [the author] is as critical in his views of the 19th-century governing system as even the most acerbic German historians of the Empire. Craig's Germany enforced conformity, suppressed socialist dissent, had an egregious record on women's rights even in an epoch where no society had a good one; it encouraged lickspittle subordination to military display and bureaucratic authority.... Finally, Craig does not spare the German resistance to Hitler: honoring its bravery, he is frank about its often romantic and conservative objectives. He also reminds us how little of it there was."

In a companion book, *The Germans*, Craig presents a more contemporary view of Germany against a historical backdrop. "His method is to take a subject—religion, say—and go as far back as necessary to explain recent developments and the position of the German churches today," according to a *New Yorker* critic. Craig deals not only with religion, but with soldiers, women, "and other modern German themes," says Amos Perlmutter in a *New Republic* piece. "The section on 'Berlin: Athens on the Spree and City of Crisis' is nostalgic and evocative, a past-and-present tour from an expert guide. *The Germans* is free-wheeling, surprisingly entertaining for a scholarly book, and extremely eloquent." Stern, in his *New York Times Book Review* article, is likewise impressed: "It is impossible to convey fully the richness of the book. It is a splendid introduction to some of the characteristics of German life, past and present."

BIOGRAPHICAL/CRITICAL SOURCES:

PERIODICALS

Los Angeles Times Book Review, July 3, 1983.
New Republic, October 7, 1978, February 24, 1982, March 7, 1983.
New Yorker, September 11, 1978, February 8, 1982.
New York Review of Books, January 25, 1979, May 31, 1984.
New York Times Book Review, January 21, 1979, March 14, 1982.
Times Literary Supplement, October 6, 1978, October 5, 1984.
Washington Post Book World, March 20, 1983, May 8, 1983.

*   *   *

CRIST, Judith (Klein) 1922-

PERSONAL: Born May 22, 1922, in New York, N.Y.; daughter of Solomon and Helen (Schoenberg) Klein; married William B. Crist (an educational public relations consultant), July 3, 1947; children: Steven Gordon. *Education:* Hunter College (now Hunter College of the City University of New York), B.A., 1941; Columbia University, M.S., 1945.

ADDRESSES Home and office—180 Riverside Dr., New York, N.Y. 10024.

CAREER: State College of Washington (now Washington State University), Pullman, instructor, 1942-44; *New York Herald Tribune*, New York City, reporter, 1945-60, associate drama critic, 1957-63, arts editor, 1960-63, film critic, 1963-66; *New York World Journal Tribune*, New York City, film critic, 1966-67; *TV Guide*, Radnor, Pa., film critic, 1966—; *Beverly Hills [213]*, Beverly Hills, Calif.; film critic, 1982—. Film commentator, "Today Show," National Broadcasting Co., 1963-73; film critic, WOR-TV, New York City, 1981—. Adjunct professor of critical writing and journalism, Columbia University, 1959—; associated with Education for the Arts, 1960-63. Organizer, Judith Crist Film Weekends, Tarrytown, N.Y.

MEMBER: New York Film Critics (past chairman), Society of Film Critics, Columbia University School of Journalism Alumni Association (president, 1967-70).

AWARDS, HONORS: George Polk Award, 1951; Education Writers Association award, 1952; Page One award, New York Newspaper Guild, 1955; New York Newswomen's Club award, 1955, 1959, 1963, 1965, and 1967; Columbia Graduate School of Journalism Alumni award, 1961; Centennial President's Medal, Hunter College, 1970.

WRITINGS:

The Private Eye, the Cowboy, and the Very Naked Girl: Movies from Cleo to Clyde (nonfiction), Holt, 1968.
(Contributor) H. H. Hart, editor, *Censorship: For and Against*, Hart, 1971.
(Contributor) Hart, editor, *Marriage: For and Against*, Hart, 1972.
(Contributor) P. Nobile, editor, *Favorite Movies*, Macmillan, 1972.
Judith Crist's TV Guide to the Movies, Popular Library, 1974.
(Editor with Shirley Sealy) *Take 22: Moviemakers on Moviemaking*, Viking, 1984.

Contributing editor and film critic for periodicals, including *Playgirl, Saturday Review*, and *New York*. Contributor of articles and reviews to periodicals.

SIDELIGHTS: In an interview with David Paletz in *Film Quarterly,* Judith Crist explained her approach to movie reviewing: "To me movies are very much a mass medium. I do not think that as a whole they can be regarded as an art form because most movies are not art, so why be concerned with the form when you haven't got any art to put into it? And they are one of the most important social factors in our society, and even more important, they are to me the one medium that is an intellectually international medium." As for what she looks for in a movie, Crist commented: "I could say you look for quality. I look for content. I am rather old-fashioned. I think that a movie has to say something."

Crist considers a reviewer's general attitude toward movies as an important factor in film criticism. "Anyone who is a movie critic can't 'hate' movies," she remarked in a *TV Guide* article. "He has, in fact, not merely to 'like' movies but to love them with a fanatic's passion.... And obviously, to subject yourself to film after film . . . you either have to be the world's foremost masochist—or else you have to be the movie-lover that any film critic worth the label is.... Why bother to criticize if you don't care? Critics are people; their opinions are personal. But their subjectivity is, hopefully, tempered by a background, an experience, a knowledge that broadens the value of their viewpoint.... We're all critics—but what separates us from the other animals is that our discriminatory reactions go beyond taste, smell and instinct and involve a bit of gray matter. And what separates the professional critic from the other reactors is essentially that he articulates the reactions that the layman is, alas, prone to put in a succinct 'Wow!' or 'Yuch!'" In short, Crist maintains, "a critic's major goal is to share the good things, to advocate what he considers quality stuff, to urge others to see what has pleasured or enriched him. There's little joy in negativism, even though, alas, it attracts the most attention."

In a review of *The Private Eye, the Cowboy, and the Very Naked Girl, New York Times Book Review* critic Richard R. Lingeman labels Crist a "good, gutsy critic, a self-styled 'preacher' with a tendency to moralize, who keeps her built-in bunk detector, zap-the-producer gun, parody-the-plot knife and other critical weapons in fine condition.... Her thinking is grooved down the middle of the intellectual road, which means it is on the *Consumer Reports,* rather than the *Partisan Review,* level of discourse." Of her book Lingeman notes that "taken in well-spaced doses . . . these collected reviews are an often sprightly running commentary on our cinematic times, of special interest to the presumably numerous movie-goers who are disciples of Crist."

More recently, Crist has organized the Judith Crist Film Weekends in Tarrytown, N.Y., to enable actors, producers, writers, directors, and other professionals to exchange views with fans and scholars on the creative and business aspects of filmmaking. The critic collected transcripts of several of these sessions for her book *Take 22: Moviemakers on Moviemaking.* This work, according to Christopher Schemering in the *Washington Post,* "alternately celebrates and bemoans the state of the art, the personality spats the creative process produces and—more often than not—the tensions between artists and the Hollywood money men." And while Schemering doubts that *Take 22* "will be read as a filmmaking primer," he concludes that Crist's book is "a gossip-filled, movie-chat binge to be read and enjoyed by fans as discerning as the unusually sharp audiences who questioned the stars."

BIOGRAPHICAL/CRITICAL SOURCES:

BOOKS

Authors in the News, Volume I, Gale, 1975.

PERIODICALS

Film Quarterly, winter, 1968.
New York Times Book Review, December 29, 1968.
Philadelphia Bulletin, November 21, 1974.
TV Guide, August 29, 1970.
Washington Post, December 18, 1984.

*   *   *

CROSS, Anthony (Glenn) 1936-

PERSONAL: Born October 21, 1936, in Nottingham, England; son of Walter Sidney and Ada (Lawson) Cross; married Margaret Elson, August 11, 1960; children: Jane Louise, Serena Claire. *Education:* Cambridge University, B.A., 1960, Ph.D., 1966; Harvard University, A.M., 1961.

ADDRESSES: Home—55 Ben Rhydding Rd., Ilkley LS29 8RN, England. *Office*—Department of Russian Studies, University of Leeds, Leeds LS2 9JT, England.

CAREER: University of East Anglia, School of European Studies, Norwich, England, lecturer, 1964-69, senior lecturer, 1969-72, reader in Russian, 1972-81; University of Leeds, Leeds, England, Roberts Professor of Russian, 1981—. Fellow of Center for Advanced Study, University of Illinois, 1968-69; visiting fellow, All Souls College, University of Oxford, 1978.

MEMBER: British Universities Association of Slavists (president, 1982-84), GB-USSR Association, British Society for Eighteenth-Century Studies.

AWARDS, HONORS: Frank Knox Memorial Fellowship, Harvard University, 1960-61; Litt.D., University of East Anglia, 1981.

WRITINGS:

Russia under Western Eyes, 1517-1825, St. Martin's, 1971.
N. M. Karamzin: A Study of His Literary Career, 1783-1803, Southern Illinois University Press, 1971.
(Editor and contributor) *Russian Literature in the Age of Catherine the Great,* Willem A. Meeuws, 1976.
(Compiler) *Anglo-Russian Relations in the Eighteenth Century: Catalogue of an Exhibition,* University of East Anglia, 1977.
(Editor and contributor) *Great Britain and Russia in the Eighteenth Century: Contacts and Comparisons,* Oriental Research Partners, 1978.
"By the Banks of the Thames": Russians in Eighteenth-Century Britain, Oriental Research Partners, 1980.
(Compiler) *The 1780s: Russia under Western Eyes,* University of East Anglia, 1981.
(Editor) *Russia and the West in the Eighteenth Century,* Oriental Research Partners, 1983.
(With G. S. Smith) *Eighteenth-Century Russian Literature, Culture and Thought: A Bibliography,* Oriental Research Partners, 1983.
The Russian Theme in English Literature: An Introductory Survey and a Bibliography, Willem A. Meeuws, 1984.

General editor of reprint series "Russia through European Eyes, 1553-1917," Cass-DaCapo. Contributor to journals specializing in Slavic studies in Europe, North America, and Soviet Union. Editor, *Study Group on Eighteenth-Century Russia Newsletter;* reviews editor, *Journal of European Studies.*

WORK IN PROGRESS: "By the Banks of the Neva": The British in Eighteenth-Century Russia.

BIOGRAPHICAL/CRITICAL SOURCES:

PERIODICALS

Times Literary Supplement, August 22, 1980.

* * *

CROSS, Ralph D(onald)   1931-

PERSONAL: Born December 31, 1931, in Quincy, Ill.; son of Raymond B. and Dorothy (a teacher; maiden name, Cook) Cross; married Madolyn Rachel Estrich (a registered nurse), June 30, 1955; children: Angela Cross Pickett, Pamela, Jeffrey, Janet Rush. *Education:* Flint Community College, A.A., 1958; Eastern Michigan University, A.B., 1960; University of Oklahoma, M.A., 1961; Michigan State University, Ph.D., 1968. *Religion:* Methodist.

ADDRESSES: Home—109 Parkwood Dr., Hattiesburg, Miss. 39401. Office—Box 5051, University of Southern Mississippi, Southern Station, Hattiesburg, Miss. 39401.

CAREER: Southeast Missouri State College (now University), Cape Girardeau, instructor in earth science, 1961-63; Michigan State University, East Lansing, assistant instructor in geography, 1963-65; Northeast Oklahoma State College, Tahlequah, assistant professor of social science, 1965-66; Oklahoma State University, Stillwater, assistant professor of geography, 1966-68; Boston University, Boston, Mass., assistant professor of geography, 1968-71; University of Southern Mississippi, Hattiesburg, associate professor, 1971-80, professor of geography, 1980—. Instructor at Flint Community College, 1964-65. Speaker at scholarly meetings. Market analyst with Paul E. Smith & Associates; air quality analyst for Leaf River Forest Products. Member of Lamar County Planning Commission. *Military service:* U.S. Navy, radar operator, 1952-55.

MEMBER: American Water Resources Association (secretary of New England district), Association of American Geographers, National Weather Association, Western Writers of America, Southeastern Association of American Geographers (member of program and steering committees), Oklahoma Academy of Science (chairman of geography section), Mississippi Academy of Sciences (section head), Phi Kappa Phi.

AWARDS, HONORS: Grants from *Southern Quarterly,* 1973, Mississippi Marine Resources Council, 1975, Mississippi Water Resources Research Institute, 1976, Southeast Mississippi Air Ambulance District, 1976, U.S. Forest Service, 1977, U.S. Fish and Wildlife Service, 1981, Mississippi Department of Natural Resources, 1982, and Victor P. Smith and Associates, 1982.

WRITINGS:

NONFICTION

(Contributor) Clifford Humphreys, editor, *Parameters of Water Quality,* Michigan State University Press, 1966.
(Contributor) Charles R. Brent and R. Norman Bailey, editors, *Effect on Environment Resulting from Conversion of South Mississippi Electric Power Association's Moselle Plant to Number 6 Fuel Oil as Auxiliary Fuel,* University of Southern Mississippi, 1973.
(Contributor) Brent and Bailey, editors, *Effect on Environment Resulting from Conversion of South Mississippi Power Electric Association's Benndale Plant Number 6 Fuel Oil as an Auxiliary Fuel,* University of Southern Mississippi, 1973.
(Editor and contributor) *Atlas of Mississippi,* University Press of Mississippi, 1974.
(Contributor) *Climate and Human Ecology,* D. Armstrong, 1979.
(Editor) *Proceedings of the National Symposium on Freshwater Inflow to Estuaries,* two volumes, U.S. Government Printing Office, 1982.

FICTION

Denton's Army (western), Tower, 1979.
The Key to Murder (mystery), Tower, 1980.
When the Old Man Died (mystery), Tower, 1980.

Also author of *The Coward* (western), 1985.

OTHER

Contributor to *Academic American Encyclopedia.* Also contributor of articles and reviews to geography and scientific journals. Regional editor of *National Weather Digest;* editor of *Hub Elks Times;* fiction reviewer for *Hattiesburg American.*

WORK IN PROGRESS: *Flint/Assignment 1: The Wolf,* a western; *Lawson's Last Shot,* a mystery.

SIDELIGHTS: Ralph D. Cross comments: "My motivation to write seems to be a compulsive need to string words together. Essentially, I write to please myself and would probably continue to do so even if I couldn't publish my work.

"I am essentially a non-violent person, so when someone has wronged me, I convert him to a villain (much disguised, of course) in one of my books where I can wreak all kinds of havoc on him. In this way, I can relieve my frustrations without anyone knowing about it. I also find it is a great help in bringing out feelings of intense emotions in my characters.

"I've always thought of myself as a writer, even back when I had never written anything. Actually, I guess, my writing career began with my master's thesis and has been diversifying ever since.

"My first book fits into my specialty field. Actually the book contains more narrative than maps or pictures. Despite all the local publicity from its publication, which included autograph parties, appearances on television talk shows, and seeing the book in bookstores, I received no thrill of any kind. It all seemed mundane.

"On the other hand, when I received the contract for my first novel—a paperback yet—I was on a high which lasted for weeks. Maybe if I work hard, I can re-experience that thrill. I'll keep trying, no matter what."

* * *

CROWLEY, Ellen T(eresa)   1943-

PERSONAL: Born March 29, 1943, in Wyandotte, Mich.; daughter of Frank R. (an accountant) and Veronica Mary (a teacher; maiden name, Marr) Crowley. *Education:* University of Detroit, A.B., 1965; additional study, Wayne State University, 1966-75.

ADDRESSES: Home—1298 South Eton Rd., Birmingham, Mich. 48008. *Office*—Gale Research Co., Book Tower, Detroit, Mich. 48226.

CAREER: Teacher at public schools in Berkley, Mich., 1965-66, Fremont, Calif., 1966-67, and Royal Oak, Mich., 1967-68; Gale Research Co., Detroit, Mich., assistant editor, 1968-69, editor, 1969-85, senior editor, 1979-84, director of Indexes and Dictionaries Division, 1984—.

WRITINGS:

ALL PUBLISHED BY GALE

(Contributing editor) *Programs in Progress Encyclopedia,* 1969.

(Editor with Robert C. Thomas) *New Acronyms and Initialisms* (companion volume to *Acronyms and Initialisms Dictionary*), 1969.

(Assistant editor) *Encyclopedia of Associations,* 6th edition, 1970, 7th edition, 1972, 8th edition, 1973, 16th edition (senior editor), 1981, 17th edition, 1982, 18th edition, 1983.

(Editor with Thomas) *Acronyms and Initialisms Dictionary,* 3rd edition, 1970, 4th edition, 1973, 5th edition (sole editor) published as *Acronyms, Initialisms, and Abbreviations Dictionary,* 1976, 6th edition, 1978, 7th edition, 1980, 8th edition, 1982, 9th edition (with Helen E. Sheppard), 1984.

(Editor with Thomas) *Reverse Acronyms and Initialisms Dictionary,* 1972, 6th edition (sole editor) published as *Reverse Acronyms, Initialisms, and Abbreviations Dictionary,* 1978, 7th edition, 1980, 8th edition, 1982, 9th edition (with Sheppard), 1984.

(Editor) *Trade Names Dictionary,* preliminary edition, 1974, 1st edition, 1976, 2nd edition, 1979, 3rd edition, 1982.

(Editor) *New Trade Names* (companion volume to *Trade Names Dictionary*), 1976, 1977, (senior editor) 1980, 1981, 1982-83.

(Editorial coordinator) *Eponyms Dictionaries Index,* 1977.

(Editor) *Trade Names Dictionary Company Index* (companion volume to *Trade Names Dictionary*), 2nd edition, 1979, 3rd edition, 1982.

(Senior editor) *Pseudonyms and Nicknames Dictionary,* 1980, 2nd edition, 1982.

(Senior editor) *New Pseudonyms and Nicknames* (companion volume to *Pseudonyms and Nicknames Dictionary*), 1981, 1983.

(Senior editor) *Periodical Title Abbreviations: By Abbreviations,* 3rd edition, 1981, 4th edition, 1983.

(Senior editor) *Periodical Title Abbreviations: By Title,* 3rd edition, 1981, 4th edition, 1983.

(Senior editor) *New Periodical Title Abbreviations* (companion volume to *Periodical Title Abbreviations: By Abbreviations* and *Periodical Title Abbreviations: By Title*), 1982-83.

(Editor) *International Acronyms, Initialisms, and Abbreviations Dictionary,* preliminary edition, 1984, 1st edition (with Sheppard), 1985.

(Editor with Sheppard) *Reverse International Acronyms, Initialisms, and Abbreviations Dictionary,* 1985.

*   *   *

CROWTHER, Duane S(wofford)   1934-

PERSONAL: Born August 16, 1934, in Takoma Park, Md.; son of Don Q. (a statistician) and Mary Irene (Swofford) Crowther; married Helen Jean Decker (a writer), March 21, 1958; children: Donald Kent, Scott Duane, Laura Jean (deceased), Lisa Marie, David Smith, William Orson, Sharon Irene, Bethany Jean. *Education:* Brigham Young University, B.A. (with high honors), 1959, M.A., 1961; additional graduate study at Utah State University, 1962; University of Utah, Ph.D., 1973. *Religion:* Church of Jesus Christ of Latter-day Saints.

ADDRESSES: Home—191 North 650 E., Bountiful, Utah 84010. *Office*—Horizon Publishers, P.O. Box 490, 50 South 500 W., Bountiful, Utah 84010.

CAREER: Mormon missionary to Central America, 1954-57; teacher and principal at Mormon seminaries in Bountiful and Lehi, Utah, and Burley and Rigby, Idaho, 1959-62; owner and manager of Crowther's Music & Book Center, Smithfield, Utah, and Logan Music & Book Co., Logan, Utah, 1962-66; Salt Lake City (Utah) public schools, music teacher, 1970-71; Horizon Publishers, Bountiful, Utah, owner and president, 1971—. Teacher of extension courses in religion at Brigham Young University, 1960-62, and in music at University of Utah, 1969-71, and Granite School District, 1972. Organized and directed a dance combo and a twelve-piece orchestra while in college; organizer and conductor of community choirs and choruses, including a choir from Guatemala City which toured Guatemala and El Salvador. Consultant and lecturer for the Institute for Retail Store Management, 1984—. Lecturer throughout the West, making more than 150 appearances a year.

MEMBER: Utah Historical Society, Utah Poetry Society, League of Utah Writers, Music Educators National Conference, Phi Kappa Phi, Phi Eta Sigma, Society for the Preservation and Encouragement of Barber Shop Quartet Singing in America.

AWARDS, HONORS: Freedom Foundation awards for both the stage and television productions of the show "This Is My Country," 1968 and 1969.

WRITINGS:

Prophecy: Key to the Future, Bookcraft, 1962.

The Prophecies of Joseph Smith, Bookcraft, 1963, revised edition, Horizon Publishers, 1983.

Gifts of the Spirit, Bookcraft, 1965, reprinted, Horizon Publishers, 1983.

Prophets and Prophecies of the Old Testament, Deseret, 1966, revised edition, Horizon Publishers, 1973.

Life Everlasting, Bookcraft, 1967.

Come unto Christ, Horizon Publishers, 1971.

God and His Church, Horizon Publishers, 1971.

The Plan of Salvation and the Future in Prophecy, Horizon Publishers, 1971.

A Guide to Effective Scripture Study, Horizon Publishers, 1972.

(Editor with wife, Jean D. Crowther) *The Joy of Being a Woman: Guidance for Meaningful Living by Outstanding LDS Women,* Horizon Publishers, 1972.

Reading Guide to the Book of Mormon: A Simplified Program Featuring Brief Outlines and Doctrinal Summaries, Horizon Publishers, 1975.

Prophetic Warnings to Modern America, Horizon Publishers, 1977.

Family Ancestral Record: Adult Genealogy Starter Kit, Horizon Publishers, 1978.

This Is My Life: Personal History Guide, Horizon Publishers, 1979.

Thus Saith the Lord: The Role of Prophets and Revelation in the Kingdom of God, Horizon Publishers, 1980.

My Family Heritage: Youth Genealogy Starter Kit, Horizon Publishers, 1981.

Teaching Choral Concepts: Simple Lesson Plans and Teaching Aids for In-Rehearsal Choir Instruction, Horizon Publishers, 1981.

Atlas and Outline of the Acts of the Apostles, Horizon Publishers, 1983.

Atlas and Outline of the Life of Christ, Horizon Publishers, 1983.

CASSETTE TAPES

Through Death unto Life Everlasting, Horizon Publishers, 1979.
World War III, Horizon Publishers, 1979.
Ye Must Be Born Again, Horizon Publishers, 1979.
Joseph Smith: A True Prophet of God, Horizon Publishers, 1979.
God Speaks through Prophets Today, Horizon Publishers, 1982.
God's Eternal Plan of Salvation, Horizon Publishers, 1982.
Biblical Proofs of the Book of Mormon, Horizon Publishers, 1983.
Biblical Proofs of the Restored Church, Horizon Publishers, 1983.
Forty Keys to Family Emergency Readiness, Horizon Publishers, 1984.
Recognizing Techniques of Deception in Anti-Mormon Literature, Horizon Publishers, 1984.
He Comes in Glory, Horizon Publishers, 1984.
Doctrinal Evidences That Mormons Are Christians, Horizon Publishers, 1984.
Why Protestants Become Mormons, Horizon Publishers, 1985.
A Mormon View of Christ and the Trinity, Horizon Publishers, 1985.
Are You Saved?, Horizon Publishers, 1985.

OTHER

Also author and producer of show "This Is My Country," presented on stage and television, 1968 and 1969; author of "Profitability Plus!," a monthly business management series for *Sew Business* and *Giftware Business* magazines, 1985—. Contributor to *Improvement Era, Instructor, Bookstore Journal, Christian Bookseller and Librarian, Sew Business* and *Giftware Business*.

WORK IN PROGRESS: A three-volume series on the Bible; a study of life-after-death experiences; a novel of America during and after a third world war; a novel on the life of Josephus; a doctrinal study of the nature of God and the Trinity.

*   *   *

CRUMMEY, Robert O(wen)   1936-

PERSONAL: Born May 12, 1936, in New Glasgow, Nova Scotia, Canada; came to United States in 1964, naturalized in 1971; son of Clarence B. (a physician) and Dorothy (MacDonald) Crummey; married second wife, Nancy Nesbit, 1980; children: (first marriage) Daniel John. *Education:* University of Toronto, B.A., 1958; University of Chicago, M.A., 1959, Ph.D., 1964.

ADDRESSES: Home—1209 Fordham Dr., Davis, Calif. 95616. *Office*—Department of History, University of California, Davis, Calif. 95616.

CAREER: University of Illinois at Urbana-Champaign, assistant professor of history, 1964-65; Yale University, New Haven, Conn., assistant professor, 1965-70, associate professor

of history, 1970-74; University of California, Davis, associate professor, 1974-79, professor of history, 1979—.

MEMBER: American Association for the Advancement of Slavic Studies.

WRITINGS:

(Editor with Lloyd E. Berry) *Rude and Barbarous Kingdom: Russia in the Accounts of Sixteenth-Century English Voyagers*, University of Wisconsin Press, 1968.
The Old Believers and the World of Antichrist: The Vyg Community and the Russian State, 1694-1855, University of Wisconsin Press, 1970.
The Reconstitution of the Boiar Aristocracy, Forsch. Osteuropaeischen Geschichte, 1973.
(Contributor) *Windows on the Russian Past*, Columbus, 1976.
(Contributor) *Russian Officialdom from the Seventeenth to the Twentieth Century*, University of North Carolina Press, 1981.
Aristocrats and Servitors: The Boyar Elite in Russia, 1613-1689, Princeton University Press, 1983.

*   *   *

CULLY, Iris V(irginia Arnold)   1914-

PERSONAL: Born September 12, 1914, in Brooklyn, N.Y.; daughter of James Aikman and Myrtle Marie (Michael) Arnold; married Kendig Brubaker Cully (a professor and clergyman), September 9, 1939; children: Melissa Iris Mueller, Patience Allegra Ecklund. *Education:* Adelphi College (now Adelphi University), B.A., 1936; Hartford Seminary Foundation, M.A., 1937; Garrett Theological Seminary, B.D., 1954; Northwestern University, Ph.D., 1955. *Politics:* Democrat. *Religion:* Episcopalian.

ADDRESSES: Home—Claremont, Calif. (winter); P.O. Box 2, Belmont, Vt. (summer). *Office*—Lexington Theological Seminary, 631 South Limestone St., Lexington, Ky. 40508.

CAREER: Garrett Theological Seminary, Evanston, Ill., part-time teacher of religious education, 1958-61; Northwestern University, Evening Division, Chicago and Evanston campuses, part-time teacher of religion, 1960, 1963; visiting professor, Chicago Lutheran Seminary, Chicago, 1963, Drew University School of Theology, 1964, and New York University, 1964-65; Yale University Divinity School, New Haven, Conn., associate professor of Christian education, 1965-72; Lexington Theological Seminary, Lexington, Ky., Alexander Campbell Hopkins Professor of Religious Education, 1976-85, professor emerita, 1985—. Visiting professor, Pacific School of Religion, summer, 1961, Union Theological Seminary, 1964-66, St. Meinrad School of Theology, 1973, 1981, and Fordham University.

MEMBER: American Academy of Religion, Religious Education Association (member of board of trustees, 1975-79), Association of Professors and Researchers in Religious Education (vice-president, 1972-73; president, 1973-74).

WRITINGS:

(With husband, Kendig Brubaker Cully) *Two Seasons: Advent and Lent*, Bobbs-Merrill, 1954.
The Dynamics of Christian Education, Westminster, 1958.
Children in the Church (Pastoral Psychology Book Club selection and Religious Book Club alternate selection), Westminster, 1960.

Imparting the Word: The Bible in Christian Education, Westminster, 1962.

(With K. B. Cully) *An Introductory Theological Wordbook,* Westminster, 1964.

Ways to Teach Children, Lutheran Church Press, 1966.

Christian Worship and Church Education, Westminster, 1967.

(Contributor) Alois Mueller, editor, *Catechetics for the Future,* Herder & Herder, 1970.

Change, Conflict and Self-Determination, Westminster, 1972.

New Life for Your Sunday School, Hawthorn, 1976.

(With K. B. Cully) *From Aaron to Zerubbabel: Profiles of Bible People,* Hawthorn, 1976.

(Editor with K. B. Cully) *Process and Relationship: Issues in Theology, Philosophy, and Religious Education,* Religious Education Press, 1978.

Christian Child Development, Harper, 1979.

(With K. B. Cully) *A Guide to Biblical Resources,* Morehouse, 1981.

Education for Spiritual Growth, Harper, 1984.

Also author of curriculum materials. Contributor of articles and book reviews to magazines. Founder and editor, with K. B. Cully, of *Review of Books and Religion,* 1971-76, and *New Review of Books and Religion,* 1976-78; *Religious Education,* associate editor, 1974-78, consulting editor, 1978-83.

SIDELIGHTS: Iris V. Cully observed and studied religious education in western Europe in 1956. She conducted similar studies in the Caribbean area, South America, and Mexico in 1962, in Asia in 1970, and in the Middle East in 1979.

*   *   *

CULLY, Kendig Brubaker 1913-

PERSONAL: Born November 30, 1913, in Millersville, Pa.; son of William Bigler and Emma Lavina (Kendig) Cully; married Iris Virginia Arnold, September 9, 1939; children: Melissa Iris Mueller, Patience Allegra Ecklund. *Education:* American International College, A.B. (cum laude), 1934; Hartford Theological Seminary, B.D., 1937; Hartford School of Religious Education, M.R.E., 1938; Hartford Seminary Foundation, Ph.D., 1939; Seabury-Western Theological Seminary, S.T.M., 1953.

ADDRESSES: Home—Claremont, Calif. (winter); P.O. Box 2, Belmont, Vt. (summer).

CAREER: Minister of Congregational churches in Southwick, Belchertown, Melrose, and Haverhill, all Mass., 1939-51; First Methodist Church, Evanston, Ill., minister of education, 1951-54; ordained Episcopal priest, 1955; Seabury-Western Theological Seminary, Evanston, professor of religious education, 1955-64; New York Theological Seminary, New York, N.Y., professor of Christian education, 1964-72, dean, 1965-72. Guest professor at Pacific School of Religion, Union Theological Seminary, Yale University, University of Pittsburgh, Lutheran School of Theology, Christian Theological Seminary, St. Michael's College, Lexington Theological Seminary, Boston University, Northwestern University, St. George's College, and Bethany Theological Seminary; visiting professor of Anglican studies, Louisville Presbyterian Theological Seminary, 1977-80; Episcopal Theological Seminary in Kentucky, dean, 1980-82, rector-dean, 1982-85.

MEMBER: Religious Education Association, American Theological Society (midwest division), Association of Professors and Researchers in Religious Education, American Academy of Religion, Tau Kappa Epsilon, Masons.

AWARDS, HONORS: S.T.D. from Episcopal Theological Seminary, 1984.

WRITINGS:

(With wife, Iris V. Cully) *Two Seasons: Advent and Lent,* Bobbs-Merrill, 1954.

(Editor) *Basic Writings in Christian Education,* Westminster, 1960.

Exploring the Bible, Morehouse, 1960.

(Contributor) *Religious Education,* Abingdon, 1960.

Sacraments: A Language of Faith, Christian Education Press, 1961.

(Editor) *Prayers for Church Workers,* Westminster, 1961.

(Editor) *Confirmation: History, Doctrine, Practice,* Seabury, 1962.

The Teaching Church, United Church Press, 1963.

(Contributor) *Preaching the Passion,* Fortress, 1963.

(Editor) *The Westminster Dictionary of Christian Education,* Westminster, 1963.

The Lord of Life, Morehouse, 1964.

(With I. V. Cully) *An Introductory Theological Wordbook,* Westminster, 1964.

The Search for a Christian Education: Since 1940, Westminster, 1965.

The Episcopal Church and Education, Morehouse, 1966.

(Editor) *Does the Church Know How to Teach?,* Macmillan, 1970.

(Editor with F. Nile Harper) *Will the Church Lose the City?,* World Press, 1970.

Decisions and Your Future, [Geneva], 1970.

(With I. V. Cully) *From Aaron to Zerubbabel: Profiles of Bible People,* Hawthorn, 1976.

(Editor with I. V. Cully) *Process and Relationship: Issues in Theology, Philosophy, and Religious Education,* Religious Education Press, 1978.

(With I. V. Cully) *A Guide to Biblical Resources,* Morehouse, 1981.

Confirmation Re-Examined, Morehouse, 1982.

General editor of eleven volumes in "The Westminster Studies in Christian Communication" series. Contributor of articles, poems and reviews to periodicals. Founder and editor, with I. V. Cully, of *Review of Books and Religion,* 1971-76, and *New Review of Books and Religion,* 1976-78.

*   *   *

CUMBERLEGE, Marcus (Crossley) 1938-

PERSONAL: Born December 23, 1938, in Antibes, France; son of Claude Michael Bulstrode (a merchant sailor and yachtsman) and Nancy Pemberton (Wooler) Cumberlege; married Ava Nicole Paranjoti, December 11, 1965 (divorced, 1972); married Maria Juliana Lefever (a teacher and librarian), November 9, 1973; children: Eunice Ava. *Education:* St. John's College, Oxford, B.A., 1961. *Politics:* None. *Religion:* Amida Buddhism. "God is best served by observance of the forms and rhythms of nature in a spirit of love and worship, to the best of one's individual ability."

ADDRESSES: Home—Westmeers 84 8000, Brugge, Belgium.

CAREER: Writer. Worked as teacher and farmer in Peru, 1957-58 and 1962-63; Ogilvy & Mather Ltd., London, England, advertising executive, 1964-67; British Travel Association, London, advertising executive, 1967-68; Lycee International, St. Germain-en-Laye, France, teacher of English, 1968-70. Lecturer in poetry at universities in the Netherlands; visiting lecturer at Universite Internationale de Manternach, Lugano, Switzerland, 1978—; official translator of Flemish tourist literature in West Flanders, Belgium, 1976—.

AWARDS, HONORS: Eric Gregory Award for Poetry from Gregory Foundation, 1967; winter champion of Royal Bruges Chess Circle, 1974.

WRITINGS:

POETRY

Oases, Anvil Press Poetry, 1968.
Poems for Quena and Tabla, Carcanet Press, 1970.
Running Towards a New Life, Anvil Press Poetry, 1973.
(With Owen Davis) *Bruges, Bruges,* Manufaktuur (Bruges), 1975.
La Nuit noire (title means "The Dark Night"), Manufaktuur, 1975.
Firelines, Anvil Press Poetry, 1977.
The Poetry Millionaire, Dollar of Soul Press, 1977.
(With Horst De Blaere) *Twintig Vriendelijke Vragen,* Ganzespel, 1977.
Northern Lights, Manufaktuur, 1981.
Vlaamse Fabels, Manufaktuur, 1982.
Sweet Poor Hobo, Manufaktuur, 1985.

OTHER

Co-editor with Scott Rollins of *Dremples,* 1977. Contributor of poems to British Broadcasting Corp. (BBC) and to periodicals, including *Crab Grass, Fuse, Honest Ulsterman, Phoenix, Poetry Review,* and *Trinity News.*

WORK IN PROGRESS: Houria, an autobiographical novel set in Spain and France, c. 1969.

SIDELIGHTS: Marcus Cumberlege told *CA:* "I have several volumes of a private journal begun in Bruges since my marriage in 1973. It records daily life, meetings, thoughts and astrological phenomena, dreams experienced in the small historic town where I have made my permanent home after many years of travel.

"My present concern is with my immediate surroundings, relationships, and life-style, in which I seek to achieve a harmony and a validity, a purity of deed and word which will inform my writing with positive values. I now strive to reduce experiential activity (paid work, travel, etc.) to a minimum, to arrest fruitless emotion, to avoid worthless involvement, to improve the quality of my life by doing everything at half speed and thus combatting the neurosis of productivity and restlessness which I feel is edging mankind towards the brink.

"I now enjoy learning difficult tasks like cooking, gardening, music study, all of which demand time and make normal life schedules impossible. I try to give up more time to yoga and meditation, but I have also installed a telephone for the use of friends. Visitors are always welcome, and though they appear to disrupt my life it is always for the better. I am impressed by Lao-tse's statement that it is not necessary to leave one's room in order to know the world.

"I am curious to see how the entry of Pluto into the sign of Scorpio in 1984 will affect the human psyche; in particular I am concerned about the abuse of parapsychological techniques and the danger to political prisoners and others who are motivated by 'alternative' ideas about power and energy.

"Although Capricorns are said to be ambitious, I view all position, fame, and authority with a sidelong glance, and write only for one person, whose identity will not be revealed to me in this life.

"In my school years I read Rimbaud and the French symbolists with passion. In answer to a letter I wrote him at fifteen, T. S. Eliot told me he thought Rimbaud's 'Le Cabaret vert' was the finest sonnet in the French language. I began as a love poet at school, but will not be remembered for my interpretation of the gentle feeling. Too many currents have crossed my soul, and my hand is zig-zagged with fire. Whether we like it or not, our future is in the air.

"My father named me after Marcus Hare, captain of the ship 'Euridice' in the poem by Gerard Manley Hopkins. My favorite title, however, is 'The Blessed Virgin Compared to the Air We Breathe'—and this despite a predilection for John Keats among the English bards and Cesar Vallejo from the rest of the world.

"An older poet warned me twenty five years ago that the decade between age forty and age fifty is crucial. I certainly find it very difficult to handle creatively. One feels that one has already said everything and nothing; that it is time to make room for the younger generation; that one has achieved one's best in some of those 'exquisitely turned lyrics,' and yet that this best has somehow only been a literary training to prepare one to handle themes of deeper and even more human significance, such as only ripeness brings.

"The vision changes, but does not fade. Is that a line from a poem I must still write or simply a throw-away thought while attempting to situate myself? Every poem I have written has been a form of hara-kiri. I mean this in the positive samurai sense, in the gesture of the pelican piercing its own breast to feed its young. I would give the same advice to aspiring writers.

"*Firelines* was written as an act of love and devotion. I honestly dreamed that book would in some way help to create peace between Saxon and Gael. In that respect, it was a political act. Futile, you may say, since I doubt whether more than a dozen copies ever found their way across the Irish Sea. Therein lies the tragedy of poetry—and the challenge!"

In a review of *Firelines,* Martin Booth noted that Cumberlege "writes with a firmness of voice, with drive and definite intentions." Martin Seymour-Smith assessed that "in [Cumberlege] we have a writer admirably unafraid of versatility, and one of refreshing honesty."

BIOGRAPHICAL/CRITICAL SOURCES:

PERIODICALS

Birmingham Post, February 2, 1974.
British Book News, December, 1977.
Irish Press, February 10, 1973.
Tribune, March 23, 1973, November 25, 1977.

D

DADIE, Bernard B(inlin) 1916-

PERSONAL: Born in 1916 in Assinie, Ivory Coast, Africa; son of Gabriel Binlin and Enouaye (Nongbou) Dadie; married Rosa Assamala Koutoua, 1950; children: Renee, Michele, Benjamin, Dominique, Claude, Claire, Andre, Paule, Pierre. *Education:* Ecole Primaire Superieure Bingerville (Ivory Coast), certificat etudes primaires superieures; Ecole Normale William Ponty (Senegal), diplome de sortie. *Politics:* PDCI-RDA (Parti Democratique de la Cote d'Ivoire-Rassemblement Democratique Africaine). *Religion:* Roman Catholic.

ADDRESSES: Home—Abidjan, Ivory Coast, Africa. *Office*—Direction des Affaires Culturelles, BP V 39 Abidjan, Ivory Coast, Africa.

CAREER: University of Dakar, Institut Fondamental d'Afrique Noir, Dakar, Senegal, librarian and archivist, 1936-47; press secretary to the Committee Director of PDCI-RDA, Ivory Coast, 1947-53; head of the Cabinet of the Ministry of National Education, Ivory Coast, 1957-59; director of Information Services, Government of the Ivory Coast, 1959-61; director of Cultural Affairs for the Ministry of National Education, Ivory Coast, 1961—. Member and vice-president of the Executive Council of UNESCO, 1964-72; director, Commission Nationale de la Fondation Felix Houphouet-Boigny (African Institute for Historical and Political Research); member, Conseil Economique et Social, 1976-77; president, Conference Generale de l'Agence de Cooperation Culturelle et Technique, 1977-79.

MEMBER: Association Internationale pour le Developpement de la Documentation des Bibliotheques et des Archives en Afrique (president), Association Generale des Arts et Lettres de Cote d'Ivoire (president), Association pour le Developpement de la Documentation, des Bibliotheques, des Archives, et des Musées de Cote d'Ivoire (president), Societe Africaine de Culture (president of Ivory Coast chapter), P.E.N. (vice-president of Ivory Coast chapter), L'Academie de l'Union Litteraire et Artistique de France, Association des Ecrivains de Langue Francaise (Mer et Outre Mer), Societe des Gens de Lettres de France, Violetti Picards et Normands (honorary member), Academie des Sciences Sociales et Politiques du Bresil (corresponding member), Academie Hispano-Americaine des Belles Lettres (corresponding member), Academie bresilienne des Arts (corresponding member).

AWARDS, HONORS: Commandeur de l'Ordre National de la Cote d'Ivoire; Commandeur de l'Ordre du Merite de l'Education Nationale; Officier du Merite National Francais; Chevalier des Arts et Lettres; Chevalier de l'Elite Francaise (bronze medal); Laureat du Grand Prix Litteraire de l'Afrique Noire, 1965, for *Patron de New-York;* gold medal of l'Academie de Trevise; silver medal of la Ville de Paris; silver medal of la Ville de Bordeaux; Prix America "Marciano Moreno" d'Argentine; Ph.D. from l'Academie Internationale de Vancouver; Ph.D. and membre d'honneur of l'Academie des Sciences et Relations Humaines de Mexico; Ph.D. from University of Sheffield; diplome d'honneur et membre protecteur du Club de la Presse de la Republique Dominicaine.

Troubadour d'Honneur du College des Troubadours; gold medal from UNESCO; gold medal of l'Academie Populaire de Guyenne et Gascogne; gold medal (St. Francois) of the Haute Academie Internationale de Lutece; Edgar Allan Poe Poetry Prize, 1975; cross from l'Academie des Sciences d'Outre-Mer; cross of honor, first class for Science and Art (Austria); medal of Alfonso X El Sabio; Officier, Ordre National des Arts et Lettres (France); Commandeur de l'Ordre du Merite Francais d'Outre-Mer, 1964; Commandeur de l'Ordre du Merite de l'Education Nationale; Commandeur de Pleiade de l'Ordre de la Francophonie et du Dialogue des Cultures; Commandeur d'Ordre National de la Legion d'Honneur (France); Grand Officier de l'Ordre de Leopold (Belgium); Grand Officier de l'Ordre National du Merite (France); Grand Officier de l'Ordre National de Cote d'Ivoire; Grand Officier de l'Ordre du Merite de la Republique Federale d'Allemagne.

WRITINGS:

FICTION

Legendes africaines (stories; also see below), Seghers, 1954.
Le Pagne noir (stories), Presence Africaine, 1955, published with stories by Andre Terrisse as *Les belles histoires de Kacou Ananze l'araignee,* F. Nathan, 1963, reprinted as *Le Pagne noir: Contes africains,* Presence Africaine, 1970.
Climbie (novel; also see below), Seghers, 1956, translation by Karen Chapman published as *Climbie,* Africana Publishing, 1971.
Un Negre a Paris (novel), Presence Africaine, 1956, second edition, 1966.
Patron de New-York (novel), Presence Africaine, 1964.

La Ville ou nul ne meurt (chronicle), Presence Africaine, 1968.
Commandant Taureault et ses negres, CEDA (Abidjan), 1980.
Les Jambes du fils de Dieu (novellas), CEDA, 1980.
Carnet de prison, CEDA, 1981.
Les Contes de Koutou-as-Samala (stories), Presence Africaine, 1982.

POETRY

Afrique debout (also see below), Seghers, 1950.
La Ronde des jours (also see below), Seghers, 1956, third edition, 1982.
Hommes de tous les continents, Presence Africaine, 1957.

PLAYS

''Les Villes,'' 1933, produced at a festival, Ivory Coast, 1934.
Assemien Dehyle, roi du Sanwi, Album officiel de la Mission Pontificale, 1936, 3rd edition, CEDA, 1979.
''Min Adja-o (C'est mon heritage!),'' first produced in 1960, published in *Le Theatre populaire en Republique de Cote d'Ivoire,* Cercle Culturel et Folklorique de Cote d'Ivoire (Abidjan), 1965.
''Serment d'amour,'' produced at Theatre Populaire en Republique de Cote d'Ivoire, Abidjan, 1965, published in *Le Theatre populaire en Republique de Cote d'Ivoire,* Cercle Culturel et Folklorique de Cote d'Ivoire, 1965.
''Situation difficile,'' produced at Theatre Populaire en Republique de Cote d'Ivoire, 1965, published in *Le Theatre populaire en Republique de Cote d'Ivoire,* Cercle Culturel et Folklorique de Cote d'Ivoire, 1965.
Monsieur Thogo-gnini (comedy; first produced, 1969), Presence Africaine, 1970.
Les Voix dans le vent (tragedy; first produced, 1969), Editions Cle, 1970.
Beatrice du Congo (three-act; first produced, 1969), Presence Africaine, 1970.
Iles de Tempete, Presence Africaine, 1973.
Papassidi maitre-escroc (comedy; first produced, 1960), Nouvelles Editions Africaines, 1975.
Mhoi-Ceul, Presence Africaine, 1979.

NONFICTION

Opinions d'un negre (essays), Nouvelles Editions Africaines, 1979.

OTHER

Legendes et Poemes (contains *Afrique debout, Legendes africaines, Climbie,* and *La Ronde des jours*), Seghers, 1966, third edition, 1979.

Also author of *Textes,* edited by R. Mercier and M. Battestini, French & European Publications, and of commentary for film, ''L'Italie vue par un africain,'' 1961.

WORK IN PROGRESS: Les Ecrivains dans la lutte pour la liberte, for CEDA.

BIOGRAPHICAL/CRITICAL SOURCES:

BOOKS

Banhma, M., editor, *African Theatre Today,* Pitman, 1976.
Battestini, Monique, *Bernard B. Dadie, ecrivain ivoirien,* F. Nathan, 1964.
Brench, A. C., *The Novelists' Inheritance in French Africa,* Oxford University Press, 1967.
Quillateau, C., *Bernard Binlin Dadie: L'Homme et l'oeuvre,* Presence Africaine, 1962.

PERIODICALS

Antioch Review, summer, 1967.

*   *   *

DAILEY, Janet (Ann)   1944-

PERSONAL: Born May 21, 1944, in Storm Lake, Iowa; daughter of Boyd (a farmer) and Louise Haradon; married William Dailey; stepchildren: two. *Religion:* Methodist.

ADDRESSES: Home—Branson, Mo. *Office*—Janbill Ltd., SR 4, Box 2197, Branson, Mo. 65616.

CAREER: Worked as a secretary in Nebraska and Iowa, 1962-74; writer, 1974—.

WRITINGS:

No Quarter Asked, Harlequin, 1976.
Boss Man from Ogallala, Harlequin, 1976.
Savage Land, Harlequin, 1976.
Land of Enchantment, Harlequin, 1976.
Fire and Ice, Harlequin, 1976.
The Homeplace, Harlequin, 1976.
After the Storm, Harlequin, 1976.
Dangerous Masquerade, Harlequin, 1977.
Night of the Cotillion, Harlequin, 1977.
Valley of the Vapors, Harlequin, 1977.
Fiesta San Antonio, Harlequin, 1977.
Show Me, Harlequin, 1977.
Bluegrass King, Harlequin, 1977.
A Lyon's Share, Harlequin, 1977.
The Widow and the Wastrel, Harlequin, 1977.
The Ivory Cane, Harlequin, 1978.
The Indy Man, Harlequin, 1978.
Darling Jenny, Harlequin, 1978.
Reilly's Woman, Harlequin, 1978.
To Tell the Truth, Harlequin, 1978.
Sonora Sundown, Harlequin, 1978.
Big Sky Country, Harlequin, 1978.
Something Extra, Harlequin, 1978.
Master Fiddler, Harlequin, 1978.
Beware of the Stranger, Harlequin, 1978.
Giant of Mesabi, Harlequin, 1978.
The Matchmakers, Harlequin, 1978.
For Bitter or Worse, Harlequin, 1979.
Green Mountain Man, Harlequin, 1979.
Six White Horses, Harlequin, 1979.
Summer Mahogany, Harlequin, 1979.
The Bride of the Delta Queen, Harlequin, 1979.
Touch the Wind, Pocket Books, 1979.
Tidewater Lover, Harlequin, 1979.
Strange Bedfellow, Harlequin, 1979.
Low Country Liar, Harlequin, 1979.
Sweet Promise, Harlequin, 1979.
For Mike's Sake, Harlequin, 1979.
Sentimental Journey, Harlequin, 1979.
A Land Called Deseret, Harlequin, 1979.
Kona Winds, Harlequin, 1980.
That Boston Man, Harlequin, 1980.
The Rogue, Pocket Books, 1980.
Bed of Grass, Harlequin, 1980.
The Thawing of Mara, Harlequin, 1980.
The Mating Season, Harlequin, 1980.
Lord of the High Lonesome, Harlequin, 1980.
Southern Nights, Harlequin, 1980.
Ride the Thunder, Pocket Books, 1980.

Enemy in Camp, Harlequin, 1980.
Difficult Decision, Harlequin, 1980.
Heart of Stone, Harlequin, 1980.
One of the Boys, Harlequin, 1980.
Night Way, Pocket Books, 1981.
Wild and Wonderful, Harlequin, 1981.
A Tradition of Pride, Harlequin, 1981.
The Traveling Kind, Harlequin, 1981.
The Hostage Bride, Silhouette Books, 1981.
Dakota Dreamin', Harlequin, 1981.
This Calder Sky (Doubleday Book Club selection), Pocket Books, 1981.
The Lancaster Men, Silhouette Books, 1981.
For the Love of God, Silhouette Books, 1981.
Northern Magic, Harlequin, 1982.
With A Little Luck, Harlequin, 1982.
Terms of Surrender, Silhouette Books, 1982.
That Carolina Summer, Harlequin, 1982.
This Calder Range (Doubleday Book Club selection), Pocket Books, 1982.
Wildcatter's Woman, Silhouette Books, 1982.
Foxfire Light, Silhouette Books, 1982.
The Second Time, Silhouette Books, 1982.
Mistletoe and Holly, Silhouette Books, 1982.
Stands a Calder Man, Pocket Books, 1983.
Separate Cabins, Silhouette Books, 1983.
Western Man, Silhouette Books, 1983.
Calder Born, Calder Bred (Doubleday Book Club selection), Pocket Books, 1983.
Best Way to Lose, Silhouette Books, 1983.
Leftover Love, Silhouette Books, 1984.
Silver Wings, Santiago Blue (Doubleday Book Club selection and Literary Guild selection), Poseidon, 1984.
The Pride of Hannah Wade (Doubleday Book Club selection), Pocket Books, 1985.
The Glory Game (Doubleday Book Club selection and Literary Guild selection), Poseidon, 1985.

Also author of a screenplay based on her novel *Foxfire Light*, 1983; composer of lyrics for country western songs. Author and publisher of *Janet Dailey Newsletter*.

WORK IN PROGRESS: A novel.

SIDELIGHTS: With over eighty novels to her credit, romance writer Janet Dailey is currently the fifth best-selling author in the world, just behind Harold Robbins, Barbara Cartland, Irving Wallace, and Louis L'Amour. In the little more than ten years that she has been writing, Dailey has seen her books sell well over 100 million copies in nineteen languages.

A voracious reader as a child, Dailey knew as a teenager that she wanted to be a writer. After high school, however, she left her hometown to work as a secretary for an Omaha construction company owned by Bill Dailey, whom she later married. After years of helping run the business, Bill made Janet a partner. In 1974, they decided to sell the company. The couple then set off to journey across America in a travel trailer.

Deciding that she could write better romance novels than the ones she had been reading to occupy her free time, Dailey, with her husband's encouragement, started to work on her first romance novel. "I kept saying to Bill that this is the kind of book I'd like to write," she remarked in *Forbes*. "He got tired of hearing that in a hurry and told me to write the book, not just talk about it." Upon its completion, the novel was immediately accepted for publication by Toronto's Harlequin Books, becoming the first of more than fifty Dailey titles brought

out by the Canadian firm; for years she was the only American romance writer Harlequin published.

One reason for Dailey's enormous literary output in such a brief period is her strict writing schedule. Six mornings a week, with only an occasional day off for promotional engagements or other business obligations, she writes from eleven to fifteen pages of manuscript. Calling herself a "workaholic," Dailey explained in *Working Woman* the motivation behind maintaining such a work schedule: "I get so involved that if I weren't sitting down at the typewriter, the story would just be going around in my head all the time anyway; once you start that first page, your life starts to revolve around the book."

According to Eliot Fremont-Smith in the *Voice Literary Supplement*, "Dailey writes two kinds of novels—150-pagers and 350-pagers—though 180-pagers and 240-pagers have at least been experimented with. . . . The 150s take her nine days to complete, the 350s between 30 and 45 days." As she declared to Linda Witt of *People*, "working two years on a novel would drive me up the wall."

This dedication to her writing, coupled with her respect for her craft, seems to be a major attraction for Dailey's multitude of readers. "My romance readers are like me," she once stated in the *New York Times Book Review*. "They are work-oriented women who are under a great deal of stress. They are very involved . . . and they need an escape." Furthermore, the author continued, "I'm not identified with Hollywood decadence. I still have too much dirt between my toes; I wear Levi's rather than Calvin Klein's. My readers know that I'm a Midwestern girl and that I hold to Midwestern values."

Even though Dailey's books are extremely popular with readers, they have generally not been well reviewed or treated very seriously by critics. Many point to the never-changing themes of romance novels, to the predictable plots, and to the similarity of characters as reasons why they virtually ignore this genre. *People*'s Margot Dougherty describes Dailey's novels as "escapist literature, smooth and shallow." The author answers this charge in *Redbook:* "It's true that they're called escape novels, but they won't work unless there's an element of reality too. I show a genuine conflict between the hero and heroine. Real or imagined, the conflict exists and they can't wish it away. The characters cope with it, find a way to resolve it, and that resolution involves change—it brings them closer together. We can all recognize that kind of pattern from our own relationships, even if the setting is idealistic and escape-oriented."

When Joseph Parisi of the *Chicago Tribune* asked Bill Dailey to explain why he felt critics tended to ignore his wife's books, he remarked: "We've talked to critics before, and they can't see any value in this [type of literature]. And, of course, our comment back is we're not trying to write the Great American Novel. We're pleasing ourselves. We got 22 million readers in this country and 53 million around the world. We couldn't care less, really. It's nice to be on the *New York Times* [best-sellers list], and we are. But if you've got 22 million readers who love the books and they can associate with Janet, that beats hell out of a dozen critics." Added Janet Dailey in *Working Woman:* "I often respond to critics with the cliche that Bob Hope isn't going to win any awards for acting, in the same way that I'm never going to win a Pulitzer. But look at the entertainment we give."

Dailey's husband serves as her manager as well as her partner in their joint business firm, Janbill Ltd. In the writing area,

Bill Dailey handles all of the research—supplying his wife with the details that make her novels as authentic as possible—helps edit her manuscripts, and organizes her schedule. As he explained to Alice Turner of *Redbook:* "I went to Jan and laid out a plan for doing these stories. She would do the writing, and I would manage her career and take care of all the research and the business. We would be a team. And that's the way we've done it." Agreeing, Janet Dailey remarked to Witt: "Bill and I are a team. You can't be Rodgers and Hammerstein when you are only Rodgers."

Janet and Bill Dailey are also involved in a variety of other ventures. Their companies include such enterprises as a television production company, a restaurant/lounge, a music publishing company, and several country music theaters. But their biggest project to date is their theme park and resort complex called Wildwood, U.S.A., located in their hometown of Branson, Missouri.

Dailey and her books generate so much interest among her readers that she and her husband began publishing the *Janet Dailey Newsletter*. With over 53,000 subscribers, the quarterly keeps Dailey's fans up-to-date on her writing, answers their questions, and informs them about her professional and personal activities.

When Dailey was asked what it is about her books that triggers such interest and loyalty, she told Joseph Parisi of the *Chicago Tribune:* "The first thing is story. The second thing is traditional values. And by that I'm talking about loyalty, fidelity, honesty in relationships. . . . It's also touching on feelings. . . . A writer must write it so the reader will feel it, to the point where he hurts and cries and he laughs and he feels the warmth in it."

In addition to her numerous romance novels, Dailey has also written books that the *Saturday Review* describes as "part modern romance, part modern western, and part modern gothic. Among these novels are her four volume multigenerational saga on the Calder family and the book *Silver Wings, Santiago Blue,* which Dailey describes in *Working Woman* as "fiction, . . . but with a nonfictional theme."

In 1984 she published her last strictly romance-type novel, saying in *Publishers Weekly,* "I quit writing category romances with the publication of *Leftover Love,* . . . I was—and am—moving on as a writer." Explaining herself further in the *Chicago Tribune,* Dailey noted that she is going to concentrate on "more historical or general fiction. But I'm going to stay with the strong love theme. . . . Pick up any best seller and you'll find it there."

One of the reviewers who has taken a serious look at Dailey's books is Eliot Fremont-Smith. Writing in a *Voice Literary Supplement* review of *Calder Born, Calder Bred,* Fremont-Smith states that Dailey's "books are about courage and grit. They are not escapes from a world that is drab, but invitations to a world that is, though conflicted, exciting, wonderful, and eventually fulfilling for those with right values and an understanding of what this thing called 'man' is. The idea is to partake, participate. The message is, you can do it, with the books as a demo. The function is to release innate bravery."

MEDIA ADAPTATIONS: The film rights to Dailey's "Calder" series have been purchased for production as a television mini-series.

AVOCATIONAL INTERESTS: Travel.

CA INTERVIEW

CA interviewed Janet Dailey by telephone on March 11, 1985, at her home in Branson, Missouri.

CA: You started writing in the mid-1970s, traveling around with your husband in a Silver Streak trailer, and quickly became America's bestselling romance novelist and one of the top five in the world. Did that set up a kind of standard that you felt you had to keep living up to?

DAILEY: Definitely. I think it's a combination. You know at the point when people are buying the book strictly by your name, without even reading the blurb to see what it's about, that they're buying out of loyalty and you'd better give them the best you can. I find I'm a very competitive person with myself. I always want to do better than the last time, and I always want to try new things. So it's a combination of the two. They both sort of push you on to jump a higher fence.

CA: You became something of a cult yourself, with readers not only enjoying your books but also subscribing to the Janet Dailey Newsletter *to find out more about your life. Is the fan mail a job in itself?*

DAILEY: It hasn't been lately, simply because of the newsletter. We still answer some of the mail individually, when it's related to some specific book. When it's something general, then we usually acknowledge it through the newsletter. From that standpoint, it hasn't been a full-time job. But we read everything that comes in; we don't just let the secretary read it and forget it. We read it personally.

CA: What kind of readers do you hear from most?

DAILEY: Strangely, there isn't any one kind. You almost feel that each book brings out different ones that it appeals to. Of course with *Silver Wings, Santiago Blue,* my first hardcover, I heard from many people who were either women pilots, WASPs, or knew one or flew with one. I had a lot of male readers on that book, and a lot of them saying something like, I was stationed at such-and-such place, and they had WASPs flying out of the base. I heard a lot in that instance from people who were relating to the material in the book directly.

But trying to say what the average writer is, I would say we're usually hearing from people who have suddenly made a change in their own lives. Whether it's that they've gone back to college or they've started writing or they've set up their own business, it seems the books have motivated them in some way to change their lives, that they weren't happy before and now they're going to try something that they've always wanted to do and they've been encouraged in some way by the books.

CA: That must give you a very good feeling.

DAILEY: Oh, yes! And the third thing, and one of the things that to me is the biggest compliment any writer can get, is hearing from the ones who say, I used to think reading was boring until I picked up one of your books. That's great because I know if they read my books they're going to read other books; they're going to go back to reading again.

CA: How many languages are your books translated into now?

DAILEY: Nineteen, I believe.

CA: Does there seem to be one country outside the United States where they are most popular?

DAILEY: It's spread around so much, I wouldn't know on population statistics. I know that Japan is one place where they're enormously popular. The Philippines is another one, and India. And obviously in Europe they're very popular.

CA: One of the ideas you and your husband came up with early was to set a book in each state, and you traveled around to do the necessary research for them. Did you have a favorite state, one that you most enjoyed researching and writing about?

DAILEY: No. I loved the traveling, but I believe very much that the setting of a book and the plot have to be married. You can't just arbitrarily say, I'm going to find a place and set a book there. You have to find a plot that fits that area, because I think the background of your book sets much of its mood. So I could never say one place, one state, was more fertile. I was always trying to do that marriage of plot and background. Some backgrounds make their own plot. I have a book coming out in June, a hardcover, that's the main Literary Guild selection. It has a polo background. There the subject matter dictated that it would be set in the United States and Europe and Argentina. It more or less dictated its own background.

CA: I've read that your husband does most of the research for you. How does that work?

DAILEY: In a variety of ways, actually. He handles it. Sometimes he physically gets the material. Sometimes, for instance, when there's library research involved, he may hire someone to do the actual library research because obviously he has other things that he does as well. When we're in an area, he may call on the Agriculture Bureau, the Bureau of Land Management, the Weather Bureau, the Farm Bureau—whatever background I'm needing, he will go to the sources. He may go to ranchers, if it's a ranching story. He will literally call on the necessary people and run down whatever information I need.

CA: So you're spared the legwork.

DAILEY: Yes. That's not one of my strong points. I like to have things at my fingertips, and I'm not the type that likes to nose it out, to go to five different sources before I find the one I want.

CA: Some of your books are far more than frothy romances—the Calder books especially. How did the Calder books come about?

DAILEY: I had originally had an idea for a story that would be of a large ranching family, but I wanted it to be in the north, where you would still have the big acreages involved. I had decided on Montana—it was wide-open country and there was a degree of isolation because of the low population level—and it was going to be a contemporary story. But even though it was going to be a contemporary story, I still had to know how the ranch got into the family and what the family's background would be, so I had asked Bill to research it. As he was working on it, he said that most of Montana was settled by Texans. I said, "Texans! You've got to be kidding. Why were Texans going north to Montana?" I'd never heard of this. He went back to find that out, then came back and told me that Montana was the last of the free grass. They were fencing in Texas, so these big cattle ranches were setting up

separate ranches in Montana. The XIT ranch, which was one of the biggest in Texas—it covered ten counties there—had a ranch in Montana, and many other famous Texas ranches were also in Montana.

Well, this was something I hadn't heard of, and I thought, this is fascinating. Then he turned around and told me of the Dust Bowl years and the homesteaders that had come to Montana. I saw then that I didn't have just a single story, I really had a generation story. When I decided to do the Calders, I knew that I had a lot more to work with.

CA: What kind of working schedule do you keep? Are you still getting up at four in the morning to write?

DAILEY: Oh yes. And I still do a certain number of pages every day. I work six days a week, usually. Of course there are occasions when I miss a day—with a book like the Calders, there's obviously no way I can set aside the three or four months it takes to write it without having an interview or having to go somewhere. So it varies, but usually I work six days a week.

CA: You must have to go to bed pretty early to get up at four—or don't you need a lot of sleep?

DAILEY: Obviously I don't need the sleep. I go to bed at ten o'clock. When I'm working a lot on a book, my tension level is such that I don't require a lot of sleep. But afterwards, I always have this enormous letdown.

CA: Between books, then, do you get away from writing entirely for a while?

DAILEY: I get away from it as far as the book writing is concerned, but I might do other writing in relation to some of our other businesses—things of that nature. But I pretty well try not to worry about the writing until it's time to write another book.

CA: Is there any one part of the writing that you feel you have to work hardest at?

DAILEY: The description. Description is the hardest for me. I never seem to have a great deal of problem with dialogue and working out speech mannerisms, but I have a great deal of difficulty with description. A lot of people have said they love the description in my books. Maybe it's because I work harder at it.

CA: Your first book was accepted without revisions. Do you revise a lot now before you turn a book in?

DAILEY: No. I have often said I do a lot of my editing in my head before I put it on paper. I really know how a scene is going to affect future scenes in the book as well as how it works with the previous scene. If I see it altering things at that point, before I ever get it down, I stop and say, do I want it to alter? Is it better if it does? If it isn't, how can we change it to keep it? When I say I don't do revisions, I mean I don't do revisions on paper. But mentally I do revisions all the time.

CA: Do you work on a word processor?

DAILEY: No, I don't, although we have one in the office. I prefer to use the typewriter.

CA: In the 1981 Sakowitz Christmas catalogue there was this $115,000 gift idea: "America's first lady of romantic novels, Janet Dailey, will write a 125-page manuscript with you starring as the hero or heroine!" Did anybody buy?

DAILEY: No. And I sort of breathed a sigh of relief!

CA: The waning romance market doesn't seem to have hurt you, since you've been coming up with bigger books.

DAILEY: No. I stopped as far as the small romances go, the Harlequin and Silhouette types; I quit writing those actually three years ago. Obviously I had books in the pipeline, so they were still being published even though I wasn't physically writing them. I had already branched out into the larger format, larger novels. And now I'm sort of making the progression into something closer to mainstream fiction.

CA: Janbill has gone far beyond just managing your career as a writer—into music publishing, recording, television production, and building a theme park. What's Janbill doing now that's especially exciting?

DAILEY: Gosh, what aren't we doing! It sounds so staggering when you list it all, but of course it doesn't feel staggering, and I guess that's what you have to judge by. We have bought a country music theater here in Branson, which we're calling Country Music World. Our show will feature an extremely talented vocal group called the Tennessee Valley Boys and a very beautiful singer named Kaye Landers. Bill is producing the show and I'm collaborating with George Horne, our musical director, to write it. Actually we have more country music shows—theaters—than there are in Nashville or the world. We have something like twenty theaters with a capacity of around 30,000 people.

CA: You're going to have a real country music center there.

DAILEY: Definitely. We already have a major recording studio here, and I think it's going to branch out considerably in the next five to ten years and be a major music center. So we're involved in that, and we're developing our Wildwood property into a total entertainment complex. Right now we're putting in roads and sewers and water, and selling some of the property that we don't want to develop personally. And we're working on several feasibility plans for some things we do want to build on the property. We're also working on some television things—some based on my books, some on original material.

CA: Are you writing the scripts for those?

DAILEY: No, I'm working as story consultant, basically. I've written a screenplay based on one of my books, *Foxfire Light*, which Bill produced. It was a great experience. I realize now why they have to change the book. As a writer, you can suddenly let go of your ego and understand that it's a different medium, that what works in a book will not necessarily work in a movie. So it was great to do it once. But to tie my time up as is needed on a screenplay, no thank you. I'm not the type that likes to rewrite, and on a screenplay that's all you do—rewrite, rewrite!

CA: You were trying your hand at song lyrics earlier too. Is that turning into something important?

DAILEY: Well, for me it's like working a crossword puzzle. You're still doing something with words, but in a different form. It almost becomes a mind exercise and a way of relaxing. It's nothing I'm really serious about or plan to do to any great extent; it's just something I play with.

CA: Do you still find time to travel?

DAILEY: Not as much. That's the way it goes, I guess. I'm glad we did all the traveling we did when we did it. I'm becoming quite a homebody. I love being here on the lake. We have twenty acres right here on the lake, and it's very quiet. I have the horses, my son has horses, and I can go riding anytime I want. It's become very nice just to be at home.

CA: What else would you like to write that you haven't tried yet?

DAILEY: Oh, everything! I think that's the one thing I have found. The challenge of writing and trying different things. I just finished what I suppose you'd call an epic, a book on Alaska which begins in 1745 and goes all the way up to 1975.

CA: That sounds *like an epic.*

DAILEY: Well, I heard Michener was doing Texas, and I thought Alaska was bigger! Even though I had done the Calders, I had done it in four books; I'd never attempted to do anything like that in one volume. That for me was a challenge. Who knows what I might try next? I've got a lot of ideas in my mind. There are a lot of books that I'd like to write. The question is deciding which one. I'd like doing something I haven't done before, but whether a mystery, suspense—who knows?

CA: How do you feel, in retrospect, about starting out with the romances?

DAILEY: They were very useful to me as a writer. They really taught me how to write; they were my college education. In the romance fiction market—or basically any category fiction market, whether you're dealing with Westerns or romance or mystery or science fiction—there are certain strictures that you have to set your story within. They're very much like the short story market, which has pretty much gone by the wayside. You learn to tell your story quickly, succinctly, draw your characters quickly, succinctly. And it teaches you the basics of writing: timing, the tempo of the story; your plot—is it tight, does it drag anywhere? It teaches you the fundamentals of writing. It's where you can perfect your craft. In anything you always have to start out with a degree of natural talent. But if you don't refine your craft and perfect it, you don't go anywhere, you just keep doing the same thing. And I feel I was blessed. I became very successful writing romance novels, but it also opened up something totally new for me. It was like a stepping stone, and I don't know where it's going to go from here. Hopefully higher!

BIOGRAPHICAL/CRITICAL SOURCES:

PERIODICALS

Booklist, March 1, 1982, December 15, 1982, September 1, 1983.
Chicago Tribune, June 12, 1983.
Cosmopolitan, September, 1984.
Detroit News, July 21, 1985.

Forbes, March 6, 1978.
Kirkus Reviews, February 15, 1982, July 15, 1983.
Library Journal, August, 1984.
Los Angeles Times, September 17, 1984.
Los Angeles Times Book Review, December 19, 1982, December 16, 1983.
New York Times Book Review, August 3, 1980, August 16, 1981, August 26, 1984, March 17, 1985.
People, July 13, 1981, September 17, 1984, March 18, 1985.
Publishers Weekly, April 2, 1979, November 28, 1980, June 12, 1981, February 26, 1982, November 26, 1982, August 24, 1984.
Redbook, June, 1983.
Saturday Review, March, 1981.
Voice Literary Supplement, October, 1983.
Washington Post Book World, March 3, 1985.
Working Woman, March, 1984.

—*Sketch by Margaret Mazurkiewicz*

—*Interview by Jean W. Ross*

*   *   *

DALLEK, Robert   1934-

PERSONAL: Born May 16, 1934, in Brooklyn, N.Y.; son of Rubin (a business-machine dealer) and Esther (Fisher) Dallek; married Geraldine Kronmal (a policy health analyst), August 22, 1965. *Education:* University of Illinois, B.A., 1955; Columbia University, M.A., 1957, Ph.D., 1964.

ADDRESSES: Home—2258 Prosser Ave., Los Angeles, Calif. 90024. *Office*—Department of History, University of California, Los Angeles, Calif. 90064.

CAREER: Columbia University, New York, N.Y., instructor in history, 1960-64; University of California, Los Angeles, assistant professor, 1964-69, associate professor, 1969-73, professor of history, 1973—. Commonwealth Fund Lecturer, University College, University of London, 1984.

MEMBER: American Historical Association, Organization of American Historians, Society of American Historians (fellow), Society for Historians of American Foreign Relations.

AWARDS, HONORS: Guggenheim fellow, 1973-74; National Endowment for the Humanities fellow, 1976-77; Bancroft Prize and American Book Award nomination in history, both 1980, both for *Franklin D. Roosevelt and American Foreign Policy, 1932-1945;* Rockefeller Foundation fellow, 1981-82.

WRITINGS:

Democrat and Diplomat: The Life of William E. Dodd, Oxford University Press, 1968.
(Editor) *1898: McKinley's Decision—War on Spain,* Random House, 1969.
(Editor) *The Roosevelt Diplomacy and World War II,* Holt, 1970.
(Contributor) Ernest May and James Thomson, editors, *American-East Asian Relations: A Survey,* Harvard University Press, 1972.
(Editor) *Dynamics of World Power: Documentary History of U.S. Foreign Policy, 1945-1973,* Volume I, Chelsea House, 1973.
Franklin D. Roosevelt and American Foreign Policy, 1932-1945, Oxford University Press, 1979.
The American Style of Foreign Policy: Cultural Policy and Foreign Affairs, Knopf, 1983.

Ronald Reagan: The Politics of Symbolism, Harvard University Press, 1984.
(With B. Bailyn, D. B. Davis, D. H. Donald, J. L. Thomas, and G. S. Wood) *The Great Republic: A History of the American People,* 3rd edition (Dallek was not associated with earlier editions), Heath, 1985.
(Contributor) Mark Garrison and Abbott Gleason, editors, *Shared Destiny: Fifty Years of Soviet-American Relations,* Beacon Press, 1985.
(Contributor) Sanford J. Ungar, editor, *Estrangement: America and the World,* Oxford University Press, 1985.

Contributor to *American Historical Review, Survey,* and other journals in his field.

WORK IN PROGRESS: Lyndon Johnson: A Biography, for Oxford University Press.

SIDELIGHTS: A historian who specializes in studies of America's relations with other members of the world community, Robert Dallek is the author of such books as *Franklin D. Roosevelt and American Foreign Policy, 1932-1945* and *The American Style of Foreign Policy: Cultural Policy and Foreign Affairs.* In addition to receiving the Bancroft Prize and an American Book Award nomination, the Roosevelt work garnered widespread critical acclaim, including Basil Rauch's comment in the *National Review* that it is "much the most detailed, thoughtful, and objective study of Roosevelt as a maker of foreign policy that we are likely to have in our time."

As Dallek notes in his survey of Roosevelt's foreign policy, the president's role during the turbulent years prior to the Japanese air attack on Pearl Harbor was to "balance the country's desire to stay out of war against its contradictory impulse to assure the defeat of Nazi power." Roosevelt "came to the fore at a moment when the American people still believed they had a valid choice between isolation from international politics and full involvement in them," says Henry F. Graff in the *New York Times Book Review.* Even while providing often covert aid to European allies, Roosevelt was able to stave off American military involvement until December 7, 1941, when the events at Pearl Harbor demanded immediate retaliation.

Some of Roosevelt's critics question his reasons for not entering the war sooner, an act they feel might have prevented the Japanese attack. But to Dallek, Roosevelt's motivation was clear, reports *New Republic* reviewer Ronald Steel: "FDR's refusal to oppose Nazi and Italian aggression in the 1930s lay not in indecisiveness, isolationism or appeasement, but in a 'determination to retain his ability to influence crucial developments at home.'" Steel also comments: "Whether or not one fully accepts Dallek's admiring view of Roosevelt as diplomatist, all students of foreign affairs must remain in his debt for the diligence of his research, the objectivity of his analysis, the thoroughness and intellectual integrity of his treatment. [*Franklin D. Roosevelt and American Foreign Policy, 1932-1945*] is diplomatic history at a very high level."

In *The American Style of Foreign Policy,* the author proposes that "foreign policy has for the most part reflected domestic anxieties and preoccupations," as Mark Garrison comments in the *Washington Post Book World.* Acknowledging the work of fellow historian Richard Hofstadter, who originally conceived this theory, Dallek "proceeds systematically and frequently mechanically through 80 years of foreign policy," remarks *New York Times Book Review* critic Gaddis Smith. "Time and again he argues American perceptions and actions had little to do with foreign reality and much to do with a felt need to cure domestic disharmony or to prove to ourselves that democracy is alive and well or to justify cultural and political conformity." Smith criticizes Dallek for going "too far in an effort to fit everything into the Iron Maiden of the Hofstadter thesis. He sees all bad policies as the result of the inappropriate and dangerous influence of internal forces or considerations. He sees good policies, congruent with external realities, as good largely by chance." However, Smith adds, "pressing an argument too far is better than blandness and therefore is no great flaw. This book should be judged not by details but by its capacity to stimulate thinking about fundamentals. By that measure it succeeds."

In *New Republic* critic Walter LaFeber's view, *The American Style of Foreign Policy* "provides more than an interesting survey of U.S. foreign policy in the twentieth century. It attempts to develop a new synthesis for understanding that policy. In doing so, Dallek raises some of the most important questions that must be asked about past and present diplomacy. He has not retreated into history to avoid current controversies, but used history to open new perspectives on them."

Dallek's next book, *Ronald Reagan: The Politics of Symbolism,* moves out of the realm of foreign policy to examine the forces that have shaped the president's outlook on life. Published just months before Reagan's election to a second term as chief executive, the book takes a psycho-sociological view of his words and actions. Dallek states that Reagan's presidency "is shaped by an obsession to recapture an idyllic childhood past, which never existed," *Atlantic* critic Robert Sherrill relates. Reagan "has a fanatical faith in 'traditional values' that, in fact, had only a secondary influence on his own life," Sherrill continues. "He preaches precepts that he has never had to live by."

Morton Kondracke, writing in the *New York Times Book Review,* takes exception to Dallek's tone in *Ronald Reagan,* saying that the author is "both morally and intellectually condescending toward the President." Furthermore, "some of [Dallek's] accusations seem contradictory," adds Kondracke. "On the one hand, Mr. Reagan is described as passive, 'the consummate expression of the organization man, the other-directed personality who lacks genuine autonomy.' On the other hand, he remains fixedly attached to his 'familiar verities'. . . which logically would seem to make him the consummate expression of the sociologist David Riesman's 'inner-directed' personality."

Dallek's recollection of Reagan's childhood, including his relationship with his alcoholic, often unemployed father, and the author's theory that this depressing experience made Reagan a champion of personal independence, makes Sherrill "uneasy." Explains the critic: "For one thing, Dallek makes too much of Reagan's rather commonplace memories. [The author] admits that 'these memories are not remarkable'; he insists, however that they are significant, because Reagan 'himself makes so much of them.' But does he really? . . . The fact that Reagan has been talking about good old Dixon, Illinois, and moaning about poor old Dad for a quarter-century does not necessarily mean that these memories lie at the center of his soul; repetition is the style of all politicians." Despite these reservations, Sherrill feels that Dallek's "probing of Reagan's skull is done in a graceful and lucid style. It is free of psychoanalytical cant, and anyone literate enough to read a ballot will have no problem following his argument." As C. Vann Woodward concludes in a *New Republic* article: "While Dallek may have overstressed the symbolic side and neglected

to some degree the hard-nosed, class-interest achievements of President Reagan's domestic policy, the same cannot be said of his treatment of foreign policy. On the whole [*Ronald Reagan: The Politics of Symbolism*] is one of the more illuminating studies of the dominant American political figure of our time."

BIOGRAPHICAL/CRITICAL SOURCES:

BOOKS

Dallek, Robert, *Franklin D. Roosevelt and American Foreign Policy, 1932-1945,* Oxford University Press, 1979.
Dallek, Robert, *Ronald Reagan: The Politics of Symbolism,* Harvard University Press, 1984.

PERIODICALS

Atlantic, March, 1984.
Los Angeles Times, March 8, 1984.
National Review, October 26, 1979.
New Republic, May 19, 1979, June 20, 1983, April 2, 1984.
New York Review of Books, October 25, 1979, May 28, 1984.
New York Times Book Review, May 20, 1979, March 27, 1983, March 4, 1984.
Times Literary Supplement, May 15, 1969, February 22, 1980, October 19, 1984.
Washington Post Book World, May 8, 1983.

—*Sketch by Susan Salter*

*   *   *

DAVIDSON, Basil   1914-

PERSONAL: Born November 9, 1914, in Bristol, England; son of Thomas and Jessie (Craig) Davidson; married Marion Ruth Young, 1943; children: Nicholas, Keir, James.

ADDRESSES: Home—Old Cider Mill, North Woolton, Somerset BA4 4HA, England. *Agent*—Curtis Brown Ltd., 575 Madison Ave., New York, N.Y. 10022.

CAREER: Economist, London, England, member of editorial staff, 1938-39; *Times,* London, Paris correspondent, 1945-47, European leader writer, 1947-49; free-lance writer. *Military service:* British Army, 1940-45; became lieutenant colonel; awarded Military Cross, Bronze Star (U.S. Army), twice mentioned in dispatches.

MEMBER: Savile Club (London).

AWARDS, HONORS: Anisfield-Wolf Award for best book concerned with racial problems in field of creative literature, 1960, for *The Lost Cities of Africa;* gold medal from Haile Selassie for his work on African history, 1970; Litt.D., University of Ibadan, 1975; Medalha Amilcar Cabral, 1976; honorary degrees from Open University of Great Britain, 1980, and from University of Edinburgh, 1981; Gold Award, International Film and Television Festival of New York, 1984, for "Africa."

WRITINGS:

Partisan Picture: Jugoslavia 1933-44, Bedford, 1946.
Highway Forty (novel), Frederick Muller, 1949.
Germany: What Now? Potsdam 1945—Partition 1949, Frederick Muller, 1950.
Report on Southern Africa, J. Cape, 1952.
Golden Horn (novel), J. Cape, 1952.
Daybreak in China, J. Cape, 1953.
The African Awakening, Macmillan, 1955.

The Rapids (novel), Houghton, 1956.

Turkestan Alive, J. Cape, 1957.

Lindy (novel), J. Cape, 1958, published as *Ode to a Young Love,* Houghton, 1959.

The Lost Cities of Africa, Little, Brown, 1959, revised edition, 1970.

Black Mother, Little, Brown, 1961, published as *The African Slave Trade,* 1965, revised and enlarged edition, Atlantic-Little, Brown, 1981.

Guide to African History, Allen & Unwin, 1963, Doubleday, 1965, revised edition, edited by Haskel Frankel, Zenith Books, 1971.

Which Way Africa?: The Search for a New Society, Penguin, 1964, 3rd edition, 1971.

(Editor) *The African Past: Chronicles from Antiquity to Modern Times,* Little, Brown, 1964.

(With F. K. Buah) *The Growth of African Civilization: West Africa, 1000-1800,* Longmans, Green, 1965, revised edition published as *A History of West Africa to the Nineteenth Century,* Doubleday Anchor, 1966, new edition published under original title, Longmans, Green, 1967.

(With the editors of Time-Life) *African Kingdoms,* Time-Life, 1966.

Africa: History of a Continent, Macmillan, 1966, revised edition, Spring Books, 1972, published as *Africa in History: Themes and Outlines,* Macmillan, 1968, revised edition, 1974.

The Andrassy Affair (novel), Whiting & Wheaton, 1966.

History of West Africa, Doubleday, 1966, revised edition, Longmans, 1978.

East and Central Africa to the Late Nineteenth Century, Longmans, Green, 1967, revised edition, Doubleday, 1969.

(With Paul Strand) *Tir a'mhurain: Outer Hebrides,* Grossman, 1968.

The Liberation of Guine: Aspects of an African Revolution, Penguin, 1969.

The Africans: An Entry to Cultural History, Longmans, Green, 1969.

The African Genius: An Introduction to African Cultural and Social History, Little, Brown, 1969.

Old Africa Rediscovered, Longmans, Green, 1970.

Walking 300 Miles with Guerrillas through the Bush of Eastern Angola, Munger Africana Library, 1971.

In the Eye of the Storm: Angola's People, Doubleday, 1972, revised edition, Penguin, 1975.

Black Star: A View of the Life and Times of Kwame Nkrumah, Allen Lane, 1973.

Growing from Grass Roots: The State of Guinea-Bissau, Committee for Freedom in Mozambique, Angola, and Guinea, 1974.

Can Africa Survive?: Arguments against Growth without Development, Little, Brown, 1974.

(With Joe Slovo and Anthony R. Wilkinson) *Southern Africa: The New Politics of Revolution,* Penguin, 1976.

Ghana: An African Portrait, Aperture, 1976.

Let Freedom Come: Africa in Modern History, Little, Brown, 1978.

Special Operations Europe: Scenes from the Anti-Nazi War, Gollancz, 1980.

The People's Course, Longman, 1981.

Modern Africa, Longman, 1982.

Also author of eight-part television series, "Africa." Contributor to journals.

WORK IN PROGRESS: Emily's People.

SIDELIGHTS: Basil Davidson is a prominent figure in the field of African history who has, in the words of Benedict Wengler, "almost singlehandedly reversed the ethnocentric trend of considering anything African inferior" and "developed a whole new school of modern African history based on archaeology rather than on presumptions." In books such as *The Lost Cities of Africa,* Davidson uses archaeological evidence to prove that, far from being primitive savages, ancient Africans lived in civilizations that were technically and culturally very sophisticated. Many reviewers have praised the book for its fresh approach to African history, for its scope, and for Davidson's fine writing style. "It is both a sound historical and archaeological work and very exciting reading, . . . systematic, scientific and thoroughly up-to-date," states Kenneth Rexroth in *Nation.* James Duffy expresses a similar opinion in the *New York Times Book Review,* writing that *The Lost Cities of Africa* is "an exciting and richly detailed book. This is an important volume for anyone seriously interested in Africa."

However, some reviewers have suggested that Davidson practices a kind of African chauvinism. "Davidson tends to see the white man as an interloper in the African Garden of Eden," observes Peter Duignan in the *San Francisco Chronicle. New York Review of Books* contributor Roland Oliver notes that Davidson's interest in Africa began with his involvement in the anti-colonial struggle there and expresses the opinion that the author's political beliefs may color the objectivity of some of his work. Even so, Oliver credits Davidson as being "the most effective popularizer of African history and archaeology outside Africa," and many reviewers agree with W. F. Albright's assessment of the author: "Not only does he write vividly and with a seldom failing sense of the dramatic, but he also knows his material."

BIOGRAPHICAL/CRITICAL SOURCES:

PERIODICALS

American Anthropologist, April, 1973.

Best Sellers, December 15, 1970.

Black World, August, 1974.

Book Forum, winter, 1977.

Business Week, July 31, 1978.

Christian Century, February 18, 1970.

Christian Science Monitor, May 17, 1969, December 16, 1974.

Current History, March, 1973.

Journal of Negro Education, summer, 1966.

Journal of Negro History, July, 1969.

Los Angeles Times, October 9, 1981.

Nation, December 26, 1959, July 31, 1967.

New Statesman, October 27, 1972.

New York Herald Tribune Book Review, November 15, 1959.

New York Review of Books, December 17, 1970.

New York Times, December 3, 1968.

New York Times Book Review, November 15, 1959, December 4, 1966.

New Yorker, June 10, 1970.

Observer, February 4, 1973.

Punch, November 23, 1966.

Saturday Review, March 22, 1969, April 25, 1970.

Times (London), December 17, 1980.

     *   *   *

DAVIDSON, Margaret 1936-
  (Mickie Compere, Mickie Davidson)

PERSONAL: Born May 14, 1936, in New York, N.Y.; daughter of Thomas Stephen (a writer) and Ruth (Davis) Compere; married Carson Davidson (a film producer), April 27, 1964. *Education:* Baylor University, B.A., 1958. *Politics:* Liberal-independent. *Religion:* None.

ADDRESSES: Home—86 Bedford St., New York, N.Y. 10014.

CAREER: Ellington Advertising Agency, New York City, employee, 1958-60; Military Publishing Institute, New York City, writer, 1960-63; elementary school teacher, New York City, 1963; author of children's books, 1963—.

AWARDS, HONORS: Junior Book Award of Boys' Clubs of America, for *Helen Keller's Teacher.*

WRITINGS:

(Under name Mickie Compere) *Dolphins!*, Four Winds, 1964.
(Under name Mickie Compere) *The Story of Thomas Alva Edison, Inventor: The Wizard of Menlo Park,* Four Winds, 1964.
(Under name Mickie Davidson) *The Adventures of George Washington,* Four Winds, 1965.
(Under name Mickie Davidson) *The Pirate Book,* Random House, 1965.
(Under name Mickie Davidson) *Helen Keller's Teacher,* Four Winds, 1966.
Frederick Douglass Fights for Freedom, Four Winds, 1968.
The Story of Eleanor Roosevelt, Four Winds, 1969.
Helen Keller, Hastings House, 1971.
Louis Braille: The Boy Who Invented Books for the Blind, Scholastic Inc., 1971.
Neighbor to Neighbor, Popular Library, 1973.
Nine True Dolphin Stories, Hastings House, 1974.
(Editor) *Abraham Lincoln,* Scholastic Inc., 1976.
The Golda Meir Story, Scribner, 1976, revised edition, 1981.
Five True Dog Stories, Scholastic Inc., 1977.
Seven True Dog Stories, Hastings House, 1977.
Five True Horse Stories, Scholastic Inc., 1979.
Seven True Horse Stories, Hastings House, 1979.
Wild Animal Families, Hastings House, 1980.

AVOCATIONAL INTERESTS: Art, reading, museums, peace work.†

*　　*　　*

DAVIDSON, Mickie
See DAVIDSON, Margaret

*　　*　　*

DAVIES, (William) Robertson 1913-
(Samuel Marchbanks)

PERSONAL: Born August 28, 1913, in Thamesville, Ontario, Canada; son of William Rupert (a publisher) and Florence Sheppard (McKay) Davies; married Brenda Matthews, February 2, 1940; children: Miranda, Jennifer (Mrs. C. T. Surridge), Rosamund (Mrs. John Cunnington). *Education:* Attended Upper Canada College, Toronto, and Queen's University at Kingston; Balliol College, Oxford, B.Litt., 1938.

ADDRESSES: Home and office—Massey College, University of Toronto, 4 Devonshire Pl., Toronto, Ontario, Canada M5S 2E1. *Agent*—Curtis Brown Ltd., 10 Astor Pl., New York, N.Y. 10003.

CAREER: Old Vic Company, London, England, teacher and actor, 1938-40; *Saturday Night,* Toronto, Ontario, literary ed-

itor, 1940-42; *Examiner,* Peterborough, Ontario, editor and publisher, 1942-62; University of Toronto, Toronto, professor of English, 1960—, master of Massey College, 1962-81. Senator, Stratford Shakespeare Festival, Stratford, Ontario.

MEMBER: Royal Society of Canada (fellow), Royal Society of Literature (fellow), American Academy and Institute of Arts and Letters (honorary member), Authors Guild, Authors League of America, Dramatists Guild, Writers' Union (Canada), P.E.N. International.

AWARDS, HONORS: Louis Jouvet Prize for directing, Dominion Drama Festival, 1949; Stephen Leacock Medal for Humour, 1954, for *Leaven of Malice;* LL.D., University of Alberta, 1957, Queen's University, 1962, University of Manitoba, 1972, University of Calgary, 1975, and University of Toronto, 1981; D.Litt., McMaster University, 1959, University of Windsor, 1971, York University, 1973, Mount Allison University, 1973, Memorial University of Newfoundland, 1974, University of Western Ontario, 1974, McGill University, 1974, Trent University, 1974, University of Lethbridge, 1981, University of Waterloo, 1981, University of British Columbia, 1983, and University of Santa Clara, 1985; Lorne Pierce Medal, Royal Society of Canada, 1961; D.C.L., Bishop's University, 1967; Companion of the Order of Canada, 1972; Governor-General's Award for fiction, 1973, for *The Manticore;* D.Hum. Litt., University of Rochester, 1983.

WRITINGS:

THE "SALTERTON TRILOGY"

Tempest-Tost, Clarke, Irwin, 1951, Rinehart, 1952, reprinted, Penguin, 1980.
Leaven of Malice (also see below), Clarke, Irwin, 1954, Scribner, 1955, reprinted, Penguin, 1980.
A Mixture of Frailties, Scribner, 1958, reprinted, Penguin, 1980.

THE "DEPTFORD TRILOGY"

Fifth Business, Viking, 1970.
The Manticore, Viking, 1972.
World of Wonders, Macmillan (Toronto), 1975, Viking, 1976.

FICTION

The Rebel Angels (novel), Viking, 1982.
High Spirits (stories), Viking, 1983.
What's Bred in the Bone (novel), Viking, 1985.

NONFICTION

Shakespeare's Boy Actors, Dent, 1939, Russell, 1964.
Shakespeare for Young Players: A Junior Course, Clarke, Irwin, 1942.
The Diary of Samuel Marchbanks (collection of newspaper pieces originally published under pseudonym Samuel Marchbanks; also see below), Clarke, Irwin, 1947.
The Table Talk of Samuel Marchbanks (collection of newspaper pieces originally published under pseudonym Samuel Marchbanks; also see below), Clarke, Irwin, 1949.
(With Tyrone Guthrie and Grant Macdonald) *Renown at Stratford: A Record of the Shakespearean Festival in Canada,* Clarke, Irwin, 1953, new edition, 1971.
(With Guthrie and Macdonald) *Twice Have the Trumpets Sounded: A Record of the Stratford Shakespearean Festival in Canada,* Clarke, Irwin, 1954.
(With Guthrie, Boyd Neal, and Tanya Moiseiwitsch) *Thrice the Brinded Cat Hath Mew'd: A Record of the Stratford Shakespearean Festival in Canada,* Clarke, Irwin, 1955.

A Voice from the Attic, Knopf, 1960 (published in England as *The Personal Art: Reading to Good Purpose,* Secker & Warburg, 1961, reprinted, Darby Books, 1983).

Le Jeu de centenaire, Comission du Centenaire, c.1967.

Samuel Marchbanks' Almanack (collection of newspaper pieces originally published under pseudonym Samuel Marchbanks; also see below), McClelland & Stewart, 1967.

The Heart of a Merry Christmas, Macmillan (Toronto), 1970.

Stephen Leacock, McClelland & Stewart, 1970.

(Editor and author of introduction) *Feast of Stephen: An Anthology of Some of the Less Familiar Writings of Stephen Leacock,* McClelland & Stewart, 1970.

(With Michael R. Booth, Richard Southern, Frederick Marker, and Lise-Lone Marker) *The Revels History of Drama in English, Volume VI: 1750-1880,* Methuen, 1975.

One Half of Robertson Davies: Provocative Pronouncements on a Wide Range of Topics, Macmillan (Toronto), 1977, published as *One Half of Robertson Davies,* Viking, 1978.

The Enthusiasms of Robertson Davies, edited by Judith Skelton Grant, McClelland & Stewart, 1979.

(Contributor) Robert G. Lawrence and Samuel L. Macey, editors, *Studies in Robertson Davies' Deptford Trilogy,* English Literary Studies, University of Victoria, 1980.

The Well-Tempered Critic: One Man's View of Theatre and Letters in Canada, edited by Grant, McClelland & Stewart, 1981.

The Mirror of Nature (lectures), University of Toronto Press, 1983.

The Papers of Samuel Marchbanks (contains portions of *The Diary of Samuel Marchbanks, The Table Talk of Samuel Marchbanks,* and *Samuel Marchbanks' Almanack*), Irwin Publishing, 1985.

PLAYS

Fortune, My Foe (first produced in Kingston, Ontario, by the International Players, 1948), Clarke, Irwin, 1949.

Eros at Breakfast and Other Plays (contains "Eros at Breakfast" [first produced in Montreal, Quebec, at the Montreal Repertory Theatre, 1948], "Overlaid" [first produced in Peterborough, Ontario, at Peterborough Little Theatre, 1947], "The Voice of the People" [also see below; first produced in Montreal at the Montreal Repertory Theatre, 1948], "At the Gates of the Righteous" [first produced in Peterborough at the Peterborough Little Theatre, 1948], and "Hope Deferred" [first produced in Montreal at the Montreal Repertory Theatre, 1948]), with introduction by Tyrone Guthrie, Clarke, Irwin, 1949, revised edition published as *Four Favorite Plays,* 1968.

At My Heart's Core (first produced in Peterborough at the Peterborough Little Theatre, 1950), Clarke, Irwin, 1952.

A Masque of Aesop (first produced in Toronto, Ontario, at Upper Canada College, May, 1952), Clarke, Irwin, 1952.

A Jig for the Gypsy (first produced in Toronto at the Crest Theatre, 1954), Clarke, Irwin, 1955.

Love and Libel (based on *Leaven of Malice;* first produced in Toronto at the Royal Alexandra Theatre, November, 1960; first produced on Broadway at the Martin Beck Theatre, December, 1960), Studio Duplicating Service, 1960.

A Masque of Mr. Punch (first produced in Toronto at Upper Canada College, 1962), Oxford University Press, 1963.

The Voice of the People, Book Society of Canada, 1968.

Hunting Stuart and Other Plays (contains "Hunting Stuart" [first produced in Toronto at the Crest Theatre, 1955], "King Phoenix" [first produced in Peterborough, 1950], and "General Confession"), New Press, 1972.

"Brothers in the Black Art," first produced on Canadian Broadcasting Corporation, 1974.

Question Time (first produced in Toronto at the St. Lawrence Center, 1975), Macmillan, 1975.

"Pontiac and the Green Man," first produced in Toronto at the Macmillan Theatre, 1977.

WORK IN PROGRESS: A novel.

SIDELIGHTS: The "Deptford Trilogy"—consisting of the novels *Fifth Business, The Manticore,* and *World of Wonders*—has brought Robertson Davies to international attention as one of Canada's leading men of letters. "These novels," Claude Bissell writes in *Canadian Literature,* "comprise the major piece of prose fiction in Canadian literature—in scope, in the constant interplay of wit and intelligence, in the persistent attempt to find a pattern in this [, as Davies states in the trilogy,] 'life of marvels, cruel circumstances, obscenities, and commonplaces.'"

The trilogy traces the lives of three Canadian men from the small town of Deptford, Ontario, who are bound together by a single tragic event from their childhood. At the age of ten, Dunstan Ramsay and Percy "Boy" Staunton are throwing snowballs at one another. Staunton throws a snowball at Ramsay which contains a rock. Ramsay ducks. The snowball strikes Mrs. Mary Dempster in the head, causing her to give birth prematurely to a son, Paul Dempster, and to have a mental breakdown that ends in her permanent hospitalization. Each novel of the trilogy revolves around this tragedy and deals primarily with one of the three men involved: *Fifth Business* with Dunstan Ramsay, who becomes a teacher; *The Manticore* with Boy Staunton, a politician; and *World of Wonders* with Paul Dempster, a stage magician. "*Fifth Business* provides the brickwork," John Alwyne writes in the *New Statesman,* "the two later volumes, the lath and plaster. But what a magnificent building is the result. [The trilogy] bears comparison with any fiction of the last decade."

Davies did not intend to write a trilogy when he first began *Fifth Business.* His initial story idea prompted him to write the novel, he tells *Time* (Canada), "but I found almost as soon as I had finished it that wasn't all I wanted to say." So Davies wrote *The Manticore* to tell more of his story. Reviewers then asked "to hear about the magician who appeared in the other two novels," Davies explains, "and I thought 'Well, I know a lot about magicians' and I wrote the third book."

Despite the unplanned development of the trilogy, it has garnered extensive critical praise and each volume has been an international bestseller. The first volume, *Fifth Business,* is, Sam Solecki maintains in *Canadian Forum,* "Davies' masterpiece and . . . among the handful of Canadian novels that count." In the form of an autobiographical letter written by Dunstan Ramsay upon his retirement, the novel delineates the course of Ramsay's life and how it was shaped by the pivotal snowball incident. Because he avoided being hit, and thereby caused Mrs. Dempster's injury, Ramsay has lived his life suffering under a tremendous guilt. This guilt inspired an interest in hagiology, the study of saints, and Ramsay becomes in later years the foremost Protestant authority on the lives of the saints. "All the lore on saints and myth," Judith Skelton Grant states in *Book Forum,* "is firmly connected to the central character, reflecting his interests, showing how he thinks, influencing his life, and playing a part in his interpretation of events." It is in terms of hagiology that Ramsay eventually comes to a realization about himself. His autobiographical letter finally "leads

Ramsay to comprehension of his own nature—which is not saintly,'' John Skow reports in *Time*.

Much of this same story is reexamined in *The Manticore*, the second novel of the trilogy, which takes place after the mysterious death of prominent Canadian politician Boy Staunton. Staunton has been found drowned in his car at the bottom of Lake Ontario, a rock in his mouth. Investigation proves the rock to be the same one that Staunton threw at Mrs. Dempster some sixty years before. Ramsay, obsessed with the incident, had saved it. But how Staunton died, and why he had the rock in his mouth, is unknown. During a performance by the magician Magnus Eisengrim (Paul Dempster's stage name), a floating brass head is featured that answers questions from the audience. Staunton's son David asks the head an explosive question, ''Who killed Boy Staunton?'' In the tumult caused by his outburst, David runs from the theater. His breakdown and subsequent Jungian psychoanalysis in Switzerland make up the rest of the novel. During his analysis, David comes to terms with his late father's career. ''The blend of masterly characterization, cunning plot, shifting point of view, and uncommon detail, all fixed in the clearest, most literate prose, is superbly achieved,'' writes Pat Barclay in *Canadian Literature*.

The life story of Paul Dempster is told in *World of Wonders*, the final volume of the trilogy. As a young boy, Dempster is kidnapped by a homosexual stage magician while visiting a travelling carnival. Dempster stays with the carnival as it makes its way across Canada, intent on becoming a magician himself by learning the secrets of the man who abducted him. While learning the trade, Dempster works inside a mechanical fortune-telling gypsy, operating the gears that make it seem lifelike. When the carnival breaks up, Dempster heads for Europe where he finds work as a double for a popular stage actor. With his knowledge of magic and the stage manner he has acquired from the theater people he knows, Dempster strikes out on his own as a magician, becoming one of the most successful acts on the continent. *World of Wonders*, Michael Mewshaw states in the *New York Times Book Review*, is ''a novel of stunning verbal energy and intelligence.'' L. J. Davis of *New Republic* believes the novel's ''situation is shamelessly contrived, and the language fairly reeks of the footlights (to say nothing of, yes, brimstone).'' Furthermore, Davis contends that *World of Wonders* ''isn't so much a novel as it is a brilliant act whose strength lies in the complexity of its symbolism and the perfection of its artifice.'' It is, Davis judges, ''a splendid conclusion'' to the trilogy.

In each of these novels the lead character undergoes a psychological transformation. Dunstan Ramsay finds the key to himself in the study of saints and myth, using these archetypes for greater self-understanding. David Staunton relies on Jungian psychoanalysis to help him in discovering his true nature and in coming to terms with his father's disreputable life and mysterious death. Paul Dempster learns from his work as a magician and his life in the theater about reality and illusion, gaining insight into his own personality. The three novels are, Bissell explains, ''essentially parts of a whole: three parallel pilgrimages.'' Grant, too, sees the essential search in which the three characters are engaged. She believes they explore different aspects of nature, however. ''Dunstan moves toward God and Boy toward the Devil,'' Grant writes, ''[while Dempster] experiences both.'' This experience of both good and evil, Grant believes, allows those dark aspects of the mind to be exposed and confronted. ''Not everything that has been labeled Evil proves to be so,'' Grant states, ''nor all that has

been repressed ought to remain so. And the genuinely evil and justifiably banished are weaker if faced and understood.'' Grant believes that ''together with the vigorous, lively and eccentric narrators of the [Deptford] trilogy, these moral, . . . mythic and psychological ideas have given these books a place among the dozen significant works of fiction published in Canada during the seventies.'' Peter S. Prescott, writing in *Newsweek*, sees the revelations of the three characters in similar terms. Davies, he writes, ''means to recharge the world with a wonder it has lost, to re-create through the intervention of saints and miracles, psychoanalysts and sleight-of-hand a proper sense of awe at life's mystery and a recognition of the price that must be paid for initiation into that mystery.''

The recurring theme of self-discovery follows the pattern established by psychologist Carl Jung, although Davies does not adhere strictly to Jungian psychology. He has explored a number of models for ''complete human identity,'' Patricia Monk writes in her *The Smaller Infinity: The Jungian Self in the Novels of Robertson Davies*, and though he has a ''deep and long-lasting affinity with Jung, . . . Davies eventually moves beyond his affinity . . . to a more impartial assessment of Jungianism as simply one way of looking at the universe, one myth among a number of others.'' Still, in common with the Jungian belief in archetypal influence on the human mind, Davies presents in his fiction characters who ''discover the meaning of their lives,'' Roger Sale writes in the *New York Review of Books*, ''by discovering the ways those lives conform to ancient patterns.'' Peter Baltensperger, writing in *Canadian Literature*, sees this as a consistent theme in all of Davies's fiction, not only in the ''Deptford Trilogy.'' This theme Baltensperger defines as ''the conquest of one's Self in the inner struggle and the knowledge of oneself as fully human.''

Commenting to *CA*, Davies clarifies the primary concern in all of his work. ''The theme which lies at the root of all my novels is the isolation of the human spirit,'' he explains. ''I have not attempted to deal with it in a gloomy fashion but rather to demonstrate that what my characters do that might be called really significant is done on their own volition and usually contrary to what is expected of them. This theme is worked out in terms of characters who are trying to escape from early influences and find their own place in the world but who are reluctant to do so in a way that will bring pain and disappointment to others.''

Many critics label Davies a traditionalist who is a bit old-fashioned in his approach to writing. I. M. Owen of *Saturday Night*, for example, places Davies ''curiously apart from the main stream of contemporary fiction.'' A critic for the *Washington Post Book World* characterizes Davies as ''a true novelist writing imagined stories, wonderful stories full of magic and incandescence, thought and literary art,'' something the critic does not find in other contemporary fiction. Davies is known as a moralist who believes in a tangible good and evil, a fine storyteller who consciously uses theatrical melodrama to enliven his plots, and a master of a wide variety of genre and styles.

Davies's strong moral sense is evident in the ''Deptford Trilogy'' where, Mewshaw finds, ''no action is without consequences.'' This unflinching explication of his characters' behavior makes for ''a constant, lively judging and damning of characters,'' as the writer for *Time* (Canada) reports. ''The habit of stern judgment is missing from most modern discourse,'' he continues, ''which tends charitably or fearfully to find excuses. But it is abundantly present in Davies's novels.'' These judgments are rooted in Davies's belief, Jean Strouse of *Newsweek* quotes him as saying, that "sin is the great unacknowledged element in modern life." It is sin which Davies explores in his novels, setting his characters to "grapple with magic, madness, mysticism, Gnosticism, miracles, freaks, saints, devils, Jung, Freud, God, mythic beasts, guilt, dominion and human nature."

Since he has written a number of plays, been a teacher and actor with the Old Vic Company, and served on the board of the Stratford Shakespeare Festival for many years, it is not surprising to find that Davies employs theatrical elements in his novels. He uses theatricality to move his story along at a quicker pace. In *World of Wonders*, a *Time* critic states, the characters "are brilliant talkers, but when they natter on too long, the highly theatrical author causes a grotesque face to appear at a window, drops someone through a trap door or stages a preposterous recognition scene." These melodramatic touches come naturally to Davies who, Davis remarks, "is a player in love with the play, and the kind of play he loves is melodrama." In his collection of lectures entitled *The Mirror of Nature*, Davies makes his case on behalf of melodrama and attempts, as Alberto Manguel writes in the Toronto *Globe & Mail*, "to save melodrama's lost honor." Davies argues in this book that "theatre is a coarse art. . . . It appeals immediately to primary, not secondary elements in human nature." Melodrama's emphasis on creating an emotional response in its audience, Davies continues, is true to theatre's fundamental purpose. Manguel concludes that Davies "succeeds" in justifying his own use of melodrama.

The range of Davies's abilities is reflected not only in the variety of genres in which he has written but in his ability to move "easily from the bawdiest humor to the loftiest abstraction, charging every character and idea with power and fascination," as Mewshaw states. Davies's work in the "Deptford Trilogy," Strouse maintains, encompasses such divergent elements as "mystery, grotesquerie, desolation and psychological sagacity." Walter E. Swayze of *Canadian Forum* notes that although Davies has written in a "diversity of styles . . . direct expression and bold colour have been constant features." Admitting that Davies is a "fine writer—deft, resourceful, diverse and . . . very funny," John Kenneth Galbraith nonetheless writes in the *New York Times Book Review* that Davies's greatest strength is "his imagination."

Calling Davies "a compellingly inventive storyteller" who has garnered an "affectionate following," James Idema of the *Chicago Tribune Book World* explains the appeal of his fiction. It lies in "his way of placing ordinary humans in the midst of extraordinary events, of bringing innocent, resolutely straight characters into contact with bonafide exotics . . . ," Idema believes. "The 'real world' interests [Davies] only as a starting point. Enigma, myth, illusion and magic are the stuff of his elegant stories." Similarly, William Kennedy observes in the *New York Times Book Review* that Davies "conveys a sense of real life lived in a fully imagined if sometimes mythical and magical world." Comparing the role of the novelist with that of the magician, because both "mean us to believe in what never happened and to this end use many conjuror's tricks," Prescott defines Davies as one writer "who takes seriously his magician's role." In doing so, Davies has become "one of the most gifted and accomplished literary entertainers now writing in English," as a writer for *Time* remarks. In a speech given at the University of Windsor and quoted by *Time* (Canada), Davies observes that "though it is

always an unwise thing to say too loudly—because you never know who may be listening—I am a happy man."

CA INTERVIEW

CA interviewed Robertson Davies by telephone on January 25, 1985, at his home near Toronto, Ontario.

CA: In "The Conscience of the Writer" (in One Half of Robertson Davies) *you said you've always been grateful for your journalistic experience because it kept your technique "in good muscular shape" and trained you to sit down and get right to the business of writing. Did working in the theater and writing plays also help in discernible ways when you began to write fiction?*

DAVIES: They gave me a very strong feeling for the importance of dialogue and the immediacy and speed with which you can convey plot though dialogue, rather than through prose descriptive passages. Also, it was something that had to do with my own childhood, when I read endlessly. I would pick up books and look through them to see if there was lots of dialogue. If there was, I thought it was a good book and wanted to read it. But if it was all description, I wasn't strong on that.

CA: The influence of Carl Jung on your writing is well known to your readers, and is now in fact the subject of a book. Do you continue to read Jung's writings and find revelations in them?

DAVIES: Oh yes, I do. Also, I'm very much involved with the Analytical Psychology Society here in Toronto, which is a flourishing one. So I'm continually attending lectures and meeting Jungian analysts and thinkers and people whose work is attached to his work. Of course he influences philosophers and writers and people outside the straight psychoanalytical world, so I meet them all the time and have most interesting conversations with them. One of my daughters edits a small paper which is involved with Jungian thought, and my oldest daughter is a Jungian analyst. So I have it very close. Jung's thought is very expansive and plays upon an enormous number of aspects of life. I know some scientists who are keenly interested in it. It is a sort of opening out of life, whereas so much psychoanalytical thinking is rather reductive; it's getting you right back to the womb and a lot of trouble.

CA: Your fiction offers the reader a factual feast—John Kenneth Galbraith referred to it as "an extraordinary range of wholly unpredictable information." Do you store in your head information on Paracelsus, obscure saints, and gypsy folklore (for starters), or do such topics grow out of your plots and sometimes require research?

DAVIES: They arise from plots and they require research, but they wouldn't arise from the plots if I wasn't already somewhat interested in that kind of thing. I always have been, because one of my continuing ideas is that people in the past were no stupider than we are. Something that they believed, like alchemy, cannot be wholly foolish, because people whom we regard as very, very great thinkers took it seriously. It may not be true, and it may not be in accord with modern scientific thinking, but I think that it was another way of reaching after a truth toward which science is only one path.

CA: Did Dunstan Ramsay's interest in saints grow out of your own?

DAVIES: I'm very much interested in saints, because of the reason I explained in *Fifth Business*. Saints are extraordinary people. Criminals are extraordinary people, and everybody's very interested in criminals. I think they might equally all be interested in saints, because saints are very strange people of amazing energy and unusual intensity of feeling.

CA: Some writers say they have trouble transforming real places into fictional ones. Were there any hurdles for you in turning Kingston into Salterton, or Thamesville, where you were born, into Deptford?

DAVIES: Well, they're not photographic portraits. They're just something that I found in the spirit of the places that was interesting to me, and which other people tell me they don't see at all. But there's no reason why they should. That's how I get my living: I show it to them.

CA: Since some of your characters go from book to book, you live with them, in a sense, for a long time. Is it ever hard to part with them when you finally have to?

DAVIES: Pretty much what a character has to say has been exhausted by the time I reach the end of a series of books, and I don't particularly recur to them. I think I've pretty well exhausted them by the time I've finished writing.

CA: No so with your readers—at least this one. When I reached the end of the "Deptford Trilogy," I started all over again.

DAVIES: That's an enormous compliment. That's the way I feel with certain books which I regard very, very highly. I'm sorry to part with the characters at the end. But there it is.

CA: There's a lovely part in Leaven of Malice *that seems to be a spoof on narrow academic specialization involving a Canadian writer named Heavysege. Tell me about Heavysege.*

DAVIES: Heavysege is a reality; he's a very well known Canadian dramatist of the nineteenth century. He was an unfortunate man, a very nineteenth-century character. He was a workman, an expert joiner, carpenter, furniture maker—an expert cabinetmaker, in fact, who immigrated to Canada and settled in Montreal. But he had a mind above his daily work, and he wrote two or three ghastly novels and a great big thumping tragedy. The extraordinary thing was that he got a lot of encouragement. Longfellow said that he was absolutely first-rate and even compared him with Dante. You know, he was blown up enormously. But it hasn't remained. It's a kind of object lesson to all writers: you can be enormously praised in your lifetime, but that doesn't really mean that your work's any good. I've read Heavysege; I'm one of the few people who has. It's hard work, I can tell you. He had a very aspiring mind, but he had no poetic feeling at all.

CA: I suspect you spend a lot of time on your characters' names. Many of them seem fraught with meaning, or at least suggestion.

DAVIES: They are attempts to find names that fit the characters, but the names themselves do not have any special meaning—not like the names of plays in Restoration drama or anything like that.

CA: In Leaven of Malice, *Pearl Vambrace reveals to Solly Bridgetower that she is also named Veronica. Solly can then see her differently. Paul Dempster in the "Deptford Trilogy" is also Faustus Legrand and Magnus Eisengrim. Is there a Jungian connection?*

DAVIES: Not really, no. But I have a feeling that virtually everybody at some time or other wishes they had a name other than the one that they have. They generally settle for the one they have because, by that time, too many things are associated with it to make a break. I think every teenager, for instance, wishes for a name of great significance and rich connotations. Most people feel that way. The giving of a new name is rather like a change of personality or the release of something which has formerly been hidden. I think that's what happens in those books. A young man who is setting out to be a conjurer would probably take a very grand name like Faustus Legrand. But it's not a good name; it hasn't got real resonance, and it's the name that would occur to a sort of ignorant tent show conjurer. Later on it is Liesl who gets down to business and calls him Magnus Eisengrim, and that is a name with much more resonance, as she explains in the book.

CA: Liesl is a wonderful character.

DAVIES: I'm very fond of her, yes.

CA: After so many years as a newspaperman, did you find it hard in any way to leave the Examiner *and go into teaching at the University of Toronto?*

DAVIES: No, I didn't, because I'd had twenty years of newspaper work. And although newspaper men are very romantic—they're among the most romantic people in the world, I think—you can't give your whole life to newspaper work and be totally contented. My father was a newspaper editor, a very good one. He used to say that there was nothing about the newspaper world that you couldn't learn in three months, but it would take you three years to learn how to apply it. But once you've learned it and learned how to apply it and done it for twenty years, you wonder, am I going to go on with another twenty years of this? You can get enough of it, because, although newspapers like to represent themselves as wonderfully romantic and hitched into world events and so forth, they are really an entertainment and manufacturing business. The press has to begin every day at exactly the same time, or you lose an awful lot of money and you run into trouble with the unions; and all these things condition what a newspaper really is. The news is what you can squeeze in before you have to go to press; it's not what's happening in the world.

CA: Do you love newspapers still? Do you read specific ones regularly?

DAVIES: Oh yes. I read a good many newspapers and try to get different views from them. I read the London *Times* airmail edition because it gives me quite a different slant on American and Canadian affairs.

CA: It's very heartening that you can be a part of academia and still poke good fun at it. Do you think it would benefit in general from taking a less serious attitude toward itself?

DAVIES: Well, in that it is just like everything else. Business would benefit from taking a less ponderous attitude toward itself. Most groups—church, newspapers, academia, the stock market—they all take themselves with a leaden seriousness. They never seem to see themselves in perspective.

CA: What are you proudest of in your tenure as Master of Massey College?

DAVIES: I was able to set it going and to establish a pattern for it, and to try to set some high standards of achievement for the young people who come there. They are a rather special group, and I'm a great believer in encouragement, you know. I feel that very clever people are often very lonely, and the people who came to that college were often very lonely. They needed people to tell them that what they had to do and what they had to give to the world was genuinely important. Later on, when they get into academic life, they sometimes exaggerate that absurdly, but at the beginning it's not easy. A great number of young people who are very brilliant come from very humble families, and they have to fight the family criticism. That is the hardest of all to overcome. I've known of many instances of brilliant young people who had to go through a lot of hard times at home: you know how hard we've worked to make you what you are and you're turning against us, you've got ideas we never had, are you sure you're right—all that kind of thing.

CA: You've been a reviewer as well as the subject of reviews. Are there reviewers or review periodicals that you feel do a responsible job?

DAVIES: I don't know, really, because, though I read a considerable number of book reviews, I'm aware of how they're done and how they have to be done. Two of the problems of book reviewers—even quite good ones—are that, first of all, they have to read too much, and next, they're awfully badly paid as the usual thing. I don't know how it is in the States, but in Canada and in England the pay for book reviews is very poor. If you pay people rotten money, you mustn't be surprised if you get slapdash, quickie results. If someone is getting $50 for a book review, he's got to write three to get the equivalent of what he would get if he was paid $150. It's just too much. Even some quite important papers pay their reviewers a not very substantial sum for a review which may take an awful lot of time. One of the worst, of course, is the area of the academic review, which is done for an academic publication where they pay nothing at all. They expect you to work yourself down to a stump to write 3,000 words under those conditions. Of course you're interested in doing it or you wouldn't do it, but it's not the way to get the best.

CA: How do you feel about the growing body of critical writing on your own work?

DAVIES: Well, of course that's very difficult to say. Very strange things happen, and people interpret books in such an extraordinary way. There was one book written about my work which was entirely looking at it from a Jungian point of view, by somebody who hadn't really absorbed much of Jungian feeling, though they'd absorbed a certain amount of Jungian knowledge. I honestly couldn't read the book through, and I don't know of anybody who did. Very often people who write reviews, particularly in the academic world, want to put you right, to tell you how you ought to write your books and so forth. That does become rather irritating, because you feel that if their knowledge of technique and style and their invention is all so excellent, why don't they give up this nonsense and write books themselves? You get pretty tired of that.

Also, there is a thing which is inevitable but which can be irritating. That is the very young academic who is trying to

gain a reputation by being a giant killer. He boos you and says what a fathead you are and how you really aren't good for anything at all. That is the way he brings himself to the attention of his superiors. It's all basically a lot of baloney, because really, the way you have to judge what you're doing in the world is by who reads your books and how many of those people there are. If you have a substantial readership, you know that you've at least got something. And you know from the letters that you get—and I get a lot of letters—what the quality of your readers is. I was astonished recently to get a note from my agent to point out that my books are now available in ten languages. That is reassuring. If people want to read my work in ten languages, it can't be as awful as some terrible little fellow tells you it is who is just writing an article for the university review.

Many writers have pretended that they do not particularly want a large audience. Virginia Woolf, for instance, was delighted when her books sold 2,000 copies. But I'll bet she'd be even more delighted if she were living now and knew how many copies they've sold. I don't really think anybody will go to the hard, hard work of writing a book unless they hope they're going to reach quite a few people who will enjoy it. They really wish to give pleasure in the truest sense—not just a kind of foolish enjoyment, like eating a lollipop, but a genuine refreshment, a genuine enlargement, a genuine new look at life. That's what they want. Of course they're pleased if they get it, and you can only get that if you have quite a few readers. I'm not a believer in mute, inglorious Miltons. If they're mute and inglorious, what the hell kind of Milton are they?

CA: Pretending not to care may be only a pose on the part of those writers who do it.

DAVIES: It's a defense, really. Poor brutes, they're so jumped on and beaten around that they have to pretend a lot.

CA: I loved the story of the seventeen-year-old whose class had been given the assignment of writing an essay on your "Deptford Trilogy." He came to interview you and asked right off the bat what you considered the greatest structural flaw of the trilogy. You said you didn't consider that it had any structural flaws; you thought it was just great.

DAVIES: You see, that's the way high school kids are taught. My books are read a lot in high schools, and they teach them that nonsense. But you know, after I published that story, I got a letter from that young man. He was absolutely furious; he said I had exposed him and mocked him and held him up to derision. I wrote back and said, "Cool down, my boy. What kind of gall have you to come to me and ask me to say what I think is wrong with my books? That's somebody else's job. I've got to believe in them or I'm through!" He was just a simple lad, a nice boy, but he honestly thought he was being very helpful. He had the vanity of youth, you know; he really thought he'd done something wonderful.

CA: You've written a lot about Canada and Canadian writing. Do you think Canada is expecting more from her writers now than when you raised the issue in a speech in 1972?

DAVIES: I don't know. It's terribly difficult to say, because in a country like Canada, with a quite small population and not as big an intelligentsia as you might get in a country with the same population in Europe, it's very difficult to know what people generally expect. A lot of people in Canada are pleased that there are writers in the country, but they regard them much as they might regard the hockey stars or somebody like that; they're somebody who does something that's unusual and is well known for it. But I think that there is a genuine change, and the change has come about because of the influx into Canada of people from Europe. We have a big immigration, and it is an immigration which, to a surprising degree, is on a high educational level. So you get all kinds of people who come here who are used to a sort of intellectual life in the countries they come from. They rather expect it here, and so it is generated by that means.

CA: Some of your writers are getting very good reviews here. Is there a consciousness there of Canadian writing as such?

DAVIES: There is a very great consciousness of Canadian writing, but in Canada there is inevitably a very painful line drawn between those who are recognized abroad and those who are not. Sometimes those who are not say that they are the real Canadians, because they don't travel! There is now a recognition of Canadian writing abroad that would have been utterly incredible thirty years ago. Just last summer I was in Vienna. While I was there, I attended a conference on Canadian writing at which thirty-eight European universities were represented. I wondered how many of them knew really anything about Canadian writing. I quickly found out, because I was sitting next to people who were quoting Canadian poets and knew all kinds of work—and flatteringly knew my own work very intimately. And you see, we're now beginning to attract attention in countries which are really more like ourselves—deeply, not superficially. We're attracting a lot of attention in South America because we're about the size of some South American countries in population. Our problems are somewhat similar, and we are interesting to them because we're strange—we live in a basically very cold country of a type unfamiliar to them. Altogether we're getting away from that image of being a British colony and not a very interesting one. In the United States we've been treated with great generosity. As you say, many Canadian writers are reviewed regularly in the United States, and with kindness and understanding much greater sometimes than they get at home.

CA: Is there rivalry between Canadian writers that keeps them from reviewing each other fairly in Canada?

DAVIES: One of the problems here is that there is a small population spread out over a gigantic land mass. We're the second largest country in the world in land mass. We've got about twenty-three million people here. So it's terribly hard to get any real notion of the whole country. Inevitably where there is any real literature there are factions and jealousies and bitternesses. But it is difficult to know how much importance to attach to them. Of course if you're near them or if you're the object of them, they seem much more important than they really are. One of the things about Canada that is difficult for writers and for the development of the literature is that there is no popular paper which circulates over the whole country which carries authoritative reviews. So it's still rather regional in feeling. And there is always the question, of course, of the writers in French, who are very good writers indeed, but they have to look toward continental France for their recognition and their appreciation. They get it, too.

CA: What kind of writing schedule do you follow now?

DAVIES: I work every day in the morning, from about 9:30 to 12:30. That's just actually at the desk. I do a lot of sitting around and thinking—it looks as though I weren't doing anything, but of course I'm working very hard.

CA: Are you still active in theater?

DAVIES: No, not really, My wife and I are great theatergoers, and we travel around a good deal to see theater and opera, but we're not ourselves actively engaged in it.

CA: Is there work in progress that you can talk about?

DAVIES: Yes, I just finished a new novel, which follows *The Rebel Angels.* Then there will be a third that will follow this one. I am making notes for it, but I haven't done any work on it yet. I'm also re-editing and getting ready for publication three books which I published really very early in my writing career. They were the imaginary writings of a man called Samuel Marchbanks. The Marchbanks books are coming out in a new edition with notes and so forth. I'm doing it in a sort of pretend-academic way, as though I were an academic let loose on the works of Marchbanks. It is very enjoyable. They will be coming out in the autumn in a single volume.

CA: Will you write an autobiography or a memoir?

DAVIES: No. There is a lady who is working on a biography of me. But, you know, it is by no means easy work being the subject of a biography. You know that, excellent though she is—and she works very hard—you wonder if she really knows you at all—because of course you know so many things about yourself you wouldn't dream of letting anyone else know!

BIOGRAPHICAL/CRITICAL SOURCES:

BOOKS

Anthony, Geraldine, editor, *Stage Voices: 12 Canadian Playwrights Talk about Their Lives and Work,* Doubleday, 1978.

Buitenhuis, Elspeth, *Robertson Davies,* Forum House Publishing, 1972.

Cameron, Donald, *Conversations with Canadian Novelists,* Part 1, Macmillan, 1973.

Contemporary Literary Criticism, Gale, Volume II, 1974, Volume VII, 1977, Volume XIII, 1980, Volume XXV, 1983.

Davies, Robertson, *Fifth Business,* Viking, 1970.

Davies, Robertson, *The Manticore,* Viking, 1972.

Davies, Robertson, *World of Wonders,* Macmillan (Toronto), 1975, Viking, 1976.

Davies, Robertson, *The Mirror of Nature,* University of Toronto Press, 1983.

Grant, Judith Skelton, *Robertson Davies,* McClelland & Stewart, 1978.

Heath, Jeffrey M., editor, *Profiles in Canadian Literature #2,* Dundurn Press, 1980.

Jones, Joseph and Johanna Jones, *Canadian Fiction,* Twayne, 1981.

Klinck, Carl F., editor, *Literary History of Canada,* University of Toronto Press, 2nd edition, 1976.

Lawrence, Robert G. and Samuel L. Macey, editors, *Studies in Robertson Davies' Deptford Trilogy,* English Literary Studies, University of Victoria, 1980.

Monk, Patricia, *The Smaller Infinity: The Jungian Self in the Novels of Robertson Davies,* University of Toronto Press, 1982.

Moore, Mavor, *Four Canadian Playwrights,* Holt, 1973.

Morley, Patricia, *Robertson Davies,* Gage Educational Publishing, 1977.

New, William H., editor, *Dramatists in Canada: Selected Essays,* University of British Columbia Press, 1972.

PERIODICALS

America, December 16, 1972.

Book Forum, Volume IV, number 1, 1978.

Book World, December 13, 1970.

Canadian Forum, June, 1950, December, 1975, October, 1977, December-January, 1981-82.

Canadian Literature, spring, 1960, winter, 1961, spring, 1973, winter, 1974, winter, 1976.

Canadian Review, fall, 1976.

Chicago Tribune Book World, January 31, 1982.

Dalhousie Review, autumn, 1981.

Financial Post, January 19, 1963.

Globe & Mail (Toronto), March 5, 1977, January 7, 1984.

Journal of Canadian Fiction, winter, 1972, winter, 1982.

Journal of Canadian Studies, February, 1977.

Library Quarterly, April, 1969.

Listener, April 15, 1971.

Los Angeles Times, January 29, 1982.

Maclean's, March 15, 1952, September, 1972.

Nation, April 24, 1982.

New Republic, March 13, 1976, April 15, 1978, March 10, 1982.

New Statesman, April 20, 1973, April 4, 1980.

Newsweek, January 18, 1971, March 22, 1976, February 8, 1982.

New York Review of Books, February 8, 1973.

New York Times, February 8, 1982, November 6, 1985.

New York Times Book Review, December 20, 1970, November 19, 1972, April 25, 1976, February 14, 1982.

Rolling Stone, December 1, 1977.

Saturday Night, April 26, 1947, December 13, 1947, February 14, 1953, November, 1967, October, 1985.

Saturday Review, December 26, 1970, April 3, 1976.

Spectator, August 21, 1982.

Tamarack Review, autumn, 1958.

Time, January 11, 1971, May 17, 1976.

Time (Canada), November 3, 1975.

Times Literary Supplement, March 26, 1982.

University of Toronto Quarterly, Number XXI, 1952.

Washington Post Book World, May 30, 1976, February 7, 1982, October 30, 1983.

—Sketch by Thomas Wiloch

—Interview by Jean W. Ross

*   *   *

DAVIS, Frederick Barton   1909-1975

PERSONAL: Born August 27, 1909, in Boston, Mass.; died March 2, 1975, in Bronxville, N.Y.; son of Ernest L. F. and Dorothy (Barton) Davis; married Charlotte Croon, October, 1940; children: Dorothy Barton (Mrs. James Franklin Truitt, Jr.). *Education:* Boston University, B.S., 1931; Harvard University, Ed.M., 1933, Ed.D., 1941. *Religion:* Unitarian Universalist.

ADDRESSES: Home—10 Kent Rd., Bronxville, N.Y. *Office*—Center for Research in Evaluation and Measurement, University of Pennsylvania, Philadelphia, Pa. 19104.

CAREER: Avon Old Farms School, Avon, Conn., psychologist, 1936-39; Cooperative Test Service, New York City, editor, 1939-42; George Peabody College for Teachers (now George Peabody College of Vanderbilt University), Nashville, Tenn., professor of psychology and head of department, 1947-49; Hunter College of the City University of New York, New York City, professor of education, 1949-64; University of Pennsylvania, Philadelphia, professor of education and director of Center for Research in Evaluation and Measurement, 1964-75. Vice-president, Educational Records Bureau, 1965-72.

Lecturer at Wellesley College, 1936-37, University of California, 1947, 1956, 1957, Harvard University, 1948, Columbia University Teachers' College, 1953-54, 1960-62, 1967-68, and Syracuse University, 1965; visiting research professor at Rutgers University, 1970-71. Director of Test Research Service, Bronxville, N.Y., and American Institute for Research, Pittsburgh, Pa. Special consultant to Secretary of War, 1941-42, and Secretary of Air Force, 1947-51; consultant to American Council on Education, 1947, and to Mayor's Commission on Manpower, New York City; research consultant to Philippine Center for Language Study, 1959-75, Ford Foundation, 1967, College Entrance Examination Board, 1970-71, and other organizations. *Military service:* U.S. Army Air Forces, 1942-46; served as aviation psychologist; became major; awarded Legion of Merit.

MEMBER: American Psychological Association (fellow; president, Division 16, 1958-59), American Educational Research Association, National Council on Measurement in Education (president, 1964-65), Psychometric Society, Bronxville Field Club.

AWARDS, HONORS: Fulbright lecturer at University of Amsterdam, 1957-58.

WRITINGS:

Item-Analysis Data: Their Computation, Interpretation and Use in Test Construction, Harvard University Press, 1946.

A.A.F. Qualifying Examination, U.S. Government Printing Office, 1947.

Utilizing Human Talent, American Council on Education, 1947.

(With Gerald S. Lesser) *The Identification and Classroom Behavior of Elementary-School Children Gifted in Five Mental Characteristics,* Hunter College Educational Clinic, 1959.

Educational Measurements and Their Interpretation, Wadsworth, 1964.

(Contributor) B. J. Wolman, editor, *Scientific Psychology,* Basic Books, 1964.

(Editor) *Modern Educational Developments: Another Look,* Educational Records Bureau, 1966.

Identification and Measurement of Reading Skills of High School Students, University of Pennsylvania, 1967.

Philippine Language Teaching Experiments, Alemar Phoeniz (Philippines), 1967.

(Editor) Martin Kling, *The Literature of Research in Reading with Emphasis on Models: Final Report,* Graduate School of Education, Rutgers University, 1971.

The Measurement of Mental Capability through Evoked-Potential Recordings, Educational Records Bureau, 1971.

Also author of the *Davis Reading Tests,* 1958 and 1962, *Comprehension Skills of Mature Readers,* 1967, and of pamphlet *Criterion-Referenced Measurement,* ERIC Clearinghouse on Tests, Measurements, and Evaluation, 1972. Editor of *Journal of the American Educational Research Association,* 1963-65, and *Psychometric Monographs.*

SIDELIGHTS: *Item-Analysis Data* has been published in French and Dutch.

OBITUARIES:

PERIODICALS

New York Times, March 3, 1975.†

* * *

De GEORGE, Richard T(homas) 1933-

PERSONAL: Born January 29, 1933, in New York, N.Y.; son of Nicholas (a beautician) and Carmelina (D'Ippolito) De George; married Fernande Melanson, June 15, 1957; children: Rebecca Marie, Anne Marie, Catherine Anne. *Education:* Attended University of Paris, 1952-53; Fordham University, B.A. (cum laude), 1954; Universite de Louvain, Ph.B. (with distinction), 1955; Yale University, M.A., 1958, Ph.D., 1959; University of Fribourg, postdoctoral study, 1962-63. *Religion:* Catholic.

ADDRESSES: *Home*—945 Highland Dr., Lawrence, Kan. 66044. *Office*—Department of Philosophy, University of Kansas, Lawrence, Kan. 66045.

CAREER: University of Kansas, Lawrence, assistant professor, 1959-62, associate professor, 1962-64, professor of philosophy, 1964-72, University Distinguished Professor, 1972—, chairman of department, 1966-72, Center for Humanistic studies, co-director, 1977-82, director, 1982-83. Senior research fellow, Columbia University, 1965-66; research fellow, Yale University, 1969-70; visiting fellow, Stanford University, 1972-73. National Endowment for the Humanities, director of project grant, 1972-73, summer seminar on contemporary Marxism, 1976, 1977, and summer interprofessional seminar, 1980, 1981, co-director of research tools grant, 1977-78, and grant on business and the humanities, 1978-81; director, Mellon Foundation grant for faculty development, 1977-83. Chairman of executive committee and program committee, Mountain Plains Philosophy Conference, 1974-75; member of organizing committee, Bicentennial Symposium of Philosophy, 1975-76; chairman of steering committee, Conference of Philosophical Societies, 1976-84. Member of editorial board, Regents Press of Kansas, 1966-69, 1973-77, and Philosophy Documentation Center, 1974—. Consultant on philosophy and education to National Endowment for the Humanities, Georgia State University, De Paul University, and other institutions. *Military service:* U.S. Army, Intelligence, 1955-57; became first lieutenant. U.S. Army Reserve, Intelligence, 1958-66; became captain.

MEMBER: International Federation of Philosophical Societies (member of governing board representing the United States, 1978—; vice-president, 1983—), International Association for Philosophy of Law and Social Philosophy (American section; vice-president, 1975-77; president, 1977-79), American Philosophical Association (member of executive committee, Western Division, 1976-79; member of national board of officers, 1982-85), Metaphysical Society of America (president, 1982-83), American Association for the Advancement of Slavic Studies, American Council of Learned Societies, American Association of University Professors, American Catholic Philosophical Association (member of executive council, 1968-71).

AWARDS, HONORS: Fulbright fellowship, 1954-55; Elizabeth Watkins faculty fellowship, summer, 1961; American Council of Learned Societies and Social Science Research Council joint grant in postdoctoral foreign area, 1962-63; Ford Foundation grant, summer, 1964; Encaenia Distinguished Alumni Award, Fordham University, 1964; HOPE Teaching Award, University of Kansas, 1965; University of Kansas research grants, 1965-70; National Endowment for the Humanities fellowship, 1969-70; Rockefeller Foundation fellowship, 1977-78.

WRITINGS:

(Editor) *Classical and Contemporary Metaphysics: A Source Book,* Holt, 1962.
Patterns of Soviet Thought: The Origins and Development of Dialectical and Historical Materialism, University of Michigan Press, 1966.
(Editor) *Ethics and Society: Original Essays on Contemporary Moral Problems,* Anchor Books, 1966.
(Co-editor and contributor) *Reflections on Man,* Harcourt, 1966.
New Marxism: Soviet and East European Marxism since 1956, Pegasus, 1968.
(Co-author) *Science and Ideology in Soviet Society,* edited by G. Fischer, Atherton, 1968.
Soviet Ethics and Morality, University of Michigan Press, 1969.
A Guide to Philosophical Bibliography and Research, Appleton, 1971.
(Co-editor) *The Structuralists from Marx to Levi-Strauss,* Anchor Books, 1972.
(Co-editor and contributor) *Marxism and Religion in Eastern Europe,* D. Reidel, 1976.
(Co-editor and contributor) *Ethics, Free Enterprise and Public Policy,* Oxford University Press, 1978.
The Philosopher's Guide to Sources, Research Tools, Professional Life and Related Fields, Regents Press of Kansas, 1980.
(Editor) *Semiotic Themes,* University of Kansas Publications, 1981.
Business Ethics, Macmillan, 1982.
The Nature and Limits of Authority, University Press of Kansas, 1985.

CONTRIBUTOR

E. Laszlo, editor, *Philosophy in the Soviet Union: A Survey of the Mid-Sixties,* D. Reidel, 1967.
Sowjetsystem und demokratische Gesellschaft: Eine vergleichende Enzyklopaedie, Herder, 1968.
R. Apostol, editor, *Human Values in a Secular World,* Humanities, 1970.
E. Pollack, editor, *Human Rights,* Jay Stewart Publications, Inc., 1971.
Marxism, Communism and Western Society, Volumes III-IV, Herder & Herder, 1972.
F. Adelmann, editor, *Authority,* Nijoff, 1974.
R. B. Harris, editor, *Authority: A Philosophical Analysis,* Alabama University Press, 1976.
T. Armstrong and K. Cinnamon, editors, *Power and Authority in Law Enforcement,* C. C Thomas, 1976.
J. Roland Pennock and John W. Chapman, editors, *Anarchism,* New York University Press, 1978.
Guidelines for Business When Societal Demands Conflict, Council for Better Business Bureaus, 1978.
Moral Philosophy and the Twenty-First Century, University of Notre Dame Press, 1978.

Law and the Ecological Challenge, William S. Hein & Co., 1978.

Also contributor to *Marxism and the Good Society*, edited by J. Burke, L. Crocker, and L. Legters, Cambridge University Press, and *On Reading Philosophy*, Harper. Also contributor to other books and proceedings.

OTHER

Member of editorial board, "Sovietica" series, D. Reidel, 1974—. Contributor of articles, reviews, and translations to several professional journals. Acting managing editor, *Review of Metaphysics*, 1958; consulting editor, *Studies in Soviet Thought*, 1967—, and *New Scholasticism*, 1970—; editorial consultant, *Philosophy Research Archives*, 1974—; advisory editor, *Southern Journal of Philosophy*, 1974—, and *Teaching Philosophy*, 1978—; member of board of editorial consultants, *American Philosophical Quarterly*, 1978-83.

WORK IN PROGRESS: Further study in the "philosophical issues pertinent to business, economics, and public policy."

*   *   *

DELL, Sidney   1918-

PERSONAL: Born December 14, 1918, in London, England. *Education:* Queen's College, Oxford, B.A., 1939, M.A., 1946.

ADDRESSES: Office—Centre on Transnational Corporations, United Nations, New York, N.Y. 10017.

CAREER: Board of Trade, London, England, economist, 1946-47; United Nations, New York, N.Y., economist, 1947—, director of New York office of Conference on Trade and Development, 1965-73, assistant administrator of development program, 1973-76, special advisor to and executive director for Centre on Transnational Corporations, 1977-84. Senior fellow at United Nations Institute for Training and Research, 1985—. *Military service:* Royal Navy, Fleet Air Arm, 1940-45; became lieutenant commander.

WRITINGS:

Problemas de un mercado comun en America Latina, Centro de Estudios Monetarios Latinoamericanos, 1959.
Trade Blocs and Common Markets, Knopf, 1963.
A Latin American Common Market?, Oxford University Press, 1966.
The Inter-American Development Bank, Praeger, 1972.
(With Roger Lawrence) *The Balance of Payments Adjustment Process in Developing Countries*, Pergamon, 1980.
On Being Grandmotherly: The Evolution of IMF Conditionality, Princeton University Press, 1981.

CONTRIBUTOR

The Common Market: Progress and Controversy, Prentice-Hall, 1964.
Werner Baer and Isaac Kerstenetzky, editors, *Inflation and Growth in Latin America*, Irwin, 1964.
Miguel S. Wionczek, editor, *Latin American Economic Integration*, Praeger, 1966.
Stefan H. Robuck and Leo M. Solomon, editors, *International Development, 1965*, Oceana, 1966.
Annual Review of United Nations Affairs, 1965, Oceana, 1966.
International Development, 1966, Oceana, 1967.
John Williamson, editor, *IMF Conditionality*, Institute for International Economics, 1983.

David Worswick and James Trevithick, editors, *Keynes and the Modern World*, Cambridge University Press, 1983.
Michael Zammit Cutajar, editor, *UNCTAD and the South-North Dialogue*, Pergamon, 1985.

OTHER

Contributor of articles to professional and financial journals.

*   *   *

del REY, Lester   1915-
(John Alvarez, Cameron Hall, Marion Henry, Philip James, Wade Kaempfert, Henry Marion, Philip St. John, Erik van Lhin, Kenneth Wright; joint pseudonyms: Edson McCann, Charles Satterfield)

PERSONAL: Name originally Ramon Felipe San Juan Mario Silvo Enrico Alvarez del Rey; born June 2, 1915, in Clydesdale, Minn.; son of Franc (a carpenter and farmer) and Jane (Sidway) del Rey; married Evelyn Harrison; married fourth wife, Judy-Lynn Benjamin (a writer and science fiction editor), March 21, 1971. *Education:* Attended George Washington University, 1931-33. *Politics:* Independent.

ADDRESSES: Home—310 East 46th St., New York, N.Y. 10017. *Agent*—Scott Meredith Literary Agency, 845 Third Ave., New York, N.Y. 10022.

CAREER: Writer and editor. Fantasy editor, Ballantine books, 1975—. Teacher of fantasy fiction at New York University, 1972-73. Author's agent, Scott Meredith Literary Agency, 1947-50. Sheet metal worker, McDonnell Aircraft Corp., 1942-44.

MEMBER: Authors Guild, Authors League of America, Society of Illustrators, Trap Door Spiders Club.

AWARDS, HONORS: Boy's Clubs of America science fiction award, 1953, for *Marooned on Mars;* guest of honor, World Science Fiction Convention, 1967.

WRITINGS:

. . . And Some Were Human, Prime Press, 1948, abridged edition, Ballantine, 1961.
It's Your Atomic Age: An Exploration in Simple Everyday Terms of the Meaning of Atomic Energy to the Average Person, Abelard Press, 1951.
(Editor and author of introduction with Cecile Matschat and Carl Cramer) *The Year after Tomorrow: An Anthology of Science Fiction Stories*, Winston, 1954.
(With Frederik Pohl under pseudonym Edson McCann) *Preferred Risk*, Simon & Schuster, 1955.
Nerves, Ballantine, 1956, revised edition, 1976.
(Under pseudonym Erik van Lhin) *Police Your Planet*, Avalon, 1956, enlarged edition published under name Lester del Rey with Erik van Lhin, Ballantine, 1975.
Robots and Changelings: Eleven Science Fiction Stories, Ballantine, 1957.
Day of the Giants, Avalon, 1959.
(Author of introduction) Hans Santesson, editor, *The Fantastic Universe Omnibus*, Prentice-Hall, 1960.
The Mysterious Earth, Chilton, 1960.
The Mysterious Sea, Chilton, 1961.
The Eleventh Commandment, Regency Books, 1962, revised edition, Ballantine, 1970.
Two Complete Novels: The Sky Is Falling [and] *Badge of Infamy*, Galaxy, 1963, reissued as *The Sky Is Falling* [and] *Badge of Infamy*, Ace, 1973.

The Mysterious Sky, Chilton, 1964.

Mortals and Monsters: Twelve Science Fiction Stories, Ballantine, 1965.

(With Paul Fairman) *The Scheme of Things,* Belmont, 1966.

Pstalemate, Putnam, 1971.

(Author of introduction) Robert Silverberg, editor, *The Day the Sun Stood Still,* Thomas Nelson, 1972.

(Editor) *Best Science Fiction Stories of the Year,* Volumes I-V, Dutton, 1972-76.

Gods and Golems, Five Short Novels of Science Fiction, Ballantine, 1973.

(Editor and author of introduction with Isaac Asimov) *John W. Campbell Anthology,* Doubleday, 1973.

(Editor and author of introduction) *The Best of Frederik Pohl,* Doubleday, 1975.

(Editor and author of introduction) *The Best of C. L. Moore,* Ballantine, 1975.

(Editor and author of introduction) *Fantastic Science Fiction Art,* Ballantine, 1975.

Early del Rey, Doubleday, 1975.

(Editor and author of introduction) *The Best of John W. Campbell,* Doubleday, 1976.

(Author of introduction) *The Best of Robert Bloch,* Ballantine, 1977.

(Author of introduction) *The Fantastic Art of Boris Vallejo,* Ballantine, 1978.

The Best of Lester del Rey, Ballantine, 1978.

(With Raymond F. Jones) *Weeping May Tarry,* Pinnacle Books, 1978.

(Editor) *The Best of Hal Clement,* Ballantine, 1979.

The World of Science Fiction: 1926-1976, Garland, 1980.

JUVENILES

A Pirate Flag for Monterey, Winston, 1952.

Marooned on Mars, Winston, 1952.

(Under pseudonym Philip St. John) *Rocket Jockey,* Winston, 1952 (published in England as *Rocket Pilot,* Hutchinson, 1955).

Attack from Atlantis, Winston, 1953.

(Under pseudonym Erik van Lhin) *Battle on Mercury,* Winston, 1953.

(Under pseudonym Kenneth Wright) *The Mysterious Planet,* Winston, 1953.

Step to the Stars, Winston, 1954.

(Under pseudonym Philip St. John) *Rockets to Nowhere,* Winston, 1954.

Mission to the Moon, Winston, 1956.

Rockets through Space: The Story of Man's Preparations to Explore the Universe, Winston, 1957, revised edition, 1960.

The Cave of Spears, Knopf, 1957.

Space Flight, Golden Press, 1959.

Moon of Mutiny, Holt, 1961.

Rocks and What They Tell Us, Whitman, 1961.

Outpost of Jupiter, Holt, 1963.

(With Fairman) *Rocket from Infinity,* Holt, 1966.

(With Fairman) *The Infinite Worlds of Maybe,* Holt, 1966.

OTHER

Also author of plot outlines for novels ghostwritten by Paul Fairman and published under name Lester del Rey, including *Siege Perilous,* Lancer, 1966, published as *The Man without a Planet,* Lancer, 1970, *Runaway Robot* (juvenile), Westminster, 1965, *Tunnel through Time* (juvenile), Westminster, 1966, and *Prisoners of Space* (juvenile), Westminster, 1966.

Contributor of short fiction, sometimes under pseudonyms John Alvarez, Marion Henry, Philip James, Wade Kaempfert, and Henry Marion, to periodicals, including *Galaxy, Analog, Amazing Stories, Fantastic Universe,* and *Fantasy and Science Fiction.* Editor of science fiction magazines, 1952-74, including *Science Fiction Adventures,* under pseudonym Philip St. John, 1952-53, *Fantasy Fiction,* 1953 (one issue appeared under pseudonym Cameron Hall), *Rocket Stories,* under pseudonym Wade Kaempfert, 1953, and *Worlds of Fantasy,* 1968-70; *Galaxy* and *If* magazines, managing editor, 1968-69, feature editor, 1969-74.

SIDELIGHTS: ''If there is a finer short story craftsman in all of [science fiction than Lester del Rey], show him to me,'' challenges Algis Budrys in the *Magazine of Fantasy and Science Fiction.* ''Don't show me the hosts of more widely admired ones, or the more popular ones, or the more ideologically accepted ones of the moment. Never mind the ones who write more elegant words. Just show me the one who knows more about communicating with the reader, and the handful of those who have endured longer than he.'' As one of the pioneer writers and editors of science fiction, Lester del Rey can claim a ''unique place in the colorful history'' of the genre, writes Greta Eisner in *Dictionary of Literary Biography.* According to Eisner, del Rey has ''been instrumental in guiding the fortunes of science fiction from the vagaries of the early pulp-magazine market to the respectability of the prestigious del Rey imprint [Ballantine Books's science fiction and fantasy imprint].

One of del Rey's most common themes is that of the relationship between man and his creations. In ''Helen O'Loy,'' a variation on the Pygmalion story, a man creates a beautiful female robot and marries her. As he ages, she also does so artificially, to preserve the illusion of her humanity. Although she could have immortality, when her creator dies, she burns out all her circuits. Though labelling this resolution somewhat sentimental, Eisner states that it ''in no way detracts from the fundamental question the story raises. . . . What can we hope for by uniting ourselves with the appearance of things as we would have them, instead of committing ourselves to the mysterious, ever-changing, and palpable reality which often eludes us?''

She continues: ''Del Rey is preoccupied with the precarious relationship between man and his creations. Often in these tales survival hinges on the sensitivity, vision, and common sense with which man, moral and mutable, handles the inorganic creatures produced by his fertile brain. The struggle between man as maker-creator and man as destroyer is a struggle for the survival of man himself—and for his humanity. This theme, effectively tapping into a primary anxiety of our age, becomes the axis of del Rey's fiction.'' Eisner criticizes some of del Rey's work—particularly his juvenile novels—as suffering from thin characterization. However, Budrys disagrees, writing, ''When [del Rey] thinks of a character, he thinks that person through to the last electron.''

Eisner concludes: ''At his best, del Rey is a sensitive and articulate spokesman for humanistic values in a world no longer able to discern properly what constitutes the uniquely human and thus no longer willing to cherish and preserve it. Del Rey balances cynicism and optimism: man, he seems to say, carries within him the seeds of his own destruction and the means of his own salvation. In the balance is all of civilization, and del Rey skillfully charts for his readers some of the crucial distance between the struggle and the promise.''

Del Rey told *CA:* "I do believe that science fiction or fantasy must entertain and must have beginning, middle and end; that stories are read for the plot and re-read for the characterization—if there is any; and that science, when used, should be accurate, and consistency and logic be observed. My knowledge of science is not formal, but is sufficient to discuss (and edit) the work of qualified scientists. I've written books on nuclear physics, rocketry, geology, oceanography, and astronomy. My best knowledge is in physics, mathematics, and electronics.

"So far as I can determine, my writing was not strongly influenced by any single science fiction writer. My reading background was always catholic, from Shakespeare (long before I ever saw a play or found that the works were supposed to be Great Literature) and Gibbon to Burroughs and Merritt. If anything influenced me, probably the Bible (as literature—at least in part) and the whole range of better pulp fiction made the strongest impression on me.

"I do *not* believe in ESP (or psi), flying saucers, Bermuda triangles, the need for relevance in science fiction (beyond the universals that exist beyond current fads), or the insignificance of man."

AVOCATIONAL INTERESTS: Cabinet making, baseball, football, hockey, cooking, typewriters, hi-fi equipment, and music (especially classical, but "even some oriental and real hillbilly-western music, and real jazz").

BIOGRAPHICAL/CRITICAL SOURCES:

BOOKS

Dictionary of Literary Biography, Volume VIII: *Twentieth-Century American Science Fiction Writers,* Gale, 1981.
Moskowitz, Sam, *Seekers of Tomorrow,* Hyperion Press, 1974.

PERIODICALS

Choice, June, 1980.
Magazine of Fantasy and Science Fiction, March, 1979.
Times (London), April 14, 1983.
Times Literary Supplement, February 2, 1973.
Washington Post Book World, December 23, 1979.

*   *   *

DEMIJOHN, Thom
See DISCH, Thomas M(ichael)

*   *   *

DENNIS, Charles   1946-

PERSONAL: Born December 16, 1946, in Toronto, Ontario, Canada; came to the United States in 1972; son of Samuel (a manufacturer) and Sade (Iscove) Dennis; married Catherine Grace Brendan Hickey (a designer), September 20, 1975. *Education:* University of Toronto, B.A., 1968.

ADDRESSES: Home—Los Angeles, Calif. *Agent*—Richard Heckenkamp, Paul Brandon & Associates, 9046 Sunset Blvd., Los Angeles, Calif. 90069.

CAREER: Toronto Telegram, Toronto, Ontario, theater and film critic, 1964-67; Colonnade Theatre, Toronto, producer and performer in his own play "Everyone Except Mr. Fontana," 1968; novelist, playwright, and screenwriter, 1969—; Rangeloff-Century, Inc. (production company), Los Angeles, Calif., president, 1975—.

MEMBER: Authors Guild, Writers Guild of America West.

WRITINGS:

Stoned Cold Soldier (novel), Bachman & Turner, 1973.
The Next-to-Last Train Ride (novel; also see below), Macmillan (England), 1974, St. Martin's, 1975.
This War Is Closed Until Spring (first novel of "The Broken Sabre Quartet"), Futura Publishing, 1975.
Somebody Just Grabbed Annie! (political thriller), St. Martin's, 1976.
A Divine Case of Murder, Macmillan (Canada), 1977.
The Periwinkle Assault (second novel of "The Broken Sabre Quartet"), Macmillan (Canada), 1978.
Bonfire (based on the radio play "To an Early Grave"), Dell, 1979.
The Deal Makers (novel), Dell, 1981.

PLAYS

"Everyone Except Mr. Fontana" (three one-act comedies), first produced in Toronto, Ontario, at Colonnade Theatre, November 12, 1968.
"Bonfire" (three-act), first broadcast on BBC-Radio, June 18, 1973.
"The Alchemist of Cecil Street" (three-act comedy), first broadcast on CBC-TV, October, 1976.

OTHER

(With Ronny Graham and Terence Marsh) "Finders Keepers" (screenplay; based on Dennis's novel *The Next-to-Last Train Ride*), Warner Brothers, 1984.

Also author of screenplay "What's a Nice Country Like You Doing in a Crisis Like This?" Creator of "Marked Personal" series for Thames Television, 1973.

WORK IN PROGRESS: Nikki Ever After, a novella; *Kashmar,* a novel.

SIDELIGHTS: "Finders Keepers," a film adapted by Charles Dennis, Ronny Graham, and Terence Marsh from Dennis's novel *The Next-to-Last Train Ride,* is set on a train headed from Oakland, California, to New York City. A comedy, its cast includes a foul-mouthed actress and a former roller derby manager, and its plot revolves around a stolen $5 million hidden in a casket that supposedly carries the remains of a Vietnam veteran.

According to Vincent Canby in the *New York Times,* the movie is "not especially graceful, but it grows increasingly funny" as it approaches its showdown in Nebraska. Canby comments that, "though the pacing of the film is uneven—its highpoints stand out like clumps of trees in the flat Nebraska landscape, 'Finders Keepers' is unexpectedly satisfying."

BIOGRAPHICAL/CRITICAL SOURCES:

PERIODICALS

Los Angeles Times, May 18, 1984.
New York Times, May 18, 1984.
Times Literary Supplement, October 4, 1974, January 9, 1976.†

*   *   *

DENTLER, Robert A(rnold)   1928-

PERSONAL: Born November 26, 1928, in Chicago, Ill.; son of Arnold E. and Jennie (Munsen) Dentler; married Helen Hosmer, 1950; children: Deborah, Eric A., Robin H. *Edu-*

cation: Northwestern University, B.S., 1949, M.A., 1950; American University, M.A., 1954; University of Chicago, Ph.D., 1960. *Religion:* Unitarian Universalist.

ADDRESSES: Home—11 Childs Rd., Lexington, Mass. 02173. *Office*—Department of Sociology, University of Massachusetts, Harbor Campus, Boston, Mass. 02125.

CAREER: Dickinson College, Carlisle, Pa., member of faculty, 1954-57; Unviersity of Chicago, Chicago, Ill, university fellow, 1957-59; University of Kansas, Lawrence, researcher, 1959-61; Dartmouth College, Hanover, N.H., assistant professor, 1961-62; Columbia University, Teachers College, New York, N.Y., associate professor, 1962-65, professor, 1966-72; Boston University, Boston, Mass., dean of education and university professor, 1972-79; Abt Associates, Cambridge, Mass., education area manager and senior sociologist, 1979-83; University of Massachusetts, Harbor Campus, Boston, professor of sociology, 1983—. Director of Center for Urban Education, 1966-72.

WRITINGS:

The Young Volunteers, National Opinion Research Center, 1959.
(Co-author) *The Politics of Urban Renewal,* Free Press of Glencoe, 1962.
(Co-author) *Hostage America,* Beacon Press, 1963.
(Co-author) *Politics and Social Life,* Houghton, 1963.
Major American Social Problems, Rand McNally, 1967, 2nd edition published as *Major Social Problems,* 1972.
(With Mary Ellen Warshauer) *Big City Dropouts and Illiterates,* Praeger, 1967.
(Co-author) *The Urban R's,* Praeger, 1967.
(Co-editor) *Readings in Educational Psychology,* Harper, 1976.
Urban Problems, Rand McNally, 1977.
(With Marvin B. Scott) *Schools on Trial,* Abt Books, 1981.
(Co-author) *University on Trial,* Abt Books, 1983.

Contributor of seventy articles to social and behavioral science journals.

WORK IN PROGRESS: A book on the baby boom generation.

BIOGRAPHICAL/CRITICAL SOURCES:

PERIODICALS

New York Times Book Review, September 6, 1981.

*   *   *

DERMAN, Sarah Audrey   1915-

PERSONAL: Born August 28, 1915, in Rock Island, Ill.; daughter of Jacob and Bessie (Meyer) Derman. *Education:* Attended Milwaukee State Teachers College (now University of Wisconsin—Milwaukee), 1930-32, and Marquette University; University of Wisconsin—Milwaukee, B.S.Ed.; additional study at Wisconsin Conservatory of Music.

ADDRESSES: Home—1725 North Prospect Ave., Apt. 611, Milwaukee, Wis. 53202.

CAREER: Teacher of primary grades at Victory School, Town of Lake, Milwaukee, Wis., 1936-50, West Allis, Wis., 1950-51, Oak Creek, Wis., 1951-54, East Granville, Wis., 1954-58, and South Milwaukee, Wis., 1958-70; currently affiliated with Indian Community School, Milwaukee.

MEMBER: International Platform Association, Association of Reading Clinicians, National Teachers Association, Wisconsin

Teachers Association, Wisconsin Pen Women, South Milwaukee Teachers Association, Allied Authors (Milwaukee), Theta Sigma Phi.

WRITINGS:

JUVENILES

The Snowman Who Wanted to Stay, illustrations by Dorcas, Whitman Publishing, 1948.
Plush, illustrations by William Gschwind, Wilcox & Follett, 1952.
Pretty Bird, illustrations by Dave Gillis, Benefic Press, 1957.
Pony Ring, illustrations by Gillis, Benefic Press, 1957.
Monkey Island, illustrations by Jack Boyd, Benefic Press, 1957.
Big Top, illustrations by Boyd, Benefic Press, 1958.
Surprise Egg, illustrations by Boyd, Benefic Press, 1958.
Poker Dog, illustrations by Boyd, Benefic Press, 1958.
A Party in the Pantry, Republic, 1963.

OTHER

Exquisitely Mine (poetry), Mr. Print, 1985.

Contributor of poetry to *Milwaukee Star Times, Milwaukee Journal,* and to magazines.

WORK IN PROGRESS: Textbooks for Beckley-Cardy; children's poetry.

MEDIA ADAPTATIONS: One of Sarah Audrey Derman's poems for children, ''Said the Snail to the Whale,'' was set to music and sung during a performance at the Milwaukee Public Museum.

*   *   *

Di CICCO, Pier Giorgio   1949-

PERSONAL: Born July 5, 1949, in Arezzo, Italy; son of Jiuseppe and Primetta (Liberatore) Di Cicco. *Education:* University of Toronto, B.A., 1972, B.Ed., 1976. *Religion:* Roman Catholic.

ADDRESSES: Home—P.O. Box 839, Station P, Toronto, Ontario, Canada M5S 2Z1.

CAREER: Bartender in Toronto, Ontario, 1972-75; *Books in Canada,* Toronto, associate editor, 1976-79; free-lance writer, 1979—. Gives readings in the United States and Canada, including television and radio broadcasts. Consultant to Ontario Arts Council.

MEMBER: League of Canadian Poets.

AWARDS, HONORS: Canada Council awards for poetry, 1974, 1976, and 1980; Italo-Canadian Literary Award from Carleton University, 1979.

WRITINGS:

POETRY

We Are the Light Turning, Missing Link Press, 1975, revised edition, Thunder City Press, 1976.
The Virgin-Maker, McClelland & Stewart, 1976.
The Sad Facts, Fiddlehead Books, 1977.
The Circular Dark, Borealis Press, 1977.
Dancing in the House of Cards, Three Trees Press, 1978.
A Burning Patience, Borealis Press, 1978.
(Editor) *Roman Candles: An Anthology of Seventeen Italo-Canadian Poets,* Hounslow Press, 1978.

Dolce-Amaro, Papavero Press, 1979.
The Tough Romance, McClelland & Stewart, 1979.
Reasons for Humanness, Intermedia Press, 1980.
Women We Never See Again, Borealis Press, 1984.
Post-Sixties Nocturne, Fiddlehead Books, 1985.

Also author of *Flying Deeper into the Century,* 1981. Work represented in anthologies, including *Storm Warning II,* edited by Al Purdy, McClelland & Stewart, *This Is My Best,* Coach House Press, *Whale Sound,* J. J. Douglas, *Italo-Canadian Voices,* Mosaic Press, *Canadian Poetry Now,* House of Anansi Press, *The Oxford Book of Canadian Verse,* edited by Margaret Atwood, *The Oxford Companion to Canadian Literature,* and *The New Canadian Poets,* McClelland & Stewart.

OTHER

Contributor of more than one hundred fifty poems to magazines, including *Tamarack Review, Critical Quarterly, Kayak, Miss Chatelaine,* and *Denver Quarterly.* Contributing editor, *Argomenti Canadesi* and *Italia-America;* past editor, *Waves, Poetry View, Poetry Toronto, Descant,* and *Grad Poet.*

*   *   *

Di FRANCO, Fiorenza   1932-

PERSONAL: Born June 19, 1932, in Budapest, Hungary; daughter of Oscarre and Olga (Czako) Di Franco. *Education:* Attended Universita di Roma, 1951-53; Western Reserve University (now Case Western Reserve University), M.A., 1965, Ph.D., 1969.

ADDRESSES: Home—Via Angelo Olivieri 91, Ostia (Roma), Italy. *Office*—Department of Humanities, John Cabot International College, Via Massaua, 7, Rome, Italy.

CAREER: Notre Dame College, Cleveland, Ohio, instructor in French and Latin, 1965-66; Kent State University, Kent, Ohio, instructor in French, 1966-67; Case Western Reserve University, Cleveland, assistant professor of French and Italian, 1968-72; University of Missouri—St. Louis, assistant professor of French and Italian, 1972-74; John Cabot International College, Rome, Italy, professor of French, Italian, and comparative literature, 1976—. Visiting professor at Oberlin College, 1969-72.

MEMBER: Modern Language Association of America.

AWARDS, HONORS: Wright-Plaisance fellowship to France, 1967-68; grant from Italian Government, for study, 1974-77.

WRITINGS:

Le Theatre de Salacrou, Gallimard, 1970.
(Contributor) Roger Johnson, editor, *Moliere and the Commonwealth of Letters,* University of Southern Mississippi Press, 1973.
Il teatro di Eduardo, Laterza, 1975.
Eduardo De Filippo, Gremese, 1978, 2nd edition, 1980.
Eduardo de scugnizzo a senatore, Laterza, 1982.
Le commedie di Eduardo, Laterza, 1984, 2nd edition, 1985.

WORK IN PROGRESS: Peppino De Filippo, for Gremese; *Pier Paolo Pasolini.*

*   *   *

DILLENBERGER, John   1918-

PERSONAL: Born July 11, 1918, in St. Louis, Mo.; son of

Charles and Bertha (Hoffman) Dillenberger; children: Eric, Paul. *Education:* Elmhurst College, B.A., 1940; Union Theological Seminary, B.D., 1943; Columbia University, Ph.D., 1948.

ADDRESSES: Home—1536 LeRoy Ave., Berkeley, Calif. 94708.

CAREER: Ordained minister, United Church of Christ, 1943; Union Theological Seminary, New York City, tutor, 1947-48; Princeton University, Princeton, N.J., instructor, 1948-49; Columbia University, New York City, 1949-54, began as assistant professor, became associate professor; Harvard University, Divinity School, Cambridge, Mass., associate professor, 1954-57, Parkman Professor of Theology, 1957-58; Drew University, Madison, N.J., professor, 1958-62; San Francisco Theological Seminary, San Francisco, Calif., professor and dean of graduate studies, 1962-64; Graduate Theological Union, Berkeley, Calif., professor, dean, and president, 1964-78; Hartford Seminary, Hartford, Conn., professor and president, 1978-83; Graduate Theological Union, professor emeritus, 1983—.

MEMBER: Society for Values in Higher Education.

AWARDS, HONORS: D.D., University of Vermont, 1957, and Elmhurst College, 1959; S.T.D., Church Divinity School of the Pacific, 1965; L.H.D., University of San Francisco, 1966.

WRITINGS:

God Hidden and Revealed, Muhlenberg, 1953.
(With Claude Welch) *Protestant Christianity: Interpreted through Its Development,* Scribner, 1954.
Protestant Thought and Natural Science, Doubleday, 1960, reprinted, Greenwood Press, 1977.
(Editor) *Martin Luther: Selections from His Writings,* Doubleday-Anchor, 1961.
(Contributor) Anderson, editor, *The Old Testament and Christian Faith,* Harper, 1963.
(Contributor) Cobb and Robinson, editors, *The New Hermeneutic,* Harper, 1964.
(Contributor) Jerry R. Tompkins, editor, *D-Days at Dayton,* Louisiana State University Press, 1965.
Contours of Faith, Abingdon, 1969.
(Editor) *John Calvin: Selections from His Writings,* Doubleday-Anchor, 1971.
(Contributor) *Humanities, Religion, and the Arts Tomorrow,* Holt, 1972.
Benjamin West: The Context of His Life's Work, Trinity University Press, 1977.
Perceptions of the Spirit in Twentieth-Century American Art, [Indianapolis], 1977.
The Visual Arts and Christianity in America, Scholars Press, 1984.

WORK IN PROGRESS: A book on the visual arts and the church.

*   *   *

DILLON, Conley Hall   1906-

PERSONAL: Born October 19, 1906, in Proctorville, Ohio; son of Elmer W. and Ottie Olive (Hall) Dillon; married Virginia Bull, December 29, 1934; children: Carol Gay, Conley Hall, Jr. *Education:* West Virginia State Normal School (now Marshall University), A.B., 1928; Duke University, A.M.,

1933, Ph.D., 1936. *Politics:* Democrat. *Religion:* United Church of Christ.

ADDRESSES: Home—1754 Overlook Dr., Silver Spring, Md. 20903. *Office*—Department of Government and Politics, University of Maryland, College Park, Md. 20740.

CAREER: Lorado Grade School, Lorado, W.Va., principal, 1928-29; Chapmanville High School, Chapmanville, W.Va., assistant principal, athletic coach, and social science teacher, 1929-32; West Virginia State Normal School (now Marshall University), Huntington, instructor, 1934-35, assistant professor, 1935-36, associate professor, 1937-41, professor of political science, 1941-60, chairman of department, 1937-41, 1946-50, 1953-60; University of Maryland, College Park, professor of government and politics, 1960-77, professor emeritus, 1977—. State price executive, U.S. Office of Price Administration, 1943-46; chief of service trades branch, Office of Price Stabilization, 1951-53. Chairman of Fiscal Stress and Public Management Project, Inc., 1979. Member of forum faculty, U.S. Office of Education, 1936-37; member of American Committee in Geneva, 1937, and of Prince Georges County Study Commission, 1966-68. Member of board of directors of Marshall Foundation. Consultant to Huntington Production Pool, 1955-79, governor of West Virginia, 1961-68, Appalachian Regional Commission, 1968-69, Kramer Associates, D. A. Lewis Associates, and Logistics Management Institute.

MEMBER: American Society for Public Administration (president of Maryland chapter, 1971-72; member of national council, 1973-76), American Association of University Professors, National Education Association, American Political Science Association, American Society of International Law, Southern Political Science Association, Alpha Sigma Phi, Pi Sigma Alpha, Phi Kappa Phi.

AWARDS, HONORS: Carnegie Endowment grant, 1937, Distingushed Service Award, Maryland Chapter, American Society for Public Administration, 1973.

WRITINGS:

(Co-author) *Government of West Virginia,* Jarrett, 1937.
International Labor Conventions: Their Interpretation and Revision, University of North Carolina Press, 1942.
Government—Labor in Action: Labor Meets Government, National Capitol Publishers, 1951.
(With Carl Leiden and Paul D. Stewart) *Introduction to Political Science,* Van Nostrand, 1958.
The Area Redevelopment Administration: New Patterns in Developmental Administration, Bureau of Governmental Research, University of Maryland, 1964.
(Editor) *Addresses and State Papers of J. Millard Tawes, Governor of Maryland,* two volumes, State of Maryland, 1967.
(Contributor) David R. Deener, editor, *De Lege Pactorum: Essays in Honor of Robert Renbert Wilson,* Duke University Press, 1970.

Also author of *Comparative Administration in the Regional Planning Process: London and Richmond,* 1976. Member of editorial board, *Southern Review of Public Administration.*

BIOGRAPHICAL/CRITICAL SOURCES:

BOOKS

Strouse, James C., Richard P. Claude, and John D. Huss, editors, *Making Government Work: Essays in Honor of Conley H. Dillon,* preface by Nesta M. Gallas, University Press of America, 1981.

di MICHELE, Mary 1949-

PERSONAL: Surname is pronounced Dee-mee-ka-*leh*; born August 6, 1949, in Lanciano, Italy; daughter of Vincent (an electrician) and Concetta (Andreacola) di Michele. *Education:* University of Toronto, B.A. (with honors), 1972; University of Windsor, M.A., 1974.

ADDRESSES: Home—103 Regina Ave., Toronto, Ontario, Canada M6A 1R5.

CAREER: Writer. Worked as clerk at Eaton's department store, chef at a restaurant in London, Ontario, and sorter with the Canadian Post Office in Scarborough, Ontario, 1972-79; Student Christian Movement Book Room, Toronto, Ontario, part-time poetry buyer, 1980—; free-lance editor; teacher. Writer-in-residence, University of Toronto, 1985-86. Gives poetry readings.

MEMBER: League of Canadian poets.

AWARDS, HONORS: Grants from Canada Council, 1979, and Ontario Arts Council, 1979-80; first prize from Canadian Broadcasting Corp. poetry competition, 1980, for poem "Mimosa"; Silver Medal, DuMaurier Award for Poetry, 1982; Air Canada Writing Award, 1983.

WRITINGS:

POETRY

Tree of August, Three Tree, 1978.
Bread and Chocolate (bound with *Marrying into the Family* by Bronwen Wallace), Oberon Press, 1980.
Mimosa and Other Poems, Mosaic, 1981.
Necessary Sugar, Oberon Press, 1983.
Anything Is Possible, Mosaic, 1984.

CONTRIBUTOR TO ANTHOLOGIES

Pier Giorgio Di Cicco, editor, *Roman Candles: An Anthology of Seventeen Italo-Candian Poets,* Hounslow Press, 1978.
M. Atwood, editor, *Oxford Book of Canadian Verse,* Oxford University Press, 1982.
Bennett and Brown, editors, *An Anthology of Canadian Literature in English,* Volume II, Oxford University Press, 1983.
Ken Norris, editor, *Canadian Poetry Now: Poets of the '80s,* Anansi, 1984.
Dennis Lee, *New Canadian Poets, 1970-85,* McClelland & Stewart, 1985.

Contributor to other anthologies, including *A Government Job at Last!,* edited by Tom Wayman, Macleod Books, and *Poems for Sale in the Street,* edited by Tom Clement and Ted Plantos, Steel Rail Publishing.

OTHER

Contributor to literary magazines, including *Toronto Life, Northern Light, Malahat Review, Dalhousie Review,* and *Clarion.*

WORK IN PROGRESS: Many Small Deaths, fiction; *Moon Sharks,* poetry.

SIDELIGHTS: Mary di Michele told *CA:* "I am a feminist. I am more interested in poems than in poetry, more interested in people than in poems. My primary ambition is to try to describe and illuminate life as experienced by women, and through writing it to participate fully in human cultural history."

DISCH, Thomas M(ichael) 1940-
(Leonie Hargrave; Thom Demijohn and Cassandra Knye, joint pseudonyms)

PERSONAL: Born February 2, 1940, in Des Moines, Iowa; son of Felix Henry and Helen (Gilbertson) Disch. *Education:* Attended New York University, 1959-62.

ADDRESSES: Agent—Barney Karpfinger, 18 East 48th St., New York, N.Y. 10017.

CAREER: Free-lance writer, 1964—. Lecturer at universities.

MEMBER: P.E.N., Writers Guild East, National Book Critics Circle.

AWARDS, HONORS: O. Henry Prize, 1975, for story "Getting into Death," and 1979, for story "Xmas"; John W. Campbell Memorial Award, 1980, for *On Wings of Song;* British Science Fiction Award, 1981, for story "The Brave Little Toaster."

WRITINGS:

NOVELS

The Genocides, Berkley Publishing, 1965.
Mankind under the Leash (also see below), Ace Books, 1966 (published in England as *The Puppies of Terra,* Panther Books, 1978).
(With John Sladek under joint pseudonym Cassandra Knye) *The House That Fear Built,* Paperback Library, 1966.
Echo Round His Bones, Berkley Publishing, 1967.
(With Sladek under joint pseudonym Thom Demijohn) *Black Alice,* Doubleday, 1968.
Camp Concentration, Hart-Davis, 1968, Doubleday, 1969.
The Prisoner, Ace Books, 1969.
334, MacGibbon & Kee, 1972, Avon, 1974.
(Under pseudonym Leonie Hargrave) *Clara Reeve,* Knopf, 1975.
On Wings of Song, St. Martin's, 1979.
Triplicity (omnibus volume), Doubleday, 1980.
(With Charles Naylor) *Neighboring Lives,* Scribner, 1981.
The Businessman: A Tale of Terror, Harper, 1984.
Amnesia (computer-interactive novel), Electronic Arts, 1985.

STORY COLLECTIONS

One Hundred and Two H-Bombs and Other Science Fiction Stories (also see below), Compact Books, 1966, revised edition published as *One Hundred and Two H-Bombs,* Berkley Publishing, 1969 (published in England as *White Fang Goes Dingo and Other Funny S. F. Stories,* Arrow Books, 1971).
Under Compulsion, Hart-Davis, 1968, published as *Fun with Your New Head,* Doubleday, 1969.
Getting into Death: The Best Short Stories of Thomas M. Disch, Hart-Davis, 1973, revised edition, Knopf, 1976.
The Early Science Fiction Stories of Thomas M. Disch (contains *Mankind under the Leash* and *One Hundred and Two H-Bombs and Other Science Fiction Stories*), Gregg, 1977.
Fundamental Disch, Bantam, 1980.
The Man Who Had No Idea, Bantam, 1982.

POETRY

(With Marilyn Hacker and Charles Platt) *Highway Sandwiches,* privately printed, 1970.
The Right Way to Figure Plumbing, Basilisk Press, 1972.
ABCDEFG HIJKLM NPOQRST UVWXYZ, Anvil Press Poetry, 1981.

Orders of the Retina, Toothpaste Press, 1982.
Burn This, Hutchinson, 1982.
Here I Am, There You Are, Where Were We, Hutchinson, 1984.

EDITOR

(Ghost editor with Robert Arthur) *Alfred Hitchcock Presents: Stories That Scared Even Me,* Random House, 1967.
The Ruins of Earth: An Anthology of Stories of the Immediate Future, Putnam, 1971.
Bad Moon Rising: An Anthology of Political Foreboding, Harper, 1975.
The New Improved Sun: An Anthology of Utopian Science Fiction, Harper, 1975.
(With Naylor) *New Constellations: An Anthology of Tomorrow's Mythologies,* Harper, 1976.
(With Naylor) *Strangeness: A Collection of Curious Tales,* Scribner, 1977.
Richard Lupoff, *Stroka Prospekt,* Toothpaste Press, 1982.

OTHER

(Librettist) "The Fall of the House of Usher" (opera), first produced in New York, N.Y., by the Bel Canto Opera Company, 1979.
(Librettist) "Frankenstein" (opera), first produced in Greenvale, N.Y., at the C. W. Post Center of Long Island University, 1982.
Ringtime (short story), Toothpaste Press, 1983.
Torturing Mr. Amberwell (short story), Cheap Street, 1985.
The Brave Little Toaster (juvenile), Doubleday, 1986.

Work appears in anthologies. Contributor to *Transatlantic Review, Playboy, Harper's,* and other periodicals. Regular reviewer for *Times Literary Supplement* and *Washington Post Book World.*

SIDELIGHTS: An author of science fiction, poetry, historical novels, opera librettos, and computer-interactive fiction, Thomas M. Disch has been cited as "one of the most remarkably multi-talented writers around" by a reviewer for the *Washington Post Book World.* Noting the diversity of Disch's work, Charles Platt writes in *Dream Makers: The Uncommon People Who Write Science Fiction* that "he has traveled widely, through almost every genre and technique. . . . And in each field [Disch] has made himself at home, never ill-at-ease or out-of-place, writing with the same implacable control and elegant manners."

Disch began his career by writing science fiction, where his unique vision—"dark, disturbing, and skeptical," as Erich S. Rupprecht calls it in the *Dictionary of Literary Biography*—made his work stand out from the rest of the genre. His first novel, *The Genocides,* concerns an alien invasion of Earth. But it differs from other such invasion novels in that the aliens win, and all human beings are exterminated. The invasion is carried out by sowing the Earth with the seeds of gigantic plants that disrupt their surroundings as they grow, eventually crowding out all other forms of life. When a few human survivors try to fight back, they are easily destroyed by the mechanical robots who tend the plants. The aliens themselves are never seen, make no attempt to contact the humans, and seem unaware of or indifferent to the destruction they have caused. When they kill the last of the humans, it is similar to the killing of insects in a farm field and just as impersonal. "The novel succeeds on several counts," Rupprecht states. "One source of its power is the utter absurdity of the humans' situation.

Like characters in a Kafka novel, they are absolutely bewildered by events outside their control. . . . The novel is also powerful in the way that it forces the reader to alter his perspective, to reexamine what it means to be human.'' Speaking to Platt, Disch explains that he found the conventional alien invasion story, in which the humans overcome great odds to win, unsatisfying. ''Let's be honest,'' Disch states, ''the real interest in this kind of story is to see some devastating cataclysm *wipe mankind out*. There's a grandeur in that idea that all the other people threw away and trivialized. My point was simply to write a book where you don't spoil that beauty and pleasure at the end.''

Camp Concentration, another early Disch novel and one of his best known, is equally uncompromising in its approach. It is set at a secret prison camp run by the U.S. Army where selected prisoners are being treated with a new drug that increases their intelligence. Unfortunately, this drug also causes the prisoners' early deaths. The novel is in the form of a diary kept by one of the prisoners. The diary's style grows more complex as the narrative develops, reflecting the prisoner's increasing intelligence. According to Robert Scholes and Eric S. Rabkin in *Science Fiction: History, Science, Vision,* the novel ''combines considerable technical resources in the management of the narrative . . . with a probing inquiry into human values.'' Rupprecht draws a parallel between *Camp Concentration* and *The Genocides.* In both novels, he argues, the characters must survive inescapable situations. Disch's continuing theme, Rupprecht summarizes, is ''charting his characters' attempts to keep themselves intact in a world which grows increasingly hostile, irrational, inhuman.''

This theme is also found in *334,* a novel set in a New York City housing project of the future. Divided into six loosely-related sections, the novel presents the daily lives of residents of the building, which is located at 334 East Eleventh Street. The characters live in boredom and poverty; their city is run-down and dirty. The world of the novel, Scholes and Rabkin believe, ''is not radically different from ours in many respects but is deeply troubling for reasons that apply to the present New York as well. Above all, the aimlessness and purposelessness of the lives chronicled is affecting.'' In his analysis of the book, Rupprecht also notes the similarity between the novel's setting and the world of the present. He finds *334* to be ''a slightly distorted mirror image of contemporary life.'' Although the *Washington Post Book World* reviewer judges the setting to be ''an interesting, plausible and unpleasant near-future world where urban life is even more constricted than now,'' he nonetheless believes that ''survival and aspiration remain possible.'' Rupprecht praises *334* as Disch's ''most brilliant and disturbing work. . . . One can think of few writers—of science fiction or other genres—who could convey a similar sense of emptiness, of yearning, of ruin with this power and grace. . . . Like all great writers, Disch forces his readers to see the reality of their lives in a way that is fresh, startling, disturbing, and moving.'' Speaking of *Camp Concentration* and *334,* David Lehman of the *Times Literary Supplement* states that these two novels ''seem to transcend their genre without betraying it; they manage to break down the barriers separating science fiction from 'literature,' and they do so by shrewdly manipulating the conventions of the former.''

On Wings of Song, winner of the John W. Campbell Memorial Award, has also been praised for its ability to transcend its science fiction trappings to work as literature. As Joanna Russ comments in the *Magazine of Fantasy and Science Fiction,*

''Science-fiction writers and readers often talk about uniting science fiction with the mainstream; Disch has done it [in *On Wings of Song*], by pushing the possibilities of science fiction to the limit.'' The novel depicts a future America where the coastal cities are decadent and decrepit, and the rest of the country is run by smothering corporate bureaucracies. In this society it is possible to ''fly'' in one's spirit body by singing with the proper amount of honest feeling. When Daniel Weinrab and his wife Boadicea attempt to fly, Boadicea is successful, leaving her physical body behind in a comatose state, but Daniel fails. The rest of the novel traces his efforts to rejoin his wife.

There is a strong satirical element in *On Wings of Song* that moves Russ to call it ''an ominous attack on the morals and good customs of Middle America'' and Hermione Lee of the *Observer* to compare it with Nathanael West's *A Cool Million.* But John Calvin Batchelor of the *Village Voice* believes that with *On Wings of Song* ''Disch achieves a blend of the conflicting mix in his oeuvre—the rebellion, silliness, despair, survival, aesthetics—to produce a novel that may be read both as a condemnation of Amerika and as an affirmation of America, of its innovative citizenry.''

In *Neighboring Lives,* Disch turns from science fiction to the historical novel, teaming with Charles Naylor to write a fictional account of nineteenth-century Chelsea, a section of London where many famous artists and writers lived at the time. It is, Elaine Kendall writes in the *Los Angeles Times,* ''a sort of group biography.'' Based on letters and journals of the principal characters, *Neighboring Lives* interweaves the life histories of such people as Thomas Carlyle, John Stuart Mill, Gabriel Rossetti, John Ruskin, Lewis Carroll, and Frederick Chopin. ''This is not pageantry—peak moments in the lives of the great—but montage of small, telling events that quietly evoke the spirit of time and place,'' Laura Geringer writes in *Saturday Review.* Chopin demonstrates to Mrs. Carlyle that her piano is out of tune; Lewis Carroll ponders over a title for his children's book about a young girl named Alice; Algernon Charles Swinburne takes George Meredith's son to look at boats on the Thames. ''There is no story here, no gathering force, none of the momentum we expect of a 'novel,' '' Cynthia King writes in the *Detroit News.* ''But that word on the cover allows this probing of minds of people long dead, this invention of actions and motives and conversations.'' Disch and Naylor, Jean Strouse writes in *Newsweek,* ''have given vivid fictional life to a wide range of mid-century characters [in *Neighboring Lives*].'' Although Strouse admits that the authors ''have taken poetic license with time and fact'' to write their novel, they ''have clearly also done their homework and have delivered a period Chelsea refined and enhanced by fiction.''

With *The Businessman: A Tale of Terror,* Disch explores the genre of horror fiction in a satirical, ironic manner. Businessman Bob Glandier murders his wife, Giselle, but she returns to haunt him. A monstrous spirit, Bob and Giselle's offspring, also haunts him. Meanwhile, the ghost of poet John Berryman is forced to haunt Minneapolis by a nineteenth-century poet who controls limbo. And heaven turns out to be equipped with television sets on which celestial residents can watch reruns of their own lives. The novel, Stephen Dobyns writes in the *Washington Post,* ''draws from a number of strange tales ranging from 'The Exorcist' to 'The Frog Prince' and one could scarcely credit any of it if Disch weren't an excellent writer.''

Glandier has denied "the possibility of a spiritual realm that can make itself wondrously felt in the here and now," David Lehman writes in *Newsweek*. "'The Businessman' is a hymn to this possibility." It is a possibility, however, that Disch handles in an ironic manner. He writes in the novel: "The source of grace—let us be honest and call it God—is also an ironist and a dweller in paradoxes." Although Glandier eventually dies as punishment for the murder he has committed, John Clute writes in the *Times Literary Supplement*, "the outcome is arbitrary. At the heart of the book there is a cruel vertigo of godlessness." This distressing tone moves Marion Zimmer Bradley to write in the *New York Times Book Review:* "It is all very elegantly satirical: none of these horrors really induce pity or terror. There's a lot of literary trivia and a lot of clever literary allusions concealed in the book, but there is no impulse to suspend disbelief."

Such negative reaction to Disch's work, Clute explains, is often due to the fact that Disch is "an ironist in a culture which tends to treat irony as suspect, frivolous, metropolitan." Fred Pfeil of the *San Francisco Review of Books* takes exception to Bradley's comment. Bradley "got one thing right," Pfeil concedes. "As a standard Stephen-King-style horror novel, *The Businessman* is all screwed up." Pfeil believes the novel combines the banal with the horrifying to create the true feeling of contemporary society. It is, Pfeil argues, both realistic and fantastic. "A realistic novel," he writes, "*because* a fantastic one; because in a fully consumerized society all the landscape is always already commodified, sloganized, in effect possessed. It is then the formal machinery of the horror novel that comes to seem slightly silly in *The Businessman*, the images of sheerest dailiness that smack of fear." Clute judges *The Businessman* to be "a *tour de force* of polished, distanced, sly narrative art."

The variety found in Disch's novels also extends to his short stories, where he has explored a number of different genres. As Disch tells Platt: "Part of my notion of a proper ambition is that one should excel at a wide range of tasks." "Getting into Death," a short story about Gothic novelist Cassandra Knye searching among her fictional characters for help in accepting her imminent death, won Disch an O. Henry Prize in 1975. (Disch and John Sladek had used the joint pseudonym Cassandra Knye in writing the Gothic novel *The House That Fear Built* in 1966.) The collection *Getting into Death: The Best Short Stories of Thomas M. Disch* exhibits a sampling of the many styles Disch has employed in his short fiction. "At times [in this collection] he sounds like a soft-spoken contributor to The New Yorker," Edmund White maintains in the *New York Times Book Review*, "at others like Jerzy Kosinski, and at still others like Jules Feiffer." "The Asian Shore," a story in which an American in Turkey gradually transforms into a Turk, is called by a reviewer for the *Times Literary Supplement* "this collection's single solid achievement." Reviewing the same collection, Paul Gray states in *Time* that "it is one thing to cerebrate; to narrate is quite another. . . . Thomas M. Disch . . . can do both." Citing the fantastic nature of many of the collection's stories, Gray points out that "fantasy makes many adults nervous. . . . Disch shows that an unfettered imagination need not be childish or frivolous. His stories show just how serious fancies can be." Writing in the *Los Angeles Times Book Review* about the collection *The Man Who Had No Idea*, Don Strachen echoes this assessment of Disch's short stories. He "reminds us," Strachen believes, "what the fantasy short story can do. His prose twists and turns down cerebral corridors; his situations entertain hosts of human

quandaries simultaneously." Speaking of the stories "The Asian Shore" and "Bodies," both collected in *Fundamental Disch*, William Boyd of the *Times Literary Supplement* describes them as "superb examples of modern short fiction."

"The distinctive qualities of Disch's prose fiction—wit, invention, and the gift of gab—are the virtues of his verse as well," Lehman writes in the *Times Literary Supplement*. "Disch has, in addition to a highly developed nose for the new, an excellent ear and a clever tongue." Disch's poetry ranges over a wide variety of forms. He writes free verse, light verse, odes, sonnets, and ballads. But whatever the form, Disch's poetry is a "lucid and accessible art," as Blake Morrison calls it in the *Times Literary Supplement*. Unlike some modern poets, Disch is concerned with being understood. This concern is evident in several of his poems, often addressed to particular poets, in which he distances himself "from prevailing fashions," as Morrison explains.

Gavin Ewart of the *Times Literary Supplement* likens Disch as a poet to "John Updike, John Fuller or X. J. Kennedy . . . somebody, that is, who is not afraid to write what used to be called Light Verse, somebody with a games-playing mind and an interest in the shapes of poems, somebody, too, who is very accomplished at writing them." Disch's interest in games-playing is reflected in Judith Moffet's comment in the *Washington Post Book World* that he displays "an interest in a dazzling surface rather than substance. . . . Disch's delight in his own dexterity is infectious at first. Before long, though, one begins to doubt whether he takes himself seriously enough." Ewart disagrees. In his review of *ABCDEFG HIJKLM NPOQRST UVWXYZ*, Ewart finds that Disch has written "serious poems of great merit." Morrison maintains that Disch is "never less than enjoyable and accomplished."

In most evaluations of his work, Disch is praised for his great imagination. In science fiction, Lehman writes in *Newsweek*, Disch enjoys a reputation as "the strongest—and surely the most fiercely literary—of the genre's recent practitioners. . . . His flights of fancy, fueled by never-failing powers of invention, succeed . . . in raising ordinary life to mythic status." In speaking to Platt, Disch emphasizes that fiction, whether fantastic or not, needs to address life in a realistic manner. "I'm not saying that every writer has to be a realist," Disch explains, "but in terms of the ethical sensibility brought to bear in a work of imagination, there has to be some complex moral understanding of the world. In the art I like, I require irony, for instance, or simply some sense that the writer isn't telling egregious lies about the lives we lead."

BIOGRAPHICAL/CRITICAL SOURCES:

BOOKS

Contemporary Literary Criticism, Volume VII, Gale, 1977.

Delany, Samuel R., *The Jewel-Hinged Jaw: Notes on the Language of Science Fiction*, Dragon (Elizabethtown, N.Y.), 1977.

Delany, Samuel R., *The American Shore: Meditations on a Tale of Science Fiction by Thomas M. Disch*, Dragon, 1978.

Dictionary of Literary Biography, Volume VIII: *Twentieth-Century American Science-Fiction Writers*, Gale, 1981.

Disch, Thomas M. *The Businessman: A Tale of Terror*, Harper, 1984.

Platt, Charles, *Dream Makers: The Uncommon People Who Write Science Fiction*, Berkley Publishing, 1980.

Scholes, Robert and Eric S. Rabkin, *Science Fiction: History, Science, Vision,* Oxford University Press, 1977.

PERIODICALS

American Book Review, July-August, 1985.
Chicago Tribune Book World, March 22, 1981.
Detroit News, April 19, 1981.
Los Angeles Times, February 3, 1981.
Los Angeles Times Book Review, November 21, 1982, July 13, 1984.
Magazine of Fantasy and Science Fiction, February, 1980.
Minnesota Review, fall, 1984.
New Statesman, June 22, 1979, May 22, 1981, July 13, 1984.
Newsweek, March 9, 1981, July 2, 1984.
New York Times Book Review, July 27, 1975, March 21, 1976, October 28, 1979, March 22, 1981, August 26, 1984.
Observer, June 24, 1979.
San Francisco Review of Books, November-December, 1984.
Saturday Review, February, 1981.
Time, July 28, 1975, February 9, 1976, July 9, 1984.
Times Literary Supplement, February 15, 1974, May 15, 1981, June 12, 1981, June 19, 1981, August 27, 1982, May 25, 1984.
Village Voice, August 27-September 2, 1980.
Virginia Quarterly Review, summer, 1976.
Washington Post, July 3, 1984.
Washington Post Book World, November 23, 1980, March 1, 1981, July 26, 1981, October 31, 1982, March 13, 1983.

—*Sketch by Thomas Wiloch*

*   *   *

DIXON, Stephen 1936-

PERSONAL: Born June 6, 1936, in New York, N.Y.; married Anne Frydman, January 17, 1983; children: Sophia Cara. *Education:* City College of New York (now City College of the City University of New York), B.A., 1958.

ADDRESSES: Office—The Writing Seminars, Johns Hopkins University, Baltimore, Md. 21218.

CAREER: Writer. Worked as fiction consultant, reporter for a radio news service, magazine editor, and assistant producer of a television show, "In Person," for the Columbia Broadcasting System; New York University, School of Continuing Education, New York, N.Y., instructor, 1979; Johns Hopkins University, Baltimore, Md., associate professor of fiction, 1980—. Wallace Stegner creative writing fellow at Stanford University, 1964-65.

AWARDS, HONORS: National Endowment for the Arts grant for fiction, 1974-75; O. Henry Award, 1977, for "Mac in Love," and 1982, for "Layaways"; Pushcart Prize, 1977, for "Milk Is Very Good for You"; American Academy-Institute of Arts and Letters prize for literature, 1983.

WRITINGS:

SHORT STORY COLLECTIONS

(Contributor) *Making a Break* (anthology), Latitudes Press, 1975.
No Relief, Street Fiction Press, 1976.
Quite Contrary, Harper, 1979.
14 Stories, Johns Hopkins University Press, 1980.
Movies, North Point Press, 1983.
Time to Go, Johns Hopkins University Press, 1984.

NOVELS

Work, Street Fiction Press, 1977.
Too Late, Harper, 1978.
Fall and Rise, North Point Press, 1985.

OTHER

Contributor of more than 150 short stories to periodicals, including *Harper's, Viva, Playboy, Paris Review, American Review, Atlantic, Pequod, Esquire, Yale Review, South Carolina Review, Triquarterly,* and *Chicago Review.*

SIDELIGHTS: "One of the short story's most accomplished if quirky practitioners," according to Patricia Blake in *Time,* Stephen Dixon has published nearly two hundred pieces of short fiction and three novels over the course of his twenty-year career. His work has appeared in a wide variety of magazines, as Blake notes, "from the venerable *North American Review* to the ephemeral *Nitty-Gritty,*" and some critics have seen the success of his five published short story collections as an indication of a "boomlet" of interest in that genre. Dixon, who worked odd jobs for years while trying to sell his fiction, admits in a *Baltimore Sun* article that he didn't really start publishing books until he was forty. "By being published late, I learned I could endure and survive and still write. If I lost my job [as associate professor of creative writing at Johns Hopkins University], . . . I would get a job as a waiter or a bartender and go on writing."

A pervasive theme in Dixon's work is the plight of "ordinary people, usually in urban settings," says John T. Irwin in the *Baltimore Sun.* A native New Yorker, Dixon often sets his fiction's action in that city. Paul Skenazy notes in the *San Francisco Chronicle* that Dixon "writes about people who live in rundown apartments, . . . he gives a reader the irritating, wearing feel of city life. He captures that rubbing of noise and excitement against the grain of one's inertia, that constant intrusion of human traffic. But at its best the tone is less tough than worn-at-the-cuffs, frayed and slightly frantic from observing people who let their pride escape while they were watching TV or doing the laundry." "Dixon's imagination sticks close to home," writes John Domini in the *New York Times Book Review.* "His principal subject is the clash of the mundane and the aberrant, those unsettling run-ins with wackos or former lovers all too familiar to anyone who's ever lived in a city." In a story in *Movies,* for example, a young man grossly disfigured by several accidents is harassed by his neighbors and even rejected by a freak show. A plastic surgeon tells him, "Wear a ski mask, they're very chic nowadays." Skenazy feels that Dixon's urban stories "frequently have a powerful impact that, while distasteful, is bracing; and there is something of the feel of that part of life too often ignored by fiction." "His stories are deceptively low-key," Irwin suggests. "They remind you of a combination of a Frank Capra comedy and a Kafka short story in their ability to be extremely funny then suddenly become terrifying and bizarre."

Much of Dixon's work also chronicles the pitfalls and problems of male-female relationships, painting "a harrowing portrait of therapeutic man and therapeutic woman trying to experience love," according to Anatole Broyard in the *New York Times.* A *Kirkus Reviews* critic writes: "Dixon's theme becomes clear: love affairs are like fiction—stories that are added to, rubbed out, obsessively changed, matters of chosen order and nuance and correction." "His male protagonists are generally so yearning and irritably hungry for sex and/or intimacy that they either don't look before they leap, or if they do look, leap anyway no matter what they see ahead,'' claims David Aitken in the *Baltimore Sun*. "As a result, their lives are almost always in uncontrollable comic disarray."

This theme is apparent in Dixon's novel *Fall and Rise,* in which the leading character tries, through a long New York night, to woo a woman he met at a party earlier in the evening. It is also the controlling idea behind Dixon's O. Henry Award-winning short story ''Mac in Love,'' in which a repulsed suitor yells wistful nonsense at his date's balcony until the beleaguered woman calls the police. The final effect in many of Dixon's male-female imbroglios is, in Aitken's opinion, ''vaguely Woody Allenish. Dixon's comedy is stronger than Allen's though, in being less stylized and drawn with a fresher eye for the particulars of life.''

Some critics find fault with aspects of Dixon's work. In his review of *Time to Go,* Aitken comments: ''One wishes Dixon didn't republish so many of his weaker stories. It dilutes the impression his best work makes.'' John Domini similarly finds that in *Time to Go,* ''all Mr. Dixon's encounters lack any but the most general physicality.... The repression of rhetoric and an emphasis on the trivial are hallmarks of many contemporary short stories. But Mr. Dixon is so unrelenting in both regards that he ends up compounding a lack of imagination with a near absence of passion.'' James Lasdun writes in the *Times Literary Supplement:* ''One has the feeling that Dixon begins most of his stories with little more in mind than a vague idea, a couple of characters, or a briefly observed scene, relying on his ready wit to transform it into a convincing piece of fiction. This is fine when it works, but occasionally the initial impulse is too flimsy and the story fails to take off.''

In general, however, Dixon's literary output has elicited considerable critical approval. Lasdun notes: ''The best of these stories have a certain manic quality about them, caused largely by Dixon's delight in speeding life up and compressing it, to the point where it begins to verge on the surreal.'' In the *Chicago Tribune Book World,* George Cohen concludes: ''Dixon's best is superb, tragic, funny, cynical. He's telling us all the bizarre things we already know about ourselves, and he's right on the mark.'' ''Every overworked adjective of praise in the lit[erary] crit[icism] business applies to Dixon's writing, beginning with 'versatile,''' comments a reviewer in the *Baltimore Sun*. And Richard Burgin, in an article for the *St. Petersburg Times,* calls Dixon ''a prolific and versatile writer whose strong vision balances anxiety and darkness with humor and compassion.... It is high time that the larger American literary community recognized that he is one of our finest writers of short fiction.''

BIOGRAPHICAL/CRITICAL SOURCES:

PERIODICALS

Baltimore Sun, January 22, 1984, July 22, 1984.
Chicago Sun Times, June 4, 1978.
Chicago Tribune Book World, July 15, 1979, January 4, 1981.
Kansas City Star, August 12, 1984.
Kirkus Reviews, May 1, 1979.
New York Times, June 9, 1979.
New York Times Book Review, July 31, 1977, May 7, 1978, October 14, 1984, July 7, 1985.
St. Petersburg Times, August 26, 1984.
San Francisco Chronicle, January 29, 1984.
Soho Weekly News, December 2, 1976.
South Carolina Review, November, 1978.
Time, August 13, 1984.

Times Literary Supplement, May 29, 1981.
Washington Post Book World, February 22, 1981, August 5, 1984, July 20, 1985.

—*Sketch by Anne Janette Johnson*

*   *   *

DONAHUE, Jack 1917-

PERSONAL: Born December 6, 1917, in Waco, Tex.; son of Jackson Washington (an engineer) and Beatrice (a horse trainer; maiden name, Knight) Donahue; married Novella Ellen Sellingsloh, June 6, 1940 (died, 1969); married Gene Hughes (a singer), December 14, 1968; children: Michael, Terence, Brian. *Education:* Attended Baylor University, 1936-37.

ADDRESSES: Home and office—15618 Fern Basin Dr., Houston, Tex. 77084.

CAREER: Houston Press, Houston, Tex., reporter, 1946-47; *Houston Chronicle,* Houston, reporter, 1947-49; *Houston Press,* city editor, 1949-57; *Houston Post,* Houston, managing editor, 1957-60; *Los Angeles Mirror,* Los Angeles, Calif., managing editor, 1960-62; free-lance writer, 1962—. *Military service:* U.S. Army, 1941-45; became master sergeant.

MEMBER: Writers Guild of America (West), Authors League of America, Authors Guild.

WRITINGS:

NOVELS

Someone to Hate, New American Library, 1962.
The Confessor, World Publishing, 1963.
Erase My Name, World Publishing, 1964.
Divorce American Style, Popular Library, 1967.
Pray to the Hustler's God, Reader's Digest Press, 1977.
The Lady Loved Too Well, McGraw, 1978.
Grady Barr, Arbor House, 1981.
The Finest in the Land, Gulf Publishing, 1984.
Hack Donavon of the Press and the Purification of Houston, Shearer, 1984.

OTHER

Wildcatter: The Story of Michael T. Halbouty and the Search for Oil (biography), McGraw, 1979.

SIDELIGHTS: Jack Donahue commented to *CA:* ''I write because I have to. I'm not good at anything else.''

BIOGRAPHICAL/CRITICAL SOURCES:

PERIODICALS

New York Times, July 20, 1979.

*   *   *

DORESKI, William 1946-

PERSONAL: Born January 10, 1946, in Stafford, Conn.; son of Lawrence Howard (a store clerk) and Mildred (McGuire) Doreski; married Jean Eddy (a stockbroker), June 24, 1967 (divorced, 1978); married Carole Kiler, 1981. *Education:* Attended University of Hartford, 1963-67; Goddard College, M.A., 1976; Boston University, Ph.D., 1980.

ADDRESSES: Home—394 Elm St., Keene, N.H. 03431. *Office*—Keene State College, Keene, N.H. 03431.

CAREER: Pratt and Whitney Aircraft Co., East Hartford, Conn., inspector, 1965; Connecticut Department of Highways, Warehouse Point, mechanic, 1966-67; John Hancock Life Insurance Co., Boston, Mass., supervisor, 1967-68; Ahab Rare Books, Boston, owner, 1970-77; Goddard College, Plainfield, Vt., teacher, beginning 1976; Keene State College, Keene, N.H., assistant professor, 1982—. Teacher at Emerson College, 1973 and 1976. Trustee, Pym-Randall Press, 1972—. Worked as volunteer fireman, 1963-67.

AWARDS, HONORS: *Poet Lore* subjective poem award, 1972, translation award, 1973; *Black Warrior Review* Poetry Prize, 1978.

WRITINGS:

POETRY

To Face the Sea, Windy Row Press, 1969.
Running the Bitch Down, Barn Dream Press, 1970.
Roxbury 1968, Beanbag Press, 1972.
The Testament of Israel Potter, Seven Woods Press, 1976.
Half of the Map, Burning Deck, 1980.

OTHER

"The Fourth Man's Work" (two-act play), first produced in Boston at Boston Dramatic Arts Workshop Theatre, March, 1970.
(Editor) *Earth That Sings: The Poetry of Andrew Glaze,* Ford-Brown, 1985.

Contributor to *Hartford Times, Antioch Review, Yale Review,* and *Massachusetts Review.*

WORK IN PROGRESS: A book of poems and a critical study of Robert Lowell.

SIDELIGHTS: William Doreski told *CA:* "I write out of necessity, which is, of course, the grandaddy of motives. Every poem has its own sub-motive, determined partly by its content, partly by the form the poem takes for itself. I subscribe to no theories, am interested in no programs, politics, etc. These things can come between the poem and its self-imposed shape, and therefore, I believe, must be avoided. That is not a comment on 'social' responsibilities; but those are outside the work—in the conscious, rather than the unconscious place where poems appear."

*   *   *

DOUBTFIRE, Dianne (Abrams)   1918-

PERSONAL: Born October 18, 1918, in Leeds, Yorkshire, England; daughter of Frederick Samuel and Etty (Heslewood) Abrams; married Stanley Doubtfire, 1946; children: Ashley Graham. *Education:* Attended Harrogate School of Art, Yorkshire; Slade School of Fine Art, University of London, diploma, 1941; Institute of Education, University of London, A.T.D., 1947.

ADDRESSES: Home—Folly Cottage, Ventnor, Isle of Wight, England. *Agent*—Curtis Brown Ltd., 162-168 Regent St., London W1R 5TA, England.

CAREER: Free-lance writer, 1952—. Adult education lecturer in creative writing for Surrey County Council and Isle of Wight County Council. *Military service:* Women's Auxiliary Air Force, 1941-46; became flight sergeant; served in the Middle East in administrative capacity, 1944-46.

MEMBER: International P.E.N., Society of Authors, National Book League, Writers' Guild of Great Britain.

WRITINGS:

Fun with Stamps, Hutchinson, 1957.
More Fun with Stamps, Hutchinson, 1958.
Lust for Innocence (novel), Morrow, 1960.
Reason for Violence (novel), P. Davies, 1961.
Kick a Tin Can (novel), P. Davies, 1964.
The Flesh Is Strong (novel), P. Davies, 1966.
Behind the Screen (novel), P. Davies, 1969.
Escape on Monday (juvenile), Macmillan, 1970.
This Jim (juvenile), Heinemann, 1974.
Girl in Cotton Wool (juvenile), Scholastic Book Services, 1975.
A Girl Called Rosemary (juvenile), Scholastic Book Services, 1977.
Girl with Wings, Scholastic Book Services, 1978 (published in England as *Sky Girl,* Macmillan, 1978).
The Craft of Novel-Writing, Allison & Busby, 1978.
Girl in a Gondola (juvenile), Macmillan, 1980.
Sky Lovers (juvenile), Macmillan, 1981.
Teach Yourself Creative Writing, Hodder & Stoughton, 1983.
The Wrong Face, W. H. Allen, 1985.

WORK IN PROGRESS: A novel.

SIDELIGHTS: "There should be no aspect of human affairs," Dianne Doubtfire told *CA,* "which the serious novelist cannot introduce, with taste and compassion, into his books. . . . I try to work six hours a day, during which I am lucky if I complete one thousand words. When I reach a temporary deadlock (a frequent occurrence) I go for a walk, talking aloud to myself, battling the thing out. I never prepare a rigid plot in advance; the story grows as the characters develop. . . . My greatest ambition is to write a novel that really satisfies *me!*"

AVOCATIONAL INTERESTS: Motoring, cinematography, cooking, travel, meditation.

BIOGRAPHICAL/CRITICAL SOURCES:

PERIODICALS

Books and Bookmen, March, 1960, September, 1961.
Everywoman, August, 1961.
Observer, December 8, 1974.
Times Literary Supplement, December 11, 1970.

*   *   *

DOUGLAS, R. M.
See MASON, Douglas R(ankine)

*   *   *

DOWNS, Robert Bingham   1903-

PERSONAL: Born May 25, 1903, in Lenoir, N.C.; son of John McLeod and Clara (Hartley) Downs; married Elizabeth Crooks, August 17, 1929 (died, 1982); married Jane B. Wilson, 1983; children: (first marriage) Clara (Mrs. William J. Keller), Roberta (Mrs. Terence A. Andre). *Education:* University of North Carolina, A.B., 1926; Columbia University, B.S., 1927, M.S., 1929.

ADDRESSES: Home—708 West Pennsylvania Ave., Urbana, Ill. 61801. *Office*—University of Illinois Library, Urbana, Ill. 61801.

CAREER: Colby College, Waterville, Me., librarian, 1929-31; University of North Carolina at Chapel Hill, assistant librarian, 1931-32, librarian and associate professor, 1932-34, librarian and professor of library science, 1934-38; New York University, New York, N.Y., director of libraries, 1938-43; University of Illinois at Urbana-Champaign, professor of library science and director of library and Library School, 1943-58, dean of library administration and director of Graduate School of Library Science, 1958-71. Visiting professor, University of Toronto, 1973, and University of North Carolina, 1975. Served on Committee on Books Abroad, U.S. Information Agency. Adviser to libraries in Japan, Turkey, Burma, Mexico, Afghanistan, Tunisia, and several South American countries.

MEMBER: American Library Association (vice president, 1951-52; president, 1952-53; honorary member, 1977—), Association of College and Research Libraries (president, 1940-41), Southeastern Library Association (honorary member), Illinois Library Association (president, 1955-56), Phi Beta Kappa, Phi Kappa Phi, Rotary Club (Urbana; president, 1962), Dial, University Club, Caxton Club (Chicago).

AWARDS, HONORS: Litt. D., Colby College, 1944; LL.D., University of North Carolina, 1949; L.S.D., University of Toledo, 1953; L.H.D., Ohio State University, 1963; Clarence Day Award, American Textbook Publishers, for outstanding work in encouraging the love of books and reading, 1963; Joseph W. Lippincott Award for distinguished service in librarianship, 1964; L.H.D., Southern Illinois University, 1970; Centennial Medal, Syracuse University, 1970; Guggenheim fellow, 1971-72; Litt. D., University of Illinois, 1973; Melvil Dewey Medal, 1974.

WRITINGS:

(With Louis R. Wilson) *Report of a Survey of the Libraries of Cornell University,* Cornell University Press, 1948.
Books That Changed the World, New American Library, 1956, 2nd edition, American Library Association, 1978.
(With others) *Family Saga and Other Phases of American Folklore,* University of Illinois Press, 1958.
Molders of the Modern Mind, Barnes & Noble, 1961.
Strengthening and Improving Library Resources for Southern Higher Education, Southern Regional Education Board, 1962.
The Kabul University Library, University of Wyoming Education Program, 1963.
(Editor) *The Bear Went over the Mountain,* Macmillan, 1964.
Famous Books, Ancient and Medieval, Barnes & Noble, 1964.
Resources of North Carolina Libraries, Governor's Commission on Library Resources, 1965.
How to Do Library Research, University of Illinois Press, 1966, 2nd edition, 1975.
Resources of Missouri Libraries, Missouri State Library, 1966.
(With Frances B. Jenkins) *Bibliography: Current State and Future Trends,* University of Illinois Press, 1967.
Resources of Canadian Academic and Research Libraries, Association of Universities of Canada, 1967.
University Library Statistics, Association of Research Libraries, 1968.
Books That Changed America, Macmillan, 1970.
Famous American Books, McGraw, 1971.
Books and History, University of Illinois Library School, 1974.
Horace Mann, Twayne, 1974.
Heinrich Pestalozzi, Twayne, 1975.
Famous Books, Littlefield, 1975.
Books That Changed the South, University of North Carolina Press, 1977.
Henry Barnard, Twayne, 1977.

Friedrich Froebel, Twayne, 1978.
Australian and New Zealand Library Resources, Mansell, 1979.
British and Irish Resources, Mansell, 1981.
Landmarks in Science, Libraries Unlimited, 1982.
(With others) *Memorable Americans,* Libraries Unlimited, 1983.
Perspectives on the Past, an Autobiography, Scarecrow, 1984.
(With John T. Flanagan and Harold W. Scott) *More Memorable Americans,* Libraries Unlimited, 1985.

PUBLISHED BY AMERICAN LIBRARY ASSOCIATION

(Editor) *Resources of Southern Libraries,* 1938.
Library Specialization, 1941.
(Editor) *Resources of New York City Libraries,* 1942.
(Editor) *Union Catalogs in the United States,* 1942.
American Library Resources, 1951, first supplement, 1962, second supplement, 1972.
(Editor) *Status of American College and University Librarians,* 1958.
(Editor) *The First Freedom: Liberty and Justice in the World of Books and Reading,* 1960.
British Library Resources, 1973.
Guide to Illinois Library Resources, 1974.
Far Horizons: Epic Tales of Exploration and Discovery, 1978.
(With Ralph E. McCoy) *The First Freedom Today,* 1984.

OTHER

Also author of numerous published surveys. Contributor to library journals.

WORK IN PROGRESS: Images of America, for University of Illinois Press.

AVOCATIONAL INTERESTS: Collecting American folklore and humor.

BIOGRAPHICAL/CRITICAL SOURCES:

BOOKS

Orne, Jerrold, editor, *Research Librarianship: Essays in Honor of Robert B. Downs,* Bowker, 1971.

PERIODICALS

Bulletin of Bibliographay, May-August, 1967.

*   *   *

DRAKE, David (Allen)   1945-

PERSONAL: Born September 24, 1945, in Dubuque, Iowa; son of Earle Charles (a maintenance foreman) and Maxine (Schneider) Drake; married Joanne Kammiller (a teacher), June 5, 1967; children: Jonathan. *Education:* University of Iowa, B.A., 1967; Duke University, J.D., 1972.

ADDRESSES: Home—P.O. Box 904, Chapel Hill, N.C. 27514. *Agent*—Kirby McCauley Ltd., 432 Park Ave. S., New York, N.Y. 10016.

CAREER: Town of Chapel Hill, N.C., assistant town attorney, 1972-80; part-time bus driver, 1981; full-time free-lance writer, 1982—. Partner of Carcosa (publisher). *Military service:* U.S. Army, 1969-71; served in Viet Nam and Cambodia.

MEMBER: International Fortean Organization, Science Fiction Writers of America, Phi Beta Kappa.

WRITINGS:

Hammer's Slammers (science fiction), Ace Books, 1979.
The Dragon Lord (fantasy novel), Putnam, 1979.

Time Safari, Tor Books, 1982.
Sky Ripper, Tor Books, 1983.
From the Heart of Darkness, Tor Books, 1984.
Forlorn Hope, Tor Books, 1984.
Birds of Prey, Baen, 1984.
Cross the Stars, Tor Books, 1984.
(With Karl Edward Wagner) *Killer,* Baen, 1984.
(With Janet Morris) *Active Measures,* Baen, 1985.
At Any Price, Baen, 1985.
Bridgehead, Tor Books, 1986.
Fortress, Tor Books, 1986.

Contributor of more than fifty stories to magazines. Assistant editor of *Whispers.*

WORK IN PROGRESS: Research for a historical novel; short stories.

SIDELIGHTS: David Drake wrote *CA:* "I am a military history buff, though with no particular affection for the military as an institution. (I was drafted out of law school to serve as an interrogator in Viet Nam and Cambodia.) I tend to write on themes of violence and to explore interplays between society on the one hand and personal values on the other; that is, friendship, love, honor, et cetera. I try to be a careful writer, seeing myself as a craftsman, rather than an artist. Writing is no longer the hobby it was for fifteen years, but it's just as much fun and I do it the same way I used to—slowly and carefully—but three hours a day, every day."

*   *   *

DRENNEN, D(onald) A(rthur) 1925-

PERSONAL: Born August 8, 1925, in New York, N.Y.; son of William Michael (an insurance specialist) and Anastasia (Kearney) Drennan; married M. Eileen Connolly, August 4, 1951; children: Maura, Deirdre, Susan, Eileen, Donald Reid, Maribeth. *Education:* Fordham University, A.B., 1947, M.F.A., 1950, M.A., 1951, Ph.D., 1958; postdoctoral study at Hebrew Union College, 1964-65, American University (Cairo), 1965, Columbia University, 1965-66, 1970, McGill University, 1967, and Southampton College, 1968. *Politics:* Democrat. *Religion:* Anglo-Catholic.

ADDRESSES: Home—57 Blue Belle Court, Lanark, Fla. 32323; and Poughkeepsie Yacht Club, Box 172, Hyde Park, N.Y. 12538 (summer). *Office*—Box 1236, Lanark, Fla. 32323.

CAREER: Fordham University, School of General Studies, New York, N.Y., lecturer, 1951-53; Marymount College, Tarrytown, N.Y., associate professor of philosophy, 1952-62; Marist College, Poughkeepsie, N.Y., professor of philosophy, 1962-82, professor emeritus, 1982—, chairman of department, 1964-82. Consulting cultural psychologist and free-lance writer, 1982—. Visiting scholar, Columbia University, 1965-66; lecturer, Catholic University of America, 1966-67; scholar-diplomat, U.S. Department of State, 1970, 1974, and 1976. Consultant, Macmillan Publishing Co., Educational Testing Service, and Editions de Paris.

MEMBER: American Philosophical Association, American Catholic Philosophical Association (member of executive council, 1969-71), Metaphysical Society of America, Society for Phenomenology and Existential Philosophy, American Association of University Professors.

AWARDS, HONORS: Rockefeller Foundation grant, 1952; New York State Foreign Area award, 1963-64; National Science Foundation award, 1965; U.S. Department of State foreign studies grant, 1965; New York State faculty fellow, 1965-66; Carnegie grant, 1968; National Defense postdoctoral award, 1970.

WRITINGS:

(Editor) *Christian Ethics,* McKay, 1952.
A Christian Preface to Modern Thought, Marycor Press, 1959.
(Editor) *Readings in Modern Thought,* Marycor Press, 1959.
A Modern Introduction to Metaphysics, Macmillan, 1962.
(Contributor) L. A. Foley, editor, *Philosophy in a Pluralistic Society,* Catholic University of America Press, 1963.
Major Themes in Modern Thought, Marist Press, Volume I, 1963, Volume II, 1964.
Philosophy and Theistic Experience, Marist Press, 1965.
The Methodical Philosophy of Rene Descartes, Barron's, 1976.
(Contributor) G. F. McLean, editor, *Philosophy and Contemporary Man,* Catholic University of America Press, 1968.
(Contributor) McLean, editor, *Current Issues in Modern Philosophy,* Catholic University of America Press, 1969.
A Cultural Introduction to Philosophy, Marist Press, 1971.
Karl Marx's Communist Manifesto, Barron's, 1972.
(Contributor) McLean, editor, *Religion in Contemporary Thought,* Alba House, 1973.
Culture, Logic, and Science, Philosophical Resources, 1976.
Ethical Structures, Philosophical Resources, 1977.
Science and Scientific Thought, Philosophical Resources, 1978.
Introductory Exercises in Logic, Philosophical Resources, 1979.
Philosophy, History and Religion, Marycor Press, 1980.
Introduction to Philosophy, Marycor Press, 1981.
Introductory Ethics, Marycor Press, 1982.

General editor of texts in Christian philosophy, for Free Press. Contributor of articles to philosophy journals, including *Thought, Review of Metaphysics,* and *Philosophy;* contributor of reviews to periodicals, including *America.* News editor, *Business Week,* 1952-55.

WORK IN PROGRESS: Manuscripts on history and culture; investigations in cultural psychology and Arabic and Hebrew language and philosophy.

*   *   *

du BOIS, William (Sherman) Pene 1916-

PERSONAL: Born May 9, 1916, in Nutley, N.J.; son of Guy Pene (an artist) and Florence (Sherman) du Bois; married Willa Kim (a theatrical designer), March 26, 1955. *Education:* Attended schools in New York, France, and New Jersey. *Politics:* Democrat. *Religion:* Protestant.

ADDRESSES: Office—c/o Viking Press, 625 Madison Ave., New York, N.Y. 10022. *Agent*—Ann Watkins, Inc., 77 Park Ave., New York, N.Y. 10016.

CAREER: Author and illustrator of children's books. Art editor and designer, *Paris Review. Military service:* U.S. Army, 1941-45, correspondent for the *Yank.*

AWARDS, HONORS: New York Herald Tribune Spring Book Prize, 1947, for *The Twenty-One Balloons,* and 1956, for *Lion;* Newbery Medal, American Library Association, 1948, for *The Twenty-One Balloons; Bear Circus* was named to the *New York Times* "Best Illustrated Book" list, 1971, and was selected a Children's Book Showcase Title, 1972.

WRITINGS:

SELF-ILLUSTRATED

Elizabeth, the Cow Ghost, Nelson, 1936, reprinted Viking, 1964.
Otto at Sea, Viking, 1936, reprinted, 1958.
The Three Policeman, Viking, 1938, reprinted, 1960.
The Great Geppy, Viking, 1940, reprinted, 1965.
The Flying Locomotive, Viking, 1941.
The Twenty-One Balloons, Viking, 1947, reprinted, Dell, 1969.
Peter Graves, Viking, 1950, reprinted, 1963.
Bear Party, Viking, 1951, reprinted, 1963.
Squirrel Hotel, Viking, 1952, revised edition, G. K. Hall, 1979.
The Giant, Viking, 1954.
Lion, Viking, 1956, reprinted, 1981.
Otto in Texas, Viking, 1959.
Otto in Africa, Viking, 1961.
The Alligator Case, Harper, 1965.
Lazy Tommy Pumpkinhead, Harper, 1966.
The Horse in the Camel Suit, Harper, 1967.
Pretty Pretty Peggy Moffitt, Harper, 1968.
Porko von Popbutton, Harper, 1969.
Call Me Bandicoot, Harper, 1970.
Otto and the Magic Potatoes, Viking, 1970.
Bear Circus, Viking, 1971.
(With Lee Po) *The Hare and the Tortoise and the Tortoise and the Hare* (text in Spanish and English), Doubleday, 1972.
Mother Goose for Christmas, Viking, 1973.
The Forbidden Forest, Harper, 1978.

Also author of *Gentleman Bear*.

ILLUSTRATOR

Rumer Godden, *The Mousewife*, Viking, 1951.
Claire Huchet Bishop, *Twenty and Ten*, Viking, 1952, reprinted, Puffin Books, 1978.
Richard Wilbur, *Digging for China: A Poem*, Doubleday, 1956, reprinted, 1970.
George Plimpton, *The Rabbit's Umbrella*, Viking, 1956.
Marguerite Clement, *In France*, Viking, 1956.
John Steinbeck, *The Short Reign of Pippin IV*, Viking, 1957.
Edward Fenton, *Fierce John, a Story*, Holt, 1959.
Edward Lear, *The Owl and The Pussy Cat*, Doubleday, 1961.
George MacDonald, *Light Princess*, Crowell, 1962.
Three Little Pigs, Viking, 1962, reprinted, Penguin, 1978.
Jules Verne, *Dr. Ox's Experiment*, Macmillan, 1963.
Rebecca Caudill, *A Certain Small Shepherd*, Holt, 1965.
Roald Dahl, *The Magic Finger*, Harper, 1966.
Betty Yurdin, *The Tiger in the Teapot*, Holt, 1968.
Isaac Bashevis Singer, *The Topsy-Turvy Emperor of China*, Harper, 1971.
Peter Matthiessen, *Seal Pool*, Doubleday, 1972.
Charlotte Shapiro Zolotow, *William's Doll*, Harper, 1972.
Norma Farber, *Where's Gomer?*, Dutton, 1974.
Zolotow, *My Grandson Lew*, Harper, 1974.
Zolotow, *The Unfriendly Book*, Harper, 1975.
Zolotow, *It's Not Fair*, Harper, 1976.
Paul-Jacques Bonzon, *The Runaway Flying Horse*, Parents' Magazine Press, 1976.
Tobi Tobias, *Moving Day*, Random House, 1976.
Mildred Hobzek, *We Came a-Marching—1, 2, 3*, Parents' Magazine Press, 1978.
Patricia MacLachlan, *The Sick Day*, Pantheon, 1979.
Mark Strand, *The Planet of Lost Things*, C. N. Potter, 1982.

Also illustrator of other books.

WORK IN PROGRESS: A series of juvenile books on the seven deadly sins.

SIDELIGHTS: William Pene du Bois' book *Porko von Popbutton* tells about a thirteen-year-old boy who weighs 274 pounds and cares for nothing but food until he is sent away to a boarding school where he develops an interest in hockey. According to a *Book World* reviewer, the story is a witty, "irrepressible performance." Du Bois "has a well-developed sense of humor," Richard F. Shepard writes in the *New York Times Book Review,* "and a style of story telling that is fresh, simple and hard-hitting."

Du Bois' *The Forbidden Forest,* a children's story set in World War I, is praised by Jean Fritz in the *New York Times Book Review,* who indicates that the illustrations in particular comprise a "meticulously executed, wonderfully topsy-turvy, exuberant world."

BIOGRAPHICAL/CRITICAL SOURCES:

BOOKS

Diana Klemin, *The Art of Art for Children's Books*, C. N. Potter, 1966.

PERIODICALS

Book World, September 10, 1967, November 7, 1971.
Christian Science Monitor, November 11, 1971.
Library Journal, May 15, 1969.
New York Times Book Review, May 4, 1969, October 18, 1970, November 7, 1971, December 31, 1978.
Times Literary Supplement, November 3, 1972.
Young Readers' Review, November, 1966.
Young Wings, June, 1947, February, 1951.†

*   *   *

DUBUS, Andre   1936-

PERSONAL: Surname is pronounced De-*buse;* born August 11, 1936, in Lake Charles, La.; son of Andre Jules and Katherine (Burke) Dubus; married Patricia Lowe, February 22, 1958 (divorced, 1970); married Tommie Gail Cotter, June, 1975 (divorced, 1977); married Peggy Rambach (a writer), December 16, 1979; children: (first marriage) Suzanne, Andre Jeb, Nicole; (third marriage) Cadence Yvonne. *Education:* McNeese State College, B.A., 1958; University of Iowa, M.F.A., 1966. *Politics:* "I believe in the principles of social justice taught by Christ." *Religion:* Roman Catholic.

ADDRESSES: Home—753 East Broadway, Haverhill, Mass. 01830. *Agent*—Philip G. Spitzer, 1465 Third Ave., New York, N.Y. 10028.

CAREER: U.S. Marine Corps, commissioned lieutenant, 1958, left service as captain, 1964; Bradford College, Bradford, Mass., teacher of modern fiction and creative writing, 1966-84. Visiting teacher at colleges and universities, including University of Alabama and Boston University.

AWARDS, HONORS: $20,000 fellowship for creative prose, National Endowment for the Arts, 1985.

WRITINGS:

The Lieutenant (novel), Dial, 1967, reprinted, Green Street Press, 1986.
(With David R. Godine) *Voices from the Moon* (novella), David Godine, 1984.

SHORT STORY COLLECTIONS

Separate Flights, David Godine, 1975.
Adultery and Other Choices, David Godine, 1977.
Finding a Girl in America, David Godine, 1980.
The Times Are Never So Bad, David Godine, 1983.
We Don't Live Here Anymore, Crown, 1984.
Land Where My Fathers Died (limited edition), Stuart Wright, 1984.
The Last Worthless Evening, David Godine, 1986.

OTHER

Also contributor of stories to four editions of *Best American Short Stories* and to *O. Henry Prize Stories.* Contributor of stories to periodicals, including *Sewanee Review, Midwestern University Quarterly, Sage, New Yorker, Viva,* and *Ploughshares.*

SIDELIGHTS: Andre Dubus's stories "explore the strange mingling of our contemporary currents: what happens to human verities in a consumerist economy and a Playboy-tinged culture," writes Richard Eder in the *Los Angeles Times.* In short story collections such as *Separate Flights, Adultery and Other Choices,* and *Finding a Girl in America,* Dubus describes the loneliness and isolation that stretch between people in modern society, focusing especially on the relationships between men and women. Although his vision is often characterized as bleak, Joyce Carol Oates declares in the *Ontario Review* that "Dubus's attentiveness to his craft and his deep commitment to his characters make the experience of reading these tales—which are almost without exception about lonely, pitiful people—a highly rewarding pleasure."

In a *Publishers Weekly* article, Robert Dahlin describes the author as "that sort of manly figure that baldly emphasizes a tough gender," but adds that "he confounds expectations by using salty language to muse on the troubling puzzles in the man-woman bonds that he portrays so movingly in his stories." In discussing his major theme with Dahlin, Dubus gave his explanation for the lack of understanding that often comes between men and women: "One of the first reasons is all the stuff a boy goes through to feel like a man, and for a girl to feel like a woman. Everything that goes into this process only increases the isolation between them. I think that's why we're all essentially lonely. People don't know about other people. Boys and girls grow up in a strained society, one that drives them apart. It's a solipsistic society.

"Add to that that we have mostly meaningless jobs today. The only thing to be gotten out of them is money. There's no satisfaction, and it's hard for a young couple, especially when both work as most have to today, to have a working life and then come home and have anything to do with the family.... When I grew up, I learned that the most important thing you can do is get married and have children.... When I got married for the first time, my wife and I had no knowledge that things could go wrong. We thought there was a set of rules and happiness followed."

Dubus's collections are filled with people who, like their creator, followed that "set of rules." They worked, married, and raised families, but did not find fulfillment. Sometimes their frustration goads them to infidelity or acts of violence; more often, however, they simply become resigned to their lot. *Washington Post Book World* contributor Michael Harris believes that this resignation marks a new era in American literature. In the past, he states, "one went down fighting, like Ahab, despairing, like Gatsby, or at least babbling, like Port-

noy; but so long as life was alleged to promise Americans everything, resignation was a rarity." Harris credits Dubus with giving voice to a new mood in America, "a painful awareness, by people who once expected better, that horizons are shrinking."

Separate Flights contains several examples of this tone. The title story, which is hailed as "brilliant" by *New Leader* reviewer Charles Deemer, ends with a woman pretending to sleep beside her husband, even though she knows he has just committed adultery. "Miranda over the Valley" tells of a pregnant college student who succumbs to parental pressure and aborts the baby she would have chosen to keep. In another story, two husbands jog companionably together after sleeping with each other's wives. Discussing *Separate Flights* in the *New York Times Book Review,* novelist Gail Godwin notes that these characters will probably "grow older without growing wiser.... Nobody goes mad in these stories."

"Dubus can write," continues Godwin. "He'll take you into his universe and show you all its corners, but he cannot show you a way out. He writes like a person with 20/20 vision who refuses to look at the mountains beyond his own backyard." This limited perspective in Dubus's work troubles some reviewers, including David Seideman, who complains in *New Republic* that the collection *Finding a Girl in America* "lacks humor, [and] the stories strike a uniform, insistently dismal refrain. This narrowness of vision is disappointing." Walter Sullivan echoes this thought, writing in *Sewanee Review* that *Separate Flights* suffers from a "sameness of characterization from one piece to the next, [an] obsession with sexual congress and crumbling affections." Sullivan points out the similarity in this respect between Dubus's work and that of British author Alan Sillitoe, but notes, "Sillitoe's people drink and fornicate because they are poor and bored and ignorant and desperate," whereas Dubus's people are not. "Has the whole world become an extension of this English hopelessness [found in Sillitoe's work]?" asks Sullivan. "Are the possibilities of literature reduced in our time to variations on a single theme?"

Charles Deemer concurs with Sullivan in *New Leader,* indicating that "no linear notes extolling Dubus' 'humanity' remove the fact that he is, by and large, depressing to read." He denies, however, that the stories are expressions of hopelessness. "What hope we find in *Separate Flights* comes from the fact that sickness must be correctly diagnosed before it can be cured. Dubus' achievement, I think, is to put love, sex and promiscuity back into the moral context they have escaped. He has no answers, nor is he a prude; he simply asks the right questions with more power and depth than any contemporary fiction writer I know."

Times Literary Supplement contributor Peter Kemp also counters the notion that Dubus's work features characters with lax morals. While acknowledging that the stories collected in *We Don't Live Here Anymore* are "at first deceptively hedonistic-seeming," Kemp believes that they are in fact strongly moral. "In all four stories, self-indulgence is shown sapping people and partnerships," he writes. "They fix their attention on the way selfishness and cynicism can slowly loosen partnerships. At first portraying infidelity as feverish excitement, each then closes in on the psychological and emotional wear and tear taken.... Effort—put into everything from relationships to household chores—is repeatedly applauded.... True to this industrious ethic, Dubus's fiction is the result of an authorial vigilance—imaginative and observant—that never allows anything to relax into the sloppy or unpredictable. Packed and powerful, his novellas are as vigorous as they are rigorous.''

The ''authorial vigilance'' mentioned by Kemp is widely praised as one of Dubus's greatest strengths; Gene Lyons declares in *Nation* that any of the stories contained in *Separate Flights* ''might serve as textbook examples of what one means by calling a fiction author a 'craftsman.''' Rather than using flashy literary devices to tell his stories, the author employs ''quick strokes, slight details that bring whole sequences into focus,'' explains Walter Sullivan. ''Minor characters, people seen briefly in bars or at filling stations, give Dubus's work an enhanced sense of reality and enriched texture.'' Charles Deemer believes that this low-key, naturalistic style heightens the stories' impact. ''The characters and events are not wrapped up in avant-garde artifices that only draw attention to themselves, and thus away from the content,'' he explains. Therefore, ''we see terror and emptiness at their most naked limits'' in Dubus's subtle tales.

The ability to convincingly portray a character's viewpoint is another aspect of Dubus's writing that is praised by many. ''His characters are resolutely ungiving and uncharming,'' according to Joyce Carol Oates in the *New York Times Book Review*, and getting readers to identify with them is a major feat. ''Most of them perform criminal actions of one kind or another,'' notes Oates, ''[but] we are allowed to see how they define themselves as other than merely 'bad' through the author's extraordinary sympathy with them; he has a gift for conveying, with a wonderful sort of clairvoyance, their interior voices.'' This same talent leads *Los Angeles Times Book Review* contributor Carolyn Banks to name Dubus ''a writer of real might.'' Banks cites the novella ''The Pretty Girl'' as an example of the author's power. In it, readers come to feel a strong sympathy for Raymond, a character who eventually rapes his wife, Polly, at knifepoint. ''Dubus is able to make us laugh *with* Raymond even after we know him as a beast. . . . Because of this moment, when our laughter puts us in cahoots with Raymond—our shame, when we read Polly's account of the rape, is enormous.'' Banks summarizes: ''Andre Dubus' mastery of his material and therefore of his readers is total. He knows exactly how he wants us to respond and we do.''

''The slices of life that [Dubus] sets forth may not be to everyone's taste, but no one can deny his talent or generosity,'' concludes Paul Gray in *Time*. Gray also notes a new direction in Dubus's latest writings. In his review of *The Times Are Never So Bad,* he writes: ''These bleak emotional landscapes will look familiar to readers of Dubus' three earlier collections of short fiction. Yet there is something new here: a religious sense, largely implicit in previous stories, that is now explicitly Roman Catholic. . . . The shift from senseless to redemptive suffering marks Dubus as a writer with a distinguished past and a promising future.''

CA INTERVIEW

CA interviewed Andre Dubus by telephone on May 10, 1985, at his home in Haverhill, Massachusetts.

CA: Most of your work has been in the short form—stories and novellas. Was that a conscious choice, or rather what seemed dictated by the nature of what you wanted to write about?

DUBUS: Really the latter. I had published a novel, *The Lieutenant,* in 1967. It's now out of print and it ought to be; it

should have been a novella, but I didn't know much about the craft. I started a second novel and I read a story by Chekhov called ''Peasants.'' I immediately reread it, because I wanted to see how he covered in thirty pages an entire year and a family and a peasant village and therefore a microcosm of the majority of Russian society after the freeing of the serfs. I studied it and learned how he did it, and then I decided it was time to learn to write. I began compressing, and nothing has been long since then. I think, too, that the ideas I work with should really be handled in the short form. I have a limited number of characters. There's usually one theme—I have a feeling that real novels have more than one. My work would be very bad if I tried to make it into novels. It seems to me it's always better to cut.

CA: You intended The Lieutenant *to be a novel, then? It didn't start out as a story and grow?*

DUBUS: No. I did it at the University of Iowa. It was based on a real incident. I kept telling the story so often at parties, somebody said, ''You ought to write that; it's a good story.'' So I wrote it. I realize now that I'm forty-eight—I was twenty-nine when I wrote it—that it would have been a nice 100-page thing. But it would not have been published either. I did have to reread it in 1968 to write a script of it, and I was not embarrassed by it.

CA: Burt Lancaster bought the movie rights, didn't he?

DUBUS: That's what happened. He had an option. He had a small company, and they asked me to do the script. It was very nice; they flew me out, interviewed me, and gave me a contract which said that doing the script would not interfere with my fiction writing or my teaching, and I could do it all at home. But you know the way they throw money around out there. From the very beginning they had doubts that they could ever do the movie. They needed a million dollars. And they felt it was the young audiences who went to movies, and because of Vietnam, how would they get a young audience to go to a movie about Marines? How could they be told it was anti-Establishment? They were sure the Navy would not co-operate when they knew what the material was, so they would have to rig up the ship. But they were very frank about it. Lancaster's producer, Roland Kibbe, a wonderful man who died last year, said, ''Kid, ninety percent of the scripts that we buy out here are never made into movies.''

That was fun, but I wouldn't want to write a script again because you don't get to write any prose. It isn't that it's easy. I loved Horton Foote's *Tender Mercies* and Nora Ephron and Alice Arlen's *Silkwood;* those things weren't easy. But I love to write prose. As Richard Yates said once, ''You know, you can start off a movie script with 'We see a World War II combat formation of bombers,' which would take a fiction writer *days* to write.'' So I'm not saying that it's a form for dumb people; it just doesn't give me the challenge I want. I wouldn't do it now anyway, because the only reason I would do it now would be for money, and I'm too old to write for money. I'm at the age where you can drop dead before supper. So I turned down what looked like a sure job for PBS last fall. I got home very happy, and twenty-four hours later I was depressed. I thought, You can't take this job writing this script; that's not your work.

CA: Voices from the Moon *has been publicized as a novel. Do you consider it a novella?*

DUBUS: I consider it a novella, and there was no skulduggery going on. They're very nice people at Godine. From the beginning they said I could dictate what would be on the cover. I said I wanted *novella* to be on the jacket; they had their obvious reasons for wanting to call it a novel, simply being that a bookstore manager would treat it differently. I said I thought it took as long to read as Joan Didion's *Play It As It Lays*, but *Play It As It Lays* is a novel and *Voices from the Moon* is a novella, and I could not explain that. The discussion lasted for about eight months. It was always friendly; they always said, whatever you want, we'll do. But they won. It's not an argument the writer can win, if both sides are friendly, because all they have to do is start listing very short books, including *The Old Man and the Sea,* that were published as novels. I finally said, what the hell, they know the business better than I do, and anybody else who knows the business will know why it's called a novel. I don't even think about it anymore. The concession they *did* make, which I didn't even ask for, was to say they would put *novel* on the dust jacket, but not the title page. At the very end, as a matter of fact, when they realized how short it really *would* be, they were going to put *a short novel,* but they had a temperamental calligrapher who refused to write s-h-o-r-t, and that was the end of that.

CA: It was a lovely approach you took, getting at the conflict of the story from the various points of view.

DUBUS: That's why it became a novella. I was just going to do it as a short story from the boy's point of view, but I realized I had written a story very much like that called "Delivering." I thought, I can't have another story about a boy overhearing something bad and dealing with it. So I decided to do each point of view. After that, it grew. It didn't become a mutant, though, and go four hundred pages. The house joke at Godine was to call it a *novelini,* which comes from a cartoon in the *New Yorker.*

CA: Does a story usually begin with an outline, either in your head or on paper?

DUBUS: Never. And I always told my students that if they had an outline, they had already killed the story, so they should throw out the outline and write something else. No, it usually begins with a "what if." An idea just comes to me. You know, I've retired from teaching, so I find that I have more time to receive ideas. At first I told my wife that I had more time to think, and then I realized that's not what it is: it's having more time with nothing on your mind. I'll use a story called "The Fat Girl" for an example. I have had many in classes, and one day I thought, What's it like to be an eighteen-year-old female and fat in one of the worst countries in the world to be female and fat? So I started to write the story and gained ten pounds. I got rid of all my diet colas.

CA: Do your stories go through several drafts?

DUBUS: They used to. I used to average five, sometimes six. A novella called "Adultery" was seven drafts, a total of 400 typed pages to get 60. But in 1980 I was writing the story called "Anna," and I didn't know anything about the girl, because I never knew anybody—at least as far as I know—who'd held up a drugstore. I thought the story was going to be about betrayal. I'd made a note from a story I'd read in the *Boston Globe* years earlier about a guy who robbed a bank in Boston by himself, then went to a phone booth and called his

woman in Florida and said he had all this money and he was on his way. She said, "Where's the phone booth?" He told her; she wrote it down for her lover, who went next-door and phoned the police; she kept the guy on the line until they got there. So I was going to write a story to see what would make a woman reach the point where she would do this, but the story was very difficult to write because I didn't understand the woman. So, instead of writing in a horizontal way—that is, trying to get from page one to page five, which I used to do—I decided to write vertically. I would actually hunch over my shoulders as I was starting to write, and say, Don't leave a sentence until you know what it feels like to be her. I went very slowly, and as a result, the story was finished more quickly. The first draft was almost the final draft, because, by going slowly, I didn't take any wrong paths.

In "Anna," the couple rob a drugstore and then they go to a bar. When they were in the bar, I realized that they were in love with each other and there was going to be no betrayal; then I didn't know what was going to happen. So I just followed them through the next few days and the story ended. Ever since then I've tried to concentrate more on each word and each line, and usually I take a long time with the longhand draft, and then I read it over and make any corrections. Then I tape it, always, and listen to it, and make some more corrections—cuttings, additions—and then it's ready to type.

CA: That's interesting. I don't think I've ever talked to a writer before who tapes his work.

DUBUS: I recommend it to everybody. I think most writers do what I do, which is to sit down every day and read everything you've written up until where you left off the day before. So some paragraphs you've read a hundred times, and you're not really reading them anymore. When you read them aloud, it involves your body and it awakens some focus, I think. You begin to see things or hear things that you've been overlooking. Then when you hear it back, you get the same effect. You will hear an unintentional interior rhyme, dialogue going on too long, repetition of words that you don't want, somebody saying something on page thirty that they said on page two. It helps a lot, and I think everybody should do it. Of course for novelists it's hard. I do tape my novellas. It's boring, but I do it—though not at one sitting.

CA: Some of your characters do really bad things, but you are nevertheless able to treat them sympathetically. Does that require a kind of distancing process in the writing?

DUBUS: No. I always try to become them; if I can't become them, I can't write them. That was my problem with "Anna." I could become her working in the store. I could become her being poor. But I couldn't become her involved with a holdup for a while. I learned a lot from Chekhov, and I guess a lot of it is in my nature anyway, although probably when I'm not writing I'm pretty judgmental and mean. Someone wrote to Chekhov about his story called "Thieves" and said it was an immoral story because he did not show that horse stealing is immoral. Chekhov wrote back saying, "Everybody knows it's immoral to steal horses. I wanted you to know what it feels like to be a man who steals horses."

CA: He was a master, wasn't he?

DUBUS: He was. He had great compassion in his personal life too, which I don't always have.

CA: How do you get to know your characters before you put them on paper?

DUBUS: I gestate for a long, long time. I make notes of things that may never get into the story. I want to know if they believe in God; if so, do they belong to an organized religion? Ever since the surgeon general's report on smoking I've thought it was important to know whether or not a character smoked, because it said something about the character.

CA: A lot of your characters do.

DUBUS: Yes. I have a fetish about that anyway. I like to watch women smoke. I'm writing a story about two guys on board a ship now, and every once in a while there's a cigarette, but it's not really very important. It's saying, You guys can smoke too, because you do, but I'm not going to really watch that.

I make notes on the age, the family. The hardest part is to get the characters' employment. I have to find them a job, and then I have to find out something about the job. I've had several jobs—I was a Marine, I was a bartender, I was a teacher—but you've got to have characters who do something besides those things. I'm gestating something now about a priest, and I've got to go spend some time with one. I'm going to ask him if I can say a mass. Robert De Niro did that for *True Confessions,* just to get the feel of it. I want to put on the vestments and do the whole thing to see what it feels like. Getting the employment is usually the biggest problem. I don't want to cop out and have characters that have inherited money or are dying, or they're writers or painters.

CA: I read that your first acceptance was a story taken by the Sewanee Review.

DUBUS: That's true.

CA: Was that, as the report goes, the impetus that got you out of the Marines and into the Iowa Writers' Workshop?

DUBUS: No. I've never told anybody that, but that's what people write. I've said that I had a quarrel with my commanding officer and I resigned and went to Iowa. I sold a story, which didn't make me think at all of getting out. What I hoped was that I wouldn't have to do over ten years in the Marines, and somehow I'd have money from writing and I could go live somewhere. That was a young man's hope. But I was ready to stay in for twenty years. You know, a writer has to have a job, and I enjoyed that one; there was no war. But no. My commanding officer and I had a difference of opinion and I resigned at once and went to Iowa. A year later I realized that I had really resigned because my father had died two months before I had resigned, and so I no longer had to show him that I was a man. That's really what set me free.

CA: Had you been writing all through the years as a Marine?

DUBUS: Oh yeah, all the time. The first two years I'd get up at 4:30 and write until 7:00. Then I went on sea duty and I was able to write at night. I had no family aboard ship, of course, and I was an officer, so I had a room with a desk. After I got home to the kids, family life just did not allow everybody to go to bed at 9:00 so Daddy could get up at 4:30. Then I had to write from 11:00 at night to 1:00 or something like that.

CA: Your wife, Peggy Rambach, is also a published writer. Does it work out well having two writers in the household?

DUBUS: I think very well. She said something which is probably wise: maybe if we were both at the same point in our careers, we might sometimes get jealous of each other. But she's twenty-seven and I'm forty-eight, and so we're not competing. I have a feeling, though, that we respect each other enough that if we were the same age, it wouldn't matter anyway. The great thing about it is that she doesn't need to be entertained, as many women of my generation did. It's not their fault—I think you know that from reading my work—but they were not brought up to do much. Sometimes it can be hard for a woman like that to live with a person who can suddenly become distracted through no will of his own but because a story has started talking to him while they're having dinner. When that happens to one of us, the other one knows it and it's no problem. We both recognize how the other is reacting to a story not going well. We both know how rejections feel, because we both get them all the time.

CA: Do you read and comment on each other's work?

DUBUS: Oh yes, always. We usually do that when the work is finished, or if one of us is having trouble. Peggy's helped me a lot with that, and I guess I've helped her some too. There's a novella called "The Pretty Girl," which began with a rape scene. When I finished that, there was nowhere to go. I gave it to her and said, "What's wrong?" Then I took a walk, and when I came back, she said, "You'd better find out about these people and why they were married and what went wrong first, instead of starting with the rape." So I started then from the point of view of the husband. I had simply wanted to write a story about a woman being assaulted and chased and terrorized, because I knew of one whose father finally sent her someplace secret; they were that worried. And that's what I wanted to write, but it didn't work that way.

CA: Do you write every day on a regular schedule?

DUBUS: Yeah. When I'm working on something, I try to work seven days a week. Usually Peggy works in the morning and I'll take care of our little daughter Cadence when she's not in play school. And then when Peggy's done, I write. I used to have to write at the same time every day, and that's where Peggy is now. But I started writing in 1954, so now I can generally write whenever. I'm not as nervous about it as I was.

CA: Time *reviewer Paul Gray, writing about the collection* The Times Are Never So Bad, *noted "the shift from senseless to redemptive suffering" in "A Father's Story," which also made its way into* The Best American Short Stories 1984. *Does that shift stem from a a change in your own outlook?*

DUBUS: I think it's not a coincidence that in 1970, when I lost my first marriage, I wrote the story "We Don't Live Here Anymore," which was very bleak. Peggy and I got married in December, 1979, and the novella I wrote at the end of the decade was "Finding a Girl in America," which had a happy ending. Except for one story, which I had started before I met Peggy—a story called "Waiting," about a woman who was going to commit suicide—I think every story I've written since I met Peggy has had an affirmative ending. I don't believe I've written a story since then in which the characters don't survive. I think Peggy's a big part of that.

Also, in my thirties, my friends and I were getting divorced, and it didn't look like we were going to make it. I was particularly worried about the women; I thought they were the ones who needed the nest. Well, they did a lot better than the men did. I did some reading and found out that men in middle age living alone did not do well at all. They had more illnesses, more alcoholism, more suicide. But then I got into my forties and looked around, and most of us had survived. So I think that experience too had something to do with the change in my work. I remember when Peggy and I got together, I wrote to the novelist Thomas Williams and said, "I think I'm probably about to die, because I've never really been a happy man, and I never thought that anyone *was* happy unless they were about to die. But every day I'm happy, and I've never experienced that." He wrote back and said, "Relax and enjoy it."

CA: Are you going to miss the teaching in any way?

DUBUS: If I weren't doing a lot of college readings, I would. But I've been in contact with students ever since I retired. I go to universities and read and talk with students. I'm going to teach one seminar at the University of Alabama in the fall of 1985, and I'm going to teach one course at Boston University the following spring. I think if I'm lucky I'll always be teaching a course somewhere. I love teaching; I simply got exhausted, that was all. I was teaching four classes and was teaching five afternoons a week. Even though I work out every day, I would come home tired. Then I'd brew up some tea, start writing. Cadence is almost three now, but then she was a little baby; by the time I finished writing, she was in bed. I never saw her. It built up and finally my blood pressure went up, and it was just a crazy way to live. Now we're a lot poorer, but we write more and we see our daughter more.

CA: Do you have any long-term goals as far as the writing goes?

DUBUS: I'd like to get better. Someday I'd like to write something as good as the best of Chekhov. I know I'll never do that, but it's a great goal for me. His novella called "My Life" is the best thing I've ever read by anybody. Besides wanting to get better, I hope Godine stays in business, because they keep my books in print, which is the main reason I stay with them. People have asked me why I don't get a bigger publisher so I can get bigger advances. I say it's because the books would go out of print in six months. This happens all the time. I'll read a book by somebody and go down to order the rest of her books (I say *her* because I tend to end up reading women more than men; maybe they write better), and they're all out of print. I don't like to go to libraries; I guess it's too much like homework. For some reason libraries depress me. They shouldn't; they probably buy more of my books than anybody else.

CA: You're a Southerner by birth—from Louisiana—but you seem pretty happy about being in Massachusetts.

DUBUS: It's given me perspective. When Jimmy Carter was first campaigning, I thought, No wonder Northerners laugh at Southerners. When I first heard the North Shore accent, it occurred to me that all regional accents sound dumb if you're not from that region. I have a Caedmon recording of Faulkner reading, and he sounds like some illiterate guy running the corner store, with tobacco in his mouth. You hear some of these people up here, and they sound like movie characters to those of us used to softer speech.

But I do love Massachusetts. We bought a lot to retire on that's surrounded by acreage that cannot be built on. There are pheasants mating among the poplars in the back, and a fox tries to cross the road in front to get to the pheasants. I've considered it home here ever since my mother died in 1980. I've been here since 1966, and I love the weather and the land. I can't stand Southern humidity anymore.

BIOGRAPHICAL/CRITICAL SOURCES:

BOOKS

Contemporary Literary Criticism, Volume XIII, Gale, 1980.

PERIODICALS

Harper's, January, 1978.
Hudson Review, autumn, 1978.
Los Angeles Times, November 7, 1984.
Los Angeles Times Book Review, July 6, 1980, August 14, 1983.
Nation, February 26, 1977.
New Leader, September 15, 1975.
New Republic, February 4, 1978, August 23, 1980.
Newsweek, July 18, 1983.
New York Times, June 25, 1980.
New York Times Book Review, August 24, 1975, June 22, 1980, June 26, 1983, November 18, 1984.
Ontario Review, fall-winter, 1976-77.
Publishers Weekly, October 12, 1984.
Saturday Review, January 21, 1978.
Sewanee Review, summer, 1975.
Time, June 16, 1980, August 15, 1983.
Times Literary Supplement, February 22, 1985.
Village Voice, November 26-December 2, 1980.
Washington Post Book World, July 20, 1975, December 18, 1977.

—Sketch by Joan E. Marecki
—Interview by Jean W. Ross

*   *   *

DUGGAN, Maurice (Noel)   1922-1974

PERSONAL: Born November 25, 1922, in Auckland, New Zealand; died December 11, 1974, in Auckland, New Zealand; married Barbara Platts, 1945; children: one. *Education:* Attended University of Auckland.

ADDRESSES: Home—58 Forrest Hill Rd., Takapuna, Auckland 10, New Zealand.

CAREER: Writer. Worked in metal stamping plant, 1943, and in advertising, beginning 1961; J. English Wright Advertising Ltd., Auckland, New Zealand, staff member, 1965-72.

AWARDS, HONORS: Hubert Church Memorial Award, 1957; Esther Glenn Award, New Zealand Library Association, 1959, for *Falter Tom and the Water Boy;* Katherine Mansfield Award, 1959; Robert Burns fellow at Otago University, 1960; New Zealand Literary Fund scholar, 1966; Freda Buckland Award, 1970, for his advancement of New Zealand literature.

WRITINGS:

Immanuel's Land: Stories, Pilgrim Press, 1956.
Falter Tom and the Water Boy (juvenile), Blackwood & Janet Paul, 1957, Criterion, 1958.
(With others) *New Authors: Short Stories I*, Hutchinson, 1961.
Summer in the Gravel Pit: Stories, Blackwood & Janet Paul, 1965.

(Contributor) *"Landfall" 80*, New Zealand Publishers, 1966.

O'Leary's Orchard, and Other Stories, Caxton Press, 1970.

The Fabulous McFanes, and Other Children's Stories, illustrated by Richard Kennedy, International Publications Service, 1974.

Collected Stories, edited and introduced by Christian Karlson Stead, Oxford University Press (Auckland), 1981.

CONTRIBUTOR TO ANTHOLOGIES

D. M. Davin, editor, *New Zealand Short Stories*, Oxford University Press, 1953.

Charles Brasch, editor, *"Landfall" Country*, Caxton Press, 1962.

J. C. Reid, editor, *A Book of New Zealand*, Collins (Auckland), 1964, revised edition, Peter Cape, 1979.

OTHER

Also contributor to *Speaking for Ourselves*, edited by Frank Sargeson, Caxton Press. Contributor to periodicals, including *Anvil* and *Landfall*.

SIDELIGHTS: As an author of short fiction, Maurice Duggan was "an unfixed writer, engaged in an endless effort to arrange selves for himself—selves that, over and over, he straightaway undoes, dissolves, and discards," wrote Valentine Cunningham in the *Times Literary Supplement*. His stories, according to R. A. Copland, consequently "display within themselves very little growth, little energy of an expanding sort, little plot and no great exploration of character." Copland found Duggan's stories to be reductions of experience to moments of crisis, written both skillfully and economically, but trimmed so much "that occasionally it seems that only the human circumstance remains, almost independently of the humans who create it."

Such a narrow range of tone and theme, though, "may become a virtue," wrote Lawrence Jacobs, "if it encourages intensity, as Joyce's *Dubliners* illustrates. Such a world as Mr. Duggan's needs to be presented in the Joycean static mode, in stories that depend more on the revelation than the resolution of conflict, more on image and mood than on plot." Jacobs felt that "to achieve intensity such stories require an economical choice of telling details that will cumulatively form a revelation of a character and his situation to the reader (and sometimes to himself). The style must be precise, close to poetry in the range and control of connotation." Judged by these criteria, Jacobs continued, "Duggan's technique is not always adequate. . . . Often the setting is beautifully evoked in vivid detail and is made quite relevant to the characters. . . . However, there is often a loss in clarity and economy through full development."

Terry Sturm, too, noted that "in almost all [Duggan's] stories there is a careful stress on meticulously observed physical detail, to establish a solidly realistic environment for his characters, but this detail is also used to create a mood and atmosphere—an emotional tone which envelops the stories as a whole." Mindful of criticism leveled against Duggan's use of detail in his short stories, Sturm observed that "one often detects, in comments about Duggan's style, an impatience that he hasn't said 'what he has to say' more directly, or more simply." Sturm called Duggan, especially in his later stories, a difficult writer: "The general development of his style has been from a relatively bare selective realism in the manner of the early Joyce, to a much denser, evocative prose working through overtones, allusion, suggestion." Sturm pointed out, however, that "the exploitation of perspective, of the angle

of vision, is crucial to the effect of a Duggan story; there is always some kind of ironic distance between Duggan's total perspective on the world he creates in his stories and the partial or limited perspective of individual characters."

Jacobs suggested that while Duggan's characters "are primarily members of the submerged society of the lonely, the repressed, and the futile that has populated much of British short fiction since Joyce's *Dubliners*, . . . the general tone . . . reminds one of Joyce's dead Dubliners and the 'young man carbuncular' of Eliot's London." But Sturm remarked about Duggan's gloomy characters: "Occasionally [they] reach a moment of self-awareness, a dim recognition which breaks through defense mechanisms and rationalizations, habitual ways of thinking and feeling and reacting. More often, though, they remain tragically or pathetically imprisoned, victims (at some crisis of commitment on which the stories characteristically focus) of a radical failure of will in themselves or in others." Sturm concluded: "Duggan's interest in this aspect of human experience has produced writing of increasing complexity and depth. It could perhaps be described as his individual variation of the theme of 'man alone.'"

BIOGRAPHICAL/CRITICAL SOURCES:

BOOKS

Duggan, Maurice, *Collected Stories*, edited and introduced by Christian Karlson Stead, Oxford University Press (Auckland), 1981.

"Landfall" 80, New Zealand Publishers, 1966.

PERIODICALS

Landfall, March, 1957, September, 1965, March, 1971.

London Magazine, September, 1970.

Times Literary Supplement, April 9, 1982.

OBITUARIES:

PERIODICALS

AB Bookman's Weekly, February 3, 1975.†

    *   *   *

DUNCAN, Frances (Mary) 1942-

PERSONAL: Born January 24, 1942, in Vancouver, British Columbia, Canada; daughter of Edgar A. S. (in business) and Frances (a social worker; maiden name, Fraser) Chowne; married Norman Duncan (a school principal), May 10, 1963; children: Kelly, Kirsten. *Education:* University of British Columbia, B.A., 1962, M.A., 1963.

ADDRESSES: Home—Vancouver, British Columbia, Canada. *Office*—Writers Union of Canada, 24 Ryerson Ave., Toronto, Ontario, Canada M5R 1K5. *Agent*—Nancy Colbert, 303 Davenport Rd., Toronto, Ontario, Canada M5R 1K5.

CAREER: Woodlands School, New Westminister, British Columbia, psychologist, 1963-65; Burnaby Mental Health Centre, Burnaby, British Columbia, psychologist, 1965-67; Metropolitan Health Department, Vancouver, British Columbia, psychologist, 1969-73; writer, 1973—.

MEMBER: P.E.N. International, Writers Union of Canada, CANSCAIP, West Coast Women and Words Society, Federation of British Columbian Writers.

WRITINGS:

Cariboo Runaway (juvenile), Burns & MacEachern, 1976.

(Contributor) *New: West Coast* (poems), Intermedia, 1977.
Kap-Sung Ferris (Children's Book Centre choice), Burns & MacEachern, 1977, Macmillan, 1980.
(Contributor) *Common Ground* (short fiction), Press Gang, 1980.
The Toothpaste Genie (juvenile fantasy; Children's Book Centre choice), Scholastic Inc., 1981.
Dragonhunt (novel), Women's Educational Press, 1981.
(Contributor) *Canadian Short Fiction Anthology,* Volume II, Intermedia, 1982.
Finding Home (novel), Avon, 1982.
(Contributor) *Baker's Dozen* (short fiction), Women's Educational Press, 1984.
(Contributor) *Anthology* (short fiction), University of British Columbia Press, 1986.

Contributor of short stories to magazines, including *Makara, Northern Journey,* and *Canadian Fiction Magazine.*

WORK IN PROGRESS: The Breeding Season and *Pattern Makers,* two novels; *No State of Grace,* a juvenile novel; a sequel to *The Toothpaste Genie.*

SIDELIGHTS: Frances Duncan commented: "I am primarily interested in individuals and how they cope with situations, external crises, and crises of their own making; also in isolation and attempts to overcome it. I am interested in Canadian identity, but within a framework of individual identity which has international applications. When I am writing, I make no distinction between 'juvenile' and 'adult' books, that is, I do not say 'Now I will write a book for children' or 'a story for adults.' I write to tell the protagonist's story and hope that it will be read by whoever is interested in her (usually her) story. I am not particularly concerned about the readers' ages, and think a lot of the categorizations used for writing are gratuitous."

AVOCATIONAL INTERESTS: Outdoor activities, travel, ("reading and conversation cannot come under this category: they are essentials").

BIOGRAPHICAL/CRITICAL SOURCES:

PERIODICALS

In Review, October, 1979.

* * *

DUNHAM, Donald Carl 1908-

PERSONAL: Born August 30, 1908, in Columbus, Ohio; son of Ray Stanley and Agnes (Jordan) Dunham; married Florence Atkins Ross, 1944; children: Robert Ross (stepson). *Education:* Yale University, Ph.B., 1930; Harvard University, graduate study, 1939-40; University of Bucharest, Ph.D., 1948.

CAREER: U.S. Department of State, Foreign Service, Washington, D.C., vice-consul in Berlin, Germany, 1931-32, Hong Kong, 1932-35, Athens, Greece, 1935-38, and Aden (now part of Yemen), 1939; museum supervisor for New York State Works Project Administration (WPA), 1940; Metropolitan Museum of Art, New York City, administrative assistant to director, 1941-42; director, East and West Association, 1942-43; editor of financial research program for National Bureau of Economic Research, 1943-45; *Life* Magazine, New York City, cable editor, 1945-46; U.S. Department of State, UNESCO relations officer, 1946-47; public affairs officer for Foreign Service in Bucharest, Rumania, 1947-50, Bern, Switzerland, 1950-52, and Trieste, Italy, 1952-55; American Committee for

Liberation, New York City, director of planning, 1955-61; United States Mission to the United Nations, New York City, director of public service, 1962-68; United Nations, New York City, representative for Australia, Papua/New Guinea, and New Zealand to Development Programme, United Nations International Children's Emergency Fund (UNICEF), and High Commissioner for Refugees, 1968-71, official at Institute for Training and Research, beginning 1971. Lecturer in international affairs, Cooper Union, 1945; adjunct associate professor, Fordham University, 1962.

MEMBER: Delta Kappa Epsilon, Dutch Treat Club.

WRITINGS:

Envoy Unextraordinary, John Day, 1944.
Die Schatten Werden Laenger, Thomas Verlag, 1950.
Kremlin Target: U.S.A., Washburn, 1961.
Zone of Violence, Belmont Books, 1962.

Contributor of articles to various publications.†

* * *

DUNHAM, Katherine 1910-
(Kaye Dunn)

PERSONAL: Born June 22, 1910, in Joliet, Ill.; daughter of Albert Millard (an operator of a cleaning and dyeing establishment, a musician, and a singer) and Annette (a teacher; maiden name, Poindexter) Dunham; married John Thomas Pratt (a theatre designer), July 10, 1941; children: Marie Christine. *Education:* University of Chicago, Ph.B.; Northwestern University, Ph.D.

ADDRESSES: Home—Residence Leclerc, Port au Prince, Haiti, West Indies. *Office*—Performing Arts Training Center, Southern Illinois University, East St. Louis, Ill. 62201.

CAREER: Director and teacher of own schools of dance, theatre, and cultural arts in Chicago, New York, Haiti, Stockholm, and Paris, beginning 1931; professional dancer, beginning 1934, with theatre experience beginning with performances in Chicago Opera, Chicago World's Fair, and eventually including world-wide tours; choreographer for theatre, opera, motion pictures, and television nationally and internationally. Lecturer nationally and internationally, beginning 1937; Southern Illinois University, artist in residence at Carbondale and Edwardsville campuses, 1967, cultural counselor and director of Performing Arts Training Center at East St. Louis campus, 1967—, university professor at Edwardsville campus, 1968—.

Member of Chicago Opera Co., 1935-36; supervisor of Chicago City Theater Project on cultural studies, 1939; dance director of Labor Stage, 1939-40; producer and director for Katherine Dunham Dance Co., 1945; established school in Port-au-Prince, Haiti, 1961. U.S. State Department adviser to First World Festival on Negro Art, 1966; artistic and technical adviser to president of Senegal, 1966-67. Productions for her own dance companies include "Bal Negre," 1946, "New Tropical Revue," 1948, "Caribbean Rhapsody," 1948, and "Bamboche," 1963. Appearances in motion pictures include "Star Spangled Rhythm," Paramount Pictures, 1943; "Stormy Weather," Twentieth Century-Fox, 1943; "Casbah," Universal-International, 1949; "Mambo," Paramount Pictures, 1966; and "The Bible," Twentieth Century-Fox, 1966.

President, Dunham Fund for Research and Development of Cultural Arts, Inc.; founder, Foundation for the Study of Arts and Sciences of the Vodun; vice-president, Foundation for the

Development and Preservation of Cultural Arts, Inc.; board member, National Institute on Aging and Illinois Arts Council; member, Illinois committee of J. F. Kennedy Center-Alliance Arts Education, American Council on Arts in Education, and Arts Worth/Intercultural Committee. Consultant, Interamerican Institute for Ethnomusicology and Folklore (Caracas, Venezuela), National Endowment for the Humanities review committee, and Organization of American States; advisory board member, Modern Organization for Dance Evolvement.

MEMBER: American Guild of Variety Artists, American Society of Composers, Authors, and Publishers (ASCAP), American Guild of Music Artists (member of board of governors, 1943-49), American Federation of Radio Artists, Screen Actors Guild, Writers Guild, Actors' Equity Association, Black Academy of Arts and Letters, Institute of the Black World (board member), Negro Actors Guild, Royal Anthropological Society, Lincoln Academy, Sigma Epsilon.

AWARDS, HONORS: Julius Rosenwald travel fellowship to West Indies, 1936-37; Haitian Legion of Honor and Merit Chevalier, 1950, Commander, 1958, Grand Officer, 1968; named honorary citizen of Port au Prince, Haiti, 1957; awarded key to East St. Louis, Ill., 1968; *Dance Magazine* award, 1969; Eight Lively Arts award, 1969; Southern Illinois University distinguished service award, 1969; St. Louis Argus Award, 1970; East St. Louis Monitor Award, 1970; International Who's Who in Poetry certificate of merit, 1970-71; American Association for Health, Physical Education, and Recreation dance division heritage award, 1972; National Center of Afro-American Artists award, 1972; Black Merit Academy award, 1972; Mather scholar, Case Western Reserve University, 1973; Black Filmmakers Hall of Fame, 1974; American Dance Guild Annual Award, 1975; Kennedy Center Board of Trustees sixth annual award, 1983; State Department of International Education Fulbright fellow; University of Chicago, professional achievement award; L.H.D., MacMurray College, Jacksonville, Ill., 1972, and Ph.D.L., Atlanta University, 1977.

WRITINGS:

Katherine Dunham's Journey to Accompong, Holt, 1946, reprinted, Greenwood Press, 1972.
A Touch of Innocence (autobiography), Harcourt, 1959, reprinted, Books for Libraries, 1980.
Island Possessed, Doubleday, 1969.
(Author of foreword) Lynne F. Emery, *Black Dance in the United States from 1619 to 1970,* Mayfield, 1972.
Kasamance: A Fantasy, Third Press, 1974.
Dances of Haiti (revised version of doctoral thesis), Center for Afro-American Studies, 1983.

Also co-author of play, "Ode to Taylor Jones," 1967-68. Author of television scripts, produced in Mexico, Australia, France, England, and Italy. Contributor of short stories, sometimes under pseudonym Kaye Dunn, to popular magazines, including *Esquire, Mademoiselle, Show, Realities,* and to anthropology, travel, and dance magazines. Consulting editor, *Dance Scope.*

SIDELIGHTS: Best known for her contributions to the world of dance, Katherine Dunham is also an accomplished anthropologist and writer. As an aspiring young student, she was equally attracted to the disciplines of science and art, and it wasn't until she abandoned her dream of classical ballet and embraced ethnic dance that she could reconcile her interests. Her investigation into the origins of Caribbean dance led to a 1936 Rosenwald travel fellowship to the West Indies. There, "she plunged into voodoo and became initiated as a way of finding herself and doing research," according to a writer for the *New York Times Book Review.* Her participation in and description of native rituals made a valuable contribution to anthropology, provided her with raw materials for original choreography, and furnished the subject matter for her doctoral thesis—later revised and published as *Dances of Haiti.* Commenting in the *Saturday Review,* dance critic Walter Terry sums up her achievements this way: "Dunham, who began dancing professionally in 1931, was among the first of her race to conceive of black dance as art as well as entertainment. Certainly she was the first to explore and use for dance the anthropological and ethnological origins of her race. With a Ph.D. in anthropology from the University of Chicago, she evolved not only a dance technique and style but a concept of black dance theatre."

Like many black artists, Dunham had to overcome racial prejudice in order to succeed, and she once suggested to an *Ebony* reporter that her greatest accomplishment had been "breaking through various social barriers." In the early 1930s, when Dunham was searching for a performing avenue, there were no black ballerinas and no Negro Ballet. Even if there had been, her acceptance would not have been assured. As her college mentor and dance instructor Mark Turbfill explained in *Dancemagazine,* Dunham came to him untrained, "an ambitious Negro girl, who had never had a lesson in her life in the art, but who wanted to become a ballet dancer."

Together Dunham and Turbyfill—a white poet and dancer with an appetite for the untried—conceived the notion of a Negro Ballet. With encouragement from prominent black citizens and a few open-minded artists, they borrowed time in an existing studio and began to recruit students. Within months, there were problems, as Turbyfill recalls in his diary, which is excerpted in *Dancemagazine:* "The manager of the building is not pleased to see Negroes coming to class. I have to give up [this] place. I look for another studio, but everywhere I go I am indignantly refused. Finally, I go to the small dingy R—— studio and succeed in renting time. Pupils lose interest and drop off. We talk of taking a place of our own. Katherine and I are forced to stand on street corners and on El platforms while making plans for the Negro Ballet."

Though Turbyfill did finally finagle a studio of his own, the new locale did not solve many problems. He discovered that some of his black pupils had been attracted, not to his classes per se, but to the access that attendance gave them to a Michigan Avenue studio. When he moved to the new location, classes became alarmingly small. To make matters worse, choreographer Agnes de Mille dropped by to visit one day and informed him "that the idea of a ballet for Negroes is all wrong. She reminds me that it has never been done, that it isn't physiologically in the picture. I tell her that I am not thinking of a physiological picture, but rather an abstract one."

Discouraged by such resistance, Dunham's interest waned, and just a year after its conception, the project was abandoned. Out of the failure of a Negro Ballet, however, grew a splendid opportunity. After observing Dunham in class one day, choreographer/dancer Ruth Page noted her potential and, in 1933, recommended Dunham for a part in *La Guiablesse,* a new ballet based on a West Indian legend.

Dunham's participation in this performance marked a turning point in her life. "After *La Guiablesse,* she turned more of her attention to the dances and culture of the displaced Africans in the West Indies,'' Page reports in *Dancemagazine*. In 1936, she won the Rosenwald grant to travel to the Caribbean, and this in turn led to the development of a long and happy relationship between Dunham and the West Indies—particularly Haiti. She returned to the area—at first by herself and later with her husband and costume designer John Pratt—and eventually established a second residence in Port au Prince, Haiti.

Out of her experiences Dunham fashioned a new style of dance that ''included anatomical bases of ballet and modern dance and emphasized the torso movements of the primitive ritual of Caribbean-African dance and jazz rhythms,'' according to an article in *Dancemagazine*. Her innovative synthesis of old and new movement brought her international acclaim as a dancer/choreographer. She made her off-Broadway debut in 1940 with *Tropics and Le Jazz Hot* and went on to star on Broadway and in several Hollywood films, including *Carnival of Rhythm*, a twenty-minute short, and *Stormy Weather*, a full-length feature.

Since her retirement from the stage in the 1960s, Dunham has devoted her energies to the Performing Arts Training Center in the predominantly black city of East St. Louis, Ill., where she was invited to teach. ''On the very day she arrived,'' reports *Ebony* contributor Lynn Norment, ''she was arrested because she protested the random arrest of young Black men. University officials criticized her for being friendly with 'militant types' and suggested that she move to the Carbondale, Ill., campus. 'I'm here now and this is where I'll stay!' the strong-willed Miss Dunham announced. 'There was something burning all the time in this city,' she recalls, 'and I decided to direct some of that energy into something useful.'''

In addition to her dance career, Dunham has published five well-received books, ranging from fantasy to autobiography to nonfiction. Most of this writing addresses some aspect of her art, but *A Touch of Innocence* is a third person chronicle of her early life that scarcely alludes to dancing. ''As a study in questing childhood and what she calls 'defeated adolescence' . . . this can be extremely touching,'' reports a *Times Literary Supplement* reviewer of her autobiography. ''As writing,'' notes Arthur Todd in the *Saturday Review*, ''it is honest, searing, graphic and touching, giving us a rather heart-breaking early view of the young American Negro who was later to make a name for herself. . . . Though it hardly has a word about dance in it, it is notable for the background it provides and what it foretells of her future.'' Writing in the *New York Times Book Review*, Elizabeth Janeway calls *A Touch of Innocence* ''one of the most extraordinary life-stories I have ever read. . . . Not one breath of sentimentality or self-pity mars or falsifies the clear picture of her girlhood, her family and her surroundings. . . . The content of this book is so heartbreaking that only the strongest artistic skill could keep it from leaking out in sobbing self-pity, but Katherine Dunham's art contains it, understands it and refuses to be overwhelmed by its terrors.'' Katherine Dunham, concludes *Time* magazine, ''writes with skill and taste.''

With *Island Possessed*, her next book, Dunham ''continues her autobiography which began with 'A Touch of Innocence','' a *Publishers Weekly* writer reports. The book describes her experiences among the people of Haiti over a period of twenty-three years and touches on such disparate topics as Haitian politics and history, as well as her participation in ancient voodoo rites. ''A rambling, often fascinating, thoroughly honest, highly personal and sometimes egocentric

monologue,'' *Island Possessed* is ''of great value,'' according to a critic for *America*. ''In her double role as devout participant and trained observer, she gained access to—as well as an understanding of—those secret services and sacrifices that other researchers know only from a distance.'' *American Anthropologist* contributor Erika Bourguignon, on the other hand, concludes that ''this book is of interest not as an ethnography, nor for what it may tell us about Haiti but as a personal document of an American Negro woman, an artist seeking identity and roots, her 'lares and penates,' as she puts it, while uprootedly traveling about the world in the exercise of her art.''

AVOCATIONAL INTERESTS: Steam baths, horseback riding, cooking, painting (her work has been shown in Australia, Italy, and England), reading, walking after midnight.

BIOGRAPHICAL/CRITICAL SOURCES:

BOOKS

Adams, Russell L., *Great Negroes, Past and Present*, Afro-American Publishing, 3rd edition, 1969.
Biemiller, Ruth, *Dance: The Story of Katherine Dunham*, Doubleday, 1969.
Buckle, Richard, editor, *Katherine Dunham: Her Dancers, Singers, and Musicians*, Ballet Publications, 1949.
Cluzel, Madeleine E., *Glimpses of the Theatre and Dance*, Kamin, 1953.
Crosland, Margaret, *Ballet Carnival*, Arco, 1955.
Dunham, Katherine, *A Touch of Innocence*, Harcourt, 1959.
Dunham, Katherine, *Island Possessed*, Doubleday, 1969.
Hurok, Solomon and Ruth Goode, *Impresario: A Memoir*, Random House, 1946.
Hurok, Solomon, *Solomon Hurok Presents*, Hermitage, 1953.

PERIODICALS

America, December 27, 1969.
American Anthropologist, October, 1970.
Dancemagazine, December, 1983.
Ebony, January, 1985.
Newsweek, May 1, 1950.
New Yorker, April 29, 1950.
New York Times Book Review, November 8, 1959, September 28, 1969.
Opera News, December 7, 1963.
Publishers Weekly, July 14, 1969.
Saturday Review, December 5, 1959, May 26, 1979.
Time, December 7, 1959.
Times Literary Supplement, November 25, 1960.†

—*Sketch by Donna Olendorf*

*   *   *

DUNN, Kaye
    See DUNHAM, Katherine

*   *   *

DURACK, Mary 1913-

PERSONAL: Born February 20, 1913, in Adelaide, Australia; daughter of Michael Patrick (a pastoralist) and Bessie Ida Muriel (Johnstone) Durack; married Horace Clive Miller (an aviator), December 2, 1938 (died, 1980); children: Patricia Mary Miller Millett, Robin Elizabeth Miller Dicks (deceased), Juliana Miller Rowney (deceased), Andrew Clive, Marie Rose Miller Megaw, John Christopher. *Education:* Attended convent school in Adelaide Terrace, Australia.

ADDRESSES: Home and office—12 Bellevue Ave., Nedlands, Western Australia 6009, Australia. *Agent*—T. Curnow, Curtis Brown Ltd., 24 Renny St., Paddington, New South Wales 2021, Australia.

CAREER: West Australian Newspapers Ltd., Perth, Australia, journalist, 1937-38; free-lance writer, 1938—. Director and patron, Stockman's Hall of Fame and Outback Heritage Centre.

MEMBER: International P.E.N. (Australia; honorary life member), Fellowship of Australian Writers (honorary life member; president of Western Australia branch, 1958-63), Australian Society of Authors, Australian Society of Women Writers, National Trust, Aboriginal Cultural Foundation (past executive member), Royal Western Australian Historical Society, Kulijak Playwrights.

AWARDS, HONORS: Commonwealth Literary Fund grants, 1973, 1977; Order of the British Empire, officer, 1966, dame commander of Civil Division, 1978; D.Letters from University of Western Australia, 1978; Australian Research grants, 1980, 1984-85; Alice Award, Australian Society of Women Writers, 1982; Literature Board of the Australia Council emeritus fellowship, 1983-85.

WRITINGS:

(With Florence Rutter) *Child Artists of the Australian Bush,* Harrap, 1952.
Keep Him My Country (novel), Constable, 1955.
Kings in Grass Castles (family history), Constable, 1959.
The Rock and the Sand, Constable, 1969.
(Editor) M. L. Skinner, *The Fifth Sparrow,* Sydney University Press, 1972.
(With Ingrid A. Drysdale) *The End of Dreaming,* Rigby, 1974.
Swan River Saga (two-act play; first produced in Perth, Australia, 1971), Service Printing Co., 1975.
To Be Heirs Forever (biography of Eliza Shaw), Constable, 1976.
Sons in the Saddle (novel), Constable, 1983.
(With Olsen, Serventy, Dutton, and Bortignon) *The Land beyond Time,* Macmillan, 1984.
(With Mahood, Williams, Willey, Sawrey, Iddon, and Ruhen) *The Stockman,* Landsdowne-Rigby, 1984.

JUVENILES

Little Poems of Sunshine by an Australian Child, R. S. Sampson, 1923.
All-About: The Story of an Aboriginal Community on Argyle Station, Kimberley, Endeavour Press, 1935.
Chunuma, Endeavour Press, 1936.
Son of Djaro, Endeavour Press, 1938.
The Way of the Whirlwind, Consolidated Press, 1941, reprinted, Angus & Robertson, 1979.
Piccaninnies (poems), Offset Printing, 1943.
The Magic Trumpet (poems), Cassell, 1944.
Kookanoo and Kangaroo (poems), Rigby, 1963, Lerner, 1966.
To Ride a Fine Horse, St. Martin's, 1963.
The Courteous Savage: Yagan of Swan River, Thomas Nelson, 1964, published as *Yagan of the Bibbulmun,* 1976.
An Australian Settler, Clarendon Press, 1964, published as *A Pastoral Emigrant,* Oxford University Press, 1964.
Tjakamarra: Boy between Two Worlds, Vanguard Service Printing Co., 1977.

UNPUBLISHED PLAYS

"The Dallying Llama" (radio play), 1959.

"Dalgerie" (libretto for one-act opera), first produced in Perth, Australia, 1966.
"The Ship of Dreams" (two-act for children), first produced in Broome, Australia, 1968.
"The Way of the Whirlwind" (two-act ballet for children), first produced in Nedlands, Australia, at Octagon Theatre, 1970.

OTHER

Author of scripts for Australian Broadcasting Corp.

SIDELIGHTS: Mary Durack told *CA:* "I was never aware of having an ambition to write books, though I seem to have been a compulsive writer from the time I could form words on paper. It now looks as though I am fated to continue this lifelong habit as long as I can push a pen or tap a typewriter. Perhaps the compulsion arose from the genes of Celtic ancestors who were frustrated by lack of opportunity, education, or encouragement.

"That the greater part of my literary output has been of a documentary or historical nature was a matter of chance rather than of choice. For preference I would have concentrated on fiction or drama, but my inheritance or chance acquisition of historical documents decided otherwise. I could, of course, have deposited this material in our state or national archives to be dealt with by some better-qualified historian, present or future, but I realized that, whereas many could produce better novels and plays than myself, no one knew as much as I of the circumstances and people with which these documents are concerned. Only I have had the opportunity, over many years, of supplementing these records with the personal recollections of those involved, who remembered the circumstances surrounding them. The majority of these, black, white, and brindle, are no longer living, and much of their story remains to be told.

"Bearing in mind Napoleon's definition of history as 'a fiction agreed upon,' I try to assure that there is as little fiction as possible in my interpretation and to remember that my characters, enmeshed in their time and circumstances, should not be casually judged by standards imposed by different backgrounds and other generations.

"The happenings and political maneuverings of my own times I see often as ideal subjects for satire and long to put history aside to interpret them in this medium. Whether the time will ever be available or the inclination persist, remains to be seen. In the meantime I look hopefully to the future while living, to a great extent, in the past."

MEDIA ADAPTATIONS

Six of Durack's "Kookanoo" stories have been recorded in an album released by Admark in 1973.

BIOGRAPHICAL/CRITICAL SOURCES:

BOOKS

Hetherington, John, *Forty-Two Faces,* F. W. Cheshire, 1962.

*   *   *

DUTTON, Geoffrey (Piers Henry) 1922-

PERSONAL: Born August 2, 1922, in Anlaby, Kapunda, Australia; son of Henry Hampden and Emily (Martin) Dutton; married Ninette Trott (an enameler), July 31, 1944 (divorced); married Robin Lucas (a writer), April 4, 1985; children: (first marriage) Francis, Teresa, Sam. *Education:* Attended University of Adelaide, 1940-41; Magdalen College, Oxford, B.A., 1949.

ADDRESSES: Home—Piers Hill, Williamstown, South Australia, Australia. *Agent*—Curtis Brown Ltd., P.O. Box 19, Paddington, New South Wales 2021, Australia.

CAREER: Writer in Europe and Australia, 1949-54; University of Adelaide, Adelaide, South Australia, Australia, lecturer, 1954-58, senior lecturer in English, 1958-62; Penguin Books Ltd., Melbourne, Victoria, Australia, editor, 1961-65; writer and farmer, 1962—; Sun Books Ltd., Melbourne, co-founder, 1966, currently editorial director. Commonwealth Lecturer in Australian Literature at University of Leeds, 1960; visiting professor at Kansas State University, 1962. Member, Australian Council for the Arts, 1968-70, Commonwealth Literary Fund Advisory Board, 1972-73, Australian Literature Board, beginning 1973, and Australian National University. Has appeared on television. *Military service:* Royal Australian Air Force, pilot, 1941-45; became flight lieutenant.

WRITINGS:

POEMS

Nightflight and Sunrise, Reed & Harris, 1944.
Antipodes in Shoes, Edwards & Shaw, 1955.
Flowers and Fury, F. W. Cheshire, 1962.
On My Island: Poems for Children, F. W. Cheshire, 1967.
Poems Soft and Loud, F. W. Cheshire, 1967.
Findings and Keepings: Selected Poems, 1940-70, Australian Letters, 1970.
New Poems to 1972, Australian Letters, 1972.
A Body of Words, Edwards & Shaw, 1977.
Selective Affinities, Angus & Robertson, 1985.

Also author of *Night Fishing,* Australian Letters.

NOVELS

The Mortal and the Marble, Chapman & Hall, 1950.
Andy, Collins, 1968.
Tamara, Collins, 1970.
Queen Emma of the South Seas, St. Martin's, 1976.

BIOGRAPHIES

Founder of a City: The Life of William Light, F. W. Cheshire, 1960.
The Hero as Murderer: The Life of Edward John Eyre, F. W. Cheshire, 1967, published as *Edward John Eyre: The Hero as Murderer,* Penguin (London), 1977.
Australia's Last Explorer: Ernest Giles, Barnes & Noble, 1970.

TRAVEL AND HISTORY

A Long Way South, Chapman & Hall, 1953.
Africa in Black and White, Chapman & Hall, 1956.
States of the Union, Chapman & Hall, 1958.
Australia since the Camera: 1901-1914, F. W. Cheshire, 1971, published as *From Federation to War,* Longman Cheshire, 1972.
Swimming Free: On and below the Surfaces of Lake, River, and Sea, St. Martin's, 1972.
A Taste of History: Geoffrey Dutton's Australia, Rigby, 1978.
Australian Heroes, Angus & Robertson, 1982.
The Beach, Oxford University Press, 1985.

JUVENILES

Tisi and the Yabby, Collins, 1965.

Seal Bay, Collins, 1966.
Tisi and the Pageant, Rigby, 1968.

CRITICISM

Patrick White, Landsdowne Press, 1961, 4th edition, Oxford University Press, 1971.
(Author of introduction and commentaries) Samuel Thomas Gill, *Paintings,* Rigby, 1962.
Russell Drysdale, Thames & Hudson, 1964, revised edition, 1969.
Whitman, Grove, 1971 (published in England as *Walt Whitman,* Oliver & Boyd, 1971).
White on Black: The Australian Aborigine Portrayed in Art, Macmillan (London), 1974.

EDITOR

The Literature of Australia, Penguin, 1964, revised edition, 1976.
Modern Australian Writing, Fontana, 1966.
Australia and the Monarchy, Sun Books, 1966.
(With Max Harris) *The Vital Decade: Ten Years of Australian Art and Letters,* Sun Books, 1968.
(With Harris) *Australia's Censorship Crisis,* Sun Books, 1970.
(With Harris) *Sir Henry Bjelke: Don Baby and Friends,* Sun Books, 1971.
The Australian Uppercrust Book, Sun Books, 1971.
Australian Verse from 1805, Rigby, 1976.
Republican Australia?, Sun Books, 1977.

TRANSLATOR

(With Igor Mezhakoff-Koriakin) Evgenii Aleksandrovich Evtushenko, *The Bratsk Station and Other Poems,* Sun Books, 1966, Doubleday, 1967.
(With Mezhakoff-Koriakin) Bella Akhmadulina, *Fever and Other Poems,* Sun Books, 1968, Morrow, 1969.
Robert Ivanovich Rozhdestvenskii, *A Poem on Various Points of View and Other Poems,* Sun Books, 1968.
Evtushenko, *Bratsk Station, The City of Yes and the City of No, and Other Poems,* Sun Books, 1970.
Andre Andreevich Voznesenskii, *Little Woods,* Sun Books, 1972.
(With Eleanor Jacka) Evtuschenko, *Kazan University and Other New Poems,* Sun Books, 1973.

OTHER

Editor, *Australian* (literary magazine); co-founder, *Literary Quarterly, Australian Letters,* 1957, and *Fortnightly Australian Book Review,* 1962.

BIOGRAPHICAL/CRITICAL SOURCES:

PERIODICALS

Best Sellers, September, 1978.
Books and Bookmen, June, 1966, March, 1970.
New Statesman, January 12, 1968.
Observer, February 1, 1970, December 19, 1976.
Spectator, June 3, 1966, January 17, 1970.
Times Literary Supplement, January 4, 1968, October 2, 1970, August 16, 1974, November 12, 1976.

*   *   *

DYKES, Jeff(erson) C(henowth)   1900-

PERSONAL: Born July 20, 1900, in Dallas, Tex.; son of George Richard and Melrose (Chenowth) Dykes; married Martha Lewin

Read (a book dealer), August 1, 1923; children: Martha Ann (Mrs. Arthur Goldsmith, Jr.). *Education:* Texas Agricultural and Mechanical College (now Texas A&M University), B.S., 1921; graduate study at Colorado Agricultural College (now Colorado State University) and Texas Agricultural and Mechanical College (now Texas A&M University). *Politics:* Democrat. *Religion:* Protestant.

ADDRESSES: Home—4511 Guliford Rd., College Park, Md. 20740. *Office*—Box 38, College Park, Md. 20740.

CAREER: Vocational agriculture teacher in Stephenville, Tex., 1921-26, and McAllen, Tex., 1926-39; Texas Agricultural and Mechanical College (now Texas A&M University), College Station, professor of agricultural education, 1929-35; U.S. Department of Agriculture, Soil Conservation Service, assistant regional administrator, Fort Worth, Tex., 1935-42, assistant administrator, Washington, D.C., 1942-65; Western Books, College Park, Md., partner, beginning 1965; currently library appraiser and bookseller by mail and appointment. President, Friends of the Texas University Library, 1979.

MEMBER: American Society of Agricultural Engineers, Soil Conservation Society of America (fellow), American Society of Range Management, Panhandle-Plains Historical Society, Westerners International (president, 1980, 1981), Texas State Historical Association, Kansas Historical Society (life member), Wyoming Historical Society, Westerners (Potomac Corral; sheriff, 1961).

AWARDS, HONORS: Superior Service Award, U.S. Department of Agriculture, 1962; Distinguished Alumnus, Texas A&M University, 1984.

WRITINGS:

Billy the Kid: The Bibliography of a Legend, University of New Mexico Press, 1952.
(Consultant and author of introduction) *Cowboys and Cattle Country,* Junior American Heritage, 1962.
(With Ovie Clark Fisher) *King Fisher: His Life and Times,* University of Oklahoma Press, 1966.
(With Ben W. Kemp) *Cow Dust and Cattle Leather,* University of Oklahoma Press, 1968.
My Dobie Collection, Friends of the Texas A&M University Library, 1971.
Fifty Great Western Illustrators: A Bibliographical Checklist, Northland Press, 1975.
Western High Spots, Northland Press, 1977.
Collecting Range Life Literature, Cedarhouse Press, 1982.
Rare Western Outlaw Books, Westerners (Albuquerque Corral), 1985.

EDITOR

Thomas Edgar Crawford, *The West of Texas Kid, 1881-1910: Recollection of Thomas Edgar Crawford, Cowboy, Gunfighter, Rancher, Hunter, Miner,* University of Oklahoma Press, 1952, reprinted, 1973.
(With Berton Wendell Allred) *Flat Top Ranch: The Story of a Grassland Venture,* University of Oklahoma Press, 1957.
Great Western Indian Fights, Doubleday, 1960.
Hiram Latham, *Trans-Missouri Stock Raising,* Old West, 1962.
William French, *Some Recollections of a Western Ranchman,* two volumes, Argosy-Antiquarian, 1965.
Ranges All! (catalogs), Western Books, 1966—.
(With William Tucker) *The Grand Duke Alexis in the U.S.A. during the Winter of 1871,* Interland, 1972.

OTHER

Also author of introductions to other books on the West. Associate editor, *Brand Book,* Westerners (Chicago Corral), 1949—. Author, originally with Allred and F. G. Renner, later with David Dary, of monthly book review column "Western Book Round-up," 1954-80. Contributor of articles on conservation and on western books to magazines.

WORK IN PROGRESS: Second volume of Billy the Kid bibliography.

SIDELIGHTS: Jeff C. Dykes appraised the J. Frank Dobie collection for the University of Texas. His own collection of western Americana at one time included sixteen thousand books, most of them concerning the Texas Rangers, outlaws, the range livestock industry, and western illustrators.

*   *   *

DYSON, Freeman J(ohn) 1923-

PERSONAL: Born December 15, 1923, in Crowthorne, England; came to the United States in 1947, naturalized citizen in 1957; son of George (a composer/conductor) and Mildred (a lawyer; maiden name, Atkey) Dyson; married Verena Esther Huber, August 11, 1950 (divorced, 1958); married Imme Jung, November 21, 1958; children: (first marriage) Esther, George; (second marriage) Dorothy, Emily, Miriam, Rebecca. *Education:* Cambridge University, B.A., 1945; graduate study with Hans Bethe at Cornell University, 1947-48, and with J. Robert Oppenheimer at Institute for Advanced Study, Princeton, N.J., 1948-49.

ADDRESSES: Home—105 Battle Road Circle, Princeton, N.J. 08540. *Office*—School of Natural Sciences, Institute for Advanced Study, Princeton, N.J. 08540.

CAREER: Cornell University, Ithaca, N.Y., professor of physics, 1951-53; Institute for Advanced Study, Princeton, N.J., professor of physics, 1953—. Research fellow, Trinity College, Cambridge University, 1946-49; Warren research fellow, University of Birmingham, 1949-51. Member of nuclear reactor design team, General Atomics Division, General Dynamics Corp., beginning 1956; chief theoretician for propulsion system, Orion Project, La Jolla, Calif., 1958-59; nuclear weapons designer, Lawrence Livermore National Laboratory, Livermore, Calif., 1959. Consultant, Arms Control and Disarmament Agency, 1962, 1963. *Wartime service:* Royal Air Force, Bomber Command, civilian statistician in operational research section, 1943-45.

MEMBER: National Academy of Sciences, Federation of American Scientists (member of council, 1960; chairman, 1962), American Physical Society, American Philosophical Society, Royal Society (London; fellow).

AWARDS, HONORS: Heineman Prize, American Institute of Physics, 1965; Lorentz Medal, Royal Netherlands Academy of Sciences, 1966; Hughes Medal, Royal Society, 1968; Max Planck Medal, German Physical Society, 1969; J. Robert Oppenheimer Memorial Prize, Center for Theoretical Studies, 1970; Harvey Prize, Israel Institute of Technology, 1977, for the application of mathematical analysis to theoretical physics; Wolf Prize, Wolf Foundation, 1981; American Book Award nomination, 1982, for *Disturbing the Universe;* Los Angeles Times Book Prize nomination, 1984, for *Weapons and Hope;* National Book Critics Circle award for general nonfiction, 1984, for *Weapons and Hope;* honorary degrees from Yeshiva University, Princeton University, and University of Glasgow.

WRITINGS:

Symmetry Groups in Nuclear and Particle Physics, W. A. Benjamin, 1966.
Neutron Stars and Pulsars, Academia Nazionale dei Lincei, 1971.
Disturbing the Universe, Harper, 1979.
Values at War, University of Utah Press, 1983.
Weapons and Hope, Harper, 1984.

SIDELIGHTS: A scientist whose professional interests include mathematics, nuclear physics, rocket technology, and astrophysics, and whose personal interests range from social and political issues to music and literature, Freeman J. Dyson has been well-suited to take on the problems that arise when technology and public policy collide. As a problem solver, Dyson relies on the diversity of his interests to inform him and lend him an appreciation of the various approaches to an issue. He recognizes the interests of the parties involved in debates of technology and public policy, and his solutions offer a means of reconciling differences. In fact, observes Jeffrey Marsh in *Commentary,* "the urge to reconciliation seems . . . to be the driving force of his personality."

Dyson first captured the attention of the scientific community, especially those in the field of theoretical physics, when at the age of twenty-four he reconciled two different approaches to explaining the interaction of electromagnetic radiation with matter. The two approaches were, as Horace Freeland Judson relates in the *New York Times Book Review,* "the stupefyingly intricate, rigorously classical mathematics of Julian Schwinger and the simple, powerful, bafflingly intuitive diagrammatic method of Richard Feynman. Mr. Dyson, by demonstrating that the two amounted to the same thing, was midwife to the birth of quantum electrodynamics." His synthesis of the two approaches was not immediately accepted by J. Robert Oppenheimer, then director of the Institute for Advanced Study in Princeton, New Jersey, and Dyson's mentor during his fellowship there. In a series of seminars, the two men debated the new approach until Dyson finally convinced Oppenheimer of the validity of his synthesis. Oppenheimer rewarded his pupil by making him a long-term member of the institute.

The position at the Institute for Advanced Study would have allowed the young scientist to develop his ideas in the field of theoretical physics. Yet, unlike conventional theoretical physicists who "sit for years with [their] whole mind concentrated upon one deep question," writes Dyson in *Disturbing the Universe,* "I followed my destiny into pure mathematics, into nuclear engineering, into space technology and astronomy, solving problems that [Oppenheimer] rightly considered remote from the mainstream of physics." In 1956, he joined Edward Teller at the General Atomic Division of the General Dynamics Corporation on a project to design a commercial nuclear reactor that would meet rigorous safety standards. The design team built TRIGA (Training Reactor, Isotopes General Atomic), a small reactor for medical use so safe that it would shut itself down during crises. Dyson also worked on the design of the safe and efficient High Temperature Graphite Reactor (HTGR) for commercial power production. With Theodore Taylor, he was a member of the Project Orion team; Orion's scientists hoped to use controlled nuclear explosions to propel a rocket to Saturn. Policy decisions and the 1963

ban on nuclear tests in space eventually undermined the project. In 1959, again under the direction of Teller, Dyson served at the Lawrence Livermore National Laboratory in its weapons lab.

While gaining experience as a practical scientist, Dyson was also developing an understanding of the relationship between science and society, an understanding that would create in him "a passion to probe the long-range moral and social fallout of today's scientific miracles," Elizabeth Peer observes in *Newsweek.* Driven by this passion, the scientist has diverted an increasing amount of his energy toward influencing public opinion and public policy. And, although Dyson's diverse interests may have distracted him from making a great scientific discovery, Peer adds that "in this diversity lies his greatest strength, for it enables him to convey the magic and terror of science to outsiders."

As an insider, Dyson has seen both the good and the bad of science, and his knowledge has made him both an educated critic and an enthusiastic supporter of its goals. He first encountered the collision of technology and policy when, as an undergraduate at Cambridge, he was recruited to serve as a civilian statistician for the Royal Air Force Bomber Command. According to Judson, "Bomber Command taught him that the coupling of a technology with a bureaucracy breeds monstrous misuse of science, stifles individual moral judgment and protest, suppresses even the inventiveness that might diversify, humanize, redeem that technology." As Stephen Jay Gould explains in the *New York Review of Books,* today Dyson "not only believes in smallness and diversity for its own sake, but he has defined his scientific ethic by it in fighting bureaucracy and institutionalized 'big' science as the agents of stultified mediocrity."

Dyson has long argued against science's tendency toward reductionism. "[He] joyfully contemplates a future in which physicists will accept the endless diversity of the universe rather than try to unify it in a set of equations," remarks John P. Wiley, Jr., in *Smithsonian.* "He looks for a new science he calls cosmic ecology in which for the first time since Newton cosmologists will think of the universe as neither dead nor empty." Dyson has also brought his expertise to bear on the United States space program's plans to study our solar system. An outspoken critic of the National Aeronautics and Space Administration (NASA), he maintains that "space-science projects have become large and inflexible," writes a contributor to *Scientific American.* "Dyson would rather see space science move in small steps, allowing each simple, specialized mission to determine the questions the next project should answer."

One project that he strongly supports is the colonization of space. "For Dyson, there is no doubt that human civilization will go into space . . . to find new possibilities for diversifying life . . . [and] to improve conditions of life on earth using the resources of the cosmos," comments Andrei Sakharov in the *Washington Post Book World.* In 1960, Dyson proposed a scheme for colonizing the solar system that would maximize both the space available and the use of the sun's energy. Using matter from Jupiter, space engineers would construct a huge spherical shell at a suitable distance from the sun. Colonists would then settle on the spacious inner surface of the shell. More recently, Dyson has become interested in asteroids as prospective new homes for space colonists. Because the transport of future colonists to space colonies will require a safe and economical means of transportation, Dyson has long been a promoter of new propulsion systems. In addition to his work on Project Orion, he has envisioned a launching system that would use a laser to place small space vessels into earth orbit; once there, the vessels would derive the power necessary to drive their jet engines from the sun's energy, collected by solar sails.

Dyson discusses science, society, and his hopes for both in his book *Disturbing the Universe*. The book has been called an intellectual autobiography, and as Marsh notes, its author "certainly succeeds in presenting a fascinating account of the mind, work and undeniable humanity of one scientist." Written in language understandable to laymen, *Disturbing the Universe* contains Dyson's views on several scientific issues, including nuclear proliferation and biogenetic engineering. "One may argue with the author, sometimes disagree with him, sometimes even consider him too naive," writes Sakharov, "but he is always consistent, logical and thoroughly honest." And although he discusses science and the problems of technology, he does not confine himself to the technical, but draws from many disciplines to complete his argument. Christopher Lehmann-Haupt comments in the *New York Times,* "What is easy to miss in the book because of the author's unassuming manner is the extent to which art, and in particular poetry, infuse Mr. Dyson's text." This characteristic blend of science, art, and autobiography offers, in the view of *Times Literary Supplement* reviewer Christopher Longuet-Higgins, "a series of glimpses into the life of a highly gifted and sensitive person, struggling to reconcile his other-worldly concerns with his obligations to a confused and pathetic humanity."

In recent years, Dyson has stepped forward as an outspoken critic of nuclear arms proliferation. His book *Weapons and Hope* is an examination of the arms race and the battle it has generated on the home front between nuclear strategists and the various arms control movements. His knowlege of both the technical and the political aspects of this issue—he has worked as both a weapons designer and a consultant to the Arms Control and Disarmament Agency—has allowed him to see the complexity of the nuclear weapons issue. His insights and suggested solutions are based upon this experience.

Dyson outlines the issue in the *New Yorker:* "The military establishment looks on the peace movement as a collection of ignorant people meddling in a business they do not understand, while the peace movement looks on the military establishment as a collection of misguided people protected by bureaucratic formality from all contact with human realities. Both these preconceptions create barriers to understanding. Both preconceptions are to some extent true." *Weapons and Hope,* comments Brad Knickerbocker in the *Christian Science Monitor,* "is intended to bridge the great and potentially dangerous gap between those who must plan for nuclear war and an increasingly disturbed public."

Dyson feels that the programs advanced by both sides to assure peace are flawed; he rejects complete disarmament and he rejects the policy of deterrence through mutual assured destruction (MAD). "What he settles on is a middle way that includes a mutually agreeable reduction in nuclear weapons and a shift toward defensive systems, although not of the 'star wars' variety," notes Knickerbocker. Dyson observes in *Weapons and Hope* that those who accept MAD "identify nuclear destructive power with national security and so become trapped in the cult of destruction." This is, he adds, a case in which public opinion and even government policy have lagged behind weapons technology. As Michael Howard writes

in the *New York Times Book Review,* Dyson points out that "the whole trend of weapons development in the past 25 years has been away from weapons of mass destruction toward those of greater accuracy, maneuverability and precision." Dyson would employ this technology to build numerous small, precise, non-nuclear defensive missiles to replace the nuclear arsenals held by the superpowers.

David A. Hoekema, contributor to the *Christian Century,* questions whether such defensive systems would be accurate and reliable enough to convince the superpowers to change their current policy and scrap their nuclear warheads. Dyson's call for defensive weapons shows, in Hoekema's opinion, "too much of the confident scientific attitude holding out technical solutions to political problems, and too little of the cautious and historical thinking that dominates the rest of [his] book." In a review of *Weapons and Hope* in the *Chicago Tribune Book World,* however, Jack Fuller writes that the author's arguments for a missile defense "are a refreshing antidote to the disarmament orthodoxy which holds that such a program is either unfeasible or dangerous or both."

Dyson also argues against the use of smaller nuclear weapons in a limited war. "He makes an eloquent and, to me, persuasive case that the United States should abandon its long-held threat to use nuclear weapons first in Western Europe, if the Soviets are winning the conventional war," finds James Fallows in the *Washington Post Book World.* Dyson reasons that because the Soviets fear another devastation of their homeland, they will launch preemptive strikes, nullifying U.S. plans to save Europe through a limited nuclear war. His ability to see both the military and personal consequences of nuclear strategies "gives his political and spiritual arguments a depth that few other accounts can match," according to Fallows.

The diversity of his experience has enabled Dyson to make *Weapons and Hope* a book that will inform experts and laymen. John Wilkes, contributor to the *Los Angeles Times Book Review* concedes that "Dyson's strategy might be too gradual for some, but it carries the technical persuasiveness—without swamping the reader—to satisfy warriors, and the political savvy to earn respect from diplomats." In the opinion of some critics, *Weapons and Hope* will also move its readers. "Instead of simply laying out an argument," comments Jim Miller in *Newsweek,* "'Weapons and Hope' offers a series of parables—stories that will stir any reader's feelings and imagination." Dyson's solution, which attempts to reconcile both the military establishment and the peace movement, offers hope to the individual living in the nuclear age. As Wilkes writes, "From a wide variety of literary sources he builds a richly affirmative moral order to replace the fatalistic resignation darkening the world today." Miller concludes, "A meditation of lyrical beauty, striking wisdom and steady moral passion, Dyson's essay is a landmark achievement—perhaps the best book yet on nuclear arms and the human predicament."

BIOGRAPHICAL/CRITICAL SOURCES:

BOOKS

Brower, Kenneth, *The Starship and the Canoe,* Holt, 1978.

PERIODICALS

Chicago Tribune Book World, November 18, 1979, June 10, 1984.
Christian Century, November 28, 1984.
Christian Science Monitor, October 9, 1984.
Commentary, January, 1980.

London Review of Books, October 18, 1984.
Los Angeles Times Book Review, April 8, 1984.
New Republic, May 28, 1984.
Newsweek, September 10, 1979, April 16, 1984.
New Yorker, February 6, 1984.
New York Review of Books, October 11, 1979, June 14, 1984.
New York Times, August 21, 1979, April 4, 1984.
New York Times Book Review, August 19, 1979, April 8, 1984.
Omni, October, 1978.
Punch, January 23, 1980.
Scientific American, January, 1985.
Smithsonian, March, 1981.
Time, June 11, 1984.
Times Literary Supplement, February 29, 1980.
Washington Post, April 9, 1984.
Washington Post Book World, September 23, 1979, April 22, 1984.

—Sketch by Bryan Ryan

E

EDDY, Samuel K(ennedy)   1926-

PERSONAL: Born November 26, 1926, in St. Louis, Mo.; son of Ernest Arthur (a manufacturer) and Annie Maude (Kennedy) Eddy. *Education:* Washington University, St. Louis, Mo., A.B., 1950, A.M., 1951; University of Michigan, Ph.D., 1958.

ADDRESSES: Home—1808 Jefferson Tower, 50 Presidential Plaza, Syracuse, N.Y. 13202. *Office*—Department of History, Syracuse University, Syracuse, N.Y. 13210.

CAREER: University of Nebraska, Lincoln, instructor, 1955-58, assistant professor of history and research associate in classical archaeology, 1958-61; University of California, Santa Barbara, assistant professor of history, 1961-64; Syracuse University, Syracuse, N.Y., associate professor, 1968-72, professor of history, 1972—. *Military service:* U.S. Navy, 1944-46.

MEMBER: American Association of University Professors.

WRITINGS:

The King Is Dead: Studies in Near Eastern Resistance to Hellenism, 334-31 B.C., University of Nebraska Press, 1961.
The Minting of Antoniniani, A.D. 238-249, and the Smyrna Hoard, American Numismatic Society, 1967.

Contributor to *American Journal of Philology, Classical Philology, American Journal of Archaeology,* and *Syracuse Scholar.*

WORK IN PROGRESS: The Origins of the War of 431 B.C.; A History of Corinth, 500-146 B.C.†

*   *   *

ELFMAN, Blossom   1925-

PERSONAL: Born in 1925 in New York, N.Y.; married Milton Elfman (a teacher); children: Richard, Daniel. *Education:* University of California, Los Angeles, B.A., 1948; University of Southern California, M.A., 1965.

ADDRESSES: Home—476 Greencraig Rd., Los Angeles, Calif. 90049. *Agent*—Arthur Pine, 1780 Broadway, New York, N.Y. 10019.

CAREER: Puppeteer, 1950-55; teacher at public schools in Los Angeles, Calif., 1962-72, and at University of California, Los Angeles, Extension.

AWARDS, HONORS: National Academy of Television Arts and Sciences (Emmy) Award, for "I Think I'm Having a Baby."

WRITINGS:

The Strawberry Fields of Heaven, Crown, 1983.

YOUNG ADULT NOVELS

The Girls of Huntingdon House, Houghton, 1972.
A House for Jonnie O., Houghton, 1977.
The Sister Act, Houghton, 1978.
The Butterfly Girl, Houghton, 1980.
The Return of the Whistler, Houghton, 1981.

TELEPLAYS

"The Making of Emma," American Broadcasting Companies (ABC-TV), 1983.

Also author of "I Think I'm Having a Baby," Columbia Broadcasting System (CBS-TV).

WORK IN PROGRESS: First Love Lives Forever, for Ballantine.

SIDELIGHTS: Blossom Elfman established her reputation with her award-winning juvenile fiction. Her first adult novel, *The Strawberry Fields of Heaven,* is as successful as her work for young adults, according to Joan Reardon in the *Los Angeles Times.* The story is set in the historic Oneida community, a religious settlement that flourished outside New York City after the Civil War. Under the leadership of John Humphrey Noyes, who founded the sect in 1847, Oneidans believed in hard manual labor, community sharing, and free love. The novel's protagonist, Peter Berger, a prosperous New York City lawyer, takes his wife and three children to the settlement in search of spiritual fulfillment. Although the Bergers leave the colony after a year, realizing that "the world inside is a vain dream of heaven, . . . they are able to deal more successfully with the complexities of their world because of the Oneidans and their belief in Complex Marriage," notes Reardon. She concludes: "Elfman's exploration of human love in all of its seasons is fascinating."

BIOGRAPHICAL/CRITICAL SOURCES:

PERIODICALS

Los Angeles Times, September 9, 1983.

*　　　*　　　*

el HAJJAM, Mohammed ben Chaib   1940-
　　(Mohammed Mrabet)

PERSONAL: Born March 25, 1940, in Tangier, Morocco; son of Chaib and Rahma bent Bouchta (Tuzani) el Hajjam; married Zohra bent Ali ben Allal, 1964; children: Mohammed Larbi, Hadija, Ahmed, Aicha. *Religion:* Muslim.

ADDRESSES: Home—Casa Zugari, Calle Ajdir, Merstakhoche, Tangier, Morocco. *Agent*—Ned Leavitt, William Morris Agency, 1350 Avenue of the Americas, New York, N.Y. 10019.

CAREER: Writer, 1967—.

WRITINGS:

UNDER NAME MOHAMMED MRABET; TRANSLATED BY PAUL BOWLES FROM THE ORIGINAL MAGHREBI

Love with a Few Hairs (novel), P. Owen, 1967, Braziller, 1968.
The Lemon (novel), P. Owen, 1969, McGraw, 1972.
M'Hashish, City Lights, 1969.
The Boy Who Set the Fire and Other Stories, Black Sparrow Press, 1974.
Look and Move On (autobiographical novel), Black Sparrow Press, 1976.
Harmless Poisons, Blameless Sins (short stories), Black Sparrow Press, 1976.
The Big Mirror (novella), Black Sparrow Press, 1977.
The Beach Cafe and the Voice, Black Sparrow Press, 1979.
(Contributor) *Five Eyes* (anthology), Black Sparrow Press, 1979.
The Chest (stories), Tombouctou Books, 1983.
Marriage with Papers (novella), Tombouctou Books, 1985.

OTHER

Also author of one-act play, *Earth,* 1980.

SIDELIGHTS: The fiction of Mohammed ben Chaib el Hajjam—better known as Mohammed Mrabet—often illustrates the disruptive influences of Western culture on the ancient patterns of Moroccan life, and the author's direct, stylistic simplicity promotes a narrative speed and efficiency comparable to "some of the most sophisticated new fiction," observes J. H. Stern in the *Saturday Review.* In Mrabet's first novel, *Love with a Few Hairs,* the "confrontation of cultures is beautifully dramatized," says Stern, involving what *New York Times Book Review* critic J. M. Edelstein describes as "a mixture of Western sophistication and ancient beliefs, of naivete and guile, of strict morality and easy promiscuity." The story concerns a young Moroccan who comes close to madness after he deserts the wife he had won with a magic love potion concocted from a few hairs. In the end, he is saved by an English hotelkeeper, Mr. David, who has loved him all the while. Calling it a somber book, Edelstein writes that it shows a "world where love is a commodity and perfunctory, where the gulfs between human beings are not only vast but are also taken for granted as permanent." And according to J. A. Phillips in *Best Sellers,* the reader glimpses "an ancient people rebelling against the ignorance, tradition, and superstition which keep them from

becoming a part of the Western sophistication they see about them."

In later works, Mrabet draws widely from traditional sources. *Harmless Poisons, Blameless Sins* is a collection of tales based on the adventures of Hadidan Aharam, a legendary picaresque hero in Moroccan folklore. Whether pitted against rich men, sheiks, animals, or wives, the wily Aharam always emerges the victor, usually by means of a clever ruse or scheme that neatly defeats his adversaries and gives him the last laugh. In another book, *The Big Mirror,* Mrabet tells of a beautiful sorceress whose malevolent occult powers are turned against her husband. "A gruesome vendetta ensues, but the catharsis is suitably mysterious and inconclusive," a *Booklist* reviewer remarks.

Look and Move On, an autobiographical novel, concerns Mrabet's own adventures with Americans in Morocco and the cultural disjunction he experiences as a visitor in the United States. "It moves from scene to scene, year to year, at tremendous speed," notes Robert Bonazzi in the *Library Journal.* "It makes for fast reading, exciting reading." As in his other writings, Mrabet's technique and direct presentation "lend an immediate appeal," maintains the reviewer for *Booklist.* And though Bonazzi believes some "gratuitous violence and melodrama need deletion," he nevertheless concludes: "[Mrabet] sums up Los Angeles' airless lifestyle perfectly, chillingly. . . . Most of it works beautifully."

BIOGRAPHICAL/CRITICAL SOURCES:

PERIODICALS

Best Sellers, March 15, 1968.
Booklist, June 1, 1976, September 1, 1977.
Library Journal, July, 1976.
New Statesman, January 27, 1967.
New York Times Book Review, September 8, 1968.
Saturday Review, April 6, 1968.
Times Literary Supplement, February 2, 1967.
Transatlantic Review, spring, 1971.

*　　　*　　　*

ELLIOTT, Robert
　　See GARFINKEL, Bernard Max

*　　　*　　　*

ELLIS, Albert   1913-

PERSONAL: Born September 27, 1913, in Pittsburgh, Pa.; son of Henry (an insurance broker) and Hettie (Hanigbaum) Ellis; married Karyl Corper (divorced, 1938); married Rhoda Winter (divorced, 1958). *Education:* City College (now City College of the City University of New York), B.B.A., 1934; Columbia University, M.A., 1943, Ph.D., 1947.

ADDRESSES: Home and office—45 East 65th St., New York, N.Y. 10021.

CAREER: Modern Age Books, Inc., New York City, reader, 1937; Distinctive Creations, Inc., New York City, personnel manager, 1938-48; Northern New Jersey Mental Hygiene Clinic, Greystone Park, clinical psychologist, 1948-49; Rutgers University, New Brunswick, N.J., instructor, 1948-49; New York University, New York City, instructor, 1949; New Jersey Diagnostic Center, Menlo Park, chief psychologist, 1949-50; New Jersey Department of Institutions and Agencies, Trenton, chief psychologist, 1950-52; private practice in psychotherapy and marriage counseling, New York City, 1943-58; Institute for Rational Emotive Therapy, New York City, executive director, 1959—. Adjunct professor, Rutgers University, 1972—, United States International University, San Diego, 1974—, Pittsburgh State University, and Kansas State University. Has conducted workshops and lectured extensively in the United States and abroad. Consultant in clinical psychology, Veterans Administration, 1961-67.

MEMBER: American Psychological Association (president, division of consulting psychology, 1962; member, council of representatives, 1964), Authors League of America, National Council on Family Relations (chairman of marriage counseling section, 1954-55), American Sociological Association (fellow), American Association for the Advancement of Science (fellow), Society for the Scientific Study of Sex (president, 1960-62), American Academy of Psychotherapists (member of executive committee, 1956-62; vice-president, 1962-64), Association for Applied Anthropology (fellow), American Association of Marriage Counselors (member of executive committee, 1958-60), American Anthropological Association, Association for the Advancement of Psychotherapy, Eastern Psychological Association, New York State Psychological Association, New York Society of Clinical Psychologists (member of executive committee, 1951-53), Mensa.

AWARDS, HONORS: Humanist of the Year award, American Humanist Association, 1971; Distinguished Sex Researcher award, Society for the Scientific Study of Sex, 1972; Distinguished Professional Psychologist award, Division of Psychotherapy, American Psychological Association, 1974; Distinguished Sex Educator and Therapist award, American Association of Sex Educators, Counselors, and Therapists, 1976; Distinguished Psychologist award, Academy of Psychologists in Marital and Family Therapy, 1982; National Academy of Practice award, 1983; Distinguished Professional Contributions to Knowledge award, American Psychological Association, 1985.

WRITINGS:

An Introduction to the Principles of Scientific Psychoanalysis, Journal Press, 1950.
Folklore of Sex, Grove, 1951, revised edition, 1961.
(With A. P. Pillay) *Sex, Society, and the Individual,* International Journal of Sexology Press, 1953.
The American Sexual Tragedy, Lyle Stuart, 1954, revised edition, 1962.
Sex Life of the American Woman and the Kinsey Report, Greenberg, 1954.
New Approaches to Psychotherapy Techniques, Journal of Clinical Psychology Press, 1955.
(With Ralph Brancale) *The Psychology of Sex Offenders,* C. C Thomas, 1956.
How to Live with a Neurotic: At Work or at Home, Crown, 1957, revised edition, 1974.
Sex without Guilt, Lyle Stuart, 1958, revised edition, 1966.
What Is Psychotherapy, American Academy of Psychotherapists, 1959.
The Place of Values in the Practice of Psychotherapy, American Academy of Psychotherapists, 1959.
Art and Science of Love, Lyle Stuart, 1960, revised edition, Dell, 1965.
Encyclopedia of Sexual Behavior, Hawthorn, 1961.
(With R. A. Harper) *Creative Marriage,* Lyle Stuart, 1961, revised edition, Tower, 1966.

(With Harper) *A Guide to Rational Living,* Prentice-Hall, 1961.
Reason and Emotion in Psychotherapy, Lyle Stuart, 1962.
If This Be Sexual Heresy, Lyle Stuart, 1963.
Sex and the Single Man, Lyle Stuart, 1963.
The Intelligent Woman's Guide to Manhunting, Lyle Stuart, 1963.
The Origins and the Development of the Incest Taboo, Lyle Stuart, 1963.
(With Edward Sagarin) *Nymphomania: A Study of the Oversexed Woman,* Gilbert Press, 1964.
The Case for Sexual Liberty, Seymour Press, 1965.
Homosexuality: Its Causes and Cure, Lyle Stuart, 1965.
Suppressed: Seven Key Essays Publishers Dared Not Print, New Classics House, 1965.
The Search for Sexual Enjoyment, Macfadden, 1966.
How to Prevent Your Child from Becoming a Neurotic Adult, Crown, 1966.
(With Roger O. Conway) *The Art of Erotic Seduction,* Lyle Stuart, 1968.
Is Objectivism a Religion?, Lyle Stuart, 1968.
Growth through Reason, Science and Behavior Books, 1971.
Executive Leadership: A Rational Approach, Citadel, 1972.
(With Flora Setuya and Susan Losher) *Sex and Sex Education: A Bibliography,* Bowker, 1972.
(With John Gullo) *Murder and Assassination,* Lyle Stuart, 1972.
How to Master Your Fear of Flying, Peter H. Wyden, 1972.
The Civilized Couple's Guide to Extramarital Adventure, Peter H. Wyden, 1972.
The Sensuous Person: Critique and Corrections, Lyle Stuart, 1972.
Humanistic Psychotherapy: The Rational-Emotive Approach, Julian Press, 1973.
(With Robert A. Harper) *A New Guide to Rational Living,* Prentice-Hall, 1975.
Sex and the Liberated Man, Lyle Stuart, 1976.
How to Live with and without Anger, Reader's Digest Press, 1977.
(With William Knaus) *Overcoming Procrastination; or, How to Think and Act Rationally in Spite of Life's Inevitable Hassles,* Institute for Rational Living, 1977.
(With Russell Grieger) *Handbook of Rational-Emotive Therapy,* Springer Publishing, Volume I, 1977, Volume II, 1985.
A Garland of Rational Songs, Institute for Rational Living, 1977.
(With Eliot Abrahms) *Brief Psychotherapy in Medical and Health Practice,* Springer Publishing, 1978.
The Intelligent Woman's Guide to Marriage and Dating, Lyle Stuart, 1979.
(With John M. Whiteley) *Theoretical and Empirical Foundations of Rational-Emotive Therapy,* Brooks/Cole, 1979.
(With Irving Becker) *A Guide to Personal Happiness,* Wilshire, 1982.
(With Michael Bernard) *Rational-Emotive Approaches to the Problems of Childhood,* Plenum, 1983.
Overcoming Resistance, Springer Publishing, 1985.
(With Bernard) *Clinical Applications of Rational-Emotive Therapy,* Plenum, 1985.

Also author of *How to Raise an Emotionally Healthy, Happy Child,* Wilshire, and *Guide to Successful Marriage,* Wilshire. Contributor of more than one hundred chapters to psychology and sociology books and anthologies. Columnist for *Independent* and *Realist;* contributor of more than three hundred articles to professional journals and of more than one hundred articles to popular periodicals, including *Pageant, This Week, Cosmopolitan, Playboy, Penthouse, Saturday Review,* and *Mademoiselle.*

WORK IN PROGRESS: Treatment of Alcoholism with Rational-Emotive Therapy; The Practice of Rational-Emotive Therapy; Rational-Emotive Therapy and Cognitive Behavior Therapy.

SIDELIGHTS: Albert Ellis is the developer of Rational-Emotive Psychotherapy, which rejects Freudian theories and advocates the belief that emotions come from conscious thought "as well as internalized ideas of which the individual may be unaware." Ellis told *CA* that he works "with psychotherapy and marriage counseling clients from 9:30 A.M. to 11:00 P.M., including the holding of sessions with eight different psychotherapy groups every week. Do most writing on Sundays, if I am not on the road somewhere here or abroad, giving workshops on RET or sex therapy."

A *Newsweek* reporter writes: "In the 1950s, Dr. Albert Ellis . . . began publishing the first widely read books that broke firmly with the tradition of marital romance and sexual piety. Ellis exhorted his readers to fearless sensuality, assuming that some form of premarital experience is not only likely but in fact beneficial. In plain, hard-headed language, he offered the inexperienced specific and pragmatic advice on everything from the first good-night kiss to some of the farther reaches of sexual experimentation—most of which he heartily endorsed. At first, Ellis was labeled a sensationalist and sexual radical by many of his colleagues. But . . . other sex manuals have appeared that either lash out or laugh at traditional guilts. . . . Ellis's 'do-it' books have turned out to be the heralds of a new era in positive sex instruction."

BIOGRAPHICAL/CRITICAL SOURCES:

PERIODICALS

Newsweek, August 24, 1970.

*   *   *

ELLIS, Henry C(arlton) 1927-

PERSONAL: Born October 23, 1927, in New Bern, N.C.; son of Henry Alford (a machinist) and Frances (Mays) Ellis; married M. Florence Pettyjohn (a manager of real estate), August 15, 1957; children: Joan, Diane Elizabeth, John Weldon. *Education:* College of William and Mary, B.S., 1951; Emory University, M.A., 1952; Washington University, St. Louis, Mo., Ph.D., 1958.

ADDRESSES: Home—1905 Amherst Dr. N.E., Albuquerque, N.M. 87106. *Office*—Department of Psychology, University of New Mexico, Albuquerque, N.M. 87131.

CAREER: University of New Mexico, Albuquerque, assistant professor, 1957-62, associate professor, 1962-67, professor of psychology, 1967—, Sigma Xi lecturer, 1966, annual research lecturer, 1978, head of department, 1975-84. Member of summer faculty at Washington University, St. Louis, Mo., 1963-67; University of California, Berkeley, visitor at Institute of Human Learning and visiting professor, 1971; visiting professor at University of Hawaii, 1977; distinguished visiting professor at U.S. Air Force Medical Center at Lackland Air Force Base, 1978; member of visiting faculty, Learning Research and Development Center, University of Pittsburgh, 1985; speaker at colleges and universities throughout the United States.

Vice-president of General Programmed Teaching Corp., 1960-62; member of advisory panel of Southwestern Cooperative Educational Laboratory, 1967; consultant to Westinghouse Corp., Sandia Corp., Kaman Aircraft Corp., New Mexico Public Defender's Office, Federal Public Defender's Office, Western Interstate Commission on Higher Education, Kuwait University, National Institute of Education, and Ford Foundation's Western States Small School Project. *Military service:* U.S. Army Air Forces, medical laboratory technician, 1946-47; became sergeant.

MEMBER: American Psychological Association (fellow; member of council of representatives, 1980-81, 1983-86; president of Division of Experimental Psychology, 1985-86), American Association for the Advancement of Science (fellow), National Council of Graduate Departments of Psychology (member of executive board, 1976-81; chairperson, 1977-79), Southwestern Psychological Association (member of council, 1971-74 and 1976-79; president, 1977-78), New Mexico Psychological Association, Rocky Mountain Psychological Association (president, 1968-69), Psychonomic Society, Sigma Xi, Phi Kappa Phi, Cosmos Club.

AWARDS, HONORS: Grants from Sandia Corp., 1959-60, National Science Foundation, 1962-63, 1963-65, 1965-66, 1965-68, 1968-71, and 1971-75, and U.S. Department of Health, Education, and Welfare, 1977-82.

WRITINGS:

The Transfer of Learning, Macmillan, 1965.
Fundamentals of Human Learning and Cognition, W. C. Brown, 1972, 2nd edition published as *Fundamentals of Human Learning, Memory, and Cognition,* 1978.
(With T. L. Bennett, T. C. Daniel, and E. J. Rickert) *Psychology of Learning and Memory,* Brooks/Cole, 1979.
(With R. R. Hunt) *Fundamentals of Human Memory and Cognition,* W. C. Brown, 1983.

CONTRIBUTOR

G. D. Ofiesh and W. C. Meierhenry, editors, *Trends in Programmed Instruction,* Volume I, National Society for Programmed Instruction and Audio-Visual Instruction, 1964.
R. M. Gagne and W. Gephart, editors, *Learning Research and School Subjects,* F. T. Peacock, 1968.
M. H. Marx, editor, *Learning: Processes,* Macmillan, 1969.
R. Bernstein, editor, *Learning, Retention, and Transfer,* Naval Training Device Center, 1969.
T. L. Bennett, editor, *Readings in the Psychology of Perception,* MSS Educational Publishing, 1971.
M. E. Meyer, editor, *Cognitive Learning,* Western Washington Press, 1972.
G. H. Bower, editor, *The Psychology of Learning and Motivation,* Volume VII, Academic Press, 1973.
Marx and M. E. Bunch, editors, *Foundations and Applications of Learning,* Macmillan, 1977.
Meyer, editor, *Foundations of Psychology,* Oxford Book Co., 1979.
M. R. Crow and R. J. Harvey, editors, *Learning and Retention of Basic Skills in Alternative Environments,* National Center for Research in Vocational Education, National Institute of Education, 1980.
R. Malatesha and L. Hartlage, editors, *Neuropsychology and Cognition,* Nijhoff, 1982.
International Union of Psychological Sciences, Trillas (Mexico), 1984.

OTHER

Contributor to *International Encyclopedia of Psychiatry, Psychoanalysis, Experimental Psychology, and Neurology.* Contributor of articles and reviews to psychology journals. Member of editorial board of *Perceptual and Motor Skills* and *Psychological Reports*, both 1963—, *Journal of Experimental Psychology*, 1967-74, *Journal of Experimental Psychology: Human Learning and Memory*, 1974-76, *Perception and Psychophysics*, 1971-78, and Journal Supplement Abstract Service's *Catalog of Selected Documents in Psychology: Human Experimental Psychology*, 1978-81.

WORK IN PROGRESS: Books on general psychology and human memory; research on encoding, storage, and retrieval processes in human memory; research on emotional factors in memory and cognition.

SIDELIGHTS: Henry C. Ellis told *CA:* "All of my writing has been either general or advanced books in psychology. *The Transfer of Learning* summarized the major findings and theories of transfer available in 1965. Since there was no single book on the topic, I was most pleased to write this book on request. *Fundamentals of Human Learning and Memory* was written at the request of Frank Logan, who had written a companion volume. This book described the basic findings of human learning and cognitive psychology at a basic readable level. It is heavily illustrated with practical everyday examples designed to clarify basic principles. *Psychology of Learning and Memory* is an advanced coverage of basic learning principles and memory and cognitive psychology. It is a comprehensive book, with considerable review of the primary literature. My most current work is on the effects of emotional mood states in memory and cognitive processes."

* * *

ELLIS, Howard W(oodrow) 1914-

PERSONAL: Born February 19, 1914, in Linton, Ind.; son of Lee (a merchant) and Effie May Ellis; married Susanna Goldsmith, August 27, 1942; children: Patricia Sue, Mary Lou. *Education:* Evansville College (now University of Evansville), A.B., 1941; Garrett Biblical Institute (now Garrett Evangelical Theological Seminary), B.D., 1946; studied art at American Art Academy, Chicago Art Institute, Peabody College, and University of Tennessee. *Politics:* Democrat.

ADDRESSES: Home—Ann Robe House, 605 Anderson St., Greencastle, Ind. 46135. *Office*—Gobin Memorial United Methodist Church, Greencastle, Ind. 46135.

CAREER: Ordained Methodist minister, Indiana Annual Conference, 1946; Methodist Church, member of staff of General Board of Evangelism, 1946-66, associate secretary and director of Cooperative Department of Youth Evangelism, 1952-64, director of unconventional evangelism, 1964-66; Central Methodist Church, Indianapolis, Ind., minister of witness and outreach, 1966-68; Main Street United Methodist Church, Booneville, Ind., senior pastor, 1968-74; Wall Street United Methodist Church, Jeffersonville, Ind., senior pastor, 1974-78; Gobin Memorial United Methodist Church, Greencastle, Ind., associate pastor for pastoral care, beginning 1978; itinerate gospel art evangelist in United States, Great Britain, Mexico, Scandinavia, and India, 1978—. Artist, with several one-man shows; work has been exhibited at Parthenon Galleries, Nashville, Tenn., 1958, Smithsonian Institute, Washington, D.C., 1960, Mexican Institute for North American

Cultural Relations, Mexico City, 1960, and at other art festivals in the United States, Korea, Mexico, and Japan.

MEMBER: Disciplined Order of Christ, Tennessee Art League, Kappa Chi, Kappa Alpha, Pi Gamma Mu.

AWARDS, HONORS: H.H.D., Evansville College, 1962; awards for graphics at Tennessee State Fair, 1959-61; other art awards from Tennessee Art League and Nashville Arts Festival; Denman Evangelism Award, South Indiana Conference, 1984.

WRITINGS:

Evangelism for Teen-Agers, Abingdon, 1958, published as *Evangelism for Teen-Agers for a New Day*, 1966.
The Witnessing Fellowship, Abingdon, 1961.
How to Draw and Speak, Warner, 1961.
(Editor and illustrator) *He Took the Cup*, Upper Room, 1961.
(With Ted McEachern) *Reflections on Youth Evangelism*, Methodist Board of Education, 1963.
The Last Supper, Upper Room, 1963.
(With Kenneth Reed) *Encounter Dialog in Art*, Upper Room, 1966.

Also author of audio-visual teaching design, "Encounter with God, Man, Christ and the Church," Tidings, 1966.

WORK IN PROGRESS: The Good Life, a poetic version of the Sermon on the Mount; *The Warner Sallman Story; Celebrating the Nativity Story; Reliving the Passion Story; The Jesus Style*, with Bruce Larson, for Word, Inc.; *Enjoy the Christ of the Beatitudes*, an experimental project; illustrations for the four gospels.

* * *

ELLIS, Mary Jackson 1916-

PERSONAL: Born March 21, 1916, in Wheeling, W.Va.; daughter of James Garfield and Bessie List (Kennedy) Jackson; married Carter Vernard Ellis, March 20, 1935; children: Susan Nan (Mrs. Charles Crutchfield), Joy List (Mrs. Jeffrey Bartlett), Carter Ellis III. *Education:* West Virginia State Dental College, dental hygienist; West Virginia State College, A.B., 1939; graduate study at University of Minnesota.

CAREER: Kindergarten teacher in Institute, W.Va., 1939; public school teacher in Minneapolis, Minn., beginning 1947. Developer of teaching aids and educational games, including See-Quees.

MEMBER: National Education Association, Delta Kappa Gamma.

AWARDS, HONORS: Alumnus of the Year, West Virginia State College, 1961.

WRITINGS:

Gobble, Gobble, Gobble, Denison, 1956.
Challenge Symbols, Denison, 1956.
Spaghetti Eddie, Denison, 1957.
Swimmer Is a Hopper, Denison, 1957.
Creative Handwork Ideas, Denison, 1958.
Community Helper Charts, Denison, 1958.
Fingerplay Approach to Dramatization, Denison, 1959.
(With Elizabeth Mechem Fuller) *Springboards to Science*, 1959.
Teaching Resources for the Kindergarten-Primary Teacher, National Education Association, 1959.
Wading into Science, Denison, 1960.

Fingerplay Time, Denison, 1960.
(With Fuller) *Learning How to Use the Five Senses,* Denison, 1960.
Creative Art Ideas, Denison, 1960.
Kindergarten Rhymes, Teachers Publishing, 1965.
Time for Rhymes, Teachers Publishing, 1965.
Manipulative Language Arts, Teachers Publishing, 1965.
(With G. L. Scholtz) *Activity and Play of Children,* Prentice-Hall, 1978.
Those Dancing Years, State Mutual Book, 1982.

"LOG" SERIES

The Kindergarten Log, Denison, 1955, reprinted, 1977.
(With Mayon Atherton) *The First Grade Log,* Denison, 1956.
(With Pearl K. Esko and Lillian F. Carlson) *The Second Grade Log,* Denison, 1957.
(With Lillian Brosi and Jane Norman) *The Third Grade Log,* Denison, 1958.
(With Brosi and George Robert Kane) *The Fourth Grade Log,* Denison, 1959.
(With Kane and Bernice I. Hills) *The Fifth Grade Log,* Denison, 1959.
(With others) *The Sixth Grade Log,* Denison, 1961.

Also author of "Kindergarten Science" series, Continental Press, 1961.

WORK IN PROGRESS: Additional "Log" books; a new series of See-Quees, for Judy Toy Co.

SIDELIGHTS: Mary Jackson Ellis was one of eight elementary instructors in the country chosen as a master teacher to demonstrate creative teaching methods at the New York World's Fair.

AVOCATIONAL INTERESTS: Carving, fishing, baseball, and golf.†

* * *

ENLOE, Cynthia H(olden) 1938-

PERSONAL: Born July 16, 1938, in New York, N.Y.; daughter of Cortez F. (a physician) and Harriett (Goodridge) Enloe. *Education:* Connecticut College, B.A. (cum laude), 1960; University of California, Berkeley, M.A., 1963, Ph.D., 1967.

ADDRESSES: Office—Department of Government, Clark University, Worcester, Mass. 01610.

CAREER: University of California, Berkeley, acting instructor in political science, 1966-67; Miami University, Oxford, Ohio, assistant professor, 1968-71, associate professor of political science, 1971-72; Clark University, Worcester, Mass., associate professor, 1972-77, professor of government, 1977—, coordinator of women's studies, 1982—. Fulbright lecturer in political science, University of Guyana, Georgetown, 1971-72.

MEMBER: American Political Science Association, National Women's Studies Association, Association for Asian Studies, Phi Sigma Alpha.

AWARDS, HONORS: National Endowment for the Humanities grant, 1969; Council on Foreign Relations fellow, 1974-75; Ford Foundation fellow, 1979-80.

WRITINGS:

Multi-Ethnic Politics: The Case of Malaysia, Center for South and Southeast Asia Studies, University of California, 1970.

Ethnic Conflict and Political Development, Little, Brown, 1973.
Politics of Pollution in a Comparative Perspective, Longman, 1975.
(Co-author) *Development and Diversity in Southeast Asia,* McGraw, 1977.
(Contributor) Ronald M. Grant and E. Spencer Wellhofer, editors, *Ethno-nationalism, Multinational Corporation, and the Modern State,* Graduate School of International Studies, University of Colorado, 1979.
Police, Military and Ethnicity: Foundations of State Power, Transaction Books, 1980.
Ethnic Soldiers: State Security in Divided Societies, University of Georgia Press, 1980.
Of Common Cloth: Women in the Global Textile Industry, Institute for Policy Studies, 1983.
Does Khaki Become You?: The Militarization of Women's Lives, Phito Press/South End Press, 1983.

Contributor of articles to journals, including *Pacific Affairs, International Studies Quarterly, Armed Forces and Society, Comparative Politics,* and *Women's Review of Books.*

WORK IN PROGRESS: A cross-national study of the ways in which women and men have experienced differently the shaping of international economic, military, and political alliances and conflicts.

* * *

ERDMAN, David V(orse) 1911-

PERSONAL: Born November 4, 1911, in Omaha, Neb.; son of Carl Morris and Myrtle (Vorse) Erdman; married Virginia Bohan, 1937; children: Heidi, Wendy. *Education:* Carleton College, B.A., 1933; Princeton University, Ph.D., 1936.

ADDRESSES: Home—58 Crane Neck Rd., Setauket, N.Y. 11733. *Office*—Department of English, State University of New York, Stony Brook, N.Y. 11794.

CAREER: Agriculture, Mechanical and Normal College (now University of Arkansas at Monticello), professor of English, 1936-37; University of Wisconsin—Madison, instructor in English, 1937-41; Olivet College, Olivet, Mich., instructor in English, 1941-42; The Citadel, Charleston, S.C., assistant professor, 1942-43; United Auto Workers-Congress of Industrial Organizations (UAW-CIO), Detroit, Mich., editor in education department, 1943-46; University of Minnesota, Minneapolis, assistant professor, 1948-54; New York Public Library, New York, N.Y., editor of publications, 1956-68, part-time editor, 1968—; State University of New York at Stony Brook, professor, 1968—. Visiting professor, Duke University, 1952-53; adjunct professor, Temple University, 1964; instructor, University of Massachusetts Summer School in Bologna, 1966; John Cranford Adams Chair, Hofstra University, 1966-67. Advisor, 1789-1989: A UCLA Bicentennial Program for the French Revolution.

MEMBER: Modern Language Association of America, Keats-Shelley Association, Shaw Society, English Institute (chairman, 1960).

AWARDS, HONORS: Guggenheim fellow, 1947, 1954; Emily S. Hamblen Memorial Award for best work on William Blake, 1955, for *Blake: Prophet against Empire;* awarded Committee on Scholarly Editions emblem, 1980, for *The Complete Poetry and Prose of William Blake.*

WRITINGS:

Blake: Prophet against Empire, Princeton University Press, 1954, 3rd edition, 1977.

(Editor) *The Poetry and Prose of William Blake,* Doubleday, 1965, revised edition published as *The Complete Poetry and Prose of William Blake,* 1980.

(Editor with Ephim Fogel and contributor) *Evidence for Authorship: Essays in Attribution,* Cornell University Press, 1966.

(Principal editor) *A Concordance to the Poetry and Prose of William Blake,* Cornell University Press, 1968.

(Editor with John E. Grant and contributor) *Blake's Visionary Forms Dramatic,* Princeton University Press, 1970.

(Editor with Donald K. Moore) *The Notebook of William Blake,* Oxford University Press, 1973, revised edition, Readex Books, 1977.

(Editor) S. T. Coleridge, *Essays on His Times,* three volumes, Princeton University Press, 1978.

(Coordinating editor) *Blake's Designs for Young's Night Thoughts,* Oxford University Press, 1980.

(Author of commentary with Cettina Tramontane Magno) *The Four Zoas Manuscript by William Blake: A Photographic Facsimile with Commentary on the Illuminations,* Bucknell University Press, 1986.

Commerce des lumieres: John Oswald and the British in Paris in 1790-1793, University of Missouri Press, in press.

Byron's Poetic Technique, Station Hill, in press.

Editor of Byron papers, *Shelley and His Circle,* Harvard University Press, Volumes III-IV, 1970, Volumes V-VI, 1973. Also contributor of over sixty articles to professional journals. Critic-reviewer of Byron and Blake studies, 1947—, and Coleridge studies, 1958—. Coordinating editor and critic-reviewer, *Annual Bibliography of the Romantic Movement,* 1963—. Editor, *Bulletin* of the New York Public Library, 1956-77, and *Bulletin* of Research in the Humanities, 1978—; guest editor, *Keats-Shelley Journal,* 1966.

WORK IN PROGRESS: Editing *Collected Essays on the English Romantics,* for Station Hill; compiling *An Annotated Critical Bibliography of Blake Studies,* for Harvester Press.

*   *   *

ERLANGER, Baba
   See TRAHEY, Jane

*   *   *

EVANS, Bennett
   See BERGER, Ivan (Bennett)

*   *   *

EVANS, David R(ussell)   1937-

PERSONAL: Born October 22, 1937, in Rochester, N.Y.; son of Ralph Merrill (a researcher and writer in color perception and photography) and Pauline (Fowler) Evans; married Judith Ann Lewis, June 12, 1965 (divorced, November, 1976); children: Daniel. *Education:* Oberlin College, B.A. (cum laude), 1959; University of Illinois, M.Sc., 1961; Makerere University, Kampala, Uganda, Diploma in Education, 1962; Stanford University, Ph.D., 1969.

ADDRESSES: Home—36 Morgan Circle, Amherst, Mass. 01002. *Office*—Center for International Education, Hills House S., University of Massachusetts, Amherst, Mass. 01003.

CAREER: Makerere Institute of Education, Kampala, Uganda, lecturer in mathematics, 1962-64, research associate, 1967-68; University of Massachusetts—Amherst, assistant professor, 1969-72, associate professor, 1973-80, professor of education, 1981—, director of Center for International Education, 1974-81. Principal investigator for projects in Indonesia, Ghana, Swaziland, Lesotho, and Ecuador. Consultant to Peace Corps, U.S. Information Agency, U.S. Agency for International Development, United Nations Development Program, UNESCO, World Bank, and Ford Foundation.

MEMBER: African Studies Association, Comparative and International Education Society, Phi Beta Kappa, Sigma Xi.

AWARDS, HONORS: Ford International Development Study fellowship, 1965-66; Ford Foreign Area fellowship, 1966-68.

WRITINGS:

Attitudes and Behavior of Teachers in Uganda: An Aspect of the Process of National Development, International Development Education Center, 1969.

(With W. A. Smith and J. Hoteng) *Nonformal Alternatives to Schooling: A Glossary of Educational Methods,* Center for International Education, University of Massachusetts, 1971.

(With Smith and A. Gillette) *Educational Innovations: Issues in Adaptation,* Center for International Education, University of Massachusetts, 1971.

Teachers as Agents of National Development: A Case Study of Uganda, Praeger, 1971.

(With G. L. Schimmel) *The Impact of a Diversified Educational Program on Career Goals: Tororo Girls' School in the Context of Girls' Education in Uganda,* Center for International Education, University of Massachusetts, 1971.

Responsive Educational Planning: Myth or Reality?, IIEP/UNESCO (Paris), 1977.

Games and Simulations in Literacy Training, Hulton Educational Publications for the International Institute for Adult Literacy Methods, 1979.

The Planning of Nonformal Education (monograph), IIEP/UNESCO, 1981.

CONTRIBUTOR

Harold Lyons, editor, *Learning to Feel—Feeling to Learn,* C. E. Merrill, 1971.

Kenneth Prewitt, editor, *Education and Political Values,* East African Publishing House, 1971.

F. H. Klassen and D. G. Imig, editors, *National and Community Needs: The Challenge for Teacher Education,* [Washington, D.C.], 1974.

T. J. LaBell, editor, *Educational Alternatives in Latin America: Social Change and Social Stratification,* Latin American Center Publications, University of California, Los Angeles, 1975.

D. W. Allen, M. A. Melmik, and C. C. Peele, editors, *Improving University Teaching: Reform, Renewal, Reward,* Clinic to Improve University Teaching (Amherst, Mass.), 1976.

J. Bock and G. Papagiannis, editors, *Nonformal Education and National Development,* Praeger, 1983.

OTHER

Contributor to *Comparative Education Review, Prospects, Canadian Journal of African Studies,* and other journals.

WORK IN PROGRESS: Research and writing on materials for nonformal education; uses of micro-computers in educational planning; computer-based models of educational systems.

AVOCATIONAL INTERESTS: Natural history (particularly the study of birds), motorcycles, travel, camping.

* * *

EWART, Gavin (Buchanan) 1916-

PERSONAL: Born in 1916 in London, England; son of George Arthur (a surgeon) and Dorothy (Turner) Ewart; married Margo Bennett (a school secretary), March 24, 1956; children: Jane Susan, Julian Robert. *Education:* Attended Christ's College, Cambridge, 1934-37. *Politics:* Labour. *Religion:* None.

*ADDRESSES: Home—*57 Kenilworth Court, Lower Richmond Rd., London S.W. 15, England.

CAREER: Assistant in book review department, British Council, 1946-52; advertising copywriter, 1952-71; free-lance writer, 1971—. *Military service:* British Army, Royal Artillery, 1940-46; became captain.

MEMBER: Royal Society of Literature (fellow), Poetry Society (chairperson, 1978-79), Society of Authors, Performing Rights Society.

AWARDS, HONORS: Cholmondeley Award, 1971, for achievement as a poet; travel scholarship from Royal Society of Literature, 1978.

WRITINGS:

POETRY

Poems and Songs, Fortune Press, 1939.
Londoners, Heinemann, 1964.
Throwaway Lines, Keepsake Press, 1964.
Two Children, Keepsake Press, 1966.
Pleasures of the Flesh, Alan Ross, 1966.
The Deceptive Grin of the Gravel Porters, London Magazine Editions, 1968.
Twelve Apostles, Ulsterman Publications, 1970.
The Gavin Ewart Show, Trigram Press, 1971.
Venus, Poem-of-the-Month Club, 1972.
The Select Party, Keepsake Press, 1972.
Alphabet Soup, Sycamore Press, 1972.
By My Guest!, Trigram Press, 1975.
An Imaginary Love Affair, Ulsterman Publications, 1975.
(With Zulfikar Ghose and B. S. Johnson) *Penguin Modern Poets 25,* Penguin, 1975.
A Question Partly Answered, Sceptre Press, 1976.
No Fool Like an Old Fool, Gollancz, 1976.
Or Where a Young Penguin Lies Screaming, Gollancz, 1977.
All My Little Ones, Anvil Press, 1978.
The Collected Ewart, 1933-1980, Hutchinson, 1980.
The New Ewart: Poems, 1980-1982, Hutchinson, 1982.
More Little Ones, Anvil Press, 1982.
Capital Letters, Sycamore Press, 1983.
Festival Nights, Other Branch Readings, 1984.
The Ewart Quarto, Hutchinson, 1984.
The Young Pobble's Guide to His Toes, Hutchinson, 1985.
Useful Information about Animals, Century/Hutchinson, 1986.

Work is also represented in James Laughlin's *New Directions* anthologies.

EDITOR

Forty Years On: An Anthology of School Songs, Sidgwick & Jackson, 1964.
The Batsford Book of Children's Verse, Batsford, 1976.
New Poems 1977-78: A P.E.N. Anthology of Contemporary Poetry, Hutchinson, 1977.
The Batsford Book of Light Verse for Children, Batsford, 1978.
The Penguin Book of Light Verse, Penguin, 1980.
Other People's Clerihews, Oxford University Press, 1983.

OTHER

(Author of introduction) E. C. Bentley, *The Complete Clerihews of E. Clerihew Bentley,* Oxford University Press, 1981.

WORK IN PROGRESS: Literary Landmarks, a book of short satirical poems on "literary" subjects.

SIDELIGHTS: "One of the few bright features about poetry in the late 1970s is that Gavin Ewart is growing old disgracefully," wrote Anthony Thwaite in a 1978 *Times Literary Supplement* review. "He grows more prolific, wider-ranging, funnier and more scabrous as the years go by." The five books of light verse Ewart has published in the 1980s—and their increasing acceptance as legitimate poetry—suggest that Thwaite's observation still applies. Reviewers find the recent flowering of this British satirist all the more remarkable because his poetic voice was silent for twenty-five years.

First published nationally at the precocious age of seventeen, Ewart had a poetry book, *Poems and Songs,* to his credit by the time he was twenty-three. T. S. Eliot, Ezra Pound, and Ronald Bottrall are all acknowledged influences in this early verse, with W. H. Auden making his presence felt later on. But just as he was establishing his own poetic voice, Ewart found his writing interrupted by the outbreak of war. "I found it very hard to write during World War II, when I was on active service in North Africa and Italy," Ewart told *CA.* And when the war was over, he pursued a different path, first becoming an assistant in the book review department of the British Council and then an advertising copywriter for eighteen years. He didn't pursue his old vocation until, as he told *CA,* "Alan Ross, editor of *London Magazine,* encouraged me to begin writing poetry again in 1959." Following what the *Times Literary Supplement* has described as his "remarkable poetic rebirth in the early 1960s," Ewart has produced an uninterrupted stream of light-hearted verse that is known for its irreverence, sexual content, and effortless technical skill.

An acknowledged master of forms who can mimic almost any style of writing, Ewart has depth as well as breadth, as a *Times Literary Supplement* reviewer explains: "What makes him different is that he isn't content with satirical pastiche or parody. He has a strong, gamey talent of his own, much concerned with the disputed territory that lies between things-as-they-are, things-as-they-might-be, and things-as-people-say-they-are." For instance, in "The Gentle Sex," which recounts how a group of Ulster Defence Association women beat a political opponent to death in Belfast, Northern Ireland, Ewart employs a metric form that Gerald Manley Hopkins used. "On the face of it what could be less apt than to tell this bleak story in the stanza form of 'The Wreck of the Deutschland'?" asks Anthony Thwaite. "But this is very precisely what Ewart does; and in the process one feels the ghostly presence of Hopkins's nuns behind the brutally vicious tale."

While Ewart's subtle literary allusions may be lost on unknowing readers, there is no mistaking his preoccupation with sex, which frequently serves as a springboard for larger concerns. "Starting off from sex, often in one of its unhappier forms, Ewart comments on ambition, middle age, life in the suburbs, the boredom of wives, office politics, children, history, etc.," writes Peter Porter in *London Magazine*. One of Ewart's earliest successes was a take-off on the Lewis Carroll classic, irreverently titled "Phallus in Wonderland," and he seems to have become even less inhibited with advancing age. In the opening poem of his more recent *Pleasures of the Flesh*, for instance, Ewart embraces his lusts joyfully: "A small talent, like a small penis, / Should not be hidden lightly under a bushel, / But shine in use, or exhibitionism. / Otherwise how should one know it was there?"

With the appearance of *Pleasures of the Flesh*, "it becomes clear how perfectly Ewart's creative life has conformed to the butterfly system," notes *Times Literary Supplement* contributor Russell Davies. "An active and noticeable caterpillar in youth, and twenty years a chrysalis, he struggles out stickily in *Londoners* and bursts forth, at last, into a gaudy maturity with *Pleasures*." In his *London Magazine* review of this volume, Porter expresses a similar view: "*Pleasures of the Flesh* establishes Ewart as an important poet . . . with something to say to us directly. The gestation which followed that early promise was a long one, but the results have been worth waiting for."

Davies believes that since the early 1970s Ewart has been "the star of his own production. The very title of *The Gavin Ewart Show* proclaims it. In a curious way, he has become the sort of poet whom one 'follows,' as one might an actor or a sportsman or a singer. Ewart never produces a tight, interlocking performance at book length, but nor do singers with their 'albums'; yet there are always one or two songs you play over and over. To have established this kind of career at all is a very considerable achievement." When reading *The Gavin Ewart Show*, David Howarth suggests in hs *Phoenix* review that rather than approaching the volume academically, it's "much better to take Ewart's advice: 'Slup me rough and homely and I'll taste fine.'"

BIOGRAPHICAL/CRITICAL SOURCES:

BOOKS

Contemporary Literary Criticism, Volume XIII, Gale, 1980.
Dictionary of Literary Biography, Volume XL: *Poets of Great Britain and Ireland since 1960*, Gale, 1985.
Ewart, Gavin, *Pleasures of the Flesh*, Alan Ross, 1966.

PERIODICALS

London Magazine, May, 1966.

Phoenix, July, 1973.
Times (London), April 25, 1985.
Times Literary Supplement, October 30, 1969, April 21, 1972, March 19, 1976, December 10, 1976, April 14, 1978, July 11, 1980, January 9, 1981, July 30, 1982, May 27, 1983, November 11, 1983, September 20, 1985.

—*Sketch by Donna Olendorf*

*   *   *

EWBANK, Walter F(rederick) 1918-

PERSONAL: Born January 29, 1918, in Poona, India; son of Sir Robert (in Indian civil service) and Frances Helen (Simpson) Ewbank; married former wife, Ida Margaret Whitworth, April 5, 1941; married second wife, Josephine Alice Williamson, October 9, 1976; children: Jane Margaret (Mrs. Andrew Colin Renfrew), Clare Caroline (Mrs. John Henry Fryer Fryer-Spedding), Anthea Mary. *Education:* Balliol College, Oxford, B.A. (with honors), 1946, B.Th., 1952.

ADDRESSES: Home—High Rigg, Castle Sowerby, Hutton Roof, Penrith, Cumbria CA11 0XY, England. *Office*—3 The Abbey, Carlisle CA3 8TZ, England.

CAREER: Ordained clergyman of Church of England, 1946; youth chaplain of Diocese of Carlisle, 1949-52; Casterton School, Westmorland, chaplain, 1952-62; administrative chaplain to Bishop of Carlisle, 1962-66; St. Cuthbert's Church, Carlisle, vicar, 1966-71; archdeacon of Westmorland and Furness and vicar of Winster, 1971-77; canon residentiary of Carlisle Cathedral, 1977-82, honorary canon, 1982—. Member of Convocation of York and the Church Assembly, 1957-70; diocesan director of ordinands, 1962-70; member of Canon Law Standing Commission, 1968-70, and Faculty Jurisdiction Commission, 1979—. Rural dean of Carlisle, 1969-71.

MEMBER: Royal Overseas League, Country Club of Carlisle.

AWARDS, HONORS: Winter War Remembrance Medal, 1940.

WRITINGS:

Salopian Diaries, Wilding & Son, 1961.
Morality without Law, World Publishing, 1969.
Charles Euston Nurse: A Memoir, World Publishing, 1982.

Contributor of articles to periodicals.

WORK IN PROGRESS: Poems: Latin and English.

AVOCATIONAL INTERESTS: Greek and Latin classical literature, walking, bird-watching, meteor-watching.†

F

FALKIRK, Richard
  See LAMBERT, Derek

*   *   *

FIRES, Alicia
  See OGLESBY, Joseph

*   *   *

FIRMIN, Peter   1928-

PERSONAL: Born December 11, 1928, in Harwich, England; son of Lewis Charles (a railway telegrapher) and Lila (Burnett) Firmin; married Joan Ruth Clapham (a bookbinder), July 29, 1952; children: Charlotte, Hannah, Josephine, Katharine, Lucy, Emily. *Education:* Colchester Art School, diploma, 1947; Central School of Art, diploma, 1952. *Politics:* Socialist.

ADDRESSES: Home—Hillside Farm, 36 Blean Hill, Blean, Canterbury, Kent, England.

CAREER: Free-lance book illustrator, writer, puppet maker, and cartoon film artist, 1952—. *Military service:* Royal Navy, 1947-49.

WRITINGS:

SELF-ILLUSTRATED CHILDREN'S BOOKS

The Winter Diary of a Country Rat, Kaye & Ward, 1982.
Chicken Stew, Pelham, 1983.
Tricks and Tales, Kaye & Ward, 1983.
The Midsummer Notebook of a Country Rat, Kaye & Ward, 1984.

SELF-ILLUSTRATED CHILDREN'S BOOKS; "BASIL BRUSH" SERIES

Basil Brush Goes Flying, Kaye & Ward, 1969, Prentice-Hall, 1977.
. . . Goes Boating, Kaye & Ward, 1969, Prentice-Hall, 1976.
. . . in the Jungle, Kaye & Ward, 1970.
. . . at the Seaside, Kaye & Ward, 1970, Prentice-Hall, 1976.
. . . and the Dragon, Kaye & Ward, 1971.
. . . Finds Treasure, Kaye & Ward, 1971.
. . . Builds a House, Kaye & Ward, 1973, Prentice-Hall, 1977.
. . . Gets a Medal, Kaye & Ward, 1973.
. . . and the Windmills, Kaye & Ward, 1979.

. . . on the Trail, Kaye & Ward, 1979.
Three Tales of Basil Brush, Books 1-2, Kaye & Ward, 1979.
Two Tales of Basil Brush, Fontana, 1982.
Basil Brush Takes Off, Kaye & Ward, 1983.

ILLUSTRATOR; CHILDREN'S BOOKS BY OLIVER POSTGATE; "SAGA OF NOGGIN" SERIES

King of the Nogs, Kaye & Ward, 1969.
The Game, Kaye & Ward, 1972.
Noggin and the Money, Kaye & Ward, 1973.
Flying Machine, Kaye & Ward, 1974.
The Omruds, Kaye & Ward, 1974.
The Blackwash, Kaye & Ward, 1975.
Nogmania, Kaye & Ward, 1977.
Noggin the Nog, Armada, 1980.
Noggin and the Flowers, Fontana, 1980.
Noggin and the Island, Fontana, 1980.
Three Tales of Noggin, Books 1-2, Kaye & Ward, 1981.

ILLUSTRATOR; CHILDREN'S BOOKS BY POSTGATE; "IVOR THE ENGINE" SERIES

Ivor the Engine: The First Story, Fontana, 1977.
. . . : The Snowdrifts, Fontana, 1977.
. . . : The Dragon, Collins, 1979.
. . . : The Elephant, Collins, 1979.
. . . : The Foxes, Armada, 1982.
Ivor's Birthday, Collins, 1984.

ILLUSTRATOR; CHILDREN'S BOOKS BY POSTGATE

Bagpuss in the Sun, Collins, 1974.
Bagpuss on a Rainy Day, Collins, 1974.
Mr. Rumbletum's Gumboot, Carousel Books, 1977.
Silly Old Uncle Feedle, Carousel Books, 1977.
The Song of the Pongo, Carousel Books, 1977.

ILLUSTRATOR; CHILDREN'S BOOKS

Biddy Baxter, *The "Blue Peter" Book of Limericks,* Pan Books, 1976.
Baxter, *The "Blue Peter" Book of Odd Odes,* BBC Publications, 1976.
Peter Meteyard, *Stanley: The Tale of the Lizard,* Deutsch, 1979.
Edith Nesbit, *The Last of the Dragons,* Macdonald & Jane's, 1980.

Nesbit, *Melisande*, Macdonald & Co., 1982.

WORK IN PROGRESS: Three books about "Pinny the Smallest Doll in the World," for Deutsch.

SIDELIGHTS: Peter Firmin writes: "Most of my work results from the partnership with Oliver Postgate. We have made films, including cartoon and puppet films. But now I write and illustrate my own books.

"I like creating books with a particular readership in mind. As I now have four grandchildren, I am writing a series for them which will be dedicated to them and the other children of my family. I like to test my books on them first."

AVOCATIONAL INTERESTS: Walking, sailing, birds, books.

*   *   *

FISHER, Aileen (Lucia) 1906-

PERSONAL: Born September 9, 1906, in Iron River, Mich.; daughter of Nelson E. and Lucia (Milker) Fisher. *Education:* Attended University of Chicago, 1923-25; University of Missouri, B.J., 1927.

ADDRESSES: Home and office—505 College Ave., Boulder, Colo. 80302.

CAREER: Women's National Journalistic Register, Chicago, Ill., director, 1928-31; Labor Bureau of the Middle West, Chicago, research assistant, 1931-32; free-lance writer, 1932—.

MEMBER: Theta Sigma Phi.

AWARDS, HONORS: Silver Medal from U.S. Treasury Department, World War II; Western Writers of America Award for juvenile nonfiction, 1967, for *Valley of the Smallest: The Life Story of a Shrew;* award for children's poetry, National Council of Teachers of English, 1978.

WRITINGS:

JUVENILE

The Coffee-Pot Face (Junior Literary Guild selection), McBride, 1933.
Inside a Little House, McBride, 1938.
Guess Again!, McBride, 1941.
Up the Windy Hill (verse), Abelard, 1953.
Runny Days, Sunny Days, Abelard, 1958.
I Wonder How, I Wonder Why, Abelard, 1962.
Cricket in a Thicket, Scribner, 1963.
In the Woods, in the Meadow, in the Sky, Scribner, 1965.
Out in the Dark and Daylight, Harper, 1980.
Rabbits, Rabbits, Harper, 1983.

JUVENILE; PUBLISHED BY THOMAS NELSON

That's Why, 1946.
Off to the Gold Fields, 1955.
All on a Mountain Day, 1956.
A Lantern in the Window, 1957.
Skip, 1958.
Fisherman of Galilee, 1959.
Summer of Little Rain, 1961.
My Cousin Abe, 1962.

JUVENILE; PUBLISHED BY ATHENEUM

Over the Hills to Nugget, 1949.
Trapped by the Mountain Storm, 1953.
Homestead of the Free: The Kansas Story, 1953.

Timber! Logging in Michigan, 1955.
Cherokee Strip: The Race for Land, 1956.
(With Olive Rabe) *We Dickinsons*, 1965.
(With Rabe) *We Alcotts*, 1968.

JUVENILE; PUBLISHED BY CROWELL

Going Barefoot, 1960.
Where Does Everyone Go?, 1961.
Like Nothing at All, 1962.
I Like Weather, 1963.
Listen, Rabbit, 1964.
In the Middle of the Night, 1965.
Arbor Day, 1965.
Best Little House, 1966.
Valley of the Smallest: The Life Story of a Shrew, 1966.
(With Rabe) *Human Rights Day*, 1966.
Skip around the Year, 1967.
My Mother and I, 1967.
We Went Looking (verse), 1968.
Up, up the Mountain, 1968.
In One Door and out the Other (verse), 1969.
Sing, Little Mouse (verse), 1969.
Clean as a Whistle, 1969.
But Ostriches, 1970.
Jeanne d'Arc, 1970.
Feathered Ones and Furry (verse), 1971.
Do Bears Have Mothers, Too?, 1973.
My Cat Has Eyes of Sapphire Blue, 1975.
I Stood upon a Mountain, 1979.
Anybody Home?, 1980.
When It Comes to Bugs, 1985.

JUVENILE; PUBLISHED BY BOWMAR/NOBLE

Animal Houses, 1972.
Animal Disguises, 1973.
Animal Jackets, 1973.
Now That Days Are Colder, 1973.
Tail Twisters, 1973.
Filling the Bill, 1973.
Going Places, 1973.
Sleepy Heads, 1973.
You Don't Look Like Your Mother, 1973.
No Accounting for Tastes, 1973.
Now That Spring Is Here, 1977.
And a Sunflower Grew, 1977.
Mysteries in the Garden, 1977.
Seeds on the Go, 1977.
Plant Magic, 1977.
Petals Yellow and Petals Red, 1977.
Swords and Daggers, 1977.
Prize Performance, 1977.
A Tree with a Thousand Uses, 1977.
As the Leaves Fall Down, 1977.

JUVENILE PLAYS

Set the Stage for Christmas, Row, Peterson & Co., 1948.
Health and Safety Plays and Programs, Plays, 1953.
Holiday Programs for Boys and Girls, Plays, 1953.
(With Rabe) *United Nations Plays and Programs*, Plays, 1954, 2nd edition, 1961.
(With Rabe) *Patriotic Plays and Programs*, Plays, 1956.
Christmas Plays and Programs, Plays, 1960.
Plays about Our Nation's Songs, Plays, 1962.
Bicentennial Plays and Programs, Plays, 1975.
Year-Round Programs for Young Players, Plays, 1985.

OTHER

Contributor to periodicals, including *Story Parade, Jack and Jill,* and *Child Life.*

SIDELIGHTS: Aileen Fisher told *CA:* "After living on a ranch in the foothills for more than thirty years, I now live in Boulder, Colo., on a dead-end street at the foot of Flagstaff Mountain. Except for rabbits, I find more wildlife here at the edge of town than on the ranch; and I still enjoy many of the pleasures of country living, including what my neighbor calls a 'wild' yard. I like an organized life of peace and quiet, and so I avoid crowds, cities, noise, airports, neon lights, and confusion. My first and chief love in writing is writing children's verse."

BIOGRAPHICAL/CRITICAL SOURCES:

BOOKS

Hopkins, Lee Bennett, *Books Are by People,* Citation Press, 1969.

PERIODICALS

New Yorker, December 14, 1968.
Young Readers' Review, November, 1968.

*   *   *

FITZGERALD, George R.   1932-

PERSONAL: Born May 15, 1932, in Jaffrey, N.H.; son of Edward Roland (an engineer) and Mary (Blanchette) Wilder. *Education:* Dartmouth College, A.B. (cum laude), 1954; St. Paul's College, Ph.B., 1961, M.A. (theology), 1965; Tufts University, M.A. (political science), 1970; also attended Columbia University, 1965, and University of Chicago, 1970-71. *Politics:* Democrat.

ADDRESSES: Home—Newman Hall, 2700 Dwight Way, Berkeley, Calif. 94704.

CAREER: Entered Missionary Society of St. Paul the Apostle (Paulist Fathers), ordained Roman Catholic priest, 1965; pastor of Roman Catholic churches in Toronto, Ontario, Boston, Mass., Berkeley, Calif., Washington, D.C., Chicago, Ill., and New York City; Tufts University, Medford, Mass., Roman Catholic chaplain and teacher of political science, 1965-70; St. Paul's College, Washington, D.C., rector, 1971-78; Paulist Press, New York City, member of editorial staff, 1978-80; University of California, Berkeley, Newman Hall—Holy Spirit Parish, pastor, 1980—. Member of faculty, Boston College, 1965-70, and Catholic University of America and Washington Theological Union, both 1971-78; guest lecturer, Virginia Theological Seminary. *Military service:* U.S. Air Force, 1954-57; became captain.

WRITINGS:

Communes: Their Goals, Hopes, and Problems, Paulist/Newman, 1971.
A Practical Guide to Preaching: Helps and Hints for Preparation and Delivery, Paulist Press, 1980.
Handbook of the Mass, Paulist Press, 1982.

Contributor to *America* and *U.S. Catholic.*

SIDELIGHTS: George R. Fitzgerald told *CA:* "I am interested in communication and the ways in which individuals translate faith into action, move from motivation to praxis. I am also interested in the various ways in which a culture is determined by the individual and common faith of its people, and the ways in which faith is shaped and determined by movements within a society."

*   *   *

FITZWILLIAM, Michael
See LYONS, J. B.

*   *   *

FLEETWOOD, Frances   1902-
(Frank Fleetwood)

PERSONAL: Surname originally Buss; name legally changed; born May 24, 1902, in London, England; daughter of Francis Fleetwood (a professor) and Elsie (Hudson) Buss. *Education:* Sorbonne, University of Paris, certificat d'etudes francaises, 1922. *Politics:* "General skepticism." *Religion:* "Freethinker."

ADDRESSES: Home—Via del Golfo 4, 04028 Scauri (Latina), Italy.

CAREER: Writer. Has worked at various times as secretary, language teacher, interpreter, stage manager and understudy in small club theatres, motion picture extra, and hostess-interpreter for a London tourist agency. Served with Civil Defense in London during World War II. Has read papers at conferences.

AWARDS, HONORS: Civil Defense Medal, 1945; silver medal from Servizio Volontariato Giovanile, 1972, for work at Caserta Castle; honorable mention, Gradara (Italy) Literary Competition, 1973, for a short story in Italian; "Friends of Gradara" medal, 1972, for writing featuring that area.

WRITINGS:

(With Betty Conquest) *Conquest: The Story of a Theatre Family,* W. H. Allen, 1953.
(Translator from the French) Maurice Dekobra, *The Seventh Wife of Prince Hassan* (novel), W. H. Allen, 1961.
(Translator from the Italian) Umberto Nobile, *My Polar Flights,* Muller, 1961.
(Translator) Dekobra, *Double or Quits* (novel), W. H. Allen, 1962.
The Elephant and the Rose: Romance of the Malatesta Family of Rimini, Ponticelli, 1968.
Concordia (novel), W. H. Allen, 1971, St. Martin's, 1973.
Concordia Errant (novel), W. H. Allen, 1973.
La Torre dei falchi (history; title means "The Falcons' Tower"), Caramanica, 1973, 2nd edition, 1977.
(With Vera Schuyler) *Beloved Upstart* (novel), W. H. Allen, 1974.
Flashback, Russo (Caserta), 1980.
(With Mario Tabanelli) *Castelli, Rocche e Torri dei Malatesti,* Magalini (Brescia), 1983.
Le Donne dei Malatesti, Magalini, 1984.
Romagna, Magalini, 1984.

UNDER PSEUDONYM FRANK FLEETWOOD

The Threshold (poems), Selwyn & Blount, 1925.
(With George Cusack) *To What Purpose?* (novel), Stanley Paul, 1929.
(Translator from the Italian) Umberto Nobile, *With the "Italia" to the North Pole,* Allen & Unwin, 1930.
(Translator with Elizabeth Dithmer) Dithmer, *The Truth about Nobile,* Williams & Norgate, 1933.

(Translator from the German with Eric Reissner) Carl Schuett, *The Elements of Aeronautics,* Pitman & Sons, 1941.

OTHER

Also ghost-writer of several books. Occasional contributor to *Times Educational Supplement* (London), *La Pie* (Italian literary journal), *Cultural Review,* and *Dove e Quando?*

SIDELIGHTS: Frances Fleetwood describes her writing habits: "For a historical novel, I spend several months visiting research libraries and stocking-up relevant photocopies. Meanwhile, on long country walks or in bed at night, I compose (in my head) the general lines of the story, so that I have a clear idea of the beginning and the end, and some notion of the main incidents. Then I make a time-schedule of the actual historical dates and the way they fit in with the private lives of my characters. When I am ready to write, I start at Chapter I and work steadily through to the end (occasionally postponing a difficult chapter, or one for which I need further factual information). The first draft is handwritten in a copybook. Having accumulated several chapters, I type a rough draft, and at this stage the major corrections and alterations are made. At the end—several weeks or months later, by which time I can criticize my work impersonally—I type the fair copy and *never touch it again,* unless I discover an anachronism, a mistake in historical fact or a stylistic blunder. I abominate the type of writer who complains: 'I've written this chapter over and over again, and it *won't* come right!' My advice in this case is uncompromising: Leave the damned chapter as it stands, and finish the book. Then go back and see if it is really necessary to the plot; if not, scrap it entirely. If so, include the requisite information, casually, in some other chapter."

Fleetwood told *CA* that she wrote her first novel at the age of nine but made no attempt to have it published. The book was entitled *The Suffragettes of the Twentieth Century.* At fifteen, she wrote a novel about the English Civil War ("strongly royalist") that was submitted to an agent who failed to place it with a publisher. Of her early interest in literature she writes: "My father had a complete collection of Walter Scott's novels, and as a child I read them all with enjoyment, but, frankly, have never opened one since! The writers who have influenced me most are (in time order) R. L. Stevenson, Rudyard Kipling, and Lawrence of Arabia. All these combine pace and elegance with a love of sounding words and heroic deeds. *Puck of Pook's Hill* was the favourite book of my childhood, and I can read it today with the same thrill. In fact, I owe to it the 'time voyage' idea on which [one of my novels] is based.

"During the past twenty years, the work of filling wide gaps in my knowledge of Italian literature, classic and modern, has prevented my following contemporary developments in English-speaking countries. I recently discovered Thom Gunn and found his work exciting, especially the early verses, where he displays a profound European culture expressed in impeccable rhyme and rhythm schemes. As novelists I like Mary Renault, Mary Stewart, and Lawrence Durrell; but to my mind the most absorbing book written in the last twenty-five years is Tolkien's *Lord of the Rings.* Irving Stone's biographical novels are all very fine, especially *The Greek Treasure.* I don't like modern drama, which is usually sordid, anti-heroic and taken up with dreary 'underdog' problems."

AVOCATIONAL INTERESTS: Gardening, weaving, cooking, swimming, long country walks, mediaeval history (especially Italian).

FLEETWOOD, Frank
See FLEETWOOD, Frances

*   *   *

FLINK, Salomon J.   1906-1983

PERSONAL: Born December 22, 1906, in Neumarkt, Germany (now Nowy Targ, Poland); died June, 1983, in Israel; son of Samuel and Frieda (Stein) Flink; married Florence Rothman, 1937; children: Naomi Zucker, Jonah, Rachael. *Education:* University of Berlin, M.B.A., 1927; Columbia University, M.A., 1928, Ph.D., 1931.

ADDRESSES: Home—Israel.

CAREER: City College (now City College of the City University of New York), New York, N.Y., teacher of economics and banking, 1929-34; University of Newark, Newark, N.J., 1934-46, began as assistant professor, became associate professor; Rutgers University, Newark Campus, Newark, N.J., professor, beginning 1946, chairman of department of economics. Fulbright professor at College of International Economics in Vienna and University of Vienna, 1955-56; visiting professor at New York University Graduate School of Business Administration, 1960; lecturer for U.S. Department of State in Austria, Germany, India, and Japan. Associate director of research, Research Institute of America, 1943-44; director of research, Housing Institute, 1944-45; U.S. representative, International Organization for European Economic Cooperation conference, Paris, 1956, 1957. Chief economic and fiscal consultant, General Assembly of New Jersey, 1958-59; consultant to several banks in New Jersey and to a Canadian mining and steel company; consultant to administrator, U.S. Small Business Administration, 1963-64.

MEMBER: American Economic Association, American Statistical Association.

WRITINGS:

The German Reichsbank and Economic Germany, Harper, 1930, reprinted, Greenwood Press, 1969.
(With B. Burn) *Codes, Cartels, National Planning,* McGraw, 1934.
(Co-editor) *Your Business after the War,* Research Institute of America, 1943.
The Coming Housing Boom, Housing Institute of America, 1945.
The American Economy, Dryden Press, 1948.
Die Roboter Kommen, Obelisk Verlag (Vienna), 1956.
Equity Financing for Small Business, Simmons-Boardman, 1962.
Equity Financing of Small New Jersey Manufacturing Companies, New Jersey Department of Economic Development, 1962, reprinted, Ayer Co., 1979.
The Role of Commercial Banks in the Small Business Investment Company Industry, American Bankers Association, 1965.
(With Donald Grunewald) *Managerial Finance,* Wiley, 1969.
(With Meyer Ungar and Meir Tamari) *Debt Capital Financing in Israel,* Bar-Ilan University Press, 1975.
Israel, Chaos and Challenge: Politics versus Economics, Turtledove Publishers, 1979.

Contributor of articles to publications in the United States, Austria, India, and Japan. Editor, *Review of New Jersey Business,* 1951-59.

AVOCATIONAL INTERESTS: Theater and ballet.

BIOGRAPHICAL/CRITICAL SOURCES:

PERIODICALS

New York Times, April 17, 1958.†

* * *

FLYNN, Leslie Bruce 1918-

PERSONAL: Born October 3, 1918, in Hamilton, Ontario, Canada; son of James A. and Agnes (Shaver) Flynn; married Bernice L. Carlson, 1945; children: Linnea, Janna, Marilee, Annilee, Donna, Carol, Susan. *Education:* Attended Moody Bible Institute, 1937-40; Wheaton College, A.B., 1942; Eastern Baptist Theological Seminary, B.D., 1944; University of Pennsylvania, A.M., 1946.

ADDRESSES: Home—32 Highview Ave., Nanuet, N.Y. *Office*—Grace Conservative Baptist Church, 22 Demarest, Nanuet, N.Y.

CAREER: Bethlehem Baptist Church, St. Clair, Pa., pastor, 1944-49; Grace Conservative Baptist Church, Nanuet, N.Y., pastor, 1949—. Instructor, Nyack College, 1951-72.

MEMBER: Evangelical Theological Society.

AWARDS, HONORS: D.D. from Conservative Baptist Theological Seminary, 1963.

WRITINGS:

Did I Say That?, Broadman, 1959.
Serve Him with Mirth, Zondervan, 1960.
Your God and Your Gold, Zondervan, 1961.
The Power of Christlike Living, Zondervan, 1962.
Did I Say Thanks?, Broadman, 1963.
Christmas Messages, Baker Book, 1964.
Day of Resurrection, Broadman, 1965.
How to Save Time in the Ministry, Broadman, 1966.
Your Influence Is Showing, Broadman, 1967.
You Can Live above Envy, Conservative Baptist Press, 1970.
A Source Book of Humorous Stories, Baker Book, 1973.
Nineteen Gifts of the Spirit, Scripture Press, 1974.
It's about Time, Timothy Books, 1974.
Now a Word from Our Creator, Scripture Press, 1976.
Great Church Fights, Scripture Press, 1976.
Man: Ruined and Restored, Scripture Press, 1978.
(With wife, Bernice Flynn) *God's Will: You Can Know It,* Scripture Press, 1979.
Joseph: God's Man in Egypt, Scripture Press, 1979.
The Gift of Joy, Scripture Press, 1980.
You Don't Have to Go It Alone, Accent, 1981.
From Clay to Rock, Christian Herald, 1981.
Dare to Care Like Jesus, Scripture Press, 1982.
The Twelve, Scripture Press, 1982.
Worship—Together We Celebrate, Scripture Press, 1983.
Your Inner You, Scripture Press, 1984.
The Sustaining Power of Hope, Scripture Press, 1985.

* * *

FOX, Douglas A(llan) 1927-

PERSONAL: Born March 20, 1927, in Mullumbimby, New South Wales, Australia; son of Cecil Edwin Madison and Lilly (Tucker) Fox; married Margaret Porter, September 12, 1958; children: Elizabeth Rachel, Michael Glenn. *Education:* University of Sydney, B.A., 1956; University of Chicago, M.A., 1958; Pacific School of Religion, S.T.M., 1958, Th.D., 1963.

ADDRESSES: Office—Department of Religion, Colorado College, Colorado Springs, Colo. 80903.

CAREER: Protestant clergyman, 1956-63; minister in New South Wales, Australia, 1956-61, and San Francisco, Calif., 1962-63; Colorado College, Colorado Springs, assistant professor, 1963-68, associate professor, 1968-74, professor of religion, 1974-83, David and Lucille Packard Professor of Religion, 1983—.

MEMBER: American Association of University Professors.

WRITINGS:

Buddhism, Christianity, and the Future of Man, Westminster, 1972.
The Vagrant Lotus: An Introduction to Buddhist Philosophy, Westminster, 1973.
Mystery and Meaning: Personal Logic and the Language of Religion, Westminster, 1976.
What Do You Think about God, Judson, 1985.
Meditation and Its Altered States of Consciousness, John Knox, in press.

Contributor to *Journal of Bible and Religion, Encounter, Philosophy East and West, Religion in Life, Contemporary Religions in Japan,* and other journals.

WORK IN PROGRESS: Oriental Philosophy: The Relation of Ideas in Christian and Oriental Philosophy; An Introduction of Mahayana and Theravada Buddhist Philosophy; Sanskrit translations of Prajnaparamita works and Sankara's philosophy.

SIDELIGHTS: Douglas A. Fox writes: "I have been concerned to explore those systems of thought and practice (generally religious) which have enabled persons in diverse cultures and times to endure and to find or make some meaning in their lives. In writing about these things I have tried both to make a small contribution to scholarship and to write clearly enough to break out of academic confinements and speak to intelligent and interested general readers. For this reason I find most encouraging the sort of review that explicitly responds to this effort. For example, John G. Kuethe in *Lutheran Quarterly* wrote about *Mystery and Meaning: Personal Logic and the Language of Religion,* 'The book is indeed a new way to approach theology that makes it rewarding for the layman as well as the initiated. . . . By all odds, one of the most rewarding books I have read this year.' Father Michael D. Mielach of Siena College wrote in *Cord,* 'I can only welcome [*Buddhism, Christianity, and the Future of Man*] as fulfilling a real need and recommend it with all possible enthusiasm, both for academic use and for the enjoyment and enlightenment of the discriminating reader.' Finally, *Washington Buddhist* reviewed *The Vagrant Lotus: An Introduction to Buddhist Philosophy* and, from a Buddhist perspective, said, 'Professor Fox's book is the best introduction to Buddhist philosophy which this reviewer has come across in his study of Buddhism to date.'

"These responses, suggesting that breadth of appeal has not been achieved at the expense of fidelity to the subject, seem to indicate that my principal goal in writing is being approached."

BIOGRAPHICAL/CRITICAL SOURCES:

PERIODICALS

Cord, December, 1972.
Lutheran Quarterly, April, 1977.
Washington Buddhist, January, 1976.

*   *   *

FOX, Robert J. 1927-

PERSONAL: Born December 24, 1927, in Watertown, S.D.; son of Aloysius John (a farmer) and Susie Emma (Lorentz) Fox. Education: Attended St. John's University, Collegeville, Minn., 1947-50; St. Paul Seminary, St. Paul, Minn., B.A., 1955.

ADDRESSES: Home—Box 158, Alexandria, S.D. 57311.

CAREER: Ordained Roman Catholic priest, 1955; pastor of churches in South Dakota, 1961-72; St. Bernard's Church, Redfield, S.D., pastor, beginning 1972; St. Mary's Church, Alexandria, S.D., pastor, 1985—. National spiritual director of Cadets of Our Lady of Fatima.

WRITINGS:

Religious Education: Its Effects, Its Challenges Today, Daughters of St. Paul, 1972.
The Catholic Prayerbook, Apostolic Publishing Co., 1972, revised edition, Our Sunday Visitor, 1974.
Renewal for All God's People, Our Sunday Visitor, 1975.
Charity, Morality, Sex and Young People, Our Sunday Visitor, 1975.
The Marian Catechism, Our Sunday Visitor, 1976.
Saints and Heroes Speak, Our Sunday Visitor, 1977.
A Prayer Book for Young Catholics, Our Sunday Visitor, 1977.
Catholic Truth for Youth, Ave Maria Press, 1978.
A World at Prayer, Our Sunday Visitor, 1979.
A Catechism of the Catholic Church: Two Thousand Years of Faith and Tradition, Franciscan Herald, 1980.
Rediscovering Fatima, Our Sunday Visitor, 1982.
The Call of Heaven: Life of Stigmatist of San Vittorino, Father Gino, Christendom Publications, 1982.
Fatima Today, Christendom Publications, 1983.
The Catholic Faith, Our Sunday Visitor, 1983.
The Work of the Holy Angels, AMI International, 1984.
Immaculate Heart of Mary: True Devotion, Our Sunday Visitor, 1986.
Human Sexuality and Young People, Our Sunday Visitor, in press.

Also author of numerous pamphlets, booklets, and cassette recordings, including a cassette album of 24 lessons on "Instructions in the Catholic Faith," produced by Sons of the Immaculate Heart of Mary, 1983, and "Sharing the Faith," produced by Sons of the Immaculate Heart of Mary, available as a 26½-hour TV program in VHS or Beta videocassette. Columnist, National Catholic Register, Twin Circle, and Soul. Contributor to periodicals, including Our Sunday Visitor, Homiletic and Pastoral Review, and Priest.

*   *   *

FOXX, Richard M(ichael) 1944-

PERSONAL: Born October 28, 1944, in Denver, Colo.; son of James Martin and Marie (Harris) Foxx; married Carolyn Crofutt, April 4, 1966; children: two. Education: University of California, Riverside, B.A., 1967; California State University, Fullerton, M.A., 1970; Southern Illinois University at Carbondale, Ph.D., 1971.

ADDRESSES: Agent—Georges Borchardt, Inc., 136 East 57th St., New York, N.Y. 10022. Office—Department of Treatment Development, Anna Mental Health and Development Center, 1000 North Main St., Anna, Ill. 62906.

CAREER: Patton State Hospital, Patton, Calif., research assistant, 1968-69; California Department of Game and Fish, Los Angeles, researcher, 1968-70; research assistant, Pacific State Hospital, 1969-70; California State University, Fullerton, instructor in psychology, 1970; Anna State Hospital, Anna, Ill., research scientist in Behavior Research Laboratory, 1970-74; University of Maryland, Baltimore County, Baltimore, assistant professor, 1974-76, associate professor of psychology, 1976-80, assistant professor in Medical School, 1975-80; Anna Mental Health and Development Center, Anna, Ill., director of department of treatment development, 1980—. Private practice of psychology, 1975-80. Adjunct professor, Southern Illinois University, 1980—.

MEMBER: American Psychological Association (fellow), American Association on Mental Deficiency (fellow), Association for the Advancement of Behavior Therapy, Behavior Research Society (fellow), Psi Chi, Phi Kappa Phi.

WRITINGS:

WITH NATHAN H. AZRIN

Rapid Toilet Training of the Retarded: Day and Nighttime Independent Toileting, Research Press, 1973.
Toilet Training in Less Than a Day, Simon & Schuster, 1974.
Increasing the Behavior of Severely Retarded and Autistic Individuals, Research Press, 1982.
Decreasing the Behavior of Severely Retarded and Autistic Individuals, Research Press, 1982.

OTHER

Contributor of articles to journals in the behavioral sciences.

WORK IN PROGRESS: Research on environmental design and social skills training.

*   *   *

FRAZIER, Kendrick (Crosby) 1942-

PERSONAL: Born March 19, 1942, in Windsor, Colo.; son of Francis Elliott (a pharmacist) and Sidney Lenore (Crosby) Frazier; married Ruth Toelle (an executive of a non-profit Indian child sponsorship program), September 10, 1964; children: Christopher Kendrick, Michele Lenore. Education: University of Colorado, B.A., 1964; Columbia University, M.S., 1966.

ADDRESSES: Home and office—3025 Palo Alto Dr. N.E., Albuquerque, N.M. 87111. Agent—Harold Matson Co., Inc., 276 Fifth Ave., New York, N.Y. 10001.

CAREER: Greeley Daily Tribune, Greeley, Colo., reporter, 1962; Colorado Transcript, Golden, news editor, 1963, 1964; United Press International (UPI), Denver, Colo., news reporter, 1964-65; National Academy of Sciences, Washington, D.C., editor of News Report, 1966-69; Science News, Washington, D.C., earth sciences editor, 1969-70, managing editor, 1970-71, editor, 1971-77, contributing editor, 1977-82; Sandia National Laboratories, Albuquerque, N.M., science writer,

1983—. Guest lecturer at George Washington University, 1974-77; adjunct instructor for University of Missouri, 1975-77. Member of editorial advisory board of Prometheus Books.

MEMBER: National Association of Science Writers, Society of Professional Journalists, American Polar Society, Society of the South Pole, Committee for Scientific Investigation of Claims of the Paranormal (fellow; member of executive council, 1977—; member of board of directors, 1978—).

AWARDS, HONORS: Pulitzer traveling fellowship, 1966; Robert E. Sherwood scholarship, 1966; George Norlin Award, University of Colorado, 1985, for outstanding achievement of alumni in their professions.

WRITINGS:

(Contributor) James Christian, editor, *Extra-Terrestrial Intelligence: The First Encounter,* Prometheus Books, 1976.
The Violent Face of Nature: Severe Phenomena and Natural Disasters, Morrow, 1979.
Our Turbulent Sun, Prentice-Hall, 1981.
(Editor) *Paranormal Borderlands of Science,* Prometheus Books, 1981.
Solar System, Time-Life, 1985.

Author of "Looking Out," a weekly astronomy column syndicated by Newspaper Enterprise Association, 1969-70. Contributor to *Encyclopaedia Britannica Yearbook of Science and the Future.* Contributor of several dozen articles to scientific journals, popular magazines, and newspapers, including *Mosaic, Smithsonian, Reader's Digest, Physics Today, Science 80,* and *Science News.* Editor of *Skeptical Inquirer,* 1977—.

WORK IN PROGRESS: People of Chaco, a book on prehistoric Indian culture in the area of Chaco Canyon, N.M., 900-1150 A.D., for Norton; editing *Scientists Confront the Paranormal,* another "book of articles of skeptical inquiries into the paranormal and fringe-sciences," for Prometheus Books.

SIDELIGHTS: Kendrick Frazier wrote: "Over the years I have covered many developments in science, including the geological revolution brought about by sea-floor spreading and plate tectonics, unmanned missions to the planets, climate change, weather prediction and modification, forecasting of severe storms, the search for superheavy elements, new discoveries about the sun, earthquake prediction, tree ring research, icebergs for fresh water, and the philosophical implications of a future discovery of extra-terrestrial intelligence.

"I have covered scientific activities in such places as Israel and Mexico. In 1973 I traveled to Antarctica and the South Pole, covering the U.S. research program there.

"I am especially interested in science as an exciting and very human intellectual quest, especially in the earth and geophysical sciences. In recent years I have also become interested in public perceptions and misperceptions of science, in public acceptance of claims of paranormal phenomena and fringe-science (UFOs, astrology, psychics) despite the absence of any convincing scientific evidence for their existence, and in the related issues of the psychology of belief and the prevalence of anti-science, anti-intellectual attitudes. I am also interested in the history of science and ideas, in natural history, and in New World archaeology and archaeoastronomy."

AVOCATIONAL INTERESTS: Hiking, camping, photography.

BIOGRAPHICAL/CRITICAL SOURCES:

PERIODICALS

Albuquerque Journal, August 2, 1978.
Albuquerque Tribune, March 1, 1982.
Los Alamos Monitor, May 8, 1980.
Los Angeles Times, March 1, 1984.
New Mexico Independent, December 14, 1979.
Rocky Mountain News, April 20, 1980, April 11, 1982.
Science News, August 27, 1977.
Scientific American, February, 1982.
Technology Review, June/July, 1980.
Village Voice, September 4, 1978.

*   *   *

FREEDBERG, S(ydney) J(oseph)   1914-

PERSONAL: Born November 11, 1914, in Boston, Mass.; married Anne Blake, 1942 (divorced, 1950); married Susan Pulitzer, 1954 (died, 1965); married Catherine Blanton, 1967; children: William Blake, Kate Pulitzer, Nathaniel Davis, Sydney Joseph, Jr. *Education:* Harvard University, A.B. (summa cum laude), 1936, A.M., 1939, Ph.D., 1940.

ADDRESSES: Home—13326 Reservoir Rd. N.W., Washington, D.C. *Office*—National Gallery of Art, Washington, D.C. 20565.

CAREER: Harvard University, Cambridge, Mass., assistant and tutor, department of fine arts, 1938-40; Wellesley College, Wellesley, Mass., assistant professor, 1946-49, associate professor of art, 1950-54; Harvard University, visiting lecturer, 1953-54, associate professor, 1954-61, professor of art, 1961-83, Arthur Kingsley Porter Professor of Fine Arts, 1979-83, professor emeritus, 1983—, chairman of department of fine arts, 1959-63, member of faculty council, 1973-76, chairman of University Museums Council, 1977-80, acting director of Fogg Art Museum, 1978-79; National Gallery of Art, Washington, D.C., chief curator, 1983—. National vice-chairman, Committee to Rescue Italian Art, 1966-74; member of board of directors, Save Venice, 1970—; member of Signet Associates; member of Council of Scholars, Library of Congress, 1983—. Member of advisory council, Guggenheim Foundation, 1976—. *Military service:* U.S. Army, 1942-46; received Order of the British Empire (military), 1946.

MEMBER: American Academy of Arts and Sciences (fellow), College Art Association of America (director, 1962-66), Phi Beta Kappa.

AWARDS, HONORS: Faculty fellow, Wellesley College, 1949-50; Guggenheim fellow, 1949-50, 1954-55; American Council of Learned Societies fellow, 1958-59, 1966-67; Harvard Press Faculty Prize, 1961, for *Painting of the High Renaissance in Rome and Florence;* Morey Book Award of College Art Association, 1963, for *Andrea del Sarto;* named Grand Officer, Star of Italian Solidarity, 1968; National Endowment for the Humanities senior fellow, 1973-74; Walter Channing Cabot fellow, Harvard University, 1973-76; Grand Officer, Order of Merit of Italian Republic, 1982.

WRITINGS:

(With J. S. Plaut) *Sources of Modern Painting,* Institute of Modern Art (Boston), 1939.
Old Master Paintings, Brandt Gallery, 1941.
New Masters from Old Holland: Less Known Painters of the Seventeenth Century, Brandt Gallery, 1941.

Parmigianino: His Works in Painting, Harvard University Press, 1950, reprinted, Greenwood Press, 1971.

Raphael, the Stanza della Segnatura in the Vatican, Metropolitan Museum of Art (New York), 1953.

Painting of the High Renaissance in Rome and Florence, two volumes, Harvard University Press, 1961, reprinted, Hacker, 1985.

Andrea del Sarto, two volumes, Harvard University Press, 1963.

Painting in Italy, 1500-1600, Penguin Books, 1971, 5th edition, 1983.

Circa 1600: A Revolution of Style in Italian Painting, Harvard University Press, 1983.

EDITOR; ALL PUBLISHED BY GARLAND

Katherine P. Erhart, *The Development of the Facing Head Motif on Greek Coins and Its Relationship to Classical Art,* 1979.

Richard E. Lamoureux, *Alberti's Church of San Sebastiano in Mantua,* 1979.

Sarah B. Landau, *Edward T. and William A. Potter, American Victorian Architects,* 1979.

Sara Lichtenstein, *Delacroix and Raphael,* 1979.

J. Russell Sale, *Filippino Lippi's Strozzi Chapel in Santa Maria Novella,* 1979.

Charles Baudelaire, *Eugene Delacroix: His Life and Works,* 1979.

Johann D. Passavant, *Raphael of Urbino and His Father Giovanni Santi,* 1979.

John Ruskin, *The Stones of Venice,* Volume I: *The Foundation,* Volume II: *The Sea-Stories,* Volume III: *The Fall,* 1979.

M. E. Chevreul, *The Principles of Harmony and Contrast of Colors and Their Applications to the Arts,* 1980.

J. A. Crowe and G. B. Cavalcaselle, *New History of Painting in Italy from the Second to the Sixteenth Century,* three volumes, 1980.

Eugene Delacroix, *The Journals of Eugene Delacroix,* 1980.

A. C. De Quincy, *History of the Life and Works of Rafaello,* 1980.

William Y. Ottley, *The Italian School of Design,* 1980.

General editor, "Outstanding Dissertations in the History of Art" series, 1984—.

OTHER

Contributor to *Encyclopedia of World Art* and to periodicals. Art exhibition reviewer, *Art News,* 1947-49.

SIDELIGHTS: According to a *Times Literary Supplement* critic, S. J. Freedberg's *Painting in Italy, 1500-1600* "presents a clearer and truer picture of the development of High Renaissance style and of the intentions and accomplishments of the great High Renaissance artists than any previous book." Freedberg "conveys a remarkable amount of information including very rich biographical references (up to 1968)," says Henri Zerner in the *New York Review of Books,* "but the information is unobtrusive because it is subservient to a powerfully controlled scheme. Freedberg very seldom describes explicitly the methods he uses; they are like an elaborate intellectual scaffolding removed after a construction is finished." The *Times Literary Supplement* reviewer adds that the book "is planned with feeling and written with great concentration, and it demands a corresponding degree of response from the reader, not because it is in any sense imperfectly

articulate but because virtually every sentence in it results from the act of thought."

Freedberg's collection of lecture-essays, *Circa 1600: A Revolution of Style in Italian Painting,* is also praised by Eugene Victor Thaw, who writes in the *New Republic* that "today we are able to look more comfortably and intelligently at Baroque painting and its sources, thanks to the work of art historians like Professor Sydney Freedberg. . . ." Freedberg, Thaw comments, "does not merely dazzle us with his immense apparatus of learning, but keeps bringing us back again and again to the works of art. He makes us look at what the artist is doing by formal analysis and by finding verbal equivalents for the mood, atmosphere, and psychological intensity of the work."

BIOGRAPHICAL/CRITICAL SOURCES:

PERIODICALS

New Republic, May 16, 1983.
New York Review of Books, August 31, 1972, May 12, 1983.
Times Literary Supplement, October 22, 1971, March 23, 1984.
Washington Post, March 1, 1983.

*   *   *

FREELING, Nicolas 1927-
(F. R. E. Nicolas)

PERSONAL: Born March 3, 1927, in London, England; married Cornelia Termes, 1954; children: four sons, one daughter. *Education:* Attended primary and secondary schools in England, Ireland, and France; attended University of Dublin. *Politics:* "Visionary." *Religion:* Catholic.

ADDRESSES: Home—Grandfontaine, 67130 Schirmeck, Bas Rhin, France. *Agent*—Curtis Brown Ltd., 10 Astor Pl., New York, N.Y. 10003.

CAREER: Professional cook in hotels and restaurants throughout Europe, 1948-60; novelist, 1960—. *Military service:* Royal Air Force, 1945-47.

MEMBER: Authors Guild, Authors League of America.

AWARDS, HONORS: Crime Writers Award, 1963, and Grand Prix de Roman Policier, 1965, for *Gun before Butter;* Mystery Writers of America Edgar Allan Poe Award, 1966, for *The King of the Rainy Country.*

WRITINGS:

NOVELS

Love in Amsterdam (also see below), Gollancz, 1961, Harper, 1962.

Because of the Cats (also see below), Gollancz, 1962, Harper, 1963.

Gun before Butter (also see below), Gollancz, 1963, published as *Question of Loyalty,* Harper, 1964.

Valparaiso, Harper, 1964 (published in England under pseudonym F. R. E. Nicolas, Gollancz, 1964).

Double Barrel (also see below), Gollancz, 1964, Harper, 1965.

Criminal Conversation, Gollancz, 1965, Harper, 1966.

The King of the Rainy Country (also see below), Harper, 1966.

The Dresden Green (also see below), Gollancz, 1966, Harper, 1967.

Strike out Where Not Applicable, Gollancz, 1967, Harper, 1968.

This Is the Castle, Hamish Hamilton, 1968, Harper, 1969.

The Freeling Omnibus: Comprising "Love in Amsterdam," "Because of the Cats," and "Gun before Butter," Gollancz, 1968.

Tsing-Boum, Hamish Hamilton, 1969, Harper, 1970.

The Lovely Ladies, Harper, 1970 (published in England as *Over the High Side*, Hamish Hamilton, 1970).

Aupres de ma blonde, Harper, 1971 (published in England as *A Long Silence*, Hamish Hamilton, 1971).

The Second Freeling Omnibus: Comprising "Double Barrel," "The King of the Rainy Country," and "The Dresden Green," Gollancz, 1972.

Dressing of Diamond, Harper, 1974.

The Bugles Blowing, Harper, 1975 (published in England as *What Are the Bugles Blowing For?*, Heinemann, 1975).

Lake Isle, Heinemann, 1976, published as *Sabine*, Harper, 1977.

Gadget, Coward, 1977.

The Night Lords, Pantheon, 1978.

The Widow, Pantheon, 1979.

Castang's City, Pantheon, 1980.

Arlette, Pantheon, 1981 (published in England as *One Damned Thing after Another*, Heinemann, 1981).

Wolfnight, Pantheon, 1982.

The Back of the North Wind, Viking, 1983.

No Part in Your Death, Viking, 1984.

A City Solitary, Viking, 1985.

WORK IN PROGRESS: A novel, *Cold Iron.*

SIDELIGHTS: Nicolas Freeling's crime novels have enjoyed a wide popularity in Great Britain and the United States since the early 1960s. Newgate Callendar of the *New York Times Book Review* calls Freeling "one of the masters of the [crime fiction] genre." Central to Freeling's books are studies of human nature and the problems of modern society; he incorporates these themes into his mysteries most often through the sensitivities of his central character. According to *Washington Post Book World* columnist Jean White, Freeling delves "into character, the malaise of society and the undercurrent of human relationships under the surface of crime and chase."

In a letter to *CA*, Freeling elaborated on his career as an author of detective novels: "I have been writing crime fiction for more than twenty-five years. There are not many around with this experience in the genre. To pretend that I have not widely influenced crime-writing would be false modesty. Since my own beginnings I have known my ideas plagiarised, material pillaged, and my manner parodied, repeatedly. This is a compliment paid to all original writers and one does not complain of it. Some have the grace to acknowledge their sources and others do not. Some are not even aware of it.

"Experience does not of itself confer wisdom. The writer's desire outruns performance. He and she approach the current work in a flare-up of excitement and a sense of discovery: in this country no one has yet set foot. And at the end it is so much less interesting than he had hoped. But he has merely surveyed this new patch of territory. Others will follow and mine it, to their profit, which he will be wise not to grudge them.

"Over the fifty years since the heyday of Dorothy Sayers, and thirty on from Chandler's *The Simple Art of Murder*, the genre 'crime novel' has expanded enormously and the antiquated categories of mystery or suspense have become meaningless. Those that have survived have invariably been (as in all fiction) those with a sense of character.

"I believe that after thirty years it will be time, concurrent with the fiction I find myself at work on, to synthesize personal thinking and individual experience. In doing so I hope to un-derstand my trade better. I hope that other writers—and readers—will find matter for thought. A critical essay? Autobiography? The portentous and self-satisfied connotations of either give pause. Elements of both will be needed: the project will be difficult. But as with fiction a notion strikes root, a crystallization occurs, and then however flawed, the books insist upon being written. My publishers will doubtless be appalled; they've been appalled before at more or less yearly intervals and they should be accustomed to the feeling by now."

One decision that Freeling made in 1971 surprised his readers as well as the critics. In his novel *Aupres de ma blonde*, he "killed off" his popular detective, Inspector Van der Valk, who had been the central character in a series of mysteries. Van der Valk, described by John R. Coyne, Jr., in the *National Review* as "a cranky, gentle, bumbling, brilliant, nonconformist student of human behavior whose primary concern is why rather than how crimes are committed," was, in the opinion of Tom Sharpe in *New Statesman*, "one of the most interesting fictional sleuths to appear in the Sixties." Freeling indicated that he needed to "switch heroes to free himself as a writer," according to White, who adds: "I still long for Van der Valk, who over a decade of mysteries grew sadder, wiser, perhaps a bit wearier but no less compassionate and tolerant of human frailties."

Van der Valk's successor in Freeling's fiction is Henri Castang, a police inspector in a French provincial city. "Castang has had a hard act to follow," notes White. "However, with each new book, Castang is growing in character." Though the hero is different, Freeling continues to use his stories as vehicles for exploring the philosophy of ideas and social or national eccentricities. "There is no doubt that Nicolas Freeling's novels, in depth, subtlety and interest, are far superior to most other examples of the genre," writes T. J. Binyon in the *Times Literary Supplement*. David Lehman similarly praises Freeling's efforts in the *Washington Post Book World*: "Freeling's idiosyncratic style makes demands on his readers but rewards them with wit and humor and with an unusual depth of feeling."

AVOCATIONAL INTERESTS: "Planting trees. Then planting more trees."

BIOGRAPHICAL/CRITICAL SOURCES:

PERIODICALS

Globe and Mail (Toronto), June 30, 1984.

National Review, August 24, 1971.

New Statesman, September 26, 1975.

New York Times Book Review, August 6, 1972.

Spectator, May 1, 1971.

Times Literary Supplement, May 30, 1980.

Washington Post Book World, May 19, 1974, February 19, 1978, November 19, 1978, July 4, 1982.

*   *   *

FREEMAN, David Hugh 1924-

PERSONAL: Born November 14, 1924, in Washington, D.C.; son of David (a minister) and Grace (a social worker; maiden name, Kern) Freeman; married Iren Klara Enyedi, 1950; children: Iren Grace, Diana Beatrice, John David Bela. *Education:* Calvin College, B.A., 1947; graduate study at University of Grenoble, summer, 1948, and Free Univeristy of Amsterdam, 1949-51; University of Pennsylvania, M.A., 1952, Ph.D., 1958;

additional graduate study at University of Cologne, summer, 1955. *Religion:* Protestant.

ADDRESSES: Home—136 Oakwood Dr., Peace Dale, R.I. 02879. *Office*—Department of Philosophy, University of Rhode Island, Kingston, R.I. 02881.

CAREER: Wilson College, Chambersburg, Pa., assistant professor of philosophy and chairman of department, 1952-57; University of Rhode Island, Kingston, professor of philosophy, 1957—, chairman of department, 1957-58, 1966-74. Chairman of Rhode Island Governor's Commission to Investigate Textbook Aid to Non-public Schools, 1962-63. Foreign book editor, Presbyterian and Reformed Publishing Co., 1952—; editor and consultant, Craig Press. *Military service:* U.S. Army, 1942-45; received Purple Heart.

MEMBER: American Philosophical Association, Metaphysical Society of America, Association for Realistic Philosophy (president, 1971-73), Philosophy of Education Society, American Association of University Professors (secretary, 1961-62).

AWARDS, HONORS: Edward J. Bok Dutch Government grant, 1949-51; Danforth Foundation teacher study grant, 1956-57.

WRITINGS:

Tillich, Presbyterian & Reformed, 1962.
Recent Studies in Philosophy and Theology, Presbyterian & Reformed, 1962.
(Co-author) *A Philosophical Study of Religion,* Craig Press, 1964.
Logic: The Art of Reasoning, McKay, 1967.
Know Your Self, Craig Press, 1976.

TRANSLATOR

J. Spier, *Christianity and Existentialism,* Presbyterian & Reformed, 1953.
(With William S. Young) Herman Dooyewerd, *New Critique of Theoretical Thought,* four volumes, Presbyterian & Reformed, 1953-58.
(General editor and translator) Spier, *Introduction to Christian Philosophy,* Presbyterian & Reformed, 1954.
(Editor and translator) Hendrick van Riessen, *Society of the Future,* Presbyterian & Reformed, 1957.
Herman Ridderbos, *Paul and Jesus,* Presbyterian & Reformed, 1958.
Gerrit Berkouwer, *Conflict with Rome,* Presbyterian & Reformed, 1958.
Sytse Zuidema, *Kierkegaard,* Presbyterian & Reformed, 1960.
John Bavinck, *An Introduction to the Science of Missions,* Presbyterian & Reformed, 1960.
B. Worth, *Christian Counseling,* Presbyterian & Reformed, 1962.
Ridderbos, *The Authority of New Testament Scriptures,* Presbyterian & Reformed, 1962.
Ridderbos, *The Coming of the Kingdom,* Presbyterian & Reformed, 1962.
Logic, McKay, 1967.

OTHER

Editor of an International Library of Philosophy and Theology series on modern thinkers, with monographs published on John Dewey, Paul Tillich, Karl Barth, Jean-Paul Sartre, Reinhold Neibuhr, Friedrich Nietzsche, and Soeren Kierkegaard.

AVOCATIONAL INTERESTS: Swimming, horseback riding, karate.†

FREEMAN, Richard Borden   1908-

PERSONAL: Born October 7, 1908, in Philadelphia, Pa.; son of Walter Jackson and Corinne (Keen) Freeman; married Barbara Ames Burditt, 1937; children: Deborah Freeman Crocker (died, 1960), Sarah Freeman Evans, Jonathan. *Education:* Yale University, A.B., 1932; Harvard University, A.M., 1934.

ADDRESSES: Home—3310 Tates Creek Rd., Lexington, Ky. 40502. *Office*—Department of Fine Art, University of Kentucky, Lexington, Ky. 40506.

CAREER: Nelson Gallery of Art, Kansas City, Mo., member of staff, 1934-36; Fogg Museum of Art, Cambridge, Mass., registrar, 1936-38; Cincinnati Art Museum, Cincinnati, Ohio, assistant curator, 1938-41; Flint Institute of Arts, Flint, Mich., director, 1941-47; San Francisco Museum of Art, San Francisco, Calif., assistant director, 1947-50; University of Alabama, Tuscaloosa, professor of art and head of department, 1950-56; Hartford Art School, Hartford, Conn., director, 1956-57; University of Kentucky, Lexington, professor of art and head of department, 1958-75, professor emeritus, 1975—. Visiting professor, Hamilton College, 1958. Member of Flint (Mich.) board of education, 1945-47.

MEMBER: American Federation of Arts, College Art Association, American Association of University Professors, Southeastern College Art Conference (president, 1953-54), Midwestern College Art Association (president, 1966-67), Kentucky Guild of Artists and Craftsmen (life member).

AWARDS, HONORS: Named fellow of University of Kentucky.

WRITINGS:

Picasso-Gris-Miro, San Francisco Museum of Art, 1948.
Ralston Crawford, University of Alabama Press, 1953.
The Lithographs of Ralston Crawford, University of Kentucky Press, 1962.
Niles Spencer, Department of Art, University of Kentucky, 1965.
Graphics '73: Ralston Crawford, Drawings and Watercolors, University of Kentucky, 1973.
Graphics '74: Spain, University of Kentucky, 1974.
Graphics '75: Watergate, the Unmaking of a President, University of Kentucky, 1975.
Graphics '76: Britain, University of Kentucky, 1976.
The Prints of Ralston Crawford, Print Review, 1985.

Also editor of *University of Kentucky Graphics, '58-66,* and *University of Kentucky Graphics, '67-76.*

Editor, *Cincinnati Art Museum Bulletin,* 1938-41; contributing editor, *Magazine of Art,* 1945-50.

*   *   *

FREID, Jacob L.   1913-

PERSONAL: Born May 29, 1913, in New York, N.Y.; son of Harry and Fanny (Axelrod) Freid; married Janet Glickman; children: Allison Ora. *Education:* City College (now City College of the City University of New York), B.A., 1937; Columbia University, M.A., 1938, Ph.D., 1950. *Religion:* Jewish.

ADDRESSES: Office—Jewish Braille Institute, 48 East 74th St., New York, N.Y.

CAREER: Office of War Information and Department of State, New York City and Washington, D.C., head of Moscow cable-wireless desk, 1942-46; New School for Social Research, New York City, senior college chairman of political science department, 1947-62; Jewish Braille Institute of America, New York City, executive director, 1952—. Formerly taught sociology at Rutgers State University and City College of the City University of New York. Chairman, Five Towns Planning Commission, 1961-62.

MEMBER: American Association of University Professors, National Federation of the Blind, American Association of Workers for the Blind, American Jewish Historical Society.

AWARDS, HONORS: Received honor award, Jewish Graduate Society of Columbia University.

WRITINGS:

EDITOR

Jews in the Modern World, two volumes, Twayne, 1962.
Judaism and the Community, Yoseloff, 1968.
Jews and Divorce, Ktav, 1968.

OTHER

Contributor of articles to journals. Former editor, "Jewish Affairs" pamphlet series.†

* * *

FRENCH, Peter A(ndrew) 1942-

PERSONAL: Born March 19, 1942, in Newburgh, N.Y.; son of Ernest C. (a Lutheran minister) and Gretchen (Schillke) French; married Sandra Schall, June 1, 1961; children: Sean Trevor, Shannon Elizabeth. *Education:* Gettysburg College, B.A., 1963; University of Southern California, M.A., 1965; University of Miami, Coral Gables, Fla., Ph.D., 1971.

ADDRESSES: Home—15807 Wolf Creek, San Antonio, Tex. 78232. *Office*—Department of Philosophy, Trinity University, 715 Stadium Dr., San Antonio, Tex. 78284.

CAREER: Northern Arizona University, Flagstaff, instructor, 1965-66, assistant professor, 1966-68; Miami-Dade Junior College, Miami, Fla., assistant professor, 1968-71, chairman, 1970-71; University of Minnesota, Morris, assistant professor, 1971-72, associate professor, 1972-76, professor of philosophy, 1976-81, coordinator of philosophy department, 1972-73, 1977-78; Trinity University, San Antonio, Tex., Lennox Distinguished Professor of the Humanities and professor of philosophy, 1981—, chairman of department of philosophy, 1982—. Visiting professor at Dalhousie University, 1976. University of Delaware, Center for the Study of Values, distinguished research professor, 1980-81, senior fellow, 1981—. Member of Minnesota Humanities Commission.

MEMBER: American Philosophical Association, Society for Philosophy and Public Affairs, Royal Institute of Philosophy, Minnesota Philosophical Society.

AWARDS, HONORS: Horace T. Morse-Amoco Foundation Award, 1979, for outstanding contributions to undergraduate education; Governor of Minnesota's certificate of honor, 1982, for outstanding contributions to education.

WRITINGS:

Exploring Philosophy, Schenkman, 1970, revised edition, 1972.
Individual and Collective Responsibility: Massacre at My Lai, Schenkman, 1972.

(Contributor) Nagel, Held, and Morgenbesser, editors, *Philosophy, Morality, and International Affairs*, Oxford University Press, 1973.
Conscientious Actions, General Learning Press, 1974.
Philosophical Explorations, General Learning Press, 1975.
Philosophers in Wonderland, Llewellyn, 1975.
(With H. K. Wettstein and T. E. Uehling) *Contemporary Perspectives in the Philosophy of Language*, University of Minnesota Press, 1978.
The Scope of Morality, University of Minnesota Press, 1979.
Ethics in Government, Prentice-Hall, 1983.
Collective and Corporate Responsibility, Columbia University Press, 1984.
(With Brent Fisse) *Corrigible Corporations and Unruly Laws*, Trinity University Press, in press.
(With Curtis Brown) *Puzzles, Paradoxes, and Problems*, St. Martin's, in press.
Shame and the Corporation, edited by Hugh Curtler, Havens Publishing, in press.

Contributor to philosophy journals, including *American Philosophical Quarterly*, *Philosophy*, and *Southern Journal of Philosophy*.

WORK IN PROGRESS: The Concept of Shame.

* * *

FRIDY, (William) Wallace 1910-

PERSONAL: Born December 25, 1910, in Hodges, S.C.; son of William Allen and Sara (Haddon) Fridy; married Martha Baskette, 1937 (died December 26, 1973); married Ellen I. Cardwell, July 19, 1975 (died May 18, 1978); married Frewil Culler Griffith, October 27, 1979; children: (first marriage) William Wallace, Jr., Martha (Mrs. Richard S. Thompson), Prentice (Mrs. Wilson O. Weldon, Jr.), Elizabeth (Mrs. Edward A. Gill III). *Education:* Clemson College (now University), B.S., 1932; Yale University, B.D., 1937; attended Union Theological Seminary.

ADDRESSES: Home and office—758 Albion Rd., Columbia S.C. 29205.

CAREER: Ordained Methodist minister, 1937. Director of Christian education at church in High Point, N.C., 1937-38; director of youth work, upper South Carolina conference of Methodist Church, 1938-42; minister and director of youth work at churches in Lyman, Inman, and Gramling, S.C., 1942-48; pastor of church in Spartanburg, S.C., 1948-54; district supervisor in Columbia, S.C., 1954-61, and Anderson, S.C., 1962-68; program director of South Carolina conference of United Methodist Church, 1968-75. Adjunct professor, Lutheran Theological Southern Seminary, 1979—. Superintendent of Charleston district, 1961-62; conductor of preaching mission at Pastor's Schools in England, 1964, and of radio program "Today Is Yours." Member of board of trustees, Scarritt College, 1946-80; former member of board of trustees, Spartanburg Junior College; former chairman of board of trustees of Columbia College; chairman of the Board of Ministers, Dean Pastor's School. Delegate to World Methodist Conference, 1961, 1971.

MEMBER: Phi Beta Kappa, Rotary Club, Spartanburg Club (former president), Columbia Club (president, 1974-75), Blue Key.

AWARDS, HONORS: H.H.D., Clemson College (now University), 1956.

WRITINGS:

A Lamp unto My Feet, Abingdon, 1952.
A Light unto My Path, Abingdon, 1953.
Devotions for Adult Groups, Abingdon, 1956.
Adults at Worship, Abingdon, 1959.
Adult Devotions, Abingdon, 1961.
Wings of the Spirit, Abingdon, 1963.
Meditations for Adults, Abingdon, 1965.
Devotions for Personal and Group Renewal, Abingdon, 1969.
Everyday Prayers, Abingdon, 1974.

Also author of "The Sanctuary," 1968-72. Contributor of articles to religious journals and magazines and to several South Carolina area newspapers. Editor of *South Carolina Methodist Advocate,* 1976-79.

AVOCATIONAL INTERESTS: Golf, photography.

* * *

FRIEDLAND, Seymour 1928-

PERSONAL: Born October 8, 1928, in New York, N.Y.; son of David and Eva (Klausner) Friedland; married Gloria Lee Tassel, August 30, 1952; married second wife, Eleanor Deborah Swartzfeld, April 27, 1980; children: (first marriage) Randall, Andrew, Sharon; stepchildren: Lorne E., Richard N. *Education:* Boston University, B.S., 1950, M.B.A., 1951; Harvard University, Ph.D., 1956. *Politics:* Democrat. *Religion:* Jewish.

ADDRESSES: Home—No. 2, 423 Avenue Rd., Toronto, Ontario, Canada. *Office*—Faculty of Administrative Studies, York University, Toronto, Ontario, Canada.

CAREER: U.S. Government, Washington, D.C., economist in Bureau of the Census, 1950-51, and Bureau of Labor Statistics, 1951; instructor in economics at Middlebury College, Middlebury, Vt., 1951-52, and Boston University, Boston, Mass., 1953-54; Northeastern University, Boston, lecturer, 1954-55; Massachusetts Institute of Technology, Cambridge, instructor, 1955-56; assistant professor of economics at Boston University, 1956-58, and Rutgers University, New Brunswick, N.J., 1958-60; Claremont Graduate School, Claremont, Calif., associate professor, 1960-64, professor of economics and business and chairman of department of business economics, 1964-67; York University, Faculty of Administrative Studies, Toronto, Ontario, professor of finance and director of capital markets research programs, 1967—. Senior consultant, Joel Dean Associates, New York, N.Y., 1965-66; visiting professor, New York University, 1966-67; president of Camar Consultants Ltd. and S. F. Research Associates, 1970—; director of Financial Research Institute, 1971-80, Koffler Stoes Ltd., and Federal Trust Co. Private consultant to government agencies and industrial clients. *Military service:* U.S. Army, 1947-48.

MEMBER: American Economic Association, American Finance Association.

AWARDS, HONORS: Gulf Oil Corp. research fellowship, 1962; National Business Writing Award from Royal Bank and Toronto Press Club, 1980.

WRITINGS:

(Contributor) *Financing Small Business,* Federal Reserve Board, 1959.
Financing Patterns of New Jersey Manufacturing Corporations, State of New Jersey, 1964.

The Economics of Corporate Finance, Prentice-Hall, 1966.
Principles of Financial Management: Corporate Finance, Investments, and Macrofinance, Winthrop, 1978.
What You Should Know about Your Personal Finances, Financial Times, 1981, 3rd edition, 1985.

Contributor to *Financial Times of Canada, New England Journal of Medicine, Mercurio* (Italy), *Engineering Economist,* and other journals.

WORK IN PROGRESS: Studying security yields and flow of funds.

* * *

FRIEDMAN, Albert B(arron) 1920-

PERSONAL: Born August 16, 1920, in Kansas City, Mo.; son of Jay and Edith (Barron) Friedman. *Education:* University of Missouri, B.A., 1941; Harvard University, M.A., 1942, Ph.D., 1952; attended Oxford University, 1939, 1946, University of London, 1951, Cambridge University, 1952, and Sorbonne, University of Paris, 1957-58.

ADDRESSES: Home—706 California Dr., Claremont, Calif. 91711. *Office*—Department of English, McManus Hall, Claremont Graduate School, Claremont, Calif. 91711.

CAREER: Harvard University, Cambridge, Mass., instructor, 1952-55, assistant professor, 1955-60; Claremont Graduate School, Claremont, Calif., associate professor, 1960-61, professor of English, 1962-69, William Starke Rosecrans Professor of English, 1969—. Visiting professor, University of California, Los Angeles, 1962-63. *Military service:* U.S. Army, 1942-46; became captain; awarded Legion of Merit Silver Star, Royal Order of George I, Order of the Phoenix (Greece), Kaiser-i-Hind, second class (India).

MEMBER: Modern Language Association of America (chairman of comparative literature, 1958-59), Mediaeval Academy of America (vice-president, 1970-72), American Folklore Society (fellow), American Association of University Professors, Early English Text Society, California Folklore Society.

AWARDS, HONORS: Guggenheim fellow, 1958-59, 1965-66; International Folklore Society Prize, 1961; American Council of Learned Societies grants, 1962, 1966; National Endowment for the Humanities senior fellow, 1971-72.

WRITINGS:

(Editor) *Folk Ballads of the English-Speaking World,* Viking, 1956, revised edition published as *The Viking Book of Folk Ballads of the English-Speaking World,* 1982.
Literary Experience of School Seniors, Illinois Teachers of English, 1957.
The Ballad Revival, University of Chicago Press, 1961.
Ywain and Gawain, Oxford University Press, 1964.
(With Milton Eisenhower and others) *Creativity in Graduate Education,* University of California Press, 1964.
The Usable Myth, University of California Press, 1970.
(Contributor) *American Folk Legend,* University of California, 1971.

Also author of *Myth and Ideology,* 1976. Contributor to *Journal of the English Folk-Song Society, Folklore* (London), and other professional journals. Associate editor, *Journal of American Folklore,* 1959-65; editor, *Western Folklore,* 1966-70.†

FRISBIE, Richard P(atrick)   1926-

PERSONAL: Born November 27, 1926, in Chicago, Ill.; son of Chauncey Osborn and Pearl (Harrison) Frisbie; married Margery Rowbottom (a writer), June 3, 1950; children: Felicity, Anne, Thomas, Ellen, Paul, Patrick, Teresa, Margaret. *Education:* Attended University of Chicago, 1944; University of Arizona, B.A., 1948. *Religion:* Roman Catholic.

ADDRESSES: Home—631 North Dunton Ave., Arlington Heights, Ill. 60004. *Office*—Frisbie Communications, 333 North Michigan Ave., Chicago, Ill. 60601.

CAREER: Chicago Daily News, Chicago, Ill., staff writer, 1948-53, assistant feature editor, 1953-55; advertising agency creative director at Wentzel, Wainwright, Poister & Poore, Chicago, 1955-58, Cunningham & Walsh, Chicago, 1958-61, Hill, Rogers, Mason & Scott, Chicago, 1961-63, and Campbell-Ewald, Chicago, 1964-66; Frisbie Communications, Chicago, editorial and advertising consultant, 1966—. Arlington Heights (Ill.) Public Library, member of board of directors, 1967-87, treasurer, 1971-73, president, 1973-79; North Suburban Library System (Ill.), member of board of directors, 1976-81, treasurer, 1978-79, president, 1979-81. Member of executive board, Cana Conference of Chicago, 1953, 1954.

MEMBER: Society of Midland Authors (treasurer, 1980-81 and 1983-85; president, 1985—).

AWARDS, HONORS: Catholic Press Association Award for best article in general interest magazine for "Let's Be Serious about the Comics."

WRITINGS:

(With wife, Margery Frisbie) *The Do-It-Yourself Parent,* Sheed, 1963.
Family Fun and Recreation, Abbey Press, 1964.

How to Peel a Sour Grape, Sheed, 1965.
Who Put the Bomb in Father Murphy's Chowder?, Doubleday, 1968.
It's a Wise Woodsman Who Knows What's Biting Him, Doubleday, 1969.
Basic Boat Building, Henry Regnery, 1975.

AUTHOR AND EDITOR OF ANNALS PUBLISHED BY MARQUIS

Bicentennial Biographies, 1976.
Looking Back, 1877-1977, 1977.
Future Gazing, 1978.
Second Starts: It's Never as Late as You Think, 1979.
Vanished Glory: Towns Where the Date Is Always Yesterday, 1980.
The Lure of the Islands: Appointments with Dreams, 1981.
Legends That Came to Life, 1982.
Speculations for Starry Nights, 1983.
Epic Escapes and Rescues, 1984.
Winners and Losers, 1985.
Traces of Adventure, 1986.

OTHER

Contributor of about 400 articles to periodicals. Former editor, *Events, Chrysler Owners' Magazine,* and *Town and Country News;* former co-editor, *Couplet;* editor, *Chicago,* 1971-72.

BIOGRAPHICAL/CRITICAL SOURCES:

PERIODICALS

Chicago Daily News, June 8, 1955.
Newsweek, December 12, 1952.
New York Times, March 2, 1965.
St. Jude, March, 1963.
Sign, April, 1963.

G

GANGEL, Kenneth O(tto) 1935-

PERSONAL: Born June 14, 1935, in Paterson, N.J.; son of Otto John (a baker) and Rose Marie (Schneider) Gangel; married Elizabeth Blackburn (a schoolteacher), September 1, 1956; children: Jeffrey Scott, Julie Lynn. *Education:* Taylor University, B.A., 1957; Grace Theological Seminary, B.D., 1960; Winona Lake School of Theology, M.A., 1960; Concordia Theological Seminary, S.T.M., 1965; University of Missouri at Kansas City, Ph.D., 1969; postdoctoral study, Florida State University, 1973. *Politics:* Republican.

ADDRESSES: Office—Department of Christian Education, Dallas Theological Seminary, 3909 Swiss Ave., Dallas, Tex. 75204.

CAREER: Clergyman of Baptist Church; Calvary Bible College, Kansas City, Mo., instructor of education, 1960-63, registrar, 1963-66, academic dean, 1966-68, vice-president and professor of education, 1969-70; Trinity Evangelical Divinity School, Deerfield, Ill., professor and director of the School of Christian Education, 1970-74; Miami Christian College, Miami, Fla., president, 1974-82; Dallas Theological Seminary, Dallas, Tex., professor and chairman of department of Christian education, 1982—. Lecturer at numerous churches, schools, and seminars throughout the United States and other countries, 1960—. Administrative assistant for academic affairs, Kansas City Regional Council for Higher Education, 1968-69. Member of advisory board, Scripture Press Ministries.

MEMBER: National Association of Evangelicals, National Association of Professors of Christian Education (former president; board member), National Christian School Education Association, American Association for Higher Education, National Education Association, Evangelical Teacher Training Association (board member).

AWARDS, HONORS: Research grant, American Association of Theological Schools, 1972-73; Distinguished Alumnus of the Year award, Grace Theological Seminary, 1973; Alumni Achievement award, University of Missouri at Kansas City, 1975; Chamber of Achievement award, Taylor University, 1976.

WRITINGS:

Understanding Teaching, Evangelical Teacher Training Association, 1968, reprinted, with teacher's guide, 1979.

Leadership for Church Education (also see below), Moody, 1970.

The Beloved Physician: A Biography of Dr. Walter L. Wilson, Moody, 1970.

The Family First, His International Service, 1972.

So You Want to Be a Leader!: An Analysis of Basic Principles and Methods of Christian Leadership, with leader's guide, Christian Publications, 1973.

(With wife, Elizabeth Gangel) *Between Christian Parent and Child,* Baker Book, 1974.

Competent to Lead (also see below), Moody, 1974.

24 Ways to Improve Your Teaching, Victor Books, 1974.

You and Your Spiritual Gifts, Moody, 1975.

The Effective Sunday School Superintendent: A Handbook for Leaders, Victor Books, 1975.

The Gospel and the Gay, Thomas Nelson, 1978.

Lessons in Leadership from the Bible, BMH Books, 1980.

Building Leaders for Church Education (contains revised and expanded editions of *Leadership for Church Education* and *Competent to Lead*), Moody, 1981.

You Can Be an Effective Sunday School Superintendent, Victor Books, 1981.

Unwrap Your Spiritual Gifts, Victor Books, 1983.

(With Warren S. Benson) *Christian Education: Its History and Philosophy,* Moody, 1983.

Thus Spake Qoheleth: A Study Guide Based on an Exposition of Ecclesiastes, Christian Publications, 1983.

(Editor) *Toward a Harmony of Faith and Learning: Essays on Bible College Curriculum,* William Tyndale College Press, 1983.

(Contributor) *Parents and Teachers,* Victor Books, 1984.

Church Education Handbook, Victor Books, 1985.

Contributor of more than 1,000 articles to periodicals. Contributing editor, *Journal of Psychology and Theology;* research editor, *Christian Education Today.*

AVOCATIONAL INTERESTS: Athletics, photography, music, world travel, reading.

*   *   *

GARFINKEL, Bernard Max 1929-
(Robert Allen, Robert Elliott, Janet Martin)

PERSONAL: Born May 3, 1929, in New York, N.Y.; son of

Max and Ida (Konwiser) Garfinkel. *Education:* University of Missouri, A.B., 1951, M.A., 1953; graduate study at Columbia University.

CAREER: Magazine Management Co., New York City, managing editor, 1958-65; Platt & Munk Co., Inc. (publishers), New York City, vice-president, beginning 1965. *Military service:* U.S. Army, 1953-55.

MEMBER: Phi Beta Kappa.

WRITINGS:

JUVENILES

The Champions, illustrations by David K. Stone, photographs by Dan Baliotti, Platt, 1972.
My Growing Up Book, illustrations by Janet Ahlberg, Platt, 1972.
They Changed the World: The Lives of Forty-Four Great Men and Women, Platt, 1973.
Marvelous Creatures: A First Book about Animals, photographs by Meryl Joseph, Platt, 1977.
(With Jules Siegel) *The Journal of the Absurd,* illustrations by Diana Bryan, Workman Publishing, 1980.

UNDER PSEUDONYM ROBERT ALLEN; JUVENILES

Things to See, Platt, 1966.
ABC: An Alphabet Book, Platt, 1966.
Jamie and the Leopard, illustrations by Yutaka Sugita, Platt, 1967.
Numbers: A First Counting Book, photographs by Mottke Weissman, Platt, 1968.
The Zoo Book: A Child's World of Animals, photographs by Peter Sahula, Platt, 1968.
Count with Me, illustrations by Edith Witt, Platt, 1969.
This Is Yellow and This Is Red, illustrations by Witt, Platt, 1969.
A Child's Book of Animals, Putnam, 1981.

UNDER PSEUDONYM ROBERT ELLIOTT; JUVENILES

Call to Glory, Platt, 1969.
Banners of Courage: The Lives of Fourteen Heroic Men and Women, illustrations by Huntley Brown, Platt, 1972.

UNDER PSEUDONYM JANET MARTIN; JUVENILES

Round and Square, illustrations by Philippe Thomas, Platt, 1965.
Fast and Slow, illustrations by Thomas, Platt, 1967.
Fur and Feathers, illustrations by Thomas, Platt, 1967.
Red and Blue, illustrations by Thomas, Platt, 1967.

OTHER

Also author of *Hot and Cold,* 1965, *Large and Small,* 1965, *Light and Heavy,* 1965, and *Songs and Silence,* 1965†

*   *   *

GARNETT, David   1892-1981
(Leda Burke)

PERSONAL: Born March 9, 1892, in Brighton, England; died February 17, 1981, in Montocq, France; son of Edward (a literary critic and editor) and Constance (a translator; maiden name, Black) Garnett; married Rachel Alice Marshall, 1921 (died, 1940); married Angelica Vanessa Bell, 1942; children: (first marriage) Richard Duncan, William Tomlin Kasper; (second marriage) Amaryllis Virginia, Henrietta Catherine Va-

nessa, Frances Olivia, Nerissa Stephen. *Education:* Imperial College of Science and Technology, A.R.C.S., 1913, D.I.C., 1915.

ADDRESSES: Agent—A. P. Watt & Son, 26/28 Bedford Row, London WC1R 4HL, England.

CAREER: Writer, bookseller, and publisher. Operated bookstore in Soho district of London, England, 1920; co-founder of Nonesuch Press, London, 1923-32; literary editor, *New Statesman,* 1932-34; Rupert Hart-Davis Ltd. (publishers), London, director. *Wartime service:* Conscientious objector during World War I; served with a Quaker relief organization in Europe and as a farm laborer; Royal Air Force, 1940; worked in intelligence section and as planning officer and historian.

AWARDS, HONORS: Commander, Order of the British Empire; James Tait Black Memorial Prize and Hawthornden Prize, both 1923, both for *Lady into Fox;* fellow, Imperial College of Science and Technology, 1956.

WRITINGS:

(Translator) Vincent Alfred Gressent, *The Kitchen Garden and Its Management,* Selwyn, Blount, 1919.
(Under pseudonym Leda Burke) *Dope-Darling: A Story of Cocaine,* T. Warner Laurie, 1919.
Lady into Fox (also see below), Chatto & Windus, 1922, Knopf, 1923.
A Man in the Zoo (also see below), Knopf, 1924.
The Sailor's Return, Knopf, 1925
Go She Must!, Knopf, 1927.
The Old Dovecote and Other Stories, Mathews & Marrot, 1928.
(Translator) Andre Maurois, *A Voyage to the Island of the Articoles,* J. Cape, 1928, Appleton, 1929.
Never Be a Bookseller, Knopf, 1929.
Lady into Fox [and] *A Man in the Zoo,* Chatto & Windus, 1929.
No Love, Knopf, 1929.
The Grasshoppers Come, Brewer, Warren & Putnam, 1931.
A Rabbit in the Air: Notes from a Diary Kept While Learning to Handle an Aeroplane, Brewer, Warren & Putnam, 1932.
A Terrible Day, William Jackson, 1932.
Pocahontas: or, The Nonpareil of Virginia, Harcourt, 1933.
Beany-Eye, Harcourt, 1935.
(Editor) T. E. Lawrence, *The Letters of T. E. Lawrence,* J. Cape, 1938, Doubleday, Doran, 1939, published as *Selected Letters of T. E. Lawrence,* Hyperion Press, 1979.
War in the Air: September, 1939-May, 1941, Doubleday, 1941.
(Editor) Henry James, *Fourteen Stories,* Hart-Davis, 1946.
(Editor) *The Novels of Thomas Love Peacock,* Hart-Davis, 1948.
(Editor) *The Essential T. E. Lawrence,* Dutton, 1951.
The Golden Echo (memoirs), Volume I: *The Golden Echo,* Chatto & Windus, 1953, Harcourt, 1954, Volume II: *Flowers of the Forest,* Chatto & Windus, 1955, Harcourt, 1956, Volume III: *The Familiar Faces,* Chatto & Windus, 1962, Harcourt, 1963.
Aspects of Love, Harcourt, 1955.
A Shot in the Dark, Little, Brown, 1958.
A Net for Venus, Longmans, Green, 1959.
(Translator) Lawrence, *338171 T. E. (Lawrence of Arabia),* Dutton, 1963.
Two by Two: A Story of a Survival, Longmans, Green, 1963, Atheneum, 1964.
Ulterior Motives, Longmans, Green, 1966, Harcourt, 1967.

An Old Master and Other Stories, Yamaguchi Shoten (Tokyo), 1967.

(Editor) *The White/Garnett Letters,* Viking, 1968.

(Editor and author of introduction) Dora de Houghton Carrington, *Carrington: Letters and Extracts from Her Diaries,* J. Cape, 1970, Holt, 1971.

First "Hippy" Revolution, San Marcos Press, 1970.

A Clean Slate, Hamish Hamilton, 1971.

The Sons of the Falcon, Macmillan, 1972.

Plough over the Bones, Macmillan, 1973.

Purl and Plain and Other Stories, Macmillan, 1973.

The Master Cat: The True and Unexpurgated Story of Puss in Boots, Macmillan, 1974.

Up She Rises, St. Martin's, 1977.

Great Friends: Portraits of Seventeen Writers, Macmillan (London), 1979, Atheneum, 1980.

SIDELIGHTS: David Garnett came by his literary career naturally. His grandfather was an author and head of the British Museum reading room. His father, Edward Garnett, was a publisher's reader who discovered and encouraged such authors as Joseph Conrad and D. H. Lawrence. His mother, Constance Garnett, was the first translator into English of Leo Tolstoy, Anton Chekhov, Fedor Mikhailovich Dostoevski, and other Russian authors of the nineteenth century. Advised by his father, according to the London *Times,* to "never try to write, but above all never have anything to do with publishing or the book trade," Garnett nevertheless became a novelist, bookstore owner, and a partner in the publishing firm of Rupert Hart-Davis. His association with the Bloomsbury Group, a circle of British writers that included E. M. Forster, John Maynard Keynes, and Virginia Woolf, and his award-winning novel *Lady into Fox,* brought Garnett to literary prominence.

After taking his degree in botany in 1915, Garnett published his first book, a translation of a gardening manual. Garnett later claimed that his second book, a novel entitled *Dope-Darling: A Story of Cocaine,* was written "deliberately badly," as Roland Dille recounted in the *Dictionary of Literary Biography.* It was published under a pseudonym in 1919. It was with his third book, *Lady into Fox,* that Garnett first attracted critical notice. The story of Mrs. Tebrick—a woman who becomes a fox, leaves her husband, and goes to live in the woods—the novel won the James Tait Black Memorial Prize and the Hawthornden Prize. It brought Garnett "popular acclaim and serious critical attention," Ann S. Johnson wrote in *Contemporary Literature.*

It is Garnett's style in *Lady into Fox* that attracted the most critical praise. Writing in *The Modern Novel in Britain and the United States,* Walter Allen remarked on the book's casual quality. Although the plot is fantastic, Garnett "merely narrates it as a true story," Allen stated, "telling it in a style a little archaic, a little mannered, suggestive of [Daniel] Defoe. . . . A triumph, if you like, of artificiality, it is also a triumph of story-telling." Frank Swinnerton, in his *The Georgian Literary Scene, 1910-1935,* argued that "the demureness of such a book as 'Lady into Fox' . . . is proper to the theme." But Swinnerton also allowed that Garnett "was telling [the] story with a false gravity which amused himself and his friends."

The perfection of the novel's narrative was remarked upon by several observers who felt it to be the novel's chief virtue. Garnett "makes not one blunder," the critic for the *International Book Review* wrote, "not a single mischance. He has written a little masterpiece of perfect art, for which ordinary praise seems almost an impertinence, so exemplary is this cu-

rious and distinguished fable." The *New York Times* critic found *Lady into Fox* to be "one of those small bright accidents of literary achievement that happen all too seldom." In his review for the *New York World,* Heywood Broun called the novel "an exceptionally adroit performance. . . . Once the major premise is accepted, everything is developed with unimpeachable logic." Allen concluded that *Lady into Fox* is "a brilliant *tour de force.*"

In his next novel, *A Man in the Zoo,* Garnett explored another whimsical situation. The novel concerns two lovers who quarrel during a visit to the city zoo. Enraged by John Cromartie's suggestion that they live together, Josephine Lackett tells John that he is nothing but an animal who deserves to be a zoo exhibit himself. He acts upon her suggestion, having himself displayed in the ape-house as an example of *homo sapiens.* At first ashamed of the scandalous attention this generates, Josephine eventually realizes her love for John and the novel ends with their reunion. By his flamboyant action, John "demonstrates that man in his natural place in the world is unencumbered by the artificialities with which society has surrounded him," Dille explained. The *Saturday Review* critic thought Garnett showed "more than a whimsical point of view and an austere style: he has a perception of the infinite sanity underlying the insane antics of mankind."

In *The Sailor's Return,* Garnett turned to a more realistic situation. William Targett, a sailor who has been to sea for many years, returns to his hometown with his black wife and child to find that the townspeople cannot accept him. An attempt is made to burn down Targett's inn. The couple is forced to remarry at the local church, having originally been married in Africa in a native ceremony the villagers refuse to recognize. Targett is eventually killed in a fight with some men who have insulted his wife. The novel, Johnson maintained, exposes "an intolerable system of racial and sexual caste." Calling it a "tragical rolling ballad," Laura Benet of *Nation* pointed out that in this novel, Garnett displayed his "poetic sense of irony and pity." Noting the brevity of these first three novels, Benet wrote: "Some day, perhaps, instead of these small, compressed prints [Garnett] will give us a powerful and heroic canvas."

These first three novels, Allen wrote, are "delightful *divertissements,* and that is how we should take them." With *Go She Must!* and *No Love,* Allen believed, Garnett "moves much closer to the naturalistic novel of character and situation." *Go She Must!* tells the story of Anne Dunnock, the daughter of a clergyman, who leaves her small village and runs off to Paris. There she falls in love and marries, but she and her husband soon return to the country. Anne finds that love is more important than the glamorous life of Paris. The book, L. P. Hartley wrote in *Saturday Review,* "has a beautiful surface and a pictorial quality which delights the eye; a style that never falters or runs riot, an outlook on life exceptionally just, sympathetic and trustworthy. It is more human than Mr. Garnett's previous books." Similarly, the *Spectator* reviewer found that the novel's "main virtues lie in the charm of its writing, in its subtle and tender analysis of a girl's emotions, and in its pictures of the spacious, quiet Fenland contrasted with glimpses of a sordid Paris interior."

No Love, the novel Garnett considered his best work, is judged by Allen to be "fully realized. The prose is as pure and formal as ever, but much more contemporary; one no longer has the impression that the characters are figures in a tapestry; one feels they have their own independent life." The novel is the story of two boys from two very different English families. Benedict's family is tolerant and open-minded, while Simon's family holds Victorian values. Simon grows up and marries a woman he does not love. When she falls in love with Benedict, Benedict gives her up, convinced that it would not be right to take his friend's wife. "The style of this book," the *Boston Transcript* critic noted, "is clear, succinct, direct. It is like a perfectly played fugue heard on a crisp morning."

These early novels show Garnett to reject many of the "conventional values that restrict human feeling," as Dille argued. But, Dille continued, "the judgment he makes of society is balanced by a melancholy that owes less to the losses imposed by the unthinking and the unfeeling than to a regret for death, separation, and the failure of love." After writing *The Grasshoppers Come,* a novel about an attempted long-distance flying record, and *Pocahontas; or, The Nonpareil of Virginia,* an historical novel, Garnett gave up the novel for some twenty years, turning his attention to editing books and writing nonfiction works. Among these items, perhaps the most important is the collection of T. E. Lawrence's letters that Garnett edited. Lawrence, better known as Lawrence of Arabia, was Garnett's close friend.

The three-volume memoirs, *The Golden Echo, Flowers of the Forest,* and *The Familiar Faces,* and the autobiographical *Great Friends: Portraits of Seventeen Writers,* trace the course of Garnett's long life. Because his parents knew many prominent literary figures, and because Garnett himself was a member of the influential Bloomsbury Group, these memoirs furnish many anecdotes and insights concerning the British literary scene over several decades. Nora Sayre wrote in the *New York Times Book Review* that in Garnett's memoirs his contemporaries "are portrayed with such natural ease that these men and women seem as accessible as one's own contemporaries." The memoirs are, Dille wrote, "a portrait of Bloomsbury and one of the best records of literary London between the wars." They are also, Dille concluded, "the self-portrait of a man who writes without malice and is revealed as tolerant, wise, and full of sympathy and affection." The three volumes begin with Garnett's childhood and end with his first wife's death in 1940.

The first volume of the memoirs, *The Golden Echo,* covers the years of Garnett's childhood and recounts some of his early memories of his parents' literary friends. Garnett's mother knew Russian authors and political leaders through her work as a translator. She served as Nikolai Lenin's translator when he visited London at the turn of the century. Garnett's father knew British authors because of his work as a publisher's reader. Their house in the English countryside was a literary gathering place. Such figures as Ford Madox Ford, D. H. Lawrence, and Joseph Conrad were frequent visitors. Garnett remembers that Ford had a propensity for embellishing his stories. Lawrence was judged by the young Garnett as not being "a gentleman." As David Stone stated in the *Spectator,* these memories are "re-created, rather than remembered . . .; we grow up with the book—an exceptional and delightful effect."

Flowers of the Forest, the second volume of memoirs, concerns the period of the First World War, when Garnett joined the Bloomsbury Group. The Bloomsbury Group began about 1906 as a casual meeting of literary friends. The association continued until the 1930s and came to include a number of prominent British writers and artists. The binding philosophy of the group was taken from a passage in George Edward

Moore's *Principia Ethica* in which it is argued that the "most valuable things" are "the pleasures of human intercourse and the enjoyment of beautiful objects." The Bloomsbury writers were, Kathleen Nott stated in the *Observer,* "probably the last group . . . able to maintain the illusion of liberal and humane influence, particularly for the artist." Writing in the *Atlantic,* Edward Weeks found Garnett's character drawings of his literary friends to be "delightfully acute. What they wore and where they lived, their likes and dislikes, their impetuosities, political opinions, and love affairs are set down with a dry, scrupulous fidelity." As a volume of reminiscences, Aileen Pippett wrote in the *New York Times, Flowers of the Forest* is "incomparable. . . . Seldom has so much been written about so many with such precision."

The Familiar Faces covers the 1920s and 1930s, a period when Garnett became a bookseller and a partner in the publishing firm of Rupert Hart-Davis. It was through his role as publisher, K. T. Willis wrote in *Library Journal,* that Garnett "knew everyone in England and America who had genius for writing." His portraits of these people are successful, the critic for the *Times Literary Supplement* believed, because "Garnett's main virtues as a writer and surely as a person, derive from his love for his fellows, men and women, whom he is able to describe with the light and shade of real life." The book is "singularly free," J. D. Scott wrote in *Saturday Review,* "from the writer's occupational diseases of malice and self-pity." It also possesses, Scott continued, "a very pleasant, likable quality, like good, friendly conversation." Scott recommended the book "if you want to read a shrewd, urbane, yet feeling account of English literary life seen from its center."

Much of the same period covered in his memoirs is also covered in *Great Friends,* a book containing extended remembrances of seventeen writers Garnett knew during his career. It is, Michael Dirda wrote in the *Washington Post Book World,* "an anecdotal, sentimental collection, and one sure to please anyone who enjoys literary gossip." One of these remembrances concerns a visit by Joseph Conrad to the Garnett residence when Garnett was five years old. To amuse the boy, Conrad fashioned a make-believe sailboat from a large laundry basket and a bedsheet, and he and Garnett "sailed" about the lawn. Garnett also remembers how Virginia Woolf entertained his own children by getting on her hands and knees and chasing them about the house. "*Great Friends,*" wrote Jonathan Raban in the *New Statesman,* "is a triumph of informal, unvarnished portraiture."

All of Garnett's writing, whether fiction or nonfiction, was marked by his distinctive, graceful style, "compounded from equal parts of [Daniel] Defoe and Jonathan Swift," as Swinnerton maintained. Writing in the *New York Herald Tribune Book Review,* Virgilia Peterson described Garnett's writing as possessing a "flawless manner, or—if you will,—[an] unfailingly civilized, . . . deceivingly simple, precise, and unimpeachable style." *Lady into Fox* and several other early novels, with their "compassion and sentimental gentleness, clarity and compression," as James Glinden characterized them in the *Saturday Review,* are the best and most lasting examples of Garnett's work. Even in his eighties, though, he was still writing and publishing "with great zest of youth and fever in his blood," the London *Times* reported. At the time of his death in 1981, Garnett was editing his correspondence with author Sylvia Townsend Warner and had several books awaiting publication.

MEDIA ADAPTATIONS: Film rights to *The Sailor's Return* have been sold.

BIOGRAPHICAL/CRITICAL SOURCES:

BOOKS

Allen, Walter, *The Modern Novel in Britain and the United States,* Dutton, 1964.
Contemporary Literary Criticism, Volume III, Gale, 1975.
Dictionary of Literary Biography, Volume XXXIV: *British Novelists, 1890-1929: Traditionalists,* Gale, 1985.
Edel, Leon, *Bloomsbury: A House of Lions,* Lippincott, 1979.
Gadd, David, *The Loving Friends: A Portrait of Bloomsbury,* Harcourt, 1974.
Garnett, David, *A Rabbit in the Air: Notes from a Diary Kept While Learning to Handle an Aeroplane,* Brewer, Warren & Putnam, 1932.
Garnett, David, *The Golden Echo,* Chatto & Windus, 1953, Harcourt, 1954.
Garnett, David, *Flowers of the Forest,* Chatto & Windus, 1955, Harcourt, 1956.
Garnett, David, *The Familiar Faces,* Chatto & Windus, 1962, Harcourt, 1963.
Garnett, David, editor, *The White/Garnett Letters,* Viking, 1968.
Garnett, David, *Great Friends: Portraits of Seventeen Writers,* Atheneum, 1980.
Heilbrun, Carolyn, *The Garnett Family,* Macmillan, 1961.
Moore, George Edward, *Principia Ethica,* Cambridge University Press, 1903.
Swinnerton, Frank, *The Georgian Literary Scene, 1910-1935,* Hutchinson, revised edition, 1969.

PERIODICALS

Atlantic, October, 1956.
Books and Bookmen, June, 1973.
Book Week, March 1, 1964, July 2, 1967.
Boston Transcript, July 13, 1929.
Commonweal, October 26, 1956, June 19, 1959.
Contemporary Literature, spring, 1973.
International Book Review, September, 1923.
Library Journal, March 1, 1963.
Los Angeles Times, May 25, 1980.
Nation, May 23, 1923, November 4, 1925, March 3, 1956.
New Republic, December 30, 1925, May 8, 1971.
New Statesman, April 26, 1924, February 26, 1927, July 21, 1968, March 22, 1977, June 15, 1979.
New Yorker, February 4, 1956.
New York Herald Tribune Book Review, June 2, 1929, May 30, 1954, January 29, 1956.
New York Times, April 15, 1923, June 15, 1924, September 2, 1956, April 10, 1980.
New York Times Book Review, April 27, 1980.
New York World, May 6, 1923, October 4, 1925.
Observer, June 24, 1979.
Saturday Review, July 17, 1954, March 2, 1963, February 8, 1964.
Saturday Review of Literature, May 10, 1924, September 19, 1925, October 17, 1925, January 29, 1927, November 19, 1935.
Spectator, November 25, 1922, September 26, 1925, January 29, 1927, October 11, 1935, December 25, 1953, June 21, 1968.
Time, May 23, 1954, September 3, 1956.

Times Literary Supplement, September 17, 1925, January 20, 1927, May 8, 1931, November 21, 1958, October 26, 1962, December 8, 1966, June 27, 1968.
Washington Post Book World, May 4, 1980.

OBITUARIES:

PERIODICALS

Publishers Weekly, March 13, 1981.
Times (London), February 19, 1981.†

—*Sketch by Thomas Wiloch*

*   *   *

GARRISON, Phil
   See BRANDNER, Gary

*   *   *

GEHERIN, David J(ohn)   1943-

PERSONAL: Born June 5, 1943, in Auburn, N.Y.; son of Alfred G. (a vocational instructor) and Margaret A. (Taylor) Geherin; married Diane A. Barresi (an educator), August 29, 1964; children: Christopher, Peter, Daniel. *Education:* University of Toronto, B.A., 1964; Purdue University, M.A., 1967, Ph.D., 1970.

ADDRESSES: Home—1453 Witmire, Ypsilanti, Mich. 48197. *Office*—Department of English, Eastern Michigan University, Ypsilanti, Mich. 48197.

CAREER: Eastern Michigan University, Ypsilanti, assistant professor, 1969-74, associate professor, 1974-79, professor of English, 1979—. Producer of "The Automobile in American Life," a series on WTVS-TV, 1976.

MEMBER: American Popular Culture Association, Private Eye Writers of America.

AWARDS, HONORS: Grant from Michigan Council for the Humanities, 1976.

WRITINGS:

Sons of Sam Spade, Ungar, 1980.
John D. MacDonald, Ungar, 1982.
The American Private Eye, Ungar, 1985.

Contributor to magazines, including *Armchair Detective* and *Critique.* Associate editor of *Journal of Narrative Technique,* 1971-77.

WORK IN PROGRESS: Essays on Robert Stone and on the contemporary American short story.

SIDELIGHTS: Sons of Sam Spade is David J. Geherin's assessment of the modern private eye, focusing on the characters created by Robert B. Parker, Roger L. Simon, and Andrew Bergman. "Geherin's thesis is that detective heroes are neither a dying breed nor watered-down versions of the tough guys of the 1930s and '40s," notes a *Booklist* reviewer, who finds the book a "fascinating" and "thoughtful analysis."

According to Geherin, writes David Wilson in the *Times Literary Supplement,* the literary prototype of the modern-day fictional private detective is James Fenimore Cooper's Natty Bumppo in *Leatherstocking Tales,* "and what better American pedigree than that? He came of age in the novels of Hammett and Chandler and Ross Macdonald" and is currently "alive and well and living (usually) in Los Angeles." Wilson, too, finds much of Geherin's narrative "perceptive."

BIOGRAPHICAL/CRITICAL SOURCES:

PERIODICALS

Booklist, February 15, 1980.
Times Literary Supplement, December 12, 1980.

*   *   *

GEORGI, Charlotte

PERSONAL: Born in Pittsburgh, Pa.; daughter of Woldemar Carl and Olga (Mehnert) Georgi. *Education:* University of Buffalo (now State University of New York at Buffalo), B.A. (magna cum laude), 1942, M.A., 1943; University of North Carolina, M.S. in L.S., 1956. *Politics:* "Disappointed Democrat."

ADDRESSES: Home—4214 Raintree Cir., Culver City, Calif. 90230-4430. *Office*—Graduate School of Management Library, University of California, Los Angeles, Calif. 90024.

CAREER: University of Buffalo (now State University of New York at Buffalo), instructor in English department, 1942-43; Stephens College, Columbia, Mo., assistant professor, 1943-49, associate professor in humanities department, 1950-54; University of North Carolina, Business Administration Library, Chapel Hill, head, 1955-57, chief of Business Administration and Social Sciences Division, 1957-59; University of California, Graduate School of Management Library, Los Angeles, chief librarian, 1959-80, librarian for management bibliography, 1980—. *Military service:* U.S. Army Air Forces, 1942-43.

MEMBER: American Library Association, American Association of University Professors (councillor and secretary, UCLA chapter, 1967-78), American Association of University Women, Special Libraries Association (director of local chapter, 1960—; secretary, business and finance division, 1961-62; division vice-chairman, 1962-63; chairman, 1963-64; member of board of directors, 1966-69), California Academic and Research Librarians/Academic Business Librarians Exchange, Los Angeles Committee of Professional Women (member of board of directors, 1970-78; member of executive board, 1979-83), Phi Beta Kappa (councillor and secretary of UCLA chapter, 1960-62), Phi Chi Theta, Pi Lambda Theta, Beta Phi Mu.

WRITINGS:

The Novel and the Pulitzer Prize, 1918-1958, University of North Carolina Library, 1958.
The Businessman in the Novel, University of North Carolina Library, 1959.
(Co-compiler) *Sources of Commodity Prices,* Special Libraries Association, 1960.
(Co-editor) *Statistics Sources,* Gale, 1962, 3rd edition, 1971.
The Literature of Executive Management, Special Libraries Association, 1963.
(Editor) *Encyclopedia of Business Information Sources,* Gale, 1965, 5th edition, 1983.
The Arts and the World of Business, Scarecrow, 1973, 2nd edition, 1979.
(Editor with Marianne Roos) *Foundations, Grants and Fund Raising: A Selected Bibliography,* Graduate School of Management, University of California, Los Angeles, 1976.
The Essential Business Library, Bro-Dart Publishing, 1978.

Current Tools for Management: Sources of Business Information, Atlantic Richfield, 1982.
(With Terry Fate) *Fund Raising, Grants, and Foundations: A Comprehensive Bibliography,* Libraries Unlimited, 1985.
(Co-editor) *Excellence in Library Management,* Haworth Press, 1985.

Editor-in-chief, "Graduate School of Management Library Reference and Information Guides" series, 1962-80. Contributor of articles and reviews to *New York Herald Tribune Book Review, College Art Journal, Antiquarian Bookman, Library Journal,* and *American Reference Books Annual.* Editor of *Newsletter* of Special Libraries Association, business and finance division, 1960-63, and of Los Angeles Committee of Professional Women *News Notes,* 1977-79.

WORK IN PROGRESS: The Businessman in the American Novel: Horatio Alger to Howard Hughes, a comprehensive bibliography; *Best Books for Business: Keeping Up-to-Date on Management; Authors and Publishers: Writing for Publication, Publishing for Profit—A Comprehensive Bibliography.*

*   *   *

GEYER, Georgie Anne 1935-

PERSONAL: Born April 2, 1935, in Chicago, Ill.; daughter of Robert George (a dairy owner) and Georgie Hazel (Gervens) Geyer. *Education:* Northwestern University, B.S., 1956.

ADDRESSES: Home and office—800 25th St. N.W., Washington, D.C. 20037.

CAREER: Chicago Daily News, Chicago, Ill., foreign correspondent, 1964-75; syndicated columnist, Los Angeles Times Syndicate, 1975-80, Universal Press Syndicate, 1980—. Television commentator on news programs. Lyle M. Spenser Professor of Journalism, Syracuse University, 1976. Member of board, Chicago Council on Foreign Relations. Trustee of American University, 1981—.

MEMBER: Overseas Writers, Overseas Press Club, Women in Communications, Sigma Delta Chi.

AWARDS, HONORS: Fulbright scholarship, University of Vienna, 1956-57; human interest award, American Newspaper Guild, Chicago, 1962; Seymour Berkson Foreign Assignment Grant, 1964; Overseas Press Club award for Latin American reporting, 1966; alumnae merit award, Northwestern University, 1966; national merit award, Theta Sigma Phi, 1967; Maria Moors Cabot Award, Columbia University, 1971; Hannah Solomon Award, National Council of Jewish Women, 1973; Illinois Special Events award, 1975.

WRITINGS:

The New Latins: Fateful Change in South and Central America, Doubleday, 1970.
The New 100 Years War, Doubleday, 1972.
The Young Russians, Education & Training Consultants, 1975.
Buying the Night Flight: The Autobiography of a Woman Foreign Correspondent, Delacorte, 1983.

Contributor of articles to *Saturday Review, Atlantic, New Republic, Progressive, Nation, Wildlife, Kiwanis Magazine, True,* and other periodicals.

WORK IN PROGRESS: A book on Central America, tentatively entitled *The First War We Can Drive To;* an historical biography of Fidel Castro.

SIDELIGHTS: An unmarried woman traveling alone as a foreign correspondent was a rarity when Georgie Anne Geyer began her career with the *Chicago Daily News* in the early 1960s. As she relates in her *Contemporary Authors* interview, professional skepticism and sexism were just two of the obstacles she had to overcome. During her years in the profession, Geyer gained enough insight and experience to produce books on international politics and society, as well as her own story, *Buying the Night Flight: The Autobiography of a Woman Foreign Correspondent.*

Her autobiography chronicles her own experiences as a journalist, concentrating on the particular circumstances that accompany being a female foreign correspondent. As Grace Lichtenstein reports in the *Washington Post,* Geyer's "major point is that being a woman enhanced her effectiveness as a foreign correspondent, even as it left her prey to special dangers." Although Carolyn See in the *Los Angeles Times Book Review* finds this viewpoint flawed, she also notes that in this "energetic crazy-making book" the author's "ignorance, her ingenuousness, is fully equal to her sense of adventure and her lust for independence. Which is no doubt why she succeeded—and why we read her book."

According to Lichtenstein, Geyer "stands as a conservative yet admirable role model for young women (or, for that matter, nonswaggering young men) who want to become reporters. Her plucky autobiography should be required reading for the next generation of foreign correspondents." *Chicago Tribune Book World* critic Ron Grossman calls it "a book I'd like my daughters to read." *Buying the Night Flight* is "predominantly hard-eyed and realistic, yet [Geyer's] story still has the sweep of romantic adventure," Edmund Fuller concludes in the *Wall Street Journal.*

CA INTERVIEW

CA interviewed Georgie Anne Geyer by telephone on February 15, 1985, at her office in Washington, D.C.

CA: You wrote in Buying the Night Flight *about how your mother gave you the curiosity about other parts of the world, and growing up in Chicago, with its power politics delineated by ethnic groups, gave you a hatred for injustice and corruption. When did you begin to realize that you could channel both the curiosity and the social concern into writing?*

GEYER: I think I really began to feel that as early as my teens in Chicago. One thing I do feel very strongly about is that growing up in a city neighborhood, a real neighborhood where there are bullies on the block and also wonderfully human and compassionate *real* people, gives you a very realistic idea of human nature. You can afford still to be idealistic, but the idealism is tempered by wisdom and by reality. I don't think people are intrinsically all good any more than they are intrinsically all evil. It inculcated in me an idea that it is decent and rational systems that must control people. That's why I believe in democracy, because I believe it's the system that gives people the greatest room for their talents and for their spirit; but it also controls their darker sides.

I was writing all the time. I wrote a little novel when I was ten and typed it on little pages to look like a book, because I loved books so much. But it wasn't until I got out of college and started working for the *Chicago Daily News* that I could see how you could really be effective, though on a very minor scale. Then I put the two together. And there were people, as

I said in *Buying the Night Flight,* who had a great influence on me, like Saul Alinsky, the great organizer in Chicago and a very dear friend. I wrote a lot about Saul and knew him very well personally. And just observing him taught me tactics, something that I hadn't learned before. That became invaluable later, particularly in the foreign work.

CA: Mike Royko said in his introduction to Buying the Night Flight, *"In 1960 a Chicago bookie might have given 1,000 to 1 against" your fulfilling your ambition to become a foreign correspondent. What gave you the courage to keep after it in the face of such professional discrimination against women?*

GEYER: A lot of people ask me that, and I have to admit that it was just so damn much fun that I never stopped to think much about being discriminated against. I'm afraid a lot of women like to nurse their grudges—I like to do away with the people who cause them! That's very Chicago, too. I don't mean physically, of course (at least, not usually!), but to expunge them from interfering with my life. But I never took these things personally, because I didn't expect life to be perfect. I expected it to be a struggle, and to me the struggle was the joyous part of it—particularly when you win. I never felt bitter. The men on the paper were wonderful once I got the job—and there were no women on the city desk then, much less the foreign desk. But once I was there, we were all the closest of friends and buddies. They're still the best group of people I've ever met.

CA: Though discrimination was obviously there in the 1950s, women then grew up loving men, which changed in the '60s.

GEYER: Exactly, and that's a very good key to women who grew up in the '60s. I see a lot more bitterness with them, although paradoxically they had a lot more opportunity. There's something else. I really do feel in many ways it was a lot easier for me than for the women today, because I was the only one. There just weren't that many women who wanted to go into journalism, particularly on the foreign staff. Once I broke through, it was like an opossum at an elks' convention. I was very noticeable, and everything I did was noticed—particularly when I did the unusual thing, like going to the mountains with the guerillas in Latin America. Today there are so many young women who want to do this—or *think* they want to do it, which is a different thing and sometimes a tormenting thing. They are so well-educated and so able, and there just isn't going to be room for them. I was very single-minded; I was thinking only of doing what I wanted to do and what I loved to do. It wasn't ambition primarily. I was ambitious, but more than that I wanted to do the things I wanted to do. And I always took great joy in them. Joy—it's important!

CA: Latin America was your first love, your first real post, and the subject of your first book. You said in Buying the Night Flight *that you weren't sure what the attraction was. Has it become any clearer to you since?*

GEYER: I think it has. I had been to Cuba with my parents when I was fifteen; I'd been to Mexico, and studied in Mexico for three months in my junior year at Northwestern; and I had gone down once to the Andean countries on vacation. I just knew at that point that I loved it. I felt more alive, I felt more fulfilled, I was endlessly fascinated, my nerves were zinging. Now I think I know what it is. It's the old attraction of the people from the North to the countries and the peoples and the cultures of the South. You know, it's the same in Europe: the Swedes and the Finns are intensely attracted to Italy, to Spain—to the darker people, to their romantic quality. It fulfills them in a different way. It's almost like finding and fulfilling the other side of your soul. I'm convinced that was the attraction. It made me feel more alive, more fulfilled. It was very satisfying—and it still is.

CA: It was interesting to read how you determined that the best way to report on Latin America was to cut through the acronyms and write about important social movements. Did you already have the historical background at your command, or was a great deal of further study required to get you established in the kind of reporting you made your reputation with?

GEYER: I'm always reading more and learning more, but I was very well versed in Latin American history. I had a very good professor at Northwestern, and it was in his history classes that I really put together how much I wanted to go down there and how much I was attracted to it. But I kept reading. For instance, when I went to live in Peru—which is an unusual place to go, and at that point our editor would have sent me to Vietnam—one of the first people I wanted to see was Victor Raul Haya de la Torre, who was the founder of the Aprista Party, the first reformist liberal democratic party in Latin America. I read so much about Peru and so much about Haya, he was the first person I dreamed of meeting.

CA: Your skill with languages has been an invaluable asset in your career. How did you learn them quickly, and how do you keep them in working order through periods of disuse?

GEYER: I do have a talent for them and learn them quickly, but it still is a lot of work. I don't think I know anybody, actually, who can "pick up" languages. I can learn a language in about three months if I'm in the country, if I have a tutor for two hours a day, and if I really work at it and practice. But that's not picking it up; that's really working hard. I learned German on my Fulbright. Spanish, I studied off and on, but I really learned it in Peru. Russian I learned in night school; and Portuguese, when I lived in Rio. But as to keeping them up, I don't try to. That would be impossible. Spanish keeps up because I've used it so much, and German pretty much keeps up. But the other two I don't try to. If I were going to Russia or Portugal, I'd spend a few weeks reviewing the language or take a good blitzkrieg course with a tutor.

CA: The roster of famous people you've interviewed is impressive indeed, including Fidel Castro, Salvador Allende, Anwar and Jihan Sadat, Yasser Arafat, Muammar Qaddafi, the Ayatollah Khomeini. Who was the most impressive person you've interviewed?

GEYER: When I came back from a trip from Argentina, I had seen Juan Peron and I had seen Jorge Luis Borges. Mike Royko asked me in the office, "Of all the people you've interviewed, who's the most impressive one?" And I said Borges. He guffawed and said, "She interviews all these leaders, and the man she admires most is this little, old, frail, blind writer." And he was. I was so impressed with the man first of all for his work, which I think is magnificent. The night I had dinner with him in Buenos Aires, I called him for an interview and he said, "Fine. Why don't you come down and we'll have dinner in my neighborhood?" He was seventy-four then, very frail, almost totally blind. He came down into the lobby of

the building where he lived, and we walked around the corner to this little restaurant where he ate almost every night. He could hardly eat anything, because he was sick in other ways as well.

But two things were so impressive to me. One was that there was not the slightest bit of self-pity in this man. He just accepted his infirmity; he said that blindness had always run in his family and he knew that he would be blind. He said that he was kept very busy with his writing and his teaching, which he still is doing, and speaking. And he said he was learning Icelandic and Old Norse. The other thing was the element of comparing him to Peron, whom I found very interesting and very physically handsome, even at eighty-two. So many of Borges's stories are about the caudillos of the pampas, the strong men and the saloon fighters—the exact antithesis of himself. And yet he made this distinction between the men who apparently live life and those who write about it but may live it in a more intense way. Everything he said and everything he's written has spoken to me in special ways.

CA: What was your most frightening interview?

GEYER: I think probably not physically frightening, but frightening in terms of what I could see was coming, was Khomeini. This was in Paris, just before he went back to Iran. I think I'm very rational, but I truly felt I was in the presence of total evil. It was a very surreal, very scary thing spiritually. I was overly kind in the columns I wrote, because realizing how strongly I felt, I wrote them very straight. Actually, my instincts were right; I should have written what I felt. I think women try to lean over backwards like that.

CA: You've written about the process of getting carried along with the story, wherever it goes and however long it takes. Did you learn early to deal with the interruptions this must cause in the rest of a reporter's life, such as work back home?

GEYER: My work wasn't interrupted so much back home, because my work in those years was mostly overseas. The first three books were written when I took a few months off every year because I was working so intensely. The autobiography got interrupted an awful lot. I'd carry it with me—I remember I was writing part of it in Baghdad during the beginning months of the war there. I lost a chapter in Caracas. That's not the way to write books.

CA: Your previous books had been mainly factual. Was it hard to make the switch to writing about yourself?

GEYER: No, it really wasn't. I think, had I had two or three months free just to write it, I could have written it very easily in that time. I didn't want to make myself look like a fool, but it's also nice to have that kind of control over your image. I was more concerned about other people, frankly. I didn't want to misrepresent people I cared about or hurt people's feelings. An autobiography, particularly at my age, was very sensitive to me in that way. I thought I might feel hesitant about writing about some of my loves or a lot of things, but I really didn't.

CA: Was there any official Russian response to your 1975 book, The Young Russians?

GEYER: Only from the one person that I got to know quite well and like immensely, Professor Vladimir Lisovsky at Leningrad University, the sociologist on youth. I'm sure they forced him to write—because it's not in his style at all—a very sarcastic and terrible review in a magazine. That was the only response I got. And *The Young Russians* was not an anti-Russian book, as I think anyone who would read it objectively would agree.

CA: That you've enjoyed traveling is absolutely clear in your writing, and you've said that you love hotels. Do you have a favorite?

GEYER: I have a couple of favorites. One is the Nile Hilton in Cairo, a wonderful hotel right (of course!) on the Nile. It was the first luxury hotel there. It's the meeting place for all the politicians, and everybody in the world goes through there. I stayed there so much that I got to know everybody, and it was always so much fun coming back there. Another one *was* the St. Georges in Beirut, which of course was burned out. It breaks your heart. It was the most beautiful place, right on the bay—a small hotel, very intimate, very classy. You could water ski off the dock, water ski around the bay, and watch people ski in the mountains at the same time. It was heaven. Foreign correspondents get very attached to their hotels, and it's just heartbreaking when you see one like that go. But there are a lot I like: there's the American Colony Hotel in Jerusalem, which is wonderful, and the Algonquin in New York, the old writer's hotel, which is where I always stay. I have them spotted around. The Sacher in Vienna, the Intercontinental in Paris. These are all my hotels.

CA: Since you've given up being a foreign correspondent and become a columnist, how much travel do you manage to work into your schedule?

GEYER: I control the situation completely. Nobody tells me what to write, where to go, when to go. So I make all the decisions. But the concomitant and rather important fact there is that I have to pay for it! That's not a problem now, because I'm doing a lot of speaking, and that's much better pay than writing columns. So I can travel as much as I want to. I'd say I'm overseas maybe thirty percent of the time, which is just about what I want now. When I was a correspondent, it was seventy-five percent. I did that for twelve years, and that was enough. This way I don't have to give it up, but I can do it at a more reasonable time.

CA: What column topic seems to bring the strongest response from readers?

GEYER: There are several. In the foreign field, there's no question: it's either the Middle East or Central America. It *was* Vietnam, of course, but that's past. On a national level, abortion—no question, that's the number one. And again Central America, which fits in both categories.

CA: Do you enjoy the television appearances?

GEYER: I do, yes. I used to be terribly nervous, but I'm not usually now. On the presidential debate, for example, I didn't feel nervous at all for some reason. But I like doing the shows I do, like ''Washington Week in Review,'' which I'm going to do tonight. They're serious and yet they're fun, and we have a really fine group of serious and professional people who are also a lot of fun. It's that colleagueship that I don't really have anymore, because I work so alone.

CA: What are your own regular sources of news?

GEYER: I read the two Washington papers, the *Post* and the *Washington Times.* I read the *New York Times* every day, the *Wall Street Journal,* some specialized magazines, newspapers from the Middle East (such as the *Jerusalem Post*), and the *Times of the Americas* for Latin American affairs. Then just a lot of different materials that I get selectively or go out and get.

CA: You've won many awards for your own newspaper work. What are your feelings about the competition fostered by journalism awards? Do you think it makes for a healthy situation?

GEYER: Well, it certainly has an unhealthy side. I think we've seen the outcome with things like Janet Cooke's stories in the *Post.* I don't work that much with the young journalists, but I hear from people that there is a real streak of doing a story to get an award and not to do the coverage. If this is true—and I'm told it is—this is certainly deplorable. And equally deplorable is what I've heard about prizes like the Pulitzer—that the big papers sort of divide them up. But I haven't been personally involved, so that's really based on what I've heard from other people.

CA: Do you think the press generally does an adequate job of policing itself?

GEYER: I don't think we do any job of policing ourselves, and I'm not sure at all that we can. I do think the editors should be more in control. There's permissive journalism just as there's permissive parenting and permissive foreign policy in this country. We don't like to control things, to control people under us. The old editors that I had on the *Daily News* certainly did control. Wow, did they! But I don't see those editors around much anymore.

CA: Is there really a great deal less discrimination against women now than there was when you were getting your start?

GEYER: Oh, absolutely. It's so different that it's almost unbelievable. I go into a newspaper office now and sometimes half of the reporters are women. You still don't see that many on the higher editorial levels, although there are a lot of them even controlling the editorial pages of the *Washington Post* and the *New York Times.* It's a situation that is almost unrecognizable from the years when I started.

CA: Are there new areas, geographical or political or otherwise, that you'd like to explore in your work?

GEYER: I'm exploring them right now, actually. I'm doing two books. I've just finished one on Central America which is very different from the others—it's much more a book of ideas, really, on what are the real roots of the conflicts there. The other one, which I'm well into, is a historical biography—it's about Fidel Castro. So along with him, and along with the interviewing, and along with the research, I'm studying how to write historical biography.

CA: What advice would you give aspiring journalists?

GEYER: Just to be curious about everything in the world, and don't think of journalism as a way to become a celebrity or to get ahead, but think of it in terms of the joy and satisfaction that it can bring to you personally, and the wisdom and information that it can bring to other people.

BIOGRAPHICAL/CRITICAL SOURCES:

BOOKS

Geyer, Georgie Anne, *Buying the Night Flight: The Autobiography of a Woman Foreign Correspondent,* Delacorte, 1983.

PERIODICALS

Chicago Tribune Book World, February 13, 1983.
Los Angeles Times Book Review, January 2, 1983.
National Review, January 7, 1977.
New York Times Book Review, January 30, 1983.
Saturday Review, September 12, 1970.
Wall Street Journal, January 17, 1983.
Washington Post, January 11, 1983.

—*Interview by Jean W. Ross*

*   *   *

GEZI, Kal
   See GEZI, Kalil I(smail)

*   *   *

GEZI, Kalil I(smail)   1930-
   (Kal Gezi)

PERSONAL: Surname rhymes with "easy"; born April 7, 1930, in Baghdad, Iraq; son of Ismail and Jamila (Nasir) Gezi; married Lou Jahrling, December 22, 1956; children: Vincent, John, Robert. *Education:* Teachers College, Iraq, B.A., 1950; Stanford University, M.A., 1955, Ph.D., 1959. *Politics:* Independent. *Religion:* Roman Catholic.

ADDRESSES: Home—4116 Crondall Dr., Sacramento, Calif. 95825. *Office*—Department of Behavioral Sciences in Education, California State University, 6000 J St., Sacramento, Calif. 95819.

CAREER: Immaculate Heart College, Los Angeles, Calif., assistant professor of education, 1960-63; Chico State College (now California State University, Chico), associate professor of education, 1963-69; California State University, Sacramento, professor of education and chairman of behavioral sciences in education, 1969—. Lecturer, University of London, 1973. Consultant to Far West Laboratory, 1966, Educational Project, Inc. and to state and national agencies; education consultant to publishers, including Holt, Rinehart & Winston, 1968—.

MEMBER: American Educational Research Association, Comparative and International Education Society, Association for Higher Education, California Educational Research Association (vice-president, 1969-71; president, 1972), California Teachers Association, United Professors of California, Phi Delta Kappa, Kappa Delta Pi.

AWARDS, HONORS: Grants from National Science Foundation and California State University, Chico, 1967.

WRITINGS:

The Acculturation of Middle Eastern Arab Students in Selected American Universities and Colleges, American Friends of the Middle East, 1960.
(With J. Myers) *Teaching in American Culture,* Holt, 1968.

Education in Comparative and International Perspectives, Holt, 1971.
(With Ann Bradford) "The Young Authors" series (children's books with cassettes), Child's World, 1975.
(With Bradford) *Beebi, the Little Blue Bell: A Story to Finish,* illustrated by Dan Siculan, Child's World, 1976.
(With Bradford) *One Little White Shoe: A Story to Finish,* illustrated by Siculan, Child's World, 1976.

UNDER NAME KAL GEZI

The Educational System of Arab Republic of Egypt, U.S. Department of Health, Education, and Welfare, Office of Education, 1979.

"THE MAPLE STREET FIVE" JUVENILE SERIES; UNDER NAME KAL GEZI, WITH ANN BRADFORD

The Mystery in the Secret Club House, illustrated by Mina McLean, Child's World, 1978.
The Mystery of the Live Ghosts, illustrated by McLean, Child's World, 1978.
The Mystery of the Missing Raccoon, illustrated by McLean, Child's World, 1978.
The Mystery at Misty Falls, illustrated by McLean, Child's World, 1980.
The Mystery of the Blind Writer, illustrated by McLean, Child's World, 1980.
The Mystery of the Square Footprints, illustrated by McLean, Child's World, 1980.
The Mystery at the Tree House, illustrated by McLean, Child's World, 1980.
The Mystery of the Midget Clown, illustrated by McLean, Child's World, 1980.
The Mystery of the Missing Dogs, illustrated by McLean, Child's World, 1980.

OTHER

Contributor of articles and reviews to professional journals. Member of educational board, *California Journal of Educational Research,* 1973—; editorial consultant, *Comparative Education Review,* 1974—.†

*   *   *

GILL, Bartholomew
   See McGARRITY, Mark

*   *   *

GILLETT, Margaret   1930-

PERSONAL: Born in 1930 in Wingham, New South Wales, Australia; daughter of Leslie Frank and Janet (Vickers) Gillett. *Education:* University of Sydney, B.A., 1950; attended University of Copenhagen, 1953; Russell Sage College, M.A., 1958; Columbia University, Ed.D., 1961.

ADDRESSES: Home—2480 Chemin du Club, Box 1693, Ste. Adele, Quebec, Canada J0R 1L0. *Office*—Faculty of Education, McGill University, Montreal, Quebec, Canada H3A 1Y2.

CAREER: New South Wales Education Department, New South Wales, Australia, teacher, 1951-53; Commonwealth Office of Education, Sydney, Australia, educational research and administration, 1954-57; Dalhousie University, Halifax, Nova Scotia, assistant professor, 1961-62; Haile Selassie I University, Addis Ababa, Ethiopia, faculty member, 1962-64; McGill University, Montreal, Quebec, associate professor, 1964-67, professor of education, 1967-83, Macdonald Professor, 1983—. Member of Canadian Research Institute for the Advancement of Women.

MEMBER: Comparative and International Education Society of Canada (president, 1977-79), Comparative Education Society, Canadian Association of University Professors, History of Education Society.

WRITINGS:

(Editor) *Plot Outlines of 101 Best Novels,* Barnes & Noble, 1962.
(With Monica Kehoe) *The Laurel and the Poppy* (novel; based on the life of Francis Thompson), Vanguard, 1965.
A History of Education: Thought and Practice, McGraw, 1966.
(Editor) *Readings in the History of Education,* McGraw, 1969.
Educational Technology: Toward Demystification, Prentice-Hall, 1973.
(Editor) *Foundation Studies in Education: Justifications and New Directions,* Scarecrow, 1973.
We Walked Very Warily: A History of Women at McGill, Eden Press, 1981.
(With Kay Sibbald) *A Fair Shake: Autobiographical Essays by McGill Women,* Eden Press, 1984.
(Contributor) Geraldine Clifford, editor, *Pioneer Women in Higher Education,* Feminist Press, 1986.

Contributor to education journals in Australia, Canada, England, and the United States. Founding editor, *McGill Journal of Education,* 1966-77.

WORK IN PROGRESS: Dear Grace: Letters of Dr. William C. Little to Grace Ritchie, 1889-1894.

SIDELIGHTS: Margaret Gillett has traveled extensively in Europe, southeast Asia, and Africa.

MEDIA ADAPTATIONS: A film, "Knowing Women," based on *We Walked Very Warily,* is in production at the Canadian National Film Board.

AVOCATIONAL INTERESTS: Tennis, skiing, swimming, the theatre.

*   *   *

GILMORE, Christopher Cook 1940-
(C. C. Parx)

PERSONAL: Born August 3, 1940, in Washington, D.C.; son of Edwin Lanier King Gilmore (a writer) and Margot (an artist; maiden name, Cook) Dawson; children: Zebedee (daughter). *Education:* Attended George Washington University, 1959-61; University of Miami, Coral Gables, Fla., B.A., 1964; attended Stanford University, 1965.

ADDRESSES: Home—8801 Atlantic Ave., Margate, N.J. 08402. *Office*—161 rue du Faubourg St. Antoine, 75011 Paris, France. *Agent*—Peter Miller Agency, 1021 Avenue of the Americas, Suite 403, New York, N.Y. 10018.

CAREER: Associated Press, bureau news staffer in Richmond, Va., and Denver, Colo., 1965-66; elementary school teacher in Absecon, N.J., 1966-68; writer, 1968—. Writer in residence, Shakespeare & Company Bookstore, Paris, France, 1983. Beachmaster of Catamaran Racers, Margate, N.J. Member of Margate Beach Patrol, 1957-67. *Military service:* U.S. Marine Corps Reserve, 1964.

MEMBER: Mensa (life member).

WRITINGS:

Atlantic City Proof (novel), Simon & Schuster, 1979.
(Under pseudonym C. C. Parx) *Slavers* (novelization of a screenplay), Charter, 1980.
The Bad Room, Avon, 1983.
Road Kills, Warner Books, 1985.

Contributor of about eighty short stories to magazines, including *Gallery, Swank, Chic, Genesis,* and *Surfer.* Contributing editor, *Atlantic City,* 1983—.

WORK IN PROGRESS: A suspense novel about insanity.

SIDELIGHTS: Christopher Cook Gilmore told *CA* that his father, Edwin "Eddy" Gilmore, who won the Pulitzer Prize in 1947, ran the Associated Press Moscow Bureau during World War II and published four novels. Regarding his own writing habits, Gilmore commented: "I write in the morning every day. By noon I'm finished and free to spend the day as I like, sailing in the summer, riding horses, walking in the winter.

"In the fall I need the city, New York, Paris, London, or Rome, and I stay three or four months depending on the action. Then, when change becomes necessary, I go to Spain, Morocco, Greece, Thailand, India, Kenya, anywhere that's warm. In the spring I head for home, Margate, and the beautiful beaches there.

"I know how to survive and writing is my only source of income. I have a Spitfire, a Hobiecat, the love of a beautiful woman, and plenty of time to enjoy them. I would trade my life for none other, but I would recommend my lifestyle to very few: artists and madmen only, people with few material needs and plenty of imagination.

"Fame and wealth may be in the future, but if they're not I won't mind, just as long as I can keep writing, keep drifting, loving my lady and our baby girl Zebedee and all the fascinating people and places there are to see. If there is one thing I'm searching for, I guess it's a good story."

Gilmore's *Atlantic City Proof,* a story set in Prohibition-era New Jersey, is described by Doris Grumbach in the *Chicago Tribune Book World* as a "fine, funny, and wholly satisfying novel." According to a *West Coast Review of Books* critic, the book leads the reader on "an adventure-filled sea coast course, skippered by an expert captain." Gilmore, indicates the critic, "is a superb story teller. Nearly each chapter contains a complete tale in itself, expertly woven into the story as a whole. Gilmore tells his tales with gentle humor and affection, about unique people and unusual events." "Clearly it is a movie on its way to being made," states Grumbach, "but that doesn't detract from its quality as a wonderful novel." The book has also been translated into Italian.

BIOGRAPHICAL/CRITICAL SOURCES:

PERIODICALS

Chicago Tribune Book World, January 14, 1979.
Los Angeles Times Book Review, July 24, 1983.
Times Literary Supplement, May 30, 1980.
West Coast Review of Books, March, 1979.

*   *   *

GIROUD, Francoise 1916-

PERSONAL: Born September 21, 1916, in Geneva, Switzerland; daughter of Salih (a journalist) and Elda (Faragi) Gourdji;

married Anatole Eliacheff, June 25, 1946 (divorced, 1961); children: Alain Danis (died, 1972), Caroline Eliacheff. *Education:* Educated in France. *Politics:* Radical Party. *Religion:* Catholic.

ADDRESSES: Office—c/o Editions Fayard, 75 rue des Saints-Peres, Paris 75007, France. *Agent*—Max Becker, 115 East 82nd St., New York, N.Y. 10028.

CAREER: Script-girl in cinema productions with Marc Allegret (''Fanny''), 1932, and Jean Renoir (''La Grande Illusion''), 1936; assistant producer, 1937; *Elle* (women's magazine), Paris, France, editor-in-chief, 1946-53; *L'Express* (news magazine), Paris, co-founder and editor in chief, 1953-74, president of Express-Union, 1970-74; served in French government as minister of women, 1974-76, and minister of culture, 1976-77; writer. Press consultant to Hachette (publishers). Vice-president of Parti Radical. *Wartime service:* Member of French Resistance.

AWARDS, HONORS: Chevalier de la Legion d'Honneur from France; Merite Civil decoration from Spain; Ordre du Drapeau decoration from Yugoslavia; D.H.L. from University of Michigan, 1976, and Goucher College, 1977.

WRITINGS:

Le Tout Paris, Gallimard, 1952.
Nouveaux Portraits (title means ''New Portraits''), Gallimard, 1953.
La Nouvelle Vague (title means ''The New Wave''), Gallimard, 1958.
Si je mens . . . , Stock, 1971, translation by Richard Seaver published as *I Give You My Word,* Houghton, 1974.
Une poignee d'eau (title means ''A Handful of Water''), Laffont, 1972.
La Comedie du pouvoir (title means ''The Comedy of Power''), Fayard, 1977.
Ce que je crois (title means ''What I Believe''), Grasset, 1978.
Une Femme honorable, Marie Curie, Fayard, 1981.
Le Bon Plaisir (also see below), Mazarine, 1983.

Also author of dialogue and adaptations for numerous films, including ''Antoine et Antoinette,'' 1947, ''La Belle que voila,'' 1950, ''L'Amour, Madame,'' 1951, ''Julietta,'' 1953, and ''Le Bon Plaisir'' (based on her book of the same title), 1984. Former contributor to *Le Monde;* contributor to *Le Nouvel Observateur.*

WORK IN PROGRESS: Un sejour a la campagne.

SIDELIGHTS: As secretary of the world's first ministry for the feminine condition, created by former French president Valery Giscard d'Estaing, Francoise Giroud captured the world's attention with her attempts to meet the ministry's goal of ''overseeing the integration of women into contemporary French society.'' In a society still largely dominated by the sexist Napoleonic Code and traditional views of women's roles, French women have continued to fill low-status, low-paying jobs and to endure discrimination because of their sex. Giroud viewed her task primarily as one of ''[changing] the mentality of the people'' in order to facilitate the adoption of various reform measures.

High on the list of her priorities were the special problems of older women, who often lacked skills necessary for entering the work force because of the years they had spent in child-rearing. Giroud also sought to encourage the development of day-care centers and the institution of more flexible working hours to enable women with families to pursue jobs outside

their homes. Despite the visible accomplishments of women in French national life, Giroud remained concerned with the *average* level of women in the society and endeavored to upgrade their status by such measures as urging professional schools to admit more women. Determined to find ways of enforcing existing legislation guaranteeing women equal pay for equal work, she also strove for more stringent legislation banning discrimination in hiring practices. Besides the issue of employment, Giroud also concentrated on other concerns of women such as the liberalization of abortion laws and the banning of exploitative television advertising.

Though she has forcefully denounced sexism in French society, both as editor of the popular magazine *L'Express* and as minister of women, Giroud has refused to ally herself with feminists or the women's liberation movement. In an interview with Marilyn Gardner of the *Milwaukee Journal,* she once said that the ''revolt'' of women ''is part and parcel of the evolution of human affairs and is right. But when it expresses itself as hatred of men, it's stupid. The best way to hurt a man, if you hate him, is to be the object of his desire, not to hustle him into the kitchen to do the dishes.'' As she once explained to *CA,* she is reluctant, or more exactly, *refractaire,* towards radical feminism.

When asked about the phenomenon of reverse discrimination, Giroud told *CA:* ''The problem of 'reverse discrimination' doesn't exist in France—or perhaps I should say, not yet. But I believe that we are far from it, even if it should come about some day. The economic crisis and the accompanying unemployment are in the process of seriously slowing down things, for one thing. Besides that, it seems to me that discrimination is felt much less in France than in the United States.''

BIOGRAPHICAL/CRITICAL SOURCES:

BOOKS

Authors in the News, Volume I, Gale, 1976.

PERIODICALS

Milwaukee Journal, November 10, 1974.
Ms., January, 1975.
Newsweek, September 22, 1975.
Oregonian, October 30, 1974.
Saturday Review, June 14, 1975.
Time, July 29, 1974.
Times Literary Supplement, October 9, 1981.

*   *   *

GLECKNER, Robert Francis 1925-

PERSONAL: Born in 1925 in Rahway, N.J.; son of Adam Francis (an insurance broker) and Frieda (Froehlich) Gleckner; married Glenda Jean Karr, February 7, 1946; children: Jeffrey Michael, Susan Frances. *Education:* Williams College, B.A., 1948; Johns Hopkins University, Ph.D., 1954. *Religion:* Episcopalian.

ADDRESSES: Home—Hickory Grove Church Rd., Route 6, Box 353, Raleigh, N.C. 27612. *Office*—Department of English, Duke University, Durham, N.C. 27706.

CAREER: Johns Hopkins University, Baltimore, Md., instructor in English, 1949-51; University of Cincinnati, Cincinnati, Ohio, instructor in English, 1952-54; University of Wisconsin—Madison, assistant professor of English, 1954-57; Wayne State University, Detroit, Mich., associate professor of English, 1957-62; University of California, Riverside, professor of English, 1962-78, chairman of department, 1962-66, associate dean of College of Letters and Science, 1968-70, dean of College of Humanities, 1970-75; Duke University, Durham, N.C., professor of English, 1978—, acting chairman of department, 1982. Manuscript referee for scholarly journals and for several university presses. Consultant, National Endowment for the Humanities, 1975-77. *Military service:* U.S. Army Air Forces, 1943-45; bombardier; became first lieutenant.

MEMBER: American Blake Foundation (member of board of directors), Byron Society (charter member of American committee), Keats-Shelley Association, Wordsworth-Coleridge Association, Phi Beta Kappa, Beta Theta Pi.

AWARDS, HONORS: Poetry Society of America, Emily Hamblen Award, 1959; National Endowment for the Humanities summer stipend, 1978; American Council of Learned Societies grant-in-aid, 1978-79; National Endowment for the Humanities senior fellowship, 1980-81; Carl and Lily Pforzheimer Foundation grants, 1969, 1984; National Endowment for the Humanities publication grant, 1984; American Philosophical Society research grant, 1984-85.

WRITINGS:

The Piper and the Bard: A Study of William Blake, Wayne State University Press, 1959.
(Editor with G. Enscoe) *Romanticism: Points of View*, Prentice-Hall, 1962, 3rd edition (sole editor), Wayne State University Press, 1975.
(Editor) *Selected Writings of William Blake*, Appleton-Century-Crofts, 1966, revised edition, 1970.
Byron and the Ruins of Paradise, Johns Hopkins Press, 1969, reprinted, Greenwood Press, 1980.
(Editor) *Complete Poetical Works of Byron*, Houghton, 1975.
Blake's Prelude: "Poetical Sketches," Johns Hopkins University Press, 1982.
Blake and Spenser, Johns Hopkins University Press, 1985.
(Editor with Mark Greenberg) *Teaching Blake's "Songs,"* Modern Language Association, 1986.

CONTRIBUTOR

Martin Magalaner, editor, *A James Joyce Miscellany*, Southern Illinois University Press, 1962.
G. E. Bentley and M. K. Nurmi, editors, *A Blake Bibliography*, University of Minnesota Press, 1964.
C. Hart and J. Dalton, editors, *Twelve and a Tilly: Essays on "Finnegans Wake,"* Faber, 1966.
D. V. Erdman and others, editors, *A Concordance to the Writings of William Blake*, Cornell University Press, 1969.
E. E. Bostetter, editor, *Twentieth-Century Interpretations of "Don Juan,"* Prentice-Hall, 1969.
A. Rosenfeld, editor, *William Blake: Essays for S. Foster Damon*, Brown University Press, 1969.
R. Paulson and A. Stein, editors, *ELH Essays for Earl R. Wasserman*, Johns Hopkins University Press, 1976.
M. H. Abrams, editor, *English Romantic Poets: Modern Essays in Criticism*, Oxford University Press, 1975.
R. J. Bertholf and A. S. Levitt, editors, *William Blake and the Moderns*, State University of New York Press, 1982.

Also contributor to *Blake: Twentieth-Century Interpretations*, edited by Northrop Frye, *Twentieth-Century Interpretations of Blake's "Songs of Innocence and of Experience,"* edited by M. D. Paley, *Balke and the Moderns*, 1980, and *A Spenser Encyclopedia*, edited by A. C. Hamilton, 1986.

OTHER

Contributor to professional journals. Member of advisory board, *Criticism: A Quarterly for Literature and the Arts, Studies in Romanticism, Romanticism Past and Present,* and *Blake Studies.*

WORK IN PROGRESS: A book on Blake's *Marriage of Heaven and Hell.*

AVOCATIONAL INTERESTS: Skiing, tennis, swimming (coach of a competitive A.A.U. swim team, 1969-78), genealogical research.

BIOGRAPHICAL/CRITICAL SOURCES:

PERIODICALS

Criticism, fall, 1968.
New York Review of Books, May 23, 1968.
South Atlantic Quarterly, autumn, 1968.
Times Literary Supplement, June 15, 1984.
Virginia Quarterly Review, summer, 1968.
Yale Review, spring, 1968.

* * *

GOLD, Herbert 1924-

PERSONAL: Born March 9, 1924, in Cleveland, Ohio; son of Samuel S. and Frieda (Frankel) Gold; married Edith Zubrin, April, 1948 (divorced, 1956); married Melissa Dilworth, January, 1968; children: (first marriage) Ann, Judith; (second marriage) Nina, Ari, Ethan. *Education:* Columbia University, B.A., 1946, M.A., 1948; Sorbonne, University of Paris, licence-es-lettres, 1951.

ADDRESSES: Home—1051-A Broadway, San Francisco, Calif. 94133.

CAREER: Full-time writer. Western Reserve University (now Case Western Reserve University), Cleveland, Ohio, lecturer in philosophy and literature, 1951-53; Wayne State University, Detroit, Mich., member of English department faculty, 1954-56; University of California, Davis, regents professor, 1973. Visiting professor, Cornell University, 1958, University of California, Berkeley, 1963 and 1968, Harvard University, 1964, and Stanford University, 1967. McGuffey Lecturer in English, Ohio University, 1971. *Military service:* U.S. Army Intelligence, 1943-46.

AWARDS, HONORS: Fulbright fellow at Sorbonne, University of Paris, 1950; Inter-American Cultural Relations grant to Haiti, 1954; *Hudson Review* fellow, 1956; Guggenheim fellow, 1957; Ohioana Book Award, 1957, for *The Man Who Was Not with It;* National Institute of Arts and Letters grant in literature, 1958; Longview Foundation Award, 1959; Ford Foundation theatre fellow, 1960; California Literature Medal Award, 1968, for *Fathers: A Novel in the Form of a Memoir.*

WRITINGS:

NOVELS

Birth of a Hero, Viking, 1951.
The Prospect before Us, World Publishing, 1954, published as *Room Clerk*, New American Library, 1955.
The Man Who Was Not with It, Little, Brown, 1956, published as *The Wild Life*, Permabooks, 1957.
The Optimist, Little, Brown, 1959.
Therefore Be Bold, Dial, 1960.
Salt, Dial, 1963.

Fathers: A Novel in the Form of a Memoir, Random House, 1967, reprinted, Arbor House, 1983.
The Great American Jackpot, Random House, 1969.
Biafra Goodbye, Twowindows Press, 1970.
My Last Two Thousand Years, Random House, 1972.
Swiftie the Magician, McGraw, 1974.
Waiting for Cordelia, Arbor House, 1977.
Slave Trade, Arbor House, 1979.
He/She, Arbor House, 1980.
Family: A Novel in the Form of a Memoir, Arbor House, 1981.
True Love, Arbor House, 1982.
Mister White Eyes, Arbor House, 1984.

STORY COLLECTIONS

(With R. V. Cassill and James B. Hall) *15 x 3*, New Directions, 1957.
Love & Like, Dial, 1960.
The Magic Will: Stories and Essays of a Decade, Random House, 1971.
Stories of Misbegotten Love (bound with *Angel on My Shoulder and Other Stories* by Don Asher), Capra, 1985.

NONFICTION

The Age of Happy Problems, Dial, 1962.
A Walk on the West Side: California on the Brink, Arbor House, 1981.

EDITOR

Fiction of the Fifties: A Decade of American Writing, Doubleday, 1959.
(With David L. Stevenson) *Stories of Modern America*, St. Martin's, 1961.
First Person Singular: Essays for the Sixties, Dial, 1963.

CONTRIBUTOR

Granville Hicks, editor, *The Living Novel*, Macmillan, 1957.
Bob Booker and George Foster, editors, *Pardon Me, Sir, but Is My Eye Hurting Your Elbow?*, Geis, 1968.

Work appears in *O. Henry Prize Stories*, 1954.

JUVENILE

The Young Prince and the Magic Cone, Doubleday, 1973.

OTHER

Contributor to *Atlantic, Playboy, New York Times Book Review, Hudson Review, Harper's, Esquire, Partisan Review,* and other publications.

WORK IN PROGRESS: A Girl of Forty; Lovers and Cohorts: Collected Stories.

SIDELIGHTS: Herbert Gold is considered one of the foremost literary chroniclers of life in modern America. His successful evocation of specific settings, the insight he shows in the presentation of personal relationships, and his skill at creating characters have been praised by many critics. Robert G. Kaiser of the *Washington Post Book World*, commenting on the realism of Gold's fiction, goes so far as to suggest including Gold's books in a time capsule so that our descendants can see clearly how people of our time actually lived. Gold, Kaiser continues, "is a gifted reporter, a writer whose characters' dilemmas are rooted in a precise cultural moment that Gold evokes supremely well."

Although his early novels are set in his native midwest, much of Gold's fiction since the 1960s is set in California, where he has lived for many years. His depictions of that state are considered to be especially accurate. Not only does Gold know California, Bruce Cook reports in the *Detroit News*, "but more important, he manages as few do to get it down on paper." Gold "is forever uncovering the latest totems and odd social byways of the Pacific shore," Peter Andrews of the *New York Times Book Review* reports, "and writing about them with grace and humor." Brook Landon of the *Dictionary of Literary Biography* agrees, calling Gold "among those American novelists and essayists best attuned to life in California."

In addition to his skill at evoking a California setting, Gold also possesses an insight into "the agonizing dynamics of contemporary male-female relationships," Landon asserts. This is evident, Landon believes, in Gold's continuing concern with the "breakdown of marriage as an American institution." In *Slave Trade,* for example, the detective Sid Kasdan is hired by an international group that supplies young Haitian boys to homosexual men in America and Europe. At first he works for the group, escorting the boys from Haiti to their buyers. But when he is to deliver a boy to a sadistic veterinarian with murderous plans, Kasdan balks. He frees the boy and takes him back to Haiti. Throughout his association with the slavers, Kasdan has been so obsessed with his ex-wife that he is insulated from the suffering around him. His own sorrow blinds him to the sorrow of others. But when he returns the boy to Haiti he finds that his former wife now works for the slavers. They kill the boy and at novel's end, Kasdan is negotiating with them for his own life. As Landon explains, Kasdan has been "a slave to the memory of his former wife [and] essentially a man paralyzed by divorce."

In *He/She*, Gold tells the story of an unnamed couple ("he" and "she") in the midst of a divorce. "She wants a life of 'unboredom,'" Anatole Broyard explains in the *New York Times*, "and her nameless husband wants their marriage to be 'a festival.'" His love for her is not the kind of love she needs. She is bored with him, but he doesn't know what the problem is. When she divorces him and lives with another man, he is heartbroken. She explains to him, Broyard writes, "that everybody's heart is broken." But after a time they become lovers. "The book is about the tenacity of relationships," Larry McMurtry writes in the *New York Times Book Review*, "as expressed in the breakup of one marriage; the impersonal nature of the tenacity is underscored by the use of pronouns instead of names." Admitting that the premise of the novel is "a slender hinge on which to hang a narrative," Cyra McFadden of the *Chicago Tribune Book World* nonetheless finds that "Gold makes of this marriage, and what becomes of it, a book that is suspenseful, touching, and sometimes darkly funny."

Throughout Gold's work he shows an understanding and sympathy for his characters and their problems. He expresses in *The Man Who Was Not with It* "a deep compassion for human suffering and bewilderment," writes W. L. Greesham in the *New York Times Book Review.* Speaking of *Fathers: A Novel in the Form of a Memoir,* Theodore Solotaroff of *Book Week* cites the strongest element in the novel as "Gold's feeling for his father." Gold argues for perseverance in the face of life's hardships. As Ihab Hassan states in *Radical Innocence: Studies in the Contemporary American Novel,* "the need to bounce with life, to take risks with its incompleteness, to celebrate the 'tin and hope' of human existence, knowing all that while that reality may be its own end . . . or, less frequently, that ambition contains its own death . . .—these are the primary concerns of Herbert Gold."

These themes are explored by Gold in a variety of styles and settings and through a wide assortment of characters. *The Prospect before Us,* for example, concerns an old hotel for the destitute whose manager comes under fire for renting a room to a black woman. In *The Man Who Was Not with It,* Gold writes of a carnival worker who is a drug addict. *Therefore Be Bold* tells the story of a young couple in 1950s Cleveland whose romance is doomed by her father's resistance. In *Fathers,* Gold draws upon his own family for inspiration, contrasting his father's generation of Jewish immigrants with his own generation.

These diverse and sometimes unsavory characters come alive because Gold is particularly adept at accurately capturing their speech patterns, whatever their social backgrounds may be. "He has a sensitivity for the nuances of speech," Harry T. Moore observes in his *Contemporary American Novelists,* "and can frequently catch the precise accent, rhythms, and tone of dialogue and dialect." In *The Man Who Was Not with It,* for example, Gold uses carnival jargon to tell his story. "He shows its tricks of insincerity, an important part of the story," Moore writes, "but also displays its force in expressing the deepest feelings of the people who speak it." Discussing *The Prospect before Us* in *Literary Horizons: A Quarter Century of American Fiction,* Granville Hicks praises Gold's "mastery of a colloquial style. The dialogue is so perfect that it seems artless. . . . The effect is to immerse the reader in the garish world of [hotel manager] Harry Bowers."

A constant factor in all of Gold's work is "his love of wordplay," George Jensen writes in the *Dictionary of Literary Biography.* Gold's wordplay, Jensen continues, "has been cited as his greatest accomplishment as a fiction writer and his greatest defect." This trait is a defect, Jensen explains, because it "is too unusual and too present to ignore; the fate of his novels rests with the acceptance or rejection of his style." Hicks acknowledges Gold's Joycean style, seeing it as a means of attaining "greater freedom and freshness in the use of words, not for the sake of shocking the reader but in order to rouse him out of lethargy in order to compel him to see more clearly and feel more strongly."

In novels where the language of his characters is colorful, Gold's style seems to be most successful. *Fathers,* for example, with its Yiddish speech, is suited to Gold's style. David J. Gordon of *Yale Review* thinks "Gold's virtues are more solidly present [in *Fathers*] than in his earlier novels. One reason may be that the constantly colorful idiom he seems to require is, in part, justified dramatically by the Yiddish-English speech of the parents. Another reason may be that his subject touches a deeper layer of feeling." In like terms *The Man Who Was Not with It,* with its carnival slang, gives Gold the opportunity to "handle colorful idiom," writes Moore, who believes, "it crackles. But the language isn't flashed just for its own sake. . . . Gold's tendency toward the bizarre in style exactly matches the subject matter in this book."

Many of Gold's talents seem to be most effective when he deals primarily in autobiographical material. Though elements of his life appear in several of his books—his divorce, childhood in Cleveland, and work as a hotel manager, for example—Gold deals directly with his life only in three novels: *Fathers, My Last Two Thousand Years,* and *Family: A Novel in the Form of a Memoir.* The first of these focuses on Gold's relationship with his father and contrasts his father's generation, and the many problems they overcame, with Gold's own generation, who had far fewer difficulties in life. *My Last Two*

Thousand Years is an "autobiography-with-a-theme," as William Abrahams describes it in the *Saturday Review of Education.* In it, Gold recounts his life with special emphasis on those moments of peak importance. *Family* concentrates on the women of the Gold family, as *Fathers* deals with the men.

Fathers traces the life of Gold's father Samuel from Czarist Russia to Cleveland, where he owned a grocery store for many years. The conflict between the father, "a man of fact and commercial action, of will and property," as Robert Garis describes him in the *Hudson Review,* and the son, whose values are opposite to his father's, creates the dramatic tension of the story. Despite their differences, Gold is instructed by his father on how to enter into the adult world. His father's struggle over the years, so foreign to Gold, is at last reflected in his own life when his marriage ends in divorce. At that time, his father understands and helps him to overcome the pain. "Gold begins to learn," Jensen states, "how to survive in an unstable world."

My Last Two Thousand Years is an exploration of Jewish history, with Gold relating the history of his people to his personal history, attempting to find his rightful place in the world. "The interests of *My Last Two Thousand Years,*" Alvin H. Rosenfeld writes in *Midstream,* "are two-fold: as a critique of the literary life and with it most of the values of cultural Modernism, and as a discovery of a more central identity through an awakening to history." Thomas R. Edwards of the *New York Times Book Review* believes the autobiographical novel to be obsessed with "incidents that carry the theme of tribal discovery" rather than with the "necessary and interesting irrelevancies of a life." He does, however, find Gold's "account of his youth and early manhood . . . often quite wonderfully funny and poignant" and concludes that "Gold makes sense of his life."

As *Fathers* examined the men in Gold's family, *Family* looks at the women. It was titled *Family,* Gold explains to Cook, because "you can't call a book *Mothers* these days without being misunderstood." The novel, although essentially unstructured, revolves around Gold's mother, "as blazingly erratic and as trivial as a child's sparkler," Penelope Mesic writes in the *Chicago Tribune Book World.* Jerome Charyn agrees that Gold's mother is "the central force of the novel." Writing in the *New York Times Book Review,* Charyn finds that *Family* "exists almost as pure song. . . . It is an homage to the loving and bullying women around [Gold]." When the novel's fact and fiction blend well, Mesic notes, they "produce a literary alloy with the strength of truth and lightness of fiction." Cook judges *Fathers, My Last Two Thousand Years,* and *Family*—all of which combine autobiography and fiction—as Gold's "three best novels."

Gold's strengths as a fiction writer include, McFadden believes, "his talent for making high drama of ordinary events, ordinary experience." Similarly, Kenneth Turan of the *Washington Post Book World* lists Gold's "ability as an observer of the social scene, his eye for cultural detail and nuance" as one of his strengths. Gold's "writing style, smooth, seductive and sly, carefully constructed to pull the reader along with a minimum of strain" is another of his assets, Turan concludes. Charyn sees Gold's "particular strength" as "the intimacy of detail that he establishes between himself and the reader. . . . In his very best work, . . . he establishes a sad but powerful voice, the wound of isolation, that slow dying within and around us." Cook describes Gold, simply, as "one of the most gifted writers in America."

BIOGRAPHICAL/CRITICAL SOURCES:

BOOKS

Allen, Walter, editor, *The Modern Novel in Britain and the United States*, Dutton, 1965.

Balakian, Nona and Charles Simmons, editors, *The Creative Present*, Doubleday, 1963.

Contemporary Fiction in America and England, 1950-1970, Gale, 1976.

Contemporary Literary Criticism, Gale, Volume IV, 1975, Volume VII, 1977, Volume XIV, 1980.

Dictionary of Literary Biography, Volume II: *American Novelists since World War II*, Gale, 1978.

Dictionary of Literary Biography Yearbook: 1981, Gale, 1982.

Fiction!: Interviews with Northern California Novelists, Harcourt, 1976.

Hassan, Ihab, *Radical Innocence: Studies in the Contemporary American Novel*, Princeton University Press, 1961.

Hicks, Granville and Jack Alan Robbins, *Literary Horizons: A Quarter Century of American Fiction*, New York University Press, 1970.

Moore, Harry T., *Contemporary American Novelists*, Southern Illinois University Press, 1964.

Nemerov, Howard, *Poetry and Fiction: Essays by Howard Nemerov*, Rutgers University Press, 1963.

Newquist, Roy, *Counterpoint*, Simon & Schuster, 1964.

Solotaroff, Theodore, *The Red Hot Vacuum and Other Pieces on the Writing of the Sixties*, Atheneum, 1970.

Weinberg, Helen, *The New Novel in America: The Kafkan Mode in Contemporary Fiction*, Cornell University Press, 1970.

Widmer, Kingsley, *The Literary Rebel*, Southern Illinois University Press, 1965.

PERIODICALS

America, April 15, 1967.
Atlantic, April, 1956.
Best Sellers, June, 1979.
Books and Bookmen, February, 1968, October, 1974.
Book Week, April 9, 1967.
Chicago Tribune Book World, June 15, 1980, October 4, 1981.
Christian Science Monitor, March 23, 1967.
Columbia, summer, 1980.
Detroit News, April 12, 1981, June 14, 1981, September 27, 1981.
Figaro Litteraire, number 20, 1965.
Harper's, February, 1970, November, 1974.
Hudson Review, summer, 1967, winter, 1974-75.
Les Langues Modernes, number 58, 1964.
Life, April 7, 1967.
Listener, September 7, 1978.
Los Angeles Times, April 13, 1981.
Los Angeles Times Book Review, June 1, 1980, October 25, 1981, December 5, 1982, October 14, 1984.
Midstream, April, 1975.
Nation, October 6, 1951, June 23, 1956, April 25, 1959, July 3, 1967.
National Observer, March 27, 1967, March 2, 1970.
New Leader, May 22, 1967.
New Republic, June 17, 1967.
Newsweek, March 27, 1967, January 26, 1970, October 16, 1972.
New York Herald Tribune Book Review, March 27, 1960.
New York Review of Books, June 1, 1967, May 21, 1970.

New York Times, February 19, 1956, October 20, 1972, June 6, 1980, September 26, 1985.
New York Times Book Review, February 14, 1954, September 4, 1966, March 19, 1967, October 19, 1969, January 25, 1970, October 15, 1972, September 15, 1974, May 22, 1977, April 22, 1979, May 25, 1980, December 13, 1981, December 12, 1982, November 11, 1984.
Saturday Review, April 2, 1960, April 20, 1963, March 25, 1967, July 23, 1977.
Saturday Review of Education, November 11, 1972.
Spectator, August 12, 1978.
Time, March 31, 1967, October 16, 1972.
Virginia Quarterly Review, summer, 1970.
Vogue, April 1, 1967.
Washington Post Book World, June 3, 1979, June 15, 1980, January 8, 1983.
Writer's Digest, September, 1972.
Yale Review, autumn, 1967.

—*Sketch by Thomas Wiloch*

*   *   *

GOODMAN, Norman 1934-

PERSONAL: Born February 19, 1934, in New York, N.Y.; son of Jack and Hannah (Hoffman) Goodman; married Marilyn Goldberg (a teacher), December 26, 1954; children: Jack, Susan Andrea, Carolyn Wendy. *Education:* Brooklyn College (now Brooklyn College of the City University of New York), B.A., 1955; New York University, M.A., 1961, Ph.D., 1963.

ADDRESSES: Home—4 Skylark Lane, Stony Brook, N.Y. 11790. *Office*—Department of Sociology, State University of New York at Stony Brook, Stony Brook, N.Y. 11794-4356.

CAREER: New York Department of Welfare, New York City, social investigator, 1957-58; Russell Sage Foundation, New York City, research assistant, 1958-60; Association for the Aid of Crippled Children (now Foundation for Child Development), New York City, research assistant, 1958-61; Columbia University, Teachers College, New York City, instructor in sociology, 1961-62; Queens College of the City University of New York, Flushing, N.Y., lecturer, 1962-63, assistant professor of sociology, 1963-64; State University of New York at Stony Brook, assistant professor, 1964-68, associate professor, 1968-73, professor of sociology and chairman of department, 1973—, assistant dean of Graduate School, 1966-67. Visiting scholar, London School of Economics and Political Science, 1970-71, 1978-79, and 1985-86. Reviewer, National Science Foundation, 1975-76, and Social Science and Humanities Research Council of Canada, 1981-83; manuscript reviewer for publishing companies, including Random House, Prentice-Hall, and Rand McNally, 1970—. Member or past member of numerous government committees and commissions. Has presented papers throughout the U.S. *Military service:* U.S. Army, 1955-56.

MEMBER: American Association of University Professors, American Sociological Association (member of committee on regulation of research, 1983-86), Society for the Study of Symbolic Interaction, Council on Family Relations, Society for Research in Child Development, Eastern Sociological Society (member of Candace Rogers Award committee, 1980-81, and committee on undergraduate education, 1984-87), Alpha Kappa Delta.

AWARDS, HONORS: Bobbs-Merrill Award in sociology, New York University, 1963; Founders Day Award, New York University, 1963, for excellence in scholarship; National Institute of Mental Health special research fellowship, 1970, to London School of Economics and Political Science; Chancellor's Award, State University of New York, 1975-76, for excellence in teaching; Student Life Award, State University of New York at Stony Brook, Student Affairs Division, 1984.

WRITINGS:

An Evaluation of the Eighth World Congress of the International Society for the Rehabilitation of the Disabled, International Society for the Rehabilitation of the Disabled, 1961.

(With Orville G. Brim, Jr., David C. Glass, and David E. Lavin) *Personality and Decision Process: Studies in the Social Psychology of Thinking,* Stanford University Press, 1962, reprinted, 1978.

(Contributor) Helmut Strasser, editor, *Fortshritte der Heilpedagogik,* Carl Marhold, 1968.

(Contributor) Billy J. Franklin and Frank J. Kohout, editors, *Social Psychology and Everyday Life,* McKay, 1973.

(Contributor) Glen H. Elder, Jr., and Sigmund E. Dragastin, editors, *Adolescence in the Life Cycle: Psychological Change and Social Context,* Hemisphere Publishing, 1975.

(With Gary T. Marx) *Society Today,* 3rd edition, Random House, 1978, 4th edition, 1982.

(Editor with Marx) *Sociology: Classic and Popular Approaches,* Random House, 1980.

(With Gary S. Belkin) *Marriage, Family, and Intimate Relationships,* Rand McNally, 1980.

(Contributor with others) Walter W. Powell and Richard Robbins, editors, *Conflict and Consensus: Essays in Honor of Lewis A. Coser,* Free Press, 1984.

(Contributor) Harvey A. Farberman and Robert Perinbanayagam, editors, *The Foundations of Interpretive Sociology: Original Essays in Symbolic Interaction,* JAI Press, 1985.

(With Belkin) *Marriage and Family, Today and Tomorrow,* Random House, in press.

Also contributor, Farberman, editor, *Social Psychology: An Introduction to Symbolic Interaction,* Harper. Contributor to numerous journals, including *American Sociological Review, Social Interaction, Journal of Social Psychology,* and *Journal of Advertising Research.* Advisory editor, *Symbolic Interaction,* 1980-82.

WORK IN PROGRESS: Research in the effects of various educational programs in family day care; research in social psychology, courtship and marriage, socialization of children and youth, identity formation and maintenance, and communication processes.

*   *   *

GOODPASTER, Kenneth E(dwin) 1944-

PERSONAL: Born October 11, 1944, in Chicago, Ill.; son of Vincent Kendall (in business) and Irene (Michalik) Goodpaster; married Harriet Houk (a software engineer), May 24, 1969; children: Elizabeth, John. *Education:* University of Notre Dame, A.B., 1967; University of Michigan, A.M., 1969, Ph.D., 1973. *Religion:* Roman Catholic.

ADDRESSES: Office—Graduate School of Business Administration, Harvard University, Boston, Mass. 02163.

CAREER: University of Notre Dame, Notre Dame, Ind., assistant professor of philosophy, 1973-80; Harvard University,

Boston, Mass., associate professor of business administration, 1980—.

MEMBER: American Philosophical Association.

AWARDS, HONORS: Woodrow Wilson fellow, 1967-68; distinguished scholar in residence at Southern Methodist University, March, 1985.

WRITINGS:

(Editor) *Perspectives on Morality,* University of Notre Dame Press, 1976.

(Editor) *Ethics and Problems of the Twenty-First Century,* University of Notre Dame Press, 1979.

(With K. M. Sayre, E. L. Maher, and others) *Values, Regulation, and the Public Interest,* University of Notre Dame Press, 1980.

Ethics in Management, Harvard Business School, Division of Research, 1984.

(With J. Matthews and L. Nash) *Policies and Persons: A Casebook in Business Ethics,* McGraw, 1985.

Contributor of articles to professional journals.

WORK IN PROGRESS: A monograph on ethical theory and its relation to corporate ethics.

SIDELIGHTS: Kenneth E. Goodpaster commented to *CA:* "My main professional interests are theoretical and applied ethics, corporate ethics, environmental ethics, and the application of ethics to energy policy. I am convinced that moral philosophy must make itself accessible to areas of major decision making in our society. For too long, philosophy has been tied to pure theory."

AVOCATIONAL INTERESTS: The game of Go.

*   *   *

GORDON, Barbara 1935-

PERSONAL: Born in 1935, in Miami, Fla.; divorced. *Education:* Attended Vassar College and Barnard College.

ADDRESSES: Home—New York City. *Agent*—Morton Janklow Associates, 598 Madison Ave., New York, N.Y. 10022.

CAREER: WCBS-TV, New York, N.Y., writer and producer of documentary films for "Eye On" series, including "Limbo People," "Superlandlord—Who Owns This Town?," and "Reading, Writing and Recruiting"; free-lance writer. Has written and produced films for National Broadcasting Co. (NBC-TV) and Public Television and contributed to television programs, including "The Great American Dream Machine" and "NET Journal." Produced "Victor Marchetti vs. United States of America," a one-hour special film for "The Fifty-First State" series. Has produced films on Jane Fonda, Studs Terkel, Jason Robards, Earl Warren, Jose Quintero, Colleen Dewhurst, Dalton Trumbo, and many other celebrities.

AWARDS, HONORS: Received two Emmy awards from National Academy of Arts and Sciences; received a number of awards for films in WCBS-TV "Eye On" series; *I'm Dancing as Fast as I Can* was nominated for an American Book Award, 1979.

WRITINGS:

I'm Dancing as Fast as I Can (Literary Guild alternate selection), Harper, 1979.
Defects of the Heart, Harper, 1982.

WORK IN PROGRESS: A third book.

SIDELIGHTS: In her autobiographical work, *I'm Dancing as Fast as I Can,* Barbara Gordon tells about her breakdown after attempting to quit Valium without assistance and her subsequent recovery. In a letter to *CA,* Gordon indicates that her book is not only about drug addiction and survival but also about "starting over, a book in which Valium was the metaphor for something outside of myself that I needed to feel whole."

Gordon began taking Valium for pain from a back injury; she resumed the drug when going through a divorce. Ten years later, as a highly respected television documentary producer with several awards to her credit, she seemed to have a rich, full life but was still taking the drug at a prescribed daily dosage that had increased over the years from five to thirty milligrams. Despite the Valium, Gordon was experiencing panic attacks at the thought of simply going out to lunch or shopping in a crowded department store, even though she had always considered herself an adventurous person.

The writer finally became determined to face her anxiety without pills. Her psychiatrist advised her to quit Valium all at once, rather than gradually decreasing the dosage as is generally recommended. The resulting symptoms included chronic insomnia, convulsions, and hallucinations, a "roaring withdrawal reaction," as Leon Gussow calls it in the *Chicago Tribune Book World.* "After the initial convulsions, all the terrors that years of tranquilizers had suppressed overwhelmed her," Gussow writes. During her subsequent mental and physical deterioration, Gordon writes in *I'm Dancing as Fast as I Can,* her then live-in boyfriend discouraged her from seeking help and became abusive. She eventually required two hospitalizations and the assistance of several psychiatrists before she could return to a new life.

After her release from the hospital, Gordon sought her old job at CBS. Not immediately successful, she began to write her story, including her impressions of the mental health profession and an account of her own analysis. As Gordon relates in *I'm Dancing as Fast as I Can,* "there I was, an ex-mental patient with no job. I didn't know what to do, so I sat down at the typewriter. I felt compelled to make myself understand who I was and where I had been." "At first," she writes, "I had no wish to tell anyone what had happened to me. I have always despaired of people who look for private salvation in the public marketplace. My book began as something to do when I got out of the hospital, something to help me process the overload of data that I had gathered about myself. . . . I had to clean the air, my air. And if along the way I could unfog someone else's atmosphere, that would be my dividend, my reward."

The author had another concern, she says in the book. "It was my realization that almost everyone I met in the hospital had been a patient of a psychiatrist outside, and that they all had taken large amounts of mind-altering drugs, generally on the advice and with the consent of their doctors. . . . They are drugs that can be anesthetics of the emotions. And their sudden withdrawal can precipitate psychosis or worse. Because of my strong feelings about medical mismanagement, because of the prevalence of drug-abuse—and the soft-core prescription-pad variety is drug abuse all the same—I felt I had to tell my story."

Apart from the issue of prescription drugs, Gordon had difficulty finding compatible psychiatric help; she feels that a patient should take the time to shop for a good psychiatrist. People "must fight for their own health care," she indicates in *I'm Dancing as Fast as I Can.* "They should say they don't want to be treated like some submissive junkie. . . . The profession needs a Ralph Nader. We give more thought to buying a car or winter coat than shopping for the right doctor."

I'm Dancing as Fast as I Can was generally praised by reviewers, although some found the author lacking in technical knowledge. Gordon "praises as she pans," Suzanne Fields says in the *Washington Post,* indicating that although Gordon writes humorously and vividly, "her powerful narrative suffers from her own limits of understanding." Gordon describes how her addiction is not surprising in view of the state of medical practice, but she "draws no distinctions," according to Fields, in the use of prescription drugs or in their benefits or side effects. And *Times Literary Supplement* reviewer Stuart Sutherland views the work in a similar light, writing that Gordon "believes that psychotropic drugs merely mask symptoms and may actually prevent patients from confronting their own emotions, which may be necessary for a proper recovery, but she fails to distinguish between different drugs and different mental disorders."

According to a *West Coast Review of Books* critic, who says that the book "is written straight out, with guts and determination," *I'm Dancing as Fast as I Can* "will stay with you, for it is a picture of mental illness unlike any that has come before. There is warmth here too—the support of [Gordon's] family and close friends, of a caring young woman psychologist, and of pathetic fellow-patients." Kay Larrieu reports in *Best Sellers:* "To her credit, Ms. Gordon never victimizes herself. She frankly reveals parts of her background with which she had come to grips, all the time acknowledging her limitations and shortcomings." Gordon "shows precisely what it is like to be in a mental institution: the way that life becomes one's only reality; the terror of moving out into the other world in new, tender skin," writes *New York Times Book Review* contributor Jill Robinson. Moreover, Gordon tells *CA,* the book appeals to a general audience: After reading *I'm Dancing as Fast as I Can* "hundreds of people who had never taken a pill in their life" wrote her that they found the book meaningful. Robinson concludes that *I'm Dancing as Fast as I Can* "is a genuine offering: it hides nothing, yet is not exploitive."

Gordon discusses a similar subject in *Defects of the Heart,* a novel in which she also draws upon the knowledge she gained during her years as a documentary film producer. The book's heroine is attempting to make a film about a pharmaceutical company's marketing of a drug that reportedly causes birth defects, but her efforts are frustrated by the station owner. And the people she tracks down and interviews "dramatically affect her own life," Gordon comments in the *Library Journal.* Critics are less enthusiastic about this book than *I'm Dancing as Fast as I Can,* but a *Chicago Tribune Book World* reviewer concludes that *Defects of the Heart* is "a good read, ending not with forever afters, but with possibilities."

MEDIA ADAPTATIONS: I'm Dancing as Fast as I Can was produced as a motion picture by Paramount Pictures.

CA INTERVIEW

CA interviewed Barbara Gordon by telephone on March 22, 1985, at her home in New York, New York.

CA: After living through the ordeal that resulted from your going off Valium cold turkey, you sat down and wrote about it in I'm Dancing as Fast as I Can. *Wasn't it difficult to relive the experience through the writing?*

GORDON: The typewriter had always been my safe place, even as a child. And even though I had never written a book before, I did work as a writer in television for a number of years, in the documentary world. When I got out of the hospital and my old work as a documentary film writer and producer wasn't available to me—for all kinds of reasons, probably having partly to do with the stigma of having the word out that I had been mentally ill, or in *that kind* of a place—I began writing as a way of organizing what had happened to me. And no, at that time it was not painful. It was a way of sorting out, and rather than reliving, a way of feeling, refeeling, and then distancing and creatively making use out of what had happened to me. I never thought it would be a book that anybody would buy, let alone a bestseller. I didn't write it to be a bestseller. I wrote it just as honestly as I could. It was difficult sometimes when the editor would say to me, "You'd better do that chapter again." Here I was writing stuff over again that had happened to me, and I wished it were a novel. But in the long run, the writing of the book had more pluses than minuses for me, in so many ways.

CA: Was the book an immediate success?

GORDON: It was. It was almost a success before it was published. The Literary Guild had made it an alternate selection long before publication date; Bantam had put in a bid for it long before publication; the movie—no matter how they trashed it—was sold long before publication date. And a few weeks after publication, when I began to tour, it hit the bestseller list. There were a lot of people behind the book. Booksellers felt very strongly about it, and the book became many people's favorite that season. Whether they had suffered from depression or not, or had had a mucked-up psychiatric experience or not, or had had an abusive man in their lives or not, people felt very keenly identified with the book in some way. "My childhood," they wrote me; "my mother"; "my dream," or whatever. And more important than the bestseller list is to have people tell you how you spoke to their inner self that had made them feel so alone for so long.

CA: You must have heard from a lot of people who were taking Valium or some other drug and wanted your advice.

GORDON: I heard from people who had never taken a pill in their lives, who wanted to say how I had spoken to things they had feared or wished or experienced, and then I heard from people who had themselves or had relatives who had been victims of over-prescribed or mis-prescribed drugs or who had been victims of rotten medicine in general. I really refused to play the part of the evangelical about anything—taking pills, not taking pills. I only gave advice to the extent of saying that we must be ombudsmen of our own health care. Women enter a doctor's office more frequently than men, by the statistics; men just don't go to doctors as often as we do, for all kinds of societal and psychological and cultural reasons. I urged people not to be as docile and passive as I was. Here I was, a woman who was inquiring and creative and investigatory and cynical with her television cameras and typewriter when it came to institutions of government that weren't serving the oppressed in society, but when it came to my personal life, I was strangely unquestioning. It was that chord that got as many letters as the Valium issue, not only across the country,

but all over Europe, because the book has been published in ten languages.

CA: All of us women who grew up before the '60s learned early to let other people tell us what to do.

GORDON: Absolutely! And doctors were gods. They were all Dr. Kildare and Marcus Welby. I lecture across the country about twelve times a year, and when I say this, people laugh. But it's true. In my house, doctors were saints.

CA: Was there ever any response from the psychiatrist who gave you the bad advice?

GORDON: No. He's still practicing medicine—his brand of medicine.

CA: As a documentary producer for television, you were accustomed to working with other people and under pressure. Writing, as you and other writers have said, is lonely work. How do you deal with that aspect of it?

GORDON: Sometimes I deal with it very well. Joan Didion has a phrase that I often use: "Writing makes order out of disorder." That's not just the pile of papers on your desk; it means out of internal disorder. Writing has always been the safe place for me. But sometimes I miss the communality—the editing room, the associate producer, the research, the camera crew. In writing, you have to be all of it. You have to be the sound, the lights, the camera. Sometimes I manage it well, particularly if I know I'm replenishing myself at the end of the day with good friends or a movie or a concert. The other night I went over to see the Matisse and Rousseau exhibits at the Museum of Modern Art, which is a few blocks from my house. You need to replenish yourself, because writing is giving in one way or another; it empties you—at least the kind of writing that I respond to, and the kind of writing that I write. It is lonely.

CA: You've said the psychiatric profession needs its own Ralph Nader. With the publicity from your first book and the movie, and the publication of more books on prescription drugs, do you think the profession is beginning to police itself?

GORDON: A little bit, from what people tell me. I got so many letters from medical students and interns and residents and psychiatric nurses who read the book and who said, boy, am I going to be mindful, after reading this, of how easy it is to become that other kind of doctor, that other kind of health-care professional. There are some indications that doctors are sedating their patients less than they were, but the main reason it's happening is not because of anything within the profession—although I tend to think the younger generation of doctors is going to be more sensitive to these issues. Ted Kennedy had hearings on the Hill about tranquilizer abuse; there are other books aside from mine. It's really coming from the people themselves. The men and women who go to a health club on their lunch hour and do an hour of aerobic dancing and eat alfalfa sprouts and yogurt are much less likely to have a three-martini lunch or to abuse themselves with a chemical without questioning what that chemical is doing to their bodies. So I really think the change is coming. We, for the first time in America—at least on this issue and possibly on others that I'm not aware of—are educating the health-care professionals that we are not going to take it anymore. We're not lazy, docile, bovine creatures. We are willing to take a shared responsiblity in our own health care. I'm happy to have been a part of this enlightenment of the American people about how to be a patient.

CA: How would you advise somebody to go about the difficult job of finding the right psychiatrist or psychologist?

GORDON: You have to audition them. Americans spend more time buying a car that doesn't guzzle gasoline, or a new winter coat, than they do in choosing somebody they're going to entrust their bodies and their psyches to, who with that arsenal of prescription drugs can alter them irrevocably, and not always for the good. We have to learn not to be lazy and not to treat any profession as gods. Doctors aren't angels and they're not demons. They're just human beings, and we're all muddling through this together. I think many of them will tell you that.

CA: Were you at all involved in the movie at the end?

GORDON: No.

CA: So much that was important to the book, to the true story, was left out of the movie.

GORDON: Not only was there so much left out, but there was this cold lady, this cold anti-heroine who went off the pills *despite* the doctor's advice not to, which was exactly the opposite of what really happened. Furthermore, there was no poet; there was a woman mayor who died of pancreatic cancer, who helped change Barbara Gordon's life. They had a loving relationship. They didn't have that fight. Barbara Gordon had a slew of wonderful friends around her in real life. She had a little love affair in the hospital with a young man who helped her feel her soul again. In the movie, everything human and warm and funny was gone. But Hollywood has always had its own world view, and I'm not the first writer or the last who's had her work violated. There are writers in writers' heaven with much bigger names than mine who had it done to them long before me. I just joined the ranks. Of course, here I am talking very philosophically about it now. At the time, I was furious. I felt violated and raped. No, I had nothing to do with that movie. And happily it failed. Here I was in the weird position of rooting for the failure of my own movie!

CA: With Defects of the Heart, *published in 1983, you became a novelist. What was it like going from autobiography to fiction?*

GORDON: That was terrifying in one respect. I had always been a reality journalist. For twenty years I had taken my cameras and my tape recorders into other people's lives. They wrote the script, and I put it together in some kind of meaningful and, I hope, feeling way. With the novel, I was playing God with people's lives—what they could do and what they couldn't do, what they did do and what they didn't do, and if they fell in love and if they quit, and how they felt. I was used to being more a reflector, and so at first it felt a little fascistic! Then I got past that, plus the usual terror that writers and agents tell me every writer has who's had a first success—what's called the second-book syndrome. You have the feeling that you know America very well, and what is America? It's a country that loves to make heroes and heroines and loves to destroy them. I'd seen it all my life, and I did not think I was exempt. Again I'm speaking from the wonderful vantage of twenty-twenty hindsight. My agent said to me as I was work-

ing my way through it, "Barbara, remember one thing: you're never going to have to write a second book again." Now I'm just finishing the outline and the first three chapters of the third book, and, believe me, it's much easier.

CA: Was your experience in television production a help in any way? Are there similarities?

GORDON: I think in one regard it was a help. The creative process is the creative process. And I love it. I would be lost and diminished without it as part of my life, whether it's on film, whether it's the picture part or the word, and whether you're starting with white paper or raw film stock and raw audio tape. The difference, of course, in writing is that you have to be all those things I said: you're the sound person, you're the music person, you're the effects person, you're the sound mixer. It was a help in that I was a creative person going into it. But they're very, very different, and the biggest difference is the absolute isolation of writing. Until you turn those chapters in and you get feedback from your editor, you don't know who you are—at least I don't.

CA: You lose all those other pairs of eyes.

GORDON: Boy, do you ever! I have a lot of girl friends who are part of writers' groups. They read each other's work and help each other. That's all over the city, and I gather it's everywhere. I have one or two people now that I do that with— one person in particular, whose sensibility and humor and brilliance I trust. She thinks like me, but she has the objectivity I don't have about my own work. And I do that for her. That way you can get a little bit of feedback before you go in to your publisher with all those pages.

CA: Are you doing any documentaries now?

GORDON: No, I'm not. I'm writing full time.

CA: When you did them, did you work from any kind of script at all?

GORDON: No. The best documentaries, I think—and there are some people in the documentary field who share my view— always require the fewest words in the script. In an ideal documentary, the people you're doing the story about should tell the story. They can tell it better than you can. But the documentary is fast becoming the dinosaur of television. Everything is a magazine show. The people who show documentaries now often want to use them to put their news people to good advantage, give them a good showcase. So they want more narration. They want to tell the American people, this is what you're going to see, and then show it to them. And then tell them what they've just seen. It's the opposite of any type of creative sensibility. Then you get into the whole thing of creativity versus journalism versus pandering. If I can write and touch people, that's what I want to do. Also, isn't there something delicious about having another career in the middle of your life? I love that.

CA: Even if you hadn't said so in your first book, it would still be obvious that you love New York very much.

GORDON: Yeah, but I think New York is a brat of a town. We pay a real price for living here. After I wrote *Dancing,* I was put in the rare position of traveling around this country about three times on publicity tours, and then again for *De-*

fects. And now with the lecturing, I really see other parts of this country that I would never see otherwise. Most people are either bi-coastal or nowhere in between. But when you lecture you go to places like Iowa and Idaho and Kansas. We do pay a price. I come back and look at New York and I love the energy and the museums, and I thrive on being in this town where so much is happening and that has drawn so many interesting people who have come here to make their fortune. I love what's here, and I do take advantage of all of it. But there are days when I walk down the street and I look up and I can't see the sky because of all the overbuilding the people have permitted to obliterate our sky. And there is no space. People brush past you and hit you with their elbows to make their way down the street and they don't say excuse me. Some people are rather shocked to hear that I've lived here for thirty years; they say I sound like I just came from Ohio, because I so resent the alienating, dehumanizing aspects of it. I love it even so. But I'm so grateful that I get away from it as much as I do.

CA: Do you need the city to write, or is it necessary to have both the city and the getting away?

GORDON: Maybe you need both. To be here all the time and subject to the lack of sky, the congested air, and when you walk out to get a newspaper, being pushed down the street—not every street; certainly there are balmy, quiet streets on the Upper East Side—that's hard. I don't need the city to write. I've written in other cities as well. I had chapters to do when I was going to be away in Florida visiting my family, and I brought my portable typewriter and worked on both *Dancing* and *Defects*. Or California, where I wrote a lot of *Defects*. But I think I tend to feel very lost without New York if I'm away too long.

CA: What kinds of groups do you lecture to?

GORDON: Universities, civic groups, mental health groups, some writers' groups, the Junior League of Rockville, Illinois, this spring. So it's different; it changes.

CA: And you enjoy it?

GORDON: I love it. I get feedback and I meet people I would never meet at my typewriter. I get to learn a little more about the country I live in, how people feel about things. And I get to see new places, which I adore. I have the most startling conversations with people in Omaha or Nebraska. The people on both coasts, whether they know it consciously or not, have a certain type of elitism or specialness that really doesn't pertain. I'm going to a place in Alabama that I have to take four planes to get to. I love lecturing because it is so vastly different—from my friends, from my typewriter. I can't tell you how enriched I am when I come back from these trips.

CA: What kind of writing schedule do you keep?

GORDON: I am very, very good in the morning and late at night. Something in the afternoon is not good for me; that's when I go do all my errands. The best part about this city for me is when it's very early and very quiet. I take two- or three-mile walks and I think about the problems that are happening in the writing, how to handle this or that. I'm looking in the windows and it's quiet and the city is just waking up and there's no congestion—I love all of that. I feel the energy of the city, and it keeps me centered. I had never been a great

walker before, and those anxiety attacks toward the end of my illness were so crushing I couldn't walk two blocks without being phobic. Now I walk two, three, four miles. Travelin' light, travelin' free—no pills, and it's wonderful!

BIOGRAPHICAL/CRITICAL SOURCES:

BOOKS

Gordon, Barbara, *I'm Dancing as Fast as I Can*, Harper, 1979.
Holden, Anton, *Prince Valium*, Stein & Day, 1982.

PERIODICALS

Best Sellers, July, 1979.
Chicago Tribune Book World, August 12, 1979, January 8, 1984.
Detroit Free Press, September 17, 1979.
Library Journal, February 1, 1983.
Los Angeles Times, March 4, 1982.
Los Angeles Times Book Review, July 24, 1983.
New York Times, March 5, 1982.
New York Times Book Review, July 1, 1979, August 5, 1979, July 3, 1983.
People, June 18, 1979
Saturday Review, July, 1983.
Times (London), March 27, 1980.
Times Literary Supplement, May 16, 1980.
Washington Post, May 28, 1979.
West Coast Review of Books, July, 1979.

—*Sketch by Candace Cloutier*
—*Interview by Jean W. Ross*

*   *   *

GOUDIE, Andrew Shaw   1945-

PERSONAL: Born August 21, 1945, in Cheltenham, England; son of William (a pharmacist) and Mary (Pulman) Goudie. *Education:* Trinity Hall, Cambridge, B.A., 1970, Ph.D., 1971. *Religion:* Christian.

ADDRESSES: Home—9 Hayfield Rd., Oxford, England. *Office*—School of Geography, Oxford University, Mansfield Rd., Oxford, England.

CAREER: Oxford University, St. Edmund Hall and Hertford College, Oxford, England, lecturer and demonstrator in geography, 1970-76, fellow of Hertford College, 1976—, professor of geography, 1984—. Honorary secretary, Royal Geographical Society.

MEMBER: Geographical Club, Institute of British Geographers, British Geomorphological Research Group.

WRITINGS:

Duricrusts of Tropical and Sub-Tropical Landscapes, Clarendon Press, 1973.
Environmental Change, Clarendon Press, 1977.
The Warm Desert Environment, Cambridge University Press, 1977.
The Prehistory and Paleo-geography of the Great Indian Desert, Academic Press, 1978.
The Human Impact, Basil Blackwell, 1981.
Geomorphological Techniques, Allen & Unwin, 1981.
Chemical Sediments and Geomorphology, Academic Press, 1983.
The Nature of the Environment, Basil Blackwell, 1984.
Discovering Landscape in England and Wales, Allen & Unwin, 1985.

Contributor to professional journals.

WORK IN PROGRESS: Research on the landforms and history of deserts.

*   *   *

GOULDNER, Alvin W(ard)   1920-1980

PERSONAL: Born July 29, 1920, in New York, N.Y.; died of a heart attack, December 15, 1980, in Madrid, Spain; son of Louis and Estelle (Fetbrandt) Gouldner; married second wife, Janet Lee Walker, February 5, 1966; children: Richard, Alan, Andrew, Alessandra. *Education:* City College (now City College of the City University of New York), B.B.A., 1941; Columbia University, M.A., 1945, Ph.D., 1953.

ADDRESSES: Home—7260 Creveling Dr., St. Louis, Mo. 63130. *Office*—Department of Sociology, Washington University, St. Louis, Mo. 63130.

CAREER: American Jewish Committee, New York, N.Y., resident sociologist, 1945-47; State University of New York College for Teachers (now State University of New York College at Buffalo), assistant professor of sociology, 1947-51; Standard Oil Co. of New Jersey, New York, N.Y., consulting sociologist, 1951-52; Antioch College, Yellow Springs, Ohio, associate professor of sociology, 1952-54; University of Illinois at Urbana-Champaign, associate professor, 1954-57, professor of sociology, 1957-59; Washington University, St. Louis, Mo., research professor of sociology, 1959-67, Max Weber Research Professor of Social Theory, 1967-80, chairman of department of sociology and anthropology, 1959-64. Visiting lecturer, Harvard University, 1956; visiting professor at Free University, Berlin, Germany, 1965, School of Economics, Stockholm, Sweden, 1965, 1977, Hebrew University, Jerusalem, Israel, 1966, Warsaw University, Poland, 1966, University of Amsterdam, Netherlands, 1972-76, University of Lund, 1972, University of Puerto Rico, 1972, Goldsmith's College, London, England, 1977, University of Copenhagen, 1977, and University of Zagreb, 1977. Chief principal investigator, Pruitt-Igoe Project, National Institute of Mental Health, 1963-67. Consulting editor, Penguin Books (London), 1969-74.

MEMBER: American Sociological Association (member of council), Society for the Study of Social Problems (president, 1960-61, 1962), Society for the Psychological Study of Social Issues, Sociological Research Association.

AWARDS, HONORS: Social Science Research Council award, 1952, research award, 1959; Fellow of the Center for Advanced Study in the Behavioral Sciences, Stanford University, 1961-62.

WRITINGS:

(Editor) *Studies in Leadership: Leadership and Democratic Action,* Harper, 1950.
Patterns of Industrial Bureaucracy, Free Press of Glencoe, 1954.
Wildcat Strike, Antioch, 1954.
(Editor) Emile Durkheim, *Socialism and Saint-Simon,* Antioch, 1958.
(With Richard Peterson) *Notes on Technology and the Moral Order,* Bobbs-Merrill, 1962.
(With H. P. Gouldner) *Modern Sociology: An Introduction to the Study of Human Interaction,* Harcourt, 1963.

Enter Plato: Classical Greece and the Origins of Social Theory, Basic Books, 1965, part 1 published as *The Hellenic World: A Sociological Analysis,* Harper, 1969.
(Editor with S. M. Miller) *Applied Sociology: Opportunities and Problems,* Free Press, 1965.
A Preliminary Report on Housing and Community Experiences of Pruitt-Igoe Residents, Social Science Institute, Washington University, 1966.
The Coming Crisis of Western Sociology, Basic Books, 1970.
For Sociology: Renewal and Critique in Sociology Today, Basic Books, 1973.
The Dialectic of Ideology and Technology: The Origins, Grammar, and Future of Ideology, Seabury, 1976.
The Future of Intellectuals and the Rise of the New Class: A Frame of Reference, Theses, Conjectures, Arguments, and an Historical Perspective on the International Class Contest of the Modern Era, Seabury, 1979.
The Two Marxisms: Contradictions and Anomalies in the Development of Theory, Seabury, 1980.
Against Fragmentation: The Origins of Marxism and the Sociology of Intellectuals, edited by Janet Gouldner and Cornelis Disco, Oxford University Press, 1984.

Editor, Bobbs-Merrill reprint series in sociology, 1960-80. Founder and editor-in-chief, *Trans-Action,* 1963-66; editor-in-chief, *New Critics Press,* St. Louis, 1969-80; co-founder and editor, *Theory and Society,* Amsterdam, 1973-80. Also associate editor of *Social Problems, Sociological Abstracts,* and *Journal of the History of the Behavioral Sciences.*

SIDELIGHTS: Turning the analytical eye of the sociologist on sociology itself, closely observing the behavior of the sociologist and the social theorist, Alvin W. Gouldner became an outspoken opponent of the convention that the sociologist could or should be an objective observer, removed from the object of study. In his book *The Coming Crisis of Western Sociology,* Gouldner advocated what he called "Reflexive Sociology." "A Reflexive Sociology means that we sociologists must . . . acquire the ingrained habit of viewing our own beliefs as we now view those held by others," he wrote.

"Many practitioners [of sociology] stress that it is a social *science* and regard its scientific side as its most distinguishing and important feature," Gouldner observed in *The Coming Crisis of Western Sociology.* "They wish to become, and to be thought of as, scientists; they wish to make their work more rigorous, more mathematical, more formal, and more powerfully instrumented. To them it is the scientific method of study itself, not the object studied or the way the object is conceived, that is the emotionally central if not the logically defining characteristic of sociology." For these sociologists, writes Bennett M. Berger in the *New York Times Book Review,* "the purpose of [social] theory is to explain the known facts of society and culture." In this view, sociology, like other natural sciences, is "value-neutral," adds Berger.

Gouldner argued in *The Coming Crisis of Western Sociology,* however, that objectivity emerged and has continued not out of a need for neutrality but as "the ideology of those who are alienated and politically homeless." Similarly, notes Berger, "Gouldner sees most of modern sociology as an effort by theorists to create social worlds they could accommodate themselves to, because they could not change the world they in fact confronted." Gouldner hoped that a "Reflexive Sociology" would convince sociologists that they use social theories to advance their own interests. He commented, "The ultimate goal of a Reflexive Sociology is the deepening of the sociologist's own awareness, of who and what he is, in a specific society at any given time, and of how both his social role and his personal praxis affect his work as a sociologist."

Unlike the scientist/sociologist, Gouldner believed that "the major significance of [social] theory is ideological," Berger indicates, "because every explanation of given social facts sustains or undermines specific political interests and the definitions of the socially 'real' in which those interests are rooted." In Gouldner's view, the sociologist should be engaged and take an active role in confronting contemporary social issues. He saw "the task of the sociologist as the establishment of a new community with its own radical critical conceptualizations, which emancipate through the understanding they give *beyond that available in everyday life,*" writes a *Times Literary Supplement* reviewer.

Even so, as Gouldner wrote, "It will be impossible either to emancipate men from the old society or to build a humane new one, without beginning here and now the construction of a total counter-culture, including new social theories; and it is impossible to do this without a critique of the social theories dominant today." Gouldner offered his critique in *The Coming Crisis of Western Sociology;* he examined Soviet Marxism and American functionalism, especially in the ideas of Talcott Parsons. "It is the most learned, the most closely reasoned, and the most eloquently written sociological history of sociological ideas to have appeared in the 20 years that I have been reading sociology," maintains Berger.

In two later books, *The Future of Intellectuals and the Rise of the New Class* and *Against Fragmentation: The Origins of Marxism and the Sociology of Intellectuals,* Gouldner examined how Marxism has been employed not by the proletariat but rather by a "New Class" to acquire and consolidate its authority. According to Gouldner, notes Norman Birnbaum in the *New York Times Book Review,* "Marx made a significant mistake when he thought that the bourgeoisie would be replaced by the proletariat. He failed to see that culture, a more important form of capital than money, would become the driving force of history." Those who control culture, the intellectuals (including sociologists) and the technical intelligentsia, form this "New Class." Gouldner suggested in *The Future of Intellectuals and the Rise of the New Class,* "The New Class believes that the world should be governed by those possessing superior competence, wisdom and science—that is, themselves. The Platonic Complex, the dream of the philosopher king with which Western philosophy begins, is the deepest wish-fulfilling fantasy of the New Class."

The posthumously published *Against Fragmentation* represents "a sociological analysis of the way [Marxism] has been used by some intellectuals and how it may be used by intellectuals in the future," Andrzej Walicki comments in the *New York Review of Books.* According to Gouldner, Karl Marx was the first to see scientific Marxism as "an ideology that intellectuals could and did use against their artisan competitors." Marxism, Gouldner indicated, "served to justify intellectuals' presence in a workers' movement in which they were all too obviously aliens." Gouldner added that Marxist socialism has provided "a strategy for optimizing the life chances of the new cultural bourgeoisie—intellectuals—by removing the moneyed class and old institutions that limit its upward mobility, and . . . a political strategy through which the New Class can attract allies to accomplish this."

"Although Gouldner's thesis is not new," Walicki points out, "his elaboration of it is certainly more thorough and impres-

sive than that of his various predecessors." He adds, "It may lead some Marxist or radical intellectuals in the West to become more aware of the implications of their own views."

BIOGRAPHICAL/CRITICAL SOURCES:

BOOKS

Gouldner, Alvin W., *The Coming Crisis of Western Sociology,* Basic Books, 1970.
Gouldner, Alvin W., *The Future of Intellectuals and the Rise of the New Class: A Frame of Reference, Theses, Conjectures, Arguments, and an Historical Perspective on the International Class Contest of the Modern Era,* Seabury, 1979.
Gouldner, Alvin W., *Against Fragmentation: The Origins of Marxism and the Sociology of Intellectuals,* edited by Janet Gouldner and Cornelis Disco, Oxford University Press, 1984.

PERIODICALS

New York Review of Books, March 11, 1971, April 25, 1985.
New York Times, April 16, 1979.
New York Times Book Review, October 25, 1970, April 15, 1979.
Times Literary Supplement, January 11, 1974, July 25, 1980, September 6, 1985.

OBITUARIES:

PERIODICALS

New York Times, January 11, 1981.†

—*Sketch by Bryan Ryan*

*　　*　　*

GRAFF, Henry F(ranklin) 1921-

PERSONAL: Born August 11, 1921, in New York, N.Y.; son of Samuel F. and Florence (Morris) Graff; married Edith Krantz, 1946; children: Iris Joan (Mrs. Andrew R. Morse), Ellen Toby. *Education:* City College (now City College of the City University of New York), B.S. in S.S., 1941; Columbia University, A.M., 1942, Ph.D., 1949.

ADDRESSES: Home—47 Andrea Lane, Scarsdale, N.Y. 10583. *Office*—Fayerweather Hall, Columbia University, New York, N.Y. 10027.

CAREER: Columbia University, New York, N.Y., 1946—, began as instructor, professor of history, 1961—, chairman of department, 1961-64. Member, National Historical Publications Commission, 1965-71. *Military service:* U.S. Army, Security Agency, 1942-46; became lieutenant; received citation.

MEMBER: American Historical Association, Organization of American Historians, Society of American Historians, Society of Historians of American Foreign Relations, Council on Foreign Relations, National Council for the Social Studies, Authors Guild, Authors League of America, P.E.N., American Council of Learned Societies (fellow), Phi Beta Kappa, Faculty House (Columbia University), Century Association (New York, N.Y.).

AWARDS, HONORS: Townsend Harris Medal from City College of the City University of New York, 1966.

WRITINGS:

Bluejackets with Perry in Japan, New York Public Library, 1952.

(With Jacques Barzun) *The Modern Researcher*, Harcourt, 1957, 4th edition, 1985.

(With John A. Krout) *The Adventure of the American People*, Rand McNally, 1959, revised edition, 1973.

(With Clifford Lord) *American Themes*, Columbia University Press, 1963.

(Contributor) John A. Garraty, editor, *Quarrels That Have Shaped the Constitution*, Harper, 1964.

Thomas Jefferson, Silver Burdett, 1966.

The Free and the Brave, Rand McNally, 1967, revised edition, 1980.

American Imperialism and the Philippine Insurrection, Little, Brown, 1969.

The Tuesday Cabinet, Prentice-Hall, 1970.

(With Paul J. Bohannan) *The Grand Experiment*, Rand McNally, Volume I: *The Call of Freedom*, 1978, Volume II: *The Promise of Democracy*, 1978.

(With Richard B. Morris) *America at Two Hundred*, Foreign Policy Association, 1979.

This Great Nation: A History of the United States (textbook), Riverside Publishing, 1983.

The Presidents: A Reference History, Scribner, 1984.

America: The Glorious Republic (textbook), with teacher's manual, Houghton, Volume I: *To 1877*, 1985, Volume II: *From 1877*, in press.

Consulting editor, *Life's* "History of the United States" (book series), 1963-65. Contributor to *New York Times* and to popular and professional periodicals.

WORK IN PROGRESS: Writing essays on the Presidency.

SIDELIGHTS: Henry F. Graff told *CA:* "The aim of good historical writing should be to orient the reader in his own time and thus to make him comfortable in the present. I would like to think that I am succeeding in this delicate and indispensable work."

*   *   *

GRANT, James Russell 1924-

PERSONAL: Born December 14, 1924, in Bellshill, Scotland; son of William Martyn (a metallurgist) and Margaret (a company secretary; maiden name, Lawson) Grant; married Olga Zarb (an occupational therapist), March 26, 1955 (divorced, 1983); children: Christopher Russell. *Education:* Univeristy of Glasgow, degree, 1945, M.B.Ch.B., 1951. *Politics:* Socialist. *Religion:* Buddhist.

ADDRESSES: Home—255 Creighton Ave., London N.2, England. *Office*—Clinic, Gatesden, Cromer St., London, W.C.1, England.

CAREER: Assistant general practitioner of medicine in London, England, 1952-53; Maudsley Hospital, London, registrar at Institute of Psychiatry, 1954-55; Provincial Guidance Clinic, Red Deer, Alberta, psychiatrist, 1955-57; medical practitioner in London, 1958—. Medical adviser to Thomas Coram Foundation (adoption agency); medical officer at King's Cross Hostel for the Homeless, London Department of Health and Social Security, 1970—. *Military service:* British Army, Scottish Rifles, 1945-47.

MEMBER: British Medical Association, Cruising Association.

WRITINGS:

Hyphens (poems), Putnam, 1958.
Poems, Botteghe Oscure, 1959.

(Translator) Guillaume Apollinaire, *Zone*, Library, Harvard University, 1961.

The Excitement of Being Sam, Outposts Publications, 1977.

Myths of My Age (poems), University of St. Pancras, 1985.

Hattonrig Road (poems), University of St. Pancras, in press.

Writer for British Broadcasting Corp. and Canadian Broadcasting Corp. Contributor to psychiatry journals.

WORK IN PROGRESS: The Silent Scream, cartoon stories; *Self and Social Realism*, essays on positive aspects of anxiety; *State of Emergency*, autobiographical sketches.

SIDELIGHTS: James Russell Grant wrote that his motivation is to "understand anxiety as a means to personal, social, and political progress. Social realism is the active presence of personality emerging in the body politic. We must *be* more than we *are*. H. Marcuse said, 'It demands the political synthesis of experience as a constitutive act.' Poetry is the written science of this so-far latent power: an awareness of universality in individuality."

He adds: "I have lived in post-war Paris, with its existentialism, gloomy tartan bars, jazz and the Bhagavad-Gita, and its other writers; in Italy and Canada; in Scotland, during the industrial depression of the thirties. I am working with problems of stress in the inner city, probing the myths by which we all live; not least the myths of politics as well as personal life."

AVOCATIONAL INTERESTS: Ocean cruising.

*   *   *

GREEN, Phyllis 1932-

PERSONAL: Born June 24, 1932, in Pittsburgh, Pa.; daughter of Victor Geyer (a plumbing contractor) and Phyllis (a teacher; maiden name, Sailer) Hartman; married Robert Bailey Green (an insurance executive), August 15, 1959; children: Sharon Ann, Bruce Robert. *Education:* Westminster College, B.S., 1953; University of Pittsburgh, M.Ed., 1955.

ADDRESSES: Home and office—Portland, Ore.

CAREER: Elementary and special education teacher in Dormont, Pa., and Newark and Wilmington, Del., 1953-59; free-lance writer, 1959—. Former band vocalist and actress in summer theater.

MEMBER: Dramatists Guild, Authors League of America, Detroit Women Writers.

AWARDS, HONORS: Playwriting fellowship, Wisconsin Arts Board, 1981; California Young Reader Medal (primary category), 1984, for *Bagdad Ate It*.

WRITINGS:

The Fastest Quitter in Town, Addison-Wesley, 1972.
Nantucket Summer, Thomas Nelson, 1974.
Ice River, Addison-Wesley, 1975.
Mildred Murphy, How Does Your Garden Grow?, Addison-Wesley, 1977.
Grandmother Orphan, Thomas Nelson, 1977.
Wild Violets, Thomas Nelson, 1977.
Walkie-Talkie, Addison-Wesley, 1978.
Nicky's Lopsided, Lumpy, but Delicious Orange, Addison-Wesley, 1978.
A New Mother for Martha, Human Sciences, 1978.
The Empty Seat, Elsevier-Nelson, 1979.

Gloomy Louie, Albert Whitman, 1980.
Bagdad Ate It, F. Watts, 1980.
Eating Ice Cream with a Werewolf, Harper, 1983.
Uncle Roland, the Perfect Guest, Four Winds Press, 1983.

Also author of stage plays "By the Beautiful Sea," first read Off-Off Broadway at Theater at St. Clement's, January, 1978, "Deer Season," produced Off-Off Broadway at Theater at St. Clement's, January, 1980, and "Physically Handicapped Singles Dance," produced Off-Off Broadway at Marquee Theater by American Line; also author of radio plays "I'll Be Home for Christmas" and "Acapulco Holiday," both produced on Wisconsin public radio stations. Contributor of short stories, poems, and articles to national magazines.

WORK IN PROGRESS: Sequels to *Wild Violets* and *Grand-mother Orphan;* novelization of play "Deer Season"; expanding play "Physically Handicapped Singles Dance" to full-length.

SIDELIGHTS: Phyllis Green told *CA:* "What I hope to accomplish as a writer: In the theater, I hope to create wonderful roles for women, roles where actresses can use their talents. In my stories for young people, I hope to please my readers. I hope I never bore them. I hope my stories make them laugh and/or cry and/or think, but mostly I hope they laugh."

BIOGRAPHICAL/CRITICAL SOURCES:

PERIODICALS

New York Times, January 23, 1980.

*   *   *

GREEN, Reginald Herbold 1935-

PERSONAL: Born May 4, 1935, in Walla Walla, Wash.; son of Reginald James (a professor and clergyman) and Marcia (Herbold) Green. *Education:* Whitman College, A.B. (summa cum laude), 1955; Harvard University, M.A., 1957, Ph.D., 1961. *Religion:* Anglican.

ADDRESSES: Office—Institute of Development Studies, University of Sussex, Falmer, Brighton BN1 9RE, England.

CAREER: Yale University, New Haven, Conn., assistant professor of economics, 1961-65; University of East Africa, Makerere University College, Kampala, Uganda, research fellow at East African Institute of Social and Economic Research, 1965-66; United Republic of Tanzania, economic adviser to the Treasury under Ford Foundation contract, 1966-75; University of Dar es Salaam, Dar es Salaam, Tanzania, honorary professor of economics, 1969-74; University of Sussex, Brighton, England, honorary professorial fellow and fellow of Institute of Development Studies, 1975—. University of Ghana, visiting lecturer, 1963-65, external examiner in economics, 1967—; faculty member of Carnegie Institute of Diplomacy, East Africa, 1965-66, and East African Staff College, 1965. Member of young adult council, National Social Welfare Assembly, 1956-63; member of education committee, Catholic Institute for International Relations, 1978—; member of liaison committee, Southern African Development Coordination Conference, 1978—. Trustee, International Center on Law in Development, 1978—. Member of Advisory Group on Economic Matters, World Council of Churches, 1978—. Economic advisor, Tanzania Treasury, 1966-74, 1980. Advisor and consultant to numerous governments and organizations, including the governments of Ghana, Uganda, Tanzania, Botswana, and Swaziland, SWAPO of Namibia, Group of 77,

International Foundation for Development Alternatives, United Nations, Commonwealth Secretariat, and African Centre for Monetary Studies, 1964—.

MEMBER: International Center for Law Development, African Studies Association (fellow), Asian Studies Association, Economic Society of Ghana, Economic Society of Tanzania, Phi Beta Kappa, Pi Kappa Delta, Delta Sigma Rho.

AWARDS, HONORS: L.H.D., Whitman College, 1975.

WRITINGS:

The College Student and the Changing South: A Consideration of the Problems of Race Relations Confronting the Southern Campus and Its Student Body: Report of the Southwide Student Human Relations Conference of November 1958, United States Student Association, c. 1958.
Responsibility in Student Affairs, United States Student Association, 1958.
(With K. G. V. Krishna) *Economic Co-Operation in Africa: Retrospect and Prospect,* Oxford University Press, 1967.
(Contributor) J. Sheffield, editor, *Education, Employment and Rural Development,* East African Publishing House, 1967.
Ghana and the Ivory Coast, 1957-67: Reflections on Economic Strategy, Structure, Implementation, and Necessity, [New York], 1967.
Stages in Economic Development, Bank of Sudan (Khartoum), 1967.
(With Ann Seidman) *Unity or Poverty: The Economics of Pan-Africanism,* Penguin, 1968.
(Contributor) C. Allen and R. W. Johnson, editors, *African Perspectives,* Cambridge University Press, 1970.
(Contributor) P. Foster and A. R. Zolberg, editors, *Ghana and the Ivory Coast: Perspectives on Modernisation,* University of Chicago, 1971.
(Contributor) Yashpal Tandon, editor, *Technical Assistance Administration in East Africa,* Almqvist & Wiksell (Stockholm), 1973.
Toward ujamma and kujitegemea: Income Distribution and Absolute Poverty Eradication Aspects of the Tanzania Transition to Socialism, Institute of Development Studies, University of Sussex, 1974.
Productive Employment in Africa: An Overview of the Challenge, Institute of Development Studies, University of Sussex, 1975.
(Contributor) Y. Ghai, editor, *Law in the Political Economy of Public Enterprise: African Perspectives,* Scandinavian Institute of African Studies, Uppsala/International Center for Law in Development, 1977.
Toward Socialism and Self Reliance: Tanzania's Striving for Sustained Transition Projected, Scandinavian Institute of African Studies, Swedish International Development Agency, 1977.
Adult Education in National Development Planning, International Council for Adult Education, 1977.
(Contributor) J. Faundez and S. Picciotto, editors, *The Nationalization of Mutinationals in Peripheral Economies,* Macmillan, 1978.
Namibia: A Political Economic Survey, Institute of Development Studies, University of Sussex, 1979.
Economic Shocks and National Policy Making: Tanzania in the 1970s, Institute of Social Studies, 1980.
From Sudwestafrika to Namibia: The Political Economy of Transition, Scandinavian Institute of African Studies, 1981.
(Editor with Kimmo Kiljunen and Marja-Liisa Kiljunen) *Namibia, the Last Colony,* Longman, 1981.

(Contributor) M. Fransman, editor, *Industry and Accumulation in Africa*, Heinemann, 1982.

(With D. de Gaspar and C. Espiritu) *World Hunger: A Christian Reappraisal*, World Council of Churches/Churches' Commission on Participation in Development, Geneva, 1982.

(Contributor with Stephany Griffith-Jones) T. Rose, editor, *Crisis and Recovery in Sub-Saharan Africa: Realities and Complexities*, Organisation of Economic Cooperation and Development, Growth Centre, 1985.

(With P. Ndegwa and L. Mureithi) *Development Options for Africa in the 1980's and Beyond*, Oxford University Press, 1985.

Also author, with Augusto C. Espiritu, of *The International Context of Rural Poverty in the Third World: Issues for Research and Action by Grassroots Organizations and Legal Activists*, 1984, and *Developing State Trading in a Peripheral Economy*. Contributor to professional journals. Member of editorial board, Economic Society of Tanzania.

WORK IN PROGRESS: A volume on Cameroun economy for "Tiers Monde" series of Presses Universitaires de France; a volume on the East African economic community, for East African Publishing House.

SIDELIGHTS: Reginald Herbold Green has traveled in twenty African and a dozen South Asian countries and in Europe and Latin America.

BIOGRAPHICAL/CRITICAL SOURCES:

PERIODICALS

Times Literary Supplement, March 5, 1982.

*   *   *

GREEN, Sheila Ellen   1934-
(Sheila Greenwald)

PERSONAL: Born May 26, 1934, in New York, N.Y.; daughter of Julius (a manufacturer) and Florence (Friedman) Greenwald; married George Green (a surgeon), February 18, 1960; children: Samuel, Benjamin. *Education:* Sarah Lawrence College, B.A., 1956. *Politics:* Democrat. *Religion:* Jewish.

ADDRESSES: Home—175 Riverside Dr., New York, N.Y. 10024.

CAREER: Writer and illustrator. Has done illustrations for *Harper's, Gourmet, The Reporter*, and other magazines.

WRITINGS:

UNDER NAME SHEILA GREENWALD; SELF-ILLUSTRATED

A Metropolitan Love Story, Doubleday, 1962.
Willie Bryant and the Flying Otis, Grosset, 1971.
The Hot Day, Bobbs-Merrill, 1972.
Miss Amanda Snap, Bobbs-Merrill, 1972.
Mat Pit and the Tunnel Tenants, Lippincott, 1972.
The Secret Museum, Lippincott, 1974.
The Secret in Miranda's Closet, Houghton, 1977.
The Mariah Delany Lending Library Disaster, Houghton, 1977.
The Atrocious Two, Houghton, 1978.
All the Way to Wits End, Little, Brown, 1979.
It All Began with Jane Eyre, Little, Brown, 1980.
Give Us a Great Big Smile Rosy Cole, Atlantic Monthly Press, 1981.
Blissfull Joy and the SATs, Atlantic Monthly Press, 1982.

Will the Real Gertrude Hollings Please Stand Up, Atlantic Monthly Press, 1983.
Valentine Rosy, Atlantic Monthly Press, 1984.
Rosy Cole's Great American Guilt Club, Atlantic Monthly Press, 1985.

ILLUSTRATOR

Marie L. Allen, *Pocketful of Poems*, Harper, 1957.
Carol Ryrie Brink, *The Pink Motel*, Macmillan, 1959.
Florence Laughlin, *The Little Leftover Witch*, Macmillan, 1960.
Miriam Dreifus, *Brave Betsy*, Putnam, 1961.
Grace V. Curl, *Come A-Witching*, Bobbs-Merrill, 1964.
Laura H. Fisher, *Amy and the Sorrel Summer*, Holt, 1964.
Barbara Rinkoff, *Remarkable Ramsey*, Morrow, 1965.
Hila Colman, *Boy Who Couldn't Make Up His Mind*, Macmillan, 1965.
Anne Mallett, *Who'll Mind Henry?*, Doubleday, 1965.
Laughlin, *Seventh Cousin*, Macmillan, 1966.
Mary J. Roth, *Pretender Princess*, Morrow, 1967.
James Playsted Wood, *When I Was Jersey*, Pantheon, 1967.
Emma V. Worstell, *Jump the Rope Jingles*, Macmillan, 1967.
Jean Bothwell, *Mystery Cup*, Dial, 1968.
M. Jean Craig, *New Boy on the Sidewalk*, Norton, 1968.

OTHER

Also contributor to *Cricket* and *New York Times*.

SIDELIGHTS: Sheila Ellen Green told *CA:* "I started drawing too far back to remember and I did it all the time, as a habit, as a way to amuse myself. After illustrating other peoples' books for a number of years, I decided to try writing my own and found this doubly rewarding. I write down ideas that appeal to me—some work out, some don't. *The Hot Day* was based on an incident from my father's childhood, *Willie Bryant and the Flying Otis* on situations my own children have experienced, and *Miss Amanda Snap* on a turn in the old fairy tale. I write and draw because I enjoy writing and drawing. My books are intended for whoever enjoys my pleasure in these things."

BIOGRAPHICAL/CRITICAL SOURCES:

PERIODICALS

Charm Magazine, August, 1959.
New York Times, May 29, 1961.

*   *   *

GREEN, Stanley   1923-

PERSONAL: Born May 29, 1923, in New York, N.Y.; son of Rudy (a businessman) and Frances (Kuschner) Green; married Catherine Hunt, August 8, 1954; children: Susan Hunt, Rudy David. *Education:* Union College (now Union College and University), Schenectady, N.Y., B.A., 1943; University of Nebraska, Army Specialized Training Program, 1943-44.

CAREER: Writer. Lynn Farnol Group, New York City, public relations account executive for American Society of Composers, Authors and Publishers, 1961-65; Radio station WBAI, New York City, music commentator, 1961-67. *Military service:* U.S. Army, 1943-46.

MEMBER: Players Club.

AWARDS, HONORS: English-Speaking Union Ambassador of Honor citation for *The Great Clowns of Broadway*.

WRITINGS:

The World of Musical Comedy: The Story of the American Musical Stage as Told through the Careers of Its Foremost Composers and Lyricists, foreword by Deems Taylor, Ziff Davis, 1960, 4th edition, A. S. Barnes, 1980.

The Rodgers and Hammerstein Story, John Day, 1963, revised edition, Da Capo Press, 1980.

Ring Bells! Sing Songs!, Arlington House, 1971, published as *Broadway Musicals of the Thirties,* Da Capo Press, 1982.

Starring Fred Astaire, Dodd, 1973.

Encyclopedia of the Musical Theatre, Dodd, 1976, revised edition, Da Capo Press, 1980.

Broadway Musical Picture Quiz Book, Dover, 1977.

Rodgers and Hammerstein Fact Book, Lynn Farnol, 1980.

Encyclopedia of the Musical Film, Oxford University Press, 1981.

The Great Clowns of Broadway, Oxford University Press, 1984.

Broadway Musicals Show by Show, Hal Leonard Co., 1985.

Contributor to *Variety, Saturday Review, Atlantic Monthly, New York Times,* and other publications. Contributing editor, *Hi/Fi Stereo Review,* 1957-63; editor, *ASCAP Biographical Dictionary,* 1966.

SIDELIGHTS: New York Times Book Review contributor Howard Teichmann writes that Stanley Green's *The Great Clowns of Broadway* "is a scholarly work, written with obvious affection and insight. He probes deeply into his subjects, wisely limiting himself to 10 headliners, most of whom started out in vaudeville and later gained fame on the legitimate stage." According to Walter Kerr in the *New Republic,* "this book reminds us of how good it felt to be one of them. It further suggests that clowns don't vanish just because the clowns themselves wander away; they vanish because the audience wanders away, fragmenting and diffusing the crazy thing that happened. What is truly sad is that twenty-five years from now no one will be able to write this sort of book." In *The Great Clowns of Broadway,* remarks Kerr, Stanley Green "has written a book about ten of these irreplaceable people who are not being replaced."

BIOGRAPHICAL/CRITICAL SOURCES:

PERIODICALS

New Republic, November 5, 1984.

New York Times Book Review, November 15, 1981, November 11, 1984.

Times Literary Supplement, May 24, 1985.

Variety, February 26, 1969.

*   *   *

GREENHILL, Basil (Jack)   1920-

PERSONAL: Born February 26, 1920, in Weston-super-Mare, Somerset, England; son of Basil Jack and Edith (Holmes) Greenhill; married Gillian Stratton, 1950 (died, 1959); married Ann Giffard, 1961; children: (first marriage) Richard Basil Stratton; (second marriage) James Giffard. *Education:* University of Bristol, B.A., 1946, Ph.D., 1981. *Religion:* Anglican.

ADDRESSES: Office—West Boetheric Farm, St. Dominic, Saltash, Cornwall, PL12 G52, England.

CAREER: British Government, Diplomatic Service, 1946-67, served in Pakistan, 1950-54, New York, N.Y., 1954, Tokyo, Japan, 1955-58, and Geneva, Switzerland, 1958, high com-

missioner in East Pakistan (now Bangladesh), 1958-59, and Ottawa, Ontario, 1961-64; National Maritime Museum, Greenwich, London, England, director, 1967-83. Member of Ancient Monuments Board for England, 1972-82; trustee, Royal Naval Museum, 1973-83; Dulwich College, member of board of governors, 1974—, chairman of picture gallery committee, 1977—; chairman of *SS Great Britain* project, 1982—; chairman of maritime monitor project, Exeter University, 1985—; chairman of government advisory committee on historic wreck sites, 1986—. Principal historical advisor for BBC television series "The Commanding Sea," 1980, and "Trade Winds," 1985, and for BBC radio series "The British Seafarer," 1981. *Military service:* British Navy, 1941-45; became lieutenant.

MEMBER: International Congress of Maritime Museums (president, 1975—), Royal Historical Society (fellow), Society for Nautical Research (vice-president, 1975—), Maritime Trust (vice-president), National Museum Directors Conference.

AWARDS, HONORS: Named Companion of St. Michael and St. George, 1967; American Association award, 1968, for *Westcountrymen in Prince Edward's Isle;* Order of the White Rose of Finland, 1980; named companion of the Bath, 1981; honorary fellowship, University of Exeter, 1985.

WRITINGS:

The Merchant Schooners, Percival Marshall, Volume I, 1951, revised edition, 1968, Volume II, 1958, revised edition, 1978.

Out of Appledore, Percival Marshall, 1959, 3rd edition, 1980.

Sailing for a Living, Percival Marshall, 1962.

(With wife, Ann Giffard) *Westcountrymen in Prince Edward's Isle,* David & Charles, 1967, revised edition, University of Toronto Press, 1975.

(With A. Giffard) *The Merchant Sailing Ship,* David & Charles, 1970.

Boats and Boatmen of Pakistan, David & Charles, 1971.

(With A. Giffard) *Women under Sail,* David & Charles, 1971.

(With A. Giffard) *Travelling by Sea in the Nineteenth Century,* A. & C. Black, 1972.

Steam and Sail, David & Charles, 1973.

A Victorian Maritime Album, Patrick Stephens, 1974.

(With W. J. Slade) *Westcountry Coasting Ketches,* Conway Maritime Press, 1974.

A Quayside Camera, David & Charles, 1975.

The Coastal Trade, Phaidon, 1975.

Archaeology of the Boat, A. & C. Black, 1976.

(With A. Giffard) *Victorian and Edwardian Sailing Ships,* Batsford, 1976.

(Editor and author of preface) Georg Kahres, *The Last Tall Ships,* Conway Maritime Press, 1978.

(With A. Giffard) *Victorian and Edwardian Ships and Harbours,* Batsford, 1978.

(With A. Giffard) *Victorian and Edwardian Steamships,* Batsford, 1979.

Schooners, Batsford, 1980.

The British Sea Farer Discovered, British Broadcasting Corp. and Hutchinson, 1980.

The Life and Death of the Sailing Ship, H.M.S.O., 1981.

(With A. Giffard) *Towards Quebec,* H.M.S.O., 1981.

Karlsson, H.M.S.O., 1983.

The Grain Races, Conway Maritime Press, 1986.

The Woodshipbuilders, Batsford, 1986.

Also author of numerous pamphlets. Contributor of more than two hundred articles and reviews on maritime history subjects to a variety of publications, including *London Times, Christian Science Monitor, Geographical Magazine, Lloyd's List,* and *Country Life.*

WORK IN PROGRESS: A research project on the Baltic fleet in the Crimean War.

SIDELIGHTS: Basil Greenhill told *CA:* "The maritime aspects of history have been greatly neglected. Most of my writing is intended to make people more widely aware of the importance and interest of the maritime dimension."

MEDIA ADAPTATIONS: Westcountrymen in Prince Edward's Isle was filmed for television.

AVOCATIONAL INTERESTS: Boating, travel.

*   *   *

GREENWALD, Sheila
See GREEN, Sheila Ellen

*   *   *

GRIBBIN, William James   1943-

PERSONAL: Born October 2, 1943, in Washington, D.C.; son of Walter James (an electrician) and Helena (Slechta) Gribbin. *Education:* Catholic University of America, B.A. 1965, M.A., 1966, Ph.D., 1968. *Politics:* Conservative. *Religion:* Roman Catholic.

ADDRESSES: Home—3800 13th St., N.E., Washington, D.C. 20017. *Office*—Senate Republican Policy Committee, U.S. Senate, 347 Russell Senate Office Bldg., Washington, D.C. 20510.

CAREER: Virginia Union University, Richmond, assistant professor of history, 1968-71; District of Columbia Teachers College (now University of District of Columbia), Washington, D.C., assistant professor of history, 1973; legislative assistant to Senator James L. Buckley, 1974-77; U.S. Senate, Senate Republican Policy Committee, Washington, D.C., senior policy analyst, 1977—, assistant director, 1982-85. Deputy director of White House Office of Legislative Affairs, 1981-82.

MEMBER: Phi Beta Kappa.

AWARDS, HONORS: Woodrow Wilson fellowship, 1965-66; Stephen Greene Press Award, 1974.

WRITINGS:

The Churches Militant: The War of 1912 and American Religion, Yale University Press, 1973.
(Editor) *Emblem of Freedom: The American Family in the 1980s,* American Family Institute, 1981.
(Editor) *The Family in the Modern World,* American Family Institute, 1982.
(Editor) *The Wealth of Families,* American Family Institute, 1982.
(Editor) *The Family and the Flat Tax,* American Family Institute, 1984.

Contributor to *New England Quarterly, Church History, Americas, Historian, Vermont History, South Atlantic Quarterly, Journal of Presbyterian History,* and many other periodicals.

GRIFFIN, Glen C.   1934-

PERSONAL: Born August 2, 1934, in Asnieres, France; U.S. citizen; son of Smith Ben and Marion (Hussey) Griffin; married Mary Ella Page, December 23, 1957; children: Janelle, Joan, Mark, Gary, Jill, Greg. *Education:* Texas Western College (now University of Texas at El Paso), B.A., 1954; University of Texas, Main University (now University of Texas at Austin), M.D., 1958. *Politics:* Republican. *Religion:* Church of Jesus Christ of Latter-day Saints (Mormon).

ADDRESSES: Home—421 Indian Springs Rd., Bountiful, Utah 84010. *Office*—575 Medical Dr., Bountiful, Utah 84010.

CAREER: Former positions include pediatrician at South Davis Medical Center, Bountiful, Utah, president of Medical Practice Systems, Inc., Bountiful, and vice-president of Child Health Centers of America, Jackson, Tenn.; currently pediatrician in private practice; University of Utah, College of Medicine, Salt Lake City, 1970—, began as clinical instructor, currently associate professor of pediatrics. Diplomate of American Board of Pediatrics. *Military service:* U.S. Army, 1961-63; became captain.

MEMBER: American Academy of Pediatrics (fellow; chairman of Utah chapter, 1982-84), American Medical Association, American Thoracic Society, American College of Allergists (associate fellow), Intermountain Pediatric Society (president, 1982-84), Utah State Medical Association, Davis County Medical Association.

WRITINGS:

About Life and Love, Deseret, 1968.
(With W. Dean Belnap) *About Marriage and More,* Deseret, 1968.
(With Lynn Eric Johnson) *What's Up?,* Deseret, 1970.
You Were Smaller than a Dot, Better Books, 1972.
About You and Other Important People, Deseret, 1979.
Not about Birds, Deseret, 1979.

Writer of patient education filmstrips and other educational materials. Author of syndicated column "Children and Teens," 1979—.

SIDELIGHTS: Glen C. Griffin told *CA* that he is an inventor and has developed numerous efficiency systems for the improvement of health care delivery, including his unique medical office for the care of children and teens. "In this office there is no waiting room," he explains. "Patients drive into a covered parking place and enter their own examining or surgery room. Closed circuit televisions and electric eye beams and thirteen tape recording units welcome patients and instruct them in interesting ways, many automatically. Even the examining rooms are unconventional—designed like mini-living rooms to avoid a 'sterile doctor's office appearance and setting.'"

*   *   *

GRIFFITH, A. Kinney   1897-

PERSONAL: Born August, 1897, in Territory of Arizona (now state of Arizona); son of Thomas Grant and Nora (Kinney) Griffith; married Edree Margaret Wilson; children: Walter Michael, Patricia Marie. *Education:* Attended Bucknell University. *Religion:* Catholic.

CAREER: U.S. Civil Service employee until retirement; currently rancher and writer. Has been technical advisor on three motion pictures dealing with Indians and on "Hell's Angels" and "Lilac Time." *Military service:* U.S. Army, 1917-20; served in Field Artillery and Air Corps; member of First Pursuit Group, American Expeditionary Force under Capt. Eddie Rickenbacker.

MEMBER: Arizona Pioneers Historical Society, Pimeria Alta Historical Society, Hollywood Professional Authors (life member), National Writers Club, Elks Club, Adventurers Club, Westerners Club (Phoenix Corral).

WRITINGS:

The Big Scalphunter, William-Frederick, 1961.
Mickey Free: Manhunter, Caxton Printers, 1969.
(With Ciye Cochise) *The First Hundred Years of Nino Cochise: The Untold Story of an Apache Indian Chief,* Abelard, 1971.

Also author of novelettes and three novels; co-author of *Arizona Bibliography of Life and Literature.* Contributor of short stories and articles to action and adventure magazines.

WORK IN PROGRESS: To Finance an Empire; The Amber Sky.

SIDELIGHTS: A. Kinney Griffith, the son of an Arizona pioneer family, was raised among the Apache Indians and is a life-long friend of Ciye (Nino) Cochise, grandson of the great Chief Cochise of the Chiricahau Apaches. In *The First Hundred Years of Nino Cochise: The Untold Story of an Apache Indian Chief,* Griffith tells the life story of his friend and details the daily life of Cochise's Apache tribe in Sonora, Mexico, where they chose to establish themselves rather than live on the San Carlos reservation. Griffith's recounting of the Apache lifestyle prompted E. A. Dooley to observe in *Best Sellers:* "An anthropologist will find the book a veritable mine salted with innumerable stories of Apache culture and tribal customs. . . . The book is well written."

Under the leadership of Nino's mother, the tribe lived without conflict and remained culturally intact. However, under Nino's leadership, the Apaches found themselves caught up in Mexican politics, and eventually war brought an end to their tribal way of life. Collin Clark comments on the book in *Library Journal:* "Compared with the memoirs of Chief Red Fox, Nino's story, though much more readable, is uneventful and does not make a great work." However, *New York Review of Books* contributor Peter Farb disagrees, observing that the book "is written with restraint, attention to detail, and modesty, and it is . . . a very good story."

BIOGRAPHICAL/CRITICAL SOURCES:

PERIODICALS

Best Sellers, January 1, 1972.
Library Journal, April 15, 1972.
New York Review of Books, December 16, 1972.†

*   *   *

GRIMES, Ronald L.   1943-

PERSONAL: Born May 19, 1943, in San Diego, Calif.; son of Milton L. and Joyce N. (Williams) Grimes; married Mary Judith Shown, May 31, 1964 (divorced); married Susan L. Scott; children: (first marriage) Trevor. *Education:* Kentucky Wesleyan College, B.A. (summa cum laude), 1964; Emory University, M.Div. (magna cum laude), 1967; Columbia University and Union Theological Seminary, Ph.D., 1970.

ADDRESSES: Home—13 Roslin Ave. N., Waterloo, Ontario, Canada N2L 2G4. *Office*—Department of Religion and Culture, Wilfrid Laurier University, Waterloo, Ontario, Canada N2L 3C5.

CAREER: Columbia University, Barnard College, New York, N.Y., instructor in religion, 1970; Lawrence University, Appleton, Wis., assistant professor of religion, 1970-74; Wilfrid Laurier University, Waterloo, Ontario, professor of religion and culture, 1974—, chairperson of department, 1985-88. Visiting professor at University of Pittsburgh, 1985-86. Has presented theological papers at conferences in the U.S. and Canada. Participant in Polish Theater Laboratory, 1980. Director of and actor in local theater productions.

MEMBER: American Academy of Religion, American Anthropological Society.

AWARDS, HONORS: Younger Humanists grant from National Endowment for the Humanities, 1973-74, for field research in Santa Fe, N.M., and library research at the University of Chicago; faculty research grants from Wilfrid Laurier University, 1975, 1976, 1982, and 1985; Social Sciences and Research Council of Canada research grant, 1977-78, fellowship, 1981-82; honorary doctor of humane letters from Kentucky Wesleyan College, 1984; Brown Memorial Award in Religion; Edward Arthur Mellinger Foundation Award.

WRITINGS:

The Divine Imagination: William Blake's Major Prophetic Visions, Scarecrow, 1972.
(Contributor) Joseph A. Wittreich and Stuart Curran, editors, *Blake's Sublime Allegory,* University of Wisconsin Press, 1973.
Symbol and Conquest: Public Ritual and Drama in Santa Fe, New Mexico, Cornell University Press, 1976.
(Contributor) Leszek Kolankiewicz, editor, *The Road to Active Culture,* Theater Laboratory Institute (Wroclaw, Poland), 1978.
(Contributor) Victor Turner, editor, *Celebration: Studies in Festivity and Ritual,* Smithsonian Institution Press, 1982.
Beginnings in Ritual Studies, University Press of America, 1982.
(Contributor) Tony Coult and Baz Kershaw, editors, *Engineers of the Imagination,* Methuen, 1983.
Research in Ritual Studies, Scarecrow, 1985.
(Contributor) Mircea Eliade, editor, *Encyclopedia of Religion,* Macmillan, in press.

Also author of "The Ronnie Stories" and of unpublished poetry and illustrations "The Book of Form and Emptiness," and "bull." Contributor of numerous articles, reviews, and poetry to academic journals, including *Face to Face, Christianity and Crisis, Classmate, Journal of the American Academy of Religion, Catholic World,* and *Union Seminary Quarterly Review.* Member of editorial board of *Congress of Social and Humanistic Studies: Culture and Performance Series,* 1983—.

WORK IN PROGRESS: Repetition and Fiction, a critical examination of the idea of repetition in modern thought.

SIDELIGHTS: Ronald L. Grimes wrote *CA:* "The center of my academic interests has been and remains the interpretation of symbolic forms. The problem of symbolization lies at the intersection of several sub-disciplines, religion and the arts, symbolic anthropology, and philosophy of religion, and it is the phenomenon of symbolization, rather than one of these sub-disciplines which constitutes my field. Because 'comparative symbology' (Victor Turner's term) is inter-disciplinary in nature, I spend much of my research teaching time dealing with methodological questions and pursuing phenomenological motifs.

"My understanding of both religion and art is strongly informed by William Blake. From him I learned what constitutes a symbol. I was also taught by him that generalizations are to be approached through the 'minute particulars.' Consequently, my work as a philosopher of religion usually occurs in the form of extended case studies of some rather carefully chosen and rigidly delimited data, for instance, a cycle of ritual and drama in Santa Fe or Blake's three major prophetic works. I think that philosophizing about religion should occur on the heels of field study, so I am more prone to search out religio-aesthetic performances than I am to read philosophical and theological texts as preludes to generalization. As a result, the metaphors which inform my method are dramatistic rather than linguistic; religion is 'performance' rather than 'text.' This is why I tend to emphasize ritual, storytelling, and meditational practice rather than ethics, theology and poetry or novel."

*   *   *

GRIMSHAW, Nigel (Gilroy) 1925-

PERSONAL: Born November 5, 1925, in Manchester, England; son of Harold C. (a scientist) and Gladys Jeanne Grimshaw; married Margarete Apell, February 25, 1950; children: Rosemary, Mark, Peter, John. *Education:* Victoria University of Manchester, B.A. (with honors), 1950; University of Nottingham, M.A., 1976.

ADDRESSES: Home and office—3 Plane Trees, Rosedale E., Pickering, North Yorkshire, England. *Agent*—Watson Little Ltd., Suite 8, Charing Cross Rd., London WC2H 0DG, England.

CAREER: Teachers Training College, Bangkok, Thailand, lecturer in English, 1958-62; Francis Bacon Grammar School, St. Albans, England, teacher of English and department head, 1962-65; Kesteven College of Education, Grantham, England, senior lecturer in English, 1965-79; writer, 1979—. *Military service:* Royal Navy, 1943-47.

MEMBER: Society of Authors.

WRITINGS:

Tiger Gold, Longmans, Green, 1964.
The Painted Jungle, Longmans, Green, 1965.
David Copperfield, by Charles Dickens, Longmans, Green, 1968.
The Sign of Indra, edited by G. C. Thornley, Longmans, Green, 1968.
The Angry Valley, Longmans, Green, 1970.
Bluntstone and the Wildkeepers (juvenile), Faber, 1974.
The Wildkeepers' Guest (juvenile), Faber, 1976.
Read and Write, five books, Cassell, 1983.

FOR CHILDREN; WITH PAUL GROVES

Up Our Way, Edward Arnold, 1972.
Living Our Way, Edward Arnold, 1973.
Join the Action, Edward Arnold, 1973.
Going Our Way, Edward Arnold, 1975.
Action Replay, Edward Arnold, 1975.

Thirteen Ghosts: A Collection of Original Ghost Stories with Suggestions for Varied Work in English, Edward Arnold, 1976.
Smudge and Chewpen: A Book of Exercises for Correction of the Common Errors Made in Writing, Edward Arnold, 1976.
The Goodbodys, Edward Arnold, 1976.
Thirteen Weird Tales: A Collection of Original Strange Stories with Suggestions for Varied Work in English, Edward Arnold, 1977.
Action Stations: Seven Plays to Read or Record, Edward Arnold, 1977.
Monsters of Myth and Legend, Edward Arnold, 1977.
Smudge and Chewpen Tests: A Book of Short Tests on the Common Errors Made in Writing, Edward Arnold, 1978.
Stops and Starts, Edward Arnold, 1978.
Call to Action: Seven Plays to Read or Record, Edward Arnold, 1978.
Thirteen Horror Stories, Edward Arnold, 1978.
Thirteen Sci-Fi Stories, Edward Arnold, 1979.
Into Action, Edward Arnold, 1979.
Smudge and Chewpen Word Book, Edward Arnold, 1980.
All Action, Edward Arnold, 1981.
Basic Speech Punctuation, Edward Arnold, 1981.
The Tufton Hill Lot, Murray, 1981.
The Smuggler and Other Stories, Murray, 1981.
Smudge and Chewpen Sentence Book, Edward Arnold, 1981.
The Glittering Seeds, Edward Arnold, 1981.
Smudge and Chewpen Letters, Edward Arnold, 1982.
Heroes and Their Journeys, Edward Arnold, 1982.
Read around One, Edward Arnold, 1983.
Six Plays for Today, Murray, 1983.
Looking after Number One, Murray, 1984.
Read around Two, Edward Arnold, 1984.
Ten Ghosts, Edward Arnold, 1984.
(And John Griffin) *Thirteen Tales of Crime,* Edward Arnold, 1984.
Thirteen Animal Stories, Edward Arnold, 1984.
Ten Strange Tales, Edward Arnold, 1985.
Sort It Out with Smudge and Chewpen, Edward Arnold, 1985.

"STEPS: BASIC ENGLISH COURSE" SERIES FOR CHILDREN; WITH GROVES AND GRIFFIN

Steps One, Longman, 1983.
Steps Two, Longman, 1983.
Steps Three, Longman, 1983.
Steps Four, Longman, 1984.
The Alphabet at Work, Longman, 1985.
Write in Sentences, Longman, 1985.
Be a Writer, Longman, 1985.

"ON YOUR MARKS" SERIES FOR CHILDREN; WITH GROVES AND GRIFFIN

On Your Marks 1, Longman, 1986.
On Your Marks 2, Longman, 1986.
On Your Marks 3, Longman, 1986.
On Your Marks 4, Longman, 1986.

WORK IN PROGRESS: Another novel for children; textbooks.

SIDELIGHTS: Nigel Grimshaw commented: "My first children's novel began as a story I told my own children during a rather wet holiday in Wales. Since that was intentionally comic, I wrote *The Wildkeepers' Guest* in a more serious mode as a companion piece."

GRIPE, Maria (Kristina) 1923-

PERSONAL: Surname is pronounced *Gree*-per; born July 25, 1923, in Vaxholm, Sweden; married Harald Gripe (an artist), 1946; children: Camilla. *Education:* Attended Stockholm University; received General Certificate of Education.

ADDRESSES: Home—Fruaengsgatan 5, 61131 Nykoeping, Sweden.

CAREER: Free-lance writer.

AWARDS, HONORS: Association of Swedish Libraries' Nils Holgersson Plaque for the best children's book of the year for *Hugo och Josefin;* Lewis Carrol Shelf Award, Wisconsin Book Conference, for *Pappa Pellerin's Daughter;* honor book, *New York Herald Tribune's* Children's Spring Book Festival, for *Pappa Pellerin's Daughter; Expressen* (Swedish evening newspaper) "Heffaklumpen" Award, 1966, for *Hugo;* Litteraturfraemjandets stipendium, 1968, for *Nattpappan;* Sveriges foerfattarfonds konstnaars stipendium, 1970-71; Astrid Lindgren-priset, 1972; Hans Christian Andersen International Children's Book Award, 1974; Sveriges foerfattarfonds premium foer litteraar foertjaanst, 1974; Hjalmar Bergman-priset, 1977; Doblougska priset, 1979; LO stipendiet, 1980; Metalls Kulturpris, 1981; Premio Nacional, utdelat av Spanska Kulturministeriet, 1982; Litteraturfraemjandets stora barnbokspris tillsammans med Harald Gripe, 1982; Jeremias i Troestloesapriset, 1983.

WRITINGS:

PUBLISHED BY BONNIERS

I vaar lilla stad, 1954.
Naar det snoeade, illustrated by husband, Harald Gripe, 1955.
Kung Laban Kommer, 1956.
Kvarteret Labyrinten, 1956.
Sebastian och Skuggan, 1957.
Stackars Lilla Q, 1957.
Tappa inte Masken, 1959.
De smaa roeda, illustrated by H. Gripe, 1960.
Glastunneln, 1969.
Tanten (based on radio play "The Aunt"; also see below), 1970.
. . . ellen dellen . . . , 1974.
Den "riktiga" Elvis, illustrated by H. Gripe, 1976.
Att vara Elvis, illustrated by H. Gripe, 1977.
Tordyveln flygeri i skymningen, 1978.
Bara Elvis, illustrated by H. Gripe, 1979.
Agnes Cecilia-en saellsam historia, 1981.
Skuggan oever stenbaenken, 1982.
. . . och de vita skuggorna i skogen, 1984.

IN ENGLISH TRANSLATION; ILLUSTRATED BY H. GRIPE

Josefin, Bonniers, 1961, translation by Paul Britten Austin published as *Josephine,* Delacorte, 1970.
Hugo och Josefin, Bonniers, 1962, translation by Austin published as *Hugo and Josephine,* Delacorte, 1969.
Pappa Pellerins dotter, Bonniers, 1963, translation by Kersti French published as *Pappa Pellerin's Daughter,* John Day, 1966.
Glasblaasarns Barn, Bonniers, 1964, translation by Sheila La Farge published as *The Glassblower's Children,* Delacorte, 1974.
I Klockornas Tid, Bonniers, 1965, translation by La Farge published as *In the Time of the Bells,* Delacorte, 1976.
Hugo, Bonniers, 1966, translation by Austin published under same title, Delacorte, 1970.

Landet utanfoer, Bonniers, 1967, translation by La Farge published as *The Land Beyond,* Delacorte, 1974.
Nattpappan, Bonniers, 1968, translation by Gerry Bothmer published as *The Night Daddy,* Delacorte, 1971.
Julias hus och Nattpappan, Bonniers, 1971, translation by Bothmer published as *Julia's House,* Delacorte, 1975.
Elvis Karlsson, Bonniers, 1972, translation by La Farge published as *Elvis and His Secret,* Delacorte, 1976.
Elvis!, Elvis!, Bonniers, 1973, translation published as *Elvis and His Friends,* Delacorte, 1976.

OTHER

Also author of screenplays for a film verison of *Hugo and Josephine,* 1968, and for a film based on the Elvis Karlsson books, 1976; author of radio plays "The Night Daddy," "Elvis Karlsson," 1973, and "Elvis! Elvis!," 1974, all based on her books of the same titles; author of six-part radio play "The Aunt," broadcast in 1969, on which *Tanten* was based; and author of a television play based on *The Night Daddy,* 1971.

SIDELIGHTS: Maria Gripe told *CA* that she had been warned by her father that there was but one person worthy to be called an *author:* Hans Christian Andersen, and that "light years behind him come all the poor wretches who were just 'writers.'" Her father, she said, told her one day, "'In order to write you need (a) to have something to write about, and (b) to know how to write. While waiting for (a) learn (b).' Such was his judgment. And so I began to wait . . . and wait. Till I had my little daughter. Then there was no getting away from it—I had something to write about—and somebody to write *for.*"

BIOGRAPHICAL/CRITICAL SOURCES:

PERIODICALS

Christian Science Monitor, November 6, 1969.
New Statesman, June 4, 1971.

                              *   *   *

GROSSER, Morton 1931-

PERSONAL: Born December 25, 1931, in Philadelphia, Pa.; son of Albert J. (an industrial realtor) and Esther (Mendel) Grosser; married Janet Zachs (an engineer and calligrapher), June 28, 1953; children: Adam. *Education:* Massachusetts Institute of Technology, S.B., 1953, S.M., 1954; Stanford University, Ph.D., 1961; National Institutes of Health postdoctoral fellow at University of California, Los Angeles, School of Medicine, 1961-62.

ADDRESSES: Home—1016 Lemon St., Menlo Park, Calif. 94025. *Agent*—Jane Gelfman, John Farquharson Ltd., 250 W. 57th St., New York, N.Y. 10107.

CAREER: Raytheon Corp., Waltham, Mass., design engineer, 1954-55; Clevite Transistor Products, Development Division, Waltham, head of design, 1955-57; Boeing Scientific Research Laboratories, Seattle, Wash., director of publication, 1964-65; independent consultant, 1967—; L. H. Alton & Co., San Francisco, Calif., general partner and managing director, 1984—. Visiting professor at Massachusetts Institute of Technology, University of California, Los Angeles, and Stanford University. Member of Gossamer Albatross Team, 1978-81. Also designer of power tools, medical transducers, missile engine components, and aircraft manufacturing machinery.

MEMBER: World Trade Club, American Institute of Aeronautics and Astronautics, American Society of Mechanical Engineers, Society of Automotive Engineers, Authors Guild, Authors League of America, Bohemian Club, M.I.T. Club, San Francisco Museum Society, San Francisco Ballet Association.

AWARDS, HONORS: Stegner creative writing fellowship at Stanford University, 1963-64.

WRITINGS:

The Discovery of Neptune, Harvard University Press, 1962.
The Hobby Shop, Houghton, 1967.
The Snake Horn (juvenile), Atheneum, 1973.
Diesel: The Man and the Engine, Atheneum, 1978.
Gossamer Odyssey: The Triumph of Human-Powered Flight, Houghton, 1981.
On Gossamer Wings, Dupont/York, 1982.

Contributor to scholarly journals and popular magazines, including *Atlantic, Harper's, New Yorker, Holiday, Saturday Evening Post, Natural History,* and *Technology Review.*

WORK IN PROGRESS: A research partnership in peripheral nerve repair which combines microsurgery and microelectronics; a novel, *The Fabulous Fifty,* about baseball, set in Philadelphia in 1921.

SIDELIGHTS: Morton Grosser told *CA:* "I currently divide my working time between writing and consulting on technology assessment, management, and corporate strategy. In 1978, I was invited by Dr. Paul MacCready to join the *Gossamer Albatross* team. Both my wife and I helped design and build components for the human-powered airplane that flew across the English Channel on June 12, 1979. I was also a member of the flight expedition, and I wrote the authorized book on the *Albatross* and its predecessor, the *Gossamer Condor.*"

According to Frances Taliaferro in the *New York Times Book Review,* Grosser's *Gossamer Odyssey* "will delight air enthusiasts." Taliaferro finds the book "often too technical to entertain the ordinary reader," but later confesses that "even a technological illiterate, making the acquaintance of the spunky Condor and Albatross, must become their affectionate partisan."

AVOCATIONAL INTERESTS: Tennis, ballet, model building, wood carving, transportation.

BIOGRAPHICAL/CRITICAL SOURCES:

PERIODICALS

New York Times Book Review, May 24, 1981.

*   *   *

GROVE, Fred(erick)   1913-

PERSONAL: Born July 4, 1913, in Hominy, Okla.; married, 1938; children: William Riley. *Education:* University of Oklahoma, B.A., 1937. *Religion:* Episcopalian.

ADDRESSES: Home—P.O. Box 1248, Silver City, N.M. 88062.

CAREER: Daily Citizen, Cushing, Okla., sports editor, 1938-39; *Morning News,* Shawnee, Okla., reporter, 1940-42; *The Star,* Harlingen, Tex., sports editor, 1942; *Morning News and Star,* Shawnee, reporter, 1943-44, managing editor, 1944-46; *Oklahoma City Times* and *Daily Oklahoman,* copyreader, 1946-47; University of Oklahoma, Norman, senior assistant in public relations, 1947-54; currently full-time writer.

MEMBER: Western Writers of America, Westerners (Silver City).

AWARDS, HONORS: National Cowboy Hall of Fame and Western Heritage Center Wrangler award, 1962, for short story "Comanche Son," and 1969, for novel *The Buffalo Runners;* Western Writers of America Spur award, 1963, for short material "Comanche Woman," 1963, for novel *Comanche Captives,* 1969, for short material "When the Caballos Came," 1977, for novel *The Great Horse Race,* and 1982, for novel *Match Race,* award finalist, 1971, for novel *War Journey,* and 1972, for novel *The Child Stealers.*

WRITINGS:

Flame of the Osage, Pyramid Books, 1958.
Sun Dance, Ballantine, 1958.
No Bugles, No Glory, Ballantine, 1959.
(Contributor) *Spurs West,* Doubleday, 1960.
Comanche Captives, Ballantine, 1961.
(Contributor) *Western Roundup,* Macmillan, 1961.
The Land Seekers, Ballantine, 1963.
(Contributor) *The Pick of the Roundup,* Avon, 1963.

PUBLISHED BY DOUBLEDAY

Buffalo Spring, 1967.
The Buffalo Runners, 1968.
War Journey, 1971.
The Child Stealers, 1973.
Warrior Road, 1974.
Drums without Warriors, 1976.
The Great Horse Race, 1977.
Bush Track, 1978.
The Running Horses, 1980.
Phantom Warrior, 1981.
Match Race, 1982.
A Far Trumpet, 1985.

SIDELIGHTS: Fred Grove studied under Lester Harris, western author and teacher, and the noted biographer and historian Walter Stanley Campbell at the University of Oklahoma. Grove later studied with Dwight V. Swain, nationally-known teacher and science fiction writer. He is a researcher on the history of the American Southwest and quarter-horse racing.

*   *   *

GROVES, Paul   1930-

PERSONAL: Born in 1930 in Oxford, England; son of Charles Hubert Warburg and Doris (Watson) Groves; married June Griggs; children: Wendy, Sally. *Education:* Royal Academy of Dramatic Art, diploma, 1950, L.R.A.M., 1955; attended College of St. Mark and St. John, 1955-57. *Politics:* Labour.

ADDRESSES: Home—Willows, Casthorpe Rd., Barrowby, Grantham, Lincolnshire, England.

CAREER: Professional actor, 1950-53; clerk for Colgate Palmolive, 1953-55; teacher at Lancastrian school in Chichester, 1957-61; teacher of English and head of department at St. Hugh's C.E. Comprehensive School, 1961-84. *Military service:* British Army, Royal Electrical and Mechanical Engineers, 1949-50.

MEMBER: National Association for the Teaching of English.

WRITINGS:

FOR CHILDREN

Mr. Egbert Nosh, Hodder & Stoughton, 1970.

The Third Climber, Hutchinson, 1977.
Not That I'm Workshy, Hutchinson, 1977.
Six Silly Plays, Longman, 1985.
Six Even Sillier Plays, Longman, 1986.

FOR CHILDREN; WITH NIGEL GRIMSHAW

Up Our Way, Edward Arnold, 1972.
Living Our Way, Edward Arnold, 1973.
Join the Action, Edward Arnold, 1973.
Going Our Way, Edward Arnold, 1975.
Action Replay, Edward Arnold, 1975.
Thirteen Ghosts: A Collection of Original Ghost Stories with Suggestions for Varied Work in English, Edward Arnold, 1976.
Smudge and Chewpen: A Book of Exercises for Correction of the Common Errors Made in Writing, Edward Arnold, 1976.
The Goodbodys, Edward Arnold, 1976.
Monsters of Myth and Legend, Edward Arnold, 1977.
Action Stations: Seven Plays to Read or Record, Edward Arnold, 1977.
Thirteen Weird Tales: A Collection of Original Strange Stories with Suggestions for Varied Work in English, Edward Arnold, 1977.
Call to Action: Seven Plays to Read or Record, Edward Arnold, 1978.
Stops and Starts, Edward Arnold, 1978.
Thirteen Horror Stories, Edward Arnold, 1978.
Smudge and Chewpen Tests: A Book of Short Tests on the Common Errors Made in Writing, Edward Arnold, 1978.
Thirteen Sci-Fi Stories, Edward Arnold, 1979.
Into Action, Edward Arnold, 1979.
Smudge and Chewpen Word Book, Edward Arnold, 1980.
All Action, Edward Arnold, 1981.
Basic Speech Punctuation, Edward Arnold, 1981.
The Tufton Hill Lot, Murray, 1981.
The Smuggler and Other Stories, Murray, 1981.
Smudge and Chewpen Sentence Book, Edward Arnold, 1981.
The Glittering Seeds, Edward Arnold, 1981.
Smudge and Chewpen Letters, Edward Arnold, 1982.
Heroes and Their Journeys, Edward Arnold, 1982.
Read around One, Edward Arnold, 1983.
Six Plays for Today, Murray, 1983.
Looking after Number One, Murray, 1984.
Read around Two, Edward Arnold, 1984.
Ten Ghosts, Edward Arnold, 1984.
(And John Griffin) *Thirteen Tales of Crime*, Edward Arnold, 1984.
Thirteen Animal Stories, Edward Arnold, 1984.
Ten Strange Tales, Edward Arnold, 1985.
Sort It Out with Smudge and Chewpen, Edward Arnold, 1985.

"TEMPO BOOK" SERIES FOR CHILDREN; WITH LESLIE STRATTA

The Swinging Kings, Longman, 1965.
The Big Drop, Longman, 1965.
Lost in the Fog, Longman, 1965.
The Club Dance, Longman, 1966.
Sandra Helps the Gang, Longman, 1966.
At the Market, Longman, 1966.
Bonfire Night, Longman, 1967.
The Trap, Longman, 1967.
The Fair, Longman, 1967.
At the Circus, Longman, 1967.
On the Mountain, Longman, 1979.
The Swindle, Longman, 1979.

Please Help, Longman, 1979.
Happy Christmas, Longman, 1979.
Tempo Plays, Longman, 1981, Volume I: *The Car Dump*, Volume II: *Death on the Railway*.

"BANGERS AND MASH" SERIES FOR CHILDREN; ILLUSTRATED BY EDWARD McLACHAN

The Hat Trick, Longman, 1975.
Eggs, Longman, 1975.
Wiggly Worms, Longman, 1975.
The Clock, Longman, 1975.
The Best Duster, Longman, 1975.
In a Jam, Longman, 1975.
Ding Dong Baby, Longman, 1975.
Red Indians and Red Spots, Longman, 1975.
The Bee and the Sea, Longman, 1975.
Wet Paint, Longman, 1975.
Toothday and Birthday, Longman, 1975.
Bikes and Broomsticks, Longman, 1975.
The Hole Story, Longman, 1975.
The Cow and Bull Story, Longman, 1975.
Bubble Bath, Longman, 1979.
Tea Break, Longman, 1979.
Jumpers, Longman, 1979.
Hatching Is Catching, Longman, 1979.
Sticky Trousers, Longman, 1979.
The C.P.O., Longman, 1979.
Snatch and Grab, Longman, 1979.
Garden Trouble, Longman, 1979.
(With Jennifer Bromley) *Workbook One*, Longman, 1979.
(With Bromley) *Workbook Two*, Longman, 1979.
(With Bromley) *Workbook Three*, Longman, 1979.
Back to School, Longman, 1982.
Knots and Knocks, Longman, 1982.
Kippers and Cleaners, Longman, 1982.
Tears and Cheers, Longman, 1982.
(With Bromley) *Bangers and Mash Alphabet Book*, Longman, 1983.
(With Bromley) *Workbook Four*, Longman, 1985.
Red Nose, Longman, 1985.
Ant Eggs, Longman, 1985.
Mud Cake, Longman, 1985.
Duck in the Box, Longman, 1985.
Pond Monster, Longman, 1985.
Lion Pit, Longman, 1985.

"STEPS: BASIC ENGLISH COURSE" SERIES FOR CHILDREN; WITH GRIFFIN AND GRIMSHAW

Steps One, Longman, 1983.
Steps Two, Longman, 1983.
Steps Three, Longman, 1983.
Steps Four, Longman, 1984.
The Alphabet at Work, Longman, 1985.
Write in Sentences, Longman, 1985.
Be a Writer, Longman, 1985.

"ON YOUR MARKS" SERIES FOR CHILDREN; WITH GRIFFIN AND GRIMSHAW

On Your Marks 1, Longman, 1986.
On Your Marks 2, Longman, 1986.
On Your Marks 3, Longman, 1986.
On Your Marks 4, Longman, 1986.

"WINNERS" SERIES FOR CHILDREN; WITH MARTIN PITTS

The Magic Football, Edward Arnold, 1983.

The Mystery of the Shadows, Edward Arnold, 1983.
Bikes in the Air, Edward Arnold, 1983.
Billy's Big Push, Edward Arnold, 1983.

"MISS WILLOW" SERIES FOR CHILDREN

Miss Willow Goes to the Zoo, Edward Arnold, 1981.
Miss Willow and the Riverboat, Edward Arnold, 1981.
Miss Willow Goes Camping, Edward Arnold, 1981.

OTHER

Also author of "Egbert Nosh" cartoon strips for BBC-TV.

SIDELIGHTS: Paul Groves comments: "As a writer, I am a leader in the use of phonics in learning to read. I am also a pioneer in the use of humor, particularly for slow-learning pupils. I have received many letters from teachers who say that pupils who had initially failed to read found the humorous approach of 'Bangers and Mash' the impetus they needed. I write a lot of realistic and fantasy stories for older pupils."

Mr. Egbert Nosh has been translated into German and Czech.

* * *

GROZNY, I. L.
   See BERGER, Ivan (Bennett)

* * *

GUELICH, Robert A(llison)   1939-

PERSONAL: Born June 20, 1939, in Charleston, W.Va.; son of Robert Stanley (a clergyman) and Agnes (Allison) Guelich; married Janet Fransen (a teacher), June 15, 1963 (divorced June 18, 1979); married Joyce Finnie Calvert, May 12, 1980; children: Scott Andrew, David Robert. *Education:* Wheaton College,Wheaton, Ill., B.A., 1961; University of Illinois, M.A., 1962; Fuller Theological Seminary, S.T.B., 1964; University of Hamburg, D.Theol., 1967. *Politics:* Independent.

ADDRESSES: Office—Colonial Church, 6200 Colonial Way, Edina, Minn. 55435.

CAREER: Ordained Baptist minister; University of Hamburg, Hamburg, West Germany, tutor and research assistant, 1966-67; Bethel College and Seminary, St. Paul, Minn., visiting lecturer in college, 1967-68, assistant professor of New Testament in seminary, 1968-70, associate professor, 1970-73; Colonial Congregational Church, Edina, Minn., teaching minister, 1973-75; Bethel Theological Seminary, professor of New Testament, 1975-79; Northern Baptist Theological Seminary, Lombard, Ill., professor of New Testament, 1980-84; Colonial Church, Edina, Minn., teaching minister and theologian in residence, 1984—. Visiting professor, University of Aberdeen, Scotland, 1973.

MEMBER: Studiorum Novi Testamenti Societas, Society of Biblical Literature.

AWARDS, HONORS: Alexander von Humboldt fellowship, 1978; American Theological Schools grant, 1978; Alexander von Humboldt and Fulbright grants, 1979-80, for research at University of Tuebingen, West Germany.

WRITINGS:

(Translator) Leonhard Goppelt, *Apostolic and Post-Apostolic Times,* Harper, 1970 (published in England as *Apostolic and Post-Apostolic Age,* A. & C. Black, 1970).

(Editor) *Unity and Diversity in New Testament Theology: Essays in Honor of George E. Ladd,* Eerdmans, 1978.
The Sermon on the Mount: A Foundation for Understanding, Word, Inc., 1982.

Contributor to *Baker's Dictionary of Christian Ethics* and *New International Standard Bible Encyclopedia.*

WORK IN PROGRESS: The Gospel of Mark: Word Bible Commentary Series, for Word, Inc.; *The Gospel of Matthew: The New International Commentary,* for Eerdmans.

AVOCATIONAL INTERESTS: Sailing, skiing, backpacking.

* * *

GULICK, Bill
   See GULICK, Grover C.

* * *

GULICK, Grover C.   1916-
   (Bill Gulick)

PERSONAL: Surname is pronounced *Gu*-lick; born February 22, 1916, in Kansas City, Mo.; son of Grover Cleveland (a veterinarian) and Golda Mae (Hall) Gulick; married Marcella Jeanne Abbott (researcher for her husband), June 30, 1946. *Education:* Attended University of Oklahoma, 1935-37, 1939-41.

ADDRESSES: Home—Route 3, Walla Walla, Wash. 99362. *Agent*—Carl Brandt, Brandt & Brandt Literary Agency, 1501 Broadway, New York, N.Y. 10036.

CAREER: Professional writer, 1941—.

MEMBER: Western Writers of America (president, 1955-56).

AWARDS, HONORS: Best Short Story Award, Western Writers of America, 1958, 1960; Western Heritage Award, Cowboy Hall of Fame, 1966, for *They Came to a Valley;* Governor's Award, Washington State Arts Commission, 1967, 1972; Pacific Northwest Booksellers Award, 1971, for *Snake River Country;* Levi's Saddleman Award, Levi Strauss Co. and Western Writers of America, 1983, for "an impressive career writing fiction, nonfiction, and drama of the West."

WRITINGS—Under name Bill Gulick:

NOVELS

Bend of the Snake (also see below), Houghton, 1950.
A Drum Calls West, Houghton, 1952.
A Thousand for the Cariboo, Houghton, 1954.
White Men, Red Men and Mountain Men, Houghton, 1955.
The Land Beyond, Houghton, 1958.
Showdown in the Sun (also see below), Popular Library, 1958.
The Shaming of Broken Horn, Doubleday, 1961.
The Moon-Eyed Appaloosa, Doubleday, 1962.
The Hallelujah Trail (also see below), Doubleday, 1963.
They Came to a Valley, Doubleday, 1966.
Liveliest Town in the West, Doubleday, 1969.
The Country Club Caper, Doubleday, 1971.
Treasure in Hell's Canyon, Doubleday, 1979.

SCREENPLAYS

"Bend of the River" (based on his novel *Bend of the Snake*), Universal Pictures, 1951.
"The Road to Denver" (based on the *Saturday Evening Post* serial "The Man from Texas"), Republic Pictures, 1955.

"Hallelujah Trail" (based on his novel of the same title), United Artists, 1965.

Also author of "Showdown in the Sun," optioned by Richmond Productions, and "Fandango," optioned by Twentieth Century-Fox.

OTHER

(With Thomas Rothrock) *Abilene or Bust* (juvenile), Cupples & Leon, 1946.

(With Rothrock) *Desolation Trail* (juvenile), Cupples & Leon, 1946.

Snake River Country (nonfiction; photographs by Earl Roberge), Caxton, 1971.

Chief Joseph Country: Land of the Nez Perce (nonfiction), Caxton, 1981.

Author of two historical pageants, "The Magic Musket," 1953, and "The First Treaty Council," 1955, both produced regionally; also author of historical outdoor drama, "Trails West," first produced in Walla Walla, Wash., July 1, 1976. Contributor of about 150 stories to magazines, including *Esquire, Argosy, Collier's, Liberty, Saturday Evening Post,* and *Adventure.*

SIDELIGHTS: Grover C. Gulick, better known to readers as Bill Gulick, has worked in the Western genre for virtually his entire writing career. His stories differ from more conventional ones, however, in that they are usually set in the Pacific Northwest rather than the Southwest or Middle West, and they emphasize character development instead of action and violence. Reviewers have praised the extensive research that makes Gulick's Westerns so much more authentic than many books in the genre. As the author commented in his *CA* interview, "I never did like what you might call the slam-bang action Western. . . . I knew a little too much about the real West."

CA INTERVIEW

CA interviewed Bill Gulick by telephone on February 25, 1985, at his home in Walla Walla, Washington.

CA: In 1983 you won the Levi's Saddleman Award for your career as a writer about the West. How did you fall in love with the American West?

GULICK: You might say I was raised in it. I was raised in central Kansas and moved to Oklahoma City when I was fourteen. I went to school in Oklahoma City and at the University of Oklahoma. And all my family had pioneered; my father and grandfather were from western Kansas. They still owned some farm property, and I used to go out there every summer. But even though I was raised in it, I really didn't get too much interested in it until I started to write.

CA: When did you know you wanted to be a writer?

GULICK: Oh, when I was in the third grade, I think. I was writing little stories, and reading always interested me. I think I sold my first piece when I was in the fifth grade: I would write book reports for twenty-five cents for other kids who were too lazy to write their own. It was my second year at the university when we had to write some poetry for a class, and my teacher wanted to enter mine in some sort of a contest. I told her to go ahead. A while later she called me in after class and she said, "I want you to be at the library this afternoon." There was a meeting of an honorary society. I said, "Well,

I'm sorry, but I have baseball practice then." She said, "You had better be there." So I went, and I had won first and third in the poetry contest. The poems were published in the university paper, and I caught it from the boys on the baseball team!

I was out of the university after my sophomore year. Times were a little tough. I had a pretty good job working on a construction crew for a couple of years and I would write on the side. But when that work petered out, I thought, well, I like to write and there are some good professional writing courses at the University of Oklahoma. I'll just sell my car and go back to school and transfer to professional writing school and see if I can make it. I gave it six months.

The courses were taught by Walter S. Campbell and Foster Harris. Campbell had been a Rhodes scholar and his father had been an Indian agent; he'd written a number of books himself on the West—histories and that sort of thing. Foster Harris had been an editor and had written a lot for the pulp magazines. They had a theory something like Ben Jonson, who said that only a fool writes for anything but money. I remember Dr. Campbell used to say, "You've come to me saying, 'I know I can write; teach me how to sell.' You've got hold of the wrong end of the stick. I can teach you how to sell, but you'll be the rest of your life learning how to write."

So I tried sports stories and this, that, and the other. Nothing sold. Finally one day Foster Harris said, "Why don't you write Westerns?" I said, "What do I know about the West?" He said, "Well, you've lived in it all your life." At that time there was a very big market for Western stories in the pulp magazines, and the fourth or fifth one I wrote—about a boy and a wild horse he captured—sold, for the great sum of thirty dollars, and I was on my way.

I started, really, just wanting to sell and get published. But I never did like what you might call the slam-bang action Western. I didn't quite believe it; I knew a little too much about the real West. So I just gradually, as I wrote, tried to make my Western stories a little more authentic. That was forty-five years ago; it was in 1940 that I sold my first story.

CA: Why do you think the history of the West is so often distorted?

GULICK: Probably because it was so popular when they first began writing about it. I take a rather broad view of what is a Western. I think A. B. Guthrie, Jr., writes Westerns. Everything from James Fenimore Cooper, the beginning of the pioneer West. The boundaries gradually moved West. I got intrigued with the mountain men, the fur trappers and traders of the Rocky Mountains in the 1820s and 1830s. Ironically, some years later, I had a story in the *Saturday Evening Post* and the editor said, "The thing I like about your stories is that they're not Westerns." This was a story about some mountain men who had invaded California in the early days. My old teacher, Foster Harris, refused to give that same story an award because, he said, "That's not a Western." So it's according to who is defining it, what is a Western.

CA: Who were your literary idols?

GULICK: Stewart Edward White was one, certainly. He wrote for about fifty years, and he was very popular when I was growing up. I read most of his things. And of course later I read Ernest Haycox and Zane Grey. I got a little tired of Zane

Grey. Ernest Haycox I admired for his style, although he was a rather dangerous man to imitate. Then the historical novelists, like Kenneth Roberts, I always loved. But more and more I turn to the more historical type of writing, the authentic type. Later Bud Guthrie, Dan Cushman, Dorothy Johnson.

CA: A great deal of research obviously goes into your work, the fiction as well as the nonfiction. Is that a process that you especially enjoy?

GULICK: I do in a way; I like to read the original diaries and that sort of thing, and I like to know my facts and have them right. But my wife, when we got married, was a secretary for Weyerhauser Steamship Company, and she got interested in the research end of things. After we moved here to Walla Walla, she went to work as a librarian at Whitman College, where they have a very fine library. She liked to do research. When I found that out, I just would turn her loose in the field that I was working on and she would do most of the research for me. That gave me my afternoons free to play golf. She doublechecks everything and she likes to dig out the facts for me. I select those that I want to use. We've built up quite a library between us. If I can't find something, she can.

CA: So she's usually in on a book from the very start?

GULICK: Yes. For example, some years ago I was writing a big historical novel, *They Came to a Valley,* about the beginnings of Idaho Territory. I happened to read an item in an early newspaper, 1867, about eighty wagons loaded with whiskey and champagne that had left Julesburg bound for Denver. I told her, ''There's a short story in this.'' I did nothing with it, and later I said, ''No, that ought to be a novelette.'' Finally I said, ''I believe there's a book in this.'' My publisher, Doubleday, wanted me to write a shorter book while I finished the long historical novel I was on, so I gave a brief outline of how I would handle it.

At that time, suffragettes were invading the West—Wyoming Territory, Colorado Territory. Treaties had just been made with the Sioux Indians. Prospectors were swarming into the area. This wagon train was obviously carrying Denver's winter drinking supply. I said to myself, what would happen if all of these elements had gotten wind of that cargo and had gone after it? So one of my characters, naturally, had to be a suffragette and temperance worker, Cora Templeton Massengale. But I wasn't satisfied with the stereotype, so Jeanne said to me, ''We have these autobiographies of some of the suffragettes at the library.'' She brought one set home; I think there were about four volumes in it. And for at least a month or two I became an expert on the suffragist temperance movement. It made my character come to life. That was *Hallelujah Trail.*

CA: That book was quite a feat of plotting, wasn't it?

GULICK: It really wrote itself. Seems like every newspaper man I've ever met wished he were a free-lance writer and had a great novel in him. So to handle that, I thought, why not have this newspaper reporter a wartime correspondent who was making a report and bringing it back to President Grant? It was a device, but it seemed to work. I think I wrote that in a flat two months.

CA: Do you normally have a novel tightly plotted before you begin to write?

GULICK: I have it pretty well planned, and usually I do work out an outline, yes, so that I know where I'm going. But I don't have any hesitancy in departing from it. Very often you see something when you finally get down to writing it that is better than what you originally conceived.

CA: In your 1981 history, Chief Joseph's Country, *you wrote from the Indian point of view. Why did you do it that way?*

GULICK: I had always been interested in the Chief Joseph story, and I'd been all over the country. My first nonfiction book was *Snake River Country,* which covered essentially the same area. But while the Indians played an important part, it was more from the white point of view. That book did very well, and a few years later, the publisher, Caxton, thought the time was right for a book on the Nez Perce and that it should be from the Indian point of view. I agreed. So you might say that the two books balanced one another. And I had worked with the Indians on a number of projects.

CA: Tell me more about those projects with the Indians.

GULICK: The first one was in 1953. They were having a Washington Territory Centennial here, and I was asked to write what was called a pageant in those days, an outdoor production to be staged at the fairgrounds. In those days a lot of Indians used to come there and camp; there would be a hundred lodges or so of them who would camp on the fairgrounds. We used them in the production.

That experience sort of intrigued me, and in 1955 there was the centennial of the Stevens Treaties, which were made here in the Walla Walla Valley and settled the fate of about five regional Indian tribes. In this case the Indians had begun to get some settlements from the government's building the dams on the Columbia River, which flooded their traditional fishing rights. An attorney friend of mine had helped them get the settlement, so he got me a transcript of the nineteen days of talks in 1855 which were recorded by two white secretaries— what the Indians said, what the whites said. I used these as a basis for the outdoor drama, which is what it actually turned out to be. We had about sixteen Indian leaders who could speak the language here, and we used them in a soundproof booth to read the lines in the Indian tongue and then translate while the actual Indians out front were pantomiming them. I was on that for four or five months, an interesting experience.

Then in 1976 I was commissioned to write an outdoor drama with a professional cast, and again we used quite a few Indians. I worked with a second generation of them. I was rather intrigued to see how few could speak the language anymore. They had lost it in twenty years. *Chief Joseph Country* was a natural outgrowth of my work with the Indians on the pageants.

CA: You've said you found in the direct accounts of the Indians' dealings with the whites that the Indians' accounts were much more to be trusted.

GULICK: They had a self-censoring device, in a way. After a battle, each warrior would get up and tell what he had done, just what he himself had done. If he tried to brag about it, if he exaggerated, everybody there would say, no, that isn't the way it happened. Walter Campbell, who wrote under the pen name Stanley Vestal, used to say—and his father was an Indian agent with the Sioux, and he used to say this too—that they never dared say anything about themselves unless it was true. I found this among the Nez Perce the same way. Where they got undependable was when you asked them what happened that they didn't observe, that they had just heard about. Then they were apt to tell you whatever they thought you wanted to hear. But when they were talking about what they did personally, it was pretty apt to be true.

CA: In addition to the Saddleman Award, you've won awards specifically for short stories, for your novels, and for nonfiction. Do you prefer one form to the others, or do you enjoy working in them all equally?

GULICK: I always liked the short story because you can write one in a week or two and be done with it. For the last fourteen years that the old *Saturday Evening Post* was in existence, that was my main market. They treated their writers so well and paid me so well that I was really spoiled for any other kind of writing. But I began to see what was going to happen to the *Post,* and I was beginning to have books published. I have missed the *Saturday Evening Post* greatly. I haven't really written any new short stories since they folded, though I have published some that were left over that I had written when they were having their fading days and weren't really buying.

There's really no market for Western short stories anymore. So I have gotten into the longer things. I'm presently in the longest one yet. It's a historical novel, and it's going to be about twice the length of *Chief Joseph Country,* it now looks like. It's over 300,000 words, and I've got another month on it.

CA: What kind of schedule do you write on? Do you work every day?

GULICK: Five days a week. I like to get to the typewriter at nine o'clock in the morning, take a break for lunch and maybe go for a walk with my wife and the dog after lunch, then come back to it until four o'clock or something like that. If I can do four or five pages a day, steady, I'm satisfied; that's good production.

CA: Some Western writers complain that their books are discriminated against by the New York publishing establishment and consequently receive far too little attention nationwide. Do you agree?

GULICK: That is true. A lot of people turn up their noses at anything that has to do with the West—it's a Western. Well, ninety percent of all music that's produced is bad. Ninety percent of all books that are written are bad. But in any kind of music and any kind of books, it's that other ten percent that counts. There are certainly some very good Western writers writing today—I think of Elmer Kelton, for example, down in Texas; and, as I said, Dan Cushman, Bud Guthrie, and Dorothy Johnson, who passed away not too long ago.

CA: You've served as president of the Western Writers of America. What does that organization do?

GULICK: It was formed in 1953, and it is an association of writers, editors, publishers, and so on who get together once a year at a convention to discuss problems of the trade. And we have a monthly publication. It's changed since the beginning. In the beginning, most of the writers were full-time writers. Now that's the exception. I think the requirements are that you have published three books for full membership, or

twenty short stories or articles. The associate members are those who have published less, or are in some allied part of the field—as publishers, editors, TV producers or directors, agents, and so on. I believe there's something like six or seven hundred members now. We see each other only once a year. When she first went to one of these conventions, my wife said, ''This shouldn't be called the Western Writers; it should be called the Western Talkers!''

CA: Does the organization do something to try to get Western writers more recognition?

GULICK: That's part of it, but there are also things like contracts, dealing with publishers who don't pay their royalties on time, and all that sort of thing. Then they started this program of giving awards every year to recognize various types of writing from the historical to the straight Western.

CA: You settled in Walla Walla many years ago, after trying several other places. Obviously you haven't regretted your choice. How did you pick that spot?

GULICK: My wife originally came from Tacoma, which is on the rainy side of the mountains out here west of the Cascades. I had come out from Oklahoma, where we had sunshine. After we got married, we went back East to New York for a year or so, then New England. We kept coming back to the Pacific Northwest. We'd go to the Southwest, but we kept coming back to the Pacific Northwest. But we just got a little tired of the rain and grayness west of the Cascades. The *Saturday Evening Post* had indicated they would be interested in a novel if I wanted to write one as a serial, but they wanted something fresh. I got interested in the inland Pacific Northwest—that is, the Snake River area, eastern Washington, Oregon, and Idaho. My first book was called *Bend of the Snake,* which was about the development of gold mining in Idaho Territory. It was all centered in Walla Walla, because this was the head of navigation. People would come up the Columbia and then go overland to the Idaho mines.

The book was too big for a serial, the *Post* said, but it was published by Houghton Mifflin and the movies bought it and made it into the movie *Bend of the River.* I remembered Walla Walla and the area from having done a little research here, so one rainy week in June we headed for sunshine and happened to hit here one day when the sun was shining. At that time I was writing mostly for the *Post.* All I needed was a post office and a library. Whitman College is a fine liberal arts college, and it did have a good library. So we decided we'd try it here for a year or so, and we've been here ever since. The other reason was that there was some historical material in the area that had not really been used a whole lot. I sort of concentrated on this area.

CA: Have you been much involved in the production of the movies?

GULICK: Very little, really. They buy something, and they are going to do what they want with it. When they were filming *Bend of the River,* down around Mount Hood, I went down on location for a day or two and just watched. That was about all. When they bought *Hallelujah Trail,* that was really a nice experience. I was invited to go down on location to Gallup, New Mexico, with the company. My wife and I spent a week there. The first thing the director, John Sturges, did was ask me if I had read the screenplay, which I hadn't. He said, ''I want you to read it and tell me what's wrong with it.'' He kind of smiled and said, ''I'm not saying we'll change it, but you tell me anyhow.'' I think there's a relationship between how much they pay for a novel and how they treat it. They treated that one with a lot of respect. I liked the screenplay. Then we went back for another week in Hollywood when they were filming, and we went down for the premiere and were quite well treated.

As the magazine market faded and I had sold some things to television—published stories—I discovered they paid the television writer about five times more to adapt my story, so I thought, why can't I do that and combine it with a winter trip south? But every time we went down to Hollywood on one of those excursions, the writers went out on strike or my favorite producer got fired, and I just decided it was too much of a hassle. I would stay here and write my stories, and if they sold, fine; if not, I didn't have a hassle.

I've had a couple of books bought by the movies that have never been produced. A producer bought one with Tyrone Power slated to star in it and had a screenplay written, and Tyrone Power died. The property was tied up in his estate for years. Then after they did *Hallelujah Trail,* this producer decided he was going to get John Sturges to direct this one with Burt Lancaster. He sent him my book and a screenplay, and Sturges said, ''Well, the book would make a good movie, but this is a lousy screenplay. Why don't you get Bill Gulick to fix it for you?'' So I went down on that, and we struck up a tentative deal. I would have gotten paid about three times as much to write a screenplay as they paid me originally. But it got hung up on financing, as those things often do, and it's never been made. You're in such a helpless state. Much as they pay for some of these productions, the writer gets usually not more than four or five percent out of the total budget. That's the way they treat you. And having had first-class treatment from markets like the *Post* and my book publishers, it just was too much of a hassle for me.

CA: Do you have a project planned beyond the big book you're finishing up now?

GULICK: I've got a tentative one in mind, but I want to get this out of the way first. As I say, it's the biggest thing I've undertaken. It didn't start out that way, but it grew. It's based on the fact that William Clark fathered a child by a Nez Perce woman while he was in this part of the country, and the child grew to manhood knowing he was Clark's son. He survived into his seventies and was with the Chief Joseph contingent that was captured and taken to Indian territory. He died there. So I've taken that as a basis, three generations of Indians and whites, but I've written it as a historical novel.

AVOCATIONAL INTERESTS: Fishing, golf, photography.

BIOGRAPHICAL/CRITICAL SOURCES:

PERIODICALS

New York Times, March 7, 1969.
New York Times Book Review, February 16, 1969, December 5, 1971.

—*Interview by Jean W. Ross*

*   *   *

GULLACE, Gino 1925-

PERSONAL: Born August 18, 1925, in Ferruzzano, Italy; son of Giovanni and Nicoletta (Audino) Gullace; married Estelle Scala, September, 1950. *Education:* Messina University, Dottore in Lettere, 1946; University of Rochester, M.A., 1952; Syracuse University, Ph.D., 1964.

ADDRESSES: Home—38 Van Ness Ct., Maplewood, N.J. 07040. *Office*—Rizzoli Publishers, 1500 Broadway, Suite 1603, New York, N.Y. 10036. *Agent*—Rizzoli Press Service, Via Angelo Rizzoli 2, 20132 Milano, Italy.

CAREER: Foreign correspondent for Italian magazines, *Oggi, Annabella,* and *Novella 2000,* 1951—. Notable assignments include the coverage of the American space program, the first heart transplant, and other medical events. Teacher at University of Rochester.

MEMBER: Overseas Press Club, Foreign Correspondents Association.

WRITINGS:

I Grandi Nomi del Ventesimo Secolo (title means *The Big Names of the Twentieth Century*), De Agostini (Italy), 1973.
Reportage 900, Rizzoli, 1982.
Back to the Roots: A View of Magna Grecia, Rizzoli, 1986.

SIDELIGHTS: Gino Gullace told *CA:* ''Writing is for me a form of catharsis. I write because I feel the need to unburden myself of thoughts, ideas and emotions. I consider the act of writing more important and exciting than having my work published.''

*   *   *

GUTEK, Gerald L(ee) 1935-

PERSONAL: Born July 10, 1935, in Streator, Ill.; son of Albert T. and Irene (Novotney) Gutek; married Patricia Ann Egan, June 12, 1965; children: Jennifer Ann, Laura Lee. *Education:* University of Illinois, B.A., 1957, M.A., 1959, Ph.D., 1964. *Religion:* Roman Catholic.

ADDRESSES: Home—437 South Edgewood Ave., LaGrange, Ill. 60525. *Office*—School of Education, Loyola University of Chicago, 820 North Michigan Ave., Chicago, Ill. 60611.

CAREER: Loyola University of Chicago, Chicago, Ill., instructor, 1963-65, assistant professor, 1965-68, associate professor, 1968-72, professor of education and history, 1972—, chairman of department of foundations of education, 1969—, dean of School of Education, 1979—. Visiting professor, summers, at Loyola University of Los Angeles (now Loyola Marymount University), 1965, University of Illinois, 1966, and Michigan State University, 1969 and 1973; visiting professor at Loyola University in Rome, Italy, 1974-75. Grotelueschen Lecturer, Concordia College, 1979; Powell Memorial Lecturer, University of Illinois at Chicago Circle, 1982; lecturer at or participant in numerous conferences, seminars, and symposia. Member of Cook County (Ill.) Board of Education, 1978-81, board of trustees of Erikson Institute for Early Childhood Education, 1979-83, and Street Law Advisory Board, Chicago, 1979—.

MEMBER: American Educational Studies Association (member of editorial review board, 1980-82; member of executive board, 1981-83), American Studies Association, American Association of Colleges for Teacher Education (Loyola University of Chicago representative, 1979—), National Historic Communal Societies Association, Society of Historians of the

Early Republic, Council for Basic Education, Comparative Education Society, History of Education Society, National Council for the Social Studies, Organization of American Historians, Philosophy of Education Society, Society for Professors of Education, Midwest Comparative Education Society, Midwest History of Education Society (president, 1970-71), Midwest Philosophy of Education Society, Illinois Council for the Social Studies, Illinois Association of Colleges for Teacher Education (Loyola University of Chicago representative, 1979—), Phi Delta Kappa.

AWARDS, HONORS: American Philosophical Society grant, 1968, for work on an annotated edition of Joseph Neef's *Sketch of a Plan and Method of Education;* National Endowment for the Humanities grant, 1970; named Educator of the Year by Loyola University of Chicago chapter, Phi Delta Kappa, 1977.

WRITINGS:

Pestalozzi and Education, Random House, 1968.
The Educational Theory of George S. Counts, Ohio State University Press, 1970.
An Historical Introduction to American Education, Crowell, 1970.
A History of the Western Educational Experience, Random House, 1972.
Philosophical Alternatives in Education, C. E. Merrill, 1974.
(Contributor) Elmer L. Towns, editor, *A History of Religious Educators,* Baker Book, 1975.
(Contributor) *Proceedings of the National Academy of Education,* National Academy of Education, 1976.
(With Jasper J. Valenti) *Education and Society in India and Thailand,* University Press of America, 1977.
(Contributor) Allan C. Ornstein, editor, *An Introduction to the Foundations of Education,* Rand McNally, 1977, 3rd edition, Houghton, in press.
Joseph Neef: The Americanization of Pestalozzianism, University of Alabama Press, 1978.
Basic Education: An Historical Perspective, Phi Delta Kappa Educational Foundation, 1981.
Education and Schooling: An Introduction, Prentice-Hall, 1983.
George S. Counts and American Civilization: The Educator as Social Theorist, Mercer University Press, 1984.
(Contributor) Glenn Smith, editor, *Lives in Education: People and Ideas in the Development of Western Education,* Education Studies Press, in press.

TAPE-RECORDED LECTURES

Pestalozzi and Education, JAB Press, 1978.
George S. Counts and a Reconstructionist Philosophy of Education, JAB Press, 1978.
The Progressive Education Movement, JAB Press, 1978.

OTHER

Contributor to *Yearbook of the American Philosophical Society,* 1969, and to proceedings; consulting editor, *Standard Education Almanac* (annual), Marquis, 1983-85. Contributor of numerous articles and reviews to periodicals, including *History of Education Quarterly, Journal of Southern History, Social Education, Journal of American History,* and *Educational Forum.*

WORK IN PROGRESS: An Educational History of the New Harmony Community: Robert Owen and William Maclure; A History of American Education, for Prentice-Hall.

SIDELIGHTS: Gerald L. Gutek told *CA:* "My interest in writing is to use the historical method to investigate educational

issues and concerns. I began my writing career as a student at Streator Township High School where I wrote essays for student publications. As a student in the College of Education and the Department of History at the University of Illinois, I worked to acquire the skill of writing clearly and directly without falling into jargon that besets many writers on educational topics. My interests lie in the examination of educational theory in its historical setting and in the writing of biographies of educators. I currently am working on an intellecutal history of the individuals who were members of Robert Owen's New Harmony community in early nineteenth-century Indiana."

* * *

GUTMANN, Joseph 1923-

PERSONAL: Born August 17, 1923, in Wuerzburg, Germany (now West Germany); came to the United States in 1936, naturalized in 1943; son of Henry (a merchant) and Selma (Eisemann) Gutmann; married Marilyn B. Tuckman (a teacher of mathematics), October 8, 1953; children: David, Sharon. *Education:* Temple University, B.S., 1949; New York University, M.A., 1952; Hebrew Union College-Jewish Institute of Religion (Cincinnati), Ph.D., 1960.

ADDRESSES: Home—13151 Winchester, Huntington Woods, Mich. 48070. *Office*—Department of Art and Art History, Wayne State University, Detroit, Mich. 48202.

CAREER: Ordained rabbi, 1957. Hebrew Union College-Jewish Institute of Religion, Cincinnati, Ohio, assistant professor, 1960-65, associate professor of art history, 1965-69; Wayne State University, Detroit, Mich., professor of art and art history, 1969—. Adjunct professor, University of Cincinnati, 1961-68; Charles Friedman Visiting Lecturer, Antioch College, 1964; visiting professor of the history of art, University of Michigan, 1985. Member of board of advisors, Wayne State University Press, 1970—; adjunct curator, Detroit Institute of Arts, 1971—. Interim associate rabbi, Temple Beth El, Detroit, 1974; rabbi, Congregation Solel, Brighton, Mich., 1979-82. *Military service:* U.S. Army Air Forces, 1943-46; interrogator and research analyst, U.S. Strategic Bombing Survey in Europe.

MEMBER: International Center of Medieval Art, World Union of Jewish Studies, Society of Biblical Literature (chairman of art and Bible section, 1970—), Central Conference of American Rabbis, College Art Association of America, Beta Gamma Sigma.

AWARDS, HONORS: Henry Morgenthau fellowships to Israel, 1957 and 1958; Memorial Foundation for Jewish Culture grants, 1959 and 1972; American Philosophical Society grant to Europe, 1965; Wayne State University faculty grants, 1971 and 1973; American Council of Learned Societies grant, 1973 and 1983; honorary degree of Doctor of Divinity, Hebrew Union College-Jewish Institute of Religion, Cincinnati, 1984.

WRITINGS:

Juedische Zeremonialkunst, Ner-Tamid-Verlag, 1963, translation by Gutmann published as *Jewish Ceremonial Art,* T. Yoseloff, 1964, revised edition, 1968.
Images of the Jewish Past: An Introduction to Medieval Hebrew Miniatures, Society of Jewish Bibliophiles, 1965.
(Editor and contributor) *Beauty in Holiness: Studies in Jewish Customs and Ceremonial Art,* Ktav, 1970.
(Editor and contributor) *No Graven Images: Studies in Art and the Hebrew Bible,* Ktav, 1971.

(With Paul Pieper) *Die Darmstaedter Pessach-Haggadah,* Propylaen Verlag, 1972.

(Editor and contributor) *The Dura-Europos Synagogue: A Re-Evaluation,* Council on the Study of Religion, 1973.

(With Stanley Chyet) *Moses Jacob Ezekiel: Memoirs from the Bath of Diocletian,* Wayne State University Press, 1975.

(Editor and contributor) *The Synagogue: Origins, Archaeology, and Architecture,* Ktav, 1975.

(Editor and contributor) *The Temple of Solomon: Archaeological Fact and Mediaeval Tradition in Christian, Islamic, and Jewish Art,* Scholars Press, 1976.

(Editor and contributor) *The Image and the Word: Confrontations in Judaism, Christianity, and Islam,* Scholars Press, 1977.

Hebrew Manuscript Painting, Braziller, 1978.

(Contributor) *Danzig, 1939: Treasures of a Destroyed Community,* Wayne State University Press, 1980.

(Editor and contributor) *Ancient Synagogues: The State of Research,* Scholars Press, 1981.

The Jewish Sanctuary, E. J. Brill, 1983.

(Contributor) *Ezekiel's Vision: Moses Jacob Ezekiel and the Classical Tradition,* National Museum of American Jewish History, 1985.

Contributor of over one hundred and fifty articles, many reprinted separately, to scholarly journals.

WORK IN PROGRESS: The Jewish Life Cycle, for E. J. Brill; *Old Testament Themes in Muslim Art,* with Vera Moreen.

AVOCATIONAL INTERESTS: Travel, reading, tennis.

*   *   *

GWYN, Richard J.   1934-

PERSONAL: Born May 26, 1934, in Suffolk, England; son of Philip Jermy and Elisabeth (Tilley) Gwyn; married Alexandra Fraser (a free-lance writer), April 12, 1958. *Education:* Attended Stonyhurst College, Blackburn, Lancashire, and Royal Military College, Sandhurst. *Religion:* Roman Catholic.

ADDRESSES: Home—457 Cole Ave., Ottawa 13, Ontario, Canada.

CAREER: Time, Inc. (Canada), Ottawa, Ontario, correspondent, 1962-67; Canadian Broadcasting Corp., Montreal, Quebec, television host, 1968—. Visiting professor, Institute of Social Communications, St. Paul University, Ottawa.

WRITINGS:

The Shape of Scandal: A Study of a Government in Crisis, Clarke, Irwin, 1965.

Smallwood: The Unlikely Revolutionary, McClelland & Stewart, 1968, 2nd revised edition, 1972.

The Northern Magus: Pierre Trudeau and the Canadians, McClelland & Stewart, 1980.

(Editor with William B. Gwyn) *Britain: Progress and Decline,* Volume XVII, Tulane Studies in Political Science, 1980.

The 49th Paradox: Canadian North America, McClelland & Stewart, 1985.

Also author of a political column published in the *Toronto Star,* 1973—.

SIDELIGHTS: Richard J. Gwyn's book *The Northern Magus: Pierre Trudeau and the Canadians* was described by *Quill & Quire* critic Peter Desbarats in 1980 as "informative and opinionated about everything and everyone of importance in Ottawa in the past 15 years. If he reads it, the Prime Minister will hate it."

BIOGRAPHICAL/CRITICAL SOURCES:

PERIODICALS

Books in Canada, October, 1980.
Canadian Forum, December/January, 1981-82.
Globe & Mail (Toronto), October 26, 1985.
Quill & Quire, October, 1980.†

H

HAHN, James (Sage) 1947-

PERSONAL: Born May 24, 1947, in Chicago, Ill.; son of James Peter (a designer and manufacturer) and Joan (Redfern) Hahn; married Mona Lynn Lowery (a writer), April 17, 1971. *Education:* Attended Wright City College, 1965-67; Northwestern University, B.A., 1970. *Politics:* Independent. *Religion:* Roman Catholic.

ADDRESSES: Home and office—2202 Sherman Ave., Evanston, Ill. 60201.

CAREER: Free-lance writer and photographer for newspapers, magazines, and books. Lecturer.

AWARDS, HONORS: Outstanding Science Books for Children award, 1975, for *The Metric System.*

WRITINGS:

CHILDREN'S BOOKS; WITH WIFE, LYNN HAHN

Reycling: Re-Using Our World's Solid Wastes, F. Watts, 1973.
Plastics: A First Book, F. Watts, 1974.
The Metric System, F. Watts, 1975.
Environmental Careers, F. Watts, 1976.
Hamsters, Gerbils, Guinea Pigs, Pet Mice, and Pet Rats, F. Watts, 1977.
Aim for a Job in the Construction Industry, Rosen Publishing, 1978.
Tracy Austin: Powerhouse in Pinafore, EMC Corp., 1978.
Rod Carew: A Promise and a Dream, EMC Corp., 1978.
Bill Walton: Maverick Cager, EMC Corp., 1978.
Franz Beckenbauer: Soccer Superstar, EMC Corp., 1978.
Franco Harris: The Quiet Ironman, EMC Corp., 1979.
Reggie Jackson: Slugger Supreme, EMC Corp., 1979.
Janet Guthrie: Champion Racer, EMC Corp., 1979.
Bjorn Borg: The Coolest Ace, EMC Corp., 1979.
Nancy Lopez: Golfing Pioneer, EMC Corp., 1979.
Aim for a Job in the Telephone Company, Rosen Publishing, 1979.
Aim for a Job in the Printing Trades, Rosen Publishing, 1979.
Aim for a Job in a Small Business Occupation, Rosen Publishing, 1980.
Exploring Careers in Home Economics, Rosen Publishing, 1981.
Pele! The Sports Career of Edson do Nascimento, Crestwood House, 1981.

Henry! The Sports Career of Henry Aaron, Crestwood House, 1981.
Tark! The Sports Career of Francis Tarkenton, Crestwood House, 1981.
Brown! The Sports Career of James Brown, Crestwood House, 1981.
Patty! The Sports Career of Patricia Berg, Crestwood House, 1981.
Thorpe! The Sports Career of James Thorpe, Crestwood House, 1981.
Zaharias! The Sports Career of Mildred Zaharias, Crestwood House, 1981.
Sayers! The Sports Career of Gale Sayers, Crestwood House, 1981.
Casey! The Sports Career of Charles Stengel, Crestwood House, 1981.
Killy! The Sports Career of Jean-Claude Killy, Crestwood House, 1981.
Chris! The Sports Career of Chris Evert Lloyd, Crestwood House, 1981.
Babe! The Sports Career of George Ruth, Crestwood House, 1981.
King! The Sports Career of Billie Jean King, Crestwood House, 1981.
Wilt! The Sports Career of Wilton Chamberlain, Crestwood House, 1981.
Ali! The Sports Career of Muhammed Ali, Crestwood House, 1981.
Aim for a Job in Appliance Repair, Rosen Publishing, 1982.

WORK IN PROGRESS: The Top Secret Radioactive Documents, ecological science fiction.

SIDELIGHTS: James Hahn told *CA:* "Young people of all ages have been the biggest motivating factors in my career. Publishers label my books 'children's books'; however, I write so young people of all ages may enjoy and learn. Writing helps me understand our world better, and I hope my work helps others. I began my writing career at our community's recycling center. I saw several young people recycling metal, glass, and paper. Their enthusiasm excited me. I wanted to find out why they were so enthusiastic. My search lasted many months and resulted in my first book, *Recycling.* My advice to aspiring writers is write about anything that excites and interests you.

Write simply and clearly so young people of all ages can understand why you're so excited.''

AVOCATIONAL INTERESTS: "Walking in the uncommon areas of large cities.''

BIOGRAPHICAL/CRITICAL SOURCES:

PERIODICALS

Evanston Review, February 21, 1974.
Reader, January 20, 1978.

*   *   *

HAHN, (Mona) Lynn   1949-

PERSONAL: Born July 3, 1949, in Cleveland, Ohio; daughter of James William (a boilermaker) and Mona Alice (Benjamin) Lowery; married James Hahn (a writer), April 17, 1971. *Education:* Northwestern University, B.S., 1971. *Politics:* Independent. *Religion:* United Church of Christ.

ADDRESSES: Home and office—2202 Sherman Ave., Evanston, Ill. 60201.

CAREER: Writer for newspapers, magazines, and books. Lecturer and photographer.

AWARDS, HONORS: Outstanding Science Books for Children award, 1975, for *The Metric System.*

WRITINGS:

CHILDREN'S BOOKS; WITH HUSBAND, JAMES HAHN

Recycling: Re-Using Our World's Solid Wastes, F. Watts, 1973.
Plastics: A First Book, F. Watts, 1974.
The Metric System, F. Watts, 1975.
Environmental Careers, F. Watts, 1976.
Hamsters, Gerbils, Guinea Pigs, Pet Mice, and Pet Rats, F. Watts, 1977.
Aim for a Job in the Construction Industry, Rosen Publishing, 1978.
Tracy Austin: Powerhouse in Pinafore, EMC Corp., 1978.
Rod Carew: A Promise and a Dream, EMC Corp., 1978.
Bill Walton: Maverick Cager, EMC Corp., 1978.
Franz Beckenbauer: Soccer Superstar, EMC Corp., 1978.
Franco Harris: The Quiet Ironman, EMC Corp., 1979.
Reggie Jackson: Slugger Supreme, EMC Corp., 1979.
Janet Guthrie: Champion Racer, EMC Corp., 1979.
Bjorn Borg: The Coolest Ace, EMC Corp., 1979.
Nancy Lopez: Golfing Pioneer, EMC Corp., 1979.
Aim for a Job in the Telephone Company, Rosen Publishing, 1979.
Aim for a Job in the Printing Trades, Rosen Publishing, 1979.
Aim for a Job in a Small Business Occupation, Rosen Publishing, 1980.
Exploring Careers in Home Economics, Rosen Publishing, 1981.
Pele! The Sports Career of Edson do Nascimento, Crestwood House, 1981.
Henry! The Sports Career of Henry Aaron, Crestwood House, 1981.
Tark! The Sports Career of Francis Tarkenton, Crestwood House, 1981.
Brown! The Sports Career of James Brown, Crestwood House, 1981.
Patty! The Sports Career of Patricia Berg, Crestwood House, 1981.
Thorpe! The Sports Career of James Thorpe, Crestwood House, 1981.

Zaharias! The Sports Career of Mildred Zaharias, Crestwood House, 1981.
Sayers! The Sports Career of Gale Sayers, Crestwood House, 1981.
Casey! The Sports Career of Charles Stengel, Crestwood House, 1981.
Killy! The Sports Career of Jean-Claude Killy, Crestwood House, 1981.
Chris! The Sports Career of Chris Evert Lloyd, Crestwood House, 1981.
Babe! The Sports Career of George Ruth, Crestwood House, 1981.
King! The Sports Career of Billie Jean King, Crestwood House, 1981.
Wilt! The Sports Career of Wilton Chamberlain, Crestwood House, 1981.
Ali! The Sports Career of Muhammed Ali, Crestwod House, 1981.
Aim for a Job in Appliance Repair, Rosen Publishing, 1982.

WORK IN PROGRESS: The Diary of a Country Music Woman, fiction.

SIDELIGHTS: Lynn Hahn told *CA:* "I started thinking about a writing career in the third grade, when an outstanding teacher, Mrs. Doris Griffith, began encouraging me. She remained a great encouragement throughout my education, and even when my first books were being published. I think I've had an added advantage in being married to another writer. All published writers have the thrill of sharing their work with others when it is completed and published, but I have the added joy of sharing it while it is in progress. It is a special feeling to share your work with another person who is as involved in and excited by the work as you are, while you are still writing it. Sharing research—discovering clues together—is another special thrill.''

AVOCATIONAL INTERESTS: Creative photography and photographic processing, designing and sewing clothing, baking.

BIOGRAPHICAL/CRITICAL SOURCES:

PERIODICALS

Evanston Review, February 21, 1974.
Reader, January 20, 1978.

*   *   *

HALL, Cameron
See del REY, Lester

*   *   *

HALL, John F.   1919-

PERSONAL: Born April 24, 1919, in Philadelphia, Pa.; son of Harry R. and Alta (Herner) Hall; married Jean Midlam, May 14, 1943; children: John. *Education:* Ohio University, B.S., 1946; Ohio State University, M.A., 1947, Ph.D., 1949.

ADDRESSES: Home—1288 Penfield Rd., State College, Pa. 16801. *Office*—Department of Psychology, Pennsylvania State University, University Park, Pa. 16802.

CAREER: Pennsylvania State University, University Park, 1949—, began as assistant professor, professor of psychology, 1958—. Visiting professor at University of Virginia, summer, 1952, University of California, Berkley, summer, 1962, University of Hawaii, summer, 1968, and Florida State University, 1975-76; research associate, University of Wisconsin, summer, 1954. Program director of psychobiology at National Science Foundation, 1966-67. *Military service:* U.S. Army Infantry, 1943-45, became technical sergeant; awarded Bronze Star.

MEMBER: American Psychological Association, American Association for the Advancement of Science, Psychonomics Society, Midwestern Psychological Association, Sigma Xi.

WRITINGS:

Psychology of Motivation, Lippincott, 1961.
Psychology of Learning, Lippincott, 1966.
(Editor) *Readings in the Psychology of Learning,* Lippincott, 1967.
Verbal Learning and Retention, Lippincott, 1971.
Classical Conditioning and Instrumental Learning: A Contemporary Approach, Lippincott, 1976.
An Invitation to Learning and Memory, Allyn & Bacon, 1982.

Contributor to professional journals in the United States and Canada. Consulting editor, *Journal of Comparative and Physiological Psychology,* 1955—.

*   *   *

HALLE, Jean-Claude 1939-

PERSONAL: Surname is pronounced Hal-*lay;* born February 26, 1939, in France; son of Jean and Heber (Emanuele) Halle; married Marie-Francoise Place, July 9, 1966; children: Olivier, Frederique. *Education:* Attended Institut d'etudes politiques, 1958-62, and Centre de formation des journalistes, 1962-64.

ADDRESSES: Home—6 Parc de Bearn, 92210 Saint-Cloud, France. *Office*—Banque Nationale de Paris, Direction de la Communication, 6 Boulevard des Capucines, 75009 Paris, France.

CAREER: L'Express, Paris, France, staff reporter, 1966-73; *Paris-Match,* Paris, staff reporter, 1974-78; *Journal du Dimanche,* Paris, editor in chief, beginning 1979; *Geo,* Paris, senior editor, beginning 1982; Banque Nationale de Paris, Direction de la Communication, Paris, senior vice-president and public relations director, 1983—. *Military service:* French Army Reserve; present rank, captain.

WRITINGS:

(Contributor) Pierre Desgraupes and Pierre Dumayet, editors, *Prague: L'Ete des tanks,* Tchou, 1968.
Guide secret des courses et du tierce, Tchou, 1969.
Francois Cevert: La Mort dans mon contrat, Flammarion, 1974, translation by Denis Frostick and Michael Frostick published as *Francois Cevert: A Contract with Death,* Kimber, 1975.
Glasgow 76: Le Defi des "Verts," Flammarion, 1976.
Football Story, Flammarion, 1978.
(With Paul Chantrel) *Le Marginal* (novel), Julliard, 1979.
L'avant-centre (novel), Flammarion, 1982.
Histoire de la Revolution Francaise, Fernand Nathan, 1983.

*   *   *

HANSEN, Ron 1947-

PERSONAL: Born December 8, 1947, in Omaha, Neb.; son of Frank L. (an electrical engineer) and Marvyl (a stenographer; maiden name, Moore) Hansen. *Education:* Creighton

University, B.A., 1970; University of Iowa, M.F.A., 1974; further graduate study at Stanford University, 1977-78.

ADDRESSES: Home—Ithaca, N.Y. *Office*—Department of English, Cornell University, Ithaca, N.Y. 14853. *Agent*—Liz Darhansoff, 1220 Park Ave., New York, N.Y. 10128.

CAREER: Stanford University, Stanford, Calif., Jones Lecturer in Creative Writing, 1978-81; affiliated with Michigan Society of Fellows, University of Michigan, Ann Arbor, 1981-84; affiliated with The Writers Workshop, University of Iowa, Iowa City, 1985, and Cornell University, Ithaca, N.Y., 1985-86.

WRITINGS:

Desperadoes, Knopf, 1979.
The Assassination of Jesse James by the Coward Robert Ford, Knopf, 1983.
The Shadowmaker, Harper, 1986.

WORK IN PROGRESS: A mystery novel.

SIDELIGHTS: "Some writers feel compelled to use contemporary settings in their novels because they need to explain their own lives to themselves or speak about public issues that are important to them," Ron Hansen explained in a letter to *CA.* "I've been too private for that sort of exploration. Historical fiction has given me the opportunity to say all I knew about the Old West and about philosophical questions I thought were important, and it kept me away from a contemporary world that I found comparatively boring or implausible. And I liked the idea of using a popular genre, such as the Western, as a way of expanding the appeal of my work to people who wouldn't otherwise pick it up." Sam Cornish remarks on the impact of Hansen's work in the *Christian Science Monitor,* indicating that in his novels Hansen has "written seriously about the West, proving himself one of our finest stylists of American historical fiction."

Hansen's first novel, *Desperadoes,* is about the notorious Dalton gang, a group of outlaws that flourished in the West during the late 1800s. The Dalton brothers started as peace officers in the Indian Territories but became disillusioned with the low wages and took up rustling. Later, they turned to robbing banks and trains. Hansen's version of the story is told in retrospect by the last of the gang's survivors, Emmett Dalton. Ironically, as Hansen reports in *Desperadoes,* Dalton has come full circle; the former outlaw is now a "real-estate broker, a building contractor, a scriptwriter for Western movies; a church man, a Rotarian, a member of Moose Lodge 29."

Some critics take exception to Hansen's recounting of the Daltons' story. For instance, Anatole Broyard in the *New York Times* regards *Desperadoes* as an "interesting but slightly improbable fictional reconstruction of the exploits of the Dalton gang." On the other hand, Geoffrey Wolff remarks in *Esquire* that the author has done an admirable job in portraying some of the Old West's most famous outlaws: "Hansen punches through the scrim of legend to make dead bones walk again. The Daltons and their sidekicks pulse with life. . . . He has elevated the Daltons to a level of history—and art—beyond their own expectations." Although Frederick Bush finds in the *Chicago Tribune* that structure and point of view are "very seriously flawed elements in this novel," he notes that *Desperadoes* should be read for its "authentic-feeling evocations of America's West."

New York Times Book Review contributor Jerome Charyn is struck by the strength of the writing in *Desperadoes,* claiming the "force of the narrative comes from Ron Hansen's ability to rein his language in. His writing is never lazy or imprecise." Wolff calls the book "one of the great prose entertainments of recent years," adding that the narrative is "supple and vigorous, witty and charming, full of surprises without straining for them." In short, concludes Charyn, Hansen's "writing is so accomplished and the book has such an authoritative tone that one finds it difficult to think of [*Desperadoes*] as a *first* novel."

In *The Assassination of Jesse James by the Coward Robert Ford*, Hansen writes about the last days of the famous Old West outlaw, Jesse James. In *Newsweek*, Peter S. Prescott calls this work a "thickly textured novel [that] seems to hover deliberately between fiction and biography." Hansen's version of the story begins in 1881 when Jesse is already a legend. He is considered the Robin Hood of the West because he never steals from southerners or clerics, and he gives to the needy. However, he is thirty-four years old, his gang is disbanding, and the governor of Missouri is offering a reward for his death. Jesse befriends a 19-year-old boy named Bob Ford and a strange, psychosexual bond develops between them. The young Ford tries to emulate Jesse's way of life and personal habits. Yet Ford is as "mentally unstable as his mentor, but more craven—he can never *be* Jesse, he can only destroy him," claims Prescott. At the end of the novel, Ford murders Jesse for a pardon and a reward.

Critics praise Hansen for the well-developed prose and attention to historical detail evident in *The Assassination of Jesse James by the Coward Robert Ford*. "The language of Hansen's novel is dense and textured, requiring careful reading," writes Cornish. "The pleasure of the book is in the eloquence of its dialogue and description, which are both literary and historically appropriate." Alan Cheuse expresses a similar viewpoint in the *Los Angeles Times Book Review*, calling the work a "first-rate piece of craftsmanship that gives off the aura of legend without ever letting us succumb to any sentimental or ignorant aspects." Prescott adds that Hansen has "crafted a very effective novel."

Hansen is now at work on a mystery novel and a ghost story. In a letter to *CA*, he commented on the expansion of his range to include mystery and the occult: "Devotees of those genres will possibly be disappointed by my not playing strictly by the rules, but I hope I'll gain something by tapping into the popular consciousness and aligning my work with the archetypes that already exist in the readers' minds."

BIOGRAPHICAL/CRITICAL SOURCES:

BOOKS

Hansen, Ron, *Desperadoes*, Knopf, 1979.

PERIODICALS

Chicago Times Book World, March 18, 1984.
Chicago Tribune, April 8, 1979.
Christian Science Monitor, December 28, 1983.
Esquire, May 8, 1979.
Los Angeles Times Book Review, November 20, 1983.
Newsweek, April 9, 1979, November 14, 1983.
New York, April 23, 1979.
New York Times, June 13, 1979.
New York Times Book Review, June 3, 1979, February 5, 1984.
Washington Post, May 4, 1979.

—*Sketch by Nancy E. Rampson*

HARDIN, Clement
See NEWTON, D(wight) B(ennett)

* * *

HARDING, Walter Roy   1917-

PERSONAL: Born April 20, 1917, in Bridgewater, Mass.; son of Roy V. (a farmer) and Mary Alice (MacDonald) Harding; married Marjorie Brook, June 7, 1947; children: David, Allen, Lawrence, Susan. *Education:* Bridgewater State Teachers College (now Bridgewater State College), B.S. Ed., 1939; University of North Carolina, M.A., 1947; Rutgers University, Ph.D., 1950.

ADDRESSES: Home—P.O. Box 115, Groveland, N.Y. 14462. *Office*—Department of English, State University of New York College, Geneseo, N.Y. 14454.

CAREER: Center School, Northfield, Mass., principal, 1939-41; Rutgers University, New Brunswick, N.J., instructor in English, 1947-51; University of Virginia, Charlottesville, assistant professor, 1951-56; State University of New York College at Geneseo, associate professor, 1956-59, professor of English and chairman of department, 1959-65, chairman of humanities division, 1965-66, university professor, 1966-71, distinguished professor, 1971-82, emeritus professor, 1982—. U.S. Department of State lecturer in Japan, 1964, and Europe, 1967. Director, Concord summer seminars, 1969—, and National Endowment for the Humanities summer seminars on transcendentalism, 1976—. Member of board of directors, State University of New York Research Foundation, 1971-83.

MEMBER: Thoreau Society (secretary, 1941—; president, 1963-64), Modern Language Association of America.

AWARDS, HONORS: American Council of Learned Societies fellow, 1962; D.Litt. from State University of New York, 1984.

WRITINGS:

Thoreau's Library, University Press of Virginia, 1957.
A Thoreau Handbook, New York University Press, 1959.
The Days of Henry Thoreau, Knopf, 1965, revised edition, Dover, 1984.
Emerson's Library, University Press of Virginia, 1967.
(With Michael Meyer) *A New Thoreau Handbook*, New York University Press, 1981.

EDITOR

Thoreau: A Century of Criticism, Southern Methodist University Press, 1954.
(And author of introduction) Charles Mayo Ellis, *An Essay on Transcendentalism*, Scholars' Facsimiles & Reprints, 1954, reprinted, Greenwood Press, 1970.
(With Carl Bode) *The Correspondence of Henry David Thoreau*, New York University Press, 1958, reprinted, Greenwood Press, 1974.
Thoreau: Man of Concord, Holt, 1960.
Amos Bronson Alcott, *Essays on Education*, Scholars' Facsimiles & Reprints, 1960.
Henry David Thoreau, *The Variorum "Walden,"* Twayne, 1962.
(With Milton Meltzer) *A Thoreau Profile*, Crowell, 1962.
Thoreau, *A Week on the Concord and Merrimack Rivers*, Holt, 1963.

Thoreau, *Journals,* Dover, 1963.
Thoreau, *Anti-Slavery and Reform Papers,* Harvest Books, 1963.
The Thoreau Centennial, State University of New York Press, 1964.
William Ellery Channing, *The Collected Poems of William Ellery Channing, the Younger: 1817-1901,* Scholars' Facsimiles & Reprints, 1967.
Thoreau, *The Variorum "Civil Disobedience,"* Twayne, 1967.
Henry David Thoreau: A Profile, Hill & Wang, 1971.
(With Jean C. Advena) *A Bibliography of the Thoreau Society Bulletin Bibliographies, 1941-1969: A Cumulation and Index,* Whitston Publishing, 1971.
(With others) *Henry David Thoreau: Studies and Commentaries,* Fairleigh Dickinson University Press, 1972.
(And author of introduction) *The Selected Works of Thoreau,* Houghton, 1975.
The Woods and Fields of Concord, Peregrine Smith, 1983.
The Journal of H. D. Thoreau, Peregrine Smith, 1984.

OTHER

Editor, "Study Guides to American Literature," Shelley, beginning 1963; editor-in-chief, "The Writings of Henry D. Thoreau," Princeton University Press, 1965-74. Contributor to *Encyclopedia Americana.* Contributor of articles and book reviews to literary magazines and to the *Chicago Tribune, Library Journal,* and *American Literature.* Editor of Thoreau Society *Bulletin* and booklets, 1941—.

SIDELIGHTS: Though much has been written about Thoreau the author, much less has been written about Thoreau the man. In *The Days of Henry Thoreau,* Walter Roy Harding's goal is to portray Thoreau "as he really was" in order to dispel the image of him as an eccentric recluse scorned by society and the critics. Sterling North of *Saturday Review* calls the book "by far the most detailed report on the complete life of Thoreau from birth to death [which] has not missed, as far as I can see, a single fact, important or otherwise." Yet he feels that this "plethora of detail" tends to make the biography "a trifle tedious" and that Harding fails to "bring alive the active nature philosopher of Walden Pond."

A critic in *Book Week,* on the other hand, writes: "Mr. Harding's prose carries the reader effortlessly forward. The writing is transparent and simple—perhaps the best style in which to record the little adventures of a genius who traveled a great deal in Concord. . . . [The author] has written what looks like the definitive biography of the man, leaving to others, perhaps wisely, the rich and difficult problem of assessing Thoreau's 'philosophy' and his influence." Carl Bode of the *New York Times Book Review* acknowledges that Harding, "by instinct, perhaps, as well as design," avoids an in-depth examination of Thoreau the author and writes instead "out of [a] single-minded devotion." The result, he concludes, "is the best biography we have had. . . . There is [however] a trace of special pleading. Thoreau finishes by looking a trifle rosier than perhaps he should . . . but only a trifle."

Harding is the owner of one of the largest, if not *the* largest, collection of books, pamphlets, articles, and manuscripts by and about Henry David Thoreau.

AVOCATIONAL INTERESTS: Bird-watching.

BIOGRAPHICAL/CRITICAL SOURCES:

PERIODICALS

Book Week, November 28, 1965.

New York Times Book Review, December 26, 1965.
Saturday Review, January 15, 1966.

* * *

HARGRAVE, Leonie
See DISCH, Thomas M(ichael)

* * *

HARRAGAN, Betty Lehan   1921-

PERSONAL: Born June 2, 1921, in Milwaukee, Wis.; daughter of Charles Joseph and Marie Ann (Caswell) Lehan; married David Joseph Harragan, January 2, 1962 (deceased); children: Kathleen Ann. *Education:* Attended Milwaukee State Teachers College, 1939-41; Marquette University, A.B., 1944; Columbia University, A.M., 1947. *Politics:* "Women's Equality."

ADDRESSES: Home and office—541 East 20th St., New York, N.Y. 10010.

CAREER: Worked for Allis Chambers, Columbia Broadcasting System, and Newell-Emmett Advertising Agency; New York Telephone Co., New York City, women's editor of employee publications, 1950-56; Ruth Lundgren Co., New York City, 1957-63, executive vice-president, 1960-63; J. Walter Thompson Co., New York City, senior public relations account executive, 1963-72; Betty Harragan & Affiliates (consultants on women's employment), New York City, principal, 1972—.

MEMBER: National Organization for Women, National Women's Political Caucus, Authors Guild, Authors League of America.

WRITINGS:

Games Mother Never Taught You: Corporate Gamesmanship for Women, Rawson Associates, 1977.
(Contributor) Henry Myers, editor, *Women at Work: How They're Reshaping America,* Dow Jones-Irwin, 1979.
Knowing the Score: Play-by-Play Directions for Women on the Job, St. Martin's, 1983.
(Contributor) Jennie Farley, editor, *The Woman in Management: Career and Family Issues,* ILK Press, 1983.

Author of monthly columns on job strategies for *Working Woman* and *Mademoiselle.* Contributor to magazines.

SIDELIGHTS: Betty Lehan Harragan writes: "My interests and expertise are solely directed toward moving women into economic power positions. Today's young women have all the qualifications for success except that nobody tells them the truth about real-life conditions in the world of business. I am a businesswoman, a writer, and an activist in the woman's rights movement, and all my writing is a reflection of those interests. So is my lecturing and public speaking, which now takes up a considerable portion of my time since my books have become classic references in the business management field." Mary M. Regan writes in *Library Journal* that *Games Mother Never Taught You: Corporate Gamesmanship for Women* is "valuable in that it gets down to concrete and workable strategies in the executive suite" and "teaches [women executives] how to compete and win."

BIOGRAPHICAL/CRITICAL SOURCES:

PERIODICALS

Library Journal, June 1, 1977.

Publishers Weekly, March 14, 1977.

*　　*　　*

HARWELL, Richard Barksdale 1915-

PERSONAL: Born June 6, 1915, in Washington, Ga.; son of Davis Gray and Helen (Barksdale) Harwell. *Education:* Emory University, A.B., 1937, A.B.L.S., 1938. *Politics:* Whig.

ADDRESSES: P.O. Box 607, Washington, Ga. 30673.

CAREER: Duke University, Durham, N.C., assistant to director of Flowers Collection of Southern Americana, 1938-40; Emory University Library, Atlanta, Ga., cataloguer of special collections, 1940-43, 1946-48, assistant librarian, 1948-55; Southeastern Library Research Facility, Atlanta, director, 1954-56; Virginia State Library, Richmond, director of publications, 1956-57; American Library Association, Chicago, Ill., executive secretary, Association of College and Research Libraries, 1957-61, associate executive director, 1958-61; Bowdoin College, Brunswick, Me., librarian, 1961-68; Smith College, Northampton, Mass., librarian, 1968-70; Georgia Southern College, Statesboro, director of libraries, 1970-75; University of Georgia, Athens, curator of rare books and manuscripts, 1975-80.

Member of board, Freedom Hall, 1958. Library administrator and building consultant, Alma College, 1958, Arizona State University, 1959, University of Rangoon and University of Mandalay, 1961, Franklin and Marshall College, 1965, University of Jordan, University of Baghdad, Bethel Academy, and St. Johns University, 1967, Bates College, 1968, and U.S. Coast Guard Academy, 1969. Archival consultant, Coca-Cola Co., Atlanta, 1953-68; consultant in Southern bibliography, University of Virginia, 1953; bibliographical consultant, Athenaeum, Boston, 1953; member of board of review, Civil War Book Club, 1957-61. *Military service:* U.S. Navy, 1943-46; became lieutenant.

MEMBER: American Library Association, American Civil War Round Table of United Kingdom (London), Association of College and Research Libraries, American Antiquarian Society, Authors Guild, Authors League of America, Southern Historical Society, Southeastern Library Association, Georgia Historical Society (board member, 1954-56), Georgia Library Association, Confederate Memorial Literary Society (Richmond), Atlanta Historical Society (member of executive board, 1955-56), Hereward the Wake Society, Alpha Beta Alpha, Beta Phi Mu, Phi Beta Kappa, Sigma Alpha Epsilon, Atlanta Civil War Round Table (founder; president, 1949-50), Grolier Club (New York).

AWARDS, HONORS: D.Lit., New England College, 1966; Distinguished Service Award, Atlanta Civil War Round Table, 1983; Nevins-Freeman Award, Chicago Civil War Round Table, 1984.

WRITINGS:

Confederates Belles Lettres, Book Farm, 1941, revised edition, Gordon Press, 1977.
Confederate Music, University of North Carolina Press, 1950.
Songs of the Confederacy, Broadcast Music, Inc., 1951.
Cornerstones of Confederate Collecting, Bibliographical Society, University of Virginia, 1952, 2nd edition, 1953.
A Union List of Holdings in Chemistry and Allied Fields at Emory University, the Georgia Institute of Technology, Florida State University, the University of Florida, the University of Georgia, and the University of Miami, Southern Regional Education Board, 1955.
Research Resources in the Georgia and Florida Libraries of Southeastern Interlibrary Research Facility, Southeastern Interlibrary Research Facility, 1955.
Virginia State Publications, Virginia State Library, 1955.
The Sweep of American History, Abraham Lincoln Book Shop, 1957.
More Confederate Imprints, two volumes, Virginia State Library, 1957.
(With Robert L. Talmadge) *The Alma College Library: A Survey*, Association of College and Research Libraries, 1958.
(With others) *The Concordia Seminary Library*, Library Building Consultants, 1958.
(With Everett T. Moore) *The Arizona State University Library*, Association of College and Research Libraries, 1959.
The War of 1861-1865 as Depicted in the Prints of Currier and Ives, Nationwide Insurance Co., 1960.
The War They Fought, McKay, 1960.
A Confederate Marine, Confederate Publishing Co., 1963.
The Confederate Hundred, Beta Phi Mu, 1964.
Confederate Imprints in the University of Georgia Library, University of Georgia Press, 1964.
Honor Answering Honor, Bowdoin College, 1965.
End of Measured Mile, Oakland University Library, 1966.
Hawthorne and Longfellow, Bowdoin College, 1966.
"The Touchstone": William Lloyd Garrison and the Declaration of the Anti-Slavery Convention, Philadelphia, 1833, Smith College, 1970.
Brief Candle: The Confederate Theatre, American Antiquarian Society, 1972.
Confederate Imprints at the Georgia Historical Society, Georgia Historical Society, 1975.
Mint Julep, Beehive Press, 1975, new edition, University Press of Virginia, 1977.
(Author of foreword) R. M. Willingham, Jr., *No Jubilee*, Wilkes Publishing Co., 1976.
In Tall Cotton, Jenkins Publishing, 1979.
(With Willingham, Jr.) *Georgiana*, Abrams, 1980.

EDITOR

John Hill Hewitt, *King Linkum the First*, Emory University Library, 1947.
Hewitt, *Recollections of Poe*, Emory University Library, 1949.
Asa G. Candler, Coca-Cola, and Emory College, Emory University Library, 1951.
Henry Hotze, *Three Months in the Confederate Army*, University of Alabama Press, 1952.
A Confederate Diary of the Retreat from Petersburg, Emory University Library, 1953.
John Wesley on the Death of Whitefield, Emory University Library, 1953.
John Esten Cooke, *Stonewall Jackson and the Old Stonewall Brigade*, University of Virginia Press, 1954.
Richard Taylor, *Destruction and Reconstruction*, McKay, 1955.
The Death of Lee, Emory University Library, 1955.
The Committees of Safety of Westmoreland and Fincastle, Virginia State Library, 1956.
Cooke, *Song of the Rebel*, Confederate Museum, 1956.
Ralph Hamor, *The Present State of Virginia*, Virginia State Library, 1957.
The Confederate Reader, McKay, 1957, 2nd edition, 1976.
The Union Reader, McKay, 1958.
Stephen F. Miller, *Ahab Lincoln*, Civil War Round Table (Chicago), 1958.

F. Ross, *Cities and Camps of the Confederate States,* University of Illinois Press, 1958.

Kate Cumming, *Kate, the Diary of a Confederate Nurse,* Louisiana State University Press, 1959, new edition, 1977.

Uniform and Dress of the Army and Navy of the Confederate States, St. Martins, 1960.

John D. Billings, *Hardtack and Coffee,* Donnelley, 1960.

Cooke, *Outlines from the Outpost,* Donnelley, 1961.

Lee (one-volume condensation of D. S. Freeman's *R. E. Lee*), Scribner, 1961.

O. J. Hollister, *Colorado Volunteers in New Mexico, 1862,* Donnelley, 1962.

Arthur J. L. Fremantle and Frank A. Haskell, *Two Views of Gettysburg,* Donnelley, 1964.

Washington (one-volume abridgement of Douglas S. Freeman's *George Washington;* Literary Guild selection), Scribner, 1968.

Sidney Lanier, *Tiger-Lillies,* University of North Carolina Press, 1969.

Philip Hofer, *Mishaps of a Compulsive Collector,* Rosemary Press, 1970.

Augustus B. Longstreet, *Georgia Scenes,* Beehive Press, 1975.

Margaret Mitchell, *Margaret Mitchell's "Gone with the Wind" Letters, 1936-1949* (Book of the Month Club alternate selection; Columbia Book Club selection), Macmillan, 1976.

Technical Adviser: The Making of "Gone with the Wind"—The Hollywood Journals of Wilbur G. Kurtz, Atlanta Historical Society, 1978.

The Confederate Constitution, Wormsloe Foundation, 1978.

GWTW: The Screenplay, Macmillan, 1980.

Marion Alexander Boggs, *The Alexander Letters,* University of Georgia Press, 1980.

"Gone with the Wind" as Book and Film, University of South Carolina Press, 1983.

Douglas S. Freeman, *The South to Posterity,* Broadfoot Broadfoot's Bookmark, 1983.

Anne and Winifred Fluker, *Confederate Gold,* Tullous, 1984.

Virginia Nirenstein, *With Kindly Voices,* Tullous, 1984.

CONTRIBUTOR

The Lasting South, Regnery, 1957.

Lincoln for the Ages, Doubleday, 1960.

The Idea of the South, University of Chicago Press, 1964.

A Bibliographical Guide to the Study of Southern Literature, Louisiana State University Press, 1969.

Encyclopedia of Library and Information Science, Dekker, 1971.

The Encyclopedia of Southern History, Louisiana State University Press, 1979.

Darden A. Pyron, editor, *Recasting "Gone with the Wind,"* University Presses of Florida, 1983.

OTHER

Associate editor, "Emory Sources and Reprints" series, 1948-55; member of editorial board, *Jefferson Davis Papers,* Rice University. Contributor of articles and reviews to numerous library and historical journals and to popular magazines. Member of editorial boards of *Emory University Quarterly,* 1948-56, and *Journal of Civil War History,* 1955-71; editor of *College and Research Libraries,* 1962-63.

SIDELIGHTS: In an interview with Charlotte Folk, Richard Barksdale Harwell was asked whether he thought of himself as a historian, bibliographer, biographer, editor, librarian, researcher, or scholar. He responded: "I think of myself as a librarian because that's where I've earned a living for the long-

est. Actually, I've worked in libraries for 44 and a half years now, except for 3 and a half years in the Navy. And I think that in relation to writing this is good, too, because writing, even though a project has been of great importance to me when I was doing it, it was still recreation from another kind of work. And the only time that it wasn't was when I was working for the Virginia State Libraries as head of their publications, and I found myself less wanting to do anything of my own because I did it all day at work. There wasn't the feeling of change and recreation in going home and working on something else."

When asked which of his writing projects he thought the most important and which he had enjoyed the most, Harwell answered: "I got deeply involved in the Margaret Mitchell letters, and I think having a hand in bringing about their publication when she herself had said she never wanted them published and her brother was uncertain whether they should be or not, was probably the most worthwhile thing I've done. But I enjoyed as much, certainly, condensing the two multi-volume biographies by Douglas Freeman of Robert E. Lee and George Washington. The Lee book has sold more, but I like the Washington book better. I didn't think I was going to like Washington when I got into it, having already done the Lee, but he was such a fabulous person that you just can't resist him once you learn something about him. . . . He did everything. He did everything he did well. He was almost faultless. And this isn't a myth, this is real. He was a very human person."

BIOGRAPHICAL/CRITICAL SOURCES:

PERIODICALS

Committee Newsletter: Reports from Committees of the University of Georgia Libraries Faculty, Volume II, number 2-3, 1978.

*   *   *

HARWICK, B. L.
   See KELLER, Beverly (Lou)

*   *   *

HATFIELD, Elaine (Catherine)   1937-
   (Elaine Walster, Elaine Hatfield Walster)

PERSONAL: Born October 22, 1937, in Detroit, Mich.; daughter of Charles E. (a police officer) and Eileen (Kalahar) Hatfield. *Education:* University of Michigan, B.A., 1959; Stanford University, Ph.D., 1963. *Religion:* None.

ADDRESSES: Home—3334 Ano'ai, Honolulu, Hawaii 96822. *Office*—334 Porteus, Honolulu, Hawaii 96822.

CAREER: University of Minnesota, Minneapolis, assistant professor, 1963, associate professor of sociology and psychology, 1963-66; University of Rochester, Rochester, N.Y., associate professor of psychology, 1966-67; University of Wisconsin—Madison, associate professor, 1969-70, professor of sociology and psychology, 1970-81; University of Hawaii at Manoa, Honolulu, professor of psychology and chairperson of department, 1981—. Guest research professor at Sonderforschungsbereich 24, Mannheim, West Germany, 1972. Research associate at Wisconsin Family Studies Institute, 1980-81. Family therapist at King Kalakaua Center, 1982—.

MEMBER: American Psychological Association (fellow; member of council, 1969-74), Association for Women Psychologists, Society of Experimental Social Psychology (member of executive committee, 1970-73), Society for the Psychological Study of Social Issues (fellow), American Association of Sex Educators and Counselors, Society for Personality and Social Psychology, American Sociological Association (fellow), Hawaii Psychological Association.

AWARDS, HONORS: Grants from National Institute of Mental Health, 1965-68, 1969-72, 1976-78, and 1982-83, National Science Foundation, 1966-68, 1967-69, 1970-72, and 1971-75, and National Institutes of Health, 1979-80; National Media Award from American Psychological Association, 1979, for *A New Look at Love.*

WRITINGS:

(Under name Elaine Hatfield Walster with Ellen Berscheid) *Interpersonal Attraction,* Addison-Wesley, 1969, 2nd edition, 1978.

(With William Griffitt) *Human Sexual Behavior,* Scott, Foresman, 1974.

(Editor with J. P. Houston, Helen Bee, and D. C. Rimm) *Introduction to Psychology,* Academic Press, 1979.

(Editor with Robert Fogel, Sara Kielser, and Ethel Shanas, and contributor) *Aging: Stability and Change in the Family,* Academic Press, 1981.

(With Susan Sprecher) *Mirror, Mirror: The Importance of Looks in Everyday Life,* State University of New York Press, in press.

UNDER NAME ELAINE WALSTER

(Editor with Leonard Berkowitz and contributor) *Advances in Experimental Social Psychology,* Volume IX: *Equity Theory: Toward a General Theory of Social Interaction,* Academic Press, 1976.

(With G. W. Walster) *A New Look at Love,* Addison-Wesley, 1978.

(With Berscheid and Walster) *Equity: Theory and Research,* Allyn & Bacon, 1978.

CONTRIBUTOR

Lauren Wispe, editor, *Altruism, Sympathy, and Helping,* Academic Press, 1978.

Bert Galaway and James Hudson, editors, *Offender Restitution in Theory and Action,* Lexington Books, 1978.

R. L. Burgess and T. L. Huston, editors, *Social Exchange in Developing Relationships,* Academic Press, 1979.

Steve Duck and Robin Gilmour, editors, *Personal Relationships I: Studying Personal Relationships,* Academic Press, 1980.

Gerhard Mikula, editor, *Justice in Social Interaction,* Hans Huber, 1980.

Gerald Greenberg and R. L. Cohen, editors, *Equity and Justice in Social Behavior,* Academic Press, 1982.

Martin Fisher and George Stricker, editors, *Intimacy,* Plenum, 1982.

E. R. Allgeier and N. B. McCormick, editors, *Changing Boundaries: Gender Roles and Sexual Behavior,* Mayfield, 1982.

S. B. Bacharach and E. J. Lawler, editors, *Perspectives in Organizational Sociology: Theory and Research,* JAI Press, 1982.

Joan Murray and Paul R. Abrahamson, editors, *Bias in Psychology,* Praeger, 1983.

H. H. Blumberg, A. P. Hare, and others, editors, *Small Groups and Social Interaction,* Volume II, Wiley, 1983.

J. D. Fisher, Arlie Nadler, and B. M. DePaulo, editors, *New Directions in Helping,* Volume I: *Recipient Reactions to Aid,* Academic Press, 1983.

William Ickes, editor, *Compatible and Incompatible Relationships,* Springer-Verlag, 1985.

Also contributor to *The Implications of Non-Clinical Research for Clinical Practice,* edited by Stricker and Robert Keisner, Plenum, *The Development of Intimate Relationships,* edited by Val Derlaga, Praeger, *Helping with the Sexually Oppressed,* edited by H. L. Gochros, J. S. Gochros, and Joel Fischer, Prentice-Hall, and *The Psychology of Cosmetic Treatments,* edited by Jean Graham and Arnold Kligman, Praeger.

CONTRIBUTOR; UNDER NAME ELAINE WALSTER

Leon Festinger, editor, *Conflict, Decision, and Dissonance,* Stanford University Press, 1964.

James Wright, editor, *Man vs. Time,* Graduate School Research Center, University of Minnesota, 1966.

Judson Mills, editor, *Experimental Social Psychology,* Macmillan, 1969.

J. R. Macaulay and L. Berkowitz, editors, *Altruism and Helping Behavior,* Academic Press, 1970.

B. I. Murstein, editor, *Theories of Attraction and Love,* Springer Publishing, 1971.

James Tedeschi, editor, *The Social Influence Process,* Aldine-Atherton, 1972.

Berkowitz, editor, *Advances in Experimental Social Psychology,* Academic Press, 1974.

T. L. Huston, editor, *Foundations of Interpersonal Attraction,* Academic Press, 1974.

Bernard Seidenberg and Alan Snadowsky, editors, *Social Psychology: An Introduction,* Free Press, 1976.

Mark Cook and Glenn Wilson, editors, *Love and Attraction: An International Conference,* Pergamon Press, 1979.

OTHER

Contributor to *Encyclopedia of Psychology.* Contributor of more than sixty articles to psychology journals.

*   *   *

HAUSMAN, Gerald   1945-
(Gerry Hausman)

PERSONAL: Born October 13, 1945, in Baltimore, Md.; son of Sidney (an engineer) and Dorothy (Little) Hausman; married Lorry Wright (a publicity director), June, 1968; children: Maria Fox, Hannah. *Education:* New Mexico Highlands University, B.A., 1968.

ADDRESSES: Home—P.O. Box 517, Tesuque, N.M. 87501. *Agent*—Mary Jane Ross, 85 Sunset Lane, Tenafly, N.J. 87574.

CAREER: Poetry teacher in Lenox, Mass., 1969-72; Bookstore Press, Lenox, editor, 1972-77; Sunstone Press, Santa Fe, N.M., vice-president, 1979-81; Santa Fe Preparatory School, Santa Fe, teacher of English, 1981-85. Poet-in-residence in public schools, 1970-76, and at Central Connecticut State College, 1973.

MEMBER: Poets and Writers.

AWARDS, HONORS: Union College poetry prize, 1965, for ''Quebec Poems.''

WRITINGS:

(With David Kherdian) *Eight Poems,* Giligia, 1968.

(Editor) *Shivurrus Plant of Mopant and Other Children's Poems*, Giligia, 1968.

New Marlboro Stage, Giligia, 1969, 2nd edition, Bookstore Press, 1971.

Circle Meadow, Bookstore Press, 1972.

The Boy with the Sun Tree Bow, Berkshire Traveller Press, 1973.

(Contributor) Kathleen Meagher, editor, *Poets in the Schools*, Connecticut Commission on the Arts, 1973.

Beth: The Little Girl of Pine Knoll, Bookstore Press, 1974.

Sitting on the Blue-Eyed Bear, Lawrence Hill, 1975.

(Under name Gerry Hausman with wife, Lorry Hausman) *The Pancake Book*, Persea Books, 1976.

(Under name Gerry Hausman with L. Hausman) *The Yogurt Book*, Persea Books, 1977.

The Day the White Whales Came to Bangor, Cobblesmith, 1977.

Night Herding Song, Copper Canyon Press, 1979.

No Witness, Stackpole, 1980.

Runners, Sunstone Press, 1984.

Meditations with Animals: A Native American Bestiary, Bear & Co., 1986.

The Woman Who Walked Away, Sunstone Press, 1986.

Contributor to anthologies, including *Contemporaries: 28 New American Poets*, Viking, *Desert Review Anthology*, Desert Review Press, and *Poetry Here & Now*, edited by Kherdian, Morrow.

AVOCATIONAL INTERESTS: Reading, athletics.

*   *   *

HAUSMAN, Gerry
See HAUSMAN, Gerald

*   *   *

HEALEY, B. J.
See HEALEY, Ben (James)

*   *   *

HEALEY, Ben (James) 1908-
(B. J. Healey; pseudonyms: J. G. Jeffreys, Jeremy Sturrock)

PERSONAL: Born June 26, 1908, in Birmingham, England; son of William Henry (an engraver) and Alice (Owen) Healey; married Muriel Rose Herd, January 15, 1951. *Education:* Attended Birmingham School of Art, 1922-23, and University of Birmingham, 1923-26. *Politics:* Conservative. *Religion:* Church of England.

ADDRESSES: Home—Windermere, Velindre, Three Cocks, Brecon, Powys LD3 0TB, England.

CAREER: Worked as stage designer for theatres, 1939-45; artist and designer in film industry, 1945-70; full-time writer, 1971—. *Military service:* Royal Air Force, 1940-45.

MEMBER: Royal Horticulture Society.

WRITINGS:

Waiting for a Tiger, Harper, 1965.

The Millstone Men, R. Hale, 1966.

The Terrible Pictures, Harper, 1967 (published in England as *Death in Three Masks*, R. Hale, 1967).

Murder without Crime, R. Hale, 1968.

The Red Head Herring, R. Hale, 1969.

The Trouble with Penelope, R. Hale, 1972.

The Vespucci Papers, Lippincott, 1972.

The Stone Baby, Lippincott, 1973.

The Horstmann Inheritance, R. Hale, 1975.

The Blanket of the Dark, R. Hale, 1976.

Captain Havoc, R. Hale, 1977.

The Snapdragon Murders, R. Hale, 1978.

Havoc in the Indies, R. Hale, 1979.

The Most Wicked Bianca, Hamlyn, 1980.

Midnight Ferry to Venice, Walker & Co., 1981 (published in England as *Last Ferry from the Lido*, R. Hale, 1981).

The Week of the Scorpion, R. Hale, 1981.

UNDER PSEUDONYM J. G. JEFFREYS; PUBLISHED IN ENGLAND UNDER PSEUDONYM JEREMY STURROCK

The Thief Taker, Walker & Co., 1972 (published in England as *The Village of Rogues*, Macmillan [London], 1972).

A Wicked Way to Die, Walker & Co., 1973, Macmillan (London), 1973.

The Wilful Lady, Walker & Co., 1975, Macmillan (London), 1975.

A Conspiracy of Poisons, Walker & Co., 1977, R. Hale (London), 1977.

Suicide Most Foul, Walker & Co., 1981, R. Hale (London), 1981.

Captain Bolton's Corpse, Walker & Co., 1982, R. Hale (London), 1982.

The Pangersbourne Murders, Walker & Co., 1984, R. Hale (London), 1984.

OTHER

"The Black Arrow" (television script for children's historical adventure), Southern Television, 1972.

(Under name B. J. Healey) *A Gardener's Guide to Plant Names*, Scribner, 1972.

(Under name B. J. Healey) *The Plant Hunters*, Scribner, 1975.

SIDELIGHTS: Ben Healey told *CA:* "I wrote my first book in 1965 for my own entertainment, and I have been writing for my own and (I hope) my readers' enjoyment ever since. I have no particular 'messages' to offer, and I do not delude myself that I am adding anything very significant to literature. I enjoy writing and I like my characters—who always seem to do pretty well as they please—so that at the end of a working day I usually feel that I have passed a pleasant time in amusing, if somewhat dubious, company. I am tending to turn away from modern crime or suspense novels, which seem to be becoming increasingly stereotyped, in favor of stories set in a historical period. But here I do take care to make the period background as accurate as possible even to the smallest details. I get atmosphere by extensive reading of newspapers, journals and biographies of the period. My main interest at present is European (particularly British) and American history from the French Revolution to 1850."

AVOCATIONAL INTERESTS: Reading crime stories, gardening.

*   *   *

HEITZMANN, William Ray 1948-
(William R. Vincent)

PERSONAL: Born February 12, 1948, in Hoboken, N.J.; son of William Henry (a truck driver) and Mary (in sales; maiden name, Tolland) Heitzmann; married Kathleen Esnes (a publisher's sales consultant), June 20, 1970; children: Richard Raymond, Mary Elizabeth. *Education:* Villanova University, B.S., 1964; University of Chicago, M.A.T., 1966; University of Delaware, Ph.D., 1974. *Politics:* Independent Republican. *Religion:* Roman Catholic.

ADDRESSES: Home—132 Sycamore Rd., Havertown, Pa. 19083. *Office*—Department of Education, Villanova University, Villanova, Pa. 19085.

CAREER: University of Chicago, Chicago, Ill., part-time social studies teacher at laboratory middle school, 1964-65; high school social studies teacher in Chicago, Ill., 1965-66; high school social studies teacher and basketball coach in North Chicago, Ill., 1966-67, and Highland Falls, N.Y., 1967-69; Villanova University, Villanova, Pa., instructor, 1969-74, assistant professor, 1974-77, associate professor of education and history, 1977—, recruiter of minority students and basketball players. Member of adjunct faculty at Thomas Jefferson University. Basketball coach, Catholic Youth Organization and high schools and colleges. Conducts and directs workshops; guest on radio programs in Texas, Pennsylvania, and New York. President, HELPS, Havertown, Pa. Consultant to Airco Corp., U.S. Naval Institute, and colleges and school districts.

MEMBER: North American Society of Oceanic Historians, American Association of University Professors, U.S. Naval Institute, National Council for the Social Studies (head of committee of editors, 1973-76), National Marine Education Association, Oceanic Society, Community College Social Science Association, Naval Historical Association, Middle States Council for the Social Studies (member of executive committee, 1978—), Pennsylvania Council for the Social Studies (member of executive committee, 1972—; member of board of directors, 1973—; vice-president, 1977-78; president-elect, 1978-79; president, 1979-80), Philadelphia Council for the Social Studies (member of executive committee, 1974-78), Kappa Delta Pi, Phi Delta Kappa, Delta Tau Kappa.

AWARDS, HONORS: Outstanding Service Award, National Council for the Social Studies; also recipient of awards from Student Pennsylvania State Education Association, Weehawken School District, National Council for the Social Studies, and Pennsylvania Council for the Social Studies.

WRITINGS:

(Editor with Patricia Stetson) *The Psychology of Teaching and Learning,* MSS Information, 1973.
(Editor with Charles Staropoli) *Student Teaching: Classroom Management and Professionalism,* MSS Information, 1974.
Educational Games and Simulations, National Education Association, 1974, 2nd edition, 1983.
American Jewish Political Behavior: History and Analysis, R & E Research Associates, 1975.
Fifty Political Cartoons for Teaching United States History, J. Weston Walch, 1975.
America's Maritime Heritage and Energy Education (student workbooks), two volumes, Con-Stran Publications, 1977.
Minicourses, National Education Association, 1977.
The Classroom Teacher and the Student Teacher, National Education Association, 1977.
(Contributor) Louis Thayer and Kent O. Beeler, editors, *Affective Education: Innovations for Learning,* University Associates, 1977.

Opportunities in Marine and Maritime Careers, National Textbook Co., 1979.
The Newspaper in the Classroom, National Education Association, 1979.
Opportunities in Sports and Physical Education, National Textbook Co., 1980, 2nd edition published as *Opportunities in Sports and Athletics,* 1985.
Political Cartoons, Scholastic Inc., 1980.
Opportunities in Sports Medicine, National Textbook Co., 1984.
Introduction to General Teaching Methods, Airco Publishing, 1984.
Guide to Introduction to General Teaching Methods, Airco Publishing, 1985.

Contributor of more than one hundred articles and reviews to newspapers, scholarly journals, sports magazines (sometimes under pseudonym William R. Vincent), and popular magazines, including *Sea World* and *Real World.* Member of editorial staff, *Beachcomber, Social Studies,* and *Current.*

WORK IN PROGRESS: Research on maritime studies, sports, and writing for publication.

SIDELIGHTS: William Ray Heitzmann comments that his interests include "a great desire to remind the American people of the nation's maritime tradition and to show that academic study (and cerebral activity) is intimately related to successful sports participation."

BIOGRAPHICAL/CRITICAL SOURCES:

PERIODICALS

Asbury Park Press, July 16, 1978.
Catholic Standard and Times, December 20, 1984.
County Press, January 30, 1985.
Delaware County Daily Times, April 23, 1985.
New York Daily News, February 18, 1979.
Philadelphia Bulletin, July 21, 1978.
Suburban and Wayne Times, August 30, 1979.
Temple Telegram, November 14, 1979.
Times Herald (Norristown, Pa.), February 11, 1985.

*   *   *

HELBIG, Alethea K.   1928-

PERSONAL: Born June 23, 1928, in Ann Arbor, Mich.; daughter of Elmer J. (a farmer) and Hilda (Goebel) Kuebler; married Harold R. Helbig (an accountant), June 12, 1948; children: Rick, Reid (deceased). *Education:* University of Michigan, B.A., 1950, M.A., 1953; further graduate study at Eastern Michigan University, Fort Hays State College, University of Michigan, and Temple University. *Politics:* Democrat. *Religion:* United Church of Christ.

ADDRESSES: Home—3640 Eli Rd., Ann Arbor, Mich. 48104. *Office*—Eastern Michigan University, 612 G Pray-Harrold, Ypsilanti, Mich. 48197.

CAREER: High school teacher of Latin and history in Manchester, Mich., 1950-52; high school teacher of Latin and English in Chelsea, Mich., 1953-54; elementary school teacher in Ann Arbor, Mich., 1966; Eastern Michigan University, Ypsilanti, instructor, 1966-69, assistant professor, 1969-76, associate professor, 1976-81, professor of English, 1981—.

MEMBER: Children's Literature Association (International), National Council of Teachers of English, National Folklore Society, Modern Language Association of America, American

Association of University Professors, Assembly on Literature for the Adolescent (founding member), Midwest Modern Language Association, Michigan Academy of Arts and Sciences, Michigan Folklore Society, Michigan Council of Teachers of English, Phi Beta Kappa, Phi Kappa Phi, Alpha Lambda Delta.

WRITINGS:

(With Agnes Perkins) *Dictionary of American Children's Fiction, 1859-1959: Books of Recognized Merit*, Greenwood Press, 1986.
(With Perkins) *Dictionary of American Children's Fiction, 1960-1984*, Greenwood Press, 1986.
Nanabozhoo, Giver of Life, Green Oak, 1986.

EDITOR; POETRY ANTHOLOGIES FOR CHILDREN

(With Helen Hill and Perkins) *Straight on Till Morning: Poems of the Imaginary World*, Crowell, 1977.
(With Hill and Perkins) *Dusk to Dawn*, Crowell, 1981.

OTHER

Author of "My Views in Reviews," a column in *Michigan English Teacher*. Contributor of articles and reviews to professional journals.

WORK IN PROGRESS: Heroes and Heroines, retellings of hero tales and a study of the traditional hero; two poetry anthologies for children, with Agnes Perkins and Helen Hill; *Dictionary of British Children's Fiction*, with Perkins.

SIDELIGHTS: Alethea K. Helbig wrote: "As far back as I can remember, I've wanted to be a teacher. Books and learning have always been important to me, and my parents strongly encouraged me to read and continue my education. Old stories, myths and hero tales, and biblical stories have always enthralled me, and poetry, too, has provided special thrills down through the years.

"My association with Helen Hill and Agnes Perkins began as a professional one, since the three of us teach together. But we have worked together on many projects, and over the years we have become good friends. We share the philosophy that only the best literature is good enough for children and young people. Working on our anthologies has given the three of us a great deal of pleasure. We sit around our dining room or kitchen tables an afternoon a week, munching cheese and crackers, drinking pots of tea, and reading the poems we have found aloud to one another. We enjoy listening to them, arguing about how good they are, re-reading the ones we especially like, and experimenting with ways in which to group them for the most interesting effects. The projects have been a lot of fun."

AVOCATIONAL INTERESTS: Reading, sewing, travel.

*   *   *

HELD, Peter
See VANCE, John Holbrook

*   *   *

HENDRICKS, William Lawrence   1929-

PERSONAL: Born March 10, 1929, in Butte, Mont.; married Lois Ann Lindsey (a teacher), June 4, 1951; children: John Lawrence. *Education:* Oklahoma Baptist University, A.B., 1951; Southwestern Baptist Theological Seminary, B.D., 1954, Th.D., 1958; University of Chicago, M.A., 1965, Ph.D., 1972. *Politics:* Democrat.

ADDRESSES: Home—3003 Sunnyside Dr., Louisville, Ky. 40206. *Office*—Southern Baptist Theological Seminary, 2825 Lexington Rd., Louisville, Ky. 40280.

CAREER: Pastor of Southern Baptist churches in Shawnee, Okla., and Dodson, Tex., 1954-57; Southwestern Baptist Theological Seminary, Fort Worth, Tex., assistant professor, 1957-59, associate professor, 1959-68, professor of theology, 1968-78; Golden Gate Baptist Seminary, Mill Valley, Calif., professor of theology and Christian philosophy, 1978-84; Southern Baptist Theological Seminary, Louisville, Ky., professor of theology and seminary director of graduate studies, 1984—. Former counselor of boys, Buckner Orphans Home, Dallas, Tex.

MEMBER: American Academy of Religion, Society of Biblical Literature.

AWARDS, HONORS: American Association of Theological Schools study grant, 1964.

WRITINGS:

(Contributor) H. C. Brown, editor, *Southwestern Sermons*, Broadman, 1960.
The Letters of John, Convention Press, 1970.
(Contributor) Clifford Ingle, editor, *Children and Conversion*, Broadman, 1970.
Resource Unlimited, Stewardship Commission of Southern Baptist Convention, 1972.
The Doctrine of Man, Convention Press, 1977.
A Theology for Children, Broadman, 1980.
Religion in an Age of Reason: Pascal and Fenelon, Broadman, 1980.
Who Is Jesus Christ?, Broadman, 1985.

Editor, *Southwestern Journal of Theology*, 1965 and 1970.

*   *   *

HENRY, Marion
See del REY, Lester

*   *   *

HENRY, Robert Selph   1889-1970

PERSONAL: Born October 20, 1889, in Clifton, Tenn.; died August 18, 1970, at his home in Alexandria, Va.; buried in Mount Olivet Cemetery, Nashville, Tenn.; son of Robert Allison and Emily James (Selph) Henry; married Lura Temple, October 30, 1929; children: Elizabeth Temple (Mrs. N. B. Musselman), Roberta Selph (Mrs. George B. Vest, Jr.). *Education:* Vanderbilt University, LL.B., 1910, B.A., 1911; postgraduate study at Queen's College, Cambridge, 1919. *Religion:* Presbyterian.

ADDRESSES: Home—813 Clovercrest Dr., Alexandria, Va. 22314.

CAREER: Nashville Tennessean and *Nashville Banner*, Nashville, Tenn., reporter, 1907-13; admitted to the Bar of Tennessee, 1911; private secretary to Ben W. Hooper, governor of Tennessee, 1913-15; private law practice, Nashville, 1915-21; assistant to vice-president, Nashville, Chattanooga & St. Louis Railway, 1921-34; Association of American Railroads, assistant to president, 1934-47, vice-president, 1947-58. Chairman of board of trustees, Ladies Hermitage Association, Nashville, 1926-34; trustee of Vanderbilt University, Nashville, and Historic Alexandria Foundation; member of Alexandria Library Co. *Military service:* U.S. Army, Field Artillery, 1917-36 (active and reserve); became lieutenant colonel.

MEMBER: Society of American Historians, Southern Historical Association (vice-president, 1956, president, 1957), Phi Beta Kappa, Phi Delta Theta, Phi Delta Phi; Army and Navy, Cosmos, and National Press Clubs (all Washington, D.C.).

AWARDS, HONORS: Litt.D. from University of Chattanooga (now University of Tennessee at Chattanooga), 1950; Gold Medal Award, Civil War Round Table, 1954.

WRITINGS:

The Story of the Confederacy, Bobbs-Merrill, 1931, revised edition, 1957.
Trains, Bobbs-Merrill, 1934.
On the Railroad, Saalfield, 1936.
Portraits of the Iron Horse: The American Locomotive in Pictures and Story, Rand McNally, 1937, reprinted, Sunstone Press, 1976.
The Story of Reconstruction, Bobbs-Merrill, 1938, reprinted, Peter Smith, 1963.
This Fascinating Railroad Business, 1942, 3rd edition, 1946.
"First with the Most" Forrest, 1944, reprinted, Greenwood Press, 1974, revised edition, McCowat-Mercer, 1969.
(Editor with Frank P. Donovan, Jr.) *Headlights and Markers: An Anthology of Railroad Stories,* Creative Age, 1946, reprinted, Golden West, 1968.
The Story of the Mexican War, Bobbs-Merrill, 1950.
(Editor) *As They Saw Forrest: Some Recollections and Comments of Contemporaries,* McCowat-Mercer, 1956.
The Armed Forces Institute of Pathlogy: Its First Century, 1862-1962, U.S. Government Printing Office, 1964.

Contributor to *The American Story* and *The Unforgettable Americans.* Guest editor of *Civil War History* for special issue on railroads in the Civil War, September, 1961.

SIDELIGHTS: Robert Selph Henry was an amateur historian noted for his dramatic style and lucid prose. He wrote a series of books spanning American history from the Mexican War to the end of Reconstruction that gained enormous popularity among a wide variety of readers for over thirty years. "Henry's strong suit was his forceful, journalistic style combined with a clear vision of the events he was relating," commented Thomas Fleming in the *Dictionary of Literary Biography.* "The result was a narrative clarity unusual among twentieth-century historians."

Henry received special praise for his book *"First with the Most" Forrest,* a biography of Nathan Bedford Forrest, a key commander for the Confederacy during the Civil War. Forrest had a charismatic personality that has been romanticized in many sources. But Henry avoided this type of treatment, said a *New Yorker* critic, and "is to be complimented for recording the facts of his hero's life instead of romanticizing about them." R. A. Brown remarked similarly in *Nation,* "[Bedford] lives and rides again in this fascinating military biography, which is as scholarly and as well written as it is interesting." *New York Times* reviewer N. K. Burger also commended this work, calling it "a comprehensive and masterful biography."

BIOGRAPHICAL/CRITICAL SOURCES:

BOOKS

Dictionary of Literary Biography, Volume XVII: *Twentieth-Century American Historians,* Gale, 1983.

PERIODICALS

Nation, December 2, 1944.
New Yorker, November 18, 1944.
New York Times, November 12, 1944.

*   *   *

HERMANN, Donald H(arold) J(ames)   1943-

PERSONAL: Born April 6, 1943, in Southgate, Ky.; son of Albert H. J. (a financier) and Helen (Snow) Hermann. *Education:* Stanford University, A.B. (with honors), 1965; Columbia University, J.D., 1968; Harvard University, LL.M., 1974; Northwestern University, M.A., 1979, Ph.D., 1981. *Politics:* Republican. *Religion:* Episcopalian.

ADDRESSES: Home—1243 Forest Ave., Evanston Il. 60202. *Office*—College of Law, DePaul University, 25 East Jackson Blvd., Chicago, Ill. 60604.

CAREER: Admitted to bars of Arizona, 1968, Washington, 1969, Kentucky, 1971, and Illinois, 1972, and to Bar of U.S. Supreme Court, 1974; University of Washington, School of Law, Seattle, assistant professor, 1968-71; University of Kentucky, Lexington, assistant professor of law, 1971-72; DePaul University, College of Law, Chicago, Ill., associate professor, 1972-73, professor of law, 1973—, director of academic planning and interdisciplinary study, 1975-76, associate dean, 1976-78. Lecturer in philosophy of law, Northwestern University, 1978-81. Counsel to DeWolfe, Poynton & Stevens (attorneys), 1984—. Fellow in law and humanities, Harvard University, 1973-74, and Stanford University, 1980; fellow in law and economics, University of Chicago, 1975-76; judicial fellow, U.S. Supreme Court, 1983-84. Cooperating attorney, American Civil Liberties Union, Seattle, Wash., 1969-71; special assistant attorney general, State of Washington, 1970. Reporter for Illinois Judicial Conference. Speaker at professional conferences.

AWARDS, HONORS: National Endowment for the Humanities fellow, 1979 and 1981.

MEMBER: International Association for Philosophy of Law and Social Philosophy, American Bar Association, American Judicature Society, American Society of International Law, American Academy of Political and Social Science, American Philosophical Association, American Society for Political and Legal Philosophy, American Association of University Professors, American Society of Writers on Legal Subjects, Society for Phenomenology and Existential Philosophy, Illinois Philosophical Society, Illinois State Bar Association, Chicago Bar Association.

WRITINGS:

Intellectuals and the New Deal (monograph), Department of Special Programs in Humanities, Stanford University, 1965.
The Suspect and the Law, University of Washington Press, 1968.
The State versus the Citizen, University of Washington Press, 1971.
Disputes in Legal Philosophy, University Press of Kentucky, 1972.
Political Trials in America, University of Washington Press, 1973.
(Contributor) Donald S. Henley and others, editors, *International Business: A Selection of Current Readings,* Michigan State University, 1973.

The Law of Economic Planning: Price and Wage Controls,
DePaul University, 1973.
Legal Education: The Next Quarter Century, DePaul University, 1974.
Legal Doctrine and Economic Theory, two volumes, DePaul University, 1975.
Law and the Legal System, 2nd edition, DePaul University, 1976.
Law and the Social Order, 2nd edition, DePaul University, 1976.
The Insanity Defense: Philosophical, Historical and Legal Perspectives, C. C. Thomas, 1982.
(Contributor) W. Haesler, editor, *Mentally Abnormal and Drug-addicted Offenders,* Verlag Ruedder, 1984.
(Contributor) D. Coyne, editor, *Representing Health Care Institutions and Professionals,* Illinois Institute for Continuing Legal Education, 1985.
Representing the Respondent in Civil Commitment Proceedings, American Bar Association, 1985.

Contributor of articles and reviews to law journals. Former member of editorial staff, *Columbia Journal of Transnational Law.*

WORK IN PROGRESS: Economic Evidence, for Wiley; *Psychiatric Evidence,* for Wiley; *Reforming the Civil Commitment Laws,* for Vanderbilt University Press; articles on amnesia and the law and compulsive gambling and the insanity defense.

*   *   *

HIEBERT, Paul (Gerhardt) 1892-

PERSONAL: Born July 17, 1892, in Pilot Mound, Manitoba, Canada; son of John (a merchant) and Maria (Penner) Hiebert; married Dorothea Cunningham, February 27, 1926. *Education:* University of Manitoba, B.A., 1916; University of Toronto, M.A., 1917; McGill University, M.Sc., 1921, Ph.D., 1923. *Religion:* Christian.

ADDRESSES: Home—Box 364, Carman, Manitoba, Canada R0G 0J0.

CAREER: University of Manitoba, Winnipeg, member of chemistry faculty, 1924-53, professor of chemistry, 1943-54; writer.

AWARDS, HONORS: Governor-General's Medal for science, 1924, for research on hydrogen peroxide; L.L.D., University of Manitoba, 1924; D.Litt., Brandon University, 1925; Stephen Leacock Memorial Award for best Canadian book of humor, 1947, for *Sarah Binks.*

WRITINGS:

Sarah Binks (humor), Oxford University Press, 1939, reprinted, New Canadian Library, 1964.
Tower in Siloam (nonfiction), McClelland & Stewart, 1966.
Willows Revisited (humor), McClelland & Stewart, 1967.
Doubting Castle (religious), Queenston Press, 1976.
For the Birds, Peguis Publishers, 1981.
Not as the Scribes, Queenston Press, 1984.

Also author of material for radio and television.

WORK IN PROGRESS: Reflections on the meaning of Christianity.

SIDELIGHTS: Paul Hiebert told *CA:* "I want merely to share with others laughter and insights into the meaning of life and the destiny of mankind. That is why I write humorous and

religious books. I am not a particularly good writer, but I have a small, dedicated group of followers."

AVOCATIONAL INTERESTS: Philosophy, gardening.

*   *   *

HIGGINBOTHAM, (Prieur) Jay 1937-

PERSONAL: Born July 16, 1937, in Pascagoula, Miss.; son of Prieur Jay (a contractor) and Vivian (Perez) Higginbotham; married Alice Louisa Martin, June 27, 1970; children: Jeanne-Felicie, Denis Prieur, Robert Findlay. *Education:* University of Mississippi, B.A., 1960; graduate study at Hunter College of the City University of New York and American University.

ADDRESSES: Home—60 North Monterey St., Mobile, Ala. 36604. *Office*—Mobile Municipal Archives, Mobile, Ala.

CAREER: State House of Representatives, Jackson, Miss., assistant clerk, 1955-61; Mobile (Ala.) Public Schools, teacher, 1962-73; Mobile Public Library, head of local history department, 1973-83; Mobile Municipal Archives, director, 1983—. *Military service:* U.S. Army Reserve, 1955-62.

MEMBER: Authors League of America, Franklin Society, Smithsonian Associates.

AWARDS, HONORS: General L. Kemper Williams Prize from the Louisiana Historical Association, 1977; award of merit from Mississippi Historical Society, 1978; Alabama Library Association nonfiction award, 1978; Gilbert Chinard Prize from Institut Francais de Washington and Society for French Historical Studies, 1978.

WRITINGS:

The Mobile Indians, Colonial Books, 1966.
Family Biographies, Colonial Books, 1967.
The Pascagoula Indians, Colonial Books, 1967.
Pascagoula: Singing River City, Gill Press, 1968.
Mobile: City by the Bay, Mobile Jaycees, 1968.
The Journal of Sauvole, Colonial Books, 1969.
Fort Maurepas: The Birth of Louisiana, Colonial Books, 1969.
Brother Holyfield, Thomas-Hull, 1972.
A Voyage to Dauphin Island, Museum of the City of Mobile, 1974.
Old Mobile: Fort Louis de la Louisiane, 1702-1711, Museum of the City of Mobile, 1977.
Fast Train Russia, Dodd, 1983.

Contributor to *Encyclopaedia Britannica.* Also contributor of articles to newspapers, magazines, and journals in the United States and abroad, including *Louisiana Studies, Alabama Review, Journal of Mississippi History, XX Century and Peace, Zvezda* (Leningrad), *Novedades de Moscu, Literaturnaya Gazeta,* and *Sovietskaya Rossia.*

WORK IN PROGRESS: One novel, six poems, two plays; a memoir, *Autumn in Petrishevo.*

SIDELIGHTS: Jay Higginbotham told *CA:* "I began writing as a child and have never stopped. I began because I came from a family of lawyers, orators and raconteurs, and I could never get any words in except by writing. I always have been, and always will be, determined to be heard on a wide variety of subjects."

Higginbotham's works have been distributed in 128 countries and translated into seventeen languages, including Arabic, Czech, Japanese, Russian, and Hungarian.

HIGGINS, George V(incent) 1939-

PERSONAL: Born November 13, 1939, in Brockton, Mass.; son of John Thompson and Doris (Montgomery) Higgins; married Elizabeth Mulkerin, September 4, 1965 (divorced January, 1979); married Loretta Lucas Cubberley, August 23, 1979; children: (first marriage) Susan, John. *Education:* Boston College, B.A., 1961, J.D., 1967; Stanford University, M.A., 1965.

ADDRESSES: Home—15 Brush Hill Lane, Milton, Mass. 02186.

CAREER: Journal and *Evening Bulletin,* Providence, R.I., reporter, 1962-63; Associated Press, bureau correspondent in Springfield, Mass., 1963-64, newsman in Boston, Mass., 1964; Guterman, Horvitz & Rubin (law firm), Boston, researcher, 1966-67; admitted to the Massachusetts Bar, 1967; Commonwealth of Massachusetts, Office of the Attorney General, Boston, legal assistant in the administrative division and organized crime section, 1967, deputy assistant attorney general, 1967-69, assistant attorney general, 1969-70; U.S. District Court of Massachusetts, Boston, assistant U.S. attorney, 1970-73, special assistant U.S. attorney, 1973-74; George V. Higgins, Inc. (law firm), Boston, president, 1973-78; Griffin & Higgins (law firm), Boston, partner, 1978-82; writer. Instructor in law enforcement programs, Northeastern University, Boston, 1969-71; instructor in trial practice, Boston College Law School, 1973-74, 1978-79. Consultant, National Institute of Law Enforcement and Criminal Justice, Washington, D.C., 1970-71.

MEMBER: Writers Guild of America.

AWARDS, HONORS: The Friends of Eddie Coyle was chosen one of the top twenty postwar American novels by the Book Marketing Council, 1985.

WRITINGS:

NOVELS

The Friends of Eddie Coyle (also see below), Knopf, 1972.
The Digger's Game, Knopf, 1973.
Cogan's Trade (also see below), Knopf, 1974.
A City on a Hill, Knopf, 1975.
The Judgement of Deke Hunter, Little, Brown, 1976.
Dreamland, Little, Brown, 1977.
A Year or So with Edgar, Harper, 1979.
Kennedy for the Defense, Knopf, 1980.
The Rat on Fire (also see below), Knopf, 1981.
The Patriot Game, Knopf, 1982.
A Choice of Enemies, Knopf, 1984.
Penance for Jerry Kennedy, Knopf, 1985.
The Friends of Eddie Coyle, Cogan's Trade, The Rat on Fire,
     Robinson, 1985.
Imposters, Holt, 1986.

The Friends of Eddie Coyle has been translated into Italian, Spanish, French, Danish, Norwegian, Finnish, German, Flemish, and Turkish; *The Digger's Game* has been translated into Spanish and Norwegian; *Cogan's Trade* has been translated into Norwegian.

OTHER

(Contributor) Martha Foley, editor, *The Best American Short
     Stories 1973* (anthology), Houghton, 1973.
(Contributor) James Ross, editor, *They Don't Dance Much*
     (anthology), Southern Illinois University Press, 1975.

The Friends of Richard Nixon (nonfiction), Little, Brown, 1975.
*Style versus Substance: Boston, Kevin White, and the Politics
     of Illusion,* Macmillan, 1984.
Old Earl Died Pulling Traps: A Story, limited edition, Bruccoli Clark, 1984.

Columnist, *Boston Herald American,* 1977-79; author of magazine criticism column, *Boston Globe,* 1979-85; author of biweekly television column, *Wall Street Journal,* 1984—. Contributor of essays and short fiction to journals and magazines, including *Arizona Quarterly, Cimarron Review, Esquire, Atlantic, Playboy, GQ, New Republic,* and *Newsweek.*

WORK IN PROGRESS: A nonfiction study of Congressional irresponsibility.

SIDELIGHTS: A lawyer who has served as a prosecutor and defense lawyer in both state and federal courts, George V. Higgins has an intimate knowledge of the criminal justice system and the political system. As a novelist, Higgins draws from his experience, creating detailed examinations of crime, justice, and politics. Higgins told Nicholas Shakespeare of the London *Times,* "The disability of much American literature is that it's written by college professors sitting on their big fat rusty-dusties who don't know anything about law, politics, or any subject in which real people make real livings." Higgins has worked with real criminals, real policemen, real lawyers, and real politicians; his fiction has been praised for its authentic depictions of these people and their lives.

As Hugh M. Ruppersburg points out in the *Dictionary of Literary Biography,* "George V. Higgins' work has two notable features: its analysis of the motives underlying human character and behavior, and its reliance on dialogue for the revelation of plot, character, and theme." Although he focuses on characters who live outside the mainstream of society, Higgins demonstrates that these people are plagued by the same ambitions and frustrations as those in more mundane walks of life. He allows each character to speak for himself and then arranges the conversations like the testimony in a trial to convey the larger story. The author uses dialogue so extensively that "the plot of a Higgins novel—suspense, humor and tragedy—is a blurrily perceived skeleton within the monsoon of dialogue," comments Roderick MacLeish in the *Washington Post Book World.* Higgins's novels are spoken, and therefore "lacking in figurative or heavily imagistic language," writes Ruppersburg. "The result is a concrete style, economical and to the point."

His first three novels—*The Friends of Eddie Coyle, The Digger's Game,* and *Cogan's Trade*—established Higgins as "an impressive chronicler of the life style of the small-time hoodlum for whom crime is the only thing that does pay," notes O. L. Bailey in the *New York Times Book Review.* Some reviewers immediately placed his fiction in the crime genre; yet, unlike the traditional crime novelist, Higgins "forgoes sentimentality, private eyes and innocent victims to write exclusively of criminals who work on each other in a community where sin is less talked of than are mistakes," relates Peter S. Prescott in *Newsweek.* The author's scrutiny of this often unseen yet real segment of society puts his novels in the company of serious mainstream fiction. Similarly, by uncovering the obscure world of the criminal, Higgins allows its comparison to mainstream society. "Money, family pressures, and the desire for a middle-class life-style motivate the behavior of the criminal as well as the average citizen," indicates Ruppersburg. "Kids grow up," J. D. O'Hara adds in *New Republic,* "customs change, new men take over from the dying or incompetent old men, power changes hands, deals succeed or fail.'' Yet the tone of this subsociety is different. ''The criminal world is . . . realistically depicted as a pitiless jungle where self-preservation depends on constant vigilance, and everyone leads a twitching knife-edge existence,'' Leo Harris observes in *Books and Bookmen.*

Higgins received immediate critical approval for his writing with the publication of *The Friends of Eddie Coyle,* ''one of the best of its genre I have read since Hemingway's 'The Killers,''' claims Christopher Lehmann-Haupt of the *New York Times.* It ''is fiction of a most convincing order,'' according to Harvey Gardner in the *New York Times Book Review.* ''The story of Eddie and his hood friends, and of the cops and lawyers who belong in their world as much as the crooks do, is told in short, beautifully-made episodes, full of nicely heard talk.'' Eddie Coyle is a struggling middleman in Boston's underworld economy whose specialty is dealing guns. ''There is nothing glamorous or humorous about Eddie Coyle, and nothing remotely adventurous about the life he leads,'' Joe McGinniss observes in the *New York Times Book Review.* ''It is seamy; it is drab.''

The Friends of Eddie Coyle introduced what would become the trademark of Higgins's fiction, a ''unique virtuosity in exploiting an uncanny ear for the argot of the underworld,'' explains Bailey. By using the language of the criminal and emphasizing dialogue, Higgins creates a book that is ''flat, toneless, and positively reeking with authenticity,'' writes McGinniss. ''Its dialogue eats at one's nerve endings,'' adds Lehmann-Haupt. However, not all reviewers praise Higgins's use of dialogue to relate his story. One complaint is that because all these criminals speak the same slang, they sound alike; character distinctions become blurred. McGinniss admits that ''all of Eddie's friends . . . seem not so much individuals as facets of the same personality.'' The reviewer adds, however, ''Rather than a weakness, I suspect that this may well be Higgins's main point.'' In Harris's opinion, *The Friends of Eddie Coyle* ''is expressed in dialogue that is perhaps just a shade too good, too redolent of Hemingway . . . and Runyon.'' Yet Harris finds that Higgins's style ''makes a literary tragedy out of a small time crook and his fate.'' McGinniss concludes, ''With 'The Friends of Eddie Coyle,' [Higgins has] given us the most penetrating glimpse yet into what seems the real world of crime.''

The Digger's Game ''confirms that Higgins writes about the world of crime with an authenticity that is unmatched,'' comments Jonathan Yardley in the *Washington Post Book World.* ''In [his first two] novels,'' adds Yardley, ''the central character is an obscure man who has done something fairly stupid but quite understandable, and is trying to pay the price without getting killed in the process.'' The Digger's mistake is gambling away eighteen thousand dollars in Las Vegas, putting him in debt to a loan shark. Higgins follows Digger; the things he does and the people he sees while trying to pay his debt tell his story. ''Higgins has done more than write a fast, gripping story about Boston's underworld,'' James Mills notes in *The New York Times Book Review.* ''He has created in the Digger a deeply touching character who . . . would be equally moving if he were out of crime and struggling for survival in a bank or an automobile factory.'' Mills adds, ''A lot of writers have taken a shot at the Vegas madness, but none has described it with more humor, sadness and pathos than Higgins.''

The critical debate surrounding Higgins's third novel, *Cogan's Trade,* has centered on the author's continued evolution toward a novel told completely through the dialogue of its characters. Understanding is difficult in the opinion of Bailey because the reader must glean information from the conversations of characters who speak in unfamiliar slang. ''The flaw in 'Cogan,''' he writes in the *New York Times Book Review,* ''is that there is not enough of our mother tongue to keep confusion at bay.'' What prose there is offers primarily physical description and very little interpretation or judgment of the criminal behavior of Higgins's characters. But a *Times Literary Supplement* reviewer maintains that ''in Higgins, violence is always committed in cold blood; people are just doing their job, and so the prose can afford to remain disinterested.''

Higgins employs dialogue for more than its realistic effect, believe some reviewers. ''Like [James] Joyce, Higgins uses language in torrents, beautifully crafted, ultimately intending to create a panoramic impression,'' writes Roderick MacLeish. Adds a contributor to the *Times Literary Supplement,* ''For all their surface authenticity, the speeches have more in common with dramatic monologues than with conversations that are merely 'overheard'; brutal and obscene though they unquestionably are, their effect is still one of stylization.'' ''He's drawing the fewest possible lines on his canvas in order to conjure up in the reader's imagination the details of the spaces in between,'' explains Lehmann-Haupt. ''Lines that provoke the imagination so actively are what entertaining art is all about.''

In summary writes MacLeish: ''As a novel, *Cogan's Trade* is a brilliant exposition of Higgins's Boston underworld as the flipside of all respectable lives of desperation. As a thriller it is that taut story whose drama is heightened by our own understanding of how it has to end.'' ''*Cogan's Trade* . . . firmly establishes [Higgins] as a novelist of wit, intelligence and disquieting originality,'' concludes a *Times Literary Supplement* reviewer.

In his fourth novel, *A City on a Hill,* Higgins ''has abandoned Boston lowlife for the more complex and intellectually treacherous milieu of Washington politics,'' Pearl K. Bell comments in the *New Leader.* The United States had entered the Watergate era and Higgins tuned his ear for the power struggles and corruption of the political arena. ''In politics as in crime, Higgins' interest lies with those who work in the shadows. He is as concerned as ever with hopes that go unrealized, prospects that never materialize, ambitions that prove excessive,'' Yardley relates in the *New Republic.* Politics has remained a major concern of Higgins's fiction; it has also been the topic of a nonfiction work, an examination of the Watergate incident entitled *The Friends of Richard Nixon.*

A City on a Hill ''may be the definitive novel of Washington at the staff level,'' Christopher Lydon writes in the *New York Times Book Review,* ''the world of driven, dependent campaign hotshots who so quickly become power junkies and then political tramps and almost never leave the capital.'' Yardley finds that although this novel ''contains many perceptive observations about the machinations of politics and political people . . . Higgins does not seem secure of his territory.'' Yardley adds: ''*A City on a Hill* simply does not have the authenticity, the sureness, of the earlier novels. When it does have authenticity, Higgins has moved from Washington back to Boston, to the people he knows.''

Higgins concentrates on the people and the city he knows best in another novel of the political scene, *A Choice of Enemies.*

The story is that of Bernie Morgan, speaker of the state house, his fall from power, and the people responsible. "Certain [is Higgins's] feeling for the corridor and cloakroom dynamics of Massachusetts politics," writes Charles Champlin in the *Los Angeles Times Book Review*. As a novel, *A Choice of Enemies* received a mixed critical response, primarily because of its form; "all information, personal background, emotion (everything but interior decoration and clothing) is expressed through dialogue," explains *National Review* contributor D. Keith Mano.

Some reviewers believe that with this novel Higgins's continuing experiment with form exceeded its limits. "Every monotonous obscenity, every dropped word, every cliche and catch phrase, has an initial ring of taped reality," Champlin concedes. He adds, however, "Like transcripts, it needs careful pruning or the sound overruns the sense and, even more damaging, grows dull." In his article in the *New York Times Book Review*, Peter Andrews is strongly critical of the book: "'A Choice of Enemies' represents the final collapse of [Higgins's] ongoing experiment in trying to create a kind of gutter prose-poetry as a vehicle for narrative storytelling." Andrews remarks, "The author has told his tale in such an opaque fashion that I could never get a handle on the story."

Higgins responded to his critics in a letter to *CA:* "What I am doing is replacing the omniscient author with the omniscient reader. The requisite suspension of disbelief consists wholly of the reader's agreement that for his money he has gotten not only a batch of search warrants valid everywhere, to listen in on what the characters say, but the remarkable good fortune to attend only those conversations in which they hatch their plots, betray themselves, and doublecross each other. If the reader is acute, the characters will tell him the story, leaving him to judge for himself the morality, ethics and decency of their actions."

Some reviewers do respond favorably to Higgins's efforts. In gradually moving toward a story told entirely by dialogue, "Higgins has pulled off a remarkable transition," writes D. Keith Mano, "from distinctive realist crime writer to serious, long-reach novelist, still distinctive." "Hemming, hawing, tortuous circumlocutions, and the endless maundering excursuses of quotidian conversation are the devices that Higgins expertly uses to build suspense and tension," explains Nick Tosches in the *Village Voice*. And according to Mano, Higgins has overcome one of the faults that weakened his earlier novels: "Where, in *Cogan's Trade* (1974), each voice sounded like the same marvelous Boston Glib Person, here you have differentiation, variety, and social ecumenism." "Higgins is the master of what he does, and *A Choice of Enemies* contains some of the most brilliant and outrageous passages he has ever brought forth," concludes Tosches.

Jerry Kennedy, the protagonist of two Higgins novels, lives at the intersection of crime, politics, justice, and middle-class America. Like Higgins, Kennedy is a Boston criminal trial lawyer. *Kennedy for the Defense* and *Penance for Jerry Kennedy* offer the expected insights into criminal behavior and political infighting, but they also examine the role of the criminal trial lawyer in the American justice system. Kennedy "makes his living providing the Constitutionally guaranteed defense for the victims and/or perpetrators of the rampant socioeconomic chaos prevalent in various levels of society in and around Boston," observes Tom McNevin in *Best Sellers*. Kennedy defends not by proving his clients innocent; his cases seldom go to trial. The offenders he represents are usually guilty, and more often than not he advises them to plead so.

Higgins explains in a *Time* article: "There is a good reason why 85% to 90% of all criminal cases brought by a competent prosecutor end up in defense pleas; nobody can win them." What Kennedy does is use the various mechanisms of justice to obtain for his clients lesser charges, reduced sentences, and accelerated probations. "Higgins argues that experts like Kennedy fill a vital function in the criminal justice system as indispensable agents of the plea bargaining in whose absence the courts would surely collapse," comments Robert Lekachman in the *Nation*. "Higgins claims further that justice is more likely to be served by the ministrations of cynical, greedy but invariably astute lawyers than by the more formal processes of trial and sentence."

Beyond their portraits of the criminal trial lawyer and the justice system, the Jerry Kennedy novels have gained attention for their characterization. As John Jay Osborn, Jr., notes in the *Washington Post Book World,* "Because the characters ruminate instead of react, there is never much tension in the novel. . . . Yet some of what is lost in the way of tension is gained in the careful depiction of character." Jeremiah Francis Kennedy is a man caught between his desire to lead a relaxed middle-class life-style and his fascination with his work. Kennedy, his colleagues, and clients make *Kennedy for the Defense* "a variegated yarn of third-rate perpetrators, second-class citizens and first-person encounters," *Time* reviewer Peter Stoler remarks. Although they may not be likable, Stoler adds that this "tangled cast is instantly credible and permanently delightful." Evan Hunter echoes Stoler's view. He writes in the *New York Times Book Review:* "George V. Higgins has created a genre of his own, in which the people are so real that it doesn't matter what they're doing or how they go about doing it; just being in their company is pleasure enough."

In *Penance for Jerry Kennedy*, Higgins presents an older Kennedy plagued by difficulties, "a decent, hard-working lawyer who has not lived up to the expectations of his professors, his clients, his colleagues or his wife, and who knows it," says Elaine Kendall in the *Los Angeles Times*. Kennedy commits a mistake that earns him the disfavor of an influential judge and makes him the object of a television reporter's investigation. Kennedy compounds his troubles by drinking to excess. He is at the depths of his personal and professional life. His values are going out of style. "*Penance for Jerry Kennedy* is a novel about a dying breed—lawyers who think on their feet rather than from behind desktop computer terminals and who fight with reasoned words instead of endless streams of documents," Douglas E. Winter remarks in the *Washington Post Book World*. "But Jerry Kennedy is unstoppable," concludes Winter, "the kind of fictional lawyer one meets all too rarely—one whose life and work are made real."

Higgins has been called by some a crime novelist and by others the creator of a new genre. He has at times been compared to major literary figures of the twentieth century. For Hugh M. Ruppersburg, "his skill in characterization and realistic dialogue, his success at portraying individuals in a crisis of identity, his understanding of the influences which form human character, and his development of a unique, effective novelistic form appropriate to his talents . . . establish George V. Higgins as a writer of considerable stature."

MEDIA ADAPTATIONS: The Friends of Eddie Coyle was filmed by Paramount, 1973.

CA INTERVIEW

CA interviewed George V. Higgins by telephone on May 16, 1984, at his home near Boston, Massachusetts.

CA: You maintain a law practice, write a weekly newspaper column, and turn out an amazing number of good novels. How do you do it all?

HIGGINS: I started by reducing the law practice to a mere shadow of its never-too-robust self. I found that in Boston self-fulfilling prophecies are quite as adequate as fully-formed intentions. Word got out on the street that I had given up practicing law. It had the effect of reducing my clientele to, I'm sorry to say, a very manageable number. And after ten years of it I looked back: I had made a profit one year, I had broken even two years, and I had lost money the other seven. I thought God was trying to tell me something. Besides, it's gotten hideously expensive to maintain an office for the private practice of law. I have a theory that the middle class is being priced out of legal services, whether providing them or purchasing them.

CA: You wrote an article about that in Boston Magazine, *I believe.*

HIGGINS: Yes. That was developed from a speech I made a couple of years previously that was printed in the *Boston Bar Journal*, to the effect that really the middle class just can't afford to hire lawyers and certainly can't afford to operate law offices because the overhead is so high. I had to collect (which is not the same thing as charging) $135 an hour in order to get a net return—after I had paid for my secretary and my law library and my office space and all the other foofaraw that I had to have—for an hour of work on a law case that I could get for an hour of writing. And I found that I just couldn't do it with any sort of regularity sufficient to meet the expense of running the office. All I really wanted to do was to net out something fairly approximate to what I'd get for writing; I couldn't do it.

CA: That really is shocking, and most people probably don't understand it.

HIGGINS: It's terrifying. We're going to be in a situation within the next ten or twenty years where we'll be forced into something a lot like Medicare, only it will be Judicare; and I venture to say it won't be any more successful as far as reducing costs is concerned.

CA: Did you really junk ten novels before The Friends of Eddie Coyle *was published?*

HIGGINS: No less than ten and no more than fourteen, depending on how you count rewrites.

CA: Were you working toward writing fiction back in your early days as a newspaper man?

HIGGINS: I wrote my first novel when I was fifteen years old. It was terrible!

CA: How did the interest in politics and law evolve?

HIGGINS: Politics from being in the newspaper business. That's the king-beat among newspaper reporters. It obviously wouldn't be among the sports-section people, but for the would-be, up-and-coming young reporter, politics and government are the things to cover. So, as a matter of self-interest, I developed a strong fascination with politics. And newspapering also led me to go to law school—from covering court cases. The people

trying those cases looked like they were having a lot of fun; it was something I thought I would like to do myself, and I was right. I did like it and I miss it today.

CA: Your law practice obviously has provided some of the inspiration and material for your fiction. Do writing and practicing law work together in other ways that might be less obvious?

HIGGINS: I suppose so, but it is somewhat obscure to me. I'm sure it does in organization: In preparing a case for trial and then trying it, you are, in effect, staging a story in a sort of primitive way. You arrange the actors—the witnesses—so as to present the story in its most coherent form, which is usually chronological if at all possible. You put your experts on last to tell the jury what they should infer from the hard evidence that they've heard, and then you get up on your hind legs and hope that you deliver a coherent summation of it. It's really a species of storytelling, albeit a cumbersome, expensive, and time-consuming one. And I suppose that had a good deal to do with the evolution of my writing style, if it has evolved at all. It made my approach to telling stories, I think, more—I want to say *pragmatic,* though that's not precisely the word that's called for. I think it leads to certain economy in writing fiction simply because that's the whole training that trial law gives you.

In addition to that, of course, I went to the best creative writing school in the country, which is the Associated Press. They teach you to get it over with quickly because fifty fine grafs on the wire five minutes after the United Press International has moved five bad grafs on the wire will mean that your story will get spiked because UPI's is running. So it's really the best training I've ever had in writing.

CA: You make more extensive and perhaps more flexible use of dialogue than any other current writer. Do you try to reproduce actual speech, or do you go beyond that in some way?

HIGGINS: That question implies a more conscientious attitude than I've even taken toward writing dialogue. The first book that I had published, *The Friends of Eddie Coyle,* I didn't plan to tell all in dialogue. And quite honestly, when I finished writing the book I wasn't particularly impressed by the fact that I had written it in dialogue. It didn't really occur to me. It was the most economical, direct, and therefore in my estimation the best way of telling that story; and that's been so with virtually all the other books except for *Dreamland, A Year or So with Edgar,* and *Kennedy for the Defense.* And, of course, it could be argued that each of those is entirely dialogue because they're first-person narrative. But I don't make a conscientious effort to mimic normal speech patterns; what I try to do is write down what I can hear the characters say. I do have that sort of hallucination that I can hear the people talking as I write.

CA: Do you overhear conversations when you're having lunch, going through the everyday routines?

HIGGINS: Oh, yes; I'm an inveterate eavesdropper. I'm a terrible snoop. I often get the donnée, as Henry James called it, from listening to other people's conversation. People have a notion when they're sitting at a table in a restaurant that they're in some sort of an isolation chamber, that nobody can hear what they're saying. I notice it too with my kids. I'll pick them up at school with their friends, and they get into the car and begin these conversations and are of the apparent assumption that I can't hear them. Unfortunately it hasn't given me very much good material, but the hope remains, you know.

CA: Do you do a lot of revision on the dialogue?

HIGGINS: No. I either print it pretty much as it comes out the first time or else I rewrite it front to back. I do very little tinkering with my fiction. It's either right when I do it or else it's terrible and I stop before I finish it. I can tell when I'm off my feed, and I don't write any more that day. I was satisfied with the first draft of what will be *Penance for Jerry Kennedy,* the sequel to *Kennedy for the Defense,* which will be published next year. But I have revised it significantly, very significantly, once. I had a 370-page manuscript that, when I had tinkered with it a little for the second draft, came out to about 470 pages, of which 70 were unchanged from the original. And when I get that back from the copyeditor I contemplate making a few more changes, but it won't be a front-to-back rewrite; it'll be rearranging some details so as to highlight material that became more important to the eventual development and resolution of the plot than I thought it would be when I put it in initially. I don't have an outline. I don't know how the book is going to come out. One of the reasons I write fast is because there is a certain amount of suspense on my side too—I don't know how a thing is going to end.

CA: So you're enjoying it as you're doing it?

HIGGINS: Yes. There seems to be a complete ignorance on the part of many biographers of writers of the fact that writing is great fun. I noticed it in Frank McShane's biography of Raymond Chandler, which I perhaps read more carefully because I'm working on a biography of Chandler. McShane never does seem to have glommed on to the fact that Chandler really liked writing. It's probably the only thing in his life that he did—except screwing secretaries and drinking too much—that he really enjoyed. He thrived on it. Faulkner was the same way. He did a certain amount of griping about writing but he said, you know, you can't drink all the time and you can't screw all the time; you have to work. And he took a great deal of satisfaction in it. So do I. I love it. I'd rather do this than anything else—including trying cases, though I like trying cases a lot.

CA: The influences that you've cited include some ground-breakers—Hemingway, Joyce, Conrad, perhaps O'Hara especially.

HIGGINS: Yes. I've just done an article on O'Hara. It's fifty years this August since *Appointment in Samarra* was published, which I didn't realize when I proposed doing the article; I discovered it only when I started reading back. What a wonderful writer he was—but vastly superior, I think, in his short stories, rather than his novels. He was much more comfortable with the short story.

CA: Did you set about your own writing with any kind of specific idea of doing something unique in fiction?

HIGGINS: No. All I wanted to do was tell stories. I thought that reading stories was an absorbing, happy way to spend your time and therefore that telling them must be even more fun, even more absorbing; and I was right. I was convinced I could never make a living at it, that I would always have to do something else. And I craved comfort, so I was a good boy

and went to college and got my graduate degree and just wrote because I liked to do it. I'm still doing it for that reason, except now I get paid for it and that's even better.

CA: Sometimes reviewers differ very widely in their response to your books, though every book has gotten plenty of positive response. How seriously do you take the reviews? Do you care about them?

HIGGINS: Well, I think I allowed myself to get seduced into a fallacy as a result of the early experience I had with the reviews. I equated a successful book with a large fistful of laudatory reviews, especially in the four journals that I think count the most—the two editions, daily and Sunday, of the *New York Times,* and *Time* and *Newsweek.* Therefore, about the time the eighth or ninth book came out, and particularly with the publication of my book about the Watergate, I found that I was more unsettled than I should have been by negative reviews or total disregard.

The fact of the matter is that one has no defense against an idiot. I drew an idiot, unfortunately, to review *A Choice of Enemies* for the *New York Times Book Review.* The man just didn't understand it. I'm sure it had a decidedly negative effect upon the sales, but fortunately for me it came out six or seven weeks after the book had been out on sale. So the damage was limited. But it was time, I decided, for me to realize that by now I have a certain number of readers who will buy what I write because they're used to the by-line; it's a known quantity. And there's a certain number of readers that I will never get. It's my misfortune to fall between the two stools: I will never sell like Harold Robbins and I will probably never enjoy the critical acclaim of John Updike. There's nothing I can do about those things. If I could I would.

CA: The people who are sophisticated enough to read reviews faithfully must realize that they can be quirky.

HIGGINS: It isn't only that. I do a lot of book reviewing, and I know that, given the demands of my schedule and the amount of money that the review brings in, the most conscientious job I can do for the author is to read the book carefully once, then write a careful review—which for my own professional satisfaction has to be an essay that will stand on its own. The essay ought to tell the reader of the review what the book is about and whether I liked it. I only get 750 or 800 words to accomplish those three objectives, which isn't very much. And I'm mindful also of the observation made by Bill Robertson, the book editor of the *Miami Herald,* who said that if one percent of the people who read the Sunday book review section of the *Miami Herald* acted upon what they read, then every book that is favorably reviewed would sell 20,000 copies in the Miami area alone. And that doesn't happen. I have had the experience repeatedly of lambasting an utter fraud of a novel and seeing it land on the bestseller list in the very newspaper in which I lambasted it—and *stay* there, showing that the vast majority of the people in the paper's circulation area totally ignored what I wrote. I thought in 1982, when *Newsweek* reviewed *The Patriot Game* so favorably, that it would sell furiously, and it didn't. And I was somewhat downcast this year when *Newsweek* was decidedly mixed about *A Choice of Enemies.* It sold like blazes. So you make sense out of it; I can't. The only thing that really affects me, as far as the reviews are concerned, are the sales; and I am no longer convinced that there is a direct correlation between favorable reviews and plentiful sales.

CA: Would you like to see more academic treatment of your work?

HIGGINS: Purely from a standpoint of greed, yes. If I got more academic attention, then the books would be placed on the required reading lists and they'd sell more copies. It would also serve the purpose that was accomplished by the editors of *Great American Short Stories* when they included "The Eighty-Yard Run" in their collection and made me a sucker for anything that has Irwin Shaw's name on it. I love his stuff. I think Irwin got a bit lax in later years, but my Lord, reading those short stories—"Sailor Off the Bremen" and the others—made me a devotee of his for life. The same thing with Graham Greene. I had a professor in college who was beserk on the subject of Graham Greene. He loved his stuff, and therefore once I read it under his tutelage, so did I. Sure, I would like to have more academic exposure than I've gotten, and I hope it comes. But John O'Hara never had very much of it and he's done reasonably well.

CA: You've been described, or described yourself, as an "apprentice curmudgeon," and in your magazine articles have expressed very strong views on such matters as gun control, education, funding for the arts, Ma Bell, and the high cost of practicing law. What are you feeling most curmudgeonly about at present?

HIGGINS: I've just taken on the assignment of doing a television column every other week for the *Wall Street Journal,* and I am continuing to do my magazine criticism every week for the *Boston Globe,* so I suppose it's those two things. Each is of course a marketplace that is absolutely wallowing in drivel, so there's almost always something about which I can get exercised. And each of them has the advantage of being accessible without too much effort or expense by the reader of the newspaper, so there are common reference points and you don't have to explain a lot of stuff.

And I've remained vexed that the natural outlet of prolific writers such as I doesn't seem to want our stuff. I'm talking about the *New Yorker.* I'm at a loss really to understand the premium that they put on what I consider to be altogether too ephemeral fiction. It's vexing to me because they come out every week and they could publish frequent contributions from prolific writers, as I say. But they don't wish to do it.

I'm a little bit distressed at the general decline of fiction in popular magazines. A friend of mine pointed out recently that if you want to read a story—you know, just a short story with a beginning and a middle and an end—you've got to go to the quarterly reviews, which is the opposite of what it was when I was in college. They're not supposed to change the rules on me like that. *TriQuarterly* has got much better fiction in it than the *New Yorker* has. In the *New Yorker* it's all these mildly disaffected, neurasthenic ladies, some of them eighteen and some of them fifty-eight, and the lot of them indistinguishable from each other except by whether they have or have not had children. That's it. I don't understand it, and it bothers me because I can see a market glimmering there. The same thing with a magazine like *Vanity Fair,* which was revived with such fanfare and hoopla and has turned into something that sounds like a party at Truman Capote's. I have the uncomfortable feeling that I may be learning more and more to make better and better buggy whips and the market for my stuff just won't be around.

CA: What's in the works that you'd like to talk about?

HIGGINS: I'm always excited about the next book that's coming out because, rightly or wrongly (and I've been wrong a couple of times), I think each one is better than the others that came before it. I'd like to believe that I've learned something, although I may have trouble topping *Enemies.* Put it this way: There's no question in my mind that *Enemies* is my best book. I mean no insult to Mister Coyle. Dead as he is, he's been good to me; but *Eddie Coyle* is not in the same room with *A Choice of Enemies.* But next year's book is—to use that word again—more accessible. It's a sequel to *Kennedy for the Defense* and life has become a lot more complicated for poor Jerry. And it's perhaps a more compassionate book. It's a lot longer. I've discovered in the five years since I wrote the first Kennedy book that life is a bit more complicated than I had imagined, at least for Jerry Kennedy. So I think it may have the potential for more popularity than *Enemies* had. *Enemies* is in its own sweet way a fairly difficult book. It repays perhaps more attention than the person reading for relaxation is inclined to give it.

CA: Is there anything you'd like to try that's completely unlike what you've done?

HIGGINS: No. I've tried most of the things that I want to try. Not all of them by any means succeeded. I'm pretty much, I think, at the point where I can do a workmanlike job with a screenplay. That was not the case when I first tried to do a screenplay back in 1973, when *The Digger's Game* came out. I thought I could do a screenplay because, after all, I'd written the novel. I found that they were vastly different media. Writing screenplays is tedious as hell, but I think I'm at the point now where if the opportunity presented itself I could do a fairly decent job of it. I might hope to ease into it by doing screen-stories, forty- or fifty-page stories from which a nuts-and-bolts screenwriter could develop the actual shooting script.

I could hope to do that simply because there's a lot of money to be made in that area. I've been fascinated by it for a long time. I worked for three and a half years on a television pilot that was never made, but those development projects can pay handsomely too. And let's face it, you have to make a living. The freedom's wonderful when you're a writer, but there ain't no security whatever. There's no pension in the racket. It's true that nobody can order you out to New Hampshire. But it's also true that if you're feeling poorly and you spend two weeks in bed, you don't get any money. That does tend to focus the attention. It makes you industrious.

CA: Do you foresee any major changes in your routine?

HIGGINS: I have the two columns, which pretty much liberates me from doing any of the other ordinary things that writers do to get regular income. I don't make that many speeches. I can foresee three or four years down the road, once my youngest child is eighteen, that I'll be a bit more free to travel than I have been for the past six or seven years. I've been extremely reluctant to take on the sort of assignment that I had with the Watergate, for example, when I was commuting to Washington. I don't know that I will *want* to do that—I'm a little older now than I was when Richard Nixon was in trouble—but I'll be *free* to do it.

I have a nonfiction book coming out from Macmillan in October about Boston politics, the sixteen years of Kevin White's administration. And I rather hope to do more nonfiction, but I'll be picking and choosing my areas. I've just completed an article for *New England Monthly* about Mayor Vincent Cianci of Providence, who was forced to resign from office when he was convicted of a felony, battering his ex-wife's lover. A friend of mine had suggested that it looks to him as though I'm trying to make a second career of specializing in the stories of mayors who make fools of themselves. But the thing of it is I'm freer now to do nonfiction than when I was trying not so successfully to do a law practice. And I think that I need to do that because I don't want to become a masochistic, navel-gazing Sensitive Writer. I want to continue to deal with the real world, and the only way to do it is to butt up against it every so often, no matter how soiled you get in the process.

BIOGRAPHICAL/CRITICAL SOURCES:

BOOKS

Contemporary Literary Criticism, Gale, Volume IV, 1975, Volume VII, 1977, Volume X, 1979, Volume XVIII, 1981.
Dictionary of Literary Biography, Volume II: *American Novelists since World War II*, Gale, 1978.
Dictionary of Literary Biography Yearbook: 1981, Gale, 1982.

PERIODICALS

Best Sellers, August, 1980.
Books and Bookmen, September, 1972.
Los Angeles Times, February 28, 1985.
Los Angeles Times Book Review, March 4, 1984.
Nation, April 26, 1980.
National Review, November 7, 1975, May 18, 1984.
New Republic, March 30, 1974, April 12, 1975.
Newsweek, March 25, 1974, April 28, 1975, September 6, 1976, March 3, 1980.
New Yorker, June 24, 1974, March 18, 1985.
New York Times, January 25, 1972, March 23, 1973, April 10, 1974, March 14, 1975.
New York Times Book Review, February 6, 1972, February 11, 1973, March 25, 1973, March 31, 1974, March 30, 1975, October 26, 1975, March 2, 1980, February 12, 1984, February 24, 1985.
Time, April 1, 1974, April 14, 1975, August 23, 1976, March 31, 1980.
Times (London), May 16, 1985.
Times Literary Supplement, August 16, 1974, November 7, 1980.
Village Voice, January 31, 1984.
Washington Post Book World, April 1, 1973, March 31, 1974, March 2, 1980, March 17, 1985.

—Sketch by Bryan Ryan

—Interview by Jean W. Ross

*   *   *

HIGGINS, Paul Lambourne   1916-

PERSONAL: Born September 1, 1916, in Long Beach, Calif.; son of Clarence F. and Minnie (Hauk) Higgins; married Ruth Paddock-Weir, 1954. *Education:* Attended University of California, Los Angeles, 1933-34; Southwestern University, LL.B., 1937; Whittier College, A.B., 1942, M.A., 1943; University of Chicago, D.B., 1945, further study, 1945-46.

ADDRESSES: Home—60 Thacher Rd., Rockport, Mass. 01966.

CAREER: Served as student pastor at Methodist churches in Dominguez, Calif., 1941-43, and Washburn, Ill., 1943-46; pastor at Washington Heights Methodist Church, Chicago, Ill.,

1946-52, Hyde Park Methodist Church, Chicago, 1952-61, Richards Street Methodist Church, Joliet, Ill., 1961-73, at churches in Sanbornville, N.H., and Newfield, Me., 1974-76, and at Tenney Methodist Church and North Salem Church, Salem, N.H., 1976-83; currently director of Rockport Colony, Rockport, Mass., and leader of religious retreats, seminars, and pilgrimages abroad. Past president, Hyde Park-Kenwood Council of Churches and Synagogues; delegate, World Methodist Conference, Oslo, Norway, 1961, and London, England, 1966.

MEMBER: Spiritual Frontiers Fellowship (co-founder; president, 1956-60, 1962-64; life member of executive council), Churches' Fellowship for Psychical and Spiritual Studies (England).

WRITINGS:

Preachers of Power, Vantage, 1950.
John Wesley: Spiritual Witness, Denison, 1960.
Encountering the Unseen, Denison, 1966, 2nd edition, Clark, 1971.
Mother of All, Denison, 1969.
Spiritual Horizons, Rockport, 1973.
Frontiers of the Spirit, Denison, 1976.
Moon over Cape Ann, Rowley, 1978.

''PILGRIMAGE'' SERIES

Pilgrimages: A Guide to the Holy Places of Europe for Today's Traveler, Prentice-Hall, 1984.
Pilgrimages USA, Prentice-Hall, 1985.
Pilgrimages to Rome and Beyond: A Guide to Holy Places of Southern Europe for Today's Traveler, Prentice-Hall, 1985.
Holy Lands Pilgrimages: A Guide to the Sacred Places of the Near East for Today's Traveler, Prentice-Hall, 1986.

OTHER

Contributor to anthologies. Contributor to periodicals, including *Spiritual Frontiers Journal*.

WORK IN PROGRESS: A book on Christianity and the Great Mother and one on spiritual healing; other books in the ''Pilgrimage'' series.

SIDELIGHTS: Paul Lambourne Higgins told *CA* his interests include religious history, travel, spiritual power centers, art and architecture, psychical research, spiritual healing, the Virgin Mary and the Mother Goddess, John Wesley, and mysticism.

*   *   *

HIGHAM, Charles   1931-

PERSONAL: Born February 18, 1931, in London, England; emigrated to Australia in 1954; came to the United States in 1969; son of Sir Charles Frederick (a publicist and author) and Josephine (Webb) Higham; married Norine Lillian Cecil (deceased). *Education:* Studied privately.

ADDRESSES: Home—Hollywood, Calif. *Agent*—Barbara Lowenstein, 250 W. 57th St, New York, N.Y. 10107.

CAREER: Literary and film critic in London, England, and then in Sydney, Australia, 1954-63; *Bulletin* (weekly), Sydney, literary editor, 1963-68; University of California, Santa Cruz, Regents Professor, 1969; KPFK Radio, Los Angeles, Calif., film critic, 1969-71; Hollywood correspondent for *New York Times*, 1970-80, and *Us* (magazine), 1977—. Official historian for audio history of the movies presented to the American Film Institute in 1973, Time-Life Books.

AWARDS, HONORS: Poetry prizes from Poetry Society of London, 1949, and *Sydney Morning Herald,* 1956; Prix des createurs for biography, Academie Francaise, 1977.

WRITINGS:

A Distant Star (poems), Hand & Flower Press, 1951.
Spring and Death (poems), Hand & Flower Press, 1953.
(Translator of poems of Marc Chagall) H. F. S. Bauman, editor, *Eight European Artists,* Heinemann, 1954.
The Earthbound and Other Poems, Angus & Robertson, 1960.
(Editor with Alan Brissenden) *They Came to Australia: An Anthology,* F. W. Cheshire, 1961.
Noonday Country: Poems, 1954-1965, Angus & Robertson, 1966.
(Editor with Michael Wilding) *Australians Abroad: An Anthology,* F. W. Cheshire, 1967.
(Editor) *Australian Writing Today,* Penguin, 1968.
(With Joel Greenberg) *Hollywood in the Forties,* A. S. Barnes, 1968.
(With Greenberg) *The Celluloid Muse: Hollywood Directors Speak,* Angus & Robertson, 1969, Regnery, 1971.
The Films of Orson Welles, University of California Press, 1970.
Hollywood Cameramen: Sources of Light, Indiana University Press, 1970.
The Voyage to Brindisi and Other Poems, 1966-1969, Angus & Robertson, 1970.
Hollywood at Sunset, Saturday Review Press, 1972.
Ziegfeld, Regnery, 1972.
The Art of the American Film, Doubleday, 1973.
Cecil B. De Mille: A Biography, Scribner, 1973.
Ava: A Life Story, Delacorte, 1974.
Kate: The Life of Katharine Hepburn, Norton, 1975.
Charles Laughton: An Intimate Biography, Doubleday, 1975.
The Adventures of Conan Doyle, Norton, 1976.
Marlene: The Life of Marlene Dietrich, Norton, 1977.
The Changeling: A Fairy Tale of Terror (novel), Simon & Schuster, 1978.
(With Hal Wallis) *Star Maker: The Autobiography of Hal Wallis,* Macmillan, 1980.
Errol Flynn: The Untold Story, Doubleday, 1980.
Bette: The Life of Bette Davis, Macmillan, 1981.
Trading with the Enemy, Delacorte, 1983.
Princess Merle: The Romantic Life of Merle Oberon, Coward, 1983 (published in England as *Merle: A Biography of Merle Oberon,* New English Library, 1983).
Sisters: The Lives of Olivia de Havilland and Joan Fontaine, Coward, 1984.
American Swastika, Doubleday, 1985.
Orson Welles: The Rise and Fall of an American Genius, St. Martin's, 1985.

CONTRIBUTOR TO POETRY ANTHOLOGIES

Rex Warner and others, editor, *New Poems, 1954: A P.E.N. Anthology,* M. Joseph, 1954.
Ronald McCuaig, editor, *Australian Poetry, 1954,* Angus & Robertson, 1955.
A. A. Phillips, editor, *Australian Poetry, 1956,* Angus & Robertson, 1956.
G. A. Wilkes, editor, *Australian Poetry, 1963,* Angus & Robertson, 1963.
Lionel Stevenson and others, editors, *Best Poems of 1962: Borestone Mountain Poetry Awards,* Pacific Books, 1963.

D. Stewart, editor, *Poetry in Australia II,* Angus & Robertson, 1964, University of California Press, 1965.
C. V. Wedgwood, editor, *New Poems, 1965: A P.E.N. Anthology of Contemporary Poetry,* Hutchinson, 1966.
David Campbell, editor, *Australian Poetry, 1966,* Tri-Ocean, 1967.
Stevenson and others, editors, *Best Poems of 1967: Borestone Mountain Poetry Awards,* Pacific Books, 1967.

OTHER

Contributor of poems, articles, reviews, and interviews to magazines and newspapers, including *London Magazine, Sight and Sound, Hudson Review, Yale Review, Cosmopolitan,* and *New York Times.*

WORK IN PROGRESS: Audrey: The Life of Audrey Hepburn; The Sailor Home from the Sea, a novel; "Nightstick," a screenplay.

SIDELIGHTS: Charles Higham told *CA* that his first love is verse. Higham is best known, however, for his biographies of Hollywood celebrities. Praised by some reviewers, these books have roused indignation in others because of their sensational nature. For example, *New York Times Book Review* contributor Foster Hirsch takes exception to Higham's *Sisters,* which chronicles the feud between movie star siblings Joan Fontaine and Olivia de Havilland. Hirsch declares that *Sisters* "implies that people who made it big in movies are of course unsavory." Yet he allows that "Mr. Higham can be droll; he knows how to keep his story moving, and he works up some tension, even if it's only wondering what petty monarch will take the next pratfall." *Bette,* Higham's book on actress Bette Davis, is a "cheesy, tattletale excuse for a biography," according to *Washington Post Book World* reviewer Elliott Ivan Sirkin, but the same book is described as "tightly focused" by a *Chicago Times Book World* writer, who adds that "from start to finish [Higham] writes a detailed, fascinating book."

Higham's most controversial work is certainly his biography entitled *Errol Flynn: The Untold Story.* The dashing Australian actor played the noble hero in many adventure films of the 1930s and 1940s, including "Captain Blood," "Robin Hood," and "The Sea Hawk." Offscreen, Flynn built a formidable reputation as a hard-drinking libertine. But Higham contends that Flynn was not only an alcoholic womanizer; he claims to have evidence proving that the actor was a Nazi spy and a homosexual. His case is built upon Flynn's connections with Dr. Hermann Friedrich Erben, an admitted member of a Nazi spy ring in Asia. Upon uncovering this friendship, Higham traced Erben to a leper colony in the Philippines and hired a Filipino associate to tape record an interview with Dr. Erben. *The Untold Story* is based on this interview and on 12,000 pages of declassified federal documents detailing government surveillance of Flynn.

The accusations of Nazism enraged many of Flynn's former companions. Nora Eddington Black, Flynn's wife during World War II, stated in Maggy Daly's *Chicago Tribune* column: "I resent Higham's book because it is a fraud. He hasn't come up with a single document about Errol's supposed tie-in with the Gestapo, but continues to go around the country saying he has." "I don't have a document that says A, B, C, D, E, Errol Flynn was a Nazi agent," Higham explained to Robert Lindsey in the *New York Times.* "But I have pieced together a mosaic that proves that he is."

Some reviewers are critical of the methods of reportage used in compiling *The Untold Story,* including Lawrence S. Dietz, who in a *New York Times Book Review* article calls the book "a standard job of celebrity scandal-mongering, in which Mr. Higham, with a certain moral fervor, details Flynn's obsessive sexual behavior and drug habits. Unfortunately, no one seems to have bothered to tell Mr. Higham that the rules for serious investigative reporting are far different from those for uncovering ancient Hollywood peccadillos." *Chicago Tribune* contributor Richard Phillips states that "documentation, . . . the litmus test of any credible scandal, is about as tangible as a hole in a doughnut. Alleged bribes are completely unsupported, an assertion of flagrant antisemitism by Flynn is backed up by only one quote in the entire book (the quote itself is of questionable harm), and the author's case for espionage is—in its most favorable light—circumstantial. Aside from that, the untold story of Errol Flynn is a 'good read.'" Higham told Phillips that he was surprised by the outcry over his book. "[Flynn's] reputation was dirt, anyway," he noted.

In a letter to *CA*, Higham described himself as "a poet, of the Romantic school, out of sympathy with most American and British verse of my period, but very much in sympathy with the poetry of Australia, where I lived for fifteen years. I deeply admire Patrick White (a poet-novelist), A. D. Hope, W. Hart-Smith, James McAuley, and other Australian poets; American poets I do warm to are Elizabeth Bishop, Howard Moss, James Dickey, and W. S. Merwin. I write biographies for a professional occupation, much as some poets might teach or practise law or medicine, but my biography of Conan Doyle provided a rare opportunity to provide a book of literary content and (I hope) quality. I like writing, and am restless and unhappy only when not busy on a new project. I have never had writer's block; writing *is* my holiday. Now I have found a way to blend my poetic and more commercial talents; I have discovered, rather in the middle of life, a gift for fiction. This has been the greatest joy of my life.

"My view of literary criticism is that like so much cultural activity today it is fighting a rearguard action against the force of mass culture. . . . The result is that literary critics are increasingly nervous, tense and mistrustful; they tend to prefer fragmented, collapsed narrative structures and books which deal in mental breakdown and disorder because, in American culture, they can identify with plights rather than triumphs, with disease rather than health. I have preferred the Victorian solution: prose is made to earn the right to the luxury of verse; all work is valuable, if seriously and sincerely intended; life and humanity are to be encouraged and nurtured; progress is a reality, though man has preferred that progress to be toward his general medical and social welfare rather than that of an intellectual elite; humankind is fundamentally a species to be optimistic about; let us write solid, worthwhile, straight-forward stories about people; let us not be cynical, disruptive, destructive, elliptical, abstruse, obscure, or inverted, when we embark on the voyage of literature. I admire the novelists of security and substance: the Bronte sisters, Dickens, Balzac, Flaubert, Svevo, rather than those of breakdown and despair, Kafka, Joyce, Virginia Woolf, Celine, Sartre.

"In 1983, I returned to writing poetry after a brief interval; poems based on Rilkean and Leopardian themes, all of which are reflective and contemplative in mode."

AVOCATIONAL INTERESTS: Rare old movies, health foods, physical fitness, Nautilus weightlifting, literary detection, old English murder cases.

BIOGRAPHICAL/CRITICAL SOURCES:

PERIODICALS

Chicago Tribune, May 11, 1980, May 28, 1980.
Chicago Tribune Book World, November 15, 1981, September 8, 1985.
Christian Science Monitor, May 14, 1971, June 26, 1975.
London Magazine, April, 1967.
Los Angeles Times Book Review, October 12, 1980, May 5, 1985.
New Statesman, November 29, 1968, February 6, 1970, January 1, 1971, November 26, 1976.
Newsweek, April 7, 1980.
New York Times, March 23, 1980.
New York Times Book Review, April 20, 1980, July 1, 1984, September 15, 1985.
Washington Post Book World, November 5, 1981, September 15, 1985.

*   *   *

HILLERT, Margaret 1920-

PERSONAL: Born January 22, 1920, in Saginaw, Mich.; daughter of Edward Carl (a tool and die maker) and A. Ilva (Sproull) Hillert. *Education:* Bay City Junior College, A.A., 1941; University of Michigan, R.N., 1944; Wayne University (now Wayne State University), A.B., 1948.

ADDRESSES: Home—Birmingham, Mich. *Office*—Whittier School, 815 East Farnum, Royal Oak, Mich. 48067.

CAREER: Primary school teacher in public schools of Royal Oak, Mich., 1948—. Poet and writer of children's books.

MEMBER: International League of Children's Poets, Society of Children's Book Writers, Emily Dickinson Society, Poetry Society of Michigan, Detroit Women Writers.

AWARDS, HONORS: Numerous awards for poems from Poetry Society of Michigan.

WRITINGS:

CHILDREN'S POETRY

Farther Than Far, Follett, 1969.
I Like to Live in the City, Golden Books, 1970.
Who Comes to Your House?, Golden Books, 1973.
The Sleepytime Book, Golden Press, 1975.
Come Play with Me, Follett, 1975.
What Is It?, Follett, 1978.
I'm Special . . . So Are You!, Hallmark Books, 1979.
Let's Take a Break, Continental Press, 1980.
Action Verse for the Primary Classroom, Denison, 1980.
Doing Things, Continental Press, 1980.
Fun Days, Follett, 1982.
Rabbits and Rainbows, Standard Publishing, 1985.

CHILDREN'S BOOKS; PUBLISHED BY FOLLETT

The Birthday Car, 1966.
The Little Runaway, 1966.
The Yellow Boat, 1966.
The Snow Baby, 1969.
Circus Fun, 1969.
A House for Little Red, 1970.
Little Puff, 1973.
Happy Birthday, Dear Dragon, 1977.
Play Ball, 1978.

The Baby Bunny, 1980.
What Am I?, 1980.
Run to the Rainbow, 1980.
I Love You, Dear Dragon, 1980.
Happy Easter, Dear Dragon, 1980.
Let's Go, Dear Dragon, 1980.
Merry Christmas, Dear Dragon, 1980.
Happy Halloween, Dear Dragon, 1980.
Away Go the Boats, 1980.
Who Goes to School?, 1981.
Big Cowboy, Little Cowboy, 1981.
City Fun, 1981.
The Witch Who Went for a Walk, 1981.
Take a Walk, Johnny, 1981.
The Purple Pussycat, 1981.
The Cow That Got Her Wish, 1981.
Let's Have a Play, 1982.
Up, Up and Away, 1982.
I Like Things, 1982.
Why We Have Thanksgiving, 1982.
The Ball Book, 1982.
The Funny Ride, 1982.

CHILDREN'S BOOKS; PUBLISHED BY MODERN CURRICULUM PRESS

Go to Sleep, Dear Dragon, 1985.
Help for Dear Dragon, 1985.
Come to School, Dear Dragon, 1985.
It's Circus Time, Dear Dragon, 1985.
A Friend for Dear Dragon, 1985.
I Need You, Dear Dragon, 1985.

CHILDREN'S STORIES RETOLD; PUBLISHED BY FOLLETT

The Funny Baby, 1963.
The Three Little Pigs, 1963.
The Three Bears, 1963.
The Three Goats, 1963.
The Magic Beans, 1966.
Cinderella at the Ball, 1970.
The Cookie House, 1978.
The Golden Goose, 1978.
Not I, Not I, 1980.
The Little Cookie, 1980.
Four Good Friends, 1980.
The Magic Nutcraker, 1982.
Pinocchio, 1982.
The Boy and the Goats, 1982.
Tom Thumb, 1982.
Little Red Ridinghood, 1982.

OTHER

Contributor to numerous magazines, including *Horn Book, Christian Science Monitor, McCall's, Saturday Evening Post, Jack and Jill*, and *Western Humanities Review*.

WORK IN PROGRESS: A collection of children's poetry and three collections of adult poetry; fifteen juveniles.

SIDELIGHTS: In *Pass the Poetry, Please*, Margaret Hillert writes: "I can't give you a glib one-line definition of poetry such as many I have seen. Poetry has been an undefined but definite part of my life, and I don't think I chose to write it at all. I have been writing it ever since the first one I did when I was eight years old, which seems to indicate it has always been a part of my nature. I read widely, from the poetry stacks in the library when I was growing up—and still do to some extent. I'm not one of those people who can say, 'Today I'll

write a poem.' I may go without writing anything for some time as a consequence, but once I get the grain of an idea, the thing must be worked through, sometimes for days, weeks, or months. Things don't usually come to me whole and full blown. It intrigues me to work generally, but not always, with traditional forms but in fresh ways.''

To *CA*, Hillert added: "I am glad to see that much is being done to interest children in poetry, but I would like to see greater interest in reading it and listening to it instead of so much writing without sufficient background; and I cannot subscribe to the current theory that whatever a child writes can be called a poem despite any sign of imagination or creativity.''

Margaret Hillert's work has been translated into Danish and Portuguese.

BIOGRAPHICAL/CRITICAL SOURCES:

BOOKS

Authors in the News, Volume I, Gale, 1976.
Hopkins, Lee B., *Pass the Poetry, Please*, Citation Press, 1972.
LeMaster, J. R., *Poets of the Midwest*, Young Publications, 1966.

*   *   *

HINE, James R.   1909-

PERSONAL: Born May 4, 1909, in Lafayette, Ind.; son of Fred R. (a postal clerk) and Nora (Niebergal) Hine; married Janet Ronald, June 24, 1938; children: Judith (Mrs. Forrest Hughes), Susan, James Ronald. *Education:* Purdue University, B.S.M.E.; McCormick Theological Seminary, M.Div. *Politics:* Democrat.

ADDRESSES: *Home*—4961 North Calle Luisa, Tucson, Ariz. 85718. *Office*—School of Family and Consumer Resources, University of Arizona, Tucson, Ariz. 85721.

CAREER: Presbyterian minister in Hanover, Ind., 1936-42, and Champaign, Ill., 1942-67; University of Arizona, Tucson, associate professor of child development and family relations, beginning 1968. Member of faculty, Hanover College, 1936-42. Director, McKinley Foundation (Champaign), 1942-67; member, Arizona Governor's Council on Children, Youth and Families.

MEMBER: American Association for Marriage and Family Therapy, Association of Couples for Marriage Enrichment.

AWARDS, HONORS: D.D., Hanover College.

WRITINGS:

(With Natalia M. Belting) *Your Wedding Workbook*, Interstate, 1955, 5th edition, 1986.
Alternative to Divorce, McKinley Foundation (Champaign, Ill.), 1957, 3rd edition, Interstate, 1978.
Grounds for Marriage, McKinley Foundation, 1957, 7th edition, Interstate, 1985.
Marriage Counseling Kit, Interstate, 1958, new edition, 1980.
Come Prepared to Stay Forever, Interstate, 1966.
Your Marriage: Analysis and Renewal, Interstate, 1966, 2nd edition, 1976.
Marriage Counseling: A Guide for Ministers, Interstate, 1966.
Will You Make a Wise Marriage Choice?, Interstate, 1978.
What Comes After You Say, "I Love You," Pacific Books, 1980.

How to Have a Long, Happy, Healthy Marriage, Interstate, 1985.
The Springtime of Love and Marriage, Judson Press, 1985.

Contributor to *Presbyterian Survey* and *Christian Home.*

* * *

HINSON, (Grady) Maurice 1930-

PERSONAL: Born December 4, 1930, in Marianna, Fla.; son of Bartlett A. and Willie (Blackman) Hinson; married Margaret Hume, June 16, 1952; children: Jane Leslie, Susan Elizabeth. *Education:* Attended Juilliard School of Music, 1947-48; University of Florida, B.A., 1952; graduate study, Conservatoire National, University of Nancy, 1953; University of Michigan, M.M., 1955, D.M.A., 1958.

ADDRESSES: Home—213 Choctaw Rd., Louisville, Ky. 40207. *Office*—School of Church Music, Southern Baptist Theological Seminary, 2825 Lexington Rd., Louisville, Ky. 40206.

CAREER: University of Michigan, Ann Arbor, teacher of piano, 1953-57; Southern Baptist Theological Seminary, School of Church Music, Louisville, Ky., professor of piano, 1957—. Guest lecturer in piano at National Music Camp, Interlochen, Mich., summers, 1960-70; lecturer and recitalist at universities, conventions, and workshops throughout the United States, Canada, England, and other countries. *Military service:* U.S. Army, 1952-54.

MEMBER: American Liszt Society, Music Teachers National Association (president of southern division, 1966-68), American Guild of Organists, Kentucky Music Teachers Association (president, 1962-64; former chairman of piano and of certification board), Greater Louisville Music Teachers Association (president, 1960-62), Pi Kappa Lambda.

AWARDS, HONORS: Medal of Excellence of the American Liszt Society; Liszt Medal of the Hungarian Liszt Society.

WRITINGS:

Keyboard Bibliography, Music Teachers National Association, 1968.
Early American Music, Belwin-Mills, 1969.
Duets of Early American Music, Belwin-Mills, 1969.
Contemporary Piano Literature, two volumes, Belwin-Mills, 1969.
Guide to the Pianist's Repertoire, edited by Irwin Freundlich, Indiana University Press, 1973.
The Piano Teacher's Sourcebook: An Annotated Bibliography of Books Related to the Piano and Piano Music, Belwin-Mills, 1974, 3rd edition, 1986.
An Adventure in Ragtime, Belwin-Mills, 1975.
The Piano in Chamber Ensemble: An Annotated Guide, Indiana University Press, 1978.
Supplement to Guide to the Pianist's Repertoire, Indiana University Press, 1979.
Music for Piano and Orchestra: An Annotated Guide, Indiana University Press, 1981.
Music for More than One Piano: An Annotated Guide, Indiana University Press, 1983.

EDITOR OF MUSICAL COMPOSITIONS

(And annotator with Anne McClenny) *A Collection of Early American Keyboard Music,* Willis Music, 1971.
Piano Music in Nineteenth-Century America, two volumes, Hinshaw Music, 1975.

Arthur Farwell, *American Indian Melodies,* Hinshaw Music, 1977.
(With McClenny) *Dances of the Young Republic,* Hinshaw Music, 1977.
Presto d'incerto autore, Hinshaw Music, 1977.
(With Charlotte Martin) *Piano Music of Viceregal Mexico,* Hinshaw Music, 1979.
Twelve by Eleven, Hinshaw Music, 1979.

Also editor of *Classical Music in the Worship Service,* two volumes, G. Schirmer, and of musical compositions by Muzio Clementi, Edward MacDowell, Alexander Reinagle, Rainor Taylor, Hector Berlioz, Samuel Coleridge-Taylor, Anton Diabelli, and Johann Anton Andre.

OTHER

Contributor to *The New Grove Dictionary of Music in the United States.* Contributor of articles to *American Music Teacher, Piano Quarterly, Clavier,* and *English Liszt Society Journal.* Editor, *Journal of the American Liszt Society;* review editor, *American Music Teacher;* contributing editor, *Piano Quarterly.*

WORK IN PROGRESS: The third and fourth volumes of the "Guide to the Pianist's Repertoire" series, dealing with music for piano and orchestra and two-piano literature.

* * *

HIRSCH, Foster (Lance) 1943-

PERSONAL: Born December 20, 1943, in New York, N.Y.; son of Harry (a real estate investor) and Etta (Goldberg) Hirsch. *Education:* Stanford University, B.A., 1965; Columbia University, M.F.A., 1966, M.A., 1967, Ph.D., 1971. *Religion:* Jewish.

ADDRESSES: Home—49 West 12th St., New York, N.Y. 10011. *Office*—Department of Film, Brooklyn College of the City University of New York, Brooklyn, N.Y. 11210. *Agent*—Lillian Friedman, 545 Madison Ave., New York, N.Y. 10022.

CAREER: Brooklyn College of the City University of New York, Brooklyn, N.Y., instructor, 1967-73, assistant professor, 1974-77, associate professor of English, 1978-85, professor of film, 1985—. New School for Social Research, lecturer, 1970-72, critic, 1970—.

MEMBER: Authors Guild, Authors League of America, National Book Critics Circle, Phi Beta Kappa.

WRITINGS:

Elizabeth Taylor, Pyramid Publications, 1973.
(Contributor) James Vinson, editor, *Contemporary Dramatists,* St. Martin's, 1973.
(Contributor) Thomas Atkins, editor, *Sexuality in Film,* Indiana University Press, 1975.
Edward G. Robinson, Pyramid Publications, 1975.
George Kelly, Twayne, 1975.
The Hollywood Epic, A. S. Barnes, 1978.
Who's Afraid of Edward Albee?, Creative Arts, 1978.
Laurence Olivier, G. K. Hall, 1979.
A Portrait of the Artist: The Plays of Tennessee Williams, Kennikat, 1979.
Joseph Losey, Twayne, 1980.
Film Noir: The Dark Side of the Screen, A. S. Barnes, 1981.
Love, Sex, Death, and the Meaning of Life: Woody Allen's Comedy, McGraw, 1981.

A *Method to Their Madness: The History of the Actors Studio,*
Norton, 1984.
Eugene O'Neill, York Press, 1986.

Contributor of film, book, and drama reviews to *Nation,
America, New York Times, Commonweal,* and *Village Voice.*

WORK IN PROGRESS: *The American Scene: Theatre in the
Twenties; Alan Schneider,* for Cambridge University Press.

SIDELIGHTS: Foster Hirsch's *A Method to Their Madness:
The History of the Actors Studio* describes the evolution of Lee
Strasberg's Actors Studio. Strasberg's method acting technique evolved from a system formulated by Konstantin Stanislavsky in Europe; the first half of Hirsch's book gives a
thorough analysis of the development of Stanislavsky's system. "Mr. Hirsch's imagination endows this history with new
life, enriched with interviews of people who participated in
the events," notes *New York Times Book Review* writer Marshal W. Mason. "Unfortunately, in Part Two, . . . Mr. Hirsch
fails to follow through on the opportunity to show the relationship of [Lee Strasberg's] Studio to its inspired predecessors. The tone degenerates from historical to anecdotal as he
switches from researched opinion to on-site observation. His
gossipy reports of operations at the Studio are based on six
months as an official observer . . . [and] can shed little light
on the question of how Stanislavsky's ideas became distorted
into Strasberg's method. Highly critical of Lee Strasberg, Mr.
Hirsch paints him as a man with a monstrous ego and destructive eccentricities." Mason concludes, however, that Hirsch's
"opinions make entertaining reading."

BIOGRAPHICAL/CRITICAL SOURCES:

PERIODICALS

New York Times Book Review, November 4, 1984.

*   *   *

HITCHCOCK, H(ugh) Wiley 1923-

PERSONAL: Born September 28, 1923; son of Hugh Wellman
(in advertising) and Charlotte (Wiley) Hitchcock; married Janet Cox (a professor), May 22, 1965; children: (previous marriage) Susan Tyler, Hugh Jarvis. *Education:* Dartmouth College, B.A., 1944; University of Michigan, M.Mus., 1948,
Ph.D., 1954. *Politics:* Independent.

ADDRESSES: *Home*—1192 Park Ave., New York, N.Y. *Office*—Conservatory of Music, Brooklyn College of the City
University of New York, Brooklyn, N.Y. 11210.

CAREER: University of Michigan, Ann Arbor, assistant professor, 1955-59, associate professor of music, 1959-61; Hunter
College of the City University of New York, New York, N.Y.,
professor of music, 1961-71; Brooklyn College of the City
University of New York, Brooklyn, N.Y., professor of music,
1971-80, distinguished professor, 1980—, director of Institute
for Studies in American Music. *Military service:* U.S. Army,
1943-46.

MEMBER: American Musicological Society, Society for Ethnomusicology, Societe de Musicologie, Music Library Association (president, 1966-67).

AWARDS, HONORS: Fulbright senior research fellowships in
Italy, 1954-55, and France, 1968-69; Guggenheim fellowship,
1968-69; National Endowment for the Humanities fellowship,
1982-83.

WRITINGS:

"Judicium Salomonis" of Marc-Antoine Charpentier, A-R
Editions, 1962.
Music in the United States: A Historical Introduction, Pren-
tice-Hall, 1969, 2nd edition, 1974.
"Le Nuove Musiche" of Giulio Caccini, A-R Editions, 1970.
(Editor) *The American Music Miscellany,* Da Capo Press, 1972.
(Editor) Supply Belcher, *The Harmony of Maine,* Da Capo
Press, 1972.
(Editor) Stephen Foster, *The Social Orchestra for Flute or
Violin: A Collection of Popular Melodies Arranged as
Duets, Trios, and Quartets,* Da Capo Press, 1973.
(Editor) Edward Riley, *Riley's Flute Melodies,* Da Capo Press,
1973.
(Author of preface) *American Music before 1865 in Print and
on Records: A Biblio-Discography,* Institute for Studies
in American Music, 1976.
Ives, Oxford University Press, 1977, revised edition, Institute
for Studies in American Music, 1983.
(Co-editor) *An Ives Celebration,* University of Illinois Press,
1977.
Marc-Antoine Charpentier's "Pestis Mediolanensis," Uni-
versity of North Carolina Press, 1979.
(Editor) *The Phonograph and Our Musical Life: Proceedings
of a Centennial Conference,* Institute for Studies in American Music, 1980.
(Area editor) Stanley Sadie, editor, *New Grove Dictionary of
Music and Musicians,* Groves Dictionaries of Music, 1980.
(With Lorraine Inserra) *The Music of Henry Ainsworth's Psal-
ter,* Institute for Studies in American Music, 1981.
(Co-editor) *New Grove Dictionary of American Music,* four
volumes, Groves Dictionaries of Music, 1986.

Also author of *Les Oeuvres de Marc-Antoine Charpentier,*
1982. Editor of "History of Music" series, eleven volumes,
Prentice-Hall, 1965-74.

*   *   *

HOFFMAN, Helmut 1912-

PERSONAL: Some sources list surname as Hoffmann; born
August 24, 1912, in Flensburg, Germany (now West Germany); son of Erich Hoffman. *Education:* University of Berlin, Ph.D., 1938.

ADDRESSES: *Office*—Department of Uralic-Atalic Studies,
343 Goodbody Hall, Indiana University, Bloomington, Ind.
47405.

CAREER: Berlin Academy, Berlin, Germany, scientific col-
laborator, 1938-45; University of Hamburg, Hamburg, Ger-
many (now West Germany), lecturer in Indology, 1945-48;
University of Munich, Munich, West Germany, professor of
Indology, beginning 1948; professor, Indiana University at
Bloomington.

MEMBER: Bavarian Academy of Sciences of Munich, Academy of Sciences and Literature (Mayence).

WRITINGS:

*Bruchstuecke des Atanatikasutra aus dem zentralasiatischen
Sanskrit-Kanon der Buddhisten,* [Leipzig, Germany], 1939.
Quellen zur Geschichte der tibetischen Bon-Religion, [Wies-
baden, West Germany], 1950.
The Religions of Tibet, Allen & Unwin, 1961, reprinted,
Greenwood Press, 1979.

(With Stanley Frye, Thubten J. Norbu, and Ho-chin Yang) *Tibet: A Handbook,* Research Center for the Language Sciences, Indiana University, 1975.

Also author of *Maerchen aus Tibet,* 1965. Editor, *Saeculum;* co-editor, *Central Asiatic Journal.*

WORK IN PROGRESS: A study on the Stupas of Nepal.

AVOCATIONAL INTERESTS: Music and sports.†

* * *

HOHENDAHL, Peter Uwe 1936-

PERSONAL: Born March 17, 1936, in Hamburg, Germany (now West Germany); son of Wilhelm F. (a businessman) and Emilie (Uelschen) Hohendahl; married I. Maria Zoetelief (a university lecturer), July 2, 1965; children: Deborah, Gwendolyn. *Education:* University of Hamburg, Ph.D., 1964. *Politics:* Independent. *Religion:* Lutheran.

ADDRESSES: Home—81 Genung Rd., Ithaca, N.Y. 14850. *Office*—Department of German, Cornell University, Ithaca, N.Y. 14853.

CAREER: Pennsylvania State University, University Park, assistant professor of German, 1965-68; Washington University, St. Louis, Mo., associate professor, 1968-69, professor of German, 1970-77, chairman of department, 1972-77; Cornell University, Ithaca, N.Y., professor of German and comparative literature, 1977—, chairman of department, 1981—. Visiting professor, University of Hamburg, 1974; visiting research professor, Free University of Berlin, 1976, and Center for Interdisciplinary Research, 1980-81.

MEMBER: Modern Language Association of America, American Association of Teachers of German.

AWARDS, HONORS: Postdoctoral fellow at Harvard University, 1964-65; research grants from Thyssen Foundation, 1975, and American Philosophical Society, 1976; Guggenheim fellow, 1983-84.

WRITINGS:

Das Bild der buergerlichen Welt im expressionistischen Drama, Winter, 1967.
Benn-Wirkung wider Willen, Athenaeum, 1971.
(Editor with Egon Schwartz and Herbert Lindenberger and contributor) *Essays on European Literature,* Washington University Press, 1972.
(Editor) *Sozialgeschichte und Wirkungsaesthetik,* Fischer-Athenaeum Verlag, 1974.
Literaturkritik und Oeffentlichkeit, Piper Verlag, 1974.
(Co-editor) *Literatur und Literaturtheorie in der D.D.R.,* Suhrkamp Verlag, 1976.
Der europaeische Roman der Empfindsamkeit, Athenaion, 1977.
(Co-editor) *Legitimationskrisen des deutschen Adell 1200-1900,* Metzlersche Verlagsbuchhandlung, 1979.
The Justification of Criticism, Cornell University Press, 1982.
Literarische Kultur im Zeitelter des Liberalismus, 1830-1870, Beck, 1985.
(Editor) *Geschichte der deutschen Literaturkritik,* Kretzler, 1985.

Contributor of articles to *Orbis Litterarum, LILI, Schiller-Jahrbuch, German Quarterly, Deutsche Vierteljahrsschrift fuer Literaturwissenschaft und Geistesgeschichte, Germanisch-Romanische-Monatsschrift, Telos,* and *New German Critique.* Associate editor, *Modern International Drama,* 1967-68;

member of board of editors, *Literaturwis-senschaft und Linguistik,* 1971—, *New German Critique,* 1981—, and *German Quarterly,* 1984—; member of council of advisers, *PMLA,* 1984—.

WORK IN PROGRESS: Studies on the aesthetic theory of the Frankfurt School.

* * *

HOLLAND, John L(ewis) 1919-

PERSONAL: Born October 21, 1919, in Omaha, Neb.; son of Edward Lewis (in advertising business) and Ellen (Dean) Holland; married Elsie M. Prenzlow, August 30, 1947; children: Kay E., Joan E., Robert D. *Education:* University of Omaha (now University of Nebraska at Omaha), B.A., 1942; University of Minnesota, M.A., 1947, Ph.D., 1952.

ADDRESSES: Office—Department of Social Relations, Johns Hopkins University, 3505 North Charles, Baltimore, Md. 21218.

CAREER: Western Reserve University (now Case Western Reserve University), Cleveland, Ohio, instructor and director of counseling center, 1950-53; U.S. Veterans Administration Hospital, Perry Point, Md., chief of vocational counseling service, 1953-56; National Merit Scholarship Corp., Evanston, Ill., director of research, 1957-63; American College Testing program, Iowa City, Iowa, vice-president for research and development, 1963-69; University of Iowa, Iowa City, professor of education and psychology, 1963-69; Johns Hopkins University, Baltimore, Md., professor of education, 1969-75, professor of social relations, 1969—, professor of psychology, 1977-80, director of Center for Study of Social Organization of Schools, 1969-75. Fellow, Center for Advanced Study in the Behavioral Sciences, 1965-66.

MEMBER: American Psychological Association (fellow), American Educational Research Association.

AWARDS, HONORS: Research award, American Personnel and Guidance Association, 1960.

WRITINGS:

Manual for the Holland Vocational Preference Inventory, Consulting Psychologists Press, 1958, 6th edition published as *Manual for the Vocational Preference Inventory,* 1967.
Explorations of a Theory of Vocational Choice, Part V, Chronical Guidance Press, 1964.
(With Clifford Abe) *A Description of College Freshmen,* Research and Development Division, American College Testing Program, 1965.
The Psychology of Vocational Choice: A Theory of Personality Types and Model Environments, Blaisdell, 1966.
Making Vocational Choices: A Theory of Careers, Prentice-Hall, 1973, 2nd edition published as *Making Vocational Choices: A Theory of Vocational Personalities and Work Environments,* 1985.
(With Gary D. Gottfredson) *Dictionary of Holland Occupational Codes,* Consulting Psychologists Press, 1982.

CONTRIBUTOR

Creativity: Its Assessment and Measurement, Educational Testing Service, 1962.
H. Borow, editor, *Man in a World of Work,* Houghton, 1964.
C. W. Taylor, editor, *Widening Horizons in Creativity,* Wiley, 1964.

J. M. Whiteley, editor, *Perspectives on Vocational Development*, American Personnel & Guidance Association, 1972.

OTHER

Writer of research reports for American College Testing Program. Contributor of more than one hundred articles to psychology and education journals. Consulting editor, *Journal of Applied Psychology*, 1961-69, and *Journal of Vocational Behavior*, 1971-77.

WORK IN PROGRESS: Revising theory of personality and occupational classification.

BIOGRAPHICAL/CRITICAL SOURCES:

PERIODICALS

Horn Book, August, 1969.

*   *   *

HOLQUIST, (James) Michael 1935-

PERSONAL: Born December 20, 1935, in Rockford, Ill.; son of Leonard (a factory worker) and Billye (Applebye) Holquist; married Lydia Landis, June 30, 1960 (divorced, 1972); married Katerina Clark, 1974; children: (first marriage) Peter Isaac, Benjamin Michael, Joshua Applebye; (second marriage) Nicholas Manning, Sebastian. *Education:* Attended Rockford College, 1954-55; University of Illinois, B.A., 1963; Yale University, Ph.D., 1968.

ADDRESSES: Office—Slavic Department, Indiana University, Bloomington, Ind. 47405.

CAREER: Factory worker, 1957-58; Yale University, New Haven, Conn., 1968-76, began as lecturer, became associate professor of Russian literature; University of Texas at Austin, chairman of department of Slavic languages, beginning 1976, professor of Russian literature, 1978-81; Indiana University at Bloomington, professor of Russian and comparative literature, 1981—. *Military service:* U.S. Army, 1958-61.

MEMBER: Modern Language Association of America, American Association of Teachers of Slavic and East European Languages, American Association for the Advancement of Slavic Studies.

AWARDS, HONORS: Morse research fellow, 1969-70; Inter-University Committee Travel Grants fellow at Leningrad University, 1969-70; American Philosophical Society fellow, 1978; National Endowment for the Humanities translation grant, 1979; American Council of Learned Societies-International Researches and Exchanges Board grant, 1983; Rockefeller humanities fellow, 1983-84.

WRITINGS:

(Contributor) *Alice in Wonderland* (critical edition), Norton, 1971.
(Compiler with Peter Brooks and Alvin B. Kerman) *Man and His Fictions: An Introduction to Fiction-Making, Its Forms and Uses*, Harcourt, 1972.
Dostoevsky and the Novel: The Wages of Biography, Princeton University Press, 1977.
(Editor and translator with Caryl Emerson) Mikhail Bakhtin, *The Dialogic Imagination: Four Essays*, University of Texas Press, 1981.
(With wife, Katerina Clark) *Mikhail Bakhtin* (biography), Belknap Press of Harvard University Press, 1985.

SIDELIGHTS: Michael Holquist's translations and studies of the Soviet scholar Mikhail Bakhtin are considered valuable additions to the field of Russian literary criticism. Tzvetan Todorov, reviewing for *Times Literary Supplement*, praises the thoroughness of the biography *Mikhail Bakhtin* by Holquist and his wife, Katerina Clark. "It is only with an infinite patience and considerable intelligence that Clark and Holquist have been able, starting from tenuous clues and from indirect evidence, to reconstruct Bakhtin's life and that of the intellectual milieu in which he moved," Todorov asserts. "Clark and Holquist's book will henceforth be an indispensable tool for all 'Bakhtinologists.'"

Holquist's *Dostoevsky and the Novel: The Wages of Biography* has also received favorable critical response. Doris Grumbach of the *New York Times Book Review* calls Holquist "a graceful, concise writer" who strives "to reduce his literary observations and insights to a manageable length and a direct, simple . . . rhetoric." In *Sewanee Review*, George Woodcock writes: "*Dostoevsky and the Novel* is . . . a valuable addition to the critical literature on Dostoevsky, which all too often has been distinguished more by enthusiasm than by sensible analysis." *Times Literary Supplement* reviewer Alex de Jonge finds "minor weaknesses" in the work but notes overall that Holquist's book "is a most stimulating work by a critic who comes to his subject dominated by one idea. When, as here, the idea really is central to the writer and his age it is an approach which can make for the most illuminating kind of criticism."

BIOGRAPHICAL/CRITICAL SOURCES:

PERIODICALS

New York Times Book Review, October 9, 1977.
Sewanee Review, summer, 1979.
Times Literary Supplement, September 8, 1978, July 17, 1981, June 14, 1985.

*   *   *

HOOK, J(ulius) N(icholas) 1913-

PERSONAL: Born December 25, 1913, in Macoupin County, Ill.; son of Charles E. and Rose (Engel) Hook; married second wife, Rachel Grace Gerhart, 1955; children: Edward N., Julian Lee. *Education:* University of Illinois, A.B., 1933, A.M., 1934, Ph.D., 1941. *Religion:* Presbyterian.

ADDRESSES: Home—R.R. 1, Waveland, Ind. 47989. *Office*—109 English Bldg., University of Illinois, Urbana, Ill.

CAREER: High school teacher in Forrest, Ill., 1934-36; Mankato State College (now University), Mankato, Minn., 1941-46, began as instructor, became associate professor of English; University of Illinois at Urbana-Champaign, professor of English, 1946-71, professor emeritus, 1971—. Teacher during summers at schools in Texas, New York, Rhode Island, Wisconsin, and Missouri. Coordinator of Project English, U.S. Office of Education, 1961.

MEMBER: National Council of Teachers of English (executive secretary, 1953-60), Conference on College Composition and Communication (treasurer, 1953-60), Modern Language Association of America, Conference on English Education (chairman, 1966-68), Illinois Association of Teachers of English (president, 1961).

AWARDS, HONORS: Twice honored by National Council of Teachers of English in 1960, with W. Wilbur Hatfield Award and by establishment of research foundation in his honor; named Illinois Author of the Year, 1981.

WRITINGS:

(With William F. Ekstrom) *Toward Better English,* Lippincott, 1941, 2nd edition, 1949.
(With Elizabeth Collette, Tom Peete Cross, and Elmer Stauffer) *Writers in America,* Ginn, 1949.
(With Collette, Cross, and Stauffer) *Writers in England,* Ginn, 1949.
Teaching of High School English, Ronald, 1950, 4th edition, 1972.
(With Max Herzberg, Florence Guild, and Robert L. Stevens) *Better English,* six volumes, Ginn, 1952-53.
(With Ekstrom) *Guide to Composition,* Lippincott, 1953.
(With E. G. Mathews) *Modern American Grammar and Usage,* Ronald, 1956.
(With others) *Literature for High Schools,* four volumes, Ginn, 1957.
How to Take Examinations in College, Barnes & Noble, 1958.
(With Guild and Stevens) *English Skills,* four volumes, Ginn, 1959.
(With Stevens) *Harbrace Guide to Sentence-Building,* Harcourt, 1961.
Guide to Good Writing, Ronald, 1961.
Writing Creatively, Heath, 1963, 2nd edition, 1967.
(With William H. Evans) *Individualized English,* Follett, 1965, 2nd edition, 1974.
(With Stevens) *Competence in English,* Harcourt, 1967, 2nd edition, 1977.
Spelling 1500, Harcourt, 1967, 3rd edition, 1985.
Testmanship, Barnes & Noble, 1967.
(Editor) *Publishers and English Teachers,* American Textbook, 1967.
The Story of American English, Harcourt, 1972.
The Story of British English, Scott, Foresman, 1974.
People Say Things Different Ways, Scott, Foresman, 1974.
History of the English Language, Ronald, 1975.
English Today, Ronald, 1976.
A Long Way Together, National Council of Teachers of English, 1979.
The Grand Panjandrum, and 1,999 Other Rare, Useful, and Delightful Words, Macmillan, 1980.
Two-Word Verbs in English, Harcourt, 1981.
Family Names: How Our Surnames Came to America, Macmillan, 1982.
The Book of Names, F. Watts, 1983.

Also author, with Ryoji Inoue, of *Determiners, Prepositions, Two-Word Verbs, and Verbs.* Contributor to professional journals. Editor, *Illinois English Bulletin,* 1949-59.

WORK IN PROGRESS: A novel about the American Revolution.

SIDELIGHTS: J. N. Hook wrote *CA:* "I believe that textbooks need not, should not, must not be dull. They should, in fact, be among the best-written books (as well as the most accurate), for each introduces to young people new and potentially exciting material. Youths' attitudes toward a branch of knowledge can be informed and shaped by the textbooks they use in school."

*　　　*　　　*

HOPKINS, Antony 1921-

PERSONAL: Born March 21, 1921, in London, England. *Education:* Royal College of Music, L.R.A.M., 1942.

ADDRESSES: Home—Woodyard, Ashridge, Berkhamsted, Hertfordshire, England.

CAREER: Composer, pianist, and conductor, 1944—, working with orchestras in England, Ireland, Japan, and Yugoslavia. Professor at Royal College of Music, 1955-70; former Gresham Professor of Music at City University, London; fellow of Robinson College, Cambridge, 1980. Director of Intimate Opera Company, 1952-64; presenter, "Talking about Music," a weekly series for British Broadcasting Corp. (distributed to forty-four foreign countries), 1953—.

MEMBER: Royal College of Music (fellow), Royal Academy of Music (honorary member).

AWARDS, HONORS: Medal of honor from the City of Tokyo, 1974; Commander of Order of the British Empire, 1976; honorary doctorate from University of Stirling, 1980.

WRITINGS:

Talking about Symphonies, Heinemann, 1961.
Talking about Concertos, Heinemann, 1964.
Music All around Me (anthology), Frewin, 1967.
Lucy and Peterkin (juvenile), Frewin, 1968.
(With Andre Previn) *Music Face to Face* (dialogues), Hamish Hamilton, 1971.
Talking about Sonatas, Heinemann, 1971.
The Downbeat Guide to Music, Oxford University Press, 1977.
Understanding Music, Dent, 1979.
The Nine Symphonies of Beethoven, Heinemann, 1980.
Beating Time (autobiography), M. Joseph, 1982.
Songs for Swinging Golfers (verse), M. Joseph, 1982.
Sounds of Music, Dent, 1982.
Pathway to Music, Dent, 1983.
The Concertgoer's Companion, Dent, Volume I, 1984, Volume II, 1986.

Also author of *Music and Musings,* 1984. Composer of operas, including "Three's Company" (one-act), first produced in 1953, "A Time for Growing" (three-act for children), first produced in Norwich, England, at St. Andrew's Hall, 1967, produced in London, England, at Royal Albert Hall, 1968, "Rich Man, Poor Man, Beggar Man, Saint" (two-act for children), first produced at Stroud Festival of Religious Drama, 1969, and "Dr. Musikus" (one-act for children), first produced in London at Arts Theatre, 1971; composer of numerous musical compositions for orchestration in motion pictures and concerts, including "Riding to Canonbie," "John and the Magic Music Man," and "Early One Morning."

SIDELIGHTS: Antony Hopkins told *CA:* "My tendency to compose for the young or for amateur music makers indicates a marked preference for tuneful and approachable music that audiences can enjoy at first hearing. It is a gift for communication, whether through music or words, that is perhaps my greatest asset; yet although my writings and broadcasts might be thought too populist in some academic circles, the fact remains that I am much admired by fellow professional musicians for my musical insights and originality of approach in analysis."

AVOCATIONAL INTERESTS: Motor sport and golf.

BIOGRAPHICAL/CRITICAL SOURCES:

PERIODICALS

Times Literary Supplement, May 1, 1981.

HOPKINS, Kenneth 1914-
(Christopher Adams, Anton Burney, Warwick Mannon, Paul Marsh, Edmund Marshall, Arnold Meredith)

PERSONAL: Born December 7, 1914, in Bournemouth, Hampshire, England; son of Reginald Marshall (a civil servant) and Elsa (Adams) Hopkins; married Elizabeth Coward, September 7, 1939; children: Edmund Marshall. *Education:* Attended school at St. Peter's, Bournemouth.

ADDRESSES: Home—12 New Rd., North Walsham, Norfolk NR28 9DF, England.

CAREER: Professional writer. Visiting lecturer in English, University of Texas, Main University (now University of Texas at Austin), 1961; visiting professor of English at Southern Illinois University at Carbondale, 1964-72, Carleton University, 1976-77, and Colgate University, 1978. Guest lecturer at St. Louis University, University of Tennessee, Colgate University, Boston College, Wake Forest College, and other schools. *Military service:* Royal Army Ordnance Corps, 1941-45.

MEMBER: Royal Society of Literature of the United Kingdom (fellow).

WRITINGS:

Twelve Poems, privately printed, 1937.
Recent Poetry , privately printed, 1937.
New Sonnets, privately printed, 1938.
Six Sonnets, privately printed, 1938.
The Younger Sister, Grasshopper Press, 1944.
Love and Elizabeth (poems), Sylvan Press, 1944.
Miscellany Poems, Grasshopper Press, 1946.
Songs and Sonnets, Grasshopper Press, 1947.
Poems on Several Occasions, Grasshopper Press, 1948.
To a Green Lizard Called Ramorino, Faun Press, 1949.
(Published anonymously) *Apes and Elderberries*, Grasshopper Press, 1950.
Walter De la Mare: A Study, Longmans, Green, 1953, revised edition, 1957.
The Corruption of a Poet (autobiography), Barrie & Rockliff, 1954.
The Poets Laureate, Library Publishers, 1955, revised and augmented edition, Barnes & Noble, 1973.
The Girl Who Died (detective novel), Macdonald, 1955.
Inca Adventure (children's fiction), Chatto & Windus, 1956.
Great Moments in Exploration (juvenile), Roy Publishers, 1956.
She Died Because (detective novel), Macdonald, 1957, Holt, 1964.
The Forty-First Passenger (detective novel), Macdonald, 1958.
Portraits in Satire, Barnes & Noble, 1959.
Dead against My Principles (detective novel), Macdonald, 1960, Holt, 1962.
Pierce with a Pin (detective novel), Macdonald, 1960.
Poor Heretic (poems), University of Texas Press, 1961.
Foundlings and Fugitives (poems), Brick Row Book Shop (Austin, Tex.), 1961.
Forty-Two Poems, Putnam, 1961.
A Trip to Texas (travel), Macdonald, 1962.
Body Blow (detective novel), Macdonald, 1962, Holt, 1965.
English Poetry: A Short History, Lippincott, 1963.
Campus Corpse, Macdonald, 1963.
Collected Poems, 1935-65, Southern Illinois University Press, 1965.

The Powys Brothers, Phoenix House, 1967, new edition, Warren House, 1972.
Poems English and American, Brick Row Book Shop (Houston), 1968.
Slivers of Syntax: More Emanations from Emily, Colgate University Press, 1969.
Bourbon and Branch: Poems, Brick Row Book Shop, 1969.
Kickshaws and Garnishings (poems), Warren House, 1970.
American Poems and Others, Rota, 1970.
The Enfant Terrible Again, Warren House, 1974.
Mood, Comment and Occasion (poems), Warren House, 1975.
Samuel Butler: Four Sonnets Concerning Miss Savage, Warren House, 1976.
A Dull Head among Windy Spaces: The Eliot Cult, Warren House, 1976.
By Invitation Only (poems), Warren House, 1977.
Hal Trovillion and the Powys Brothers, Warren House, 1978.
The Dead Slave and Other Poems, Catalyst, 1978.
Collected Poems, 1966-1977, Warren House, 1978.
Llewelyn Powys, an Essay, Enitharmon, 1979.
Gamel and Rex (a poem), Warren House, 1979.
Introits and Indulgences (poems), Warren House, 1982.
The Man Who Built the Pyramids, Warren House, 1984.
The End of a Golden String (poems), Warren House, 1984.
Book Collecting for the Financially Unstable, Amtmann Circle (Toronto), 1985.

UNDER PSEUDONYM CHRISTOPHER ADAMS

Helen of Troy (film story), Beverley Books, 1956.
English Literature for Fun, Hutchinson, 1957.
(Author of introduction and notes) *The Worst English Poets*, Wingate, 1958.
Amateur Agent, Boardman, 1964.

UNDER PSEUDONYM ANTON BURNEY

The Liberace Story, Beverley Books, 1957.

UNDER PSEUDONYM WARWICK MANNON

Vice Versa, World Film Publications, 1946.
Spring in Park Lane, World Film Publications, 1948.
Miranda, World Film Publications, 1948.
No Room at the Inn, World Film Publications, 1948.
Bond Street, World Film Publications, 1948.

UNDER PSEUDONYM PAUL MARSH

Safari (film story), Beverley Books, 1956.

UNDER PSEUDONYM EDMUND MARSHALL

Tales of Ambledown Airport, Hutchinson, Number 1: *Colin's Lucky Day*, 1960.
The Missing Viscount, Hutchinson, 1960.

UNDER PSEUDONYM ARNOLD MEREDITH

The Guinea Pig, World Film Publications, 1948.

BOOKS EDITED, OR WITH INTRODUCTION, BY HOPKINS

The English Lyric: A Selection, De Visscher, 1945.
Edmund Blunden: A Selection of His Poetry and Prose, Hart-Davis, 1950, Horizon, 1962.
Llewelyn Powys: A Selection from His Writings, Macdonald, 1952, Horizon, 1961.
H. M. Tomlinson: A Selection from His Writings, Hutchinson, 1953.
Walter De la Mare: A Selection from His Writings, Faber, 1953.

Guy de Maupassant, *Bel Ami,* Folio Society, 1954.
Emily Eden, *The Semi-Attached Couple,* Folio Society, 1955.
R. S. Surtees, *Hawbuck Grange,* Folio Society, 1956.
Walter De la Mare, *Ghost Stories,* Folio Society, 1956.
Surtees, *Hillingdon Hill,* Folio Society, 1956.
Henry Fielding, *Tom Jones,* Folio Society, 1959.
Daniel Defoe, *Journal of the Plague Year,* Folio Society, 1960.
O. Henry, *Selected Stories,* Folio Society, 1960.
Thomas Love Peacock, *Crotchet Castle,* Folio Society, 1963.
A Little Treasury of Familiar Verse, John Baker, 1963.
A Little Treasury of Love Lyrics, John Baker, 1963.
A Little Treasury of Familiar Prose, John Baker, 1964.
A Little Treasury of Religious Verse, John Baker, 1964.
John Cowper Powys: Selected Poems, Macdonald, 1964, Colgate University Press, 1965.
The Search: Fourth Series, Southern Illinois University Press, 1965.
Crusade against Crime, Boardman, 1966.
Second Crime Crusade, Boardman, 1966.
The Poetry of Railways, Frewin, 1966.
Louis Wilkinson, *Blasphemy and Religion,* Colgate University Press, 1969.
Wilkinson, *Bumbore, a Romance,* Colgate University Press, 1969.
William Allan, *Kit, the Courier,* Warren House, 1969.
Wilkinson, *Welsh Ambassadors,* Colgate University Press, 1971.
Jacob Mountain, *Poetical Reveries 1977,* Warren House, 1977.
Gamel Woolsey, *Twenty-Eight Sonnets,* Warren House, 1977.
Woolsey, *The Last Leaf Falls,* Warren House, 1978.
Frederick Locker-Lampson and A. E. Gathorne-Hardy, *An Exchange of Compliments,* Warren House, 1978.
Letters of Gamel Woolsey to Llewelyn Powys, 1930-1939, Warren House, 1983.

CONTRIBUTOR

For Those Who Are Alive, Fortune Press, 1946.
Women, an Anthology, Spottiswoode Ballantyne, 1947.
Holidays and Happy Days, Phoenix House, 1948.
The Pick of "Punch" 1950, Chatto & Windus, 1951.
The Pick of "Punch" 1951, Chatto & Windus, 1952.
The Pleasure Ground, Macdonald, 1952.
Considered Trifles, Werner Laurie, 1955.
Peninsula, an Anthology of West Country Verse, Macdonald, 1959.
Dawn and Dusk, Brockhampton, 1962.
Theodore: Essays on T. F. Powys, St. Albert's Press, 1964.
The Second Bed Post, Macdonald, 1964.
Across a Crowded Room, Frewin, 1965.

Also contributor to *The Children's Book of Famous Lives,* Odhams, and to numerous other anthologies.

OTHER

Contributor to *Encyclopaedia Britannica* and *Dictionary of National Biography;* contributor to *New Statesman, Punch, Spectator, Times Literary Supplement, Argosy, South Carolina Review, Russell, Samuel Butler Newsletter, Texas Studies in Literature and Language,* and many other magazines and newspapers in the United States and England. Literary editor, *Everybody's,* 1949-54; editor, at various times, of *Literary Digest, Go, Preview,* and other journals.

WORK IN PROGRESS: Editing the letters of Gamel Woolsey; collecting material for a memoir.

SIDELIGHTS: The bulk of Kenneth Hopkins' manuscripts, a selection of his literary correspondence, and other material relating to his work is at the Humanities Research Center in the University of Texas. Much of Hopkins' library is housed at the University of Tulsa.

BIOGRAPHICAL/CRITICAL SOURCES:

BOOKS

Blackmore, R. L., editor, *Advice to a Young Poet: The Correspondence of Llewelyn Powys and Kenneth Hopkins,* Farleigh Dickinson University Press, 1969.
Hopkins, Kenneth, *The Corruption of a Poet* (autobiography), Barrie & Rockliff, 1954.
Hopkins, *A Trip to Texas,* Macdonald, 1962.

*   *   *

HORSMAN, Reginald 1931-

PERSONAL: Born October 24, 1931, in Leeds, Yorkshire, England; U.S. citizen; son of Alfred William (an engineer) and Elizabeth (Thompson) Horsman; married Lenore McNabb, September 3, 1955; children: John Reginald, Janine Lenore, Mara Eileen. *Education:* University of Birmingham, B.A., 1952, M.A., 1955; Indiana University, Ph.D., 1958.

ADDRESSES: Home—3548 North Hackett Ave., Milwaukee, Wis. 53211. *Office*—Department of History, University of Wisconsin, Milwaukee, Wis. 53201.

CAREER: University of Wisconsin—Milwaukee, instructor, 1958-59, assistant professor, 1959-62, associate professor, 1962-64, professor of history, 1964—, distinguished professor, 1973—, associate dean of letters and science, 1962.

MEMBER: Society of American Historians, Society for Historians of the Early American Republic, American Historical Association, Organization of American Historians.

AWARDS, HONORS: William H. Kiekhofer award of the University of Wisconsin, 1961, for excellence in teaching; Guggenheim fellow, 1965-66.

WRITINGS:

The Causes of the War of 1812, University of Pennsylvania Press, 1962.
(Contributor) Philip P. Mason, editor, *After Tippecanoe: Some Aspects of the War of 1812,* Michigan State University Press, 1963.
Matthew Elliott: British Indian Agent, Wayne State University Press, 1964.
(Contributor) Howard Quint, Dean Albertson, and Milton Cantor, editors, *Main Problems in American History,* Dorsey, 1964.
Expansion and American Indian Policy, 1783-1812, Michigan State University Press, 1967.
The War of 1812, Knopf, 1969.
Napoleon's Europe: The New America, Paul Hamlyn, 1970.
The Frontier in the Formative Years, 1783-1815, Holt, 1970.
Race and Manifest Destiny: The Origins of American Racial Anglo-Saxonism, Harvard University Press, 1981.
The Diplomacy of the New Republic, 1776-1815, Harlan Davidson, 1985.

Contributor of articles to *Encyclopaedia Britannica, Collier's Encyclopedia,* and to professional journals.

WORK IN PROGRESS: A biography of Josiah C. Nott.

SIDELIGHTS: Reginald Horsman "is well established in this country as an authority on frontier history," writes C. Vann

Woodward in a *New Republic* review of Horsman's *Race and Manifest Destiny: The Origins of Racial Anglo-Saxonism.* Woodward adds: "He writes with an easy familiarity with sources here and abroad." *Race and Manifest Destiny* explores the "scientific" theories of Anglo-Saxon superiority that in part paved the way for the nineteenth-century pioneer expansion into the American West and Southwest. According to Horsman's view, the belief in natural Anglo-Saxon dominance eased the guilt of American settlers as they ousted American Indians from their lands and enslaved black Africans. Kenneth S. Lynn, reviewing the book for the *Times Literary Supplement,* feels that Horsman's treatment is overly simplistic, and that he "displays his unwillingness to deal with historical complexity" by ignoring religious doctrines and popular literature of the times that promoted egalitarian ideas. Woodward, however, finds Horsman's approach satisfactory: "*Race and Manifest Destiny* has pushed back and multiplied the origins of racial Anglo-Saxonism to an earlier era than it has been generally assumed to exist. [Horsman] has also demonstrated how a major burden of historic national guilt was incurred in the age of innocence and revealed much about the underlying foundations and the fragility of that innocence."

BIOGRAPHICAL/CRITICAL SOURCES:

PERIODICALS

Book World, March 9, 1969.
New Republic, March 17, 1982.
New York Times Book Review, November 16, 1969.
Times Literary Supplement, March 12, 1982.

*   *   *

HOSKING, Eric (John) 1909-

PERSONAL: Born October 2, 1909, in London, England; son of Albert (an accountant) and Margaret Helen (Steggall) Hosking; married Dorothy Sleigh, April 15, 1939; children: Margaret Hosking Woodward, Robin, David. *Education:* Attended trade school, 1919-25. *Religion:* Baptist.

ADDRESSES: Home—20 Crouch Hall Rd., London N8 8XH, England.

CAREER: Photographer, 1929—, work exhibited by Royal Photographic Society and throughout the world. Ornithologist; director and leader of expeditions to Spain, Bulgaria, Hungary, Jordan, Pakistan, the Galapagos, Bangladesh, Antarctica, the Seychelles, Israel, Sri Lanka, Alaska, and Africa; member of Laboratory of Ornithology at Cornell University, 1961—. Broadcaster.

MEMBER: Royal Photographic Society (fellow; member of council, 1950-56), Royal Society for the Protection of Birds (vice-president), British Trust for Ornithology, British Naturalists Association (vice-president), British Ornithologists Union (vice-president), Nature Photographic Society (president), Nature Conservancy Council (chairman of photographic advisory committee), Zoological Society (scientific fellow), Zoological Photographic Society, British Institute of Incorporated Photographers (fellow), London Natural History Society (honorary vice-president).

AWARDS, HONORS: Cherry Kearton Award from Royal Geographic Society, 1968; gold medal from Royal Society for the Protection of Birds, 1974; silver medal from Zoological Society, 1975; member of Order of the British Empire, 1977.

WRITINGS:

ALL SELF-ILLUSTRATED

(With Cyril W. Newberry) *Intimate Sketches from Bird Life* (introduction by Julian Huxley), Country Life, 1940.
(With Newberry) *The Art of Bird Photography,* Country Life, 1944, revised edition, Trans-Atlantic, 1948.
(With Newberry) *Birds of the Day,* Collins, 1944.
(With Newberry) *Birds of the Night,* Collins, 1945.
(With Newberry) *More Birds of the Day,* Collins, 1946.
(With Newberry) *The Swallow,* Collins, 1946.
(Editor with Harold Lowes) *Masterpieces of Bird Photography,* Collins, 1947.
(With Newberry) *Birds in Action,* Collins, 1949.
(With Stuart Grayston Smith) *Birds Fighting: Experimental Studies of the Aggressive Displays of Some Birds,* Faber, 1955.
Summer Migrants (stamps based on his photographs), Educational Productions, 1956.
(With Newberry) *Bird Photography as a Hobby,* Stanley Paul, 1961, McBride Books, 1962.
(With Winwood Reade) *Nesting Birds: Eggs and Fledglings,* Blandford, 1967, 3rd edition, 1971.
(With Frank W. Lane) *An Eye for a Bird: The Autobiography of a Bird Photographer,* with foreword by Prince Philip, Hutchinson, 1970, Paul Eriksson, 1973.
(With John Gooders) *Wildlife Photography: A Field Guide,* Hutchinson, 1973, Praeger, 1974.
(With H. E. Axell) *Minsmere: Portrait of a Bird Reserve,* Hutchinson, 1977.
A Passion for Birds: Fifty Years of Photographing Wildlife, Coward, 1979.
(With Bryan Sage) *Antarctic Wildlife,* Croom Helm, 1982.
(With Jim Flegg) *Eric Hosking's Owls,* Pelham Books, 1982.
(With W. G. Hale) *Eric Hosking's Waders,* Pelham Books, 1983.
(With R. M. Lockley) *Eric Hosking's Seabirds,* Croom Helm, 1983.
(With Janet Kear) *Eric Hosking's Wildfowl,* Croom Helm, 1985.
(With Peter France) *An Encyclopedia of Bible Animals,* Croom Helm, 1985.

Also author of *Birds of Britain,* with H. E. Axell, 1978.

ILLUSTRATOR

Norman Ellison, *Our British Birds and Beasts,* Open Air Publications, 1947.
Garth Christian, editor, *Wings of Light: An Anthology,* Newnes, 1965.
Guy Mountford, *The Vanishing Jungle: The Story of the World Wildlife Fund Expeditions to Pakistan,* Collins, 1969.

Also illustrator of more than eight hundred other books.

OTHER

Photographic editor of "New Naturalist," a book series, Collins, 1942—. Photographic editor of *British Birds,* 1960-76.

*   *   *

HOWARD, Roger 1938-

PERSONAL: Born June 19, 1938, in Warwickshire, England; married Anne Mary Zemaitis (a teacher), August 13, 1960; children: Bjorn Axel. *Education:* Attended Royal Academy of

Dramatic Art, 1956-57, and University of Bristol, 1958; University of Essex, M.A., 1976.

ADDRESSES: Home—Church Rd., Little Waldingfield, Sudbury, Suffolk CO10 0SN, England. *Office*—Department of Literature, University of Essex, Wivenhoe Park, Colchester CO4 3SQ, England.

CAREER: Poet, playwright, novelist, and biographer. Nankai University, Tientsin, People's Republic of China, teacher of English, 1965-67; Collets Bookshop, Peterborough, England, manager, 1967-68; Bookshop 85, London, England, manager, 1968-72; Peking University, Peking, People's Republic of China, lecturer in English literature, 1972-74; Mercury Theatre, Colchester, England, playwright-in-residence, 1976; University of York, York, England, fellow in creative writing, 1976-78; University of East Anglia, Norwich, England, Henfield Writing Fellow, 1979; University of Essex, Colchester, lecturer in literature, 1979—. Founder and director, The Theatre Underground, 1979—. *Military Service:* Royal Armoured Service Corps, 1958; sentenced to imprisonment after refusing to wear uniform; dishonorably discharged.

MEMBER: British Theatre Institute, Society of Anglo-Chinese Understanding (member of council of management, 1971-72), Union of Theatre Writers.

AWARDS, HONORS: Playwright's bursary from Arts Council of Great Britain, 1975-76.

WRITINGS:

Phantastic Satire (novel), Chapple, 1960.
From the Life of a Patient (novel), Chapple, 1961.
Four Stories (bound with *Twelve Sketches* by Tony Astbury), Mouthpiece, 1964.
To The People (poems), Mouthpiece, 1966.
Praise Songs (poems), Mouthpiece, 1966.
The Technique of the Struggle Meeting (nonfiction), Clandestine, 1968.
The Use of Wall Newspapers (nonfiction), Clandestine, 1968.
The Hooligan's Handbook (essay), Action Books, 1971.
(Editor) *Culture and Agitation: Theatre Documents*, Action Books, 1972.
Method for Revolutionary Writing, Action Books, 1972.
Mao Tse-Tung and the Chinese People (biography), Allen & Unwin, 1976, Monthly Review Press, 1977.
Contemporary Chinese Theatre, Heinemann, 1976.
Ancient Rivers (short stories), Greville Press, 1984.
(Translator with Estella Schmid) Stefan Schutz, *Sappa*, Playback, 1984.
(Contributor) *Contradictory Theatres*, Theatre Action Press, 1985.

PLAYS

"Bewitched Foxes Rehearsing Their Roles," first produced in London, England, 1968.
Fin's Doubts (first produced in London, 1968), privately printed, 1968.
"The Love Suicides at Havering" (also see below), first produced in London, 1969.
"Season," first produced in London, 1969.
"Simon Murdering His Deformed Wife with a Hammer," first produced in London, 1969.
"Seven Stages on the Road to Exile" (also see below), first produced in Carlisle, England, 1970.
"The Carrying of X From A to Z" (also see below), first produced in Papua, New Guinea, 1971.

"Dis" (also see below), first produced in York, England, 1971.
"The Meaning of the Statue" (also see below), produced in London, 1971.
"Writing on Stone" (also see below), first produced in London, 1971.
"The Auction of Virtues," first produced in London, 1972.
"Sunrise," first produced at Peking University, 1973.
"The Travels of Yi Yuk-sa to the Caves at Yenan" (also see below), produced in Colchester, England, 1976.
"The Drum of the Strict Master" (also see below), first produced in Colchester at Essex University Theatre, February, 1976.
"Klong 1, Klong 2, and the Partisan," first produced in Colchester, 1976.
"Notes for a New History," first produced in Colchester at Essex University Theatre, February, 1976.
"The Tragedy of Mao in the Lin Piao Period," first produced, under title "History of the Tenth Struggle," in London at ICA Theatre, September, 1976.
"The Great Tide," first produced in Colchester at Mercury Theatre, 1976.
"A Feast during Famine," first produced by Wakefield Tricycle Co., 1977.
"Travelling Players of the Dawn," first produced in York, 1977.
"Women's Army," first produced by Omoro Theatre Co., 1978.
"Margery Kempe," first produced in London at ICA Theatre, May, 1978.
"Joseph Arch," public reading in London by Royal Shakespeare Company, 1978.
"Korotov's Ego-Theatre" (also see below), first produced in Edinburgh, Scotland, by Cambridge Mummers' Theatre, 1978.
"Report from the City of Reds in the Year 1970" (also see below), first produced in Cambridge, England, by Cambridge Mummers' Theatre, 1978.
"Episodes from Fighting in the East" (also see below), first produced in Edinburgh by Cambridge Mummers' Theatre, 1978.
"Queen," first produced in Alsager, England, at Alsager College, March, 1979.
"The Society of Poets" (also see below), first produced in Edinburgh, 1979.
"Memorial of the Future" (also see below), first produced in Norwich, England, 1979.
The Society of Poets [and] *Memorial of the Future*, Action Books, 1979.
A Break in Berlin (first produced in Colchester at the Theatre Underground, 1979), Theatre Action Press, 1980.
The Seige (first produced in Colchester at Mercury Theatre, 1981), Theatre Action Press, 1982.
"White Sea," first produced in Colchester at the Theatre Underground, 1982.
Partisans (first produced in Colchester at the Theatre Underground, 1982), Actual Size Press, 1983.

Also author of forty-five plays as yet neither published or produced, including "The Berserk Joe Brown Junior," "Cage," "Hiss Play," "Still Birth," "Testimony of the Accused X23Z," and "The Use of Burning."

PLAY COLLECTIONS

(Contributor) *New Short Plays* (includes "Dis," "The Carrying of X From A to Z," "The Love Suicides at Havering,'' and ''Seven Stages on the Road to Exile''), Methuen, 1968.

Slaughter Night and Other Plays (contains ''Slaughter Night,'' ''The Meaning of the Statue,'' ''The Travels of Yi Yuksa to the Caves at Yenan,'' ''Returning to the Capital,'' ''Writing on Stone,'' ''Korotov's Ego-Theatre,'' ''Report from the City of Reds in the Year 1970,'' ''The Drum of the Strict Master,'' ''Episode from the Fighting in the East,'' ''A New Bestiary,'' and ''The Play of Iron''), Calder & Boyars, 1971.

OTHER

Contributor of poems, stories, and reviews to magazines and journals, including *Fireweed, Stand, Bananas, Transatlantic Review, Times Literary Supplement, New Poetry,* and *Play and Players.* Member of editorial committee of *China Now,* 1968-72, and *Platform,* 1977-82.

WORK IN PROGRESS: A book on the idea content of new English theatre writing; a full-length play about Goethe's meeting with Napoleon at Erfurt.

SIDELIGHTS: Though Roger Howard is the author of a ''sympathetic biography'' of Mao Tse-Tung, he earned his ''Maoist'' label long before his study of the revolutionary Chinese leader. His plays, as he says, fall under a number of headings, but the recurring theme of revolution reinforces his belief that the purpose of art is to ''divide and agitate.'' Having raised their class consciousness to the point of overcoming fear of action, the heroes of Howard's plays are revolutionaries. Howard relies on his heroes to shake the ''great sleep'' encouraged by society's oppressors—those that preserve its class divisions.

But the ''Maoist'' label may be misleading. An outline of some of Howard's plays, while it reveals his preoccupation with the revolutionary theme, also shows his roots in English popular tradition. Manifest in the revolutionary theme is the author's belief in the ability of individuals to influence the conditions under which they live. ''My early short plays are most of them highly stylised abstractions,'' Howard remarks.

''They have a rather international subject matter—decolonisation in Africa, the Cultural Revolution in China, ancient Britain, modern Ireland. The recent long plays include a series of plays dealing with moments in English history, in the lives of people struggling. 'The Earth-Founding' is about slaves and farmers in St. Edmund's time. 'Margery Kempe' is about an unorthodox medevial mystic and brewer. 'Bread, Meat and Higher Learning' deals with the Catholic suppression of the Protestants during Mary's reign. 'The Weight of Many Masters' traces the rise of the agricultural workers' union in the late nineteenth century and the career of one of its first leaders, Joseph Arch. . . . A number of my plays on contemporary England, like 'Still Birth' and 'Women's Army,' deal with people who, as it were, resist 'fitting in.' ''

Closely related to an understanding of Howard's definition of socialism is the difference between what is and what could be. In ''A Break in Berlin,'' for example, a German woman realizes there are two sides to the invading Red Army. First, explains Howard, when she ''sees the easy informality between officers and men and listens to their optimistic ideas, she is struck by the contrast between the Nazi propaganda version of the Red Army, raping, looting and killing, and the actuality.'' Eventually this woman finds that the Red Army does indeed rape, loot and kill, but, ironically, in a socialist way. ''This lonely, prejudiced, and suffering middle-class woman had her first experience of the realities of 'actually-existing socialism' lying on her back,'' notes Howard.

The subject matter of ''A Break in Berlin'' ''draws attention to the primary matter I'm dealing with in all my plays,'' the author continues. ''It is that I am concerned to show the person, from whatever class, in a material way, from many angles, containing a multitude of facets—expressed in anguish, suffering, sorrow, hopes, happiness, joy—from a personal point of view and a social point of view simultaneously, so that the person's private self is shown in relation to that person's public persona.''

Howard's plays are considered easily stagable, but he has had little success in having them widely performed in larger theatres. One reason, he speculates, is the current state of socialist theatre: ''As we are not yet free to operate in properly based socialist theatre companies and not yet free, as writers, to write completely as socialists, we must still usually put our meaning in obliquely, sometimes hide behind conundrums, often compromise, resort to prevarication and occasionally be agitationally bold in order to get our plays performed at all.''

In a letter to *CA,* Howard described his recent work: ''I am developing a theory and practice of a Theatre of Contradiction and a dialectical drama deriving in part from the ideas of Brecht's last three years in East Germany. This work is preparing the ground for a theory of tragedy which will take tragedy away from its metaphysical origins and will allow for the integration of a materialist philosophy, a process which began with my 'The Tragedy of Mao in the Lin Piao Period' in 1976. The Theatre Underground's production of my 'White Sea' was an attempt to present an ironic tragedy, with music, about the forced labour and re-education programme at the construction site of the White Sea Canal in the Soviet Union in the early thirties. This study of Stalinism was followed by Theatre Underground's production of 'Partisans' in which I examined the history of a dissident actress in England's 'alternative' theatre, from the counter-culture upheavals of the sixties, through the terrorism of the seventies to the peace camps of the eighties. This play took the idea of a democratic Theatre of Contradiction into the very workings of the production process, in that the play's script demands that the actors fantasize upon their roles and develop them beyond the script to 'contradict' the author.''

BIOGRAPHICAL/CRITICAL SOURCES:

PERIODICALS

Times Literary Supplement, November 10, 1978.

*   *   *

HSIA, C(hih)-T(sing) 1921-

PERSONAL: Born January 11, 1921, in Soochow, China; son of Ta-tung and Yun-chih (Ho) Hsia; married Della Wang, 1969; children: Joyce Lynn, Natalie Tzu-chen, Ming Jiao. *Education:* University of Shanghai, B.A., 1942; Yale University, M.A., 1949, Ph.D., 1952.

ADDRESSES: Home—415 West 115th St., Apt. 22, New York, N.Y. 10025. *Office*—Department of East Asian Languages, Columbia University, New York, N.Y. 10027.

CAREER: University of Michigan, Ann Arbor, visiting lecturer in Chinese, 1955-56; State University College of Education (now State University of New York College at Potsdam), associate professor of English, 1957-61; University of

Pittsburgh, Pittsburgh, Pa., associate professor of Chinese, 1961-62; Columbia University, New York, N.Y., associate professor, 1962-69, professor, 1969—.

MEMBER: Association for Asian Studies.

AWARDS, HONORS: Guggenheim fellow, 1969-70; National Endowment for the Humanities senior fellow, 1982-83.

WRITINGS:

A History of Modern Chinese Fiction, Yale University Press, 1961, revised edition, 1971.
The Classic Chinese Novel: A Critical Introduction, Columbia University Press, 1968.
(Editor) *Twentieth-Century Chinese Stories,* Columbia University Press, 1971.
(Co-editor) *Modern Chinese Stories and Novellas, 1919-1949,* Columbia University Press, 1981.

CONTRIBUTOR

Cyril Birch, editor, *Chinese Communist Literature,* Praeger, 1963.
William Theodore de Bary, editor, *Self and Society in Ming Thought,* Columbia University Press, 1970.
Birch, editor, *Studies in Chinese Literary Genres,* University of California Press, 1974.
Joseph S. M. Lau, editor, *Chinese Stories from Taiwan,* Columbia University Press, 1976.
Andrew Plaks, editor, *Chinese Narrative: Critical and Theoretical Essays,* Princeton University Press, 1977.
Adele Austin Rickett, editor, *Chinese Approaches to Literature from Confucius to Liang Ch'i-ch'ao,* Princeton University Press, 1978.
Jeannette L. Faurot, editor, *Chinese Fiction from Taiwan: Critical Perspectives,* Indiana University Press, 1980.
Jaroslav Prusek, *The Lyrical and the Epic,* Indiana University Press, 1980.
Peter H. Lee, editor, *Critical Issues in East Asian Literature,* International Cultural Society of Korea (Seoul), 1983.

OTHER

Also contributor to *Journal of Asian Studies, China Quarterly, Criticism, Harvard Journal of Asiatic Studies, Renditions,* and other periodicals.

*   *   *

HUBBELL, Jay B(roadus)   1885-1979

PERSONAL: Born May 8, 1885, in Smyth County, Va.; died February 13, 1979; son of David Shelton and Ruth (Eller) Hubbell; married Lucinda Smith, June 1, 1918; children: Jay B., Jr., David Smith. *Education:* University of Richmond, B.A., 1905; Harvard University, M.A., 1908; Columbia University, Ph.D., 1922.

ADDRESSES: Home—121 Pinecrest Rd., Durham, N.C.

CAREER: Bethel College, Kentucky, instructor in Latin and Greek, 1905-06; University of North Carolina at Chapel Hill, instructor in English, 1908-09; Wake Forest College (now University), Wake Forest, N.C., associate professor, 1911-14; Southern Methodist University, Dallas, Tex., 1915-27, began as assistant professor, became Lilly Professor of English and head of department; Duke University, Durham, N.C., professor of American literature, 1927-54, emeritus professor, 1954-79. Visiting professor of American literature, University of Vienna, 1949, 1950; Fulbright professor of American litera-

ture and civilization, University of Athens, 1953; visiting professor of English, University of Virginia, 1954-55, Clemson University, 1956, Columbia University, 1957-58, Texas Tech University, 1960, and University of Kentucky, 1961. Honorary consultant in American cultural history to Library of Congress, 1965-67. *Military service:* U.S. Army Field Artillery, Officers Reserve Corps, 1919-24; became first lieutenant.

MEMBER: Modern Language Association of America (member of executive council, 1946-49; vice-president, 1951), South Atlantic Modern Language Association, North Carolina Folklore Society, Masons, Phi Beta Kappa, Andiron Club (New York), Faculty Club and Erasmus Club (both Duke University).

AWARDS, HONORS: Mayflower Cup of Mayflower Descendants in North Carolina for best nonfiction book by a North Carolinian, 1955, for *The South in American Literature, 1607-1900;* Jay B. Hubbell Silver Medallion of the Modern Language Association of America was established and first awarded to Hubbell, 1964, "for distinguished service to scholarship in the field of American literature; Litt.D. from Southern Methodist University, 1951, University of Richmond, 1956, and Clemson University, 1961; the Jay B. Hubbell Center for American Literary Historiography was established in the William R. Perkins Library at Duke University, 1976.

WRITINGS:

(With John Owen Beaty) *An Introduction to Poetry,* Macmillan, 1922, revised edition, 1936.
(With Beaty) *An Introduction to Drama,* Macmillan, 1927.
The Enjoyment of Literature, Macmillan, 1929.
American Life in Literature (anthology for college students), two volumes, Harper, 1936, revised edition, 1949, reprinted, Books for Libraries Press, 1971, abridged edition, Harper, 1951.
The Last Years of Henry Timrod, 1864-1867, Duke University Press, 1941, reprinted, AMS Press, 1978.
The South in American Literature, 1607-1900, Duke University Press, 1954.
Southern Life in Fiction, University of Georgia Press, 1960.
South and Southwest: Literary Essays and Reminiscences, Duke University Press, 1965.
(Author of introduction) Edgar Allan Poe, *"Tales," and "The Raven and Other Poems,"* C. E. Merrill, 1969.
Who Are the Major American Writers?: A Study of the Changing American Literary Canon, Duke University Press, 1972.

EDITOR

Robert Louis Stevenson, *Treasure Island,* Macmillan, 1927.
Kennedy, *Swallow Barn,* Harcourt, 1929.

CONTRIBUTOR

Culture in the South, University of North Carolina Press, 1934.
American Studies in Honor of William K. Boyd, Duke University Press, 1940.
Elizabethan and Other Essays in Honor of George F. Reynolds, University of Colorado Press, 1945.
Anglo-Americana, Wilhelm Braumuller (Vienna), 1955.
Floyd Stovall, editor, *Eight American Authors,* Modern Language Association of America, 1956, revised edition, 1971.

OTHER

Also author of *Lucinda: A Book of Memories,* 1975. Editor, *Southwest Review,* 1924-27. Chairman of board of editors (and founding editor), *American Literature,* 1928-54.

SIDELIGHTS: Jay B. Hubbell once wrote *CA:* "At Harvard, Columbia, and other universities, it was my good fortune to know some very able scholars and teachers, notably George Lyman Kittredge, Bliss Perry, William P. Trent, and Ashley H. Thorndike. I have been fortunate enough also to know a number of important American poets: Witter Bynner, Vachel Lindsay, Robert Frost, Carl Sandburg, and John Hall Wheelock. The literary renaissance of the 1920s and 1930s was accompanied by a remarkable upsurge of interest in American literature on the part of a small but very able group of younger scholars determined to replace the usual amateurish books then in circulation by books and articles as good as the best that dealt with the literature of the British Isles. As editor of *American Literature* for a quarter of a century, I had something like a central role in that development."

Hubbell's peers considered him "a pre-eminent authority of Southern and American writing," according to Rayburn S. Moore in *Southern Literary Journal.* In honor of Hubbell's contributions to the field of American literature, the Modern Language Association of America created the Jay B. Hubbell Medallion in 1964. Hubbell himself was the first recipient of that award. Duke University honored him further by giving his name to its Center for American Literary Historiography, a depository for the papers of American literature scholars, and also by publishing a *Festschrift* entitled *Essays on American Literature in Honor of Jay B. Hubbell* in 1967.

In *Southern Literary Journal,* Moore says of Hubbell's works: "*An Introduction to Poetry* and *An Introduction to Drama* are true pioneering efforts to present the work of new poets and playwrights." Reviewing *South and Southwest: Literary Essays and Reminiscences* in *Georgia Review,* Moore notes, "*South and Southwest* is an important book. The fruit of a lifetime's work, it is also in many ways a complement to *The South in American Literature.* Between them these volumes form an imposing monument to an illustrious career." *New York Times* writer Christopher Lehmann-Haupt finds *Who Are the Major American Writers?* "a valuable historiographical study of how the American literary canon arrived where it is today, and an awesome reminder of how little we know where it's headed." Lehmann-Haupt also writes that while Hubbell's book "can hardly be recommended as entertainment for a general audience, it nonetheless has much to teach, particularly to those of us who think that literary history began yesterday or that the books we find deathless today have much chance of enduring tomorrow."

BIOGRAPHICAL/CRITICAL SOURCES:

BOOKS

Essays on American Literature in Honor of Jay B. Hubbell, Duke University Press, 1967.

PERIODICALS

Georgia Review, winter, 1967.
New York Times, March 30, 1972.

OBITUARIES:

PERIODICALS

Southern Literary Journal, fall, 1979.†

*   *   *

HUDNUT, Robert K(ilborne)   1934-

PERSONAL: Born January 7, 1934, in Cincinnati, Ohio; son

of William Herbert (a clergyman) and Elizabeth (Kilborne) Hudnut; married Constance Conklin, September 12, 1957; married Janet Lee Morlan; children: (first marriage) Heidi, Robert, Jr., Heather, Matthew. *Education:* Princeton University, B.A. (summa cum laude), 1956; Union Theological Seminary, New York, N.Y., B.D., 1959.

ADDRESSES: Home—1078 Elm St., Winnetka, Ill. 60093. *Office*—1225 Willow Rd., Winnetka, Ill. 60093.

CAREER: Ordained Presbyterian minister, 1959; Westminster Presbyterian Church, Albany, N.Y., assistant pastor, 1959-62; St. Luke Presbyterian Church, Wayzata, Minn., pastor, 1962-73; Minnesota Public Interest Research Group, Minneapolis, executive director, 1973-75; Winnetka Presbyterian Church, Winnetka, Ill., pastor, 1975—. Fusion candidate for mayor of Albany, 1961; member of board of directors for Minnesota Council of Churches, 1964-70; co-chairman of Minneapolis Board of Welfare Task Force on Homeless Alcoholics, 1967, and Minnesota Joint Religious Legislative Committee, 1970-75; chairman of Democratic Party, 33rd Senatorial District, Minn., 1970-72, and Minnetonka Democratic Party, 1970-72; president, Greater Metropolitan Federation of Twin Cities, 1970-72; national chairman of Presbyterians for Church Renewal, 1971; trustee, Princeton University, 1972-76, and Asheville (N.C.) School, 1979—.

MEMBER: Phi Beta Kappa.

AWARDS, HONORS: Rockefeller Foundation Fellow, 1956; Distinguished Service Award, Minnetonka Teachers Association, 1969.

WRITINGS:

Surprised by God—What It Means to Be a Minister in Middle-Class America Today, Association Press, 1967.
A Thinking Man and the Christ, Fortress, 1971.
The Sleeping Giant: Arousing Church Power in America, Harper, 1971.
A Sensitive Man and the Christ, Fortress, 1971.
An Active Man and the Christ, Fortress, 1972.
Arousing the Sleeping Giant: How to Organize Your Church for Action, Harper, 1973.
Church Growth Is Not the Point, Harper, 1975.
The Bootstrap Fallacy: What the Self-Help Books Don't Tell You, William Collins, 1978.

Contributor to *Our Sunday Visitor* (Catholic weekly), *Christian Century, Presbyterian Life, Minneapolis Star,* and other publications.

*   *   *

HUMBLE, Richard   1945-

PERSONAL: Born January 17, 1945, in London, England; son of Joseph Graeme (a professor of hematology) and Elsie May (Hunt) Humble. *Education:* Oriel College, Oxford, M.A. (with honors), 1966. *Politics:* Liberal.

ADDRESSES: Home and office—Manor Mead, 2a Laureston Rd., Newton Abbot, Devon, England.

CAREER: B.P.C. Publishing Ltd., London, England, deputy executive editor, 1966-68, assistant editor, 1968-69, editor, 1969-72; Orbis Publishing Ltd., London, managing editor of military publications, 1971-73.

MEMBER: Oriel Tortoises Boat Club, Leander Club.

WRITINGS:

Hitler's High Seas Fleet, Ballantine, 1971.
Japanese High Seas Fleet, Ballantine, 1973.
Hitler's Generals, Arthur Barker, 1973.
Napoleon's Peninsular Marshals, Macdonald & Jane's, 1973, Taplinger, 1975.
The Fall of Saxon England, Arthur Barker, 1975, St. Martin's, 1976.
Marco Polo, Putnam, 1975.
Before the Dreadnought, Macdonald & Jane's, 1976.
Captain Bligh, Arthur Barker, 1976.
Tanks, Weidenfeld & Nicolson, 1977.
The Explorers, Time-Life, 1978.
Famous Land Battles: From Agincourt to the Six Day War, Little, Brown, 1979.
Warfare in the Ancient World, Cassell, 1980.
The Saxon Kings, Weidenfeld & Nicolson, 1980.
Undersea Warfare, Basinghall, 1981.
Aircraft-Carriers: The Illustrated History, M. Joseph, 1982.
(Editor) Naval Warfare, Orbis, 1983.
Fraser of North Cape, Routledge & Kegan Paul, 1983.
Battleships and Battle-Cruisers, Chartwell Press, 1983.
U.S. Fleet Carriers of World War II, Blandford, 1984.
English Castles, Weidenfeld & Nicolson, 1984.
Submarines, C. A. Watts, 1985.

Contributor to History of the Second World War, History of the Twentieth Century, New English Encyclopedia, and History of the English-Speaking Peoples.

WORK IN PROGRESS: Crusader: Eighth Army's Forgotten Victory, for Secker & Warburg; The Rise and Fall of British Sea Power, 1509-1985, for Queen Anne Press; Operation Corporate: The Fleet Air Arm and the Reconquest of the Falklands, for Picton.

BIOGRAPHICAL/CRITICAL SOURCES:

PERIODICALS

Times Literary Supplement, April 20, 1984.

*   *   *

HUNT, John Dixon   1936-

PERSONAL: Born January 18, 1936, in Gloucester, England; son of Sydney H. and Marjorie (Dixon) Hunt; married Phyllis Marie DuBois (an academic librarian), February, 1973. Education: Attended English School of Languages, La Tour de Peliz, Switzerland, 1954; King's College, Cambridge, B.A. (with honors), 1957, M.A., 1961; University of Bristol, Ph.D., 1964.

ADDRESSES: Home—Norfolk, England. Office—School of English and American Studies, University of East Anglia, Norwich, England.

CAREER: Vassar College, Poughkeepsie, N.Y., instructor in English, 1960-62; University of Exeter, Exeter, England, assistant lecturer, 1962-63, lecturer in English, 1963-64; University of York, Heslington, England, lecturer in English, 1964-75, deputy provost of Langwith College, 1971-72; University of London, Bedford College, London, England, reader, 1975-79, professor of English, 1979-82; University of Leiden, Leiden, Netherlands, professor of English, 1983-85; University of East Anglia, Norwich, England, professor of English, 1985—. Visiting professor at Johns Hopkins University, summer, 1968, 1972-73, autumn, 1977; senior tutor at Open Uni-

versity, summer, 1971; Franklin Jasper Walls Lecturer at Pierpont Morgan Library, New York City, 1981; lecturer at universities in the United States and France. Member of Institute for Advanced Study (Princeton, N.J.), 1977-78. Broadcaster for British Broadcasting Corp.-Third Programme. Participant in international conferences.

AWARDS, HONORS: Fulbright scholarship and English-Speaking Union fellowship, both 1959-60, for study at University of Michigan; Hopwood Awards from University of Michigan, all 1960, for poems All These Ithacas, novel The Sad Probation, and essays American Collage, and Other Pieces; fellow of Folger Shakespeare Library, 1966, 1968; senior fellow of Leverhulme Trust, 1973-74, in Italy; British Academy European exchange grant, 1973-74; senior fellow in landscape architecture, 1985, at Dumbarton Oaks in Washington, D.C.

WRITINGS:

The Pre-Raphaelite Imagination, 1848-1900, Routledge & Kegan Paul, 1968.
(Editor and author of introduction) Pope's "The Rape of the Lock": A Selection of Critical Essays, Macmillan, 1968.
A Critical Commentary on Shakespeare's "The Tempest," Macmillan, 1968.
(Editor and author of introduction) Tennyson's "In Memoriam": A Selection of Critical Essays, Macmillan, 1970.
(Editor and contributor) Encounters: Essays on Literature and the Visual Arts, Studio Vista, 1971.
(Editor) Ronald Paulson, Rowlandson: A New Interpretation, Studio Vista, 1972.
(Editor) Wycherly, The Country Wife, Benn, 1973.
(Editor with Peter Willis) The Genius of the Place: The English Landscape Garden, 1620-1820, Elek, 1975.
The Figure in the Landscape: Poetry, Painting, and Gardening during the Eighteenth Century, Johns Hopkins Press, 1976.
Andrew Marvell: His Life and Writings, Elek, 1978.
(Editor and author of introductions) The English Landscape Garden, thirty volumes, Garland Publishing, 1980.
The Wider Sea: A Life of John Ruskin, Viking, 1982.
(Editor with Faith M. Holland) The Ruskin Polygon: Essays on the Imagination of John Ruskin, Manchester University Press, 1982.
Garden and Grove: The Italian Renaissance Garden and the English Imagination, 1600-1750, Dent, 1985.

CONTRIBUTOR

A. E. Dyson, editor, English Poetry: Select Bibliographical Guides, Oxford University Press, 1971.
Malcolm Bradbury and David Palmer, editors, Victorian Poetry, Edward Arnold, 1972.
Bradbury and Palmer, editors, Shakespearean Comedy, Edward Arnold, 1972.
Palmer, editor, Tennyson and His Background, G. Bell, 1973.
J. B. Broadbent, editor, John Milton: Introductions, Cambridge University Press, 1973.
A. D. Moody, editor, The Waste Land in Different Voices, Edward Arnold, 1974.
James Sambrook, editor, Pre-Raphaelites, University of Chicago Press, 1974.
C. A. Patrides, editor, Aspects of Time, University of Toronto Press, 1976.
(Author of introduction) William Gilpin, Dialogue upon the Gardens at Stowe, Augustan Reprint Society, 1976.

David Bevington and Jay H. Halio, editors, *Shakespeare: Pattern of Excelling Nature*, University of Delaware Press, 1978.

Patrides, editor, *Approaches to Marvell: The York Tercentenary Lectures*, Routledge & Kegan Paul, 1978.

Proceedings of the Ashmolean Museum Tercentenary Symposium on Cabinets of Curiosities, Clarendon Press, 1985.

Litz, editor, *Jane Austen Handbook*, Scribner, in press.

OTHER

Also author of *All These Ithacas, The Sad Probation*, and *American Collage, and Other Pieces*. Work represented in anthologies, including *Modern European Poetry*, edited by Willis Barnstone, Bantam, 1966. Contributor of more than thirty articles, poems, and reviews to language and literature journals, literary magazines, including *Ambit* and *Michigan Quarterly Review*, and newspapers. Editor of *Journal of Garden History*, 1981—; senior editor of *Word and Image: A Journal of Verbal/Visual Enquiry*, 1985—.

WORK IN PROGRESS: A book on the social history of the English garden.

SIDELIGHTS: John Dixon Hunt writes: "Trained in English literature, I have worked increasingly in the history of art and architecture and firmly believe that literary studies need to reach out and relate words to images. I also think that academics need to use their expertise in larger arenas, which is why I have always enjoyed, for example, reviewing books in the London *Times* or for British Broadcasting Corp., and why I chose to write a life and works study of Andrew Marvell for non-specialists.

"I love travelling (especially in France, Italy, and Greece; I speak French, Italian, and Greek more or less well—modern Greek painfully) and am fascinated by writers and artists who did travel—Marvell again, Ruskin, Turner, and the English travellers in the seventeenth and eighteenth centuries who visited Italy.

"My life is centred largely around my teaching and I resent even research work that takes me too far from those necessary classroom encounters; what is strangely called 'private work' feeds, for me, at least, directly into what I have to teach. I have always enjoyed teaching in the United States: both the students and courses are different and require different approaches—the changes they force in one stop the mental arteries from hardening.

"What spare time *is* left over goes into walking, especially in mountains, but not, positively *not*, into gardening, which I detest but engage in with manic abandon once in a while."

BIOGRAPHICAL/CRITICAL SOURCES:

PERIODICALS

Times Literary Supplement, March 12, 1982.
Washington Post Book World, August 12, 1982.

J

JACKINS, Harvey 1916-

PERSONAL: Born June 28, 1916, in Spirit Lake, Idaho; son of Harvey Wilson (a farmer) and Caroline (a teacher; maiden name, Moland) Jackins; married Dorothy Diehl, September 3, 1939; children: Gordon, Tim, Sarah, Christopher. *Education:* University of Washington, Seattle, B.A., 1960. *Religion:* Methodist.

ADDRESSES: *Home*—719 Second Ave. N., Seattle, Wash. 98109. *Office*—Personal Counselors, Inc., 2327 Fourth Ave., Seattle, Wash. 98121.

CAREER: Personal Counselors, Inc., Seattle, Wash., president, 1952—. International reference person for Reevaluation Counseling Communities, 1971—.

MEMBER: American Association for the Advancement of Science, American Mathematical Society, Mathematical Association of America, American Geophysical Union, Amonii Socii, Phi Beta Kappa, Phi Lambda Upsilon, Pi Mu Epsilon.

WRITINGS:

The Human Side of Human Beings: The Theory of Re-Evaluation Counseling, Rational Island, 1965.
The Meaningful Holiday: Poems, Rational Island, 1970.
Fundamentals of Co-Counseling Manual, Rational Island, 1970.
The Human Situation, Rational Island, 1973.
Zest Is Best: Poems, Rational Island, 1973.
Quotes from Harvey Jackins, Rational Island, 1975.
Guidebook for Re-Evaluation Counseling, Rational Island, 1975.
Rough Notes from Liberation I and II, Rational Island, 1976.
(With others) *Rough Notes from La Scherpa I,* Rational Island, 1977.
The Upward Trend, Rational Island, 1978.
Rough Notes from Buck Creek I, Rational Island, 1979.
The Benign Reality, Rational Island, 1981.
(With others) *Rough Notes from Calvinwood I,* Rational Island, 1983.
The Reclaiming of Power, Rational Island, 1983.

MONOGRAPHS

Communications of Important Ideas, Rational Island, 1963.
Complete Appreciation of Oneself, Rational Island, 1964.
Co-Counseling for Married Couples, Rational Island, 1965.
Flexible Human in the Rigid Society, Rational Island, 1965.

Logic of Being Completely Logical, Rational Island, 1965.
Who's in Charge, Rational Island, 1965.
Nature of the Learning Process, Rational Island, 1966.
Uses of Beauty and Order, Rational Island, 1967.
Multiplied Awareness: The Intermediate Co-Counseling Group, Rational Island, 1969.
Is Death Necessary?, Rational Island, 1970.
Letter to a Respected Psychiatrist, Rational Island, 1970.
Necessity of Long-Range Goals, Rational Island, 1972.
The Distinctive Characteristics of Re-Evaluation Counseling, Rational Island, 1973.
(With Mary McCabe) *A New Kind of Communicator,* Rational Island, 1974.

Also author of *The Good and Great Art,* Rational Island.

WORK IN PROGRESS: *The Rest of Our Lives.*

SIDELIGHTS: Harvey Jackin's books have been translated into seventeen languages.

* * *

JACKSON, Norman 1932-

PERSONAL: Born March 4, 1932, in Hull, Yorkshire, England; son of Wilfred (an engineer) and Elsie (Dutton) Jackson; married; wife's name, Margaret Elizabeth. *Education:* Attended Hull College of Technology, 1948-54, Hull College of Arts and Crafts, 1954-57, Fircroft College, 1960-61, and University of Hull, 1962-63. *Politics:* Socialist. *Religion:* Church of England.

ADDRESSES: *Home*—64 Auckland Ave., Cottingham Rd., Hull, Yorkshire, England. *Agent*—Bertha Klausner International Literary Agency, Inc., 71 Park Ave., New York, N.Y. 10016. *Office*—Department of English, Wolverhampton Polytechnic, Wolverhampton, England.

CAREER: Apprenticed to the building trades as a bricklayer, 1946-54; painter, 1957-60, exhibiting from time to time at Ferens Gallery in Hull, England, and at other galleries in northern England; *Tribune,* London, England, book reviewer, 1963-66; poetry editor, British Broadcasting Corp.; University of Iowa, Iowa City, Fulbright lecturer in English and creative writing, 1966-67; University of Keele, Keele, England, Gulbenkian fellow in poetry and teacher of creative writing, 1967-

68; Wolverhampton Polytechnic, Wolverhampton, England, lecturer in modern literature and creative writing 1968—. Lecturer in adult education department, Staffordshire Education Authority, Newcastle under Lyme, 1968—. Producer of series of poetry programs for National Broadcasting Co.

AWARDS, HONORS: Robert Frost fellowship in poetry at Bread Loaf Writers' Conference, 1967; writer's grant from Arts Council, 1976.

WRITINGS:

Selected Poems, J. A. Allen, 1963.
12 Poems (pamphlet), Northern Poetry Publications, 1964.
Faulkner: The Novelist behind the Man, University of Mississippi Press, 1966.
Beyond the Habit of Sense (poems), Villiers Publications, 1968.
Sexy Europe, Pinnacle Books, 1976.
Ways and Means, Lincolnshire and Humberside Arts, 1977.
Waking in the Dark, Paston, 1980.
Fieldwalking, Bran's Head Books, 1983.

Also author of material for British Broadcasting Corp. program he helped found, "The Northern Drift," and for BBC "Today" columns. Contributor of poems and other writings to *New Yorker, Observer, Saturday Review, Poetry Review, Outposts, Reporter, Tracks,* and other periodicals. Editor, *Torchnight.*

BIOGRAPHICAL/CRITICAL SOURCES:

PERIODICALS

Books and Bookmen, July, 1968.
Observer Review, June 30, 1968.†

*   *   *

JACOBS, Louis   1920-

PERSONAL: Born July 17, 1920, in Manchester, England; son of Harry and Lena (Myerstone) Jacobs; married Shulamith Lisagorsky, 1944; children: Ivor, Naomi, David. *Education:* University College, London, B.A. (honors), 1946, Ph.D., 1952; Manchester Talmudical College, Rabbinical Diploma, 1941.

ADDRESSES: Home—27 Clifton Hill, St. John's Wood, London NW8 0QE, England.

CAREER: Central Synagogue, Manchester, England, rabbi, 1948-52; New West End Synagogue, London, England, rabbi, 1952-60; Jews' College, London, tutor, 1960-62; New London Synagogue, London, rabbi, 1964—. Visiting professor of Jewish thought at Harvard University Divinity School, 1985-86.

WRITINGS:

We Have Reason to Believe, Vallentine, Mitchell, 1959, 3rd edition, 1965.
Jewish Values, Vallentine, Mitchell, 1960, 2nd edition, Hartmore, 1969.
Studies in Talmudic Logic, Vallentine, Mitchell, 1962.
(Translator) Dobh Baer Schneor Zalman, *Tract on Ecstasy,* Vallentine, Mitchell, 1963.
Principles of the Jewish Faith, Basic Books, 1964.
Seeker of Unity: The Life and Works of Aaron of Starosselje, Basic Books, 1966.
Jewish Law, Behrman, 1968.
Faith, Basic Books, 1968.
(Editor) *Jewish Ethics, Philosophy and Mysticism,* Behrman, 1969.

Jewish Thought Today, Behrman, 1970.
Hasidic Prayer, Schocken, 1972.
What Does Judaism Say About . . .?, Quadrangle, 1973.
Jewish Biblical Exegesis, Behrman, 1973.
A Jewish Theology, Behrman, 1973.
Theology in the Responsa, Routledge & Kegan Paul, 1975.
Hasidic Thought, Behrman, 1976.
Jewish Mystical Testimony, Schocken, 1977.
TEKYU: The Unsolved Problem in the Babylonian Talmud, Cornwell, 1981.
A Tree of Life: Divinity, Flexibility and Creativity in Jewish Law, Oxford University Press, 1984.
The Talmudic Argument, Cambridge University Press, 1984.
The Book of Jewish Belief, Behrman, 1984.

Contributor to theological publications.

WORK IN PROGRESS: Talmudic reasoning and literary analysis of the Talmud; theological studies.

SIDELIGHTS: Louis Jacobs told *CA:* "In my works I have tried to follow the style of English theological writing, ever mindful of the warning addressed to those who imagine that obscurity is evidence of depth: 'You don't have to be fat to drive fat oxen'! Some of my books are technical but often belong to the *genre* of popular theology. To engage in which I do not consider to be unworthy or embarrassing; quite the opposite."

BIOGRAPHICAL/CRITICAL SOURCES:

PERIODICALS

Judaism, winter, 1979.
Times Literary Supplement, February 2, 1967.

*   *   *

JAFFE, Dan   1933-

PERSONAL: Born January 24, 1933, in Elizabeth, N.J.; son of Samuel Herbert and Sally (Friedman) Jaffe; married Robin Gale Goldstein; children: Michael Adam, Sara Ann, Anna Gabrielle, Tamar, Marina. *Education:* Rutgers University, B.A., 1954; University of Michigan, M.A., 1958. *Politics:* Independent. *Religion:* Jewish Orthodox.

ADDRESSES: Home—5725 Wyandotte, Kansas City, Mo. 64113. *Office*—Department of English, University of Missouri, 5100 Rockhill Rd., Haag Hall, Kansas City, Mo. 64110.

CAREER: University of Nebraska, Lincoln, instructor, 1958-60; Willamette University, Salem, Ore., assistant professor, 1960; University of Missouri—Kansas City, instructor, 1961-65, assistant professor, 1965-68, associate professor, 1968-77, professor of English, 1977—. Editor-in-chief, BkMk Press, 1972—. Former director of American Poets Series, Kansas City Jewish Community Center; former administrator of Devins Memorial Award for Kansas City poetry contests. *Military service:* U.S. Air Force, 1955-57; became first lieutenant.

AWARDS, HONORS: Avery and Jule Hopwood Award (major) in poetry, University of Michigan, 1958; Bread Loaf Writers' Conference fellowship, 1958; first and second prize in *Kansas City Star* poetry contest, 1964.

WRITINGS:

Dan Freeman (biography in poetry and prose), University of Nebraska Press, 1967.
Archibald MacLeish: Mapping the Tradition in the Thirties, Everett/Edwards, 1967.

First Tuesday in November, BkMk Press, 1971.
(Editor) *Kansas City Outloud*, BkMk Press, 1975.
The Muscles and Bones That Carry Us to Love (chorale series of music and poems), Walton Music Corp., 1975.
(Editor with Sylvia Wheeler) *For Kids by Kids: A Book of Poems and Pictures*, BkMk Press, 1977.
(Editor with John Knoepfle) *Frontier Literature: Images of the American West*, McGraw, 1979.

Librettist for "Without Memorial Banners," jazz opera with music by Herb Six, produced in 1965. Contributor of essay to *Black American Writer*, 1972, and of critical essays to anthologies. Former reviewer for *Kansas City Star*; occasionally wrote "Poetry Roundup" for *Saturday Review*. Contributor of articles and poetry to *Prairie Schooner, Saturday Review, Mademoiselle, New York Times, Vortex, Poetry Bag*, and other periodicals. Poetry editor, *Focus Midwest*, 1973—; former poetry editor, *Fine Arts Calendar*.

WORK IN PROGRESS: Seasons of the River, a multimedia theatrical presentation; a book on "communal poetry"; an anthology of literature of the west.

SIDELIGHTS: Dan Jaffe was the subject of the film "Poets Are People."

*   *   *

JAMES, Allen
See ALLEN, James L(ovic), Jr.

*   *   *

JAMES, P. D.
See WHITE, Phyllis Dorothy James

*   *   *

JAMES, Philip
See del REY, Lester

*   *   *

JAMES, Philip
See MOORCOCK, Michael (John)

*   *   *

JAVITS, Jacob K(oppel)   1904-

PERSONAL: Born May 18, 1904, in New York, N.Y.; son of Morris and Ida (Littman) Javits; married Marian Ann Borris, 1947; children: Joy, Joshua, Carla. *Education:* Attended Columbia University; New York University, LL.B., 1926. *Politics:* Republican. *Religion:* Jewish.

ADDRESSES: Office—1211 Avenue of the Americas, New York, N.Y. 10036.

CAREER: Admitted to Bar of State of New York, 1927; member of law firm, Javits & Javits, New York City, 1927-54; began political career as active campaigner in reform movement of Mayor Fiorello La Guardia, New York City, 1937; elected to U.S. House of Representatives and served four terms as representative from Twenty-first Congressional District, 1946-54; attorney general of state of New York, 1954-56; U.S. senator from State of New York, 1956-81; Parker, Chapin, Flattau & Klimpl (law firm), New York City, special counsel, 1984—.

Ranking minority member of Senate Foreign Relations Committee; member of Labor and Human Resources Committee, Government Affairs Committee, and Joint Economic Committee. Member of numerous Senate subcommittees, including European Affairs Subcommittee, Education, Arts, and Humanities Subcommittee, and International Economic Policy Subcommittee. Chairman of economic committee, Parliamentarians Conference, North Atlantic Treaty Organization (NATO); U.S. delegate to United Nations General Assembly, 1970; member of National Commission on Marijuana and Drug Abuse, 1971-73. Special (civilian) assistant to chief of Chemical Warfare Service, U.S. Army, 1941-42. Commissioner, Anti-Defamation League of B'nai B'rith. *Military service:* U.S. Army, Chemical Warfare Service, 1942-45; served in European and Pacific Theaters; became lieutenant colonel; received Legion of Merit. New York National Guard, 1946-64; became colonel.

MEMBER: American Legion, Veterans of Foreign Wars, Jewish War Veterans (honorary national commander), Harmonie Club (New York City).

AWARDS, HONORS: Has received honorary degrees from forty colleges and universities, including New York University, Yeshiva University, Dartmouth College, Jewish Theological Seminary, and Colgate University.

WRITINGS:

Discrimination, U.S.A., Harcourt, 1960.
Order of Battle: A Republican's Call to Reason, Atheneum, 1964.
(With Donald Kellerman) *Who Makes War: The President versus Congress*, Morrow, 1973.
(With Rafael Steinberg) *Javits: The Autobiography of a Public Man*, Houghton, 1981.

Contributor to periodicals, including *Reporter, Esquire, New York Times Sunday Magazine*, and *Look*.

SIDELIGHTS: Liberal Republican Jacob K. Javits served eight terms in the U.S. Congress—four as a district representative and four as a senator from New York—before losing his first election at age seventy-six to a conservative (and much younger) challenger. The following year, 1981, he published a reminiscence of his thirty-four years of service entitled *Javits: The Autobiography of a Public Man*. Written with Rafael Steinberg, a former *Time* and *Newsweek* correspondent, the book itemizes Javits's political accomplishments, skimming over the details of his private life and confirming what discerning observers had long ago surmised: "politics was his whole life," to use the *New Republic*'s words.

Born to an immigrant Jewish family in a ghetto of New York City, Javits forged his success through a combination of "pluck, perseverance, and talent," according to Haynes Johnson in the *Washington Post Book World*. Though he practiced law for almost twenty years before assuming public office at age forty-two, Javits, once elected, devoted himself entirely to his congressional posts. In addition to progressive health and housing legislation, he promoted civil liberties and civil rights, helping to enact the Civil Rights Bill of 1964. More recently, he successfully sponsored the War Powers Resolution, which limits the chief executive's war-making powers and restores to Congress its constitutional prerogatives.

Javits discusses some of his favorite issues in two early books, *Discrimination, U.S.A.*, a history of racial prejudice in the United States and its effect on several minority groups, and

Who Makes War: The President versus Congress, a history of executive and legislative use of war-making powers since the country was first formed. In *Javits: The Autobiography of a Public Man,* the former senator reveals the impact of his public commitments on his private life as *New Republic* contributor Andy Logan explains: "Javits makes it clear that his wife, Marian, whom he married in 1947, was so tangential to the Washington world that absorbed him that she had no alternative but to make a life of her own in New York. The three children of the marriage, now grown, are faceless figures in his autobiography mentioned only in passing."

Logan believes that *Javits*'s style and tone clearly reflect the politician's priorities, and he describes the book as "undiluted Javits: measured, intelligent, self-important, humorless, and in command of more detail than many readers will care to follow." Writing in the *New York Times Book Review,* Maurice Carroll acknowledges that Javits's "book skimps on anecdote," but then suggests, "when the public man unbends and tells about the private person, the book is better." One place where Javits does reveal his personal side is in the coda, which describes his return to the Lower East Side neighborhood where he was raised: "As I shook hands with so many people there on the street corner where it all began for me, I realized that they knew what I was and that they knew what I had accomplished for them and for all of us, and I saw that one defeat meant little on the long road I have traveled."

Despite what he views as Javits's "unnecessary need for reassurance," Johnson concludes his review by saying that "you finish these pages wishing we had more like him."

AVOCATIONAL INTERESTS: Tennis, squash, swimming.

BIOGRAPHICAL/CRITICAL SOURCES:

BOOKS

Javits, Jacob K., *Javits: The Autobiography of a Public Man,* Houghton, 1981.

PERIODICALS

Commonweal, June 12, 1964.
National Review, June 30, 1964.
New Republic, June 27, 1981.
New York Herald Tribune Book Review, October 2, 1960.
New York Times, June 17, 1981.
New York Times Book Review, October 2, 1960, April 26, 1964, October 14, 1973, May 17, 1981.
Saturday Review, May 23, 1964.
Times Literary Supplement, April 7, 1961.
Washington Post Book World, May 31, 1981.

*   *   *

JEFFREYS, J. G.
   See HEALEY, Ben (James)

*   *   *

JOHNSGARD, Paul A(ustin)   1931-

PERSONAL: Born June 28, 1931, in Fargo, N.D.; son of Alfred Bernard (a sanitarian) and Yvonne (Morgan) Johnsgard; married Lois Lampe, June 24, 1956; children: Jay, Scott, Ann, Karin. *Education:* North Dakota State University, B.S., 1953; Washington State University, M.S., 1956; Cornell University, Ph.D., 1959.

ADDRESSES: Home—7341 Holdrege, Lincoln, Neb. 68505. *Office*—School of Biological Sciences, University of Nebraska, Lincoln, Neb. 68588-0118.

CAREER: University of Nebraska, Lincoln, instructor, 1961-62, assistant professor, 1962-64, associate professor, 1964-68, professor of zoology, 1968-80, Foundation Professor of Life Sciences, 1980—.

MEMBER: American Ornithologists Union (fellow), Wilson Ornithological Society, Cooper Ornithological Society, Sigma Xi.

AWARDS, HONORS: National Science Foundation fellow, University of Bristol, 1959-60; U.S. Public Health Service fellow, 1960-61; National Science Foundation research grant, 1963-66; top honor book award, Chicago Book Clinic, 1969, for *Waterfowl: Their Biology and Natural History;* Guggenheim fellowship, 1971; outstanding book publication award, Wildlife Society, 1974, for *Grouse and Quails of North America;* Mari Sandoz Award, Nebraska Library Association, 1984, for natural history writings; University of Nebraska Outstanding Research and Creative Activity Award, 1984.

WRITINGS:

Handbook of Waterfowl Behavior, Cornell University Press, 1965.
Animal Behavior, W. C. Brown, 1967, 2nd edition, 1972.
Waterfowl: Their Biology and Natural History, University of Nebraska Press, 1968.
Grouse and Quails of North America, University of Nebraska Press, 1973.
Song of the North Wind: A Story of the Snow Goose, Doubleday, 1974.
American Game Birds of Upland and Shoreline, University of Nebraska Press, 1974.
Waterfowl of North America, Indiana University Press, 1975.
(Editor) *The Bird Decoy: An American Art Form,* University of Nebraska Press, 1976.
Ducks, Geese, and Swans of the World, University of Nebraska Press, 1978.
A Guide to North American Waterfowl, Indiana University Press, 1979.
Birds of the Great Plains: Breeding Species and Their Distribution, University of Nebraska Press, 1979.
Plovers, Sandpipers, and Snipes of the World, University of Nebraska Press, 1981.
Those of the Gray Wind: The Sandhill Cranes, St. Martin's, 1981.
Teton Wildlife: Observations of a Naturalist, Colorado Associated University Press, 1982.
(With daughter, Karin Johnsgard) *Dragons and Unicorns: A Natural History,* St. Martin's, 1982.
Hummingbirds of North Carolina, Smithsonian Institution Press, 1983.
Cranes of the World, Indiana University Press, 1983.
Grouse of the World, University of Nebraska Press, 1983.
The Platte: Channels in Time, University of Nebraska Press, 1984.
Pheasants of the World, Oxford University Press, in press.
Prairie Children, Mountain Visions, Media Productions, in press.
Birds of the Rocky Mountains, Colorado Associated University Press, in press.

WORK IN PROGRESS: Auks, Grebes and Loons of North America, for University of Nebraska Press; a book on the quails, partridges, and francolins of the world.

SIDELIGHTS: Paul A. Johnsgard has conducted field work in North and South America, Australia, and Europe. *Song of the North Wind: A Story of the Snow Goose* has been translated into Russian and Latvian.

AVOCATIONAL INTERESTS: Photography, art (especially line illustration).

*   *   *

JOHNSON, Diane   1934-

PERSONAL: Born April 28, 1934, in Moline, Ill.; daughter of Dolph and Frances (Elder) Lain; married B. Lamar Johnson, Jr., July, 1953; married second husband, John Frederic Murray (a professor of medicine), May 31, 1968; children: (first marriage) Kevin, Darcy, Amanda, Simon. *Education:* Attended Stephens College, 1951-53; University of Utah, B.A., 1957; University of California, M.A., 1966, Ph.D., 1968.

ADDRESSES: Home—24 Edith Pl., San Francisco, Calif. 94133. *Office*—Department of English, University of California, Davis, Calif. 95616. *Agent*—Helen Brann, 157 West 57th St., New York, N.Y. 10019.

CAREER: University of California, Davis, 1968—, began as assistant professor, currently professor of English.

MEMBER: International P.E.N., Modern Language Association of America.

AWARDS, HONORS: National Book Award nomination, 1973, for *Lesser Lives,* and 1979, for *Lying Low;* Guggenheim fellowship, 1977-78; Rosenthal Award, American Academy and Institute of Arts and Letters, 1979; Pulitzer Prize nomination in general nonfiction, 1983, for *Terrorists and Novelists; Los Angeles Times* book prize nomination in biography, 1984, for *Dashiell Hammett: A Life.*

WRITINGS:

NOVELS

Fair Game, Harcourt, 1965.
Loving Hands at Home, Harcourt, 1968.
Burning, Harcourt, 1971.
The Shadow Knows (also see below), Knopf, 1974.
Lying Low, Knopf, 1978.

BIOGRAPHY

Lesser Lives: The True History of the First Mrs. Meredith, Knopf, 1973 (published in England as *The True History of the First Mrs. Meredith and Other Lesser Lives,* Heinemann, 1973).
Dashiell Hammett: A Life (also see below), Random House, 1983.

SCREENPLAYS

(With Stanley Kubrick) "The Shining" (based on the Stephen King novel of the same title), Warner Bros., 1980.

Also author of unproduced screenplays "Grand Hotel," "The Shadow Knows" (based on her novel of the same title), and "Hammett" (based on her biography *Dashiell Hammett: A Life*).

OTHER

(Author of preface) John Ruskin, *King of the Golden River* [and] Charles Dickens, *A Holiday Romance* [and] Tom Hood, *Petsetilla's Posy,* Garland Publishing, 1976.

(Author of preface) Margaret Gatty, *Parables of Nature,* Garland Publishing, 1976.
(Author of preface) George Sand, *Mauprat,* Da Capo Press, 1977.
Terrorists and Novelists (collected essays), Knopf, 1982.

Also author of preface to *Frankenstein* by Mary Shelley, c. 1979. Contributor of essays and book reviews to periodicals, including the *New York Times, New York Review of Books, San Francisco Chronicle,* and *Washington Post.*

WORK IN PROGRESS: A novel set in Iran.

SIDELIGHTS: In an age when writers tend to be pigeonholed, Diane Johnson remains a difficult author to categorize. Perhaps best known as an essayist and biographer, she got her start as a novelist and continues to write successfully in this vein. She is a teacher and scholar, with an expertise in nineteenth-century literature, yet she also lent a hand in writing "The Shining," a popular horror film. And while her initial focus was on women and their problems in society, she has since written sympathetically of a man who faced similar difficulties in *Dashiell Hammett: A Life.* Even her early works, which have been claimed as the province of feminists, were intended to cast a wider net, as Johnson explained to Susan Groag Bell in *Women Writers of the West Coast:* "The kinds of crises, the particular troubles that I assign to my women characters, these are not necessarily meant to be feminist complaints. . . . In my mind, they may be more metaphysical or general. That sounds awfully pretentious, but I guess what I mean is that I'm not trying to write manifestos about female independence, but human lives."

Like many serious artists, Johnson sees herself as a craftsman whose work should be judged on its merits as literature, not—as is often the case with women writers—on moral or extra-literary grounds. In her highly acclaimed collection of book reviews and essays, *Terrorists and Novelists,* Johnson addresses the particular problems faced by female novelists, chiding those male critics who "have not learned to read books by women and imagine them all to be feminist polemics." As she told Bell: "The writer wants to be praised for the management of formal and technical aspects of the narrative and wide-ranging perceptions about society and perhaps the quality of her sensibility, not her own character, and, mainly you want your book to be a success on its own terms."

Though all her novels and one of her biographies have California settings, Johnson was born and raised in Moline, Illinois. Her childhood was untroubled: the first child of middle-aged parents, she lived in the same house surrounded by neighboring aunts and uncles until she went away to college at seventeen. She describes herself as a "puny, bookish little child, with thick glasses" and told *Los Angeles Times* reporter Beverly Beyette that she was "the kind of whom you say, 'Let's take her to the library on Saturday.' I was typecast, but I was a type." When she was nineteen, Johnson married her first husband, then a UCLA medical student, and relocated to the West Coast where she has remained.

Despite her long residence in California, Johnson told Bell that "a certain view of life, which I very much obtained from my Illinois childhood, does inform my work. In a couple of my books I have put a middle-western protagonist, always somebody who's displaced like I am, looking at the mess of today. This person remembers an orderly society from which subsequent events have seemed to depart." She maintains that it is the turmoil of modern society, rather than a personal preoccupation with disorder, that leads to the prevalence of violence in her books. "She is not sensational, sentimental, nor simple-minded," suggests *Critique: Studies in Modern Fiction* contributor Marjorie Ryan, who points out that Johnson writes in "the satiric-comic-realistic tradition, in a mode that may not appeal to readers nurtured on the personal, subjective, and doctrinaire."

In her early fiction, *Fair Game, Loving Hands at Home,* and *Burning,* Johnson employs "a comic tone" as well as "a central female character who is uncertain about how to conduct her life," according to Judith S. Baughman in the *Dictionary of Literary Biography Yearbook.* In each of these novels, a woman who has ventured outside the boundaries of convention "has a shocking experience which sends her back inside, but only temporarily until another experience . . . either sends her outside again or changes her whole perspective," Ryan explains.

As is so often the case with a writer's first fruits, these early novels largely escaped the notice of critics—at least initially. By the time *Burning* appeared, there were flickers of interest, though it was Johnson's potential as a novelist rather than the work at hand that attracted praise. Much criticism was leveled at Johnson's choice of subject. A Southern California story of disaster, *Burning* was viewed as a genre novel that had been approached in the same fashion many times before. As R. R. Davies put it, "Group therapy and the drug-induced self-analysis of depressed citizens have been done to death as satirical material." Though *Newsweek*'s Peter Prescott finds her "witty and serious," he points out that she "tries to be both at once and doesn't make it. Her book should have been either much funnier, or much grimmer or, failing that, she should have been much better." *Book World* contributor J. R. Frakes compares the crowded canvas of her apocalyptic tale to "a twelve ring circus" and welcomes its disastrous ending "almost as a relief," but then goes on to praise Johnson's style, noting that she "superintends this asylum with cool disdain and a remarkable neo-classic elegance of phrase, sentence, and chapter. It is comforting to know that someone competent is in charge."

Her competence established, Johnson began to attract more serious attention, and her fourth novel, *The Shadow Knows,* was widely reviewed. Originally set in Los Angeles, the story was relocated to Sacramento because, as Johnson explained to Susan Groag Bell, "I decided after the reception of *Burning* that Los Angeles was too loaded a place in the minds of readers." The novel takes its title from an old radio melodrama (which featured the line, "Who knows what evil lurks in the hearts of men? The Shadow knows.") and focuses on one terror-filled week in the life of a young divorcee and mother of four known simply as N. When someone slashes her tires, leaves a strangled cat on her doorstep, threatens her over the telephone, and beats up her babysitter in the basement laundry room, N. becomes convinced that she is marked for murder. But who is the assailant? Her spiteful former husband? The wife of her married lover? The psychotic black woman who used to care for her children? Her jealous friend Bess, who comes to visit with a hunting knife in her purse? Or, worst of all, is it some nameless stranger, an embodiment of evil she does not even know? N.'s attempt to identify her enemy, and her imaginary dialogue with the Famous Inspector she conjures up to help her, make up the heart of the book.

Writing in the *New Statesman,* A. S. Byatt describes the novel as a "cunning cross between the intensely articulate plaint of the under-extended intelligent woman and a conventional mystery, shading into a pyschological horror-story." *Nation* contributor Sandra M. Gilbert calls it "a sort of bitter parody of a genre invented by nineteenth-century men: the detective novel." Though it masquerades as a thriller, most reviewers acknowledge that *The Shadow Knows* is really a woman's story in which N. abandons what she calls her "safe" life to follow one that is "reckless and riddled with mistakes."

"In her attempts to create a fresh, true identity unconfined by the usual social and familial influences, N. must penetrate the evils which lurk in the hearts of men, even in her own heart in order to find her 'way in the dark,'" writes Baughman. "Thus, she has not only to uncover her potential murderer but also to deal with her own considerable problems and confusions. . . . Because the pressures upon her are so great, the possibility arises that N.'s terrors are powerful projections of her own sense of guilt and confusion rather than appropriate responses to the malevolent acts of an outside aggressor." Some reviewers go so far as to suggest that N.'s problems are more imagined than real. "Understandably, N. would like to know who's doing all these bad things to her, if only to be sure that she's not making it all up," writes Thomas R. Edwards in the *New York Review of Books.* "And since we also wonder if she may not be doing that, we share her desire for knowledge."

In her interview with Bell, Johnson makes it clear that such disbelief stems more from readers' biases than from the way the protagonist is portrayed. "There's [a] problem that comes from having as your central character a female person," says Johnson. "The male narrative voice is still accorded more authority. The female narrative voice is always questioned— is she crazy? Are the things she's saying a delusion, or reality? The narrator in *The Shadow Knows* was intended as an exact and trustworthy reporter of what was happening to her. But many reviewers, while in general liking her, also questioned her about her hysteria, her paranoia, her untrustworthiness. Is she mad or sane? So I began to notice that female narrators, if they're of a sexual age, of a reproductive age, of an age to have affairs, aren't considered trustworthy. . . . Nonetheless, I write about women of childbearing age, because I like to fly in the face of these prejudices and hope that I can make them authoritative and trustworthy reporters."

While women still figure prominently in Johnson's next novel, *Lying Low,* the focus has shifted from psychological to political concerns and from one protagonist to several. The book, which covers four days in the lives of four characters who inhabit a boarding house in Orris, California, is a "mosaic-like juxtaposition of small paragraphs, each containing a short description, a bit of action, reflections of one of the principal characters, or a mixture of all three," according to Robert Towers in the *New York Times Book Review.* Praising its artful construction, elegant style, and delicate perceptions, Towers calls it "a nearly flawless performance. . . . Despite the lack of any headlong narrative rush, one's interest in the working out of the story is maintained at a high level by the skillful, unobtrusive distribution of plot fragments." *Newsweek*'s Peter Prescott says it "represents a triumph of sensibility over plot" and observes that, like other feminist novels, it is "most convincing when least dramatic. Condition, not action, is [its] true concern: the problems of women confronting, or trying to ignore, their desperate lot."

Johnson's skill at rendering domestic crises makes *Saturday Review* contributor Katha Pollitt "wish Diane Johnson had kept her canvas small, a comedy or tragicomedy of manners for our decade of extreme political bewilderment. . . . When Johnson aims for a grander drama, though, she is not convincing. . . . The end, [in which a bomb explodes, killing one of the main characters], seems a failure of imagination, an apocalypse produced ex machina so that we all get the point about the violence that smolders beneath the American surface.'' A *New Yorker* critic pronounces the conclusion ''an awkward attempt to endow a cerebral narrative with the action of a thriller.'' And the *New Republic* likens the ending to ''one of those simple-minded 1960s films in which the source of all evil is 'Amerika''' and concludes that it ''seems much too jarring in a novel as full of subtleties of observation and atmosphere as this one.''

In addition to novels, Johnson has written two biographies. Her portrait of the first Mrs. George Meredith, *Lesser Lives: The True History of the First Mrs. Meredith,* grew out of her doctoral dissertation. ''In biographies of Meredith, there would always be this little paragraph about how he was first married to Mary Ellen Peacock who ran off and left him and then, of course, died, deserted and forlorn—like the woman in a Victorian story,'' Johnson told Bell. ''I always thought, I bet there is her side of it too. This was when my own marriage was breaking up, and I was particularly interested in the woman's side of things.''

Working from evidence she exhumed from letters and diaries, Johnson hypothesizes that the real Mary Ellen was a strong-willed, intelligent, free spirit, whose main sin was being out of step with her times. Raised by her father in the tradition of eighteenth-century individualism, she incited the wrath of her decidedly Victorian second husband, the famous novelist George Meredith, when she abandoned their loveless marriage to lead a life of her own. The portrait that survives of her as a crazed adulterer who lured a much younger man into marriage is more a reflection of Meredith's vindictiveness than an indication of who she was.

Though some critics felt the biography was lacking in evidence, many praised its artful style. ''Jump cutting from scene to scene, she shows what she thinks to be true, what she thinks might be true, and what, in all candor, she thinks no one can prove to be either true or false,'' writes Catharine R. Stimpson in *Ms.* ''Like a historian, she recovers pellets of the past. Like a psychologist, she applies theory and common sense to human behavior. Like a novelist, she takes imaginative liberties and worries about the internal coherence of her work of art. . . . *Lesser Lives* has the buoyant vitality of a book in which a writer has taken risks, and won.''

Even when her subject is a contemporary figure, about whom concrete facts and anecdotes are readily available, Johnson prefers an artistic to an exhaustive approach. ''A biography has a responsibility which is to present the facts and get all of them straight, so that people can get the basic outlines of a person's life,'' Johnson explained to Miriam Berkley in *Publishers Weekly.* ''And then, I think, it has to have a point of view and a shape which has to come out of the biographer as artist. I guess I am arguing for the interpretive biography, you might call it an art biography, as opposed to a compendious . . . presentation of a lot of facts.''

Johnson's commitment to biography as art presented especial challenges in her study of mystery writer Dashiell Hammett and the writing of *Dashiell Hammett: A Life.* The first ''authorized'' Hammett biographer, Johnson had access to all his personal papers and the cooperation of his family and friends.

But in exchange for these privileges, Hammett's executrix and long-time companion Lillian Hellman insisted that she be shown the final manuscript and granted the right to decide whether or not the quoted material could stand.

''She set out to be pleasant and wonderful, then, when she stopped being wonderful, I stopped going to see her,'' Johnson told Beverly Beyette in the *Los Angeles Times.* The problem was one of vision: ''She saw him very much as her guru, this wonderfully strong, terrifically honest, fabulously intelligent dream man. I saw him as an intelligent, troubled man, an alcoholic with terrible writer's block. She didn't like to think of his life having been painful, unsuccessful.'' Johnson eventually obtained Hellman's permission to use Hammett's letters in her own way. ''She had to agree, I guess, that it *was* the best way of presenting Hammett,'' Johnson told Berkley. ''He was a difficult man and not entirely sympathetic, but he was certainly at his most sympathetic in his own voice.''

Using a novelistic approach, Johnson intersperses excerpts from Hammett's letters with short stretches of narrative that sometimes reflect her viewpoint, sometimes that of his family and friends. *New York Times Book Review* contributor George Stade compares the technique to one Hammett perfected in his own novels, ''the method of the camera eye. We see what the characters do, hear what they say, note their gestures and postures, watch them assume positions toward each other, record their suspect attempts to account for themselves and each other.'' But just as Hammett's readers had to decipher for themselves his protagonists' motives, so, too, must Johnson's readers ''decide for themselves what made Hammett tick.''

Because so much is left to the reader, some critics suggest that Johnson is withholding judgement; others conclude that she cannot reveal what she does not know. As *New York Times* reviewer Christopher Lehmann-Haupt puts it: ''Silence was Hammett's weapon—silence turned against all bullies and lovers, against his readers and himself. At the bottom of that silence was an ocean of anger: that much this biography makes very clear. The mystery that remains—that will probably remain forever—is the true source of that anger.'' Characterizing Hammett as ''a fundamentally passive individual who drifted through life with no clear motivations or deep impulses,'' *Washington Post Book World* critic Jonathan Yardley wonders if Johnson's inability to ''penetrate through to the inner man'' might just reflect the fact that there was nothing there. ''Perhaps,'' Yardley speculates, ''when you come right down to it, the 'mystery' lies within us rather than him: for expecting more of him, since he wrote good books, than was actually there, and for feeling frustrated when those expectations go unmet.''

Ralph B. Sipper, on the other hand, finds Johnson's ''tracking of Hammett's inner life . . . the most revealing to date'' and speculates in the *Los Angeles Times Book Review* that perhaps her ''most delicate accomplishment is the fine line between iffy psychologizing and creative analysis.'' Describing the interpretative approach to biography as one in which the writer ''studies the facts and filters them through her own sensibility,'' Sipper concludes that ''Diane Johnson has done just that with her multifaceted subject and the result is pure light.''

CA INTERVIEW

CA interviewed Diane Johnson by telephone on April 5, 1985, at her former home in Oakland, California.

CA: Your writing seems to dovetail so neatly with the rest of your life, and it seems to have been accomplished almost from the start without the anxiety and struggle so often associated with writers. Is that an overly simple perception? Has it been difficult to fit the work in and get the books done?

JOHNSON: I wonder what gives that impression. It's true that I haven't had insupportable obstacles or else I wouldn't have gotten any work done. I had small children—at one point in my work all my children were under six. That was a difficult time, and I think my writing suffered. But also I was just beginning and learning about writing so if I'd had unbounded leisure, would I have known what to do with it? And even then I had household help and I was able to seclude myself from time to time. I also had the support of friends, other women who were writing, and we would babysit for each other. I think that maybe I would be a better writer if I had been more single-minded and not had a lot of distractions. On the other hand, I have gotten pretty much done.

CA: You maintain a separate house or apartment for doing your writing in. Does the work in some form spill over to the other places, or can you leave it behind when you lock the door?

JOHNSON: I can't leave it behind. I drag it around with me in an L. L. Bean bag. And now I have a wonderful little typewriter, a little Canon electronic one which is really light, so I take that too.

CA: But the other place must be nice for an escape.

JOHNSON: Yes, it really is. A lot of women do it. And men often have a studio out in the backyard that they can go to. I spoke of these other women. When I lived in Los Angeles, Alison Lurie would babysit my children and I would babysit hers. And Aljean Harmetz, another friend, wasn't really into babysitting, but she would go over to still another friend's house in the morning, the other friend having gone to work. That's how she got out of her house. She did her writing in Robin's living room while Robin went to medical school.

CA: Are there sometimes long rests between books when you can shut out the writing altogether?

JOHNSON: Not really, no. I prefer to be working, and I tend to start thinking about the next thing before I've finished the last one so that I won't have any traumatic blank interval in between.

CA: What kind of schedule do you work on?

JOHNSON: When I'm working on something, I work every day, as long as I can. I should say I work every day I *can;* life always seems to be full of obstacles of the kind we were talking about. Right now we're remodeling an old house in San Francisco, and you can imagine what kind of an intrusion that is. I work best in the mornings, and that's when I work, until I run out. I don't feel obliged to work every day whether I'm working on something or not, and detest staring at a blank page.

CA: You've spoken of racing along to the ending of a novel when you're writing, in the anticipation of seeing the book as a whole. How much sense of plot or structure do you have at the beginning of the work?

JOHNSON: Quite a strong sense. At least for my last three novels, including the one I'm writing now, I've made very careful outlines. They change quite a bit as I go along, but I have a plan and I like to work with an outline. I like to look at it in its structural, skeletal form and I can move the parts around or think about thematic or other kinds of developments, or the plot, without being burdened by the particulars of the text. Then the text itself develops its own qualities, and that may dictate changes in the form, but I feel happier with a formal plan to begin with.

CA: Do you have a favorite among your fictional characters?

JOHNSON: I don't know. I guess I like N. in *The Shadow Knows.*

CA: One of your characters that I find extremely interesting is Ouida Sensa in Lying Low, *partly because of her kind of desperate hope and partly because of her linguistic problems.*

JOHNSON: Oh, I loved Ouida. Ouida is a real person, and I love the real person too. I almost don't seem to distinguish between the two.

CA: One day English became clear to the fictional Ouida all at once, as if by magic.

JOHNSON: I had that experience with French, so I could identify with her linguistic problems. One day French became clear to me; I could understand what the people were saying on the bus. Of course they were saying the same things that people would be saying on a bus here. That was sort of disappointing.

CA: You spoke to Susan Groag Bell (for Women Writers of the West Coast) *about the misinterpretation of N.'s rape in* The Shadow Knows. *Would you end the book differently if you were doing it again?*

JOHNSON: I think I might. Or maybe I wouldn't, but I would make it clearer that this was not a women-enjoy-and-invite-rape kind of statement, but rather meant to say that everyone participates in violence. And also that there is evil in one's self—that kind of thing. Maybe I would substitute another kind of violent act, just to avoid the particular political things that are associated with rape.

CA: You've talked about the challenge of creating a female narrator who would be regarded as a trustworthy reporter of the novel's events. Having now done the biography of Dashiell Hammett, would you like to write a novel with a male central character?

JOHNSON: Each time I write a novel, I think of doing that and then I lose courage. In the novel I'm writing now, there is a male character whose point of view I write from, as I did in *Lying Low,* where there are little sections that are slightly from the point of view of a man. This one has slightly more; actually there are two men. Yet I still don't know that I would write a whole novel about a man, I guess because I don't know men's stories. In the case of Dashiell Hammett, I took over his story, to resolve my insecurity, and to learn about a man from within.

CA: Was it difficult starting on the Hammett biography without more of a feeling of sympathy for Hammett in the beginning?

JOHNSON: I didn't really start until I had found a way of relating to him sympathetically. I think that may have delayed the beginning of the writing some, but by the time I began to write I had this view of the sad life and the form of courage that Hammett had. Even though I at first didn't find him entirely sympathetic, I sort of respected him and I liked his sweetness. Then I could start to write, and I hoped to capture some of those qualities just by using a lot of quotations.

CA: Did Lillian Hellman's cooperation impose more constraint than you would have liked?

JOHNSON: Yes, it really did. In fact, I've just written a fairly long piece about that for Vanity Fair. In it, I tried not to complain too much, but just to tell how it was. It was mostly that she became afraid of the biography, so that although ostensibly she was cooperating, she began to undermine it. You could see that she was, in a way, afraid that it would show that their love wasn't true or something like that. I never was entirely sure what she was afraid of; she didn't articulate it. But you could see that she wanted it presented as a great love story, and she was afraid, I think, that when she read it she was going to find something out. So she began to create difficulties. Certain material didn't show up, and she was always firing letters off to me about this or that, or wishing I wouldn't go talk to certain people, or getting the sulks and refusing to believe that somebody in Hammett's past had existed at all. What she did mostly was complain to Random House all the time, and they complained to me. It wasn't that she would call me up and berate me, exactly, although finally it came to that.

CA: You're interested in the writing of biography as an art form, you told Miriam Berkley for Publishers Weekly (September 9, 1983). Can you elaborate on that idea, what it means to you?

JOHNSON: What it means to me is something about dramatization. I won't say fictionalization, because I've never written a fictionalized biography and I wouldn't; I think everything has to be true in a biography, or clearly indicated if not, as I did in imaginary patches in Lesser Lives. But biography works with the same materials as fiction and gives them a kind of dramatic emphasis and/or understands the themes and patterns of a real life. For me, novel writing becomes hard, and then I think, oh, if only I didn't have to make up everything: if I had the facts to go on, it would be wonderful. Then I start a biography and I think, how wonderful if I could just write a novel and sit home and not have to go to the library! It's kind of a change of pace, and it is interesting to have the givens of a life to work with. Again, maybe it's just another way of accepting formal constraints within which to work, either devising them yourself or finding them in real life. And it's exciting getting into unexpected material. I think I grew from writing Hammett. There I was writing from a male point of view, with a male main character. Perhaps now I will feel more comfortable and competent doing that. Certainly I would never have thought of writing a novel about an American private detective in the 1920s, but a biography opened the way.

CA: Are there any models you would cite for biography as an art form?

JOHNSON: I've been influenced in a way by Lytton Strachey, although my books aren't at all like his. He's somebody who took a definite position and wrote wonderfully. I like Andre

Maurois for his Disraeli. And Boswell, because his Life of Samuel Johnson is so adorable, though I wouldn't ever try to do anything like that. Much of contemporary biography is too long and too shapeless for my taste.

CA: Often one biography provides the subject for another. Did either Lesser Lives or Hammett give you a future subject?

JOHNSON: Lesser Lives did. I still haven't written it, but it's a future subject. It's Mrs. Meredith's first father-in-law, a wonderful character called "Fighting Nicolls," whose life was a sequence of events in which he found himself in every major event of his particular epoch, which was around 1800 to 1860 or so. He was in New Zealand and tried to become the governor there. He issued an emancipation proclamation to free the American slaves when he was in Florida, where he had landed for some reason in about 1811. And he had something to do with the arrival of the steamship. He kept losing parts of his body in battles; I think he was a marine. Nothing turned out, but he was always in the forefront of history, always had a great idea for improving things. If his ideas had been enacted, history would have changed. But they never were. Instead he would get his arm lopped off. I thought he was great, and I'd like to do a little arty biography about history with him in it.

CA: As a book reviewer yourself and a writer whose books are reviewed, what's your feeling about the quality of book reviewing in general?

JOHNSON: I don't think it's very good, in general. I'm not usually interested in book reviews. But there are some reviewers who write consistently interesting reviews, and I always read them. I guess that's what everyone thinks. I've done a lot of critical writing. I like doing it and I'm surprised that more novelists don't do it, because it gives you a chance to think theoretically about writing. I think novelists might upgrade reviewing, or at least make it a little more thoughtful. Writers might be more understanding about other writers, would tend to have more ability to see what problems the writer was up against and understand how he was trying to approach things.

CA: Do you feel, as many writers do, that West Coast writers are at a disadvantage because of being across the country from New York?

JOHNSON: Yes.

CA: You wrote the screenplay for The Shining. What other screenplays have you done?

JOHNSON: I've done a couple of others, but they haven't been produced. I wrote a screenplay with Mike Nicols which was going to be a remake of "Grand Hotel." It would have been wonderful, but it didn't come about, as these things often don't. I also wrote a script for United Artists, although they eventually dropped it, for The Shadow Knows. And I wrote a script of Hammett, a sort of sequel to "Julia." That's in the second draft, being written by Alvin Sargent, who wrote "Julia," and more recently "Ordinary People." He's a very distinguished real screenwriter. That film may be produced sometime. I don't know if any vestiges of my first draft will be left, but they may.

CA: Do you enjoy writing the screenplays?

JOHNSON: I do, although I wouldn't want to do it all the time; I wouldn't want to be *a screenwriter*. But I certainly have enjoyed the ones I've done.

CA: How much teaching are you doing now?

JOHNSON: Less and less. Right now I'm pledged to go up to Davis one quarter a year, or I can even cut back from that a little bit. I haven't been there for about two years and I won't go until next spring. I've been stringing leaves and sabbaticals and every other thing together. I find that when I'm in the middle of a project, teaching is the hardest thing to combine with writing.

CA: You're working on a novel set in Iran?

JOHNSON: Yes, at last.

CA: Do you have plans beyond that, or is it too early to be thinking that far ahead?

JOHNSON: I do have one little project planned. I'm going to write a short biography of Chanel for a Penguin series that an English editor is getting up on lives of modern women. It will be a hundred pages.

CA: Are you interested in doing short stories or poetry?

JOHNSON: No, not really. I have a short story that I've been working on for years. I keep thinking I'll get it out and finish it. I've only written one other short story, ''An Apple, an Orange.'' It's had a nice life; it was originally published in *Epoch*, and it got put on television and is being made into a play. Obviously a short story can have the kind of life a novel does. But I find them very hard to write; I don't think I'm very good at it.

CA: Is there anything you'd like to do in your writing that you haven't tried yet?

JOHNSON: I don't know. One always hopes to get better. My novels always fall short, by the end, of what I had hoped for them starting out. I'd like to think more about plot and try to rehabilitate the idea of plot in novels, because I think it's valuable and I don't know that I'm very good at it. There are some formal experiments I'd like to try. One has these vague ambitions, but they always get modified by the task at hand.

BIOGRAPHICAL/CRITICAL SOURCES:

BOOKS

Contemporary Literary Criticism, Gale, Volume V, 1976, Volume XIII, 1983.
Dictionary of Literary Biography Yearbook: 1980, Gale, 1981.
Johnson, Diane, *Terrorists and Novelists,* Knopf, 1982.
Yalom, Marilyn, editor, *Women Writers of the West Coast: Speaking of Their Lives and Careers,* Capra, 1983.

PERIODICALS

America, March 19, 1983.
Best Sellers, September 1, 1971.
Book World, October 13, 1968, September 5, 1971.
Chicago Tribune Book World, January 9, 1983.
Critique: Studies in Modern Fiction, Volume XVI, number 1, 1974.
Los Angeles Times, October 6, 1982, April 27, 1983.

Los Angeles Times Book Review, October 30, 1983.
Ms., May, 1974, November, 1978.
Nation, June 14, 1975, November 11, 1978, December 17, 1983.
New Republic, November 11, 1972, November 18, 1978.
New Statesman, November 19, 1971, June 6, 1975.
Newsweek, December 23, 1974, May 5, 1975, October 16, 1978, October 17, 1983.
New Yorker, March 3, 1975, November 13, 1978, November 14, 1983.
New York Review of Books, November 2, 1972, February 20, 1975, November 23, 1978.
New York Times, November 27, 1974, May 23, 1980, October 16, 1982, October 5, 1983.
New York Times Book Review, September 5, 1971, December 31, 1972, December 22, 1974, November 19, 1978, October 31, 1982, October 16, 1983.
Publishers Weekly, September 9, 1983.
Saturday Review, October 28, 1978.
Time, November 7, 1983.
Times Literary Supplement, June 6, 1975, November 23, 1979.
Village Voice, January 8, 1979.
Washington Post Book World, December 22, 1974, November 26, 1978, September 29, 1982, October 9, 1983.

—*Sketch by Donna Olendorf*

—*Interview by Jean W. Ross*

*   *   *

JOHNSON, W(endell) Stacy 1927-

PERSONAL: Born December 27, 1927, in Kansas City, Mo.; son of Amos Vernon and Vera (Reese) Johnson. *Education:* University of Kansas City (now University of Missouri—Kansas City), B.A., 1948; Ohio State University, M.A., 1949, Ph.D., 1952. *Politics:* Democrat. *Religion:* Episcopalian.

ADDRESSES: Home—65 Hampton St., Southampton, N.Y. 11968. *Office*—Department of English, Graduate School and University Center of the City University of New York, 33 West 42nd St., New York, N.Y. 10036.

CAREER: Smith College, Northampton, Mass., 1952-62, began as instructor, became associate professor of English; City University of New York, New York, N.Y., 1962—, began as associate professor at Hunter College, currently professor of English at Graduate School and University Center.

MEMBER: American Society for Aesthetics, American Association of University Professors, Modern Language Association of America, American Civil Liberties Union.

AWARDS, HONORS: Fulbright fellowship, 1952; Elizabeth Clay Howald research fellowship, 1961; American Council of Learned Societies grants, 1961, 1977; Guggenheim fellowship, 1965; Huntington Library grant, 1976; National Endowment for the Humanities research fellowship, 1979; Clark Library grant (University of California, Los Angeles), 1982.

WRITINGS:

The Voices of Matthew Arnold: An Essay in Criticism, Yale University Press, 1961.
(With M. K. Danziger) *An Introduction to Literary Criticism,* Heath, 1962.
(With Danziger) *An Introduction to the Study of Literature,* Heath, 1965.
Gerard Manley Hopkins: The Poet as Victorian, Cornell University Press, 1968.

(With Danziger) *A Poetry Anthology,* Random House, 1968.
Sex and Marriage in Victorian Poetry, Cornell University Press, 1975.
Words, Things, and Celebrations, Harcourt, 1975.
(With Danziger) *The Critical Reader,* Ungar, 1978.
Living in Sin, Nelson-Hall, 1979.
Charles Dickens: New Perspectives, Prentice-Hall, 1982.
Sons and Fathers, Peter Lang, 1985.

Also contributor to *The Critical Temper,* 1969, and other collections of essays. Contributor of articles and consultant to various scholarly journals. Editor, *Victorian Poetry* and *Browning Institute Studies.*

WORK IN PROGRESS: Words Cannot Stop: Unpublished Auden, 1929-1930.

SIDELIGHTS: W. Stacy Johnson told *CA:* "I am interested in writing as a form of teaching. Textbooks, of course, represent a direct mode, but scholarly books and articles also teach. My personal life is hardly separable from the vocation of teaching and writing."

The Critical Reader has been translated into Portuguese and published in Brazil.

BIOGRAPHICAL/CRITICAL SOURCES:

PERIODICALS

Criticism, Volume XI, number 3, 1969.

*   *   *

**JONES, Sanford W.
    See THORN, John**

*   *   *

JOSEPH, Joan   1939-

PERSONAL: Born July 13, 1939, in Tel Aviv, Israel; daughter of Philip (a lawyer) and Dena (Shapiro) Joseph; divorced; children: Robert Evan. *Education:* McGill University, B.A. (with honors), 1959; attended University of Aix-Marseilles, University of Paris, University of Southern California, and University of Miami, Coral Gables. *Politics:* Democrat. *Religion:* Jewish.

ADDRESSES: Home—10 West 66th St., New York, N.Y. 10023. *Agent*—Henry Morrison, Inc., P. O. Box 235, Bedford Hills, N.Y. 10507.

CAREER: High school teacher of French in Miami, Fla., 1965-66; U.S. Department of Commerce, Bureau of Standards, New York, N.Y., French translator for Joint Publications Research Service, 1966-67.

MEMBER: American Society of Journalists and Authors, American Historical Association, Authors Guild, Authors League of America, Phi Alpha Theta.

AWARDS, HONORS: Grants from Littauer Foundation and Dropsie University Center for Manuscript Research; Spertus College research fellow.

WRITINGS:

YOUNG ADULT BOOKS

Peter the Great, Messner, 1968.
South African Statesman: Jan Christiaan Smuts, Messner, 1969.
Folk Toys around the World and How to Make Them, Parents' Magazine Press, 1972.
Black African Empires, F. Watts, 1973.
Henry Hudson, F. Watts, 1974.
Political Corruption, Pocket Books, 1974.
Pet Birds, F. Watts, 1975.
Alcohol and Alcoholism, F. Watts, 1976.
(With Robert Levy) *Robert Levy's Magic Book,* M. Evans, 1976.
(Research editor) *La Jeunesse Encyclopedia,* Grolier, 1967.

ADULT BOOKS

For Love of Liz, Manor Books, 1976.
Love's Frantic Flight, Fawcett, 1980.
In Joy and Sorrow, Dell, 1982.
A World for the Taking, Dell, 1983.
Now Is the Hour, Dell, 1985.

OTHER

Contributor to *Encyclopedia of World Drama,* McGraw, *Medical Encyclopedia for Home Use, Would You Believe It, 1000 Great Events,* and *New American Bible.*

WORK IN PROGRESS: A social study of medieval England, for Bantam.

SIDELIGHTS: Joan Joseph has traveled extensively in western Europe. She spent three months doing research in Asian countries in 1969 and three months in New Zealand and the South Pacific in 1982. Joseph has a reading knowledge, adequate for research purposes, in medieval Latin, Old, Medieval, and modern French, Old English, Braide Scot, German, and Dutch; she also has studied Japanese.

AVOCATIONAL INTERESTS: Piano (plays about two hours daily), swimming, sailing, water skiing, and scuba diving.

BIOGRAPHICAL/CRITICAL SOURCES:

PERIODICALS

Jewish Week, April 28, 1982.
Montreal Star, June 4, 1965.

K

KAEMPFERT, Wade
See del REY, Lester

*   *   *

KAIN, Malcolm
See OGLESBY, Joseph

*   *   *

KALINS, Dorothy (G.)   1942-

PERSONAL: Born October 9, 1942, in White Plains, N.Y.; daughter of Joseph M. and Gertrude (Gillery) Kalins. *Education:* Attended Skidmore College, 1960-62, and Sorbonne, University of Paris, 1962-63; Columbia University, B.A., 1965.

ADDRESSES: Office—Metropolitan Home, 750 Third Ave., New York, N.Y. 10017.

CAREER: Grolier, Inc., New York City, researcher for *Book of Knowledge,* 1965-66; Fairchild Publications, New York City, writer and an editor, *Home Furnishings Daily,* 1966-68; freelance writer and design researcher, 1969-74; *Apartment Life,* New York City, executive editor, 1974-78, editor-in-chief, 1978-81; *Metropolitan Home* (formerly *Apartment Life*), New York City, editor-in-chief, 1981—.

MEMBER: American Society of Magazine Editors (member of executive board).

WRITINGS:

(Self-illustrated) *Researching Design in New York: Interiors, Furniture, Decorative Arts,* Fairchild, 1967.
Cutting Loose: A Civilized Guide for Getting Out of the System, Saturday Review Press, 1973.
(With others) *The Apartment Book,* Crown, 1979.
(With others) *The New American Cuisine,* Crown, 1981.
(With others) *Renovation Style,* Random House, 1986.

Contributor of articles to magazines, including *New York Magazine, Cosmopolitan,* and *Town and Country.*

*   *   *

KANYA-FORSTNER, A(lexander) S(ydney)   1940-

PERSONAL: Born October 24, 1940, in Budapest, Hungary; married Jane Beattie, June 7, 1962; children: Nicholas, Susan, Martha, Charlotte. *Education:* Trinity College, University of Toronto, B.A., 1961; King's College, Cambridge, Ph.D., 1965.

ADDRESSES: Home—177 Sheldrake Blvd., Toronto, Ontario, Canada. *Office*—Department of History, York University, Downsview, Ontario, Canada M3J 1P3.

CAREER: Cambridge University, Gonville and Caius College, Cambridge, England, research fellow, 1965-69, college lecturer in history, 1969-72; York University, Downsview, Ontario, associate professor, 1972-82, professor of history, 1982—, director of graduate programme in history, 1980-84, associate dean of faculty of graduate studies, 1983—. Visiting scholar, Corpus Christi College, Cambridge University, 1977-78.

MEMBER: Royal Historical Society, Canadian Historical Society, French Colonial Historical Society, Cambridge Historical Society.

WRITINGS:

The Conquest of the Western Sudan: A Study in French Military Imperialism, Cambridge University Press, 1969.
(Contributor) *France and Britain in Africa,* Yale University Press, 1971.
(Contributor) *Studies in the Theory of Imperialism,* Longman, 1973.
(With C. M. Andrew) *The Climax of French Imperial Expansion, 1914-1924,* Stanford University Press, 1981 (published in England as *France Overseas: The Great War and the Climax of French Imperial Expansion,* Thames & Hudson, 1981).

Contributor of articles to numerous periodicals, including *Historical Journal, Journal of African History,* and *Journal of Imperial and Commonwealth History.*

*   *   *

KARLINS, Marvin   1941-
(Robert Browne)

PERSONAL: Born October 4, 1941, in Minneapolis, Minn.; son of Arnold A. (a lawyer) and Miriam (Zipp) Karlins; married Nancy Flaun Green, July 27, 1968 (divorced); married Edyth M. Hargis, May 28, 1977. *Education:* University of

Minnesota, B.A. (summa cum laude), 1963; Princeton University, M.A., 1965, Ph.D., 1966.

ADDRESSES: Office—Department of Management, University of South Florida, 4202 Fowler Ave., Tampa, Fla. 33620. *Agent*—Paul R. Reynolds, Inc., 12 East 41st St., New York, N.Y. 10017.

CAREER: Princeton University, Princeton, N.J., instructor, 1966-67, lecturer in psychology, 1967-68; University of Pittsburgh, Pittsburgh, Pa., assistant professor of psychology, 1968-69; City College of the City University of New York, New York, N.Y., assistant professor, 1969-70, associate professor of psychology, 1970-72; Southern Illinois University at Edwardsville, visiting associate professor, 1972-73, professor of business administration, 1973-74; University of South Florida, professor of business administration, 1974—.

MEMBER: Authors Guild, Authors League of America.

WRITINGS:

The Last Man Is Out (novel), Prentice-Hall, 1969.
(With Herbert I. Abelson) *Persuasion: How Opinions and Attitudes Are Formed*, 2nd edition (Karlins was not associated with first edition), Springer Publishing, 1970.
(With Lewis M. Andrews) *Requiem for Democracy?*, Holt, 1971.
(Editor) *Psychology and Society: Readings for General Psychology*, Wiley, 1971.
(With Andrews) *Biofeedback: Turning on the Power of Your Mind*, Lippincott, 1972.
(Editor with Andrews) *Man Controlled: Readings in the Psychology of Behavior Control*, Macmillan, 1972.
(With Andrews) *Psychology: What's in It for Us?*, Random House, 1973, 2nd edition, 1975.
(With Harold Schroder) *Education for Freedom*, Wiley, 1973.
(Editor) *Psychology in the Service of Man: A Book of Readings*, Wiley, 1973.
(With Andrews) *Gomorrah*, Doubleday, 1974.
The Human Use of Human Resources, McGraw, 1981.
The Other Way to Better Grades, Fawcett, 1981.
Psyching out Vegas, Lyle Stuart, 1983.

UNDER PSEUDONYM ROBERT BROWNE

The New Atom's Bombshell, Ballantine, 1980.

OTHER

Author of column "The Psychological Edge," *Gambling Times*, 1982—. Contributor of articles to professional journals. Senior editor, *Gambling Times*, 1982—.

AVOCATIONAL INTERESTS: Folksinging, guitar playing.

BIOGRAPHICAL/CRITICAL SOURCES:

PERIODICALS

Christian Science Monitor, September 18, 1969.
Personnel Psychology, winter, 1984.

*   *   *

KATZENSTEIN, Peter J(oachim) 1945-

PERSONAL: Born February 17, 1945, in Wesermuende, Germany (now Bremerhaven, West Germany); came to the United States in 1964, naturalized citizen, 1979; son of Gerhard (in business) and Gerda (Hertz) Katzenstein; married Mary Fainsod (a professor), June 18, 1970; children: Tai, Suzanne. *Ed-*

ucation: Swarthmore College, B.A. (with highest honors), 1967; London School of Economics and Political Science, London, M.Sc. (with distinction), 1968; Harvard University, Ph.D., 1973.

ADDRESSES: Home—623 Highland Rd., Ithaca, N.Y. 14850. *Office*—Department of Government, Cornell University, Ithaca, N.Y. 14853.

CAREER: University of Massachusetts—Boston, instructor in politics, 1972-73; Cornell University, Ithaca, N.Y., assistant professor, 1973-77, associate professor, 1977-80, professor of government, 1980—. Fellow of Center for Advanced Study in the Behavioral Sciences, 1981-82.

MEMBER: International Studies Association, European Consortium for Political Research, American Political Science Association, Conference Group on German Politics, Council on European Studies, Phi Beta Kappa.

AWARDS, HONORS: Helen Dwight Reid Award from American Political Science Association, 1974, for doctoral dissertation; Ford Foundation grant, 1974-77; U.S. Office of Education grant, 1975-77; fellowship from Andrew W. Mellon Foundation and Aspen Institute for Humanistic Studies, 1976-77; Rockefeller Foundation fellowship, 1977-79; German Marshall Fund fellowship, 1979-81.

WRITINGS:

From Many, One and from One, Many: Political Unification, Political Fragmentation, and Cultural Cohesion in Europe since 1815 (monograph), Cornell University, 1974.
(With Douglas Ashford and T. J. Pempel) *Bibliography of Comparative Public Policy in Britain, West Germany, Japan, and France*, American Society for Public Administration, 1976.
Disjoined Partners: Austria and Germany since 1815, University of California Press, 1976.
(Contributor) Richard Rosecrance, editor, *America as an Ordinary Country: United States Foreign Policy and the Future*, Cornell University Press, 1976.
(Contributor) Milton J. Esman, editor, *Ethnic Conflict in the Western World*, Cornell University Press, 1977.
(With Ashford and Pempel) *Comparative Public Policy: A Cross-National Bibliography*, Sage Publications, 1978.
(Editor with Sidney Tarrow and Luigi Graziano and contributor) *Territorial Politics in Industrial Nations*, Praeger, 1978.
(Editor and contributor) *Between Power and Plenty: Foreign Economic Policies of Advanced Industrial States*, University of Wisconsin Press, 1978.
Corporatism and Change: Austria, Switzerland and the Politics of Industry, Cornell University Press, 1984.
Small States in World Markets, Cornell University Press, 1985.

Contributor of articles and reviews to political science journals. *International Organization*, member of editorial board and executive committee, 1976—, editor, 1980—.

*   *   *

KAUFMAN, Barry Neil 1942-

PERSONAL: Born March 28, 1942, in New York, N.Y.; son of Abraham (a business executive) and Bertha Kaufman; married Suzi Lyte (a therapist, teacher, and writer), June, 1963; children: Bryn (daughter), Thea, Raun (son), Tayo (son), Ravi (son), Sage (daughter). *Education:* Ohio State University, B.A.,

1962; Hunter College of the City University of New York, M.A., 1963; further graduate study at New School for Social Research. *Politics:* "Citizen of the planet without judgments." *Religion:* "Trust in the inner voice."

ADDRESSES: Office—The Option Institute and Fellowship, R.D. No. 1, Box 174a, Sheffield, Mass. 02157. *Agent*—Jane Rotrosen Agency, 226 East 32nd St., New York, N.Y. 10016.

CAREER: Communications Quorum, Inc., New York, N.Y., president, 1968-74; writer, teacher, and therapist, 1974—. Director of The Option Institute and Fellowship, Sheffield, Mass.; guest lecturer at universities, hospitals, and in mass media.

MEMBER: Writers Guild of America (East), Authors Guild, Authors League of America.

AWARDS, HONORS: Humanitas Award and Christopher Medal, for the screenplay adaptation of *Son-Rise.*

WRITINGS:

Son-Rise (also see below), Harper, 1976.
To Love Is to Be Happy With, Coward, 1977.
Giant Steps, Coward, 1979.
The Book of Wows and Ughs, Option Indigo Press, 1979.
(Co-author) "Son-Rise" (screenplay based on his book of the same title), first broadcast by NBC-TV, May, 1979.
A Miracle to Believe In, Doubleday, 1980.
A Land beyond Tears, Doubleday, 1981.
A Sense of Warning, Delacorte, 1983.

SIDELIGHTS: Barry Neil Kaufman wrote: "I work with people others view as 'hopeless,' and also with plain folk, teaching an alternative life style of love and acceptance without judgments. My books document real people—ordinary people pushing their own boundaries and achieving extraordinary results. These stories reflect the fruits of our teaching process at The Option Institute and demonstrate the power of trust and healing that comes from an accepting attitude—whether we are dealing with autism, cancer, marital problems or parenting. Attitude can be the facilitating process with any and every situation."

*   *   *

KAVANAUGH, James J(oseph)   1934-
(Father Stephen Nash)

PERSONAL: Born September 17, 1934 (some sources cite 1929 or 1932), in Kalamazoo, Mich.; son of Frank P. (a salesman) and Hazel Ann (Wendell) Kavanaugh. *Education:* Xavier University, Cincinnati, Ohio, B.A., 1954; Catholic University of America, M.A., 1963, Ph.D., 1966; U.S. International University, Ph.D., 1973.

ADDRESSES: Home—P.O. Drawer 1719, Laguna Beach, Calif. 92652. *Office*—15001 National Ave., Los Gatos, Calif. 95030.

CAREER: Ordained Roman Catholic priest, 1956, resigned priesthood, 1967. Flint Intercollegiate Newman Club, Flint, Mich., chaplain, 1958-64; Catholic University of America, Washington, D.C., taught at nursing school, 1961-63, instructor in theology, 1964; Trinity College, Washington, D.C., instructor in theology, 1964-66; Human Resources Institute, La Jolla, Calif., marriage counselor and educational director, 1966-72; U.S. International University, San Diego, Calif., professor of graduate psychology, 1970-72; private practice of clinical psychology in Los Gatos, Calif., 1974—. Visiting professor of religious studies, University of Alberta; seminar

instructor, 1970—. Licensed clinical psychologist in state of California, 1971. Gives poetry readings; guest on television and radio programs; actor on stage and television.

WRITINGS:

There's Two of You, Newman, 1964.
Man in Search of God, Paulist Press, 1967.
A Modern Priest Looks at His Outdated Church, Trident, 1967.
The Struggle of the Unbeliever, Trident, 1968.
The Birth of God, Trident, 1969.
The Crooked Angel (for children), Nash, 1970.
There Are Men Too Gentle to Live among Wolves (poems; also see below), Dutton, 1971.
Will You Be My Friend? (poems), Nash, 1971.
(With Everett L. Shostrom) *Between Man and Woman,* Nash, 1971.
Faces in the City (poems), Nash, 1972.
Celebrate the Sun (poems), Nash, 1973.
The Poetry of James Kavanaugh, Nash, 1974.
(With Darrell Fetty) "Street Music" (musical review), first performed in Los Angeles, Calif., at Theatre 40, 1974.
Sunshine Days and Foggy Nights (poems), Dutton, 1975.
America (poems), Dutton, 1976.
Winter Has Lasted Too Long (poems), Dutton, 1977.
Walk Easy on the Earth (poems), Dutton, 1979.
A Coward for Them All (novel; also see below), Bantam, 1979.
A Fable, Dutton, 1980.
Maybe If I Loved You More, Dutton, 1982.
Laughing Down Lonely Canyons, Harper, 1984.
The Celibates (novel), Harper, 1985.
Search: A Guide for Those Who Dare to Ask of Life Everything Good and Beautiful, Harper, 1985.

Also author of screenplays "A Coward for Them All," based on his novel of the same title, 1980, and "The Metamorphosis of Mort Meekin"; author of lyrics for Burt Bacharach album "Futures," 1979. Contributor to psychology journals and popular magazines, including *Look, Playboy, Psychology Today,* and *Ladies' Home Journal;* contributor to *Saturday Evening Post,* under the pseudonym Father Stephen Nash, 1966.

SIDELIGHTS: Expanded from an article James J. Kavanaugh originally published in the *Saturday Evening Post* in 1966 under the pseudonym Father Stephen Nash, *A Modern Priest Looks at His Outdated Church* is a critique of Catholicism as it existed during the 1960s. In the controversial 1967 bestseller, says John Leo in the *New York Times Book Review,* Kavanaugh "argues that [Catholic] ideals have been frozen into law, abstractions have been given primacy over persons, arbitrary traditions (such as compulsory clerical celibacy) have trampled the uniqueness of the individual, and produced misery and guilt on a systematic basis."

A *Time* reviewer feels that "many Catholics who hope and pray for renewal may have cause to suspect that Kavanaugh's angry and oversimplified criticism can only hurt rather than help the forces of change within the church." But in the opinion of C. M. Smith in *Christian Century,* "the book is highly readable and liberally laced with illustrative case histories, and it has a force and impact that is almost physical. Fr. Kavanaugh does not write with sweet reasonableness, but then neither did Luther. And, like Luther, he insists he is interested not in destroying the church but in saving it."

Daniel Callahan agrees in the *Saturday Review* that Kavanaugh "undeniably loves the Church. His denunciation is expressive more of a priest unable to bear the discrepancy between Christian ideal and Catholic reality than of a man trying to evaluate the Church dispassionately. For just that reason Father Kavanaugh's book has a compelling power. It cuts not only through the pretensions of an antiquated Church, but also through the Church of Vatican II.'' As Callahan states, Kavanaugh ''symbolizes the real drama of reform.'' Shortly after completing his book, Kavanaugh left the priesthood.

A Modern Priest Looks at His Outdated Church was followed by other Kavanaugh works, including several volumes of poetry and *The Birth of God,* which the author describes to *CA* as a challenge to contemporary religious myths. In 1972, Kavanaugh recorded poems from his book *There Are Men Too Gentle to Live among Wolves.* Released by Karo, the recording features an original score by Elmer Bernstein.

AVOCATIONAL INTERESTS: Tennis, golf, and the theatre.

BIOGRAPHICAL/CRITICAL SOURCES:

BOOKS

Kavanaugh, James J., *A Modern Priest Looks at His Outdated Church,* Trident, 1967.
Kavanaugh, James J., *Search: A Guide For Those Who Dare to Ask of Life Everything Good and Beautiful,* Harper, 1985.

PERIODICALS

Best Sellers, July 1, 1967.
Christian Century, August 2, 1967.
Christian Science Monitor, July 6, 1967.
Commonweal, July 28, 1967.
Critic, August, 1976.
Los Angeles Times, November 7, 1980.
New York Times Book Review, July 30, 1967.
Saturday Review, July 29, 1967.
Time, July 7, 1967.
Washington Post, May 14, 1967.

*   *   *

KELLER, Beverly (Lou)
(B. L. Harwick)

PERSONAL: Born in San Francisco, Calif.; daughter of Wearne E. and Ruth (Burke) Harwick; married William Jon Keller, June 18, 1949 (died, 1964); children: Lisa, Kristen, Michele. *Education:* University of California, Berkeley, B.A., 1950.

ADDRESSES: Home—Davis, Calif. *Agent*—Edite Kroll, 31 E. 31st St., 2E, New York, N.Y. 10016.

CAREER: Author, newspaper columnist, and feature writer.

AWARDS, HONORS: Harcourt, Brace & World fellow, University of Colorado, 1969; ''Best Book'' citation from the *School Library Journal,* for *Fiona's Bee* and *No Beasts! No Children!;* American Library Association ''Notable Book'' citation, 1981, for *The Sea Watch;* ''Pick of the Lists'' citation from *American Bookseller,* for *A Small, Elderly Dragon.*

WRITINGS:

ADULT FICTION

The Baghdad Defections (novel), Bobbs-Merrill, 1973.

JUVENILE FICTION

Fiona's Bee (Junior Literary Guild selection), Coward, 1975.
The Beetle Bush (Junior Literary Guild selection), Coward, 1976.

Don't Throw Another One, Dover!, Coward, 1976.
(Under name B. L. Harwick) *The Frog Prints,* Raintree Editions, 1976.
The Genuine, Ingenious Thrift Shop Genie, Clarissa Mae Bean and Me, Coward, 1977.
Pimm's Place (Junior Literary Guild selection), Coward, 1978.
The Sea Watch, Four Winds Press, 1980.
Fiona's Flea (Junior Literary Guild selection), Coward, 1981.
The Bee Sneeze (Junior Literary Guild selection), Coward, 1982.
My Awful Cousin Norbert, Lothrop, 1982.
No Beasts! No Children!, Lothrop, 1983.
A Small, Elderly Dragon, Lothrop, 1984.
When Mother Got the Flu (Junior Literary Guild selection), Coward, 1984.
A Garden of Love to Share, Parker Brothers, 1984.
Rosebud, with Fangs, Lothrop, 1985.
Hide and Seek, Scott, Foresman, 1985.
Animal Trackers, Lothrop, 1986.

CONTRIBUTOR TO ANTHOLOGIES

Edward Ferman, editor, *The Best from Fantasy and Science Fiction,* Doubleday, 1974.

OTHER

Author of column for *Hayward Review;* contributor to ''Rose Petal Place,'' a television special, 1984. Contributor of short stories to *Atlantic, Fantasy and Science Fiction, Cosmopolitan,* and other magazines, and of articles and reviews to *San Francisco Chronicle, Atlantic, Women's News Service, Rome Daily American, California Mental Health News,* and Peninsula Newspapers, Inc.

WORK IN PROGRESS: A novel.

SIDELIGHTS: Beverly Keller has lived in Baghdad, Beirut, and Rome and has travelled throughout Europe.

AVOCATIONAL INTERESTS: Politics and animals' rights.

BIOGRAPHICAL/CRITICAL SOURCES:

PERIODICALS

Chicago Tribune Book World, June 9, 1985.
Washington Post Book World, May 13, 1984.

*   *   *

KEMPHER, Ruth Moon   1934-

PERSONAL: Born January 23, 1934, in Red Bank, N.J.; daughter of Leslie Guy (employed in public relations) and Bella (Kruskol) Moon; married Joseph Henry Kempher (president of Kem-San, Inc.), June 23, 1951 (divorced, 1971). *Education:* Attended Purdue University Extension; Flagler College, B.A., 1972; Emory University, M.A., 1976.

ADDRESSES: P.O. Box 2224, St. Augustine, Fla. 32084.

CAREER: Writer. Instructor at St. Johns River Community College. Part owner of White Lion Tavern, 1965-72.

WRITINGS:

The White Guitar (poetry), Olivant, 1967.
Carnival at Seaside (poetry), South & West, 1968.
Porpoise in the Beer (poetry), Olivant, 1970.
The Carnal Musings of Sylvia Savage, Windless Orchard, 1980.
Three Ring Circus: Poems from a Life, Plumbers Ink, 1982.

Also author of a novel, *Jeremiah and the Blue Motel*, published serially in *Weid*. Contributor of more than 400 poems to magazines and anthologies.

BIOGRAPHICAL/CRITICAL SOURCES:

PERIODICALS

Florida Educational Journal, December, 1966.†

*   *   *

KERSLAKE, Susan   1943-

PERSONAL: Born April 20, 1943, in Chicago, Ill.; daughter of Youart (a lawyer) and Martha E. (a teacher; maiden name, Muckley) Kerslake. *Education:* Attended Montana State University, 1960-61, and Beloit College, 1961.

ADDRESSES: Home—5713 Victoria Rd., Halifax, Nova Scotia, Canada B3H 2Y3.

CAREER: Kroch's and Brentano's Bookstore, Chicago, Ill., sales clerk, 1962-66; Dalhousie University, Halifax, Nova Scotia, library assistant, 1966-73, archives apprentice at Medical Library, 1972-73; St. Joseph's Children's Centre, Halifax, child care worker, 1974-79; affiliated with child life department of I.W.K. Hospital for Children, 1980—.

MEMBER: Writers Union of Canada, Writers Federation of Nova Scotia.

WRITINGS:

Middlewatch (magic-realism adult novel), Oberon Press, 1976.
Penumbra (novel), Aya Press, 1984.
The Book of Fears (short stories), Ragweed Press, 1984.

WORK IN PROGRESS: An untitled novel.

SIDELIGHTS: Susan Kerslake told *CA:* "Having begun writing when I was five years old, I feel that it is just what I do: living one life on a level that is unlike another one, that shows; thinking about things on paper, though story and impression, mood and word are what emerge. Achievement is personal, as I do not seem to begin a book with anything particular to say, but rather find out myself, as the book progresses (admitting to unconsciousness!). I tend to work in the evening, it being a time when distractions cease, and, of course, indulge in the little rituals that accompany the descent into blessed solitude and isolation. Always, the writing itself is the best part.

"I am influenced by anyone who loves words (some favorite authors: Joyce Carol Oates, Loren Eiseley, Christopher Fry, Dylan Thomas, Norman Cousins, Sylvia Ashton-Warner, Toni Morrison, Mark Helprin). My advice to anyone who wants to write is simply to do so, and read. The current 'scene' is discouraging to me, but not everyone is being lost. Lofty age of goals, courtesy of Robinson Jeffers: '. . . for to equal a need / Is natural, animal, mineral: but to fling / Rainbows over the rain. . . .'"

AVOCATIONAL INTERESTS: "Making stuff," being with children, Gund bears.

BIOGRAPHICAL/CRITICAL SOURCES:

PERIODICALS

Toronto Globe & Mail, June 1, 1985.

KILBY, Peter   1935-

PERSONAL: Born May 4, 1935, in Buffalo, N.Y.; married, 1960; children: three. *Education:* Harvard University, B.A., 1957; Johns Hopkins University, M.A., 1959; Oxford University, D.Phil., 1967.

ADDRESSES: Office—Department of Economics, Wesleyan University, Middletown, Conn. 06457.

CAREER: Agency for International Development, industrial economist in Nigeria, 1960-62; Wesleyan University, Middletown, Conn., assistant professor, 1965-69, associate professor, 1970-75, professor of economics, 1976—, co-chairman of College of Social Studies, 1969-72, chairman, 1982-85. Consultant to International Labor Organization, Geneva and West Africa, 1964, Agency for International Development, Washington, D.C., 1966, U.S. State Department, 1967, National Investment Bank, Accra, Ghana, 1968, Innotech, 1973, Economic Planning Unit, Government of Malaysia, 1975, and World Bank, 1978-82. Senior advisor, ILO World Employment Programme, Geneva, 1975-76. Manuscript consultant to numerous university presses and publishers, including Cambridge University Press and W. W. Norton.

AWARDS, HONORS: Fulbright research fellowship in Nigeria, 1959-60; foreign area fellow at St. Antony's College, Oxford University, 1962-65; senior fellow, East-West Center, Hawaii, 1973.

WRITINGS:

African Enterprise: The Nigerian Bread Industry, Hoover Institution, Stanford University, 1965.
Technical Education in Nigeria, 1945-65: A Critical Survey, Office of Program Coordination, United States Agency for International Development, 1966.
Industrialization in an Open Economy: Nigeria, 1945-1966, Cambridge University Press, 1969.
(Editor) *Entrepreneurship and Economic Development*, Free Press, 1970.
(With Bruce Johnston) *Agricultural Strategies, Rural-Urban Interactions and the Expansion of Income Opportunities*, Organization for Economic Cooperation and Development (Paris), 1973.
(With Johnston) *Agriculture and Structural Transformation: Economic Strategies in Late-Developing Countries*, Oxford University Press, 1975.
Small Scale Industry in Kenya, Off-Farm Employment Project, 1982.

Author of reports on economics and industry. Contributor of articles and reviews to periodicals, including *Economic Journal, Quarterly Journal of Economics, Commonweal, New Leader, Choice, Journal of Developing Areas,* and *West Africa*. Manuscript consultant to journals, including *Journal of Developing Areas* and *Journal of Economic Inquiry*.

WORK IN PROGRESS: Benefit-Cost Analyses of Microenterprise Promotion; The Impact of Oil Revenues on OPEC Economies.

*   *   *

KINGMAN, Russ   1917-

PERSONAL: Born August 8, 1917, in Ferrisburg, Vt.; son of Ray A. (a milk plant manager) and Lucy (Kimball) Kingman; married Winifred Harris, November 1, 1941. *Education:* Baylor University, B.A., 1952, M.A., 1955; further graduate study at San Francisco State University, 1961-63. *Politics:* ''Best qualified.''

ADDRESSES: Home and office—14300 Arnold Dr., Glen Ellen, Calif. 95442.

CAREER: U.S. Navy, 1935-49, acting chaplain at Naval Air Station, Alameda, Calif., 1940, catapult chief at Naval Aircraft Factory, Philadelphia, Pa., 1942-43, chief master-at-arms at Tacoma Receiving Barracks, Tacoma, Wash., 1943, Pierce County deputy fire chief, Tacoma, 1944, aviation chief machinist's mate on U.S.S. *Currituck*, 1945, photographic chief of the Marianas Islands, 1946-47, fire marshal of the Marianas Islands, 1946-48, island fire chief on Guam, 1946-48, chief-in-charge of Link trainers at Naval Air Station, Alameda, 1948, fire chief of Naval Air Station, Pensacola, Fla., 1948-49, left service as aviation chief machinist's mate; ordained Southern Baptist minister, 1949; pastor of Southern Baptist churches in Millview and Bellview, Fla., and in Cego, Cottonwood, and Waco, Tex., 1949-61; Sears, Roebuck & Co., Inc., San Rafael, Calif., in outside sales, 1961-62; Wyckoff & Associates Advertising Agency, San Francisco, Calif., account executive, 1963-68; Russ Kingman Advertising, Oakland, Calif., owner, 1968-73; Jack London Bookstore and Research Center, Glen Ellen, Calif., owner, 1971—. Executive director of Jack London Foundations, Inc., 1971—. Lecturer at schools, churches, and clubs.

MEMBER: Jack London Square Association (executive director, 1968-72), Veterans of Foreign Wars, American Legion, Western Writers of America.

WRITINGS:

(Editor and author of introduction) Jack London, *The Valley of the Moon,* Peregrine Press, 1976.
(Editor and author of introduction) *Jack London: Tales of the North,* Castle Books, 1979.
(Editor and author of introduction) *Jack London: Stories of Adventure,* Castle Books, 1980.
A Pictorial Life of Jack London, Crown, 1980.
(Editor and author of introduction) *The Best of Jack London,* Castle Books, 1984.
(Editor) *A Collector's Guide to Jack London First Editions,* Jack London Bookstore and Research Center, 1985.
(Editor) *A Collector's Guide to Jack London First Appearances,* Jack London Bookstore and Research Center, 1985.
(Editor) *A Collector's Guide to Jack London's Non-Fictional Work,* Jack London Bookstore and Research Center, 1985.
(Editor and author of introduction) Jack London, *''War,''* Jack London Bookstore and Research Center, 1985.
(Editor and author of foreword) *Jack London: A Trilogy,* Jack London Bookstore and Research Center, 1985.

Contributor to newspapers and magazines, including *Air California, Jack London Newsletter, Jack London Echoes, Jack London Update, Pacific Historian,* and *Pacific Islands Monthly.*

WORK IN PROGRESS: Wolf: A Biography of Jack London; Jack London: The Agnostic Christian Atheist; The Crowd; Jack London's ''The Heathen''; Jack London's Klondike Adventures; Jack London's South Sea Adventures; a completion of the book Jack London was working on at the time of his death, *Cherry.*

SIDELIGHTS: Russ Kingman told *CA:* ''The majority of my work is in the Jack London field. For many years I deplored the fact that nearly everything written about Jack London was poorly researched and loaded with errors and misconceptions

of the life and work of Jack London. None of the nineteen biographies of Jack London were reliable so I have dedicated my life and work to the task of 'putting the record straight.' These errors have crept into encyclopedias, textbooks and articles in magazines and newspapers.

''I lecture all over the United States on Jack London and other Western authors (mainly from the San Francisco area). My literary work stems from the influence of Irving Stone's *Sailor on Horseback* and London's *Martin Eden.*

''In 1969 I led an expedition to the Klondike to bring back the cabin in which Jack London lived during the gold rush. In 1970 I followed his trail in London, England. In 1979 I retraced his 1911 farm horse trip to Oregon and in 1980 researched London in Australia and Hawaii. My motivation is to give Jack London the place in the world that his life and works deserve.

''From my first reading of *Sailor on Horseback* in 1968 to the present day, I have been constantly researching the life and works of Jack London. During this period I have been utterly amazed that none of the London biographers were willing to adequately research before sitting down to write. As a result, the world has been unable to know the real Jack London. For instance, one leading biography had over two hundred errors, and a recent biography was a vicious caricature of him and so poorly researched that I wondered who the author was talking about.

''I started writing only after having read everything available by or about Jack London and amassing a cross-indexed, thirty-five-thousand-card file on his life and work. This research will also be used for my books now in progress on London, his times and his friends. It is my firm belief that an author of biographies owes his subject and his descendants an honest portrayal. And this requires a lot of 'dig,' as London put it.

''Jack London is still the most popular American writer in the world, but paradoxically he is the most neglected major American writer in his own country. However, American scholars are now beginning to rediscover London's work and courses on Jack London are now being taught in many schools, colleges and universities in the United States. Professors have discovered that student interest in Jack London courses is intense. The most interesting books being taught are *Martin Eden, The Call of the Wild, The Sea-Wolf, Before Adam, The People of the Abyss, The Star Rover,* and *White Fang*—all classics of American literature.''

BIOGRAPHICAL/CRITICAL SOURCES:

PERIODICALS

American Collector, April, 1980.
Antique Trader, June 14, 1978.
Baylor Line, June, 1974.
Buffalo Evening News, March 31, 1980.
Hobbies, January, 1974.
Los Angeles Times, February 13, 1980.
Milwaukee Journal, April 1, 1980.
Norfolk Virginian-Pilot, April 1, 1980.
Sacramento Bee, March 30, 1980.
St. Louis Globe-Democrat, April 2, 1980.
Saturday Evening Post, December, 1976.
Sonoma Index Tribune, April 30, 1980.
Sunday Oregonian, March 30, 1980.
Vallejo Times Herald, March 27, 1980.
Vancouver Sun, April 3, 1980.

KLEIN, Herbert Sanford 1936-

PERSONAL: Born January 6, 1936, in New York, N.Y.; son of Emil A. and Florence (Friedman) Klein; married Harriet E. Manelis (an anthropologist), September 3, 1956; children: Rachel, Daniel, Jacob. *Education:* University of Chicago, A.B., 1957, M.A., 1959, Ph.D., 1963.

ADDRESSES: Home—157 Ames Ave., Leonia, N.J. 07605. *Office*—Department of History, Columbia University, New York, N.Y. 10027.

CAREER: University of Chicago, Chicago, Ill., instructor, 1962-63, assistant professor, 1963-67, associate professor of history, 1967-69; Columbia University, New York, N.Y., associate professor, 1969-71, professor of history, 1971—.

MEMBER: Conference on Latin American History.

AWARDS, HONORS: Henry L. and Grace Doherty fellow in Bolivia, 1960-61; Fulbright grant for Bolivia, summer, 1963; Social Science Research Council fellow in Spain, 1964-65, 1971-72; Ford Foundation fellow in Argentina and Brazil, 1965-67; American Council of Learned Societies fellow, 1973; grants from National Science Foundation, 1974-76; grant from National Endowment for the Humanities, 1975-77; grant from Tinker, 1975-77; Simon F. Guggenheim fellow, 1980-81; Woodrow Wilson fellow at Smithsonian Institution, 1980-81; senior Fulbright lecturer at Hebrew University, Jerusalem, 1983.

WRITINGS:

Slavery in the Americas: A Comparative Study of Cuba and Virginia, University of Chicago Press, 1967.
Parties and Political Change in Bolivia, 1880-1952, Cambridge University Press, 1970.
The Middle Passage: Comparative Studies in the Atlantic Slave Trade, Princeton University Press, 1978.
(With J. Kelley) *Revolution and the Rebirth of Inequality: A Theory Applied to the National Revolution of Bolivia,* University of California Press, 1981.
Bolivia: The Evolution of a Multi-Ethnic Society, Oxford University Press, 1982.
(With J. TePaske) *Royal Treasures of the Spanish Empire in America, 1580-1825,* three volumes, Duke University Press, 1982.

Contributor of numerous articles and reviews to professional journals.

*   *   *

KLEJMENT, Anne M. 1950-

PERSONAL: Surname is pronounced *Klem*-ment; born April 27, 1950, in Rochester, N.Y.; daughter of Z. Henry (a coremaker) and Alice (Wegner) Klejment. *Education:* Nazareth College of Rochester, B.A. (cum laude), 1972; State University of New York at Binghamton, M.A., 1974, Ph.D., 1981.

ADDRESSES: Home—St. Paul, Minn. *Office*—Department of History, Box 4188, College of St. Thomas, St. Paul, Minn. 55105.

CAREER: State University of New York at Binghamton, lecturer in history, 1975; Vassar College, Poughkeepsie, N.Y., instructor in history, 1978-79; State University of New York College at New Paltz, instructor in innovative studies program, summer, 1979; Cornell University, Ithaca, N.Y., administra-

tor of historians-in-residence program at New York Historical Resources Center, 1979-81; State University of New York College at Plattsburgh, visiting assistant professor, 1981-82, assistant professor of history and coordinator of women's studies, 1982-83; College of St. Thomas, St. Paul, Minn., assistant professor of history, 1983—. Affiliated with Center for the Study of American Catholicism at University of Notre Dame.

MEMBER: Organization of American Historians, American Society of Church Historians, U.S. Catholic Historical Society, American Catholic Historical Association, Radical Historians Association, Immigration Historical Society, Women Historians of the Midwest (WHOM).

WRITINGS:

The Berrigans: A Bibliography of Published Writings of Daniel, Philip, and Elizabeth McAlister Berrigan, Garland Publishing, 1979.
Dorothy Day and "The Catholic Worker": A Bibliography and Index, Garland Publishing, 1986.
(Contributor) Charles DeBenedetti, editor, *Peace Heroes in Twentieth-Century America,* Indiana University Press, 1986.

Contributor to journals.

WORK IN PROGRESS: Dorothy Day and the Vietnam War; The Nonviolence of Dorothy Day; "The Catholic Worker" and the Berrigans.

SIDELIGHTS: Anne M. Klejment told *CA* that her major interests include U.S. Catholic social history, women and work, and the Vietnam-era peace protests. She added, "Radical Catholic movements of the 1930s to the 1960s in the United States have been fueled in part by a determination to restore the church of the apostles."

*   *   *

KLIMA, Ivan 1931-

PERSONAL: Born September 14, 1931, in Prague, Czechoslovakia; son of Ing Vilem and Marta (Synkova) Klima; married Helena Mala (a sociologist), September 24, 1958; children: Michal, Hana. *Education:* Graduate of Charles University.

ADDRESSES: Agent—Dilia, Vysehradska 28, Prague 2, Czechoslovakia.

CAREER: Writer. Ceskoslovensky Spisovatel (publishers), Prague, Czechoslovakia, editor, 1959-63; *Literarni noviny* (weekly publication of Union of Writers), Prague, editor, 1963-69; University of Michigan, Ann Arbor, visiting professor, 1969-70.

MEMBER: Union of Writers (member of central committee), P.E.N.

AWARDS, HONORS: Awards from Ministry of Culture, 1960, 1965, and from Ceskoslovensky Spisovatel, 1963.

WRITINGS:

Mezi tremi hranicemi (book on Slovakia), Ceskoslovensky Spisovatel (Prague), 1960.
Bezvadny den (short stories; title means "The Wonderful Day"), Ceskoslovensky Spisovatel, 1962.
Karel Chapek (essay), Ceskoslovensky Spisovatel, 1962.
Hodina ticha (fiction; title means "The Hour of Silence"), Ceskoslovensky Spisovatel, 1963.

Milenci na jednu noc (short stories; title means "Lovers for One Night"), Ceskoslovensky Spisovatel, 1964.
Ein Schloss, Baerenreiter-Verlag, 1969.
Lod jmenem nadeje, Ceskoslovensky Spisovatel, 1969, translation by Edith Pargeter published as *A Ship Named Hope,* Gollancz, 1970.
Milostne leto, Sixty-Eight Publishers, 1973.
Ma vesela jitra, Sixty-Eight Publishers, 1979, translation by George Theiner published as *My Merry Mornings: Stories from Prague,* Readers International, 1985.

PLAYS

"Zamek," first produced in Prague, Czechoslovakia, at Theatre Na Vinohradech, 1964, produced as "The Castle" in Ann Arbor, Mich., at Lydia Mendelssohn Theatre, University of Michigan, December 3, 1968, produced for television in Austria, Finland, and the Netherlands.
"Porota," first produced in Prague, April 17, 1969, adaptation for radio produced by NDR Radio, West Germany, English radio version produced by the BBC, London, England, 1970.
"Zenich pro Marcelu," translation by Ruth Willard first produced Off-Broadway at La Mama Experimental Theatre Club, spring, 1969, produced for television in Austria and West Germany.
"Klara," translation by Willard first produced Off-Broadway at La Mama Experimental Theatre Club, spring, 1969, produced for television in Austria and West Germany.

Also author of play "Cukrarna Myriam" (title means "Sweetshop Myriam").

AVOCATIONAL INTERESTS: Lawn tennis, picking mushrooms.

BIOGRAPHICAL/CRITICAL SOURCES:

BOOKS

Kienzle: *Modernes Welttheatre,* Kroner Verlag, 1966.

PERIODICALS

Los Angeles Times, June 19, 1985.
Times Literary Supplement, July 5, 1985.†

*   *   *

KNIGHT, Damon (Francis) 1922-
(Donald Laverty, a joint pseudonym)

PERSONAL: Born September 19, 1922, in Baker, Ore.; son of Frederick Stuart (a high school principal) and Leola LaDorie (a teacher; maiden name, Damon) Knight; married Gertrud Werndl; married Helen Schlaz; married Kate Wilhelm (a writer), February 23, 1963; children: Valerie, Christopher, Leslie; (third marriage) Jonathan. *Education:* Attended high school in Hood River, Ore.; attended Salem WPA Art Center, Salem, Ore., 1940-41.

ADDRESSES: Home—1645 Horn Lane, Eugene, Ore. 97404.

CAREER: Science fiction writer and editor. Assistant editor, Popular Publications, 1943-44, 1949-50; Milford Science Fiction Writers' Conference, co-founder, 1956, director, 1956-76; visiting lecturer, Clarion Workshop, 1968—; adjunct professor, Michigan State University, 1979.

MEMBER: Science Fiction Writers of America (founding president, 1965-67).

AWARDS, HONORS: Hugo Award from World Science Fiction Convention, 1956, for best science fiction criticism; Pilgrim Award, 1975, for contributions to science fiction; Jupiter Award, 1976, for short story "I See You."

WRITINGS:

NOVELS

Hell's Pavement, Lion Press, 1955, published as *Analogue Men,* Berkley Publishing, 1962, reprinted under original title, Avon, 1980.
Masters of Evolution, Ace Books, 1959.
The People Maker, Zenith Books, 1959, published as *A for Anything,* Berkley Publishing, 1965, reprinted, Avon, 1980.
The Sun Saboteurs (bound with *The Light of Lilith* by Wallis G. McDonald), Ace Books, 1961.
Beyond the Barrier, Doubleday, 1964.
Mind Switch, Berkley Publishing, 1965, published as *The Other Foot,* Whiting & Wheaton, 1965, M-B Publishing, 1971.
The Rithian Terror, Ace Books, 1965.
Three Novels: Rule Golden, Natural State, [and] *The Dying Man,* Doubleday, 1967.
The World and Thorinn, Berkley Publishing, 1981.
The Man in the Tree, Berkley Publishing, 1984.
CV, Tor Books, 1985.

SHORT STORY COLLECTIONS

Far Out: 13 Science Fiction Stories, Simon & Schuster, 1961.
In Deep, Berkley Publishing, 1963.
Off Center: A Scintillating Science Fiction Collection, Ace Books, 1965.
Turning On: Thirteen Stories, Doubleday, 1966 (published in England as *Turning On: Fourteen Stories,* Gollancz, 1967).
World without Children [and] *The Earth Quarter,* Lancer Books, 1970.
The Best of Damon Knight, Pocket Books, 1974.
Rule Golden and Other Stories, Avon, 1979.
(With wife, Kate Wilhelm) *Better Than One,* New England Science Fiction Association, 1980.

EDITOR OF ANTHOLOGIES

A Century of Science Fiction, Simon & Schuster, 1962.
First Flight, Lancer Books, 1963, published as *Now Begins Tomorrow,* 1969.
A Century of Great Short Science Fiction Novels, Dial, 1964.
A Century of Great Science Fiction Novels, Delacorte, 1964.
Tomorrow x 4, Fawcett, 1964.
The Shape of Things, Popular Library, 1965.
(And translator) *Thirteen French Science-Fiction Stories,* Bantam, 1965.
The Dark Side, Doubleday, 1965.
Beyond Tomorrow: Ten Science Fiction Adventures, Harper, 1965.
Cities of Wonder, Doubleday, 1966.
Nebula Award Stories 1965, Doubleday, 1966.
Worlds to Come: Nine Science Fiction Adventures, Harper, 1967.
Science Fiction Inventions, Lancer Books, 1967.
Toward Infinity: Nine Science Fiction Tales, Simon & Schuster, 1968 (published in England as *Towards Infinity: Nine Science Fiction Adventures,* Gollancz, 1970).
One Hundred Years of Science Fiction, Simon & Schuster, 1968.
The Metal Smile, Belmont Books, 1968.

Dimension X: Five Science Fiction Novellas, Simon & Schuster, 1970 (published in England as *Elsewhere x 3,* Coronet, 1974).

First Contact, Pinnacle Books, 1971.

(And contributor) *A Pocketful of Stars,* Doubleday, 1971.

Perchance to Dream, Doubleday, 1972.

A Science Fiction Argosy, Simon & Schuster, 1972.

Tomorrow and Tomorrow: Ten Tales of the Future, Simon & Schuster, 1973.

A Shocking Thing, Pocket Books, 1974.

The Golden Road, Simon & Schuster, 1974.

Happy Endings: 15 Stories by the Masters of the Macabre, Bobbs-Merrill, 1974.

Best Stories from Orbit, Volumes 1-10, Putnam, 1975.

Science Fiction of the Thirties, Bobbs-Merrill, 1975.

Westerns of the Forties, Bobbs-Merrill, 1977.

(And contributor) *Turning Points: Essays on the Art of Science Fiction,* Harper, 1977.

Western Classics from the Great Pulps, Barnes & Noble, 1978.

(With Martin H. Greenberg and Joseph D. Olander) *First Voyages,* Avon, 1981.

The Clarion Awards, Doubleday, 1984.

EDITOR OF "ORBIT" ANTHOLOGY SERIES

Orbit 1, Putnam, 1966.

Orbit 2, Putnam, 1967.

Orbit 3, Putnam, 1968.

Orbit 4, Putnam, 1968.

Orbit 5, Putnam, 1969.

Orbit 6, Putnam, 1970.

Orbit 7, Putnam, 1970.

Orbit 8, Putnam, 1970.

Orbit 9, Putnam, 1971.

Orbit 10, Putnam, 1972.

Orbit 11, Putnam, 1972.

Orbit 12, Putnam, 1973.

Orbit 13, Putnam, 1974.

Orbit 14, Harper, 1974.

Orbit 15, Harper, 1974.

Orbit 16, Harper, 1975.

Orbit 17, Harper, 1975.

Orbit 18, Harper, 1976.

Orbit 19, Harper, 1977.

Orbit 20, Harper, 1978.

Orbit 21, Harper, 1980.

OTHER

In Search of Wonder: Essays on Modern Science Fiction, Advent Publishing, 1956, 2nd edition, 1967.

(Translator) Rene Barjavel, *Ashes, Ashes,* Doubleday, 1967.

Charles Fort: Prophet of the Unexplained (biography), Doubleday, 1970.

The Futurians (biography), John Day, 1977.

Creating Short Fiction, Writers Digest, 1981.

Editor, *Worlds Beyond,* 1950-51, and *If,* 1958-59; book editor, *Science Fiction Adventures,* 1953-54, and *Magazine of Fantasy and Science Fiction,* 1959-60; founding editor, *Science Fiction Writers of America Bulletin,* 1965-67.

SIDELIGHTS: A writer, editor, translator, and critic, Damon Knight is best known for his well-informed, intelligent reviews of science-fiction literature. In fact, Knight is described as the "inventor of serious science fiction criticism" in *The Issue at Hand,* written by James Blish under the pseudonym William Atheling, Jr. "If it's decent criticism of science fiction that we're looking for," Blish maintains, "there is at the moment only one place to find it within our microcosm: in the book reviews of Damon Knight." Blish expands upon the historical impact of Knight's criticism in *More Issues at Hand,* indicating that his work promptly made the "mutual-admiration-society or notice-of-availability kind of review look fatuous, and encouraged several other practitioners toward greater severity."

Along with his reviews, Knight's book *In Search of Wonder: Essays on Modern Science Fiction,* is "generally considered a classic," according to Spider Robinson in *Analog.* He adds that it is "one of the most stimulating and provocative books about SF I've ever read." Blish elaborates in *More Issues at Hand* on the power of *In Search of Wonder,* calling it "a useful book for both scholar and practitioner." "But its virtues do not end there," he observes. "In addition, it is so frequently funny, and the engaging personality of its author so unreservedly informs every page of it, that it might well delight readers who have never encountered a line by any of the writers Knight examines."

"Science fiction is a field of literature worth taking seriously," Knight comments in *In Search of Wonder.* He feels that it should be judged as is mainstream fiction: by the quality of the prose as well as the plot. However, he realizes that his views are often not shared by many readers. "I was interested to find out that a lot of science-fiction fans are aware of what I call literary value, but they don't *want* that in science-fiction," Knight told Charles Platt in *Dream Makers.* "They don't want prose that demands close attention, they want something they can read carelessly and quickly, for what you call 'the story.' It would actually annoy them if the same story were written very carefully . . . because it would slow them down, make them pay more attention to the sentences and phrases than they want to." In spite of this propensity in readers, he writes in *In Search of Wonder:* "It is clear that science fiction has gone through more than half a century of concentrated development . . . in the ghetto world created by publishers. . . . There are some indications that it is now emerging from this microcosm into the mainstream." Deborah Schneider Greenhut concludes in the *Dictionary of Literary Biography* that Knight is a "persistent advocate of [science-fiction] literature."

AVOCATIONAL INTERESTS: Cooking, travel.

BIOGRAPHICAL/CRITICAL SOURCES:

BOOKS

Aldiss, Brian W., and Harry Harrison, editors, *Hell's Cartographers: Some Personal Histories of Science Fiction Writers,* Harper, 1976.

Amis, Kingsley, *New Maps of Hell: A Survey of Science Fiction,* Harcourt, 1960.

Atheling, William, Jr., *The Issue at Hand,* Advent, 1964.

Atheling, William, Jr., *More Issues at Hand,* Advent, 1970.

Davenport, Basil, editor, *The Science Fiction Novel: Imagination and Social Criticism,* Advent, 1959.

Dictionary of Literary Biography, Volume VIII: *Twentieth-Century American Science Fiction Writers,* Gale, 1981.

Knight, Damon, *In Search of Wonder: Essays in Modern Science Fiction,* Advent, 1956.

Platt, Charles, *Dream Makers: The Uncommon People Who Write Science Fiction,* Volume I, Berkley Publishing, 1980.

PERIODICALS

Amazing Stories, August, 1961.

America, April 23, 1977.
Analog, June, 1964, November, 1979.
Books and Bookmen, June, 1972, September, 1973.
Galaxy, September, 1955.
Luna Monthly, April/May, 1972.
Magazine of Fantasy and Science Fiction, November, 1964, December, 1967.
National Review, March 10, 1970, January 19, 1973.
New Worlds, January, 1965.
New York Times Book Review, November 14, 1965, April 24, 1977.
Science Fiction Review, October, 1970, November/December, 1978.
Times Literary Supplement, June 11, 1971, October 13, 1972, March 7, 1975, August 30, 1985.
Washington Post Book World, March 22, 1981, March 25, 1984.

*   *   *

KNIGHT, G(ilfred) Norman   1891-1978

PERSONAL: Born September 12, 1891, in England; died August 17, 1978; son of William Frederick and Annie Louise (Adams) Knight. *Education:* Attended Bradfield College; Balliol College, Oxford, B.A., 1913, M.A., 1920. *Politics:* Tory. *Religion:* Church of England.

ADDRESSES: Home—Scio House, Portsmouth Rd., Roehampton, London SW15 3TD, England. *Agent*—Russell Stevens, 177 Bedford Hill, London SW12, England.

CAREER: Called to the Bar, Lincoln's Inn, London, England, 1918. West India Committee, Inc., London, assistant secretary, 1919-27, 1938-39; tutor to Alfred Duggan (later the novelist), son of Marchioness Curzon, on world tour, 1927; tutor and guardian to Heir Apparent of Rapur, Uttar Pradesh, India, 1931; civil servant in British Censorship Office, London, 1939-42, and British War Office, London, 1942-56. Secretary to West Indian and Atlantic Group, British Empire Exhibition, 1923, 1924, and to Company of London, 1927. *Military service:* British Army, World War I; served with East Surrey Regiment in France, 1915; severely wounded at Battle of Loos; instructor and adjutant with Officer Cadet Battalion, 1917-18; on Judge Advocate General's staff, 1918-19; became captain.

MEMBER: National Book League, Society of Indexers (founder and secretary, 1957; chairman, 1962; vice-president, 1966; president, 1970-78), Freemasons, Balliol Society, Oxford Society, Civil Service Club, Hastings Chess Club, Barnet Chess Club (honorary life president, 1972).

AWARDS, HONORS: Wheatley Gold Medal, Library Association, for outstanding index of 1967, for his index to Volume II of *Winston S. Churchill;* Carey Award, Society of Indexers, 1977.

WRITINGS:

Chess Pieces: An Anthology, Low, 1949, 2nd edition, Chess Magazine, 1968.
(With Fred Lomax Pick) *The Pocket History of Freemasonry,* Muller, 1953, 7th edition, revised by Frederick Smyth, 1983.
(With Pick) *The Freemason's Pocket Reference Book,* Muller, 1955, 7th edition, revised by Smyth, 1983.
(Editor) *Training in Indexing: A Course of the Society of Indexers,* M.I.T. Press, 1969.

(With Will Guy) *King, Queen and Knight: A Chess Anthology,* Batsford, 1975.
Indexing, The Art of: A Guide to the Indexing of Books and Periodicals, Allen & Unwin, 1979.

Also author with R. Stevens of *Modern Outlandish Proverbs,* 1977, and with Frederick Smyth of *The Pocket Cyclopedia of Freemasonry,* 1978. Compiler of indexes to about 150 books and periodicals. Contributor to *Balliol College Record;* also contributor of articles and reviews to periodicals and newspapers, including *West Indies Chronicle, Masonic Record,* and *Indexer.*

SIDELIGHTS: G. Norman Knight wrote: "My belief is that virtually no work of nonfiction is complete without an index (a good one), while many classical novels (e.g. Don Quixote, and the works of Dickens, Thackeray, and Mark Twain) are greatly improved by this useful adjunct."

AVOCATIONAL INTERESTS: Chess, book reviewing.†

*   *   *

KNOPF, Terry Ann   1940-

PERSONAL: Born in 1940 in New York, N.Y.; daughter of Albert A. (a physician) and Irene (Kaufman) Knopf. *Education:* Queens College of the City University of New York, B.A., 1962; Harvard University, M.A., 1963. *Politics:* Independent. *Religion:* None.

ADDRESSES: Home—205 Walden St., Apt. 5L, Cambridge, Mass. 02140.

CAREER: Curriculum specialist, Educational Development Corp., 1963-65; research coordinator, Senatorial campaign of Edward W. Brooke, 1966-67; Brandeis University, Waltham, Mass., research associate for Lemberg Center for the Study of Violence, 1967-73; WCVB (television station), Needham, Mass., associate producer, 1973-76; *Miami Herald,* Miami, Florida, television writer, 1977-78; *Boston Globe,* Boston, Mass., daytime television critic, 1978-82; *Patriot Ledger,* Quincy, Mass., television critic, 1982—.

WRITINGS:

(Compiler) *U.S. Race-Related Civil Disorders,* Lemberg Center for the Study of Violence, Brandeis University, 1968.
Youth Patrols: An Experiment in Community Participation, Lemberg Center for the Study of Violence, Brandeis University, 1969.
Rumors, Race and Riots, Transaction Books, 1975.

Contributor to journals and newspapers. Editor, *Riot Data Review.*

WORK IN PROGRESS: A book on television.

*   *   *

KNYE, Cassandra
See DISCH, Thomas M(ichael)

*   *   *

KONIGSBURG, E(laine) L(obl)   1930-

PERSONAL: Born February 10, 1930, in New York, N.Y.; daughter of Adolph (a businessman) and Beulah (Klein) Lobl; married David Konigsburg (a psychologist), July 6, 1952; children: Paul, Laurie, Ross. *Education:* Carnegie Institute of

Technology (now Carnegie-Mellon University), B.S., 1952; graduate study, University of Pittsburgh, 1952-54. *Religion:* Jewish.

ADDRESSES: c/o Atheneum Publishers, 115 Fifth Ave., New York, N.Y. 10003.

CAREER: Writer. Shenago Valley Provision Co., Sharon, Pa., bookkeeper, 1947-48; Bartram School, Jacksonville, Fla., science teacher, 1954-55, 1960-62.

AWARDS, HONORS: Jennifer, Hecate, Macbeth, William McKinley, and Me, Elizabeth was chosen as an honor book in *Book Week* Children's Spring Book Festival, 1967, and as a Newbery Honor Book, 1968; Newbery Medal, 1968, and William Allen White Award, 1970, both for *From the Mixed-Up Files of Mrs. Basil E. Frankweiler;* Carnegie-Mellon Merit Award, 1971; American Library Association notable children's book and National Book Award nomination, both 1974, both for *A Proud Taste for Scarlet and Miniver;* American Library Association best book for young adults, for *The Second Mrs. Giaconda,* and *Father's Arcane Daughter;* American Library Association notable children's book and American Book Award nomination, 1980, both for *Throwing Shadows.*

WRITINGS

SELF-ILLUSTRATED JUVENILES

Jennifer, Hecate, Macbeth, William McKinley, and Me, Elizabeth, Atheneum, 1967.
From the Mixed-Up Files of Mrs. Basil E. Frankweiler, Atheneum, 1967.
About the B'nai Bagels, Atheneum, 1969.
(George), Atheneum, 1970.
A Proud Taste for Scarlet and Miniver, Atheneum, 1973.
The Dragon in the Ghetto Caper, Atheneum, 1974.

JUVENILES

Altogether, One at a Time (short stories), illustrated by Gail E. Haley, Mercer Meyer, Gary Parker, and Laurel Schindelman, Atheneum, 1971.
The Second Mrs. Giaconda, illustrated with museum plates, Atheneum, 1975.
Father's Arcane Daughter, Atheneum, 1976.
Throwing Shadows (short stories), Atheneum, 1979.
Journey to an 800 Number, Atheneum, 1982 (published in England as *Journey by First Class Camel,* Hamish Hamilton, 1983).
Up from Jericho Tel, Atheneum, 1986.

OTHER

Also author of promotional pamphlets for Atheneum.

SIDELIGHTS: E. L. Konigsburg is best known as the author and illustrator of humorous juvenile books. Konigsburg's books are not simply amusing, however; almost every story contains an element of seriousness, usually in the form of a child's search for identity. "Questions of identity—'What kind of person can I become?'—are fundamentally serious ideas, even if the surface is comedy, and they are present in nearly all Elaine Konigsburg's stories," observes David Rees in *Horn Book.* Konigsburg's ability to incorporate humor into serious subject matter makes her "a lively, amusing and painlessly educational storyteller," writes Alice Fleming in the *New York Times Book Review.*

Konigsburg's original intention was to write books that reflected the middle-class background of her own children. Her

Newbery Award-winning book, *From the Mixed-Up Files of Mrs. Basil E. Frankweiler,* for example, was directly influenced by her children's behavior on a family picnic. Konigsburg writes in *Forty Percent More than Everything You Want to Know about E. L. Konigsburg* that after listening to her children complain about ants, warm milk, and melted cupcake icing, "I thought to myself that if my children ever left home, they would never become barbarians even if they were captured by pirates. Civilization was not a veneer to them; it was a crust. They would want at least all the comforts of home plus a few dashes of extra elegance. Where, I wondered, would they ever consider running to if they ever left home? They certainly would never consider any place less elegant than the Metropolitan Museum of Art."

From the Mixed-Up Files of Mrs. Basil E. Frankweiler tells the story of two children who do just that. Claudia, tired of being big sister to three siblings and bored with suburbia, decides to run away from home. She takes along Jamie, her thrifty brother, for financial assistance. Their temporary home is the New York Metropolitan Museum of Art, where they bathe in the fountain and sleep in a musty, nineteenth-century bed. While exploring the museum, they become intrigued by an angel reputed to have been sculpted by Michelangelo. Claudia, determined to establish her identity before she returns home, is convinced the discovering the origin of the statue will help her accomplish this goal. Their search leads them to Mrs. Frankweiler, the original owner of the statue, who teaches them "that true individuality is interior—and often secret at that," writes Elva Harmon in the *Library Journal.*

Claudia and Jamie "are wholly and refreshingly recognizable and real," comments a *Times Literary Supplement* reviewer, who later states that Mrs. Frankweiler, on the other hand, "one appreciates but does not wholly believe in. She is a little too fancy-baked, from smart New Yorker-land." Rees shares the same reservations about Frankweiler. He describes her as "a kind of fairy godmother and *deus ex machina,* who sorts out the problem and the children, whereas the children should have sorted out both the problem and themselves on their own."

The children's disregard for the museum rules and lack of concern for their family has caused some reviewers to question the book's appropriateness for children. A *Times Literary Supplement* critic, however, calls it a "particularly honest observation . . . that it never occurs to the children to worry about their parents, to imagine the agonies through which they must be going." A similar opinion is shared by Harmon who maintains that anyone rejecting the book on the basis of the children's misbehavior "would be denying their patrons the reading pleasure of an unusual book, extremely well written."

In *(George),* one of Konigsburg's later books, the protagonist's identity crisis is much more serious than that of the average child. Ben has had an alter ego, George, since he was a young boy. Until Ben's twelfth year, George had been known only to Ben and his immediate family. But when Ben, an exceptional student, is placed in a high school chemistry class, George begins to vocalize, thus disturbing the class. Consequently, Ben is sent to a psychiatrist who helps him merge the two personalities. George's presence has prompted some reviewers to label Ben as schizophrenic. Konigsburg told *CA,* however, that she prefers to think of George as Ben's "inner self." This "decision to treat the darker, more socially unacceptable side of [Ben] . . . as a real, separate person" greatly contributes to the success of *(George),* comments Rees, who also praises "the skill with which Mrs. Konigsburg turns this apparently formidable material into a light-hearted, genuinely comic novel.''

Compared to Konigsburg's first three books, *(George)* is "far more complex, demanding more from the reader and giving away less," notes a *Times Literary Supplement* reviewer, who also observes that *(George)* is the first novel in which Konigsburg "writes as herself, and somehow her own voice is not as consistent or as beguiling as the voices of the personae she invented." The critic nevertheless concludes that "Konigsburg could not write a dull book if she tried, but it should be made clear that this . . . book . . . is strictly for older readers, who are prepared to accept a foreign idiom, who will be intrigued by the notion of symbiosis, and who like being made to think."

Konigsburg's books have been marketed by her publisher as being appropriate for the middle-aged child. Konigsburg at first found the terms "middle-aged" and "child" contradictory, but after researching the Middle Ages, she began to find parallels between the characteristics of that period and the pre-adolescent child. Konigsburg writes in *The Genesis of ''A Proud Taste for Scarlet and Miniver''*: "Examine the art of the Middle Ages, and you find literal interpretations of 'the light of God' and the 'mouth of Hell.' A middle-aged child listens literally and interprets literally, too. Look at a painting or a piece of sculpture from the Middle Ages, and it is hard to find perspective. A middle-aged child lacks perspective in his philosophy as well as his art."

By the time she was convinced that the term middle-aged child was really quite apt, Konigsburg had developed a love for the Middle Ages. Wishing to express her interest in this period, she wrote *A Proud Taste for Scarlet and Miniver,* a portrait of Eleanor of Aquitaine, wife of Louis VII of France and Henry II of England. The story is told in flashbacks by Eleanor, Henry's mother Empress Matilda, Abbot Suger, and others as they sit in heaven awaiting the arrival of Henry, who has been temporarily detained in hell.

Konigsburg departs from her usual choice of a protagonist in this book but not without good reason, as she explains in *The Genesis of ''A Proud Taste for Scarlet and Miniver''*: "I wanted to write about this queen, this woman's libber, for children. I wanted to do it accurately, but I didn't want to invent a small child character and plop him into the twelfth century. I felt I didn't need to do that. Eleanor of Aquitaine already had an age in common with children: the Middle Ages." In addition, Eleanor has "a certain ruthlessness" that is common to Konigsburg's other protagonists as well, writes Penelope Farmer, who also remarks in the *Times Literary Supplement* that, consequently, "the gap between Eleanor and Mrs. Konigsburg's previous heroines is perhaps not after all so great. Eleanor as seen here is nothing if not the prototype of Claudia, Jennifer, et al." Konigsburg's portrayal of "Eleanor—ambitious, intelligent, energetic—will delight youngsters who crave an emancipated heroine," declares Jennifer Farley Smith in the *Christian Science Monitor*.

In addition to novels, Konigsburg has written two collections of short stories for juveniles. The stories in the second collection, *Throwing Shadows,* "with their high humor, easy pace and sharp social comment" are reminiscent of stories by William Saroyan and Langston Hughes, according to Cynthia King in the *New York Times Book Review*. In each of the four stories, "a child encounters an adult, and both are changed," writes King. In "At the Home," for example, young Philip's awareness of the horrors of war is heightened by the stories

of a Hungarian refugee who was imprisoned at Auschwitz during World War II. When the refugee complains that the people in the nursing home are boring, Philip, in turn, instructs her by saying, "You have to overcome your prejudice about old people." Although the characters and settings are different, *Throwing Shadows* contains a familiar voice, observes King. "It is the voice of . . . a skeptic who . . . can make you laugh while illuminating the poignancies, inequities and paradoxes of contemporary life."

Many of Konigsburg's books have been published in England, including *From the Mixed-Up Files of Mrs. Basil E. Frankweiler, (George)*, and *Journey to an 800 Number* (published in England as *Journey by First Class Camel*). Konigsburg's books are undeniably American, a fact that has not diminished her popularity with British readers. Rather, "her books which are more specifically American . . . have been the most successful in England," comments Rees, who also explains that Konigsburg's "value to British readers is that she can make something universal out of a setting that is specifically American; in other words, though her writing at its finest may use language and present material and viewpoints that seem thoroughly transatlantic, her children and teenagers could be found in any place; their problems in coming to terms with themselves and with an adult world that at best is messy and at worst corrupt are the problems of the young everywhere."

CA INTERVIEW

CA interviewed E. L. Konigsburg by telephone on March 4, 1985, at her home in Jacksonville, Florida.

CA: You were a chemist before you became a writer. How did the change come about?

KONIGSBURG: To answer that, I have to tell you why I became a chemist. I became a chemist because I was good at it. We had no guidance department in my high school at the time I went there, and I was the first one in my family to go to college. In the town I lived in, a small mill town in northwestern Pennsylvania, I knew no one who made his living from the arts—I knew no writers, no artists. At that time, a person went away to college to *be* something; you went away to be a teacher, or you went away to be an engineer, or you went away to be a chemist. So I went away to be a chemist because I was good at it and that was the sort of thing that you did. I'm convinced that, had I not been such a disaster in the lab, I could have made a contribution to chemistry, something creative. I had the mind for it, but not the temperament. There was all that awful lab work to get through. And there was no one to tell me that it is only in the higher reaches that science and art are one.

When we moved South, I had not finished my master's degree and I had no credentials for teaching. There was not then and there is not now any place here where you can get a master's degree in chemistry. I had done all of the course work and had passed the language requirement for a master's degree, but I was such a disaster in the lab that my research kept going awry. I thought I could teach, and I did. I went to teach at a private girls' school because I had no certification. I did not know that they would have taken me in a public school, because chemistry teachers were as scarce then as they are now.

But going to teach in this private girls' school gave me remarkable insight into girls. I had gone to the school with a prejudice against private schools, thinking that they catered to spoiled young women who had it all. They *had* all the creature comforts of the world, but I soon learned that they were just as uncomfortable inside as I was when I was growing up. I came to realize that if you strip kids of the need for creature comforts, you can begin to discuss some pretty basic problems.

Then I retired for a while and had the three children within four years. We moved to the Northeast, and at that point I realized that there was much more alike in my children's life than was different. I wanted to write something that reflected their kind of growing up, because I felt, growing up in small towns, that my sort of life was never reflected. I would pick up a book that promised me I would meet typical kids in a typical small town, but the story would have heroines who took naps and whose mothers had household help, and it was not at all related to anything that I knew in all these small towns that I had lived in. So when I realized that my kids' growing up was very different from my own, but was related to this middle-class kind of child that I had seen when I had taught at the private girls' school, I recognized that I wanted to write something that reflected their kind of growing up, something that addressed the problems that come about even though you don't have to worry if you wear out your shoes whether your parents can buy you a new pair, something that tackles the basic problems of who am I? What makes me the same as everyone else? What makes me different?

CA: Not only does art figure in the content of some of your books, but you also illustrate many of them yourself, and very sensitively. How long have you been drawing and painting?

KONIGSBURG: I started drawing when I was in grade school, and then when I was in science I did none of it. When my daughter was born, I needed desperately to do something to get my hands out of dishwater, and I started taking art lessons at night. So there were people who knew me at a certain period in my life—say, when I was in college and when I was working in the field of science—that had no idea at all that I had an interest in drawing. During those years we lived in New York, I took Saturdays off, and David would babysit while I went to art lessons in the morning at the Art Students League, then explored New York in the afternoon.

CA: Your own children have been models for your illustrations. Have they also served as a first audience for the stories?

KONIGSBURG: Most definitely. They still do, on an entirely different level, of course. I just completed a manuscript, and before I did revisions, I sent it to my children to get their reactions to it. I used to read them what I had written, but now they read for themselves!

CA: Do you find that some of your books reach adult readers as well as younger ones?

KONIGSBURG: Yes, I do get a lot of mail from that audience. I'm always very pleased because I think that a person can communicate through literature, and when one of my books is appealing to an adult as well as to a child, or a child has thrust it into his parents' hands—very often I hear that—I feel particularly pleased.

CA: You've received several important awards and honors for your writing, including the Newbery Medal. Do you feel the

existing awards for children's writers provide adequate recognition, or should there be more?

KONIGSBURG: I think that when there are too many awards, you whittle away their importance. There was a time when the American Book Awards had so many categories that in those particular years, I don't think anyone can remember who won. So if the idea of an award is to single something out, by its very definition, I think that a proliferation diminishes the reason for having an award.

CA: Do you get a lot of fan mail?

KONIGSBURG: Yes. The mail comes in two general categories. One is that a class of kids is doing a unit on Newbery writers, and they have been asked to do a book report, the nature of which is to write a letter to an author. The other kind of mail is this very distinctive letter that comes from a kid who says, I just read something you wrote and I loved it and just wanted to let you know. I got a very wonderful phone call at 11:15 the other night from a kid in Oregon who did not realize the time difference. It was only 8:15 at his home. But he just had finished a book and wanted to talk to the author. I don't think there's a more flattering kind of phone call a person can get. I said, ''Did you want me to send you something?'' ''No, no,'' he said. ''I just wanted to say hello.''

CA: Do you try to answer all your mail?

KONIGSBURG: I try, but I am always, always behind, and I don't want to be responsible for getting a kid's assignment in on time.

CA: What kind of writing schedule do you keep?

KONIGSBURG: I'm at my desk every day when I'm here at home. I get up, get dressed, and go to my office, which is my son's old bedroom. I used to be very rigid about my mornings and not even answer the phone. My kids and my husband used to have a signal to give me if I needed to pick up the phone. But now that my children are gone from home, I do take necessary calls. My friends are all very nice; they know that I don't like to take personal calls in the morning. I find now that I go back in the afternoon; it splashes over. A lot of that is catching up with mail. I travel a lot—I enjoy speaking, and there's always mail connected with that and mail connected with other things.

CA: What kinds of audiences do you like to speak to?

KONIGSBURG: Because I work alone in that office that once was my son's bedroom, I can go for months at a time without having a good talk about books—good talk to me always implies a certain amount of gossip—so I like to talk to people to whom books are important. Very often those are people who get books into the hands of children. In their passage to the reader, children's books pass through one, and sometimes two, more filters than do adult books. Besides the editor at the publishing house and the reviewer in the media, there is the teacher or the librarian or the parent who controls what a child has available to read. That control can be one of purse strings; there is not enough money in any household or in any institution to buy everything that is published. I like to talk to these people about the creative process as it applies to children's fiction. Now that many more children's books are in paperback, children themselves have greater control over what they have access to read. Now that my books are coming out in mass-market paperback, I see from the mail that is coming in that with more titles available, more are being read.

CA: Have books always been important to you?

KONIGSBURG: They have been important to me in ways that they can never be to children being raised in the age of television. Books represented a kind of reality to me that I never questioned. Going to see a movie of the life of Thomas Edison, say, or Alexander Graham Bell—you remember Spencer Tracy and Don Ameche?—I would come home and want to read about them. It never occurred to me that a book might be as slanted a version as a movie. Books represented a kind of accuracy. Kids nowadays have the evening news for accuracy. But books can represent a kind of truth. I think that good fiction is the best kind of truth. In my newest book, *Up from Jericho Tel,* the old actress Tallulah is full of epigrams. They appear at the beginnings of the chapters. In one of them she says: "If ever you want to learn the difference between accuracy and truth, look at a photograph of Gertrude Stein and then look at Picasso's portrait of her." For years, books represented the photograph to me. Now that I am a writer, I know that they are the portrait.

CA: Is there a certain kind of reader you like to reach?

KONIGSBURG: I think that reading is something between a talent and a skill. I have known kids who seem to be born readers, kids who learn to read without being taught, the way I imagine Mozart played the piano. I have a niece and a nephew like this. To these kids, reading is a form of pleasure, of entertainment. There are other kids who are skilled readers who want to read only for information, and there are still others to whom reading will never be anything but a chore, something that they may even be able to do well but that they do only because it needs doing, like cleaning the kitchen is to me. I can tell you that there is no greater compliment than having your work cherished by one of the first kind of reader, someone who has read a lot and chooses your book out of a vast experience of reading. There is also no greater compliment than hearing from a young man in Pennsylvania, "I never liked reading until I read you." And in that middle category—those kids that are skilled but who do not take great pleasure in reading—imagine, the joy of being *chosen* by someone who otherwise reads only assignments. So I guess you could say that I love all my readers, for I do. I think they are wonderful, and I like it when they think that I am. Don't we all want to be wonderful to someone?

CA: Do you ever teach or do any workshops?

KONIGSBURG: No.

CA: History, art, and biography come into your books a lot. Do you enjoy the research?

KONIGSBURG: Extremely. So much that there's a point at which I have to say to myself, enough. I know the point when it happens. You begin with the research in a wide circle, and then you begin homing in on a certain period and certain people. And when you find yourself going back to primary sources—or as primary as I can get, I have to say, since I don't read Middle English or French or Italian—and all of your references are leading you back to the same references, then you know it's time to begin the actual writing.

CA: Father's Arcane Daughter deals with not only the problems but also the possibilities of a handicapped child, and with her brother's difficulties in finding his own identity apart from hers—all this with a mystery in the plot. Can you tell me something about how the book was conceived?

KONIGSBURG: It was based on a situation that I knew, and I had to disguise a great deal. I made up Heidi's handicap and called a woman who is a neighbor, who deals with handicapped children; she's involved with testing handicapped and learning disabled children. I said, "Does this possibility exist?" and described the handicap that I had developed for the character. She said, "If you have any combination of problems, I have witnessed it." At that time there was a young woman, who had temporarily retired as a secretary to raise two young children, who used to type for me. I took the book to her to type, and she stopped dead at a certain point and said, "Do you know, I have a sister who has exactly this handicap?" I got such chills because I knew then that it was vital, that something had really rung true. She told me that her sister, by the way, was one of twins and had been so sheltered by herself and by the mother that the child could not roll her hair. She had coordination problems. And if she was in an automobile, the hum of the car or any kind of background noise would prevent her from hearing anything that was said. She couldn't filter out the background sounds, just like Heidi in *Father's Arcane Daughter.*

CA: In (George) you tackle paranoid schizophrenia. Was your husband, as a psychologist, helpful to you on that book?

KONIGSBURG: Extremely. But I don't really think that Ben is a schizophrenic. It's a very strong feeling I have that when you're a youngster, you're much more in touch with your inner self. The peer pressure begins about sixth grade—sometimes now about fifth grade—to pull you toward what is socially acceptable to that group. You have to stay in touch with this inner self. I think the most difficult thing about writing for children, probably, is getting back to this inner self.

CA: Living in Florida now, do you miss the proximity to New York City that you had earlier?

KONIGSBURG: Yes, I miss New York; I sometimes long for it. I try to get up a couple of times a year. I just think it's a very stimulating place.

CA: Do you miss the library facilities in doing research for your books?

KONIGSBURG: The libraries here are very helpful. When I was doing research on *The Second Mrs. Giaconda,* I needed an old book on Beatrice d'Este. I called New York and was able to locate it in a used book store there; it wasn't available here. But it's not that I miss; I think it's the sense of what happens to you as you walk along the street in New York. I miss hearing foreign accents; that's one thing. When you ride the subway or a bus in New York, you hear this glut of accents. I love that, and I love the expansiveness with which clothing is worn. There's just an awful lot of diversity that I miss.

CA: What are you working on now?

KONIGSBURG: It's a combination of several of my books, in a way. It's called *Up from Jericho Tel,* and it's being told by one of the heroines, whose name is Jeanmarie Troxell. She begins it by saying, "There was a time when I was eleven years old—between the start of a new school year and Midwinter's Night—when I was invisible. I was never invisible for long, and I always returned to plain sight, but all my life has been affected by the people I met and the time I spent in a world where I could see and not be seen." She and this young man, Malcolm Soo, begin burying dead animals. One day they fall through the ground into a lighted area where there's this old actress called Tallulah. Tallulah says she's going to send them on a mission, but first she sends them through two trials. Malcolm is upset because, he says, "There's always three trials." But she says that she feels confident that they know enough, that they have learned to distinguish the real from the phony and that they have learned that sometimes doing nothing is doing something. So she's satisfied and she wants to send them for her necklace, the Regina Stone. In the course of their search, they meet some street performers that Tallulah knew, one of whom has possibly taken the Regina Stone. They find out who took the necklace and why as well as what it takes to be a star.

CA: Would you like to do other kinds of writing—maybe something for television, or just other kinds of fiction?

KONIGSBURG: I don't know. I will think about it, probably, in a little while. Periodically I *have* thought about it, but then another idea for a children's book comes up!

BIOGRAPHICAL/CRITICAL SOURCES:

BOOKS

Children's Literature Review, Volume I, Gale, 1976.
Konigsburg, E. L., *The Genesis of "A Proud Taste for Scarlet and Miniver"* (pamphlet), Atheneum, 1973.
Konigsburg, E. L., *Forty Percent More Than Everything You Want to Know about E. L. Konigsburg* (pamphlet), Atheneum, 1974.
Konigsburg, E. L., *Throwing Shadows,* Atheneum, 1979.
Townsend, John Rowe, *A Sounding of Storytellers: Essays on Contemporary Writers for Children,* Penguin Books, 1979.

PERIODICALS

Christian Science Monitor, May 1, 1974.
Horn Book, December, 1970, April, 1973, February, 1978, April, 1980.
Learning Today, fall, 1981.
Library Journal, October 15, 1967.
New York Times Book Review, November 5, 1967, March 30, 1969, November 8, 1970, May 30, 1971, October 14, 1973, November 4, 1973, October 5, 1975, November 7, 1976, December 9, 1979, May 30, 1982.
Saturday Review, November 14, 1970.
Times (London), June 16, 1983.
Times Literary Supplement, October 3, 1968, April 3, 1969, July 2, 1971, April 4, 1975, March 25, 1977, June 16, 1983.
Washington Post Book World, April 11, 1982.

—*Sketch by Melissa J. Gaiownik*

—*Interview by Jean W. Ross*

*   *   *

KONTOS, Peter G(eorge)   1935-1977

PERSONAL: Born April 21, 1935, in Cleveland, Ohio; died April 3, 1977, in Atlanta, Ga.; son of George Peter and Angelina (Scocos) Kontos; married Cecille Adair Pittenger (a writer), March 9,1957; children: David G., Philip G. *Education:* Ohio University, B.S. in Ed., 1958; Kent State University, M.A., 1966. *Religion:* Methodist.

CAREER: Cleveland (Ohio) public schools, secondary teacher, 1958-62, coordinator of instruction for senior high schools, 1962-65, coordinator of in-service education for teachers of disadvantaged youth, 1965-66; Princeton University, Office of Educational Programs, Princeton, N.J., senior staff member and director of Upward Bound Program, 1966-67; Educational Research Council of America, assistant director of Greater Cleveland Social Science Program (for disadvantaged youth), 1967-68; EDR Corp., Cleveland and Atlanta, Ga., founder, president, and chairman of the board, 1968-74; Protestant Radio and Television Center, Atlanta, president, 1974-76; EDR Corp., chairman of the board, 1976-77. Co-founder and former member of board of directors and editorial committee, Portal Press, Inc. (subsidiary of John Wiley & Sons); president and executive director, Institute for Contemporary Curriculum Development, 1969-77. Panelist, President's National Conference on Education of the Disadvantaged, 1966; trustee, Plan of Action for Citizens in Education. Consultant, Educational Projects, Inc., U.S. Office of Economic Opportunity, U.S. Office of Education, and University of Minnesota.

MEMBER: American Historical Association, National Council for the Social Studies, Blue Key.

AWARDS, HONORS: John Hay fellow in the humanities, 1975.

WRITINGS:

(Co-author and editorial consultant) "Springboard Learning Program," fourteen units, Portal Press, 1965.
(Editor with James J. Murphy) *Teaching Urban Youth: A Source Book for Urban Education,* Wiley, 1967.
(Author with wife, Cecille P. Kontos, of viewpoints) "Readings in the Humanities" series, six books, Follett, 1968-69.
(Contributor) A. Harry Passow, editor, *Developing Programs for the Educationally Disadvantaged,* Teachers College Press, Columbia University, 1968.
(Contributor) *Reaching the Disadvantaged Learner,* Columbia University, 1970.
(Contributor) *Teaching Social Studies to Culturally Different Children,* Addison-Wesley, 1971.
(With others) *Patterns of Civilization: America,* Cambridge Book Co., 1973.
(With others) *Patterns of Civilization: Europe,* Cambridge Book Co., 1973.
(With others) *Patterns of Civilization: Asia,* Cambridge Book Co., 1974.
(With others) *Patterns of Civilization: Africa,* Cambridge Book Co., 1974.
The United States: Past and Present, Cambridge Book Co., 1974.
The City: Promise and Problem, Cambridge Book Co., 1974.
(With others) *Achieve with Mathematics,* Cambridge Book Co., 1975.
(With others) *Succeed with Mathematics,* Cambridge Book Co., 1976.

Also co-author of two plays, "Broad Axe in the Wilderness," produced by American Heritage Theatre Association, 1964, and "Rock Candy Mountain."†

KORFKER, Dena 1908-

PERSONAL: Born April 6, 1908, in Grand Rapids, Mich.; daughter of Henry William and Diena (DeHaan) Korfker. *Education:* Calvin College, A.B., 1943. *Religion:* Christian Reformed-Calvinist.

ADDRESSES: Home—1720 Plymouth Rd. S.E., Grand Rapids, Mich. 49506.

CAREER: Oakdale Christian School, Grand Rapids, Mich., kindergarten teacher, 1927-73. Secretary, Denominational Sunday School Committee, 1955-61. Sunday school teacher, 1927-73; Bible storyteller at a community hospital for the elderly, 1980—.

MEMBER: Christian Teacher's Educators' Club, West Michigan Teachers' Institute, Grand Rapids Christian Teachers' Club, Phisio Philia Club.

AWARDS, HONORS: First prize, Zondervan's Juvenile Fiction Contest, 1954, for *Ankie Comes to America;* honored as the children's author of the quarter century in Zondervan's twenty-fifth anniversary celebration; distinguished alumni award, Calvin College, 1978.

WRITINGS:

Can You Tell Me?, Zondervan, 1950, revised edition, 1970.
Questions Children Ask, Zondervan, 1951.
My Bible ABC Book, Zondervan, 1952.
Ankie Comes to America, Zondervan, 1954.
Story of Jesus for Boys and Girls, Zondervan, 1954.
My Picture Story Bible, Zondervan, 1960.
My Favorite Picture Stories from the Bible, Zondervan, 1961.
Mother of Eighty (biography of Mrs. J. B. Brittell), J. C. Choate, 1970.
Good Morning Lord: A Devotion Book for Children, Baker Book, 1973.

Also author of *Shepherd of My People;* author and editor of Sunday school papers and course for preschool children.

SIDELIGHTS: Dena Korfker has travelled to Jordan and Israel and throughout the United States and Europe. Her book *My Picture Story Bible* has sold over 215,000 copies and has been translated into Portuguese.

AVOCATIONAL INTERESTS: Travel, nature, photography, giving book reviews.

* * *

KORNBLUTH, Jesse 1946-

PERSONAL: Born January 4, 1946, in New York, N.Y.; son of Samuel and Pearl (Greenwald) Kornbluth. *Education:* Harvard University, A.B. (magna cum laude), 1968.

ADDRESSES: Office—Department of Film and Television, New York University, Washington Square, New York, N.Y. 10003.

CAREER: Look, New York, N.Y., editorial assistant, 1966-68; affiliated with department of film and television, New York University; free-lance writer. Founder with Stephen Saltonstall of Paradise Manufacturing Co.; president, Georgica Productions.

WRITINGS:

(Editor and author of introduction) *Notes from the New Underground* (anthology of articles from underground newspapers), Viking, 1968.

(With Jack R. Osborn) *Winning Croquet: From Backyard to Greensward*, Simon & Schuster, 1983.

Contributing editor, *New York*.

BIOGRAPHICAL/CRITICAL SOURCES:

PERIODICALS

Books, February, 1968, June, 1968.
Newsweek, January 13, 1969.

* * *

KRAMER, Leonie Judith 1924-

PERSONAL: Born October 1, 1924, in Melbourne, Australia; daughter of Alfred Leonard (a banker) and Gertrude Isobel (Walker) Gibson; married Harold Kramer (a pathologist), April 2, 1952; children: Jocelyn Anne, Hilary Lorraine. *Education:* University of Melbourne, B.A., 1945; Oxford University, D.Phil., 1953.

ADDRESSES: Office—Department of English, University of Sydney, Sydney, New South Wales 2006, Australia.

CAREER: Canberra University College (now Australian National University), Canberra, Australia, lecturer in English, 1954-56; University of New South Wales, Sydney, Australia, 1958-68, began as lecturer, became associate professor of English; University of Sydney, Sydney, professor of Australian literature, 1968—. Visiting professor, Harvard University, 1981-82. Vice-president of Australian Council for Educational Standards; member of Universities Council. Chairman of Australian Broadcasting Commission, 1981-83. Member of board, Western Mining Corp.

MEMBER: Australia-Britain Society (national president), Australian College of Education (fellow), Australian Society of Authors (fellow), Australian Academy of the Humanities (fellow), English Teachers Association, Royal Historical Society of Victoria.

AWARDS, HONORS: Dame, Order of the British Empire, 1983; recipient of honorary degrees from University of Melbourne, Australian National University, and University of Tasmania.

WRITINGS:

Henry Handel Richardson and Some of Her Sources, Melbourne University Press, 1954.
James McAuley: Tradition in Australian Poetry (bound with *The Misfortunes of Henry Handel Richardson* by T. Inglis Moore), Canberra University College, 1957.
(Editor) *Australian Poetry*, Angus & Robertson, 1961.
A Companion to Australia Felix, Heinemann (Australia), 1962.
(Editor) *Coast to Coast, 1963-64*, Angus & Robertson, 1965.
Myself When Laura: Fact and Fiction in Henry Handel Richardson's School Career, Heinemann (Australia), 1966.
Henry Handel Richardson, Oxford University Press, 1967.
(Editor) Hal Porter, *Selected Stories*, Angus & Robertson, 1971.
(With Robert D. Eagleson) *Language and Literature: A Synthesis*, Thomas Nelson, 1976.
(With Eagleson) *A Guide to Language and Literature*, Thomas Nelson, 1977.
A. D. Hope, Oxford University Press, 1979.
(Editor and author of introduction) *Oxford History of Australian Literature*, Oxford University Press, 1981.
(Editor with Adrian Mitchell) *The Oxford Anthology of Australian Literature*, Oxford University Press, in press.

Editorial adviser, *Quadrant, Poetry Australia,* and *Australian Literary Studies.*

*   *   *

KRAMER, Mark (William) 1944-

PERSONAL: Born April 14, 1944, in New York, N.Y.; son of Sidney B. (an attorney and publisher) and Esther (a book store operator; maiden name, Schlansky) Kramer. *Education:* Brandeis University, B.A., 1966; Columbia University, M.A., 1967; graduate study at Indiana University, 1967-68.

ADDRESSES: Office—Smith College, Northampton, Mass. 01063. *Agent*—Georges Borchardt, Inc., 136 East 57th St., New York, N.Y. 10022.

CAREER: Farmer in western Massachusetts, 1969-81; Smith College, Northampton, Mass., writer in residence, 1980—. Visiting lecturer at University of Massachusetts, 1976-79.

AWARDS, HONORS: Rockefeller Foundation humanities fellowship, 1976-78; blue ribbon from American Film Festival, 1979, for writing and co-directing "Crisis in Yankee Agriculture"; Ford Foundation fellowship for nonfiction, 1980-81.

WRITINGS:

Mother Walker and the Pig Tragedy, Knopf, 1972.
(Author of introduction) Benjamin Butterworth, editor, *The Growth of Industrial Art* (picture book), Knopf, 1973.
Three Farms: Making Milk, Meat, and Money from the American Soil, Atlantic Monthly Press, 1980.
Invasive Procedures: A Year in the World of Two Surgeons, Harper, 1983.
(Contributor) Norman Sims, editor, *The Literary Journalists,* Ballantine, 1985.

Contributor of articles and reviews to *Atlantic Monthly, New York Times,* and *National Geographic.* Also author of documentary film "Crisis in Yankee Agriculture," released by Cambridge Media Resources.

WORK IN PROGRESS: A book on business, people, and changing technology, for Houghton.

SIDELIGHTS: Mark Kramer told *CA:* "I am writing about people whose lives are tangled up with changing technology and new businesses. I am as interested in style and structure as I am in my topics." Kramer's *Three Farms: Making Milk, Meat, and Money from the American Soil* examines the economic pressures that are besieging the American farm industry. In order to research the book, Kramer spent several years visiting the farms he chose to profile—a small dairy farm in Massachusetts, a larger hog farm in Iowa, and an extensive corporate farm in California. In all three cases, he found a concern for updating technology in order to expand production and profitability. Noel Perrin, reviewing *Three Farms* in the *New York Times Book Review,* feels that Kramer's background as a small farmer helped to formulate "an enthralling book." "Mr. Kramer does two remarkable things in this book," Perrin writes. "One is to capture the true feel of country life in a high-technology era. . . . Kramer's other triumph is to see what scarcely anyone else has seen so clearly: that the villain in the destruction of rural life is not . . . cold-hearted agri-businessmen or greedy distributors, but simply the capital-intensive nature of technology itself."

In *Invasive Procedures: A Year in the World of Two Surgeons,* Kramer continues his technique of writing based upon long-term observations. Having followed two doctors on their rounds, into the operating rooms, and even into their homes, Kramer reports on the quality of life his subjects achieve within their demanding professions. William A. Nolen, himself a surgeon, says in the *Washington Post Book World:* "Kramer's book gives, I think, a realistic view of how surgeons in private practice live and work. His descriptions of operating-room scenes, including the interplay between the nurses, anesthetists and doctors, [are] vivid and dramatic, but the drama isn't grossly exaggerated as is so often the case when the medical world is portrayed." In the *New York Times Book Review,* Joe McGinniss calls Kramer's work "frequently engrossing, though naggingly uneven," and goes on to comment that Kramer's "reportorial skill, combined with a prose style that . . . is as clean and sharp as one of his subjects' scalpel blades, has produced a book that gives an intriguing and often insightful look behind the scenes of a world that both fascinates and repels."

BIOGRAPHICAL/CRITICAL SOURCES:

PERIODICALS

New York Times Book Review, March 30, 1980, September 18, 1983.
Washington Post Book World, August 28, 1983.

*   *   *

KRUZAS, Anthony T(homas) 1914-

PERSONAL: Born July 23, 1914, in Brooklyn, N.Y.; son of John and Petrona (Rickes) Kruzas; married Florence A. Massulis, September 25, 1947; children: Mary Patricia. *Education:* Attended Polytechnic Institute of Brooklyn, 1931-37; City College (now City College of the City University of New York), B.B.A. (magna cum laude), 1950; University of Michigan, A.M.L.S., 1951, Ph.D., 1960.

ADDRESSES: Home and office—2125 Nature Cove Ct., Apt. 301, Ann Arbor, Mich. 48104.

CAREER: University of Kansas, Medical Center, Kansas City, associate librarian, 1951-52; State University of New York College of Ceramics, Alfred, associate librarian, 1952-56; University of Michigan, School of Library Science, Ann Arbor, 1956-74, currently professor emeritus; Gale Research Co., Detroit, Mich., editor and consulting editor, 1974—. *Military service:* U.S. Army Air Forces, 1942-46; became sergeant.

MEMBER: Special Libraries Association, Medical Library Association, Beta Gamma Sigma.

WRITINGS:

PUBLISHED BY GALE

(Co-editor) *Statistics Sources,* 1962.
(Editor) *Directory of Special Libraries and Information Centers,* 1963, 3rd edition, 1974, 4th edition, Volume II (with Margaret Young), 1977.
(Joint editor) *Research Centers Directory,* 1965.
Special Libraries and Information Centers: A Statistical Report on Special Library Resources in the U.S., 1965.
(Editor) *Encyclopedia of Information Systems and Services,* 1971, 3rd edition, 1978.
(Editor) *Encyclopedia of Governmental Advisory Organizations,* 1973, 2nd edition (with Linda Sullivan), 1975.
(Editor) *Medical and Health Information Directory,* 1977, 2nd edition, 1980, 3rd edition, Volume I, 1985.

(Editor with Robert Thomas) *Business Organizations and Agencies Directory*, 1980, 2nd edition, 1985.
(Editor with Kay Gill) *Government Research Centers Directory*, 1980, 2nd edition, 1982.
(Editor) *Health Services Directory*, 1981.
(Editor) *Social Service Organizations and Agencies*, 1982.
(Editor with Gill) *International Research Centers Directory*, 1982, 2nd edition, 1985.
(Editor) *Encyclopedia of Medical Organizations and Agencies*, 1983.
(Editor with Gill) *Government Programs and Projects Directory*, 1983.
(Editor with Gill) *Research Activities and Funding Programs*, 1983.

OTHER

Business and Industrial Libraries in the United States, 1840-1940, Special Libraries Association, 1965.

*   *   *

KYGER, Joanne (Elizabeth) 1934-

PERSONAL: Born November 19, 1934, in Vallejo, Calif.; daughter of Jacob Holmes (a career navy officer) and Anne (Lamont) Kyger; married Gary Snyder (a poet), 1960 (divorced, 1964); married John Boyce (a painter), 1966 (died, 1972). *Education:* Attended Santa Barbara College (now University of California, Santa Barbara), 1952-56.

ADDRESSES: Home—Box 688, Bolinas, Calif. 94924.

CAREER: Poet. Performer and poet in an experimental television project, 1967-68.

AWARDS, HONORS: Grant from National Endowments for the Arts, 1968.

WRITINGS:

POETRY

The Tapestry and the Web, Four Seasons Foundation, 1965.
The Fool in April: A Poem, Coyote Books, 1966.
Places to Go, Black Sparrow Press, 1970.
Joanne, Angel Hair Books, 1970.
Desecheo Notebook, Arif, 1971.
Trip Out and Fall Back, Arif, 1974.
All This Every Day, Big Sky, 1975.
The Wonderful Focus of You, Z Press, 1980.
Up My Coast, Floating Island, 1979.
The Japan-India Journals, Tombouctou Books, 1981.
Mexico Blonde, Evergreen Press, 1981.

Going On: Selected Poems 1958-80, Dutton, 1983.

CONTRIBUTOR

George Plimpton and Peter Ardery, editors, *The American Literary Anthology*, Random House, 1969.
Anne Waldman, editor, *The World Anthology*, Bobbs-Merrill, 1969.
Laura Chester and Sharon Barba, editors, *Rising Tides*, Pocket Books, 1973.

OTHER

Contributor of poems to periodicals, including *Poetry, Coyote's Journal, Paris Review, World, Turkey Buzzard Review*, and *Rockey Ledge*.

SIDELIGHTS: A leading figure in San Francisco poetry circles, Joanne Kyger was a member of some of the groups that formed around senior poets Robert Duncan and Jack Spicer in the late 1950s and fostered such writers as Richard Brautigan, Michael McClure, and George Stanley.

From 1970 on, notes Bill Berkson in the *Dictionary of Literary Biography*, "Kyger's poems have dealt with a number of set themes: Buddhist and American Indian figures and myths, the relationship of the individual psyche to the social-political life of the town, love and marriage, and travel." According to Berkson, during a 1974 panel discussion at Kent State University Kyger "spoke of her change from what she termed 'the linear line': 'at this point the kind of space that interests me is the kind of space that vibrates its meaning. It's the one-liner or the sampler on the wall. . . . It just stays there for a long time. You can go back into that one line and it will keep giving off overtones, so it doesn't have to sit there and be connected. It's connected but it's a different kind of space.'"

Kyger's papers are deposited at the Archive for New Poetry, University of California, San Diego.

BIOGRAPHICAL/CRITICAL SOURCES:

BOOKS

Dictionary of Literary Biography, Volume XVI: *The Beats: Literary Bohemians in Postwar America*, Gale, 1983.

PERIODICALS

Credences 4, Volume II, number 1, 1977.
Los Angeles Times Book Review, November 13, 1983.
Occident, spring, 1974.
Partisan Review, spring, 1972.
San Francisco Review of Books, February, 1976.
Tomales Bay Times, July 16, 1976.

L

LABBE, John T.

PERSONAL: Born in Portland, Ore. *Education:* Attended Dartmouth College and University of Oregon.

ADDRESSES: Home—11210 Southwest Marylyn Pl., Beaverton, Ore. 97005.

CAREER: Logger and lumberman; writer. *Military service:* U.S. Army, machine gunner in Infantry.

WRITINGS:

(With Vernon Goe) *Railroads in the Woods,* Howell North Books, 1961.
(With Lynwood Carranco) *Logging the Redwoods,* Caxton, 1975.
Fares Please: Those Portland Trolley Years, Caxton, 1980.
(Editor) Dave Bohn and Rodolpho Petschek, *Kinsey, Photographer: The Locomotive Portraits,* Volume III, Chronicle Books, 1984.

WORK IN PROGRESS: Portland Trolleys, a sequel to *Fares Please: Those Portland Trolley Years,* for Caxton; with Peter Replinger, *Logging to the Salt Chuck,* a history of logging railroads in Mason County, Wash.; with Lynwood Carranco, *Logger Language,* a lexicon, for University of Oklahoma Press.

SIDELIGHTS: John T. Labbe grew up surrounded by loggers and their families, and during the Depression he became a logger himself. Throughout his career he tried nearly every job within the industry, but generally preferred free-lance work to jobs with the major companies.

Labbe told *CA:* "It is my hope to provide an accurate record of the history of northwest logging, and to this end I have compiled what is probably the most extensive collection of facts and photos on the subject in the West. My library is open to any serious historian, and I have cooperated on numerous projects besides my own in an effort to provide as many reliable reference sources for the future as possible."

*   *   *

LAMBERT, Derek   1929-
(Richard Falkirk)

PERSONAL: Born October 10, 1929, in London, England; son of William Albert (a banker) and Kathleen (Riddick) Lambert; married Diane Joan Brunet; children: four. *Education:* Attended Epsom College, Surrey, England. *Politics:* None. *Religion:* None.

ADDRESSES: Agent—J. Friedmann, Julian Friedmann Literary Agency, 15 Catherine St., London WC2B 5J2, England.

CAREER: Writer. Reporter for *Dartmouth Chronicle, Eastern Daily Press,* and *Sheffield Star,* all British provincial newspapers; reporter for *Daily Mirror,* London, England, for five years, then foreign correspondent first in Africa then in Moscow, for *Daily Express,* London, for six years. *Military service:* Royal Air Force, 1947-49.

WRITINGS:

The Sheltered Days (autobiography), Deutsch, 1964.
Angels in the Snow (novel; Literary Guild choice in England), Coward, 1969.
The Kites of War (novel), Coward, 1969.
For Infamous Conduct, Coward, 1970, Arlington, 1984.
The Red House, Coward, 1972.
The Yermakou Transfer, Saturday Review Press, 1974.
Touch the Lion's Paw, Saturday Review Press, 1976.
The Great Land, Arlington, 1977.
Don't Quote Me . . . But, Arlington, 1979.
The Memory Man, Arlington, 1979.
And I Quote, Arlington, 1980.
I, Said the Spy, Arlington, 1980.
Trance, Arlington, 1981.
Unquote, Arlington, 1981.
The Red Dove, Hamilton, 1982.
The Saint Peter's Plot, Corgi, 1982.
The Judas Code, Hamilton, 1983.
The Lottery, Piatkus, 1983.
The Golden Express, Hamilton, 1984.

Also author of *Grand Slam.*

UNDER PSEUDONYM RICHARD FALKIRK

The Twisted Wire, Doubleday, 1971.
Chill Factor, M. Joseph, 1971.
Blackstone, Methuen, 1972, Bantam, 1974.
Beau Blackstone, Methuen, 1973, Stein & Day, 1974.
Blackstone's Fancy, Methuen, 1973.
Blackstone and the Scourge of Europe, Stein & Day, 1974.
Blackstone on Broadway, Methuen, 1977.

WORK IN PROGRESS: A book about Alaska and its growth from 1943 to 1976.

SIDELIGHTS: Derek Lambert once told *CA* that he has an "inescapable urge to write, but will use any excuse not to. I attempt ten pages a day, often succeed." He added that "the idea for my next novel after *Infamous* came while under fire on the Suez Canal." He has traveled in the Soviet Union, Ireland ("with draught Guinness in my pen"), Gibraltar, Spain, and Israel. "But," he admitted, "I must move on. My feet and my typewriter are restless already."

Lambert's spy thriller set in Moscow, *Angels in the Snow,* has accorded him favorable critical attention. In a *New York Times Book Review* report on the book, Martin Levin suggests: "So convincingly oppressive and claustrophobic does Mr. Lambert render life in Moscow, even among the privileged foreigners in the international enclave, that it could conceivably hinder recruiting for the Foreign Office and the State Department." A reviewer for the *New Yorker* notes that the "theme is sad, and the picture is grimly significant, but all in all this is a jolly novel, and long enough to take up the slack of a week of winter nights.... Mr. Lambert has a sure hand with detail.... The writing is direct and flat and quite free of inner meanings, and also of flourishes, and it is exactly right for the really complete, closely packed story Mr. Lambert tells."

BIOGRAPHICAL/CRITICAL SOURCES:

PERIODICALS

Best Sellers, March 1, 1969.
New Statesman, March 14, 1969.
New Yorker, March 1, 1969.
New York Times Book Review, March 2, 1969, November 22, 1970, March 4, 1973, January 5, 1975, September 25, 1983.†

* * *

LANE, David (Stuart) 1933-

PERSONAL: Born April 24, 1933, in England; son of Reginald and Mary (Maud) Lane; married Christel Noritzsch, 1962; children: Christopher, Julie. *Education:* University of Birmingham, B.Soc.Sc., 1960; Nuffield College, Oxford, D.Phil., 1966. *Politics:* Labour Party.

ADDRESSES: Office—Department of Sociology, University of Birmingham, Birmingham B15 2TT, England.

CAREER: University of Essex, Colchester, England, lecturer and reader in sociology, 1967-73, chairman of department, 1973; Cambridge University, Cambridge, England, lecturer and fellow of Emmanuel College, 1974-81; University of Birmingham, Birmingham, England, professor of sociology, 1981—. *Military service:* Royal Air Force, 1951-53.

MEMBER: Association of University Teachers, British Sociological Association, American Sociological Association, British Political Studies Association, British National Association of Soviet and East European Studies.

WRITINGS:

Roots of Russian Communism: A Social and Historical Study of Russian Social-Democracy, 1898-1907, Van Gorcum, 1969, Humanities, 1970.
Politics and Society in the U.S.S.R., Weidenfeld & Nicolson, 1970, Random House, 1971.

The End of Inequality?: Social Stratification under State Socialism, Penguin, 1971, published as *The End of Social Inequality?: Class, Status, and Power under State Socialism,* Allen & Unwin, 1982.
(With G. Kolankiewicz) *Social Groups in Polish Society,* Macmillan, 1973.
The Socialist Industrial State, Allen & Unwin, 1976.
(Contributor) R. Scase, editor, *Studies in Industrial Society,* Allen & Unwin, 1977.
(With Felicity Ann O'Dell) *Soviet Industrial Worker: Social Class, Education and Control in the U.S.S.R.,* Martin Robertson, 1978.
The Work Needs of Mentally Handicapped Adults, Disability Alliance, 1980.
Leninism: A Sociological Interpretation, Cambridge University Press, 1981.
Inequality, Socialism, and Sociology, Birmingham University, 1983.
(With Michael Tidball) *Quiet Evolution,* Macmillan, 1983.
State and Politics in the U.S.S.R., New York University Press, 1985.
Soviet Economy and Soviets, New York University Press, 1985.

Contributor to sociology, political science, and Soviet studies journals.

WORK IN PROGRESS: Labour and Employment under Socialism.

AVOCATIONAL INTERESTS: Music, soccer, travel.

BIOGRAPHICAL/CRITICAL SOURCES:

PERIODICALS

Times Literary Supplement, October 16, 1969.

* * *

LANG, David Marshall 1924-

PERSONAL: Born May 6, 1924, in Chislehurst, Kent, England; son of David Marshall (a medical doctor) and May Rena (Wilson) Lang; married Janet Sugden (a physiotherapist), February 11, 1956; children: David (deceased), Andrew, Caroline, Elizabeth. *Education:* St. John's College, Cambridge University, B.A., 1945, M.A., 1948, Ph.D., 1949. *Politics:* Liberal. *Religion:* Anglican.

ADDRESSES: Home—The Willows, Stocking Pelham, Hertfordshire, England. *Office*—School of Oriental and African Studies, University of London, London, England.

CAREER: British Foreign Office, vice-consul at Tabriz, Iran, 1944-46; Cambridge University, St. John's College, Cambridge, England, fellow, 1946-52; University of London, London, England, lecturer in Georgian, 1949-58, reader in Caucasian studies, 1958-64, professor, 1964-84, warden of Connaught Hall, 1955-84. Senior fellow of Russian Institute, Columbia University, New York, N.Y., 1952-53; visiting professor of Caucasian languages, University of California, Los Angeles, 1964-65. Member of council, 1963 Campaign for Education (Great Britain). *Military service:* British Army, 1943-45; became sergeant.

MEMBER: Philological Society, Royal Asiatic Society (member of council; secretary, 1962-64), Royal Numismatic Society (twice member of council), Association of University Teachers, Leander Club.

AWARDS, HONORS: Rotary Foundation fellow, 1948-49; D.Lit., University of London, 1958; Litt.D., Cambridge University, 1963; D. of Philological Sciences, Tbilisi State University, 1966; Prix Bremond, 1972.

WRITINGS:

Studies in the Numismatic History of Georgia, American Numismatic Society, 1955.
Lives and Legends of the Georgian Saints, Macmillan, 1956.
The Last Years of the Georgian Monarchy, Columbia University Press, 1957.
The Wisdom of Balahvar: A Christian Legend of the Buddha, Macmillan, 1957.
The First Russian Radical: Alexander Radishchev, Allen & Unwin, 1959.
A Modern History of Soviet Georgia, Praeger, 1962.
(Compiler) *Catalogue of the Georgian and Caucasian Books in the British Museum,* British Museum, 1962.
(Translator) *The Balavariani,* University of California Press, 1966.
The Georgians, Praeger, 1966.
Armenia, Cradle of Civilization, Allen & Unwin, 1970.
(Editor with D. R. Dudley) *The Penguin Companion to Classical, Oriental and African Literature,* McGraw, 1971.
(With Charles Burney) *The Peoples of the Hills: Ancient Ararat and Caucasus,* Praeger, 1971.
The Bulgarians, Thames & Hudson, 1976.
The Armenians: A People in Exile, Allen & Unwin, 1980.

Contributor to *Encyclopaedia Britannica, Encyclopaedia of Islam,* and *Cassell's Encyclopaedia of World Literature.* Contributor to professional journals, including *Numismatic Chronicle, Museum Notes, Revue des Etudes Slaves.*

*   *   *

LANGAN, Thomas   1929-

PERSONAL: Born March 20, 1929, in St. Louis, Mo.; son of Don T. (a steel company executive) and Lee (Mennemeyer) Langan; married Janine Devys, June 8, 1956; children: Marc, Claire, Noelle, Brigitte, Anne-Marie. *Education:* St. Louis University, A.B., 1951, M.A., 1952; Institut Catholique de Paris, Ph.D., 1956. *Religion:* Roman Catholic.

ADDRESSES: Home—137 Strathallan Rd., Toronto, Ontario, Canada. *Office*—Department of Philosophy, University of Toronto, Toronto, Ontario, Canada M5S 1A1.

CAREER: St. Louis University, St. Louis, Mo., assistant professor of philosophy, 1956-60; Indiana University at Bloomington, associate professor, 1960-66, professor of philosophy and chairman of department, 1965-68; University of Toronto, Toronto, Ontario, professor of philosophy, 1968—.

MEMBER: Metaphysical Society of America (president, 1981-82), American Catholic Philosophical Association (president, 1973-74).

AWARDS, HONORS: Fulbright grants to France, 1954-56, to Germany, 1962-63, and to Argentina, summer, 1965.

WRITINGS:

The Meaning of Heidegger, Columbia University Press, 1959, published as *The Meaning of Heidegger: A Critical Study of an Existentialist Phenomenology,* Greenwood, 1983.
(With Etienne Gilson) *Modern Philosophy,* Random House, 1963.

(With Gilson and Armand Maurer) *Recent Philosophy,* Random House, 1966.
Merleau-Ponty's Critique of Reason, Yale University Press, 1966.
Self-Discovery, Golden Phoenix, 1985.

American representative of Italian journal *Filosofia.*

*   *   *

LAVERTY, Donald
See KNIGHT, Damon (Francis)

*   *   *

LAZEROWITZ, Alice Ambrose   1906-
(Alice Ambrose)

PERSONAL: Born November 25, 1906, in Lexington, Ill.; daughter of Albert Lee (a florist) and Bonnie Belle (Douglass) Ambrose; married Morris Lazerowitz (a writer and professor emeritus of philosophy), June 15, 1938. *Education:* Millikin University, A.B., 1928; University of Wisconsin, M.A., 1929, Ph.D., 1932; Cambridge University, Ph.D., 1938.

ADDRESSES: Home—126 Vernon St., Northampton, Mass. 01060. *Office*—Department of Philosophy, Smith College, Northampton, Mass. 01060.

CAREER: University of Michigan, Ann Arbor, instructor in philosophy, 1935-37; Smith College, Northampton, Mass., beginning 1937, assistant professor, 1943-51, professor, 1951-64, Sophia and Austin Smith Professor of Philosophy, 1964-72, professor emeritus, 1972—. Distinguished visiting professor of philosophy, University of Delaware, 1975; visiting professor of philosophy, Hampshire College, 1977, 1979, and 1981; Cowling Professor of Philosophy, Carleton College, 1979; lecturer in philosophy, Smith College, 1981. Member of board, Northampton Community Chest; co-chairperson, Smith College drive for Community Chest.

MEMBER: American Philosophical Association (vice-president of Eastern Division, 1966; president, 1975), American Association of University Professors, Phi Kappa Phi.

AWARDS, HONORS: LL.D., Millikin University, 1958.

WRITINGS:

UNDER NAME ALICE AMBROSE

Essays in Analysis, Allen & Unwin, 1966.
(Editor) *Wittgenstein's Lectures: Cambridge, 1932-1935* (from the notes of Alice Ambrose and Margaret Macdonald), Rowman & Littlefield, 1979.

UNDER NAME ALICE AMBROSE; WITH HUSBAND, MORRIS LAZEROWITZ

Fundamentals of Symbolic Logic, Holt, 1948, revised edition, 1962.
Logic: The Theory of Formal Inference, Holt, 1961, revised edition, Scientia, 1972.
(Editor) *G. E. Moore: Essays in Retrospect,* Allen & Unwin, 1970.
(Editor) *Ludwig Wittgenstein: Philosophy and Language,* Allen & Unwin, 1972.
Philosophical Theories, Mouton, 1976.
Essays in the Unknown Wittgenstein, Prometheus Books, 1984.
Necessity and Language, Croom Helm, 1985.

Necesidad y filosofia (translation of the original English manuscript; title means "Necessity and Philosophy"), University of Mexico Press, 1985.

OTHER

Contributor to proceedings and to professional journals. Editor of *Journal of Symbolic Logic*, 1953-68.

WORK IN PROGRESS: Research on the philosphy of mathematics.

SIDELIGHTS: In a *Times Literary Supplement* review of *Ludwig Wittgenstein: Philosophy and Language*, a book Alice Ambrose edited with her husband, Morris Lazerowitz, a critic writes that "Ambrose's recollections of her experiences as a student of Wittgenstein have considerable anecdotal interest." Moreover, he points out, "Ambrose gives a much-needed explication of Wittgenstein's paradoxical assertion that arithmetical propositions say nothing about numbers."

BIOGRAPHICAL/CRITICAL SOURCES:

PERIODICALS

Times Literary Supplement, July 14, 1972.
Washington Post Book World, July 13, 1980.

*   *   *

LAZEROWITZ, Morris   1907-

PERSONAL: Surname originally Laizerowitz; born October 22, 1907, in Lodz, Poland; son of Max (a businessman) and Etta (Plochinsky) Laizerowitz; married Alice Ambrose (a professor of philosophy at Smith College), June 15, 1938. *Education:* Attended University of Nebraska, 1928-30; University of Michigan, A.B., 1933, Ph.D., 1936; Harvard University, postdoctoral study, 1936-37.

ADDRESSES: Home—126 Vernon St., Northampton, Mass. 01060. *Office*—Neilson Library, Smith College, Northampton, Mass. 01063.

CAREER: Smith College, Northampton, Mass., 1938-73, Sophia and Austin Smith Professor of Philosophy, 1964-73. Fulbright lecturer, Bedford College, University of London, 1951-52; distinguished professor of philosophy, University of Delaware, 1975; taught at Hampshire College, 1977, 1979, and 1981; Cowling Professor of Philosophy, Carleton College, 1979.

MEMBER: American Philosophical Association.

AWARDS, HONORS: Alfred H. Lloyd postdoctoral fellowship from Horace H. Rackham School of Graduate Studies, University of Michigan, 1937-38.

WRITINGS:

(With wife, Alice Ambrose) *Fundamentals of Symbolic Logic*, Rinehart, 1948, revised edition, Holt, 1962.
The Structure of Metaphysics, Routledge & Kegan Paul, 1955, Humanities, 1963.
(With Ambrose) *Logic: The Theory of Formal Inference*, Holt, 1961, revised edition, Scientia, 1972.
Studies in Metaphilosophy, Humanities, 1964.
(Editor with William E. Kennick) *Metaphysics: Readings and Reappraisals*, Prentice-Hall, 1966.
Philosophy and Illusion, Humanities, 1968.
(Editor and contributor with Ambrose) *G. E. Moore: Essays in Retrospect*, Humanities, 1970.
(Editor and contributor with Charles Hanly) *Psychoanalysis and Philosophy*, International Universities Press, 1970.

(Editor with Ambrose) *Ludwig Wittgenstein: Philosophy and Language*, Humanities, 1972.
(With Ambrose) *Philosophical Theories*, Mouton, 1976.
The Language of Philosophy, D. Reidel, 1977.
(With Ambrose) *Essays in the Unknown Wittgenstein*, Prometheus Books, 1984.
(With Ambrose) *Necessity and Language*, Croom Helm, 1985.
(With Ambrose) *Necesidad y Filosofia* (translation of the original English manuscript; title means "Necessity and Philosophy"), University of Mexico Press, 1985.

Contributor of articles and reviews to philosophical journals.

*   *   *

LEAN, Garth Dickinson   1912-
(Tenax)

PERSONAL: Born December 26, 1912, in Cardiff, Wales; son of Frederick John and Myra (Dickinson) Lean; married Margaret Mary Appleyard, June 29, 1946; children: Geoffrey Kenneth, Jenifer Mary. *Education:* Worcester College, Oxford, B.A., 1934, M.A., 1950. *Religion:* Church of England.

ADDRESSES: Home—48 Jack Straw's Lane, Oxford OX3 ODW, England.

CAREER: Free-lance journalist and editor; writer of political column in *Time and Tide*, under pseudonym Tenax, 1965-75. Member of council of management of Moral Re-Armament, Britain.

MEMBER: Institute of Journalists.

WRITINGS:

Brave Men Choose, Blandford, 1961.
John Wesley, Anglican, Blandford, 1964.
(With Arnold Henry Moore Lunn) *The New Morality*, Blandford, 1964, revised and enlarged edition, 1967.
The Cult of Softness, Blandford, 1965.
(With Lunn) *Christian Counter-Attack*, Arlington House, 1969.
(With Sydney Cook) *The Black and White Book: A Handbook of Revolution*, Blandford, 1972.
Good God, It Works!: An Experiment in Faith, Blandford, 1974.
Rebirth of a Nation?, Blandford, 1976.
Strangely Warmed, Tyndale House, 1979.
God's Politician: William Wilberforce's Struggle, Darton, Longman & Todd, 1980.
Frank Buchman: A Life, Constable, 1985.

Also editor of more than sixty books.

SIDELIGHTS: Garth Dickinson Lean tells *CA* that several of his books have been translated into other languages, most notably *The Black and White Book*, which has appeared in thirty-two languages. The book *Frank Buchman* is the first full-length biography of Buchman, and Lean anticipates an American publication.

BIOGRAPHICAL/CRITICAL SOURCES:

BOOKS

Gordon, Anne Worige, *Peter Howard: Life and Letters*, Hodder & Stoughton, 1969.
Howard, Peter, *Innocent Men*, James Heineman, 1941.

LEAVITT, Jerome E(dward) 1916-

PERSONAL: Born August 1, 1916, in Verona, N.J.; son of Thomas Edward (a painter) and Clara (Sonn) Leavitt. *Education:* Newark State Teachers College (now Kean College of New Jersey), B.S., 1938; Columbia University, graduate study, 1938-39; New York University, M.A., 1942; University of Colorado, graduate study, 1949-50; Northwestern University, Ed.D., 1952.

ADDRESSES: Home and office—5402 East Ninth St., Tucson, Ariz. 85711.

CAREER: Heights Elementary School, Roslyn Heights, N.Y., teacher, 1938-42; Sperry Gyroscope Co., Inc., Brooklyn, N.Y., instructor, 1942-45; Canyon Elementary School, Los Alamos, N.M., principal, 1945-49; Northwestern University, Evanston, Ill., instructor, 1950-52; Portland State University, Portland, Ore., assistant professor, 1952-55, associate professor, 1955-58, professor of education and executive assistant to the dean, School of Education, 1958-66; University of Arizona, Tucson, professor of education, 1966-69; California State University, Fresno, professor of education, 1969-81, chairman of department, 1969-71, coordinator of central California section of Region IX Child Abuse Project, 1975-81; Jerome Leavitt, Inc. (training and consulting firm), Tucson, 1981—. Visiting scholar, University of Arizona, 1959. Research associate for evaluation of Arkansas experiment in teacher education; American specialist in education in Cyprus for U.S. State Department.

MEMBER: International Society for Prevention of Child Abuse, National Committee for Prevention of Child Abuse, American Humane Association, National Organization for Victim Assistance, Association for Childhood Education, National Education Association, National Society of College Teachers of Education, Association for Supervision and Curriculum Development, California Teachers Association, Phi Delta Kappa, Kappa Delta Pi, Epsilon Pi Tau.

WRITINGS:

Tools for Building, Children's Press, 1955.
(Editor) *Nursery-Kindergarten Education,* McGraw, 1958.
Carpentry for Children, Sterling, 1959.
(With Huntsberger) *Terrariums and Aquariums,* Children's Press, 1961.
America and Its Indians, Children's Press, 1961.
(Editor) *Readings in Elementary Education,* W. C. Brown, 1961.
(With Salot) *The Beginning Kindergarten Teacher,* Burgess, 1965, revised edition, 1971.
The Complete Reference Handbook, Stravon Education Press, 1966.
By Land, by Sea, by Air, Putman, 1969.
(Editor) *The Battered Child: Selected Readings,* General Learning Press, 1974.
Herbert Sonn: Yosemite's Birdman, privately printed, 1975.
(Co-author) *Training Manual in Child Abuse for California Peace Officers,* Peace Officer Standards and Training, 1979.
(Editor) *Child Abuse and Neglect: Research and Innovation,* Nijhoff, 1983.

General editor, "Twayne Juveniles" series, Twayne, 1971-76. Also contributor to "Webster's New Reference Library," Thomas Nelson, 1984. Contributor of over one hundred articles to magazines and professional journals. *Education,* contributing editor, 1954-58, member of editorial board, 1973-79; editor, *NSCTE Newsletter,* 1964-65; member of board of contributing editors, *Our World* (encyclopedia), Taylor Publishing, 1971; member of board of consultants, *Modern Century Illustrated Encyclopedia,* McGraw-Hill, 1972; editorial consultant, *Primaid,* 1972-75; western regional coordinating news editor, *Education Professor,* 1975-77.

WORK IN PROGRESS: A slide program, filmstrip, and cassette based on *Child Abuse and Neglect: Research and Innovation.*

SIDELIGHTS: Jerome E. Leavitt told *CA:* "Most of my writing is a result of a felt need on my part. In some cases this is to provide informational material that is lacking, which was true in the case of *Nursery-Kindergarten Education.* With *America and Its Indians* the objective was to provide accurate up-to-date material for children on our Native Americans."

The Beginning Kindergarten Teacher has been translated into Japanese.

AVOCATIONAL INTERESTS: Reading, solar energy, gardening, remodeling houses, carpentry.

BIOGRAPHICAL/CRITICAL SOURCES:

PERIODICALS

National Elementary Principal, June, 1949.

*　　*　　*

LEE, Wayne C. 1917-
(Lee Sheldon)

PERSONAL: Born July 2, 1917, in Lamar, Neb.; son of David Elmer (a farmer) and Rosa (Deselms) Lee; married Pearl Sheldon, March 17, 1948; children: Wayne Sheldon, Charles Lester. *Education:* Graduated from high school in 1935. *Religion:* Disciples of Christ.

ADDRESSES: Home—Lamar, Neb.

CAREER: Farmer in Lamar, Neb., 1935-51; rural mail carrier, 1951-77; full-time writer, 1977—. Teacher and board member, Disciples of Christ Church. *Military service:* U.S. Army, Signal Corps, 1945.

MEMBER: Western Writers of America (president, 1970-71), Nebraska State Historical Society (member of foundation board), Nebraska Writers Guild (president, 1974-76), Toastmasters Club (former president).

AWARDS, HONORS: Historian of the Year, High Plains Preservation of History Commission, 1981.

WRITINGS:

Prairie Vengeance, Arcadia House, 1954.
Broken Wheel Ranch, Arcadia House, 1956.
Slugging Backstop, Dodd, 1957.
His Brother's Guns, Arcadia House, 1958.
Killer's Range, Arcadia House, 1958.
Bat Masterson, Whitman Publishing, 1960.
Gun Brand, Arcadia House, 1961.
Blood on the Prairie, Arcadia House, 1962.
Thunder in the Backfield, F. Watts, 1962.
Stranger in Stirrup, Arcadia House, 1962.
The Gun Tamer, Arcadia House, 1963.
Devil Wire, Arcadia House, 1963.
The Hostile Land, Arcadia House, 1964.
Gun in His Hand, Arcadia House, 1964.

Warpath West, Ace Books, 1965.
Fast Gun, Avalon, 1965.
Mystery of Scorpion Creek, Abingdon, 1966.
Brand of a Man, Avalon, 1966.
Trail of the Skulls, Bouregy, 1966.
Showdown at Julesburg Station, Bouregy, 1967.
Return to Gunpoint, Ace Books, 1967.
Only the Brave, Bouregy, 1967.
(Under pseudonym Lee Sheldon) *Doomed Planet,* Bouregy, 1967.
Sudden Guns, Bouregy, 1968.
Trouble at the Flying H, Bouregy, 1969.
Stage to Lonesome Butte, Bouregy, 1969.
Showdown at Sunrise, Bouregy, 1971.
The Buffalo Hunters, Bouregy, 1972.
Suicide Trail, Lenox Hill, 1972.
Wind over Rimfire, Lenox Hill, 1973.
Son of a Gunman, Ace Books, 1973.
Law of the Prairie, Lenox Hill, 1974.
Scotty Philip: The Man Who Saved the Buffalo (biography), Caxton Printers, 1975.
Die Hard, Ace Books, 1975.
Law of the Lawless, Ace Books, 1977.
Skirmish at Fort Phil Kearny, Avalon, 1977.
Gun Country, Ace Books, 1978.
Petticoat Wagon Train, Ace Books, 1978.
The Violent Man, Ace Books, 1978.
Ghost of a Gun Fighter, Zebra Books, 1979.
McQuaid's Gun, Avalon, 1980.
Trails of the Smoky Hill (nonfiction), Caxton Printers, 1980.
Shadow of the Gun, Zebra Books, 1981.
Guns at Genesis, Leisure Books, 1981.
Putnam's Ranch War, Avalon, 1982.
Barbed Wire War, Avalon, 1983.
The Violent Trail, Avalon, 1984.
White Butte Guns, Avalon, 1984.
War at Nugget Creek, Avalon, 1985.
Massacre Creek (tentative title), Avalon, 1985.

PLAYS

Bachelor Bait, Eldridge Publishing, 1951.
Lightly Turn toward Love, Schubert, 1952.
Poor Willie, Denison, 1954.
Hold the Phone, Denison, 1955.
Deadwood, Denison, 1956.
For Evans Sake, Denison, 1957.
Big News, Denison, 1957.

Also author of numerous other plays.

OTHER

Short stories have appeared in numerous anthologies. Contributor of over 600 short stories to more than thirty periodicals.

WORK IN PROGRESS: Wild Towns of Nebraska, for Caxton Printers; novels.

SIDELIGHTS: Wayne C. Lee told *CA:* "My writing day begins at 5 a.m. and runs until noon with time out for breakfast and news, weather and sports. Being a sport nut, I have to hear how the leagues in all sports are doing. I find that, by starting my day while the house and the world around me are quiet, I can become submerged in my writing before outside activity has an opportunity to encroach on my thinking. Once 'into' my story, it is not difficult to hold my concentration. The result is twice as much work done as when, years ago, I waited until 7 a.m. to begin. The remainder of my day, in summer, is devoted to my orchard and truck garden; in winter, to any outdoor activities that the weather will permit, reading, revision, and research."

Several of Lee's books have been translated into Swedish, Norwegian, Spanish, Portuguese, Danish, and other foreign languages.

AVOCATIONAL INTERESTS: Sports, especially community boys' sports.

*　　　*　　　*

LEIBER, Justin Fritz 1938-

PERSONAL: Born July 8, 1938, in Chicago, Ill.; son of Fritz (a writer) and Jonquil (a writer; maiden name, Stephens) Leiber; married Leslie Dunmore, July 10, 1964 (divorced May 30, 1982); married June 19, 1983; wife's name, Barbara; children: (second marriage) Katherine. *Education:* University of Chicago, B.A., 1959, M.A., 1961, Ph.D., 1967; Oxford University, B.Phil., 1972. *Religion:* Atheist.

ADDRESSES: Home—523 Bayland, Houston, Tex. 77009. *Office*—Department of Philosophy, University of Houston, Houston, Tex. 77004. *Agent*—Virginia Kidd, Box 278, Milford, Pa. 18337.

CAREER: Herbert H. Lehman College of the City University of New York, Bronx, N.Y., assistant professor of philosophy, 1968-76; Massachusetts Institute of Technology, Cambridge, visiting scientist in linguistics and philosophy, 1976-78; University of Houston, Houston, Tex., associate professor of philosophy, 1978—.

WRITINGS:

In Respect of Liking, Analysis, 1968.
Noam Chomsky: A Philosophical Overview, Twayne, 1975.
Structuralism, G. K. Hall, 1978.
Beyond Rejection (novel), Ballantine, 1980.
The Sword and the Eye, Tor Books, 1985.
The Sword and the Tower, Tor Books, 1985.
Can Animals and Machines Be Persons: A Dialogue, Hackett, 1986.

Also author of a novel, *Beyond Humanity.*

Contributor to philosophy journals and *Algol-Starship.* Co-editor of *Southern Journal of Philosophy,* 1962-63.

WORK IN PROGRESS: Research on cognitive and linguistic activity in apes.

SIDELIGHTS: Justin Fritz Leiber told *CA:* "Though I have written academic books and articles for nearly two decades, I have taken up popular writing and fiction only since 1978. It has been a curious experience. I think that my academic work and writing has helped. I wrote my first novel, *Beyond Rejection,* by drawing on a basic theme in philosophy, psychology, and linguistics—the mind-body problem: the book uses kinds of people, places, animals, and issues with which I am familiar, though they are displaced some two hundred years into the future. My second novel has my protagonist interacting with an ape and a computer. This parallels my current academic interests in the issue of ape linguistic and cognitive abilities, and the issues of whether computers can think and whether human thinkers should bear the same kinds of characterizations as computers. And so both modes of expression reinforce each other. It is perhaps obvious that I think truth an important element in fiction, and that the novel of ideas is a profitable mode.''

*   *   *

LENS, Sidney 1912-

PERSONAL: Born January 28, 1912, in Newark, N.J.; married Shirley Ruben, October, 1946. *Education:* Attended public schools in New York, N.Y.

ADDRESSES: Home—Chicago, Ill. *Agent*—Blassingame, McCauley & Wood, 432 Park Ave. S., New York, N.Y. 10016.

CAREER: Writer and activist. Active in labor unions for more than forty-five years; United Service Employees Union, AFL-CIO, Local 329, Chicago, Ill., director, 1941-66. Lecturer in foreign affairs and labor at University of Chicago, Roosevelt University, University of Illinois, DePaul University, and other universities. Candidate for U.S. Congress from 2nd Illinois district, 1962; candidate for Illinois Legislature, 1964; candidate for U.S. Senate from Illinois, 1980.

MEMBER: Institute of Social Studies (chairman), National Committee to End War in Vietnam (co-chairman), New Mobilization Committee to End War in Vietnam (former co-chairman), Coalition against Military Escalation (chairman), Impeach Nixon Committee (chairman), Justice, Action, and Peace in Latin America (chairman), Mobilization for Survival (founder and member of steering committee), Chicago Council on Foreign Relations (member of board of directors).

AWARDS, HONORS: Patron Saints Award, Society of Midland Authors, 1970; Institute for Policy Studies fellow.

WRITINGS:

Left, Right and Center, Regnery, 1949.
The Counterfeit Revolution, Beacon Press, 1952.
A World in Revolution, Praeger, 1956.
The Crisis of American Labor, Sagamore Books, 1959.
Working Men, Putnam, 1961.
Africa: Awakening Giant, Putnam, 1962.
A Country Is Born, Putnam, 1964.
The Futile Crusade, Quadrangle, 1964.
Radicalism in America: Great Rebels and the Causes for Which They Fought, 1620 to the Present, Crowell, 1966.
What Unions Do, Putnam, 1968.
Poverty: America's Enduring Paradox, Crowell, 1969.
The Military Industrial Complex, Pilgrim, 1970.
The Forging of the American Empire, Crowell, 1972.
The Labor Wars, Doubleday, 1973.
Poverty: Yesterday and Today, Crowell, 1973.
The Promise and Pitfalls of Revolution, Pilgrim, 1974.
The Day before Doomsday: An Anatomy of the Nuclear Arms Race, Beacon Press, 1978.
Unrepentent Radical: An American Activist's Account of His Five Turbulent Decades (autobiography), Beacon Press, 1980.
The Bomb (young adult), Lodestar, 1982.
The Maginot Line Syndrome: America's Hopeless Foreign Policy, Ballinger, 1982.
Strikemakers and Strikebreakers (juvenile), Lodestar, 1985.

Columnist for *National Catholic Reporter.* Contributor of articles to numerous magazines and newspapers, including *Harvard Business Review, New Republic, Nation, L'Express, New York Times,* and *Christian Science Monitor.* Senior editor, *Progressive;* co-editor, *Liberation;* contributing editor, *Dissent* and *New Politics.*

WORK IN PROGRESS: The Militarization of America.

SIDELIGHTS: Sidney Lens told *CA:* ''As I view it, a writer must be (a) a nonconformist, (b) socially-conscious, and his works should be aimed at giving readers an insight beyond the mundane and conventional. It is no accident that most of the best-known writers in the country were at one time or another associated with radical causes, for it is only those who question that which is who can understand humankind's innermost strivings.

''I was born in what was then China-town Newark. My father died when I was three. My mother, a beautiful immigrant who worked for $2.50 a week—for seventy-two hours a week—when she first arrived here in 1907, never rose appreciably beyond the poverty level. During my formative years in the Great Depression, I had the same feelings of frustration that my mother probably did, but I can not say that I ever *felt* poor, even when I had only a dime in my pocket, which was more often than not. I became dedicated to causes. I organized unemployed, organized factory workers, led demonstrations and strikes, headed a crusade against gangsters in the Chicago union that I eventually led, participated in the Detroit sitdown strikes, then in the 1950's and 1960's became one of the leaders of the antiwar movement. I was co-chairman of the New Mobilization Committee to End the War in Vietnam, Illinois chairman of the Impeach Nixon Committee, and founder of Mobilization for Survival—among many other things.

''My writings reflect these experiences, and while some people would argue that a writer should detach himself from his life and biases, I would counter-argue that first and foremost every writer is a proselytizer. And if he isn't, he is only a stylist, not a writer. In any case, I never have believed—though I've written twenty-two books and hundreds of articles—that anyone should be a writer just to be a writer, acquiring hoped-for fame and fortune. He should be a writer to translate what he is doing in the world beyond, on paper.''

BIOGRAPHICAL/CRITICAL SOURCES:

BOOKS

Lens, Sidney, *Unrepentent Radical: An American Activist's Account of His Five Turbulent Decades,* Beacon Press, 1980.

PERIODICALS

Chicago Tribune, May 4, 1980.

*   *   *

LEON, Pierre R. 1926-

PERSONAL: Born March 12, 1926, in Ligre, France; son of Roger and Marie Louise (Cosson) Leon; married Monique Maury (a university professor), April 18, 1949; children: Francoise. *Education:* University of Paris, Licence es Lettres, 1951; University of Besancon, Doctorat, 1960, Doctorat es Lettres, 1972.

ADDRESSES: Home—150 Farnham Ave., No. 504, Toronto, Ontario, Canada M4V 1H5. *Office*—Department of French, University of Toronto, Toronto, Ontario, Canada M5S 1A8.

CAREER: University of Paris, Sorbonne, Paris, France, attache at Institute of Phonetics, 1950-58; Ohio State University, Columbus, assistant professor of French, 1958-60; University of Besancon, Besancon, France, director of language laboratory at Center for Applied Linguistics, 1960-63; Ohio State

University, associate professor of French, 1963-64; University of Toronto, Toronto, Ontario, associate professor, 1964-65, professor of French, 1965—, director of Experimental Phonetics Laboratory, 1966—. Universite de Pau, maitre de conferences, 1978—, professor titulaire, 1980. *Military service:* French Army, 1948-49, Reserve, 1949—; became lieutenant.

MEMBER: International Phonetic Association, International Society of Phonetic Sciences (fellow), Speech Association of America, Modern Language Association of America, Association Canadienne Francaise pour l'Avancement des Sciences, Societe Linguistique (Paris), Union des Ecrivains Quebecois.

AWARDS, HONORS: Prize of the French Academy, 1966, for *Introduction a la phonetique corrective;* Canada Council grants, 1965-85; Palmes academiques, 1978.

WRITINGS:

Aide-memoire d'orthoepie, Didier, 1961, new edition published as *Prononciation du francais standard: Aide-memoire d'orthoepie,* 1966, 2nd edition, 1972.
Laboratoire de langues et correction phonetique: Essai methodologique, Didier, 1962, 2nd edition, 1976.
(With wife, Monique Leon) *Introduction a la phonetique corrective a l'usage des professeurs de francais a l'etranger,* Hachette-Larousse, 1964, 4th edition, 1971.
(Contributor) *Recherches et techniques au service de l'enseignement,* Conseil de la Cooperation Culturelle (Strasbourg), 1964.
(Contributor) Albert Valdman, editor, *Trends in Language Teaching,* McGraw, 1966.
(With others) *Le Francais international,* two volumes, Centre Educatif et Culturel (Montreal), 1967.
(With Philippe Martin) *Prolegomenes a l'etude des structures intonatives,* Didier, 1970.
Essais de phonostylistique, Didier, 1971.
(With Allan Grundstrom) *Interrogation et intonation en francais standard et en francais canadien,* Didier, 1973.
(Editor with Henri Mitterand) *L'Analyse du discours,* Centre Educatif et Culturel, 1976.
Applied and Experimental Linguistics, Didier, 1979.
(With Martin) *Toronto English,* Didier, 1979.
(With Ivan Fonagy) *L'Accent en francais contemporain,* Didier, 1980.
Animots croises, Nathan (Paris), 1980.
(With Mario Rossi) *Problemes de prosodie,* Didier, Volume I: *Approches theoriques,* 1981, Volume II: *Experimentations, modeles et fonctions,* 1982.
Grepotame (collection of drawings and nursery rhymes), Nathan, 1981.
Les Voleurs d'etoiles de St. Arbroussepoil, Lemeac (Montreal), 1982.
(With Jack Yashinsky) *Options nouvelles en didactique des langues,* Didier, 1982.
(With Bieler, Haac, and M. Leon) *Perspectives de France,* Prentice-Hall, 1982.
(With F. Carton and M. Rossi) *Les Accents des francais,* Hachette-Larousse, 1983.
Les Mots d'Arlequin (poems), Naaman, Sherbrooke, 1983.
(With R. Baligand and C. Tatilon) *Interpretations orales,* Hachette-Larousse, 1984.
(With P. Perron) *Le Dialogue,* Didier, 1985.
(Translator) *Chants de la toundra* (poems), La Decouverte/Maspero (Paris), 1985.

EDITOR AND CONTRIBUTOR

Applied Linguistics and the Teaching of French/Linguistique appliquee et enseignement du francais, Centre Educatif et Culturel, 1967.
Recherches sur la structure phonique du francais canadien, Didier, 1969.
(With Georges Faure and Andre Rigault) *Prosodic Feature Analysis/Analyse des faits prosodiques,* Didier, 1970.
(With others) *Problemes de l'analyse textuelle/Problems of Textual Analysis,* Didier, 1971.
(With others) *Hommages a Pierre Delattre,* Mouton, 1972.
(With Henry Schogt and Edward Burstynsky) *La Phonologie,* Klincsieck (Paris), 1976.

OTHER

Contributor of articles and art reviews to *L'Express* (Toronto).

SIDELIGHTS: Pierre R. Leon told *CA:* "As a university professor, I write articles and books in order to share my research findings with colleagues in the same fields. I have written on many different subjects, because I don't like to stay with the same problems for very long.

"As a creative writer, I started to write titles for paintings I used to do as a hobby. My paintings were highly stylized or somewhat abstract and one of my colleagues at the university, also a good friend—the late Marshall McLuhan—suggested that I write a few lines of poetry for each of my visual works. I enjoyed this kind of language play and some of my lines became small poems. One day a publisher noted these small pieces of poetry in a gallery where I was exhibiting banners (made of applique on large pieces of material). He asked me to give him my poems, demanding eighty pieces within three months. I accepted the challenge and published my first booklet of poems, *Les Mots d'Arlequin.*"

* * *

LESHER, Phyllis A(senath Bayers)　1912-

PERSONAL: Born May 19, 1912, in Kake, Alaska; daughter of Philip Lloyd (a sea captain) and Neenah (Sobeleff) Bayers; married Charles R. Lesher (a commercial fisherman), May 5, 1930; children: Robert, Philip, Vickie, Ethyle; foster children: Shirley Brogdon. *Education:* Attended University of Alaska, 1930-32, 1956-60, Portland State University, 1970-73, and Juneau-Douglas Community College. *Politics:* "Have always been a Democrat—like many Americans now believe I am an Independent." *Religion:* Church of Christ.

CAREER: Worked in accounting and secretarial positions for many sessions of the Alaska Legislature, both before and after statehood; member of staff of Bureau of Indian Affairs, Juneau, Alaska, 1951-53, and Office of U.S. Marshal and Office of District Attorney, Juneau, 1953-56; supervising secretary and accountant for Alaska Deparmtent of Public Works, Juneau, 1960-63, and Coastal Ellis Airlines, Juneau, 1963-64; statistician for Wilbur Smith & Associates, Juneau, 1965; secretary at Channel Branch, First National Bank of Anchorage, Juneau, 1965-67; member of crew of husband's fishing vessel, trolling for salmon, 1967—. Correspondent for *Oregon Journal,* 1973-76; poet-in-residence, Lincoln County Public School System, 1972-74. Creative writing instructor, Northwest Community College and Lynn-Benton Community College, 1980—. Organizer of poetry workshops.

MEMBER: National League of American Pen Women, National Secretaries Association, National Federation of Press

Women, Alaska Press Women, Poetry Society of Alaska (charter member), Oregon State Poetry Association, Central Oregon Coast Writers (president).

AWARDS, HONORS: Alaska Press Women's Award for best poetry, 1966 and 1975; other awards for poetry from *American Haiku* and Soroptimists Club of Anchorage.

WRITINGS:

99801, Juneau (haiku), Olivant, 1968.
The Ah-ness of Things (haiku-senryu), Olivant, 1970, revised edition, 1978.
Forever Alaska, Olivant, 1978.
Intimately Oregon, Olivant, 1980.

Contributor of poetry to various periodicals.

WORK IN PROGRESS: Windows: The Pacific Northwest, for Crossington Press.†

*   *   *

LesSTRANG, Jacques 1926-

PERSONAL: Born June 13, 1926, in Pittsburgh, Pa.; son of Jacques E. and Ada Marie (Mehaffey) LesStrang; married Barbara Louise Hills; children: Michelle LesStrang Cortwright, Diane LesStrang Mathias, Paul, David, Christian; stepchildren: Steven Marcks, Linda Keefer. *Education:* George Washington University, A.A., 1949; University of Michigan, A.B., 1951.

ADDRESSES: Home—Harbor Island, Mich. (summer); and Rancho Mirage, Calif. (winter). *Office*—221 Later St., Boyne City, Mich. 49712. *Agent*—International Creative Management, 40 West 57th St., New York, N.Y. 10019.

CAREER: LesStrang Advertising, Inc., Ann Arbor, Mich., and London, England, president and creative director, 1952-68; *Seaway Review* (magazine), Ann Arbor, senior editor and publisher, 1969—. Consultant to Great Lakes Commission, U.S. Army Corps of Engineers, Province of Ontario, and various other branches of the U.S. and Canadian governments. *Military service:* U.S. Army Air Forces, 1945-47.

MEMBER: National Press Club.

AWARDS, HONORS: Named maritime writer of the year by U.S. Propeller Club, 1985, for contributions to the U.S. maritime industry through published works.

WRITINGS:

Seaway (Book-of-the-Month Club alternate selection; also see below), Superior, 1979.
The Lake Carriers, Superior, 1980, published as *Cargo Carriers of the Great Lakes,* Crown, 1981.
Giants of the Lakes, Harbor House, 1984.
The Great Lakes-St. Lawrence System, Harbor House, 1985.

Also author of several books on international marketing and of federal reports on Great Lakes matters; author of "Inward Passage," a film adaptation of *Seaway,* for the Canadian government.

WORK IN PROGRESS: A novel set in Jamaica.

*   *   *

LEVIN, Ira 1929-

PERSONAL: Born August 27, 1929, in New York, N.Y.; son

of Charles (a toy importer) and Beatrice (Schlansky) Levin; married Gabrielle Aronsohn, August 20, 1960 (divorced January, 1968); married Phyllis Finkel, 1979 (divorced, 1981); children: (first marriage) Adam, Jared, Nicholas. *Education:* Attended Drake University, 1946-48; New York University, A.B., 1950.

ADDRESSES: Home—New York, N.Y. *Agent*—Harold Ober Associates, 40 East 49th St., New York, N.Y. 10017.

CAREER: Novelist and playwright. *Military service:* U.S. Army, Signal Corps, 1953-55.

MEMBER: Dramatists Guild, Authors Guild, Authors League of America, American Society of Composers, Authors and Publishers.

AWARDS, HONORS: Edgar Allan Poe Award, Mystery Writers of America, 1953, for *A Kiss before Dying,* and 1980, for *Deathtrap.*

WRITINGS:

NOVELS

A Kiss before Dying, Simon & Schuster, 1953.
Rosemary's Baby, Random House, 1967.
This Perfect Day (Literary Guild selection), Random House, 1970.
The Stepford Wives, Random House, 1972.
The Boys from Brazil, Random House, 1976.

PLAYS

No Time for Sergeants (adapted from the novel by Mac Hyman; first produced on Broadway at the Alvin Theatre, October 20, 1955; produced on the West End at Her Majesty's Theatre, August 23, 1956), Random House, 1956.
Interlock (first produced on Broadway at the ANTA Theatre, February 6, 1958), Dramatists Play Service, 1958.
Critic's Choice (first produced on Broadway at the Ethel Barrymore Theatre, February 14, 1960; produced in London, England,1961), Random House, 1961.
General Seeger (first produced on Broadway at the Lyceum Theatre, February 28, 1962), Dramatists Play Service, 1962.
"Drat!, The Cat," with music by Milton Schafer, first produced on Broadway at the Martin Beck Theatre, October 10, 1965.
"Dr. Cook's Garden," first produced on Broadway at the Belasco Theatre, September 26, 1967.
Veronica's Room (first produced on Broadway, 1973), Random House, 1974.
Deathtrap (first produced on Broadway at the Music Box Theatre, February 26, 1978), Random House, 1979.
Break a Leg (first produced on Broadway at the Palace Theatre, April 29, 1979), Samuel French, 1981.

OTHER

Also author of scripts for the television series "Clock," "Lights Out," and "U.S. Steel Hour."

SIDELIGHTS: In his plays and novels, Ira Levin exhibits "a continuing preoccupation with dark matters," as James Lardner states in the *Washington Post Book World.* Levin's first novel, *A Kiss before Dying,* is a murder mystery; *Rosemary's Baby* is a horror novel, as are *This Perfect Day* and *The Stepford Wives; The Boys from Brazil* is a thriller about the resurgence of a Nazi underground; and Levin's most successful play, "Deathtrap," is a mystery comedy. Despite his dark themes, Levin's many popular successes have shown him to be "a professional writer with an ear attuned to the elusive tempo of the times," Robert Lima writes in *Studies in American Fiction.*

Levin began his career by writing for television in the early 1950s, scripting for some of the era's top programs. His first novel, a mystery entitled *A Kiss before Dying,* appeared in 1953 to rave reviews. The novel is told in three parts: the first part from the point of view of the supposed killer of a young girl; the other parts from the point of view of the girl's two sisters as they attempt to track down the killer. Writing in the *Chicago Sunday Tribune,* Drexel Drake describes *A Kiss before Dying* as a "remarkably constructed story depicting an inconceivably vicious character in episodes of chilling horror." Anthony Boucher of the *New York Times Book Review* maintains that "Levin combines great talent for pure novel writing—full bodied characterization, subtle psychological exploration, vivid evocation of locale—with strict technical whodunit tricks as dazzling as anything ever brought off." James Sandoe of the *New York Herald Tribune Book Review* was moved to call *A Kiss before Dying* "the most striking debut of the year." The Mystery Writers of America were inclined to agree with Sandoe. They awarded the novel an Edgar Allan Poe Award as the best first novel of 1953.

It was fourteen years before Levin wrote another novel. With the success of his stage adaptation of Mac Hyman's *No Time for Sergeants* in 1955, which ran for over 700 performances on Broadway and launched the career of actor Andy Griffith, Levin devoted many years to writing exclusively for the theatre. But in 1967 he returned to the novel with *Rosemary's Baby,* the story of a young couple in the clutches of a modern cult of devil-worshippers. The Satanists want Rosemary, the young wife, to give birth to the son of the Devil, hoping that he may "overcome the influence of God's son, Christ," Lima relates. But Rosemary is a recently lapsed Catholic who may only be hallucinating the devil-worshippers out of religious guilt. She is unsure whether she is truly threatened or merely fantasizing her danger. "One by one, untoward events happen . . . .," a writer for *Time* reports. "Dark signs and other-worldly hints occur; black candles, 'tannis root' or Devil's fungus, missing articles of clothing." "The delicate line between belief and disbelief is faultlessly drawn . . . .," writes Thomas J. Fleming in the *New York Times Book Review.* "We are with [Levin] entirely, admiring his skill and simultaneously searching out possible, probable and improbable explanations of how he is going to extricate his heroine."

The setting for the novel, a gloomy Manhattan apartment building, is based on a building where Levin once lived. It "had a laundry room kind of like the one in the book," Levin explained to a writer for *Publishers Weekly.* "I would never let my wife go down there alone." Other details in the book are based on items from the daily newspaper. For the time period covered in the novel, some nine months during 1965 and 1966, Levin worked appropriate newspaper stories into *Rosemary's Baby* to make it more realistic. Coincidentally, Pope Paul VI's visit to New York occurred at the same time that Rosemary would have conceived her baby, so Levin worked it into his story. "The contrast between the Papal visit and what was happening to Rosemary produced some highly effective and quite unexpected drama," according to the *Publishers Weekly* article.

Critical appraisal of *Rosemary's Baby* was generally favorable. Barbara Nelson of *Library Journal,* for example, compares Levin's writing in the novel to the work of Shirley Jackson. Both authors, she claims, suggest a "veneer of normality with hideous evil forces busy just beneath the surface." Peter Corodimas of *Best Sellers* also praises the novel, calling it "an exercise in sheer terror and tight craftsmanship" that is "superb." Fleming, however, ultimately judges *Rosemary's Baby* to be "just another Gothic tale" because of its literal resolution. But in her conclusion, Nelson argues that Levin "suspends disbelief so effectively that the unwary reader may well be converted to belief in the supernatural."

Ironically, Levin himself is not a believer in the supernatural. "It's not something I gave much serious attention to," he told Lardner. But the huge success of *Rosemary's Baby*—with over five million copies sold—and of the subsequent film adaptation by director Roman Polanski inspired other writers to turn to the occult thriller genre. Throughout the 1970s there was "a small tidal wave of other tales of evil and the supernatural," Lardner writes. Levin finds his book so disturbing that he refused to allow his own wife, pregnant at the time he worked on the manuscript, to read it. "I don't think any pregnant woman should read it," he declared in *Publishers Weekly.*

Levin's next two novels, *This Perfect Day* and *The Stepford Wives,* have similarly chilling premises. In *This Perfect Day,* a huge subterranean computer regulates all human behavior. In *The Stepford Wives,* the wives in a suburban community are turned into obedient robots. Alex Keneas of *Newsweek* finds that, in *This Perfect Day,* Levin "knows how to handle plot, twisting here and turning there, so that his story breezes along. . . . For a quick couple of hours it takes you away." Speaking of *The Stepford Wives,* Webster Schott of *Saturday Review* complains that it "is written with a grade school vocabulary, a high school version of syntax, and a best-selling author's understanding of what mass audiences want." But Martin Levin of the *New York Times Book Review* finds a "broad current of humor beneath the horrific surface of this little ambush of Women's Lib, life and the pursuit of happiness."

The Boys from Brazil, Levin's next novel, postulates a Nazi underground in South America led by the infamous Josef Mengele, the doctor who performed hideous experiments at the Auschwitz concentration camp. Mengele's experiments with cloning lead him to attempt a cloning of Adolf Hitler and thereby restore the Nazi movement. He clones 94 babies from Hitler's genes and places the children with parents similar in age and occupation to Hitler's own parents, hoping that at least one of the children will grow up with Hitler's driving ambition for political power. In his review of *The Boys from Brazil,* the critic for the *New Yorker* finds that "the writing is smooth and suspense-inducing, the characters are wafer-thin but plausible, and Mr. Levin once again proves himself to be an author who can tell a fairly farfetched, silly story with surprising grace."

Many of the characters in the novel are based on actual people. Mengele, for example, is the real doctor from Auschwitz who was long rumored to be hiding in South America. And the novel's hero, Yakov Libermann, who tracks down fugitive Nazis and exposes the cloning plot, is based on the actual Nazi hunter Simon Weisenthal. This use of actual people as fictional characters moves R. Z. Sheppard of *Time* to criticize Levin. Sheppard thinks that "the turning of Josef Mengele into a mad scientist from the pages of a 1940s comic book requires more than a suspension of disbelief. It also requires a suspension of taste. Exploiting such a monster for entertainment and profit is enough to give evil a bad name."

But most reviews of *The Boys from Brazil* judge it to be an entertaining novel. Valentine Cunningham of *New Statesman*, for example, finds that "the plot unfolds utterly enthrallingly to make a superior read in this genre." And Gary Arnold of the *Washington Post* calls it "a snappy pop entertainment synthesis of accumulating suspense, detective work, pseudoscientific speculation and historical wish fulfillment." Writing in *Newsweek*, Peter S. Prescott admits that a Levin novel "is like a bag of popcorn: utterly without nutritive value and probably fattening, yet there's no way to stop once you've started."

The idea for *The Boys from Brazil* came from a newspaper article on cloning in which Hitler and Mozart were given as examples of the wide range of cloning possibilities. "Needless to say," Lardner observes, "Levin never gave much thought to a novel about the cloning of Mozart." Levin's ideas for books and plays "are not so much born as incubated," Alfred Gillespie writes in *People*. A story idea is first jotted down in one of Levin's many notebooks and will, over a period of years, be added to and mulled over until it coalesces into a complete plot. The process of writing, too, takes time. Levin admits to being a slow writer. "Drat!, The Cat" took ten years to reach the stage; *Rosemary's Baby* was six years in the making; and *Deathtrap* took six years from initial idea to full production.

Levin's playwriting efforts since his initial success with "No Time for Sergeants" have been only moderately fruitful. Besides "No Time for Sergeants," only "Critic's Choice" enjoyed a substantial run on Broadway. The folding of "Drat!, The Cat" after only a week, Levin told Gillespie, "succeeded only in sending me back to novels." But in 1978, Levin returned to the stage with "Deathtrap," a comedy mystery involving Sidney Bruhl, a failed playwright who toys with the idea of murdering a young playwright and stealing his play. Filled with twists and turns that keep the audience guessing as to the protagonist's real intentions, "Deathtrap" ran on Broadway for over four years—from February 26, 1978, to June 27, 1982—making it the fourth-longest-running play in Broadway history.

The play's structure—"as convoluted as an artichoke," Richard F. Shepard writes in the *New York Times*—has garnered the most critical attention. Levin succeeds in turning inside-out many cliche mystery situations so that the audience is always surprised by the unexpected. A psychic character, neighbor to the Bruhls, even predicts various plot twists in advance, but her predictions only serve to mislead the audience. According to Walter Kerr of the *New York Times*, Levin "engages us all in an open-handed, evening-long game of hide-and-seek.... [He] has brazenly opted for revealing all, showing us the naked machinery, inviting us to compete in putting the pieces into the jig-saw. And surprised us anyway. The sheer cockiness of his method compounds our delight." Sylvie Drake of the *Los Angeles Times* calls the play "two hours of escapist fun, a roller-coaster ride through convolutions of plot and psyches."

"Deathtrap" provides as many laughs as chills, following in the tradition of *Arsenic and Old Lace* and other Broadway thrillers. Sidney Bruhl's witty remarks about the writer's life and the writing of mysteries are a running commentary on the play itself. "All the way through," Shepard remarks, "['Deathtrap'] is laughing at itself and perhaps at the genre on which it is a takeoff, although at its moment of murder it wipes the smile off your face." Levin, Lardner writes, "is

after laughs as well as screams.... 'Deathtrap' is capable of generating both responses, sometimes all but simultaneously." Speaking to Gillespie, Levin defends the thriller tradition in theatre. "Thrillers are satisfying deep down," Levin says, "because they give you the chance to deal safely with violence and murder.... They're horror stories with happy endings." "Deathtrap," too, has a happy ending. In addition to its record-breaking run on Broadway, the play was performed by four national touring companies, was made into a film, and won an Edgar Allan Poe Award.

Levin's books have enjoyed sales in the millions of copies, his novels and plays have been made into popular films, and his work has been translated into many languages. His publisher, Random House, prints a minimum of 100,000 copies of every new book he writes. It is no surprise, then, to hear Levin tell Lardner that his primary purpose "will always be to entertain.... I really in general tend to resent works of art that make a moral point. In a way, when you write something sheerly to entertain, that's making a moral point, too."

MEDIA ADAPTATIONS: A Kiss before Dying was filmed by United Artists in 1956, *No Time for Sergeants* by Twentieth Century-Fox in 1959, *Critic's Choice* by Warner Bros. in 1962, *Rosemary's Baby* by Paramount in 1968, "Dr. Cook's Garden" by the American Broadcasting Co. in 1970, *The Stepford Wives* by Columbia in 1975, *The Boys from Brazil* by Twentieth Century-Fox in 1978, and *Deathtrap* by Warner Bros. in 1982.

BIOGRAPHICAL/CRITICAL SOURCES:

BOOKS

Contemporary Literary Criticism, Gale, Volume III, 1975, Volume VI, 1976.

PERIODICALS

Best Sellers, April 15, 1967.
Books and Bookmen, December, 1972.
Chicago Sunday Tribune, October 25, 1953.
Christian Science Monitor, September 27, 1972.
Library Journal, April 15, 1967.
Los Angeles Times, March 29, 1979.
National Observer, June 12, 1967, February 24, 1969.
New Republic, June 20, 1981.
New Statesman, April 16, 1976.
Newsweek, April 17, 1967, March 16, 1970, November 5, 1973, February 23, 1976.
New Yorker, November 21, 1953, November 5, 1973, March 8, 1976.
New York Herald Tribune Book Review, October 18, 1953.
New York Magazine, November 12, 1973.
New York Times, October 25, 1953, March 5, 1978, April 30, 1979, August 17, 1981, June 8, 1982, April 23, 1985.
New York Times Book Review, April 30, 1967, October 15, 1972, March 14, 1976.
People, May 15, 1978.
Publishers Weekly, May 22, 1967.
Punch, April 15, 1970.
Saturday Review, April 15, 1967, October 7, 1972.
Studies in American Fiction, autumn, 1974.
Time, June 23, 1967, November 12, 1973, February 23, 1976.
Times Literary Supplement, June 1, 1967.
Village Voice, November 8, 1973.
Washington Post, October 5, 1978, July 22, 1979, July 26, 1979.

Washington Post Book World, February 15, 1975.
World, October 10, 1972.

—*Sketch by Thomas Wiloch*

*   *   *

LEYNARD, Martin
   See BERGER, Ivan (Bennett)

*   *   *

LIEBERSON, Stanley   1933-

PERSONAL: Born April 20, 1933, in Montreal, Quebec, Canada; son of Jack (a garment worker) and Ida (Cohen) Lieberson; married Patricia Beard, 1960; children: Rebecca, David, Miriam, Rachel. *Education:* Attended Brooklyn College (now Brooklyn College of the City University of New York), 1950-52; University of Chicago, M.A., 1958, Ph.D., 1960.

ADDRESSES: Home—560 Valle Vista Ave., Oakland, Calif. 94610. *Office*—Department of Sociology, University of California, Barrows 442, Berkeley, Calif. 94720.

CAREER: State University of Iowa, Iowa City, 1959-61, began as instructor, became professor of sociology; University of Wisconsin—Madison, assistant professor, 1961-63, associate professor, 1963-66, professor of sociology, 1966-67; University of Washington, Seattle, professor of sociology and director of Center for Demography and Ecology, 1967-71; University of Chicago, Chicago, Ill., professor of sociology and associate director of Population Research and Training Center, 1971-74; University of Arizona, Tucson, professor of sociology, 1974-83; University of California, Berkeley, professor of sociology, 1983—. Claude Bissell Visiting Professor, University of Toronto, 1979-80. Associate director, Iowa Urban Community Research Center, 1959-61.

MEMBER: International Population Union, American Sociological Association, Population Association of America, Pacific Sociological Society.

WRITINGS:

(With Otis Dudley Duncan, W. Richard Scott, Beverly Duncan, and Hal H. Winsborough) *Metropolis and Region,* Johns Hopkins Press, 1960.
Ethnic Patterns in American Cities, Free Press of Glencoe, 1963.
(Editor) *Explorations in Sociolinguistics,* Indiana University Press, 1967.
Language and Ethnic Relations in Canada, Wiley, 1970.
(With Beverly Duncan) *Metropolis and Region in Transition,* Sage Publications, 1970.
A Piece of the Pie: Blacks and White Immigrants since 1880, University of California Press, 1980.
Language Diversity and Language Contact, Stanford University Press, 1981.
Making It Count: The Improvement of Social Research and Theory, University of California Press, 1985.

WORK IN PROGRESS: A monograph on ethnic groups in the United States.

*   *   *

LIMBACHER, James L.   1926-

PERSONAL: Born November 30, 1926, in St. Marys, Ohio; son of F. J. and Edith (Smith) Limbacher. *Education:* Bowling

Green State University, B.A., 1949, M.A., 1954; Indiana University, M.S. in education, 1955; Wayne State University, M.S. in Library Science, 1972. *Religion:* Unitarian Universalist.

ADDRESSES: Home—21800 Morley Ave., Apt. 1201, Dearborn, Mich. 48124.

CAREER: Bowling Green State University, Bowling Green, Ohio, assistant director of news bureau, 1949-53; Dearborn Public Library, Dearborn, Mich., audio-visual director, 1955-83.

MEMBER: American Federation of Film Societies (president, 1962-65), Educational Film Library Association (vice-president, 1963-65; president, 1966-70), Society for Cinema Studies, American Library Association, Alpha Tau Omega, Theta Alpha Phi, Omicron Delta Kappa, Beta Phi Mu.

WRITINGS:

Four Aspects of the Film, Brussel & Brussel, 1966.
(Editor) *Making Films Work for Your Community,* Educational Film Library Association, 1966.
(Editor) *Using Films: A Handbook for the Program Planner,* Educational Film Library Association, 1967.
A Reference Guide to Audiovisual Information, Bowker, 1972.
Film Music: From Violins to Video, Scarecrow, 1972.
Library Film Ratings, Pierian, 1972.
The Song List, Pierian, 1974.
Haven't I Seen You Somewhere Before?, Pierian, 1979.
Keeping Score, Scarecrow, 1980.
Sexuality in World Cinema, Scarecrow, 1984.

PUBLISHED BY DEARBORN PUBLIC LIBRARY

A Short History of the Sound Film, 1962.
(Editor) *Theatrical Events, 1900-1962,* 1962.
(Editor) *A Selected List of Recorded Musical Scores from Radio, Television and Motion Pictures,* 1962.
A Historical Study of the Color Motion Picture, 1963.
A Historical Study of the Widescreen Motion Picture, 1963.
Perspective on the Third Dimensional Film, 1964.
A Handbook for American Film Societies, 1965.
Movies before 1920, 1965.

OTHER

Also author of seventeen produced plays, including "A Lazy Afternoon," "The Rocking Chair," "My Wife Ruthie," "It Takes One to Know One," "Voices in the Hall," and "Summer B.O." Author of musical comedies "Barbara of Seville," 1949, "Swing It, Shakespeare," 1951, "Fancy Meeting You Here," 1959, and "Come As You Are," 1960, and of opera librettos "Masquerade" (English version of "Die Fledermaus"), "Hansel and Gretel," and "Turkish Delight" (English version of "Abu Hassan").

Author of filmscripts, including "The Man Called Edison," "The Gold Rush—'68," "The Lost World Revisited," and "Had You Lived Then: Midwest Family Life in 1910." Author of material for and host of television series "See Here," 1955, "Vista," 1956, "Number Please," 1957, "Shadows on the Wall," 1974, "The Screening Room," 1978, and "Talking Pictures," 1984. Author of over one hundred radio scripts for "The School of the Sky" at Indiana University.

Editor of biennial publication *Feature Films on 8, 16, and Videotape,* Bowker. Contributor of chapters to *Non-Book Librarianship, Hollywood Kids, Educational Media Yearbook,* and *International Dictionary of Films and Filmmakers.* Film and theatre critic, "Seen and Heard" column, *Dearborn Press,* 1956-73. Contributor to *Film Society Review, Variety,* and other periodicals. Editor of "The Recorded Word" column, *Library Journal;* member of editorial board, *Media Review Digest* and *Journal of Popular Film and Television.*

WORK IN PROGRESS: A revised edition of *Four Aspects of the Film; A Century of Movies.*

SIDELIGHTS: James L. Limbacher told *CA:* "After eighteen books in twenty years, I would like to turn them over to young film scholars for updating and revision and spend time editing."

*   *   *

LINDOP, Edmund   1925-

PERSONAL: Born August 31, 1925, in Chicago, Ill.; son of Edmund Frank (a realtor) and Sarah (Vaughn) Lindop; married Esther Crabtree (a writer and teacher), July 29, 1962. *Education:* University of Southern California, B.A. (summa cum laude), 1947, M.A., 1950; additional study at National University of Mexico and University of California, Los Angeles. *Religion:* Methodist.

ADDRESSES: Home—920 Las Pulgas Rd., Pacific Palisades, Calif.

CAREER: Social studies teacher in Torrance, Calif., 1948-49, and Los Angeles, Calif., 1949-56; University High School, Los Angeles, history and government teacher, 1957—, chairman of social studies department, 1959-60, 1971—; University of California, Los Angeles, training teacher, 1957—.

MEMBER: American Academy of Political and Social Studies, National Council for the Social Studies, Phi Beta Kappa, Phi Delta Kappa, Chi Phi.

WRITINGS:

(With others) *Understanding Latin America,* Ginn & Co., 1960, new edition, 1967.
Jumbo, King of Elephants, Little, Brown, 1960.
Hubert, the Traveling Hippopotamus, Little, Brown, 1961.
Life in Latin America, Ginn & Co., 1962.
Pelorus Jack, Dolphin Pilot, Little, Brown, 1964.
George Washington and the First Balloon Flight, Albert Whitman, 1964.
(With Jospeh Jares) *White House Sportsmen,* Houghton, 1964.
War Eagle: The Story of a Civil War Mascot, Little, Brown, 1966.
The First Book of Elections, F. Watts, 1968, revised edition, 1972.
Modern America: The Dazzling Twenties, F. Watts, 1970.
Modern America: The Turbulent Thirties, F. Watts, 1970.
An Album of the Fifties, F. Watts, 1978.
Our Neighbors in Latin America, Ginn & Co., 1980.
Cuba, F. Watts, 1980.
Latin America, Ginn & Co., 1983.
All about Republicans, Enslow Publications, 1985.
(With Joy Thornton) *All about Democrats,* Enslow Publications, 1985.

Contributor to professional journals.

SIDELIGHTS: Edmund Lindop told *CA:* "Why is history the source for much of my writing? It is because I see the past as an exciting drama performed by colorful, intriguing people, whose adventures and accomplishments were far more fascinating than anything recorded in fiction."

LIPSEY, Richard G(eorge)   1928-

PERSONAL: Born August 28, 1928, in Victoria, British Columbia, Canada; son of Richard A. (a company manager) and Faith (Ledingham) Lipsey; married Assia Gutman, 1952 (divorced); married Diana Louise Smart (a free-lance editor), October 3, 1960; children: Mark (stepson), Mathew, Joanna, Claudia. *Education:* Attended Victoria College, 1946-48; University of British Columbia, B.A. (with first class honors), 1951; University of Toronto, M.A., 1953; London School of Economics and Political Science, Ph.D., 1957.

ADDRESSES: Office—Department of Economics, Queen's University, Kingston, Ontario, Canada K7L 3N6.

CAREER: British Columbia Provincial Government, Bureau of Economics and Statistics, Victoria, British Columbia, research assistant, 1950-53; University of London, London School of Economics and Political Science, London, England, assistant lecturer, 1955-58, lecturer, 1958-60, reader, 1960-61, professor of economics, 1961-63, head of department, 1961-63; University of California, Berkeley, visiting professor of economics, 1963-64; University of Essex, Colchester, England, professor of economics, 1964-70, head of department, 1964-68, dean of School of Social Studies, 1964-67; Queen's University, Kingston, Ontario, Sir Edward Peacock Professor of Economics, 1970—, on leave, 1983—; C. D. Howe Institute, Toronto, Ontario, senior economic advisor, 1983—.

Visiting professor at University of British Columbia, 1969-70, University of Colorado, 1974-75, and City University, London, England, 1979; Simon Visiting Professor at Victoria University of Manchester, 1973; Irving Fisher Visiting Professor at Yale University, 1979-80. Senior economic adviser to National Economic Development Council, 1961-63; member of council and planning committee of National Institute of Economic and Social Research, 1962-72; founding member of Social Science Research Council, 1966-69; member of selection committee of Killam Foundation, 1978-80. Member of policy analysis group of Canada's Department of Consumer and Corporate Affairs.

MEMBER: Canadian Economic Association (president-elect, 1979-80), Econometric Society (fellow), Economic Study Society (chairman, 1965-69), Royal Economic Society (member of council, 1967-71), United Kingdom Association of University Teachers of Economics (member of council, 1967-70).

AWARDS, HONORS: Lister Lecturer Award from British Association for the Advancement of Science, 1961; Killam Foundation senior fellowship, 1974-75; honorary LL.D., McMaster University, 1984; honorary LL.D., University of Victoria, 1985.

WRITINGS:

An Introduction to Positive Economics, Weidenfeld & Nicolson, 1963, 6th edition, 1983.
(With P. O. Steiner) *Economics: An Introductory Analysis,* Harper, 1966, 7th edition, 1984.
An Introduction to a Mathematical Treatment of Economics, Weidenfeld & Nicolson, 1967, 3rd edition, 1977.
The Theory of Customs Unions: A General Equilibrium Analysis, Weidenfeld & Nicolson, 1973.
(With G. C. Archibald) *Mathematical Economics: Methods and Applications,* Harper, 1976.
(With C. Harburg) *An Introduction to the United Kingdom Economy,* Pitman, 1983, 2nd edition, 1985.
(With F. Flatters) *Common Ground for the Canadian Common Market,* Institute for Research on Public Policy, 1984.

(With M. Smith) *Canada's Trade Options,* C. D. Howe Institute, 1985.

CONTRIBUTOR

A. M. Ross, editor, *Employment Policy and the Labor Market,* University of California Press, 1965.

Harry M. Trebing, editor, *Essays on Public Utility Pricing and Regulation,* Michigan State University Press, 1971.

B. A. Corry and M. H. Peston, editors, *Essays in Honor of Lionel Robbins,* Weidenfeld & Nicolson, 1972.

Fritz Machlup, editor, *Economic Integration: Worldwide, Regional, and Sectorial,* Macmillan, 1976.

Michael Walker, editor, *Which Way Ahead,* Fraser Institute, 1977.

A. R. Bergstrom and other editors, *Stability and Inflation,* Wiley, 1977.

M. J. Artis and A. R. Nobay, editors, *Studies in Modern Economics,* Basil Blackwell, 1977.

Options Canada: Proceedings of the Conference on the Future of the Canadian Federation, University of Toronto Press, 1977.

David Smith, editor, *Essays in Honour of John Deutsch,* C. D. Howe Institute, 1980.

G. Lermer, *Probing,* Leviathan, 1984.

Also contributor to *After Monetarism,* edited by J. Cornwall, 1983, and to *Encyclopedia of Social Sciences.*

OTHER

Contributor of about thirty articles to academic journals. Editor of *Review of Economic Studies,* 1962-64.

WORK IN PROGRESS: Spatial Relations in Value Theory; Economics for the Millions, on the "economics that every intelligent layman ought to know but probably doesn't"; research on spatial economics and oligopoly theory; research on issues in Canadian macro-economic theory.

SIDELIGHTS: Richard G. Lipsey told *CA* that his "writings on policy include 'The Relation between Political and Economic Separatism: A Pessimistic View,' an analysis of some possible consequences to Quebec of political separation; *Appendix* to the *Legal Factum* submitted by the Canadian Labour Congress to the Supreme Court of Canada in the matter of the constitutionality of Canadian wage-price controls, which argued that, according to economic evidence, there was *not* a major emergency or crisis situation existing in the Canadian economy in the fall of 1975, and which was the first 'expert' (non-legal) evidence ever admitted to and commented on by the Canadian Supreme Court; and one of the early attempts to measure statistically the effectiveness (or what turned out to be the lack of effectiveness) of wage-price controls in Britain.

"Major theoretical and empirical studies include 'The Relation between Unemployment and the Rate of Change of Money Wage Rates in the U.K., 1862-1957' which, when published in 1960, provided the original theoretical explanation of the famous Phillips curve that related inflation to unemployment.

"I am currently on three years leave from Queen's University and am working on current policy issues with the C. D. Howe Institute in Toronto. My major activity has been to write a book analysing Canada's trade options and advocating the formation of a Free Trade Association between Canada and the United States."

Lipsey's books have been translated into Portuguese, Spanish, German, Italian, Greek, Hebrew, French, Giyarati, Sinhala, Tamil, Japanese, and Hindi.

AVOCATIONAL INTERESTS: Filmmaking, skiing, deep sea sailing.

*   *   *

LOCHER, Frances C(arol)

PERSONAL: Born in Colon, Panama; American citizen born abroad; daughter of Frank Joseph and Carol E. (Engels) Locher; married Joseph F. Freiman, July 2, 1976; children: Jonathan Locher Freiman, Matthew Locher Freiman. *Education:* Attended Mount Mercy College (now Carlow College), La Roche College, Duquesne University, and Wayne County Community College; received A.B. from University of Michigan—Dearborn.

ADDRESSES: Home—1520 Linwood Ave., Royal Oak, Mich. 48067. *Office*—Gale Research Co., Book Tower, Detroit, Mich. 48226.

CAREER: Transcriber of physicians' orders at hospital in Lincoln Park, Mich., 1971-75; Gale Research Co., Detroit, Mich., editorial assistant, 1974-75, assistant editor, 1975-76, associate editor, 1976-77, editor, 1977-82, consulting editor, 1982—. Volunteer worker at state hospital in Sewickley, Pa., 1970.

MEMBER: Association for Research and Enlightenment.

WRITINGS:

Contemporary Authors, Gale, Volumes 13-16 revised (editorial assistant), 1975, Volumes 53-56 (editorial assistant), 1975, Volume 1 permanent series (editorial assistant), 1975, Volumes 17-20 revised (assistant editor), 1976, Volumes 21-24 revised (assistant editor), 1977, Volumes 65-68 (associate editor), 1977, Volume 2 permanent series (contributing editor), 1978, Volumes 69-72 (associate editor), 1978.

EDITOR

Contemporary Authors, Gale, Volumes 73-76, 1978, Volumes 77-80, 1979, Volumes 81-84, 1979, Volumes 85-88, 1980, Volumes 89-92, 1980, Volumes 93-96, 1980, Volumes 97-100, 1981, Volume 101, 1981, Volume 102, 1981, Volume 103, 1982, Volume 104, 1982, Volume 105, 1982, Volume 106, 1982.

CONSULTING EDITOR

Contemporary Authors, Gale, Volume 107, 1983, Volume 108, 1983, Volume 109, 1983, Volume 110, 1984, Volume 111, 1984, Volume 112, 1985, Volume 113, 1985, Volume 114, 1985, Volume 115, 1985, Volume 116, 1986.

OTHER

Contributor to magazines.

*   *   *

LOGAN, Ford
See NEWTON, D(wight) B(ennett)

*   *   *

LONGGOOD, William (Frank) 1917-

PERSONAL: Born September 12, 1917, in St. Louis, Mo.; son of William F. and Grace (Turner) Longgood; married Margaret Henning, 1948; children: Bret. *Education:* University of Missouri, B.J., 1940.

ADDRESSES: Home—Box 152, Truro, Mass. 02666.

CAREER: WHLD-Radio, Niagara Falls, N.Y., writer-salesman, 1940-42; KDB-Radio, Santa Barbara, Calif., writer-salesman, 1942-43; *Newark News*, Newark, N.J., reporter, 1946-48; *New York World-Telegram and Sun*, reporter and feature writer, 1948-65; Time-Life Books, Alexandria, Va., text editor, 1965-68; free-lance writer specializing in nature writing and environmental concerns, 1968—; *New York Times*, New York, N.Y., Cape Cod correspondent, 1973—. Teacher of feature writing, New School for Social Research, 1966-72, and Columbia University Graduate School of Journalism, 1973. *Military service:* U.S. Army Air Forces, 1942-45.

AWARDS, HONORS: Pulitzer Prize; Polk Award for newspaper work; New York Newspaper Guild award; National Headliners award for feature writing; Newspaper Reporters Association of New York City award.

WRITINGS:

The Suez Story, Greenburg, 1956.
(With Ed Wallace) *The Pink Slip*, McGraw, 1958.
The Poisons in Your Food, Simon & Schuster, 1960.
Talking Your Way to Success: The Story of the Dale Carnegie Course, Association Press, 1962.
Ike: A Pictorial Biography, Time-Life, 1969.
Write It Right, Scholastic Book Services, 1970.
Write with Feeling, Scholastic Book Services, 1970.
The Darkening Land, Simon & Schuster, 1972.
(Contributor) *Family Encyclopedia of American History*, Reader's Digest Association, 1975.
The Queen Must Die: And Other Affairs of Bees and Men, Norton, 1984.

Contributor to numerous magazines.

WORK IN PROGRESS: A nature book.

SIDELIGHTS: William Longgood wrote *CA:* "Why do we write? That question endlessly fascinates me. For glory? Fortune? Ego satisfaction? Out of boredom or frustration? To find in fantasy that which is denied us in this mechanistic-materialistic world? To convert the 'heathen'? Whatever force commands us, whether personal, social, political or monetary—and each of us has his own inspiration or demons—all of us, individually and collectively, probably want to pass along some small part of that which is uniquely us.

"My own greatest writing satisfaction came from my book *The Queen Must Die: And Other Affairs of Bees and Men.* The real and enduring reward is when readers write or say it has given them a new perspective on another form of life. If I change another person's life view, even in a small respect, or add a dimension to their being, then the written word has once more wrought its age-old miracle: making it possible for distant worlds to touch, merge and reshape—reason enough to keep me, and others like me, plugging away in pursuit of our own dreams and elusive life goals."

AVOCATIONAL INTERESTS: Chess, fencing, tennis, reading, gardening, and carpentry.

BIOGRAPHICAL/CRITICAL SOURCES:

PERIODICALS

Cultural Information Service, March 9, 1984.
Los Angeles Times Book Review, January 13, 1985.
Newsweek, March 25, 1985.
New York Times Book Review, November 19, 1972.

Rocky Mountain News (Denver, Colo.), April 28, 1985.
Yankee, August, 1985.

*　　*　　*

LOVEMAN, Brian E(lliot)　1944-

PERSONAL: Born in 1944 in Los Angeles, Calif.; son of Bernard J. and Rosalie Loveman; married Sharon Ann Siem; children: Taryn, Mara, Carly, Ryan, Ben. *Education:* University of California, Berkeley, A.B., 1965; Indiana University, M.A., 1969, Ph.D., 1973.

ADDRESSES: Office—Department of Political Science, San Diego State University, San Diego, Calif. 92182.

CAREER: U.S. Peace Corps, Washington, D.C., community development volunteer in southern Chile, 1965-67; San Diego State University, San Diego, Calif., assistant professor, 1973-76, associate professor, 1976-79, professor of Latin American politics, 1979—, chairman of Latin American studies program and co-director of Latin American Studies Center, 1979-81. Visiting assistant professor at University of California, San Diego, summer, 1974. Conducted field research in Mexico and Chile. Speaker at national seminars and meetings. Research consultant, U.S. Department of Agriculture's Economic Research Service and International Development Research Center, Indiana University at Bloomington.

MEMBER: Phi Beta Kappa, Phi Kappa Phi.

AWARDS, HONORS: Woodrow Wilson fellow, 1965, 1971-72.

WRITINGS:

El campesino chileno le escribe a su excelensia (title means "The Chilean Peasant Writes to 'His Excellency,'"), Instituto de Capacitacion e Investigacion en Reforma Agraria, 1971.
El mito de la marginalidad: Participacion y represion del campesinado chileno (title means "The Myth of Marginality: Participation and Repression of the Chilean Peasantry"), Instituto de Capacitacion e Investigacion en Reforma Agraria, 1971.
Antecedentes para el estudio del movimiento campesino chileno: Pliegos de peticiones, huelgas y sindicatos agricolas, 1932-1966 (title means "Data for the Study of The Chilean Rural Labor Movement: Labor Petitions, Strikes, and Agricultural Unions"), two volumes, Instituto de Capacitacion e Investigacion en Reforma Agraria, 1971.
Struggle in the Countryside: Politics and Rural Labor in Chile, 1919-1973, Indiana University Press, 1976.
Struggle in the Countryside: A Documentary Supplement, International Development Research Center, Indiana University, 1976.
(Editor with Thomas M. Davies, Jr., and contributor) *The Politics of Antipolitics: The Military in Latin America*, University of Nebraska Press, 1978, 2nd edition, in press.
Chile: The Legacy of Hispanic Capitalism, Oxford University Press, 1979.
(Author of introduction and case studies with Davies) *Che Guevara on Guerrilla Warfare*, University of Nebraska Press, 1985.

CONTRIBUTOR

Arturo Valenzuela and J. Samuel Valenzuela, editors, *Chile: Politics and Society*, Transaction Books, 1976.

Foreign Investment in U.S. Real Estate, Economic Research Service, U.S. Department of Agriculture, 1976.

John Booth and Mitchell Seligson, editors, *Political Participation in Latin America,* Volume II, Holmes & Meier, 1979.

Albert Blum, editor, *International Handbook of Industrial Relations,* Greenwood Press, 1981.

Research Guide to Andean History, Duke University Press, 1981.

Harrell Rodgers, Jr., editor, *Public Policy and Social Institutions,* JAI Press, 1984.

OTHER

Contributor to *Handbook of Contemporary Development in World Industrial Relations* and *Andean Research Guide.* Contributor of about fifteen articles and reviews to Latin American studies, public administration, journalism, political science, and history journals.

WORK IN PROGRESS: Policy Consequences on Military Rule in Latin America.

SIDELIGHTS: Brian E. Loveman's current research interests include Latin American labor movements, agrarian reform and peasant organizations, recent military regimes, national development strategies, and local politics in Latin America, internal migration in Mexico (with special reference to Baja California), and the policy consequences of military rule in Latin America.

*   *   *

LOWNEY, Paul Benjamin   1922-

PERSONAL: Born March 25, 1922, in Butte, Mont.; son of Mark (a plumbing contractor) and Bessie (Wicks) Lowney; children: Ivy (Mrs. Steven Holt). *Education:* Montana State University, B.A., 1943; also attended Cornish School of Music, 1950, and University of Washington, Seattle, 1950-52, 1954-56. *Politics:* Republican.

ADDRESSES: Home—1808 40th Ave. E., Seattle, Wash. 98112. *Office*—1219 Westlake Ave. N., Seattle, Wash. 98109.

CAREER: American National Red Cross, Washington, D.C., staff writer, 1946; Seattle Port of Embarkation, Seattle, Wash., public information officer, 1947-54; Photo Publishing Co., Seattle, owner, 1956-82; Lowney Advertising, Seattle, owner, 1968—. *Military service:* U.S. Army Reserve, Military Intelligence, 1948-54; became first lieutenant.

MEMBER: Alpha Tau Omega (president, 1941).

AWARDS, HONORS: Port of Seattle Maritime Editorial Award, 1951, 1955.

WRITINGS:

Washington: America's Most Scenic State, privately printed, 1957.
This Is Hydroplaning, privately printed, 1959.
Offbeat Humor, Peter Pauper, 1962.
The Best in Offbeat Humor, Peter Pauper, 1968.
Gleeb, Dodd, 1973.
The Big Book of Gleeb, Dodd, 1975.
The Best of Gleeb, Columbia Publishing, 1983.
The Love Game, Columbia Publishing, 1984.

Also author and publisher of pamphlet *Seattle: The Nation's Most Beautiful City,* 1973. Author of cartoon strips "The Poo-

kas," Los Angeles Times Syndicate, 1977-78, and "Gleeb," syndicated by Copley News Service, 1980—.

SIDELIGHTS: Paul Benjamin Lowney writes: "*Gleeb* is the culmination of my search for a substantive and challenging type of humor—one in which I am able to deal with the nonsensical and frivolous aspects of human existence, as well as the fascinating data found in the physical sciences, philosophy, psychology, and sociology.

"Humor writing has always intrigued me. My first attempt was a column for my high school newspaper. I went through the usual juvenile addiction to word play, and then proceeded to a love affair with 'offbeat humor' with its wildly incongruous situations. After writing two books in this vein, I evolved the ideal format for my particular brand of humor—*Gleeb.*

"This format is a short dialogue form, usually running from six to eighteen lines. A 'gleebism' most always ends with a humorous line and, with only one exception, each has been confined to a single book page; and no paragraph—no matter how long—ever contains more than one sentence.

"I have arrived at a point in my life where I see little purpose in writing—or for that matter, engaging in any of the art forms—unless there is something in it for human knowledge and human betterment. It is not enough simply to entertain. I want the additional ingredient of saying something which informs, gives insight, and provokes thought. I like to believe that I succeed in this goal with each book I write."

*   *   *

LUKACS, John (Adalbert)   1923-

PERSONAL: Born in 1923 in Budapest, Hungary; son of Paul (a doctor) and Magdalena (Gluck) Lukacs; married Helen Elizabeth Schofield, 1953 (died, 1970); married Stephanie Harvey, 1974; children: (first marriage) Paul, Annemarie. *Education:* Cambridge University, certificate of proficiency, 1939; Budapest University, Ph.D., 1946.

ADDRESSES: Home—Pickering Close, Valley Park Rd., Phoenixville, Pa. 19460. *Office*—Department of History, Chestnut Hill College, Philadelphia, Pa. 19118.

CAREER: Chestnut Hill College, Philadelphia, Pa., associate professor of history, 1947—. Visiting professor, Columbia University, 1954-55, University of Pennsylvania, 1964, Johns Hopkins School of Advanced International Studies, 1970-71, and Fletcher School of Law and Diplomacy, 1971, 1972; Fulbright professor, University of Toulouse, 1964-65.

MEMBER: American Catholic Historical Association (president, 1977).

WRITINGS:

The Great Powers and Eastern Europe, American Book Co., 1953.
(Editor and translator) Alexis de Tocqueville, *European Revolution* [and] *Correspondence with Gobineau,* Doubleday, 1959.
A History of the Cold War, Doubleday, 1961, 3rd edition published as *A New History of the Cold War,* 1966.
Decline and Rise of Europe, Doubleday, 1965.
Historical Consciousness, Harper, 1968, new and enlarged edition, Schocken, 1985.
The Passing of the Modern Age, Harper, 1970.
The Last European War: September 1939-December 1941, Doubleday, 1976.

1945: Year Zero, Doubleday, 1978.
Philadelphia: Patricians and Philistines, 1900-1950, Farrar, Straus, 1981.
Outgrowing Democracy: A History of the United States in the Twentieth Century, Doubleday, 1984.

Also author of *A History of Chestnut Hill College, 1924-74,* 1975. Contributor to encyclopedias and periodicals.

SIDELIGHTS: John Lukacs's histories of the years of World War II and the decades since that conflict have earned him the title "philosophical historian" among reviewers of his works. According to Daniel Yergin in the *New York Times Book Review,* Lukacs's book *1945: Year Zero,* a series of profiles of five national leaders of that year, "is not really a history so much as a brisk meditation on, and memoir of, the era." John Ratte raises the same point in *Commonweal* about Lukacs's study of European involvement in World War II, *The Last European War:* "Because Lukacs is a philosophical historian, he is able to make plausible to us—with condemnation or praise as he sees appropriate—the realities of the late 1930s and early 1940s." Leonard Bushkoff, reviewing *1945: Year Zero* for the *Washington Post Book World,* affirms that Lukacs's memoirs are "compelling," but adds, "Raw emotion, however much it benefits Lukacs the memoirist, undercuts Lukacs the historian." Yergin, however, finds Lukacs's philosophical approach thought-provoking. "Lukacs's is a rigorous intelligence making strong arguments in clear language," Yergin notes. "I wish other writers on the right would ponder Mr. Lukacs's insight."

Outgrowing Democracy: A History of the United States in the Twentieth Century, perhaps Lukacs's most controversial work, "is an engaging intellectual surprise party," writes Naomi Bliven in the *New Yorker.* The book suggests that democracy in the United States is being replaced by a paper-pushing bureaucracy of corporations and big government, and that a weakening of diplomatic influence, productivity, and wealth have signalled the nation's decline. "Lukacs's insights can be reliable," J. C. Furnas asserts in the *New York Times Book Review,* "and he is not gingerly in making a statement." This plain-spoken statement of opinion does not find universal approval among critics, however. Peter Lowenberg, for example, writes in the *Los Angeles Times Book Review* that Lukacs's "view of our situation is pessimistic, pungent and often witty; but also flip, impertinent, nostalgic and dinosaurian." Bliven concludes her review by commenting: "Were American history—never mind American dominance—to cease tomorrow, our contribution to the process of advancement would deserve a more generous assessment than Mr. Lukacs's." Nevertheless, reviewer Edwin M. Yoder, Jr., praises Lukacs's work in the *Washington Post Book World:* "This eloquent, provocative but disturbing book is vulnerable . . . to the usual fate of meta-historical works—it will be easy enough to pluck the more cranky and curmudgeonly passages out of context. . . . That would be an injustice to a valuable and thoughtful work; and it would obscure a warning that may be timelier than we like to think."

BIOGRAPHICAL/CRITICAL SOURCES:

PERIODICALS

Best Sellers, December 1, 1970, July, 1978.
Book World, November 10, 1968, November 15, 1970.
Christian Science Monitor, March 1, 1976.
Commonweal, January 10, 1969, July 30, 1976.
Los Angeles Times Book Review, April 15, 1984.

National Review, November 5, 1968, October 20, 1970, April 30, 1976, May 12, 1978.
New Republic, November 16, 1968, October 20, 1970, December 12, 1970, January 27, 1982.
New Yorker, July 16, 1984.
New York Times Book Review, March 21, 1976, April 23, 1978, June 14, 1981, September 30, 1984.
Saturday Review, March 1, 1969.
Washington Post Book World, April 2, 1978, May 6, 1984.

*   *   *

LUNDBERG, Erik F(ilip)   1907-

PERSONAL: Born August 13, 1907, in Stockholm, Sweden; son of Filip and Astrid (Stedt) Lundberg; married Gertrud Nebelung, March 28, 1937; children: Britta Lundberg Tschinkel, Klas, Gunnar. *Education:* University of Stockholm, D.Phil, 1937; attended University of Chicago, 1981-82, and Columbia University, 1982-83.

ADDRESSES: Home—Syrenparken 13, S-13300 Saltsjoebaden, Sweden. *Office*—Skandinavisker, Enskilda Banken, 10322 Stockholm, Sweden.

CAREER: Government Ecomomic Research Institute, Stockholm, Sweden, head, 1937-55; University of Stockholm, Stockholm, professor of economics, 1946-65; Stockholm School of Economics, Stockholm, professor of economics, 1965-76, professor emeritus, 1976—. Visiting professor at University of Washington, Seattle, 1950, and University of California, Berkeley, 1960-61. Head of World Bank Mission to Portugal, 1964; president of Royal Swedish Academy of Sciences, 1973-76; chairman of Nobel Committee for Economics, 1974-79. Member of State Power Board, Stockholm, 1946—, and Swedish Government Planning Council, 1960—. Member of board of directors, Fagersta Steel Co., 1948-68, and Dagens Nyheters Publishing Co., 1964-72. Economic advisor to government of Iceland, 1935, Central Bank of Australia, 1955-56, and government of Portugal, 1974-77; scientific advisor to Scandinavian Bank, 1955—.

MEMBER: International Economic Association (president, 1969-79), American Economic Association.

AWARDS, HONORS: Arnberg Prize, 1946, and Soederstrom Prize, 1980, both from the Royal Swedish Academy of Sciences; Bernhard Harms Prize, Institut fuer Weltwirtschaft an der Universitaet Kiel, 1980.

WRITINGS:

Studies in the Theory of Economic Expansion, P. S. King & Son, 1937, reprinted, Kelley, 1970.
Konjunkturer och ekonomisk politik, 1953, translation published as *Business Cycles and Economic Policy,* Allen & Unwin, 1955.
Produktivitet och Raentabilitet (title means "Productivity and Profitability"), Norstedts, 1961.
Instability and Economic Growth, Yale University Press, 1968.
Svensk finanspolitik i teori och praktik (title means "Swedish Fiscal Policy in Theory and Practice"), Aldus/Bonnier, 1971.
(With Lars Calmfors) *Inflation och arbetsloeshet* (title means "Inflation and Unemployment"), Studiefoerbundet Naeringsliv och samhaelle, 1974.
(With Bengt Ryden) *Svensk ekonomisk politik: laerdomar fran 70-talet,* Studiefoerbundet Naeringsliv och samhaelle, 1980.

Ekonomiska Kriser foer och nu (title means "Economic Crisis in Past Times and Now"), Studie foerbundet Naeringsliv och samhaelle, 1983.

Also author of *Wages in Sweden, 1860-1930*, 1933.

EDITOR

Richard Stone and others, *Income and Wealth: Series One*, Bowes & Bowes, 1951.
The Business Cycle in the Post-War World: Proceedings of a Conference Held by the International Economic Association, St. Martin's, 1955.
Ekonomisk politik i foervandling, Norstedt, 1970.
Inflation Theory and Anti-Inflation Policy: Proceedings of a Conference Held by the International Economic Association at Saltsjoebaden, Sweden, Westview, 1977.
(With Sven Grassman) *The World Economic Order: Past and Prospects*, St. Martin's, 1981.

AVOCATIONAL INTERESTS: Tennis, swimming, hiking.

BIOGRAPHICAL/CRITICAL SOURCES:

BOOKS

On Incomes Policy: Papers and Proceedings from a Conference in Honor of Erik Lundberg, Studiefoerbundet Naeringsliv och samhaelle/Industrial Council for Social and Economic Studies, 1969.
Seligman, Ben, *Main Currents in Modern Economics*, Macmillan, 1962.

*   *   *

LUNDWALL, Sam J(errie)   1941-

PERSONAL: Born February 24, 1941, in Stockholm, Sweden; son of Thore (a master mechanic) and Sissi (Kuehn) Lundwall; married Ingrid Olofsdotter, June 16, 1972; children: Karin Beatrice Christina. *Education:* University of Stockholm, E.E., 1967.

ADDRESSES: Home—Storskogsvaegen 19, S-161 39 Bromma, Sweden. *Office*—Box 17030, S-16117 Bromma, Sweden. *Agent*—Spectrum Literary Agency, 60 East 42nd St., New York, N.Y. 10017.

CAREER: SSTA (Stockholm Technical Night-School), Stockholm, Sweden, electronics engineer, 1956-60; University of Stockholm, Stockholm, professional photographer, 1964-67; Christer Christian Photographic School, Fox Amphoux, France, professional photographer, 1967-68; Swedish Broadcasting Corp., Stockholm, television producer, 1968-69; Askild & Kaernekull Foerlag AB (publishers), Stockholm, editor for science fiction, 1970-73; Delta Foerlags AB (publishers), Bromma, Sweden, president, 1973-80. Judge, John W. Campbell Award, World Science Fiction Convention. Has directed television films; made short animated film based on his song "Waltz with Karin"; has recorded his own songs for Philips and Knaeppupp recording companies; has appeared on television, radio, and film as singer and artist throughout the Scandinavian countries. *Military service:* Swedish Air Force, 1960-61; electronics engineer.

MEMBER: World Science Fiction Society (president; member of board, European society), Science Fiction Writers of America.

AWARDS, HONORS: "Waltz with Karin" was named Sweden's best short film by Swedish Film Institute, 1967; Alvar award as Scandinavia's leading science fiction author from Futura (science fiction organization), 1971; Finnish Designer's Award for best book cover, 1971; Harrison Award, 1983.

WRITINGS:

Bibliografi oever Science Fiction och Fantasy (title means "Bibliography of Science Fiction and Fantasy"), Fiktiva, 1964, revised edition, 1984.
Visor i Vaar Tid (title means "Songs of Our Times"), Sonora, 1965.
Science Fiction: Fraan Begynnelsen till vaara dagar (title means "Science Fiction: From the Beginning to Our Days"), Sverges Radio Foerlag, 1969.
Alice's World, Ace Books, 1971.
No Time for Heroes, Ace Books, 1971.
Science Fiction: What It's All About, Ace Books, 1971.
Bernhard the Conqueror, DAW Books, 1973.
Den Fantastiska Romanen, four volumes (textbooks on fantastic stories and novels), Gummessons Grafiska, 1973-74.
King Kong Blues, DAW Books, 1974.
Bibliografi oever Science Fiction och Fantasy: 1741-1971, Lindqvist Foerlag, 1974.
Wat Is Science Fiction?, Meulenhoff, 1974.
Bernhards magiska sommar (title means "Bernhard's Magic Summer"), Lindqvist, 1975.
Alltid lady MacBeth (title means "Always Lady Macbeth"), Delta, 1975.
Moerkrets furste (title means "The Prince of Darkness"), Delta, 1975.
Mardroemmem (title means "The Nightmare"), Lindqvist, 1976.
Gaest i Frankensteins hus (title means "Guest in the House of Frankenstein"), Delta, 1976.
Utopia-Dystopia, Delta, 1977.
Science fiction pa svenska (title means "Science Fiction in Swedish"), Delta, 1977.
Science Fiction: An Illustrated History, Grosset, 1978.
Faengelsestaden (title means "The Prison City"), Norstedt, 1978.
Flicka i foenster vid vaerldens kant (title means "Girl in Window at the Edge of the World"), Norstedt, 1980.
Crash, Norstedt, 1982.
Tiden och Amelie (title means "Time and Amelie"), Fakta & Fantasy, 1985.

Editor of numerous science fiction anthologies and of collected works of Jules Verne; translator into Swedish of more than 150 novels and of poems by Francois Villon and George Brassens; author, producer, and director of television script from Frank Robinson's *The Hunting Season* and of other television films; author and composer of more than two hundred songs. Contributor of cartoons to Swedish edition of *Help!* and *Mad*. Contributor of articles to Swedish edition of *Popular Photography*. Editor-in-chief of *Jules Verne—Magasinet*, 1972—; editor, *Science Fiction-Serien*, 1973—.

WORK IN PROGRESS: Ygor, a novel.

*   *   *

LURIE, Alison   1926-

PERSONAL: Born September 3, 1926, in Chicago, Ill.; daughter of Harry and Bernice (Stewart) Lurie; married Jonathan Peale Bishop (a professor), September 10, 1948 (divorced,

1985); children: John, Jeremy, Joshua. *Education:* Radcliffe College, A.B., 1947.

ADDRESSES: Office—Department of English, Cornell University, Ithaca, N.Y. 14850.

CAREER: Cornell University, Ithaca, N.Y., lecturer, 1969-73, associate professor, 1973-76, professor of English, 1976—. Has also worked as a ghostwriter and librarian.

AWARDS, HONORS: Yaddo Foundation fellow, 1963, 1964, 1966; Guggenheim grant, 1965-66; Rockefeller Foundation grant, 1967-68; New York State Cultural Council Foundation grant, 1972-73; American Academy of Arts and Letters award in literature, 1978; American Book Award nomination in fiction, 1984, National Book Critics Circle Award nomination for best work of fiction, 1984, and Pulitzer Prize in fiction, 1985, all for *Foreign Affairs.*

WRITINGS:

V. R. Lang: A Memoir, privately printed, 1959.
V. R. Lang: Poems and Plays, Random House, 1974.
The Heavenly Zoo (juvenile), Farrar, Straus, 1980.
Clever Gretchen and Other Forgotten Folk Tales (juvenile), Crowell, 1980.
Fabulous Beasts (juvenile), Farrar, Straus, 1981.
The Language of Clothes (nonfiction), Random House, 1981.

NOVELS

Love and Friendship, Macmillan, 1962.
The Nowhere City, Coward, 1965.
Imaginary Friends, Coward, 1967.
Real People, Random House, 1969.
The War between the Tates, Random House, 1974.
Only Children, Random House, 1979.
Foreign Affairs, Random House, 1984.

OTHER

Also editor, with Justin G. Schiller, of "Classics of Children's Literature, 1631-1932" series, Garland Publishing. Contributor of articles and reviews to periodicals, including *New York Review of Books, New York Times Book Review, New Statesman,* and *New Review.*

SIDELIGHTS: Although she has written children's books and several works of nonfiction, Alison Lurie is best known for her novels, especially *The War between the Tates* and *Foreign Affairs,* each one a finely structured comedy of manners about people from an academic milieu. As Sara Sanborn states in a *New York Times Book Review* critique of *The War between the Tates,* from the beginning of her career Lurie "has regularly produced insightful and witty novels about The Way We Live Now, drawing on a large talent for social verisimilitude." Her work has been praised by a London *Times* reviewer as "formidably well made," while Christopher Lehmann-Haupt declares in the *New York Times* that Lurie "has quietly but surely established herself as one of this country's most able and witty novelists."

In the opinion of several critics, *The War between the Tates* and Lurie's Pulitzer Prize-winning *Foreign Affairs* are examples of the author at her best. A London *Times* reviewer explains that *The War between the Tates,* a comic novel about the marital difficulties of a professor and his wife in an era of campus unrest, "caught, just on the instant, the conflict between radical passions and more conventional moralities that raged like foreign wars in the early 1970s. It could now seem a period piece, its targets, with the hindsight of the 1980s and the new conservatism, almost too easy to pick off. But, reread, its toughness and satirical precision hold it together; its satirical object is not just the age but contradictory human nature." *Foreign Affairs,* the story of two American academics on sabbatical in England, "should help propel Alison Lurie into the forefront of American novelists, where she clearly belongs," according to William French in the Toronto *Globe and Mail.*

Lurie's characters are usually well-educated, sophisticated members of the upper middle class. Everett Wilkie and Josephine Helterman describe her in the *Dictionary of Literary Biography* as "a highly intelligent writer, perhaps too intelligent for popular tastes since much of her satire is of a cerebral sort aimed at persons in academic life, especially those in prestigious colleges." As Sanborn relates, "Miss Lurie's protagonists are always academics or writers, well-read and well-controlled, thoughtful and successful, people of good taste—and hence people especially susceptible to the Call of the Wild and the perfectly rational processes of self-deception. In each case, their carefully constructed lives and self images, glowing with conscious enlightenment, break up on the rocks of the irrational, to which they have been lured by the siren song of sheer sexual energy."

Extramarital sex is a recurring element in the tendency of Lurie's characters to depart from the carefully controlled, rational path; it figures prominently in almost every novel. *Love and Friendship* is a comedy set in academia that centers around the dissolution of a young couple's marriage, just as *The Nowhere City* contrasts the values of the northeastern United States with those of California against the backdrop of another marriage that is coming apart. In *Imaginary Friends,* described by the London *Times* reviewer as "a classic comedy about the desire to command knowledge," a sociologist becomes influenced by a millenarian cult he has infiltrated, while *Real People* satirizes Illyria, a pastoral artists' retreat. In each book, Sanborn writes, "the protagonists leave home and journey into the bizarre, where they learn their own mettle or come to terms with their lack of it. Thus each of these novels is marked to a greater or lesser degree by a certain laboriousness of invention, an intrusive quality of the special case."

In *The War between the Tates,* however, Lurie raises "The Way We Live Now into the Human Comedy" with "the effortless grace of a real ironic gift," to use Sanborn's words. The book examines the midlife crisis of Brian Tate, a professor of political science at Corinth University who is just beginning to realize that he will never be a great man outside of his department. He becomes involved with a student whom he later impregnates, and this affair precipitates the rebellion of his wife, Erica, who experiments briefly with sex, drugs, and Eastern philosophy.

The Tates' marital difficulties and the student's pregnancy are not the only sources of discontent in the Tate household, however. Their best friends, Danielle and Leonard Zimmern, have just weathered their own divorce and are adopting radically different ways of life—Danielle is becoming an abrasive feminist, and Leonard is turning into an outspoken bachelor with an apartment in New York City—and Brian and Erica are forced to align themselves against one or the other. Furthermore, the much-glorified Tate children are growing into unpleasant, rebellious adults. Well into the novel Lurie draws an elaborate parallel between the war in Vietnam and the continuing battle between sexes and generations that is taking place in the Tate household. "This metaphor, of Miltonic grandeur and epic absurdity, ascends from the embattled Tate home and floats over the campus of Corinth University like a majestic balloon,'' Walter Clemons claims in *Newsweek*. The book climaxes with a feminist demonstration during which Brian Tate has to rescue a colleague from the wrath of his girlfriend and the other protesters.

Overall, reviewers have high praise for the novel. The book ''represents a breakthrough into ease in the handling of the author's favorite themes,'' says Sanborn. Many of the incidents in the book are exaggerated or heightened for comic effect, with the plot often bordering on the preposterous, but unlike many of Lurie's earlier works, ''no one goes anywhere; the Tates meet their destiny and the truth about themselves in their own back yard, on their daily rounds,'' Sanborn observes. ''The whole plot unfolds, with the inevitability of a round dance once the first steps are taken in the college of Corinth.''

Roger Sale adds in the *New York Review of Books* that Lurie ''cheerfully takes on the standard plot—an ambitious professor, his well-educated wife, their domestic boredom and strain, a student mistress for the husband, futile attempts at retaliation and freedom by the wife, and whenever these figures and actions move into the surrounding community, we have clarity and brightness where others usually have managed murky expositions and cute tricks.'' In *The War between the Tates,* agrees Doris Grumbach in the *Washington Post Book World,* Lurie ''has taken a set of ordinary characters, or at least not exceptional ones, submitted them to the strains and battles of time, sex, legal alliances, generation gaps, politics and work: all the ingredients of a popular novel. But her sensibility and talent are so superior that she has given us an artistic work, which every one will read because it is 'common' to us all, but which some will perceive to have the crafted look and feel of a first-rate work.''

Some reviewers criticize Lurie's tendency to distance herself from the characters in *The War between the Tates,* finding various portraits overly satirical and unsympathetic. In general, however, most regard the novel as a real accomplishment, primarily due to the author's familiarity with her subject matter. Lurie is a professor of children's literature at Cornell University, the campus that is the source of much of her inspiration, and as Sale sums up, Lurie creates a convincing fictional world ''by means of her quickness, her efficiency, her lightness of touch, with lots of subjects that others manage only with ponderousness or self-regarding wit: The Department, The Book, The Cocktail Party, the Young, both children and students.'' Sanborn points out that the book is ''a novel not only to read, but to reread for its cool and revealing mastery of a social epoch.''

Only Children concerns itself with some of the same subjects as *The War between the Tates,* most notably the conflict between the sexes and the generations, but whereas *The War between the Tates* depicts children as rude interlopers, *Only Children* takes a more sympathetic view in that the story unfolds through the eyes and voices of two eight-year-old girls. The novel also reflects Lurie's interests in children's literature and gender discrimination, like her book *Clever Gretchen and Other Forgotten Folk Tales,* a collection of retold fairy tales that present women in a positive light.

Only Children relates the events of a Depression-era Fourth of July holiday that two couples and their daughters spend on a farm owned by the headmistress of the progressive school the girls attend. (Leonard Zimmern also appears in the story as the adolescent son from a previous marriage of one of the

adults.) The author's preoccupation in *Only Children* is with sexual role dynamics and the flirtations that occur among the parents as observed and puzzled over by their daughters. In the process, notes *Time* critic John Skow, Lurie also depicts ''the narrow range of adult female behavior that was on view to a girl of four decades ago.'' During the course of the long weekend, the adults' actions become more and more childish, while the girls' sensibilities take on a more mature awareness. Only the headmistress, independent and manless, but sexually experienced, remains an adult.

The book has garnered significant praise from reviewers. An *Atlantic* critic calls it Lurie's ''gentlest, most sympathetic satire,'' while Mary Gordon describes it in the *New York Review of Books* as ''the most interior of Lurie's novels, the most reflective, the most lyrical.'' And in the opinion of Ann Hulbert in the *New Republic,* ''this novel about love and its disorderly ways in unexamined lives is a thoughtfully crafted and traditionally unified comic drama. In *Only Children* Lurie draws deftly from her academic literary discipline, without cramping her ironic and sympathetic imagination, which ranges as easily and fruitfully as ever.''

Lurie's work ''is triumphantly in the comic mode, and she knows its contours and idiosyncrasies and its meticulous pacing exceptionally well,'' agrees Joyce Carol Oates in a *New York Times Book Review* critique of the novel. The *Atlantic* reviewer adds that Lurie's ''lovely evocations of the natural world nicely offset the minutely observed artificiality of her adult characters, and she deftly avoids the obvious pitfalls of writing about children.''

Other critics also laud the author's descriptive abilities in *Only Children.* Gabriele Annan comments in the *Listener* that ''Lurie is superb at describing nature, weather, interiors, sandwich cutting, stewing in a traffic jam, swimming in a sand-bottomed creek,'' while a *West Coast Review of Books* critic remarks that ''one can almost feel the Unguentine as it spreads over a firecracker burn, or taste the homemade lemon-coconut cake (and later the baking soda for the indigestion), or smell the insides of the new DeSoto sedan, or see the designs made with the Gyro Art machine.''

Some reviewers find the style of *Only Children* didactic and the work less fulfilling as a novel than *The War between the Tates,* but still noteworthy. Gordon feels that the attempt to tell the story through the eyes of children is not always successful, but maintains that Lurie ''is doing something different from what she has already done successfully, and has tried to go deeper.'' As Lynne Sharon Schwartz in *Saturday Review* indicates, ''one must admire her willingness to risk this quite different and difficult conception.'' *Only Children* ''is not so free-wheeling and inventive as 'The War between the Tates,''' Oates concludes, ''but it is a highly satisfactory achievement and should be read with enthusiasm by Miss Lurie's many admirers.''

Lurie's Pulitzer Prize-winning comedy of manners *Foreign Affairs* returns to more familiar subject matter for the author, as it ''reassemble[s] her Corinth cast in a new setting,'' states James McGrath Morris in the *Washington Post.* Two members of the faculty of Corinth University's English department, 54-year-old Vinnie Miner and young, handsome Fred Turner, ''spend a semester in London and learn a great deal more about love than about their intended scholarly pursuits,'' says Morris.

As the book opens, Vinnie Miner has boarded the plane and is settling into her seat in preparation for an uneventful flight to England. Vinnie is a professor of children's literature, single, childless, and plain-looking, who is researching the difference between American and English playground rhymes for a forthcoming book. She is a selfish woman, but also afflicted with self-pity; she realizes that, though she has been married and has always had an active sex life, she has never really been loved, probably because she is not pretty, and now she is growing too old. Furthermore, her work, which is funded by a not-so-secure grant, has just been ridiculed in a national magazine by a critic she has never heard of (Leonard Zimmern from *The War between the Tates* and *Only Children*). As Charles Champlin relates in the *Los Angeles Times Book Review,* "Vinnie Miner is accompanied by a small invisible dog that is the tangible embodiment of her self-pity (an allowable conceit in an imaginative 54-year-old academic, I expect, although I didn't so much accept it as admire Lurie's daring in making it almost credible)." Despite the fact that Vinnie feels sorry for herself, she is still excited about the trip, being an Anglophile with a wide circle of friends in London.

Seated next to Vinnie on the plane is Chuck Mumpson, a loud, retired waste disposal engineer from Tulsa, dressed cowboy-style and accompanied by a group of noisy tourists on a package tour. Though Vinnie initially finds Chuck annoying, he and Vinnie eventually become friends and passionate lovers. (Mumpson even develops an interest in researching his genealogy.) He dies of a heart attack before Vinnie figures out a way to make him fit in with her English friends and reconcile him with her career, but she gradually comes to the conclusion that, with Mumpson, she has finally loved and been loved in return.

Alternating chapters relate in counterpoint the experiences of youthful and handsome Fred Turner, who is an untenured member of Vinnie's faculty. Fred is in London researching John Gay, the 18th-century poet and playwright, and he's having a considerably worse time than Vinnie. Penniless between paychecks and recently separated from his feminist wife, Roo (Leonard Zimmern's daughter), he spends some of his time with a poor, complaining university couple who are having an equally miserable time in London. He has an affair with a spoiled, titled English actress who introduces him to her trendy friends, but it does not improve the quality of the time he spends in London wrapped up in his personal problems.

The book examines the differences between the English and the Americans while at the same time exploring a recurring theme in Lurie's novels, the line between illusion or appearance and reality. "For the real inspiration of Miss Lurie's entertaining fables is her fascination with levels of truth, with the war between fact and fantasy," says a *Times Literary Supplement* reviewer. According to William French in the Toronto *Globe and Mail,* "the characters in the novel of both nationalities simultaneously have their illusions shattered and prejudices confirmed, proving that generalizations about national traits are superficial and dangerous." And as French reports, Lurie "is sardonic, droll, intelligent and literary, in the best sense of that word, with a sure grasp of her characters and the social and cultural conditioning that has made them what they are."

The novel contains references to novelist Henry James and echoes of his work. And as Annan points out, even the fable itself is Jamesian: "Against a background of alluring, repellent London society a sophisticated American learns from an unsophisticated one that, contrary to appearances, true goodness exists and matters more than beauty, wit or grace." But Joel

Conarroe adds in the *Washington Post Book World* that "although her plot is concerned with the confrontation of American naivete and European sophistication, a major Jamesian theme, she resists the temptation to explore various levels of ironic correspondence."

Foreign Affairs also has some elements of the fairy tale; *Voice Literary Supplement* writer Maureen Corrigan finds extensive borrowings from "The Frog Prince" in the love story of Vinnie and Chuck. A more direct theme of the narrative, though, is the extent to which it is assumed that only the young and the beautiful have sex lives. Although some reviewers believe that the author states this a little too forthrightly in the novel, and others regard the portrait of Chuck Mumpson as more of a caricature than a characterization, Dorothy Wickenden in the *New Republic* indicates that "Lurie is as deft as ever when she turns to the mortifications of romance. She is an uncannily accurate observer of the ambivalent emotions that enter into unconventional sexual alliances."

Another criticism of the novel is its busy, formulaic, and often incredible plot, as *Chicago Tribune Book World* reviewer Peter Collier describes it. Lurie's novels tend to be "programmatic," with the author relying upon "formal contrivances to heighten irony, to create startling juxtapositions, and to make a larger point about the individual's accomodations to the demands of society," says Wickenden, who considers *Foreign Affairs* to be an extreme case. And Anne Bernays in the *New York Times Book Review* would have preferred a less intrusive omniscient narrator. But Collier disagrees, claiming that "this narrative voice—by turns wicked and insightful, ironic and aloof—is the primary source of pleasure" in the novel. Wickenden also qualifies her criticism as she points out that when Lurie "abandons her gimmicky plot devices and moral posturing, *Foreign Affairs* is funny, touching, and even suspenseful."

In the opinion of some reviewers, the novel is perfectly constructed. "Besides amusing us with its story," Lehmann-Haupt writes, "[*Foreign Affairs*] is wonderfully stimulating for its sheer performance as a novel. Perhaps by stressing this I'm admitting nostalgia for a classical approach to literature, but as I read 'Foreign Affairs' I couldn't help visualizing a diagram with the rise of Vinnie's fortunes superimposed on the decline of Fred Turner's. There's something almost musical in the way the two plots interplay, like two bands marching toward each other playing consonant music." The book's construction "is so neat, so ingenious and satisfying, with no loose ends anywhere, that you barely notice its two stories operating on different levels of truth and entertainment," agrees Annan.

Writing in the *Times Literary Supplement,* Lorna Sage also refers to the novel's classical structure, indicating that *Foreign Affairs* is "warm, clever and funny—the kind of novel that elicits a conspiratorial glow from the start because it flatters the reader unmercifully. You're assumed to be witty and literate, you're told (indirectly, of course) how very wide awake you are, and you're congratulated for being (on the other hand and after all) so sensible as to prefer your metafiction in traditional form." The book is "one of those rare novels," remarks French, "in which the author's vision is perfectly realized, and the reader finishes it with a sense of shared triumph and generous benediction." According to Conarroe, "it also earns the gratitude of all of us who admire literacy, wit, and the underrated joys of ironic discourse." And as Anthony Thwaite declares in the *Observer,* "let no one suppose that

[Lurie's] field of social observation is a restricted one, or in any way slight: she makes a world, commands it, and is a mistress not only of wit but of passion.''

Lurie's manuscripts are collected at Radcliffe College Library.

MEDIA ADAPTATIONS: The War between the Tates was filmed for television.

BIOGRAPHICAL/CRITICAL SOURCES:

BOOKS

Contemporary Literary Criticism, Gale, Volume IV, 1975, Volume V, 1976, Volume XVIII, 1980.
Dictionary of Literary Biography, Volume II: *American Novelists since World War II,* Gale, 1978.

PERIODICALS

America, August 10, 1974, October 18, 1975.
Atlantic, September, 1974, May, 1979, December, 1981.
Best Sellers, March 1, 1966, November 15, 1967, September 1, 1974.
Book Week, January 23, 1966.
Books and Bookmen, April, 1970.
Book World, September 24, 1967, May 18, 1969.
Chicago Sunday Tribune, April 8, 1962.
Chicago Tribune Book World, November 4, 1984.
Christian Science Monitor, October 26, 1967, May 22, 1969, September 18, 1974, May 14, 1979, May 12, 1980.
Commentary, August, 1969, January, 1975.
Commonweal, January 12, 1968.
Encounter, August, 1979.
Globe and Mail (Toronto), September 15, 1984.
Harper's, July, 1979.
Hudson Review, spring, 1966, spring, 1975.
Life, November 24, 1967, May 23, 1969.
Listener, February 19, 1970, June 20, 1974, April 19, 1979, May 6, 1982.
London Magazine, December, 1974-January, 1975.
Los Angeles Times Book Review, October 21, 1984.
Nation, November 21, 1981.
National Review, December 7, 1979.
New Leader, September 2, 1974.
New Republic, August 10-17, 1974, December 21, 1974, May 12, 1979, December 7, 1979, December 23, 1981, October 8, 1984.
New Statesman, February 5, 1965, June 30, 1967, June 21, 1974, April 20, 1979.
Newsweek, January 10, 1966, November 6, 1967, May 26, 1969, August 5, 1974, December 30, 1974, April 23, 1979, September 24, 1984.
New Yorker, March 23, 1968, October 11, 1969, August 19, 1974, May 14, 1979, November 5, 1984.
New York Review of Books, February 3, 1966, December 7, 1967, August 8, 1974, June 14, 1979, April 15, 1982, October 11, 1984.
New York Times, May 27, 1969, November 18, 1981, September 13, 1984.
New York Times Book Review, April 1, 1962, January 16, 1966, October 15, 1967, May 25, 1969, July 28, 1974, April 22, 1979, April 27, 1980, July 13, 1980, January 17, 1982, June 6, 1982, November 7, 1982, September 16, 1984.
Observer, May 16, 1965, February 15, 1970, June 16, 1974, July 31, 1977, April 16, 1978, July 23, 1978, April 15, 1979, December 9, 1979, January 20, 1985.
Progressive, April, 1975, September, 1979.

Publishers Weekly, August 19, 1974.
Punch, February 17, 1965.
Saturday Review, January 29, 1966, June 9, 1979, November, 1981, November, 1984.
Spectator, July 7, 1967, February 21, 1970, June 29, 1974, April 21, 1979, January 26, 1985.
Time, March 4, 1966, June 6, 1969, July 29, 1974, June 11, 1979, November 30, 1981, October 15, 1984.
Times (London), May 27, 1982, January 19, 1985, January 31, 1985.
Times Literary Supplement, February 4, 1965, July 6, 1967, February 10, 1970, February 19, 1970, June 21, 1974, November 23, 1979, July 18, 1980, November 20, 1981, May 14, 1982, February 1, 1985.
Village Voice, August 8, 1974.
Voice Literary Supplement, October, 1984.
Wall Street Journal, October 30, 1967.
Washington Post, April 25, 1985.
Washington Post Book World, August 11, 1974, September 7, 1975, April 29, 1979, July 13, 1980, November 29, 1981, September 30, 1984.
West Coast Review of Books, September, 1979.
Yale Review, October, 1979.

—*Sketch by Candace Cloutier*

*   *   *

LYNCH, Frances
See COMPTON, D(avid) G(uy)

*   *   *

LYONS, J. B. 1922-
(Michael Fitzwilliam)

PERSONAL: Born July 22, 1922, in Kilkelly, Ireland; son of John (a physician) and May (Higgins) Lyons; married Muriel Jones (a nurse), December 2, 1950; children: David, Kate, Jane. *Education:* National University of Ireland University College, Dublin, M.B., 1945, M.D., 1949. *Religion:* Roman Catholic.

ADDRESSES: Home—Claydon, Coliemore Harbour, Dalkey, County Dublin, Ireland. *Office*—St. Michael's Hospital, Dun Laoghaire, County Dublin, Ireland.

CAREER: Ship's surgeon for Peninsular & Oriental Steam Navigation Co. (a steamship line) and Royal Mail Shipping Line, 1949-50; Mercer's Hospital, Dublin, Ireland, consulting neurologist, beginning 1955; currently physician at St. Michael's Hospital, Dun Laoghaire, County Dublin, Ireland. Professor at Royal College of Surgeons in Ireland, Arnold K. Henry Lecturer, and William Doolin Lecturer for Irish Medical Association, 1980.

MEMBER: International P.E.N. (Irish branch), Irish Epilepsy Association (president), Irish Medical Association, Irish Neurological Association, Royal Irish Academy of Medicine (fellow), James Joyce Foundation.

WRITINGS:

The Citizen Surgeon: A Biography of Sir Victor Horsley, F.R.S., F.R.C.S., 1857-1916, Peter Dawnay, 1966.
James Joyce and Medicine, Dolmen Press, 1973.
A Primer of Neurology, Butterworth & Co., 1974.
Oliver St. John Gogarty (monograph), Bucknell University Press, 1976.

Brief Lives of Irish Doctors, 1600-1965, Blackwater Press, 1978.

The Mystery of Oliver Goldsmith's Medical Degree, Carrig Books, 1978.

Oliver St. John Gogarty: The Man of Many Talents, Blackwater Press, 1980.

The Enigma of Tom Kettle, Glendale Press, 1983.

Scholar and Sceptic, Glendale Press, 1985.

UNDER PSEUDONYM MICHAEL FITZWILLIAM; NOVELS

A Question of Surgery, Jarrolds, 1960.

South Downs General Hospital, Jarrolds, 1961.

When Doctors Differ, Jarrolds, 1963, reprinted as *A Matter of Medicine*, Arrow Books, 1965.

OTHER

Contributor to medical journals and literary magazines, including *James Joyce Quarterly* and *Dublin*.

WORK IN PROGRESS: Biographical studies in the areas of Irish medicine and Anglo-Irish literature; a collection of essays on James Joyce, for Glendale Press.

SIDELIGHTS: J. B. Lyons told *CA:* "The background to my career in writing is medical practice and I am often asked how I manage to do both. The short answer is that there are twenty-four hours in the day, many of them unused. The real explanation is that I have sold my boat (we live by the sea) and no longer fish or play golf.

"As to my method of writing—the theme is usually in my mind for a long time before anything is set down. The first sentences are scribbled on the back of an envelope or on scrap paper. A fair copy is then written and my secretary deals with this. I rarely use the typewriter myself.

"My holidays are often arranged to enable me to visit libraries abroad, including the British Library in London, the New York Public Library, and Haughton Library, Harvard. It gives me a pang of envy, not to say anger, to see so many Irish manuscripts in foreign libraries.

"My main problem in writing has been unreceptive editors. Exceptions have been Cherry Kearton of Jarrolds, who accepted my first novel, and Tom Turley of the Glendale Press, whom I have found extremely helpful."

M

MACK SMITH, Denis 1920-

PERSONAL: Born March 3, 1920, in London, England; son of Wilfrid and Alti (Gauntlett) Mack Smith; married Catharine Stevenson, March 18, 1963; children: Sophie, Jacintha. *Education:* Cambridge University, M.A., 1948; Oxford University, M.A., 1961. *Politics:* "Floating voter, never far from the center."

ADDRESSES: Home—White Lodge, Osler Rd., Headington, Oxford, England. *Office*—All Souls College, Oxford University, Oxford, England.

CAREER: Cambridge University, Cambridge, England, senior lecturer in history, 1953-61, fellow of Peterhouse, 1946-61, tutor of Peterhouse, 1948-58; Oxford University, All Souls College, Oxford, England, senior research fellow, 1962—, dean of visiting fellows, 1971—, sub-warden, 1984—. Commentator of the Order of Merit for Italy. Official orator of San Marino, 1982.

AWARDS, HONORS: Thirwall award, 1949; Serena award, 1960; Elba award, 1972; Villa di Chiesa award, 1973; Mondello award, 1975; Nove Muse award, 1976; Duff Cooper Memorial award, 1977; Wolfson Literary award, 1977; Rhegium Julii award, 1983.

WRITINGS:

Cavour and Garibaldi, 1860, Cambridge University Press, 1954, revised edition published as *Cavour and Garibaldi, 1860: A Study in Political Conflict*, 1985.
Garibaldi: A Great Life in Brief, Knopf, 1956.
(With D. C. Watt) *British Interests in the Middle East*, Oxford University Press, 1958.
Italy: A Modern History, University of Michigan Press, 1959, enlarged edition, 1969.
Medieval Sicily, Chatto & Windus, 1968.
Modern Sicily, Chatto & Windus, 1968.
The Making of Italy, 1796-1870, Harper, 1968.
Da Cavour a Mussolini, Bonanno, 1968.
Storia d'Italia dal 1861 al 1958, con documenti e testimonianze, two volumes, Edizioni Labor (Milan), 1968.
(Editor) *Garibaldi*, Prentice-Hall, 1968.
Victor Emanuel: Cavour and the Risorgimento, Oxford University Press, 1971.
Vittorio Emanuele II, Laterza, 1972.

Mussolini's Roman Empire, Viking, 1976.
Storia di Centro Anni di Vita Italiana visti attraverso il "Corriere della Sera," Rizzoli, 1978.
Mussolini, Knopf, 1982.
Cavour, Weidenfeld and Nicholson, 1985.

Also editor of E. Quinet, *Le Rivoluzioni d'Italia*, 1970, G. La Farina, *Scritti Politici*, 1972, G. Bandi, *I mille: Da Genova a Capua*, 1981, F. De Sanctis, *Un Viaggio Elettorale*, 1983, and *Nelson History of England*. Also author of *Un Monumento al Duce*, 1976, and *L'Italia del Ventesimo Secolo*, 1978.

WORK IN PROGRESS: Research on Italian fascism and the Risorgimento.

SIDELIGHTS: Denis Mack Smith is an Italian historian whose work is characterized by its "smooth, readable style," according to Edward Mortimer in the London *Times*. He is chiefly known for his work on Camille de Cavour, the first prime minister of Italy in the late 1800s, and Benito Mussolini, fascist dictator of the World War II era. Mack Smith's exceptional work has led Mortimer to call him the "leading British historian of Italy."

Mack Smith's biography of Benito Mussolini, *Mussolini*, is termed "solid and persuasive" by Gerald Clarke in *Time*. Mack Smith portrays Italy's dictator as severe, showing the "sinister side of fascism and its leader—the bullying intimidation, the rigged elections, the political murders—that lay beneath [Mussolini's] exterior," comments Jack Dierks in the *Chicago Tribune Book World*. Andrew Rolle of the *Los Angeles Times* takes exception to the writing, calling it "flat in tone and one-dimensional." He also faults Mack Smith's approach: "Like a vacuum cleaner, Mack Smith has swept up new facts about Mussolini's terroristic and clandestine activities, but deeper analysis of the dictator's motivation and of the wellsprings of his character defects is missing." However, Adrian Lyttelton takes a different viewpoint in the *Times Literary Supplement*, praising the documentation and research in the book and indicating that Mack Smith's biography will "certainly make all earlier biographies in English obsolete. . . . *Mussolini* will be remembered, I think, for the exceptional clarity and brilliance of the writing."

Mack Smith's authoritative work on Camille de Cavour, first prime minister of Italy, has been called "provocative as well as brilliant," by Derek Beales in the *Times Literary Supple-*

ment. Cavour was a complex man, who was known by his contemporaries as practical and well-educated but an unscrupulous politician. In this biography, Mack Smith unearths a fully-rounded vision of Cavour, showing that although he was a successful politician, he made many covert political maneuvers that merely alienated his allies. In spite of these mistakes, Mack Smith still considers him one of the most outstanding politicians of the nineteenth century. Beales concludes that Mack Smith's book "brings together for the first time in a single volume [the] major revisions of the story of unification [in Italy]."

Mack Smith has long been considered a expert in Italian history. Beales comments on his achievements: "When he published *Cavour and Garibaldi* in 1954, Denis Mack Smith turned the historiography of Italian unification on its head." He now says that Mack Smith's two works—*Cavour and Garibaldi, 1860* and *Cavour*—together rank "as a major achievement of modern historical writing."

BIOGRAPHICAL/CRITICAL SOURCES:

PERIODICALS

Chicago Tribune Book World, July 11, 1982.
Los Angeles Times, May 27, 1982.
Time, June 7, 1982.
Times (London), April 11, 1985.
Times Literary Supplement, April 9, 1982, May 10, 1985.
Washington Post Book World, July 4, 1982.

*   *   *

MACUMBER, Mari
See SANDOZ, Mari(e Susette)

*   *   *

MALBIN, Michael J(acob)   1943-

PERSONAL: Born June 9, 1943, in Brooklyn, N.Y.; son of Irving (a salesman) and Mae (a secretary and bookkeeper; maiden name, Levin) Malbin; married Susan Rothberg (a historian), June 14, 1969; children: Joshua Henry, David Alexander, Rachel Elizabeth. *Education:* Cornell University, B.A., 1964, Ph.D., 1973; attended University of Chicago, 1964-66.

ADDRESSES: Home—500 Dartmouth Ave., Silver Spring, Md. 20910. *Office*—American Enterprise Institute for Public Policy Research, 1150 Seventeenth St. N.W., Washington, D.C. 20036.

CAREER: New York University, New York, N.Y., visiting instructor in political science, 1971-72; Brooklyn College of the City University of New York, Brooklyn, N.Y., instructor in political science, 1972-73; *National Journal*, Washington, D.C., staff correspondent, 1973-77; American Enterprise Institute for Public Policy Research, Washington, D.C., resident fellow, 1977—. Associate professorial lecturer at George Washington University, spring, 1976; Catholic University of America, lecturer, 1976-79, adjunct associate professor, 1979—.

MEMBER: American Political Science Association.

WRITINGS:

Religion and Politics: The Intentions of the Authors of the First Amendment, American Enterprise Institute for Public Policy Research, 1978.
Unelected Representatives: Congressional Staff and the Future of Representative Government, Basic Books, 1980.
(Coauthor and editor) *Parties, Interest Groups and Campaign Finance Laws*, American Enterprise Institute for Public Policy Research, 1980.
(Coauthor and editor) *Money and Politics in the United States: Financing Elections in the 1980s*, American Enterprise Institute for Public Policy Research, 1984.

Contributor of more than one hundred articles and reviews to magazines, newspapers, and professional journals. Contributing editor, *National Journal*, 1977—.

WORK IN PROGRESS: Congress in Perspective, for Basic Books.

SIDELIGHTS: In *Unelected Representatives: Congressional Staff and the Future of Representative Government*, author Michael J. Malbin "provides some detailed examples of how Congressional staffs have assumed broad authority as the elected representatives have taken on more issues and responsibilities than they can possibly handle," observes John Herbes in the *New York Times Book Review*. "[This book is] a solid explanation of how staffers have assumed and exercised authority." And Elliott Abrams remarks in *Commentary*: "Malbin notes that Congress's enormous staff ends up creating work rather than simply handling it. To keep busy, to keep interested, to be powerful, staffs develop bills, arrange hearings, set up meetings, and above all generate paper.... And this situation contains a subtle political bias of its own, leading to ever more active intervention by government.... The debate over the size and role of government is now rightly a key issue in American politics. To this debate, *Unelected Representatives* makes a distinct contribution."

BIOGRAPHICAL/CRITICAL SOURCES:

PERIODICALS

Commentary, December, 1980.
Library Journal, November 1, 1980.
New York Times Book Review, September 14, 1980.
Washington Post Book World, August 31, 1980.

*   *   *

MALLET-JORIS, Francoise   1930-

PERSONAL: Born July 6, 1930, in Antwerp, Belgium; became French citizen; daughter of Albert (Belgian Minister of Justice) and Suzanne (a dramatist; maiden name, Verbist) Lilar; married Robert Amadou (divorced); married Alain Joxe (marriage ended); married Jacques Delfau (a painter); children: (first marriage) Daniel; (third marriage) Vincent, Alberte, Pauline. *Education:* Attended Bryn Mawr College, and Sorbonne, University of Paris. *Religion:* Roman Catholic.

ADDRESSES: Home—7 rue Jacob, 75006 Paris, France. *Office*—Editions Grasset, 61 rue des Saints-Peres, 75006 Paris, France.

CAREER: Writer. Director of "Nouvelle" collection, Editions Julliard (publishers), Paris, France, 1960-65; member of reading committee, Editions Grasset (publishers), Paris, 1965—. Member of jury for Prix Femina, 1969-70; Goncourt Academy, member of prize jury, 1970-73, vice-president, 1973—.

AWARDS, HONORS: Prix Femina, 1958, for *L'Empire Celeste*; Grand Prix Litteraire de Monaco, 1965.

WRITINGS:

NOVELS

Le Rempart des Beguines (also see below), Julliard, 1951, translation by Herma Briffault published as *The Illusionist*, Farrar, Straus, 1952 (published in England as *Into the Labyrinth*, W. H. Allen, 1953).

La Chambre rouge, Julliard, 1955, translation by Briffault published as *The Red Room*, Farrar, Straus, 1956.

Cordelia (short novels), Julliard, 1956, translation by Peter Green published as *Cordelia and Other Stories*, Farrar, Straus, 1965.

Les Mensonges, Julliard, 1956, translation by Briffault published as *House of Lies*, Farrar, Straus, 1957.

L'Empire Celeste, Julliard, 1958, translation by Briffault published as *Cafe Celeste*, Farrar, Straus, 1959.

Les Personnages, Julliard, 1961, translation by Briffault published as *The Favourite*, Farrar, Straus, 1962.

Marie Mancini: Le Premier amour de Louis XIV (historical novel), translation by Patrick O'Brien published as *The Uncompromising Heart: A Life of Marie Mancini, Louis XIV's First Love*, Farrar, Straus, 1966.

Les Signes et les prodigies, B. Grasset, 1966, translation by Briffault published as *Signs and Wonders*, Farrar, Straus, 1966.

Trois ages de la nuit: Histoires de sorcellerie, B. Grasset, 1968, translation by Briffault published as *The Witches: Three Tales of Sorcery*, Farrar, Straus, 1969.

Le Jeu du souterrain, B. Grasset, 1973, translation by Briffault published as *The Underground Game*, W. H. Allen, 1974.

MEMOIRS

Lettre a moi-meme, Julliard, 1963, translation by O'Brien published as *A Letter to Myself*, Farrar, Straus, 1964.

La Maison de papier, B. Grasset, 1970, translation by Derek Coltman published as *The Paper House*, Farrar, Straus, 1971.

BIOGRAPHY

(With Michel Grisolia) *Juliette Greco*, Seghers, 1975.

Jeanne Guyon, Flammarion, 1978.

AUTHOR OF INTRODUCTION

Marie Sevigne, *Lettres de Madame de Sevigne*, Le Club des classiques, 1969.

Attali (photographs), A. Balland, 1971.

OTHER

Poemes du dimanche (title means "Sunday Poems"), 1947.

(Editor) *Nouvelles* (stories), Julliard, 1957.

(Compiler) *Le Rendez-vous donne par Francois Mallet-Joris a quelques jeunes ecrivans*, Julliard, 1962.

Le Roi qui aimait trop les fleurs, Casterman, 1971.

Les Feuilles mortes d'un bel ete, B. Grasset, 1973.

J'aurais voulu jouer de l'accordeon, Julliard, 1975.

Allegra, B. Grasset, 1976.

Dickie-roi, B. Grasset, 1979.

Also author of screenplays, "Le Gigolo," 1962, and "Le Rempart des Beguines" (adaptation of her novel of the same title), 1972.

SIDELIGHTS: Francoise Mallet-Joris wrote her first novel, *Le Rempart des Beguines*, while still in her teens. The book, published in the United States as *The Illusionist*, was a *succes de scandale*, as it dealt with the seduction of a fifteen-year-old girl by her father's mistress. Some critics immediately compared the young author to Francois Sagan, whose work often deals with themes of lesbianism. But Rima Drell Reck, contributor to *Yale French Studies*, feels that Mallet-Joris's early novels, including *Le Rempart des Beguines* and its successor, *La Chambre rouge*, have more in common with the works of Pierre de Laclos or the Marquis de Sade. She states: "Combining a striking command of novelistic technique with scandalous subject matter, Mme. Mallet-Joris revealed a preoccupation with the politics of conflicting wills which could not fail to recall these masters of the eighteenth century."

Charles Managhan compares Mallet-Joris to another French master, Marcel Proust. Discussing *Les Signes et les prodigies*, a love story set during the French-Algerian war, Managhan writes: "Francoise Mallet-Joris is the sort of novelist who makes young French intellectuals apoplectic. . . . *Signs and Wonders*, a beautifully constructed novel abrim with wisdom is a good indication why. Mallet-Joris is the master of an art that walks in the footsteps of Proust, an art one generation old. That is both her strength and her weakness. Her art lives in awe of Proust's incredible demonstration that unraveling a love affair can reveal all a writer would want to reveal: passion, venality, fun, stupidity, class antagonisms, tenderness." *Les Signes et les prodigies* examines many of the questions raised by war. In particular, it probes the personal compromises that are often necessary during war. The novel follows Nicholas Leclusier through his efforts to come to terms with himself and with compromise. In the end, he fails, saying, "Everything becomes transformed beneath my eyes, becomes polluted in my hands; God is my malady."

Mallet-Joris is a devout Catholic convert, and critics often point to her religion as an important force in her work. For example, Managhan feels that in *Les Signes et les prodigies* she has created "a Roman Catholic's art—a very contemporary Roman Catholic, that is, working within a philosophical framework close to those of Graham Greene and Muriel Spark, reacting against the soppy tide of uplift that dominated Catholic writing in the '20s and 30s. For . . . Mallet-Joris, the hallmark of the seriously religious man is continuous reappraisal."

The author's next novel, *Trois ages de la nuit*, differed radically in plot from the reflective love story offered in *Les Signes et les prodigies*. *Trois ages de la nuit* is based on three documented witch trials from the Renaissance. Mallet-Joris presents the accused women's life histories, their eventual denunciations as witches, and their ensuing trials. In the preface to the novel, the author states that while the women she chose to portray were actual historical figures, she departed from strict adherence to the available facts regarding them and their trials in order to explore the "spirit" of the witch trial phenomenon.

Pierre Courtines comments: "Each of the three short stories could be called a case history in abnormal psychology with emphasis on the struggle between good and evil, and the religious obsessions of her characters, their families, and relations. In doing so, she involves the reader, for the three heroines, in spite of their personal demons, are very close to the norm in their reactions to their environment, their families, and townsfolk. What is particularly fascinating is the intuitive knowledge of psychology revealed by the three women, who seem to manipulate those around them in a manner not unworthy of today's most subtle hidden persuaders."

A reviewer for *Time* praises Mallet-Joris's gift for historic imagination: "Statistics and dry records are unlikely to convey . . . any idea of the atmosphere that hangs for days, according to the author, in a town square after a witch has been burned. Is the smell, for instance, reassuring, since it signifies that evil has been expunged? Or is it unsettling, because it calls to mind a dreadful spectacle too heartily enjoyed? Such questions elude the historian. Novelist Mallet-Joris, however, seems imaginatively sure of the answers. . . . It is not frivolous to say that she learned the feel of the late 16th and early 17th centuries by writing these novels, and that she wrote them in order to learn."

Genevieve Delattre concludes in *Yale French Studies* that the themes of isolation, free will, and the hidden self unify the body of Mallet-Joris's work. "When we look at Francoise Mallet-Joris' characters . . . our eyes are met by their appearance only, that is by what they are willing to let us see. Their truth hides behind the fortress of lies they have erected. . . . The dream of what one pretends to be, the reality of what one is: nearly all Francoise Mallet-Joris' characters are torn by this conflict between lucidity and complacency, between a longing for and a fear of authenticity."

BIOGRAPHICAL/CRITICAL SOURCES:

BOOKS

Contemporary Literary Criticism, Volume II, Gale, 1974.
Curley, Dorothy Nyren and Arthur Curley, *Modern Romance Literatures,* Ungar, 1967.
Mallet-Joris, Francoise, *Lettre a moi-meme,* Julliard, 1963, translation by Patrick O'Brien published as *A Letter to Myself,* Farrar, Straus, 1964.
Mallet-Joris, Francoise, *La Maison du papier,* B. Grasset, 1970, translation by Derek Coltman published as *The Paper House,* Farrar, Straus, 1971.

PERIODICALS

Atlantic, September, 1969.
Books Abroad, spring, 1969.
Commonweal, December 27, 1968, January 16, 1970.
National Observer, October 9, 1967.
New Statesman, August 27, 1965.
Newsweek, September 22, 1969.
New Yorker, July 11, 1964, July 31, 1971.
New York Times Book Review, May 29, 1971, August 24, 1975.
Saturday Review, April 28, 1962, May 23, 1964.
Time, October 31, 1969.
Times Literary Supplement, May 4, 1973.
Yale French Studies, Number 24, 1959, Number 27, 1961.†

*   *   *

MALONE, Elmer Taylor, Jr.   1943-
(Ted Malone)

PERSONAL: Born December 18, 1943, in Wilson, N.C.; son of E. Taylor and Mildred (Winborne) Malone; married Lynda Cyrus, June 15, 1969; children: Anna Richmond, Edward Winborne. *Education:* Campbell College, B.S., 1967; University of Maryland, graduate study in Europe, 1967-68; University of North Carolina, M.A., 1975.

ADDRESSES: Home—103 Carl Dr., Route 4, Chapel Hill, N.C. 27514. *Office*—Historical Publications Section, North Carolina Division of Archives and History, Raleigh, N.C.

CAREER: Raleigh Times, Raleigh, N.C., reporter, 1969; *Dunn Dispatch,* Dunn, N.C., editor, 1970; *Harnett County News,* Lillington, N.C., editor, 1972-74; U.S. Environmental Protection Agency, Technical Publications Division, Durham, N.C., member of staff, 1974; *Durham Sun,* Durham, assistant news editor and drama critic, 1974-77; North Carolina Central University, Durham, visiting lecturer in English, 1977-84; North Carolina Division of Archives and History, Raleigh, editor in historical publications section, 1984—. *Military service:* U.S. Army, 1967-68.

MEMBER: North Carolina Folklore Society (president, 1984, 1985), North Carolina Literary and Historical Society, North Carolina Genealogy Society, Chapel Hill Historical Society.

WRITINGS:

UNDER NAME TED MALONE

The Cleared Place of Tara (poems), Pope Printing, 1970.
The Tapestry Maker (poems), Blair, 1972.
(Contributor) Guy Owen and Mary Williams, editors, *Contemporary Poets of North Carolina,* Blair, 1977.
The View from Wrightsville Beach (poems), St. Andrews Press, 1985.
(With Richard Walser) *Literary North Carolina: A Brief Historical Survey,* 2nd edition, North Carolina Division of Archives and History, 1986.

Contributor to numerous periodicals, including *Journal of the American Medical Association, North Carolina Folklore Journal, Crucible, Tar River Poets, Lyricist, North Carolina Historical Review,* and *Communicant.*

WORK IN PROGRESS: Harnett County Historical Places; Edwin W. Fuller: His Life and Times; Pictures of Structures That Don't Exist; a book of poems; *In Search of Little C.D.: An Anecdotal Genealogy.*

SIDELIGHTS: Elmer Taylor Malone, Jr. wrote *CA:* "I am very much interested in the concept of 'sense of place' and, as a former archaeology student, how place and person shape one another. I see North Carolina as 'my place' and all its people, black, white, and red, somehow part of my tribe."

AVOCATIONAL INTERESTS: The Irish dramatic movement and Irish history, history of the Episcopal Church in North Carolina.

*   *   *

MALONE, Ted
See MALONE, Elmer Taylor, Jr.

*   *   *

MANNON, Warwick
See HOPKINS, Kenneth

*   *   *

MAPLES, Evelyn Palmer   1919-

PERSONAL: Born February 7, 1919, in Ponce de Leon, Mo.; daughter of Thomas Sherman and Bertie (Dalby) Palmer; married William E. Maples, December 23, 1938; children: Norman Francis, Billi Jo, Matthew McBride. *Education:* Attended Southwest Missouri State College (now University), 1936-38. *Politics:* Republican. *Religion:* Reorganized Church of Jesus Christ of Latter-day Saints (Mormon).

ADDRESSES: *Home*—Route 1, Box 137, Niangua, Mo. 65713.

CAREER: Greene County (Mo.) schools, rural school teacher, 1938-39; Herald House, Independence, Mo., proofreader, 1953-63, copy editor, 1963-81; writer.

MEMBER: Missouri Writers Guild, Springfield Writers Guild.

WRITINGS:

What Saith the Scripture?, Herald House, 1960.
Norman Learns about the Sacraments, Herald House, 1961.
Jomo, the Missionary Monkey, Herald House, 1966.
That Ye Love (poetry), Herald House, 1971.
Norman Learns about the Scriptures, Herald House, 1972.
Lehi, Man of God, Herald House, 1972.
Brass Plates Adventure, Herald House, 1972.
The Many Selves of Ann-Elizabeth, Independence Press, 1973.
A Story about You, Herald House, 1983.
What Do You Think of That?, Herald House, 1983.
Big Tree, Herald House, 1983.
Friends Come to the Door, Herald House, 1983.
Mr. Red Ears, Herald House, 1983.
Jesus, Herald House, 1983.
The First Christmas, Herald House, 1983.

Contributor of a story to an anthology published by Herald House, 1956; also contributor of poetry to *Poetic Voices of the Restoration* (anthology), 1960. Contributor of children's stories, poems, plays, adult fiction, and articles to religious journals.

WORK IN PROGRESS: A second volume of poetry; *From Crosspatch*, a book of daily devotionals.

SIDELIGHTS: Evelyn Palmer Maples told *CA:* "Crafting a poem has been my great joy since the first was published in 1942. To distill the essence of a newly perceived truth or a significant moment and make it sparkle in six to ten lines is most gratifying. The directness and simplicity required in writing for children help me to refine my poetry."

* * *

MARCHBANKS, Samuel
See DAVIES, (William) Robertson

* * *

MARCUS, Mordecai 1925-

PERSONAL: Born January 18, 1925, in Elizabeth, N.J.; son of Sidney (a bookdealer) and Mary (Swerdlow) Marcus; married Erin Jenean Gasper, June 3, 1955; children: Paul, Emily. *Education:* Brooklyn College (now Brooklyn College of the City University of New York), B.A., 1949; New York University, M.A., 1950; University of Kansas, Ph.D., 1958. *Politics:* "Desperate." *Religion:* "Uncertain."

ADDRESSES: *Home*—822 Mulder Dr., Lincoln, Neb. 68510. *Office*—Department of English, University of Nebraska, Lincoln, Neb. 68588-0333.

CAREER: University of Kansas, Lawrence, instructor in English, 1953-58; Purdue University, West Lafayette, Ind., instructor, 1958-60, assistant professor of English, 1960-65; University of Nebraska, Lincoln, assistant professor, 1965-66, associate professor, 1966-72, professor of English, 1972—. Has given poetry readings at Hastings College, 1978, Wayne State College, 1979, and University of Nevada, Reno, 1979.

WRITINGS:

(Editor with Henry F. Salerno) *Cross-Section: Essays on Contemporary America*, Holt, 1963.
Five Minutes to Noon (poems), Best Cellar Press, 1971.
Return from the Desert (poems), Newedi Press, 1977.
Conversational Basketball (poems), Nebraska Review, 1980.
Talismans (chapbook of poems), Sparrow Press, 1981.
Emily Dickinson: Selected Poems (monograph), Cliff's Notes, 1982.

CONTRIBUTOR

Richard Lettis, Robert F. McDonnell, and William E. Morris, editors, *The Red Badge of Courage: Text and Criticism*, Harcourt, 1960.
Scully Bradley, Richmond Croom Beatty, and E. Hudson Long, editors, *The Red Badge of Courage: An Annotated Text, Backgrounds and Sources, Essays in Criticism*, Norton, 1962, 2nd edition revised by Donald Pizer and published as *The Red Badge of Courage: An Authoritative Text, Backgrounds and Sources, Criticism*, 1976.
James E. Miller, Jr., and Bernice Slote, editors, *The Dimensions of the Short Story: A Critical Anthology*, Dodd, 1964.
Charles Child Walcutt and J. Edwin Whitesell, editors, *The Explicator Cyclopedia*, Quadrangle Books, 1966.
Miller and Slote, editors, *The Dimensions of Literature: A Critical Anthology*, Dodd, 1967.
Shiv Kumar and Keith McKean, editors, *Critical Approaches to Fiction*, McGraw, 1968.
William Coyle, editor, *The Young Man in American Literature: The Initiation Theme*, Odyssey Press, 1969.
E. Rubinstein, editor, *Twentieth-Century Interpretations of "Pride and Prejudice": A Collection of Critical Essays*, Prentice-Hall, 1969.
Thomas A. Gullason, editor, *Stephen Crane's Career: Perspectives and Evaluations*, New York University Press, 1972.
Borestone Mountain Poetry Awards: Best Poems of 1971, Pacific Books, 1972.
Stanley Schatt, editor, *Bartleby, the Scrivener: A Casebook for Research*, Kendall/Hunt, 1972.
Broken Hoops and Plains People, Nebraska Curriculum Development Center, 1976.
Charles E. May, editor, *Short Story Theories*, Ohio University Press, 1976.
M. T. Inge, editor, *Bartleby, the Inscrutable*, Archon Books, 1979.
K. G. Harris, editor, *Robert Frost: Studies in the Poetry*, G. K. Hall, 1979.
H. Schwartz, editor, *Voices from within the Ark*, Dell, 1980.
Alan F. Pater, editor, *Anthology of Magazine Verse and Yearbook of American Poetry*, 1980 and 1981 editions, Monitor Book, 1981.
R. McGovern, editor, *Seventy on the Seventies*, Ashland Poetry Press, 1981.

OTHER

Contributor of articles, poems, and book reviews to more than sixty magazines, including *Journal of Popular Culture, Prairie Schooner, Massachusetts Review, Journal of English and German Philology, Southern Poetry Review*, and *Western Poetry*.

WORK IN PROGRESS: Poems; studying the theme of love-and-death in literature for possible articles.

BIOGRAPHICAL/CRITICAL SOURCES:

PERIODICALS

Nantucket Review, May, 1975.

*   *   *

MARIL, Nadja   1954-

PERSONAL: Born March 24, 1954, in Baltimore, Md.; daughter of Herman (an artist) and Esta (a psychiatric social worker; maiden name, Cook) Maril; married Cyril J. Patrick (in business), August 26, 1978. *Education:* Attended Smith College, 1972-73; University of California, Santa Barbara, B.A. (cum laude), 1975.

ADDRESSES: Home—2 Steele Ave., Annapolis, Md. 21401. *Office*—Panamacy, Inc., P.O. Box 6180, Annapolis, Md. 21401.

CAREER: Community Council, Isla Vista, Calif., communications coordinator, 1975-76; Tres Condados Girl Scout Council, Santa Barbara, Calif., secretary, 1976-77; free-lance writer in Baltimore, Md., 1977-78; Gryphon Gifts and Gallery, Provincetown, Mass., manager, beginning 1979; Panamacy, Inc. (antique dealer and appraiser), Annapolis, Md., director, 1980—. Former manager of antiques, gifts, and art work at J. C. Patrick Ltd.; director of Cottage Gallery, summer, 1979. Literary secretary to Kenneth Rexroth, 1976. Member of board of directors of Isla Vista Food Cooperative, 1974; secretary of Provincetown Democratic Town Committee, beginning 1979.

MEMBER: Women Writers Guild, Lower Cape League of Women Voters (member of board of directors, 1978-79).

WRITINGS:

Me, Molly Midnight, the Artist's Cat (juvenile), Stemmer House, 1977.
Runaway Molly Midnight: The Artist's Cat, Stemmer House, 1981.
(With Jonas Rappaport and Anise Mercer) *Ask Mom: A Guide to Child Abuse Prevention,* Family Time Products, 1985.

Special writer, *Provincetown Magazine,* 1983—; author of column, "Know Your Antiques." Contributor to newspapers.

SIDELIGHTS: Nadja Maril comments: *"Me, Molly Midnight, the Artist's Cat* is a true story inspired by my interest in conveying the artist's point of view in formulating his work—in this case, paintings. My goal in writing for children is to instruct and entertain at the same time.

"Ask Mom provides a means for parents and children to prevent sexual child abuse by dealing with the subject in a constructive, positive manner. The book is written in collaboration with psychiatrists Jonas Rappaport and Anise Mercer."

BIOGRAPHICAL/CRITICAL SOURCES:

PERIODICALS

Baltimore Sun, December 18, 1977.

*   *   *

MARION, Henry
See del REY, Lester

MARK, Jan   1943-

PERSONAL: Born June 22, 1943, in Welwyn, England; daughter of Colin Denis and Marjorie Brisland; married Neil Mark (a computer operator), March 1, 1969; children: Isobel, Alexander. *Education:* Canterbury College of Art, N.D.D., 1965. *Politics:* Labour. *Religion:* None.

ADDRESSES: Home—10 Sydney St., Ingham, Norfolk NR12 9TQ, England. *Agent*—Murray Pollinger, 4 Garrick St., London WC2E 9BH, England.

CAREER: Southfields School, Gravesend, England, teacher of art and English, 1965-71; full-time writer, 1975—. Writer-fellow, Oxford Polytechnic, 1982-84.

AWARDS, HONORS: Penguin/*Guardian* Award, 1975, for *Thunder and Lightnings;* Carnegie Medal from the Library Association, 1976, for *Thunder and Lightnings,* and 1983, for *Handles;* Rank/*Observer* award for teenage fiction, 1982, for *Aquarius;* Angel Award for fiction, 1983, for *Feet;* British nominee for Hans Andersen Award, 1984.

WRITINGS:

FICTION

Thunder and Lightnings, Kestrel, 1976, Crowell, 1979.
Under the Autumn Garden, Kestrel, 1977, Crowell, 1979.
The Ennead, Crowell, 1978.
Divide and Rule, Kestrel, 1979, Crowell, 1980.
The Short Voyage of the Albert Ross, Granada, 1980.
Nothing to Be Afraid Of, Kestrel, 1980.
Hairs in the Palm of the Hand, Kestrel, 1981.
The Dead Letter Box, Hamilton, 1981.
The Long Distance Poet, Dinosaur, 1981.
Aquarius, Kestrel, 1982, Atheneum, 1984.
Out of the Oven, Kestrel, 1982.
Feet, Kestrel, 1983.
Handles, Kestrel, 1983.
Bold as Brass, Hutchinson, 1983.
Trouble Halfway, Kestrel, 1985.

Also author of *Childermas,* 1984, and *At the Sign of the Dog and Rocket,* 1985.

OTHER

Author of television plays and radio dramas. Contributor of stories and articles to magazines.

SIDELIGHTS: British author Jan Mark is a two-time recipient of England's Carnegie Medal for children's fiction. Her work, which the *New York Times Book Review* describes as "suitable for adolescents and adults," often explores the potential of the human imagination, both in everyday situations and in the realm of science fiction. "Jan Mark has achieved an archetypal image of the good place of fantasy in a physically, socially and emotionally realistic framework," notes Allan Mackie in the *Times Literary Supplement.* Mark is praised, too, for her ability to give "the child's eye view," in the words of Colin Mills for the *Times Literary Supplement.* Mills comments: "Jan Mark has . . . shown that she can combine the direct voice with the storyteller's art to depict sharper issues." Judith Elkin, also writing for the *Times Literary Supplement,* expresses a similar opinion: "Jan Mark has a wonderful eye for just the right detail and a real feeling for character and narrative."

Mark told *CA:* "I believe reading and writing is the nearest most of us will ever come to telepathy. If I write stories about children they are normally read by children—I do not otherwise aim at any particular audience. I write about people, the ways in which they use each other and allow themselves to be used. I am not interested in victims, only in the men and women who are authors of their own downfalls. There can be no external intervention. The forces of evil currently fashionable are not supernatural, but human ignorance and complacency.

"My prime motive in becoming a professional writer was the need to earn a living. Although writing gives me more pleasure than does anything else, I do not write for pleasure: I write for money. I am singularly fortunate in getting both, but I fear that if I did not have to choose between writing and starving I should have begun self-indulgent and made no subsequent progress. I started well by winning a competition for new fiction but this has imposed on me the challenge to produce always something at least as good as the first book. I dare not fall below that standard.

"I did not begin writing seriously until I was in my thirties and am in retrospect glad of it, since I had by then developed a voice of my own, an intelligible one, moreover. One writer I know of, who was published very young, describes herself as having 'learned to write in public.' I was spared that, but only through lack of self-confidence.

"When writing about children I like to present readers with a situation they may recognize and supplement with their own experience. In novels for older readers I prefer to place a character in an unfamiliar environment and watch him struggle (or in one case disintegrate) in the best traditions of tragedy, through his own shortcomings. They tend to be studies in failure. *The Ennead* dealt with the results of total self-absorption; *Divide and Rule* with the liberal conscience under attack from extremists and unable to defend itself. Exploitation is always rife."

BIOGRAPHICAL/CRITICAL SOURCES:

PERIODICALS

Guardian, July 17, 1975.
New York Times Book Review, January 20, 1985.
Publishers Weekly, December 11, 1978.
Times Educational Supplement, November 24, 1978.
Times Literary Supplement, September 19, 1980, July 24, 1981, July 23, 1982, January 13, 1984, June 7, 1985.
Washington Post, December 12, 1978.

*   *   *

MARLATT, Daphne (Buckle) 1942-

PERSONAL: Born July 11, 1942, in Melbourne, Australia; daughter of Arthur Charles (an accountant) and Edrys (Lupprian) Buckle; married Gordon Alan Marlatt (a clinical psychologist); divorced; children: Christopher Alan. *Education:* University of British Columbia, B.A., 1964; Indiana University, M.A., 1968.

ADDRESSES: Office—c/o Turnstone Press, 99 King St. No. 201, Winnipeg, Manitoba Canada R3B 1H7.

CAREER: Capilano Community College, North Vancouver, British Columbia, instructor in English, 1968, 1973-76. Writer-in-residence, University of Manitoba, fall, 1982, University of Alberta, 1985-86.

MEMBER: Writers Union of Canada, West Coast Women and Words.

AWARDS, HONORS: Canada Council arts grants, 1969-70, 1973-74, and 1985.

WRITINGS:

Frames of a Story, Ryerson, 1968.
leaf leafs (poems), Black Sparrow Press, 1969.
Rings (poem narrative), Vancouver Community Press, 1971.
Vancouver Poems, Coach House Press, 1972.
Steveston (poems), Talonbooks, 1974, revised edition, Longspoon Press, 1984.
Our Lives (poem narrative cycle), Truck Press, 1975, revised edition, Oolichan, 1979.
(Editor) *Steveston Recollected: A Japanese-Canadian History,* Provincial Archives of British Columbia, 1975.
Zocalo, Coach House Press, 1977.
The Story, She Said, b. c. Monthly Press, 1977.
(Co-editor) *Opening Doors: Vancouver's East End,* Provincial Archives of British Columbia, 1979.
What Matters, Coach House Press, 1980.
Selected Writing: Net Work, edited by Fred Wah, Talonbooks, 1980.
Here and There, Island Writing Series, 1981.
(Editor) Maxine Gadd, *Lost Language,* Coach House Press, 1982.
How Hug a Stone, Turnstone Press, 1983.
Touch to My Tongue, Longspoon, 1984.

Contributor of poetry to small magazines, including *Origin, Imago, Center, Truck, Is, Writing, periodics, Canadian Forum, Tessera,* and *Capilano Review;* contributor of criticism to *Open Letter.* Poetry editor, *Capilano Review,* 1973-76; co-editor, *periodics,* 1977-80; associate editor, *Island,* 1980-83; member of editorial collective, *Tessera,* 1983—.

SIDELIGHTS: Daphne Marlatt's *Selected Writing: Net Work* "is aimed at students, and for students is an excellent demonstration of Marlatt's prosody and her particular attitude toward the poet's role," according to Anne Collins in *Books in Canada. Canadian Materials* reviewer Boh Kinczyk comments that "the patient reader who cares about the poet's struggle with language and is willing to give Marlatt a chance will be amply rewarded. The gorgeous prose-poem 'Listen' is alone worth the price of the book."

BIOGRAPHICAL/CRITICAL SOURCES:

PERIODICALS

Books in Canada, June/July, 1981.
Canadian Materials, number 1, 1982.

*   *   *

MARSH, Dave 1950-

PERSONAL: Born March 1, 1950, in Pontiac, Mich.; son of O. K. (a railroad worker) and Mary (Evon) Marsh; married Barbara Carr (a recording executive), July 21, 1979; stepchildren: Sasha, Kristen. *Education:* Attended Wayne State University, 1968-69.

ADDRESSES: Office—*Rock & Roll Confidential,* P.O.Box 1073, Maywood, N.J. 07607.

CAREER: Creem (magazine), Birmingham, Mich., editor, 1969-73; *Real Paper,* Boston, Mass., music editor, 1974; *Newsday,* Garden City, N.Y., staff member, 1974-75; *Rolling Stone,* New York, N.Y., record reviews editor and writer, 1975-78; free-lance writer, 1978—; *Rock & Roll Confidential,* Maywood, N.J., editor and publisher, 1983—.

AWARDS, HONORS: Born to Run: The Bruce Springsteen Story made the "Best Books for Young Adults 1979" list compiled by the American Library Association, 1979.

WRITINGS:

Born to Run: The Bruce Springsteen Story, Doubleday, 1979.
(Editor with John Swenson) *Rolling Stone Record Guide: Reviews and Ratings of Almost Ten Thousand Currently Available Pop, Rock, Soul, Country, Blues, Jazz, and Gospel Albums*, Random House, 1980, revised edition published as *The New Rolling Stone Record Guide*, 1984.
(With Kevin Stein) *The Book of Rock Lists*, Dell, 1980.
Elvis, Times Books, 1981.
Before I Get Old: The Story of the Who, St. Martin's, 1982.
(With Sandra Charon and Deborah Geller) *Rocktopicon*, Contemporary, 1984.
Fortunate Son: The Best of Dave Marsh, Random House, 1985.
The First Rock & Roll Confidential Report: Inside the World of Rock & Roll, Pantheon, 1985.

Author of "American Grandstand," a column in *Rolling Stone*, 1976-79. Contributor to magazines and newspapers, including *New York Daily News, Los Angeles Times, Look, Film Comment, Boston Phoenix*, and *Village Voice;* music critic for *Playboy* magazine, 1985—.

WORK IN PROGRESS: A book about Michael Jackson.

SIDELIGHTS: "Rock and roll is not just music," Dave Marsh told *Publishers Weekly.* "It's one of the most important things that's ever happened in American culture." As a former writer for *Rolling Stone* magazine, a music critic for *Playboy* magazine, and an author of books about rock and roll greats such as Elvis Presley, Bruce Springsteen, and the Who, Marsh has tried to approach rock writing with a "straightforward and emotionally honest" style. Despite the fact that his book *Born to Run: The Bruce Springsteen Story* was a trade-paperback best seller, Marsh has found a cold attitude in the publishing industry towards rock writing. "I know that lots of people in the publishing business think, 'Well, we publish stuff about this trash because it subsidizes the serious work'; it's not supposed to *be* the serious work," he told *Publishers Weekly.* "And people are going to pay some very heavy dues for that kind of thinking, no doubt about it. It's just very insulting and debilitating."

Marsh told *CA:* "Professionally despised though it may be, writing about pop music continues to be what I most want to do. Rock is the cultural experience that defines my generation, much as the novel and movies were for earlier ones. Such views do not lend one much credibility in the conventional city room, and they preclude much of the respectability and prestige that normally accrue to people who write intelligently about a cultural phenomenon. Fortunately, prestige and respectability are things which rock and roll teaches one to live without."

BIOGRAPHICAL/CRITICAL SOURCES:

PERIODICALS

Choice, June, 1980.
Los Angeles Times, May 15, 1983, December 11, 1983, February 5, 1984.
New Statesman, September 24, 1982.
Newsweek, October 31, 1983.
New York Times, November 16, 1979.
New York Times Book Review, December 30, 1979, November 28, 1982, July 28, 1985.

Publishers Weekly, October 21, 1983.
Time, January 7, 1980.
Times Educational Supplement, December 24, 1982.
Washington Post Book World, September 11, 1982.

*   *   *

MARSH, Paul
See HOPKINS, Kenneth

*   *   *

MARSHALL, Bill   1937-

PERSONAL: Born May 16, 1937, in Mampong Akwapim, Ghana; son of Albert Obiri and Hilda (Amene) Marshall; married Clara Jackson-Davies, October 21, 1969 (died April, 1977); married Elizabeth Odei, 1980; children: (first marriage) Beulah, Bill, Jr., Aida; (second marriage) Martin, Nana Addo. *Education:* Guildhall School of Music and Drama, L.G.S.M., 1964; City Literary Institute, London, A.D.B., 1964; School of Television Production, London, certificate, 1965. *Religion:* Christian.

ADDRESSES: Home and office—Pen Lodge, Box 140, Achimota, Accra, Ghana.

CAREER: Writer and film producer, Lintas, Ghana, 1973-77; Studio Africain, Accra, Ghana, creative director, 1977—; director, National Film and Television Institute, 1984—.

MEMBER: National Drama Association, Ghana Association of Writers (vice-president).

AWARDS, HONORS: Best drama award from Hollywood Festival of World Television, 1972; best television producer award from Ghana Broadcasting Corp., 1973; Ghana book award, 1979; Manilows fellow, 1983.

WRITINGS:

PLAYS

Stranger to Innocence [and] *Shadow of an Eagle*, Ghana Publishing Corp., 1969, Panther House, 1970.
The Son of Umbele (three-act), Ghana Publishing Corp., 1973.

Also author of *The Queue, No Time for Tears*, and *Strange Neighbours*, all published by Ghana Publishing Corp., and of *The Oeuve and Other Plays*, 1979, and *The Crow*, 1979.

NOVELS

Bukom, Longman, 1979.
Permit for Survival, Educational Press, 1981.

TELEVISION DRAMAS

"Midnight Strangers," Ghana Broadcasting Corp. (GBC-TV), 1968.
"A Matter of Class," GBC-TV, 1972.
"Naki," GBC-TV, 1976.

RADIO PLAYS

"Trial by Dice," GBC-Radio, 1968.

WORK IN PROGRESS: A play, "Goat Street."

SIDELIGHTS: Bill Marshall told *CA:* "I write as I please. And what pleases me is the mind, for I think it is that which belies man's behaviour. I do not, ever, attempt to impose my personal 'mind' in any of my works. Any form of philosophy or 'mind' that may emerge or be observed in my writing is not subjective but that of the people or the situations I write about. In this respect, I think a writer should be wickedly fair. He must be an impartial observer of Society and present it as a discussion, a debate and without drawing conclusions. I pray that freedom for creative expression be preserved for all times throughout the world. I also pray that the writer recognizes the need for some form of ethics and to resist the temptation to abuse this freedom or to indulge in dirt-splashing simply for the sake of art.''

* * *

MARSHALL, Edmund
See HOPKINS, Kenneth

* * *

MARSHALL, Thomas Archibald   1938-
(Tom Marshall)

PERSONAL: Born April 9, 1938, in Niagara Falls, Ontario, Canada; son of Douglas Woodworth (a chemical engineer) and Helen (Kennedy) Marshall. *Education:* Queen's University, B.A., 1961, M.A., 1965.

ADDRESSES: Home—Kingston, Ontario, Canada. *Office*—Department of English, Queen's University, Kingston, Ontario, Canada.

CAREER: Queen's University, Kingston, Ontario, instructor, 1964-66, lecturer, 1966-69, assistant professor, 1969-73, associate professor of English, 1973—.

WRITINGS:

ALL UNDER NAME TOM MARSHALL

(With Tom Eadie and Colin Norman) *The Beast with Three Backs* (poems), Quarry Press, 1965.
The Silences of Fire (poems), Macmillan, 1969.
The Psychic Mariner (critical study of poems by D. H. Lawrence), Viking, 1970.
A. M. Klein (criticism), Ryerson, 1970.
Magic Water (poems), Quarry Press, 1971.
(Editor with David Helwig) *Fourteen Stories High* (anthology), Oberon, 1971.
The Earth-Book (poems), Oberon, 1974.
The White City (poems), Oberon, 1976.
Rosemary Goal (novel), Oberon, 1978.
Harsh and Lovely Land (critical study), University of British Columbia Press, 1979.
The Elements (poems), Oberon, 1980.
Playing with Fire (poems), Oberon, 1984.
Dance of the Particles (poems), Quarry Press, 1984.
Glass Houses (fiction), Oberon, 1985.

Former chief editor of *Quarry;* poetry editor of *Canadian Forum,* 1973-78.

WORK IN PROGRESS: A book of literary essays.

SIDELIGHTS: Thomas Archibald Marshall wrote *CA:* ''A poet attempts to make sense of the world, to discover what is real, for himself and others.'' He continues, ''I am very concerned about Canada's national identity and the future of Canada, but more optimistic about it than some of my contemporaries seem to be. I am also interested in foreign countries and cultures, and enjoy travelling.''

MEDIA ADAPTATIONS: With David Helwig, Gail Fox, and Stuart MacKinnon, Marshall has made a sound recording of

his own work, ''Four Kingston Poets,'' Quarry Recordings, 1972.

* * *

MARSHALL, Tom
See MARSHALL, Thomas Archibald

* * *

MARTIN, Ged
See MARTIN, Gerald Warren

* * *

MARTIN, Gerald Warren   1945-
(Ged Martin)

PERSONAL: Born May 22, 1945, in Hornchurch, England; son of Percival Joseph Willing (a hospital administrator) and Edith Dorothy (Wheel) Martin. *Education:* Magdalene College, Cambridge, B.A. (with first class honors), 1967, Ph.D., 1972.

ADDRESSES: Office—Centre of Canadian Studies, 21 George Square, University of Edinburgh, Edinburgh E48 9LO, Scotland.

CAREER: Cambridge University, Magdalene College, Cambridge, England, Charles Kingsley Bye Fellow in History, 1969-70, research fellow, 1970-72; Australian National University, Canberra, Australia, research fellow in history, 1972-77; University College, Cork, Ireland, lecturer in modern history, 1977-83; University of Edinburgh, Centre of Canadian Studies, Edinburgh, Scotland, director, 1983—. Has made broadcasts in Great Britain, North America, and New Zealand.

MEMBER: Historical Association (England), Australian Society for the Study of Labour History, Cambridge Historical Society.

AWARDS, HONORS: Riddell Prize, Ontario Historical Society, 1981.

WRITINGS:

UNDER NAME GED MARTIN

A Visitor's Guide to Magdalene College, Cambridge, Magdalene College, Cambridge University, 1971.
Durham Report and British Policy: A Critical Essay, Cambridge University Press, 1972.
(With Ronald Hyam) *Reappraisals in British Imperial History,* Macmillan, 1975.
(Editor) *The Founding of Australia,* Hale & Iremanger, 1978.
Episodes of Old Canberra, Australian National University Press, 1978.
Bunyip Aristocracy, Croom Helm, 1985.
(With Jeffrey Simpson) *The Canadian Guide to Britain,* Volume I, Macmillan, 1985.

Contributor to *Historical Journal, Journal of American Studies, Journal of Imperial and Commonwealth History, Albion, Irish Historical Studies, New Zealand Journal of History, Ontario History, Australian Economic History Review, Higher Education Review,* and *Sunday Times.*

WORK IN PROGRESS: Research on British attitudes to constitutional development in British North America between 1837 and 1867 and on British imperial history; a biography of Sir Francis Bond Head.

BIOGRAPHICAL/CRITICAL SOURCES:

PERIODICALS

Globe & Mail (Toronto), May 25, 1985.

* * *

MARTIN, Janet
See GARFINKEL, Bernard Max

* * *

MARTIN, Kenneth R(obert)   1938-

PERSONAL: Born February 12, 1938, in Upper Darby, Pa.; son of Kenneth Edward (a chemist) and Evelyn (Rankin) Martin; married Pamela Ann Miller (a college professor), December 19, 1968 (divorced, 1977). *Education:* Dickinson College, A.B., 1959; University of Pennsylvania, M.A., 1961, Ph.D., 1965.

ADDRESSES: Home—Days Ferry, Me. *Office*—P.O. Box 284, Woolwich, Me. 04579.

CAREER: Gettysburg College, Gettysburg, Pa., instructor, 1965-66, assistant professor of history, 1966-68; Slippery Rock State College, Slippery Rock, Pa., associate professor of history, 1968-74; Kendall Whaling Museum, Sharon, Mass., director, 1974-80; currently senior historian, History Associates, Inc., Rockville, Md. Instructor at University of California Extension, Hawaii, 1976-78, and American Field Studies, 1984—. Reviewer, National Endowment for the Humanities, 1979-81. *Military service:* U.S. Army Reserve, 1959-67; became first lieutenant.

MEMBER: Society for Marine Mammalogy.

AWARDS, HONORS: Hagley Foundation research grant-in-aid, 1972.

WRITINGS:

Delaware Goes Whaling, Eleutherian Mills-Hadley Foundation, 1973.
Whalemen and Whaleships of Maine, Harpswell Press, 1975.
"Naked and a Prisoner": Captain Edward Barnard's Journal of Shipwreck in Palau, Kendall Whaling Museum/Pacific Trust Territory, 1980.
Home Port: A History of the Navy Federal Credit Union, Dorrance, 1983.
Whalemen's Paintings and Drawings, Associated University Presses, 1983.
(Editor) *In the Way of the Whale: The Journal of John F. Martin,* David R. Godine, 1985.
(Co-author) *The Maine Lobster Fishery,* Maine Maritime Museum, in press.

Also author of *Management at Texas Instruments, 1926-1976.* Editor, Kendall Whaling Museum series, 1977-80. Contributor of articles and reviews to numerous periodicals, including *Gettysburg Times, Mankind, Victorian Studies, Journal of Popular Culture, Pennsylvania History, Hawaiian Journal of History,* and *Technology and Culture.* Editor, *Mercer County History,* 1970-72.

WORK IN PROGRESS: Co-authoring *A Singleness of Purpose: Skolfield Ships and Seaman,* for Maine Maritime Museum.

AVOCATIONAL INTERESTS: Travel, American primitive antiques and folk art, American jazz, and working with watercolors.

MARTINEAU, Gilbert

PERSONAL: Born in Rochefort, Charente-Maritime, France; son of Roger and Bertha (Bourlat) Martineau. *Religion:* Roman Catholic.

ADDRESSES: Home and office—Consul of France, Island of St. Helena, South Atlantic Ocean; and 15 rue du Corneau, 17590 Ars-en-Re, France.

CAREER: French Navy, served with Fleet Air Arm squadron attached to U.S. Navy, 1944-45; French Diplomatic Service, 1956—, consul on the Island of St. Helena, 1957—.

MEMBER: Society of Authors (England).

AWARDS, HONORS: Knight, Legion of Honor; Order of Merit (France); Croix de Guerre; Officer of the Order of the British Empire.

WRITINGS:

(Translator into French) Gore Vidal, *The City and the Pillar,* Deux Rives, 1948.
La Vie quotidienne a Sainte-Helene au temps de Napoleon, Hachette, 1966, translation by Frances Partridge published as *Napoleon's St. Helena,* J. Murray, 1968, Rand McNally, 1969.
(Co-author) *Napoleon et l'empire,* Hachette, 1968.
Napoleon se rend aux anglais, Hachette, 1969, translation by Partridge published as *Napoleon Surrenders,* J. Murray, 1971.
Napoleon's Last Journey, J. Murray, 1976.
Madame Mere, Napoleon's Mother, J. Murray, 1977.
Le Roi de Rome, France Empire, 1982.
Napoleon a Sainte-Helene, Tallandier, 1982.
L'Entente cordiale, France Empire, 1984.
Lord Byron, la malediction du genie, Tallandier, 1984.
Malrie-Louise, France Empire, 1985.

Also author of scripts for French radio and British Broadcasting Corp. programs.

WORK IN PROGRESS: A biography of Franz Liszt; essays on Pauline Bonaparte and Joseph, King of Spain; an historical novel set in the nineteenth century.

AVOCATIONAL INTERESTS: Filmmaking.

BIOGRAPHICAL/CRITICAL SOURCES:

PERIODICALS

Le Figaro, May 31, 1967.

* * *

MARTINSON, Ruth A(lice)   1915-

PERSONAL: Born July 27, 1915, in Joplin, Mont. *Education:* Western Washington State College (now Western Washington College), B.A., 1941; University of California, Los Angeles, M.A. in Ed., 1946, Ed.D., 1949.

ADDRESSES: Home—Laguna Hills, Calif. 92653.

CAREER: Elementary and junior high school teacher, 1941-47; Los Angeles County Schools, Los Angeles, Calif., coordinator of research and guidance, 1947-49; University of California, Los Angeles, psychologist in university elementary school, 1949-51, lecturer, 1950-51; California State College (now University), Long Beach, 1951-64, began as assistant professor, became professor; California State University, Dominguez Hills, professor of education and psychology and director of teacher education programs, beginning 1964, currently professor emeritus. Visiting professor at University of California, Los Angeles, 1963-64; visiting summer professor at University of Washington, Seattle, 1962, 1972. Production supervisor of film "Understanding the Gifted," Churchill Films, 1964. Consultant to school systems and commissioned advisor for California State Department of Education and U.S. Office of Education.

MEMBER: Association for the Gifted (president, 1962-63), Council for Exceptional Children, American Psychological Association, National Education Association, American Association of University Professors, California Association of School Psychologists and Psychometrists (chairman, committee on the gifted), Association of California State College Professors (secretary, 1956-59), Pi Lambda Theta.

AWARDS, HONORS: Awards from Association for the Gifted, California Association for the Gifted, and U.S. Office of Education.

WRITINGS:

(With Harry Smallenburg) *Guidance in Elementary Schools,* Prentice-Hall, 1958.
Curriculum Enrichment for the Gifted in the Primary Grades, Prentice-Hall, 1968.
(With Jean Wiener) *The Improvement of Teaching Procedures with Gifted Elementary and Secondary School Students,* Bureau of Research, U.S. Office of Education, 1968.
(With Jeanne L. Delp) *A Handbook for Parents of Gifted and Talented,* National/State Leadership Training Institute on Gifted and Talented, 1975, 2nd edition, 1977.
A Guide toward Better Teaching for the Gifted, National/State Leadership Training Institute on Gifted and Talented, 1975.
The Identification of the Gifted and Talented, Council for Exceptional Children, 1975.

Author of monographs and bulletins on the gifted child for the U.S. Office of Education and of sections of Commissioner's Report to Congress. Contributor to yearbooks, textbooks, symposia, and journals.

WORK IN PROGRESS: Research on intelligence and creativity.†

*   *   *

MASON, Douglas R(ankine)   1918-
(R. M. Douglas, John Rankine)

PERSONAL: Born September 26, 1918, in Hawarden, England; son of Russell (an engineer) and Bertha (Greenwood) Mason; married Norma Eveline Cooper (a social worker), May 26, 1945; children: Keith, Patricia (Mrs. Richard Morris), John, Elaine. *Education:* University of Manchester, B.A., 1947, teacher's diploma, 1948. *Politics:* "Liberal by inclination, Conservative sometimes by observation of policies." *Religion:* Methodist.

ADDRESSES: Home—The Byre, Hollens Farm, Grasmere, Cumbria, England. *Agent*—Lesley Flood, Romneybury Bungalow, New Old Harlow, Essex, England.

CAREER: Taught in primary and secondary schools in Cheshire, England, 1950-67; St. George's Primary School, Wallasey, England, headmaster, 1967-78. *Military service:* British Army, Royal Signals Corps, 1939-46; served in Africa; became lieutenant.

MEMBER: National Association of Head Teachers, Wallasey Association of Head Teachers (president, 1973-74).

WRITINGS:

From Carthage Then I Came, Doubleday, 1966, published as *Eight against Utopia,* Paperback Library, 1967.
Ring of Violence, R. Hale, 1968, Avon, 1969.
Landfall Is a State of Mind, R. Hale, 1968.
The Tower of Rizwan, R. Hale, 1968.
The Janus Syndrome, R. Hale, 1969.
Matrix, Ballantine, 1970.
Satellite 54-0, Ballantine, 1971.
Horizon Alpha, Ballantine, 1971.
Dilation Effect, Ballantine, 1971.
The Resurrection of Roger Diment, Ballantine, 1972.
The Phaeton Condition, Putnam, 1973.
The End Bringers, Ballantine, 1973.
Pitman's Progress, Elmfield Press, 1976.
The Omega Worm, R. Hale, 1976.
Euphor Unfree, R. Hale, 1977.
Mission to Pactolus R, R. Hale, 1978.
The Typhon Intervention, R. Hale, 1981.

Also author of *Links over Space* and *The Vort Programme.*

UNDER PSEUDONYM R. M. DOUGLAS

The Darkling Plain (historical novel), R. Hale, 1979.

UNDER PSEUDONYM JOHN RANKINE

The Blockade of Sinitron: Four Adventures of Dag Fletcher, Thomas Nelson, 1964.
Interstellar Two Five, Dobson, 1966.
Never the Same Door, Dobson, 1967.
One Is One, Dobson, 1968.
Moons of Triopus, Dobson, 1968, Paperback Library, 1969.
Binary Z, Dobson, 1969.
The Weizman Experiment, Dobson, 1969.
The Plantos Affair, Dobson, 1971.
The Ring of Garamas, Dobson, 1972.
Operation Umanaq, Ace Books, 1973.
The Bromius Phenomenon, Ace Books, 1973.
The Fingalnan Conspiracy, Sidgwick & Jackson, 1973.
Astral Quest, Futura Publishing, 1975.
Moon Odyssey, Futura Publishing, 1975.
Lunar Attack, Futura Publishing, 1975.
Android Planet, Futura Publishing, 1976.
The Thorburn Enterprise, Dobson, 1977.
The Star of Hesiock, Dobson, 1980.
Last Shuttle to Planet Earth, Dobson, 1980.

WORK IN PROGRESS: A historical novel of the Saxon period, entitled *Sturmer;* science fiction novels.

*   *   *

MASON, Robert E(mmett)   1914-

PERSONAL: Born December 10, 1914, in Blissfield, Mich.; son of Harold C. and Alta (McFate) Mason; married Nell Jean Wood, 1938; children: Jean Roberta. *Education:* Huntington College, A.B., 1935; Indiana University, A.M., 1937; Columbia University, Ph.D., 1949.

ADDRESSES: Office—Division of Education, Southern Illinois University, Edwardsville, Ill. 62025.

CAREER: New York College for Teachers (now State University of New York at Albany), assistant professor of education, 1947-49; Brooklyn College (now Brooklyn College of the City University of New York), Brooklyn, N.Y., assistant professor of education, 1949-52; Western Reserve University (now Case Western Reserve University), Cleveland, Ohio, professor of education, 1952-58; University of Pittsburgh, Pittsburgh, Pa., professor of education, 1958-69; Southern Illinois University at Edwardsville, professor, 1969—. Visiting professor at University of Illinois, Columbia University, University of Missouri, Occidental College, and Northern Iowa University.

MEMBER: American Association of University Professors (president, Western Reserve University chapter, 1957-58), American Historical Association, National Education Association, History of Education Society (secretary-treasurer, 1960—), John Dewey Society (member of commission on publications, 1962—), Kiwanis Club, University of Pittsburgh Faculty Club.

WRITINGS:

Moral Values and Secular Education, Columbia University Press, 1950.
(Co-author) *John Dewey: Master Educator,* Society for the Advancement of Education, 1959.
(Contributor) *Dictionary of Education,* McGraw, 1959.
Educational Ideals in American Society, Allyn & Bacon, 1960.
Education in the Culture of Great Cities, University of Pittsburgh, 1967.
Contemporary Educational Theory, McKay, 1972.
The Community of the Young, Society of Professors of Education, 1975.

Editor, *Proceedings of the National Philosophy of Education Society,* 1961-62. Contributor to professional journals. Member of editorial board, *History of Education Quarterly.*†

*   *   *

MATTSON, Lloyd   1923-

PERSONAL: Born August 29, 1923, in Duluth, Minn.; son of David J. (a police officer) and Beatrice L. Mattson; married Elsie E. Heaton (a nurse), November 19, 1942; children: Sally Mattson Rogers, Keith, Joel, David, Kevin. *Education:* Bethel Theological Seminary, St. Paul, Minn., Th.B., 1947; also attended John Wesley College. *Politics:* Republican.

ADDRESSES: Home and office—5118 Glendale St., Duluth, Minn. 55804.

CAREER: Ordained Baptist minister; pastor of Baptist congregations in Wisconsin, Michigan, and Alaska, 1947-62; Baptist General Conference, Evanston, Ill., executive, 1962-72; free-lance writer, editor, photographer, and camp consultant in Minnesota, 1972-77; North Shore Baptist Church, Duluth, Minn., pastor, 1977—; Camping Guideposts (publisher), Duluth, founder and editor, 1981—, editor of *Guidepost* (newsletter). Producer of filmstrips; outdoor editor, WWJC-Radio, Duluth, Minn., 1978—.

MEMBER: Outdoor Writers Association of America.

WRITINGS:

Camping Guideposts, Moody, 1964, revised edition, 1972.
Wilderness Way, Baptist Men's Board, 1971, revised edition, Accent Books, 1979.

Family Camping, Moody, 1973.
Foul-up or Follow-up?, Victor Books, 1974.
Work with Boys Successfully, Victor Books, 1975.
Devotions for Men: Good Morning, Lord, Baker Book, 1979.
(Co-editor) *Introduction to Christian Camping,* Moody, 1979.
Rediscover Your Family Outdoors, Victor Books, 1980.
The Camp Counselor, Camping Guideposts, 1981.
The Apples in a Seed, Camping Guideposts, 1983.
Build Your Church through Camping, Camping Guideposts, 1984.
New Life in Alaska, Camping Guideposts, 1985.

Also author of *Way to Grow* and *Camping with Families,* both published by Victor Books. Contributor to religious and camping journals. Editor of *Journal of Christian Camping,* 1970-73.

SIDELIGHTS: "The world is full of preachers writing about religion. Not many give themselves to writing about the outdoors, where the Christian religion had its roots. I count it an honor to be one of the few. I am persuaded the Christian cause would be far better off if more time was spent in the outdoors and less in church. Any who doubt this should drop in some Sunday at our small church on the shores of Lake Superior the week after a camping retreat or caravan. If the object of the gospel is to help people love one another, then we're on the right track. The burden of my writing is to persuade more people that this is so, and to equip outdoor leaders for effective service.

"Three of my books have found their way into other languages. Our files contain notes from people around the world who have found my unreligious approach to Christian thought refreshing. It is gratifying to reach that age when one cares little or nothing about the wrath of bishops or their Baptist counterparts."

*   *   *

MAVES, Paul B(enjamin)   1913-

PERSONAL: Born April 21, 1913, in Burwell, Neb.; son of Benjamin C. and Ellen Alverda (Craun) Maves; married Mary Carolyn Hollman (a writer), September 10, 1939; children: Margaret Alverda Maves Hansell, David Hollman. *Education:* Nebraska Wesleyan University, A.B., 1936; Drew University, B.D., 1939, Ph.D., 1949; also attended New York University, 1945-46, and Harvard University, 1957-58. *Politics:* Democrat.

ADDRESSES: Home—10200 Edelweiss Cir., Merriam, Kans. 66203. *Office*—5218 Oak St., Kansas City, Mo. 64112.

CAREER: Pastor of Methodist churches in Albany, N.Y., 1940-42, and Middlebury, Vt., 1942-45; New York University, New York City, instructor in education, 1945-46; Federal Council of Churches of Christ in America, research associate, 1946-48, acting executive secretary of department of pastoral services, 1948-49; Drew University, Madison, N.J., adjunct professor of human relations, 1948-49, assistant professor, 1949-51, associate professor, 1951-56, George T. Cobb Professor of Religious Education, 1956-67; National Council of Churches of Christ, New York City, associate executive director of department of educational development, 1967-70; St. Paul School of Theology, Kansas City, Mo., director of field education, 1970-75; Kingsley Manor, Los Angeles, Calif., administrator, 1975-78; National Shepherd's Center Development Project, Kansas City, Mo., director, 1978-84, Shepherd's Center International, director of training, 1984—.

Past director of Mid-America Resource and Training Center on Aging, Kansas City. Visiting scholar, Columbia University, 1964-65. Staff associate, National Training Laboratories, Inc., 1960-70; delegate to White House Conference on Aging, 1961. Member of board of directors, National Council on Aging, 1950-58; member of certification council, Board of Health and Welfare Ministries of United Methodist Church, 1964-72.

WRITINGS:

(With J. Lennart Cedarleaf) *Older People and the Church* (Religious Book Club selection), Abingdon, 1949.
Christian Service to Older People (pamphlet), Women's Division of Christian Services, Methodist Church, 1949.
(Editor) *The Practical Field in Theological Education* (pamphlet), Department of Pastoral Services, Federal Council of Churches of Christ in America, 1949.
The Christian Religious Education of Older People, Department of Pastoral Services, Federal Council of Churches of Christ in America, 1950.
(Editor) *Anxiety in Religious Work and Medical Practice* (pamphlet), Clifton Springs Sanitarium, 1950.
(Contributor) J. Richard Spoon, editor, *Pastoral Care*, Abingdon, 1951.
They Shall Bring Forth Fruit in Age (pamphlet), National Council of the Protestant Episcopal Church, 1951.
The Best Is Yet to Be, Westminster, 1951.
(Editor) *The Church and Mental Health* (Religious Book Club selection), Scribner, 1953.
Understanding Ourselves as Adults, Abingdon, 1959.
(Contributor) Marvin Taylor, editor, *Religious Education: A Comprehensive Survey*, Abingdon, 1960.
(Contributor) Clark Tibbitts, editor, *A Handbook of Social Gerontology*, University of Chicago Press, 1960.
On Becoming Yourself (for seventh grade students), Graded Press, 1962.
(With Charles Stewart) *Christian Faith and Emotional Health*, Abingdon, 1962.
(With wife, Mary Carolyn Maves) *Finding Your Way through the Bible*, Graded Press and Abingdon, 1971.
(With M. C. Maves) *Learning More about the Bible*, Abingdon, 1973.
(With M. C. Maves) *Exploring How the Bible Came to Be*, Abingdon, 1973.
(With M. C. Maves) *Discovering How the Bible Message Spread*, Abingdon, 1973.
A Faith for Growing: A Manual for Working with Older Volunteers, Judson, 1980.
A Place to Live in Your Later Years, Augsburg, 1983.
Faith for Growing Older, Augsburg, 1985.

Also author of curriculum materials for the Methodist church. Contributor to *Encyclopedia for Church Group Leaders*. Contributor of about fifty articles and reviews to church publications and theology and other journals, including *International Journal of Religious Education*, *Church School*, *Child Guidance*, *Workers on Youth*, *Adult Teacher*, and *Mature Years*. Guest editor, *Pastoral Psychology*, September, 1954.

SIDELIGHTS: Paul B. Maves's book *The Best Is Yet to Be* was translated into Norwegian in 1956.

AVOCATIONAL INTERESTS: Writing poetry.

*   *   *

McCALL, Virginia Nielsen 1909-
(Virginia Nielsen)

PERSONAL: Born June 14, 1909, in Idaho Falls, Idaho; daughter of Jesse Hans (a sheep rancher and teacher) and Florence (Kingston) Nielsen; married Robert M. Pressey, April 4, 1938 (deceased); married Joseph R. McCall (a park ranger), April 21, 1943. *Education:* Attended University of Idaho, 1927-29, and Utah State Agricultural College (now Utah State University), 1931.

ADDRESSES: Home and office—9028 Talisman Dr., Sacramento, Calif. 95826. *Agent*—Curtis Brown Ltd., 10 Astor Pl., New York, N.Y. 10003.

CAREER: Free-lance writer. Member of staff of writers' conferences in California, Utah, Washington, and Texas.

MEMBER: National League of American Penwomen, Inc., Authors Guild, Authors League of America, California Writers Club.

WRITINGS:

Navy Nurse (Junior Literary Guild selection), Messner, 1968.
(With husband, Joseph R. McCall) *Your Career in Parks and Recreation*, Messner, 1970, revised edition, 1974.
(With J. R. McCall) *Outdoor Recreation, Forest, Park, and Wilderness*, Glencoe, 1977.
Civil Service Careers, F. Watts, 1977.
A Faraway Love, Gold Medal, 1982.
The House of Three Sisters, Scholastic Inc., 1982.
Traitor for Love, Avon, 1983.
Mirror, Mirror, Scholastic Inc., 1983.
Trusting, Harlequin, 1984.
Weekend of Fear, Scholastic Inc., 1984.
Moonlight on Snow, Harlequin, 1985.

UNDER NAME VIRGINIA NIELSEN

Try to Forget Me, Doubleday, 1942.
Cadet Widow, Doubleday, 1942.
Bewildered Heart, Arcadia House, 1946.
The Golden One, Arcadia House, 1947.
Journey to Love, Bouregy, 1959.
Remember Me, Bouregy, 1960.
Dangerous Dream, Bouregy, 1961.
The Road to the Valley, McKay, 1961.
The Mystery of Fyfe House, Bouregy, 1962.
The Whistling Winds, McKay, 1964.
Keoni, My Brother, McKay, 1965.
Kimo and Madame Pele (Junior Literary Guild selection), McKay, 1966, published as *The House on the Volcano*, Scholastic Inc., 1966, new edition, 1985.
The Mystery of Secret Town, McKay, 1969.
Adassa and Her Hen, McKay, 1971.
Seven Tides, Bantam Books, 1972.
Yankee Lover, Doubleday, 1978.
The Marriage Contract, Doubleday, 1980.

WORK IN PROGRESS: Sorcery, a historical novel for Dell; *The Crimson Serpent*, a contemporary novel for Harlequin.

SIDELIGHTS: Virginia Nielsen McCall told *CA:* "I love a good story, one that holds the reader spellbound because he is genuinely interested in the characters and their interrelationships. I believe such a reading experience can contribute to a young person's emotional development as well as his understanding of the world he, or she, will enter.

"It pleases me that my romantic suspense and historical novels appeal to young people abroad as well as in America. And it pleases me that so many fine books are being issued in paperback form, enabling children to buy and build their own individual libraries.''

AVOCATIONAL INTERESTS: Travel, swimming, young writers.

*   *   *

McCANN, Edson
  See del REY, Lester

*   *   *

McCLURE, Michael (Thomas)   1932-

PERSONAL: Born October 20, 1932, in Marysville, Kan.; son of Thomas and Marian (Dixie Johnston) McClure; married Joanna Kinnison, 1954; children: Katherine Jane. *Education:* Attended Wichita State University, 1951-53, and University of Arizona, 1953-54; San Francisco State University, B.A., 1955.

ADDRESSES: Home—264 Downey St., San Francisco, Calif. 94117. *Agent*—Helen Merrill, 361 West 17th St., New York, N.Y. 10011.

CAREER: California College of Arts and Crafts, Oakland, Calif., assistant professor, 1962-77, associate professor, beginning 1977, currently professor of humanities. Lecturer, State University of New York at Buffalo, 1979; associate fellow, Pierson College, Yale University, 1982.

AWARDS, HONORS: National Endowment for the Arts grant, 1967 and 1974; Guggenheim fellow, 1973; Alfred Jarry Award, Magic Theatre, 1973; Rockefeller fellow for the theatre, 1975; Obie Award, 1979, for *Josephine, the Mouse Singer;* California Arts Council award, 1980.

WRITINGS:

(Author of foreword) Charles Olson, *Maximus from Dogtown-I,* Auerhahn Press, 1961.
Meat Science Essays, City Lights, 1963, revised edition, 1966.
(With Frank Reynolds) *Freewheelin' Frank, Secretary of the Angels,* Grove, 1967.
The Mad Cub (novel), Bantam, 1970.
The Adept (novel), Delacorte, 1971.
(Author of introduction) Sam Shepard, *Mad Dog Blues: The Collected Plays of Sam Shepard,* Winter House, 1972.
(Author of afterword) Jerry Hopkins and Daniel Sugarman, *No One Here Gets Out Alive,* Warner Books, 1980.
Scratching the Beat Surface (essays), North Point Press, 1982.

POETRY

Passage, Jonathan Williams, 1956.
Peyote Poem (broadside), Semina, 1958.
For Artaud, Totem Press, 1959.
Hymns to St. Geryon and Other Poems (also see below), Auerhahn Press, 1959.
Dark Brown (also see below), Auerhahn Press, 1961.
The New Book/A Book of Torture, Grove, 1961.
Ghost Tantras, privately printed, 1964, Four Seasons Foundation, 1969.
Two for Bruce Conner, Oyez, 1964.
Love Lion, Lioness (poem poster), Oyez, 1964.
Double Murder! Vahrooooooohr!, Semina, 1964.
Thirteen Mad Sonnets, [Milan, Italy], 1965.
Poisoned Wheat, Oyez, 1965.
Mandalas, Dave Haselwood, 1965.

Unto Caesar, Dave Haselwood, 1965.
Dream Table, Dave Haselwood, 1965.
(With Bruce Conner) *(The Mandala Book),* Dave Haselwood, 1966.
Hail Thee Who Play: A Poem, Black Sparrow Press, 1968, revised edition, Sand Dollar Press, 1974.
Muscled Apple Swift, Love Press, 1968.
Love Lion Book, Four Seasons Foundation, 1968.
The Sermons of Jean Harlow and the Curses of Billy the Kid, Four Seasons Foundation, 1969.
Plane Pomes, Phoenix Bookshop, 1969.
Oh Christ God Love Cry of Love Stifled Furred Wall Smoking Burning, Auerhahn Press, c.1969.
Hymns to St. Geryon [and] *Dark Brown,* Cape Goliard Press, 1969, 3rd edition, Grey Fox Press, 1982.
The Surge: A Poem, Frontier Press (Columbus, Ohio), 1969.
Lion Fight, Pierrepont Press, 1969.
Star, Grove, 1970.
99 Theses, Tansy Press, 1972.
The Book of Joanna, Sand Dollar Press, 1973.
Transfiguration, Pomegranate Press, 1973.
Rare Angel (writ with raven's blood), Black Sparrow Press, 1974.
September Blackberries, New Directions, 1974.
Solstice Blossoms, Arif Press, 1974.
Fleas, 189-195, Aloe Editions, 1974.
A Fist-Full (1956-1957), Black Sparrow Press, 1974.
On Organism, Institute of Further Studies (Buffalo, N.Y.), 1974.
Flea 100, Frank Hallman, 1975.
Jaguar Skies, New Directions, 1975.
Man of Moderation: Two Poems, Frank Hallman, 1975.
Antechamber, Poythress Press, 1977, revised edition published as *Antechamber and Other Poems,* New Directions, 1978.
Fragments of Perseus, New Directions, 1983.
Fleas (180-186), Les Ferriss, 1985.

PLAYS

''!The Feast!,'' produced in San Francisco, Calif., at the Batman Gallery, December 22, 1960.
''Pillow'' (also see below), first produced in New York, N.Y., at the American Theatre for Poets, 1961.
The Blossom; or, Billy the Kid (also see below; first produced in New York at the American Theatre for Poets, 1964), Great Lakes Books, 1967.
The Beard (also see below; first produced in San Francisco at the Encore Theatre, December 18, 1965; produced in New York, 1967; produced in London, England, 1968), privately printed, 1965, revised edition, Grove, 1967.
The Cherub (also see below; first produced in Berkeley, Calif., at the Magic Theatre, May, 1969), Black Sparrow Press, 1970.
Little Odes, Poems, and a Play, ''The Raptors,'' Black Sparrow Press, 1969.
''The Charbroiled Chinchilla: The Pansy, The Meatball, Spider Rabbit'' (also see below), first produced together in Berkeley at the Magic Theatre, 1969; ''Spider Rabbit'' and ''The Meatball'' produced together in London, 1970, and in New York, 1976.
The Shell (also see below; first produced in San Francisco, 1970; produced in London, 1975), Cape Goliard Press, 1968.
''The Brutal Brontosaurus: Spider Rabbit, The Meatball, The Shell, Apple Glove, The Authentic Radio Life of Bruce Conner and Snoutburbler'' (also see below), first pro-

duced together in Berkeley at the Magic Theatre, May, 1970; "The Authentic Radio Life of Bruce Conner and Snoutburbler" produced separately in London, 1975.

Gargoyle Cartoons (contains "The Shell," "The Pansy," "The Meatball," "The Bow," "Spider Rabbit," "Apple Glove," "The Sail," "The Dear," "The Authentic Radio Life of Bruce Conner and Snoutburbler," "The Feather" [also see below], and "The Cherub"; first produced together in Philadelphia, Pa., at the Open Theatre, 1970), Delacorte, 1971.

"Polymorphous Pirates: The Pussy, The Button, The Feather" (also see below), first produced together in San Francisco at the Magic Theatre, January 21, 1972.

"The Growl," produced in Berkeley at the Magic Theatre, June, 1971.

The Mammals (contains "The Blossom," "The Feast," and "Pillow"), Cranium Press, 1972.

"McClure on Toast," first produced in Los Angeles, Calif., at the Company Theatre, 1973.

"The Pussy, The Button, and Chekhov's Grandmother; or, The Sugar Wolves," first produced together in New York, December, 1973.

"Music Piece" (also see below), first produced in San Francisco at the Magic Theatre, 1974.

Gorf; or, Gorf and the Blind Dyke (first produced in San Francisco at the Magic Theatre, July, 1974), New Directions, 1976.

"One Acts by Michael McClure," produced in New York at the Theatre Genesis, 1974.

"The Derby," first produced in Los Angeles at the Company Theatre, 1974; new version produced in New York at the Stage Company, 1981.

"General Gorgeous," first produced in San Francisco at the American Conservatory Theatre, November, 1975; produced in Edinburgh, Scotland, 1976.

"Sunny-Sideup: The Pink Helmet and The Masked Choir" (also see below), produced together in Los Angeles at the Company Theatre, March, 1976.

"Range War," produced in Tucson, Ariz., 1976.

"Two for the Tricentennial: The Pink Helmet and The Grabbing of the Fairy" (also see below), first produced together in San Francisco at the Magic Theatre, 1976.

"Goethe: Ein Fragment," produced in San Francisco at the Julian Theatre, January, 1978.

"Minnie Mouse and the Tap-Dancing Buddha," produced in San Francisco at the Magic Theatre, May, 1978.

The Grabbing of the Fairy (first produced in Los Angeles at the Company Theatre, January, 1973), Truck Press, 1978.

Josephine, the Mouse Singer (adaptation of a story by Franz Kafka; produced in New York at the W.P.A. Theatre, November 20, 1978), New Directions, 1980.

"The Red Snake," produced in San Francisco at the Magic Theatre, January 11, 1979; produced in New York at the Public Theatre Workshop, 1980.

"The Mirror," produced in Los Angeles at the Odyssey Theatre, 1979.

"Coyote in Chains," produced in San Francisco, 1980.

The Beard and VKTMS, Grove, 1985.

Also author of television play, "The Maze," 1967 and of a radio play, "Music Peace," 1974.

CONTRIBUTOR

Daisy Alden, editor, *A New Folder: Americans: Poems and Drawings*, Folder Editions, 1959.

Elias Wilentz, editor, *The Beat Scene*, Corinth, 1960.

Lawrence Ferlinghetti, editor, *Beatitude Anthology*, City Lights, 1960.

Donald M. Allen, editor, *The New American Poetry, 1945-1960*, Grove, 1960.

Reidar Ekner, editor, *Helgon & Hetsporrar*, Raben & Sjogren (Stockholm), 1960.

Gregory Corso and Walter Hollerer, editors, *Junge Amerikanische Lyrik*, Carl Hanser, 1961.

Lyle E. Linville, editor, *Tiger*, Linville-Hansen Associates, 1961.

Gene Baro, editor, *"Beat" Poets*, Vista, 1961.

Thomas Parkinson, editor, *A Casebook on the Beat*, Crowell, 1961.

Fernando Pivano, editor, *Poesi degli Ultimi Americani*, Feltrinelli, 1964.

Walter Lowenfels, editor, *Poets of Today*, International Publishers, 1964.

Donald M. Allen and W. Tallman, editors, *The Poetics of the New American Poetry*, Grove, 1964.

Paris Leary and Robert Kelly, editors, *A Controversy of Poets*, Anchor, 1965.

David Meltzer, editor, *The San Francisco Poets*, Ballantine, 1971.

Lynda Rosen Obst, editor, *The Sixties*, Rolling Stone Press, 1977.

(And author of foreword) Gene Anthony, *The Summer of Love: Haight-Ashbury at Its Height*, Celestial Arts, 1980.

The Postmoderns, Grove, 1982.

OTHER

Contributor to magazines, including *Poetry, Semina Two, Life, Chicago Review, Black Mountain Review, Jabberwock, Beatitude, Yugen, Big Table, Kulchur, Nation, City Lights Journal, Imago*, and *Rolling Stone*. Editor, *Ark II/Moby I*, 1957; co-editor, *Journal for the Protection of All Beings*, 1961.

SIDELIGHTS: The term "spiritmeat" was coined by poet and playwright Michael McClure to designate the body and mind united. McClure, drawing inspiration from biology and mysticism, sees writing as a process whereby this unity can be achieved. His work, a reviewer for the *Times Literary Supplement* explains, "is one of the more remarkable achievements in recent American literature, a record of a man's attempt to find the terms he needs for a vital balance, for some kind of homeostasis of body and psyche." "It is this fusion of mind and body as a single principle that is the particular stamp of the man," David Kherdian writes in *Six Poets of the San Francisco Renaissance: Portraits and Checklists*, "and it is this concept that has determined the flow of his work, which is of constant change, growth, and expansion."

McClure first began writing in the 1950s and came to public attention as one of San Francisco's Beat poets. Influenced not only by such literary figures as Theodore Roethke and Charles Olson but by the ideas then prevalent in biology and other natural sciences, McClure's poetry was meant to be an expression of the whole man. "For McClure," Kherdian writes, "there can be no distinction between the man and the writer—one being condemned to serve the other—nor can there be a differentiation between the mind and the body, for if the mind is in error it will be reflected by a gesture of the body." McClure explains that "a poem is as much of me as an arm. Measure, line, etc. is interior and takes an outward shape, is not pre-destined or logical but immediate."

In *Meat Science Essays*, McClure develops some of his ideas about poetry and biology. He speaks of the need for man to be aware that he is an animal. This awareness results in the "intellect as we know it [subsiding] and mammalian intelligence—acknowledgement of the senses as organs of knowing—[returning]," writes Michael Lynch in *Parnassus: Poetry in Review*. This idea is also raised in the collection *Scratching the Beat Surface*. In this book, Beverly Bouwsma of the *Berkeley Gazette* explains, McClure recounts how the Beat poets of the 1950s were "concerned with nature, mind and biology.... They thought they could bring new life to poetry and save humanity from civilization, technology and emotional bankruptcy by reminding us of the integrity in the lives of animals and in the processes of nature." Writing in the *Dictionary of Literary Biography*, William R. King points out that McClure sees the Beat movement as an "intense awakening of a 'bio-alchemical' consciousness" and calls for human beings "to achieve the clearest perceptions and to attune themselves to the inner voice or genetic being (the voice of the universe, which speaks from many centers) in order to transform society and restore the planet." From this biological awareness, then, emerges an essentially mystical revelation. "To McClure," King writes, "the universe—all that can be sensed or intuited—is in a sense the messiah, leading us to witness its miraculous unfolding."

McClure's writing seeks to be an expression of the enlightened state of consciousness he hypothesizes. His work is, above all, a personal expression rather than a form of communication with an audience. Speaking of how he came to this approach, McClure states in *Scratching the Beat Surface* that "communication was not as important to me as expression. To speak and move was the most important thing." McClure carries this idea to the physical structure of his poetry. His poems are centered on the page and move across and down in a flowing motion meant to approximate the actual speaking voice. Influenced by poet Charles Olson and his theory of projective verse and by the painter Jackson Pollock, who created action painting, McClure sees a poem as "a calligram of the moment of creation or experience, an artifact entirely representing the perceptions it contains in a highly compressed image," King explains. As McClure tells Jhan Hochman and Todd Grimson of the *Portland Review*, "What we write, or what we paint, or what we sing or do, must actually, literally, be an extension of ourselves, or it is meaningless." Because of the Beats' emphasis on raw expression as a means to reveal the essential self, McClure, speaking to Hochman and Grimson, calls the Beat writers "the literary wing of the environmental movement."

McClure's poetic language—combining Biblical phrasing, scientific terms, mantras, and meaningless yet powerful sounds—gives his poetry a freewheeling energy praised by many critics. Francis Crick, writing in *Margins*, claims, "What appeals to me most about [McClure's] poems is the fury and imagery of them. I love the vividness of his reactions and the very personal turns and swirls of the lines." Similarly, Robert Peters states in *Margins* that "McClure's writing is like action painting: spontaneous. The reader is to re-experience the excitement McClure felt writing the poems. The energy ... is as important as any direct poetic statement the reader might receive, of a traditional sort.... McClure's beast (mammal) language is LOVE: we are to form these strange sounds with abandon and pleasure, with love-explosives, love-verbal-fun-ejaculations." At its best, Geoffrey Thurley writes in *The Beats: Essays in Criticism*, McClure's poetry "achieves a poise and a sinewy delicacy rarely to be found in recent American writing."

McClure's plays also display an intense energy. In the tradition of such avant-garde playwrights as Antonin Artaud, McClure's work combines wildly divergent elements into dreamlike sequences. His play "The Beard" brought him notoriety when it was produced in San Francisco and Berkeley, California, in 1965. Because of the simulated sex act at play's end, the cast was arrested at each nightly performance. (The play was later judged not to be obscene when finally brought to trial.) A production in Los Angeles was also met with police resistance, but "The Beard"'s New York performance won Obie Awards for its director and lead actress.

Featuring the characters Billy the Kid and Jean Harlow, who meet in the hereafter, "The Beard" explores American sexual attitudes as embodied in two cultural representatives of sex and violence. As Richard Gilman writes in his *Common and Uncommon Masks: Writings on Theatre, 1961-1970*, "The whole point of the couple's being dead and legendary is that they may now serve as exemplary figures of the American confusion between orders of being, of our perpetual conversion of sexuality into one kind of art—the popular mythology of archetypal surrogates, the blonde bombshell, the steely outlaw—and the consequent depletion of the sexual by being turned into emblem and shady metaphor."

Critical reaction to "The Beard" was generally favorable, with the play's "offensive" material deemed to be integral to its message. The language, the *Newsweek* reviewer admits, is "without question the 'filthiest' ever heard on a commercial stage in the English speaking nations." But "the proper reaction is neither shock nor a bland pretense of not being shocked . . . ," continues the reviewer. "McClure raises profanity to a comic passion. He has written a brilliant little monster of a play." Harold Clurman, while calling "The Beard" "inconsequential as art," nevertheless finds the play "a mockery of sex, a 'milestone' on the road to nonentity. We need not despise it. It shows us that our myths ... are in the process of dissolution."

For "Josephine, the Mouse Singer," a play produced in New York in 1980, McClure won the coveted Obie Award. Unusual in that all the characters are mice, the play concerns the singer Josephine, who defends the freedom of the artist in modern society. It is in "the tradition of the fable, with all the grace and poise of La Fontaine along with his social astuteness," writes Peter Clothier in the *Los Angeles Times Book Review*.

Speaking of McClure's work as a playwright, Mel Gussow of the *New York Times* judges him to be "something of a comic book fantasist, projecting larger-than-life images on an imaginary silver screen." But Arthur Sainer acclaims him as "one of the best playwrighting minds now working in America" and finds "The Beard" to be "a small masterpiece."

Speaking again to Hochman and Grimson, McClure defines the relationship between his poetry and plays. "They're quite different," he says, "and they're complimentary. And they certainly come from different aspects of my character; poetry being subjective, [it has to] do with perception, and theatre being a social probing—more like doing sculptures with bodies to create hallucinations on stage, to see the effect of the reflection of my hallucinations on the universe and on other people. I *think* with my poetry, and I *experience* with my poetry, and I'm really *probing* with my theatre."

MEDIA ADAPTATIONS: McClure and his wife, Joanna McClure, made a color video of poems from *September Black-*

berries for KQED-TV, 1973; a film of scenes from "The Blossom" was made by George Herms.

BIOGRAPHICAL/CRITICAL SOURCES:

BOOKS

A Bibliography of the Auerhahn Press and Its Successor, Dave Haselwood Books, Poltroon Press, 1976.

Allen, Donald M., editor, *The New American Poetry, 1945-1960,* Grove, 1960.

Bartlett, Lee, editor, *The Beats: Essays in Criticism,* McFarland, 1981.

Bertholf, Robert J. and Ian W. Reid, editors, *Robert Duncan: Scales of the Marvellous,* New Directions, 1979.

Clements, Marshall, *A Catalog of Works by Michael McClure, 1957-1965,* Phoenix Bookshop, 1965.

Contemporary Literary Criticism, Gale, Volume VI, 1976, Volume X, 1979.

Cook, Bruce, *The Beat Generation,* Scribner, 1971.

Dictionary of Literary Biography, Volume XVI: *The Beats: Literary Bohemians in Postwar America,* Gale, 1983.

Ferlinghetti, Lawrence and Nancy Peters, *Literary San Francisco: A Pictorial History from Its Beginnings to the Present Day,* City Lights/Harper, 1980.

Gilman, Richard, *Common and Uncommon Masks: Writings on Theatre, 1961-1970,* Random House, 1971.

Kherdian, David, *Six Poets of the San Francisco Renaissance: Portraits and Checklists,* Giligia Press, 1967.

Leary, Paris and Robert Kelly, editors, *A Controversy of Poets,* Anchor, 1965.

Lipton, Lawrence, *The Erotic Revolution,* Sherbourne Press, 1965.

Meltzer, David, *The San Francisco Poets,* Ballantine, 1971.

PERIODICALS

Berkeley Gazette, July 8, 1982.
Big Table, spring, 1960.
Booklist, May 1, 1978.
Books, September, 1967, October, 1967.
Book World, August 15, 1971.
Christian Century, January 17, 1968.
Credences, Number 1, 1980.
Los Angeles Free Press, February 2, 1982.
Margins, March, 1975.
Nation, November 13, 1967, July 20, 1970.
Newsweek, November 6, 1971.
New York Times, October 3, 1981.
New York Times Book Review, June 20, 1971.
Parnassus: Poetry in Review, spring-summer, 1976.
Poetry Information, spring, 1975.
Portland Review, Volume 28, number 1, 1982.
San Francisco Review of Books, December, 1977.
San Francisco Theatre, summer, 1977.
Show, May, 1970.
Times Literary Supplement, March 25, 1965.
Village Voice, October 5, 1967, November 2, 1967, November 16, 1967, January 22, 1970, January 3, 1974.
Yugen, Number 7, 1961.

—*Sketch by Thomas Wiloch*

*   *   *

McCORD, John H(arrison) 1934-

PERSONAL: Born December 22, 1934, in Oceanside, N.Y.; son of John Francis (an accountant) and Elsie (Powers) McCord; married Maureen Maclean (an attorney), December 31, 1961; children: John F. X., Paul V., David G., Maureen E. *Education:* Fordham University, A.B., 1957; St. John's University, Jamaica, N.Y., LL.B. (since changed to J.D.), 1960; University of Illinois, LL.M., 1965. *Politics:* Independent. *Religion:* Roman Catholic.

ADDRESSES: Home—15 Sherwin Dr., Urbana, Ill. 61801. *Office*—231 Law Building, University of Illinois at Urbana-Champaign, Urbana, Ill. 61801.

CAREER: U.S. Department of Justice, Washington, D.C., attorney, 1960-61; University of Illinois at Urbana-Champaign, College of Law, assistant professor, 1964-67, associate professor, 1967-68, professor of law, 1968—. Visiting professor, University of North Carolina, 1975, University of Hawaii, 1976. Academic consultant, Illinois Institute for Continuing Legal Education, 1968-72; advisory council member, University of Miami Institute for Estate Planning. *Military service:* U.S. Air Force, 1961-64; became captain.

MEMBER: American Bar Association (member of committee for continuing legal education), American Arbitration Association (member of national panel of arbitrators, 1969—), Association of American Law Schools (member of federal taxation roundtable council, 1969-72), U.S. Navy League, American Association of University Professors, American Judicature Society, American Trial Lawyers Association, Illinois State Bar Association (member of executive council of federal tax section, 1966-73; section chairman, 1971-72), Champaign County Bar Association, Chicago Bar Association, Eastern Illinois Estate Planning Council (president, 1971-72), Order of the Coif, Sierra Club.

WRITINGS:

(Editor with R. E. Keeton and J. O'Connell) *Crisis in Car Insurance,* University of Ilinois Press, 1968.

(Editor) *With All Deliberate Speed: Civil Rights Theory and Reality,* University of Illinois Press, 1969, reprinted, 1985.

(With J. C. O'Byrne) *Deskbook for Illinois Estate Planners,* Bobbs-Merrill, 1969.

(Contributor) John J. Vassen, *Professional Corporations,* Illinois Institute for Continuing Legal Education, 1970.

(With Albert C. O'Neill, Ronald A. Pearlman, and Robert E. Stroud) *Course Materials on Buying, Selling and Merging Businesses: Study Outline,* American Law Institute-American Bar Association Joint Committee on Continuing Professional Education, 1971.

The Study of Federal Tax Law, Commerce Clearing House, 1972.

(With Charles Lowndes and Robert Kramer) *Federal Estate and Gift Taxes,* 3rd edition, West Publishing, 1974.

Federal Income Taxation, Bracton Press, 1976.

1976 Estate and Gift Tax Reform: Analysis, Explanation, and Commentary, West Publishing, 1977.

Estate and Gift Tax, 10th edition, Harcourt and Gilbert Law Summaries, 1979.

Also author of *Buying and Selling Small Businesses,* 1969, and *Closely Held Corporations,* 1971; co-author with McKee of *Federal Income Taxation: A Summary Analysis,* 1975, and with Kramer of *Problems for Federal Estate and Gift Taxes,* 1976. Editor of *Dimensions and Academic Freedom,* 1969. Contributor to law reviews. Editor, *University of Illinois Law Forum.*†

McCORMACK, Mark H(ume) 1930-

PERSONAL: Born November 6, 1930, in Chicago, Ill.; son of Ned H. (a publisher) and Grace (Wolfe) McCormack; married Nancy Breckenridge, October 9, 1954; children: Breck Breckenridge, Todd Hume, Mary Leslie. *Education:* Attended Princeton University, 1948; William and Mary College, B.A., 1951; Yale University, LL.B., 1954.

ADDRESSES: Home—2830 Lander Rd., Pepper Pike, Ohio 44124. *Office*—International Management Group, Inc., No. 1300, One Erieview Plaza, Cleveland, Ohio 44114.

CAREER: Admitted to the Bar of Ohio, 1957; Arter & Hadden (law firm), Cleveland, Ohio, associate, 1957-63, partner, 1964—; International Management Group, Inc., Cleveland, chairman and chief executive officer, 1960—. Commentator for televised golf tournaments, British Broadcasting Corp., 1960—. Publisher, *Golf International* (England), 1972-74, and *Tennis World* (England). *Military service:* U.S. Army, 1954-56.

MEMBER: Cleveland Bar Association, Union Club, Country Club of Cleveland.

WRITINGS:

The World of Professional Golf 1967, Cassell, 1967, subsequent annual volumes published by World Publishing, 1968, International Literary Management, 1969-71, Collins, 1972-74, Atheneum, 1975-78, published as *Dunhill Golf Yearbook*, Doubleday, 1979-80, published as *The Dunhill World of Professional Golf*, A. S. Barnes, 1981-83, published as *The Ebel World of Professional Golf*, Acropolis Books, 1984—.
Arnie: The Evolution of a Legend, Simon & Schuster, 1967 (published in England as *Arnold Palmer: The Man and the Legend*, Cassell, 1968).
The Wonderful World of Professional Golf, Atheneum, 1973.
What They Don't Teach You at Harvard Business School: Notes from a Street-Smart Executive, Bantam, 1984.

SIDELIGHTS: Mark H. McCormack owns and directs International Mangement Group (IMG), Inc., a sports and entertainment management corporation touted by *People* magazine as "the undisputed heavyweight champ of sports marketing." Considered a pioneer in the relatively new industry, McCormack launched his multi-million dollar company without formal education in management. He describes his successful business techniques in the best-selling *What They Don't Teach You at Harvard Business School: Notes from a Street-Smart Executive*.

In 1960, McCormack, an attorney by vocation, began to act as business representative for professional golfer Arnold Palmer. Over the first two years of their association, Palmer's earnings jumped from $60,000 to more than $500,000 per year, primarily because McCormack marketed Palmer's name as an endorsement for a number of commercial products. Since then, the use of professional athletes as spokespersons for consumer goods, corporations, and charities has become commonplace, in large part due to McCormack's early efforts in the field. His company now represents such notables as tennis players Bjorn Borg, Martina Navratilova, and Chris Evert-Lloyd, runners Sebastian Coe and Mary Decker Slaney, football star Herschel Walker, basketball player John Havlicek, baseball outfielder Jim Rice, and the London Symphony Orchestra. IMG, which employs over four hundred people in fifteen worldwide offices, also negotiates television packages and merchandising rights for interests as diverse as the Nobel prize ceremonies and the Olympic games. McCormack has also created dozens of widely-publicized sporting events and television shows like the popular "Superstars" specials.

Having achieved success without the graduate-level business courses some in industry feel are so essential, McCormack writes in *What They Don't Teach You at Harvard Business School* about what he calls "street-smart thinking." The term he has coined, as he explains in *People* magazine, means "the ability to make active, positive use of your instincts, insights and even gut feelings when it comes to other people." McCormack practices this "applied people sense" by conducting business meetings over breakfast or lunch, or otherwise negotiating in a more relaxed atmosphere. The *Wall Street Journal* quotes him on his philosophy: "If I say to somebody, 'Come to a meeting in Cleveland,' they say, 'Maybe.' If I say, 'Come to Wimbledon,' they say, 'Sure.'"

BIOGRAPHICAL/CRITICAL SOURCES:

PERIODICALS

Cleveland Plain Dealer, February 2, 1969.
Fortune, January, 1970.
Newsweek, July 4, 1983.
New York Times Book Review, October 21, 1984.
People, October 8, 1984.
Saturday Evening Post, May, 1968.
Signature, October, 1972.
Time, August 27, 1984.
Times Literary Supplement, June 2, 1972, May 31, 1985.
Wall Street Journal, June 27, 1985.

*   *   *

McCOY, Alfred W. 1945-

PERSONAL: Born June 8, 1945, in Concord, Mass.; son of Alfred Mudge (an Army officer and electronic engineer) and Margarita (an urban planner; maiden name, Piel) McCoy. *Education:* Columbia University, B.A., 1968; University of California, Berkeley, M.A., 1969; Yale University, Ph.D., 1977.

ADDRESSES: Home—Glenhaven Pl., Oyster Bay, New South Wales, Australia. *Office*—Department of History, University of New South Wales, Sydney, New South Wales, Australia.

CAREER: University of New South Wales, Sydney, Australia, associate professor of history, 1977—.

MEMBER: Association of Asian Studies.

WRITINGS:

(With Nina S. Adams) *Laos War and Revolution*, Harper, 1970.
The Politics of Heroin in Southeast Asia, Harper, 1972.
(Contributor) Luis Simmons and Abdul Said, editors, *Drugs, Politics and Diplomacy: The International Connection*, Sage Publications, 1974.
Drug Traffic: Narcotics and Organized Crime in Australia, Harper, 1980.
(Editor) *Southeast Asia under Japanese Occupation*, Yale University Press, 1980.
(With Ed de Jesus) *Philippine Social History*, University of Hawaii Press, 1982.
Priests on Trial, Penguin, 1984.
Philippine Cartoons: Political Caricature of the American Era, Vera-Reyes, 1985.

Contributor to numerous periodicals.

* * *

McCRAW, Thomas K(incaid) 1940-

PERSONAL: Born September 11, 1940, in Corinth, Miss.; son of John Carey (an engineer) and Olive (Kincaid) McCraw; married Susan Morehead, September 22, 1962; children: Elizabeth, Thomas. *Education:* University of Mississippi, B.A., 1962; University of Wisconsin—Madison, M.A., 1968, Ph.D., 1970.

ADDRESSES: Office—Baker Library, Graduate School of Business Administration, Harvard University, Soldiers Field, Boston, Mass. 02163.

CAREER: University of Texas at Austin, assistant professor, 1970-74, associate professor of history, 1974-78; Harvard University, Graduate School of Business Administration, Boston, Mass., professor of business administration, 1978—. Visiting associate professor of business administration, Harvard Business School, Harvard University, 1976-78. *Military service:* U.S. Navy, 1962-66; became lieutenant.

MEMBER: American Historical Association, Organization of American Historians.

AWARDS, HONORS: William P. Lyons Master's Essay Award from Loyola University of Chicago and Loyola University Press, 1969; Harvard-Newcomen resident fellowship in business history at Harvard University, 1973-74; Pulitzer Prize in history, 1985, for *Prophets of Regulation*.

WRITINGS:

Morgan vs. Lilienthal: The Feud within the TVA, Loyola University Press, 1970.
TVA and the Power Fight, 1933-1939, Lippincott, 1971.
(Contributor) Lewis L. Gould, editor, *The Progressive Era,* Syracuse University Press, 1974.
(Editor) *Regulation in Perspective: Historical Essays,* Division of Research, Graduate School of Business Administration, Harvard University, 1981.
Prophets of Regulation: Charles Francis Adams, Louis D. Brandeis, James M. Landis, Alfred E. Kahn, Belknap Press of Harvard University Press, 1984.
(Contributor) Harvard Sitkoff, editor, *Fifty Years Later: The New Deal Evaluated,* Knopf, 1985.

Also contributor to scholarly journals and popular magazines, including *Business History Review, California Management Review, The American Scholar, Journal of Policy Analysis and Management,* and *American Heritage.*

WORK IN PROGRESS: Research on business-government relations in twentieth-century America and Japan; a book of essays, tentatively entitled *America versus Japan,* for Division of Research, Harvard Business School.

SIDELIGHTS: Thomas K. McCraw's Pulitzer Prize-winning history book, *Prophets of Regulation,* profiles four men who were instrumental in the move for regulatory policy in the American marketplace. The working lives of these men— Charles Francis Adams, Louis D. Brandeis, James M. Landis, and Alfred E. Kahn—span the decades from the nineteenth-century railroad boom to the deregulation of the airline industry in the early 1980s. As Peter Schuck explains in the *Washington Post Book World,* "By tracing the careers and economic-political ideas of four central figures in the evolution

of the administrative state . . . , McCraw hopes to illuminate some relationships between individuals and regulatory change, between ideas and regulatory techniques, that have previously been neglected and obscure."

Reviewers such as Merin Wexler in the *New York Times Book Review* praise McCraw for his ability to explain "sophisticated economic theory in accessible terms." Schuck, appreciative of McCraw's "novel, stimulating approach," notes that McCraw's effort "to clarify the nature of regulation by carefully integrating biography, history of ideas and regulatory strategy pays handsome dividends." Eliot Janeway, commenting in the *Los Angeles Times Book Review,* reaches a similar conclusion. "McCraw . . . has done an absorbing job of applying the Plutarchian art [of unfolding history in terms of trenchant personalities] to what might seem to be the tedious, Pecksniffian, barren subject of regulation in the United States," Janeway writes. " 'Prophets of Regulation' is a scholarly and provocative job of bringing Schumpeter's definition of economics as 'historical sociology' to life, presenting four regulators as role models in action."

BIOGRAPHICAL/CRITICAL SOURCES:

PERIODICALS

Business History Review, summer, 1985.
Journal of Economic History, spring, 1985.
Los Angeles Times Book Review, October 28, 1984.
New York Times Book Review, October 21, 1984.
Washington Post Book World, October 7, 1984.

* * *

McCULLOUGH, Colleen 1938(?)-

PERSONAL: Born c. 1938 in Wellington, New South Wales, Australia; married Ric Robinson (a housepainter), April 13, 1984. *Education:* Attended University of Sydney.

ADDRESSES: Home—Norfolk Island, Australia. *Agent*—Frieda Fishbein Ltd., 353 West 57th St., New York, N.Y. 10019.

CAREER: Worked as a teacher, a library worker, and a bus driver in Australia's Outback; journalist; Yale University, School of Internal Medicine, New Haven, Conn., associate in research neurology department, 1967-76; writer, 1976—.

WRITINGS:

NOVELS

Tim, Harper, 1974.
The Thorn Birds (Literary Guild selection), Harper, 1977.
An Indecent Obsession, Harper, 1981.
A Creed for the Third Millenium, Harper, 1985.

OTHER

An Australian Cookbook, Harper, 1982.

Contributor to magazines.

SIDELIGHTS: "I always write books with peculiar themes: I don't like writing about boy meets girl, boy loses girl, boy gets girl," best-selling author Colleen McCullough told Kay Cassill in a *Publisher's Weekly* interview. The plots of McCullough's novels back her statement: in *Tim,* a middle-aged businesswoman becomes romantically linked with a twenty-five-year old, mentally retarded man; *The Thorn Birds* turns on a frustrated love between a young woman and a Roman Catholic cardinal; *An Indecent Obsession*'s heroine, a war nurse to battle-fatigued soldiers, is tacitly engaged to one of her patients and sexually attracted to another. Such ingenious story lines, combined with a talent for what Christopher Lehmann-Haupt calls in the *New York Times* "good old-fashioned story telling," have made McCullough's books appeal to millions of readers.

McCullough, a native of Australia, first aspired to a career as a physician but could not afford the necessary tuition. She taught in the Outback, drove a school bus, worked as a librarian and finally qualified as a medical technician specializing in neurophysiology. It was in this position that she eventually came to work at Yale University. In the evenings, she wrote—but not with an eye toward publication. "I always wrote to please myself," she told Cassill. "I was a little snobby about it—that way I could write entirely as I wished. To write for publication, I thought, was to prostitute myself." Once McCullough decided to approach writing commercially, however, she did so very systematically. "I sat down with six girls who were working for me. They were very dissimilar types, and not especially avid readers. Yet, they were all mad about Eric Segal's *Love Story.* I thought it was bloody awful and couldn't see what girls so basically intelligent could love about it. I asked them what they wanted most out of a book. First, they liked the idea that *Love Story* was about ordinary people. They didn't want to read about what was going on in Hollywood and all that codswallow, and they wanted something with touches of humor. Yet they enjoyed books that made them cry. . . . If you didn't cry the book wasn't worth reading. . . . So, I said, 'That's it, mate. No matter what else you do in a book, don't forget the buckets of tears.'" McCullough had a story in mind that would conjure 'buckets of tears,' a grand romance set mostly on a sheep ranch. She knew, however, that this tale—which would eventually be published as *The Thorn Birds*—would be lengthy, and that "no one would publish such a long book as a first novel. So I wrote *Tim.*"

Tim is a "novel of awakenings," according to a *Publisher's Weekly* writer, "a lovely and refreshing addition to tales of love." Its two central characters are Mary Horton and Tim Melville. In her climb from an orphanage to success as a mining executive, forty-five year old Mary has developed her discipline and self-sufficiency to a high degree but has ignored her emotions. Tim arrives at her home one day to do some yard work. He catches her eye, for he is strikingly handsome. Eventually she learns that this attractive young man is "without the full quid"—that is, he is mentally retarded. First Tim's beauty, then his gentle innocence draw Mary to him, unsettling her rigidly ordered world. This unusual pair experience first love together. When Tim faces being left without a family to care for him, Mary realizes that marriage could be fulfilling and practical for both of them. She must then decide if she has the courage to take such an unconventional step.

Tim was well-received by critics. A *New York Times Book Review* contributor praises the story's "delightful freshness," and Margaret Ferrari, writing in *America,* remarks upon McCullough's sensitive treatment of her subject matter: "There are many genuinely touching moments in the novel. . . . Its language is clear and direct, full of colorful Australian slang. McCullough's feeling for character, from major to minor, is compassionate yet concise. They are without exception well-rounded and believable. Her delicacy is perfectly suited to the story. . . . *Tim* is a warm book to read, reassuring about goodness in human nature and about the power of love to overcome worldly obstacles and to make us care more for another person's interests than for our own." A *Publisher's Weekly* re-

viewer calls Colleen McCullough's "telling of the story . . . accomplished, sensitive, and wise." The author herself is less generous than most reviewers in describing her first novel. "It's an icky book," she told Cassill, "a saccharine-sweet book." In spite of this negative assessment, she was pleased by its success. "I made $50,000 out of *Tim,* which wasn't bad for a first novel, and I thought I'd always be a middle of the road, modest selling, respectable novelist," said McCullough to Phillipa Toomey in the London *Times.*

Having established herself as a good risk in the publishing world, she began to work intensely at getting that long novel she had already "written in her head" down on paper. It was *The Thorn Birds,* a multi-generational saga of the Cleary family and their life on an Australian sheep station named Drogheda. McCullough focuses on three Cleary women: Fiona, her daughter, Meggie, and Meggie's daughter, Justine. Meggie is loved by Ralph de Bricassart, an ambitious Catholic priest who has known her since her childhood. When he leaves the Outback for the Vatican, Meggie enters into an unhappy marriage that produces one child, Justine. When Father Ralph visits Drogheda many years later, he and Meggie consummate their love. Her second child, a son named Dane, is born nine months later. Meggie keeps the knowledge that she has borne Ralph's son her secret, but it makes the boy especially beloved to her. When the child grows up, he, like his father, becomes a priest and leaves Drogheda for Rome; Justine goes to England to become the toast of the London stage.

McCullough was still working full-time at Yale while drafting this story and so had to confine her writing to the evenings. She spent such long hours sitting at the typewriter that her legs became swollen; she took to wearing elbow-length evening gloves to keep her fingers from blistering and her arms from chafing against her desk. These efforts paid off: she wrote the first two drafts of *The Thorn Birds* in three months, churning out 15,000-word blocks of prose nightly. After working at this pace for a year, the final draft was completed. It was 1,000 pages long and weighed ten pounds. McCullough felt that its hefty size was justified; in her interview with Cassill, she declared, "If an editor had seen *Thorn Birds* in manuscript and 'just loved it,' but suggested it would make a better book if I cut it to a nice 300-page story, I'd have simply said, 'Get stuffed, mate.'"

Her editors made no such suggestion. Sensing that *The Thorn Birds* had the potential to be a major best seller, they prepared its release carefully and backed it with an extensive publicity campaign. By the time the book became available to the general public, the publishing industry was abuzz with excitement over its prospects; paperback rights had been sold for a then-record price of $1.9 million. This faith and investment in the book were well-rewarded, for *The Thorn Birds* has sold over a half-million copies in hardcover and more than seven million copies in paperback. The book was clearly a hit with the reading public.

Some reviewers quickly dismissed the popularity of *The Thorn Birds* as a tribute to marketing rather than a reflection of the book's worth. Amanda Heller denounces McCullough's novel as "awesomely bad" in *Atlantic Monthly.* "The writing is amateurish, all adjectives and exclamation points. The dialogue is leaden. . . . The characters are mechanical contrivances that permit the plot to grind along without encountering much resistance." And Paul Gray, while admitting in *Time* that "McCullough knows how to stage convincing droughts, floods and fires,'' declares that she ''has not made literature. For a season or so, her book will make commercial history.''

Alice K. Turner counters negative assessments of *The Thorn Birds* with praise for the novel's value as entertainment. ''To expect *The Thorn Birds* to be a Great Book would be unfair,'' she suggests in the *Washington Post.* ''There are things wrong with it, stock characters, plot contrivances and so forth. But to dismiss it would also be wrong. On its own terms, it is a fine, long, absorbing popular book. It offers the best heart-throb since Rhett Butler, plenty of exotic color, plenty of Tolstoyan unhappiness and a good deal of connivance and action. Of its kind, it's an honest book.'' Eliot Fremont-Smith further praises McCullough's engaging style in the *Village Voice:* ''Her prose, even when stately, owes little to any formula; it is driven by a curiosity of mind, a caring for the subject, and some other great energy within the author that in turn, at one remove, spurs the reader on. *The Thorn Birds* didn't make me laugh and weep, and I could put it down. It is, after all, a romance, and very long. But then I kept picking it up again, more times than can be accounted for by any sense of duty. A fine book.''

Both Fremont-Smith and Turner express admiration for McCullough's vivid characterizations. ''McCullough does make her characters and their concerns come alive,'' asserts Fremont-Smith. ''She gives them (the leads particularly, and Ralph most of all) intelligence and complexity and dimension. Even the minor characters are not dull.'' Elaborating on the priest's role in the story, Turner writes, ''Very few novels spotlight a Roman Catholic priest as a sex symbol, but Father Ralph's bravura performance in this one rivals the landscape for originality. Father Ralph is simply yummy. . . . And, of course, he is out of the running, which gives the author plenty of opportunity to dangle him as an erotic tease.'' ''Actually, Ralph was supposed to be a minor character,'' explained McCullough in her *Publisher's Weekly* interview. ''Yet, when I was planning it in my head I was aware I didn't have a dominant male lead. The minute the priest walked into the book I said, 'Ah ha, this is it. This is the male character I've lacked!' But I had to keep him in the story and, logically, he didn't belong in it. The only way I could do it was to involve him emotionally with Meggie, the only woman available. It worked beautifully because again it made more interesting reading to have a love that couldn't be fulfilled. It kept the reader going.''

The solid success of *The Thorn Birds* made it almost inevitable that McCullough's next books would be compared with it. ''When you produce a book which is well loved—and people do love it—it's a very hard book to bury,'' noted the author in the London *Times.* Although she believes ''a lot of writers keep feeding people the same book,'' McCullough stated in a *New York Times Book Review* interview with Edwin McDowell that she had ''decided long ago . . . to have a bash at different kinds of books.'' Her third novel, *An Indecent Obsession,* certainly differs from its predecessor in many ways; while *The Thorn Birds* spanned three continents and most of a century, *An Indecent Obsession* is set entirely within the confines of a ward of a South Pacific army hospital near the end of World War II. The drama centers on the tension between Honour Langtry, Ward X's nurse, and her group of ''troppo'' patients—soldiers who have snapped under the strain of tropical jungle fighting. Many reviewers characterized *An Indecent Obsession* as a more serious work than *The Thorn Birds.*

Despite these differences, *Chicago Tribune Book World* reviewer Julia M. Ehresmann finds that *An Indecent Obsession* ''has McCullough's fingerprints all over it.'' Comparing the themes of *Tim, The Thorn Birds,* and *An Indecent Obsession,* Ehresmann observes that ''in these times when personal gratification is valued so highly, Colleen McCullough is writing about old-time moral dilemmas and largely discarded qualities: self-denial, self-control, and notions of duty, honor, and love as self-displacing virtues.'' Joanne Greenberg agrees in the *New York Times Book Review* that *An Indecent Obsession* is ''a very old-fashioned novel, with its focus on the conflict between duty and love, a rare concern in contemporary fiction.'' McCullough's well-drawn characterizations and powerfully-evoked setting once again gained praise from many critics, with Greenberg crediting the author's ''attention to detail'' as the factor that ''makes one feel the discomfort of the sweltering tropical nights as well as appreciate the awesome beauty of the sea, the torrential rains and the sunsets.'' Finally, in his *Washington Post Book World* article, William A. Nolen addresses ''the question a lot of potential readers will want answered: Is *An Indecent Obsession* as good as McCullough's *The Thorn Birds?* The question can't be answered. It's like asking if a nice, ripe orange is as tasty as a nice, ripe apple; it depends on your mood and your taste buds. I enjoyed both books, but I thought *An Indecent Obsession* was more intriguing, more thought provoking, than was *The Thorn Birds.*''

Christopher Lehmann-Haupt, however, finds fault with the book in the *New York Times.* ''We turn the pages,'' he acknowledges. ''I do not mean to make light of Colleen McCullough's already best-selling successor to her gigantically successful 'The Thorn Birds'. . . . Miss McCullough is a natural story-teller, more than merely clever at getting up a head of emotional steam. . . . But if [she] expects to be taken seriously as a novelist—and, to judge from the improvement of this book over 'The Thorn Birds,' there's no reason why she shouldn't be—she's going to have to write just a little less slickly.'' McCullough's glibness, continues Lehmann-Haupt, ''makes one want to say that 'An Indecent Obsession' is merely a gilded version of what I believe teen-age readers used to refer to as a nurse book. It isn't really. But far too often, its faults reduce it to medical soap opera.''

McCullough responds to such criticism calmly. ''Only time tells,'' she philosophized in her interview with Cassill. ''If it lasts, it's good literature. If it dies, it's just another book. Very often the books the critics like today are gone tomorrow.'' She says that the greatest change that her phenomenal success has brought to her life has been a feeling of increased security and freedom. While working at Yale, she expected to ''have to go home and look after mother when I was 50, and try to hold down a job at the same time—then at 70 I'd be living in a cold-water, walk-up apartment, just about able to afford a 60-watt light bulb.'' She now owns several homes, spending most of her time on tiny Norfolk Island, some 1,000 miles off the east coast of Australia. This South Pacific island is inhabited mostly by descendants of the *Bounty* mutineers. Life there suits McCullough perfectly. ''It isn't what you are, it's who you are in a place like this,'' she told Phillipa Toomey in the London *Times,* ''It's incredibly beautiful and peaceful and remote. . . . I get a heck of a lot of work done because there is nothing much else to do.''

MEDIA ADAPTATIONS: Tim was released as a film starring Piper Laurie and Mel Gibson, directed and produced by Michael Pate, in 1981. *The Thorn Birds* was broadcast as a ten-hour miniseries on ABC-TV, in March, 1983.

AVOCATIONAL INTERESTS: Photography, music, chess, embroidery, painting, and cooking.

BIOGRAPHICAL/CRITICAL SOURCES:

BOOKS

Contemporary Literary Criticism, Volume XXVII, Gale, 1984.

PERIODICALS

America, August 10, 1974.
Atlantic Monthly, June, 1977.
Best Sellers, May 15, 1974.
Chicago Tribune Book World, October 11, 1981.
Christian Century, March 31, 1982.
Los Angeles Times Book Review, October 25, 1981.
National Observer, June 20, 1977.
New Leader, July 4, 1977.
Newsweek, April 25, 1977.
New York Times, May 2, 1977, March 25, 1979, September 17, 1981, October 29, 1981, March 26, 1983, March 27, 1983.
New York Times Book Review, April 21, 1974, May 8, 1977, October 25, 1981, November 15, 1981.
People, May 7, 1984.
Publisher's Weekly, March 7, 1977, February 22, 1980, February 18, 1984.
Saturday Review, April 16, 1977.
Time, May 9, 1977, May 20, 1985.
Times (London), November 30, 1981.
Times Literary Supplement, October 7, 1977, December 11, 1981.
Village Voice, March 28, 1977.
Washington Post, April 24, 1977, November 26, 1981, March 27, 1983.
Washington Post Book World, October 11, 1981, January 20, 1985, April 28, 1985.
Writer's Digest, March, 1980.†

—*Sketch by Joan E. Marecki*

*   *   *

McELROY, Colleen J(ohnson)   1935-

PERSONAL: Born October 30, 1935, in St. Louis, Mo.; daughter of Jesse O. (an army officer) and Ruth (Long) Johnson; married David F. McElroy (a writer), November 28, 1968 (divorced); children: Kevin D., Vanessa C. *Education:* Attended University of Maryland, 1953-55; Harris Teachers College, A.A., 1956; Kansas State University, B.S., 1958, M.A., 1963; graduate study at University of Pittsburgh, 1958-59, and Western Washington State College (now Western Washington University), 1970-71; University of Washington, Ph.D., 1973.

ADDRESSES: Home—2616 4th St. N., Apt. 406, Seattle, Wash. 98109. *Office*—Department of English, University of Washington, Seattle, Wash. 98105.

CAREER: Rehabilitation Institute, Kansas City, Mo., chief speech clinician, 1963-66; Western Washington State College (now Western Washington University), Bellingham, assistant professor of English, 1966-73; University of Washington, Seattle, 1973—, began as assistant professor, currently professor of English. Affiliate member of speech faculty, University of Missouri—Kansas City, 1965-66; summer instructor, Project Head Start and Project New Careers. Moderator of "Out-

look," KVOS-TV, 1968-72. Watercolors and pen-ink sketches displayed at gallery exhibit, 1978. Member of board, Washington State Commission for the Humanities.

MEMBER: American Speech and Hearing Association, National Council of Teachers of English, Conference on College Composition and Communication, Writers Guild of America East, United Black Artists Guild (Seattle).

AWARDS, HONORS: Carnation teaching incentive award, 1973; Breadloaf scholarship for fiction, 1974; Best of Small Presses award for poetry, Pushcart Book Press, 1976; National Endowment for the Arts fellowship in creating writing, 1978; Matrix Women of Achievement Award, 1985; Before Columbus American Book Award, 1985, for *Queen of the Ebony Isles.*

WRITINGS:

Speech and Language Development of the Preschool Child: A Survey, C. C Thomas, 1972.
The Mules Done Long since Gone (poems), Harrison-Madronna Press, 1973.
Music from Home: Selected Poems, Southern Illinois University Press, 1976.
(Contributor) *Iron Country* (anthology), Copper Canyon Press, 1978.
(Contributor) Dexter Fisher, editor, *The Third Woman* (anthology), Houghton, 1980.
(Contributor) *Backbone 2* (anthology), Seal Press, 1980.
Winters without Snow (poems), I. Reed, 1980.
A Country under Its Original Name (poems), Blue Begonia Press, 1985.
Queen of the Ebony Isles (poems), Wesleyan University Press, 1985.

Also author of *Lie and Say You Love Me* (poems), Circinatum Press and, with Virginia Chappell, *Continuity: Writing Effective Paragraphs,* Random House; author of stories and scripts for television and of educational film scripts, including "Tracy Gains Language" and "Introduction to Clinical Practicum," distributed by the Bureau of Faculty Research, Western Washington University. Also contributor to *Black Sister: Poems by Black American Women, 1946-1980,* 1981, and other anthologies.

Contributor of poems and short fiction to numerous literary reviews and little magazines, including *Wormwood Review, Poetry Northwest, Choice, Seneca Review, Southern Poetry Review, Confrontation, Massachusetts Review, Georgia Review, Southern Poetry Review,* and *Black Warrior Review.*

WORK IN PROGRESS: A short fiction collection, *Ain't Nobody's Business;* a poetry collection, *Bone Flames;* a novel, *Long Way from St. Louie.*

*   *   *

McEWAN, Peter J(ames) M(ichael)   1924-

PERSONAL: Born November 16, 1924, in London, England; son of James Albert N. (an economics consultant) and Violet K. (Rose) McEwan; married Dorothy A.W. Wilson (a fine art dealer), August 1, 1949; children: Feona Mary, Malcolm P.S., Rhoderick N.T. *Education:* University of Edinburgh, M.A., 1949, Ph.D., 1963. *Politics:* Liberal (British). *Religion:* Humanist.

ADDRESSES: Home—Glengarden, Ballater, Aberdeenshire AB3 5UB, Scotland.

CAREER: Farmed 2,000-acre estate in the Scottish Highlands, 1952-58; director of research team studying white society in Rhodesia, 1959-62; State University of New York at Albany, visiting professor of African studies, 1963-64; Harvard University, Cambridge, Mass., director of family research unit, 1965-68; University of Sussex, Falmer, Brighton, England, director of Centre for Social Research, 1968-73. Liberal candidate for Parliament for Caithness and Sutherland, 1951.

MEMBER: Royal Commonwealth Society (fellow), British Sociological Association, Society for Psychical Research, American Sociological Association, American Public Health Association.

WRITINGS:

(With R. B. Sutcliffe) *The Study of Africa,* Crowell, 1967.
(Editor and compiler) *Readings in African History,* Oxford University Press, Volume I: *Africa from Early Times to 1800,* 1968, Volume II: *Nineteenth-Century Africa,* 1968, Volume III: *Twentieth-Century Africa,* 1968.
(Editor with Frank B. Baker and Alan P. Sheldon) *Industrial Organizations and Health: Selected Readings,* Barnes & Noble, Volume I, 1969.
(With Sheldon and Carol P. Ryser) *Retirement: Patterns and Predictions,* National Institute of Mental Health, 1975.
(Editor) *Social Science and Medicine: International Conference Background Papers,* Social Science and Medicine, 1981.
(Editor) *Some Case Studies in Latin America,* Pergamon, 1983.

Editor in chief, *Social Science and Medicine.*

SIDELIGHTS: Peter J. M. McEwan says that he has a ''strong and passionate attachment to isolated, under-populated places.''

* * *

McGARRITY, Mark 1943-
(Bartholomew Gill)

PERSONAL: Born July 22, 1943, in Holyoke, Mass.; son of Hugh F. and Cecilia (Gill) McGarrity; married Margaret Wellstood Dull (a photographer), October 10, 1966. *Education:* Brown University, B.A., 1966; Trinity College, Dublin, M.Litt., 1971.

ADDRESSES: Home and office—159 North Shore Road, Andover, N.J. 07821. *Agent*—Robin Rue, Anita Diamant Agency, 310 Madison Ave., New York, N.Y. 10017.

CAREER: Has worked as speech writer, public relations and annual report writer, and financial reporter; teacher and freelance writer, 1969—. Writer-in-residence, Dover Public Schools, Dover, N.J., 1984-85.

AWARDS, HONORS: First prize, critical writing, New Jersey Press Association Competition, 1984.

WRITINGS:

Little Augie's Lament (novel), Grossman, 1973.
Lucky Shuffles (novel), Grossman, 1973.
A Passing Advantage (novel), Rawson, Wade, 1980.
(Contributor) Dilys Winn, *Murderess Ink,* Workman Publishing, 1980.

UNDER PSEUDONYM BARTHOLOMEW GILL; ''McGARR'' SERIES

McGarr and the Politician's Wife, Scribner, 1976.
. . . and the Sienese Conspiracy, Scribner, 1977.
. . . on the Cliffs of Moher, Scribner, 1978.
. . . at the Dublin Horse Show, Viking, 1980.
. . . and the P. M. of Belgrave Square, Viking, 1983.
. . . and the Method of Descartes, Viking, 1984.
. . . and the Wrath of a Woman Scorned, Viking, 1985.

OTHER

Also contributor to *New Jersey Herald.*

WORK IN PROGRESS: Lake House, a generational novel of an American family.

SIDELIGHTS: Under his pseudonym Bartholomew Gill, Mark McGarrity is the creator of a well-received addition to the world of international crime and mystery literature—Peter McGarr, chief superintendent of detectives of the Irish police. In the *Washington Post Book World,* Jean White assures readers that McGarr ''is no imitation. [The author] has created a solid, original character.'' A *New York Times Book Review* critic agrees. Commenting on *McGarr and the Politician's Wife,* he writes that ''there is no caricature or stage-Irishman stuff—Gill knows his people and treats them with dignity.''

As for McGarrity's writing style, Newgate Callendar notes in *New York Times Book Review* that ''everything [in *McGarr and the Sienese Conspiracy*] is nicely relaxed. . . . Yet there is a great deal of tension, and also enough action to satisfy the reader who demands gore. McGarr . . . sort of ambles through everything. . . . There is never any feeling of heavy breathing. Gill paces everything beautifully. *McGarr and the Sienese Conspiracy* is very well plotted, very civilized and very, very good.''

McGarr on the Cliffs of Moher evokes a similar response in a *New Republic* reviewer. After admitting that McGarrity's novels ''grow upon one,'' he states that ''the pace is relaxed, the clues are planted with almost stodgy care, the author's intelligence is evident throughout, and Ireland comes alive, bit by bit. McGarr will not keep one up all night but he will not let one loose either. . . . Gill is a writer to watch.''

MEDIA ADAPTATIONS: The ''McGarr'' series has been optioned by film producer Barry Levinson.

BIOGRAPHICAL/CRITICAL SOURCES:

PERIODICALS

New Republic, June 10, 1978.
New York Times, December 13, 1984.
New York Times Book Review, April 8, 1973, May 1, 1977, February 12, 1978.
Washington Post Book World, August 20, 1978.

* * *

McGEE, Reece (Jerome) 1929-

PERSONAL: Born October 19, 1929, in St. Paul, Minn.; son of Reece J. (an attorney) and Vivien (McFarland) McGee; married Betty Ann Enns (a psychological therapist), June 10, 1950 (divorced); married Sharron Ann Cavness (a high school media specialist), 1978; children: (first marriage) Kaelin, Jon, Beth. *Education:* Attended Macalester College, 1947-49; University of Minnesota, B.A., 1952, M.A., 1953, Ph.D., 1956. *Politics:* Liberal Democrat. *Religion:* Anglo-Catholic.

ADDRESSES: Home—R.R. 1, Box 225, Monon, Ind. 47959. *Office*—Department of Sociology and Anthropology, Purdue University, West Lafayette, Ind. 47907.

CAREER: University of Minnesota, Minneapolis, research fellow, 1954-56, research associate, 1957; University of Texas, Main University (now University of Texas at Austin), assistant professor, 1957-61, associate professor of sociology, 1961-64, executive secretary of department, 1958-59; Macalester College, St. Paul, Minn., visiting associate professor, 1964-65, professor of sociology, 1965-67; Purdue University, West Lafayette, Ind., professor of sociology, "master teacher," and coordinator of introductory sociology program, 1967—. Visiting assistant professor, Humboldt State Teachers College (now Humboldt State University), fall, 1956; visiting associate professor, University of California, Berkeley, summer, 1968; visiting professor, University of North Carolina at Chapel Hill, 1976. Invited participant, Lilly Seminar on the Liberal Arts, 1982.

Advisory editor in sociology to Dryden Press, 1970-76, Praeger Publishers, Inc., 1977, and Holt, Rinehart & Winston, 1977-79. Member of editorial board of Glendessary Press, 1967-75, and Purdue University Press, 1967-74; consulting editor to Wadsworth Publishing Company, 1979-81. Consultant to Southern Regional Education Board, Association for Higher Education, the president of Eastern Illinois University, and University of Kentucky department of sociology; departmental consultant for the American Sociological Association Teaching Services Program to numerous colleges and universities. Field reader, Bureau of Research, Office of Education, Department of Health, Education, and Welfare, 1966-71. *Military service:* U.S. Army, Artillery, 1948-58, became first lieutenant.

MEMBER: American Sociological Association (member of numerous sections and committees), American Association of University Professors, Midwest Sociological Society, North Central Sociological Society (council member-at-large), Phi Beta Kappa.

AWARDS, HONORS: Distinguished Contributions to Undergraduate Education Award from the American Sociological Association, 1982.

WRITINGS:

(With Theodore Caplow) *The Academic Marketplace,* Basic Books, 1958.
(Contributor) *Current Issues in Higher Education,* Association for Higher Education, 1961.
Social Disorganization in America, Chandler Publishing, 1962.
(Contributor) R. Sutherland and others, editors, *Personality Factors on the College Campus,* Hogg Foundation for Mental Health, 1962.
(Contributor) *The Role of Institutional Planning,* Office of Institutional Studies, University of Wisconsin, 1963.
(Contributor) D. Hansen and J. Gerstl, editors, *On Education: Sociological Perspectives,* Wiley, 1967.
(Contributor) W. T. Tucker, editor, *Foundations for a Theory of Consumer Behavior,* Holt, 1967.
(Contributor) E. Kronovet and E. Shirk, editors, *In Pursuit of Awareness: The College Student in the Modern World,* Appleton-Century-Crofts, 1967.
(Contributor with Irving Tallman) Erwin Smigel, editor, *Handbook on the Study of Social Problems,* Rand McNally, 1971.
Academic Janus: The Liberal Arts College and Its Faculty, Jossey-Bass, 1971.
Points of Departure: Basic Concepts of Sociology, Dryden, 1972.

(With Charlene S. Knuckman) *The Mind's Eye: Basic Readings,* Dryden, 1973.
Sociology: An Introduction, Holt, 1977.
(Contributor with others) *Knowledge Available and Knowledge Needed to Improve Instruction in Sociology,* American Sociological Association, 1979.
(Editor with Frederick L. Campbell and Hubert M. Blalock) *Teaching Sociology: The Quest for Excellence,* Nelson-Hall, 1984.

Also author, with others, of *Bulletins of the Purdue Experiment in Mass Instruction.* Contributor of articles and reviews to professional journals. Member of editorial board, *Teaching Sociology,* 1972—, and *Sociological Focus,* 1974-80.

*   *   *

McHALE, John   1922-1978

PERSONAL: Born August 19, 1922, in Glasgow, Scotland; died of cardiac arrest, November 2, 1978, in Houston, Tex.; married Magda Cordell. *Education:* Attended Nelson Hall College and Yale University; Southern Illinois University, Ph.D.

ADDRESSES: c/o Magda Cordell McHale, Center for Integrative Studies, School of Architecture and Environmental Design, Room 108, Hayes Hall, State University of New York at Buffalo—Main Campus, Buffalo, N.Y. 14214.

CAREER: Artist, designer, filmmaker, writer, and lecturer in London, England, 1947-62; Southern Illinois University at Carbondale, executive director of World Resources Inventory, 1962-68; State University of New York at Binghamton, director of Center for Integrative Studies, 1968-77; University of Houston, Houston, Tex., professor of sociology and director of Center for Integrative Studies, 1977-78. Work has been exhibited in Europe at one-man shows at the Institute of Contemporary Arts, London, 1956 and 1962, and Steendrukkerij de Jong & Co., Hilversum, Holland, 1960, and at numerous group shows. Special fellow, Yale University School of Art, 1955-56; senior research fellow, East-West Center, University of Hawaii, 1973; presidential fellow, Aspen Institute for Humanistic Studies, 1977. Consultant to the United Nations, U.S. national and state governments, and private organizations. *Military service:* Royal Navy, 1941-46.

MEMBER: World Future Studies Federation (vice-president and member of board), World Academy of Art and Science (fellow; former executive secretary), World University Council, Continuing Committee of the World Future Research Congress, World Future Society, Royal Society of Arts (fellow), Institute of Ecology, Society for Advancement of General Systems Theory, Society for the History of Technology, American Sociological Association, American Geographical Society (fellow), New York Academy of Sciences (fellow). *Awards, honors:* Medaille d'Honneur en Vermeil from Societe d'Encouragement au Progres, 1966; knight commander's cross, Order of St. Dennis; LL.D., Ripon College, 1977.

WRITINGS:

R. Buckminster Fuller, Braziller, 1962.
(With R. Buckminster Fuller and others) *World Design Science Decade, 1965-1975: Five Two Year Phases of a World Retooling Design Proposed to the International Union of Architects for Adoption by World Architectural Schools,* Southern Illinois University, 1963-68.
The Future of the Future, Braziller, 1969.

(Contributor) Gillo Dorfles, *Kitsch: The World of Bad Taste,* Universe Books, 1969.

The Ecological Context, Braziller, 1970.

World Facts and Trends, P. F. Collier, 1972.

(With Magda Cordell McHale and Guy F. Streatfield) *Women in World Terms: Facts and Trends,* Center for Integrative Studies, University of Houston, 1975.

(With M. C. McHale) *Future Studies: An International Survey,* United Nations Institute for Training and Research, 1975.

(Editor with Boris Pregel and Harold D. Lasswell) *Environment and Society in Transition: World Priorities,* American Division of the World Academy of Art and Science and New York Academy of Sciences, 1975, published as *World Priorities,* Transaction Books, 1977.

The Changing Information Environment, Elek, 1976.

(With M. C. McHale) *Human Requirements, Supply Levels and Outerbounds: A Framework for Thinking about the Planetary Bargain,* Program in International Affairs, Aspen Institute for Humanistic Studies, 1976.

(With M. C. McHale, Streatfield, and Laurence Tobias) *The Futures Directory,* Westview, 1977.

(With M. C. McHale) *Basic Human Needs: A Framework for Action,* Transaction Books, 1978.

(With M. C. McHale and Streatfield) *Children in the World,* Population Reference Bureau, 1979.

Member of international editorial board, *Futures*; member of editorial board of numerous publications, including *Technological Forecasting and Social Change.*

SIDELIGHTS: John McHale was the author of *The Future of the Future,* a look at what must be done if, as William H. Stringer noted in the *Christian Science Monitor,* "we are to cope, in time, with the threat of an over-exploited, chemically-poisoned, burned-out earth." The author based his discussion on the concept of the world as an integrated environmental system in which man is faced with two alternatives: collaborating with nature to create a better life for everyone or abusing and destroying nature and, ultimately, all of humanity. McHale also believed that man's will to survive is more powerful than his urge to destroy and that the misuse (or underuse) of technology, not technology itself, is what jeopardizes the future. His book, generally optimistic, even "cheerful" (to use *New York Times* critic John Leonard's word), contends that man has never been in a more fortunate position to manipulate his environment and make important decisions about the human condition in the years to come. In short, declared McHale, "the future of the future is what we determine it to be, both individually and collectively."

Commenting in *Christian Century,* Tommy W. Rogers described *The Future of the Future* as "a wide-ranging and broadly informative" study that "is couched not so much in philosophic terms as in terms of the specifics of global ecology and world resources." Stringer also found that McHale "goes beyond the customary facts and figures cited by ecologists." Futhermore, the reviewer continued, being "more textbook than polemicist in tone," *The Future of the Future* contains "no idealistic call for 'One World,' no sentimental appeal for a wilderness-oriented conservation." Instead, it "sounds a practical, pragmatic warning that unless men everywhere are more alert to the accelerating despoliation of Planet Earth, reform could come too late."

"McHale supplies us with an enormous amount of information and an exciting vision,"observed Leonard, a view that was shared by Hugh Kenner, who went on to remark in the *New York Times Book Review* that "correlating masses of research" occasionally left the author "with a bemused expression, one half of a zipper in each hand." Nevertheless, concluded Kenner, "[*The Future of the Future* is] easy, jargon-free, a book to put into the hands of students, high-school and older, who are being harassed by assertions that the world is closing its automated doors."

In addition to his writings, McHale was an artist of note, one of the leaders of the innovative British Pop Art movement of the 1950s. Here, too, his futurist bent found a means of expression, primarily via collages. Reflecting his fascination with the mechanized world, his collages ususally featured images of modern machines, especially audio-visual equipment. Following a visit to the United States in the middle of the decade, McHale also began to make extensive use of glossy pictures clipped from the pages of popular magazines, catalogues, and other materials in mass circulation. These pictures, often arranged into human shapes with a robot-like appearance, were designed to convey positive, non-threatening messages about technology, echoing the artist's belief in the ability of automation to free mankind from a restrictive and stagnant society.

In her introduction to *The Expendable Ikon,* a catalogue of an exhibition of works by John McHale, Charlotta Kotik remarked: "John McHale was at once a visual artist, writer, educator and organizer; but most important, he was a humanist philosopher endowed with relentless energy to pursue innovations which were ultimately to result in changes beneficial to mankind. He looked toward the future with a mixture of optimism and skepticism, but above all with a great deal of realistic wisdom, making possible a clear formulation of our predicament, and the consequences of our own behavior well in advance of the mainstream."

BIOGRAPHICAL/CRITICAL SOURCES:

BOOKS

Hasiotis, Georgette M., editor, *The Expendable Ikon: Works by John McHale* (exhibition catalogue), Albright-Knox Art Gallery/Buffalo Fine Arts Academy (Buffalo, N.Y.), 1984.

McHale, John, *The Future of the Future,* Braziller, 1969.

PERIODICALS

Christian Century, October 15, 1969.
Christian Science Monitor, September 9, 1969.
New York Times, August 21, 1969.
New York Times Book Review, April 20, 1969.

OBITUARIES:

PERIODICALS

New York Times, November 8, 1978.†

*   *   *

McINTYRE, Vonda N(eel)   1948-

PERSONAL: Born August 28, 1948, in Louisville, Ky.; daughter of H. Neel (an electrical engineer) and Vonda Keith (a volunteer worker) McIntyre. *Education:* University of Washington, Seattle, B.S., 1970, graduate study, 1970-71.

ADDRESSES: Home—P.O. Box 31041, Seattle, Wash. 98103-1041. *Agent*—Frances Collin, Marie Rodell-Frances Collin Literary Agency, 110 West 40th St., New York, N.Y. 10018.

CAREER: Writer, 1969—.

MEMBER: Authors Guild, Authors League of America, Science Fiction Writers of America, Planetary Society, Space Studies Institute, National Organization for Women, Cousteau Society.

AWARDS, HONORS: Nebula Award from Science Fiction Writers of America, 1974, for best science fiction novelette, "Of Mist, and Grass, and Sand"; Hugo Award from World Science Fiction Convention and Nebula Award, both 1979, both for best science fiction novel, *Dreamsnake;* American Book Award nomination for best paperback science fiction novel, 1980, for *Dreamsnake.*

WRITINGS:

The Exile Waiting (novel), Fawcett, 1975.
(Editor with Susan Janice Anderson) *Aurora: Beyond Equality,* Fawcett, 1976.
Dreamsnake (novel), Houghton, 1978.
Fireflood and Other Stories (includes novelettes "Of Mist, and Grass, and Sand" and "Aztecs"), Houghton, 1979.
(Contributor) Ursula K. Le Guin and Virginia Kidd, editors, *Interfaces* (short stories), Ace Books, 1980.
The Entropy Effect (novel), Timescape, 1981.
Star Trek II: The Wrath of Khan (novelization), Pocket Books, 1982.
Superluminal (novel), Houghton, 1983.
Star Trek III: The Search for Spock (novelization), Pocket Books, 1984.

Contributor to science fiction magazines, including *Analog: Science Fiction/Science Fact.*

WORK IN PROGRESS: Starfarers, a novel; *Barbary,* a young adult novel; three screenplays, "The Zero Level," "Raith," and "Dreamsnake."

SIDELIGHTS: Vonda N. McIntyre is the author of award-winning science fiction, including short stories, novelettes, and novels. Like Ursula Le Guin, to whom she has been favorably compared, McIntyre "portrays positively and optimistically the realization of individual human potential in a variety of characters," in the words of *Science Fiction and Fantasy Review* contributing critic Philip E. Smith II. In a letter to *CA,* McIntyre explains her fascination with the genre this way: "I write science fiction because its boundaries are the only ones wide enough for me to explore experiences people have not had—*yet;* and because it allows my characters to develop as far as their ability will take them, unlimited by the crippling demands and unambitious expectations our society puts on us."

McIntyre's commitment to the unlimited development of her mostly female characters has earned her the reputation of being a feminist writer. In her novelette "Of Mist, and Grass, and Sand," first published in *Analog: Science Fiction/Science Fact,* McIntyre portrays Snake, a healer who cures with venomous snakes. Two of her three snakes, Mist and Sand, are genetically modified to produce a healing venom when fed the proper drug. The bite of the third, an alien dreamsnake named Grass, delivers a peaceful death to the incurably ill. The story ends with Grass being killed by the frightened parents of a boy Snake is trying to heal. "Snake is as complex and sympathetic a character as SF has realized in some years: tough, tender, bitter, forgiving, afraid, daring, independent and loving," comments Bud Foote in the *Detroit News.* Carolyn Wendell concurs, declaring in *Extrapolation* that Snake is a departure

from "the cliched science-fiction female who may feel, but only the gentler emotions, and who certainly never thinks."

In *Dreamsnake,* a continuation of the successful novelette, Snake quests for a new dreamsnake, without which she risks the loss of her self-respect and the disparagement of her peers. "This is a superbly crafted s.f. adventure story," writes Gerald Jonas in the *New York Times Book Review.* Jonas also observes that "everything about this world, from its wild animals to its people, is described with luminous clarity." Alex de Jonge in *Spectator* praises *Dreamsnake* as "a gentle, moving and feminine book in the good sense of that word."

Many of the writings in McIntyre's next book, *Fireflood and Other Stories,* illustrate her theme of unlimited human development by presenting individuals who have been biologically altered in unusual ways. Some fly, others breathe underwater, and still others burrow through the earth. *Village Voice* reviewer Eve Ottenberg believes McIntyre's preoccupation with biological change "comes from her feminism, her desire to show a future in which sex roles have been radically changed by evolution." Yet other critics claim that these biological changes result not in freedom for either sex, but in the alienation of people in general. McIntyre "describes people isolated on genetic islands of intellectual, physiological, and technical specialization, and the grotesque mistakes possible to mere humans trying to invent better humans," writes Carolyn F. Ruffin in the *Christian Science Monitor.* Ruffin's view is shared by *Washington Post Book World* contributor Joanna Russ, who declares, "Critics have noted McIntyre's feminism, but (at least in this collection) alienation—usually literal—is her real subject, and alien(ated) beings her heroes."

One such alien being, who appears in the novelette "Aztecs," is starship pilot Laenea Trevelyan. The pilots are set apart from the rest of their species, not only because they hold a highly respected position, but also because they have had their hearts replaced with electronic pumps. These pulseless hearts allow them to travel at velocities surpassing the speed of light. Unfortunately, they also make the pilots incompatible with normal humans, which Laenea discovers when she falls in love with Radu Dracul, a starship crew member. Since Laenea is unwilling to renounce her profession and be returned to her normal state, and Radu is ineligible to become a pilot, the two must part. Praising "Aztecs" and the collection as a whole in the *Magazine of Fantasy and Science Fiction,* Thomas M. Disch writes that McIntyre "seems to be moving from strength to strength. In the concluding novella, 'Aztecs,' she is able finally to write 'paid' to an emotional theme dealt with obsessively, but never quite successfully, in many of the other stories—the need to renounce a love that is in conflict with personal growth."

In *Superluminal,* an expansion of "Aztecs," the paths of Radu and Laenea cross again when Laenea is lost on her training flight and Radu sets out to find her. Although the two are eventually reunited, Radu decides to stay with Orca, the underwater inhabitant who helped him search for Laenea. In this novel, "McIntyre has several point-of-view characters and tries to establish individual perspectives and backgrounds for each, but not always successfully," writes Smith in *Science Fiction and Fantasy Review.* Some of the more successful characterizations are of Orca and the divers, according to *New York Times Book Review* contributing critic Gerald Jonas, who finds their adventures "much more vivid" than those of Laenea and the pilots. "Perhaps Miss McIntyre is simply more at home with cultures whose 'technology' is based on biology rather than physics," he observes. In a review published in *Analog: Science Fiction/Science Fact*, Tom Easton expresses a similar view, predicting that "any sequel to this book will dwell far more on the world of divers. . . . Wonders loom in their lives, unpreempted by cosmology." Despite his reservations about parts of the narrative, Easton concludes: "I enjoyed the book. McIntyre's characters live. Her vision enchants and intrigues. Her world beckons. Follow, and enjoy."

BIOGRAPHICAL/CRITICAL SOURCES:

BOOKS

Contemporary Literary Criticism, Volume XVIII, Gale, 1981.

PERIODICALS

Analog: Science Fiction/Science Fact, March, 1984.
Christian Science Monitor, January 23, 1980.
Detroit News, March 16, 1980.
Extrapolation, winter, 1979.
Magazine of Fantasy and Science Fiction, January, 1979, July, 1980.
New York Times Book Review, June 25, 1978, November 6, 1983.
Pacific Northwest Review of Books, June, 1978.
Science Fiction and Fantasy Review, March, 1984.
Spectator, August 26, 1978.
Village Voice, March 3, 1980.
Washington Post Book World, February 24, 1980.

—*Sketch by Melissa J. Gaiownik*

*　　*　　*

McKENDRICK, Melveena (Christine)   1941-

PERSONAL: Born March 23, 1941, in Glamorgan, Wales; daughter of James Powell (a teacher) and Catherine Letitia Jones; married Neil McKendrick (a historian), March 18, 1968; children: Olivia, Cornelia. *Education:* King's College, London, B.A. (with first class honors), 1963; Girton College, Cambridge, Ph.D., 1967.

ADDRESSES: Home—Howe House, Huntingdon Rd., Cambridge CB3 0LX, England. *Office*—Girton College, Cambridge University, Cambridge CB3 0JG, England.

CAREER: Cambridge University, Girton College, Cambridge, England, fellow, 1967-70, tutor, 1970-74, senior tutor, beginning 1974, lecturer in Spanish, 1970—.

WRITINGS:

Ferdinand and Isabella, American Heritage, 1968.
A Concise History of Spain, McGraw, 1972.
Woman and Society in the Spanish Drama of the Golden Age, Cambridge University Press, 1974.
Cervantes, Little, Brown, 1982.
(Contributor) Beth Miller, editor, *Women in Hispanic Literature: Icons and Fallen Idols*, University of California Press, 1983.

Also contributor to *Calderon: Critical Studies*, edited by J. E. Vasey, 1973, and to language and Spanish studies journals.

WORK IN PROGRESS: A composite edition of Calderon's *El magico prodigioso* with A. A. Parker; *The Spanish Stage in the Sixteenth and Seventeenth Centuries*, for Cambridge University Press.

SIDELIGHTS: Melveena McKendrick's *Cervantes* is described by Alan Cheuse in the *Los Angeles Times Book Review*

as a "scrupulously researched and extremely well-written biography of the Spanish master." He indicates that "documentation of the life of the giant is, as McKendrick impresses upon us, shadowy and not always available. But the portrait she works up of the man, his work and the age that produced them, belongs on a shelf alongside our favorite studies of Shakespeare and Faulkner." In *Cervantes*, as E. C. Riley comments in the *Times Literary Supplement*, "known facts and uncertainties are handled in a measured and sensible way, and from time to time useful second thoughts are prompted about things often taken for granted." The book's utility as a scholarly work is limited by the fact that a list of source references has been omitted, Riley observes, but, "aside from this deficiency—which will not worry the average reader much—the next British or American biographer of Cervantes will have to work hard to better this one."

BIOGRAPHICAL/CRITICAL SOURCES:

PERIODICALS

Los Angeles Times Book Review, May 31, 1981.
Times Literary Supplement, July 3, 1981.

*　　*　　*

McKIM, Donald K(eith)   1950-

PERSONAL: Born February 25, 1950, in New Castle, Pa.; son of Keith B. (an accountant) and Mary (a teacher; maiden name, Leslie) McKim; married LindaJo Horton (a United Presbyterian minister), February 28, 1976; children: Stephen, Karl. *Education:* Westminster College, New Wilmington, Pa., B.A. (cum laude), 1971; Pittsburgh Theological Seminary, M.Div. (magna cum laude), 1974; University of Pittsburgh, Ph.D., 1980.

ADDRESSES: Home—3405 Dove St., Dubuque, Iowa 52001. *Office*—Theological Seminary, University of Dubuque, 2000 University Ave., Dubuque, Iowa 52001.

CAREER: Ordained United Presbyterian minister, 1975; Friendship United Presbyterian Parish, Slippery Rock, Pa., student pastor, 1970-74, supply pastor, 1975-80; University of Dubuque, Theological Seminary, Dubuque, Iowa, associate professor of theology, 1981—. Visiting member of faculty at Westminster College, New Wilmington, Pa., 1979.

MEMBER: Karl Barth Society of North America (charter member), American Society of Church History, Presbyterian Historical Society, Calvin Studies Society, American Academy of Religion.

WRITINGS:

The Church: Its Early Life, Cooperative Uniform Series, 1978.
(With Jack B. Rogers) *The Authority and Interpretation of the Bible: An Historical Approach*, Harper, 1979.
(With Rogers) *Biblical Inerrancy*, Harper, 1980.
What Christians Believe about the Bible, Nelson, 1985.

EDITOR

The Authoritative Word: Essays on the Nature of Scripture, Eerdmans, 1983.
Readings in Calvin's Theology, Baker Book, 1984.
A Guide to Contemporary Hermeneutics, Eerdmans, in press.
How Karl Barth Changed My Mind, Eerdmans, in press.

OTHER

Contributor to *International Standard Bible Encyclopedia*.

Contributor of articles and reviews to history and theology journals.

SIDELIGHTS: Donald K. McKim told *CA:* "The Authority and Interpretation of the Bible: An Historical Approach was written to fill a pressing scholarly need. Until now there has been no detailed study of the history of the doctrine of Scripture in the Christian church from the early church to the present. Specialists have provided much help with specific historical periods or with the doctrine of certain theologians. But co-author Jack B. Rogers and I saw that a much broader picture was needed. So we tried to draw it.

"Our book is the result of over ten years of individual and joint study. I built on Jack's 1967 doctoral dissertation, *Scripture in the Westminster Confession,* with several articles. Our individual research and published pieces through the years formed the initial basis for our book. But for three years we worked specifically to 'fill in the cracks.' We needed to flesh out our story, to reassess what we had already learned in light of new research, and to tie together the themes we found running through the church's understandings of Scripture from the earliest times till the present. Our collaboration was carried on long-distance: Jack in Pasadena, Calif.; I in Pittsburgh, Pa. Several chances to meet personally in those 'research' years helped us gain perspective and plot our future course.

"We wrote with scholars in mind. But we were most aware of the difficulties of Christian people faced with multiple options of belief about the Bible and the nature of its authority and means of interpretation. Some have claimed the church has always seen the Scriptures as an errorless (inerrant) source of information on topics ranging from astronomy to geography and philosophy. We found that this was not the case. Instead there is a central tradition extending from the early church through the Protestant reformers of the sixteenth century and extending to our own times that has regarded the Bible rather as the primary way by which people are informed about salvation—how to have a right relationship with God. The Bible *is* an infallible source about this. So Jack and I wanted to set the historical record straight. We wanted lay people in the church as well as scholars to realize that their trust in the Scriptures as the real word of God does not have to rest on whether or not the Bible presents totally accurate scientific information on any topic under the sun! So we wrote our book to bring the insights of the best of the church's past thinking to present problems. Our next book [tells] this same story in a non-technical fashion. It [is] aimed at a much wider reading public.

"It was hard work. But it was thrilling to see our project progress and to trace the story of the development of the doctrine of Scripture in the church. It's much like detective work. At many points, various historical and philosophical influences caused some to turn away to an extreme position regarding Scripture, rather than following the church's central tradition. Our job was to pinpoint what these influences were and who led people in that direction. Both Jack and I grew up in the Presbyterian or Reformed tradition of theology. So part of our emphasis was to see how this tradition's understanding of the Bible has developed—especially in America. And we found some startling information! But our study, we hope, will also aid people in other theological traditions. It was a real attempt to discover 'roots' and to anchor our attitudes for the present in the richness and depth of our understandings in the past."

AVOCATIONAL INTERESTS: Reading, chess, sports.

McLAURIN, R(onald) D(e) 1944-

PERSONAL: Born October 8, 1944, in Oakland, Calif.; son of Lauchlin De and Marie (Friedman) McLaurin; married Joan Adcock (a nurse), June 11, 1966; children: Leila, Cara. *Education:* Attended Universite de Tunis, 1964-65; University of Southern California, B.A., 1965; Fletcher School of Law and Diplomacy, Tufts University, A.M., 1966, M.A.L.D., 1967, Ph.D., 1973. *Politics:* Independent.

CAREER: Merrimack College, North Andover, Mass., instructor in political science, 1966-67; Office of Assistant Secretary of Defense, Washington, D.C., management assistant, 1967-68, assistant for Africa, 1968-69; American Institutes for Research, Washington, D.C., research scientist in social science, 1969-75; Abbott Associates, Inc. (social science researchers), Alexandria, Va., senior research staff scientist, beginning 1975. Partner, Ajamaaw Enterprises, 1977—. Member of Triangle Civic Association, 1975—. Consultant to U.S. Department of Defense, 1972—, Center for Advanced International Studies, University of Miami, 1973, A. R. Wagner & Co., 1975—, and American Institutes for Research, 1975.

MEMBER: International Political Science Association, International Studies Association, American Political Science Association, American Academy of Political and Social Science, American Civil Liberties Union, American Philatelic Society, Policy Studies Association, National Capital Area Political Science Association.

WRITINGS:

(Contributor) D. M. Condit and Bert H. Cooper, Jr., editors, *United States Military Response to Overseas Insurgencies,* American Institutes for Research, 1970.
(Contributor) Condit and Cooper, editors, *Population Protection and Resources Management in Internal Defense Operations,* American Institutes for Research, 1971.
(With Arnold E. Dahlke, Jane Meyer, Richard H. Orth, and Carl F. Rosenthal) *Dissent in the Military,* American Institutes for Research, 1971.
(With Mohammed Mughisuddin) *The Soviet Union and the Middle East,* American Institutes for Research, 1974.
The Middle East in Soviet Policy, Heath, 1975.
(With Mughisuddin) *Cooperation and Conflict: Egyptian, Iraqi, and Syrian Objectives and U.S. Policy,* American Institutes for Research, 1975.
(With Edward E. Azar, Thomas Havener, Craig Murphy, Thomas Sloan, and Charles Wagner) *Early Warning of Strategic Crisis in the Middle East,* American Institutes for Research, 1975.
(With Jon Cozean, Suhaila Haddad, Phillip P. Katz, and Charles Wagner) *The Arab Elite Worldview,* American Institutes for Research, 1975.
(With James M. Price) *Soviet Middle East Policy since the October War,* Abbott Associates, 1976.
(Editor with Daniel C. Pollock, Rosenthal, and Sarah A. Skillings) *The Art and Science of Psychological Operations,* U.S. Government Printing Office, 1976.
(With Mughisuddin and Abraham R. Wagner) *Foreign Policy Making in the Middle East: Domestic Influences on Policy in Egypt, Iraq, Israel, and Syria,* Praeger, 1977.
(With Haddad) *The Political Impact of U.S. Military Force in the Middle East,* American Institutes for Research, 1977.
(Editor) *The Political Role of Minority Groups in the Middle East,* Praeger, 1979.

(With Paul Jureidini) *Beyond Camp David: Emerging Alignments and Leaders in the Middle East,* Syracuse University Press, 1981.

Middle East Foreign Policy: Issues and Processes, Praeger, 1982.

(Editor) *Military Propaganda: Psychological Warfare and Operations,* Praeger, 1982.

(With Jureidini) *Jordan: The Impact of Social Change on the Role of the Tribes,* Praeger, 1984.

Contributor to *Maghreb Digest* and to newspapers. Member of board of consulting editors of *Asia-Pacific Defense Forum.*†

* * *

McRAE, Kenneth D(ouglas) 1925-

PERSONAL: Born January 20, 1925, in Toronto, Ontario, Canada; son of Douglas Archibald and Constance (Dingle) McRae; married Dorothea Annette Simon, 1950; children: Patricia, Sandra, Karen, Susan. *Education:* University of Toronto, B.A., 1946; Harvard University, A.M., 1947, Ph.D., 1954.

ADDRESSES: Office—Department of Political Science, Carleton University, Ottawa, Ontario, Canada K1S 5B6.

CAREER: University of Toronto, Toronto, Ontario, lecturer, 1950-52; Carleton University, Ottawa, Ontario, assistant professor, 1955-57, associate professor, 1957-64, professor of political science, 1964—. Research supervisor, Canadian Royal Commission on Bilingualism and Biculturalism, 1964-69.

MEMBER: Royal Society of Canada (fellow; honorary secretary, 1980-83), Canadian Political Science Association (president, 1978-79).

WRITINGS:

(Editor) Jean Bodin, *The Six Bookes of a Commonweale,* Harvard University Press, 1962, reprinted, Arno, 1979.

Switzerland: Example of Cultural Coexistence, Canadian Institute of International Affairs, 1964.

(Contributor) Louis Hartz and others, editors, *The Founding of New Societies,* Harcourt, 1964.

(Editor) *The Federal Capital: Government Institutions,* Queen's Printer, 1969.

(With others) *Consociational Democracy: Political Accommodation in Segmented Societies,* McClelland & Stewart, 1974.

Conflict and Compromise in Multilingual Societies, Humanities, Volume I: *Switzerland,* 1983, Volume II: *Belgium,* 1985.

* * *

MEANS, Richard K(eith) 1929-

PERSONAL: Born February 26, 1929, in Morristown, Ind.; son of Louis E. (a teacher) and Mary T. (Correll) Means; divorced; children: Mary C., Carolyn K., Christopher E. *Education:* University of Minnesota, B.S., 1952, M.A., 1954; University of California, Los Angeles, Ed.D., 1961. *Politics:* Republican. *Religion:* Congregationalist.

ADDRESSES: Home—619 Tanglewood Ave., Auburn, Ala. 36830. *Office*—School of Education, Auburn University, Auburn, Ala. 36849.

CAREER: Public school teacher of health education and biology in Long Beach, Calif., 1954-57; University of Califor-

nia, Santa Barbara, associate in health and physical education, 1957-58; University of California, Los Angeles, associate in health education, 1958-61; Temple University, Philadelphia, Pa., associate professor of health education, 1961-64; Auburn University, Auburn, Ala., professor of health education, 1964—, director of health education. Member of writing team, National School Health Education Study, 1964-71. *Military service:* U.S. Air Force, 1952-54; became first lieutenant.

MEMBER: National Education Association (life member), Association for the Advancement of Health Education, American School Health Association (fellow; chairman of research council, 1964-66), American Public Health Association (fellow), American Alliance for Health, Physical Education, Recreation, and Dance, Alabama Education Association, Alabama Association for Health, Physical Education and Recreation, Alabama Health Educators Organization, Phi Delta Kappa.

AWARDS, HONORS: Scholar Award, Association for the Advancement of Health Education, 1985.

WRITINGS:

A History of Health Education in the United States, Lea & Febiger, 1962.

Methodology in Education, Merrill, 1968.

Foundations of Health Science, Allyn & Bacon, 1968, 3rd edition, 1977.

Instructor's Resource and Methods Handbook for Health Education, Allyn & Bacon, 1971, revised edition, 1977.

Teaching Health Today, J. Weston Walch, 1973, revised edition, 1979.

Historical Perspectives on School Health, Charles B. Slack, 1975.

Personal Health: Confronting Your Health Behavior, Allyn & Bacon, 1977.

Personal Health: Appraising Behavior, Wiley, 1985.

Instructor's Manual for Personal Health, Macmillan, 1985.

CONTRIBUTOR

Synthesis of Research in Selected Areas of Health Instruction, National Education Association, 1963.

School Health Services, Joint Committee on Health Problems in Education, National Education Association and American Medical Association, 1963.

Health Education: A Conceptual Approach to Curriculum Design, 3M Co., 1967.

Health Education in Alabama Schools: Into the 1980s, American Lung Association of Alabama, 1981.

Final Reports: Health Education Risk-Reduction Program, Bureau of Health Education, Centers for Disease Control, Volume I, 1981, Volume II, 1982.

OTHER

Contributor to other symposia and study reports. Contributor of more than seventy articles to professional journals.

WORK IN PROGRESS: A Treasury of Quotations on Health, Science and Medicine.

AVOCATIONAL INTERESTS: Sports, travel, reading.

* * *

MEREDITH, Arnold
See HOPKINS, Kenneth

METCALF, Paul 1917-

PERSONAL: Born November 7, 1917, in East Milton, Mass.; son of Henry K. and Eleanor M. (Thomas) Metcalf; married Nancy Harman Blackford, May 31, 1942; children: Anne (Mrs. Gary Westmoreland), Adrienne (Mrs. Alan Weinman). *Education:* Attended Harvard University, 1936.

ADDRESSES: Home—R.F.D. 1, Box 26, Chester, Mass. 01011.

CAREER: Writer and teacher. Visiting professor at University of California, San Diego, State University of New York at Albany, University of Kansas, and Simon's Rock Early College. Has lectured, given readings, and conducted workshops at high schools, colleges, art centers, and writers' conferences throughout the United States. Panelist for literature division of National Endowment for the Arts; reader and judge for National Endowment fellowships; reader and judge for private and state fellowships in Massachusetts, Wisconsin, Pennsylvania, and Minnesota.

AWARDS, HONORS: Ford Foundation grants, 1970, 1971, for a stage adaptation of *Genoa* for use by National Theater of the Deaf.

WRITINGS:

Will West, Jargon Press, 1956, reprinted, Book Store Press, 1973.
Genoa, Jargon Press, 1965.
Patagoni (poem), Jargon Press, 1971.
Apalache (poem), Turtle Island Foundation, 1976.
The Middle Passage (poem), Jargon Press, 1976.
Willie's Throw (poem), Five Trees Press, 1979.
Zip Odes (poems), Tansy Press, 1979.
U.S. Department of the Interior, Gnomon, 1980.
The Island, Tansy Press, 1982.
Both, Jargon Society, 1982.
Waters of Potowmack, North Point Press, 1982.
Louis the Torch, Cross Country, 1983.

CONTRIBUTOR TO ANTHOLOGIES

LeRoi Jones, editor, *The Moderns,* Corinth Books, 1963.
Katherine Newman, editor, *The American Equation: Literature in a Multi-Ethnic Culture,* Allyn & Bacon, 1971.
Gerald Hausman and David Silverstein, editors, *A Berkshire Anthology,* Bookstore Press, 1972.
Mark Canner and Dana Collins, editors, *The Second Berkshire Anthology,* Bookstore Press, 1975.
David Emblidge, editor, *The Third Berkshire Anthology,* Berkshire Writers, 1982.

OTHER

Contributor of articles, poems, and reviews to literary magazines, including *Monk's Pond, Lillabulero, Isthmus, Toucan, Granite,* and *Io.*

WORK IN PROGRESS: Golden Delicious; I-57; Firebird; Collected Essays.

SIDELIGHTS: Paul Metcalf wrote *CA:* "Having been published for twenty-nine years in small presses, I continue to write for this medium, and to believe that the best in both poetry and fiction will find its way to the public through these obscure, noncommercial outlets. What I take to be the 'great tradition in America' stems from Poe, Dickinson, Melville, Whitman, Dreiser, Anderson, Pound, and Williams. This tradition has been betrayed by the big commercial novelists, but

its inheritors are very much alive, and may be found in the best of the small presses. . . . Success is not the criterion. It is well to remember that, at one time or another in their lives, Thoreau, Melville, and Whitman were self-published.''

Metcalf is the great-grandson of Herman Melville.

BIOGRAPHICAL/CRITICAL SOURCES:

PERIODICALS

Credences 8/9, March, 1980.
Lillabulero 12, winter-spring, 1973.
Review of Contemporary Fiction, summer, 1981.

*　　*　　*

METZGER, Walter P. 1922-

PERSONAL: Born May 15, 1922; son of Herman and Rae (Zuckerbrod) Metzger; married Loya Ferguson (a sociologist), June 23, 1961; children: Hilary, Gillian. *Education:* City College (now of the City University of New York), B.S.S., 1942; Columbia University, M.A., 1945; State University of Iowa, Ph.D., 1950.

ADDRESSES: Home—460 Riverside Dr., New York, N.Y. 10027. *Office*—Department of History, Columbia University, New York, N.Y. 10027.

CAREER: State University of Iowa, Iowa City, instructor in history, 1947-50; Columbia University, New York, N.Y., 1950—, began as instructor, professor of history, 1963—. Lecturer at Salzburg Seminar, summer, 1956; member of faculty of Danforth Foundation workshops, summers, 1968-70, 1974. Director of training program in social history, National Institute of Mental Health, 1967—. Fellow of Center for Advanced Study in the Behavioral Sciences, 1956-57; member of board of scholars of Higher Education Research Institute (at University of California, Los Angeles), 1974—. Co-chairman of Council on Teaching and Learning of Myerson Commission (Ford Foundation), 1969-71; member of panel on benefits of higher education of National Academy of Sciences, 1972-75; member of panel on human resources of National Research Council, 1975—. Member of advisory panel to Public Broadcasting System, 1974—, consultant in higher education to National Endowment for Humanities, 1977—; member of advisory council to Danforth Foundation.

MEMBER: American Association of University Professors, American Historical Association, American Academy of Arts and Sciences (fellow), Phi Beta Kappa.

AWARDS, HONORS: Grants from Louis Rabinowitz Foundation, 1952-53, Social Science Research Council, 1963, and Carnegie Corp., 1960, 1970.

WRITINGS:

(With George L. Mosse) *Outline and Sources: History of Western Civilization,* W. C. Brown, 1948.
(With May Brodbeck and James Grey) *American Non-fiction, 1900-1950* (interpretive essays), Henry Regnery, 1952.
(With Richard Hofstadter) *Development of Academic Freedom in the United States,* Columbia University Press, 1955, Part II (sole author) published separately as *Academic Freedom in the Age of the University,* Columbia University Press, 1955.
(With Paul Goodman and John R. Searle) *Freedom and Order in the University,* Western Reserve Press, 1967.

(With Fritz Machlup) *Neutrality or Partisanship: A Dilemma of Academic Institutions,* Carnegie Foundation for the Advancement of Teaching, 1971.

CONTRIBUTOR

R. M. MacIver, editor, *Dilemmas of Youth,* Harper, 1961.

Louis Gottschalk, editor, *Generalizations in the Writing of History,* University of Chicago Press, 1963.

Owen A. Knorr and W. John Miner, editors, *Freedom and Order on the Campus,* Western Interstate Commission for Higher Education, 1965.

John McCord, editor, *Dimensions of Academic Freedom,* University of Illinois Press, 1968.

Immanuel Wallerstein and Paul Starr, editors, *University Crisis Reader II,* Vintage Book, 1971.

Robert A. Altman and Carolyn M. Nyerly, editors, *The Public Challenge and the Campus Response,* Western Interstate Commission for Higher Education, 1971.

William Keast, editor, *Faculty Tenure,* Jossey-Bass, 1973.

EDITOR; "THE ACADEMIC PROFESSION" SERIES, PUBLISHED BY ARNO PRESS, 1977

The Constitutional Status of Academic Tenure: An Original Anthology.

The Financial Status of the Professor in America and in Germany, Number 2.

Professors on Guard: The First AAUP Investigations.

The Constitutional Status of Academic Freedom.

The American Concept of Academic Freedom in Formation: A Collection of Essays and Reports.

Reader on the Sociology of the Academic Profession.

Noel G. Annan, *Leslie Stephen: His Thought and Character in Relation to His Time.*

Robert O. Berdahl, *British Universities and the State.*

Hans P. Bleuel, *Deutschlands Bekenner: German Men of Knowledge: The Professiate from the Rule of the Kaiser to the Rise of Hitler.*

Claude C. Bowman, *The College Professor in America: An Analysis of Articles Published in the General Magazines, 1890-1938.*

Alexander Busch, *Die Geschicht des Privatdozenten: Eine sociologische Studie zur grossbetrieblichen Entwicklung der deutschen Universitaten.*

J. McKeen Cattell, *University Control.*

Edward P. Cheney, *History of the University of Pennsylvania, 1740-1940.*

Theodore Caplow and J. McGee Reece, *The Academic Marketplace.*

Orrin Leslie Elliot, *Stanford University: The First Twenty-Five Years.*

Richard T. Ely, *Ground under Our Feet: An Autobiography.*

Johannes Flach, *Der Deutsche Professor der Gegenwart: The German Professor Today.*

G. Stanley Hall, *Life and Confessions of a Psychologist,* 1977.

Godfrey H. Hardy, *Bertrand Russell and Trinity: A College Controversy of the Last War.*

Alexander Kluge, *Die Universitats-Selbstwerwaltung: Ihre Geschichte und Gegenwartige Rechtsform.*

Walter M. Kotsching, *Unemployment in the Learned Professions: An International Study of Occupational and Educational Planning.*

Paul F. Lazarsfeld and Wagner Thielens, Jr., *The Academic Mind: Social Scientists in Time of Crisis.*

Mary M. McLaughlin, *Intellectual Freedom and Its Limitations in the University of Paris in the Thirteenth and Fourteenth Centuries.*

Edwin Mims, *History of Vanderbilt University.*

Wolfgang Mitsch and others, *Hochschule in der Demokratie: Kritische Beitrage zur Erbschaft und Reform der Deutschen Universitat.*

Franz L. Neumann, *The Cultural Migration: The European Scholar in America.*

Mark Pattison, *Suggestions on Academical Organisation with Especial Reference to Oxford.*

Lucille A. Pollard, *Women on College and University Faculties: A Historical Survey and a Study of Their Present Academic Status.*

Mortimer R. Proctor, *The English University Novel: University of California Publications,* Number 15.

Joseph Quincy, *The History of Harvard University,* two volumes.

Edward A. Ross, *Seventy Years of It: An Autobiography.*

S. Willis Rudy, *The College of the City of New York: A History, 1847-1947.*

Edwin E. Slosson, *Great American Universities.*

Goldwin Smith, *A Plea for the Abolition of Texts in the University of Oxford,* 2nd edition (Metzger was not associated with the first edition).

Malcolm W. Wiley, *Depression: Recovery and Higher Education.*

D. A. Winstanley, *Unreformed Cambridge: A Study of Certain Aspects of the University in the Eighteenth Century.*

Winstanley, *Early Victorian Cambridge.*

Winstanley, *Later Victorian Cambridge.*

OTHER

Contributor of articles and reviews to academic journals.

*   *   *

MIKDASHI, Zuhayr 1933-

PERSONAL: Born in 1933 in Beirut, Lebanon; son of Ramez and Fatima (Tayara) Mikdashi; married Ghada el-Sayed, 1969; children: Bilal, Louay (both sons). *Education:* University of Lyon, certificat d'Etudes Litteraires Generales, 1953; American University of Beirut, M.A., 1954, B.A., 1956; Oxford University, B.Litt., 1958, D.Phil., 1971; Stanford University, diploma, 1963.

ADDRESSES: Home—17, avenue de la Dole, CH-1005 Lausanne, Switzerland. *Office*—Ecole des Hautes Etudes Commerciales, University of Lausanne, Dorigny, CH-1015 Lausanne, Switzerland; and European Management Forum, 19, ch. des Hauts-Crets, CH-1223 Cologny/Geneva, Switzerland.

CAREER: Economist for Planning Board, government of Lebanon, 1955-56; American University of Beirut, Beirut, Lebanon, professor of business administration until 1976; University of Lausanne, Lausanne, Switzerland, professor of business administration, 1976—. Visiting lecturer at Arab Institute of Higher Studies and Research, 1966; visiting scholar at Institut Francais du Petrole, summer, 1967, and Resources for the Future, 1971-72; associate visiting professor of international business, Graduate School of Business Administration, Indiana University, 1970-71; research fellow at Harvard University, 1971-72; visiting fellow at Japan's Institute of Developing Economies, summer, 1972; guest lecturer at colleges, universities, and government agencies around the world; guest on television and radio programs; planner and director of seminars. Secretary-general of Arab-European Business Cooperation Committee; adviser to United Nations (elected to Commission on Transnational Corporations, 1983-86), Kuwait's minister of oil and finance, government of Liberia, and adviser to and member of United Arab Emirates; consultant to Organization of Petroleum Exporting Countries (OPEC), International Bank for Reconstruction and Development, and Organization for Economic Cooperation and Development.

AWARDS, HONORS: Ford Foundation travel and study grant to United States, 1970-73; Orden Francisco de Miranda from president of Venezuela, 1971.

WRITINGS:

A Financial Analysis of Middle East Oil Concessions, 1901-1965, Praeger, 1966.
(With others) *Continuity and Change in the World Oil Industry*, Middle East Research and Publishing Center, 1970.
The Community of Oil Exporting Countries: A Study in Governmental Cooperation, Cornell University Press, 1972.
The International Politics of Natural Resources, Cornell University Press, 1976.
(Editor and contributor) *Arab-European Business Cooperation: Partners in Development through Resources and Technology*, Kommentator Verlag, 1978.
(With others) *Der Islam in der Weltpolitik*, Fischer Verlag, 1982.
Investment Options, International Banking and Behaviour of Energy Exporters, Industrial Bank of Kuwait, 1983.

CONTRIBUTOR

The Economic Development of Libya, Johns Hopkins Press, 1960.
Middle East Economic Papers, Johns Hopkins Press, 1969.
M. A. Cook, editor, *Studies in the Economic History of the Middle East from the Rise of Islam to the Present Day*, Oxford University Press, 1970.
Report of the Ad Hoc Panel of Experts on Projections of Demand and Supply of Crude Petroleum and Products, United Nations, 1971.
Raymond Vernon, editor, *Enterprise and Government in Western Europe*, Harvard University Press, 1974.
Le Nouvel Ordre petrolier: The New Petroleum Order, Presses de l'Universite Laval, 1976.
N. Sherbiny and M. Tessler, editors, *Arab Oil: Impact on the Arab Countries and Global Implications*, Praeger, 1976.
Vernon, editor, *The Oil Crisis*, Norton, 1976.
International Organizations in World Politics: Yearbook 1975, Croom Helm, 1976.
A. Kapoor, editor, *Asian Business and Environment in Transition: Selected Readings and Essays*, Darwin Press, 1977.
W. Daueber and K. Wohlmuth, editors, *Transnationale Konzerne und Weltwirtschaftsordnung*, Nomos Verlagsgesellschaft, 1978.
Natural Resource Policies in Economic Development and International Cooperation, Volume I, University of Wisconsin—Madison, 1978.
Natural Resources Forum, Reidel Publishing, 1980.
Revision interne dans les etablissements de credit, H. Tschudy & Cie, 1980.
Islam in World Politics, Graduate Institute of International Studies (Geneva), 1980.
R. N. Farmer, editor, *Advances in International Comparative Management*, Volume I, JAI Press, 1984.

Also contributor to *Needs and Interests of Developing Countries*, edited by L. M. Alexander, 1973. Chairman of and contributor to *Energy in the Eighties*, from a meeting of the Ad Hoc Group of Energy and Petroleum Experts, United Nations, 1983.

CONTRIBUTOR TO PROCEEDINGS

Proceedings of the Third Arab Petroleum Congress, League of Arab States, 1961.
Proceedings of the United Nations Interregional Seminar on Petroleum Refining in Developing Countries, Indian Oil Corporation of the Government of India, 1973.
Transportation and Communication, Simon Fraser University Publications, 1984.

OTHER

(Author of foreword) Edmond Voelker, editor, *Euro-Arab Cooperation*, Sijthoff, 1976.

Also author of two monographs, *Major Protagonists in Natural Resources and Their Views of Benefits*, Institute of Developing Economies (Tokyo, Japan), 1973, and *An Analysis of World Energy Demand and Supply, 1974-1985*, Research Institute of Overseas Investment, Export-Import Bank of Japan, 1975. Author of a booklet, *Oil Revenues*, United Nations Regional Project for Public Finance and Administration in Beirut, 1974. Contributor to *Middle East Economic Papers*, 1961 and 1965. Also contributor of more than thirty articles and reviews to professional journals, including *Journal of Energy and Development, Journal of Business Administration, Foreign Policy, Journal of World Trade Law, Journal of Public Opinion*, and *Chemical Economy and Engineering Review*.

SIDELIGHTS: With *The International Politics of Natural Resources*, Zuhayr Mikdashi achieved "an admirable blend of sympathetic understanding for the Third World's sense of injustice and inequity," commented critic Susan Strange in *International Affairs*.

BIOGRAPHICAL/CRITICAL SOURCES:

PERIODICALS

International Affairs, October, 1977.

        *   *   *

MILES, T(homas) R(ichard) 1923-

PERSONAL: Born March 11, 1923, in Sheffield, England; son of Richard (an engineer) and Alice (Miller) Miles; married Elaine Armstrong (a teacher of dyslexic children), August 21, 1951; children: P. J. R. *Education:* Magdalen College, Oxford, M.A., 1945; University College of North Wales, Ph.D., 1963. *Religion:* Society of Friends (Quaker).

ADDRESSES: Home—Llys-y-Gwynt, Llandegfan, Menai Bridge, Gwynedd, Wales. *Office*—Department of Psychology, University College of North Wales, Bangor, Wales.

CAREER: University College of North Wales, Bangor, assistant lecturer, 1949-52, lecturer, 1952-63, professor of psychology, 1963—.

MEMBER: Royal Institute of Philosophy (member of council), British Psychological Society (fellow), British Dyslexia Association, Cheshire and North Wales Dyslexia Association (president).

WRITINGS:

Religion and the Scientific Outlook, Allen & Unwin, 1959.
Eliminating the Unconscious, Pergamon, 1966.
On Helping the Dyslexic Child, Methuen Educational, 1970.

Religious Experience, Macmillan, 1972.
The Dyslexic Child, Priory Press, 1974.
(With wife, Elaine Miles) *More Help for Dyslexic Children,* Methuen, 1975.
Understanding Dyslexia, Hodder & Stoughton, 1978.
(With P. Harzem) *Conceptual Issues in Operant Psychology,* Wiley, 1978.
(Editor with G. T. Pavlidis) *Dyslexia Research and Its Applications to Education,* Wiley, 1981.
The Bangor Dyslexia Test, Learning Development Aids, 1982.
(With E. Miles) *Help for Dyslexic Children,* Methuen, 1983.
Dyslexia: The Pattern of Difficulties, Granada Collins, 1983.

Contributor to *Quarterly Journal of Experimental Psychology, Mind, Philosophy, British Journal of Educational Psychology, British Journal for the Philosophy of Science, Journal of Child Psychology and Psychiatry, Religious Studies, Annals of Dyslexia,* and other professional journals.

WORK IN PROGRESS: Further research on dyslexia.

SIDELIGHTS: T. R. Miles writes *CA:* "For the last two decades my main research interest has been the study of dyslexia. Originally this was a sideline, but it soon became clear that I had—almost inadvertently—stumbled on something which was of major significance to many people. I have been particularly impressed by the courage displayed by many families despite the fact that dyslexic children are sometimes mistakenly dubbed as 'lazy' or 'careless' and their parents as 'over-fussy'; and in many cases the diagnosis itself can bring overwhelming relief. It therefore seems to me that the spreading of knowledge about dyslexia is important both theoretically and practically. My other interests include the theoretical bases of behaviourism and problems in the relationship between psychology and religion."

AVOCATIONAL INTERESTS: Lawn tennis (former international and Wimbledon player), golf, playing the cello.

*　　　*　　　*

MILLER, E(ugene) Willard　1915-

PERSONAL: Born May 17, 1915, in Turkey City, Pa.; son of Archie H. (a petroleum engineer) and Tessie (Master) Miller; married Ruby M. Skinner (a librarian), June 28, 1941. *Education:* Clarion State College, B.S., 1937; University of Nebraska, M.A., 1939; Ohio State University, Ph.D., 1942. *Religion:* United Church of Christ.

ADDRESSES: Home—845 Outer Dr., State College, Pa. *Office*—Department of Geography, Pennsylvania State University, University Park, Pa. 16802.

CAREER: Ohio State University, Columbus, instructor in geography, 1942-43; Western Reserve University (now Case Western Reserve University), Cleveland, Ohio, assistant professor of geography and geology, 1943-44; Office of Strategic Services, Washington, D.C., geographer, 1944-45; Pennsylvania State University, University Park, associate professor, 1945-49, professor of geography, 1949—, department head, 1945-63, assistant dean, 1964-72, associate dean for resident instruction, 1972—. Geographic editor, Thomas Y. Crowell Co.; U.S. member of committee on natural resources of the Commission of Geography, Pan American Institute of Geography and History; president, Geographical Slide Service.

MEMBER: American Association for the Advancement of Science (fellow), American Geographical Society (fellow), National Council for Geographic Education (fellow), Association of American Geographers, American Association of University Professors (president, Pennsylvania State University chapter, 1958-59), American Society for Professional Geographers (president, 1948), Pennsylvania Council for Geographic Education (president, 1962), Pennsylvania Academy of Science (president, 1966-68).

AWARDS, HONORS: Ray Hughes Whitbeck Award, 1950, for outstanding article on economic geography in *Journal of Geography;* Certificate of Merit from Office of Strategic Services; National Science Foundation travel grant, 1960, 1963; meritorious service award, Pennsylvania Department of Commerce, 1975; citation for service to the commonwealth, Governor of Pennsylvania, 1975.

WRITINGS:

Careers in Geography, Institute for Research, 1948, 2nd edition, 1955.
(Contributor) *Conservation of Natural Resources,* Wiley, 1950, 2nd edition, 1958.
(Contributor) *Outside Readings in Geography,* Crowell, 1955.
(Editor) *Global Geography,* Crowell, 1957.
(With others) *The World's Nations: An Economic and Regional Geography,* Lippincott, 1958.
A Geography of Manufacturing, Prentice-Hall, 1962.
An Economic Atlas of Pennsylvania, Pennsylvania State Planning Board, 1964.
Exploring Earth Environments: A World Geography, Crowell, 1964.
Mineral Resources of the United States, Rand McNally, 1968.
Energy Resources of the United States, Rand McNally, 1968.
A Geography of Industrial Location, William C. Brown, 1970.
Socioeconomic Patterns of Pennsylvania: An Atlas, Bureau of Management Services, Commonwealth of Pennsylvania, 1975.
Manufacturing: A Study of Industrial Location, Pennsylvania State University Press, 1977.
(With wife, Ruby M. Miller) *Economic, Political, and Regional Aspects of the World's Energy Problems,* Vance Bibliographies, 1979.
(Editor with S. K. Majumdar) *Hazardous and Toxic Wastes,* Pennsylvania Academy of Science, 1984.
(Editor with Majumdar) *Liquid and Solid Wastes,* Pennsylvania Academy of Science, 1984.
(With R. M. Miller) *Industrial Location and Planning: Theory, Models and Factors of Localization, a Bibliography,* Vance Bibliographies, 1984.
(With R. M. Miller) *Industrial Location and Planning: Localization, Growth and Organization, a Bibliography,* Vance Bibliographies, 1984.
(With R. M. Miller) *Industrial Location and Planning: Regions and Countries, a Bibliography,* Vance Bibliographies, 1984.
(With R. M. Miller) *Industrial Location and Planning: Industries, a Bibliography,* Vance Bibliographies, 1984.
(Editor with Majumdar) *Radioactive Materials and Wastes,* Pennsylvania Academy of Science, 1985.
Physical Geography: Earth Systems and Human Interactions, C. E. Merrill, 1985.
(With R. M. Miller) *Environmental Hazards: Air Pollution, a Bibliography,* Vance Bibliographies, 1985.
(With R. M. Miller) *Environmental Hazards: Water Pollution, a Bibliography,* Vance Bibliographies, 1985.
(With R. M. Miller) *Environmental Hazards: Solid Wastes, a Bibliography,* Vance Bibliographies, 1985.

(With R. M. Miller) *Environmental Hazards: Liquid Wastes, a Bibliography*, Vance Bibliographies, 1985.
(With R. M. Miller) *Environmental Hazards: Industrial and Toxic Wastes, a Bibliography*, Vance Bibliographies, 1985.
(With R. M. Miller) *Environmental Hazards: Radioactive Materials and Wastes, a Bibliography*, Vance Bibliographies, 1985.

Also author, with R. M. Miller, of *Industrial Location: A Bibliography*, 1978, and *The American Coal Industry*, 1980. Contributor to proceedings. Contributor to *Journal of Geography, Economic Geography, Scientific Monthly*, and other periodicals. Associate editor, *Producers Monthly*, 1948-68; associate editor, *Pennsylvania Geographer*, 1965—; general editor, *Earth and Mineral Sciences Bulletin*, 1966-68.

*   *   *

MILLER, Richard Ulric 1932-

PERSONAL: Born September 6, 1932, in New York, N.Y.; son of Luther C. (a publicist) and Frances (Wells) Miller; married Louise O'Donnell, January 6, 1954; children: Elizabeth Louise, Richard Christopher. *Education:* University of Miami, B.B.A. (cum laude), 1958; Cornell University, M.S., 1960, Ph.D., 1966.

ADDRESSES: Home—11 Glenway St., Madison, Wis. 53705. *Office*—Graduate School of Business, University of Wisconsin, Madison, Wis. 53706.

CAREER: University of Miami, Coral Gables, Fla., employment interviewer for placement service, 1957-58; University of Arizona, Tucson, instructor in economics and business administration, 1960-62; State University of New York at Buffalo, assistant professor of industrial relations, 1965-66; University of Wisconsin—Madison, assistant professor, 1966-68, associate professor, 1968-71, professor of business administration, 1971—, assistant director of Center for International Business Research, 1966-71, associate director of Industrial Relations Research Institute, 1968-71, director, 1973-77. Visiting professor of business administration, Institute of Latin American Studies, University of Texas, 1971-72. *Military service:* U.S. Navy, 1951-55.

MEMBER: Industrial Relations Research Association (president of Wisconsin chapter, 1970-71; national secretary-treasurer, 1973-77), Phi Kappa Phi, Beta Gamma Sigma, Delta Sigma Pi.

AWARDS, HONORS: Doherty fellowship for study in Latin America, 1964-65.

WRITINGS:

(Editor with A. F. Isbester and contributor) *Canadian Labour in Transition*, Prentice-Hall, 1971.
(Contributor) David Chaplin, editor, *Population Politics and Growth in Latin America*, Heath, 1972.
(Contributor) S. M. A. Hameed, editor, *The Canadian Industrial Relations System*, Butterworth & Co., 1975.
(With James Stern, Steven Rubenfield, Craig Olson, and Brian Heshizer) *Labor Relations in Urban Transit*, Industrial Relations Research Institute, University of Wisconsin, 1977.
(With Brian Becker and Edward Krinsky) *Collective Bargaining in Hospitals*, Praeger, 1979.
(Contributor) Gerald Somers, editor, *Collective Bargaining: Contemporary American Experience*, Industrial Relations Research Association, 1979.

Contributor of articles and reviews to business journals, including *Industrial Relations, Arbitration Journal, Industrial and Labor Relations Review, Labor Law Journal, Employee Relations Law Journal, Labor History, International Journal of Public Administration*, and *Arizona Review of Business and Public Administration*.

WORK IN PROGRESS: Conflict Resolution in Public Employment; Collective Bargaining by Healthcare Professionals; Labor Relations in Urban Mass Transit.

SIDELIGHTS: Richard Ulric Miller has resided and studied in Cuba, Mexico, Chile, Peru, Barbados, Canada, and Switzerland.

*   *   *

MILLER, William Alvin 1931-

PERSONAL: Born January 1, 1931, in Pittsburgh, Pa.; son of Christ William and Anna Ernestine (Wilhelm) Miller; married Marilyn Mae Miller, August 8, 1953; children: Mark William, Eric Michael. *Education:* Capital University, B.A., 1953; Lutheran Theological Seminary, Columbus, Ohio, M.Div., 1957; Andover Newton Theological School, M.S.T., 1958, D.Ministry, 1974.

ADDRESSES: Home—2005 Xanthus Lane, Plymouth, Minn. 55447. *Office*—Fairview Hospital, 2312 South Sixth St., Minneapolis, Minn. 55454.

CAREER: St. James Lutheran Church, Baltimore, Md., pastor, 1958-66; Fairview Hospital, Minneapolis, Minn., chaplain, 1966-73, director of department of religion and health, 1973—. Instructor at Fairview School of Nursing, 1967-75, and Luther Theological Seminary (St. Paul, Minn.), 1973—. President, Woodland Publishing Co., Inc., 1977—. Partner, Professional Pastoral Resources, 1978—; owner, Woodland Pastoral Services, 1981—. Public speaker and lecturer in the U.S. and Europe, 1974—.

MEMBER: Association for Clinical Pastoral Education (certified supervisor), American Protestant Hospital Association (fellow of College of Chaplains; president, 1985-86), Association of Mental Hospital Clergy (fellow).

WRITINGS:

Why Do Christians Break Down?, Augsburg, 1973.
Big Kids' Mother Goose, Augsburg, 1976.
When Going to Pieces Holds You Together, Augsburg, 1976.
You Count, You Really Do, Augsburg, 1976.
Mid Life; New Life, Woodland, 1978.
Conversations, Woodland, 1980.
Make Friends with Your Shadow, Augsburg, 1981.
Prayers at Mid Point, Augsburg, 1983.

Contributor to *Lutheran Standard, Contact, Covenant Companion*, and *Bond*.

Associate editor of the *Journal of Pastoral Care*, 1984—; member of editorial board of *Cura Animarum*, 1984—.

WORK IN PROGRESS: Eleven Keys to Wellness, for Augsburg.

AVOCATIONAL INTERESTS: Cabinetmaking, boating, skiing, mountain climbing.

MILLMAN, Lawrence 1946-

PERSONAL: Born January 13, 1946, in Kansas City, Mo.; son of Daniel S. (a lawyer) and Zelma (an artist; maiden name, Lawrence) Millman. *Education:* Washington University, St. Louis, Mo., B.A., 1968; Rutgers University, M.A., 1971, Ph.D., 1974. *Politics:* Agrarian. *Religion:* None.

ADDRESSES: Home—Box 1582, Cambridge, Mass. 02238. *Agent*—Amanda Urban, International Creative Management, 40 West 57th St., New York, N.Y. 10019.

CAREER: University of New Hampshire, Durham, assistant professor of English, 1973-74; writer in western Ireland, 1974-77; University of Minnesota, Minneapolis, assistant professor of English, 1977-78; Tufts University, Medford, Mass., lecturer in English, 1979-80; Vermont College, Montpelier, faculty advisor for Goddard M.F.A. in Writing program, beginning 1981; University of Iceland, Reykjavik, Fulbright fellow, 1982; affiliated with Harvard University Extension Program, Cambridge, Mass., 1985; writer.

AWARDS, HONORS: Grant from International P.E.N., 1977; Bush Foundation fellowship, 1979-80; Guggenheim fellowship, 1983-84; finalist, Hemingway Award, 1983.

WRITINGS:

Our Like Will Not Be There Again (nonfiction), Little, Brown, 1977.
St. Kilda Amen, Ashplant Press, 1979.
Hero Jesse (novel), St. Martin's, 1982.
Smell of Earth and Clay (Eskimo translations), White Pine, 1985.
Ultimate Thule (nonfiction), Random House, in press.

Contributor of stories, poems, and reviews to journals and newspapers. Former reviewer of fiction, *Minneapolis Tribune*.

SIDELIGHTS: Lawrence Millman writes: "I tend to react eternally against a shady past: a Ph.D. in English. My point of view was formed when I lived in Ireland for two years, among old story-tellers, and learned the verbal eloquence with which uneducated and illiterate people can speak. Since then I have tried to capture in my writings the stark and beautiful rhythms of this kind of speech, speech that lived before the onslaught of television."

BIOGRAPHICAL/CRITICAL SOURCES:

BOOKS

Brown, George Mackay, *Under Brinkie's Brae*, Gordon Wright, 1980.

PERIODICALS

Chicago Tribune Book World, April 18, 1982.
Kansas City Star, June 5, 1977.
New York Times Book Review, June 19, 1977.
Orcadian, August 9, 1977, September 6, 1979.

*   *   *

MINOT, Stephen 1927-

PERSONAL: Born May 27, 1927, in Boston, Mass.; son of William (a real estate manager) and Elizabeth (Chapman) Minot; married second wife, Virginia Stover; children: (first marriage) Stephen Reid; (second marriage) Nicholas William, Christopher Bailey. *Education:* Harvard University, A.B., 1953; Johns Hopkins University, M.A., 1955. *Politics:* Democrat.

ADDRESSES: Home—69 Hickory Hill Rd., Simsbury, Conn. 06070. *Agent*—Emilie Jacobson, Curtis Brown Ltd., 10 Astor Pl., New York, N.Y. 10003.

CAREER: Bowdoin College, Brunswick, Me., instructor, 1955-57, assistant professor of English, 1957-58; University of Connecticut, Hartford, visiting assistant professor of English, 1958-59; Trinity College, Hartford, 1959-81, began as visiting lecturer, became professor of English; full-time writer, 1981—. Writer-in-residence, Johns Hopkins University, 1974-75. *Military service:* U.S. Army Air Forces, 1945-46.

MEMBER: Authors Guild, Authors League of America, American Civil Liberties Union, National Association for the Advancement of Colored People, National Committee for an Effective Congress.

AWARDS, HONORS: "Atlantic First" award from *Atlantic*, 1962, for short story "Sausage and Beer"; Saxton Memorial Foundation fellowship, 1963-64; National Endowment for the Arts fellow, 1976-77, and 1981-82.

WRITINGS:

Chill of Dusk (novel), Doubleday, 1964.
Three Genres: The Writing of Fiction, Poetry, and Drama (college text), Prentice-Hall, 1965, 3rd edition, 1982.
(Editor with Robley Wilson, Jr.) *Three Stances in Modern Fiction*, Winthrop, 1972.
Crossings and Other Stories, University of Illinois Press, 1974.
Ghost Images (novel), Harper, 1979.
Surviving the Flood (novel), Atheneum, 1981.
Reading Fiction, Prentice-Hall, 1985.

CONTRIBUTOR TO ANTHOLOGIES

Mark Schorer, editor, *The Story: A Critical Anthology*, 2nd edition, Prentice-Hall, 1967.
James Burl Hogins and Robert E. Yarber, editors, *Phase Blue*, Science Research Associates, 1970.
Prize Stories 1971: The O. Henry Awards, Doubleday, 1971.
Christopher Reaske and John Knott, editors, *Mirrors: An Introduction to Literature*, Canfield Press, 1972.
Cyril Gulassa, editor, *The Fact of Fiction: Social Relevance in the Short Story*, Canfield Press, 1972.
Martha Foley, editor, *The Best American Short Stories 1974*, Houghton, 1974.
Foley, editor, *The Best American Short Stories 1976*, Houghton, 1976.
Foley, editor, *The Best American Short Stories 1977*, Houghton, 1977.
Prize Stories 1977: The O. Henry Awards, Doubleday, 1977.

OTHER

Author of radio scripts for Voice of America, including "Nathanael West and Tragic Farce" and "The Vibrant World of Saul Bellow." Contributor of short stories to *Atlantic, Kenyon Review, Virginia Quarterly Review, Harper's, Redbook, Ladies' Home Journal, North American Review, Quarterly Review of Literature, Carleton Miscellany, American Poetry Review, Ploughshares*, and *Playboy*; contributor of articles to *Poet and Critic, North American Review*, and other periodicals. Contributing editor, *North American Review*, 1969—.

WORK IN PROGRESS: A new novel.

SIDELIGHTS: Stephen Minot's *Surviving the Flood* is the story of Noah's son Ham after the biblical flood. In Minot's story, Noah's grandfather Methuselah shocks everyone by saying the family is descended from Cain and not Seth, and names Ham, who is not the eldest, his legitimate heir. An unlikely spokesperson, Ham rebels against his father and sets out to found a new society. Lewis Jones writes in the *Times Literary Supplement* that ''in a self-consciously low style and with considerable gusto and ingenuity [Minot] has turned his chosen myth on its head. . . . *Surviving the Flood* is . . . an effective entertainment.''

Minot, who has strong political beliefs, commented on his career path in a letter to *CA:* ''After twenty-one rewarding years at Trinity College, I have resigned to concentrate on my own writing. I have not abandoned my concern for society, and more specifically for politics, but increasingly those commitments are expressed in fiction. *Surviving the Flood* is as much about this country as it is about Noah and the Ark.''

BIOGRAPHICAL/CRITICAL SOURCES:

PERIODICALS

New York Times, June 23, 1979.
New York Times Book Review, July 1, 1979.
Times Literary Supplement, March 11, 1983.

*   *   *

MITCHUM, Hank
    See NEWTON, D(wight) B(ennett)

*   *   *

MODIANO, Patrick (Jean)   1945-

PERSONAL: Born July 30, 1945, in Boulogne-Billancourt, France; son of Albert (a financier) and Luisa (an actress; maiden name, Colpyn) Modiano; married Dominique Zehrfuss, 1970; children: Zenaide, Maria. *Education:* Attended high school in Thones, France.

ADDRESSES: Home—Paris, France. *Agent*—Georges Beaume, 3 quai Malaquais, 75006 Paris, France.

CAREER: Novelist, 1968—.

AWARDS, HONORS: Prix Roger Nimier, 1968, and Prix Felix Feneon, 1969, both for *La Place de l'etoile;* Grand Prix Roman from L'Academie Francaise, 1972, for *Les Boulevards de ceinture;* Prix Goncourt, 1978, for *Rue des boutiques obscures.*

WRITINGS:

La Place de l'etoile (novel), Gallimard, 1968.
La Ronde de nuit, Gallimard, 1969, translation by Patricia Wolf published as *Night Rounds,* Knopf, 1971.
Les Boulevards de ceinture, Gallimard, 1972, translation by Caroline Hillier published as *Ring Roads,* Gollancz, 1974.
(With Louis Malle) *Lacombe Lucien* (screenplay; released by Louis Malle, 1974), Gallimard, 1974, translation by Sabine Destree published as *Lacombe Lucien,* Viking, 1975.
Villa Triste (novel), Gallimard, 1975, translation by Hillier published as *Villa Triste,* Gollancz, 1977.
(With Emmanuel Berl) *Interrogatoire par Patrick Modiano suivi de Il fait beau, allons au cimetiere* (title means ''Examination'' and ''The Weather Is Fine, To the Cemetery''), Gallimard, 1976.
Livret de famille (novel; title means ''Family Book''), Gallimard, 1977.
Rue des boutiques obscures (novel), Gallimard, 1978, translation by Daniel Weissbort published as *Missing Person,* J. Cape, 1980.

Une Jeunesse (novel; title means ''A Youth''), Gallimard, 1981.
Memory Lane (novel), Hachette, 1981.
De si braves garcons (title means ''Such Good Fellows''), Gallimard, 1982.
Poupee blonde (title means ''Blonde Doll''), P. O. L., 1983.
Quartier perdu, Gallimard, 1985.

SIDELIGHTS: ''What did the last generation get up to when it was the present generation? That is the simple yet unsettling question out of which Patrick Modiano has . . . made . . . expert and intriguing novels,'' writes John Sturrock in the *Times Literary Supplement.* French novelist Modiano published his first book at the age of twenty-three, in 1968. Since then his work has won several major French awards, including the Grand Prix Roman from the Academie Francaise and the Prix Goncourt. Modiano, described by Joyce Carleton in the *French Review* as ''a young author particularly haunted by the grey years of the nineteen-forties,'' has set many of his novels, as well as the highly-acclaimed screenplay he co-authored, ''Lacombe Lucien,'' in Occupied France. His technique, notes Anne Duchene in the *Times Literary Supplement,* relies upon ''delicately superimposing past upon present, grafting the 'then' on the 'now,' in a thin yet infinitely hurtful threnody.''

Although Modiano is too young to have directly experienced France during the Occupation, John Weightman suggests in the *Times Literary Supplement* that ''something romantically mysterious in his past,'' perhaps ''some unhappy family link,'' ties him to that period. Weightman feels that Modiano is ''obsessed with Jewishness'' and the dubious or ambiguous roles French Jews assumed to survive the Occupation. Indeed, Modiano's novel that won the Grand Prix Roman, *Les Boulevards de ceinture,* tells the story of a young man whose father is a Jew in Occupied France. Jewish characters also play central roles in the movie ''Lacombe Lucien,'' a film that Weightman praises as ''possibly the most brilliant imaginative evocation of wartime France that has yet appeared, and a very delicate account of a certain kind of relationship between Jews and non-Jews.''

If, as Weightman suggests, an obsession with Jewishness motivates Modiano, the idea does not serve as Modiano's sole fictive theme. The author is also fascinated by the casual attitudes of some of those who cooperated with the Nazis during the Occupation. ''His characters are chiefly the Nazi occupiers and their French and international hangers-on,'' notes Francis Steegmuller in the *Times Literary Supplement.* This is particularly evident in ''Lacombe Lucien'' when the teenaged Lucien is attracted to the Nazis chiefly because they are well-dressed and living in sumptuous comfort. Jay Cocks writes in *Time* magazine: ''As with Lucien, the foundation for national tragedy is laid quietly, and is built upon with a terrible ease.''

Several of Modiano's novels have dealt with another recurring theme, that of looking back to Paris of the early 1960s. In *Une Jeunesse,* a ''flagrantly nondescript bourgeois'' couple, Louis and Odile, are ''rejoined by their past,'' according to Sturrock, who comments: ''*Une Jeunesse* has the trappings of naturalism, with the brevity of a fable; it is a more devious story than it seems. Louis and Odile's past does not explain their present; its apparent recovery invests them merely with the pathos of a third dimension, of time.'' *Quartier perdu,* too, traces the mysterious memories of an expatriate Frenchman returning to Paris after an absence of twenty years. His memories revolve around boyhood friends, described by Duchene: ''They were a fairly dispirited group, compulsively aimless, aware that the mythic Paris was dead, that 'le temps de monde fini' had begun, but still nightly seeking what passed for pleasure." In *Villa Triste*, the character Victor Chamara describes his eighteenth summer, and, as David Leich notes in the *Times Literary Supplement*, "it is not all that long ago: but the tone is one of infinite distance, infinite regret. It might be the memoir of a very old man striving painfully to re-create a moment of youth or some vanished Edwardian season lost in the mists of half a dozen decades."

Critics such as Duchene occasionally suggest that through the repetition of Modiano's themes, his technique is becoming "rather dangerously sleek, . . . at moments a matter of formula." "Patrick Modiano . . . has only a few suits which are beginning to look a little threadbare," comments Barbara Wright in the *Times Literary Supplement*. "All [his] heroes are a variation on those in his first two books." Critical consensus, however, accords Modiano high praise for his contributions to modern French letters. Steegmuller writes: "Modiano is one of the few young novelists writing today in any language to whose new books one looks forward; and whose past work, reread, does not disappoint." His method, as a *Times Literary Supplement* reviewer describes it, is "both delicate and cunning: it is to sidle up to subjects of mystery and horror, indicating them without broaching them, as if gingerly fingering the outer surface of a poison bottle." "Modiano's way," claims Sturrock, "has always been to open dark doors into the past out of a sunlit present."

BIOGRAPHICAL/CRITICAL SOURCES:

BOOKS

Contemporary Literary Criticism, Volume XVIII, Gale, 1981.

PERIODICALS

French Review, March, 1979.
Time, October 14, 1974.
Times Literary Supplement, January 1, 1969, December 4, 1969, May 5, 1972, December 15, 1972, December 12, 1975, July 15, 1977, October 27, 1978, September 5, 1980, May 8, 1981, August 2, 1985.

*   *   *

MOFFAT, Mary Jane 1933-

PERSONAL: Born April 3, 1933, in Seattle, Wash.; daughter of Robert A. (in sales) and Mary Esther (a secretary; maiden name, Laakso) Pitts; married John Paul Moffat, Jr. (an arc lamp authority), December 21, 1951 (died, 1979); children: Peter William, Michael Robert. *Education:* University of California, Los Angeles, B.A. (with honors), 1954; Stanford University, M.A., 1968. *Politics:* Democrat.

ADDRESSES: Home and office—453 Cypress Dr., Los Altos, Calif. 94022. *Agent*—Maxine Groffsky, 2 Fifth Ave., New York, N.Y. 10011.

CAREER: Stanford University, Stanford, Calif., lecturer in creative writing, 1968-71; University of California, Santa Cruz, extension lecturer in women's studies, 1971-76; Foothill College, Los Altos, Calif., instructor in creative writing, 1976—. Extension instructor at University of California, Berkeley, 1975-80; instructor at San Francisco State University, 1983. Lecturer and community organizer.

WRITINGS:

(Editor with Charlotte Painter) *Revelations: Diaries of Women*, Random House, 1974.

(Editor) *In the Midst of Winter: Selections from the Literature of Mourning*, Random House, 1982.
The Times of Our Lives: A Guide to Writing Autobiography and Memoir, Ponce Press, 1985.
Small Occasions (short stories), Ponce Press, 1986.

*   *   *

MOLLOY, Paul (George) 1924-

PERSONAL: Born July 4, 1924, in Winnipeg, Manitoba, Canada; came to the United States in 1950, naturalized in 1956; son of Thomas Boniface (a member of parliament) and Marie (Dubuc) Molloy; married Helen Kennedy, November 18, 1944 (divorced, 1982); children: Paul, Jr., Georgia Molloy Sahs, Shonagh, Nelda Molloy Siemion, Marcia Molloy Angsten, Lisa Molloy Yow, Barbara, Mark. *Education:* University of Manitoba, B.A., 1941. *Religion:* Roman Catholic.

ADDRESSES: Home—101 Lemon St. W., Tarpon Springs, Fla. 33589. *Agent*—Arthur Pine, 1780 Broadway, New York, N.Y. 10019.

CAREER: Worked as laborer in Canadian gold and copper mines; affiliated with *Montreal Herald*, Montreal, Quebec, 1941-45; United Press International, bureau manager in Quebec City, Quebec, and Winnipeg, Manitoba, 1946-50; *Tulsa Daily-Tribune*, Tulsa, Okla., feature writer, 1950-51; *Time*, New York, N.Y., writer-editor, 1951-53; *Commercial Appeal*, Memphis, Tenn., columnist, 1953-57; *Chicago Sun-Times*, Chicago, Ill., television and radio critic, 1957-70, feature writer, 1970-75; writer. Producer of numerous radio and television programs. *Military service:* Served in the Canadian Army during World War II.

MEMBER: National Headliners Club, Society of Midland Authors.

AWARDS, HONORS: National Headliner Award, National Headliners Club, 1960, for outstanding achievement in radio and television criticism; outstanding journalist award, Chicago Festival of Merit, 1960; James J. Haines Award, Friends of American Writers, 1964, for *A Pennant for the Kremlin*; George Washington Honor Medal, Freedoms Foundation, 1965 and 1972; two nominations for Pulitzer Prize.

WRITINGS:

And Then There Were Eight, Doubleday, 1961.
A Pennant for the Kremlin, Doubleday, 1964.
All I Said Was . . ., Doubleday, 1966.
Where Did Everybody Go?, Doubleday, 1981.

Also author of *The Man with Three Hearts* and *The Town the World Forgot*; author of numerous radio and television programs. Contributor of articles to a variety of popular magazines, including *Life* and *Saturday Evening Post*.

SIDELIGHTS: In *Where Did Everybody Go?*, Paul Molloy, a former television and radio critic and feature writer for the *Chicago Sun-Times*, discusses alcoholism and his personal experience as an alcoholic. The book, writes Robert Cromie in the *Chicago Tribune Book World*, "is a moving and painfully honest account of how the author's grim love affair with the bottle began, the desperate stratagems he adopted in attempting to end it, and how he believes that he finally has conquered that passion, at tremendous personal and professional cost." "Molloy writes with almost clinical detachment of his own struggle," adds Cromie. For a reviewer writing in the *Critic*, this detachment weakens the book: "[Molloy] doesn't elicit the reader's compassion." "What seems to be missing," observes this reviewer, "is the pain an alcoholic suffers."

Yet as Judith Weightman points out in *Best Sellers,* "Molloy correctly describes alcoholism as a disease which ruins many lives: both that of the alcoholic and those of the people surrounding him." Molloy's account offers insights into the nature of both the victim and the disease. "Molloy knows," Clarence Peterson notes in the *Chicago Tribune Book World,* "and appears to have practiced, every self-deception in the alcoholic's trick bag and describes them in lucid detail." The author also illustrates the extent of this disease, affecting doctors, the clergy, and young people in ever increasing numbers.

MEDIA ADAPTATIONS: Paul Molloy's book *A Pennant for the Kremlin* has been adapted for the theater by David Rogers and has been optioned to Universal.

BIOGRAPHICAL/CRITICAL SOURCES:

BOOKS

Molloy, Paul, *And Then There Were Eight,* Doubleday, 1961.
Molloy, Paul, *All I Said Was . . . ,* Doubleday, 1966.
Molloy, Paul, *Where Did Everybody Go?,* Doubleday, 1981.

PERIODICALS

Best Sellers, July, 1981.
Catholic Digest, February, 1962.
Chicago Tribune Book World, April 12, 1981, August 8, 1982.
Critic, May 15, 1981.

*   *   *

MONTGOMERY, Ruth Shick

PERSONAL: Born in Sumner, Ill.; daughter of Ira Whitmer and Bertha (Judy) Shick; married Robert H. Montgomery (a former businessman), December 26, 1935. *Education:* Attended Baylor University, 1930-33, and Purdue University, 1934. *Religion:* Methodist.

ADDRESSES: Home and office—2101 Connecticut Ave. N.W., Washington, D.C. 20008.

CAREER: Women's editor, *Louisville Herald-Post,* Louisville, Ky.; feature writer, *St. Louis Post-Dispatch,* St. Louis, Mo., and *Indianapolis Star,* Indianapolis, Ind.; reporter with *Detroit News,* Detroit, Mich., *Detroit Times,* Detroit, and *Waco News-Tribune,* Waco, Tex.; *Chicago Tribune,* Chicago, Ill., reporter, 1943-44; *New York Daily News,* New York, N.Y., correspondent in Washington, D.C., 1944-55; special correspondent in Washington, D.C., for International News Service, 1956-58; syndicated political columnist in Washington, D.C., for Hearst Headline Service, King Feature Syndicate, 1956-68. Occasional foreign correspondent in Europe, South America, Far East and Middle East, beginning 1946.

MEMBER: National Press Club, Washington Press Club (president, 1950-51; member of board of governors, 1951-54), Alpha Chi Omega, Kappa Kappa Kappa, Theta Sigma Phi.

AWARDS, HONORS: Pall Mall Journalism award, 1947; LL.D., Baylor University, 1956, and Ashland College, 1958; Front Page Award, Indianapolis Press Club, 1957; George R. Holmes Journalism award, 1958; best nonfiction book of the year award, Indiana University, 1966, for *A Gift of Prophecy;* Most Valuable Alumna award, Baylor University, 1966.

WRITINGS:

Once There Was a Nun, Putnam, 1962.

Mrs. LBJ, Holt, 1964.
A Gift of Prophecy: The Phenomenal Jeane Dixon, Morrow, 1965.
Flowers at the White House, Morrow, 1966.
Here and Hereafter, Coward, 1966.
A Search for the Truth, Morrow, 1967.
Hail to the Chiefs, Coward, 1970.
A World Beyond, Coward, 1971.
Born to Heal, Coward, 1973.
Companions along the Way, Coward, 1974.
The World Before, Coward, 1976.
Strangers among Us, Coward, 1979.
Threshold to Tomorrow, Coward, 1982.
Aliens among Us, Coward, 1985.

Contributor to *Look, Good Housekeeping, Cosmopolitan,* and other popular magazines.

WORK IN PROGRESS: An autobiography, for Doubleday.

SIDELIGHTS: Ruth Shick Montgomery began her writing career as a newspaper reporter. In that capacity, she traveled to every continent except Australia, filing stories from the Orient, the Middle East, Russia, Siberia, Poland, Europe, and South America. "Her stories filed from Havana in 1947 reportedly changed Cuban national politics of that time," claims Phyllis Theroux in *Washington Post Book World.* In addition, Montgomery regularly covered presidential press conferences and the national conventions of the Republican and Democratic parties during the 1940s, 1950s, and 1960s. She was also the only woman selected to cover the funeral of Franklin Delano Roosevelt.

In 1958, Montgomery wrote a series of articles on the occult as a break from her usual political columns. She approached her subject skeptically, but her research and experiences convinced her that there was a great deal of validity to the unseen world of which psychics spoke. Little by little, she reduced her journalistic duties until she was free to write and speak exclusively on psychic phenomena. She has now written books on her investigations into psychic healing, reincarnation, extrasensory perception, and extraterrestrials.

In a letter to *CA,* she explained what motivated her to abandon political writing in favor of books in the psychic field: "My principal reason for writing books in the psychic field is to awaken readers to the reality of a vibrant world beyond our five senses and three-dimensional earth plane. I want to dispel all fear of death. What we mistakenly call death is simply a transition to a different vibratory level, and I have presented a great deal of evidence that communication regularly exists between the living and the so-called dead. Spiritual growth, rather than monetary gain, should be our goal, and the way to achieve this is through helping others. After all, since each of us is a part of our Creator, we are all one."

BIOGRAPHICAL/CRITICAL SOURCES:

BOOKS

Authors in the News, Volume I, Gale, 1976.

PERIODICALS

Best Sellers, March 15, 1967, November 15, 1970.
Miami Herald, March 30, 1973.
New York Times Book Review, February 11, 1973.
Washington Post Book World, February 21, 1983.

MOORCOCK, Michael (John) 1939-

(Bill Barclay, William Ewert Barclay, Edward P. Bradbury, James Colvin; Michael Barrington and Philip James, joint pseudonyms; Desmond Reid, house pseudonym)

PERSONAL: Born December 18, 1939, in Mitcham, Surrey, England; son of Arthur and June (Taylor) Moorcock; married Hilary Bailey (a writer), September, 1962 (divorced April, 1978); married Jill Riches (divorced); married Linda Mullens Steele, September, 1983; children: (first marriage) Sophie, Katherine, Max.

ADDRESSES: Home—c/o Sheil, 43 Doughty St., London WC1, England. *Agent*—Wallace & Sheil, 177 East 70th St., New York, N.Y. 10021.

CAREER: Writer. Has worked as an office junior, singer-guitarist, and farm worker; editor, *Tarzan Adventures* (juvenile magazine), 1956-58; editor and writer, Sexton Blake Library, 1959-61; editor and pamphleteer, Liberal Party, 1962-63; *New Worlds* (science fiction magazine), London, England, editor and publisher, 1964-78; works with rock and roll band Hawkwind; member of rock and roll band Michael Moorcock and the Deep Fix.

MEMBER: Authors Guild.

AWARDS, HONORS: Nebula Award, Science Fiction Writers of America, 1967, for *Behold the Man;* British Science Fiction Association award and Arts Council of Great Britain award, both 1967, both for *New Worlds;* August Derleth Award, British Fantasy Society, 1972, for *The Knight of the Swords,* 1973, for *The King of the Swords,* 1974, for *The Jade Man's Eyes,* 1975, for *The Sword and the Stallion,* and 1976, for *The Hollow Lands;* International Fantasy Award, 1972 and 1973, for fantasy novels; *Guardian* Literary Prize, 1977, for *The Condition of Muzak;* John W. Campbell Memorial Award, 1978, and World Fantasy Award, World Fantasy Convention, 1979, both for *Gloriana; or, The Unfulfill'd Queen.*

WRITINGS:

(With James Cawthorn, under house pseudonym Desmond Reid) *Caribbean Crisis,* Sexton Blake Library, 1962.

The Sundered Worlds, Compact Books, 1965, Paperback Library, 1966, published as *The Blood Red Game,* Sphere Books, 1970.

The Fireclown, Compact Books, 1965, Paperback Library, 1966, published as *The Winds of Limbo,* Sphere Books, 1970.

(Under pseudonym James Colvin) *The Deep Fix,* Compact Books, 1966.

The Wrecks of Time (bound with *Tramontane* by Emil Petaja), Ace Books, 1966 (revised edition published separately in England as *The Rituals of Infinity,* Arrow Books, 1971).

The Twilight Man, Compact Books, 1966, Berkley Publishing, 1970 (published in England as *The Shores of Death,* Sphere Books, 1970).

(Under pseudonym Bill Barclay) *Printer's Devil,* Compact Books, 1966, published under name Michael Moorcock as *The Russian Intelligence,* Savoy Books, 1980.

(Under pseudonym Bill Barclay) *Somewhere in the Night,* Compact Books, 1966, revised edition published under name Michael Moorcock as *The Chinese Agent,* Macmillan, 1970.

The Ice Schooner, Sphere Books, 1968, Berkley Publishing, 1969, revised edition, Harrap, 1985.

(With Hilary Bailey) *The Black Corridor,* Ace Books, 1969.

The Time Dweller, Hart-Davis, 1969, Berkley Publishing, 1971.

(With James Cawthorn under joint pseudonym Philip James) *The Distant Suns,* Unicorn Bookshop, 1975.

Moorcock's Book of Martyrs, Quartet Books, 1976, published as *Dying for Tomorrow,* DAW Books, 1978.

Sojan, Savoy Books, 1977.

Epic Pooh, British Fantasy Society, 1978.

Gloriana; or, The Unfulfill'd Queen, Allison and Busby, 1978, Avon, 1979.

The Golden Barge, DAW Books, 1980.

My Experiences in the Third World War, Savoy Books, 1980.

The Retreat from Liberty, Zomba Books, 1983.

Letters from Hollywood, Harrap, 1986.

"ELRIC" SERIES

The Stealer of Souls, and Other Stories (also see below), Neville Spearman, 1963, Lancer Books, 1967.

Stormbringer, Jenkins, 1965, Lancer Books, 1967.

The Singing Citadel (also see below), Berkley Publishing, 1970.

The Sleeping Sorceress, New English Library, 1971, Lancer Books, 1972, published as *The Vanishing Tower,* DAW Books, 1977.

The Dreaming City, Lancer Books, 1972 (revised edition published in England as *Elric of Melnibone,* Hutchinson, 1972).

The Jade Man's Eyes, Unicorn Bookshop, 1973.

Elric: The Return to Melnibone, Unicorn Bookshop, 1973.

The Sailor on the Seas of Fate, DAW Books, 1976.

The Bane of the Black Sword, DAW Books, 1977.

The Weird of the White Wolf (contains some material from *The Stealer of Souls, and Other Stories* and *The Singing Citadel*), DAW Books, 1977.

Elric at the End of Time, DAW Books, 1985.

"MICHAEL KANE" SERIES; UNDER PSEUDONYM EDWARD P. BRADBURY

Warriors of Mars (also see below), Compact Books, 1965, published under name Michael Moorcock as *The City of the Beast,* Lancer Books, 1970.

Blades of Mars (also see below), Compact Books, 1965, published under name Michael Moorcock as *The Lord of the Spiders,* Lancer Books, 1971.

The Barbarians of Mars (also see below), Compact Books, 1965, published under name Michael Moorcock as *The Masters of the Pit,* Lancer Books, 1971.

Warrior of Mars (contains *Warriors of Mars, Blades of Mars,* and *The Barbarians of Mars*), New English Library, 1981.

"THE HISTORY OF THE RUNESTAFF" SERIES

The Jewel in the Skull (also see below), Lancer Books, 1967.

Sorcerer's Amulet (also see below), Lancer Books, 1968 (published in England as *The Mad God's Amulet,* Mayflower Books, 1969).

Sword of the Dawn (also see below), Lancer Books, 1968.

The Secret of the Runestaff (also see below), Lancer Books, 1969 (published in England as *The Runestaff,* Mayflower Books, 1969).

The History of the Runestaff (contains *The Jewel in the Skull, Sorcerer's Amulet, Sword of the Dawn,* and *The Secret of the Runestaff*), Granada, 1979.

"JERRY CORNELIUS" SERIES

The Final Programme (also see below), Avon, 1968, revised edition, Allison & Busby, 1969.

A Cure for Cancer (also see below), Holt, 1971.

The English Assassin (also see below), Allison & Busby, 1972.

The Lives and Times of Jerry Cornelius, Allison & Busby, 1976.

The Adventures of Una Persson and Catherine Cornelius in the Twentieth Century, Quartet Books, 1976.

The Condition of Muzak (also see below), Allison & Busby, 1977, Gregg, 1978.

The Cornelius Chronicles (contains *The Final Programme, A Cure for Cancer, The English Assassin*, and *The Condition of Muzak*), Avon, 1977.

The Great Rock 'n' Roll Swindle, Virgin Books, 1980.

The Entropy Tango, New English Library, 1981.

The Opium General, Harrap, 1985.

"KARL GLOGAUER" SERIES

Behold the Man, Allison & Busby, 1969, Avon, 1970.

Breakfast in the Ruins: A Novel of Inhumanity, New English Library, 1972, Random House, 1974.

"CORUM" SERIES

The Knight of the Swords (also see below), Mayflower Books, 1970, Berkley Publishing, 1971.

The Queen of the Swords (also see below), Berkley Publishing, 1971.

The King of the Swords (also see below), Berkley Publishing, 1971.

The Bull and the Spear, Berkley Publishing, 1973.

The Oak and the Ram, Berkley Publishing, 1973.

The Sword and the Stallion, Berkley Publishing, 1974.

The Swords Trilogy (contains *The Knight of the Swords, The Queen of the Swords*, and *The King of the Swords*), Berkley Publishing, 1977.

The Chronicles of Corum, Berkley Publishing, 1978.

"THE ETERNAL CHAMPION" SERIES

The Eternal Champion, Dell, 1970, revised edition, Harper, 1978.

Phoenix in Obsidian, Mayflower Books, 1970, published as *The Silver Warriors*, Dell, 1973.

The Dragon in the Sword, Granada, 1986.

"OSWALD BASTABLE" SERIES

The Warlord of the Air (also see below), Ace Books, 1971.

The Land Leviathan (also see below), Quartet Books, 1974.

The Steel Tsar (also see below), DAW Books, 1983.

The Nomad of Time (contains *The Warlord of the Air, The Land Leviathan*, and *The Steel Tsar*), Granada, 1984.

"THE DANCERS AT THE END OF TIME" SERIES

An Alien Heat (also see below), Harper, 1972.

The Hollow Lands (also see below), Harper, 1974.

The End of All Songs (also see below), Harper, 1976.

Legends from the End of Time, Harper, 1976.

The Transformations of Miss Mavis Ming, W. H. Allen, 1977, published as *A Messiah at the End of Time*, DAW Books, 1978.

The Dancers at the End of Time (contains *An Alien Heat, The Hollow Lands*, and *The End of All Songs)*, Granada, 1981.

"CASTLE BRASS" SERIES

Count Brass (also see below), Mayflower Books, 1973.

The Champion of Garathorm (also see below), Mayflower Books, 1973.

The Quest for Tanelorn (also see below), Mayflower Books, 1975, Dell, 1976.

The Chronicles of Castle Brass (contains *Count Brass, The Champion of Garathorm*, and *The Quest for Tanelorn)*, Granada, 1985.

"VON BEK FAMILY" SERIES

The Warhound and the World's Pain, Timescape, 1981.

The Brothel in Rosenstrasse, New English Library, 1982, Tigerseye Press, 1986.

The City in the Autumn Stars, Ace Books, 1986.

"COLONEL PYAT" SERIES

Byzantium Endures, Secker & Warburg, 1981, Random House, 1982.

The Laughter of Carthage, Random House, 1984.

SCREENPLAYS

"The Final Programme" (based on his novel of the same title; removed name from credits after dispute with director), EMI, 1973.

"The Land That Time Forgot," British Lion, 1975.

EDITOR

(And contributor under name Michael Moorcock and under pseudonym James Colvin) *The Best of "New Worlds,"* Compact Books, 1965.

Best SF Stories from "New Worlds," Panther Books, 1967, Berkley Publishing, 1968.

The Traps of Time, Rapp & Whiting, 1968.

(And contributor under pseudonym James Colvin) *The Best SF Stories from "New Worlds" 2*, Panther Books, 1968, Berkley Publishing, 1969.

(And contributor under pseudonym James Colvin) *The Best SF Stories from "New Worlds" 3*, Panther Books, 1968, Berkley Publishing, 1969.

The Best SF Stories from "New Worlds" 4, Panther Books, 1969, Berkley Publishing, 1971.

The Best SF Stories from "New Worlds" 5, Panther Books, 1969, Berkley Publishing, 1971.

(And contributor) *The Best SF Stories from "New Worlds" 6*, Panther Books, 1970, Berkley Publishing, 1971.

The Best SF Stories from "New Worlds" 7, Panther Books, 1971.

New Worlds Quarterly 1, Berkley Publishing, 1971.

New Worlds Quarterly 2, Berkley Publishing, 1971.

New Worlds Quarterly 3, Sphere Books, 1971.

(With Langdon Jones and contributor) *The Nature of the Catastrophe*, Hutchinson, 1971.

New Worlds Quarterly 4, Berkley Publishing, 1972.

New Worlds Quarterly 5, Sphere Books, 1973.

New Worlds Quarterly 6, Avon, 1973.

Before Armageddon: An Anthology of Victorian and Edwardian Imaginative Fiction Published before 1914, W. H. Allen, 1975.

England Invaded: A Collection of Fantasy Fiction, Ultramarine, 1977.

New Worlds: An Anthology, Fontana, 1983.

RECORDINGS; UNDER NAME "MICHAEL MOORCOCK AND THE DEEP FIX"

"The New Worlds Fair," United Artists, 1975.

"Dodgem Dude/Starcruiser" (single), Flicknife, 1980.

"The Brothel in Rosenstrasse/Time Centre" (single), Flicknife, 1982.

(With others) "Hawkwind Friends and Relations," Flicknife, 1982.

(With others) "Hawkwind & Co.," Flicknife, 1983.

Also composer of songs recorded by others, including "Sonic Attack," "The Black Corridor," "The Wizard Blew His Horn," "Standing at the Edge," "Warriors," "Kings of Speed," "Warrior at the End of Time," "Psychosonia," "Coded Languages," "Lost Chances," "Choose Your Masks," and "Arrival in Utopia," recorded by Hawkwind; "The Great Sun Jester," "Black Blade," and "Veteran of the Psychic Wars," recorded by Blue Oyster Cult.

OTHER

Contributor, sometimes under pseudonyms, to *Guardian, Punch, Ambit,* London *Times,* and other publications.

SIDELIGHTS: Michael Moorcock was associated with the New Wave science fiction of the 1960s that introduced avant-garde literary techniques, along with a wider range of subject matter and style, to the science fiction field. As editor of *New Worlds,* the most prominent of the New Wave publications, Moorcock promoted the movement and provided a showcase for its writing.

The New Wave, Donald A. Wollheim writes in his *The Universe Makers,* was an "effort to merge science fiction into the mainstream of literature. . . . The charges brought against old-line science fiction were on the basis of both structure and content. Structurally, the charge was made that too much of the writing retained the flavor of the pulps [and] that science fiction writers were not keeping up with the experimental avant-garde. . . . Internally, the charge was made that science fiction actually was dead—because the future was no longer credible. The crises of the twentieth century . . . were obviously insurmountable. We would all never make it into the twenty-first century." In an interview with Ian Covell of *Science Fiction Review,* Moorcock says of the New Wave: "We were a generation of writers who had no nostalgic love of the pulp magazines, who had come to SF as a possible alternative to mainstream literature and had taken SF seriously. . . . We were trying to find a viable literature for our time. A literature which took account of science, of modern social trends, and which was written not according to genre conventions but according to the personal requirements of the individuals who produced it."

Moorcock's own writing covers a wide range of science fiction and fantasy genres. He has written science fiction adventures in the style of Edgar Rice Burroughs's Mars novels, sword and sorcery novels, comic and satirical science fiction, and time-traveling science fiction. Some of these books, Moorcock admits, were written for the money. *New Worlds* was an influential magazine in the science fiction field, but it was never a financial success. When creditors needed to be paid it was Moorcock, as editor and publisher, who was held responsible. He was often forced to write a quick novel to pay the bills. Even so, Charles Platt recounts in his *Dream Makers: The Uncommon People Who Write Science Fiction,* "it was not unusual for the magazine's staff to be found cowering on the floor with the lights out, pretending not to be home, while some creditor rang the bell and called hopefully through the mail slot in the front door—to no avail."

The genre books that brought Moorcock to critical attention, and those that he considers among his most important, combine standard science fiction trappings with experimental narrative structures. His *Breakfast in the Ruins: A Novel of Inhumanity,* for instance, contains a number of historical vignettes featuring the protagonist Karl Glogauer. In each of these, Karl is a different person in a different time, participating in such examples of political violence as the French Revolution, the Paris Commune, a Nazi concentration camp, and a My Lai-style massacre. Interwoven with these vignettes is a homosexual love scene, involving Karl and a black Nigerian, that takes on a mystical connotation as the two lovers seem to merge into each other's identities. Helen Rogan of *Time* describes the book as "by turns puzzling, funny, and shocking" and Moorcock as "both bizarrely inventive and highly disciplined." Writing in the *New York Times Book Review,* John Deck calls the book "a dazzling historical fantasy."

In the books and stories featuring Jerry Cornelius, Moorcock has experimented with character as well as with narrative structure. Cornelius has no consistent character or appearance. He is, as Nick Totton writes in *Spectator,* "a nomad of the territories of personality; even his skin color and gender are as labile as his accomplishments." Cornelius' world is just as flexible, containing a multitude of alternative histories, all contradictory, and peopled with characters who die and resurrect as a matter of course. Within this mutable landscape, Cornelius travels from one inconclusive adventure to another, trapped in an endless existence. As Colin Greenland maintains in the *Dictionary of Literary Biography,* Cornelius is "an entirely new kind of fictional character, a dubious hero whose significance is always oblique and rarely stable, equipped to tackle all the challenges of his time yet unable to find a satisfactory solution to any of them."

The Condition of Muzak, completing the Jerry Cornelius tetralogy, won the *Guardian* Literary Prize in 1977, bringing Moorcock acceptance by a wider literary world. At the time of the award, W. L. Webb of the *Guardian* wrote: "Michael Moorcock, rejecting the demarcation disputes that have reduced the novel to a muddle of warring sub-genres, recovers in these four books a protean vitality and inclusiveness that one might call Dickensian if their consciousness were not so entirely of our own volatile times." Moorcock, according to Angus Wilson in the *Washington Post Book World,* "is emerging as one of the most serious literary lights of our time. . . . For me his Jerry Cornelius quartet [of novels] assured the durability of his reputation."

Moorcock's literary standing has been substantially enhanced with the publication of *Byzantium Endures* and *The Laughter of Carthage.* These two novels are the closest Moorcock has come to conventional literary fiction, being the autobiography of Russian emigre Colonel Pyat. Pyat was born on January 1, 1900, and so the story of his life is a history of the twentieth century. Pyat survived the Russian Revolution, travelled throughout Europe and America, and participated in a number of important historical events. But he is a megalomaniac who imagines himself to be both a great inventor, the equal of Thomas Edison, and a major figure on the stage of world history. He is also an anti-Semite who sees true Christianity, as embodied in the Russian Orthodox Church, in a battle against the Jews, Orientals, Bolsheviks, and other destroyers of order. He likens Western Christianity to Byzantium, his enemies to Carthage. Naturally, Pyat's account of his life is self-aggrandizing and inaccurate.

Byzantium Endures focuses on the first twenty years of Pyat's life, telling his opportunistic role in the Russian Revolution. Pyat survives the upheaval of the revolution and the subsequent civil war by working first for one side and then another. As Frederic Morton writes in the *New York Times Book Review,* his mechanical skills are put to good use "repairing the rifles of anarchist guerrillas, fixing the treads of White Army tanks [and] doctoring the engine in one of Trotsky's armed trains.'' Pyat claims to have invented the laser gun on behalf of Ukrainian nationalists fighting against the Red Army, but when the electrical power failed so did his gun. ''Pyat's self-serving recollections,'' Bart Mills states in the *Los Angeles Times Book Review,* ''contain a vivid picture of the events of 1917-1920, down to menus, street names and the color of people's moustaches.'' The novel, writes Robert Onopa in the *Chicago Tribune Book World,* is ''utterly engrossing as narrative, historically pertinent, and told through characters so alive and detail so dense that it puts to shame all but a few writers who have been doing this kind of work all along.''

The Laughter of Carthage covers Pyat's life from 1920 to 1924, detailing his escape from Communist Russia and subsequent travels in Europe and America. His activities are sometimes unlawful, requiring him to change his residence and name frequently. He meets everyone from Dylan Thomas to Tom Mix and lives everywhere from Constantinople to Hollywood. Because of the scope of Pyat's adventures, *The Laughter of Carthage* is a sweeping picture of the world during the 1920s. ''Moorcock provides an exotic itinerary, a robust cast of opportunists and scoundrels, and a series of dangerous adventures and sexual escapades,'' notes R. Z. Sheppard of *Time.* ''This is epic writing . . . ,'' Valentine Cunningham of the *Times Literary Supplement* writes. ''As [D. W.] Griffith stuffed his movies with vast throngs and Promethean matter so Pyat's narration feeds hugely on the numerous people he claims to have met, the history he makes believe he has helped to shape, the many places his traveller's tales take him to.''

Pyat's narration, because it is colored by his eccentric, offensive views and his distorted sense of self-importance, gives a fantastic sheen to the familiar historical events he relates. ''This is Moorcock's achievement: he has rewritten modern history by seeing it in the distorting mirror of one man's perceptions so that the novel has the imaginative grasp of fantasy while remaining solidly based upon recognizable facts,'' Peter Ackroyd writes in the London *Times.* ''Moorcock has here created a fiction,'' writes Nigel Andrew in the London *Times,* ''that is seething with detailed life at every level—in the headlong narrative, in the bravura passages of scene-setting description, and, particularly, in the rendering of Pyat's vision of the world.'' Although Richard Eder of the *Los Angeles Times* finds Pyat's narrative an ''extremely long-winded unpleasantness'' because of his political views, the *New York Times Book Review's* Thaddeus Rutkowski forgives the ''sometimes tedious'' nature of Pyat's narration. ''Most often, . . . ,'' he finds, ''Pyat's tirades are beguiling. They are the pronouncements of a singularly innocent intelligence gone awry.''

Moorcock's move from science fiction to mainstream fiction is welcomed by several critics. Observes Gregory Sandow in the *Village Voice:* ''It's wonderful to see Moorcock grow from a genre writer into, simply, a writer. . . . A mainstream novel gives him far more scope to nourish the obsessions (and also the passion, zaniness, and eye for detail) that made his science fiction both fun and worthwhile.'' Moorcock, Andrew allows, ''has had to come the long way to literary recognition. But now, with *The Laughter of Carthage,* he can surely no longer be denied his due; this enormous book—with its forerunner, *Byzantium Endures*—must establish him in the front rank of practising English novelists.''

Speaking of his writing, Moorcock told *CA:* ''Most of my work recently has been in terms of a moral and psychological investigation of Imperialism (Western and Eastern) seen in terms of fiction. Even my fantasy novels are inclined to deal with moral problems rather than magical ones. I'm turning more and more away from SF and fantasy and more towards a form of realism used in the context of what you might call an imaginative framework. Late Dickens would be the model I'd most like to emulate.''

Moorcock also continues his work with English rock and roll band Hawkwind, which plays science fiction-oriented music. The band took its name from a character in one of his novels. He has also formed his own band, Michael Moorcock and the Deep Fix, and has made several recordings. The League of Temporal Adventurers, based in Memphis, Tennessee, is the official Michael Moorcock society.

MEDIA ADAPTATIONS: The character Elric is featured in role-playing games from the Avalon Hill Game Company and Chaosium, in comic books published by Pacific Comics and by Star Reach Productions, and in miniature figures marketed by Citadel Miniatures; the character Oswald Bastable is featured in a computer game.

BIOGRAPHICAL/CRITICAL SOURCES:

BOOKS

Bilyeu, R., *Tanelorn Archives,* Pandora's Books, 1979.
Callow, A. J., compiler, *The Chronicles of Moorcock,* A. J. Callow, 1978.
Carter, Lin, *Imaginary Worlds,* Ballantine, 1973.
Contemporary Literary Criticism, Gale, Volume V, 1976, Volume XXVII, 1984.
Dictionary of Literary Biography, Volume XIV: *British Novelists since 1960,* Gale, 1983.
Greenland, Colin, *The Entropy Exhibition: Michael Moorcock and the British ''New Wave'' in Science Fiction,* Routledge & Kegan Paul, 1983.
Harper, Andrew and George McAulay, *Michael Moorcock: A Bibliography,* T-K Graphics, 1976.
Platt, Charles, *Dream Makers: The Uncommon People Who Write Science Fiction,* Berkley Publishing, 1980.
Walker, Paul, editor, *Speaking of Science Fiction: The Paul Walker Interviews,* Luna Publications, 1978.
Wollheim, Donald A., *The Universe Makers,* Harper, 1971.

PERIODICALS

Amazing Stories, May, 1971.
Analog, February, 1970.
Books and Bookmen, June, 1971, September, 1971, October, 1972, May, 1974, August, 1978.
Chicago Tribune Book World, January 31, 1982.
Commonweal, August 1, 1975.
Detroit News, February 24, 1985.
Encounter, November, 1981.
Guardian Weekly, April 10, 1969.
Harper's Bazaar (British edition), December, 1969.
Ink, August, 1971.
Kensington News, April 18, 1969.
Kensington Post, April 4, 1969.
Los Angeles Times, January 9, 1985.
Los Angeles Times Book Review, March 7, 1982.
Luna Monthly, November, 1975.
New Republic, June 15, 1974.
New Statesman, April 4, 1969, May 18, 1973, June 18, 1976, April 15, 1977.
New Worlds, March, 1969.

New York Times Book Review, April 5, 1970, May 19, 1974, April 25, 1976, February 21, 1982, February 10, 1985.
Observer, April 4, 1976.
Punch, January 16, 1985.
Saturday Review, April 25, 1970.
Science Fiction Monthly, February, 1975.
Science Fiction Review, January, 1971, January, 1979.
Spectator, April 11, 1969, August 10, 1974, November 20, 1976, April 9, 1977, December 24, 1977, June 27, 1981, February 9, 1985.
Speculation, May, 1970, August, 1970.
Time, August 5, 1974, January 28, 1985.
Time Out, September 17, 1971.
Times (London), September 6, 1984, November 25, 1984.
Times Literary Supplement, October 27, 1972, November 9, 1973, May 31, 1974, May 7, 1976, June 30, 1978, July 3, 1981, September 7, 1984.
Village Voice, March 2, 1982.
Virginia Quarterly Review, spring, 1975.
Washington Post Book World, March 21, 1982, December 23, 1984.

—*Sketch by Thomas Wiloch*

*   *   *

MOORE, Clayton
See BRANDNER, Gary

*   *   *

MOORE, Rayburn Sabatzky   1920-

PERSONAL: Born May 26, 1920, in Helena, Ark.; son of Max Sabatzky (a wholesale grocer) and Sammie Lou (Rayburn) Moore; married Margaret Elizabeth Bear, August 30, 1947; children: Margaret Elizabeth, Robert Rayburn. *Education:* Hendrix College, A.A., 1940; Vanderbilt University, A.B., 1942, M.A., 1947; Duke University, Ph.D., 1956. *Religion:* Presbyterian.

ADDRESSES: Home—106 St. James Dr., Athens, Ga. 30606. *Office*—Department of English, 130 Park Hall, University of Georgia, Athens, Ga. 30602.

CAREER: Interstate Grocer Co., Helena, Ark., vice-president, 1947-50; Hendrix College, Conway, Ark., 1954-59, began as assistant professor, became professor of English; University of Georgia, Athens, associate professor, 1959-65, professor of English, 1965—, director of graduate studies in English, 1964-69, chairman of American Studies Program, 1968—, chairman of Division of Language and Literature, 1975—. *Military service:* U.S. Army, 1942-46; served in Pacific Theater; became captain.

MEMBER: Modern Language Association of America (member of executive committee, General Topics VI, 1972-74), Poe Studies Association, South Atlantic Modern Language Association (member of executive council, 1975-77), Southeastern American Studies Association, Southern Historical Association, Society for the Study of Southern Literature (member of executive council, 1968, 1974-80; vice-president, 1981-82; president, 1983-84), Virginia Historical Society, Phi Beta Kappa.

WRITINGS:

Constance Fenimore Woolson, Twayne, 1963.

(Editor) Constance Fenimore Woolson, *"For the Major" and Selected Short Stories of Constance Fenimore Woolson,* College & University Press, 1967.
Paul Hamilton Hayne, Twayne, 1972.
(Editor) *A Man of Letters in the Nineteenth-Century South: Selected Letters of Paul Hamilton Hayne,* Louisiana State University Press, 1982.
(Senior editor) *A History of Southern Literature,* Louisiana State University Press, 1985.

CONTRIBUTOR

Essays in Honor of Walter Clyde Curry, Vanderbilt University Press, 1954.
Paul J. Carter and George K. Smart, editors, *Literature and Society: A Selective Bibliography,* University of Miami Press, 1967.
Louis D. Rubin, Jr., editor, *A Bibliographical Guide to the Study of Southern Literature,* Louisiana State University Press, 1969.
Edward James and others, editors, *Notable American Women, 1607-1950,* two volumes, Harvard University Press, 1971.
James Woodress and others, editors, *Essays Mostly on Periodical Publishing in America: A Collection in Honor of Clarence Gohdes,* Duke University Press, 1973.
James B. Meriwether, editor, *South Carolina Journals and Journalists,* Southern Studies Program, University of South Carolina, 1975.
Rubin and C. Hugh Holman, editors, *Southern Literary Study: Problems and Possibilities,* University of North Carolina Press, 1975.
J. Albert Robbins, editor, *American Literary Manuscripts,* 2nd edition (Moore was not associated with earlier edition), University of Georgia Press, 1977.
Gerald Nemanic, editor, *A Bibliographical Guide to Midwestern Literature,* University of Iowa Press, 1979.
Joel Myerson, editor, *Dictionary of Literary Biography,* Volume III: *Antebellum Writers in New York and the South,* Gale, 1979.
James Vinson, editor, *Writers of the English Language,* three volumes, St. Martin's Press, 1979.
Rubin and others, editors, *A Biographical Guide to Southern Literature,* Louisiana State University Press, 1979.
Kenneth Coleman and Charles S. Gurr, editors, *Dictionary of Georgia Biography,* two volumes, University of Georgia Press, 1983.
Edward Chielens, editor, *American Literary Magazines: The Eighteenth and Nineteenth Centuries,* Greenwood Press, 1985.
Robert Bain and Joseph Flora, editors, *Fifty Southern Authors before 1900,* Greenwood Press, 1985.

OTHER

Contributor of articles and book reviews to scholarly and critical journals.

WORK IN PROGRESS: Henry James's Letters to Edmund Gosse: A Selected Edition; a long article on Henry James and Constance F. Woolson; a long sketch of Paul Hamilton Hayne as a critic.

*   *   *

MORONEY, John R.   1939-

PERSONAL: Born January 29, 1939, in Dallas, Tex.; son of John R. (a lawyer) and Irene (Lewis) Moroney; married Margaret Kearny, May 30, 1959; children: John, Stephen, Helen,

Michael. *Education:* Southern Methodist University, B.A., 1960; Duke University, Ph.D., 1964.

ADDRESSES: Home—2105 Briar Oaks, Bryan, Tex. 77802. *Office*—Department of Economics, Texas A & M University, College Station, Tex. 77843.

CAREER: Florida State University, Tallahassee, assistant professor of economics, 1964-66; Michigan State University, East Lansing, associate professor of economics, 1966-69; Tulane University, New Orleans, La., professor of economics, 1969-81; Texas A & M University, College Station, professor of economics and chairman of department, 1981—. Visiting professor of economics, Massachusetts Institute of Technology, 1975-76.

MEMBER: American Economic Association, Royal Economic Society, Econometric Society, Southern Economic Association.

AWARDS, HONORS: Relm Foundation fellow, 1966; Institute of Public Utilities fellowship, 1968; Social Science Research Council faculty research fellow, 1969; National Science Foundation, faculty research grant, 1975-76, grant for research applied to national needs, 1976-78.

WRITINGS:

The Structure of Production in American Manufacturing, University of North Carolina Press, 1972.

EDITOR

Income Inequality: Trends and International Comparisons, Lexington Books, 1979.
Economic Aspects of New Technology, JAI Press, 1980.
Formal Models of Energy and Resources, JAI Press, 1982.
Econometric Models of the Demand for Energy, JAI Press, 1984.

OTHER

Contributor of articles to numerous journals, including *Journal of Political Economy, Southern Economic Journal, Journal of Money, Credit, and Banking, Western Economic Journal, American Economic Review, Economic Journal, International Economic Review,* and *Bell Journal of Economics.*

WORK IN PROGRESS: Study of production relations among capital, labor, and natural resources; study of the growth and cyclical stability of the American economy; study of income distribution and earnings of men and women in capitalistic and socialistic economies; study of formal models of the demand for and supply of natural resources (energy components and nonfuel materials).

*   *   *

MORRIS, Suzanne   1944-

PERSONAL: Born January 27, 1944, in Houston, Tex.; daughter of Frank M. (a commercial artist) and Ruth (McMickle) Page; married J. C. Morris (a company president), August 17, 1963; children: Quentin Phillip. *Education:* Attended University of Houston, 1962-64. *Religion:* Episcopalian.

ADDRESSES: Home—4819 Woodford, Baytown, Tex.

CAREER: Writer. Lecturer; has participated in numerous university seminars and workshops.

AWARDS, HONORS: First novel award from critic Evelyn Oppenheimer, 1976, and Literary East Texas Award, 1979, both for *Galveston.*

WRITINGS:

Galveston (novel), Doubleday, 1976.
Keeping Secrets (novel), Doubleday, 1979.
Skychild (novel), Doubleday, 1981.
The Browns of Ashton Villa: A Six Part History, Ashton Villa, 1981.

WORK IN PROGRESS: A novel about Houston, 1887-1960.

SIDELIGHTS: Suzanne Morris wrote *CA:* "My editor at Doubleday once assured me as I struggled to make time for continued writing at a difficult period in my life, 'You are a writer; you will write.' How true I find that statement, yet chilling in a way. Writing is a compulsive activity. The only thing harder than writing is not writing. Perhaps it is difficult to know when one has no more fresh stories to tell."

*   *   *

MOSS, John   1940-

PERSONAL: Born February 7, 1940, in Blair, Ontario, Canada; son of George F. (a poet and businessman) and Mary (Clare) Moss; married Virginia Lavin (a psychologist), May 29, 1965; children: Julie, Laura. *Education:* University of Western Ontario, B.A., 1961, M.A., 1969; University of Waterloo, M.Phil., 1970; University of New Brunswick, Ph.D., 1973.

ADDRESSES: Home—Bellrock R.R.1, Verona, Ontario, Canada K0H 2W0.

CAREER: Royal Shakespeare Company, London, England, technician, 1962; Canadian Broadcasting Corp. (CBC), Toronto, Ontario, studio director, 1963-64; high school teacher of English in Toronto, Ontario, 1965-67; University of Waterloo, Waterloo, Ontario, lecturer in English, 1969; Concordia University, Montreal, Quebec, associate professor of English, 1973-76; University of British Columbia, Vancouver, visiting professor of English, 1977-78; Queen's University, Kingston, Ontario, associate professor of English, 1978-80; University of Ottawa, Ottawa, Ontario, professor of English, 1980—. Founder and managing editor of *Journal of Canadian Fiction,* 1972-76.

MEMBER: Writers' Union of Canada, Association of Canadian University Teachers of English, Association of Canadian and Quebec Literatures.

AWARDS, HONORS: Canada Council fellowship, 1971-72, 1972-73; Ontario Arts Council grants.

WRITINGS:

Patterns of Isolation (criticism), McClelland & Stewart, 1974.
The Ancestral Present: Sex and Violence in the Canadian Novel, McClelland & Stewart, 1977.
(Editor and author of introduction) *Here and Now* (criticism), NC Press, 1978.
(Editor and author of introduction) *Beginnings* (criticism), NC Press, 1980.
A Reader's Guide to the Canadian Novel (criticism), McClelland & Stewart, 1981.
Modern Times (criticism), NC Press, 1982.
Bellrock (autobiography), NC Press, 1983.
Present Tense (criticism), NC Press, 1985.

Contributor of articles and reviews to literary journals.

WORK IN PROGRESS: A study of language, consciousness, and literary expression.

SIDELIGHTS: John Moss told *CA:* "Literary criticism is a creative process. Criticism concerned with a national literature is a political act. To be socially responsible, the critic must be a revolutionary. The critic must be a poet, an artist, for the peace of his own mind. It helps me to live in a hand-built log house on an island with my wife and daughters and a variety of animals. The most important thing I've written is the story of Bellrock, and how we've made it home."

Of Moss's book *Bellrock,* William French writes in the *Globe and Mail,* "John Moss has invented a new literary genre with *Bellrock.* It could be called the self-interview-while-driving, and kind of auto-biography, or two-cylinder memoir." Moss wrote the book during a long drive from Kingston, Ontario, to Vancouver, British Columbia, recording it on a tape recorder. "A kind of free-form rambling," observes French, "it's intensely personal and self-indulgent." He adds, "If there is a coherent theme in [*Bellrock*], it's metamorphosis: everything evolves into something else, sometimes for the better, sometimes not."

BIOGRAPHICAL/CRITICAL SOURCES:

PERIODICALS

Globe and Mail (Toronto), January 14, 1984.

*   *   *

MOSSMAN, Jennifer 1944-

PERSONAL: Born September 8, 1944, in Melksham, England; came to the United States in 1951, naturalized citizen in 1956; daughter of Joseph and Ella (Piper) Berger; married Richard Mossman (an attorney), January 2, 1978. *Education:* University of Michigan, B.A., 1966, M.L.S., 1968.

ADDRESSES: Office—Gale Research Co., Book Tower, Detroit, Mich. 48226.

CAREER: San Francisco Public Library, San Francisco, Calif., librarian, 1968-69; Eastern Michigan University, Ypsilanti, librarian, 1970-72; Gale Research Co., Detroit, Mich., assistant editor, 1973-77, associate editor, 1977-79, editor, 1979—.

WRITINGS:

(Associate editor) *Eponyms Dictionaries Index,* Gale, 1977, supplement (editor with James A. Ruffner), 1984.
(Editor) *Pseudonyms and Nicknames Dictionary,* Gale 1980, 2nd edition, 1982, inter-edition supplements published as *New Pseudonyms and Nicknames,* 1981 and 1983.
(Editor with Donna Wood) *Business Firms Master Index,* Gale, 1985.

WORK IN PROGRESS: Editing the 4th edition of *Encyclopedia of Geographic Information Sources.*

*   *   *

MOULY, George J(oseph) 1915-

PERSONAL: Born September 16, 1915, in Saskatchewan, Canada; came to the United States in 1947, naturalized in 1955; son of Paul J. and Louise (France) Mouly; married Gertrude M. Dubois, August 20, 1940; children: Paul, Michael, Eileen. *Education:* University of Saskatchewan, B.A., 1945, B.Ed., 1946, M.Ed., 1947; University of Minnesota, Ph.D., 1949.

ADDRESSES: Home—8121 Erwin Rd., Coral Gables, Fla. 33143. *Office*—Department of Educational Psychology, University of Miami, Coral Gables, Fla.

CAREER: Saskatchewan Public Schools, teacher and principal, 1934-42; University of Saskatchewan, Saskatoon, instructor in mathematics, 1946-47; University of Miami, Coral Gables, Fla., 1949—, began as director of testing bureau, professor of education, 1956—, chairman of department of educational psychology, 1968-70. *Military service:* Canadian Army, 1942-44; became lieutenant.

MEMBER: American Psychological Association, American Educational Research Association, Phi Delta Kappa.

WRITINGS:

Psychology for Effective Teaching, Holt, 1960, 4th edition published as *Psychology for Teaching,* Allyn & Bacon, 1982.
(With L. E. Walton) *Test Items in Education,* McGraw, 1962.
The Science of Educational Research, American Book Co., 1963, 3rd edition published as *Educational Research: The Art and Science of Investigation,* Allyn & Bacon, 1978.
(Editor) *Readings in Educational Psychology,* Holt, 1971.

AVOCATIONAL INTERESTS: Reading, sports.†

*   *   *

MOWRY, George E(dwin) 1909-1984

PERSONAL: Born September 5, 1909, in Washington, D.C.; died May 12, 1984; son of James Reilly and Ibby (Green) Mowry; married La Verne Raasch, 1938. *Education:* Miami University, A.B., 1933; University of Wisconsin, M.A., 1934, Ph.D., 1938.

ADDRESSES: Office—Department of History, University of North Carolina, Chapel Hill, N.C. 27514.

CAREER: University of North Carolina at Chapel Hill, assistant professor, 1938-42; Mills College, Oakland, Calif., May Treat Morrison Professor of American History, 1944-47; University of Iowa, Iowa City, professor, 1947-50; University of California, Los Angeles, professor of American history, 1951-67, chairman of history department, 1955-56 and 1958-67, dean of social sciences, 1959-67; University of North Carolina at Chapel Hill, Kenan Professor of American History, 1967-84. Harmsworth Professor, Oxford University, 1960-61. Visiting professor, summers, at University of Strasbourg, 1950-51, University of Rennes, 1951, Hebrew University of Jerusalem, 1953-54, University of Marseilles, Nice, 1958, University of Wisconsin, University of California, Western Reserve University (now Case Western Reserve University), and Columbia University. Lecturer on American history in Italy, Japan, and India. Policy analyst for Army Q.M. Corps and W.P.B., 1942-44.

MEMBER: American Association of University Professors, American Historical Association, Society of American Historians (fellow), Organization of American Historians (president, 1965), Mississippi Valley Historical Society, Sigma Alpha Epsilon.

AWARDS, HONORS: Silver Literary Medal, California Commonwealth Club, 1946, 1956, 1959; M.A., Oxford University, 1961.

WRITINGS:

Theodore Roosevelt and the Progressive Movement, University of Wisconsin Press, 1946.
The California Progressives, University of California Press, 1951.
(With John Donald Hicks) *A Short History of American Democracy,* Houghton, 1956, 3rd edition published as *A History of American Democracy,* 1966.
The Era of Theodore Roosevelt: 1900-1912, Harper, 1958.
(With Hicks) *The American Nation,* Houghton, 1963.
(Editor) *The Twenties: Fords, Flappers, and Fanatics,* Prentice-Hall, 1963.
The Federal Union, Houghton, 1964.
(Editor with Judson A. Grenier) David Graham Phillips, *The Treason of the Senate,* Quadrangle, 1964.
The Urban Nation: 1920-1960, Hill & Wang, 1965.
Another Look at the Twentieth-Century South, Louisiana State University Press, 1972.
The Progressive Era, 1900-1920: The Reform Persuasion, American Historical Association, 1972.

Also contributor to *War as a Social Institution,* 1941, and co-author of *American Society and the Changing World,* 1942. Member of editorial board, *Mississippi Valley Historical Review,* 1949.

BIOGRAPHICAL/CRITICAL SOURCES:

PERIODICALS

Times Literary Supplement, February 8, 1968.
University Bookman, autumn, 1967.†

*   *   *

MOYLES, R(obert) Gordon   1939-

PERSONAL: Born June 5, 1939, in Newfoundland, Canada; married Ada K. Brown; children: Robert, Kathy, Susan. *Education:* Memorial University of Newfoundland, B.A. (education), 1962, B.A. (with honors), 1965, M.A., 1967; University of London, Ph.D., 1969.

ADDRESSES: Home—3904 117th St., Edmonton, Alberta, Canada T6J 1T1. *Office*—University of Alberta, Edmonton, Alberta, Canada.

CAREER: University of Alberta, Edmonton, professor of English literature, 1969—, associate chairman of department of English, 1975-79, associate dean of arts, 1979—.

MEMBER: Canadian Association of University Teachers, Association of Canadian University Teachers of English.

AWARDS, HONORS: Canada Council awards, 1967-69, 1974-75.

WRITINGS:

(Contributor) Carl F. Klinck, editor, *Literary History of Canada,* University of Toronto Press, 1965, revised edition, 1976.
English-Canadian Literature: A Student Guide and Annotated Bibliography, Athabascan Publishing, 1972.
"*Complaints Is Many and Various, but the Odd Divil Likes It*": *Nineteenth-Century Views of Newfoundland,* Peter Martin Associates, 1975.
English-Canadian Literature to 1900, Gale, 1976.
(Editor) *From Duck Lake to Dawson City: The Diary of Eben McAdam's Journey to the Klondike, 1898-1899,* Prairie Book, 1977.

The Blood and Fire in Canada: A History of the Salvation Army, 1882-1976, Peter Martin Associates, 1977.
British Law and Arctic Men, Prairie Book, 1979.
(Co-editor) *From Instruction to Delight: An Anthology of Children's Literature to 1850,* Oxford University Press, 1982.
Words, Sentences, Paragraphs, Essays, Holt, 1982.
On Editing Paradise Lost: A Study in Editorial Procedure, University of Toronto Press, 1985.

General editor of *The Collected Works of E. J. Pratt.* Associate editor of *Modernist Studies;* managing editor of *English Studies in Canada.*

WORK IN PROGRESS: Research on immigrant views in Canadian children's literature.

AVOCATIONAL INTERESTS: "Fly-fishing with a Silver Doctor appetizingly skimming the surface of an inland British Columbia lake."

*   *   *

MRABET, Mohammed
See el HAJJAM, Mohammed ben Chaib

*   *   *

MULESKO, Angelo
See OGLESBY, Joseph

*   *   *

MULLEN, Edward John, Jr.   1942-

PERSONAL: Born July 12, 1942, in Hackensack, N.J.; son of Edward John (an accountant) and Elsie (Powell) Mullen; married Helen Braley (a cellular immunologist), April 3, 1971. *Education:* West Virginia Wesleyan College, B.A. (magna cum laude), 1964; Northwestern University, M.A., 1965, Ph.D., 1968.

ADDRESSES: Home—207 Edgewood Ave., Columbia, Mo. 65201. *Office*—Department of Romance Languages, University of Missouri, Columbia, Mo. 65211.

CAREER: Purdue University, Lafayette, Ind., assistant professor of modern languages, 1967-71; University of Missouri—Columbia, associate professor, 1971-77, professor of Romance languages, 1977—.

MEMBER: American Association of Teachers of Spanish and Portuguese, Modern Language Association of America.

WRITINGS:

La Revista contemporaneos: Seleccion y prologo, Editorial Anaya, 1972.
Encuentro: Ensayos de la actualidad, Holt, 1974.
Lecturas Basicas: A Literary Reader, Holt, 1976, 2nd edition (with G. Castillo-Felin), 1977.
Carlos Pellicer, Twayne, 1977.
Langston Hughes in the Hispanic World, Archon Books, 1977.
Carlos Pellicer: Interpretaciones Criticas, Universidad Nacional Autonoma, 1979.
El Cuento hispanico, Random House, 1980, 2nd edition, 1984.
The Life and Poems of a Cuban Slave: Juan Francisco Manzano 1797-1854, Archon Books, 1981.
Critical Essays on Langston Hughes, G. K. Hall, in press.

Contributor of articles and reviews to language and drama journals.

WORK IN PROGRESS: Various essays on Afro-Cuban literature.

* * *

MUNSEY, Cecil (Richard, Jr.) 1935-
(C. Richardson)

PERSONAL: Born May 21, 1935, in Portsmouth, N.H.; son of Cecil Richard (a ship repairer) and Alma (Northup) Munsey; married Dolores Jean Murray (an elementary school teacher), February 18, 1965; children: Cecil Richard III. *Education:* Attended Sacramento City College (now Sacramento Community College), 1956-58; San Diego State College (now University), A.B., 1962, Teaching Credential, 1963, M.A., 1969; United States International University, Ph.D., 1973.

ADDRESSES: Home—13541 Willow Run Rd., Poway, Calif. 92064. *Office*—Munsey Enterprises and Accelerated Worldwide Moving, Inc., 4452 Park Blvd., Suite 309, San Diego, Calif. 92116-4039; and San Diego County Office of Education, 6401 Linda Vista Rd., San Diego, Calif. 92111-7399.

CAREER: San Diego City Schools, San Diego, Calif., elementary school teacher, 1963-66, teacher of gifted elementary school children, 1966-69, teacher in model school program, 1970-71, curriculum resource teacher for gifted secondary school students, 1971-74; San Diego County Office of Education, San Diego, coordinator of Community Educational Resources, 1974-78, coordinator of Leadership Development Center, 1979-83, coordinator of Planning, Research and Evaluation, 1983—. President, Munsey Enterprises and Accelerated Worldwide Moving, Inc., both San Diego, both 1984—. Writer, photographer and editor, 1968—; partner, Nostalgia Publishing Co., Hackensack, N.J., 1978—; Rancho Bernardo Spirits Shop, San Diego, proprietor, 1978-83, secretary/treasurer, 1983—; partner, Video Games Plus, San Diego and Orange Counties, 1981-84; general partner, REM Associates (does business as Plaza Wash), Vista, Calif. Adjunct professor of education, Alfred North Whitehead College, University of Redlands, 1976-79. Historical glass consultant, Owens-Illinois Glass Co., 1973-74. Commentator for weekly radio program "Let's Talk about Antiques," KFSD-FM, 1975-76. *Military service:* U.S. Air Force, 1954-58.

MEMBER: National Education Association, National Association for Gifted Children, Association for the Gifted, U.S. International University Doctoral Society, Authors Guild, Authors League of America, America Cetacean Society, American Revenue Association, National Association of Newsletter Editors, American Institute of the History of the Pharmacy, Owens-Illinois Historical Bottle Collectors Guild (director), Federation of Historical Bottle Clubs, National Writers' Club, Les Amis du Vin, Society of Wine Educators, National Liquor Stores Association, Society to Preserve and Encourage Radio Drama, Variety, and Comedy, Toastmasters International, Americans for Wine, Popular Culture Association/West, Household Goods Forwarders Association of America, National Moving and Storage Association, California Household Goods Forwarders Association, California Retail Liquor Dealers Association, California Teachers Association, Association of California School Administrators, California Association for the Gifted (member at large), San Diego Teachers Association, Association of San Diego Educators for the Gifted, San Diego Association for the Gifted Children, San Diego County Office of Education Management Association, San Diego State University Alumni Association, San Diego His-

torical Society, San Diego Zoological Society, Green Valley Civic Association, Rancho Bernardo Chamber of Commerce (founding board member), Phi Delta Kappa.

AWARDS, HONORS: Valley Forge Teachers Medal from Freedoms Foundation, 1965; Distinguished Cub Scout Leader Award from Boy Scouts of America, 1967.

WRITINGS:

Handbook for Elementary Principals and Teachers of Programs for the Gifted, San Diego City Schools, 1968.
Would You Believe: A Compilation of Unusual Facts Pertaining to Bottle Collecting, Neyenesch, 1968.
(With Millicent Holmberg) *Handbook and Price Guide to Avon Bottles*, Western World, 1969.
(Self-illustrated) *The Illustrated Guide to Collecting Bottles* (Book-of-the-Month Club and Better Homes and Gardens Book Club selection), Hawthorn, 1970.
(Self-illustrated) *The Illustrated Guide to the Collectibles of Coca-Cola*, Hawthorn, 1972.
(Co-author) *Resource Directory for Teachers of the Gifted*, San Diego City Schools, 1973.
Disneyana: Walt Disney Collectibles (Better Homes and Gardens Book Club selection), Hawthorn, 1974.
(Co-author) *Mentally Gifted Minors Program Models*, California Association for the Gifted, 1976.
Price Guide to Collectibles of Coca-Cola, Nostalgia Publishing, 1980.

Author of brochures and curriculum materials for San Diego City Schools. Contributor of several hundred articles to professional journals, occasionally under pseudonym C. Richardson. Editor, *Bottleneck*, 1966-68, *National Bottle Gazette*, 1968-69, *Western Collector*, 1968-70, *USIU Doctoral Society Journal* (of U.S. International University Doctoral Society), 1970-71, *Human Behavior Research Journal*, 1971-72, *Programs for the Gifted Bulletin*, 1971-73, *Journal of the Federation of Historical Bottle Clubs*, 1972-77, and *CAG Communicator* (of California Association for the Gifted), 1973-77. Book review editor, *Old Bottle Magazine*, 1972-83; antique bottles price guide editor, *Antique Trader*; Coca-Cola memorabilia editor, *Bottle News*, 1976-78.

WORK IN PROGRESS: That Disease Called Collecting; Corporate Collectibles; Interviewing Successfully for a School Principalship (and Other Jobs in Educational Administration).

SIDELIGHTS: Cecil Munsey wrote *CA:* "I began serious writing after discovering that a book is merely an organized collection of articles called chapters. I write to relax—it's a hobby with me. I have an ever-changing variety of activities that keep me from making my avocation of writing my vocation. Life is probably not worth living if one only exists from day to day with no challenges and/or excitement. Boredom would seem a form of death to me.

"The surname Munsey is not an unfamiliar one to the world of letters. Frank Andrew Munsey, my great-uncle, is well-remembered in history books as owner of one of the three most important newspaper chains around the turn of the century. Uncle Frank also published a wide variety of periodicals throughout his forty-year career and can be given credit for helping numerous now-famous writers during the early stages of their careers. He has been a big influence on my various careers and a main reason for my lasting interest in writing history.

"My histories for collectors have guided the development of several hobby groups and are well-recognized reference works both nationally and internationally."

AVOCATIONAL INTERESTS: Photography, swimming, running, hiking, bicycling, tennis, sailing, collecting antiques.

BIOGRAPHICAL/CRITICAL SOURCES:

BOOKS

Deming, Bonnie J., *The San Diego Gifted and Talented Education Program,* San Diego City Schools, 1984.
Sanderlin, Owenita, *Creative Teaching,* A. S. Barnes, 1971.
Sanderlin, Owenita, *Teaching Gifted Children,* A. S. Barnes, 1973.

*   *   *

MURRAY, Donald M(orison) 1924-

PERSONAL: Born September 16, 1924, in Boston, Mass.; son of John William and Jean Edith (Smith) Murray; married Ellen Pinkham, January, 1946 (divorced, 1948); married Minnie Mae Emmerich, December 28, 1951; children: Anne, Lee, Hannah. *Education:* University of New Hampshire, A.B., 1948; Boston University, additional study, 1949-51.

ADDRESSES: Home—39 Mill Pond Rd., Durham, N.H. 03824. *Office*—Department of English, University of New Hampshire, Durham, N.H. 03824.

CAREER: Boston Herald, Boston, Mass., reporter, 1948-51; editorial writer, 1951-54; *Time,* New York, N.Y., contributing editor, 1954-56; full-time free-lance writer, 1956-63; University of New Hampshire, Durham, professor of English, 1963—, chairman of department, 1975-77. Instructor in journalism, Boston University, 1953-54. Conductor of weekly book review program, WENH-TV, 1964—. *Military service:* U.S. Army, Airborne Division, 1943-46.

MEMBER: National Council of Teachers of English, American Association of University Professors.

AWARDS, HONORS: New England award from Associated Press, 1951; Pulitzer Prize for editorial writing, 1954.

WRITINGS:

Man against Earth, Lippincott, 1961.
The Man Who Had Everything (novel), New American Library, 1964.
The World of Sound Recording, Lippincott, 1965.
A Writer Teaches Writing: A Practical Method of Teaching Composition, Houghton, 1968, 2nd edition, 1985.
(With T. W. Wong) *Noodle Words,* Tuttle, 1971.
Learning by Teaching: Selected Articles on Writing and Teaching, Boynton Cook, 1982.
Writing for Your Readers, Globe Pequot, 1983.
Write to Learn, Holt, 1984.
Read to Write, Holt, 1985.

Also author of two books under an undisclosed pseudonym; ghost writer of several books.

Contributor of several hundred magazine articles to various periodicals.

WORK IN PROGRESS: Textbooks and a novel.

MUSAPHIA, Joseph 1935-

PERSONAL: Surname is pronounced Muss-*afe*-ee-a; born April 8, 1935, in London, England; son of Solomon (a tailor) and Lillian (a dressmaker; maiden name, Rubens) Musaphia; married Marie Beder, 1966; children: Grant Harry, Leanne. *Education:* Attended boys' high school in Christchurch, New Zealand.

ADDRESSES: Home—75 Monro St., Wellington 3, New Zealand. *Agent*—Playmarket, P.O. Box 9767, Wellington, New Zealand.

CAREER: Shop assistant in Christchurch, New Zealand, 1950-51; mechanic in Christchurch, New Zealand, 1951-54; Stuart Wearn, Christchurch, New Zealand, commercial artist, 1954-55; Wood & Braddock, Wellington, New Zealand, commercial artist, 1955; John Haddon, London, England, commercial artist, 1956-57; commercial artist for agencies in Wellington, New Zealand, 1958-60; playwright, 1960—. Writer for television series "Joe's World" and "In View of Circumstances." Owner of restaurant in Wellington, New Zealand, 1971-73. Performed in television revues.

MEMBER: International P.E.N., Actors Equity Association.

AWARDS, HONORS: Grants from New Zealand Literary Fund, 1963, and New Zealand Arts Council, 1974, 1976; writing fellowship at Victoria University of Wellington, 1979; New Zealand Arts Council special projects grant.

WRITINGS:

PUBLISHED PLAYS

The Guerilla (one-act; first produced in Sydney, Australia, at Hayes Gordon's Ensemble Theatre, 1968), Currency Press, 1976.
Mothers and Fathers (three-act; first produced in Wellington, New Zealand, at Fortune Theatre, 1975), Currency Press, 1977.

UNPUBLISHED PLAYS

"Free" (one-act), first produced in Wellington at Memorial Theatre, 1962.
"Virginia Was a Dog" (one-act), first produced in Wellington at Stagecraft Theatre, 1968.
"Victims" (three-act), first produced in Wellington at Downstage Theatre, 1973.
"Obstacles" (two-act), first produced in Wellington at Downstage Theatre, 1974.
"Hunting" (two-act), first produced in Wellington at Circa Theatre, 1979.
"Shotgun Wedding," first produced in Wellington at Circa Theatre, 1980.
"The Hangman," first produced in Wellington at Depot Theatre, 1983.

OTHER

"Don't Let It Get You" (screenplay), Pacific Films, 1966.

Also author of more than a hundred radio plays, including "The Listener with the Pop-Up Toaster," "Think," "Has Anybody Here Seen Christmas?," "Jolly Roger," and "Sounds Furious."

Author of "By the Way," a column in *Wellington Dominion,* and "The Arts," a column in *Wellington Sunday Times,* both 1974—. Cartoonist for *New Zealand Listener,* 1958-60. Contributor to *Landfall 68, Act 20* and *Act 25.*

WORK IN PROGRESS—Plays: "Mates," a comedy on the theme of equal rights for women and men; "A Fair Go for Charlie Wellman," a comedy on contemporary morality; and "The Rub," a comedy on the contrast between dreams and "reality."

SIDELIGHTS: Joseph Musaphia writes: "I left school at the age of fifteen, which is the legal age one can leave. As Mark Twain said, 'My education began when I left school.'

"I cannot write anything that does not feature laughter, which I see as the best emotional release and the sharpest means of commenting on the foibles of human nature. I insist that the audience be the one to laugh at the onstage character, not at the actor, otherwise the actor loses the character and the audience, as well as the point I am presumptuous enough to think I am making. I genuinely try to say something 'serious' in my comedy, believing that the core of all comedy—all good comedy—is tragedy. Besides, an audience roaring with laughter is the sweetest sound in a theatre. In the world?"

* * *

MYRICK, Robert D(eWayne) 1935-

PERSONAL: Born May 13, 1935, in Wayne, Neb.; son of Wayne J. (a salesman) and Mary Ann (Roberts) Myrick; children: Mark, Susan, Karen, Kaylen. *Education:* Southern Oregon State College, B.S., 1957, M.S., 1961; Arizona State University, Ph.D., 1967.

ADDRESSES: Home—4108 Alpine Dr., Gainesville, Fla. 32605. *Office*—Department of Counselor Education, University of Florida, 1212 Norman Hall, Gainesville, Fla. 32611.

CAREER: Social studies teacher and dean of boys in high school in Phoenix, Ore., 1957-61; counselor in high school in Medford, Ore., 1963-65; University of Florida, Gainesville, assistant professor, 1967-70, associate professor, 1970-72, professor of education, 1972—. Visiting professor at Arizona State University, 1967, University of Miami, Coral Gables, 1969, and C. W. Post Center of Long Island University, 1983-85. Counselor, Upward Bound Program, Phoenix, Ariz., 1967; co-director of Drive-in Elementary School Guidance Conference, Gainesville, 1974, and National Elementary School Guidance and Counseling Conference, Tampa, 1974-75. Consultant to Division of College Programs, U.S. Office of Education, 1970—; consultant to numerous school systems in the United States, Canada, and overseas.

MEMBER: National Education Association, American Association for Counseling and Development (formerly American Personnel and Guidance Association; chairman of media committee, 1976-77), American School Counselors Association, Association for Counselor Education and Supervision, Florida Association for Counseling and Development (president, 1978-79), Florida Association for Practicing Psychologists, Florida Personnel and Guidance Association (member of executive board, 1977-79; president, 1978-79), Florida Association for Counselor Education and Supervision (member of executive committee, 1968-69; treasurer, 1969-70; member of board of directors, 1971-73), Northern Florida Personnel and Guidance Association (president, 1969-70), Phi Delta Kappa.

AWARDS HONORS: Florida Educational Research and Development grant, 1972; U.S. Office of Education grant, 1973; outstanding member award, Florida Personnel and Guidance Association, 1974-75; U.S. Department of Health, Education, and Welfare grant, 1976-77; outstanding service award, Florida Association of Counselor Educators and Supervisors, 1977-78; Texas Governor's Honorary Citizenship Award, 1978; Creative Leadership Award, University of Florida, 1979; outstanding service and leadership award, American School Counselor Association, 1980.

WRITINGS:

(With Joe Wittmer) *School Counseling: Problems and Methods,* Goodyear Publishing, 1972.

(Contributor) *The Status of Guidance and Counseling in the Nation's Schools,* American Personnel and Guidance Association, 1973.

(Contributor with R. Johnson) D. Dinkmeyer, *Developing Understanding of Self and Others,* American Guidance Service, 1973.

(With Wittmer) *Facilitative Teaching: Theory and Practice,* Goodyear Publishing, 1974, revised edition, Educational Media, 1980.

(With Johnson) *The Occupational Specialist in Florida* (monograph), Florida Department of Education, 1975.

Consultation as a Counselor Intervention (monograph), American School Counselors Association, 1977.

(With T. Errey) *Caring and Sharing: Becoming a Peer Facilitator,* Educational Media, 1978.

(With Errey) *Youth Helping Youth: A Handbook for Training Peer Facilitators,* Educational Media, 1978.

Children Helping Children, Educational Media, 1981.

Becoming a Friendly Helper, Educational Media, 1981.

Author, with Wittmer, of *The VEG: Does It Make a Difference?,* 1977; author of six monographs and two educational kits. Also author, with D. Sorenson, of five film scripts, including "Peer Facilitators: Youth Helping Youth," 1976, "Developmental Counseling in the Elementary School," 1976, "The Middle School Years: Guidance for Transition," 1977, and "Leading Group Discussion," 1977. Contributor to *The Florida Elementary School Counselor's Handbook,* 1979. Author of column "The Counselor's Workshop" in *Elementary School Guidance and Counseling Journal,* 1971-73. Contributor of over eighty articles to professional journals. *Elementary School Guidance and Counseling Journal,* member of editorial board, 1970-72, editor, 1972-78.

N

NAHAL, Chaman 1927-

PERSONAL: Born August 2, 1927, in Sialkot, India (now Pakistan); son of Gopal Das and Jamuna (Devi) Nahal; married Sudarshna Rani (a school principal), 1955; children: Ajanta (daughter), Anita. Education: Delhi University, M.A., 1948; University of Nottingham, Ph.D., 1961.

ADDRESSES: Home—2/1 Kalkaji Extension, New Delhi 110019, India. Office—Department of English, University of Delhi, Delhi 110007, India. Agent—John Farquharson Ltd., Bell House, Bell Yard, London WC2, England; and Paul R. Reynolds, 12 East 41st St., New York, N.Y. 10017.

CAREER: Delhi University, Institute of Postgraduate Studies, Delhi, India, 1963—, began as chairman of department of English, currently professor of English. Associate professor of English, Long Island University, 1968-70.

AWARDS, HONORS: British Council scholar, University of Nottingham, 1959-61; Fulbright fellow, Princeton University, 1967-68; Ford Foundation exchange visitor to the United States, 1974 and 1982; cultural exchange visitor to Australia, 1983; Sahitya Akademi (national academy of letters) awards and Federation of Indian Publishers' award for excellence in creative writing, 1977, both for Azadi; Federation of Indian Publishers Award, 1979, for The English Queens.

WRITINGS:

A Conversation with J. Krishnamurti, Arya, 1965.
The Weird Dance (short stories), Arya, 1965.
(Editor) Drugs and the Other Self, Harper, 1970.
D. H. Lawrence: An Eastern View, A. S. Barnes, 1970.
The Narrative Pattern in Ernest Hemingway's Fiction, Fairleigh Dickinson University Press, 1971.
My True Faces (novel), Hind Books, 1973.
Azadi (novel; title means "Freedom"), Houghton, 1975.
Into Another Dawn (novel), Sterling Publishers, 1977.
The English Queens (novel), Vision Books, 1979.
The Crown and the Loincloth (novel), Vikas, 1981.
The New Literatures in English, Allied Publishers, 1985.

WORK IN PROGRESS: A novel on the expatriate Indians, especially those settled in Fiji.

SIDELIGHTS: Chaman Nahal told CA: "My novel The Crown and the Loincloth offers the first-ever fictional account of Ma-hatma Gandhi and our freedom movement (long before the Attenborough film came out). I continue to remain preoccupied with the under-privileged. There is no room for the metaphysical novel these days. With millions living below the poverty line, the novelist owes it to himself and to his community to write about the social problems of his time.''

BIOGRAPHICAL/CRITICAL SOURCES:

BOOKS

Harrison, Barbara J., Learning about India, State University of New York Press, 1977.
Singh, Amritjit, Rajiva Verma, and Irene M. Joshi, editors, Indian Literature in English, 1827-1979: A Guide to Information Sources, Gale, 1981.

PERIODICALS

D. H. Lawrence Review, fall, 1971.

*   *   *

NAHAS, Gabriel G(eorges) 1920-

PERSONAL: Born March 4, 1920, in Alexandria, Egypt; came to United States in 1947, naturalized in 1962; son of Bishara and Gabrielle (Wolff) Nahas; married Marilyn Cashman, February 13, 1954; children: Michele, Anthony, Christiane. Education: University of Toulouse, B.A., 1937, M.D. (cum laude), 1944; University of Rochester, M.S., 1949; University of Minnesota, Ph.D., 1953.

ADDRESSES: Home—114 Chestnut St., Englewood, N.J. 07631. Office—630 West 168th St., New York, N.Y. 10032.

CAREER: Hospital Marie Lannelongue, Paris, France, chief of laboratory of experimental surgery, 1954-55; University of Minnesota, Minneapolis, assistant professor of physiology, 1955-57; Walter Reed Army Institute of Research, Department of Cardiorespiratory Disease, Washington, D.C., chief of respiratory section, 1957-59; George Washington University, Medical School, Washington, D.C., lecturer in physiology, 1957-59; Columbia University, College of Physicians and Surgeons, New York City, associate professor, 1959-62, professor of anesthesiology, 1962—, department director of research, 1959-62; Presbyterian Hospital, New York City, attending anesthesiologist, 1967—. Adjunct professor at Institute of Anesthesiology, University of Paris, 1968—. Mili-

tary service: French Underground, special agent, 1941-44; French Army, Medical Corps, 1944-45; became first lieutenant; received Presidential Medal of Freedom with gold palm, Legion of Honor, and Croix de Guerre with three palms.

MEMBER: Association des Pharmacologistes, Association des Physiologistes de Langue Francaise, American Physiological Society, American Heart Association (fellow; member of advisory board of Council on Circulation and Basic Sciences), American Society for Pharmacology and Experimental Therapeutics, American Society of Clinical Pharmacology, American Association for the Advancement of Science (fellow), National Hypertension Association (vice-chairman), British Pharmacological Society, Undersea Medical Society, National Research Council (member of committee on trauma, 1963-66), Cousteau Society (member of council of advisors), Harvey Society, New York Academy of Science (fellow), Sigma Xi.

AWARDS, HONORS: Member of Order of Orange Nassau, 1947, and Order of the British Empire, 1948; Fulbright scholar, 1966; silver medal from City of Paris, 1972; laureate, French Academy of Medicine, 1978; George Washington Medal of Freedom, 1981.

WRITINGS:

(Editor) *In Vitro and In Vivo Effects of Amine Buffers,* Annals of New York Academy of Science, 1961.
(Editor) *Regulation of Respiration,* Annals of New York Academy of Science, 1963.
(Editor with D. V. Bates) *Respiratory Failure,* Annals of New York Academy of Science, 1965.
(Editor) *Current Concepts of Acid-Base Measurements,* Annals of New York Academy of Science, 1966.
(Editor with Charles Fox) *Body Fluid Replacement in the Surgical Patient,* Grune, 1970.
(Editor with Alan Robison and Lubos Triner) *Cyclic AMP and Cell Function,* Annals of New York Academy of Science, 1973.
Marihuana: Deceptive Weed, Raven Press, 1973.
(Editor with Karl Schaeffer and Nicholas Chalazonitis) *CO2 and Metabolic Regulation,* Springer-Verlag, 1974.
Marihuana: Chemistry, Biochemistry, Cellular Effects, Springer-Verlag, 1976.
Keep off the Grass, Reader's Digest Press, 1976, revised edition, 1979.
Hashish, Cannabis, Marihuana, Presses Universitaires, 1976.
(Editor with W. D. M. Paton) *Marihuana: Biological Effects,* Pergamon, 1979.
Histoire du Hash, Laffont, 1979.
(Editor with H. C. Frick) *Drug Abuse in the Modern World,* Pergamon, 1981.
La Filiere du Rail, France-Empire, 1983.
Marihuana in Science and Medicine, Raven Press, 1984.
The Escape of the Genie: A History of Hashish throughout the Ages, Raven Press, 1985.
(With Andre Rojo) *Une Epidemie d'Amour,* France-Empire, 1985.

* * *

NASH, Father Stephen
See KAVANAUGH, James J(oseph)

* * *

NELSON, David Moir 1920-

PERSONAL: Born April 29, 1920, in Detroit, Mich.; son of James and Elizabeth (Dickie) Nelson; married Shirley Risburg, 1943; children: Amy, Benn, Eric. *Education:* University of Michigan, B.S., 1942, M.S., 1946, graduate study, 1948.

ADDRESSES: Home—114 Briar Lane, Newark, Del. *Office*—College of Physical Education, Athletics, and Recreation, University of Delaware, Newark, Del. 19716.

CAREER: Hillsdale College, Hillsdale, Mich., director of physical education and athletics, 1946-48; Harvard University, Cambridge, Mass., football backfield coach, 1948-49; University of Maine, Orono, head football coach, 1949-51; University of Delaware, Newark, professor of physical education, 1951-60, director of division of health, physical education and athletics, 1951—. *Military service:* U.S. Navy, over three years; became lieutenant; awarded Presidential Unit Citation with three battle stars.

MEMBER: National Collegiate Athletic Association (secretary of football rules committee, 1962; chairman of rules changes committee, 1959-60; member of Hall of Fame committee, 1959-62, editorial committee, 1960, and numerous other committees), American Football Coaches Association (trustee), National Association of College Directors, American Association of Health, Physical Education and Recreation, Eastern Collegiate Athletic Conference (member of executive council, 1951-53; vice-president, 1958-59; president, 1959-60), Middle Atlantic Athletic Conference (member of executive committee, 1954-56), Phi Kappa Phi.

WRITINGS:

(With Forest Evashevski) *Scoring Power with the Winged-T Offense,* W. C. Brown, 1957.
The Modern Winged-T Play Book, W. C. Brown, 1961.
Football: Principles and Play, Ronald, 1962.
(Contributor) *Championship Football by Twelve Great Coaches,* Prentice-Hall, 1962.
Illustrated Football Rules, Doubleday, 1976.

Also author of scripts and narration for National Collegiate Athletic Association films "Football Code," 1962, "Best Plays," 1963, "Monday Morning Quarterback," 1967, "Two Platoon Football," 1968, "Scrimmage Kick Rule," 1968, and "Pass Interference," 1973. Contributor to professional journals.

SIDELIGHTS: David Moir Nelson was coach of the North-South Shrine Game in 1959 and the All-American Bowl in 1960, 1961, and 1962. He has participated in one hundred sports clinics.

* * *

NELSON, James B(ruce) 1930-

PERSONAL: Born May 28, 1930, in Windom, Minn.; married Wilys Claire Coulter (a hospital chaplain), January 31, 1953; children: Stephen Joseph, Mary Elizabeth. *Education:* Macalester College, B.A. (summa cum laude), 1951; Yale University, B.D. (magna cum laude), 1957, M.A., 1959, Ph.D., 1962; postdoctoral study, Oxford University, 1969-70, and Cambridge University, 1976-77.

ADDRESSES: Office—United Theological Seminary of the Twin Cities, 3000 Fifth St. N.W., Brighton, Minn. 55112.

CAREER: Ordained Congregational minister, 1958; First Congregational Church, West Haven, Conn., assistant minister, 1957-59; First Congregational Church (United Church of Christ),

Vermillion, S.D., minister, 1960-63; United Theological Seminary of the Twin Cities, New Brighton, Minn., associate professor, 1963-68, professor of Christian ethics, 1968—. Visiting lecturer at Luther Theological Seminary, fall, 1966, Yale Divinity School, spring, 1969, and Hennepin County Medical Center, Minneapolis, 1974—; visiting professor at St. John's University, fall, 1968, University of Minnesota, 1972—, University of Minnesota Medical School, winter, 1973, spring, 1974, Iliff School of Theology, summer, 1980, and Vancouver School of Theology, summer, 1981. Member of board of directors, Sex Information and Education Council of the U.S. (SIECUS); member of Institute for Society, Ethics and the Life Sciences. *Military service:* U.S. Army, 1952-54.

MEMBER: American Academy of Religion, Society of Christian Ethics (member of board of directors), Society for the Scientific Study of Religion, Society for Values in Higher Education, Phi Gamma Mu.

AWARDS, HONORS: Distinguished Citizen Citation, Macalester College, 1982; S.T.D., Dickinson College, 1985.

WRITINGS:

The Responsible Christian, United Church Press, 1969.
Moral Nexus: Ethics of Christian Identity and Community, Westminster, 1971.
Human Medicine: Ethical Perspectives on New Medical Issues, Augsburg, 1973, revised and expanded edition (with JoAnne S. Rohricht), 1984.
Rediscovering the Person in Medical Care, Augsburg, 1976.
Embodiment: An Approach to Sexuality and Christian Theology, Augsburg, 1978.
Quality or Sanctity (booklet), Office for Church Life and Leadership, United Church of Christ, 1979.
Between Two Gardens: Reflections on Sexuality and Religious Experience, Pilgrim Press, 1983.

CONTRIBUTOR

Harvey Cox, editor, *The Situation Ethics Debate,* Westminster, 1968.
Human Sexuality: A Preliminary Study, United Church Press, 1977.
Warren Reich, editor, *Encyclopedia of Bio-Ethics,* Macmillan, 1978.
Edward Batchelor, editor, *Homosexuality and Ethics,* Pilgrim Press, 1980.
John M. Holland, editor, *Religion and Sexuality: Judaic-Christian Viewpoints in the U.S.A.,* Association of Sexologists, 1981.
John C. Gonsiorek, editor, *Homosexuality and Psychotherapy: A Practitioner's Handbook of Affirmative Models,* Haworth Press, 1982.
George Albee, Sol Gordon, and Harold Leitenberg, editors, *Promoting Sexual Responsibility and Preventing Sexual Problems,* University Press of New England, 1983.
James W. Maddock, Gerhard Neubeck, and Marvin B. Sussman, editors, *Human Sexuality and the Family,* Haworth Press, 1983.
(With Christine Gudorf and Wilson Yates) *The Annual of the Society of Christian Ethics, 1983,* Society of Christian Ethics, 1983.
Jane A. Boyajian, editor, *Ethical Issues and Ministry,* United Theological Seminary, 1984.
Justin M. Joffee, Albee, and Linda D. Kelly, editors, *Readings in Primary Prevention of Psychopathology,* University Press of New England, 1984.

James F. Childress, editor, *The Dictionary of Christian Ethics,* Westminster, 1985.
Rodney J. Hunter, editor, *The Dictionary of Pastoral Care and Counseling,* Abingdon, 1985.
Earl E. Shelp, editor, *Theology and Bioethics: Exploring the Foundations and Frontiers,* D. Reidel, 1985.

Also author of cassette tapes on theology and sexuality. Contributor of numerous reviews and articles to periodicals, including *Theology and Life, Philosophy Forum, U.S. Catholic, SIECUS Report, Theological Markings, Journal of Ecumenical Studies,* and *Religious Studies Review.*

*   *   *

NEWMAN, Joseph   1912-

PERSONAL: Born December 11, 1912, in Pittsfield, Mass.; son of Jacob and Ida (Greenburg) Newman; married Lucia Meza Barros, 1949; children: Lucia, Jr., Consuelo, Pia, Joseph, Jr. *Education:* Williams College, B.A., 1935.

ADDRESSES: Home and office—3204 Highland Place N.W., Washington, D.C. 20008.

CAREER: New York Herald Tribune, New York City, bureau chief in Tokyo, Japan, 1940-41, general reporter in New York City, 1942-43, bureau chief in Latin America, based in Buenos Aires, Argentina, 1943-46, in Moscow, U.S.S.R., 1947-49, in Berlin, Germany, 1949-50, in London, England, 1950-55, in Latin America, 1955-58, and at United Nations in New York City, 1958-62, member of editorial board, 1962-66; *U.S. News & World Report,* Washington, D.C., assistant to publishing director, 1966-67, co-founder and directing editor of Book Division, 1967-79; free-lance writer, editor, and book producer, 1979—. Creator, producer, and moderator of "Editorial Page Conference," a weekly program on Radio-Keith-Orpheum television stations, and a daily radio news program; television producer and interviewer for special documentary programs aired by American Broadcasting Co., Metromedia, and Educational Television Network; radio correspondent in Buenos Aires, Argentina.

MEMBER: National Press Club (Washington, D.C.), Overseas Press Club (New York City).

AWARDS, HONORS: Awards from Overseas Press Club, 1948-49, for correspondence from Moscow, from English-Speaking Union, 1953-54, for correspondence from London, and from Sigma Delta Chi, 1961, for series on Castro's Cuba; Guggenheim fellow, 1957.

WRITINGS:

Goodbye, Japan, L. B. Fischer, 1942.
Cuba S.S.R., New York Herald Tribune, 1961.
A New Look at Red China, U.S. News & World Report, 1971.
(Editor) Paul Watson and Warren Rogers, *Sea Shepherd: My Fight for Whales and Seals,* Norton, 1982.
(Editor) *Help Your Baby Build a Healthy Body,* Crown, 1984.

EDITOR; ALL PUBLISHED BY U.S. NEWS & WORLD REPORT

The United States on the Moon: What It Means to Us, 1969.
Social Security and Medicare Simplified: What You Get for Your Money, 1969.
Investments, Insurance, Wills Simplified: Planning for Your Family's Future, 1969, 2nd edition, 1972.
Inflation Simplified: What It Means to You, 1969.
Communism and the New Left: What They're Up to Now, 1969.

What Everyone Needs to Know about Drugs, 1970.
Good Things about the United States Today, 1970.
Our Poisoned Planet, 1970.
How to Buy Real Estate: Profits and Pitfalls, 1970.
U.S. News & World Report's Book on Income Taxes: How to Save Money and Avoid Trouble, 1971 edition, 1970, 1972 edition, 1972.
U.S. Politics: Inside and Out, 1970.
What Everyone Needs to Know about Law, 1971.
Wiring the World, 1971.
Guide to the '72 Elections, 1972, juvenile supplement, 1972.
Our Country (picture book), 1972.
Crime in America: Causes and Cures, 1972.
Teach Your Wife How to Be a Widow, 1973.
Two Hundred Years: A Bicentennial Illustrated History of the United States, two volumes, 1973.
Stocks, Bonds, Mutual Funds, 1973, revised edition, 1976.
A Bicentennial Portrait of the American People, 1973.
Famous Soviet Spies: The Kremlin's Secret Weapon, 1973.
How to Buy Insurance and Save Money, 1974.
How to Live with Inflation: A Guide to Saving Money When Buying, 1974.
(With Richard H. Rush and others) *Techniques of Becoming Wealthy,* 1977.
(With Eleanor Goldstein) *A Watch on World Affairs* (textbook), 1978.
(With Goldstein) *A Watch on the Economy* (textbook), 1978.
(With Goldstein) *A Watch on Government* (textbook), 1978.
(With Goldstein) Ann Gazourian and Marta Tarbell, *What Citizens Need to Know about Government,* revised edition, 1983.

SIDELIGHTS: Joseph Newman's assignments have included interviews with Fidel Castro, Juan Peron, Golda Meier, Madame Nhu, and Averell Harriman. In Buenos Aires he covered the rise and fall of Juan Peron; in Moscow, the cold war waged by Stalin; in Berlin, the Soviet attempt to expel the Western powers; in London, Winston Churchill's return to power; and at the United Nations, Khruschev's histrionics.

MEDIA ADAPTATIONS: Film rights to *Sea Shepherd: My Fight for Whales and Seals* have been sold to Warner Brothers.

*   *   *

NEWSOME, David Hay   1929-

PERSONAL: Born June 15, 1929, in Leamington Spa, England; married Joan Florence Trist, 1955; children: Clare, Janet, Louise, Cordelia. *Education:* Emmanuel College, Cambridge, B.A. and M.A. (with first class honors), 1954, Litt.D., 1976.

ADDRESSES: Home—The Retreat, Thornthwaite, Keswick, Cumbria, United Kingdom. *Office*—The Master, Wellington College, Crowthorne, Berkshire, England.

CAREER: Assistant history master at private boys school in Wellington, England, 1954-59, head of department, 1956-59; Cambridge University, Cambridge, England, fellow of Emmanuel College, 1959-70, senior tutor, 1965-70, assistant lecturer, 1961-66, lecturer in ecclesiastical history, 1966-70, Bishop Westcott Memorial Lecturer, 1968; Christ's Hospital, Horsham, England, headmaster, 1970-79; Wellington College, Crowthorne, Berkshire, England, master, 1980—. Gore Memorial Lecturer at Westminster Abbey, 1965; Birkbeck Lecturer at Cambridge University, 1972. *Military service:* Royal Army Education Corps, 1948-50; became captain.

MEMBER: Royal Historical Society (fellow), Royal Society of Literature (fellow), Athenaeum Club, Marylebone Cricket Club.

WRITINGS:

A History of Wellington College, 1859-1959, J. Murray, 1959.
Godliness and Good Learning: Four Studies in a Victorian Ideal, J. Murray, 1961.
The Parting of Friends: A Study of the Wilberforces and Henry Manning, J. Murray, 1966.
Two Classes of Men: Platonism and English Romantic Thought, J. Murray, 1974.
(Editor) *On the Edge of Paradise: A. C. Benson, the Diarist,* J. Murray, 1979.
(Editor) *Edwardian Excursions: Diaries of A. C. Benson, 1898-1902,* J. Murray, 1981.

Also author of *Bishop Westcott and the Platonic Tradition,* 1969. Contributor to history and theology journals.

AVOCATIONAL INTERESTS: Music, fell-walking.

BIOGRAPHICAL/CRITICAL SOURCES:

PERIODICALS

Times (London), July 10, 1980.
Times Literary Supplement, September 5, 1980, August 28, 1981.

*   *   *

NEWTON, D(wight) B(ennett)   1916-
(Dwight Bennett, Clement Hardin, Ford Logan, Hank Mitchum, Dan Temple)

PERSONAL: Born January 14, 1916, in Kansas City, Mo.; son of Otis L. and Grace (Thompson) Newton; married Mary Jane Kregel, 1941; children: Jennifer, Janet. *Education:* University of Kansas City, M.A., 1942.

ADDRESSES: Home—11 Northwest Kansas Ave., Bend, Ore. 97701.

CAREER: Full-time writer. *Military service:* U.S. Army, Corps of Engineers, 1942-46.

MEMBER: Western Writers of America (charter member; secretary-treasurer, 1953-58, 1967-71).

WRITINGS:

Guns of the Rimrock, Phoenix Press, 1946.
The Gunmaster of Saddleback, Phoenix Press, 1948.
Range Boss, Pocket Books, 1949.
Shotgun Guard, Lippincott, 1950.
Six-Gun Gamble, Lippincott, 1951.
Guns along the Wickiup, Gold Medal, 1953.
Rainbow Rider, Macdonald & Co., 1954.
The Outlaw Breed, Gold Medal, 1955.
Maverick Brand, Monarch, 1962.
On the Dodge, Berkley Publishing, 1962.
Guns of Warbonnet, Berkley Publishing, 1963.
The Savage Hills, Berkley Publishing, 1964.
Bullets on the Wind, Berkley Publishing, 1964.
Fury at Three Forks, Berkley Publishing, 1964.
The Manhunters, Berkley Publishing, 1966.
Hideout Valley, Berkley Publishing, 1967.
The Tabbart Brand, Berkley Publishing, 1967.
Shotgun Freighter, Berkley Publishing, 1968.
Wolf Pack, Berkley Publishing, 1968.

The Judas Horse, Berkley Publishing, 1969.
Syndicate Gun, Berkley Publishing, 1972.
Range Tramp, Berkley Publishing, 1973.
Massacre Valley, Curtis Books, 1973.
Bounty on Bannister, Berkley Publishing, 1975.
Trail of the Bear, Popular Library, 1975.
The Land Grabbers, Popular Library, 1975.
Broken Spur, Berkley Publishing, 1977.
Triple Trouble, Ace Books, 1978.

UNDER PSEUDONYM DWIGHT BENNETT

Stormy Range, Doubleday, 1951.
Lost Wolf River, Doubleday, 1952.
Border Graze, Doubleday, 1952.
Top Hand, Permabooks, 1955.
The Avenger, Permabooks, 1956.
Cherokee Outlet, Doubleday, 1961.
The Oregon Rifles, Doubleday, 1962.
Rebel Trail, Doubleday, 1963.
Crooked River Canyon, Doubleday, 1966.
Legend in the Dust, Doubleday, 1970.
The Big Land, Doubleday, 1972.
The Guns of Ellsworth, Doubleday, 1973.
The Cheyenne Encounter, Doubleday, 1976.
West of Railhead, Doubleday, 1977.
The Texans, Doubleday, 1979.
Disaster Creek, Doubleday, 1981.

UNDER PSEUDONYM CLEMENT HARDIN

Hellbent for a Hangrope, Ace Books, 1954.
Cross Me in Gunsmoke, Ace Books, 1957.
The Lurking Gun, Ace Books, 1961.
The Badge Shooters, Ace Books, 1962.
Outcast of Ute Bend, Ace Books, 1965.
The Ruthless Breed, Ace Books, 1966.
The Paxman Feud, Ace Books, 1967.
The Oxbow Deed, Ace Books, 1967.
Ambush Reckoning, Ace Books, 1968.
Sheriff of Sentinel, Ace Books, 1969.
Colt Wages, Ace Books, 1970.
Stage Line to Rincon, Ace Books, 1971.

UNDER PSEUDONYM FORD LOGAN

Fire in the Desert, Ballantine, 1954.

UNDER PSEUDONYM HANK MITCHUM; "STAGECOACH" SERIES

Stagecoach Station #1: Dodge City, Bantam, 1982.
. . . *#2: Laredo*, Bantam, 1982.
. . . *#4: Tombstone*, Bantam, 1983.
. . . *#6: Santa Fe*, Bantam, 1983.
. . . *#11: Deadwood*, Bantam, 1984.
. . . *#13: Carson City*, Bantam, 1984.
. . . *#20: Leadville*, Bantam, 1985.
. . . *#27: Tulsa*, Bantam, in press.

UNDER PSEUDONYM DAN TEMPLE

Outlaw River, Popular Library, 1955.
The Man from Idaho, Popular Library, 1956.
Bullet Lease, Popular Library, 1957.
Gun and Star, Monarch, 1964.

OTHER

Author of television scripts. Story consultant and staff writer for "Wagon Train," 1957, and "Death Valley Days," 1958.

NICHOLS, (John) Beverley   1898-1983

PERSONAL: Born September 9, 1898, in Bristol, England; died after a fall, September 15, 1983, in Kingston-upon-Thames, England; son of John (a solicitor) and Pauline (Shalders) Nichols. *Education:* Balliol College, Oxford, B.A., 1921.

ADDRESSES: Home—Sudbrook Cottage, Ham Common, Surrey, England.

CAREER: Journalist, novelist, playwright, and composer. Gossip columnist for *Sunday Chronicle*, London, England, for fourteen years; press correspondent in India, 1939-45.

MEMBER: Oxford Union Debating Society (president, c. 1922).

WRITINGS:

NOVELS

Prelude, Chatto & Windus, 1920.
Patchwork, Chatto & Windus, 1921, Holt, 1922.
Self, Chatto & Windus, 1922.
Crazy Pavements, G. H. Doran, 1927.
Evensong (also see below), Doubleday, 1932.
Revue, Doubleday, 1939.
Men Do Not Weep, J. Cape, 1941, Harcourt, 1942.
No Man's Street, Dutton, 1954.
The Moonflower Murder, Dutton, 1955 (published in England as *The Moonflower*, Hutchinson, 1955).
Death to Slow Music, Dutton, 1956.
The Rich Die Hard, Hutchinson, 1957, Dutton, 1958.
Murder by Request, Dutton, 1960.

PLAYS

The Stag (also see below; first produced in London, England, in 1929), P. Smith, 1933.
Avalanche (also see below; first produced in Edinburgh, Scotland, in 1931; produced in London in 1932), P. Smith, 1933.
(With Edward Knoblock) *Evensong* (three-act; based on own novel of the same title; first produced in London in 1932; produced in New York, N.Y., in 1933), Samuel French, 1933.
When the Crash Comes (also see below; first produced in Birmingham, England, in 1933), P. Smith, 1933.
Failures: Three Plays (contains "The Stag," "Avalanche," and "When the Crash Comes"), P. Smith, 1933.
Mesmer (first produced in London in 1938), J. Cape, 1937.
Shadow of the Vine (three-act; first produced in London in 1954), J. Cape, 1949.

JUVENILES

The Tree That Sat Down (also see below), J. Cape, 1945.
The Stream That Stood Still (also see below), J. Cape, 1948.
The Mountain of Magic, J. Cape, 1950.
The Wickedest Witch in the World, W. H. Allen, 1971.

NONFICTION

Twenty-five: Being a Young Man's Candid Recollections of His Elders and Betters, G. H. Doran, 1926.
Are They the Same at Home?, G. H. Doran, 1927.
The Star Spangled Manner, Doubleday, 1928.
Women and Children Last, Doubleday, 1931.
Down the Garden Path, Doubleday, 1932, reprinted, Norwood Editions, 1978.
For Adults Only, J. Cape, 1932, Doubleday, 1933.
Cry Havoc!, Doubleday, 1933.
A Thatched Roof, Doubleday, 1933.

A Village in a Valley, Doubleday, 1934, reprinted, Arden Library, 1980.

(With others) *How Does Your Garden Grow?* (broadcast talks), Doubleday, 1935.

The Fool Hath Said, Doubleday, 1936, reprinted, Norwood Editions, 1978.

No Place Like Home, Doubleday, 1936.

News of England; or, A Country without a Hero, Doubleday, 1938.

Green Grows the City, Harcourt, 1939.

Verdict on India, Harcourt, 1944.

All I Could Never Be: Some Recollections, J. Cape, 1949, Dutton, 1952.

(With Monica Dickens) *Yours Sincerely,* G. Newnes, 1949.

Uncle Samson, Evans Brothers, 1950.

Merry Hall (also see below), J. Cape, 1951, Dutton, 1953.

A Pilgrim's Progress, J. Cape, 1952.

Laughter on the Stairs (also see below), J. Cape, 1953, Dutton, 1954, reprinted, Dynamic Learning Corp., 1979.

The Queen's Coronation Day: The Pictorial Record of the Great Occasion, Pitkin Pictorials, 1953.

Beverley Nichols' Cat Book, T. Nelson, 1955.

Sunlight on the Lawn (also see below), Dutton, 1956.

The Sweet and Twenties, Weidenfeld & Nicolson, 1958.

Cats A. B. C. (also see below), Dutton, 1960.

Cats X. Y. Z. (also see below), Dutton, 1961.

Garden Open Today, Dutton, 1963.

Forty Favourite Flowers, Studio Vista, 1964, St. Martin's, 1965.

Powers That Be, St. Martin's, 1966.

A Case of Human Bondage, Award Books, 1966.

The Art of Flower Arrangement, Viking, 1967.

Garden Open Tomorrow, Heinemann, 1968, Dodd, 1969.

The Sun in My Eyes; or, How Not to Go around the World, Heinemann, 1969.

Father Figure (autobiography), Simon & Schuster, 1972.

Down the Kitchen Sink, W. H. Allen, 1974.

The Unforgiving Minute: Some Confessions from Childhood to the Outbreak of the Second World War, W. H. Allen, 1978.

The Romantic Garden, Gordon-Cremonesi, 1980.

Twilight: First and Probably Last Poems, Bachman & Turner, 1982.

COLLECTIONS

The Tree That Sat Down [and] *The Stream That Stood Still,* St. Martin's, 1966.

The Gift of a Garden; or, Some Flowers Remembered, edited by John E. Cross, W. H. Allen, 1971, Dodd, 1972.

The Gift of a Home (contains condensed versions of *Merry Hall, Laughter on the Stairs,* and *Sunlight on the Lawn*), W. H. Allen, 1972, Dodd, 1973.

Beverley Nichols' Cats A-Z (contains *Cats A. B. C.* and *Cats X. Y. Z.*), W. H. Allen, 1977.

OTHER:

(Author of introduction) Charles Sedley, *The Faro Table; or, The Gambling Mothers,* Nash & Grayson, 1931.

(Contributor) *Official Handbook of the Corporation of Brighton,* Corporation of Brighton, 1933.

(Compiler) *A Book of Old Ballads,* Hutchinson, 1934.

(Author of foreword) *The Making of a Man,* Nicholson & Watson, 1934.

(Author of preface) *Receipt Book,* Woolf, 1968.

(Author of preface) Jan Styczynski, *Cats in America,* A. Deutsch, 1962.

Founder and editor of *Oxford Outlook;* editor of *American Sketch,* 1928-29, and *Isis;* contributor to newspapers and periodicals.

SIDELIGHTS: Precocious and multi-faceted talent made Beverley Nichols a celebrity by the time he was old enough to attend Oxford University. His first novel, *Prelude,* was written before his eighteenth birthday; his second, *Patchwork,* was published before he finished his degree. While in school he founded a literary magazine, the *Oxford Outlook,* and edited it along with an already-established magazine, *Isis.* He was president of the famous Oxford Union Debating Society and was also known as a gifted pianist. Following school, he quickly established a reputation as a brilliant and daring interviewer and journalist. ''Witty, elegant, and ruinously good-looking,'' according to the London *Times,* he was an intimate of Noel Coward, Winston Churchill, George Bernard Shaw, D. H. Lawrence, and Somerset Maugham, among others. His sparkling wit and his connections made him a natural candidate for the job of columnist for the *Sunday Chronicle,* and for fourteen years he filled page two of that newspaper with ''glossy gossip and name-dropping anecdotes,'' according to Victoria Glendinning in the *Times Literary Supplement.*

Nichols's books and plays were consistent best-sellers, and thanks to his column he was known to millions, but ''as the years went by he never quite developed as a writer in the way forecast by his contemporaries in the 1920s,'' noted a London *Times* writer. ''His was the kind of success, showy and obviously remunerative, which it was easy to denigrate, and Nichols had his share of denigration where a comparable talent exercised in diligent obscurity would have earned approval. His readers had to wait more than 50 years for the key to what had struck some of the author's contemporaries as a compulsive seeking after success rather than a more serious reputation.''

That key was found in Nichols's 1972 autobiography, *Father Figure.* It describes a desperately unhappy childhood dominated by a sadistic, alcoholic father, who constantly mistreated his wife, humiliated his family, and ridiculed his son's musical abilities. A London *Times* contributor suggested that Beverley Nichols's adult life was made up of ''running . . . from the squalor and unhappiness of his home . . . from seediness, and from poverty. He had an overwhelming desire to make money, and make money he did,'' but perhaps at the cost of fully realizing his considerable gift for writing.

Publication of *Father Figure* caused some scandal because of Nichols's confession in it that he had made three sincere but unsuccessful efforts to murder his father. At age fifteen, Nichols had dissolved a bottle of aspirin in his father's soup; some months later, upon finding his father sprawled at the bottom of a steep hill, he climbed to the top of the slope, aimed a heavy lawn roller at the unconscious body below, and gave it a push. Years later, at the age of thirty-one, Nichols returned to his own home one winter night to find that his hated parent had let himself in, become dead drunk, wrecked the house, and passed out. The younger Nichols dragged his father outside and dumped him in a snowbank to freeze. But the man survived, eventually dying quite peacefully of natural causes. Commenting in the *New York Times Book Review,* Guy Davenport called *Father Figure* a ''painful but wholly interesting confession.''

Nichols's sentimental, witty musings on gardening, country life, and cats have proved to be his most enduring books. His style is personal and highly tangential; an essay about gardens may lead to an anecdote about a backstage encounter with an opera diva, then to an impassioned statement on pacifism, and then back to the garden. This style prompted a *New York Times Book Review* writer to call Nichols's most famous book, *Down the Garden Path,* "a charming and amusing book that you can read with much enjoyment, whether or not you care anything about gardens."

BIOGRAPHICAL/CRITICAL SOURCES:

BOOKS

Nichols, Beverley, *Twenty-five: Being a Young Man's Candid Recollections of His Elders and Betters,* G. H. Doran, 1926.
Nichols, Beverley, *Father Figure* (autobiography), Simon & Schuster, 1972.
Nichols, Beverley, *Beverley Nichols' Cats A-Z,* W. H. Allen, 1977.
Nichols, Beverley, *The Unforgiving Minute: Some Confessions from Childhood to the Outbreak of the Second World War,* W. H. Allen, 1978.

PERIODICALS

New York Times Book Review, February 28, 1923, October 23, 1932, December 17, 1944, October 8, 1972.
Times Literary Supplement, March 10, 1972, September 8, 1978.

OBITUARIES:

PERIODICALS

Los Angeles Times, September 17, 1983.
Times (London), September 17, 1983.
Washington Post, September 17, 1983.†

*   *   *

NICOLAS, F. R. E.
   See FREELING, Nicolas

*   *   *

NIDA, Eugene A(lbert)   1914-

PERSONAL: Born November 11, 1914, in Oklahoma City, Okla.; son of Richard Eugene (a chiropractor) and Alma Ruth (McCullough) Nida; married Althea Lucille Sprague, 1943. *Education:* University of California, Los Angeles, A.B., 1936; University of Southern California, M.A., 1939; University of Michigan, Ph.D., 1943.

ADDRESSES: Home—33 Husted Lane, Greenwich, Conn. *Office*—American Bible Society, 1865 Broadway, New York, N.Y. 10023.

CAREER: Ordained Baptist minister, 1943. University of Oklahoma, Summer Institute of Linguistics, Norman, professor of linguistics, 1937-53; American Bible Society, New York City, executive secretary for translations, 1943-79, consultant, 1979—; United Bible Societies, New York City, translations research coordinator, 1972-79.

MEMBER: Linguistic Society of America (vice-president, 1960; president, 1968), American Anthropological Association, Society of New Testament Studies, Society of Biblical Literature,

Semiotic Society of America, Linguistic Circle of New York, Phi Beta Kappa, Pi Gamma Mu.

AWARDS, HONORS: Gutenberg Award, 1967; Diamond Jubilee Medal, Institute of Linguistics, 1976; Alexander Gode Medal, American Translators Association, 1977. Honorary Degrees: D.D., Eastern Baptist Seminary, 1956, and Southern California Baptist Seminary, 1959; Th.D., University of Muenster, 1966; Litt. D., Heriot-Watt University, 1974; Phil.D., Brigham Young University, 1979, and University of Chile.

WRITINGS:

Bible Translating, American Bible Society, 1947, 2nd edition, United Bible Societies, 1961.
Linguistic Interludes, Summer Institute of Linguistics of University of Oklahoma, 1947.
Morphology: The Descriptive Analysis of Words, University of Michigan Press, 1949.
Learning a Foreign Language, Friendship, 1950.
God's Word in Man's Language, Harper, 1952.
Customs and Cultures, Harper, 1954, reprinted, William Carey Library, 1975.
(With William A. Smalley) *Introducing Animism,* Friendship, 1959.
Message and Mission, Harper, 1960.
A Synopsis of English Syntax, Summer Institute of Linguistics of University of Oklahoma, 1960.
(With Robert G. Bratcher) *A Translator's Handbook on Mark,* E. J. Brill, 1961.
Toward a Science of Translating, E. J. Brill, 1964.
Religions across Cultures, American Bible Society, 1968.
(Editor with Charles R. Taber) *The Theory and Practice of Translation,* E. J. Brill, 1969.
(With B. M. Newman, Jr.) *Translator's Handbook on the Acts of the Apostles,* United Bible Societies, 1972.
(With Newman) *Translator's Handbook on Paul's Letter to the Romans,* United Bible Societies, 1973.
(With J. De Waard) *Translator's Handbook on the Book of Ruth,* United Bible Societies, 1973.
Understanding Latin Americans, William Carey Library, 1973.
Translator's Notes on Literacy Selections, two parts, American Bible Society, 1974.
(With P. Ellingworth) *Translator's Handbook on Paul's Letter to the Thessalonians,* United Bible Societies, 1975.
Componential Analysis of Meaning, [The Hague], 1975.
Exploring Semantic Structures, [Munich], 1975.
Language Structure and Translation: Essays by Eugene A. Nida, Stanford University Press, 1975.
(With D. C. Arichea, Jr.) *Translator's Handbook on Paul's Letter to the Galatians,* United Bible Societies, 1976.
(With I. Loh) *Translator's Handbook on Paul's Letter to the Philippians,* United Bible Societies, 1977.
Good News for Everyone, Word Books, 1977.
Meaning across Cultures, Orbis Books, 1981.
Style and Discourse, Bible Society of South Africa, 1983.
Signs, Sense, and Translation, Bible Society of South Africa, 1984.

Also author of *A Book of a Thousand Tongues.* Contributor of more than twenty articles to professional journals. Former editor, *The Bible Translator;* associate editor, *Practical Anthropology.*

WORK IN PROGRESS: A translator's wordbook of New Testament vocabulary.

SIDELIGHTS: Eugene A. Nida has travelled in more than eighty-five countries doing linguistic work and checking translations in more than 200 languages.

AVOCATIONAL INTERESTS: Wood sculpturing, designing and making furniture, gardening, hiking.

*   *   *

NIELSEN, Virginia
See McCALL, Virginia Nielsen

*   *   *

NISBET, Robert A(lexander)   1913-

PERSONAL: Born September 30, 1913, in Los Angeles, Calif.; son of Henry S. and Cynthia (Jenifer) Nisbet; married Emily Heron, July 15, 1936 (divorced); married Caroline Burks Kirkpatrick, December 15, 1970; children: (first marriage) Martha (Mrs. R. Fred Rehrman), Constance (Mrs. Gordon Field); (second marriage) Ann Kirkpatrick. *Education:* University of California, Berkeley, A.B., 1936, M.A., 1937, Ph.D., 1939.

ADDRESSES: Home—2828 Wisconsin Ave. N.W., Washington, D.C. 20007.

CAREER: University of California, Berkeley, instructor, 1939-43, assistant professor of social institutions, 1943-48, associate professor of sociology, 1948-53, assistant dean of College of Letters and Science, 1942-43, 1946; University of California, Riverside, professor of sociology, 1953-72, dean of College of Letters and Science, 1953-63, vice-chancellor, 1960-63; University of Arizona, Tucson, professor of sociology and history, 1972-74; Columbia University, New York, N.Y., Albert Schweitzer Professor in the Humanities, 1974-78, professor emeritus, 1978—; American Enterprise Institute, Washington, D.C., resident scholar, 1978-80, adjunct scholar, 1980—. Visiting professor at Columbia University, 1949, and University of Bologna, 1956-57; Rieker Lecturer, University of Arizona, 1956; distinguished lecturer at Swarthmore College, 1960, University of California, Berkeley, 1962, and Cornell University, 1969; Cooper Lecturer, Swarthmore College, 1966; John Dewey Lecturer, John Dewey Society, 1970; Blazer Lecturer, University of Kentucky, 1971; William A. Nielson Research Professor, Smith College, 1971-72; W. G. Sumner Lecturer, Yale University, 1976; Leon Lecturer, University of Pennsylvania, 1982; Penrose Lecturer, American Philosophical Society, 1982. Visiting fellow, Princeton University, 1963-64; visiting scholar, Phi Beta Kappa National, 1971-72; Johns Hopkins Centennial Scholar, 1975-76. Member of board of directors of council of academic advisers, American Enterprise Institute, 1972—; member of board of directors, American Council of Learned Societies, 1974-79; member of National Council of Humanities, 1975-78; member of Parkman Prize Commission, 1978-80. Member of New York State Governor's Health Advisory Commission, 1978-80. Consulting editor, Random House, 1965-68, and Appleton-Century-Crofts, 1968-72. *Military service:* U.S. Army, 1943-45; became staff sergeant; served in the Pacific.

MEMBER: Institut Internationale de Sociologie (fellow), American Academy of Arts and Sciences (fellow), American Philosophical Society (fellow), Society of American Historians (fellow), Societe de Culture Europeene (fellow), Columbia Society of Fellows, Phi Beta Kappa, Golden Bear Society.

AWARDS, HONORS: Award of Merit of Republic of Italy for work in higher education in Italy, 1957; Guggenheim fellow, 1963-64; Berkeley Citation, University of California, Berkeley, 1970; L.H.D. from Hofstra University, 1974; Rockefeller Foundation grant, 1975-78; Richard M. Weaver Award for Scholarly Letters, Ingersoll Foundation, 1985.

WRITINGS:

The Quest for Community, Oxford University Press, 1953.
Human Relations in Administration, Zanichelli (Bologna), 1956.
(Editor with Robert K. Merton) *Contemporary Social Problems,* Harcourt, 1961, 4th edition, 1976.
Emile Durkheim, Prentice-Hall, 1965.
The Sociological Tradition, Basic Books, 1967.
Tradition and Revolt: Historical and Sociological Essays, Random House, 1968.
Social Change and History: Aspects of the Western Theory of Development, Oxford University Press, 1969.
The Social Bond, Knopf, 1970, 2nd edition, 1977.
The Degradation of the Academic Dogma, Basic Books, 1971.
The Social Philosophers, Crowell, 1973.
The Sociology of Emile Durkheim, Oxford University Press, 1974.
Twilight of Authority, Oxford University Press, 1975.
Sociology as an Art Form, Oxford University Press, 1976.
(Editor with Tom Bottomore) *A History of Sociological Analysis,* Basic Books, 1978.
History of the Idea of Progress, Basic Books, 1980.
The Social Group in French Thought, Arno Press, 1980.
Prejudices: A Philosophical Dictionary, Harvard University Press, 1982.
Conservatism: Dream and Reality, Open University Press, 1986.

CONTRIBUTOR

Alvin Gouldner, editor, *Studies in Leadership,* Harper, 1950.
Maurice Stein and Arthur Vidich, editors, *Sociology on Trial,* Prentice-Hall, 1963.
Werner Cahnman and Alvin Boskoff, editors, *Sociology and History,* Free Press, 1964.
Robert Lee and Martin Marty, editors, *Religion and Social Conflict,* Oxford University Press, 1964.
Irving Horowitz, editor, *The Rise and Fall of Project Camelot,* MIT Press, 1967.
Horowitz, editor, *Sociological Self-Images,* Sage Publications, 1969.
Philip Rieff, editor, *On Intellectuals: Theoretical Studies/Case Studies,* Doubleday, 1969.
Irving Stone, editor, *There Was Light,* Doubleday, 1970.
Stephen Tonsor, editor, *America's Continuing Revolution,* Doubleday/Anchor, 1975.
Lewis Coser, editor, *Idea of Social Structure,* Harcourt, 1975.
Charles Frankel, editor, *Social Science Controversies,* American Academy of Arts and Sciences, 1976.
Seymour M. Lipset, editor, *The Third Century,* Hoover Institution Press, 1979.
Joseph Epstein, editor, *Masters: Portraits of Great Teachers,* Basic Books, 1981.
Russell Kirk, editor, *The Portable Conservative Reader,* Viking, 1982.
Irving Howe, editor, *1984 Revisited: Totalitarianism in Our Century,* Harper, 1983.
D. J. Enright, editor, *Fair of Speech: The Uses of Euphemism,* Oxford University Press, 1985.

OTHER

Contributor to professional, scholarly, and general interest journals. Member of board of editors, *American Journal of*

Sociology, 1970-74; member of editorial board, *American Scholar,* 1975-80; member of publishing committee, *Public Interest,* 1976-85.

SIDELIGHTS: The author of such studies as *The Quest for Community, History of the Idea of Progress,* and *Prejudices: A Philosophical Dictionary,* Robert A. Nisbet is not easily categorized into one academic discipline. Although he is a sociologist by profession, most of his writings have explored areas where sociology, intellectual history, philosophy, and political science intersect, Walter Goodman explains in *Newsweek.* "In a period when sociologists have often doggedly restricted themselves to the analysis of contemporary problems," Frank E. Manuel comments in the *New York Times Book Review,* "Professor Nisbet has never failed to examine their profound historical roots." Gertrud Lenzer, also writing in the *New York Times Book Review,* calls Nisbet simply "a learned historian of ideas."

Nisbet is generally thought of as a political conservative, but his writings often contain apparent philosophical contradictions. For example, his affinity for the pluralistic values and localism of the Middle Ages often causes him to view some liberal trends in a favorable light, but he also says in *Prejudices* that the Moral Majority might provide a "real counterforce to the liberalism of statism and cultural licence." Although a firm believer in the importance of community, Nisbet proposes in *History of the Idea of Progress* a return to an emphasis on the dogma of progress, despite his quarrel with the individualism inherent in the philosophy of some of its proponents and apart from his belief in its fallaciousness as a method of historical analysis. And, although in *Prejudices* he vigorously defends abortion as the traditional prerogative of the family, he believes that the *Roe versus Wade* decision, which nationally legalized first trimester abortion, was divisive because it removed responsibility for the issue from the local sphere. Nonetheless, Robert Dawidoff points out in the *Los Angeles Times Book Review,* Nisbet "believes the anti-abortion forces to be even more perniciously attacking freedom and privacy."

Nisbet has been criticized by Lenzer for switching from the role of social analyst to that of ideologue, but Nisbet claims in *The Sociological Tradition* that "most of what has gone under the heading of 'sociology' has ratified the victory of the Toquevillean over the Marxian assessment," Peter L. Berger explains in *Commentary.* "Put crudely, this means that sociological thought has tended to conservatism rather than revolution, to a more or less dour contemplation of the modern world rather than a burning desire to transform it." Nisbet's aim in *The Sociological Tradition* is "to call attention to the conservative pedigree of sociology," agrees *Commentary* critic Dennis H. Wrong, who indicates that Nisbet pursues this theme by elucidating the views of conservative sociological theoreticians "while casting Marx as the heavy, the naive exponent of Enlightenment progressivism." Nisbet further explores this issue in *History of the Idea of Progress* and *Prejudices.*

In *Social Change and History,* Nisbet again examines the various theories of social change, including cyclical views, the Christian belief in the Fall and redemption, eighteenth-century beliefs in unilinear progress, nineteenth-century evolutionism, Hegelian-Marxist dialectical theories, and neo-evolutionary views of contemporary functionalist sociologists. According to Wrong, Nisbet argues that "this diversity is less profound than the underlying similarities stemming from the pervasive hold on men's minds of the metaphor of growth transferred

from the biological realm to human life and history." And, although Nisbet later deems the idea of progress useful and beneficial, in *Social Change and History* he claims that all developmental theories are fallacious, since they view "the totality of the past from the vantage point of the thinker's present location and discern a continuous movement divisible into stages or phases," to quote from Wrong's paraphrase. "The continuity the thinker discerns, and the stages and phases he identifies are *ex post facto* intellectual ordering devices which have nothing to do with the unique, contingent events that are the actual substance of history as it is lived by mortal men." As Gertrude Himmelfarb states in *Commentary, Social Change and History* reflects the suspicion of Nisbet's teacher Frederick Teggart of any idea "which tried to impose an artificial unity upon either history or society, thus violating the particularity of historical events and the multiplicity and complexity of social institutions."

Nisbet's own views have been significantly modified over time. According to Goodman, Nisbet was a New Dealer until the late 1930s, when "he encountered the works of Edmund Burke and Alexis de Toqueville and was redeemed. They taught him to prize common human relationships and to be wary of excessive power whether it is exercised by the elite or the mob." The author has also been influenced by the French sociologist Emile Durkheim (1858-1917), described in *America* by James R. Kelly as "par excellence the sociologist of social structure and social disorganization." According to Kelly, "no major sociologist shows more convincingly than Durkheim the mirroring of social dislocations in individual psyches and the enduring need for intermediate group structures that might protect the individual from the fragility of the isolated ego and the impersonal power of the state." Central to Nisbet's writing is the belief that many of today's social and political difficulties are the result of the loss of traditional communities since the Middle Ages and the consequent rise of totalitarian societies.

Nisbet's work *Prejudices: A Philosophical Dictionary,* a collection of brief essays on seventy subjects, may most represent his viewpoint, since, as Goodman points out, it is "unencumbered by scholarly apparatus." "Prejudice, in Nisbet's sense," writes Dawidoff, "exists somewhere between opinion and philosophy." The book's title was influenced by Edmund Burke's belief that "prejudices, in fact, are things we all have and perhaps need to get on in life and should, therefore, as Burke wrote, be examined for 'the latent wisdom' that they contain," says Dawidoff. Nisbet's *Philosophical Dictionary* is "like Voltaire's," according to Dawidoff, in that it "is 'neither philosophical nor a dictionary.'" Instead, *Prejudices* is a series of "lively takes," declares Goodman, short essays with titles such as "Anomie," "Chain of Being," "Crime and Punishment," "Environmentalism," and "Renaissancism." In these essays, Nisbet deplores popular history's denigration of the Middle Ages in favor of the Renaissance and analyses the shortcomings of the philosophies that set the French Revolution in motion, beliefs that he finds responsible for many current societal problems.

In a review of *Prejudices, New York Review of Books* critic Ian Hacking describes Nisbet's outlook, saying that the collection's overall theme is suggested by the title of an earlier work, *Twilight of Authority:* "The rot of our times must be traced back to the better times when we had a multitude of interconnecting social structures each of which exerted its own authority on its members. Family, village, and parish are often recited by way of example in Nisbet's lists of such institutions

..., but so also are town, voluntary association, class, trade union, and corporation." Hacking further explains Nisbet's beliefs: "As the authority of these rival organizations was diminished, we created the giant bureaucracies that have eaten away at democracy—or else we got, more suddenly, the totalitarian state. In either case the individual has diminished to the vanishing point, and the end of civilization is near."

The essay "Authoritarianism" is a conventional rendering of conservative theory, Paul Robinson relates in the *New York Times Book Review,* since, as Hacking explains, it "defends the doctrine of Jeane Kirkpatrick that we are to distinguish authoritarian from totalitarian regimes, accepting that the former may be our allies but the latter must in the end be our foes." According to Nisbet, who cites Elizabethan England as an example of an authoritarian society, such societies are buffered by the institutions of religion, guild, and family upon which they are based and can easily make a later transition to more democratic forms, while totalitarian societies inherently seek to eliminate such institutions.

Occasionally, Nisbet's "celebration of family and community leads to unexpected conclusions," says Robinson, pointing to his essay on abortion as the most striking example. Here, Nisbet's "conclusions favor legalized abortion," in Dawidoff's opinion, "but his arguments, based on history and theology and also a secularist prudential view of politics, are as important as his conclusion." Opposed to a national policy of any kind on the issue, Nisbet maintains that abortion has always been the natural prerogative of the family. Not until the nineteenth century, according to Nisbet, have pregnancy and the fetus been so romanticized. And, in Nisbet's opinion, "when it is said that all life is sacred and that therefore the life of the fetus may not be terminated under any circumstances whatever ... one of the oldest of mankind's perspectives is being violated, that of the scale or chain of being."

Not surprisingly the book has met with opposition from the critics. In the *New Republic,* Charles Krauthammer calls the work "a long, sometimes elegant, often repetitive polemic against the French revolution." And, as Robinson states, "only by virtually ignoring the economic realm can Mr. Nisbet place all the blame for our woes on the utopian aspirations of political philosophers.... At the same time, he is inclined to romanticize the traditional communal order from which we have supposedly been uprooted. A life dominated by locality, guild and family is, after all, a life of provincialism, dull routine and petty oppression."

Nisbet had stated similar themes in his first work, *The Quest for Community.* In that book, Currin V. Shields remarks in the *American Political Science Review,* Nisbet seems to "sound a warning for all democrats: If you do not want to slip into a totalitarian morass, you must deliberately build a pluralist society. Only in a pluralist society can we have both freedom and democracy. The author elaborates his plea for 'pluralist democracy' in the now familiar sociological terms of 'community.'" Before the rise of liberalism, according to Nisbet, local associations such as the family, parish, village, and guild formed the basis for society, performing meaningful functions for citizens and fulfilling man's psychological need for community. These ties were severed when the idea of individualism became a societal force and governmental responsibilities became centralized, placing the individual in direct confrontation with the state with no associations in between.

Here, too, Nisbet was criticized. Arthur K. Davis in the *American Sociological Review* indicates that, although Nisbet's "analysis of family roles and small group values is brilliant," he "comes perilously close to a one-factor theory of change," and "his identification of freedom with cultural diversity and decentralized groups is philosophically legitimate but sociologically parochial." Moreover, Davis states, "Nisbet's conception of the modern mass revolutions abroad is unfortunately patterned after Orwell's *1984.* A more Olympian view would reveal that there is confidence and reconstruction in the present era as well as pessimism and destructiveness."

In *Twilight of Authority,* which Nisbet wrote in the wake of Watergate, he argues that we are in the midst of a twilight age like others that have appeared in Western history, an era in which processes of decline and erosion are more apparent than those of "genesis and development." In Nisbet's opinion, the Renaissance was also a twilight age in that it signified the death of the Middle Ages. The present twilight age, he writes, also seems to mark the beginning of a Reformation, "this time, however, one that has the political state rather than the church as the central object of its force; a force that ranges from the slow drip of apathy to the more hurricane-like intensities of violence and terror." The first great Reformation, according to Nisbet, "was terminated by the rise of the national state and the gradual retreat of church, kinship, guild, and hereditary class. Today we are present, I believe, at the commencement of the retreat of the state as we have known this institution for some five centuries, though what the consequences will be no one can be certain."

In "twilight" eras, explains Nisbet, traditional religious symbols and organizations no longer hold sway, and people seek solace in the occult, mysticism, and worship of the self. Politics is no longer seen as a "civilized pursuit," and political parties become indistinguishable from each other as each group subordinates principles for means. Such a decline, he believes, is accompanied by a "cultivation of power that becomes increasingly military, or paramilitary, in shape" as opposed to a reaffirmation of traditional respect for authority.

Furthermore, Nisbet comments, the presidency has become surrounded with the pomp that used to be associated with royalty, and in attempts to expedite policies, the chief executive has sought methods to avoid the traditional checks and balances that have been established to preserve the democracy. Less reliance is placed upon elected and appointed White House officials as the president turns to his own personal assistants for aid. Nisbet believes that this process escalated during Franklin D. Roosevelt's administration and that it is not an outgrowth of conservatism or the Nixon White House but can be traced instead to a liberal tendency to seek centralized governmental solutions for difficulties that were previously taken up on a local level.

Nisbet "locates 'the heart of our problem with the state and its governing agencies' in the cultural and social spheres of modern society," says Lenzer. "In his view, the idea and the desire for equality 'at the present time undoubtedly represents the greatest single threat to liberty and social initiative.'" And, as Robert H. Bork declares in the *National Review,* "it is here that Nisbet is at his best: demonstrating the connection between centralization of power and the ideal of equality of condition as contrasted with equality of opportunity; pointing out the affinity of modern left-liberal intellectuals for both central power and egalitarianism; showing the increasing legalization of our culture and our individual relationships, ... delineating the growth of state power in new, softer, and hence less resistable forms; linking the current wave of subjectivism and irrationality, manifested in occultism and the state of the arts, to the decline of the political community.''

Some reviewers find fault with Nisbet's argument. Lenzer points out that ''in choosing to find the chief source of our present peril in the idea of equality, Nisbet is promoting a point of view that is representative of a particular state of ideological mind.'' Moreover, indicates Lenzer, ''no high rhetoric will make Nisbet's ideal self-governing societies of the past into anything but hypothetical constructs, just as the state of nature was for earlier philosophers.''

Writing in the *Nation,* Victor Lebow notes that Nisbet has some ''blind spots,'' particularly regarding his belief that ''the rise of militarism in a society means the twilight of authority in the civil sphere.'' As the critic explains, ''Nisbet appears to see no connection between capitalist enterprise and war. And yet a certain career officer, later president of Columbia University and President of the United States, saw it plainly enough to give it a lasting label. He called it the 'military industrial complex' and his name was Eisenhower.''

Of all Nisbet's works, *History of the Idea of Progress* has probably fared the best with reviewers. In that work, Nisbet traces the dogma of progress, the idea, as J. H. Plumb relates in the *New Republic,* that ''history is progressive, that the story of mankind is one of betterment,'' or in Nisbet's own words, ''that mankind has advanced in the past . . . is now advancing, and will continue to advance through the forseeable future.'' Nisbet considers the idea so valuable ''that in the present volume he has reviewed its status over 2,500 years of history,'' writes Christopher Lehmann-Haupt in the *New York Times.* ''The result is a stimulating intellectual survey that elegantly summarizes a complex body of thought.''

Nisbet examines the idea of progress apart from his thoughts on its coincidence with reality and despite his quarrel with the philosophies of some of its proponents; he considers the dogma ''essential to the well-being of society,'' says Himmelfarb. According to Robert Kirsch in the *Los Angeles Times,* Nisbet calls the idea of progress ''an idea as basic and important as any which has come out of the Greek and Christian West, one which validates other notions: liberty, justice, equality, community.''

Nisbet refutes the accepted wisdom that the idea of progress was not a part of Greek and Roman thought, that ''the ancient philosophers believed in the cyclical nature of human life; that death and decay and destruction were as inherent in society's as in a person's life,'' says Plumb. Furthermore, the author rejects the belief that the idea of progress is more to be associated with the Renaissance than the Christian Middle Ages, maintaining that ''the idea of progress is not to be found in the Renaissance—the humanists' preoccupation with chance, witches, the occult, cyclical ideas of history and their contempt for medieval culture precluded it,'' according to Peter S. Prescott in *Newsweek.* As Himmelfarb explains Nisbet's point of view, the Renaissance, ''in denying its own immediate past, demeaning it as the Dark Ages, broke the chain of progress.''

In Nisbet's schema, says Frank E. Manuel in the *New York Times Book Review,* ''Saint Augustine is the Church Father who becomes the richest source for major elements in the idea of *terrestrial* progress.'' And despite his disagreement with the individualism espoused by some of its philosophers, Nisbet finds that the Enlightenment ''witnessed the 'triumph' of the idea of progress, and that a dominant motif of the idea as it then developed was secularization, the liberation of progress

from any reliance upon providence,'' Himmelfarb says. For the purposes of his discussion, Nisbet divides the leaders of the Enlightenment into two groups: those who sought to use progress to achieve freedom and those who saw it as a means to gain power.

Although the book was generally praised by reviewers, several critics took issue with some of Nisbet's premises. Kirsch indicates that he doesn't ''see that subjectivism, the seeking for other ways of knowing, or even interest in the spiritual, the occult, is necessarily damaging to the idea of progress. The notion is not a monopoly of rationalism and science as Nisbet's history clearly shows.'' And in Nisbet's analysis of St. Augustine's *The City of God,* ''the dubiety of the notion that the idea of progress secularized or, as some might say, merely secularized Christian hope of Heaven becomes apparent if we turn the notion around and imagine transcendentalizing Marxism,'' points out *Intercollegiate Review* critic R. F. Baum. ''Would not that elicit a roar of rightful rage from old Karl himself? To transcendentalize the one or secularize the other is to subvert and contradict it.''

Manuel agrees, commenting that ''I fear that in more than one instance Professor Nisbet reads back into Augustinian phrases (although I grant that they are temptingly suggestive) ideas of a later age that used the same words but imparted to them a very different tone and meaning.'' Moreover, Plumb relates, ''it is not only with St. Augustine that by tearing some concepts from their ideological matrix a distortion is created; it occurs elsewhere in the book. This is, of course, a pitfall almost impossible to avoid in a book that covers so many centuries, so many different worlds of thought and feeling.''

Himmelfarb argues, however, that a highly secularized interpretation of Augustine ''prepares the way for a more religious view of the Enlightenment itself—and of all philosophies which claim to be truly progressive. . . . If the 18th-century *philosophes* were merely reconstructing Augustine's City of God, and if Augustine himself derived his 'raptured picture of the future' from the dialectical relationship between the City of God and the City of Man, then the idea of progress—the modern idea as much as the ancient—must be infused with an authentic spirit of religiosity, a sense of man's worth that is predicated upon a transcendent reality.'' In Himmelfarb's estimation, ''the shadow of Augustine appears again and again [in *History of the Idea of Progress*], illuminating, by contrast or comparison, a variety of later figures, and in the process fleshing out Augustine himself. It is his ghostly presence that helps explain some of the other revisionist highlights of the book—most notably the reversal of the conventional interpretations of the Renaissance and Reformation.''

Overall, ''this remains a very impressive book,'' Plumb observes. ''It seems churlish to criticize so admirable an achievement.'' In Manuel's opinion, ''Nisbet's book is by all odds the finest general account of the history of the idea of progress in any language. It is an exemplar of a well-proportioned study—compact, succinct, lucid.'' And as Prescott stresses, ''Nisbet's book may help revive the idea of progress, if only because it explains with grace, authority and clarity what the idea has meant to the West. In achieving this, Nisbet has made an impressive and significant contribution to our understanding of the past.''

CA INTERVIEW

CA interviewed Robert A. Nisbet by telephone on May 8, 1985, at his home in Washington, D.C.

CA: Are there any new trends in the last twenty or thirty years in the development of sociological analysis?

NISBET: The single trend that has been most pronounced in American sociology in the last twenty-five or thirty years has been toward a higher and higher degree of quantification, the use of mathematics as well as statistics in the largest possible measure. That has been, I think, nationwide the most marked trend. But there is still a very strong commitment, especially among the young sociologists, to the kinds of value-oriented, value-laden sociology that we identify with Karl Marx, Max Weber, Emile Durkheim, Georg Simmel, and, in this country, Charles Horton Cooley and Margaret Mead. In a way, these two aspects have always existed and have been in tension with each other in American sociology, but I would say that the mainstream of sociology today is more committed to the quantitative than it ever has been before.

CA: Are more and more courses in sociology being taught now in this country?

NISBET: Oh, yes. When I was at the University of California at Berkeley in the 1930s, there was no sociology department as such. And there were still a fair number especially of colleges, smaller institutions, that saw no reason to have sociology in the curriculum. That's changed remarkably, though. It's present now in the vast majority of colleges in the country, and it's not likely to disappear.

CA: What is there in the philosophy of Emile Durkheim that especially appeals to you? You have devoted considerable attention to his writings.

NISBET: Yes, he has been an influence in my life. I suppose it was because I liked the strong emphasis in his work on the social group, on social ties, social attachments among individuals. It was not a strongly individualistic sociology, and I found some interest in that. I have been much more influenced, though, by Alexis de Tocqueville, who preceded him. He has been a much, much larger influence in my life. And almost equally large an influence over the years has been that of my teacher at Berkeley, Frederick J. Teggart. I think Teggart and Tocqueville have been much stronger influences in what I've written. But I was very interested in Durkheim; I did write a book on him.

CA: You've said that it was a long time before Durkheim caught on in this country.

NISBET: That's right. American sociologists prior to the very late 1930s just couldn't tie onto any of his central concepts. There was such a strong individualistic bias in American sociology that Durkheim seemed tortuously metaphysical to them when he talked about society as a reality. They thought of him as a kind of medieval realist to their nominalism.

CA: Wasn't it someone at the University of Chicago who brought him to the attention of the academic community?

NISBET: Yes, it was the great English anthropologist A. R. Radcliffe-Browne. It was his residence at the University of Chicago in the early 1930s that probably had the most to do with getting Durkheim really understood in this country. He taught people how you could use Durkheim as the basis for field research to produce results that couldn't otherwise be had. That was the turnaround. And then in 1936 Talcott Par-

sons's book *The Structure of Social Action* came out, and he gave a great deal of illuminating attention to Durkheim and to Weber, among others. That helped get European sociology into American sociology in a significant way.

CA: To what extent did you model your 1982 book, Prejudices: A Philosophical Dictionary, *after Voltaire's* Philosophical Dictionary?

NISBET: Back about 1977 or 1978 the publisher at Harvard University Press invited me to do a book along the line of Voltaire's *Philosophical Dictionary*. I had my history, [*History of*] *the Idea of Progress,* to finish, and I told him it would be two or three years before I could really think about it seriously, but nevertheless it sounded interesting. That is why part of the title is *Philosophical Dictionary* in the Voltairean sense. It is not a real dictionary; it contains a lot of animadversions and preferences and foibles. The *Prejudices* part, as I indicated just beyond the title page with a quotation from Edmund Burke, is from Burke's famous treatment of prejudice in his *Reflections on the Revolution in France* that I took as my model or point of departure rather than H. L. Mencken's famous six-part series called *Prejudices.*

CA: How did you decide on the terms to write essays about?

NISBET: They were mostly interests of my own, things I knew something about and thought I could write reasonably entertainingly on. In a few cases friends made suggestions. One of the editors at Harvard, at my request, sent a list of topics that he thought would be interesting, and two or three of those attracted me. But mostly I just found myself jotting down my ideas. Then once I started, I would find myself thinking of another subject and turn to it. When I finished the manuscript, I had, I suppose, about a hundred items. Then I begged for a first-class, hard-hitting editor, and I got one. I told her that I thought a hundred was too many, but that I had written a hundred deliberately and would like her ideas on which ones to weed out. We wound up with about seventy-five or eighty.

CA: It's very entertaining reading.

NISBET: Thank you. It's the hardest writing I think I've ever done, because you're thrown back on yourself; you're trying to be knowledgeable and at the same time put some spark into it. I did a good deal of rewriting while it was being edited. My editor was great, as I say, and never hesitated to be blunt and sharp, so I found myself doing a lot of rewriting when I'd get some of those copyedited pages back.

CA: You say in your History of the Idea of Progress *(1980) that many prominent people have thought that the idea of progress is a relatively new concept.*

NISBET: A modern concept. That's the conventional view, which was first advanced by rationalists in the nineteenth century. Auguste Comte and almost all of the positivist, rationalist minds were absolutely intoxicated by the idea of the philosophy of progress, that everything by its own forces, its own powers, is advancing, improving, perfecting. Their conceit was that no one before the moderns could have known such a magnificent idea.

In 1920 J. B. Bury, an English historian, wrote a history of the idea of progress, and the book was so good for its time that it had the effect that very good books can often have of freezing thought on the matter. Bury summed up that position that the idea of progress is strictly and exclusively modern, that the ancient Greeks and Romans did not have the idea, that the Middle Ages and Christianity did not have it. And he wrote his book so well that even today it has to be reckoned with. I reviewed a book in the *New York Times* recently and had to point out that it was sixty-five years ago that Bury wrote his book. Since then there's been a whale of a lot of scholarship by classicists, medievalists, theologians, and religious historians which makes it blindingly clear that the Greeks and the Romans had a full-blown philosophy of progress. And you cannot find a better statement of the philosophy of mankind's progress anywhere than in St. Augustine's *City of God*. It became one of the two or three mainsprings of Christianity, the idea of mankind advancing, advancing, advancing until the beginning of the millennium, or into the millennium.

My book got a lot of reviews, including a favorable lead review in the *New York Times Book Review,* and it was reviewed widely in England, but I don't think there were more than three or four reviewers who had any awareness of the fact that the idea of progress was not modern. Most people are just not comfortable with the thought that the Greeks and Romans and the Christian Middle Ages could have had this strong conviction that mankind is an evolving, progressing, perfecting entity. They think this only came after Christianity had been kicked into the backyard and classicism had been overcome and the spirit of modernity burst on the world. It's a great pain in the neck to me, but there it is.

CA: Do you think most scholars are going to accept your thesis?

NISBET: In time, in time. And that's more than just an aging male's conceit or optimism, because there are only two general histories of the idea of progress in print. One is J. B. Bury's, published sixty-five years ago, and the other is mine. I see mine referred to occasionally in a footnote here and there, or as a reference, but it's apparently more than you can expect, even now, for people to break with that wholly conventionalized position that Bury wrote up so illuminatingly, so well. As I said at the beginning, this sometimes is a negative aspect of major books: they can freeze thought.

CA: In J. H. Plumb's positive review of your book in the New Republic, *February 23, 1980, he says that since many people in Western Europe and especially in this country have as much as they want in material terms, the idea of progress is beginning to fade. Do you agree with that?*

NISBET: Yes. The two final chapters of my book deal with the patterns in contemporary thought which reflect a serious disenchantment or disillusionment with the belief that mankind is progressing. There's a lot of that, no question about it. But when I was doing all the heavy reading for the book, I found myself increasingly surprised by the amount of contemporary writing that is just as firmly committed to the idea of progress as at any point in the past. So for reasons of edification, since I was out to do as full and objective a history of this idea as I possibly could, I simply balanced them in two final chapters. But there's no question that belief in progress is not as strong among the American people today as I think it was up until fifty years ago, say. Even during the Great Depression—and I can look back on that easily and vividly—it's remarkable how the faith in progress stayed strong in this country.

CA: You also said in your History of the Idea of Progress *that you think the study of history is beginning to die out.*

NISBET: It certainly is in the schools, and I'm afraid that it will in time in the colleges and universities. You really almost have to go to prep schools today to find bona fide courses in history—the history of Europe, the history of the United States, the history of this or that. In so many of the public schools, under the great pressures of the National Education Association, they've replaced history with social studies. I lament this; I think it takes something important out of the human mind if history isn't strongly emphasized. It's still strong in the colleges and universities, no question of that, but what I fear is that in another twenty-five or thirty years it'll be very much like the classics.

I went to a small-town California high school in the later 1920s, and there were available—and I took—four years of Latin. There is no Latin taught in that high school today. Up until a year or two before I started to high school, there had been two years of Greek offered there. This was not exceptional. There was still lots of Greek and Latin in the colleges; now there's damn little Greek and Latin in the colleges. I fear that the same thing will happen in history.

CA: What courses in history were taught when you were in school?

NISBET: We had a full year in ancient history, and this was common. I took that. There was also European history, and there was American history, and I took those. This was a high school that had anywhere from 150 to 250 pupils total at any given time. That has changed utterly.

CA: It seems that a lot of the history being taught now is very contemporary.

NISBET: Very contemporary, almost indistinguishable from what we used to call civics and social studies—very, very pop stuff.

CA: What would you recommend to the intelligent reader who'd like to begin an informal study of sociology?

NISBET: Durkheim's work is high among the classics. There are some splendid anthologies out. There's a very good anthology of Max Weber edited by C. Wright Mills that is most attractive for starters. And there's a volume of Simmel edited by Kurt Wolff. Those are very good for someone who wants to hit the classics. There's a history called *Masters of Sociology* by Lewis Coser. It's extremely well written and organized and has all the masters, American as well as European. That's one I would recommend.

CA: In an article in Newsweek, *September 27, 1982, Walter Goodman mentioned that until about the outbreak of World War II, you were pretty much a New Dealer and then you began reading Tocqueville and Burke and became a conservative. Is that accurate?*

NISBET: I guess I was a strongly committed liberal up until about 1938. I say I *guess* I was because I remember voting for Franklin Delano Roosevelt twice and being caught up in the whole New Deal spirit. And then I began to feel more and more disenchanted with New Deal liberalism. This was partly the result of a lot of reading; I was a graduate student in the late '30s and doing a great deal of reading of European philosophers including Tocqueville but also Nietzsche and Schopenhauer and Burckhardt and others. And then after the war I wrote *The Quest for Community*, which was a kind of agonizing process for me; it was my first book and I had to do a lot of thinking. When the book finally came out, it was from the beginning labeled a conservative book. So I just sort of said, Oh, hell, I guess I *am* a conservative and decided willy-nilly not to appeal the judgment. You have to be labeled something if you're going to be writing all the time, and I'd just as soon have that label as any other. But I do think my reputation for being a conservative is a lot wider and a lot stronger than my beliefs justify. And I must say there are a lot of self-advertised, self-described conservatives at the present time who drive me up the wall.

CA: Are you a supporter of the Reagan administration?

NISBET: I voted for Reagan and I don't regret it. I think the administration is going to be in for very, very hard times this second term. The trouble is that during the last ten or fifteen years the word *conservative* took on a kind of prestige quality which it had never had before in this country, so that a lot of people who really are not conservatives adopted the label.

Reagan is a kind of phenomenon in the same way that Franklin Roosevelt was. When Roosevelt was elected in 1932, he had accomplished almost the impossible: he had put under one big coalition tent the big-city Roman Catholics and Jews, the political machines, the very conservative solid South, the big landowners in the Southwest and the Middle West, organized labor—there was this terrific assortment that he brought together. Reagan has done pretty much the same sort of thing. When he ran in 1980, he attracted people who were not really conservatives; many of them were interested solely in a bigger defense. Others were really populists—that is, they want as much direct action on the part of the people as possible. There was the Far Right just out for power. There were the religious fundamentalists, who have never been particularly conservative. You've got a whole motley crew in there, and I think the pressures, the tensions, are beginning to show up pretty decisively.

CA: So you think some of these groups may not continue to support the Reagan administration?

NISBET: Yes. If World War II hadn't come along, I don't think FDR would ever have been elected to a third term; he was beginning to lose his coalition visibly in the latter part of his second term. When war was impending and finally broke out in Europe, everybody in this country got caught up in that worry, which helped Roosevelt. I don't expect Reagan to have that kind of luck, if that's the word. I don't foresee any major war coming along. So I think he's going to have very serious problems.

CA: Some time ago you were noting signs of a religious awakening in this country.

NISBET: Yes. I began noting that in articles and lectures back in the early '60s; it was evident to me then that it was coming. It's here. There *has* been a religious awakening. I don't know how long it will last. We've had several major awakenings in American history ever since the late seventeenth century; they come and they go. This one is still very much around, with figures like Jerry Falwell and Cardinal O'Connor, who matter a great deal to a lot of people today. And there are the moral issues—abortion and school prayer, for example. But they've come up before and they will go away. I would say right now we're at the peak, even the beginning of the downslope, of the whole religious, moral awakening. Already it's beginning to subside.

CA: Are you working on a new book now?

NISBET: Yes. In it I've tried to get across some of the things that I've just been mentioning to you. It was commissioned by an English publisher and I've already sent it away, though there may be more work to do before it's published; I'm not sure when it will be out. The title is *Conservatism: Dream and Reality* (Open University Press, 1986).

BIOGRAPHICAL/CRITICAL SOURCES:

BOOKS

Contemporary Issues Criticism, Volume I, Gale, 1982.
Nisbet, Robert A., *The Quest for Community*, Oxford University Press, 1953.
Nisbet, Robert A., *The Sociological Tradition*, Basic Books, 1967.
Nisbet, Robert A., *Twilight of Authority*, Oxford University Press, 1975.
Nisbet, Robert A., *History of the Idea of Progress*, Basic Books, 1980.
Nisbet, Robert A., *Prejudices: A Philosophical Dictionary*, Harvard University Press, 1982.

PERIODICALS

America, May 11, 1974, November 1, 1975, March 19, 1977.
American Historical Review, December, 1969, June, 1981.
American Journal of Sociology, September, 1969, March, 1970.
American Political Science Review, June, 1953, December, 1967, March, 1981.
American Sociological Review, August, 1953, December, 1965, August, 1967, February, 1970, April, 1970.
Atlantic, January, 1976, February, 1980.
Chicago Sunday Tribune, February 22, 1953.
Christian Science Monitor, March 25, 1971.
Commentary, November, 1969, March, 1976, June, 1980.
Commonweal, January 1, 1954, February 17, 1967, September 5, 1969, October 24, 1980.
Contemporary Sociology, March, 1972, January, 1981.
Critic, June, 1980.
Economist, November 6, 1971, March 13, 1976.
Encounter, March, 1970.
Ethics, April, 1977.
Harper's, November, 1982.
Intercollegiate Review, spring-summer, 1981.
Journal of Philosophy, December 3, 1953.
Los Angeles Times, March 19, 1980.
Los Angeles Times Book Review, November 2, 1980, February 13, 1983.
Nation, December 27, 1975.
National Review, May 18, 1971, October 27, 1972, October 11, 1974, November 21, 1975, February 18, 1977, November 25, 1977, June 27, 1980, October 15, 1982.
New Republic, February 23, 1980, January 24, 1983.
New Statesman, September 15, 1967, April 2, 1976.
Newsweek, March 31, 1980, September 27, 1982.
New Yorker, May 12, 1980.
New York Review of Books, February 26, 1970, February 5, 1976, April 17, 1980, February 17, 1983.

New York Times, December 22, 1975, September 29, 1976, April 21, 1980.
New York Times Book Review, August 20, 1967, June 15, 1969, May 16, 1971, April 21, 1974, October 5, 1975, December 7, 1975, October 31, 1976, March 16, 1980, September 26, 1982.
Phi Delta Kappan, October, 1983.
Political Science Quarterly, December, 1971.
San Francisco Chronicle, February 11, 1953.
Saturday Review, July 17, 1971, October 4, 1975.
Science, December 19, 1969.
Social Studies, November, 1971.
Teacher's College Record, September, 1971.
Times Literary Supplement, January 14, 1972, July 26, 1974, September 20, 1974, June 4, 1976, March 4, 1983.

—*Sketch by Candace Cloutier*

—*Interview by Walter W. Ross*

*　　*　　*

NISH, Ian Hill 1926-

PERSONAL: Born June 3, 1926, in Edinburgh, Scotland; son of David C. and Marion (Hill) Nish; married Rona Speirs, 1965; children: two daughters. *Education:* University of Edinburgh, M.A., 1951; University of London, M.A., 1958, Ph.D., 1961.

ADDRESSES: Home—Oakdene, Charlwood Dr., Oxshott, Surrey, England. *Office*—London School of Economics and Political Science, University of London, London WC2A 2AE, England.

CAREER: University of Sydney, Sydney, New South Wales, Australia, lecturer in history, 1958-62; University of London, London School of Economics and Political Science, London, England, senior lecturer, 1963-72, reader, 1972-80, professor of history, 1980—. *Military service:* British Army, 1944-48; became captain.

WRITINGS:

The Anglo-Japanese Alliance: The Diplomacy of Two Island Empires, 1894-1907, Athlone Press, 1966, reprinted, 1985.
Short History of Japan, Praeger, 1968 (published in England as *The Story of Japan,* Faber, 1968).
Alliance in Decline: A Study in Anglo-Japanese Relations, 1908-23, Athlone Press, 1972.
Britain and Japan, 1600-1975, Information Centre, Embassy of Japan, 1975.
Japanese Foreign Policy, 1869-1942: Kasumigaseki to Miyakezaka, Routledge & Kegan Paul, 1977.
(With David Steeds) *China, Japan and 19th-Century Britain,* Irish University Press, 1977.
(Editor with Charles Dunn) *European Studies on Japan,* Norbury Publications, 1979.
(Editor) *Anglo-Japanese Alienation, 1919-1952: Papers of the Anglo-Japanese Conference on the History of the Second World War,* Cambridge University Press, 1982.
The Origins of the Russo-Japanese War, Longman, 1985.

*　　*　　*

NORTHROP, Filmer S(tuart) C(uckow) 1893-

PERSONAL: Born November 27, 1893, in Janesville, Wis.; son of Marshall Ellsworth and Ruth (Cuckow) Northrop; married Christine Johnston, August 6, 1919 (died, 1969); married

Marjorie Carey, 1969; children: (first marriage) Filmer Johnston, Stuart Johnston. *Education:* Beloit College, B.A., 1915; Yale University, M.A., 1919; Harvard University, M.A., 1922, Ph.D., 1924; graduate study at University of Freiburg, Imperial College of Science and Technology, London, and Trinity College, Cambridge, 1922-23; postdoctoral study at Trinity College, Cambridge, and University of Goettingen, 1932-33. *Politics:* Independent.

CAREER: International Young Men's Christian Association, Hong Kong and Canton, China, educational secretary, 1919-20; Yale University, New Haven, Conn., instructor, 1923-26, assistant professor, 1926-29, associate professor, 1929-32, professor of philosophy, 1932-47, master of Sillman College, 1940-47, Sterling Professor of Philosophy and Law, 1947-62, Sterling Professor Emeritus, 1962—. Visiting professor at University of Iowa, 1926, University of Michigan, 1932, National University of Mexico, 1949, Rollins College, 1963, Boston College, 1976, University of Virginia, and University of Hawaii; professor extraordinaire, National Autonomous University of Mexico, 1949—. Wenner-Gren Foundation for Anthropological Research, corporate member, member of board of directors, and first vice-president, 1955-63, life research associate, 1964—; member of national board, World Federalists; member of advisory board, International World Federalists. Founding fellow of several conferences and foundations. *Military service:* U.S. Army, Tank Corps, 1917-19; became second lieutenant.

MEMBER: Association for the History and Philosophy of Science (president, 1947), American Philosophical Association (president, 1952), American Association for Advancement of Science (fellow; representative on national board), American Physical Society, American Society of Cybernetics, American Academy of Arts and Sciences (fellow), American Academy of Political and Social Science (fellow), American Council of Learned Societies, Connecticut Academy of Arts and Sciences, Delta Sigma Rho, Phi Beta Kappa, Sigma Xi, Elizabethan Club, Berzelius Club, Lawn Club, Century Club, Yale Club (New York).

AWARDS, HONORS: Guggenheim fellow, 1932-33; Litt.D., Beloit College, 1946; LL.D., University of Hawaii, 1949, and Rollins College, 1955; H.H.D., Pratt Institute, 1961; American Council of Learned Societies prize, 1962; William Clyde De Vane Phi Beta Kappa award, 1968; William L. Cross Yale Graduate School award, 1968; Order of Aztec Eagle, Government of Mexico; Wendell Willkie Freedom House Award; Fund for Adult Education prize.

WRITINGS:

Science and First Principles, Macmillan, 1931, reprinted, Ox Bow, 1979.
The Meeting of East and West, Macmillan, 1946, reprinted, Ox Bow, 1979.
The Logic of the Sciences and the Humanities, Macmillan, 1947, reprinted, Greenwood Press, 1983.
The Taming of the Nations, Macmillan, 1952.
European Union and United States Foreign Policy, Macmillan, 1954.
The Complexity of Legal and Ethical Experiences, Little, Brown, 1959, reprinted, Greenwood Press, 1978.
Philosophical Anthropology and Practical Politics, Macmillan, 1960.
Man, Nature and God, Simon & Schuster, 1962.
(Contributor) *Contemporary American Philosophy,* Macmillan, 1970.

(With J. Sinoes da Fonseca) *Interpersonal Relations in Neuropsychological and Legal Science,* Macmillan, 1975.

EDITOR AND CONTRIBUTOR

Ideological Differences and World Order, Yale University Press, 1949, reprinted, Greenwood Press, 1971.
(With Mason Gross) *Alfred North Whitehead: An Anthology,* Macmillan, 1953.
(With Helen Livingston) *Cross-Cultural Understanding: Epistemology in Anthropology,* Harper, 1964.

WORK IN PROGRESS: The Meanings of Traditional and Contemporary Art; The Existential Import of Scientific Objects; An Analysis of Semitic Theistic Religious Doctrine.

AVOCATIONAL INTERESTS: Baseball, landscape, impressionistic art, travel.†

*   *   *

NULL, Gary

PERSONAL: Son of Robert C. and Blandenia J. (Whitehead) Null.

CAREER: Director of Nutrition Institute of America, New York, N.Y., 1976—.

WRITINGS:

How to Turn Ideas into Dollars, Pilot Books, 1969.
The Conspirator Who Saved the Romanovs, Prentice-Hall, 1971.
Profitable Part-Time Home Based Businesses: How You Can Make up to $150 a Week Extra Income, Pilot Books, 1971, revised edition, 1978.
Surviving and Settling in New York on a Shoestring, Pilot Books, 1971.
(With Steve Null) *The Complete Handbook of Nutrition,* Speller, 1972.
(With others) *The Complete Question and Answer Book of General Nutrition,* Speller, 1972.
Grow Your Own Food Organically, Speller, 1972.
(With S. Null) *Herbs for the Seventies,* Speller, 1972.
The Natural Organic Beauty Book, Speller, 1972.
Body Pollution, edited by James Dawson, Arco, 1973.
Protein for Vegetarians, Pyramid Publications, 1974, revised and enlarged edition, 1975.
Foodcombing Handbook, Pyramid Publications, 1974.
Biofeedback, Fasting, and Meditation, Pyramid Publications, 1975.
Black Hollywood: The Negro in Motion Pictures, Citadel, 1975.
Alcohol and Nutrition, Pyramid Publications, 1976.
Whole Body Health and Nutrition Book, Pinnacle Books, 1976.
Successful Pregnancy, Pyramid Publications, 1976.
Handbook of Skin and Hair, Pyramid Publications, 1976.
Italio-Americans, Stackpole, 1976.
Man and His Whole Earth, Stackpole, 1976.
How to Get Rid of the Poisons in Your Body, Arco, 1977.
(With S. Null) *The New Vegetarian: Building Your Health through Natural Eating,* Morrow, 1978.

(With S. Null) *Why Your Stomach Hurts: A Handbook of Digestion and Nutrition,* Dodd, 1979.
The New Vegetarian Cookbook, Collier Books, 1980.
Gary Null's Nutrition Sourcebook for the Eighties, Macmillan, 1983.
Complete Guide to Health and Nutrition, Delacorte, 1984.

*   *   *

NURMI, Martin Karl   1920-

PERSONAL: Born September 4, 1920, in Duluth, Minn.; son of Kalle Alexander and Maiju (Onkka) Nurmi; married Ruth Elizabeth Swanson, 1944 (divorced, 1979); married Mary Ellen Gilpatric, 1979; children: (first marriage) Michael, Katherine, Susan. *Education:* University of Chicago, A.M., 1948; University of Minnesota, Ph.D., 1954. *Politics:* Democrat.

ADDRESSES: Home—1400 Ridgecrest, Kent, Ohio. *Office*—Department of English, Kent State University, Kent, Ohio. 44242.

CAREER: Raytheon Electronics Corp., Chicago, Ill., engineer, 1944-46; Florence State College (now University of North Alabama), Florence, Ala., instructor, 1948-49; instructor and research assistant, University of Minnesota, 1950-52; University of North Dakota, Grand Forks, instructor, 1952-54; Kent State University, Kent, Ohio, assistant professor, 1955-58, associate professor, 1958-63, professor of English, 1963—, dean of graduate school, 1964-68. Visiting associate professor, University of Washington, Seattle, summer, 1962; visiting lecturer, University of Minnesota, 1962-63; visiting professor, Michigan State University, summer, 1966, and University of British Columbia, summer, 1967.

MEMBER: American Association of University Professors, Modern Language Association of America.

AWARDS, HONORS: Ford Foundation faculty fellow in literature and philosophy at Princeton University, 1954-55; President's Medal, Kent State University.

WRITINGS:

Blake's ''Marriage of Heaven and Hell'': A Critical Study, Kent State University, 1957.
(With G. E. Bentley, Jr.) *A Blake Bibliography,* University of Minnesota Press, 1964.
(With C. S. Felver) *Poetry: An Introduction,* Merrill, 1967.
William Blake, Hutchinson, 1975, Kent State University Press, 1976.

Also author of libretto for ''The Legend of Sleepy Hollow,'' produced at Kent State University, 1962. Contributor to professional journals.

WORK IN PROGRESS: Writing on Romantic poetry and music.

AVOCATIONAL INTERESTS: Music, making musical instruments, photography, electronics.†

O

O'BRIEN, Andrew William 1910-
(Andy O'Brien)

PERSONAL: Born February 11, 1910; son of William John and Mary Anne (McMahon) O'Brien; married Frances Galvin, June 3, 1936. *Education:* Loyola College, Montreal, Quebec, B.A., 1931. *Religion:* Roman Catholic.

ADDRESSES: Home—4581 Cumberland Ave., Montreal H4B 2L5, Quebec, Canada.

CAREER: Staff writer for *Montreal Standard* and its successor, *Weekend* (magazine), Montreal, Quebec, 1932-78, covered police and fire departments for *Standard* in earlier days, sports editor of *Weekend,* 1951-78. War correspondent, 1939-45.

MEMBER: Canadian War Correspondents Association, Montreal Amateur Athletic Association.

AWARDS, HONORS: Award from Canadian Amateur Sports Federation for contribution to amateur sports, 1967.

WRITINGS:

UNDER NAME ANDY O'BRIEN

Rocket Richard, Ryerson, 1961.
Headline Hockey, Ryerson, 1963.
Daredevils of Niagara, Ryerson, 1965.
Hockey Wingman, Norton, 1967.
Fire-Wagon Hockey: The Story of the Montreal Canadiens, Follett, 1967.
Young Hockey Champions, Norton, 1969, 2nd edition, McGraw, 1971.
Superstars: Hockey's Greatest Players, McGraw, 1973.
The Jacques Pante Story, McGraw, 1973.
My Friend the Hangman, McGraw, 1974.

Contributor of feature stories to almost fifty newspapers in the past thirty years.

SIDELIGHTS: Andrew William O'Brien has flown about two million miles covering Olympic and other sports events throughout the world since the 1940s.

*   *   *

O'BRIEN, Andy
See O'BRIEN, Andrew William

O'CONNOR, Patricia Walker 1931-

PERSONAL: Born April 26, 1931, in Memphis, Tenn.; daughter of Shade Wilson (a college president) and Lillie (Mullins) Walker; married David Evans O'Connor, April 4, 1953 (divorced, 1965); married Anthony M. Pasquariello, February 11, 1978; children: (first marriage) Michael Peter, Erin Anne. *Education:* Attended Florida State University, 1949-51, and University of Havanna, summer, 1949; University of Florida, B.A.E., 1953, M.A., 1954, Ph.D., 1962.

ADDRESSES: Home—727 Dixmyth Ave., Cincinnati, Ohio 45220. *Office*—Department of Romance Languages, University of Cincinnati, Cincinnati, Ohio 45221.

CAREER: University of Cincinnati, Cincinnati, Ohio, instructor, 1962-63, assistant professor, 1963-67, associate professor, 1967-72, professor of Romance languages, 1972—.

MEMBER: Modern Language Association of America, American Association of Teachers of Spanish and Portuguese, American Association of University Professors, Midwest Modern Language Association, Phi Beta Kappa.

AWARDS, HONORS: Taft grants, 1965 and 1972; American Philosophical Society grant, 1971.

WRITINGS:

Women in the Theater of Gregorio Martinez Sierra, American Book Co., 1967.
Gregorio and Maria Martinez Sierra, Twayne, 1977.
(Editor with husband, Anthony M. Pasquariello) Antonio Buero Vallejo, *El tragaluz,* Scribner, 1977.
(Editor with Pasquariello) *Contemporary Spanish Theater,* Scribner, 1980.
Plays of Protest from the Franco Era, SGEL, 1981.
Contemporary Spanish Theater: The Social Comedies of the Sixties, SGEL, 1983.

Contributor to Spanish literature journals. Member of editorial staff, *Modern International Drama, Hispanofila,* and *Anales de la novela de posguerra;* editor, *Estreno* (Spanish theater journal).

WORK IN PROGRESS: Research on contemporary Spanish theater, women dramatists, problems of post-Franco theater, women novelists, images of women in Spanish literature, and the contemporary Spanish novel.

SIDELIGHTS: Patricia Walker O'Connor told *CA* that her father was a positive influence in her life. "He was delighted to have a daughter (only child) and never saw—or let me see—gender as a barrier to accomplishment. These are exciting times to be a woman!"

AVOCATIONAL INTERESTS: Tennis (competitive), piano, minor arts and crafts, play directing, and travel.

*   *   *

OGLESBY, Joseph 1931-
(Alicia Fires, Malcolm Kain, Angelo Mulesko, Lewis Vale, Jeff Woodson)

PERSONAL: Born August 14, 1931, in Louisville, Ky.; son of Joseph (a businessman) and Mary (an artist; maiden name, Wigginton) Oglesby; married Mary Bachmann (a writer), 1971; children: Joshua. *Education:* University of Louisville, B.A., 1953.

ADDRESSES: Home and office—416 Belgravia Ct., Louisville, Ky. 40208. *Agent*—Joan Daves, 59 East 54th St., New York, N.Y. 10022.

CAREER: Louisville Times, Louisville, Ky., staff writer and assistant financial editor, 1954-56; *New Albany Tribune,* New Albany, Ind., city editor, 1956-59; *Jeffersonville Evening News,* Jeffersonville, Ind., managing editor, 1960; *Frankfort Crusader,* Frankfort, Ky., editor and publisher, 1961; *Greensboro News,* Greensboro, N.C., copy editor, 1961-62; *Tonawanda News,* North Tonawanda, N.Y., police reporter, 1963-64; Scripps-Howard Newspapers, St. Matthews, Ky., executive editor of *Voice* newspapers, 1964-70; National Kitchen Cabinet Association, Louisville, public relations director, 1970-72; full-time writer, 1972—. Vice-chairman of board of managers of Young Men's Christian Association (YMCA) in St. Matthews, 1970.

MEMBER: American Newspaper Guild, Mystery Writers of America, Western Writers of America, Society of Children's Book Writers, Pi Delta Epsilon, Optimist Club (St. Matthews).

AWARDS, HONORS: Best feature story award, 1967, and best news story award, 1968, from Kentucky Press Association; Pulitzer Prize nomination, 1968; commissioned Kentucky Colonel, 1979; American Society of Journalists and Authors grant, 1983, 1985; P.E.N. International Center grant, 1983.

WRITINGS:

(Under pseudonym Jeff Woodson) *The Fires Down Below,* Orpheus Books, 1974.
(Under pseudonym Lewis Vale) *Model for Hire,* Orpheus Books, 1974.
(Under pseudonym Malcolm Kain) *The Sensuous Rebel,* Orpheus Books, 1975.
(Under pseudonym Malcolm Kain) *Camera Girls,* Carlyle, 1975.
(Under pseudonym Malcolm Kain) *Three-Ring Circus,* Carlyle, 1975.
(Under pseudonym Malcolm Kain) *Beach Ball Blonde,* Carlyle, 1976.
(Under pseudonym Angelo Mulesko) *Silky,* Carlyle, 1976.
The Marvelous Kingdom of Wee, Parnassus, 1976.

The Devil's Disciple, Bladkompaniet (Oslo, Norway), 1977.
Ghost Riders of the Staked Plains, Tower, 1980.
(Contributor) *Family Circle Hints Book,* Times Books, 1982.
The Lost Island, Carlyle, 1983.
(Under pseudonym Alicia Fires) *Sex Marks the Spot,* Carlyle, 1984.

Contributor of short stories, articles, and book reviews to numerous periodicals, including *Roundup, Prairie Schooner, Views, Courier-Journal Sunday Magazine, Chicago Sun-Times,* and *Western Magazine.*

WORK IN PROGRESS: A screenplay based upon one of his novels.

SIDELIGHTS: Joseph Oglesby told *CA:* "My motivation for writing fiction has shifted over the years. At first I wrote genre fiction—I've published novels in five genres—to satisfy a creative drive, to vent fantasies. Now I'm writing to preserve some of my memories, often fragile, of real events in my own life, though placed in a fictitious framework.

"The novel form not only allows me to reshape, redefine, and even burnish my own past, but to make it far more interesting and illuminating than it actually was. It's also a great deal of fun to go poking into one's past, shaking skeletons, remembering happy times, sometimes discovering entirely new perspectives.

"When I'm not writing, I take long walks with my wife and son, Joshua, or I read. I love the novels of Frederic Prokosch, Truman Capote, Philip Roth, William Styron, and a host of French novelists, including Andre Gide, Albert Camus and Georges Simenon. My favorite book, curiously enough, is not a novel but Ernest Hemingway's odyssey, *A Moveable Feast.* I'm also a great film buff and have done considerable research on the life and works of David Wark Griffith, whose mother was my great-great aunt.

"Travel is among my other interests, and I would love to lead an expedition to some of the more remote Mayan sites in Guatamala or to retrace T. E. Lawrence's path when he studied crusade fortifications in northern Africa. Also, the pyramids and the Nile and anything Egyptian fascinate me."

*   *   *

OLD, Bruce S(cott) 1913-

PERSONAL: Born October 21, 1913, in Norfolk, Va.; son of Edward H. H. (an officer in the Medical Corps, U.S. Navy) and Eugenia (Smith) Old; married Katharine Day, October 7, 1939; children: Edward, Randolph, Lansing, Ashlee, Barbara. *Education:* University of North Carolina, B.S., 1935; Massachusetts Institute of Technology, Sc.D., 1938. *Religion:* Episcopalian.

ADDRESSES: Home—351 Hemlock Cir., Lincoln, Mass. 01773. *Office*—Bruce S. Old Associates, Inc., P.O. Box 706, Concord, Mass. 01742.

CAREER: Bethlehem Steel Corp., Bethlehem, Pa., research engineer, 1938-41; Arthur D. Little, Inc., Cambridge, Mass., metallurgist, 1946-51, director, 1949-51, vice-president, 1951-60, senior vice-president, 1960-78; Bruce S. Old Associates, Inc., Concord, Mass., president, 1979—. Cambridge Corp., president, 1951-53, chairman of the board, 1953-55; president of Nuclear Metals, Inc., 1954-57. Atomic Energy Commission, chief metallurgist, 1947-49, consultant, 1949-55. Chairman of Concord Community Chest, 1952, and National Conference on Administrative Research, 1966. Member of science advisory committee, Executive Office of the President, 1951-54, and Concord School Committee, 1954-59. *Military service:* U.S. Naval Reserve, 1941-46; became commander; awarded commendation ribbon.

MEMBER: National Academy of Engineering, American Institute of Mining, Metallurgical and Petroleum Engineers, American Society for Metals (fellow), American Nuclear Society, American Association for the Advancement of Science (fellow), New York Academy of Science, Union Club (Boston), Cosmos Club (Washington, D.C.), Concord Country Club.

WRITINGS:

WITH WILLIAM F. TALBERT

The Game of Doubles in Tennis, diagrams by Stephen P. Baldwin, Lippincott, 1956, 4th edition, 1977.
The Game of Singles in Tennis, illustrations by wife, Katharine D. Old, and Ed Vebell, diagrams by Baldwin, Lippincott, 1962, revised edition, 1977.
Stroke Production in the Game of Tennis, illustrations by K. Old, Lippincott, 1971.
Tennis Tactics: Singles and Doubles, Harper, 1983.

EDITOR

(With Lawrence W. Bass) *Formulation of Research Policies: Collected Papers from an International Symposium,* American Association for the Advancement of Science, 1967.

OTHER

Contributor of technical articles to professional journals.

*   *   *

OLEKSY, Walter   1930-

PERSONAL: Born June 24, 1930, in Chicago, Ill.; son of John Joseph (an elevated motorman) and Pauline (Standacher) Oleksy. *Education:* Michigan State University of Agriculture and Applied Sciences (now Michigan State University), B.A., 1955. *Politics:* Independent. *Religion:* Roman Catholic.

ADDRESSES: Home and office—2106 Maple Ave., Evanston, Ill. 60201. *Agent*—Adele Leone, 52 Riverside Dr., Apt. 6-A, New York, N.Y. 10024.

CAREER: City News Bureau, Chicago, Ill., reporter and rewriter, 1958; *Chicago Tribune,* Chicago, reporter, writer, and editor, 1958-65; Geyer, Oswald (advertising agency), Chicago, editor and writer, 1965-67; *Chicago Land* (magazine), Chicago, editor, 1968; Allstate Insurance Co., Northbrook, Ill., editor of *Discovery* (motor club travel magazine), 1968-71; free-lance writer, 1971—. *Military service:* U.S. Army, 1955-57; served in Germany.

WRITINGS:

ADULT NONFICTION

One Thousand Tested Money-Making Markets for Writers, Parker Publishing, 1973.
The Old Country Cook Book, Nelson-Hall, 1974.
Bicentennial Vacation Guide, Rand McNally, 1976.
Reach for the Stars: Helping Yourself with Personal Astrology, Parker Publishing, 1980.

Magic Dimes-to-Dollars Wealth Secrets, Parker Publishing, 1980.
The Power of Concentration, Argus Press, 1981.
Builders' and Contractors' Guide to New Methods and Materials in Home Construction, Prentice-Hall, 1983.
(Contributor) *The Complete Guide to Writing Non-Fiction,* Writers Digest, 1983.
Employee Benefit Programs: A Guide to Benefit Cost-Effectiveness, Prentice-Hall, 1985.
Complete Guide to Modular Residential Construction Materials and Techniques, Prentice-Hall, 1986.

BOOKS FOR YOUNG ADULTS

The Universe Is within You, Messner, 1977.
Visitors from Outer Space?, Putnam, 1978.
Careers in the Animal Kingdom, Messner, 1980.
It's Women's Work, Too!, Messner, 1980.
Treasures of the Land, Messner, 1981.
The Black Plague, F. Watts, 1982.
Nature Gone Wild!, Messner, 1982.
Up from Nowhere, Jove, 1982.
The Pirates of Dead Man's Cay, Westminster, 1982.
One-Way Trip, Jove, 1983.
Paramedics, Messner, 1983.
UFO: Teen Sightings, Messner, 1984.
Treasures of the Deep, Messner, 1984.
The Final Act, Jove, 1984.

Also author of *Easy Way Out,* Jove.

BOOKS FOR PRETEENS

Laugh, Clown, Cry: The Story of Charlie Chaplin, Raintree, 1976.
If I'm Lost, How Come I Found You?, (novel), McGraw, 1978.
The Golden Goat, Baker Book, 1981.
Quacky and the Haunted Amusement Park, McGraw, 1982.
Quacky and the Crazy Curve-Ball, McGraw, 1982.
Bug Scanner and the Computer Mystery, Walker & Co., 1983.
The Nuclear Arms Race, F. Watts, 1986.
Miracles of Genetics, Children's Press, 1986.
The Video Revolution, Children's Press, 1986.
Laser Technology, Children's Press, 1986.
''Be Aware Books'' series, four volumes, Modern Publishing, 1986.

OTHER

Contributor of articles to magazines. Former managing editor of Third Armored Division newspaper; former editor of *Progress* and *Discovery* magazines.

SIDELIGHTS: Walter Oleksy told *CA:* ''I enjoy researching and writing books and articles for adults and juveniles on just about any subject, but I enjoy most writing nutsy adventures for kids that also have a message tossed in—like it's wrong to steal, or it's good to be helpful to others. I just wish publishers and editors weren't so conservative. They tend to think only in categories and are reluctant to accept new ideas. I'm glad to be writing, but I wish I were writing twenty or thirty years ago, when more was being published and there was more respect for good fiction for adults and kids. Publishing today is a matter of follow the leader, not let's start a trend. It's sad for readers and writers.''

AVOCATIONAL INTERESTS: Photography and microphotography, music, gardening, cooking, home improvement projects, dinners with friends, swimming, tennis, wilderness canoe trips, long walks.

* * *

OLIVER, James Henry 1905-

PERSONAL: Born April 26, 1905, in New York, N.Y.; son of James Henry and Louise (McGratty) Oliver; married Janet Carnochan, 1936. *Education:* Yale University, B.A., 1926, Ph.D., 1931; University of Bonn, additional study, 1927-28; American Academy in Rome, fellow, 1928-30.

CAREER: Yale University, New Haven, Conn., instructor, 1930-32; American Mission for the Excavation of the Ancient Athenian Agora, Athens, Greece, epigraphist and excavator, 1932-36, 1939-40; Columbia University, New York, N.Y., assistant professor, 1936-42; Johns Hopkins University, Baltimore, Md., professor of classics, 1946-57, Francis White Professor of Greek, 1957-70. Senior fellow, Center for Hellenic Studies, Washington, D.C., 1962-71. Member of various committees, American School of Classical Studies at Athens, 1938-69. Member of organizing committee, 3rd International Congress of Greek and Latin Epigraphy, Rome, 1958; participant in colloquium concerning Roman emperors of Spain, Madrid, 1964. *Military service:* U.S. Army, 1942-45; became major.

MEMBER: American Philological Association (vice-president, 1973-74; president, 1975), Society for the Promotion of Roman Studies, Archaeological Institute of America (chairman of monograph committee, 1960-64), Austrian Archaeological Institute (honorary member).

WRITINGS:

The Greek Inscriptions of Hibis, Metropolitan Museum, 1938.
The Sacred Gerusia, American School of Classical Studies at Athens, 1941, reprinted, Swets & Zeitlinger, 1975.
The Temple of Hibis in El Khargeh Oasis, Metropolitan Museum of Art, 1941, reprinted, 1973.
The Athenian Expounders, Johns Hopkins Press, 1950.
The Ruling Power: A Study of the Roman Empire in the Second Century after Christ through the Roman Oration of Aelius Aristides, American Philosophical Society, 1956.
Demokratia, the Gods, and the Free World, Johns Hopkins Press, 1960, reprinted, Arno, 1979.
The Civilizing Power, American Philosophical Society, 1968.
Marcus Aurelius: Aspects of Civic and Cultural Policy in the East, American School of Classical Studies at Athens, 1970.
The Civic Tradition and Roman Athens, Johns Hopkins University Press, 1983.

Member of editorial board, *American Journal of Philology;* advisor to *Greek, Roman and Byzantine Studies,* 1958—.†

* * *

OLSON, Richard G(eorge) 1940-

PERSONAL: Born November 4, 1940, in St. Paul, Minn.; married, 1962. *Education:* Harvey Mudd College, B.S., 1962; Harvard University, A.M., 1963, Ph.D., 1967.

ADDRESSES: Office—Department of History, Harvey Mudd College, Claremont, Calif. 91711.

CAREER: Harvard University, Cambridge, Mass., tutor in history and science, 1964-66; Tufts University, Medford, Mass.,

instructor in history, 1966-67; University of California, Santa Cruz, 1967-76, assistant professor, 1967-72, associate professor of history and head of history board of studies, 1972-74; Harvey Mudd College, Claremont, Calif., professor of history and Willard J. Keith Fellow in the Humanities, both 1976—, chairman of department of humanities and social sciences, 1982—. Directs and participates in scholarly meetings.

MEMBER: West Coast History of Science Society.

AWARDS, HONORS: Woodrow Wilson fellowship, 1962; National Endowment for the Humanities younger humanist fellowship, 1971-72; grants from Lilly Foundation, 1977, 1978; Arnold L. and Lois S. Graves Award, 1979-80.

WRITINGS:

(Editor) *Science as Metaphor: The Historical Roles of Scientific Theories in Forming Western Culture,* Wadsworth, 1971.
Scottish Philosophy and British Physics, 1750-1850: Foundations of the Victorian Scientific Style, Princeton University Press, 1975.
Science Deified and Science Defied, University of California Press, 1982.
The Uses of Science in the Age of Newton, University of California Press, 1983.

Contributor to *Tradition and Transformation in the History of Science: Essays in Honor of I. Bernard Cohen,* Cambridge University Press. Contributor of more than thirty articles and reviews to scientific journals.

WORK IN PROGRESS: Understanding and Undermining: An Interpretation of Scientism in Western Culture.

SIDELIGHTS: Richard Olson's *Science Deified and Science Defied* examines the effect of the rise of scientific attitudes and practices on our culture. In a *Los Angeles Times* review, David Linsey observes that the book "studies not only obvious material impacts but also more subtle, pervasive influences."

BIOGRAPHICAL/CRITICAL SOURCES:

PERIODICALS

Los Angeles Times, March 1, 1983.

* * *

OPPENHEIMER, Joan L(etson) 1925-

PERSONAL: Born January 25, 1925, in Ellendale, N.D.; daughter of Maurice Devillo (a teacher) and Lola (Jones) Letson; married Robert Gridley, April 10, 1943 (divorced, 1953); married Elwyn S. Oppenheimer, June 19, 1953; children: (first marriage) Donald B., Jeffrey L.; (second marriage) Debra L. *Education:* Attended Northwestern University, 1944, and Southwestern College, 1966-70. *Politics:* Democrat. *Religion:* Protestant.

ADDRESSES: Home—1663 Mills St., Chula Vista, Calif. 92010. *Agent*—Dorothy Markinko, 475 Fifth Ave., New York, N.Y. 10017.

CAREER: First National Bank, Chicago, Ill., clerk, 1942-43; Federal Bureau of Investigation (FBI), Chicago, stenographer, 1943-45; U.S. Gauge Co., Chicago, secretary, 1945; Lever Brothers, Chicago, secretary, 1946; Rohr Corp., secretary, 1952-53; Southwestern College, Chula Vista, Calif., instructor in creative writing, 1977-84; University of California, San Diego, La Jolla, Calif., instructor in creative writing, 1982—.

MEMBER: Society of Children's Book Writers (associate), Santa Barbara Writers Conference.

WRITINGS:

FOR YOUNG PEOPLE

The Coming Down Time, Transition Press, 1969.
Run for Your Luck, Hawthorn, 1971.
The Nobody Road, Scholastic Inc., 1974.
On the Outside, Looking In, Scholastic Inc., 1975.
Francesca, Baby, Scholastic Inc., 1976.
The Lost Summer, Scholastic Inc., 1977.
It Isn't Easy Being a Teenaged Millionaire, Scholastic Inc., 1978.
Walk beside Me, Be My Friend, Scholastic Inc., 1978.
One Step Apart, Tempo Books, 1978.
No Laughing Matter, Tempo Books, 1978.
The Voices of Julie, Scholastic Inc., 1979.
Which Mother Is Mine?, Bantam, 1980.
Working on It, Harcourt, 1980.
Gardine versus Hanover, Harper, 1982.
Second Chance, Scholastic Inc., 1982.
The Missing Sunrise, Scholastic Inc., 1983.
Stepsisters, Archway, 1983.

CONTRIBUTOR TO ANTHOLOGIES

Today's Stories from "Seventeen," Macmillan, 1971.
Short Story Scene, Globe, 1974.
Dreamstalkers, Economy Co., 1975.
Oceans and Orbits, Laidlaw Brothers, 1977.

OTHER

Contributor to popular magazines, including *Redbook, Woman's Day, Seventeen, Ingenue, Boy's Life,* and *Alfred Hitchcock Mystery Magazine.*

SIDELIGHTS: Joan L. Oppenheimer told *CA:* "I began writing for young people [ages 10 to 18] because it is a group facing so many serious problems in today's world. I felt strongly that a young reader might be interested in a fictional character facing a problem, learning to cope and perhaps gaining some insight into possible solutions.

"Whenever I can, I go to the young people involved with the problems I cover in fiction (drugs, alcohol, broken homes, foster homes, etc.) and get their own views. This can cover anything from family to friends to school to the way they see the world today. When I have enough material to live comfortably in a teenaged mind for several months, I am ready to write the book already in rough outline.

"The feedback from these books has been tremendous. My young readers seem to appreciate honesty in the handling of problems they are already familiar with. They develop a greater understanding of these problems and of others who struggle with them—and they write to tell me so. In my opinion, these letters are one of the greatest rewards in writing for young people."

Oppenheimer is especially pleased with the reaction to *Francesca, Baby.* The story of two young girls and their alcoholic mother, it is being distributed as an educational tool by Walt Disney Productions. "It is marvelous to know that it can help children cope with this tremendous problem," Oppenheimer commented. "And it obviously helps children understand others who are less fortunate than they in such home situations. I am, therefore, a writer who frequently weeps over her fan mail!"

MEDIA ADAPTATIONS: Francesca, Baby, It Isn't Easy Being a Teenaged Millionaire, and *Which Mother Is Mine?* have been filmed; each has appeared as an "ABC Afterschool Special."

BIOGRAPHICAL/CRITICAL SOURCES:

PERIODICALS

Philadelphia Inquirer, January 9, 1972.
Star News (National City, Calif.), August 21, 1969.

*   *   *

OSLER, Robert Willard   1911-1984

PERSONAL: Born March 29, 1911, in Indianapolis, Ind.; died September 13, 1984, in Indianapolis, Ind.; son of Harry Francis and Mary (Ludwig) Osler; married Aurzella Magel, 1932; children: Aurzella Ann, Alice Elaine. *Education:* De Pauw University, A.B.; graduate study at Butler University, 1933-34, and Indiana University, 1935-37.

ADDRESSES: Home—1431 Clay Dr., Carmel, Ind. 46032.

CAREER: Research and Review Service of America, Indianapolis, Ind., associate editor, 1937-39, 1942-48; Acacia Mutual Life Insurance Co., Washington, D.C., advertising director, 1939-40; Dartnell Corp., Chicago, Ill., member of editorial staff, 1940-42; Rough Notes Co., Indianapolis, vice president and editor, 1948-60; Underwriters National Assurance Co., Indianapolis, founder, president, and chief executive officer, 1960-64; consultant to insurance companies, 1964-76. Director of Disability Insurance Training Council, 1960-76.

MEMBER: International Health Underwriters Association (member of board, 1959-60), General Agents and Managers Conference of National Association of Life Underwriters, American Risk and Insurance Association (editor, committee on health insurance terminology), National Association of Life Underwriters, Indiana Health Underwriters (secretary-treasurer, 1953-58), Indianapolis General Agents and Managers Association, Indianapolis Association of Underwriters, Indianapolis Health Underwriters Association (president, 1965-66), Delta Tau Delta, Masons.

AWARDS, HONORS: Elizur Wright Award for outstanding original contribution to literature of insurance, American Risk and Insurance Association, 1956, for *Modern Life Insurance;* citations for service to industry from International Health Underwriters, Indiana Life Underwriters, and General Agents and Managers Conference of National Association of Life Underwriters; Harold R. Gordon Award, International Association of Health Underwriting, 1962.

WRITINGS:

Modern Life Insurance, Macmillan, 1948.
Guide to Life Insurance, Rough Notes, 1949, 6th edition, 1968.
Guide to Health Insurance, Rough Notes, 1952, reprinted, 1972.
Business Uses of Health Insurance, American College of Life Underwriters, 1960.
Programming Health Insurance, American College of Life Underwriters, 1960.
Nine Business Uses of Health Insurance, Research and Review Service, 1961.
Fifteen Ways to Increase Production, Rough Notes, 1965.
Disability Income Selling: Approach to App, Rough Notes, 1970.

(Editor with John S. Bickley and O. D. Dickerson) *Glossary of Insurance Terms,* Insurors Press, 1972.

Also author of *Disability Income Insurance* and *101 Direct Mail Letters,* both 1973. Contributor to professional journals. Editor, *Insurance Salesman,* 1948-60.

OBITUARIES:

PERIODICALS

Insurance Industry Newsletter, October 19, 1984.†

*   *   *

OUELLETTE, Fernand 1930-

PERSONAL: Surname is pronounced wel-*let;* born September 24, 1930, in Montreal, Quebec, Canada; son of Cyrille (a carpenter) and Gilberte (Chalifour) Ouellette; married Lisette Corbeil, July 9, 1955; children: Sylvie, Andree, Jean. *Education:* Universite de Montreal, License en sciences sociales, 1952. *Religion:* Catholic.

ADDRESSES: Home—37, Terrasse Paquin, Laval, Quebec, Canada H7G 3S2. *Office*—Societe Radio-Canada, 1400 boulevard Dorchester est, Montreal, Quebec, Canada.

CAREER: Societe Radio-Canada, Montreal, Quebec, producer, 1960—. Director of creative writing workshops, University of Ottawa and Universite Laval, 1977—; visiting professor at University of Turin, 1984. Member of commission d'enquete sur l'enseignement des arts a Quebec, 1966-68; co-founder of Rencontre Quebecoise Internationale des Ecrivains, 1972.

MEMBER: Union des Ecrivains Quebecois.

AWARDS, HONORS: Prix France-Quebec, 1967, for *Edgard Varese;* Prix du Gouverneur general, 1971, for *Les Actes retrouves: Essais* (refused); Prix France-Canada, 1972, for *Poesie: 1953-1971; Etudes francaises* (magazine) award, 1974, for *Journal denoue.*

WRITINGS:

Ces Anges de sang (poems; title means "These Angels of Blood"), l'Hexagone (Montreal), 1955.
Sequences de l'aile (poems; title means "Wing Sequences"), l'Hexagone, 1958.
(Editor and contributor) *Visages d'Edgard Varese* (title means "Aspects of Edgard Varese"), l'Hexagone, 1959.
Le Soleil sous la mort (poems; title means "The Sun under Darkness"), l'Hexagone, 1965.
Edgard Varese (biography), Seghers (Paris), 1966, translation by Derek Coltman published under same title, Orion Press, 1968.
Dans le sombre (poems; title means "In the Dark"), l'Hexagone, 1967.
Les Actes retrouves: Essais (title means "Recovered Acts"), HMH, 1970.
Poesie: 1953-1971, l'Hexagone, 1972, revised edition, 1979.
Depuis Novalis: Essai (title means "From Novalis"), HMH, 1973.
Journal denoue (autobiography), Presses de l'Universite de Montreal, 1974, revised edition, 1975.
Errances (poems), Editions Bourguignon, 1977.
Ici, ailleurs, la lumiere (poems), l'Hexagone, 1977.
Tu regardais intensement Genevieve (novel), Editions Quinze, 1978, revised edition, 1980.
A decouvert (poems), Editions Paralleles, 1979.

Ecrire en notre temps (essays), HMH, 1979.
La Mort vive (novel), Quinze Editeur, 1980.
En la nuit, la mer (poems), l'Hexagone, 1980.
Eveils (poems), Editions de l'Obsidienne, 1982.
Ahimsa, Andre Prevost, 1984.
Lucie; ou, Un Midi en novembre (novel), Boreal Express (Montreal), 1985.

Also author of film commentaries for l'Office National du Film, 1955-59; author of text for cantata by Pierre Mercure, "Psaume pour abri" (title means "Psalm for a Shelter"), produced by Radio Canada, 1963. Work is represented in more than a dozen anthologies, including *How Do I Love Thee: Sixty Poets of Canada (and Quebec) Select and Introduce Their Favourite Poems from Their Own Work,* edited by John Robert Colombo, M. G. Hurtig, 1970, *The Poetry of French Canada in Translation,* edited by J. Glassco, Oxford University Press, 1970, and *Anthology of Contemporary French Poetry,* edited by Granham D. Martin, Edinburgh University Press, 1972. Contributor to numerous periodicals. *Liberte,* co-founder and editor, 1958, member of editorial board, 1958—.

SIDELIGHTS: Fernand Ouellette told *CA:* "I write poems only in order to try to comprehend that which cannot be said.

"The essay, in its various forms, as an effort of language, allows me to think or to put into concrete form what I think.

"The novel makes clear my difficulty in living and the nature of my quest, which is inseparable from the deeply rooted desire in my memory.

"After having seen many paintings in various European and American museums, I am more and more fascinated by the space of the canvas, by the correspondence between poetry and painting. I have begun a project in which poems will be organically linked with pictorial or musical works and essays with paintings or artists. This link between poetry and painting is very strong in French literature. It is as if their concerns were of the same nature.

"The poet who has influenced me the most is Pierre Jean Jouve. He has helped me to concretize the constellation of sound-meaning-energy emanating from the world and from womankind. He was the first, in an unpublished letter, to support me in my writing endeavors by insisting on the necessity of maintaining a tragic vision in poetry."

AVOCATIONAL INTERESTS: Music, painting, travel.

BIOGRAPHICAL/CRITICAL SOURCES:

BOOKS

Brindaud, Serge, *La Poesie francaise contemporaine depuis 1945,* Editions Saint-Germain-des-Pres (Paris), 1973.
de Grandpre, Pierre, *Histoire de la litterature francaise du Quebec,* Beauchemin, 1969.
Dictionnaire des oeuvres litteraires du Quebec, Fides, Volume III, 1982, Volume IV, 1984.
Haeck, Philippe, *L'Action restreinte de la litterature,* Editions de l'Aurore, 1975.
Mailhot, Laurent, *La Litterature quebecoise,* Presses Universitaires de France, 1974.
Malenfant, Paul Chanel, *La Partie et le tout,* Presses de l'Universite Laval, 1983.
Marcotte, Gilles, *Le Temps des poetes,* HMH, 1969.
Nepveu, Pierre, *Les Mots a l'ecoute,* Presses de l'Universite Laval, 1979.
Robert, Guy, *Litterature du Quebec,* Volume I, Deom, 1964.

Tougas, Gerard, *Histoire de la litterature canadienne-fran-
caise*, Presses Universitaires de France, 1960.
Voix et images du pays, Volume III, Presses de l'Universite
du Quebec, 1970.

PERIODICALS

Ellipse, Number 10, 1972.
Esprit, June, 1973, April, 1975.
Etudes francaises, May, 1975.
Europe, February-March, 1969.
La Barre du jour, Number 11, 1973.
L'Actualite, December, 1978.
Livers et auteurs quebecois (annual publication), 1969-70, 1972-
75, 1977-79.
Magazine litteraire, September, 1978.
Osiris, June, 1985.
Relations, December, 1975, October, 1978.
Voix et Images, May-June, 1980.

P

PACHAI, Bridglal 1927-

PERSONAL: Born November 30, 1927, in Ladysmith, Natal, South Africa; son of Sukrani (Mardan) Pachai; married Leelawathie Ramnath (a dental assistant), December 28, 1952; children: Jairaj, Indira, Santosh, Ansuya, Pradeep. *Education:* University of South Africa, B.A., 1954, B.A. (with honors), 1956, M.A., 1958; University of Natal, Ph.D., 1962. *Religion:* Hindu.

ADDRESSES: *Office*—Black Cultural Centre of Nova Scotia, P.O. Box 2128, East Dartmouth, Nova Scotia, Canada B2W 3Y2.

CAREER: High school teacher of English and history in Ladysmith, Natal, South Africa, 1958-62; University College of Cape Coast, Cape Coast, Ghana, lecturer in history, 1962-65; University of Malawi, Zomba, professor of history, 1965-75; Dalhousie University, Halifax, Nova Scotia, and Mount Saint Vincent University, Halifax, professor of history, 1976-77; Saint Mary's University, Halifax, director of International Education Centre, 1977-79; University of Sokoto, Sokoto, Nigeria, professor of history, 1979-85; Black Cultural Centre of Nova Scotia, East Dartmouth, director, 1985—.

AWARDS, HONORS: Senior Killam fellow at Dalhousie University, 1975-76.

WRITINGS:

History of Indian Opinion, Government Printer (Cape Town, South Africa), 1963.
(Editor with R. K. Tangri and G. W. Smith) *Malawi, Past and Present,* Christian Literature Association of Malawi, 1970.
(Editor) *The Memoirs of Lewis Mataka Bandawe,* Christian Literature Association of Malawi, 1971.
(Editor) *Early History of Malawi,* Longman, 1971.
The International Aspects of the South African Indian Question, Struik, 1971.
Malawi: The History of the Nation, Longman, 1973.
(Editor) *Livingstone, Man of Africa: Memorial Essays,* Longman, 1973.
Land and Politics in Malawi, 1875-1975, Limestone Press, 1978.
South Africa's Indians: The Evolution of a Minority, University Press of America, 1979.

(Editor with Surendra Bhana) *A Documentary History of Indian South Africans, 1860-1982,* Hoover Institution, 1984.

Also author of a biography on Dr. William Pearly Oliver, Nova Scotia Museum. Contributor to scholarly journals.

WORK IN PROGRESS: *History of the Malawi Ngoni.*

SIDELIGHTS: Bridglal Pachai comments: ''My upbringing in South Africa has created a deep awareness of the experiences of black persons and minorities, and the relevance of objective studies in race relations. I have written articles on multiculturalism in Canada and the experience of blacks in Nova Scotia, and these have flowed spontaneously from my background in Africa and my entry into North American society as a new Canadian.

''My publications on South Africa examine the experiences of persons of Indian origin in the context of the total situation in that country. They draw attention to the extremely difficult position in which South African Indians find themselves, surrounded as they are by pressures emanating from many quarters. In spite of their extreme vulnerability, my studies show that this minority community has adapted—and responded—with resilience.

''My decade in Malawi was most enjoyable, rewarding, and memorable. My writings bear evidence of the growth situation in which the academic fraternity found itself in a newly independent country and in a brand new university. In many ways, it is fair to consider my historical studies on Malawi to be part of the pioneering products of a difficult and trying period.

''My five and one-half years of work in Sokoto, in northern Nigeria, have added to my insights on Africa. This area has a character of its own, vibrating with the historical traditions of Islamic Africa. My future writings will surely reflect my return to Canada, as I pick up the threads of multiculturalism and race relations.''

*   *   *

PALMS, Roger C(urtis) 1936-

PERSONAL: Born September 13, 1936, in Detroit, Mich.; son of Nelson C. and Winifred J. Palms; married Andrea Sisson, 1959; children: Grant Curtis, Andrea Jane. *Education:* Wayne

State University, B.A., 1958; Eastern Baptist Theological Seminary, B.D., 1961, M.Div., 1971, D.D., 1977; Michigan State University, M.A., 1971; graduate study at Princeton Theological Seminary.

ADDRESSES: Home—8719 19th Ave. S., Bloomington, Minn. 55420. *Office—Decision*, 1300 Harmon Place, Minneapolis, Minn. 55403.

CAREER: Ordained American Baptist minister, 1961; pastor of Baptist churches in Ronceverte, W.Va., 1961-64, and Highland Park, N.J., 1964-67; Michigan State University, East Lansing, chaplain of American Baptist Student Foundation, 1967-73; *Decision,* Minneapolis, Minn., assistant editor, 1973-74, associate editor, 1975-76, editor, 1976—. Lectures extensively; reads for radio.

WRITINGS:

The Jesus Kids, Judson, 1971.
The Christian and the Occult, Judson, 1972.
God Holds Your Tomorrows, Augsburg, 1976.
God's Promises for You, Revell, 1977.
Upon a Penny Loaf, Bethany Fellowship, 1978.
The Pleasure of His Company, Tyndale, 1982.
First Things First, Scripture Press, 1983.
Living under the Smile of God, Tyndale, 1984.

SIDELIGHTS: Roger C. Palms told *CA:* "Teaching other writers is important to me. I teach college and seminary classes, lecture at schools of writing and other workshops. I've written and taught on six continents. The Northwestern College Radio Network airs my readings on 'Something for You.' This is also carried on other stations throughout the United States."

*　　*　　*

PARK, Bill
See PARK, W(illiam) B(ryan)

*　　*　　*

PARK, W(illiam) B(ryan) 1936-
(Bill Park)

PERSONAL: Born June 12, 1936, in Sanford, Fla.; son of Charles Lanier, Sr. (a physician), and Geneva (Whitehead) Park; married Eva Kratzert (a director of a weekday school), December 28, 1961; children: William Bryan II, Robert Christopher, Anne-Marie. *Education:* University of Florida, B.A., 1959; graduate study at School of Visual Arts, New York City, 1960-61, and Rollins College, 1967-77. *Politics:* Democrat. *Religion:* Presbyterian.

ADDRESSES: Office—Park-Art Studio, 110 Park Ave. S., Winter Park, Fla. 32789.

CAREER: McGraw-Hill Book Co., New York City, staff artist, 1960-61; Tucker Wayne Advertising, Atlanta, Ga., assistant art director, 1961-63; Park-Art Studio (free-lance service for advertisers and agencies), Winter Park, Fla., owner and manager, 1963-76; free-lance illustrator, writer, and cartoonist, 1968—. Exhibitions of artwork include "The Artist as a Journalist" for Time, Inc., in New York City, 1977, a one-man show at University of Central Florida, 1979, "Cartoon '85" for Cartoonists Association in New York City, 1985, and Society of Illustrators Show in New York City, 1985.

MEMBER: Authors Guild, Society of Illustrators, Cartoonists Association.

AWARDS, HONORS: Honored for artwork in *Denzu 08,* 1978, Tokyo, *Art Direction,* 1984, New York City, and *Graphia,* 1985, Switzerland.

WRITINGS:

SELF-ILLUSTRATED JUVENILES

The Pig in the Floppy Black Hat, Putnam, 1973.
Jonathan's Friends, Putnam, 1977.
Charlie-Bob's Fan, Harcourt, 1981.
The Costume Party, Little, Brown, 1981.
Who's Sick!, Houghton, 1983.
Bakery Business, Little, Brown, 1983.

ILLLUSTRATOR

William Kottmeyer and Audrey Claus, *Basic Goals in Spelling,* McGraw, 1972.
R. N. Peck, *King of Kazoo,* Knopf, 1976.
Peck, *Basket Case,* Doubleday, 1979.
Junior Great Books, Series Two, Series Three—Volume I, Series Four—Volume II, Great Books Foundation, 1984.

CONTRIBUTOR TO ANTHOLOGIES

Holmes and Lehman, editors, *A Parade of Lines,* Canfield Press, 1971.
Ingraham, editor, *Survival,* Holbrook Press, 1971.
Weber and Lloyd, editors, *The American City,* West Publishing, 1975.

OTHER

Author of daily cartoon feature, "Off the Leash," published worldwide by United Feature Syndicate, 1985—. Contributor of articles, stories, and illustrations (including cover illustrations) to national magazines, including *Smithsonian, Travel and Leisure, Saturday Review, Time, Sports Illustrated, Fortune,* and *New Yorker.*

SIDELIGHTS: W. B. Park told *CA:* "The world has become an abysmally serious place. The hard-eyed realists have taken over, casting the romantics and poets and dreamers into outer darkness. Machine-like, the realists click and whir through life, expertly cutting up the wild flowers of fun and fantasy, and leaving a perfectly trimmed, barren, golf-green of a lawn.

"I don't want to live on a golf green. I want to wander through the wild flowers and uncut grasses and unswept leaves and yes, weeds, too. Weeds can be beautiful.

"Childhood is full of wild flowers and weeds, and the realists especially want to cut those. If they can create a golf green out of childhood, they can count on a veritable assembly line of little realists, brittle and hard-eyed as they are, marching up into adulthood.

"So they sweep the children's books of fun and innocence from the shelves and replace them with serious books about anger and truth and success and justice; and as soon as they can, they reduce Santa Claus and E. Bunny and all the other fantasies of childhood to jokes. They do this by 'enlightening' children.

"To step on those first fragile, intoxicating dreams and hopes, and click on the searing light of the 'real world' is not only unnecessary, it is destructive. Fantasy is the stretching of young wings; clip those wings and they may never grow back.

"A child's belief in the fantasies of childhood need never be broken. Parents who nurture and share these things with their children reap breathtaking treasures. If the believing is defended and encouraged in the face of a world of cynics, young and old, it will gradually mature into a higher intellectual and spiritual understanding. And then it will be discovered that the fantasies *are* real, and that the reality is in the love and fun and hope of them.

"I refuse to let the realists cancel childhood. My book *Jonathan's Friends* is a celebration of faith, and the importance of holding onto it."

BIOGRAPHICAL/CRITICAL SOURCES:

PERIODICALS

Communication Arts, Volume XIX, number 6, 1978.
Communication World, November, 1984.
Floridian, February 27, 1972.
Orlando Sentinel Star, October 11, 1977.
Print, September/October, 1985.
Winter Park-Maitland Sun Herald, October 6, 1977.

*　　*　　*

PARSONS, Howard L(ee)   1918-

PERSONAL: Born July 9, 1918, in Jacksonville, Fla.; son of Howard Lee and Edna (Powell) Parsons; married Helen Brummall (a psychiatric social worker), March 31, 1946; children: Deborah, Margaret, Susan. *Education:* Attended University of Missouri, 1936-39, 1940-41; University of Chicago, B.A., 1942, Ph.D., 1946.

ADDRESSES: Office—Department of Philosophy, University of Bridgeport, Bridgeport, Conn. 06601.

CAREER: University of Southern California, Los Angeles, visiting assistant professor of philosophy of religion, 1946-47; University of Illinois, Galesburg Campus, instructor in philosophy, 1947-49; University of Tennessee, Knoxville, assistant professor of philosophy, 1949-57; Coe College, Cedar Rapids, Iowa, associate professor, 1957-60, professor of philosophy, 1960-65, chairman of department of philosophy and religion, 1959-65; University of Bridgeport, Bridgeport, Conn., Bernhard Professor of Philosophy and chairman of department, 1965—. Member of advisory board, Center for Creative Exchange.

MEMBER: World Federation of Scientific Workers, World Peace Council (member of presidential committee), International Institute for Peace (member of scientific council), American Philosophical Association, Society for Values in Higher Education, Society for the Philosophical Study of Dialectical Materialism (president, 1962-63; vice-president, 1963), American Institute for Marxist Studies (founding sponsor; member of board, 1964—), Foundation for Philosophy of Creativity (member of board, 1957—), Societe Europeenne de Culture, American Association of University Professors, Iowa Philosophical Society (president, 1964-65).

AWARDS, HONORS: Wenner-Gren Foundation grant, 1956; Kavir Institute grant, 1963-64; American Council of Learned Societies travel grant, 1975-76.

WRITINGS:

Ethics in the Soviet Union Today, American Institute for Marxist Studies, 1967.
Humanistic Philosophy in Poland and Yugoslavia, American Institute for Marxist Studies, 1968.
Humanism and Marx's Thought, C. C Thomas, 1971.

Man, East and West, B. R. Gruener (Amsterdam), 1973.
Man Today, B. R. Gruener, 1973.
(Editor with John Somerville) *Dialogues on the Philosophy of Marxism*, Greenwood Press, 1974.
(Editor with Somerville) *Marxism, Revolution, and Peace*, B. R. Gruener, 1974.
Self, Global Issues, and Ethics, B. R. Gruener, 1977.
Marx and Engels on Ecology, Greenwood Press, 1977.
The Soviet People and the Soviet Union, B. R. Gruener, 1980.
Marxism, Christianity, and Human Values, B. R. Gruener, 1981.
Buddhism as Humanism (in Japanese), Keiso-Shobo, 1982.
Man in the Contemporary World (in Russian), Progress Publishers, 1985.

Contributor to *Praxis, Comprendre, Voprosy Filosofii,* and other philosophy journals.

WORK IN PROGRESS: Creativity.

*　　*　　*

PARULSKI, George R(ichard), Jr.   1954-
(Alan B. Brian, George Taylor)

PERSONAL: Born December 5, 1954, in Rochester, N.Y., son of George R. (an engineer) and Beatrice (Calleramie) Parulski; married Carolyn M. Iachetta (an artist), November 8, 1975; children: Jaclyn, Charles. *Education:* Attended Eisho-Ji School of Zen, 1973; St. John Fisher College, B.A., 1975.

ADDRESSES: Home—Webster, N.Y. *Office*—P.O. Box 321, Webster, N.Y. 14580.

CAREER: St. John Fisher College, Rochester, N.Y., instructor in Eastern philosophy and martial arts, 1976-78 and 1984—; free-lance writer and photographer, 1978—. Owner, Yama-ji: School of Traditional Martial Arts, Webster, N.Y.

MEMBER: International Martial Arts Federation (East Coast director of judo, 1985—), American Society of Magazine Writers and Photographers, Independent Press Association, American Society of Classical Judoka (secretary general, 1984), All-Japan Seibukan Martial Arts and Ways Association (U.S. representative, 1983—), Japan Karate Association, Chinese Kung-fu/Wu-shu Federation.

AWARDS, HONORS: Quasar Award from American Society of Fantasy Writers, 1974, for story "October's Children"; named East Coast Amateur Athletic Union judo champion by Amateur Athletic Union of the United States, 1974; named Master Kata Champion and Black Belt Weapons Champion, 1983.

WRITINGS:

A Path to Oriental Wisdom, Ohara Publications, 1976.
The Adventure of Tim Amulet (children's fantasy poetry), Sol III Publications, 1976.
Twilight Reflections (poetry), R. G. King, 1977.
Complete Book of Judo, Contemporary Books, 1984.
Art of Karate Weapons, Contemporary Books, 1984.
Secrets of Kung-fu, Contemporary Books, 1984.
(With Mark McCarthy) *Taekwon-do*, Contemporary Books, 1984.
Black Belt Judo, Contemporary Books, 1985.
Karate Power, Contemporary Books, 1985.
The Sword of the Samurai, Paladin Press, 1985.
Exotic Weapons of the Samurai, Paladin Press, 1985.
Karate's Modern Masters, Contemporary Books, 1985.

Karate for Kids, Sterling Publishing, 1985.

Contributor to *Inside Karate, Official Karate, Black Belt, Muscle-up,* and *Warriors.*

WORK IN PROGRESS: A second volume of *Karate for Kids,* for Sterling; *Japan's Modern Ninja,* for Paladin Press; and a second volume of *Secrets of Kung-fu,* for Contemporary Books.

SIDELIGHTS: George R. Parulski, Jr., told *CA* that he is an authority on the techniques, history, and philosophy of the martial arts. He holds black belt ranks in several different karate, judo, and martial arts organizations. In the early 1970s he attempted to organize his own martial arts system called "bukido" (way of the spirit warrior). The system was recognized in Japan but never perfected.

Regarding his career as an author, Parulski told *CA:* "I began writing at an early age—I think I was nine years old when I won a scholastic award for a poem entitled 'Mist.' My interest continued and in the eighth grade I edited, produced and wrote for a school science fiction magazine, *The Inner Mind.* I sold my first professional article, 'Zen and Japanese Gardens,' to *Rosicrucian Digest* in 1974, and this began a love affair between me and the written word.

"When I began doing investigative features for *Police Products News* I was told I could earn more money by supplying pictures with my features. I took an intense interest in the camera, and in addition to supplying photos with my stories I also opened up an extremely successful photography business that took me to New York City, where I worked and studied martial arts religiously. I later gave up the photo business to concentrate on my writing and martial arts. During those photo years I also took a position on a local police force which gave me insights into true combat realism and the true worth of the martial arts philosophy. My writing and photography to date have netted some two hundred articles with two dozen magazine covers.

"All my writing, which I consider philosophical by nature, has an underlying theme: The betterment of the individual for the betterment of mankind; or learning to gain peace within to be at peace with all around you. This is where 'budo' (martial arts) comes in. 'Budo' is at the heart of my consciousness and therefore of my writings.

"Philosophy is for everyone, because we are all in pursuit of knowledge of ourselves and our environment. To ignore philosophy is to ignore the basic question, WHY? Knowledge is like music; it is found in the rhythm and cadence of a song. Some sing it well, but others never learn its melody and therefore never find its harmony."

*   *   *

PARVIN, Betty 1916-

PERSONAL: Born October 10, 1916, in Cardiff, Wales; daughter of John (a brass founder and engineer) and Amelia (a dressmaker; maiden name, Hill) Ledsam; married Daniel Frederick McKenzie Parvin (a solicitor), July 5, 1941; children: Roger. *Education:* Attended convent school in Cardiff, Wales, 1927-33. *Politics:* Conservative. *Religion:* None.

ADDRESSES: Home—"Bamboo" Bunny Hill Top, Costock, near Loughborough, Leicestershire LE12 6UX, England.

CAREER: Poet and painter. Worked as a civil service secretary, 1940-43. Lecturer; guest on radio shows.

MEMBER: Royal Society for the Protection of Birds, National Trust, Nottingham Poetry Society (vice-chairman; life president, 1980—), Nottingham Society of Artists, London Poetry Society, Schools Poetry Association, Leicester Poetry Society, New Mechanics Club.

AWARDS, HONORS: Albert Ralph Korn Award for poetry, c. 1958; Manifold Scholarship Award, 1968; Lake Aske Memorial Awards, 1968, 1971, and 1979; diplomas from the Scottish Arts Association, 1977 and 1978; D.Litt. from University of Gdansk, 1977; Scottish Open Poetry first prize, 1980; South Wales Eisteddfod first prize, 1983; commendations from the York and Stroud Festivals.

WRITINGS:

POETRY

A Stone My Star, Outposts Publications, 1961.
The Bird with the Luck: Twelve Poems, introduction by G. S. Fraser, Byron Press, 1968.
Sketchbook from Mercia, Manifold Press, 1968.
(Editor) *Poetry Nottingham,* Nottingham Poetry Society, 1970.
Guernsey's Gift, Griffin Press, 1972.
(Self-illustrated) *A Birchtree with Finches,* Nottingham Poetry Society, 1974.
(Self-illustrated) *Country Matters,* Em-Press, 1979.
The Book of Daniel, Em-Press, 1980.
Prospect, Em-Press, 1981.
The Book of Oliver, Em-Press, 1984.
It's All Ours, Em-Press, 1985.

OTHER

Contributor of poetry and short stories to various journals, anthologies, and textbooks.

SIDELIGHTS: Betty Parvin has gained a reputation extending beyond her English Midland locale. Predominantly a small-press poet, she has nonetheless earned the acclaim of some of Britain's prominent critics, most notably G. S. Fraser. Parvin recalled the encouragement Fraser once gave her: "When in the sixties I first began to submit my poems to expert scrutiny, G. S. Fraser, distinguished poet and literary critic, later to become revered mentor and friend, told me: 'You have a Parnassian gift. Don't lose it!'

"I was striving then to discard my schoolhood yoke of the *Golden Treasury* and emulate 'up-to-date' poets. I returned willingly to rhyme and meter, my subjects the rural landscape which surrounds my hill-top home, not far, and not so different, from the countryside of John Clare. Over the years, wide reading of gifted modern poets has loosened my style, but the rhythm is still marked."

In his introduction to *The Bird with the Luck: Twelve Poems,* Fraser outlined his impressions of Parvin's work: "Her feeling for the flavour of words in the mouth comes from her Welsh roots but she is a very unbardic poet, and the coolness and poise of the poems comes from her Midland setting; from Mercia, the calm part of England, its surface not easily stirred, its deeper currents not easily deflected. . . . She could never become a poet of the asphalt jungle. She needs gulls, old stone, rocks, 'shivering grasses.' Yet she is not a romantic poet for she leans, I think, on the great inanimate world and the nonhuman life in it as something that gives us moral support because it gives us the sense of our own scale, because it is at once alien, admirable, necessary and permanent."

In addition to her poetry writing, Parvin also paints. She told *CA* that "acquaintances wonder at my persistence with the two arts, in view of the fact that I have been severely assailed by rheumatoid arthritis for many years. It is hard to explain to those who do not write or paint that this activity, plus a sublime family life, make it possible to accept, even to ignore, a painful progressive disease. My pleasure in living is heightened by the many invitations I receive from groups, clubs, and poetry societies to read my poems and talk about the way it is done.''

BIOGRAPHICAL/CRITICAL SOURCES:

BOOKS

Parvin, Betty, *The Bird with the Luck: Twelve Poems,* introduction by G. S. Fraser, Byron Press, 1968.

*   *   *

PARX, C. C.
See GILMORE, Christopher Cook

*   *   *

PASSERON, Rene (Jean) 1920-

PERSONAL: Born January 31, 1920, in Casablanca, Morocco; son of Joseph (a professor) and Germaine (Chabaud) Passeron; married Suzanne Allen, December 16, 1943; married Isabelle Solomon-Koechlin, October 4, 1969; children: Aube, Amelie, Juliette, Agnes, Ludovic. *Education:* Sorbonne, University of Paris, License de philosophie, 1943, Diplome d'Etudes superieures, 1943, Docteur d'etat, 1970.

ADDRESSES: Home—Champrond, Vinneuf, 89140 Pont-Sur-Yonne, France. *Office*—Centre National de la Recherche Scientifique, 15 quai Anatole France, 75700 Paris, France.

CAREER: E. D. Julliard (publisher), Paris, France, reader, 1946-55; Centre National de la Recherche Scientifique, Paris, researcher, 1955—, director of research, 1976—. University of Paris, Paris, assistant lecturer at the Sorbonne, 1968—, director of Institut d'Esthetique, 1972-83. Has shown own works in various expositions in Paris, including Breteau gallery, and in Athens, 1981, and London, 1982, both at the Institut Francais.

MEMBER: Association Internationale des Critiques d'Art.

WRITINGS:

Io lourde: Notes pour une legende, Julliard, 1952.
L'Oeuvre picturale et les fonctions de l'apparence, Vrin, 1962, revised edition, 1980.
Histoire de la peinture surrealiste, Librairie Generale Francaise, 1968.
Clefs pour la peinture, Seghers, 1969.
Rene Magritte, Filipachi, 1970.
Encyclopedie du surrealisme, Somogy, 1975, translation by John Griffiths published as *Phaidon Encyclopedia of Surrealism,* Phaidon Press, 1978.
Andre Masson et les puissances du signe, Denoel, 1975.
Salvador Dali, Filipachi, 1978.
(General editor) *Dictionaire general du surrealisme et de ses environs,* Presses Universitaires de France, 1982.
Gustav Klimt, Flammarion, 1983.
(General editor) *Recherches poietiques,* Volume V, Centre National de la Recherche Scientifique, 1985.

Member of editorial committee for *Revue d'Esthetique.*

PATTON, Bobby R(ay) 1935-

PERSONAL: Born December 18, 1935, in Fort Worth, Tex.; son of Elton Guy (a shopkeeper) and Violet (Daniels) Patton; married Bonnie Ritter (a government executive), June 1, 1958 (divorced, 1976); married Eleanor Nyquist (a theatre costumer), July 4, 1978. *Education:* Texas Christian University, B.F.A. (magna cum laude), 1958; University of Kansas, M.A., 1962, Ph.D., 1966. *Politics:* Democrat. *Religion:* Unitarian Universalist.

ADDRESSES: Home—3017 Riverview Rd., Lawrence, Kan. 66044. *Office*—Department of Communication and Theatre, 356 Murphy Hall, University of Kansas, Lawrence, Kan. 66045.

CAREER: High school teacher of speech in Hutchinson, Kan., 1958-61; Wichita State University, Wichita, Kan., instructor, 1961-62, assistant professor of speech, 1962-65; University of Kansas, Lawrence, assistant professor, 1966-69, associate professor, 1969-74, professor of speech, 1974—, chairman of department of communication and theatre, 1972—.

MEMBER: International Communication Association, Speech Communication Association, Kansas Speech Association (president, 1961-63).

AWARDS, HONORS: Named outstanding college speech teacher in the state, Kansas Speech Association, 1968.

WRITINGS:

(With Bonnie Ritter) *Living Together: Female-Male Communication,* C. E. Merrill, 1976.

WITH KIM GIFFIN

Fundamentals of Interpersonal Communication, with instructor's manual, Harper, 1971, 2nd edition, 1976.
(Compiler) *Basic Readings in Interpersonal Communication: Theory and Application,* Harper, 1971, 2nd edition, 1976.
Problem-Solving Group Interaction, Harper, 1973, 2nd edition published as *Decision-Making Group Interaction,* 1978.
(Compiler) *Interpersonal Communication: Basic Text and Readings,* with instructor's manual, Harper, 1974, 2nd edition published as *Interpersonal Communication in Action: Basic Text and Readings,* 1977, 3rd edition, 1981.
Personal Communication in Human Relations, C. E. Merrill, 1974.
(And Wil A. Linkugel) *Responsible Public Speaking,* Scott Foresman, 1982.
(And Bonnie Weaver Duldt) *Interpersonal Communication in Nursing,* F. A. Davis, 1984.

*   *   *

PEMBERTON, Margaret 1943-

PERSONAL: Born April 10, 1943, in Yorkshire, England; daughter of George Arthur (an architect) and Kathleen (an artist; maiden name, Ramsden) Hudson; married Mike Pemberton (an advertising executive), October 13, 1968; children: Amanda, Rebecca, Polly, Michael, Natasha Christina. *Education:* Attended girls' school in Bradford, Yorkshire, England. *Politics:* ''Variable.''

ADDRESSES: Home—13 Manor Lane, London S.E.13, England. *Agent*—Carol Smith Agency, 25 Hornton Court, Kensington High St., London W8 7RT, England.

CAREER: Free-lance writer, 1974—. Has worked as secretary, actress, model, nurse, overseas telegraphist, and catering manager.

MEMBER: Romantic Novelists Association, Crime Writers Association.

WRITINGS:

Rendezvous with Danger, Macdonald & Jane's, 1974.
The Mystery of Saligo Bay, Macdonald & Jane's, 1975.
Shadows over Silver Sands, Berkeley, 1976.
The Guilty Secret, R. Hale, 1979.
The Lion of Languedoc, Mills & Boon, 1980.
Harlot, Arrow, 1981.
Pioneer Girl, Mills & Boon, 1981.
Some Distant Shore, Pocket Books, 1981.
African Enchantment, Mills & Boon, 1982.
The Flower Garden, F. Watts, 1982.
Flight to Verechencko, Mills & Boon, 1983.
Forever, Fontana, 1983.
The Devil's Palace, Mills & Boon, 1984.
Silver Shadows, Golden Dreams, Macdonald, 1985.

WORK IN PROGRESS: A book on lace-making in late medieval France.

SIDELIGHTS: Margaret Pemberton writes: "My main passions in life are Mike Pemberton, smaller Pembertons, Shakespeare, theatre, acting, and travel, in that order. I am a keen amateur actress and will travel anywhere at the slightest excuse. I write because I love it, because it is the only thing I can do!"

* * *

PEN, Jan 1921-

PERSONAL: Born February 15, 1921, in De Lemmer, The Netherlands; son of Jurjen and Sipkje (de Vries) Pen; married Judith de Rook, 1946; children: Jurjen Sipke, Tiesse. *Education:* University of Amsterdam, Dr.Econ., 1950.

ADDRESSES: Home—21 Kerklaan, Haren, The Netherlands. *Office*—Faculteit der Rechtsgeleerdheid, Rijksuniversiteit, Turftorenstraat 13, 9712 BM Groningen, The Netherlands.

CAREER: Ministry of Economic Affairs, The Hague, The Netherlands, economist, 1947-52, director of economic policy, 1952-56; State University, Groningen, The Netherlands, professor of economics, 1956—.

WRITINGS:

Theorie der Collectieve Loononderhandelingen, Stenfert Kroese, 1950, translation by T. S. Preston published as *The Wage Rate under Collective Bargaining,* Harvard University Press, 1959.
Welvaart en Verdeling, Nijhoff, 1956.
Moderne Economie, Het Spectrum (Utrecht), 1958, translation published as *Modern Economics,* Penguin, 1970, 2nd edition, 1980.
Het Aardige van de Economie, Het Spectrum, 1962.
Harmonie en Conflict, De Bezige Bij, 1962, translation published as *Harmony and Conflict in Modern Society,* McGraw, 1965.
(Editor and contributor) *Wij en de Welvaart,* Het Spectrum, 1964.
A Primer on International Trade, Random House, 1967.
Income Distribution, Allen Lane, 1971, Penguin, 1974.

Wat Zijn Maatschappelijke Structuren?, Noord-Hollandsche Uitgevers Maatschappij, 1974.
Dat Stomme Economenvolk met Zijn Heilige Koeien, Het Spectrum, 1976.
Macro-Economie: Wat Wij Weten en Wat Wij Niet Weten, Het Spectrum, 1977.
Naar een Rechtvaardiger Inkomensverdeling, Elsevier, 1977.
Kijk, Economie: Over Mensen, Wensen, Werk en Geld, Het Spectrum, 1979.
Visies op Onderzoek in Enkele Sociale Wetenschappen, Staatsuitgeverij (Gravenhage), 1982.
Among Economists, North Holland Publishing Co., 1985.

Also contributor of articles to *De Economist, Het Parool* (newspaper), and other professional periodicals.

SIDELIGHTS: Jan Pen's works have been translated into Portuguese, Polish, Italian, Swedish, Greek, and Japanese.

* * *

PENNER, Jonathan 1940-

PERSONAL: Born May 29, 1940, in Bridgeport, Conn.; son of Sidney (a physician) and Leonore (Koskoff) Penner; married Lucille Recht (a writer), April 21, 1968; children: Benjamin, Daniel. *Education:* University of Bridgeport, B.A., 1964; University of Iowa, M.F.A., 1966, Ph.D., 1975.

ADDRESSES: Office—Department of English, University of Arizona, Tucson, Ariz. 85721.

CAREER: New School for Social Research, New York, N.Y., instructor in English, 1968; Housatonic Community College, Stratford, Conn., lecturer in English, 1968-70; Southern Illinois University at Carbondale, lecturer in English, 1976-77; University of Arizona, Tucson, assistant professor, 1978-84, associate professor of English, 1984—.

MEMBER: American Association of University Professors, P.E.N. American Center, Modern Language Association of America, Authors Guild, Authors League of America, Associated Writing Programs, National Book Critics Circle.

AWARDS, HONORS: National Endowment for the Arts fellowship, 1976-77 and 1983-84; first novel award from Great Lakes Colleges Association and distinguished recognition award from Friends of American Writers, both 1977, for *Going Blind;* Guggenheim fellowship, 1977-78; Arizona Commission on the Arts creative writing fellowship, 1981-82; Galileo Press Short Novel Award, 1983, for *The Intelligent Traveler's Guide to Chiribosco;* Drue Heinz Literature Prize and Louisiana State University/*Southern Review* Short Fiction Prize, both 1983, for *Private Parties;* Fulbright fellowship, 1984.

WRITINGS:

FICTION

Going Blind, Simon & Schuster, 1977.
The Intelligent Traveler's Guide to Chiribosco, Galileo, 1983.
Private Parties, University of Pittsburgh Press, 1983.

OTHER

Contributor to periodicals, including *Triquarterly, Prairie Schooner,* and *Literary Review.*

SIDELIGHTS: Jonathan Penner's fiction has received warm reviews from a number of critics who praise, among other things, his "simplicity, clarity, and lucidity." His first novel, *Going Blind,* concerns a university professor stricken with slowly failing eyesight. The portrayal of this character attracted favorable notice from Michael Harris, writing for the *Washington Post Book World:* "[Penner's] prose is restrained, witty, balanced in tone. After reading *Going Blind,* in short, it's hard to believe the author hasn't been there himself." *Newsweek* reviewer Walter Clemons comments: "As good books do, 'Going Blind' expands in one's head. Penner says something valuable about the alternatives of acceptance and resistance in any tight corner."

Penner's *Private Parties,* a short story collection, and *The Intelligent Traveler's Guide to Chiribosco,* a novella, have contributed further to his status as an able fiction writer. In a review of both books for the *Washington Post Book World,* Stephen Goodwin writes: "Penner can make you see, and he can also make you hear. A single line of dialogue often tells you everything you need to know about a character." Edith Milton, in the *New York Times Book Review,* finds the comic undertones in Penner's serious works particularly effective. "Mr. Penner's style is conversational and informal—a style for comedy," she writes. "And some of these stories are very funny indeed. But behind their comic surface there is always the deeply serious proposition that life is both mad and heroic." Goodwin phrases his praise even more succinctly: "Jonathan Penner knows how to turn a sentence. . . . He's not flashy, just confident."

BIOGRAPHICAL/CRITICAL SOURCES:

PERIODICALS

Newsweek, April 18, 1977.
New Yorker, June 13, 1977.
New York Times, May 6, 1977.
New York Times Book Review, May 29, 1977, January 15, 1984.
Washington Post Book World, March 27, 1977, February 19, 1984.

*   *   *

PETER, Laurence J.   1919-

PERSONAL: Born September 16, 1919, in Vancouver, British Columbia, Canada; son of Victor (an actor) and Vincenta (Steves) Peter; married Nancy Bailey (marriage ended); married Irene Howe, February 25, 1967; children: John, Edward, Alice, Margaret. *Education:* Attended University of British Columbia, 1938-54; Western Washington State College (now Western Washington University), B.A., 1957, M.Ed., 1958; Washington State University, Ed.D., 1963.

ADDRESSES: Home and office—2332 Via Anacapa, Palos Verdes Estates, Calif. 90274.

CAREER: Teacher of industrial arts in British Columbia, 1941-47; Provincial Prison Department, Burnaby, British Columbia, instructor, 1947-48; Vancouver School Board, Vancouver, British Columbia, mental health coordinator and special counselor, 1948-64; University of British Columbia, Vancouver, assistant professor of education, 1964-66; University of Southern California, Los Angeles, associate professor, 1966-69, professor of education, 1969-70, director of Evelyn Frieden Center for Prescriptive Teaching, 1967-70; John Tracy Clinic, Los Angeles, Calif., professor in residence, 1970-73; University of California, Stanislaus, adjunct professor of education, 1975-79; writer and lecturer. Psychologist, British Columbia Vocational Counselling Service, 1959. Panel member of review board, Department of Health, Education, and Welfare,

1969-70. Consultant to other British Columbia health and service organizations.

MEMBER: National Autistic Association, American Association of University Professors, Canadian Mental Health Association, Canadian Association of University Teachers, P.E.N., American Federation of Television and Radio Artists, Northwest Writers Conference, Association for Retarded Children, British Columbia Teachers Association, British Columbia Mental Health Association (member of executive committee, 1958-61), Greater Los Angeles Big Brother Association (member of board), Phi Delta Kappa.

AWARDS, HONORS: The Peter Principle: Why Things Always Go Wrong was named to the bestseller lists of the *New York Times* and *Publishers Weekly,* 1969; Phi Delta Kappa research award, University of Southern California, 1970; alumni awards from Western Washington State College (now Western Washington University) and Washington State University; Canadian University Associated Alumni award; Will Rogers Top Hand award; D.H.L., Heidelberg College, 1982.

WRITINGS:

Prescription Teaching, McGraw, 1965.
(With Raymond Hull) *The Peter Principle: Why Things Always Go Wrong,* Morrow, 1969.
The Peter Prescription and How to Make Things Go Right, Morrow, 1972.
The Peter Plan: A Proposal for Survival, Morrow, 1975.
Competencies for Teaching, four volumes, Wadsworth, 1975.
Peter's Quotations: Ideas for Our Times, Morrow, 1977.
Peter's People and Their Marvelous Ideas, Morrow, 1979.
Peter's Almanac, Morrow, 1982.
(With Bill Dana) *The Laughter Prescription,* Ballantine, 1982.
Why Things Go Wrong, Morrow, 1984.

Contributor to *Education Panorama* (published in five languages) and other education journals; contributor to magazines, including *Psychology Today, Human Behavior,* and *Reader's Digest.*

WORK IN PROGRESS: The Peter Pyramid; or, Will We Ever Get the Point; Processes of Teaching (textbook).

SIDELIGHTS: In 1969, psychologist and author Laurence J. Peter introduced the world to his Peter Principle: "In a hierarchy individuals tend to rise to their levels of incompetence." As Marshall Berges notes in the *Los Angeles Times,* "Peter's world overflows with incompetents. They have swarmed around him throughout his life. . . . [He] finds incompetents in all shapes and sizes and in practically every field of endeavor. Although they are too numerous to be captured by even the widest lens of a camera, Peter has made copious notes on their activities. At intervals when the stack of notes grows too high, he assembles his findings into a book." To date, Peter has produced several books on his subject, with titles like *The Peter Principle: Why Things Always Go Wrong, The Peter Prescription and How to Make Things Go Right,* and *The Peter Plan: A Proposal for Survival.*

More than one critic has suggested, in view of Peter's many similar books, that the author himself has reached his own level of incompetence. But other reviewers find humor in the continuing parade of useless laws, bad ideas, and misleading quotes that Peter chronicles. "No one is immune to Peter's corollaries, not even their lexicographer," declares *Time* critic Stefan Kanfer. In a passage of his book *Why Things Go Wrong,* the author admits, "It was never my intention to decry the sins, mistakes, vanities and incompetence of my fellow human beings. I am at least as guilty as they.'' The proof, reports Kanfer, ''lies in [Peter's] vain attempts to back a California education center. 'I realized I had reached my level of incompetence as a fund raiser when all my requests from government agencies and private foundations were rejected.' Undismayed, Peter obeyed his own dictum: 'Quit while you're behind.' ''

BIOGRAPHICAL/CRITICAL SOURCES:

BOOKS

Peter, Laurence J., *Why Things Go Wrong,* Morrow, 1984.

PERIODICALS

Christian Science Monitor, March 6, 1969.
Los Angeles Times, October 4, 1979, February 16, 1984.
New York Times Book Review, August 13, 1972, February 8, 1976.
Time, November 26, 1984.

* * *

PETERSON, Robert 1924-

PERSONAL: Born June 2, 1924, in Denver, Colo.; son of Ernest F. and Alice (Morris) Peterson; married and divorced twice. *Education:* Attended University of Nevada, 1940-41; University of California, Berkeley, A.B., 1948; San Francisco State College (now University), M.A., 1958.

ADDRESSES: Home—P.O. Box 1213, Capitola, Calif. 95010.

CAREER: Major employment in youth and college days was at Fielding Hotel, San Francisco, Calif., where he was later a clerk and then assistant manager, 1948-56; began writing poetry in 1957 (''before that I had not been good at much of anything''). *Military service:* U.S. Army, medical corpsman, 1943-46; served in Germany and the Philippines; received battle star and Combat Medical Badge.

MEMBER: Poetry Society of America.

AWARDS, HONORS: Recipient of one of the first grants for poetry awarded by National Foundation on the Arts and Humanities; Amy Lowell travelling fellowship, 1972-73.

WRITINGS:

POETRY

Home for the Night, Binweed Press, 1962.
The Binnacle, Lillabulero Press, 1967.
Wondering Where You Are, Kayak, 1968.
Lone Rider, Dingo Press, 1976.
Under Sealed Orders, Cloud Marauder Press, 1976.
Vietnam Blues, Bindweed Press, 1977.
Leaving Taos (National Poetry Series selection), compiled by Carolyn Kizer, Harper, 1981.
The Only Piano Player in La Paz, Black Dog Press, 1985.

Poems anthologized in *Students in Revolt, 1963,* 1963, *17 Love Poems,* 1966, and *Where Is Vietnam?,* Doubleday, 1967.

OTHER

Contributor to numerous journals and magazines, including *Poetry, Odyssey, Kayak, Choice, Nation, Carolina Quarterly, Ironwood,* and *New Letters.* Poetry editor, *Contact,* 1958-60.

SIDELIGHTS: Robert Peterson told *CA:* ''When I did begin to write poems, I felt that I had been wasting a lot of time up to then and could not afford to 'study' poetry. I decided to

rely on my own experience and say what I had to say in ways that were satisfying to me and might amuse some of my friends. I don't take much interest in theories. In order to discuss my motivations for writing poetry, I'd have to go back to the beginning. To someone like Peking man, I mean.

''The most important single event in my becoming a poet was a period of nine months I spent (in 1956) with a psychiatrist named David Farber. He was deaf, and so I had to write down my thoughts for him, and I learned that I could be happy that way. He's dead now. He was a great man and a dear man.''

BIOGRAPHICAL/CRITICAL SOURCES:

PERIODICALS

New York Times Book Review, September 6, 1981.

* * *

PETTIT, Philip 1945-

PERSONAL: Born December 20, 1945, in Ballinasloe, Ireland; son of Michael Anthony (a company director) and Bridget Christina Pettit; married Eileen Theresa McNally (a social worker), July 1, 1978. *Education:* National University of Ireland, B.A., 1966, M.A., 1967; Queen's University, Belfast, Ph.D., 1970. *Politics:* ''Liberal Left.''

ADDRESSES: Home—46 Southwell St., Weetangera, Canberra, ACT 2614, Australia. *Office*—Research School of Social Sciences, Australian National University, Canberra, ACT 2601, Australia.

CAREER: National University of Ireland, University College, Dublin, lecturer in philosophy, 1968-72; Cambridge University, Trinity Hall, Cambridge, England, fellow in philosophy, 1972-75; National University of Ireland, University College, Dublin, lecturer in philosophy, 1975-77; University of Bradford, Bradford, England, professor of philosophy, 1977-83; Australian National University, Institute of Advanced Studies, Canberra, professorial fellow, 1983—.

MEMBER: Mind Association, Australian Philosophy Association, Australian Political Science Association.

WRITINGS:

On the Idea of Phenomenology, Humanities, 1969.
(Editor) *The Gentle Revolution,* Scepter (Dublin), 1969.
The Concept of Structuralism, University of California Press, 1975, revised edition, 1977.
(Editor with Christopher Hookway) *Action and Interpretation,* Cambridge University Press, 1978.
Judging Justice, Routledge & Kegan Paul, 1980.
(With Graham MacDonald) *Semantics and Social Science,* Routledge & Kegan Paul, 1981.
(Editor with John McDowell) *Subject, Thought and Context,* Oxford University Press, in press.

WORK IN PROGRESS: ''Further thought in the wake of *Semantics and Social Science,* on the significance of social science, humanistically understood, and on the methodological strategies available to it. Also work on ethics and political philosophy.''

SIDELIGHTS: Philip Pettit told *CA:* ''My philosophical outlook is that of a soft naturalist. I am a naturalist in rejecting the idea that the human being is set apart metaphysically from the rest of nature, say, by the possession of a non-physical mind. I am a soft naturalist in holding that there is substance still in the traditional marks of human distinctiveness: in rationality, freedom, creativity, moral insight, and so on.''

*   *   *

PHILLIPS, Gene D(aniel)   1935-

PERSONAL: Born March 3, 1935, in Springfield, Ohio; son of Ira Granville (a factory foreman) and Johanna (Davoran) Phillips. *Education:* Loyola University of Chicago, A.B., 1957, M.A., 1959; West Baden College, Ph.L., 1959; Bellarmine School of Theology, S.T.L., 1966; Fordham University, Ph.D., 1970.

ADDRESSES: Home—Faculty Residence, Loyola University, 6525 North Sheridan Rd., Chicago, Ill. 60626. *Office*—Department of English, Loyola University of Chicago, Chicago, Ill. 60626.

CAREER: Entered Society of Jesus (Jesuits), 1952, ordained priest, 1965; Loyola University of Chicago, Chicago, Ill., 1970—, began as assistant professor, associate professor, 1975-81, professor of film history, fiction, and drama, 1981—.

MEMBER: Society for Cinema Studies, Modern Language Association of America.

AWARDS, HONORS: American Philosophical Society grant, 1971; named Teacher of the Year, Loyola University, 1979.

WRITINGS:

The Movie Makers: Artists in an Industry, Nelson-Hall, 1973.
Graham Greene: The Films of His Fiction, Teachers College Press, 1974.
Stanley Kubrick: A Film Odyssey, Popular Library, 1975, enlarged edition, 1977.
Evelyn Waugh's Officers, Gentlemen, and Rogues: The Fact behind His Fiction, Nelson-Hall, 1975.
Ken Russell, Twayne, 1979.
The Films of Tennessee Williams, Associated University Presses, 1980.
Hemingway and Film, Ungar, 1980.
John Schlesinger, Twayne, 1981.
George Cukor, Twayne, 1982.
Alfred Hitchcock, Twayne, 1984.

CONTRIBUTOR

Samuel Hynes, editor, *Graham Greene: A Collection of Critical Essays,* Prentice-Hall, 1973.
Thomas Atkins, editor, *Sexuality in the Movies,* Indiana University Press, 1975.
Stuart Kaminsky, editor, *Ingmar Bergman: Essays in Criticism,* Oxford University Press, 1975.
Atkins, editor, *Science Fiction Films,* Simon & Schuster, 1976.
Atkins, editor, *Ken Russell,* Simon & Schuster, 1976.
Frank Magill, editor, *Contemporary Literary Scene II,* Salem Press, 1979.
Christopher Lyon, editor, *The International Dictionary of Films and Filmmakers,* St. James Press, 1984.

OTHER

Contributor to *Focus on Film* (England), *America, Literature/Film Quarterly, Sequences* (Canada), and other journals.

WORK IN PROGRESS: Fitzgerald and Film.

SIDELIGHTS: Gene D. Phillips comments: ''Interviews both here and in England, with directors ranging from Cukor and Kubrick to Losey and Schlesinger, enabled me to write my first book, *The Movie Makers,* about the difficulty of an artist functioning in an industry. (I have since developed the chapters on Kubrick, Russell, Schlesinger, and Cukor into separate books.) Graham Greene's personal cooperation was most helpful in my doing the book on his fiction and films. The publication of Waugh's diaries, and interviews with his family, sparked the book *Evelyn Waugh's Officers, Gentlemen, and Rogues.''*

*   *   *

PIERARD, Richard Victor   1934-

PERSONAL: Born May 29, 1934, in Chicago, Ill.; son of Jack P. and Diana F. (Russell) Pierard; married Charlene Burdett, June 15, 1957; children: David Edward, Cynthia Kay. *Education:* Los Angeles State College of Applied Arts and Sciences (now California State University, Los Angeles), B.A., 1958, M.A., 1959; additional graduate study at University of Hamburg, 1962-63; University of Iowa, Ph.D., 1964. *Politics:* Democrat. *Religion:* Baptist.

ADDRESSES: Home—550 Gardendale Rd., Terre Haute, Ind. 47803. *Office*—Department of History, Indiana State University, Terre Haute, Ind. 47809.

CAREER: University of Iowa, Iowa City, instructor in history, 1964; Indiana State University, Terre Haute, assistant professor, 1964-67, associate professor, 1967-72, professor of history, 1972—. Visiting professor at Bibelschule Bergstrasse, 1971, Greenville College, 1972-73, Regent College, 1975, and Trinity Evangelical Divinity School, 1982; research fellow, University of Aberdeen, 1978; Fulbright professor, University of Frankfurt, 1984-85. Democratic Party precinct committeeman, 1978—; member of board of Evangelicals for Social Action, 1978-82; Indiana delegate to White House Conference on Libraries and Information Services, 1979. *Military service:* U.S. Army, 1954-56; served in Japan.

MEMBER: American Historical Association, Conference on Faith and History (secretary-treasurer, 1967—), Evangelical Theological Society (president, 1985), American Society of Church History, American Society of Missiology, Phi Alpha Theta.

AWARDS, HONORS: Fulbright scholar at University of Hamburg, 1962-63.

WRITINGS:

(With Robert G. Clouse and Robert D. Linder) *Protest and Politics: Christianity and Contemporary Affairs,* Attic Press, 1968.
The Unequal Yoke: Evangelical Christianity and Political Conservatism, Lippincott, 1970.
(With Clouse and Linder) *The Cross and the Flag,* Creation House, 1972.
(With Linder) *Politics: A Case for Christian Action,* Inter-Varsity Press, 1973.
(With Linder) *The Twilight of the Saints: Christianity and Civil Religion in Modern America,* Inter-Varsity Press, 1977.
(With Clouse) *Streams of Civilization,* Volume II, Mott Media, 1980.
Bibliography on the New Christian Right, Department of History, Indiana State University, 1981.

CONTRIBUTOR

T. Dowley, editor, *The Lion Handbook of Christian History,* Lion Press, 1977.

P. Cotham, editor, *Christian Social Ethics*, Baker Book, 1979.

R. A. Wells, editor, *The Wars of America*, Eerdmans, 1981.

H. B. Clark, editor, *Freedom of Religion in America*, Transaction Books, 1982.

R. A. Rutyna and J. W. Kuehl, editors, *Concerned in Conscience*, Donning, 1983.

J. E. Wood, editor, *Religion and Politics*, Baylor University Press, 1983.

D. G. Bromley and A. Sharpe, editors, *New Christian Politics*, Mercer University Press, 1984.

G. Marsden, editor, *Evangelicalism and Modern America*, Eerdmans, 1984.

M. J. Selvidge, editor, *Fundamentalism Today*, Brethren Press, 1984.

Wood, editor, *Religion and the State*, Baylor University Press, 1985.

S. D. Johnson and J. B. Tamney, editors, *Political Role of Religion in the United States*, Westview, 1985.

Also contributor to *Baker's Dictionary of Christian Ethics*, 1973, *The New International Dictionary of the Christian Church*, 1974, *Eerdmans Handbook to the History of Christianity*, *Brethren Encyclopedia*, 1983, *Baker Dictionary of Theology*, 1984, and *The American Conservative Press*, in press.

OTHER

Contributor to periodicals, including *Eternity, Reformed Journal, Christianity Today, Christian Century, Journal of Church and State, Journal of Ecumenical Studies, Review of Religious Research, Christian Scholars Review, Choice, Fides et Historia,* and *Covenant Quarterly*.

WORK IN PROGRESS: Writing on the German colonial society, the relationship between theological and political conservatism, social concern and Christianity, and civil religion.

* * *

PLANO, Jack Charles 1921-

PERSONAL: Born November 25, 1921, in Merrill, Wis.; son of Victor James and Minnie (Hass) Plano; married Ellen L. Ruehlow, June 25, 1954; children: Jay Charles, Gregory Victor, Vicki Lynn. *Education:* Ripon College, A.B., 1949; University of Wisconsin, M.A., 1950, Ph.D., 1954. *Politics:* Independent. *Religion:* Lutheran.

ADDRESSES: Home—705 Weaver Circle, Kalamazoo, Mich. *Office*—Department of Political Science, Western Michigan University, Kalamazoo, Mich.

CAREER: Rock Island Arsenal, Rock Island, Ill., civilian clerk, 1940-42; Western Michigan University, Kalamazoo, 1952—, currently professor of political science, chairman of department, and editor for New Issues Press. Visiting fellow, University of Sussex. Assistant state director, Michigan Citizenship Clearing House, 1957-60. *Military service:* U.S. Army, Engineer Corps, 1942-45; served two years in European Theater; became technical sergeant; received Northern France Battle Star.

MEMBER: International Studies Association, American Association for the United Nations (president of Kalamazoo chapter, 1959), American Political Science Association, American Academy of Political and Social Science, Academy of Political Science, African Studies Association, American Society of International Law, Midwest Political Science Association, Pi Gamma Mu.

AWARDS, HONORS: Ford Foundation grant for teaching of international politics; Western Michigan University fellowship; Hubert Herring Award for best reference book in Latin American studies, Pacific Coast Council on Latin American Studies, 1981.

WRITINGS:

(With Jack Wann) *The American Federation of Labor in International Affairs*, School for Workers, University of Wisconsin, 1952.

The Content of the Introductory International Politics Course: Basic Framework and Concepts, Emory University Press, 1958.

(With Milton Greenberg) *The American Political Dictionary*, Holt, 1962, 5th revised and enlarged edition, 1979.

Instructor's Manual: Governing America, Dodd, 1962.

Michigan State Government, Associated Educators, 1963.

The United Nations and the India-Pakistan Dispute, University of Manila Press, 1966.

(With Robert Riggs) *Forging World Order: The Politics of International Organization*, Macmillan, 1967, 2nd edition, 1971.

(With R. Olton) *International Relations Dictionary*, Holt, 1969, 3rd edition, American Bibliographical Center-Clio Press, 1982.

International Approaches to the Problems of Marine Pollution, University of Sussex, 1972.

(With Riggs) *Dictionary of Political Analysis*, Dryden, 1973.

(With Greenberg, Olton, and Riggs) *Political Science Dictionary*, Dryden, 1973.

(With Marjon Vashti Kamara) *United Nations Capital Development Fund: Poor and Rich Worlds in Collision*, New Issues Press, Western Michigan University, 1974.

(With Ernest E. Rossi) *The Latin American Political Dictionary*, American Bibliographic Center-Clio Press, 1980.

(With Barbara McCrea and George Klein) *The Soviet and East European Political Dictionary*, American Bibliographical Center-Clio Press, 1984.

Also editor of "Clio Dictionaries in Political Science" series, American Bibliographical Center-Clio Press, 1980-85.

SIDELIGHTS: Jack Charles Plano writes *CA:* "As a social science author and professor over the past thirty-five years, I have often been bothered—sometimes appalled—by the lack of precision in the vocabulary of the disciplines that comprise the social sciences. This is especially true for political science, as contrasted with the natural sciences. For me, precise language is the primary tool of every scientific discipline, and, as a result of a behavioral revolution that has swept the discipline in recent times, political science is striving to become a scientific discipline. My contribution has been lexicographical in nature. As I have proceeded, I have enlisted the services of more than twenty other political scientists, and together we have sought through a political dictionary series to encourage greater precision in the language of our discipline. Fields covered in these political dictionaries include general political science, international relations, political analysis, two volumes on constitutional law, international law, public administration, public policy, state and local government, presidential-congressional, and the following geographical regions: Africa, Asia, Europe, Latin America, Middle East, United States, and Eastern Europe. These books have been published by Holt, John Wiley, and ABC-Clio in both cloth editions for the libraries and general public usage, and in paperback for college classrooms. One of them—*The American Political Dictio-*

nary—has been used by more than 1 million college students over the years since 1962 when it appeared in its first edition.''

AVOCATIONAL INTERESTS: Tennis, billiards.

BIOGRAPHICAL/CRITICAL SOURCES:

PERIODICALS

Times Literary Supplement, April 20, 1973.

*   *   *

PLATT, Gerald M.   1933-

PERSONAL: Born February 13, 1933, in Brooklyn, N.Y.; son of Samuel (a shop foreman) and Rose (Perlman) Platt; children: Lucas, Genevieve. *Education:* Brooklyn College (now Brooklyn College of the City University of New York), B.A., 1955, M.A., 1957; attended Harvard University, 1963-64; University of California, Los Angeles, Ph.D., 1964.

ADDRESSES: Office—Department of Sociology, University of Massachusetts, Thompson Hall, Amherst, Mass. 01003.

CAREER: University of California, Riverside, instructor in social science, 1960-61; University of California, Los Angeles, instructor in anthropology and sociology, 1961-63; Harvard University, Cambridge, Mass., lecturer in sociology, 1964-70; University of Massachusetts—Amherst, associate professor, 1970-74, professor of sociology, 1974—. Visiting associate professor at Johns Hopkins University, autumn, 1973; academic visitor at London School of Economics and Political Science, autumn, 1977; visiting professor at University of California, Santa Cruz, winter-spring, 1978; visiting professor at University of California, Los Angeles, 1979-80. Panel member of National Academy of Sciences.

MEMBER: American Sociological Association, Group for the Use of Psychology in History.

AWARDS, HONORS: Fellow of Social Science Research Council, 1963-64; grant from Carnegie Corp., 1973-74.

WRITINGS:

(With Fred Weinstein) *The Wish to Be Free: Society, Psyche, and Value-Change,* University of California Press, 1969.
(With Weinstein) *Psychoanalytic Sociology: Contributions to Historical Phenomena and Collective Behavior,* Johns Hopkins University Press, 1973.
(With Talcott Parsons and Neil Smelser) *The American University,* Harvard University Press, 1973.
The American Academic System, Harvard University Press, 1973.
(Editor with Jerome Rabow and Marion Goldman) *Advances in Psychoanalytic Sociology,* Robert E. Krieger, in press.

CONTRIBUTOR

Carlos E. Kruytbosch and Sheldon Messinger, editors, *Authority and Change in the University,* Sage Publications, 1970.
Edward A. Tiryakian, editor, *The Phenomenon of Sociology: A Reader in the Sociology of Sociology,* Appleton-Century-Crofts, 1971.
Matilda W. Riley, Marilyn E. Johnson, and Anne Foner, editors, *Aging and Society,* Volume III, Russell Sage, 1972.
Lewis Solman and Paul Taubman, editors, *Does College Matter?: Higher Education, Policy Implications, and Future Directions,* Academic Press, 1973.

Nicholas H. Steneck, editor, *Science and Society: A Symposium Marking the Five-Hundredth Anniversary of the Birth of Nicholas Copernicus (1473-1543),* University of Michigan Press, 1975.
Robert T. Blackburn, editor, *Studies on Academics and Modes of Inquiry,* Center for the Study of Higher Education, University of Michigan, 1978.
Mel Albin, editor, *New Directions in Psychohistory: The Adelphi Papers in Honor of Erik H. Erikson,* Lexington Press, 1980.
Rom Harre and Roger Lamb, editors, *The Encyclopedic Dictionary of Psychology,* Basil Blackwell, 1983.
Michael Lewis and JoAnn Miller, editors, *Social Problems and Public Policy,* Volume III, JAI Press, 1984.
Adam Kuper and Jessica Kuper, editors, *The Social Science Encyclopedia,* Routledge & Kegan Paul, in press.
Jerome Rabow, Gerald M. Platt, and Marion Goldman, editors, *Advances in Psychoanalytic Sociology,* Robert E. Krieger, in press.

OTHER

Editor of ''Sociological Series,'' Ablex Publishing. Contributor of more than twenty articles and reviews to journals in history and the social sciences.

WORK IN PROGRESS: Research on theory and revolutions.

SIDELIGHTS: Gerald M. Platt told *CA:* ''I did not intend to become a writer; it sneaked up on me. I wanted to be a college teacher but then learned that teachers also publish. I had some ideas about which to write and I put them down on paper. An editor at the University of California Press was mistaken enough to believe the ideas were worthy of publication. He made my first manuscript a published reality. The rest just followed.''

Psychoanalytic Sociology has been translated into German and Italian.

*   *   *

PLAUT, W(olf) Gunther   1912-

PERSONAL: Born November 1, 1912, in Muenster, Germany (now West Germany); son of Jonas and Selma (Gumprich) Plaut; married Elizabeth Strauss, 1938; children: Jonathan, Judith. *Education:* Attended University of Heidelberg; University of Berlin, LL.B., 1933, Doctor juris utriusque, 1934; Hebrew Union College, Cincinnati, Ohio, M.H.L. and Rabbi, 1939.

ADDRESSES: Office—Holy Blossom Temple, 1950 Bathurst St., Toronto, Canada M5P 3K9.

CAREER: Rabbi of temples in Chicago, Ill., 1939-48, and St. Paul, Minn., 1948-61; Holy Blossom Temple, Toronto, Ontario, senior rabbi, 1961-77, senior scholar, 1978—. Visiting lecturer in philosophy, Macalester College, 1952-54; visiting lecturer in Jewish thought, Haifa University, 1978—. Member, Minnesota Governor's Committee on Human Rights, 1949-61; chairman, Minnesota Governor's Committee on Ethics in Government, 1958-61; vice-chairman, Ontario Human Rights Commission, 1977-85. National president, World Federalists of Canada, 1966-69, and Canadian Jewish Congress, 1977-80. One-person federal commission to redraft refugee determination in Canada, 1984-85. Former vice-president, St. Paul Council of Arts and Sciences; president, St. Paul Gallery and School of Art, 1953-59. *Military service:* U.S. Army, chaplain, 1943-46; became captain; received Bronze Star.

MEMBER: Central Conference of American Rabbis (member of executive committee, 1954-56; chairman of committee on new literature, 1959-61; chairman of Sabbath committee, 1965-70; chairman of committee on reform practices, beginning 1970; president, 1983-85), Minnesota Rabbinical Association (president, 1955-56), Oakdale Golf and Country Club, Maple Downs Country Club, Primrose Club.

AWARDS, HONORS: D.D., Hebrew Union College, Cincinnati, 1964; Officer of the Order of Canada, 1978; LL.D., University of Toronto, 1978; Litt.D., Cleveland College of Jewish Studies, 1979.

WRITINGS:

Materielle Eheungueltigkeit, Risse, 1934.
High Holyday Services for Children, [St. Paul], 1950, revised edition, 1964.
Mount Zion: The First Hundred Years, North Central, 1956.
The Jews in Minnesota, American Jewish Historical Society, 1959.
The Book of Proverbs: A Commentary, Union of American Hebrew Congregations, 1961.
Judaism and the Scientific Spirit, Union of American Hebrew Congregations, 1962.
The Rise of Reform Judaism, World Union of Progressive Judaism, 1963.
The Growth of Reform Judaism, World Union for Progressive Judaism, 1965.
The Case for the Chosen People, Doubleday, 1965.
Your Neighbour Is a Jew, McClelland & Stewart, 1967, United Church Press, 1968.
Page 2, [Toronto], 1971.
Genesis: A Commentary, Union of American Hebrew Congregations, 1974.
Time to Think, [Toronto], 1977.
Hanging Threads, Lester & Orpen, 1978, published as *The Man in the Blue Vest, and Other Stories,* Taplinger, 1980.
Numbers: A Commentary, Union of American Hebrew Congregations, 1979.
Exodus: A Commentary, Union of American Hebrew Congregations, 1980.
(Principal author with Bernard J. Bamberger and William W. Hallo and editor) *The Torah: A Modern Commentary,* Union of American Hebrew Congregations, 1981.
Unfinished Business (autobiography), Lester & Orpen, 1982.
Deuteronomy: The Torah, Union of American Hebrew Congregations, 1983.
Exodus: A Modern Commentary, Union of American Hebrew Congregations, 1983.

Regular contributor to *Journal* of Central Conference of American Rabbis and to *Globe and Mail* (Toronto); contributor to other professional journals, magazines, and newspapers.

SIDELIGHTS: Near the end of World War II, W. Gunther Plaut was the first rabbi to bring a Sefer Torah back to Germany and held the first free service in the burned-out shell of Cologne Synagogue in March, 1945. He also was present when the Allies liberated the first concentration and extermination camp in Nordhausen. Now beyond the age of seventy, he reports, "I left the pulpit to devote myself primarily to writing and lecturing. Has the elusive craft thereby become easier? Not at all; if anything, my standards have become such that I have more trouble than before writing something that satisfies me. But I wouldn't have it otherwise.

"After writing my first full-length novel, I wonder why I have discovered this marvellous medium so late in life; for fiction, and especially historical fiction, weds imagination to reality in a wonderfully satisfying fashion. I may become an addict yet."

AVOCATIONAL INTERESTS: Tennis, chess, golf, and sculpture.

*   *   *

PONDER, Catherine   1927-

PERSONAL: Born February 14, 1927, in Hartsville, S.C.; daughter of Roy Charles (an electrical engineer) and Kathleen (Parrish) Cook; married Robert Stearns, June 19, 1970; children: (previous marriage) Richard. *Education:* Attended University of North Carolina, 1946; Worth Business College, graduate, 1948; Unity School of Christianity, Ministerial School, B.S., 1956.

ADDRESSES: Agent—Bertha Klausner International Literary Agency, 71 Park Ave., New York, N.Y. 10016. *Office*—P.O. Drawer 1278, Palm Desert, Calif. 92261.

CAREER: Licensed into Unity ministry, 1957; ordained, 1958. Federal Bureau of Investigation, Washington, D.C., staff member of Identification Division, 1944-46; worked as private secretary in Fayetteville, N.C., 1948-56; minister of Unity churches in Birmingham, Ala., 1956-61, Austin, Tex., 1961-70, and San Antonio, Tex., 1969-73; founder-minister of Unity Church Worldwide, Palm Desert, Calif., 1973—.

MEMBER: International New Thought Alliance, International Platform Association, Unity Ministers' Association, Los Angeles Club, Bermuda Dunes Country Club, Palm Springs Racquet Club.

WRITINGS:

The Dynamic Laws of Prosperity: Forces That Bring Riches to You, Prentice-Hall, 1962, revised edition, De Vorss, 1985.
The Prosperity Secret of the Ages, Prentice-Hall, 1964, revised edition, De Vorss, 1986.
The Dynamic Laws of Healing, Parker Publishing, 1966, revised edition, De Vorss, 1985.
The Prospering Power of Love, Unity Books, 1966, revised edition, De Vorss, 1984.
The Healing Secret of the Ages, Parker Publishing, 1967, revised edition, De Vorss, 1985.
The Secret of Unlimited Supply, Unity Books, 1967, revised edition, De Vorss, 1981.
Pray and Grow Rich, Parker Publishing, 1968, revised edition published as *The Dynamic Laws of Prayer,* De Vorss, 1986.
Open Your Mind to Prosperity, Unity Books, 1971, revised edition, De Vorss, 1984.
The Millionaires of Genesis, De Vorss, 1976.
The Millionaire Moses, De Vorss, 1977.
The Millionaire Joshua, De Vorss, 1978.
The Millionaire from Nazareth, De Vorss, 1979.
Open Your Mind to Receive, De Vorss, 1983.
Dare to Prosper!, De Vorss, 1983.
The Prospering Power of Prayer, De Vorss, 1983.

Contributor to professional journals, including Unity publications and *New Thought* magazine.

POPOWSKI, Bert (John)   1904-

PERSONAL: Born February 15, 1904, near Grafton, N.D.; son of John Frank and Anna (Prondzinski) Popowski; married Harriet Isabel Seymour, September 30, 1930; children: John Seymour, Jerome Bert. *Education:* State College of Agriculture and Mechanic Arts (now South Dakota State University), B.S., 1926; graduate study in journalism at University of Minnesota; additional study at Purdue University and Indiana University.

ADDRESSES: Home and office—Star Route 3, Custer, S.D. 57730.

CAREER: High school instructor in Java, S.D., 1926-28, Indianapolis, Ind., 1928-30, and Aberdeen, S.D., 1931-39; *Look,* Des Moines, Iowa, associate editor, 1939-41; worked in advertising and sales, Aberdeen, S.D., 1942-43; college professor, Pittsburgh, Pa., 1946-47; printing and editorial supervisor, Dayton, Ohio, 1947-49; State College of Agriculture and Mechanic Arts (now South Dakota State University), Brookings, professor of printing, 1949-50; free-lance writer, photographer, and lecturer, 1950—.

MEMBER: North American Outdoor Writers Association (charter member), National Rifle Association (life member).

WRITINGS:

Crow Hunting, privately printed, 1942.
Crow Shooting, A.S. Barnes, 1946.
Hunting Small Game, Macmillan, 1948.
Calling All Game, Stackpole, 1952.
Calling All Varmints, Stackpole, 1952.
South Dakota Brags, privately printed, 1953.
Hunting Pronghorn Antelope, Stackpole, 1959.
The Varmint and Crow Hunter's Bible, Doubleday, 1962.
Varmint Hunting, Garcia Sports Library, 1971.
Saga of "Sans": A Log Cabin, privately printed, 1979.
The Hunter's Book of the Pronghorn Antelope, Winchester Press, 1982.

Contributor to numerous hunting and fishing anthologies. Contributor of more than twelve hundred articles to magazines, including *Sports Afield, Outdoor Life, Field and Stream, National Sportsman, Hunting and Fishing, American Home, Guns,* and *Guns and Hunting.* Contributing editor, *American Rifleman,* 1956—.

WORK IN PROGRESS: Planning two books and doing research for outdoor articles.

SIDELIGHTS: Bert Popowski began his writing career by reporting sports for a dozen newspapers while he was attending college in South Dakota. He was North American crow shooting champion in 1949, using calls he developed and still sells. He has also made a Columbia recording of crow calling and instructions.

*   *   *

PORTEUS, Stanley D(avid)   1883-

PERSONAL: Born April 24, 1883, in Melbourne, Victoria, Australia; naturalized U.S. citizen, 1932; son of David (a clergyman) and Katherine (Hebden) Porteus; married Frances Mainwaring Evans, July 13, 1909; children: David Hebden, John Ruxton. *Education:* Attended Melbourne Educational Institute and Melbourne University, 1910-16.

ADDRESSES: Home—1434 Punahou St., Honolulu, Hawaii 96822.

CAREER: Superintendent of Special Education in Melbourne, Australia, 1913-18; University of Melbourne, Melbourne, lecturer in experimental education, 1915-18; Psychological Laboratory, Vineland, N.J., director of research, 1919-26; University of Hawaii, Honolulu, professor of clinical psychology, 1922-48, professor emeritus, 1949—, director of psychological and psychopathic clinic, 1922-48, consultant to Psychological Research Center, 1958—. Leader of National Research Council expedition to central and northwest Australia, 1929, and of South African Council expedition to Kalahari Desert, 1934.

MEMBER: American Psychological Association, American Association of Consulting Psychologists, Phi Beta Kappa.

AWARDS, HONORS: D.Sc., University of Hawaii, 1932; prize for best book on Hawaii, 1947, for *And Blow Not the Trumpet;* Distinguished Contributions Award, Clinical Psychology Division of American Psychological Association, 1962.

WRITINGS:

Studies in Mental Deviations, Smith Printing House, 1923.
Guide to the Porteus Maze Test, Smith Printing House, 1924.
(With Marjorie E. Babcock) *Temperament and Race,* Richard Badger, 1926.
(With F. Wood Jones) *The Matrix of the Mind,* Edward Arnold, 1930.
Psychology of a Primitive People: A Study of the Australian Aborigine (Scientific Book Club selection), Edward Arnold, 1931, Longmans, Green, 1932, reprinted, Books for Libraries, 1972.
Porteus Maze Test and Mental Difference, Smith Printing House, 1933, 2nd edition published as *The Porteus Maze Test and Intelligence,* Pacific Books, 1950.
Primitive Intelligence and Environment (Scientific Book Club selection), Macmillan, 1937.
The Practice of Clinical Psychology, American Book Co., 1942.
Calabashes and Kings: An Introduction to Hawaii, Pacific Books, 1946.
And Blow Not the Trumpet, Pacific Books, 1947.
The Restless Voyage, Prentice-Hall, 1948.
Providence Ponds, Harrap, 1950.
The Maze Test and Clinical Psychology, Pacific Books, 1958.
A Century of Social Thinking in Hawaii, Pacific Books, 1962.
Streamlined Elementary Education, Pacific Books, 1964.
Porteus Maze Tests: Fifty Years' Application, Pacific Books, 1965.
A Psychologist of Sorts: The Autobiography and Publications of the Inventor of the Porteus Maze Tests, Pacific Books, 1969.

Also author of thirteen monographs and a manual on the maze tests published in England. Contributor of more than seventy articles to scientific journals in the fields of neurology and psychology.†

*   *   *

PORUSH, David H(illel)   1952-

PERSONAL: Born October 23, 1952, in New York, N.Y.; son of Abraham (in business) and Judith (in business; maiden name, Gudin) Porush. *Education:* Massachusetts Institute of Technology, B.S., 1973; State University of New York at Buffalo, M.A. and Ph.D., both 1977.

ADDRESSES: Home—Latham, N.Y. 12110. *Office*—Department of Language, Literature, and Communication, Rensselaer Polytechnic Institute, Troy, N.Y. 12181.

CAREER: Golden Alligator, Inc., New York, N.Y., antiques dealer, 1971; Maclean's Hospital, Belmont, Mass., mental hospital aide, 1972; College of William and Mary, Williamsburg, Va., assistant professor of English, 1977-81; Rensselaer Polytechnic Institute, Troy, N.Y., associate professor, 1981—.

WRITINGS:

Rope Dances (short fictions), Fiction Collective, 1979.
The Soft Machine: Cybernetic Fiction, Methuen, 1985.

Contributor to *Spree* and *American Book Review*.

WORK IN PROGRESS: Astonishment of Heart; or, The Blind Woman Tapes, a novel; research for *Paras.*

SIDELIGHTS: David H. Porush comments: "I write because it is what I do best; indeed, it is the only thing I do well. At present, the idea most important to me is that the world is a dissipative structure, in the sense that it is a momentary aberration of order building on the general dissipation of the universe. I have traveled all through Europe and the Middle East and discovered this is generally true, though more true in some places than in others. I would describe my fictions as dissipative structures as well."

*   *   *

POWELL, Ivor   1910-

PERSONAL: Born April 22, 1910, in Crosskeys, Monmouth, Wales; son of James (a mine examiner) and Hephzibah (Terrell) Powell; married Margaret Betty Davies (an evangelist), July 8, 1940. *Education:* Attended South Wales Bible Training Institute.

ADDRESSES: Home and office—612 Surf View Dr., Santa Barbara, Calif. 93109.

CAREER: Ordained minister of Baptist Union of Wales, 1934; Prince's Street Mission, Barry, Glamorganshire, Wales, pastor, 1936-44; went abroad to serve as official evangelist of Baptist churches in South Africa and Southern Rhodesia, 1948-51, Australia, 1951-54, New Zealand, 1955-56, Canada, 1957-60, and California, 1960—, with current headquarters in Santa Barbara; founder of the Ivor Powell Evangelistic Crusades, Inc., 1967. Producer of more than twenty travel films on mission work.

AWARDS, HONORS: D.D., Trinity College, Dunedin, Fla., 1973.

WRITINGS:

We Saw It Happen, Marshall, Morgan & Scott, 1948.
Black Radiance, Marshall, Morgan & Scott, 1949.
Silent Challenge, Zondervan, 1950.
Bible Cameos, Marshall, Morgan & Scott, 1951, Zondervan, 1960, reprinted, Kregel, 1985.
Bible Pinnacles, Marshall, Morgan & Scott, 1952, Zondervan, 1960, reprinted, Kregel, 1985.
Bible Treasures, Marshall, Morgan & Scott, 1953, Zondervan, 1960, reprinted, Kregel, 1985.
Bible Windows, Marshall, Morgan & Scott, 1954, Zondervan, 1960, reprinted, Kregel, 1985.

Broad Horizons, Marshall, Morgan & Scott, 1955.
God's Little Ones, Marshall, Morgan & Scott, 1956.
This I Believe: The Essential Truths of Christianity, Marshall, Morgan & Scott, 1957, Zondervan, 1961.
Bible Highways, foreword by Thomas B. McDormand, Zondervan, 1959, reprinted, Kregel, 1985.
Don't Lose That Fish!, Zondervan, 1960.
John's Wonderful Gospel, Zondervan, 1962, reprinted, Kregel, 1983.
Luke's Thrilling Gospel, Zondervan, 1965, reprinted, Kregel, 1984.
Disillusion by the Nile: What Nasser Has Done to Egypt, Solstice Productions, 1967.
The Rising of the Son, Ivor Powell Evangelistic Crusades, 1973.
Mark's Superb Gospel, Kregel, 1985.
What in the World Will Happen Next?, Kregel, 1985.
Matthew's Majestic Gospel, Kregel, in press.

WORK IN PROGRESS: Bible Messages and *The Acts of the Apostles*, both for Kregel.

AVOCATIONAL INTERESTS: Cinematography and video tape productions.

SIDELIGHTS: Ivor Powell's books have been translated into Telagu, Japanese, and German.

*   *   *

POWERS, Thomas (Moore)   1940-

PERSONAL: Born December 12, 1940, in New York, N.Y.; son of Joshua Bryant (a publisher) and Susan (Moore) Powers; married Candace Molloy, August 21, 1965; children: Amanda, Susan, Cassandra. *Education:* Yale University, B.A., 1964.

ADDRESSES: Home and office—Broad Brook Rd., South Royalton, Vt. 05068. *Agent*—Susan P. Urstadt, 125 East 84th St., New York, N.Y. 10028.

CAREER: Rome Daily American, Rome, Italy, reporter, 1965-67; United Press International, New York, N.Y., reporter, 1967-70; free-lance writer, 1970—. Lecturer.

MEMBER: P.E.N. American Center, Council on Foreign Relations.

AWARDS, HONORS: Pulitzer Prize for national reporting, 1971, for five-part series on Diana Oughton and Weatherman; American Book Award nomination, 1980, for *The Man Who Kept the Secrets: Richard Helms and the CIA*; Olive Branch Award for outstanding coverage of the nuclear arms issue, 1984, for "What Is It About" in *Atlantic*.

WRITINGS:

Diana: The Making of a Terrorist, Houghton, 1971.
The War at Home: Vietnam and the American People, 1964-68, Grossman, 1973.
The Man Who Kept the Secrets: Richard Helms and the CIA, Knopf, 1979.
Thinking about the Next War, Knopf, 1982.

Contributor of essays to periodicals, including *Commonweal, Atlantic, New York Review of Books*, and *Rolling Stone*. Contributing editor, *Atlantic*.

WORK IN PROGRESS: The Ultimate Weapon, for Knopf.

SIDELIGHTS: Piecing together interviews, public records, newly released documents and other published accounts as well as personal insights, journalist and author Thomas Powers constructs thorough examinations of recent history and current events. His books confront contemporary issues—radicalism in the late 1960s, the 1960s antiwar movement, the Central Intelligence Agency (CIA), and the threat of nuclear war—and reveal how people act and react within these contexts. In each study, Powers's investigation has allowed him to add new information to the available material on his chosen topic and to draw new conclusions—conclusions sometimes contrary to previously accepted analyses.

In 1971, Powers and Lucinda Franks earned a Pulitzer Prize for their series of articles on a young upper-middle-class student turned revolutionary. Powers's first book, *Diana: The Making of a Terrorist,* is his expansion of those articles. Born in 1942, Diana Oughton was the daughter of an influential landowner, banker, restauranteur, and prominent citizen of Dwight, Illinois. She prepared for college at a private school in Virginia, completed her undergraduate study at Bryn Mawr, and pursued a graduate degree at the University of Michigan. Her social concern led her to work in Guatemala and then teach at a special school in the Philadelphia ghetto. She joined the Students for a Democratic Society (SDS) and later became a member of its Weatherman faction. Oughton died March 6, 1970, when the Greenwich Village townhouse in which she and other Weatherman members were manufacturing bombs exploded.

Diana provides a study of the young middle class in the late 1960s and the social currents that moved them. Their background offered them the freedom to pursue higher education, education that informed them of inequality and injustice; their background also placed them among the oppressors. "Revolutionary ardor became a kind of absolution from class," writes Susan Brownmiller in the *New York Times Book Review.* They organized to push for social reforms and policy changes. Dissatisfied with the results of nonviolent protest, however, many became increasingly radical and some formed splinter groups given to extreme tactics. These splinter groups "came to embrace the fantasy that by violent action they could precipitate revolution," notes Fred J. Cook in the *Saturday Review.* What they did not understand, says Cook, is that "in America, wedded to a democratic system, violence has always been self-defeating."

Powers reveals this progression through Diana Oughton and her involvement with Weatherman, a violent offshoot of the SDS. "At [Weatherman's] center (with Diana as a paradigm) was a consuming desire both to eradicate their privileged pasts and transform their impotent presents," George Abbott White observes in *Commonweal.* The group turned to "obliterating the past with exemplary bombs and the present with obsessive sexuality that was finally as cruel and brutal and barbaric as the evils they were fighting," adds White.

Through focusing on the individual, Powers hopes to illuminate a larger picture—the groups, movements, and issues of that period of recent history. And as Susan Brownmiller comments, "It works, and brilliantly, for Diana's story *is* the evolution of Weatherman, and by placing her in a political, rather than a personal or psychological, context, her inexorable descent into the basement workshop of the townhouse becomes a history lesson of critical importance, a tragedy of alienated rage performed by some of America's most brilliant, sensitive and privileged youth." In the 1960s, protest accelerated much positive social reform and policy change, as Powers demonstrates in his second book, *The War at Home: Vietnam and*

the American People, 1964-68. But where the protest turned violent, it went wrong. Of *Diana,* Fred J. Cook writes: "Thomas Powers's moving reconstruction of [Diana Oughton's] life leaves us with our own burden of infinite sorrow that so much that could have been so fine was so pitifully wasted."

Again in his third book, *The Man Who Kept the Secrets: Richard Helms and the CIA,* Powers addresses larger issues by first focusing on the individual. A biography of former Central Intelligence Agency (CIA) director Richard Helms, the book also offers a history of the CIA and a discussion of the agency's relationship with other government branches. "It is an intelligent collection of mostly well-told tales about the CIA—its cold war origins, oddball personalities, plots against Castro, connections with Watergate—culled from private interviews, public records . . . and previously published works about intelligence and Watergate by more than 80 authors," observes David M. Alpern in *Newsweek.*

During World War II, Richard Helms worked for the Office of Strategic Services (OSS), a CIA precursor; he joined the CIA at its inception in 1947. In 1952, Helms became a chief of operations and in 1966, director of the CIA. President Nixon dismissed him in December, 1972. Powers offers a portrait of this career agent who rose to the top. "He gives us a patriotic bureaucrat," comments John le Carre in the *New York Times Book Review,* "and a man of determined plainness, who loved his service and his country and preferred to obey 'one President at a time' rather than puzzle over the fine print of the Constitution." Helms was, according to *Best Sellers* contributor Joseph A. Cawley, "the very model of a secret agent."

In 1975, Helms was indicted for perjury for testimony he had given a Senate committee inquiring into CIA operations. He was found guilty of lesser charges: not offering complete and accurate answers to Senate questions. Powers finds that Helms's choice not to divulge any agency secrets was not surprising. "For Helms . . . secrecy was not just second nature, it was his element, the very basis of his personality," explains John le Carre. Adds Alpern: "In the end, Powers concludes, Helms kept the CIA's secrets to protect himself, salvage what he could of public trust in the CIA and maintain that curtain of illusion essential to intelligence operations."

The Man Who Kept the Secrets also "includes the personalities (careers, dreams) of the people on the first and second levels who ran the agency, how they performed, how they regarded themselves and each other," points out Eliot Fremont-Smith in the *Village Voice.* What Powers found was not a group of cloak-and-dagger spys or sophisticated "James Bond" agents; nor was there mystery and intrigue at the heart of the agency. Powers "has written an excellent book on blankness and banality," contends John Leonard in the *New York Times,* "the best book on the C.I.A. ever written. The blankness at the middle is a blankness of character, of careerism."

Through Helms and these other agents emerges the history of the CIA. "[Powers] came away from the effort respecting the quality and caliber of the spymasters but questioning the evolution of the CIA's role," Charles Madigan writes in the *Chicago Tribune.* At the time Powers was writing this book, the CIA was under great pressure to account for its involvement in plots to remove foreign heads of state from power. Assassination plots against General Kassem of Iraq, Lumumba of the Congo, and Fidel Castro of Cuba as well as schemes to overthrow Sukarno of Indonesia and Allende of Chile had been uncovered. The prevailing view was that the CIA had gotten out of control, devising and implementing its own foreign policy with no regard for government policy. As Michael Ledeen writes in *Commentary,* "Powers effectively demolishes this demonology and focuses our attention where it belongs: on the ideology and conduct of the President and his colleagues in the executive branch."

"The problem, according to Powers, is that the CIA has become so closely tied to the Oval Office and subordinate to its demands that the agency often finds itself trying to bend the world to please the President instead of pursuing its intended goal: the collection of unbiased, accurate information," explains Charles Madigan. Powers maintains that Eisenhower, Kennedy, Johnson, and Nixon each used the CIA to pursue their personal policy interests when overt actions were too risky. In Powers's analysis, the plots against foreign leaders represent not the independent actions of a "rogue elephant" (in Senator Frank Church's words) but rather the pet projects of presidents and their staffs.

The conclusion that the President was ultimately responsible for the misdeeds of the CIA raised controversy in some circles. In one issue of *Commonweal,* Arthur Schlesinger, Jr., voices his objections to Powers's analysis. Schlesinger writes: "Every executive agency of course is nominally accountable to the President. But government agencies develop interests, purposes, constituencies, commitments, codes of their own. . . . This is an elementary rule of bureaucracy." Schlesinger suggests that Powers's conclusion indicates a shift in public perception influenced by the events of the day. "No doubt the inordinately uncritical reception accorded the Powers book reflects a widespread desire to believe that the CIA's past excesses were due to the iniquity of Presidents and not to the internal dynamism of over-financed and under-supervised intelligence organizations," he concludes.

Powers's response in a subsequent *Commonweal* article cites a Senate investigation to substantiate the author's analysis. "In its study of the covert operations conducted by the CIA," writes Powers, "the Church Committee focused, in exhausting detail, on Indonesia, Cuba, and Chile. In all three cases the Committee found that presidents and their advisors had pressed the CIA relentlessly for results. In every instance CIA complaints were the same: they were being pressed to do too much, too quickly, by men with too little understanding of what really might be accomplished by covert action." In a specific case—President Kennedy's involvement in the many CIA plots to assassinate Fidel Castro—Powers offers his interpretation of the situation's dynamics. "It is conceivable that a failure to say no [to a Castro assassination] was taken by the CIA as permission to go ahead. . . . But I think it more likely that Kennedy allowed himself to say yes, shrank back from the details, and then absorbed this seemingly small assent as one more of those awful freedoms which power cannot justify, but allows."

In the face of the nuclear threat posed by the superpowers' arms race, some analysts see the fear of mutual assured destruction as a powerful and adequate deterrent; some believe it makes nuclear conflict highly unlikely. Thomas Powers suggests in his book *Thinking about the Next War* that a limited nuclear war not only can happen but will happen. Powers explains: "Since 1945, the United States and the Soviet Union have been preparing to fight each other in a big war, and eventually they are going to do it." Nuclear weapons may inhibit some hostile actions, but as Joseph S. Nye notes in the *New York Times Book Review,* "Mr. Powers argues that deterrence of rational acts of aggression cannot prevent wars that

no one really intends." And Powers adds, "The next [war] will probably involve the use of nuclear weapons."

As in his previous books, Powers uncovers the details of this issue through its impact on people. "Powers approaches genocidal warfare from an intensely human perspective," observes David C. Morrison in the *Progressive,* "zeroing in on some unhappy truths along the way." *Thinking about the Next War* examines "the forces that drive us in this direction [toward nuclear war], the effect of this fearful prospect on our psychology (and, in the most moving essay in the book, on the minds of our children), the kind of war that is likely to occur and the consequences." Thomas Powers's "writing is without cliches or pretentions," concludes David Corn in the *Nation,* "full of pessimism and, probably, truth."

CA INTERVIEW

CA interviewed Thomas Powers by telephone on April 19, 1985, at his office in South Royalton, Vermont.

CA: You began your journalism career with two years as a reporter on the Rome Daily American. *Was that a good training ground?*

POWERS: That was not a very serious newspaper, but from a distance it *looked* like a serious newspaper, so for somebody who was just starting out in life, it was OK. And living in Rome for two years was good for my soul.

CA: How early had you decided to go into journalism?

POWERS: I don't know that I ever really did decide; it just sort of happened. I left college for a year and worked in a bookstore for a while. That was a surpassingly boring way to spend the day. An opening on a newspaper as a police reporter came available, and that sounded to me a lot more interesting. My father had been a journalist. I thought this way I would see something of life, and I had always thought I might like to be a writer. So it seemed like a natural and inevitable thing to do. Then after I left college I needed to get some kind of a job, and newspapers seemed like a logical place to begin since I had already worked on them. I figured that would be a good way to learn something about the world and get some experience of life and maybe grow up enough to have some ideas to justify writing something someday.

CA: In telling the story of Diana Oughton in your first book, Diana: The Making of a Terrorist *(1971), you also told the story of the Weathermen. How much help did you get from the Weathermen themselves in putting together the events that led to Diana's death?*

POWERS: The Weather people were not very forthcoming, but they were the residue of a political organization that had been much broader in scope; when they decided to become underground terrorists, they left behind a lot of people who were their intimate friends up until just fifteen minutes ago—kids who thought going underground and trying to topple the U.S. government with a campaign of terrorism was absolutely crazy. So most of the information came from people who were friends of Diana and the other Weather people. I never talked to Bernadine Dorn or Bill Ayers or Mark Rudd after they went underground.

CA: Was it hard to get the story?

POWERS: It was very difficult to find out what happened inside the political organization she'd belonged to. Basically the way we did it was to establish two chronologies. One was a personal chronology that we got from members of Diana's family and her friends at school and so on; they had seen her at regular times and intervals, and they remembered these occasions all very vividly, as a rule. Then if you matched up that chronology with what was happening politically in SDS (Students for a Democratic Society), you could see there was an obvious correspondence there. Certain kinds of things would happen in SDS and Diana would be in quite a state. For example, her father bailed her out of jail after the Days of Rage in October, 1969. That was a violent demonstration that they had spent the previous summer working on and that they hoped would trigger a mass uprising of high school students. It was a dumb idea, but they did it anyway, and Diane was arrested along with everybody else. Then her father went up to Chicago and bailed her out. He talked to her at that time, and she came home for a couple of days and people in the family all talked to her. You could find out what had been going on, in effect, in her political life by this brief window provided by members of her family. If you just went through the history of SDS and her personal history and meshed those chronologies, then you had an awful lot of it. At that point, if you went and asked some people who were close to SDS and the Weathermen and they told you anything at all, it would always fit very cleanly into the whole pattern.

CA: Diana seemed such unlikely terrorist material, coming from a well-to-do, conservative background. Did you find that true of many of the young people you came in contact with or heard about while you were working on that book?

POWERS: It was very common at that time for upper-middle-class kids who thought it was important to have opinions and important to care about the world and important to feel compassion for the poor and the downtrodden. Those were all attitudes and emotions that for the most part were the product of expensive educations, so it was natural that they came from the kind of background that can provide an expensive education. But if you go back and look at that period, the thing that's really remarkable is not the pattern in the United States, but the fact that the pattern was repeated elsewhere throughout the world. In Japan, Italy, France, and Germany very, very similar histories took place where you had a student population—upper-middle-class, liberal in sentiment—from political organizations that got increasingly hard-line, turning into Marxist-Leninist vanguard parties and going underground to try and foment revolution. But in Germany, with the Bader-Meinhoff Gang and in Italy with the Feltrinelli group and in Japan with the Red Army faction and in France with the Maoists, things tended to go a lot further. The Weather people set off a couple of bombs. The very first one they set off, of course, was the one that killed Diana and her friends. That was a very bad experience for them, and they pretty much backed out of the violence business right away. But there were other groups—the Bader-Meinhoff Gang, for example, that really went a long way in that line.

CA: In The War at Home *(1973), again you dealt with current and recent events, and with the social and political movements of the 1960s and early 1970s that were changing American life in profound ways. If you were doing that book now, would the perspective of time change any of your observations?*

POWERS: It would change one. In the introduction to that book, I mentioned that the opposition to the war was in danger of being written out of history. I can remember very clearly my feeling when I wrote that. It seemed to me an obviously exaggerated opinion, and I said it and wrote it down there simply in order to draw attention to the fact that the opposition was a real thing and played a central role in our whole involvement in Vietnam, but that it was a hard thing for historians to grapple with. Historians, you know, like to burrow down in the basement of a library somewhere with a huge pile of documents. That inclines them to spend all of their time trying to figure out what has been happening in the White House and the Pentagon, because that's where all the documents get created; those organizations produce mountains of paper, and historians like mountains of paper. But the opposition to the war was a thing that had to do with the atmosphere of the times and the intellectual and moral climate of the country. It's very hard to get a grasp on, and it doesn't leave clear documents; it's hard to assess and easy to dismiss if you're so inclined. At any rate, I thought I was exaggerating when I wrote that the opposition was in danger of being written out of history. Now, fifteen years later, it has been. It's absolutely missing from the standard histories of Vietnam. It's treated in a sentence or in passing: "rising public discontent" or "increasing disenchantment with the war"—that kind of thing, not even a chapter.

CA: Are you interested in doing a social history of that period, since you've dealt with it so much?

POWERS: I don't think so. It would be an interesting subject to write about, but I've read a bunch of pieces of the ten-years-after-Vietnam variety lately, and I find that I don't really have a strong feeling. I'm quite bewildered by what that all meant. I was absolutely positive at the time, but now I look at it and it doesn't make any sense.

CA: When did you leave newspaper work to write privately full-time?

POWERS: Fairly early on, actually. I worked for UPI in New York from the fall of 1967 until the fall of 1970, and I've been freelancing ever since. In fact I had quit UPI before I got the assignment to work on the piece about Diana Oughton. I was on my way out and they came and asked me if I wouldn't work on this project. I said OK, because they really wanted to do it and they needed somebody who had already learned something about the student movement. And besides, it seemed like kind of a good project.

CA: How did The Man Who Kept the Secrets *(1979) grow from a* Rolling Stone *article to a book?*

POWERS: I owed something—an article of some kind—to Mary Ann Partridge, who was the editor of *Rolling Stone* that I worked with on that project. We'd had a couple of other projects. She wanted me to do one about the Rockefeller cousins, and I started working on that a bit and found it really unpleasant. I didn't like going around and trying to find out what all these kids were doing, talking to their nannies and stuff like that; I had no appetite for it. After she had invested some time, and not very much money but some, in this project, I said I just couldn't do it. So I owed her something.

Then she asked me to do a profile of Richard Helms, who was much in the news at that time because of his fibs to the Congress about Chile. I said OK. I thought, when I started out, that I was going to find out very little and I was going to end up writing a story of how come you can't find out anything about the CIA. In fact, when I started going around to see people in Washington, I found that they were in a very talkative mood. I had come along at exactly the right moment; a whole generation of CIA people had either retired or been fired in '72 and '73. By the time I started, three years later, they had been sitting around in their living rooms with nothing to do and reading newspaper headlines and were in an angry and dispeptic mood. They felt they had a lot to explain, that nobody understood them and they were being given a raw deal. Then here comes some fellow who wants to ask them a lot of questions and has never heard any of their favorite stories before. So it was an ideal moment for that kind of a project.

CA: How much did your feelings about Helms and the CIA change as the research went along?

POWERS: Quite a lot. I would say I started off with an instinctively hostile attitude towards the CIA and probably towards Helms too. It wasn't based on anything in particular, but just kind of a general sentiment that he and it were wrapped up in a whole lot of public endeavors that I didn't like. It turned out that in some ways they were. But I began to understand things a lot better once I really started to pay attention to what the CIA had been doing all these years. And I began to understand a lot more about the way nations deal with each other. The question of whether or not you like the CIA began to seem increasingly beside the point—like saying, do you like an income tax service. Whether you like it or not is quite irrelevant to whether or not you're going to be paying taxes to one. That is just a standard given in civilized life. Nations collect taxes; that's it. If you don't like it, you'd just better not earn any money. It's the same with intelligence services.

CA: The Man Who Kept the Secrets must have been disconcerting to many government officials. Did you hear from any of them personally in response to the book?

POWERS: I heard quite a lot about it, and occasionally somebody would be upset or make a fuss because I had betrayed a secret that they thought ought to remain hidden. But for the most part, they liked it. They felt that it was serious and that it sort of described the world that they knew. Recently I went out to the Conference on World Affairs at the University of Colorado at Boulder, and I ran across a lot of CIA people there. They had uniformly read that book and all went out of their way to say that they liked it. Two or three of them also expressed horror at the idea that former employees of the agency would tell me all this stuff, but at the same time, they thought it was a good book.

CA: How well do you think books like yours—books of fact and opinion on current topics—are reviewed generally?

POWERS: When you've written one, generally speaking, you've learned something about the subject, and you have this deep fear that you're going to be found out, that you're going to be trounced as being superficial and having missed all the obvious points and things of that sort. But when the reviews actually appear, you discover, first to your delight and then later to your dismay, that nobody knows anything about it. You could have left the House of Representatives out of a book about Congress and nobody would notice. It made it seem like sort

of an uphill task and even a little bit futile to try and educate the public about these matters.

Having set that aside, I can say that reviews of nonfiction books are almost always not about the way the book is written, but about the subject. They serve as an occasion for general reflections on whatever the book is about. The reviewer tells you what he thinks about World War II or Vietnam or the politics of welfare in the United States or whatever else it may be. The review itself tends to be rather thin, so the writer really doesn't get much help from the reviews; people don't really tell him anything about what he's done or how he's done it. So when I review a book of that sort, which I often do, I try to remember that somebody put a lot of time and effort into it and that practically nobody's ever going to tell him anything about how he did, which he would like to hear. I try and tell him.

CA: In Thinking About the Next War *(1982), a collection of essays that originally appeared in* Commonweal, *you say that another war seems inevitable if we continue to prepare for one as we are doing. Do you think the peace movement has much hope of effecting any real change?*

POWERS: Well, I really hate being asked that question, because you hate to discourage people who are working very hard to change things. And at the same time you have a certain obligation to the facts of the matter. It seems to me that the facts of the matter suggest that both the United States and the Soviet Union are embarked on a course of action that they find it very, very difficult to alter. There's tremendous inertia behind our way of dealing with these matters. And I believe that both sides are very sober and cautious about the danger of a big war with each other, but they seem to be incapable of handling their relationship in any other way than by preparation for a big war and occasionally issuing threats or challenges. If you have a long period of preparation for war and periodic crises where you approach to the edge of war, you can naturally assume that at some point you're going to fall over the edge.

CA: One of the questions you raise in that collection is what to tell the kids. Do you find from your own experience with three daughters that they absorb a great deal of information on the subject from television, magazines, and other sources?

POWERS: I think with kids it's pretty much as it is with anybody else. When you start talking about nuclear weapons, everybody right away gets a long face. If you go around and give speeches about it, as I do, the first thing you see, everywhere you go, is a room full or an auditorium full of long faces. From that and similar experiences, I have concluded that deep down inside, everybody knows. You don't really have to explain to anybody that this is a serious matter and that we've got ourselves into real hot water here. Ordinary people know this much more clearly than members of the government or professional defense consultants or military officers. And kids are more or less the same. They sort of know; it's part of the general knowledge you acquire in growing up. It's part of understanding man's fate in the world. They're pretty good at forgetting it and pushing it to one side and putting it into that special category of things that grownups are supposed to deal with. But at the same time, they all know.

CA: What publications do you read for information and opinion?

POWERS: I read the *New York Review of Books* and the *Times Literary Supplement.* I read the *New York Times* in order to find out what happened in the world yesterday. And I read books. I don't read as many magazines as I used to. I read *Fine Woodworking* and a couple of publications like that, but for the most part, I guess I don't read periodicals. And I very rarely watch television. I don't have anything against television, I just don't do it; I read books instead.

CA: Are you living in Vermont year-round now?

POWERS: Yes, I am.

CA: Do you find it easier to write there than you did in New York City?

POWERS: No, not really. I don't find it hard to write, in the usual ways, anywhere. That is to say, I don't hate writing; I don't hate sitting down to do it. I like it. And after I've learned a lot about a subject, I find that the process of bringing it back out again onto the page is really very intensely pleasurable. It's what my life is for. But having said that, I should add that I've been working for the last several years on a history of strategic weapons, and I find that very hard to write. It's because every time you're brought to reach some kind of a general conclusion or to describe the way things are, it has a quality of terrible bleakness about it. You have to ask yourself, how did I ever come to be appointed to bring all this bad news to people? Why do I have to do this? I find myself really loath to do it.

CA: How much lecturing do you do?

POWERS: I get asked simply because people have to fill up their lecture schedules, and when I get asked, I try to say yes. It comes and goes. I'd say on the average around the year, maybe once a month. But sometimes it's more often than that.

CA: Do you go all over the country?

POWERS: East of the Mississippi. Boulder, Colorado, was the furthest west I've ever gone. It's a curious fact: there's a real divide in the middle of the country, and the kinds of things that people are interested in are different on both sides. The kinds of people that they listen to about those subjects are different on both sides. For example, that book about the CIA sold well and attracted a lot of attention in the East, and zero in the West.

CA: Do you have plans beyond the book on strategic weapons?

POWERS: I do, but it's still too early to unveil them.

BIOGRAPHICAL/CRITICAL SOURCES:

PERIODICALS

Best Sellers, January, 1980, March, 1983.
Books and Bookmen, June, 1980.
Chicago Tribune, November 8, 1979.
Chicago Tribune Book World, December 12, 1982.
Commentary, January, 1980.
Commonweal, October 22, 1971, February 29, 1980, March 14, 1980.
Los Angeles Times Book Review, December 19, 1982.
Ms., January, 1983.
Nation, January 29, 1983.

National Review, March 7, 1980.
Newsweek, October 22, 1979.
New York Times, April 12, 1971, October 11, 1979.
New York Times Book Review, April 11, 1971, October 14, 1973, October 14, 1979, January 30, 1983.
Progressive, February, 1980, May, 1983.
Saturday Review, May 1, 1971.
Time, November 12, 1979.
Times (London), April 3, 1980.
Village Voice, September 17, 1979, June 21, 1983.

—*Sketch by Bryan Ryan*

—*Interview by Jean W. Ross*

*   *   *

POYER, Joe
See POYER, Joseph John (Jr.)

*   *   *

POYER, Joseph John (Jr.)   1939-
(Joe Poyer)

PERSONAL: Born November 30, 1939, in Battle Creek, Mich.; son of Joseph John (a salesman) and Eileen (Powell) Poyer; married Susan Pilmore; children: Joseph John III, Geoffrey. *Education:* Kellogg Community College, A.A., 1959; Michigan State University, B.A., 1961. *Politics:* Independent. *Religion:* None.

ADDRESSES: Home—Orange, Calif. *Agent*—Diane Cleaver, Inc., Literary Agent, 55 Fifth Ave., New York, N.Y. 10003; and Anthony Sheil Associates Ltd., 2-3 Morewell St., London WC1B 3AR, England.

CAREER: Michigan Tuberculosis and Respiratory Disease Association, Lansing, assistant director of public information, 1961-62; Pratt & Whitney Aircraft, East Hartford, Conn., proposals writer, 1963-65; Beckman Instruments, Fullerton, Calif., proposals writer, 1965-67; Bioscience Planning, Anaheim, Calif., manager of interdisciplinary communications, 1967-68; Allergan Pharmaceuticals, Irvine, Calif., senior project manager and research administrator, 1968-77; full-time novelist, 1977—. Teacher of writing course at Golden West College, 1974-76.

WRITINGS:

UNDER NAME JOE POYER; NOVELS

Operation Malacca, Doubleday, 1968.
North Cape (Book-of-the-Month Club selection in England), Doubleday, 1969.
The Balkan Assignment, Doubleday, 1971.
The Chinese Agenda (Junior Literary Guild selection; Book-of-the-Month Club selection in Sweden), Doubleday, 1972.
The Shooting of the Green, Doubleday, 1973.
Day of Reckoning, Weidenfeld & Nicolson, 1976.
The Contract, Atheneum, 1978.
Tunnel War, Atheneum, 1979.
Vengeance 10, Atheneum, 1980.
Devoted Friends, Atheneum, 1982.

UNDER NAME JOE POYER; "A TIME OF WAR" SERIES

A Time of War: The Transgressors, Sphere, 1983.
. . . : Come Evil Days, Sphere, 1985.

UNDER NAME JOE POYER; EDITOR

Instrumentation Methods for Predictive Medicine, Instrument
Society of America, 1966.
Biomedical Sciences Instrumentation, Plenum, 1967.

OTHER

Contributor of about a dozen short stories and articles to magazines. Field editor of *International Combat Arms: Journal of
Defense Technology.*

WORK IN PROGRESS: A four-volume novel on World War
II; a sequel to *North Cape;* a nonfiction survey of the problems
involved in terrorism/counter-terrorism in the world today; additional novels in "A Time of War" series, for Sphere.

AVOCATIONAL INTERESTS: Travel, photography, antique
firearms.

BIOGRAPHICAL/CRITICAL SOURCES:

PERIODICALS

Los Angeles Times Book Review, December 9, 1979, Novem-
ber 24, 1980.
Spectator, February 28, 1970.
Washington Post, November 30, 1979.

*   *   *

PRATT, John Clark   1932-

PERSONAL: Born August 19, 1932, in St. Albans, Vt.; son
of John Lowell (a publisher) and Katharine (Jennison) Pratt;
married second wife, Doreen K. Goodman, June 28, 1968;
children: Karen, Sandra, Pamela, John Randall; stepchildren:
Lynn Goodman, Christine Goodman. *Education:* Attended
Dartmouth College, 1950-53; University of California, Berkeley, B.A., 1954; Columbia University, M.A., 1960; Princeton
University, Ph.D., 1965. *Politics:* Variable.

ADDRESSES: Office—Department of English, Colorado State
University, Ft. Collins, Colo. 80523.

CAREER: U.S. Air Force, regular officer; commissioned second lieutenant, retired as lieutenant colonel, 1974. U.S. Air
Force Academy, Colorado Springs, Colo., assistant professor,
1960-68, associate professor, 1968-73, professor of English,
1973-74; Colorado State University, Ft. Collins, chairman of
department of English, 1974-80, professor of English, 1980—.
Served in Vietnam, 1969-70. Fulbright lecturer, University of
Lisbon, 1974-75, and Leningrad State University, 1980. Consultant in remedial English, United States Industries, Inc.

MEMBER: Coffee House (New York).

WRITINGS:

The Meaning of Modern Poetry, Doubleday, 1962.
John Steinbeck, Eerdmans, 1970.
(Editor) Ken Kesey, *One Flew Over the Cuckoo's Nest,* Vi-
king, 1973.
The Laotian Fragments, Viking, 1974.
(Contributor) *Hemingway in Our Time,* Oregon State Univer-
sity, 1974.
(Author of introduction) *Kesey,* Northwest Review Books, 1977.
(Editor with Victor A. Neufeldt) *George Eliot's "Middle-
march" Notebooks: A Transcription,* University of Cali-
fornia Press, 1979.
(Compiler) *Vietnam Voices: Perspectives on the War Years,
1941-1982,* Viking, 1984.

*From the Fiction, Some Truths: The Literature of the Vietnam
War* (monograph), Asia Society, 1986.

Contributor of articles, poems, and reviews to journals in his
field.

WORK IN PROGRESS: A novel, *American Affairs;* a screenplay, *War Story;* a writing manual, *Comptext;* a musical.

SIDELIGHTS: As an Air Force lieutenant, John Clark Pratt
spent a year serving in Southeast Asia during the Vietnam
War. This experience motivated him first to write a novel, *The
Laotian Fragments,* then to compile a nonfiction book concerning the war. In this later work, entitled *Vietnam Voices:
Perspectives on the War Years, 1941-1982,* Pratt has "created
a sort of historical montage: an assemblage of more than 400
brief excerpts intended . . . to provide a 'comprehensive introduction' to the issues of the war," writes Arnold R. Isaacs in
the *Washington Post Book World.* The author organized his
book by arranging the entries—which include diaries, press
releases, poems, journalism, and graffiti—in chronological order with brief, written links. Isaacs observes that there "is no
connecting narrative. The only voices of the book belong to
the writers of the excerpted material."

The assemblage of these excerpts provides a complex framework that has been both praised and criticized by reviewers.
Isaacs maintains that the book gives a fragmented sense of
time. "Rather than reaching any new level of coherent understanding," he explains, "one reads *Vietnam Voices* with
the sensation of viewing the war years through the windows
of a high-speed train." Yet Isaacs admits that Pratt's method
is effective "when it seeks to convey aspects of experience,
rather than information. Thus, with a few exceptions, his most
meaningful images and sensations are those recording images
and sensations set down by individual soldiers." Charles True-
hart indicates in the *New York Times Book Review* that Pratt's
technique of excerpting entries makes his book a "cacaphony
of voices, and it could not be otherwise. . . . 'Vietnam Voices'
does suggest the enormous scope of the material that must be
reckoned with to appreciate what now seems a distant memory."

Pratt remarked in a letter to *CA* that in assembling his book
as a collage "I don't claim to have *created* a new art form,
but I certainly tried to adapt the visual medium to the printed
page in a way that no one else has yet accomplished." Commenting on the general quality of the book, Ralph Smith writes
in the *Times Literary Supplement:* "Few readers will come
away [from *Vietnam Voices*] without learning something from
it." Peter Loewenberg expresses a similar viewpoint in the
Los Angeles Times Book Review, declaring that *Vietnam Voices*
is a "valuable book, well worth reading."

BIOGRAPHICAL/CRITICAL SOURCES:

BOOKS

Stephens, Michael, *The Dramaturgy of Style,* Southern Illinois
University Press, 1986.

PERIODICALS

Impact (magazine of the *Albuquerque Journal*), July 30, 1985.
Los Angeles Times Book Review, December 9, 1984.
Modern Fiction Studies, spring, 1984.
New York Times Book Review, October 7, 1984.
Playboy, January, 1985.
Times Literary Supplement, August 15, 1980, February 15,
1985.

Washington Post Book World, September 23, 1984.

*   *   *

PRIDDY, Fran(ces Rosaleen)   1931-

PERSONAL: Born October 25, 1931, in Decatur, Ill.; daughter of Chester T. and Helen (Murphy) Priddy. *Religion:* Roman Catholic.

CAREER: Writer and lecturer.

MEMBER: Simian Society of America (treasurer, 1959; vice-president, 1960; director, 1961-63).

WRITINGS:

The Grand Rogue, Dodd, 1958.
TV Bandstand, Westminster, 1959.
Barbie, Westminster, 1960.
Let's Go Steady, Westminster, 1961.
The Social Swim, Westminster, 1962.
Challenge for Angel, Westminster, 1963.
Pretty as a Princess, Arcadia, 1963.
Shell Beach Mystery, Westminster, 1963.
The Ghosts of Lee House, Doubleday, 1968.
Sam's Country, McGraw-Hill, 1969.
Escape to Adventure, Woodhill, 1979.
Monster in the Boat, Woodhill, 1979.
Bridge to Love, Thomas Nelson, 1985.

Editor, Simian Society *News Graph* and its successor, *Monkey Business*, 1960.

WORK IN PROGRESS: A teenage mystery.

AVOCATIONAL INTERESTS: Travel, wild and domestic animals.†

*   *   *

PRIDHAM, Geoffrey   1942-

PERSONAL: Born January 29, 1942, in Guildford, England; son of C. E. and Marian S. Pridham; married Pippa Mason (an education writer), June 15, 1974 (divorced, 1982). *Education:* Trinity Hall, Cambridge, B.A., 1964, M.A., 1968; London School of Slavonic and East European Studies, London, Ph.D., 1969.

ADDRESSES: Office—Department of Politics, University of Bristol, Bristol, England.

CAREER: Foreign Office, London, England, research assistant, 1964-67; Institute of Contemporary History, London, research assistant, 1967-69; University of Bristol, Bristol, England, reader in European politics, 1969—. Member of Conference Group on Italian Politics and European Consortium for Political Research.

MEMBER: Political Studies Association, Association for the Study of German Politics, University Association for Contemporary European Studies, Association for the Study of Modern Italy, Societa Italiana di Studi Elettorali.

WRITINGS:

Hitler's Rise to Power: The Nazi Movement in Bavaria, 1923-33, Harper, 1973.
(Editor with Jeremy Noakes) *Documents on Nazism, 1919-45*, Viking, 1974.
Christian Democracy in Western Germany: The CDU/CSU in Government and Opposition, 1945-76, Croom Helm, 1977.

(With Pippa Pridham) *Transnational Party Cooperation and European Integration: The Process towards Direct Elections*, Allen & Unwin, 1981.
The Nature of the Italian Party System: A Regional Case-Study, Croom Helm, 1981.
(With Noakes) *Nazism, 1919-45: A Documentary Reader*, Exeter University Press, Volume I, 1983, Volume II, 1984.
The New Mediterranean Democracies: Regime Transition in Spain, Greece and Portugal, Frank Cass, 1984.

WORK IN PROGRESS: Comparative research on coalitional behavior political parties in Western Europe, West Germany, Italy, and transnationally in the European Community; new democracies in Southern Europe.

AVOCATIONAL INTERESTS: Travel, reading political thrillers, rambling, music.

*   *   *

PROSSER, Michael H.   1936-

PERSONAL: Born March 29, 1936, in Indianapolis, Ind.; son of Marshall H. and Clydia C. (O'Dea) Prosser; married Carol Hogle, November 27, 1958 (divorced, 1983); children: Michelle Ann, Leo Michael, Louis Mark. *Education:* Ball State Teachers College (now Ball State University), B.A., 1958, M.A., 1960; University of Illinois, Ph.D., 1964.

ADDRESSES: Home—11 Georgetown Green, Charlottesville, Va. 22901. *Office*—Department of Rhetoric and Communication Studies, University of Virginia, One Dawson Row, Charlottesville, Va. 22903.

CAREER: Urbana Junior High School, Urbana, Ill., teacher of Latin, 1960-63; State University of New York at Buffalo, assistant professor of speech communication, 1963-69; Indiana University at Bloomington, associate professor of speech and theatre, 1969-72; University of Virginia, Charlottesville, professor of rhetoric and communication studies, 1972—, chairman of department, 1972-77. Visiting lecturer, Queens College of the City University of New York, summers, 1966-67; visiting associate professor, California State College, Hayward (now California State University, Hayward), summer, 1971; visiting professor, Memorial University of Newfoundland, St. John's, third semester, 1972, St. Paul University, summer, 1975, and University of Ottawa, summer, 1975; distinguished visiting professor, Kent State University, 1978; distinguished lecturer in intercultural communication in Singapore and South Korea, U.S. Information Agency, 1980. Chair of International Communication Development Council of the Midwest Universities Consortium for International Activities, 1971-72. Coordinator, twenty-three program radio series "Academic Forum," for world-wide broadcast on Voice of America, 1979-80. Consultant in intercultural communication, U.S. Information Agency, 1977.

MEMBER: International Communication Association, International Society for Intercultural Education, Training, and Research (president, 1984-86), Speech Communication Association, American Foreign Students International-Intercultural Programs (president of Charlottesville-Albemarle chapter, 1982-86).

AWARDS, HONORS: Distinguished Alumni Award, Ball State University, 1978, for "notable contributions to mankind and alma mater."

WRITINGS:

(Editor and author of introduction and commentary) *An Ethic for Survival: Adlai Stevenson Speaks on International Affairs, 1936-1965,* Morrow, 1969.

(Editor with Thomas W. Benson) *Readings in Classical Rhetoric,* Allyn & Bacon, 1969, published as *Readings in Ancient Rhetoric,* Indiana University Press, 1972.

(Editor) *Sow the Wind, Reap the Whirlwind: Heads of State Address the United Nations,* two volumes, Morrow, 1970.

(Editor) *Intercommunication among Nations and Peoples,* Harper, 1973.

(Editor with Joseph M. Miller and Benson) *Readings in Medieval Rhetoric,* Indiana University Press, 1973.

(Editor) *Syllabi in Intercultural Communication: 1974,* Speech Communication Department, University of Virginia, 1974.

(Editor with Nemi C. Jain and Melvin H. Miller) *Intercultural Communication: Proceedings of the Speech Communication Summer Conference,* Volume X, Speech Communication Association, 1974.

The Cultural Dialogue: An Introduction to Intercultural Communication, Houghton, 1978.

(Editor) *USIA Intercultural Communication Course: 1977 Proceedings,* U.S. Information Agency, 1978.

An Intercultural Journal: An Individual Perception of Cultural Reality, Intercommunication Press, 1986.

Editor, *Today's Speech* (journal of Speech Association of the Eastern States), 1968-70.

BIOGRAPHICAL/CRITICAL SOURCES:

BOOKS

Asante, Molefi, Cecil Blake, and Eileen Newmark, *A Handbook of Intercultural Communication,* Sage Publications, 1979.

Cha, Bae Keun, *An Introduction to Communication,* [Seoul, Korea], 1979.

Lundberg, Per, *International and Intercultural Communication,* [Lund, Sweden], 1983.

Mauviel, Maurice, *Intercultural Communication,* [Paris, France], 1983.

Prosser, Michael H., *An Intercultural Journal: An Individual Perception of Cultural Reality,* Intercommunication Press, 1986.

Sitaram, K. S. and Roy T. Cogdell, *Foundations of Intercultural Communication,* C. E. Merrill, 1976.

PERIODICALS

Books in America, April 21, 1969.
Choice, October, 1973.
Christian Science Monitor, July 24, 1969.
Communication Education, January, 1979.
Current Views on Books, May 18, 1969.
Harper's, February, 1969.
Journal of Communication, autumn, 1974.
Lethbridge Herald, May 28, 1970.

*　　*　　*

PRPIC, George J(ure) 1920-

PERSONAL: Surname is pronounced Per-pich; born November 16, 1920, in Djala, Banat, Yugoslavia; son of Tomislav and Isabella (Toldy) Prpic; married Hilda Hermann, January 20, 1951; children: Francis Thomas, Mary Teresa. *Education:* Real Gymnasium, Pozega, Croatia, Baccalaureate, 1939; Croatian University, Zagreb, Diploma in Jurisprudence (M.A. equiva-

lent), 1944; University of Graz, further study, 1945-49; John Carroll University, M.A., 1956; Georgetown University, Ph.D., 1959. *Religion:* Roman Catholic.

ADDRESSES: Home—2615 Charney, University Heights, Ohio 44118. *Office*—Department of History, John Carroll University, University Heights, Ohio 44118.

CAREER: John Carroll University, University Heights, Ohio, instructor, 1958-60, assistant professor, 1960-65, associate professor, 1965-70, professor of history, 1970—.

MEMBER: American Historical Association, American Association for the Advancement of Slavic Studies, American Association for Southeast European Studies, Croatian Academy of America, Donau Institut (Vienna), Institutum Chroatorum Historicum (Rome), American Croatian Academic Society, Phi Alpha Theta.

AWARDS, HONORS: Faculty fellowship award, John Carroll University, 1968-69.

WRITINGS:

Maksimilijan Vanka, La Revista Croata (Buenos Aires), 1958.
French Rule in Croatia: 1806-1813, Institute for Balkan Studies (Salonika), 1964.
Eastern Europe and World Communism, Institute for Soviet and East European Studies, John Carroll University, 1966.
Fifty Years of World Communism, 1917-1967, Institute for Soviet and East European Studies, John Carroll University, 1967.
(Contributor) Joseph P. O'Grady, editor, *The Immigrants' Influence on Wilson's Peace Policies,* University of Kentucky, 1967.
The Croatian Publications Abroad after 1939: A Bibliography, Institute for Soviet and East European Studies, John Carroll University, 1969.
The Croatian Immigrants in America, Philosophical Library, 1970.
A Century of World Communism, Barron's, 1970, revised edition, 1974.
(Contributor) F. H. Eterovich and Christopher Spalatin, editors, *Croatia: Land, People, Culture,* Volume II, University of Toronto Press, 1970.
Posljednji Svibanj (title means "The Last May"; self-illustrated poetry in Croatian), Izdanja Ranjeni Labud (Rome), 1973.
(With wife, Hilda Prpic) *Croatian Books and Booklets Printed in Exile,* Institute for Soviet and East European Studies, John Carroll University, 1973.
(With Karl Bonutti) *Selected Ethnic Communication of Cleveland,* Cleveland Urban Observatory, 1974.
The Croatians in Greater Cleveland, Ethnic Heritage Studies Development Program, Cleveland State University, 1976.
South Slavic Immigration in America, Twayne, 1978.
Croatia and the Croatians: An Annotated Bibliography, Associated Book Publishers, 1982.

WORK IN PROGRESS: Translating the poetry of Walt Whitman into Croatian; *The Immigrants and the American Revolution; The Saga of Joe Magarac; Baklja u Luci—The Torch in the Harbor,* self-illustrated poetry in Croatian.

AVOCATIONAL INTERESTS: Painting and drawing.

*　　*　　*

PRUCHA, Francis Paul 1921-

PERSONAL: Born January 4, 1921, in River Falls, Wis.; son

of Edward J. (a teacher) and Katharine (Schladweiler) Prucha. *Education:* River Falls State Teachers College (now University of Wisconsin—River Falls), B.S., 1941; University of Minnesota, M.A., 1947; Harvard University, Ph.D., 1950; graduate study at St. Louis University, 1952-54, and St. Mary's College, 1954-58. *Politics:* Democrat.

ADDRESSES: Home—1404 West Wisconsin Ave., Milwaukee, Wis. 53233. *Office*—Department of History, Marquette University, Milwaukee, Wis. 53233.

CAREER: Entered Jesuit Order, 1950, ordained Roman Catholic priest, 1957; Marquette University, Milwaukee, Wis., 1960—, professor of American history, 1966—, chairman of department of history, 1962-69. *Military service:* U.S. Army Air Forces, 1942-46; became first lieutenant.

MEMBER: American Historical Association, Organization of American Historians (member of executive board, 1980-83), Western History Association (member of council, 1975-78, 1982-85; president, 1983).

AWARDS, HONORS: Social Science Research Council faculty research grant, 1959-60; Guggenheim fellow, 1967; National Endowment for the Humanities senior fellow, 1970, 1981.

WRITINGS:

Broadax and Bayonet: The Role of the United States Army in the Development of the Northwest, 1815-1860, State Historical Society of Wisconsin, 1953.
(Editor) G. Croghan, *Army Life on the Western Frontier,* University of Oklahoma Press, 1958.
(Translator and editor with G. Ellard) *Simple Rite of the Restored Order of Holy Week,* Bruce Publishing, 1958.
American Indian Policy in the Formative Years, Harvard University Press, 1962.
A Guide to the Military Posts of the United States, 1789-1895, State Historical Society of Wisconsin, 1964.
The Sword of the Republic, Macmillan, 1968.
Indian Peace Medals in American History, State Historical Society of Wisconsin, 1971.
(Editor) *The Indian in American History,* Holt, 1971.
(Editor) *The Dawes Act and the Allotment of Indian Lands,* University of Oklahoma Press, 1973.
(Editor) *Americanizing the American Indians: Writings by the "Friends of the Indian," 1880-1900,* Harvard University Press, 1973.
(Editor) *Documents of United States Indian Policy,* University of Nebraska Press, 1975.
American Indian Policy in Crisis: Christian Reformers and the Indian, 1865-1900, University of Oklahoma Press, 1976.
A Bibliographical Guide to the History of Indian-White Relations in the United States, University of Chicago Press, 1977.
United States Indian Policy: A Critical Bibliography, Indiana University Press, 1977.
The Churches and the Indian Schools, 1888-1912, University of Nebraska Press, 1979.
(Editor) Jeremiah Evarts, *Cherokee Removal: The "William Penn" Essays and Other Writings,* University of Tennessee Press, 1981.

Indian Policy in the United States: Historical Essays, University of Nebraska Press, 1981.
Indian-White Relations in the United States: A Bibliography of Works Published 1975-1980, University of Nebraska Press, 1982.
The Great Father: The United States Government and the American Indians, two volumes, University of Nebraska Press, 1984.
The Indians in American Society: From the Revolutionary War to the Present, University of California Press, 1985.

Contributor to professional publications.

*　　*　　*

PURCELL, H(ugh) D(ominic)　1932-

PERSONAL: Born March 18, 1932, in Singapore; son of Victor (a colonial official and lecturer) and Norah (Burbury) Purcell; married Suzanne Lennon, 1956; married second wife, Diana Beames (a lecturer at a technical college), September 4, 1961; children: Hugh William, Guy Roland. *Education:* Jesus College, Oxford, B.A. (with honors in Spanish), 1953; University of London, B.A. (external; with honors in English), 1963; Trinity College, Cambridge, Ph.D., 1967. *Politics:* European Unionist. *Religion:* "Nil."

ADDRESSES: c/o The British Council, P.O. Box 2274, Benghazi, Libya. *Office*—Department of English, University of Garyounis, Benghazi, Libya.

CAREER: British Institute of Rome, Rome, Italy, teacher, 1957-58; Middle East Technical University, Ankara, Turkey, lecturer in English, 1958-60; University of Chiraz, Chiraz, Iran, lecturer in English literature, 1960-63; Queen's University of Belfast, Belfast, Northern Ireland, lecturer in English literature, 1966-70; University of Garyounis, Benghazi, Libya, assistant professor of English, 1970—. Announcer, Ankara Radio, 1959-60. *Military service:* British Army of the Rhine, 1953-55; became second lieutenant.

MEMBER: East India and Sports Club.

WRITINGS:

Cyprus: A Microcosm, Praeger, 1969.
The Spanish Civil War, Putnam, 1973.
Charles I, Wayland, 1974.
Fascism, Hamish Hamilton, 1977.
Mao Tse-tung, St. Martin's, 1977.
Revolutionary War: Guerrilla War and Terrorism in Our Time, Hamish Hamilton, 1980.

Contributor to Hispanic and other journals, especially *International Affairs.*

WORK IN PROGRESS: A history of English literature in relation to the Middle East.

AVOCATIONAL INTERESTS: Climbing in remote areas of Turkey, Persia, Spain, and Italy; judo (holder of brown belt).†

Q

QUACKENBUSH, Robert M(ead) 1929-

PERSONAL: Born July 23, 1929, in Hollywood, Calif.; son of Roy Maynard (an engineer) and Virginia (Arbogast) Quackenbush; married Margery Clouser, July 3, 1971; children: Piet Robert. *Education:* Art Center College of Design, B.A., 1956.

ADDRESSES: Home—460 East 79th St., New York, N.Y. 10021. *Office*—223 East 78th St., New York, N.Y. 10021.

CAREER: Scandinavian Airlines System, advertising art director in United States and Stockholm, Sweden, 1956-61; freelance illustrator, painter, and writer, 1961—; Robert Quackenbush Gallery, New York, N.Y., owner and teacher of art classes, 1968—. *Military service:* U.S. Army, 1951-53.

MEMBER: Authors Guild, Authors League of America, Mystery Writers Club of America, Society of Children's Book Writers, Holland Society.

AWARDS, HONORS: American Institute of Graphic Arts Fifty Best Books award, 1963, for *Poems for Galloping;* Society of Illustrators citations, 1965, for *The Selfish Giant,* 1967, for *If I Drove a Truck,* 1969, for *Little Hans, the Devoted Friend* and *The Pilot,* and 1985, for *The Scarlet Letter;* American Flag Institute Award for outstanding contribution in the field of children's literature, 1976, 1977, and 1984; Edgar Allan Poe Special Award, 1981, for *Detective Mole and the Halloween Mystery.*

WRITINGS:

SELF-ILLUSTRATED CHILDREN'S BOOKS

Old MacDonald Had a Farm, Lippincott, 1972.
Go Tell Aunt Rhody, Lippincott, 1973.
She'll Be Comin' 'round the Mountain, Lippincott, 1973.
Clementine, Lippincott, 1974.
There'll Be a Hot Time in the Old Town Tonight, Lippincott, 1974.
Skip to My Lou, Lippincott, 1975.
The Man on the Flying Trapeze, Lippincott, 1975.
Too Many Lollipops, Parents' Magazine Press, 1975.
Animal Cracks, Lothrop, 1975.
Pop! Goes the Weasel and Yankee Doodle, Lippincott, 1976.
Detective Mole, Lothrop, 1976.
Pete Pack Rat, Lothrop, 1976.

Take Me Out to the Airfield! How the Wright Brothers Invented the Airplane, Parents' Magazine Press, 1976.
Detective Mole and the Secret Clues, Lothrop, 1977.
Sheriff Sally Gopher and the Haunted Dance Hall, Lothrop, 1977.
The Holiday Song Book, Lothrop, 1977.
Pete Pack Rat and the Gila Monster Gang, Lothrop, 1978.
Mr. Snow Bunting's Secret (Junior Literary Guild selection), Lothrop, 1978.
Calling Doctor Quack, Lothrop, 1978.
Detective Mole and the Tip-Top Mystery, Lothrop, 1978.
Along Came the Model T! How Henry Ford Put the World on Wheels, Parents' Magazine Press, 1978.
The Most Welcome Visitor, Windmill, 1978.
The Boy Who Dreamed of Rockets: How Robert Goddard Became the Father of Space Travel, Parents' Magazine Press, 1979.
Who Threw That Pie? The Birth of Movie Comedy, Whitman, 1979.
Moose's Store, Lothrop, 1979.
Detective Mole and the Seashore Mystery, Lothrop, 1979.
Piet Potter's First Case, McGraw, 1980.
Piet Potter Returns, McGraw, 1980.
Detective Mole and the Circus Mystery, Lothrop, 1980.
Movie Monsters and Their Masters, Whitman, 1980.
Henry's Awful Mistake, Parents' Magazine Press, 1980.
Detective Mole and the Halloween Mystery, Lothrop, 1981.
Pete Pack Rat and the Christmas Eve Surprise, Lothrop, 1981.
Piet Potter Strikes Again, McGraw, 1981.
Piet Potter to the Rescue, McGraw, 1981.
Henry's Important Date, Parents' Magazine Press, 1981.
The Boy Who Waited for Santa Claus, F. Watts, 1981.
No Mouse for Me, F. Watts, 1981.
City Trucks, Whitman, 1981.
Sheriff Sally Gopher and the Thanksgiving Caper, Lothrop, 1982.
Piet Potter on the Run, McGraw, 1982.
Piet Potter's Hot Clue, McGraw, 1982.
Henry Goes West, Parents' Magazine Press, 1982.
First Grade Jitters, Lippincott, 1982.
I Don't Want to Go, I Don't Know How to Act, Lippincott, 1983.
Henry Babysits, Parents' Magazine Press, 1983.
Investigator Ketchem's Crime Book, Avon, 1984.

Funny Bunnies, Clarion Books, 1984.
Detective Mole and the Haunted Castle Mystery, Lothrop, 1985.

SELF-ILLUSTRATED HUMOROUS BIOGRAPHIES FOR CHILDREN; PUBLISHED BY PRENTICE-HALL

Oh, What an Awful Mess! A Story of Charles Goodyear, 1980.
What Has Wild Tom Done Now?!!!, 1981.
Ahoy! Ahoy! Are You There? A Story of Alexander Graham Bell, 1981.
Here a Plant, There a Plant, Everywhere a Plant, Plant! A Story of Luther Burbank, 1982.
Watt Got You Started, Mr. Fulton? A Story of James Watt and Robert Fulton, 1982.
The Beagle and Mr. Flycatcher: A Story of Charles Darwin, 1983.
Quick, Annie, Give me a Catchy Line! A Story of Samuel F. B. Morse, 1983.
Mark Twain? What Kind of Name Is That? A Story of Samuel Clemens, 1984.
Don't You Dare Shoot That Bear! A Story of Theodore Roosevelt, 1984.
Who Said There's No Man on the Moon? A Story of Jules Verne, 1985.
Once Upon a Time! A Story of the Brothers Grimm, 1985.
Old Silver Leg Takes Charge! A Story of Peter Stuyvesant, 1986.

SELF-ILLUSTRATED CHILDREN'S BOOKS; "MISS MALLARD MYSTERY" SERIES

Express Train to Trouble, Prentice-Hall, 1981.
Cable Car to Catastrophe, Prentice-Hall, 1982.
Dig to Disaster, Prentice-Hall, 1982.
Gondola to Danger, Prentice-Hall, 1983.
Stairway to Doom, Prentice-Hall, 1983.
Rickshaw to Horror, Prentice-Hall, 1984.
Taxi to Intrigue, Prentice-Hall, 1984.
Stage Door to Terror, Prentice-Hall, 1985.
Bicycle to Treachery, Prentice-Hall, 1985.
Surfboard to Peril, Prentice-Hall, 1986.

OTHER CHILDREN'S BOOKS

(Compiler) *Poems for Counting*, Holt, 1963.
(Compiler) *Poems for Galloping*, Holt, 1963.
(Contributor) *Daisy Days*, Scott, Foresman, 1978.
(Contributor) *The New York Kid's Book*, Doubleday, 1979.
(Contributor of illustrations) *The Bird Book*, edited by Richard Shaw, 1974.

ILLUSTRATOR; CHILDREN'S BOOKS

Derrick, Schramm, and Spiegler, editors, *Adventures for Americans*, Harcourt, 1962.
Inez Rice, *A Long, Long Time*, Lothrop, 1964.
Hans Christian Andersen, *The Steadfast Tin Soldier*, Holt, 1964.
Oscar Wilde, *The Selfish Giant*, Holt, 1965.
My City, Macmillan, 1965.
Marie Halun Bloch, *The Two Worlds of Damyan*, Atheneum, 1966.
Robin McKown, *Rakoto and the Drongo Bird*, Lothrop, 1966.
McKown, *The Boy Who Woke Up in Madagascar*, Putnam, 1966.
Guy de Maupassant, *The Diamond Necklace*, F. Watts, 1967.
Mary K. Phelan, *Election Day*, Crowell, 1967.
Anthony Rowley, *A Sunday in Autumn*, Singer, 1967.
Margaretha Shemin, *Mrs. Herring*, Lothrop, 1967.
Miriam B. Young, *If I Drove a Truck*, Lothrop, 1967.

Lilian L. Moore, *I Feel the Same Way* (Junior Literary Guild selection), Atheneum, 1967.
Young, *Billy and Milly*, Lothrop, 1968.
Irma S. Black, *Busy Winds*, Holiday House, 1968.
Eleanor L. Clymer, *Horatio* (Junior Literary Guild selection), Atheneum, 1968.
Stephen Crane, *The Open Boat*, F. Watts, 1968.
Herman Melville, *Billy Budd, Foretopsman*, F. Watts, 1968.
Mariana Prieto, *When the Monkeys Wore Sombreros*, Harvey House, 1969.
Natalie S. Carlson, *Befana's Gift*, Harper, 1969.
Era K. Evans, *The Dirt Book: An Introduction to Earth Science*, Little, Brown, 1969.
Wilde, *Little Hans, the Devoted Friend*, Bobbs-Merrill, 1969.
Luther L. Terry and Daniel Horn, *To Smoke or Not to Smoke*, Lothrop, 1969.
Georgess McHargue, *The Baker and the Basilisk* (Junior Literary Guild selection), Bobbs-Merrill, 1970.
Young, *If I Flew a Plane*, Lothrop, 1970.
Leonore Klein, *D is for Rover*, Harvey House, 1970.
Irma S. Black, *Busy Seeds*, Holiday House, 1970.
Charlotte Zolotow, *You and Me*, Macmillan, 1970.
John Stewart, *The Key to the Kitchen*, Lothrop, 1970.
Young, *Beware the Polar Bear*, Lothrop, 1970.
Guy Daniels, translator, *The Peasant's Pea Patch*, Delacorte, 1971.
Lini R. Grol, *The Bellfounder's Sons*, Bobbs-Merrill, 1971.
Rosemary Pendery, *A Home for Hopper*, Morrow, 1971.
Harry S. George, *Demo of 70th Street*, Walck, 1971.
Jeanette S. Lowrey, *Six Silver Spoons*, Harper, 1971.
Julian May, *Blue River*, Holiday House, 1971.
Young, *If I Drove a Car*, Lothrop, 1971.
Young, *If I Sailed a Boat*, Lothrop, 1971.
George Mendoza, *The Scribbler*, Holt, 1971.
Young, *If I Drove a Train*, Lothrop, 1972.
Ann Cooke, *Giraffes at Home*, Crowell, 1972.
Mindel Sitomer and Harry Sitomer, *Lines, Segments and Polygons*, Crowell, 1972.
Young, *If I Drove a Tractor*, Lothrop, 1973.
Young, *If I Rode a Horse*, Lothrop, 1973.
Berniece Freschet, *Prong-Horn on the Powder River*, Crowell, 1973.
Jane Yolen, *Wizard Islands*, Crowell, 1973.
John F. Waters, *Steal Harbor*, Warne, 1973.
Young, *If I Drove a Bus*, Lothrop, 1973.
Young, *If I Rode an Elephant*, Lothrop, 1974.
Eleanor Clymer, *Leave Horatio Alone*, Atheneum, 1974.
Young, *If I Rode a Dinosaur*, Lothrop, 1974.
Clymer, *Engine Number Seven*, Holt, 1975.
Natalie Donna, *The Peanut Cookbook*, Lothrop, 1976.
Clymer, *Horatio's Birthday*, Atheneum, 1976.
F. N. Mongo, *House on Stink Alley*, Holt, 1977.
Clymer, *Horatio Goes to the Country*, Atheneum, 1978.
Walter D. Meyers, *The Pearl and the Ghost or One Mystery after Another*, Viking, 1980.
Clymer, *Horatio Solves a Mystery*, Atheneum, 1980.

ILLUSTRATOR; ADULT BOOKS

James Fenimore Cooper, *The Pilot*, Limited Editions Club, 1968.
Ann Cornelisen, *Torregreca*, Reader's Digest Condensed Books, 1969.
Mason Weems, *Life of Washington*, Limited Editions Club, 1974.

Pierre Loti, *An Iceland Fisherman*, Reader's Digest Condensed Books, 1978.

Stephen Crane, *Stories*, Franklin Library, 1982.

Norah Lofts, *The Possession of Sister Jeanne*, Reader's Digest Condensed Books, 1983.

Nathaniel Hawthorne, *The Scarlet Letter*, Reader's Digest Assn., 1984.

FILM SCRIPTS

"She'll Be Comin' 'round the Mountain," Weston Woods Studios, 1975.

"Clementine," Weston Woods Studios, 1975.

"The America Songfest," Weston Woods Studios, 1976.

"The Boy Who Waited for Santa Claus," Westport Communications Group, 1982.

OTHER

"On Tour with Robert Quackenbush" (video tape), Robert Quackenbush Studios, 1985.

"Robert Quackenbush School Program Excerpts Plus His Reading of His Book 'Stairway to Doom'" (audio tape), Robert Quackenbush Studios, 1985.

SIDELIGHTS: Robert M. Quackenbush commented to *CA* about his books for young readers: "A great number of my books for children were written with my young son, Piet (named after the first Quackenbush ancestor to arrive in America in 1660) in mind. From the day he was born, he put me in contact with a wealth of material—my own childhood experiences—that had been masked and nearly forgotten by time. These early memories and the people involved in them became the basis for such books as *Animal Cracks* and *Detective Mole* [that I] dedicated to Piet. The books seemed to take on a life of their own and the characters in them went on to individual series books that focused on humor.

"While it is true that Piet has been a major source of inspiration for my books for young readers, many other children have given me ideas for books. That is why I am in frequent contact with children of all ages. One way [I do this] is through after school art classes that I offer at my studio. Another is through school visits across the country. [Children's] thoughts, language, and interests change from month to month. So it is very important for me to be in touch with them. I like listening to them, hearing their ideas, and using their language in my books.

"Each book [I have written] required some kind of library research, some more involved than others. [For example,] extensive research was required for a biography of Jules Verne called *Who Said There's No Man on the Moon? A Story of Jules Verne*. This involved reading nearly all of Verne's writings to achieve a clear picture of this great writer, since little is known about his personal life. I became so familiar with his character that I came to understand the psychological motivations in his personal life and as a result was able to write about them in a way children would understand. Without this research the book would have [seemed] false. And children would be the quickest to pick that up.

Quackenbush concludes: "One cannot really guess about what kind of books to make for children to meet children's maturational needs. A lot of inspection must be done these days before proceeding with a project based on the information accumulated from librarians, teachers, editors, parents, booksellers, etc. if our goal is to reach children with our books, via the adults who buy the books for them. As children's

educators, we are required to do this—and we most certainly are children's educators the moment a child picks up a book of ours and pours over it. It's a wonderful feeling. One of my favorite ways of doing this is through humor. And I am the first to admit that my motives are purely selfish. To me, there is no sound more enjoyable than the sound of children's laughter."

*   *   *

QUIGLEY, Martin, Jr.   1917-

PERSONAL: Born November 24, 1917, in Chicago, Ill.; son of Martin and Gertrude (Schofield) Quigley; married Katherine J. Dunphy, 1946; children: Mark, Elin, William, Kevin, Karen, Patricia, John, Mary, Peter, Katherine. *Education:* Georgetown University, A.B. (magna cum laude), 1939; Columbia University, M.A., 1973, Ed.D., 1975. *Religion:* Roman Catholic.

ADDRESSES: Home—1 Locust Ave., Larchmont, N.Y. 10538. *Office*—Quigley Publishing Co., 159 West 53rd St., New York, N.Y. 10019.

CAREER: Motion Picture Herald, New York City and Hollywood, Calif., reporter, 1939-41; U.S. Office of War Information, New York City, film specialist, 1941-42; Motion Picture Producers and Distributors of America, representative in England, Ireland and Italy, 1943-45; Quigley Publishing Co., New York City, editor, 1946—, president, 1964—; QWS, Inc. (educational consultants), New York City, president, 1975—. Village of Larchmont (N.Y.), trustee, 1977-79, mayor, 1980-84. Teachers College, Columbia University, member of staff in department of higher and adult education, 1974-75, adjunct professor, summers, 1979-80; adjunct professor of education at Bernard M. Baruch College of the City University of New York, 1977—, and Seton Hall University, 1981-82. Lecturer on motion pictures and on family life issues. Founder and chairman of New York Independent Schools Opportunity Project, 1965-77; member of board of directors of Will Rogers Institute. Consultant to superintendent of schools for New York City Archdiocese, 1962-70.

MEMBER: Foundation for International Cooperation (president, 1960-65; director, 1960—), Religious Education Association (treasurer, 1976-80; chairman, 1981-84), Motion Picture Pioneers (member of board of directors), Christian Family Movement (member of executive committee, 1959-62; president of New York chapter, 1960-62; member of national executive committee, 1960-65), Larchmont Yacht Club.

WRITINGS:

Great Gaels, Quigley, 1943.

Roman Notes, Quigley, 1945.

Magic Shadows: The Story of the Origin of Motion Pictures, Georgetown University Press, 1948, reprinted, Biblo & Tannen, 1969.

(Editor) *New Screen Techniques*, Quigley, 1953.

(With Edward M. Connors) *Catholic Action in Practice*, Random House, 1963.

(With Richard Gertner) *Films in America, 1929-1969*, Golden, 1970.

Government Relations of Five Universities in Washington, D.C., University Microfilms, 1975.

Contributor to *Encyclopaedia Britannica*. Editor, *Motion Picture Herald*, 1949-66.

AVOCATIONAL INTERESTS: Sailing.

QUILL, Barnaby
  See BRANDNER, Gary

*   *   *

QUINN, Kenneth (Fleming)   1920-

PERSONAL: Born December 25, 1920, in Greymouth, New Zealand; son of Joseph (a policeman) and Emily (Fleming) Quinn; married Herta Reiner, December 20, 1946. *Education:* Emmanuel College, Cambridge, B.A., 1947, M.A., 1952; University of Melbourne, M.A., 1961.

ADDRESSES: Office—Department of Classics, University College, University of Toronto, Toronto, Ontario, Canada M5S 1A1.

CAREER: Victoria University of Wellington, Wellington, New Zealand, lecturer, 1948-55; University of Melbourne, Melbourne, Victoria, Australia, senior lecturer, 1955-60, reader in classics, 1960-65; University of Otago, Dunedin, New Zealand, professor of classics and head of department, 1965-69; University of Toronto, University College, Toronto, Ontario, professor of classics, 1969—. Fellow, St. John's College, Cambridge University, 1957-58; George A. Miller Centennial Lecturer, University of Illinois, 1968; Charles Beebe Martin Lecturer, Oberlin College, 1975. Member of Australian Humanities Research Council, 1963-65, and American Philo-logical Association Colloquium on the Classics in Education, 1964-65. *Military service:* New Zealand Army, 1942-45; served in North Africa and Italy.

MEMBER: Canadian Classical Association, Classical Association of Great Britain, Societe des Etudes Latines.

WRITINGS:

The Catullan Revolution, Cambridge University Press, 1959.
Latin Explorations, Routledge & Kegan Paul, 1963.
Virgil's ''Aeneid'': A Critical Description, University of Michigan Press, 1968.
Catullus: The Poems (commentary), St. Martin's, 1970, 2nd edition, 1973.
Approaches to Catullus, Barnes & Noble, 1972.
Catullus: An Interpretation, Batsford, 1972, Barnes & Noble, 1973.
Texts and Contexts: The Roman Writers and Their Audience, Routledge & Kegan Paul, 1979.
(Editor) *The Odes,* St. Martin's, 1980.
But the Queen: Conceptual Fields in Virgil's ''Aeneid,'' University of Exeter Press, 1981.
How Literature Works, Australian Broadcasting Commission, 1982.

Contributor of articles on Roman literature to *Encyclopaedia Britannica* and learned journals.†

R

RABAN, Jonathan 1942-

PERSONAL: Born June 14, 1942, in Fakenham, Norfolk, England; son of Peter (an Anglican clergyman) and Monica (Sandison) Raban; divorced. Education: University of Hull, B.A., 1963, additional study, 1963-65. Politics: "Reluctantly Socialist." Religion: None.

ADDRESSES: c/o Collins Harvill, 8 Grafton St., London W1, England. Agent—Gillon Aitken, 17 South Eaton Pl., London SW1, England.

CAREER: University College of Wales, Aberystwyth, lecturer in English literature, 1966-67; University of East Anglia, Norwich, England, lecturer in English literature, 1967-69; writer, 1969—. Visiting lecturer, Smith College, 1972.

MEMBER: Royal Society of Literature (fellow), Society of Authors, Royal Geographical Society (fellow).

AWARDS, HONORS: Old Glory: An American Voyage won the Heinemann Award from the Royal Society of Literature and the Thomas Cook Award.

WRITINGS:

The Technique of Modern Fiction: Essays in Practical Criticism, Edward Arnold, 1968, University of Notre Dame Press, 1969.
Mark Twain: Huckleberry Finn, Barron's, 1968.
The Society of the Poem, Harrap, 1971.
Soft City, Dutton, 1974.
(Editor) Robert Lowell's Poems: A Selection, Faber, 1974.
"The Sunset Touch" (play), first produced in Bristol, England, at the Old Vic Theatre, 1977.
Arabia: A Journey through the Labyrinth, Simon & Schuster, 1979.
Old Glory: An American Voyage, Simon & Schuster, 1981.
Foreign Land (novel), Viking, 1985.

TELEVISION PLAYS

"Square," Granada, 1971.
"Snooker," BBC-TV, 1975.
"The Water Baby," BBC-TV, 1975.

Also author of "Mother," BBC-TV.

RADIO PLAYS

"A Game of Tombola," BBC Radio 3, 1972.

"At the Gate," BBC Radio 3, 1973.
"The Anomaly," BBC Radio 3, 1974.
"The Daytrip," BBC Radio 3, 1976.

OTHER

Contributor to periodicals, including Times (London), New York Times Book Review, New York Review of Books, and Atlantic.

WORK IN PROGRESS: Coasting: A Voyage around the British Isles.

SIDELIGHTS: "When Jonathan Raban was seven, and the nearest water was a slip of a stream at the bottom of the street, he read Huckleberry Finn and dreamed of a Norfolk [England] transformed into the Mississippi Valley," writes Geoffrey Moorhouse in the London Times. "Of such juvenile inspirations are big adventures sometimes made." Some thirty years later, after launching his career as a lecturer, journalist, and author of several books, among them the critically acclaimed Arabia: A Journey through the Labyrinth, Raban realized his dream with a four-month trip down the Mississippi in a sixteen-foot craft. What this Englishman learned about the American land and its people is chronicled in his book Old Glory: An American Voyage.

As influenced as he was by Huckleberry Finn, however, Raban was not a natural candidate for river travel. A self-proclaimed city dweller, the author packed a minimum of supplies for his trip (including such essentials as two pipes with a tin of Captain Black Smoking Tobacco, a Zippo lighter, a corkscrew, and a thermos flask). No seasoned boater, Raban was at first naive enough to not recognize any danger in the Mississippi. "I assumed boats are much like small cars," the author told Washington Post writer James T. Yenckel. "I can drive a car; I assumed I could drive a boat. I was wrong."

Raban also didn't look forward to any challenging hardships. "Huck and Jim sleep on the raft, catch catfish, drink river water," elaborates Noel Perrin in a New York Times Book Review article on Old Glory. The author "stays in hotels and motels all the way down the Mississippi, except on the frequent occasions when inhabitants of the river towns bear him off to their homes. The one time when neither a hotel nor an invitation seems to be forthcoming, he decides that if worst comes to worst, he'll beg for a bed in the Prairie du Chien, Wis., jail; anything rather than curl up in his boat or camp on

Jackson's Island. Similarly, the one time he forgets a packed lunch and actually pulls a catfish out of the river, he is overwhelmed with disgust at the 'sad, spotty, limp-whiskered thing.' He forces himself to clean and cook it—and then eats exactly one bite: 'Mild hunger seemed far preferable to dead catfish.'''

But single-handedly conquering the river wasn't the author's aim. Raban's "passion was people," as *Newsweek*'s Jim Miller notes, "and this book takes them on the run, in a parade of one-page snapshots that glance over modern life on the Mississippi. A connoisseur of offbeat businessmen and faded barflies, he collects a motley crew of river-front civic figures, from bikers and bibulous tarts to Vicksburg's Lebanese bank president." Raban's talent, indeed, was in becoming acquainted with the people he met throughout the southward trip, attending barbeques, becoming involved in a Memphis, Tennessee, mayoral campaign, even pausing for a two-week romantic interlude in St. Louis with a woman he calls Sally.

In this respect, Yenckel finds it troubling "that this ostensibly charming guy can write so harshly about many of the unsophisticated citizens of the bleak river towns who befriended the foreign visitor, took him coon hunting and served up a special meal of squirrel." To illustrate his point, Yenckel singles out Raban's description of a Minnesota lockmaster's wife: "She looked like a retired lady wrestler. Slack-jawed, her eyes hidden behind the thick lenses of her glasses, she filled her outside stretch pants to the very last stitch." Yet as Raban responds in a *Washington Post* article: "How are you going to report life if you report it as a series of wonderful people? Some people are repulsive. Some are lovable. The book is subjective. It is how one sweaty traveler happened to find the people on his travels. If there's a real villain in the book, it's the person represented by me—the villain, the victim and the hero. My own justification for writing satirically is that I came out worse off."

In contrast, Diane Johnson, commenting in the *New York Review of Books*, finds Raban "a wonderful writer, with great powers of description, and above all the ability to interpret with elegant tact and lightness in the sort of tone one might use to criticize someone else's child without giving offense." And while Perrin says that Raban, a "master of the quick sketch," nevertheless "cannot do an extended scene," the critic also feels that "one of [the author's] triumphs is that he deals with the river in entirely fresh language. There is not a scrap of borrowed rhetoric in the book, with the exception of one sentence near the end where he deliberately echoes Huck."

The critical and popular success of *Old Glory* made Raban a temporary media figure in the United States; he was photographed for television re-creating some of his voyage, "with voice-over passages from the book," says Johnson. For the television piece, she continues, "Raban stares glumly at weather reports on the motel TV, Raban revisits a couple of nice folks on their cabin cruiser. With becoming embarrassment, he sports a duplicate of the funny hat he lost. The media are full of wonder. He praises the bird life along the Mississippi; the camera finds birds." Concludes Johnson: "It's like a Twain story all right—the mysterious European stranger comes and sells to the locals something that's been theirs all along. The Midwest has been ours all along, after all, but for those who haven't known this, Raban's book makes a continuously interesting pitch."

BIOGRAPHICAL/CRITICAL SOURCES:

BOOKS

Raban, Jonathan, *Old Glory: An American Voyage*, Simon & Schuster, 1981.

PERIODICALS

Detroit News, October 11, 1981.
Newsweek, October 5, 1981.
New York Review of Books, November 19, 1981.
New York Times, September 26, 1979, September 10, 1981.
New York Times Book Review, September 6, 1981.
Saturday Review, September, 1981.
Times (London), October 22, 1981, June 13, 1985.
Times Literary Supplement, June 28, 1985.
Washington Post, October 30, 1979, October 31, 1981.

—*Sketch by Susan Salter*

* * *

RADICE, Giles 1936-

PERSONAL: Surname is pronounced Rad-*ee*-che; born October 4, 1936, in London, England; son of Lawrence and Pat (Heneage) Radice; married Penelope Jean Angus, April 10, 1959; children: Adele, Sophie. *Education:* Attended Magdalen College, Oxford, 1957-60. *Politics:* Socialist.

ADDRESSES: Home—22 Dartmouth Park Rd., London NW5, England. *Office*—House of Commons, London S.W.1, England.

CAREER: House of Commons, London, England, legislative assistant to Francis Noel-Baker, member of Parliament, 1960-64; General and Municipal Workers Union, Claygate, Esher, Surrey, England, research officer and head of research department, 1965-73; House of Commons, member of Parliament representing Chester-le-Street district (Durham), 1973-83, member of Parliament representing Durham North, 1983—. Front Bench spokesman on foreign affairs, 1981, on employment, 1981-83, and on education, 1983—. Labour candidate for Chippenham, 1964, 1966; member of Fabian Society, 1966; chairman of Young Fabian Group, 1967-68; member of council of Policy Studies Institute. *Military service:* British Army, Coldstream Guards, second lieutenant, 1955-57.

WRITINGS:

Democratic Socialism, Longmans, Green, 1965.
(Editor with Brian Lapping) *More Power to the People: Young Fabian Essays on Democracy in Britain*, Humanities, 1968.
(With John Edmonds) *Low Pay*, Fabian Society, 1968.
(With J. O. N. Vickers) *Divide and Rule: The Industrial Relations Bill*, Fabian Society, 1971.
(Editor) *Working Power: Politics for Industrial Democracy*, Fabian Society, 1974.
(With Lisanne Radice) *Will Thorne, Constructive Militant: A Study in New Unionism and New Politics*, Allen & Unwin, 1974.
The Industrial Democrats: Trade Unions in an Uncertain World, Allen & Unwin, 1978.
Community Socialism, Fabian Society, 1979.

Regular contributor to British Socialist journals.†

* * *

RANKINE, John
See MASON, Douglas R(ankine)

RAPOPORT, Robert Norman 1924-

PERSONAL: Born November 1, 1924, in Brockton, Mass.; son of Herman and Fanny (Snyder) Rapoport; married Rhona Ross (a social psychologist), 1957; children: Lorna Carmen, Alin Joseph. *Education:* University of Chicago, M.A., 1948; Harvard University, Ph.D., 1951.

ADDRESSES: Home—7a Kidderpore Ave., London NW3 7SX, England. *Office*—Institute of Family and Environmental Research, 877A Finchley Rd., London NW11, England.

CAREER: Cornell University, Ithaca, N.Y., assistant professor, 1951-53; Belmont Hospital, Sutton, Surrey, England, director of social science research, 1953-57; Harvard University, Cambridge, Mass., lecturer in social anthropology, 1957-63; Northeastern University, Boston, Mass., research professor of sociology and anthropology, 1963-65; Boston College, Boston, professor of anthropology, 1964-65; Tavistock Institute of Human Relations, London, England, senior social scientist, 1965-73; Institute of Family and Environmental Research, London, co-director, 1973—. William T. Grant Foundation, vice president, 1981-83, senior consultant, 1984-85. *Military service:* U.S. Army, Signal Corps; became first lieutenant.

MEMBER: American Anthropological Association, American Sociological Society, Society for Applied Anthropology, Royal Anthropological Society (Great Britain).

WRITINGS:

Changing Navaho Religious Values, Peabody Museum, Harvard University, 1952, reprinted, Kraus Reprint, 1973.
(With wife, Rhona Rapoport, and Irving Rosow) *Community as Doctor: New Perspectives on a Therapeutic Community*, C. C Thomas, 1960.
(With others) *People of Cove and Woodlot*, Basic Books, 1961.
Mid-Career Development: Research Perspectives on a Developmental Community for Senior Administrators, Tavistock, 1970.
(With R. Rapoport) *Dual Career Families*, Penguin, 1971.
(With Michael Patrick Fogarty) *Sex, Career and Family*, Sage Publications, Inc., 1971.
(With R. Rapoport and Ziona Strelitz) *Leisure and the Family Life Cycle*, Routledge & Kegan Paul, 1975.
(With R. Rapoport) *Dual-Career Families Re-Examined: New Integrations of Work and Family*, M. Robertson, 1976, Harper, 1977.
(With R. Rapoport, Strelitz, and Stephen Kew) *Fathers, Mothers, and Society: Towards New Alliances*, Basic Books, 1977 (published in England as *Fathers, Mothers, and Others: Towards New Alliances*, Routledge & Kegan Paul, 1977).
(Editor with R. Rapoport) *Working Couples*, Harper, 1978.
(With R. Rapoport) *Growing through Life*, Harper, 1980.
(Editor with Michael Fogarty and R. Rapoport) *Families in Britain*, Routledge & Kegan Paul, 1982.

Also editor of *Children, Youth and Families: The Action-Research Relationship*, Cambridge University Press.

SIDELIGHTS: Robert Norman Rapoport told *CA:* "Many of my writings are collaborative with my wife, Rhona Rapoport. This has been accomplished with a mixture of pleasure and pain. We complement one another both in the fields of study we have worked at and in our writing styles. I write as the words come to mind and then edit what I read on the sheet—rather like sculpture. She will not write a word until it's all thought out, and edits minimally. The kinds of tensions this can generate are obvious—but they force us to work things through to reconcile the differences, and at best we both feel that what emerges is better than either of us could do alone."

AVOCATIONAL INTERESTS: Music.

*   *   *

REID, Desmond
See MOORCOCK, Michael (John)

*   *   *

REID, William J(ames) 1928-

PERSONAL: Born November 14, 1928, in Detroit, Mich.; son of James MacKnight and Sophie Amelia Reid; married wife, Jean, April 2, 1954 (divorced); married Audrey Smith (a professor), 1972; children: Valerie, Steven. *Education:* University of Michigan, B.A., 1951, M.S.W., 1953; Columbia University, D.S.W., 1963.

ADDRESSES: Home—R.D. 1, Rensselaer, N.Y. 12144. *Office*—135 Western Ave., Albany, N.Y. 12222.

CAREER: University of Chicago, Chicago, Ill., professor, beginning 1962, George Herbert Jones Professor, 1975; currently professor at State University of New York at Albany. Visiting professor at Smith College. Director of Center for Casework Research of Community Service Society (New York City), 1965-68.

MEMBER: National Association of Social Workers, Council on Social Work Education, Phi Beta Kappa.

WRITINGS:

(With Anne Shyne) *Brief and Extended Casework*, Columbia University Press, 1969.
(With Laura Epstein) *Task-Centered Casework*, Columbia University Press, 1972.
(With Epstein) *Task-Centered Practice*, Columbia University Press, 1977.
The Task-Centered System, Columbia University Press, 1978.
(With Charles Garvin and wife, Audrey Smith) *The Work Incentive Experience*, Allanheld & Osmun, 1978.
(With A. Smith) *Research in Social Work*, Columbia University Press, 1981.
(With Eleanor Tolson) *Models of Family Treatment*, Columbia University Press, 1981.
(With A. Smith) *Role Sharing Marriage*, Columbia University Press, 1985.
Family Problem Solving, Columbia University Press, 1985.

Editor-in-chief of "Social Work Research and Abstracts," Council on Social Work Education. Associate editor of *Social Science Review*.

SIDELIGHTS: William J. Reid commented: "Most of my books concern methods of short-term individual and family counseling, particularly one such approach—the task-centered model—developed by my colleagues and me."

*   *   *

REST, Friedrich Otto 1913-

PERSONAL: Born August 28, 1913, in Marshalltown, Iowa; son of Karl and Bertha (Leisy) Rest; married Dorothy Schumacher, 1940; children: Paul, Betty, John. *Education:* Elmhurst College, A.B., 1935; Eden Theological Seminary, B.D., 1937; Mission House Theological Seminary, D.D., 1961.

ADDRESSES: Home—827 West Merriweather, New Braunfels, Tex. 78130. *Office*—172 West College St., New Braunfels, Tex. 78130.

CAREER: Minister of United Church of Christ churches in Jasper, Ind., 1937-41, Dayton, Ohio, 1941-48, Hermann, Mo., 1948-55, Evansville, Ind., 1955-64, Rochester, N.Y., 1964-70, and Houston, Tex., 1970-75; First Protestant United Church of Christ, New Braunfels, Tex., associate pastor, 1975-85; interim pastor of Puula Church in Hawaii, 1985. Vice-president, Evangelical and Reformed Church, Missouri Valley Synod, 1954; member of department of worship and arts, National Council of Churches, beginning 1955; president, Evansville Council of Churches, 1962; moderator, South Texas Assocation, United Church of Christ, 1978-79. Host pastor on television series "Pastor's Study," WFIE-TV, 1957-63, WROC-TV, beginning 1964; has appeared on San Antonio, Tex., television programs.

MEMBER: New Braunfels Clergy Association.

WRITINGS:

Worship Aids for Fifty-two Services, Westminster, 1951.
Our Christian Symbols, Christian Education Press, 1954.
Worship Services for Church Groups, Christian Education Press, 1962.
A Topical Index of Bible Readings, Church Management, Inc., 1962.
Cross in Hymns, Judson, 1969.
Our Christian Worship: Resources from Palm Sunday through Easter, C.S.S. Publishing, 1977.
Funeral Handbook, Judson, 1982.
Fourteen Messages of Hope: Thoughts for Funerals and Other Occasions, Baker Book, 1985.
Our Christian Worship: Resources for Advent and Christmastide, C.S.S. Publishing, 1985.

Contributor to *Westminster Dictionary of Christian Education,* 1964.

WORK IN PROGRESS: A wedding manual.

BIOGRAPHICAL/CRITICAL SOURCES:

PERIODICALS

Evansville Courier, February 2, 1962.
Salem Outlook, September 26, 1963, January 12, 1964.

*   *   *

REYNOLDS, (Arthur) Graham   1914-

PERSONAL: Born January 10, 1914, in London, England; son of Arthur Thomas and Eva (Mullins) Reynolds; married Daphne Dent (an artist), February 6, 1943. *Education:* Attended Highgate School, London, England; Queens' College, Cambridge, B.A. (with honors), 1935; University of Cologne, graduate study, 1935-36.

ADDRESSES: Home—The Old Manse, Bradfield St. George, Bury St. Edmunds, Suffolk, England.

CAREER: Victoria and Albert Museum, London, England, assistant keeper of prints and drawings, 1937-39; Ministry of Home Security, assistant principal, 1939-42, principal, 1942-45; Victoria and Albert Museum, deputy keeper of paintings, 1945-59, keeper of department of prints, drawings and paintings, 1959-74; full-time writer, 1974—. Member of Board of Studies in the History of Art, University of London, 1963-66. Trustee of William Morris Gallery, 1972-75, and William Blake Trust, 1977—. Member of advisory council of Paul Mellon Centre for Studies in British Art, 1977-85.

MEMBER: Gainsborough's House Society (chairman, 1977-79), Walpole Society (member of executive and editorial committees, 1963-67).

AWARDS, HONORS: Mitchell Prize in art history, 1984, for *The Later Paintings and Drawings of John Constable;* member, Order of the British Empire, 1984, for services to art.

WRITINGS:

Twentieth-Century Drawings, Pleiades Books, 1947.
Van Gogh, Lindsay Drummond, 1947.
Nicholas Hilliard and Isaac Oliver (Victoria and Albert Museum Handbook), H.M.S.O., 1947.
Nineteenth-Century Drawings, Pleiades Books, 1949.
Thomas Bewick, Art and Technics, 1949.
An Introduction to English Water-Colour Painting, Country Life, 1950.
Gastronomic Pleasures, Art and Technics, 1950.
Elizabethan and Jacobean Costume, Harrap, 1951.
English Portrait Miniatures, A. & C. Black, 1952.
Painters of the Victorian Scene, Batsford, 1953.
Catalogue of the Constable Collection in the Victoria and Albert Museum, H.M.S.O., 1960, revised edition, 1973.
(Editor) *Handbook to the Department of Prints and Drawings and Paintings, Victoria and Albert Museum,* H.M.S.O., 1964.
Constable: The Natural Painter, McKay, 1965, reprinted, 1980.
Victorian Painting, Studio Vista, 1966, Macmillan, 1967.
(Editor) *The Engravings of S. W. Hayter,* H.M.S.O., 1967.
The Etchings of Anthony Gross, H.M.S.O., 1968.
Turner, Abrams, 1969.
A Concise History of Watercolours, Oxford University Press, 1971.
Tudor and Jacobean Miniatures, H.M.S.O., 1973.
Catalog of Portrait Miniatures, Wallace Collection, Trustees of the Wallace Collection, 1980.
Constable with His Friends in 1806, Genesis Publications, 1981.
Constable's England, Braziller, 1983.
The Later Paintings and Drawings of John Constable, two volumes, Yale University Press, 1984.

Editor of "English Masters of Black and White" series, Art and Technics, 1948-50, and of museum picture books on British water colors, French paintings, Victorian paintings, and other collections. Writer of verse in experimental forms, with palindromes published in *New Departures 1960,* and in *Listener* and *Times Literary Supplement;* contributor of articles to encyclopedias and to *Burlington Magazine, Connoisseur,* and *Apollo;* contributor of reviews to *Times Literary Supplement.*

WORK IN PROGRESS: Catalogue of Tudor and Stuart Portrait Miniatures in the Collection of Her Majesty the Queen, for Cambridge University Press; *Catalogue of Miniatures in the Collection of Fritz Lugt,* for Institut Neerlandais (Paris).

SIDELIGHTS: Called the "outstanding book of the year" by Mitchell Prize chairman Michael Jaffe in the *New York Times,* Graham Reynolds's *The Later Paintings and Drawings of John Constable* won the $10,000 Mitchell Prize for a book on art history. Reynolds's study of English landscape painter John Constable emphasizes that while Constable is considered one of the best-loved painters of the nineteenth century, much of the work of others has been misattributed to him.

Reynolds's book brings together the discussion of more than one thousand works. John Gage indicates in the *Times Literary Supplement* that "there are some signs that the [book] would have profited from a longer period of gestation," but he concedes that Reynolds's discussion on the later works of Constable is "solidly based."

BIOGRAPHICAL/CRITICAL SOURCES:

PERIODICALS

Apollo, July, 1964.
Burlington Magazine, March, 1985.
New York Times, November 15, 1984.
Times (London), November 15, 1984.
Times Literary Supplement, January 18, 1985.

*   *   *

RICHARDS, Alun   1929-

PERSONAL: Born October 27, 1929, in Pontypridd, Wales; married Barbara Helen Howden; children: three sons, one daughter. *Education:* Earned Diploma in Social Science and Diploma in Education at University College of Wales.

ADDRESSES: Home—326 Mumbles Rd., West Cross, Swansea, Wales. *Agent*—Curtis Brown Ltd., 1 Craven Hill, London W2 3EW, England.

CAREER: Probation officer in London, England, 1954-55; schoolmaster in Cardiff, Wales, 1955-66; writer, 1966—. *Military service:* Royal Navy, instructor, 1949-53; became lieutenant.

MEMBER: Writers Guild of Great Britain (chairman in Wales), Savage Club.

AWARDS, HONORS: Arts Council Prize, 1974, for *Dai Country.*

WRITINGS:

(Contributor) John Pudney, editor, *Pick of Today's Stories,* Putnam, 1962.
The Elephant You Gave Me (novel), M. Joseph, 1963.
The Home Patch, M. Joseph, 1966.
A Woman of Experience, Dent, 1969.
God—Alive!, Westminster Press, 1973.
Dai Country (stories), M. Joseph, 1973.
Home to an Empty House, J. D. Lewis, 1973.
Plays for Players, J. D. Lewis, 1975.
(Editor) *The Penguin Book of Welsh Short Stories,* Penguin, 1975.
The Former Miss Merthyr Tydfil: Stories, M. Joseph, 1976.
(Editor) *Collected Plays,* J. D. Lewis, 1976.
Ennal's Point (novel), M. Joseph, 1977.
(Editor) *The Penguin Book of Sea Stories,* Penguin, 1977, 2nd edition published as *Against the Waves,* M. Joseph, 1978.
Barque Whisper, St. Martin's, 1979.
A Touch of Glory: 100 Years of Welsh Rugby, M. Joseph, 1980.

Also editor of *The Second Penguin Book of Sea Stories.*

PLAYS

"The Big Breaker" (three-act), first produced in Coventry, England, at Belgrade Theatre, 1963.
"The Victualler's Ball" (three-act), first produced in Leatherhead, England, at Leatherhead Repertory Theatre, 1967.
"The Snow Dropper" (two-act), first produced at Hampstead Theatre, 1973.

Also author of television plays, including "Ready for the Glory," "Albinos in Black," "The Straight and the Narrow," "Going Like a Fox," "O Captain, My Captain," "Nothing to Pay," "Hear the Tiger, See the Bay," "The Hot Potato Boys," "Who Steals My Name," "Taffy Came to My House," "Under the Carpet," "The Princely Gift," "Harry Lifters," and "Ennal's Point" series.

WORK IN PROGRESS: Television scripts, "The Onedin Line," "Orson Welles Great Mysteries," and "Henry VII," for British Broadcasting Corp. (BBC-TV); adaptations of work by Georges Simenon, H. G. Wells, and Somerset Maugham.

AVOCATIONAL INTERESTS: Angling, oceanography, travel.

BIOGRAPHICAL/CRITICAL SOURCES:

PERIODICALS

Times Literary Supplement, August 17, 1973, November 16, 1973, February 1, 1974, February 20, 1976, February 13, 1981.†

*   *   *

RICHARDSON, C.
See MUNSEY, Cecil (Richard, Jr.)

*   *   *

RICHEY, Robert W(illiam)   1912-1978

PERSONAL: Born August 14, 1912, in Russellville, Ohio; died May 1, 1978; son of Robert Homer (a businessman) and Mabel May Richey; married Beatrice Eloise Huffman, December 26, 1942; children: Robert W., Jr. *Education:* Wilmington College, B.S. and B.S. in Ed., 1933; Ohio State University, M.A., 1937, Ph.D., 1941. *Politics:* Republican. *Religion:* Methodist.

ADDRESSES: Home—714 Meadowbrook Ave., Bloomington, Ind. 47401. *Office*—School of Continuing Studies, Owen Hall, Indiana University, Bloomington, Ind. 47401.

CAREER: New Antioch Elementary School, Wilmington, Ohio, principal, 1933-35; Wilmington public schools, head of department and critic teacher of science, 1935-37; Ohio State University, Columbus, placement and research assistant, 1937-41; University of Tennessee, Knoxville, assistant professor of education, 1941-42; Indiana University at Bloomington, assistant professor, 1946-49, associate professor, 1949-53, professor of education, 1953-78, director of elementary school student teaching, 1949-53, director of summer sessions, 1959-78, dean of School of Continuing Studies, 1975-78. Chief of advisory party at Chulalongkorn University and College of Education, Bangkok, Thailand, 1956-59. *Military service:* U.S. Army Air Forces, rated navigator, 1942-46; assistant executive of Academic Divison, American Army University Center, Biarritz, France, 1945-46; became captain.

MEMBER: Association of University Summer Sessions (vice-president, 1967; president, 1968), National Association of

Summer Sessions, American Association of Colleges for Teacher Education, National Science Teachers Association, National Education Association, National Society for the Study of Education, National Aerospace Education Council, American Association of University Professors, American Association for the Advancement of Science, North Central Conference on Summer Sessions (president, 1968), Indiana Schoolmasters Club, Phi Delta Kappa, Blue Key (honorary member), Rotary International.

AWARDS, HONORS: Distinguished Alumni Award from Wilmington College.

WRITINGS:

Planning for Teaching: An Introduction to Education (also see below), McGraw, 1952, 5th edition with *Instructor's Resource Book* and five correlated films, McGraw, 1973, 6th edition, 1979.
(Contributor) Paul R. Grim and John J. Michaelis, editors, *The Student Teacher in the Secondary School*, Prentice-Hall, 1953.
(Contributor) Grim and Michaelis, editors, *The Student Teacher in the Elementary School*, Prentice-Hall, 1953.
Handbook for Supervisors of Student Teaching, College of Education, University of Bangkok, 1956.
(With Gerald E. March, Marion Martz, and John R. Kittle) *Year-Around Operation in American Universities*, University of Colorado Press, 1963.
Preparing for a Career in Education: Challenges, Changes, and Issues (contains chapters from *Planning for Teaching: An Introduction to Education*), McGraw, 1974.

Also author of material for films, including "Let's Look at Leaves" and "Trees: How They Grow through the Years," both Coronet Instructional Films, 1968; co-author of bulletins issued by School of Education, Indiana University. Chairman of editorial committee, *Expanding Experiences in the Elementary School*, Indiana Department of Public Instruction, 1953. Contributor to journals.

SIDELIGHTS: Robert W. Richey traveled in Mexico, the Middle East, Africa, Europe, and the Far East.†

*   *   *

RICHMAN, Barry M(artin)   1936-1978

PERSONAL: Born March 18, 1936, in Montreal, Quebec, Canada; died June 5, 1978; son of Edward and Belle (Cohen) Richman; married Vivian Freedman, June 5, 1960; children: Viana, Stuart. *Education:* McGill University, B.Comm., 1958; Columbia University, M.S., 1959, Ph.D., 1962.

ADDRESSES: Home—20755 Seaboard Rd., Malibu, Calif. 90265. *Office*—Graduate School of Management, University of California, Los Angeles, Calif. 90024.

CAREER: University of California, Los Angeles, assistant professor, 1962-64, associate professor, 1965-66, professor of management and international business, beginning 1967, chairman of Graduate School of Management, 1975-77. Dean of Faculty of Administrative Studies, York University, 1972-73. Consultant to governmental, industrial, and educational organizations, 1958—; consulting editor, Random House and Alfred Knopf.

MEMBER: American Economic Association, International Academy of Management (fellow), American Sociological Association.

AWARDS, HONORS: Various research fellowships and grants, including a Ford Foundation grant, 1966-69.

WRITINGS:

Soviet Management, with Significant American Comparisons, Prentice-Hall, 1965.
(With Richard N. Farmer) *Comparative Management and Economic Progress*, Irwin, 1965.
(With Farmer) *International Business*, Irwin, 1966, 3rd edition, Cedarwood Press, 1980.
(With Farmer) *Incidents in Applying Management Theory*, Wadsworth, 1966.
Management Development and Education in the Soviet Union, Bureau of Business and Economic Research, Michigan State University, 1967.
A Firsthand Study of Industrial Management in Communist China, Graduate School of Business Administration, University of California, Los Angeles, 1967.
Industrial Society in Communist China, Random House, 1969.
A Firsthand Study of Industrial Management and Economic Development in India, University of California, Los Angeles, 1969.
(With Melvyn Copen) *International Management and Economic Development*, McGraw, 1972.
(With Farmer) *Leadership Goals and Power in Higher Education*, Jossey-Bass, 1974.
(With Farmer) *Management and Organizations*, Random House, 1975.

Contributor of articles on management and economic development in the Soviet Union, India, and China to journals.†

*   *   *

RIDGELY, Beverly S(ellman)   1920-

PERSONAL: Born December 16, 1920, in Baltimore, Md.; son of Irwin Oliver (a physician) and Virginia (Sellman) Ridgely; married Barbara Tomkins, May 20, 1944; children: Robert Stirling, Peter Tomkins and Virginia Sellman (twins). *Education:* Princeton University, A.B., 1943, A.M., 1949, Ph.D., 1953. *Politics:* Independent (liberal). *Religion:* Episcopalian.

ADDRESSES: Home—28 Everett Ave., Providence, R.I. 02906. *Office*—Department of French Studies, Brown University, Providence, R.I. 02912.

CAREER: Brown University, Providence, R.I., instructor, 1950-54, assistant professor, 1954-57, associate professor, 1957-64, professor of French, 1964-80, professor emeritus, 1980—. Visiting professor of French literature, Princeton University, 1969. *Military service:* U.S. Naval Reserve, active duty, 1943-46; became lieutenant junior grade.

MEMBER: Renaissance Society of America, American Association of University Professors, American Association of Teachers of French, Modern Language Association of America, Audubon Society of Rhode Island (member of board of directors, 1956-59), Phi Beta Kappa.

AWARDS, HONORS: M.A. from Brown University, 1957; Howard Foundation fellow, 1959-60.

WRITINGS:

(Editor) *La Fontaine: Fables choisies*, Prentice-Hall, 1967.
(With Willard F. Stanley and Gustavs E. Eglajs) *Birds of the World on Stamps*, American Topical Association, 1974, revised edition published as *Birds of the World in Philately*, 1984.

A Guide to the Birds of the Squam Lakes Region, New Hampshire, Squam Lakes Association, 1977.

Contributor of articles on sixteenth- and seventeenth-century French literature to professional journals in America and England. Assistant editor, *French Review,* 1968-71.

WORK IN PROGRESS: A book on La Fontaine and science and philosophy; continuing work on the French Renaissance and seventeenth-century cosmic voyages.

SIDELIGHTS: Beverly S. Ridgely has traveled extensively in western Europe and in East Africa.

AVOCATIONAL INTERESTS: Conservation, hiking, bird-watching, collecting postage stamps depicting birds and animals of the world.†

*   *   *

RIKHYE, Indar Jit   1920-

PERSONAL: Surname is pronounced "*Rickh*-ee"; born July 30, 1920, in Lahore, India; came to United States in 1960; son of Madan Lal (a physician) and Raj (Rani) Rikhye; married second wife, Cynthia de Haan (a former United Nations staff member), February 13, 1974; children: (first marriage) Ravi Indar Lall, Bhalinder. *Education:* Attended Government College, Lahore, India, 1935-38, and Defence Services Staff College, Wellington, India, 1951-52. *Religion:* Hindu.

ADDRESSES: Home—27 Normandy Terrace, Bronxville, N.Y. 10708; and "Oakland," Dhalli, Simla H.P., India. *Office*—International Peace Academy, 777 United Nations Plaza, New York, N.Y. 10017.

CAREER: Indian Army, 1939-67, served in Middle East and Italy, 1941-45, commander of Indian contingent and chief of staff of United Nations Emergency Force in Gaza, 1957-60, commander of independent infantry brigade group in Ladakh, India, 1960, military adviser to secretary-general of United Nations in New York City, 1960-66, commander of United Nations Emergency Force, 1966-67, retiring as major general; United Nations, New York City, military adviser to secretary-general, 1967-69; International Peace Academy, New York City, president, 1970—. Chairperson of Symphony for the United Nations, 1975-79. Consultant to Earthsat, Velsicol Corp., and Sungold International.

MEMBER: International Institute of Strategic Studies, India International Centre, India Institute of World Affairs, Royal Institute of International Affairs, Defense Services Club (New Delhi), Amateur Dramatic Club, Cavalry and Guards Club (London), English Speaking Union (London; member of governing board), Army and Navy Club (Washington, D.C.).

WRITINGS:

Preparation and Training of United Nations Peacekeeping Forces, International Institute of Strategic Studies, 1964.
United Nations Peacekeeping Operations Higher Conduct, International Information on Peace-Keeping Operations, 1964.
(Editor) *Peacekeeping in the Oceans,* Pacem in Maribus Publications, 1972.
(With Michael Harbottle and Bjorn Egge) *Thin Blue Line,* Yale University Press, 1973.
(With John Volkmar) *The Middle East and the New Realism,* International Peace Academy, 1975.
The Sinai Blunder, Frank Cass, 1978.

Negotiating the End of Conflicts: Namibia and Zimbabwe, International Peace Academy, 1979.
(Contributor) Henry Wiseman, editor, *Peacekeeping: Appraisals and Proposals,* Pergamon, 1983.
The Theory and Practice of Peacekeeping, St. Martin's, 1984.
Gulf Security: Quest for Regional Cooperation, International Peace Academy, 1985.

Contributor to international affairs and military journals.

WORK IN PROGRESS: Military Adviser to Hammarskjold and Thant, for C. Hurst; research on the use of technology for peacekeeping, third party roles in international peacekeeping in the Middle East, Cyprus, Kampucea, and Central America, negotiating the end of South African conflicts, and developing skills for third party international mediation and negotiation.

SIDELIGHTS: Indar Jit Rikhye writes: "During my United Nations service I led several special missions for the secretary-general, including the Spinelli-Rikhye mission to Israel and Jordan in 1965 to deal with border raids. I was an observer in the Dominican Republic in 1965 and special adviser to U Thant during the Cuban missile crisis. I have traveled extensively to crisis areas in Cyprus, the Middle East, Southeast Asia, Africa, and Latin America.

"I am motivated by Gandhi's philosophy for nonviolent social change, Nehru's doctrine of *Panch Sheel* (non-alignment), and Hammarskjold's advocacy of the role of international organizations in promoting peaceful settlement of disputes and strengthening international systems for the maintenance of peace and security."

*   *   *

ROBERTSON, Heather Margaret   1942-

PERSONAL: Born March 19, 1942, in Winnipeg, Manitoba, Canada; daughter of Harry (a teacher) and Margaret (Duncan) Robertson; married David Hildebrandt, May 16, 1968 (divorced, 1974); married Andrew Marshall (a broadcaster and publisher), July 11, 1975; children: (second marriage) Aaron. *Education:* University of Manitoba, B.A., 1963; Columbia University, M.A., 1964. *Religion:* None.

ADDRESSES: Home—175 Sherwood Ave., Toronto, Ontario, Canada M4P 2A9. *Agent*—Nancy Colbert, 303 Davenport Rd., Toronto, Ontario, Canada.

CAREER: Winnipeg Tribune, Winnipeg, Manitoba, reporter and critic, 1964-66; radio producer in public affairs for Canadian Broadcasting Corp., 1967-71; *Maclean's* magazine, author of television column, "Television," television critic, and feature writer, 1971-75; free-lance writer, 1971—.

MEMBER: Periodical Writers Association of Canada (president, 1977-78), Association of Canadian Radio and Television Artists.

AWARDS, HONORS: Woodrow Wilson fellow, 1963-64; Books in Canada first novel award, 1984; fiction prize from Canadian Authors' Association, 1984; best "talking" book prize from Canadian National Institute for the Blind, 1984.

WRITINGS:

Reservations Are for Indians (nonfiction), James Lorimer, 1970.
Grass Roots (nonfiction), James Lorimer, 1973.
Salt of the Earth (nonfiction), James Lorimer, 1974.
A Terrible Beauty: The Art of Canada at War, James Lorimer, 1977.

The Flying Bandit (nonfiction), James Lorimer, 1981.
Willie: A Romance (fiction), James Lorimer, 1983.
A Gentleman Adventurer: The Arctic Diaries of Richard Bonnycastle (nonfiction), Lester, Orpen & Dennys, 1984.
Willy-Nilly (tentative title), James Lorimer, 1986.

Contributor to Canadian magazines.

SIDELIGHTS: Heather Margaret Robertson comments: "I am fascinated by the literary potential of real people and real events, the attempt to render the raw material of specific human experience into words which not only capture its truth but reveal its meaning. I like to explore the boundaries between journalism and fiction, the point at which a real human being becomes a 'character' in a book."

BIOGRAPHICAL/CRITICAL SOURCES:

PERIODICALS

Christian Science Monitor, January 19, 1985.

*   *   *

RODERUS, Frank   1942-

PERSONAL: Born September 21, 1942, in Pittsburgh, Pa.; son of Frank James (in sales) and Alice (Hollenshead) Roderus; married Kay Marsh, March 27, 1965 (divorced August, 1977); married Betty Richardson, June 10, 1978; children: Melisse, Franklin, Stephen, Amanda. *Education:* Attended Emory-at-Oxford Junior College (now Oxford College of Emory University), 1958-60, and St. Petersburg Junior College, 1964-65. *Religion:* Associate Reformed Presbyterian.

ADDRESSES: Home—Cripple Creek, Colo.

CAREER: Free-lance writer, 1975—. *Military service:* U.S. Army, 1960-63.

MEMBER: Western Writers of America, Author's Guild, Author's League of America, Private Eye Writers of America.

AWARDS, HONORS: Spur Award, Western Writers of America, 1983, for *Leaving Kansas.*

WRITINGS:

WESTERN NOVELS

The 33 Brand, Doubleday, 1977.
Journey to Utah, Doubleday, 1977.
Duster (juvenile), Independence Press (Independence, Mo.), 1977.
Easy Money, Doubleday, 1978.
The Keystone Kid, Doubleday, 1978.
Home to Texas, Ace Books, 1978.
Hell Creek Cabin, Doubleday, 1979.
The Name Is Hart, Ace Books, 1979.
Sheepherding Man, Doubleday, 1980.
Jason Evers: His Own Story, Doubleday, 1980.
Old Kyle's Boy, Doubleday, 1981.
Cowboy, Doubleday, 1981.
The Ordeal of Hogue Bynell, Doubleday, 1982.
Leaving Kansas, Doubleday, 1983.
The Oil Rig, Bantam, 1984.
The Rain Rustlers, Bantam, 1984.
Reaching Colorado, Doubleday, 1984.
The Video Vandals, Bantam, 1985.
The Turn-Out Man, Bantam, 1985.
The Coyote Crossing, Bantam, 1985.
Finding Nevada, Doubleday, 1985.

WORK IN PROGRESS: Another western novel, for Doubleday.

SIDELIGHTS: Frank Roderus comments: "I wrote my first fiction (a western) at age five and never wanted to do anything else. I enjoy researching the American West as well as my travels in the area. My novels are built around my characters, who I like to think are representative of the people who still raise livestock in this great country."

*   *   *

ROGAL, Samuel J.   1934-

PERSONAL: Born August 3, 1934; married Susan Litchfield, August 14, 1965; children: Geoffrey C., James P. *Education:* Clarion State College (now Clarion University of Pennsylvania), B.S.Ed., 1956; University of Pittsburgh, M.A., 1960.

ADDRESSES: Home—18 Linda Lane, Normal, Ill. 61761. *Office*—Division of Humanities and Fine Arts, Illinois Valley Community College, 2578 E. 350th Rd., Oglesby, Ill. 61348.

CAREER: Instructor in English at Waynesburg College, Waynesburg, Pa., 1960-62, and Iowa State University of Science and Technology, Ames, 1962-66; State University of New York College at Oswego, assistant professor, 1966-68, associate professor of English, 1968-78; Mary Holmes College, West Point, Miss., chairman of department of English and reading, 1978-81; Illinois State University, Normal, assistant professor of English, 1981-84; Illinois Valley Community College, Oglesby, chairman of division of humanities and fine arts, 1984—. Visiting instructor at Tuskegee Institute, summer, 1966, and Miss Hall's School, Pittsfield, Mass., 1972-73. *Military service:* U.S. Army, 1957-59.

MEMBER: Modern Language Association of America, American Society for Eighteenth-Century Studies, Hymn Society of America, Augustan Reprint Society.

WRITINGS:

Teaching Composition in the Senior High School, Littlefield, 1966.
Preparing the Research Paper, Educators Publishing Service, 1967.
The Paragraph, Dickenson, 1968.
(Editor) Isaac Watts, *Reliquiae Juveniles,* Scholars' Facsimiles & Reprints, 1968.
The Student-Critic: An Aid to Writing, Educators Publishing Service, 1968.
(Contributor) James Helyar, editor, *Gilbert and Sullivan,* University of Kansas Libraries, 1971.
(Contributor) Ronald C. Rosbottom, editor, *Studies in Eighteenth-Century Culture,* University of Wisconsin Press, 1976.
A Chronological Outline of British Literature, Greenwood Press, 1980.
Sisters of Sacred Song: Selected Listing of Women Hymnodists in Great Britain and America, Garland Publishing, 1981.
The Children's Jubilee: A Bibliographical Survey of Hymnals for Infants, Youth, and Sunday Schools Published in Britain and America, Greenwood Press, 1983.
John and Charles Wesley, Twayne, 1983.
Business and Professional Correspondence, Amidon, 1984.

Contributor of articles on rhetoric, hymnology, bibliography, and eighteenth-century British literature to professional journals.

WORK IN PROGRESS: A Guide to the Hymns and Tunes of American Methodism; A Chronological Outline of American Literature.

*   *   *

ROGERS, Barbara 1945-

PERSONAL: Born September 21, 1945, in Huddersfield, England; daughter of George Theodore (a government official) and Mary Katherine (a nurse; maiden name, Stedman) Rogers. *Education:* University of Sussex, B.A. (with honors), 1968. *Politics:* Labour.

ADDRESSES: Home—10 Inner Park Rd., London S.W.19, England. *Office*—School of Development Studies, University of East Anglia, Norwich NR4 7JT, England.

CAREER: Progress Publishing House, Moscow, U.S.S.R., translator and editor, 1968; Foreign and Commonwealth Office, London, England, third secretary, 1969-70; War on Want, London, education officer, 1970-71; University of East Anglia, Norwich, England, research fellow, 1976—. Consultant to U.S. Congressman Charles C. Diggs and to the United Nations.

MEMBER: Anti-Apartheid Movement, Namibia Support Committee.

WRITINGS:

South Africa's Stake in Britain, Africa Bureau (London, England), 1971.
South Africa: The Bantu Homelands, Christian Action Publications for the International Defence and Aid Fund, 1972.
(Contributor) Olav Stokke and Carl Widstrand, editors, *Southern Africa: The UN-OAU Conference,* Volume II, Scandinavian Institute of African Studies, 1973.
Foreign Investment in Namibia, United Nations Council for Namibia, 1974.
(Contributor) Mohamed El-Khawas and Francis Kornegay, editors, *American-South African Relations: Bibliographical Essays,* Greenwood Press, 1975.
Divide and Rule: South Africa's Bantustans, International Defence and Aid, 1976, revised edition, 1980.
White Wealth and Black Poverty: American Investments in Southern Africa, Greenwood Press, 1976.
(Contributor) Hajo Hasenpflug and Karl Sauvant, editors, *The New International Economic Order: Analysis, Documents, Statistics,* Westview, 1977.
(With Zdenek Cervenka) *The Nuclear Axis: Secret Collaboration between West Germany and South Africa,* Times Books, 1978.
The Domestication of Women: Discrimination in Developing Societies, St. Martin's, 1979.
Race: No Peace without Justice, World Council of Churches, 1980.

Contributor to African studies journals in England and the United States and to *Guardian.* Editor of *X-Ray,* 1970-71.

SIDELIGHTS: Barbara Rogers once wrote *CA:* "While continuing to work on southern Africa, a major new topic of research is women in the poorest areas of the world. The two issues are quite different, but the principle is the same: liberty, equality and comradeship! Or, an end to 'home arrest.'"†

ROSKOLENKO, Harry 1907-1980
(Colin Ross)

PERSONAL: Born September 21, 1907, in New York, N.Y.; died of cancer, July 17, 1980, in New York, N.Y.; son of Barnett (a tailor, presser, and farmer) and Sara (Goldstein) Roskolenko; married Diana Chang, May 10, 1948 (divorced August, 1955); children: Deborah Crozier Harris. *Education:* "Self-educated via hoboing and extensive travel as a sailor between 1920-1927." *Religion:* Pantheist.

ADDRESSES: Home—463 West St., New York, N.Y. 10014.

CAREER: Writer. Went to work in a factory at age of nine; at thirteen, swearing he was eighteen, he shipped as a seaman on an oil tanker bound for Mexico; worked on a WPA Writers Project during the Depression; had been a law clerk, patent researcher, second mate in the Merchant Marine, and a drawbridge operator; correspondent in China, Japan, Indochina, and East Asia, 1946-47; traveled extensively via scooter, motorcycle, and station wagon for material for his books; traveled the Nile River from source to mouth. *Military service:* U.S. Army, 1942; became sergeant. U.S. Army Transport Service, 1942-45; became second officer.

MEMBER: P.E.N.

WRITINGS:

(Editor with Helen Neville) *Exiles Anthology: British and American Poets,* Press of James A. Decker, 1940.
Baedeker for a Bachelor (travel book), Padell Books, 1952.
Black Is a Man (novel), Padell Books, 1954.
Poet on a Scooter (travel book), Dial, 1958.
Lan-Lan (novel), New American Library of Canada, 1962.
White Man Go (travel book), Regency, 1962.
When I Was Last on Cherry Street (autobiography), Stein & Day, 1965.
The Terrorized: 1945-1950 (autobiography), Prentice-Hall, 1968.
The Time That Was Then: The Lower East Side, 1900-1914 (autobiography), Dial, 1971.
(Contributor) Thomas C. Wheeler, editor, *The Immigrant Experience,* Dial, 1971.
(Editor) *Solo: Great Adventures Alone,* Playboy Press, 1973.
Sensuous Eating, Manor Books, 1973.
(Editor) *Great Battles and Their Great Generals,* Playboy Press, 1974.
(Under pseudonym Colin Ross, with James T. Haight) *New York after Dark—San Francisco after Dark,* Manor Books, 1977.
(Under pseudonym Colin Ross) *Sex and Incestuous Behavior,* Manor Books, 1978.

Also author of *My Father! My Father* (libretto), 1978, and *Miracles* (play), 1978.

POETRY

Sequence on Violence, Signal Press, 1938.
I Went into the Country, Decker Press, 1940.
A Second Summary, Reed & Harris (Australia), 1944.
Notes from a Journey, and Other Poems, Meanjin Press (Australia), 1946.
Paris Poems [France], 1950.
American Civilization, National Press (Melbourne, Australia), 1971.
Is, National Press, 1971.

Also author of *Baguio Poems*, 1976, and *A Third Summary*, 1978.

OTHER

Also author of radio serial on Chinese-American relations for Voice of America, 1950. Contributor to *Prairie Schooner, New Republic, New York Times Book Review, Partisan Review, Sewanee Review,* and others. Editor, *Quadrant* (American edition), 1973.

WORK IN PROGRESS: A novel, *The Life and Death of a Building.*

SIDELIGHTS: The thirteenth of fourteen children, eight of whom died before his parents moved from the Ukraine to New York, Harry Roskolenko was well acquainted with the poverty of the lower east side of New York City (described in his book *When I Was Last on Cherry Street*). He finally ran away to become a poet and a Trotskyite, and later gave up both. Of his life as a radical he wrote: "We were so serious we couldn't tolerate each other's views." Late in his life he referred to his politics as a "private affair."

Roskolenko once told *CA:* "I travel—and usually in odd ways, to odd places. I prefer the wilderness to the City. I need wild green places, deserts, mountains, etc. The City will kill all of us, soon enough. The pollutions are as physical as they are social and spiritual. My books stem from this situation. We are over-gadgeted and breathless, incapable of free-wheeling anymore. We are locked in by highways going to a place called NOWHERE, U.S.A. Any attempt by the U.S. Government to beautify this country—can only be as disastrous as our current duplicity. Doomsday, U.S.A., is a permanent program called Progress. We have abdicated all the way home.

"I gave up poetry because it no longer is a valid art in our society. It is as empty as the American way of non-life." He later expanded on this statement: "Poetry is not valid *for me* because my world, our world, this world, this inhuman society—has *consciously* eradicated every moral and sensual basis for poetry as an art form. A simple example is a quote from my book *When I Was Last on Cherry Street:* 'The new Barbarians, circa 1964, were at work on the City . . . and even the symbols of poetry were demolished. Whitman's house on Cranberry and Fulton streets, where Whitman had set the type for *Leaves of Grass,* was torn down one bright day in June by the Able Demolition Company.'

"What is valid for me is one's natural irony and the continual criticism of the New Barbarism. That is my poetry—to expose the terror of bureaucratic stupidity; the mechanisms that rob all of us of basic human dignity; the City, now re-made, that encases us, dulls us, pollutes us. We are boxed in by skies without air, in cities without water, and a pastoral scene that has killed NATURE. It may make some sort of poetry for some poets; but God and Pantheism save me from that sort of poetry."

BIOGRAPHICAL/CRITICAL SOURCES:

PERIODICALS

New York Herald Tribune, May, 1965.
New York Times, May 14, 1965.
New York Times Book Review, September 28, 1958, May 23, 1965.
Washington Evening Star, May 13, 1965.

OBITUARIES:

PERIODICALS

New York Times, July 19, 1980.†

*   *   *

ROSS, Colin
    See ROSKOLENKO, Harry

*   *   *

ROSS, Stephen David   1935-

PERSONAL: Born May 4, 1935, in New York, N.Y.; son of Allan (a printer) and Bessie (Schlosberg) Ross; married Marilyn Gaddis Rose (a professor of comparative literature), November 16, 1968; children: David Gaddis. *Education:* Columbia University, A.B., 1956, M.A., 1957, Ph.D., 1961.

ADDRESSES: *Home*—4 Johnson Ave., Binghamton, N.Y. 13905. *Office*—Department of Philosophy, State University of New York, Binghamton, N.Y. 13901.

CAREER: Queens College of the City University of New York, Flushing, N.Y., instructor in mathematics, 1961-63; University of Wisconsin—Milwaukee, assistant professor of philosophy, 1963-65; University of Colorado, Boulder, assistant professor of philosophy, 1965-67; State University of New York at Binghamton, assistant professor, 1967-69, associate professor, 1969-73, professor of philosophy, 1973—, director of accelerated programs, 1971—, chairman of department, 1979—.

MEMBER: American Philosophical Association, Phi Beta Kappa.

AWARDS, HONORS: University of Wisconsin summer research grant, 1964; State University of New York summer research fellowships, 1968, 1969; Rockefeller Foundation humanities fellowship, 1975-76.

WRITINGS:

The Meaning of Education, Nijhoff, 1966.
Literature and Philosophy: An Analysis of the Philosophical Novel, Appleton, 1969.
The Scientific Process, Nijhoff, 1971.
Moral Decision, Freeman, Cooper, 1972.
The Nature of Moral Responsibility, Wayne State University Press, 1973.
In Pursuit of Moral Value, Freeman, Cooper, 1973.
Transition to an Ordinal Metaphysics, State University of New York Press, 1980.
Philosophical Mysteries, State University of New York Press, 1981.
Learning and Discovery, Gordon & Breach, 1981.
A Theory of Art: Inexhaustibility by Contrast, State University of New York Press, 1982.
Perspective in Whitehead's Metaphysics, State University of New York Press, 1983.
(Editor) *Art and Its Significance: An Anthology of Aesthetic Theory,* State University of New York Press, 1984.

Contributor to scholarly journals.

*   *   *

ROSSI, Alice S(chaerr)   1922-

PERSONAL: Born September 24, 1922, in New York, N.Y.,

daughter of William A. (an experimental machinist) and Emma Clara (Winkler) Schaerr; married second husband, Peter Henry Rossi, September 29, 1951; children: (second marriage) Peter Eric, Kristin Alice, Nina Alexis. *Education:* Brooklyn College (now Brooklyn College of the City University of New York), B.A., 1947; Columbia University, Ph.D., 1957. *Politics:* Independent. *Religion:* None.

ADDRESSES: Home—34 Stagecoach Rd., Amherst, Mass. 01002. *Office*—Department of Sociology, University of Massachusetts, Amherst, Mass. 01003.

CAREER: Cornell University, Ithaca, N.Y., research associate in sociology and anthropology, 1951-52; Harvard University, Cambridge, Mass., research associate at Russian Research Center, 1952-54, research associate in Graduate School of Education, 1954-55; University of Chicago, Chicago, Ill., lecturer in sociology, 1959-61, research associate in anthropology, 1961-62, research associate in sociology, 1963-64, research associate at National Opinion Research Center, 1964, research associate for Committee on Human Development, 1964-67; Johns Hopkins University, Baltimore, Md., research associate in social relations, 1967-69; Goucher College, Towson, Md., associate professor, 1969-71, professor of sociology and anthropology, 1971-74; University of Massachusetts—Amherst, professor, 1974—.

Worked for War Manpower Commission, Lend Lease, and municipal nursery and day care center, 1942-46. Social Science Research Council, member of board of directors, 1971, chairman of board of directors, 1976-78; member of board of directors, Schlesinger Library (of Harvard University), 1972-75. Member of task force, Citizens Council on Status of Women, Family Law and Policy, 1967-68; member of advisory council of fellowship program for married women, Danforth Foundation, 1967-69; member of advisory board of committee on marriage and divorce, National Conference of Commissioners on Uniform State Laws, 1968-71; member of academic advisory council, Kirkland College, 1968-71; member of National Commission for the Observance of International Women's Year, 1977-78.

MEMBER: American Sociological Association (vice-president, 1974-76; president, 1982-83), Sociologists for Women in Society (president pro tempore, 1971-72), American Council on Education, American Association of University Professors (vice-president, 1974-76), National Academy of Sciences (member of committee on ability testing, 1978-80), National Association for Repeal of Abortion Laws (member of board of directors, 1969-72), National Organization for Women (member of governing board, 1966-70), Eastern Sociological Society (president-elect, 1972-73; president, 1973-74), Washington Opportunities for Women (member of board of directors, 1971—).

AWARDS, HONORS: Career development awards, National Institute of Mental Health, 1965-67, 1967-69; Ford Foundation faculty fellowship, 1976; University of Massachusetts faculty research fellowship, 1983-84. Honorary degrees: D.H.L. from Towson State College (now University), 1973; Dr. Sci. from Rutgers University, 1975 and Northwestern University, 1984; Dr. L.L. from Simmons College, 1977, and Goucher College, 1982.

WRITINGS:

(Contributor) Robert K. Merton and Paul F. Lazarsfeld, editors, *Continuities in Social Research*, Free Press of Glencoe, 1950.

(Contributor) Robert Lifton, editor, *The Woman in America*, Beacon Press, 1965.
(Contributor) Jacquelyn A. Mattfeld and Carol G. Van Aken, editors, *Women and the Scientific Professions*, M.I.T. Press, 1965.
(Contributor) Robert Hall, editor, *Abortion in a Changing World*, Volume I, Columbia University Press, 1970.
(Editor and contributor) John Stuart Mill and Harriet Taylor Mill, *Essays on Sex Equality*, University of Chicago Press, 1970.
(Contributor) Joseph Zubin and John Money, editors, *Critical Issues in Contemporary Sexual Behavior*, Johns Hopkins Press, 1972.
(Editor) *The Feminist Papers: From Adams to de Beauvoir*, Columbia University Press, 1973.
(Editor with Ann Calderwood) *Academic Women on the Move*, Russell Sage, 1973.
(Editor with J. Kogan and T. Hareven) *The Family*, Norton, 1978.
Feminists in Politics: A Panel Analysis of the First National Women's Conference, Academic Press, 1982.
(Editor) *Gender and the Life Course*, Aldine, 1985.
(Editor) *Sociology and Anthropology in the People's Republic of China*, National Academy Press, 1985.

Contributor to symposia. Contributor of about forty articles to journals, including *American Journal of Psychiatry*, *Psychology Today*, *Dissent*, *Atlantic Monthly*, *American Sociological Review*, *Signs: A Journal of Women in Society and Culture*, *American Sociologist*, and *Humanist*. Member of editorial board, *American Sociological Review*, 1969-72, *Social Science Quarterly*, 1981—, *Annual Review of Sociology*, 1982-86, and *Journal of Family Issues*, 1984—.

*   *   *

ROUSMANIERE, John   1944-

PERSONAL: Surname is pronounced Ru-ma-*near;* born March 10, 1944, in Louisville, Ky.; son of James A. (a fundraiser) and Jessie (Pierce) Rousmaniere; children: William Pierce, Dana Starr. *Education:* Attended University of Pennsylvania, 1962-63; Columbia University, B.S. (with honors), 1967, M.A., 1968; student at Union Theological Seminary, 1984—.

ADDRESSES: Home and office—100-23 Hope St., Stamford, Conn. 06906. *Agent*—Russell & Volkening, Inc., 50 West 29th St., New York, N.Y. 10001.

CAREER: U.S. Military Academy, West Point, N.Y., assistant professor of history, 1970-72; *Yachting*, New York City, associate editor, 1972-77; *Natural History*, New York City, senior editor, 1978; free-lance writer, editor, and consultant, 1978—. Member of editorial committee, Dolphin Book Club (Book-of-the-Month-Club), 1982—. Adjunct assistant professor of writing, College of New Rochelle, 1980-83. *Military service:* U.S. Army, 1969-72; became first lieutenant.

MEMBER: Authors Guild, Authors League of America, C. G. Jung Foundation, New York Yacht Club.

WRITINGS:

A Glossary of Modern Sailing Terms, Dodd, 1975.
(With Dennis Conner) *No Excuse to Lose*, Norton, 1978.
(Editor) *The Enduring Great Lakes*, Norton, 1979.
Fastnet, Force 10, Norton, 1980.
The Luxury Yachts, Time-Life, 1981.
The Annapolis Book of Seamanship, Simon & Schuster, 1983.

America's Cup Book, Norton, 1983.
Study Guide to the Annapolis Book of Seamanship, American Sailing Association, 1984.
The Sailing Lifestyle: A Guide to Sailing and Cruising for Pleasure, Simon & Schuster, 1985.

Also author of numerous articles for major boating periodicals.

WORK IN PROGRESS: A history of yachting; a manuscript on the religious and psychological symbolism of the boat.

SIDELIGHTS: John Rousmaniere told *CA:* "I am one of the very few freelancers in the country who makes a living writing about boats. My books have covered history, journalism, and techniques of sailing and, I am pleased to say, have been well-received by reviewers as well as by readers. Now a student at Union Theological Seminary in New York City, I continue to write about sailing, but I am preparing a gradual shift of interest that, I'm sure, will be fascinating and productive."

Rousmaniere's *Fastnet, Force 10* chronicles the disastrous Fastnet race along the coasts of Great Britain and Ireland in August of 1979. Severe weather during the race killed fifteen sailors, sank five yachts and capsized nineteen more, and caused more than half of the field of three hundred participating yachts to retire. Rousmaniere himself was aboard one of the ships during the storm, so he was able to report on the incident with the authority of an observer. Robert Krisch, book critic for the *Los Angeles Times,* calls *Fastnet, Force 10* "a narrative worthy of the best sea literature." Peter Jay, in an article for the *Washington Post Book World,* notes: "Rousmaniere's book is a useful, readable and thoroughly sane introduction to the basic facts, individual experiences and underlying issues of the 1979 Fastnet disaster.... [It] is written in the good muscular style of a competent journalist with all the necessary sailing experience and specialist knowledge."

BIOGRAPHICAL/CRITICAL SOURCES:

BOOKS

Rousmaniere, John, *Fastnet, Force 10,* Norton, 1980.

PERIODICALS

Los Angeles Times, May 16, 1980, July 6, 1980.
Los Angeles Times Book Review, May 5, 1985.
New York Times, August 9, 1980.
Washington Post Book World, May 25, 1980.

*   *   *

RUBENS, Jeff(rey Peter) 1941-

PERSONAL: Born April 24, 1941, in Brooklyn, N.Y.; son of Morris M. (a school principal) and Leonora (Tashman) Rubens; married Beth Massey (a teacher), May 8, 1967; children: Peter Paul. *Education:* Cornell University, A.B., 1961; Brandeis University, M.A., 1963.

ADDRESSES: Home—5A 771 West End Ave., New York, N.Y. 10025. *Office*—Department of Mathematics, Pace University, New York, N.Y.; and *Bridge World,* 39 West 94th St., New York, N.Y. 10025.

CAREER: Bridge Journal, New York City, editor, 1963-66; Pace University, New York City, instructor in mathematics, 1965—; *Bridge World,* New York City, co-editor, 1967—. Writer for National Lexicographic Board, New York City, 1965-67.

MEMBER: International Bridge Academy, International Bridge Press Association, Mathematics Association of America, Authors Guild, Authors League of America, National Puzzler's League, American Cryptogram Association, American Association of University Professors, American Mathematical Society, Greater New York Bridge Association (member of board of directors), Phi Beta Kappa.

AWARDS, HONORS: National Science Foundation fellow, 1962-65; national contract bridge champion, 1965.

WRITINGS:

Win at Poker, Funk, 1968, 2nd edition, Dover, 1984.
(With Alvin Roth) *Modern Bridge Bidding Complete,* Funk, 1968.
The Secrets of Winning Bridge, Grosset, 1970, 2nd edition, Dover, 1980.
(With wife, Beth Rubens) *Crostics for the Connoisseur,* Grosset, 1970.
(With Roth) *Bridge for Beginners,* Funk, 1970.
(With Paul Lukacs) *Test Your Play as Declarer,* Hart Associates, 1977.

WORK IN PROGRESS: With Lukacs, *Test Your Bridge.*†

*   *   *

RUBENSTEIN, Richard L(owell) 1924-

PERSONAL: Born January 8, 1924, in New York, N.Y.; son of Jesse George (an industrial engineer) and Sara (Fine) Rubenstein; married Ellen van der Veen, April 3, 1947 (divorced, 1963); married Betty Rogers Alschuler, August 21, 1966; children: (first marriage) Aaron, Hannah, Jeremy, Nathaniel (deceased). *Education:* University of Cincinnati, A.B., 1946; Jewish Theological Seminary, M.H.L., ordained Rabbi, 1952; Harvard University, S.T.M., 1955, Ph.D., 1960. *Politics:* Democrat.

ADDRESSES: Home—751 Lake Shore Dr., Tallahassee, Fla. 32312. *Agent*—George Borchardt, 145 East 52nd St., New York, N.Y. 10022. *Office*—Department of Religion, Florida State University, Tallahassee, Fla.; and Suite 910, 1333 New Hampshire Ave. N.W., Washington, D.C. 20036.

CAREER: Temple Beth Emunah, Brockton, Mass., rabbi, 1952-54; Temple Israel, Natick, Mass., rabbi, 1954-56; Harvard University, Cambridge, Mass., interim director of B'nai B'rith Hillel Foundation, 1956-58; University of Pittsburgh and Carnegie-Mellon Institute, Pittsburgh, Pa., chaplain to Jewish students, 1958-70; Florida State University, Tallahassee, professor of religion and director of Center for the Study of Southern Culture and Religion, 1970—, Robert O. Lawton Distinguished Professor of Religion, 1977—. Co-director, Humanities Institute, 1980—; president, Washington Institute for Values in Public Policy Studies, 1981—. Charles E. Merrill Adjunct Professor of Humanities, University of Pittsburgh, 1964-70; Edgar M. Bronfman Visiting Professor, University of Virginia, 1985. Lecturer at Korean, Japanese, U.S., and Canadian universities, and at Albert Schweitzer College, Switzerland, 1963, University of Edinburgh, 1964, Catholic University of Lublin and other Catholic institutions in Poland, 1965, and University of Mainz, University of Bonn, and University of Heidelberg, 1972. John Phillips Fellow, Phillips Exeter Academy, 1970; fellow, National Humanities Institute, Yale University, 1976-77; research scholar, Nanzan University, Nagoya, Japan, summer, 1984.

MEMBER: Rabbinical Assembly of America, American Academy of Religion, Society for the Scientific Study of Religion, Society for the Arts, Religion, and Contemporary Culture (fellow), Society for Values in Higher Education (fellow), Professors' World Peace Academy of America (president, 1981-83), Springtime Tallahassee, Cosmos Club (Washington, D.C.), Governors' Club (Tallahassee).

AWARDS, HONORS: Portico d'Ottavia Literary Prize (Rome), 1977, for Italian translation of *The Religious Imagination.*

WRITINGS:

After Auschwitz: Radical Theology and Contemporary Judaism, Bobbs-Merrill, 1966.
The Religious Imagination, Bobbs-Merrill, 1967.
Morality and Eros, McGraw, 1970.
My Brother Paul, Harper, 1972.
Power Struggle: An Autobiographical Confession, Scribner, 1974.
The Cunning of History: Mass Death and the American Future, Harper, 1975.
Dimensions of the Holocaust Past and Future, National Humanities Institute, 1977, revised edition, 1983.
(Editor) *Modernization: The Humanist Response to Its Promise and Problems,* Paragon House, 1982, 2nd edition, 1985.
The Age of Triage: Fear and Hope in an Overcrowded World, Beacon Press, 1983.
(With John Roth) *Approaches to Auschwitz,* John Knox, 1986.

CONTRIBUTOR

Werner Cahnmann, editor, *Intermarriage and Jewish Life in America,* Herzl Press, 1963.
D. Gianella, editor, *Religion and Public Order,* University of Chicago Press, 1963.
Ira Eisenstein, editor, *The Varieties of Jewish Experience,* Reconstructionist Press, 1966.
America and the Future of Theology, Westminister, 1966.
The Condition of Jewish Belief: A Symposium, Macmillan, 1966.
Daniel Callahan, editor, *The Secular City Debate,* Macmillan, 1967.
Joseph Havens, editor, *Psychology and Religion: A Contemporary Dialogue,* Van Nostrand, 1968.
Donald Cutler, editor, *The Religious Situation, 1968,* Beacon Press, 1969.
John Cobb, editor, *The Theology of Thomas Altizer: Critique and Response,* Westminister, 1970.
Louis Jacobs, editor, *Jewish Thought Today,* Behrman, 1970.
Martin Marty and Dean Peerman, editors, *New Theology: No. 8,* Macmillan, 1971.
Walter Capps and Donald Capps, editors, *The Religious Personality,* Wadsworth Publishing, 1971.
Jacob Neusner, editor, *American Judaism: Adventure in Modernity,* Prentice-Hall, 1972.
Jerry V. Diller, *Ancient Roots and Modern Meanings: A Contemporary Reader in Jewish Identity,* Bloch & Co., 1978.
Giles Gunn, editor, *New World Metaphysics: Readings on the Religious Meaning of the American Experience,* Oxford University Press, 1981.

OTHER

Contributor of numerous articles and reviews to journals and magazines, including *Cross Currents, Psychoanalytic Review, Playboy, Christian Century, Commonweal, Psychology To-* *day,* and *New York Times.* Member of advisory board, *Washington Times* and *Reconstructionist.*

WORK IN PROGRESS: A book on genocide, theology, and political theory.

SIDELIGHTS: Richard L. Rubenstein's writings address various forms of theology, political theory, and sociology, ranging from a study of the Apostle Paul to an explanation of the Holocaust and other instances of mass extermination. His first work *After Auschwitz: Radical Theology and Contemporary Judaism* is a collection of essays on "various issues of significance in contemporary Judaism," according to S. W. Wojtowicz in the *Library Journal.* As a reviewer in *Christian Century* states, "It represents a very wise, sober, humane assessment of the human condition as it appears in a turbulent and often chaotic history." And Rubenstein's *The Religious Imagination* is described by Walter Arnold in the *New York Times Book Review* as "a sustained application of psychoanalytic insight to Biblical religion and its traditions."

Among Rubenstein's most acclaimed books is *The Cunning of History: Mass Death and the American Future,* a work that compares the horrors of life and death at Auschwitz to that of the American slavery years. One of the book's most ardent admirers is William Styron, who included a discussion of *The Cunning of History* in his best-selling novel *Sophie's Choice* and had this to say about the work in a 1978 *New York Review of Books* article: "Few books possess the power to leave the reader with that feeling of awareness which we call a sense of revelation. *The Cunning of History* seems to me to be one of these. It is a very brief work—a long essay—but it is so rich in perception and it contains so many startling—indeed, prophetic—insights that one can only remain baffled at the almost complete absence of attention it suffered when it was first published in 1975."

"As near in time as Auschwitz is to us," continues Styron, "it is nonetheless a historical event, and one of the excellences of Rubenstein's book is the audacious and original way in which the author has confronted the event, wringing from its seeming incomprehensibility the most subtle and resonant meanings. . . . [In *The Cunning of History* the author] is forcing us to reinterpret Auschwitz—especially, although not exclusively, from the standpoint of its existence as part of a continuum of slavery which has been engrafted for centuries onto the very body of Western civilization. Therefore, in the process of destroying the myth and the preconception, he is making us see that that encampment of death and suffering may have been more horrible than we had ever imagined. It was slavery in its ultimate embodiment. He is making us understand that the etiology of Auschwitz . . . is actually embedded deeply in a cultural tradition which stretches back to the Middle Passage from the coast of Africa, and beyond, to the enforced servitude in ancient Greece and Rome. Rubenstein is saying that we ignore this linkage, and the existence of the sleeping virus in the bloodstream of civilization, at risk of our future."

In a sequel, *The Age of Triage: Fear and Hope in an Overcrowded World,* Rubenstein examines the economic and social circumstances that caused the mass exterminations of so-called "surplus" citizens during different phases of history. (The *Triage* of the title derives from the French *trier,* meaning to pick and assort according to quality.) Among the examples the author cites are the Irish potato famine, in which Ireland lost a quarter of its population, the three million Armenians lost to a Turkish purge in World War I, and, of course, the Holocaust. In each case, the seemingly total disregard for the victims was rationalized by a concern for the "greater good" of the country or culture involved. This rational approach, suggests a *Harper's* critic, "was born in monotheist religions, Malthusian economics, and Social Darwinism, and results in either relentless possessive individualism (in capitalist societies) or tribal xenophobia (in communist societies), both of which lead, inevitably, to rationales for human extermination."

Most reviewers agree on the importance of the book's subject but criticize Rubenstein's analysis. The *Harper's* critic, for example, thinks that the book is "oversimplified" and finds fault with Rubenstein's academic style but concludes that the book's "apocalyptic theory is too disturbing and grim to ignore." *Los Angeles Times Book Review* writer John Patrick Diggins comments that "for all his admirable research [the author] cannot establish the precise cause, or even causes, of genocide." But Diggins also finds that Rubenstein "succeeds in forcing upon our attention what we would otherwise prefer to leave unknown—suffering, terror, death, the evil done by man to man." Gene G. James in the *International Journal on World Peace* believes that Rubenstein's "analysis of the ills affecting modern society is much more illuminating than his suggestions for dealing with them."

But James remains convinced that in *The Cunning of History* and *The Age of Triage*, Rubenstein "has succeeded better than any other writer in laying bare the factors which have produced so much social upheaval and violence in the 20th century." After reading *The Age of Triage*, concludes Diggins, "we need all the more to listen to the tragedies of history."

Rubenstein's books have been translated into a number of foreign languages, including Italian, Dutch, Japanese, Polish, Hebrew, and Korean.

CA INTERVIEW

CA interviewed Richard L. Rubenstein by telephone on March 23, 1985, at the UN Plaza Hotel in New York City.

CA: Do you feel it was a great shortcoming in your education that you were not exposed to continental philosophy until quite late in your intellectual training?

RUBENSTEIN: Yes. I majored in philosophy at the University of Cincinnati between 1942 and 1945. There, the emphasis was on Anglo-Saxon and Anglo-American philosophy with a certain kind of empiricist bias to it. We did have a marvelous course in the history of philosophy, and a great teacher, Julius R. Weinberg, but the course went from the pre-Socratics to Immanuel Kant and there it stopped. The whole tradition of European dialectic philosophy—thinkers like Hegel, Schelling, Kierkegaard, Marx, Engels, Weber—were people of whom we were totally unaware. So, my philosophic training was a good start, but it was woefully incomplete.

CA: Later on, when you went to graduate school at Harvard, you were exposed to some continental philosophy?

RUBENSTEIN: Yes. At Harvard I took a course in classical German philosophy under Paul Tillich. It was so important to me that in my autobiography, *Power Struggle*, I entitled a chapter "Tillich and Harvard." Tillich's course constituted a veritable intellectual revolution in my life. I had already had a course at Harvard in Hegel's *Phenomenology of the Spirit*,

but I did not really begin to grasp its significance until Tillich, who had been trained in Germany and who knew how both Germans and Americans thought, was able to instruct me and many other students. By the way, Union Theological Seminary in Richmond, Virginia, recently made available cassette tapes of the Tillich lectures, and I have had the pleasure of hearing again the lectures that I got so much from over twenty-five years ago. I never thought I'd be able to recapture that kind of experience.

CA: What do you think you gained most from Tillich?

RUBENSTEIN: His course enabled me to think in systematic terms and to integrate theology with social thought. I gained a sense of what I would call a "system of continuity" as opposed to a "system of gaps"—that is, I came to think of all branches of human thought and experience as intrinsically related to one another. Gradually I began to look for connections between various domains of human experience, social movements, and historical periods and the art, religion, and thought that came out of them.

I also gained from Tillich a different perspective on theology than the one I had had previously. I had been trained as a rabbi and came to Harvard with a rabbinical ordination and a Master of Hebrew Literature degree. I had worked for and received a Master of Theology at Harvard Divinity School with a strong emphasis on Protestant theology. But I wasn't able to understand the way Christians—I'm talking about sophisticated, intellectual Christians—saw themselves and their tradition until the encounter with Tillich.

I might also add that I was never all that close to him personally. I had the feeling that he was a great man and that he might swallow me up intellectually and spiritually if I ever got too close to him. At that time in my life I felt it was extremely important to develop on my own.

CA: In addition to the insights you gained from Tillich, didn't you also learn a great deal from psychoanalysis?

RUBENSTEIN: My basic reason for going into psychoanalysis was an urgent and impelling need to find out what it was in myself and my past that was limiting my ability to function well in such roles as clergyman and pastor as well as husband and father. The psychoanalysis was of long duration. It lasted from '53 to '58. I resumed psychoanalysis in '63 when I finally realized that my first marriage was untenable. I was living in Pittsburgh at the time. I went back for a year or two and came to understand that, in order to be myself and to work more fully, I had to put aside some of the things I had been doing. I came to the conclusion that it was my vocation to be an academic and a thinker, with a certain practical interest in social and public issues. I decided that I wasn't really a pastor, although I think that's a very important role. Those were some of the benefits that I got from psychoanalysis.

CA: Had you studied Jungian psychology?

RUBENSTEIN: I had studied Jungian psychology, and I respect Jungian thought. I sometimes teach it in my courses on the psychology of religion. But I have found that at the practical level of discovering whatever it is that makes me comfortable with myself or finding out what my true vocation in life is, Freudian psychology seemed to work better. I felt more comfortable with it, although I'm not a narrow Freudian. I'm too interested in the political, economic, and social aspects of any human problem simply to see any problem solely in individual or Freudian terms.

CA: In Power Struggle *you devote considerable attention to the submissive side of the Jewish mentality. What role has submissiveness played in Jewish history?*

RUBENSTEIN: I believe Jewish submissiveness was altogether functional during most of the period of the European diaspora. After the defeat of the Jews by the Romans in the years 70 and 132, the power equation was a hundred-to-one against the Jews. Therefore, no act of retaliation or aggression on the part of the Jews against the dominant power would have made any sense whatsoever. The Jews were wholly dependent upon the people among whom they lived. I regard submissiveness under such circumstances as functional. However, in *Power Struggle* I argued that Jewish submissiveness was functional only as long as Jews were living among people who were not interested in using official governmental means to exterminate them. And, from the defeat of the Jews by the Romans in ancient times until the National Socialist regime in Germany, no Christian government ever had as its policy the extermination of Jews. Under those circumstances, Jewish submissiveness made a great deal of sense.

Submissiveness ceased to be functional in National Socialist Germany when Jews were faced with a government that had as its non-negotiable aim the extermination of every last Jew anywhere. Submissiveness then helped to facilitate the National Socialist program, although, at the time, the Jews had no idea that the Germans wanted to exterminate them until it was too late. The Jews mistakenly thought that they were confronted by a hostile government rather than with one which had as its aim neither persecution nor expulsion but annihilation. Hitler's *Reich* was a radically novel kind of government.

I also feel that submissiveness in contemporary Israel would not be functional because the Israelis are in a situation of more or less permanent war. The Israelis have turf to defend and they have to play the game of life the way any other warring people does. Briefly stated, my analysis of Jewish submissiveness was that it made sense as long as a hostile government did not have the aim of exterminating them; it made no sense whatsoever when they were faced with the twentieth century's politics of extermination.

CA: How did the experience of the Second World War change the Jewish consciousness?

RUBENSTEIN: Once a group has been targeted for a program of extermination, it can no longer rule out the politics of extermination as a possible future scenario. Therefore, World War II has had a radically transformative effect on Jews. I tried to say in *Power Struggle* that, in fact, this transformation was more typical of the consciousness of Jews in Israel than of American Jews, because American Jews, unlike the Israelis, do not currently have to confront a potential politics of extermination. Nevertheless, as a result of the Holocaust, in the back of the mind of every Jew there is the thought that one government tried to exterminate them; who knows if another government, anywhere in the world, might not try it again? Once extermination has been introduced, it can never again be ruled out.

Let me also add that one of the reasons the United States has a huge defense budget is because the Germans fought a war of extermination against the Russians during World War II.

As a result, the Russians will never again trust the Germans to be an independent people. No matter how much the Germans change their behavior, fear of another German war of extermination will now and forever more be a Russian policy calculation. So the Russians are in the middle of Germany, and we don't dare let them take all of Germany—which they might conceivably do, if they could. Nor would the demise of the communist regime in Russia make any difference. Even a Christian, conservative Russian government would not tolerate a united Germany.

Therefore we are locked in a tragic situation in which both the Russians and Americans find themselves as cold-war adversaries armed to the teeth with nuclear weapons. The way I sometimes put it is that World War II let the evil genie out of the bottle and no man can put it back in again. That is, until World War II, no Christian nation in Europe practiced a politics of extermination against either a portion of its own population or against another nation in Europe. That's all been changed by National Socialism, and countless unborn generations on both sides of the Iron Curtain are destined to live out their lives, if they are lucky, in a peace of mutual nuclear terror.

CA: Wouldn't you agree that one of the most distressing aspects of what happened during the Nazi regime was the extent to which the Jews cooperated in their own destruction?

RUBENSTEIN: I don't regard all the Jews as having cooperated in their own destruction. I think most Jews tragically misperceived their situation. The assumption on which Jewish life had rested for 2000 years can be stated as follows: "We are strangers who are governed by rulers who for one reason or another don't trust us. If they decide they do not want to permit us to remain in their midst, the worst they will do to us will be to expel us." It must be stressed that until 1939 no government with a Christian inheritance ever sought to exterminate the Jews, no matter how harshly the Jews were treated. Under the circumstances, the most important thing that a minority people could do was to demonstrate to the rulers that they were law-abiding and not a source of rebellion. When the Nazis entered Eastern Europe, the Jews made the mistake—a very understandable mistake—of assuming that they were dealing with another such ruler.

You also have to understand that the Jewish experience of the German armies in Eastern Europe from 1914 to 1918 was of a military force that behaved very well. When the German army returned to Poland and western Russia during World War II, it was inconceivable to the Jews that the Germans would now behave in a totally different manner. This was true not only in Poland, but even more so in Russia, where the Stalinist government prevented any real knowledge of the Nazi plan of extermination from ever reaching the Jews.

Therefore, I don't believe that most Jews knowingly cooperated in their own destruction. I think that they tragically misinterpreted the situation. There is, however, one chapter in *The Cunning of History* where I suggest that some Jews could not shift gears quickly enough and did cooperate in their own destruction without fully realizing what they were doing. That was in Hungary in 1944.

CA: Do you think the uprising at Warsaw was an example of shifting gears?

RUBENSTEIN: Absolutely. By that time, the Jews realized the situation was hopeless. Incidentally, there were many such revolts in Eastern Europe, although none as spectacular as the Warsaw ghetto. Part of the problem facing the Jewish resistance was this: if you were French and decided to resist the Germans, you could always count on the support of French peasants; unfortunately, in Eastern Europe, Jewish partisans could not count on the support of Polish peasants. They could not live off the land as did the other partisans. They could not count on any support except themselves. Even the Allies refused to parachute supplies, as they did for other partisans. Not only were they facing the German enemy alone; they were surrounded by people who were quite content to let the Germans exterminate them. Not all Poles felt that way, but most Polish peasants had no interest in giving the Jews any help whatsoever.

CA: Do you think the Holocaust is being taught satisfactorily in our schools?

RUBENSTEIN: I don't really know how it's being taught in the schools; I can't offer an opinion on that. When I teach the Holocaust, I do so as an event in European history. It has to be seen in the context of economic, social, and demographic trends that were occurring in Europe. Therefore I tend to try to interpret the Holocaust in the larger historical context. I believe it was part of a larger trend of genocide which has killed millions of people in the twentieth century, many of whom were not Jewish. There are other scholars who try to stress the absolute uniqueness of the Holocaust. While I believe the Holocaust has unique features, I do not believe that justifies teaching it outside the context of world history.

Nor am I interested in entering into a debate as to who should or should not learn about the Holocaust. At Florida State the course is offered as an elective. Those who feel that it is interesting and important for what it reveals about the twentieth century will take it, and those who don't will not. Certainly I'm not interested in making it a compulsory course either in my university or elsewhere.

CA: Do you find that many non-Jews are moved by your books?

RUBENSTEIN: I have the feeling that more non-Jews than Jews read my books. As a matter of fact, I think that's been true ever since I wrote *After Auschwitz*. First of all, I know where my books tend to sell. Generally speaking, insofar as they catch on, they catch on with academics who think they should be studied in courses. For example, when *After Auschwitz* came out, the fact that a lot of professors decided to use it prompted Bobbs-Merrill to make it a short-discount textbook. They kept on reprinting it for nineteen years because it was being used. And I happen to know that the majority of the students who were studying *After Auschwitz* were studying it in American and foreign universities. Jewish students studied it, but I would say that the majority of people studying the book were not Jewish.

When you come to *The Cunning of History* and *The Age of Triage*, the same thing happened. *The Cunning of History* was ignored at first. It sold, I believe, 900 copies in the first two years. Then William Styron read the book and was excited about it. He discussed it in *Sophie's Choice* and reviewed it in the *New York Review of Books*. Then a lot of people in

history, sociology, and quite a number of criminology courses used the book. Just yesterday I came from Babson College in New England, which is a school with an overwhelmingly Protestant student body. There are a number of courses in history and humanities and ethics where they're using both *The Cunning of History* and *The Age of Triage*. That is also true in many other colleges and universities throughout North America. So I believe that the majority of my readers are not Jewish, and I'm conscious of that when I write.

CA: A lot of your work has been translated into foreign languages as well.

RUBENSTEIN: Yes. I've been fortunate. There is a Swedish translation of *The Cunning of History* as well as a Japanese translation. I won a literary prize in Italy for the Italian translation of *The Religious Imagination*. Gallimard put out the French translation of *The Religious Imagination*, and *After Auschwitz* is also in Dutch. After twenty years, there still is an audience for *After Auschwitz*. I am currently preparing a wholly revised, greatly enlarged twentieth-anniversary edition of the book for another publisher. I've had articles in German, Russian, Polish, Chinese, Japanese, and Korean. There's even a translation of *The Cunning of History* in Hungarian. So I've had a fairly large number of foreign translations of books and articles, and there again the majority of people who read my works are not Jewish.

CA: Do you have a following among the black population?

RUBENSTEIN: I don't have a following, but I don't have the sense of any great tension. One of my good friends and colleagues at Florida State University is professor William Jones, who wrote a book called *Is God A White Racist?*, which was published by Doubleday. He took on *After Auschwitz* and discussed it critically. I liked the way he criticized me, and he is now a senior professor in our department. Some blacks have realized the relevance of what I've written to their situation, but I would say that my audience is predominantly non-black.

CA: You have said that you want to devote your life, in addition to religion, to politics. What were you thinking of?

RUBENSTEIN: I'm the president of a Washington-based think tank, the Washington Institute for Values in Public Policy, in addition to serving as a professor at Florida State University. This is a public-policy research institution with a well-established publications program and a research budget of about two million dollars a year. I'm not responsible for the administrative side of the institute. I am responsible for its academic side. I am immensely gratified that, starting out as a Jewish theologian asking the question how can we understand God and the Holocaust, I then proceeded to the question how shall we understand the Holocaust in the context of twentieth-century civilization. And I have finally come to the point where I'm asking, how can I use my research and how can I help others in research to influence decision-makers in government to help make this a better world?

Many of my current activities involve helping political scientists, sociologists, economists, and experts in international affairs to address problems for a decision-making audience. We make their ideas available to government officials at our seminars and conferences, as well as in the books and monographs we publish. That's become a very important aspect of my work. One might say that it is partly the sublimation of my preaching instinct. Instead of telling people from the pulpit what they ought to believe, I've tried to engage in disciplined inquiry using the social sciences as a tool with which to examine the kind of world we live in and the kind of world we might live in, and to make these insights, both mine and the other scholars', available to decision-makers in government.

The other direction in which I've moved is that I have visited the Far East many times in the last four or five years. Last summer I was a research scholar at Nanzan University in Nagoya, Japan. And I'm going to be going back to Japan this summer, although not at Nanzan. I've visited Taiwan, Korea, and the Philippines; I've lectured in all these places. I find it fascinating that, starting out asking questions about the Holocaust and then coming to the conclusion in *The Age of Triage* and *The Cunning of History* that the Holocaust was a modernization phenomenon, I've now discovered that I have an Asian audience interested in my work on modernization. I'm hoping to do some research and perhaps to write a book on the special characteristics of Japanese capitalism. As a matter of fact, in the back of my mind I even have the title of this book. If I write it—and there's a strong possibility that I will, provided that I find the right Japanese co-author to help me with the language—it will be called *Samurai Capitalism*. So, I've moved in this direction, but I've never ceased to be a theologian and a religious thinker. I've taken a cue from my teacher, Paul Tillich. Like him, I believe that religion is a matter of ultimate concern, and there is no aspect of human endeavor that is alien to it.

BIOGRAPHICAL/CRITICAL SOURCES:

BOOKS

Rohmann, Klaus, *Vollendung in Nichts? Eine dokumentation der Amerikanischon Gott-ist-tot Theologie*, Benziger Verlag (Cologne), 1977.
Rubenstein, Richard L., *Power Struggle: An Autobiographical Confession*, Scribner, 1974.
Walliman, Isidore and Michael Dobkowski, editors, *The Age of Genocide*, Greenwood Press, 1985.

PERIODICALS

America, September 21, 1974.
Christian Century, May 10, 1967, August 17, 1983.
Commonweal, November 17, 1967, May 17, 1968, January 3, 1975.
Conservative Judaism, summer, 1974.
Harper's, January, 1983.
International Journal on World Peace, winter, 1985.
Journal of the American Academy of Religion, September, 1978.
Library Journal, November 15, 1966.
Los Angeles Times Book Review, February 20, 1983.
New Republic, October 5, 1974.
New York Review of Books, June 29, 1978.
New York Times Book Review, March 15, 1970, May 7, 1972.
Saturday Review, February 25, 1967.
Washington Post Book World, September 8, 1974.

—Sketch by Susan Salter

—Interview by Walter W. Ross

S

SADDHATISSA, Hammalawa   1914-

PERSONAL: Born May 28, 1914, in Hammalawa, Ceylon (now Sri Lanka); son of Bandara (a physician) and Ukkumenike (Mapa) Banneheka. *Education:* Vidyodaya College, Pandit, Tripitakacharya (with honors), 1939; Banaras Hindu University, B.A. (with honors), 1954, M.A., 1957; attended London School of Oriental and African Studies, 1958-61; University of Edinburgh, Ph.D., 1963.

ADDRESSES: Home and office—British Mahabodhi Society, London Buddhist Vihara, 5, Heathfield Gardens, London W4 4JU, England; and Mahabodhi Society, 130 Maligakanda Rd., Colombo 10, Sri Lanka.

CAREER: Ordained a Buddhist monk, 1926; attained rank of Mahathera; leader of Buddhist Vihara, London, England, 1957—; appointed Mahanayaka Thera, Buddhist Primate of the United Kingdom, 1980—. Vikramashila College, Pallewela, Ceylon (now Sri Lanka), senior staff member and principal, 1940-44; Mahabodhi College, Sarnath, India, senior lecturer in Pali, 1950-53; Banaras Hindu University, Varanasi, India, professor of Pali, 1956-57; University of London, London, lecturer, 1958-60; University of Toronto, Toronto, Ontario, professor, 1966-69.

Visiting lecturer at Oxford University, 1973; conducts lecture tours in Europe, the United States, and Japan. Buddhist chaplain to University of London. President of Sangha Council of Great Britain, 1966—; has established Theravada centers throughout the world.

MEMBER: Mahabodhi Society, British Mahabodhi Society (president, 1963—), Pali Text Society (vice-president, 1963—), American Oriental Society.

AWARDS, HONORS: D. Litt. from University of Kelaniya, Sri Lanka, 1979, University of Peradeniya, Sri Lanka, 1981, and University of Sri Jayewardenpura, Sri Lanka, 1981.

WRITINGS:

IN ENGLISH

Upasakajanalankara: A Critical Edition and Study, Pali Text Society, 1965.
(Editor) *Pali Tipitaka Concordance,* Volume III, Parts 2-4, Pali Text Society, 1968-70.
Buddhist Ethics, Allen & Unwin, 1970.

The Buddha's Way, Allen & Unwin, 1971.
Handbook for Buddhists, 2nd edition, Mahabodhi Society of India, 1973.
The Birth-Stories of the Ten Bodhisattas and the Dasabodhisattuppattikatha, Pali Text Society, 1975.
The Life of the Buddha, Allen & Unwin, 1976.
A Buddhist Manual, British Mahabodhi Society, 1976.
(Contributor) *Malasekera Commemoration Volume,* [Colombo], 1976.
(Translator into English) *Suttanipata,* Curzon Press, 1985.

OTHER

Saral-Pali-Siksa (Pali grammar; in Hindi), Mahabodhi Society of India, 1948.
Gunaganga, Buddhist Publication Society, 1973.
Vidyayugayata Budusamaya, Ratnavalie, 1974.
Buddha: Jivani aur Darsan, Sasta Sahitya Mahdal (New Delhi), 1981.
Buddha Margaya, Gunasema & Co., 1985.

Also contributor to *Buddhist Studies in Honour of I. B. Hornor,* 1974, and *Studies in Pali and Buddhism: A Memorial Volume in Honour of Jagdish Kashyap,* 1979. Contributor to learned journals. Co-editor of *Buddhist Quarterly* and *Mahabodhi.*

WORK IN PROGRESS: The Way to Enlightenment, an English translation of *Bodhicaryavatara; Abhidhammatthasangaha,* an English translation and critical edition; *Vibhavinitika,* an English translation and critical edition; *Pali Literature of Indo-China;* an English translation of *The Namarupa-samasa.*

SIDELIGHTS: Hammalawa Saddhatissa's life has been devoted to establishing Theravada centers throughout Europe and the rest of the Western world. He is engaged in translating Sanskrit and Pali works into English, and is also proficient in Sinhalese, Sanskrit, Hindi, and Pali.

BIOGRAPHICAL/CRITICAL SOURCES:

BOOKS

Buddhist Studies in Honour of Hammalawa Saddhatissa, University of Sri Jayewardenpura, 1984.

PERIODICALS

Colombo Sunday Observer, December 23, 1979.

St. JOHN, Philip
  See del REY, Lester

*   *   *

SALMONSON, R(oland) F(rank)   1922-

PERSONAL: First syllable of surname rhymes with "call"; born August 12, 1922, in Lake Norden, S.D.; son of Frank Oscar (a pharmacist) and Laura (Thompson) Salmonson; married Josephine Kurz, August 16, 1946; children: Linda Lou (Mrs. Ralph V. Guthrie), Sherry Lynn, Judy Kay, Lee Frank. *Education:* University of Minnesota, B.B.A., 1948, M.B.A., 1949; University of Michigan, Ph.D. 1956. *Religion:* Protestant.

ADDRESSES: Home—5144 Park Lake Rd., East Lansing, Mich. 48823.

CAREER: University of Michigan, Ann Arbor, instructor in business, 1949-55; Michigan State University, East Lansing, instructor, 1955-56, assistant professor, 1956-59, associate professor, 1959-63, professor of accounting, 1963-82. Educational consultant, Touche, Ross, Bailey & Smart, 1960; faculty resident, Arthur Andersen & Co. (certified public accountants), 1962-63. *Military service:* U.S. Navy, 1943-46.

MEMBER: American Institute of Certified Public Accountants, American Accounting Association (vice-president, 1972-73), Michigan Association of Certified Public Accountants, Beta Gamma Sigma, Beta Alpha Psi.

AWARDS, HONORS: Elijah Watt Sells Gold Medal, 1962.

WRITINGS:

(With J. D. Edwards) *Four Accounting Pioneers,* Michigan State University Press, 1961.
(With Edwards and R. H. Hermanson) *Financial and Management Accounting: A Programmed Text,* Irwin, 1965.
(Member of editorial committee) *A Statement of Basic Accounting Theory,* American Accounting Association, 1966.
Basic Financial Accounting Theory, Wadsworth, 1969.
(With Edwards and Hermanson) *Accounting: A Programmed Text,* two volumes, Irwin, 1967, 4th edition of Volume I published as *Financial Accounting: A Programmed Text,* 1978, 4th edition of Volume II published as *Managerial Accounting: A Programmed Text,* 1978.
(With Edwards and Hermanson) *A Survey of Basic Accounting,* Irwin, 1973, 4th edition, 1985.
(With Edwards and Hermanson) *Programmed Learning Aid for the Basic Accounting Cycle,* Learning Systems, 1975.
(With Edwards and Hermanson) *Accounting Principles,* Business Publications, 1980, revised edition, 1983.
(With Edwards, Hermanson, and Kensicki) *How Accounting Works: A Guide to the Perplexed,* Dow Jones-Irwin, 1983.

Contributor to business periodicals.

SIDELIGHTS: Basic Financial Accounting Theory has been translated into Japanese.

AVOCATIONAL INTERESTS: Golf and bowling.

*   *   *

SAMELSON, William   1928-

PERSONAL: Born September 21, 1928, in Sosnowiec, Poland;

son of Harry and Balbina (Stibel) Samelson; married Rosa Salinas (a ballet dancer), August 22, 1954; children: James, Regina Faye, Henry, Morris. *Education:* University of Heidelberg, B.S., 1948; Western Reserve University (now Case Western Reserve University), B.A., 1950; Kent State University, M.A., 1954; University of Illinois, additional study, 1954-55; University of Texas, Ph.D., 1960.

ADDRESSES: Office—San Antonio College, 1300 San Pedro Ave., San Antonio, Tex. 78284.

CAREER: San Antonio College, San Antonio, Tex., professor of foreign languages, 1956—, Piper Professor, 1982—. *Military service:* U.S. Army, 1951-53.

MEMBER: American Teachers Association, Modern Language Association of America, Authors Guild, Authors League of America.

WRITINGS:

Gerhart Herrmann Mostar: A Critical Profile, Mouton, 1966.
(Editor) *Der Sinn des Lesens* (anthology), Odyssey, 1968.
All Lie in Wait (novel), Prentice-Hall, 1969.
The Sephardi Heritage: Romances and Songs of The Sephardim (monograph), Valentine, Mitchell, 1972.
English as a Second Langue (textbook), Reston, *Phase One: Let's Converse,* 1973, 2nd edition, 1980, *Phase Two: Let's Read,* 1974, 2nd edition, 1982, *Phase Three: Let's Write,* 1975, 2nd edition, 1982, *Phase Four: Let's Continue,* 1979, *Phase Zero Plus,* 1981.

Contributor of short stories to magazines, including a series in *Jewish Forum.*

WORK IN PROGRESS: The Blessing, a novel.

SIDELIGHTS: William Samelson explained to *CA* that his writing has been motivated for the most part by World War II experiences (*All Lie in Wait* is a war book). He speaks German, French, Yiddish, Spanish, Russian, Polish, and Hebrew.

AVOCATIONAL INTERESTS: Playing tennis, running several miles every day.

BIOGRAPHICAL/CRITICAL SOURCES:

PERIODICALS

Reconstructionist, May 23, 1969.

*   *   *

SAMUEL, Alan E(douard)   1932-

PERSONAL: Born July 24, 1932, in Queens, N.Y.; son of Edgar Aaron and Hortense (Kesner) Samuel; married Deborah Hobson, June 13, 1964 (divorced, 1973); married Valerie Stevens, February 15, 1975; children: (first marriage) Deborah Joan, Jean Carol, Katharine Ann, Elizabeth Rose, Alexandra Whitney; (second marriage) Fraser, Roderick John, Kristen Ellen Jessica, Marion Catherine. *Education:* Hamilton College, B.A., 1953; Yale University, M.A., 1957, Ph.D., 1959.

ADDRESSES: Home—64 Alexandra Blvd., Toronto, Ontario, Canada M4R 1L9.

CAREER: Yale University, New Haven, Conn., instructor, 1959-63, assistant professor of classics, 1963-66; University of Toronto, University College, Toronto, Ontario, associate professor, 1966-67, professor of ancient history, 1967—. President of Samuel Stevens & Co. *Military service:* U.S. Naval Reserve, 1953-56; became lieutenant.

MEMBER: Comite Internationale de Papyrologie, American Philological Association (former director), Archaeological Institute of America, American Society of Papyrologists (secretary-treasurer, 1968; president, 1973).

AWARDS, HONORS: Guggenheim fellow, 1983-84.

WRITINGS:

Ptolemaic Chronology, Beck (Munich), 1962.
Alexander's Royal Journals, Historia, 1965.
The Mycenaeans in History, Prentice-Hall, 1966.
(With John F. Oates and C. Bradford Welles) *Yale Papyri in the Beinecke Rare Book and Manuscript Library,* American Society of Papyrologists, 1967.
(With W. Keith Hastings) *Death and Taxes: Ostraka in the Royal Ontario Museum,* A. M. Hakkert, 1971.
Greek and Roman Chronology: Calendars and Years in Classical Antiquity, Beck, 1972.
(With R. S. Bagnall) *Ostraka in the Royal Ontario Museum II,* Samuel Stevens, 1976.
Treasures of Canada, Samuel Stevens, 1980.
From Athens to Alexandria: Hellenism and Social Goals in Ptolemaic Egypt, Studia Helenistica, Louvain, 1983.

Contributor of articles to professional journals. Editor of *Bulletin of American Society of Papyrologists.*

*   *   *

SANDOZ, Mari(e Susette)   1896-1966
(Mari Macumber)

PERSONAL: Born May 11, 1896, in Sheridan County, Neb.; died March 10, 1966; daughter of Jules Ami and Mary Elizabeth (Fehr) Sandoz; married Wray Macumber (a rancher), 1914 (divorced, 1919). *Education:* Attended business college for nine months and University of Nebraska, 1922-31.

ADDRESSES: Home—New York, N.Y.

CAREER: Held various positions, including country school teacher in Nebraska for five years, assistant in a drug laboratory, a university English reader, and proofreader and researcher on Sioux Indians for the Nebraska State Historical Society; *The School Executive,* Lincoln, Neb., associate editor, 1927-29; *Star and Nebraska State Journal,* Lincoln, proofreader, 1929-34; Nebraska State Historical Society, Lincoln, director of research and associate editor of *Nebraska History* magazine, 1934-35; writer, teacher, lecturer, Lincoln, 1935-40, Denver, Colo., 1940-43, New York, N.Y., 1943-66. Staff leader for writers' conferences and director of short courses in writing. Cartographer.

MEMBER: Authors Guild, Authors League of America, Nebraska State Historical Society.

AWARDS, HONORS: Atlantic Monthly Press, nonfiction award, 1935, for *Old Jules;* Litt.D., University of Nebraska, 1950; award for distinguished service, Native Sons and Daughters of Nebraska, 1954; National Achievement Award of The Westerners, Chicago Corral, 1955; Headliner Award, Theta Sigma Phi, 1957; The Buffalo of the New York Posse, The Westerners, 1959, for *The Cattlemen;* Oppie Award, 1962, for *These Were the Sioux,* and 1964, for *The Beaver Men;* Western Heritage Award, 1962, for article on last frontier published in *American Heritage; The Story Catcher* was co-winner of Spur Award, 1963; Levi Straus Award for best novel on the west, 1963, for *The Story Catcher.*

WRITINGS:

These Were the Sioux (nonfiction), Hastings House, 1961.
Love Song to the Plains (nonfiction), Harper, 1961.
(Author of introduction) George Bird Grinnell, *The Cheyenne Indians: Their History and Ways,* Cooper Square, 1962.
The Battle of the Little Bighorn, Lippincott, 1966.
(Author of introduction) Amos Bad Heart Bull and Helen Blish, *A Pictographic History of the Oglala Sioux,* University of Nebraska Press, 1967.

"GREAT PLAINS" SERIES; ALL NONFICTION

Old Jules (biography; Book-of-the-Month Club selection), Atlantic, 1935, revised edition, Hastings House, 1975.
Crazy Horse: The Strange Man of the Oglalas (biography), Knopf, 1942, reprinted, Hastings House, 1975.
Cheyenne Autumn, McGraw, 1953, reprinted, Avon, 1975.
The Buffalo Hunters: The Story of the Hide Men (Outdoor Life Book Club selection), Hastings House, 1954, published in England as *The Buffalo Hunters: The Slaughter of the Great Buffalo Herds,* Eyre & Spottiswoode, 1960, reprinted, University of Nebraska Press, 1978.
The Cattlemen: From the Rio Grande across the Far Marias, Hastings House, 1958, reprinted, University of Nebraska Press, 1978.
The Beaver Men: Spearheads of Empire, Hastings House, 1964.

FICTION

Slogum House (novel), Atlantic, 1937.
Capital City (novel), Atlantic, 1939.
The Tom-Walker (novel), Dial, 1947.
Winter Thunder (novella), Westminster, 1954.
Miss Morissa: Doctor of the Gold Trail (novel), McGraw, 1955, reprinted, Hastings House, 1975.
The Horsecatcher (novella), Westminster, 1957.
Son of the Gamblin' Man: The Youth of an Artist (novel), C. N. Potter, 1960, reprinted, University of Nebraska Press, 1976.
Christmas of the Phonograph Records (novel), University of Nebraska Press, 1966.
The Story Catcher (novella), Westminster, 1973.

COLLECTIONS

Hostiles and Friendlies: Selected Short Writings of Mari Sandoz, University of Nebraska Press, 1959, reprinted, 1975.
"Old Jules" Country: A Selection from "Old Jules" and Thirty Years of Writing since the Book Was Published, Hastings House, 1965.
Sandhill Sundays and Other Recollections, University of Nebraska Press, 1970.

OTHER

Contributor of more than thirty short stories and articles to anthologies and magazines, including *Scribner's, Saturday Evening Post, Blue Book,* and *Prairie Schooner.*

Many of Sandoz's books have been published in Swiss and German editions. *Old Jules* was serialized and issued in half a dozen editions in Scandinavian countries. The author's correspondence and working papers are collected at the University of Nebraska Archives, along with her maps, genealogies, manuscripts, and library. The Mamie Meredith Collection of the Nebraska State Historical Society also has material by and about Mari Sandoz, her father, and the Sandoz family.

SIDELIGHTS: Mari Sandoz's writings, which explored nearly every aspect of life in the old west, were based on extensive research and personal knowledge. Born in the Sand Hills cattle country of northwest Nebraska, Sandoz was nine before she began attending school, and she knew the difficult circumstances of pioneer life from first-hand experience. When Sandoz was about fourteen, she became snowblind and later lost the use of one eye after she and her brother spent a day digging their cattle out of a blizzard snowdrift. Of her childhood responsibilities, Sandoz once told the *New York Times* that by the time she was ten she "could bake up a 49-pound-sack of flour, but would let the bread sour and the baby cry if there was anything to read."

After Sandoz completed the eighth grade, she passed the teacher's examination and skipped high school to teach in the countryside. She later entered the University of Nebraska and began writing. Her first book was *Old Jules*, a biography of her father, a foul-tempered Swiss immigrant who came from the east in the 1880s to settle in the high plains of the trans-Missouri area after quarreling with his own father. In his attempts to tame the land, Sandoz's father became a leading figure in the region. Helen Stauffer explained in the *Dictionary of Literary Biography* that *Old Jules* is not only a biography of Sandoz's father, but also a chronicle of the author's home community and the surrounding area.

As *New Republic* reviewer B. E. Bettinger characterized the book upon publication, it is "a wise and memorable saga of American pioneering, recited with the expansive Western gesture, bitter and fragrant as soil and prairie growth," while K. C. Kaufman in the *Christian Science Monitor* considered *Old Jules* to be "a powerful, distinctively American history of a man, a region and an epoch." A *Boston Transcript* writer reported that "as a biography of [Sandoz's] father it has great success," commenting that the character of Jules "is clearly and warmly defined." And although a *Books* writer indicated that "the old man's virtues—his toughness, perseverance and unexpected intellectual interests—didn't seem to us to compensate for his insensitiveness, even brutality, toward his family and neighbors," a critic in *Forum* pointed out that "*Old Jules* is the kind of flamboyant character whom most novelists would give their eyeteeth to create." The biography is "a vigorous, devastating, and often brutal chronicle which nevertheless achieves a certain grandeur," the *Forum* reviewer concluded.

In 1935, after fourteen rejections and revisions, *Old Jules* won the Atlantic Nonfiction Prize of $5,000. Despite her father's disapproval of the writing profession, "Sandoz's life from then on was dedicated to writing and research," Stauffer noted. Although many of the events in *Old Jules* happened during Sandoz's lifetime, Stauffer pointed out that "she spent years researching published and private memoirs, using local and state historical society collections, listening to the old storytellers in her region, and interviewing those involved" to create the book. Sandoz then used the narrative technique of fiction to tell the story. As Stauffer observed, "This combination of meticulous historical research and narrative style became the pattern for her writing."

Throughout the rest of Sandoz's writing career, her primary goals "were to preserve history and present it accurately and to bring attention to the western frontier," said Stauffer. All of her twenty-one books, along with her articles and short stories, deal with the trans-Missouri region; Sandoz is best known for her six-book Great Plains series (also sometimes referred to as the Trans-Missouri series), a nonfiction study of

man on the plains from the Stone Age to the present. Included in the series are the biographies *Old Jules* and *Crazy Horse: Strange Man of the Oglalas*, as well as *Cheyenne Autumn*, which are widely held to be Sandoz's finest works.

Both *Cheyenne Autumn* and *Crazy Horse*, the biography of the Sioux war chief and mystic, are told from the Indian point of view. Although not all reviewers found Sandoz's Indian sympathies appealing, particularly in her attempts to incorporate Indian speech patterns into the nonfictional narrative, most thought the books were well written. Discussing *Crazy Horse* in the *New Yorker*, Clifton Fadiman stated that "unquestionably, her book, the product of studious labor, will rank among the important records of the history of the American Indian," while David Lowe in the *Prairie Schooner* considered *Crazy Horse* probably Sandoz's "finest" book. In his words, "no one has written more movingly of the hopelessness of the Indian after he had seen every treaty broken, the buffalo wantonly slaughtered, the tribes decimated by the white man's disease" than Mari Sandoz in *Crazy Horse*.

Cheyenne Autumn relates the story of the 1878 fall flight of a small band of Cheyenne Indians from Indian Territory in Oklahoma, where they had been sent by the American army, to their ancestral home in Montana. Sandoz gathered some of the information for the book from the personal accounts of Indians who had participated in the journey as well as from traditional research sources. And as August Derleth commented in the *Chicago Sunday Tribune*, Sandoz did more than tell the story in *Cheyenne Autumn*: "With her customary skill, she manages to recreate a man, a scene, an event, a page from history, so that through her prose [the tale] takes on the stature of an American epic." J. F. Dobie reported in the *New York Herald Tribune Book Review* that Sandoz's "story of the flight is as poignant in realism as her biography of her father but in the eighteen years between 'Old Jules' and 'Cheyenne Autumn' her sympathy for the tears that are in human affairs have deepened, and her art now gives the strength, vividness and unity to complexity that it began by giving to simplicity."

Sandoz also produced three novellas, *Winter Thunder, The Horsecatcher,* and *The Story Catcher,* although Stauffer remarked that "Sandoz's fiction is not as a rule as well written as her nonfiction." Sandoz was able to use fictional techniques in her historical work, but Stauffer said that she was less successful with true fiction, since her novels are often allegorical or intended to instruct and are frequently cluttered with historical digressions. "Because of her tendency toward instruction," Scott L. Greenwell indicated in *Western American Literature*, "she found much of American fiction—particularly romantic Western novels—thin, 'without anything of the push and throb of life, totally inconsequential.'" Greenwell reports that Sandoz "liked bone and muscle in literature," blaming "what she considered the poor quality of domestic fiction on the American writers' tendency to conform to the commercial market" and waging her own continuing battle to write as she felt necessary.

Sandoz expressed her political beliefs through some of her novels, particularly *Capital City*, an unflattering portrait of a state capital around election time, and *Slogum House*. In Stauffer's opinion, the publication of *Capital City* may have been a factor in Sandoz's decision to move from Lincoln to Denver in 1940, since many of the Nebraska capital's residents became hostile towards the author after the book was circulated, perhaps finding the subject matter too familiar for comfort. *Slogum House*, written directly following the publication of *Old Jules*, is generally regarded to be the better novel.

In contrast to the biography of Sandoz's father, *Slogum House* portrays the darker side of the pioneer ethic. The book's protagonist, Gulla Slogum, was described by Stauffer as a "ruthless woman whose will to power leads her to use her daughters as prostitutes in her roadhouse to extend her influence over others." Gulla, maintained Margaret Wallace in the *New York Times Book Review*, is "the rugged individualist—the very archetype of the unscrupulous builders of empire to whom the West offered, in the past century, such golden opportunity." Although, according to Greenwell the book was not overwhelmingly well-received, particularly in Nebraska where it was banned from several libraries, Wallace claimed that *Slogum House* was "a remarkably sweeping novel and ironic picture of America's last frontier during a period of half a century." Sandoz also "intended the novel as an allegorical study of a nation exerting its will to power by using force to overcome opposition," Stauffer said, indicating that Sandoz wrote the book in reaction to some of Hitler's ideas, fearing that some Americans might find them attractive.

Although Sandoz frequently used her work to convey opinion, her nonfiction, in particular, also reflects "her awareness of the power and beauty of the natural world" and man's relationship to that world, Stauffer reported. "As is true with the writings of many Western writers, Sandoz's work is closely tied to nature. She had an intimate knowledge of the land she grew up in, and all her works are based on her close association with the natural world." Some of what Stauffer called Sandoz's "finest, most lyrical" writing can be found in *Love Song to the Plains*, the Nebraska volume for Harper and Row's series on the states. "Although she sometimes uses wry humor or satire she expresses her great affection for Nebraska and the Great Plains in language at times poetic," noted Stauffer. "Some of the same information, of necessity, is repeated from earlier works, but her storytelling [in her use of anecdotal information] is never better."

One of Sandoz's final works of nonfiction, *The Battle of the Little Bighorn*, investigates the circumstances of Custer's last stand. In 1966, A. M. Josephy commented in the *New York Times Book Review* that the book was "probably the best account of the battle ever written." The book "is written more from the white man's point of view than was the case in 'Crazy Horse,'" Josephy pointed out, but he said that "there is enough knowledgeable interrelation of the Indian's outlook and actions to give proper understanding to all that was transpiring." According to Stauffer, *The Battle of the Little Bighorn* "drew the ire of those who objected to the author's claims that Custer's actions were based on his White House aspirations; this motive had not been suggested in many previous accounts. Other reviewers praised her ability to fit the enormous jigsaw puzzle of the day's events into recognizable order; several considered this the apogee of her works."

MEDIA ADAPTATIONS: Cheyenne Autumn was adapted into a motion picture that was released by Warner Brothers in December, 1964.

AVOCATIONAL INTERESTS: Young writers, human justice, justice for the American Indian, motion pictures, television, and satirical drama.

BIOGRAPHICAL/CRITICAL SOURCES:

BOOKS

Contemporary Literary Criticism, Volume XXVIII, Gale, 1984.
Dictionary of Literary Biography, Volume IX: *American Novelists, 1910-1945*, Gale, 1981.
Pifer, Caroline Sandoz, *Making of an Author*, Gordon Journal Press, 1972.
Sandoz, Mari, *Old Jules*, Atlantic, 1935, revised edition, Hastings House, 1975.
Sandoz, Mari, *Hostiles and Friendlies: Selected Short Writings of Mari Sandoz*, University of Nebraska Press, 1959, reprinted, 1975.
Sandoz, Mari, *These Were the Sioux*, Hastings House, 1961.
Sandoz, Mari, *"Old Jules" Country: A Selection from "Old Jules" and Thirty Years of Writing since the Book Was Published*, Hastings House, 1965.
Sandoz, Mari, *Sandhill Sundays and Other Recollections*, University of Nebraska Press, 1970.
Stauffer, Helen Winter, *Story Catcher of the Plains*, University of Nebraska Press, 1982.

PERIODICALS

America, July 16, 1966.
American West, spring, 1965.
Atlantic, January, 1943.
Atlantic Bookshelf, November, 1935.
Baltimore Bulletin of Education, May-June, 1958.
Best Sellers, July 15, 1966.
Booklist, November, 1935, January 15, 1938, December 1, 1939, January 15, 1943, January 1, 1954, January 15, 1954, September 1, 1954.
Books, November 3, 1935, November 10, 1935, November 28, 1937, December 3, 1939, November 29, 1942.
Boston Transcript, November 6, 1935, November 27, 1937.
Chicago Daily Tribune, November 2, 1935.
Chicago Sunday Tribune, November 22, 1953, August 26, 1954, August 29, 1954, May 12, 1957, October 22, 1961, December 17, 1961.
Christian Science Monitor, October 30, 1935, August 26, 1954, May 9, 1957, December 13, 1961.
Nation, December 16, 1939, December 5, 1953.
New Republic, December 25, 1935, December 13, 1939.
New Yorker, December 2, 1939, December 5, 1942.
New York Herald Tribune, October 31, 1935.
New York Herald Tribune Book Review, December 13, 1953, September 5, 1954, May 12, 1957.
New York Herald Tribune Books, November 28, 1937, November 29, 1942, November 12, 1961.
New York Times, November 10, 1935, November 28, 1937, December 3, 1939, December 20, 1942, November 22, 1953, August 22, 1954, June 2, 1957.
New York Times Book Review, November 28, 1937, November 22, 1953, August 22, 1954, November 20, 1955, July 3, 1966.
Prairie Schooner, spring, 1968, summer, 1971.
San Francisco Chronicle, August 29, 1954, March 4, 1962.
Saturday Review, December 12, 1953, August 21, 1954, June 28, 1958, December 16, 1961.
Saturday Review of Literature, November 2, 1935, November 27, 1937, December 2, 1939, January 2, 1943.
Springfield Republican, November 10, 1935, December 19, 1937, December 14, 1942, September 26, 1954.
Time, November 29, 1937, December 11, 1939.
Western American Literature, summer, 1977.

Wisconsin Library Bulletin, October, 1954, July, 1957.
Yale Review, December, 1935, winter, 1936.

OBITUARIES:

PERIODICALS

Antiquarian Bookman, April 11, 1966.
Books Abroad, spring, 1967.
New York Times, March 11, 1966.
Publishers Weekly, March 21, 1966.†

—*Sketch by Candace Cloutier*

*   *   *

SARTORI, Giovanni   1924-

PERSONAL: Born May 13, 1924, in Florence, Italy; son of Dante and Emilia (Quentin) Sartori. *Education:* University of Florence, doctor in political and social sciences, 1946.

ADDRESSES: Home—285 Central Park W., New York, N.Y. 10024. *Office*—1430 International Affairs Bldg., Columbia University, New York, N.Y. 10027.

CAREER: University of Florence, Florence, Italy, associate professor of modern philosophy, 1950-57, associate professor of political science, 1957-65, professor of sociology, 1962-65, professor of political science, 1965-76, dean of Faculty of Political Science, 1969-71; Stanford University, Stanford, Calif., professor of political science, 1976-79; Columbia University, New York, N.Y., Albert Schweitzer Professor in the Humanities, 1979—.

MEMBER: American Academy of Arts and Sciences.

WRITINGS:

Democrazia e Definizioni, Il Mulino, 1957, 6th edition, 1985, translation by the author published as *Democratic Theory,* Wayne State University Press, 1962, new edition, Praeger, 1965.
A Teoria da Representacao no Estado Representativo Moderno, Universidade de Minas Gerais, 1962.
Il Parlamento Italiano, 1946-1963, Edizioni Scientifiche Italiane, 1963.
Stato e Politica nel Pensiero di B. Croce, Moltano, 1966.
Parties and Party Systems, Cambridge University Press, 1976.
La Politica, SugarCo, 1979.
Teoria del Partiti e Caso Italiano, SugarCo, 1982.
(Editor and co-author) *Social Science Concepts: A Systematic Analysis,* Sage Publications, 1984.
The Theory of Democracy Revisited, Chatham House, 1985.

Also contributor to books and to *International Encyclopedia of the Social Sciences.* Contributor to journals. Managing editor, *Rivista Italiana di Scienza Politica,* 1971—.

*   *   *

SATTERFIELD, Charles
See del REY, Lester

*   *   *

SAVITT, Sam

PERSONAL: Born March 22, in Wilkes-Barre, Pa.; son of Hyman (a salesman) and Rose (Eskowitz) Savitt; married Bette Orkin, March 28, 1946; children: Dara Vickery, Roger Scott.

Education: Pratt Institute, graduate, 1941; attended Art Students League, 1950-51.

ADDRESSES: Home—One-Horse Farm, North Salem, N.Y. 10560.

CAREER: Free-lance writer and illustrator. Official artist for United States equestrian team, 1956—. Artwork represented in permanent collection at Old Time Galleries, San Diego, Calif.; artwork featured in one-man shows at Aqueduct Art Gallery, Jamaica, N.Y., 1966, Concourse Gallery, Boston, Mass., 1969, Piccolo Mondo, Palm Beach, Fla., 1974, and International Sports Core, Oak Brook, Ill., and in several group exhibitions. Designer of "Sam Savitt Horse Charts." *Military service:* U.S. Army, 1942-46; served in China-Burma-India Theater; became first lieutenant.

MEMBER: American Academy of Equine Art (director of painting), Society of Animal Artists, Society of Illustrators, Authors Guild, Authors League of America, Graphic Artists Guild.

AWARDS, HONORS: Boys' Clubs of America junior book award, 1958, for *Midnight, Champion Bucking Horse.*

WRITINGS:

Step-a-Bit, Dutton, 1956.
(Self-illustrated) *Midnight, Champion Bucking Horse,* Dutton, 1958.
There Was a Horse, Dial, 1960.
Around the World with Horses, Dial, 1962.
(Self-illustrated) *Rodeo: Cowboys, Bulls, and Broncos,* Doubleday, 1963.
Sam Savitt Guide to Horses, Black Horse Press, 1963.
(Self-illustrated) *Vicki and the Black Horse,* Doubleday, 1964.
(Self-illustrated) *Day at the LBJ Ranch,* Random House, 1965.
(Self-illustrated) *America's Horses,* Doubleday, 1966.
Equestrian Olympic Sketchbook, A. S. Barnes, 1968.
(Self-illustrated) *Sam Savitt's True Horse Stories,* Dodd, 1971.
(Self-illustrated) *Wild Horse Running* (Junior Literary Guild selection), Dodd, 1973.
(With Suzanne Wilding) *Ups and Downs,* St. Martin's, 1973.
(With Herb Marlin) *How to Take Care of Your Horse until the Vet Comes,* Dodd, 1975.
(Self-illustrated) *Vicki and the Brown Mare,* Dodd, 1976.
(With William Steinkraus) *Great Horses of the United States Equestrian Team,* Dodd, 1977.
The Dingle Ridge Fox and Other Stories, Dodd, 1978.
Draw Horses with Sam Savitt, Viking, 1981.
(Self-illustrated) *One Horse, One Hundred Miles, One Day: The Story of the Tevis Cup Endurance Ride,* Dodd, 1981.
(Self-illustrated) *A Horse to Remember,* Viking, 1984.

ILLUSTRATOR

Bold Passage, Simon & Schuster, 1950.
Learning to Ride and Hunt, Doubleday, 1950.
Tiger Roan, Pocket Books, 1950.
Trailing Trouble, Holiday House, 1952.
Desert Dog, Holiday House, 1956.
Wildlife Cameraman, Holiday House, 1957.
Horsemanship, A. S. Barnes, 1958.
Black Beauty, Scholastic Book Services, 1958.
Gimmery, Dodd, 1958.
Wild Horse Tamer, Scholastic Book Services, 1958.
Witch's Colt, Dodd, 1958.
Dark Colt, Light Filly, Scholastic Book Services, 1959.
Fury, F. Watts, 1959.

Long Trail Drive, Scholastic Book Services, 1959.
Mountain Pony, Scholastic Book Services, 1959.
Shasta and Gimmery, Dodd, 1959.
A Saddlebag of Tales, Dodd, 1959.
Blizzard Rescue, F. Watts, 1959.
Born to Race, St. Martin's, 1959.
Challenger, Coward, 1959.
Pets at the White House, Dutton, 1959.
The Torch Bearer, F. Watts, 1959.
Up and Away, Harcourt, 1960.
The Top Hand of Lone Tree Ranch, Crowell, 1960.
Johnny's Island Ark, F. Watts, 1960.
Diving Horse, Coward, 1960.
Fury and the Mustangs, Holt, 1960.
Horse in Her Heart, Coward, 1960.
Horseback Riding, Lippincott, 1960.
Daughter of the Silver Brumby, Dutton, 1960.
Gun Law at Laramie, Pocket Books, 1960.
Spook the Mustang, Lippincott, 1960.
Wild Horses of Tuscanny, F. Watts, 1960.
Alcatraz the Wild Stallion, Pocket Books, 1961.
Animal Anthology, Scholastic Book Services, 1961.
Training Your Dog, Doubleday, 1961.
White Fang, Scholastic Book Services, 1961.
Little Smoke, Coward, 1961.
Loco the Bronc, Coward, 1961.
The Snow Filly, Dutton, 1961.
Thudding Hoofs, St. Martin's, 1961.
Wilderness Renegade, F. Watts, 1962.
The Horse Trap, Coward, 1962.
Teddy Koala, Dodd, 1962.
Albert P. Terhune, *Lad, a Dog,* Dutton, 1962.
Fawn in the Forest, Dodd, 1962.
Dream Pony for Robin, St. Martin's, 1962.
Dinny and the Dreamdust, Doubleday, 1962.
Buffalo Bill, Garrard, 1962.
American Girl Book of Horse Stories, Random House, 1963.
Boy's Life Book of Horse Stories, Random House, 1963.
Care and Training of Dogs, Random House, 1963.
Forever the Wild Mare, Dodd, 1963.
Horse of Your Own, Doubleday, 1963.
No Love for Schnitzle, St. Martin's, 1963.
Patrick Visits the Zoo, Dodd, 1963.
Show Ring Rouge, Coward, 1963.
Wild Heart, Doubleday, 1963.
Two Dogs and a Horse, Dodd, 1964.
Old Quarry Fox Hunt, Washburn, 1964.
Horse in the House, Coward, 1964.
P. C. Braun, editor, *Big Book of Favorite Horse Stories,* Platt, 1965.
Big Jump for Robin, St. Martin's, 1965.
Ghost Hound of Thunder Valley, Dodd, 1965.
Redhead and the Roan, Van Nostrand, 1965.
Christy Finds a Rider, Norton, 1965.
Star Bright, Norton, 1965.
Encyclopedia of Horses, Crowell, 1966.
Star Lost, Norton, 1966.
If You Want a Horse, Coward, 1966.
James Arthur Kjelgaard, *Dave and His Dog Mulligan,* Dodd, 1966.
Star, the Sea Horse, Norton, 1968.
George McMillan, *Golden Book of Horses,* Golden Press, 1968.
The Pony That Didn't Grow, Washburn, 1968.
The Lord Mayor's Horse Show, Doubleday, 1969.
Great Stories for Young Readers, Reader's Digest Press, 1969.

Harlequin Horse, Van Nostrand, 1969.
Horses, Golden Press, 1969.
Bruce Grant, *Ride, Gaucho,* World Publishing, 1969.
Margaret Cabell Self, *Sky Rocket: The Story of a Little Bay Horse,* Dodd, 1970.
Horses, Horses, Horses, Van Nostrand, 1970.
Elementary Dressage, A. S. Barnes, 1970.
Horseman's Almanac, Agway, 1971.
Bryan O'Donoghue, *Wild Animal Rescue,* Dodd, 1971.
Hundred Horse Farm, St. Martin's, 1972.
Horses in Action, St. Martin's, 1972.
Kurt Unkelbach, *How to Bring up Your Pet Dog,* Dodd, 1973.
Gift of Gold, Dodd, 1973.
Summer Pony, Macmillan, 1973.
The Art of Painting Horses, Grumbacher Library, 1973.
A Boy and a Pig, but Mostly Horses, Dodd, 1974.
Gallant Grey Trotter, Dodd, 1974.
Grand Prix Jumping, Aberdeen Press, 1974.
Backyard Pony, F. Watts, 1975.
Horses: A First Book, F. Watts, 1975.
Riding Teacher's Manual, Doubleday, 1975.
Horse Tales, St. Martin's, 1976.
The Tale of the Horse, Walter Field, 1976.
Springfellow, Windmill Books, 1977.
Anne Colver, *Pluto: Brave Lipizzaner Stallion,* Garrard, 1978.
Lee B. Hopkins, editor, *My Mane Catches the Wind: Poems about Horses,* Harcourt, 1979.
Run Hiboy Run, Garrard, 1980.
The Horses of San Simeon, Morrow, 1985.

OTHER

Contributor of "Draw Horses with Sam Savitt" series of articles to *Western Horseman,* 1966; contributor of articles to magazines, including *Equus* and *Western Horseman.*

WORK IN PROGRESS: A book of short stories; a book about a thoroughbred farm.

SIDELIGHTS: Sam Savitt told *CA:* "I began my career as an illustrator in the magazine and book field. I am a creative person and I found that painting pictures did not completely satisfy this creative urge. I turned to writing as an extension of what I felt. As an artist I think in pictures, which carries over into my writing. Sometimes I find it easier to 'say dog than to draw dog' and I write to take a break from the problems of color, tone, value and getting a three-dimensional effect on a flat surface.

"I enjoy talking to school groups. I encourage questions and often try out stories and get a lot of feedback from these audiences. One of my main interests is horses. I have schooled and trained them and know a great deal about them. Through this close association I combine experiences with an active imagination to tell a story. When I write I never start a story unless I know how it is going to end. This gives me direction and helps me stay on course."

AVOCATIONAL INTERESTS: Sculpture, fox hunting with golden bridge hounds, schooling horses, swimming, hiking.

BIOGRAPHICAL/CRITICAL SOURCES:

PERIODICALS

Eastern Horse World, July, 1984.
Horse Play, April, 1974.
Lead Line (Bedford, N.Y.), March, 1978.
New York Times, November 11, 1984.
Palm Beach Daily News, February 7, 1974.

Patent Trader (Mt. Kisco, N.Y.), November 23, 1984.
Polo Magazine, Volume XXVI, number 7, 1960.
Reporter Dispatch (White Plains, N.Y.), April 1, 1974.
Sun (Baltimore, Md.), July 17, 1962.
Sunday Independence (Wilkes-Barre, Pa.), January 17, 1960.
Sun Sentinel (Pompano Beach, Fla.), February 14, 1974.

*   *   *

SCHECHNER, Richard   1934-

PERSONAL: Born August 23, 1934, in Newark, N.J.; son of
Sheridan and Selma (Schwarz) Schechner; children: Samuel
MacIntosh. *Education:* Cornell University, B.A., 1956; graduate study at Johns Hopkins University, 1956-57; University
of Iowa, M.A., 1958; Tulane University, Ph.D., 1962.

ADDRESSES: Office—Department of Performance Studies,
Tisch School of the Arts, New York University, New York,
N.Y. 10003.

CAREER: Tulane University, New Orleans, La., assistant professor, 1962-65, associate professor of drama, 1965-67; New
York University, New York, N.Y., professor of drama, 1967-
81, professor of performance studies, 1981—. Co-artistic director, East End Players, Provincetown, Mass., 1958 and 1961;
co-producing director, Free Southern Theater, 1964-65; co-
director, New Orleans Group, 1965-67; founder and executive
artistic director, The Performance Group, 1967-80.

Director with The Performance Group of plays "Commune,"
1970-72, "The Tooth of Crime," 1972-74, "Mother Courage
and Her Childen," 1973-76, "The Marilyn Project," 1975-
76, "Oedipus," 1977, "Cops," 1978-79, and "The Balcony," 1979-80; also director of "The Red Snake," 1981,
and "Cherry Ka Baghicha," 1983. Adviser to International
Theatre Institute, 1975-77; member of board of directors of
Theatre Communications Group, 1977-78. *Military service:*
U.S. Army, 1958-60.

MEMBER: American Theater Association, American Association for the Advancement of Science, American Anthropological Association.

AWARDS, HONORS: Rockefeller third fellow, 1971-72; Guggenheim fellow, 1976; Fulbright senior fellow, 1976, fellow,
1983; Indo-American fellow, 1978; grant from Social Science
Research Council, 1982; Smithsonian research award, 1983.

WRITINGS:

Public Domain, Bobbs-Merrill, 1968.
(Editor with Gilbert Moses and Tom C. Dent) *Free Southern
    Theater,* Bobbs-Merrill, 1969.
Environmental Theater, Hawthorn, 1973.
(With Brooks McNamara and Jerry Rojo) *Theatres, Spaces
    and Environments: Eighteen Projects,* Drama Book Spe-
    cialists, 1975.
Essays on Performance Theory, 1970-1976, Drama Book Spe-
    cialists, 1976.
(Editor with Mady Schuman) *Ritual, Play, and Performance:
    Readings in the Social Sciences—Theatre,* Seabury, 1976.
The End of Humanism, Performing Arts Journal, 1982.
Performative Circumstances, South Asia Books, 1983.

PLAYS

"Blessing of the Fleet," first produced in Provincetown, Mass.,
    by East End Players, 1958.
"Briseis and the Sergeant," first produced in New Orleans at
    Tulane University, 1962.

(Editor and director) *Dionysus in 69* (based on group impro-
    visation, composition by The Performance Group, and
    Euripides's "Bacchae"; first produced in New York City
    by The Performance Group, 1968), Farrar, Straus, 1970.
(Editor and director) *Makbeth* (first produced in New York
    City by The Performance Group, 1969), I. E. Clark, 1978.

Also author and director of "Richard's Lear," 1981, and "The
Prometheus Project," 1985.

OTHER

Author of *Performative Possibilities,* 1984, *Between Theater
and Anthropology,* 1985, and with Willa Appel, *By Means of
Performance.* Editor with Brooks McNamara of "Performance
Studies" series, Performing Arts Journal, 1982—. Contributor
of essays, stories, and poetry to various publications; contributor to periodicals, including *Educational Theatre Journal,
Yale French Studies,* and *Salmagundi. Drama Review* (formerly *Tulane Drama Review*), editor, 1962-69, contributing
editor, 1969—; advisory editor of *Performing Arts Journal,*
1980—, and *Studies in Visual Communication,* 1983—.

*   *   *

SCHEER, Wilbert E.   1909-

PERSONAL: Born February 8, 1909, in Chicago, Ill.; son of
Christ F. (a teacher) and Clara (Jessen) Scheer; married Erna
Blumenschein, September 7, 1935 (died May, 1975); children:
Arlene (Mrs. Michael J. Tharp), Stephany I. (Mrs. Keith L.
Oestreich). *Education:* Took courses through the years at
Northwestern University, University of Illinois, University of
Chicago, and University of Michigan. *Politics:* Republican.
Religion: Lutheran.

ADDRESSES: Home—804 Austin Ave., Park Ridge, Ill. 60068.

CAREER: McKesson & Robbins, Inc., Chicago, Ill., office
manager and assistant operations manager, 1928-46; Illinois
Agricultural Association, Chicago, personnel director for association and its nineteen affiliated companies, 1946-51; Blue
Cross/Blue Shield, Chicago, director of personnel, 1951-69,
editorial and research assistant, 1969-74. Teacher in adult evening program, Central YMCA, 1956-66; member of faculty,
Northwestern University, beginning 1967. Speaker at meetings and conferences in Canada, Mexico, South America, and
throughout the United States. Member, Illinois Private Business School State Board, 1954-58. *Military service:* U.S. Army,
1943-45; served in New Guinea.

MEMBER: Administrative Management Society, American
Management Association, Mensa.

AWARDS, HONORS: Award of Merit, Research Institute of
America, 1954, 1955, 1956; Diamond Award, Administrative
Management Society, 1961.

WRITINGS:

You Can Improve Your Communications, Personnel Journal,
    1962.
(Author of introduction) *Leadership in the Office,* American
    Management Association, 1963.
(Contributor) *How to Manage Yourself,* Cities Service Co.,
    1964.
The Art of Successful Self-Expression and Communications,
    Motivation Associates, 1966.
(Editor) *The Dartnell Personnel Director's Handbook,* Dart-
    nell, 1969, revised edition, 1979.

Corporate Growth through Internal Management Development, Dartnell, 1972.

How to Develop an Effective Company Growth Plan: The Fundamentals of Corporate Long- and Short-Range Planning, Dartnell, 1975.

People Policies: Successful Personnel Management, Pluribus, 1984.

Personnel Administration Handbook, Dartnell, 1985.

Contributor of several hundred articles to management journals in the United States, Canada, Argentina, and Belgium.†

*　　*　　*

SCHEICK, William J(oseph)   1941-

PERSONAL: Born July 15, 1941, in Newark, N.J.; son of Joseph Edward (an engineer) and Irene (Corvil) Scheick; married Marion Ruth Voorhees, August 3, 1963 (divorced February 29, 1980); children: Jessica Holly, Nathan Andrew. *Education:* Montclair State College, B.A., 1963; University of Illinois, M.A., 1965, Ph.D., 1969.

ADDRESSES: Home—9901 Oak Run Dr., Austin, Tex. 78758. *Office*—Parlin Hall, University of Texas, Austin, Tex. 78712-1164.

CAREER: University of Texas at Austin, assistant professor, 1969-74, associate professor, 1974-79, professor of English, 1979—.

WRITINGS:

The Will and the Word: The Poetry of Edward Taylor, University of Georgia Press, 1974.

(Editor and author of introduction) Increase Mather, *The Life and Death of That Reverend Man of God, Mr. Richard Mather,* York Mail-Print, Inc., 1974.

The Writings of Jonathan Edwards: Theme, Motif, and Style, Texas A & M University Press, 1975.

Seventeenth-Century American Poetry, G. K. Hall, 1977.

The Slender Human Word: Emerson's Artistry in Prose, University of Tennessee Press, 1978.

The Half-Blood: A Cultural Symbol in Nineteenth-Century American Fiction, University Press of Kentucky, 1979.

(Editor) *Critical Essays on Jonathan Edwards,* G. K. Hall, 1979.

The Splintering Frame: The Later Fiction of H. G. Wells, University of Victoria, 1984.

(Editor) *Contemporary American Women Writers: Narrative Strategies,* University Press of Kentucky, 1985.

Contributor of over 125 articles and book reviews to academic and literary journals. Member of editorial board of *English Literature in Transition,* 1970—. Editor of *Texas Studies in Literature and Languages,* 1975—.

WORK IN PROGRESS: A study of the relation between fictional structure and ethics.

*　　*　　*

SCHMITT, Abraham   1927-

PERSONAL: Born August 7, 1927, in Saskatchewan, Canada; came to the United States in 1951, naturalized citizen in 1960; son of Jacob (a farmer) and Maria (Friesen) Schmitt; married Dorothy Stover, August 14, 1954; children: Mary Lou, Ken Fath, Ruth Ann, David Dean, Lois Lynn. *Education:* Goshen College, B.A., 1953, B.Ed., and B.D., both 1955; University

of Pennsylvania, M.S.W., 1958, D.S.W., 1966. *Politics:* Democrat. *Religion:* Mennonite.

ADDRESSES: Home—165 South Fourth St., Souderton, Pa. 18964.

CAREER: Philadephia State Hospital, Philadelphia, Pa., director of psychology training, 1963-68; University of Pennsylvania, Philadelphia, assistant professor of social work, 1968-75; marriage counselor and therapist, 1975—.

MEMBER: American Association of Marriage and Family Therapists.

WRITINGS:

Dialogue with Death, Word, Inc., 1977.

The Art of Listening with Love, Word, Inc., 1978.

Before I Wake: Listening to God in Your Dreams, Abingdon, 1984.

When a Congregation Cares: A New Approach to Crisis Ministries, Herald Press, 1984.

Renewing Family Life, Herald Press, 1985.

*　　*　　*

SCHONFELD, William R(ost)   1942-

PERSONAL: Born August 28, 1942, in New York, N.Y.; son of William A. (a psychiatrist) and Louise (Rost) Schonfeld; married Elena Beortegui, January 23, 1964; children: Natalie Beortegui, Elizabeth-Lynn Beortegui. *Education:* Attended Cornell University, 1960-61; New York University, B.A. (cum laude), 1964; Universite de Bordeaux, additional study, 1964-65; Princeton University, M.A., 1968, Ph.D., 1970.

ADDRESSES: Home—29 Rocky Knoll, Irvine, Calif. 92715. *Office*—School of Social Sciences, University of California, Irvine, Calif. 92717.

CAREER: Princeton University, Center of International Studies, Princeton, N.J., assistant in research, 1966-69, research associate, 1969-70, visiting lecturer in politics department, 1970; University of California, Irvine, assistant professor, 1970-75, associate professor, 1975-81, professor of political science, 1981—, director of graduate studies in School of Social Sciences, 1970-73, co-director of Focused Research Program in Authority Studies, 1981-84, dean of School of Social Sciences, 1982—. Visiting assistant professor at University of California, Berkeley, summer, 1972. Senior lecturer, Fondation Nationale des Sciences Politiques, Paris, 1973-74; researcher, Centre de Sociologie des Organisations, Paris, 1976-78. Fulbright senior lecturer in France, 1973-74. Referee for projects submitted to Political Science and Sociology Divisions of National Science Foundation. Has presented numerous conference papers and invited talks throughout the world.

MEMBER: American Political Science Association, Phi Beta Kappa, Pi Sigma Alpha.

AWARDS, HONORS: Fulbright fellow in France, 1964-65; Danforth fellow, 1964-69; summer faculty fellow, University of California, 1971; National Science Foundation-Centre National de la Recherche Scientifique Exchange of Scientists Program fellow, France, 1976-78; grant, Ford Foundation, 1978-79; Distinguished Teaching Award, University of California, Irvine, 1984; Professor of the Year finalist, Recognition Program of the Council for Advancement and Support of Education, 1984.

WRITINGS:

Toward Understanding the Bases of Democratic Political Instability: A Case Study of French Social Authority Patterns, Center of International Studies, Princeton University, 1969.

Youth and Authority in France: A Study of Secondary Schools, Sage Publications, 1971.

Obedience and Revolt: French Behavior toward Authority, Sage Publications, 1976.

(Contributor) William G. Andrews and Stanley Hoffman, editors, *The Fifth Republic at Twenty,* State University of New York Press, 1981.

(Contributor) J. Howorth and P. G. Cerny, editors, *Elites in French Society and Politics: Origins, Reproduction and Power,* Frances Pinter, 1981.

Scenes de la vie des parties politiques: Les Socialistes et les Gaullistes, Economica, 1984.

Contributor of articles and reviews to numerous periodicals, including *Political Studies, World Politics, Tocqueville Review, New Republic, American Journal of Political Science, Social Science Quarterly,* and *American Journal of Sociology.* Manuscript reviewer for *American Journal of Political Science, American Political Science Review, Comparative Political Studies, Comparative Politics,* and *Journal of Politics.*

WORK IN PROGRESS: Comparative study of political parties.

*   *   *

SCHRAFF, Anne E(laine) 1939-

PERSONAL: Born September 21, 1939, in Cleveland, Ohio; daughter of Frank C. and Helen (Benninger) Schraff. *Education:* Pierce Junior College, A.A., 1964; San Fernando Valley State College (now California State University, Northridge), B.A., 1966, M.A., 1967. *Politics:* Republican. *Religion:* Roman Catholic.

ADDRESSES: Home—P.O. Box 1345, Spring Valley, Calif. 92077.

CAREER: Academy of Our Lady of Peace, San Diego, Calif., teacher of social studies, 1967-77; full-time writer, 1977—.

MEMBER: California Social Studies Council, Society of Children's Book Writers.

WRITINGS:

(With brother, Francis N. Schraff) *Jesus Our Brother* (children's book), Liguori Publications, 1968.

Black Courage: Sagas of Pioneers, Sailors, Explorers, Miners, Cowboys—21 Heros of the American West (nonfiction), Macrae, 1969.

North Star (novel), Macrae, 1972.

The Day the World Went Away (novel), Doubleday, 1973.

Faith of the Presidents (nonfiction), Concordia, 1978.

(With F. N. Schraff) *The Adventures of Peter and Paul: Acts of the Apostles for the Young,* Liguori Publications, 1978.

Tecumseh: The Story of an American Indian, Dillon, 1979.

Christians Courageous (nonfiction), Concordia, 1980.

You Can't Stop Me, So Don't Even Try (novel), Perfection Form Co., 1980.

(With F. N. Schraff and Suzanne Hockel) *Learning about Jesus: Stories, Plays, Activities for Children,* Liguori Publications, 1980.

Caught in the Middle (novel), Baker Book, 1981.

JUVENILE NOVELS; "PASSAGES READING PROGRAM" SERIES

Don't Blame the Children, with workbook, Perfection Form Co., 1978.

Please Don't Ask Me to Love You, with workbook, Perfection Form Co., 1978.

An Alien Spring, with workbook, Perfection Form Co., 1978.

The Vandal, with workbook, Perfection Form Co., 1978.

The Ghost Boy, with workbook, Perfection Form Co., 1978.

Haunting of Hawthorne, with workbook, Perfection Form Co., 1978.

JUVENILE NOVELS; "RACEWAY DOUBLES READING PROGRAM" SERIES

That's What Friends Are For, with workbook and cassette, Perfection Form Co., 1981.

The Crook at Cleveland High, with workbook and cassette, Perfection Form Co., 1981.

The Coward, with workbook and cassette, Perfection Form Co., 1981.

Escape, with workbook and cassette, Perfection Form Co., 1981.

The Ghost of Sulphur Ridge, with workbook and cassette, Perfection Form Co., 1981.

Stranger at Windbreak Mountain, with workbook and cassette, Perfection Form Co., 1981.

Julia, with workbook and cassette, Perfection Form Co., 1981.

Jeremy, with workbook and cassette, Perfection Form Co., 1981.

You'll Never Get out Alive, with workbook and cassette, Perfection Form Co., 1981.

The Journey, with workbook and cassette, Perfection Form Co., 1981.

Time of Terror, with workbook and cassette, Perfection Form Co., 1981.

Shearwaters, with workbook and cassette, Perfection Form Co., 1981.

JUVENILE NOVELS; "TALETWISTERS READING PROGRAM" SERIES

Fantastic Fortune, Perfection Form Co., 1982.

The Storm, Perfection Form Co., 1982.

The Most Amazing Amusement Park in the World, Perfection Form Co., 1982.

The Pirate House, Perfection Form Co., 1982.

Lost in the Wilds, Perfection Form Co., 1982.

The Wizards Web, Perfection Form Co., 1982.

Mystery of Bat Cave, Perfection Form Co., 1982.

OTHER

Also author of interactive fiction for Homecomputer, 1984. Contributor of reviews to *Scholastic Teacher.*

WORK IN PROGRESS: A history textbook featuring anecdotes about famous and little-known Americans who have influenced history, for J. Weston Walch; several young adult novels, as yet untitled.

SIDELIGHTS: Anne E. Schraff writes *CA:* "I've been motivated by a powerful desire to write that made it impossible to do otherwise. I began my writing career at the age of eight when I wrote a love story for the *Saturday Evening Post* titled, "Orchids for Linda." I told all my friends it would soon be published and thus learned very early not to count chickens yet unhatched. I sold my first story, *Stage to Hell,* while a college freshman. It sold to *Ranch Romances,* and constituted one of the rare truly glorious experiences available to people.

"In my books, chiefly for young people, I hope to enable my readers to share the magic and adventure of life that I enjoyed in the books I devoured as a child. I also hope to convey the powerful beliefs that life is worth living and goodness is worth achieving.

"I wrote the 'Passages' novels to create exciting stories to interest reluctant teenaged readers who usually didn't read. Some letters from kids have told me my books were the first they ever read straight through. That pleased me greatly."

AVOCATIONAL INTERESTS: Music, hiking.

* * *

SCHUERER, Ernst 1933-

PERSONAL: Born September 13, 1933, in Germany; naturalized U.S. citizen, 1961; son of Josef (a craftsman) and Hermine (Ahlbrink) Schuerer; married Margarete Richter, June 20, 1964; children: Frank, Norbert, Anne. *Education:* University of Texas, B.A., 1960; Yale University, M.A., 1962, Ph.D., 1965. *Politics:* Democratic.

ADDRESSES: Home—705 East Foster Ave., State College, Pa. 16801. *Office*—Department of German, Pennsylvania State University, S-323 Burrowes Bldg., University Park, Pa. 16802.

CAREER: Yale University, New Haven, Conn., instructor, 1965-67, assistant professor, 1967-70, associate professor of German, 1970-73, director of undergraduate studies, 1969-71, director of graduate studies, 1971-73; University of Florida, Gainesville, professor of German, 1973-78, chairman of department, 1977-78; Pennsylvania State University, University Park, professor of German and head of department, 1978—.

MEMBER: International Association for Germanic Philology and Literature, International Brecht Society, Modern Language Association of America, American Association of Teachers of German, American Comparative Literature Association, American Association of Teachers of Foreign Languages, Kafka Society of America, Phi Beta Kappa.

AWARDS, HONORS: Woodrow Wilson fellowship, 1960-61; Morse fellowship, Yale University, 1968-69; Alexander von Humboldt fellowship, 1973; American Council of Learned Societies travel grant, 1980; German Academic Exchange Service fellowship, 1984.

WRITINGS:

(Editor) *Lebendige Form,* Wilhelm Fink, 1970.
Georg Kaiser, Twayne, 1971.
Georg Kaiser und Bertolt Brecht, Atheneum, 1971.
Georg Kaiser: Nebeneinander, Reclam (Stuttgart), 1978.
Carl Sternheim: Tabula rasa, Reclam, 1978.
Ernst Toller: Hoppla, wir leben!, Reclam, 1980.

CONTRIBUTOR

Horst Denkler, editor, *Gedichte der "Menschheitsdaemmerung,"* Wilhelm Fink, 1971.
Manfred Durzak, editor, *Die deutsche Exilliteratur 1933-1945,* Reclam, 1973.
Wolfgang Rothe, editor, *Die deutsche Literatur der Weimarer Republik,* Reclam, 1974.
Dietrich Papenfuss and Juergen Soering, editors, *Rezeption der deutschen Gegenwarts-literatur im Ausland,* Kohlhammer (Stuttgart), 1976.
Holger A. Pausch and Ernest Reinhold, editors, *Georg Kaiser Symposium,* Agora (Berlin), 1980.

Armin Arnold, editor, *Georg Kaiser,* Klett (Stuttgart), 1980.
John M. Spalek and Robert F. Bell, editors, *Exile: The Writer's Experience,* University of North Carolina Press, 1982.
Klaus Siebenhaar and Hermann Haarmann, editors, *Preis der Vernunft,* Medusa (Berlin/Vienna), 1982.
Jost Hermand, editor, *Zu Ernst Toller: Drama und Engagement,* Klett, 1982.
Paul Michael Luetzeler, *Brochs "Verzauberung,"* Suhrkamp (Frankfurt), 1983.

Contributor to anthologies.

OTHER

Contributor to *Monatshefte, Books Abroad, Journal of English and German Philology, German Studies, German Quarterly, Modern Austrian Literature,* and *Colloquia Germanica.*

WORK IN PROGRESS: Research on Post-Expressionistic drama and German literature in exile.

SIDELIGHTS: Ernst Schuerer told *CA:* "Reading and writing are as essential to a full life as eating and sleeping. They open us up and make us aware of new and unknown worlds."

AVOCATIONAL INTERESTS: Philosophy and archeology.

* * *

SCHULTZ, Donald O. 1939-

PERSONAL: Born October 25, 1939, in Mount Vernon, N.Y.; son of Emil H. (a bosun in the Merchant Marine) and Lillian (Schalm) Schultz; married Patricia Gail Omilak (a registered nurse), December 27, 1969; children: Donald O., Jr., Christopher Paul. *Education:* Long Beach State College (now California State University, Long Beach), B.S., 1963; University of Southern California, M.P.A., 1967; Orange County Police Academy, basic training, 1963; also attended various other police training institutes. *Politics:* Democrat. *Religion:* Lutheran.

ADDRESSES: Home—9500 Listow Ter., Boynton Beach, Fla. 33437. *Office*—Broward Community College, Davie Rd., Fort Lauderdale, Fla. 33314.

CAREER: Mobile Oil Co., Terminal Island, Calif., ordinary seaman, summers, 1957, 1958; Cal Stores, Long Beach, Calif., clerk-manager, 1958-59; Autonetics, Anaheim, Calif., clerk-accountant, 1959-61; Orange (Calif.) Police Department, motor officer-patrolman, 1962-67; Universal Armed Guard, Orange, management employee, 1967-68; Pacific Plant Protection, Fullerton, Calif., director of industrial relations, 1968; assistant professor of law enforcement at University of Nebraska, 1969-70; Broward Community College, Fort Lauderdale, Fla., instructor in law enforcement and coordinator of criminal justice program, 1970—. Member of Orange County Police Academy staff, Orange Coast College, 1964-67. Management consultant, International Association of Chiefs of Police, 1979—. Member, California Republican Assembly.

MEMBER: National Police Officers Association of America, Masons, Gold Coast Shrine Club, New York State Federation of Police.

AWARDS, HONORS: Outstanding Achievement award, Orange County Police Officers Association, 1965; awards from National Police Officers Association of America, 1968, 1972, from United States Federation of Police, 1968, from Police Conference of New York, 1970, and from Fort Lauderdale Police Department, 1971.

WRITINGS:

(With Loran A. Norton) *Police Operational Intelligence*, C. C Thomas, 1968.
Special Problems in Law Enforcement, C. C Thomas, 1971.
Principles of American Law Enforcement and Criminal Justice, C. C Thomas, 1972.
(With William J. Bopp) *A Short History of American Law Enforcement*, C. C Thomas, 1972.
The Subversive, C. C Thomas, 1973.
Police Unarmed Defense Tactics, C. C Thomas, 1973.
Police Traffic Enforcement, W. C. Brown, 1975.
(Editor) *Critical Issues in Criminal Justice*, C. C Thomas, 1975.
Crime Scene Investigation, Prentice-Hall, 1977.
Criminal Investigation Techniques, Gulf Publishing, 1978.
Principles of Physical Security, Gulf Publishing, 1978.
Police Pursuit Driving Handbook, Gulf Publishing, 1979.
(Editor) *Modern Police Administration*, Gulf Publishing, 1979.
(With J. Gregory Service) *The Police Use of Force*, C. C Thomas, 1981.
Security Litigations and Related Matters, C. C Thomas, 1982.
Traffic Investigation and Enforcement, Custom Publishing, 1983.
The Police as the Defendant, C. C Thomas, 1984.

Also author of police correspondence courses sponsored by the National Police Academy. Contributor of numerous articles on law and order to newspapers, magazines, and police journals. Senior editor, *Enforcement Journal*, 1970; police editor, *Guns and Ammo*, 1970.

* * *

SCHUMAN, David Feller 1942-

PERSONAL: Born April 24, 1942, in Tulsa, Okla.; son of Joseph Joel and Sophie (Feller) Schuman; married Barbara Meyer; children: Tamara Meadow, Amy Meadow, Benedict, Tuyet. *Education:* University of Tulsa, B.A., 1964; University of California, Berkeley, M.A., 1966, Ph.D., 1971. *Religion:* Jewish.

ADDRESSES: Home—276 Elm, Northampton, Mass. 01060. *Office*—Department of Higher Education, University of Massachusetts, Amherst, Mass. 01003.

CAREER: University of Washington, Seattle, assistant professor of political science, 1970-75; University of Massachusetts—Amherst, 1975—, began as associate professor, became professor of education.

AWARDS, HONORS: Distinguished Teaching Award, University of Massachusetts, 1980-81.

WRITINGS:

Preface to Politics, Heath, 1973, 4th edition, 1986.
Bureaucracies, Organizations, and Administration, Macmillan, 1976.
The Ideology of Form, Lexington Books, 1978.
Policy Analysis, Education and Everyday Life, Heath, 1982.
American Government: The Rules of the Game, Random House, 1984.

WORK IN PROGRESS: A textbook on public administration.

SIDELIGHTS: David Feller Schuman told *CA:* "It is almost as if I am followed by this evil spirit. No matter what I study or think about, ideas about organization always seem to ap-

pear. What makes that so difficult for me is that I really dislike highly structured, formal organizations a great deal. Maybe simply thinking through it again, while writing this book on administration, will help me get rid of the evil spirit."

* * *

SCHUR, Norman W(arren) 1907-

PERSONAL: Born October 7, 1907, in Boston, Mass.; son of Isaac H. (a banker) and Martha (Reinherz) Schur; married Marjorie Tas, December 31, 1941; children: Joanna (Mrs. Eric Weber), Christopher, Moira (Mrs. Kevin J. Craw), Geoffrey. *Education:* Harvard University, A.B. (summa cum laude), 1926; Columbia University, LL.B., 1930; also attended University of Rome and Sorbonne, University of Paris. *Politics:* "Honesty." *Religion:* "No preference."

ADDRESSES: Home—37 Davis Hill Rd., Weston, Conn. 06883.

CAREER: Attorney. Proskauer, Rose & Paskus, New York City, associate, 1930-33; private practice of law, 1933-50; partner of law firms in New York City, Simons, Schur & Straus, 1950-53, Diamond, Schur, Perl & Sewel, 1953-56, Schur & Perl, 1956-58, and Schur, Rubin & Montgomery, 1960-65; counsel to Bernton, Hoeniger, Freitag & Abbey, New York City, 1965-74, and King & Plotkin, Stamford, Conn., beginning 1965; private practice of law, 1976—. Former consultant on American law and taxation in England.

MEMBER: Phi Beta Kappa, Wig and Pen Club (London), Marylebone Cricket Club (London), Kent County Cricket Club (Canterbury, England), Hawkhurst Cricket Club (Hawkhurst, England).

AWARDS, HONORS: Franklin Medal and Derby Medal from Boston Latin School, 1923; Sheldon fellowship (Harvard), 1926.

WRITINGS:

British Self-Taught: With Comments in American, Macmillan, 1972, revised and enlarged edition published as *English English*, Verbatim, 1980.
1000 Most Important Words, Ballantine, 1982.
Practical English: 1000 Most Effective Words, Ballantine, 1983.
1000 Most Practical Words, Facts on File, 1984.

WORK IN PROGRESS: 1000 Most Challenging Words, for Ballantine.

SIDELIGHTS: Norman W. Schur writes in the *Westport News* that he has "always been a word buff." Language, he maintains, is "a living, breathing, expanding and contracting thing, changing all the time." While living in England, Schur was struck by the sometimes confusing variations between British English and American English. His notes on the subject led to his first book, *British Self-Taught*. Revised some years later and republished as *English English*, the book received favorable reviews from both British and American critics.

Besides words, notes Leonard Feather in the *Los Angeles Times*, "subtle differences of punctuation, syntax, spelling, pronunciation and the uses of preposition are examined." In addition, social and political distinctions are discussed, "sometimes briefly, occasionally in long, fascinating essays." Feather calls the "splendidly researched, wittily written" book "as much entertainment as education, especially for those of us who have lived both in the United Kingdom and the United States." And although British reviewer E. S. Turner suggests in a *Times*

Literary Supplement review that the differences in the two varieties of English may be somewhat exaggerated by Schur, he praises the book as "informative, discursive, idiosyncratic, amused and amusing."

BIOGRAPHICAL/CRITICAL SOURCES:

PERIODICALS

Los Angeles Times, April 5, 1981.
Times Literary Supplement, March 20, 1981.
Westport News, February 4, 1981.

*   *   *

SCHWARTZ, Douglas W(right)   1929-

PERSONAL: Born July 29, 1929, in Erie, Pa.; son of Harry and Vernon (Schaaf) Schwartz; married Rita Juanita Hartley (a nurse), October 4, 1950; children: Steven, Susan, Kelsey. *Education:* University of Kentucky, B.A., 1950; Yale University, Ph.D., 1955.

ADDRESSES: Office—School of American Research, P.O. Box 2188, Santa Fe, N.M. 87501.

CAREER: University of Kentucky, Lexington, field archaeologist, 1951; University of Oklahoma, Norman, instructor in anthropology, 1955-56; University of Kentucky, assistant professor, 1956-58, associate professor, 1958-62, professor of anthropology, 1962-67, director of anthropology museum, 1956-67; School of American Research, Santa Fe, N.M., director, 1967—. Chairman of anthropology panel, Fulbright-Hayes Postdoctoral Awards. Director, American National Bank of Santa Fe; president, Witter Bynner Foundation for Poetry, Inc.; vice chairman, Harvard University Overseers Committee on Peabody Museum; trustee, Jane Goodall African Wildlife Research Center; vice-chairman, Archaeological Conservancy; council member, National Park Service.

MEMBER: American Anthropological Association, Society for American Archaeology (advisory board member; president, 1973-74), Kiva Club, Harvard Club, Century Archaeology Club.

AWARDS, HONORS: American Association for State and Local History award, 1968, for *Conceptions of Kentucky Prehistory: A Case Study in the History of Archaeology;* research grants from Yale University, University of Oklahoma, National Park Service, Carnegie Corp., Southern Regional Education Board, Grand Canyon Natural History Association, National Geographic Society, and University of Kentucky.

WRITINGS:

(Contributor) *The Cohonina Culture of Northwestern Arizona,* University of Illinois Press, 1951.
The Tinsley Hill Site: A Late Prehistoric Stone Grave Cemetery in Lyon County, Kentucky, University of Kentucky Press, 1961.
(With Martha A. Rolinson) *Late Paleo-Indian and Early Archaic Manifestations in Western Kentucky,* University of Kentucky Press, 1965.
Conceptions of Kentucky Prehistory: A Case Study in the History of Archaeology, University of Kentucky Press, 1968.
Arroyo Hondo Field Report, School of American Research Press, 1972.

"GRAND CANYON ARCHAEOLOGICAL SERIES"

(With Michael P. Marshall and Jane Kepp) *Archaeology of the Grand Canyon: The Bright Angel Site,* School of American Research Press, 1979.

(With Kepp and Richard C. Chapman) *Archaeology of the Grand Canyon: Unkar Delta,* School of American Research Press, 1980.
(With others) *Archaeology of the Grand Canyon: The Walhalla Plateau,* School of American Research Press, 1981.

OTHER

Also author of brochures for the National Park Service. Editor of "University of Kentucky Studies in Anthropology" series, 1960-67. Contributor of more than thirty articles and reviews to *American Antiquity, Scientific American,* and anthropology journals. Memoir editor, Society for American Archaeology.†

*   *   *

SCHWARTZ, George R.   1942-

PERSONAL: Born January 2, 1942, in Caribou, Me; children: Ruth, Rebekah, Rachel, Moses. *Education:* Hobart College (now Hobart and William Smith Colleges), B.S. (with honors), 1963; State University of New York Downstate Medical Center, M.D. (magna cum laude), 1967.

ADDRESSES: Office—Healing Research, Inc., 301 Dartmouth N.E., Albuquerque, N.M. 87106. *Agent*—Clyde Taylor, Curtis Brown Ltd., 10 Astor Pl., New York, N.Y. 10003.

CAREER: King County Hospital, Seattle, Wash., intern, 1967-68; Hillside Hospital, Glen Oaks, N.Y., resident in psychiatry, 1968-69; St. Joseph Hospital, Albuquerque, N.M., part-time emergency physician, 1970-71; Indiana University, Medical Center, Indianapolis, resident in surgery, 1971-72; Medical College of Pennsylvania, Philadelphia, instructor and director of emergency services, 1972-74, clinical assistant professor of emergency medicine, 1974-76; private practice of medicine, 1976—; currently affiliated with Healing Research, Inc., Albuquerque.

Instructor at University of Washington, Seattle, 1967-68; associate professor and director of Division of Emergency Medicine at University of New Mexico, 1976—. Admitting and emergency physician at Coney Island Hospital, 1968-69; member of emergency department staff of Presbyterian Hospital, Albuquerque, N.M., 1970-71, and Johnson County Memorial Hospital, 1972; director of emergency medicine at West Jersey Hospital, 1974-76. Co-founder of Albuquerque Free Clinic, 1971; chief of medical services at Pocono International Raceway, 1973; director of Camden County Poison Center, 1974-76. Certified by American Board of Family Practice and American Board of Emergency Medicine. Instructor in diving and high altitude physiology. Expert medical witness in national trials. *Military service:* U.S. Air Force, flight surgeon, chief of aerospace medicine, and director of base medical services, 1969-71.

MEMBER: International Emergency Care Association, American Medical Association, American College of Emergency Physicians, American Association for the Advancement of Science, Alpha Omega Alpha.

AWARDS, HONORS: Fellowship for study in France, 1966; grant from U.S. Department of Health, Education and Welfare, 1976.

WRITINGS:

(Editor and contributor) *Principles and Practices of Emergency Medicine,* Saunders, 1978, 2nd edition, 1986.

Food Power: How Foods Can Change Your Mind, Your Personality, and Your Life, McGraw, 1979, published as *The New Food Power*, McGraw, 1986.
Geriatric Emergencies, Robert Brady, 1984.
Emergency Medicine: Clinical Update, Medical Examination Publishing, 1985.
Minna Bernays (biography), HRI Press, 1986.

Editor of "Emergency Therapy Conference," a bimonthly column in *Journal of the American College of Emergency Physicians*, 1973-74; co-editor of "Trauma Rounds," a monthly column in *Emergency Medicine*, 1973-75. Contributor of more than fifty articles and reviews to medical journals, popular magazines, and newspapers; editor of *Healing Today*, 1985—.

SIDELIGHTS: George R. Schwartz told *CA:* "I began writing in earnest somewhat later than most—in fact, after I had become established as a doctor of medicine. Starting with medical works, I decided to develop a comprehensive textbook of my chosen specialty field. Up until that time there were only handbooks and manuals. I developed a vision of something richer and deeper. Seven years later the book, 1600 pages, was published with a gratifying response. Physicians using the book found it helpful in treating patients. Before long it had become the standard reference work in the field. Once this opus was finished I began to feel that I was ready to move on to other areas. With a burning desire to seek out the true events of the beginnings of psychoanalysis, I became fascinated with Sigmund Freud and even more intrigued with his sister-in-law, Minna Bernays. With avidity that I now look at as nothing less than obsession, I lived in Vienna and meticulously sought out every detail which shaped Minna's life and began to see that she had probably helped write some of the seminal works in psychoanalysis. Her biography was written as I was also engaged in revising my textbook and writing in other areas of my interest in medicine. Why did I do it? Why write at all? These have been questions I have asked myself many times, but the answer is really simple. An idea takes root and then assumes tremendous psychic proportions. I wrote a book about 'food power' and how diets affect behavior. During the writing I became fascinated by the far-reaching implications and became convinced that it was of vital importance. Some years later I looked back on my impassioned state with some awe at the intensity.

"Emotional crises proved to be a potent stimulus. Unlike some authors who find money to be a stimulus, I have never been motivated by lucre, though it is sheer pleasure to see royalty checks and to see my books in different languages. The emotional works, mostly articles, combined psychology with medicine and expressed the deepest experiences in which I found myself. This sort of writing was to some extent cathartic but also represented a need to tell others what I had learned from the turmoil. Suffering has humorously been called the vitamin of growth, a statement with which I am in agreement. Once the growth occurred and I entered a world of another perspective, I felt it important to communicate these observations and insights to others, in some way giving further life to what would otherwise have been limited experiences.

"I find myself less interested in large causes and more concerned with the loving conduct of everyday life. I have written some works of a spiritual nature after going through a profound conversion experience at the relatively advanced age of forty-one.

"What is next? I have kept my hand in medicine. The practice keeps me humble, but I have also become more interested in

the ways of fiction—a terribly hard road for a nonfiction writer. The business aspects have made me realize the plight of many aspiring fiction writers who cannot survive with family, so have to supplement income with other jobs. Screenwriting is certainly a challenge, which I am attempting to enter. Not every writer can have the freedom of a Rilke who balked at any family entanglements. To do that seems to me to cut oneself off from some of life's most difficult and rewarding experiences. I suppose that if it were not difficult it would not be as rewarding.''

*   *   *

SCHWARTZ, S.
   See STARR, S(tephen) Frederick

*   *   *

SCIPIO
   See WATSON, (John Hugh) Adam

*   *   *

SCOTT, Latayne Colvett   1952-
   (Latayne Colvett)

PERSONAL: Born March 11, 1952, in Santa Fe, N.M.; daughter of Bennie Leo and Rose Anne Cates (Hensley) Colvett; married Daniel Gene Scott (an insurance specialist), December 28, 1973; children: Ryan, Celeste. *Education:* Attended Brigham Young University, 1970-73; University of New Mexico, B.S., 1979. *Religion:* Church of Christ.

ADDRESSES: Home—1080 Tantra Park Cir., Boulder, Colo. 80303.

CAREER: Writer. Tutor of creative writing to gifted children.

MEMBER: New Mexico State Poetry Society (first vice-president, 1979-80; president, 1980-81).

AWARDS, HONORS: The Mormon Mirage was a finalist for *Campus Life*'s Book of the Year Award, 1980.

WRITINGS:

The Mormon Mirage, Zondervan, 1980.
Open Up Your Life: A Woman's Workshop on Hospitality, Lamplighter, 1984.
To Love Each Other: A Woman's Workshop on 1 Corinthians 13, Lamplighter, 1985.

Contributor of articles and translations to magazines, sometimes under the name Latayne Colvett.

WORK IN PROGRESS: Three books for Zondervan; books on Christian stewardship and the parables of Jesus, for Lamplighter; poems; religious tracts and tapes.

SIDELIGHTS: Latayne Colvett Scott told *CA:* "Writing a researched book like *The Mormon Mirage* is like being pregnant. While you're doing all the work and experiencing all the discomfort, people only ask about your 'project' to be polite. But when the book is published or the baby arrives, everyone is so excited! And you're mostly just tired.

"*The Mormon Mirage* is about why I left Mormonism to become 'just a Christian.' It deals with the history and doctrines of the Mormon church, as well as with my experiences as a faithful Mormon.''

SHAW, Luci N(orthcote) 1928-

PERSONAL: Born December 29, 1928, in London, England; came to the United States in 1953; daughter of John Northcote (a surgeon) and Gladys Mary Deck; married Harold F. Shaw (a publisher), August 20, 1953; children: Robin Shaw Schramer, Marian (Mrs. K. Kussro), John, Jeffrey, Kristin. *Education:* Wheaton College, Wheaton, Ill., B.A. (magna cum laude), 1953. *Religion:* "Christian believer."

ADDRESSES: Home—2N734 Wayne Oaks Lane, West Chicago, Ill. 60185. *Office*—Harold Shaw Publishers, Box 567, 388 Gundersen Dr., Wheaton, Ill. 60187.

CAREER: Moody Press, Chicago, Ill., free-lance editor, 1953-56; *Christian Medical Society Journal,* Oak Park, Ill., editor, 1967-69; free-lance editor for Tyndale House, Wheaton, Ill.; Harold Shaw Publishers, Wheaton, 1967—, began as editor-in-chief, currently vice-president and senior editor. Lecturer at colleges and poetry workshops; conducts study groups.

MEMBER: Wheaton Scholastic Honor Society (director, 1973-76; president, 1976-79), Wheaton Alumni Association (member of board of directors).

AWARDS, HONORS: Book of the year award from *Campus Life,* 1977, for *The Secret Trees.*

WRITINGS:

Listen to the Green (poems), Harold Shaw, 1971.
(Editor) *Sightseers into Pilgrims* (anthology), Tyndale, 1973.
The Risk of Birth (anthology), Harold Shaw, 1974.
The Secret Trees (poems), Harold Shaw, 1976.
(Editor) Corrie Ten Boom, *Prayers and Promises for Every Day from the Living Bible: With Corrie Ten Boom,* Harold Shaw, 1977.
The Sighting (poems), Harold Shaw, 1981.
(Contributor) Ann Spangler, editor, *Bright Legacy,* Servant Publications, 1983.
(Editor) *A Widening Light,* Harold Shaw, 1984.
Postcard from the Shore (poems), Harold Shaw, 1985.

Also editor of *My Living Counselor,* 1977. Contributor of poems, articles, and reviews to magazines, including *Campus Life, Moody Monthly, Decision,* and *Christianity Today.* Contributing editor, *Radix.*

WORK IN PROGRESS: A prose book on the imagination.

SIDELIGHTS: Luci N. Shaw writes: "I was brought up in a family to whom words and their precise meanings were very important. Moreover, I had a British education that made the kind of demands on me which are lacking in most American education systems. Studies in Latin, French, and Greek added to my understanding of language and gave me the insight into word meaning and word play essential to good poetry. With that solid foundation, the expression of an imaginative gift became almost second nature.

"My exposure to different climates and cultures supplied me with a broad backdrop for creative and original expression. But it has been my years in the American Midwest that have given me roots and a foundation in the same way that Andrew Wyeth's art is an outgrowth of his environment in Pennsylvania and Maine. Though I have a British background, I identify myself as an American poet.

"I see poets today as having an essential and vital, but often neglected, role to play in an increasingly technological world. They fulfill the function that the biblical prophets had in an earlier age. Where most scientists, politicians, business executives, and technicians in most fields, even most philosophers, are taxed to keep pace with the ever-increasing input of ideas and information, and therefore develop tunnel vision, unable to see beyond their own narrow field of expertise, the poet can take the broader view of a universe packed with meaning and value and integrate it, pulling it together by saying, 'Yes, *this* is like *that*!' The poet's vision encompasses the subtle correspondences and connections that link every part of the created universe with the others and with God and ultimate significance.

"As a Christian poet I emphatically reject a relativistic value system. I am convinced that everything means something, that we are all given enough intuitive wisdom to set us squarely on the road that leads to God's truth. I see Christianity not as a legalistic, obscurantist bondage, but as a structure of archetypal significance that frees us to see clearly, much as bones and muscles free us to move. It is up to the Christian poet to interpret the world in terms of these archetypes and symbols in such a way as to involve the reader both cerebrally and emotionally in this structure of significance."

AVOCATIONAL INTERESTS: Entertaining; growing and freezing vegetables; knitting fisherman sweaters.

*   *   *

SHELDON, Lee
See LEE, Wayne C.

*   *   *

SHENTON, Edward H(eriot) 1932-

PERSONAL: Born July 5, 1932, in Philadelphia, Pa.; son of Edward (an artist and writer) and Barbara (also an artist and writer; maiden name, Webster) Shenton; married Karyl Mader (a commercial artist), December 22, 1957; children: Amy Webster. *Education:* Colby College, A.B., 1954; Texas A&M University, M.S., 1957.

ADDRESSES: Office—Research Institute of the Gulf of Maine, 96 Falmouth St., Portland, Me. 04103.

CAREER: Texas A&M Research Foundation, College Station, research scientist, 1957-58; U.S. Fish and Wildlife Service, Bureau of Commercial Fisheries, fishery aide, 1958; Smithsonian Astrophysical Observatory, Cambridge, Mass., chief of satellite tracking stations, 1958-62; Geraldine's Laboratories, Annapolis, Md., staff oceanographer, 1962-64; Westinghouse Electric Co., Underseas Division, Annapolis, oceanographer and lecturer, 1964-68; Oceans General, Inc., Miami, Fla., oceanographer, 1968-69; Dillingham Applied Oceanography, La Jolla, Calif., staff oceanographer, 1969-70; consultant, Plessey Environmental Systems, 1970-72; Research Institute of the Gulf of Maine, Portland, deputy director, 1972—. Marine research scientist II, Maine Department of Marine Resources, 1974. Consultant to Maine environmental groups, 1976—.

MEMBER: Marine Technology Society (charter member), U.S. Naval Institute.

WRITINGS:

Exploring the Ocean Depths: The Story of the Cousteau Diving Saucer in the Pacific, Norton, 1968.
Diving for Science: The Story of the Deep Submersible, Norton, 1972.
(With Donald B. Horton and the Research Institute of the Gulf of Maine) *Literature Review of the Marine Environmental Data for Eastport, Maine*, revised edition, Pittston, 1973.

Contributor to *Proceedings* of U.S. Naval Institute, *Skin Diver* (magazine), and *Explorers Journal*.

WORK IN PROGRESS: Oil and the Offshore Fisheries: Is It Inevitable?, for Maine Commercial Fisheries; *Coastal Ecology of Maine's Rock Shores*.

SIDELIGHTS: As an undergraduate, Edward H. Shenton studied geology, and it was this interest in science that led to his profession of oceanography. He traveled in Europe, South Africa, Middle East, and South America for Smithsonian tracking stations from 1958 to 1962 and accompanied the Cousteau diving saucer expedition to Baja, California. He believes it is vital that man inhabit the sea.

AVOCATIONAL INTERESTS: Sailing, scuba diving, motorcycles.†

*   *   *

SHERROD, Jane
   See SINGER, Jane Sherrod

*   *   *

SHOESMITH, Kathleen A(nne)   1938-

PERSONAL: Born July 17, 1938, in Keighley, Yorkshire, England; daughter of Roy and Lilian Shoesmith. *Education:* Avery Hill Teachers' Training College, Diploma, 1956.

ADDRESSES: Home—351 Fell Lane, Keighley BD22 6DB, Yorkshire, England.

CAREER: Teacher in Keighley, Yorkshire, England, 1958—, at Lees County Primary School, 1973—.

WRITINGS:

HISTORICAL ROMANCES

Jack O'Lantern, R. Hale, 1969, Ace Books, 1973.
Cloud over Calderwood, R. Hale, 1969, Ace Books, 1973.
The Tides of Tremannion, R. Hale, 1970, Ace Books, 1973.
Mallory's Luck, R. Hale, 1971, Ace Books, 1974.
Return of the Royalist, R. Hale, 1971.
The Reluctant Puritan, R. Hale, 1972, Ace Books, 1973.
The Highwayman's Daughter, R. Hale, 1972, Ace Books, 1974.
Belltower, R. Hale, 1973, Ace Books, 1974.
The Black Domino, R. Hale, 1975.
Elusive Legacy, R. Hale, 1976.
The Miser's Ward, R. Hale, 1977.
Smuggler's Haunt, R. Hale, 1978.
Guardian at the Gate, R. Hale, 1979.
Brackenthorpe, R. Hale, 1980.
Autumn Escapade, R. Hale, 1981.
Rustic Vinyard, R. Hale, 1982.
A Minor Bequest, R. Hale, 1984.

JUVENILE SERIES

"Playtime Stories," six books, E. J. Arnold, 1966.

"Judy Stories," four books, Charles & Son, 1968.
"Easy to Read," six books, Charles & Son, 1968.
"How Do They Grow?," four books, Charles & Son, 1969.
"Do You Know About?," sixteen books, Burke Publishing, 1970-75.
"Use Your Senses," five books, Burke Publishing, 1973.

WORK IN PROGRESS: A historical romance set in Yorkshire in 1856.

SIDELIGHTS: Most of Kathleen A. Shoesmith's historical romances have been published in paperback in France, Italy, and the Netherlands, as well as in America.

AVOCATIONAL INTERESTS: Reading and touring by car in the Yorkshire countryside.

*   *   *

SIDER, Ronald J(ames)   1939-

PERSONAL: Born September 17, 1939, in Stevensville, Ontario, Canada; came to the United States in 1962, naturalized in 1974; son of James Peter (a minister) and Ida (Cline) Sider; married Arbutus Lichti, August 19, 1961; children: Theodore Ronald, Michael Jay, Sonya Maria. *Education:* Waterloo University, B.A. (with honors), 1962; Yale University, M.A., 1963, B.D., 1967, Ph.D., 1969. *Religion:* Brethren in Christ; Mennonite.

ADDRESSES: Home—312 West Logan St., Philadelphia, Pa. 19144. *Office*—Department of Theology, Eastern Baptist Theological Seminary, Lancaster Ave. at City Line, Philadelphia, Pa. 19151.

CAREER: Messiah College, Philadelphia, Pa., instructor, 1968-70, assistant professor, 1970-74, associate professor of history and religion, 1974-78, dean, 1971-75; Eastern Baptist Theological Seminary, Philadelphia, associate professor, 1978-84, professor of theology, 1984—. Co-chairperson of National Workshop on Race and Reconciliation, 1975. Member of board of directors of Mennonite Central Committee, 1978-80, and Bread for the World, 1978-84.

MEMBER: National Association of Evangelicals, Evangelicals for Social Action (member of board of directors, 1973; chairperson of board, 1973-75, 1985—; president, 1978-84), World Evangelical Fellowship (convenor of unit on ethics and society, 1978—).

AWARDS, HONORS: Fellow of Institute for Advanced Christian Studies, 1976.

WRITINGS:

Andreas Bodenstein von Karlstadt, E. J. Brill, 1974.
(Editor and contributor) *The Chicago Declaration*, Creation House, 1974.
Rich Christians in an Age of Hunger: A Biblical Study, Inter-Varsity Press, 1977, revised edition, 1984.
Evangelism, Salvation, and Social Justice, Grove, 1977.
(Editor) *Karlstadt's Battle with Luther: Documents in a Liberal-Radical Debate*, Fortress, 1978.
Christ and Violence, Herald Press, 1979.
(Editor) *Cry Justice: The Bible on Hunger and Poverty*, Paulist Press, 1980.
(Editor) *Living More Simply*, Inter-Varsity Press, 1980.
(Editor) *Evangelicals and Development: Toward a Theology of Social Change*, Westminster, 1982.
(Editor) *Lifestyle in the Eighties: An Evangelical Commitment to Simple Lifestyle*, Westminster, 1982.

(Editor with Darrel Brubaker) *Preaching on Peace,* Fortress, 1982.

(With Richard K. Taylor) *Nuclear Holocaust and Christian Hope,* Inter-Varsity Press, 1982, published as *Nuclear Holocaust and Christian Hope: A Book for Christian Peacemakers,* Paulist Press, 1983.

(With Oliver O'Donovan) *Peace and War: A Debate about Pacifism,* Grove Books, 1985.

CONTRIBUTOR

Paul Hostetler, editor, *Perfect Love and War: A Dialogue on Christian Holiness and the Issues of War and Peace,* Evangel, 1974.

Craig Ellison, editor, *The Urban Mission,* Eerdmans, 1974.

Alton M. Motter, editor, *Preaching on National Holidays,* Fortress, 1976.

Mary Evelyn Jegen and Bruno V. Manno, editors, *The Earth Is the Lord's: Essays on Stewardship,* Paulist Press, 1978.

Donald E. Hoke, editor, *Evangelicals Face the Future,* William Carey Library, 1978.

Hans-Jurgen Goertz, editor, *Radikale Reformatoren,* Verlag C. H. Beck, 1978.

Carl F. H. Henry and Robert Lincoln Hancock, editors, *The Ministry of Development in Evangelical Perspective,* William Carey Library, 1979.

C. Norman Kraus, editor, *Evangelicalism and Anabaptism,* Herald Press, 1979.

Kenneth S. Kantzer and Stanley N. Gundry, editors, *Perspectives on Evangelical Theology,* Baker Book, 1979.

Robert Rankin, editor, *The Recovery of Spirit in Higher Education,* Seabury, 1980.

Dale W. Brown, editor, *What about the Russians?,* Brethren Press, 1984.

John A. Bernbaum, editor, *Perspectives on Peacemaking: Biblical Opinions in the Nuclear Age,* Regal Books, 1984.

Contributor to *Baker's Dictionary of Christian Ethics.*

OTHER

Contributor of over thirty-five articles to theology journals, including *Christianity Today, Christian Century,* and *New Testament Studies.* Member of editorial board of *Other Side* and co-editor of *Transformation: An International Dialogue on Evangelical Social Ethics,* 1984—.

WORK IN PROGRESS: Can We Defend Democracy without (Nuclear) Weapons? and *What Does It Mean to Be Pro-Life?*

SIDELIGHTS: Ronald J. Sider told *CA:* "I love tennis, jog to stay in shape, and try desperately to kindly decline most speaking invitations in order to stay home with my family. Discipleship begins at home. So does peace and reconciliation. It is a farce to write and speak about peace, love, and justice unless, by God's grace, it is becoming a reality in one's own home and church."

BIOGRAPHICAL/CRITICAL SOURCES:

PERIODICALS

Buzz, February, 1979.
Eternity, April, 1979.
Wittenberg Door, October-November, 1979.

*   *   *

SIGBAND, Norman Bruce   1920-

PERSONAL: Born June 27, 1920, in Chicago, Ill.; son of Max

H. and Bessie (Gitlitz) Sigband; married Joan C. Lyons, August 3, 1944; children: Robin, Shelley, Betsy. *Education:* University of Chicago, B.A., 1940, M.A., 1941, Ph.D., 1954. *Religion:* Jewish.

ADDRESSES: Home—3109 Dona Susana Dr., Studio City, Calif. 91604. *Office*—Graduate School of Business, University of Southern California, University Park, Los Angeles, Calif. 90007.

CAREER: DePaul University, Chicago, Ill., professor of business communication, 1946-65; University of Southern California, Los Angeles, professor of business communications in Graduate School of Business, 1965—. Industrial consultant to Western Electric Co., Brunswick Corp., Illinois Central Railroad, United Parcel Service, Chicago Police Department, Illinois Bell Telephone Co., Lockheed Aircraft Co., Bank of America, Commonwealth Edison, and other businesses and organizations. *Military service:* U.S. Army, 1942-46; served in European theater; became captain; awarded Bronze Star.

MEMBER: International Communication Association, Academy of Management, American Business Communication Association (president, 1964-65), National Council of Teachers of English, American Association of University Professors, Beta Gamma Sigma, Alpha Kappa Psi, Blue Key.

AWARDS, HONORS: Kellogg Foundation grant, 1954; Excellence in Teaching Award and Dean's Award, both from University of Southern California; Honored Educator Award from State of Illinois, 1979; Creative Excellence in Film Award, 1981, for "Listening: A Key to Problem Solving."

WRITINGS:

Practical English for Everyday Use, American School, 1955.
Effective Report Writing for Business, Industry, and Government, Harper, 1960.
Communication for Management, Scott, Foresman, 1969, 2nd edition published as *Communication for Management and Business,* 1976, 4th edition, 1985.
Communicating for Results, Scott, Foresman, 1980.
(With David N. Bateman) *Communicating in Business,* Scott, Foresman, 1981, 2nd edition, 1985.
(With others) *Successful Business English,* Scott, Foresman, 1983.
Business Communication, Harcourt, 1984.

Also author of filmscripts, including "Listening: A Key to Problem Solving" and "Barriers and Gateways to Communication," both Paramount Communications, and "Company Communications: The Grapevine." Author of more than seventy-five articles in the field of communications in industry.

WORK IN PROGRESS: Communications in Industry.

*   *   *

SILBERSCHLAG, Eisig   1903-

PERSONAL: Born in 1903 in Styrj, Austria; son of David and Blume (Pomeranz) Silberschlag; married Milka Antler, 1938. *Education:* University of Vienna, Ph.D., 1926.

ADDRESSES: Home—1801 Lavaca, Austin, Tex. 78701. *Office*—Center for Middle Eastern Studies, University of Texas, Austin, Tex. 78712.

CAREER: Author, educator, and lecturer. Jewish Theological Seminary, Teachers' Institute, New York, N.Y., instructor in Jewish history, 1930-31; Hebrew College, Brookline, Mass., instructor, 1932-44, professor of Hebrew literature, 1944—, dean, 1947-68, president, 1968-70; University of Texas at Austin, visiting Gale Professor of Judaic Studies, 1973-77, visiting professor of comparative studies, 1977—. Visiting professor, Emmanuel College, 1970-73. Visiting scholar, Oxford University, 1978-79. Chairman of sessions, World Congress of Jewish Studies, 1977. Trustee, Hebrew College, Boston.

MEMBER: Middle East Studies Association (fellow), American Academy for Jewish Research (fellow), National Association of Professors of Hebrew (former president), P.E.N.

AWARDS, HONORS: Lamed Prize, 1943; Saul Tschernichowsky Prize, Municipality of Tel Aviv, 1951; Florence and Harry Kovner Memorial Award, 1960, 1972; golden doctorate, University of Vienna, 1976; Doctor of Humane Letters, Hebrew Union College—Jewish Institute of Religion, 1977; first recipient of Abraham Friedman Prize for contributions to Hebrew culture in the United States.

WRITINGS:

BOOKS IN ENGLISH

Hebrew Literature: An Evaluation, Herzl Institute, 1959.
Saul Tschernichowsky: Poet of Revolt, Cornell University Press, 1968.
From Renaissance to Renaissance: Hebrew Literature from 1492-1967, Ktav, 1972.
An Exhibition of Judaica and Hebraica, University of Texas Humanities Research Center, 1973.
Hebrew Literature in the Land of Israel, 1870-1970, Ktav, 1977.

BOOKS IN HEBREW

Bi-Shebilim Bodedim (poetry; title means "In Lonely Paths"), Ogen, 1931.
Tehiyah u-Tehiyah be-Shirah (title means "Revolt and Revival in Poetry"), Abraham Joseph Stybel, 1938.
(Co-editor) *Sefer Touroff* (title means "Touroff Book"), [Boston], 1938.
Bi-Yeme Isabella (play; title means "In the Days of Isabella"), [New York], 1939.
Sheva Panim le-Havah (play; title means "Eve Has Seven Faces"), [Tel Aviv], 1942.
Ale Olam be-Shir (poetry; title means "Arise, Oh World, in Song"), Ogen, 1946.
(Co-editor) *Hatekufah*, Volumes XXX-XXXI, XXXII-XXXIII, [New York], 1946-47.
Kimron Yamai (poetry; title means "Dome of Days"), Kiryat Sefer, 1959.
Iggerotai El Dorot Aherim (title means "Letters to Other Generations"), [Jerusalem], 1971.
Yesh Reshit Le-Kol Aharit (title means "Each End Has a Beginning"), [Jerusalem], 1976.
Ben Allimut U-Ben Adishut (title means "Violence and Indifference"), [Jerusalem], 1981.

TRANSLATOR

Paulus Silentiarius, *Poems of Love*, [New York], 1945.
Carl de Hass, *Berenice: A Tragedy in Five Acts*, [New York], 1947.
The Eleven Comedies of Aristophanes, [Tel Aviv], 1967.

CONTRIBUTOR

Alexander Altman, editor, *Studies and Texts*, Harvard University Press, 1965.

Oscar I. Janowsky, editor, *The American Jew: A Reappraisal*, Philadelphia, 1966.
Alex Preminger, editor, *Encyclopedia of Poetry and Poetics*, Princeton University Press, 1965.
Yearbook of Comparative Criticism, Pennsylvania State University Press, 1971.
Hagut Ivrit ba-Amerika (title means "Hebrew Thought in America"), [Tel Aviv], 1972.

OTHER

Contributor to proceedings of the American Academy for Jewish Research. Contributor to journals and periodicals, including *Commentary, Judaism, World Literature Today,* and *Jewish Social Studies*. Editor, *Poet Lore*, 1939.

WORK IN PROGRESS: An autobiography; *Me-Ever La-Hayyim, Me-Ever La-Maret,* a book of poetry (title means "Beyond Life, Beyond Death").

SIDELIGHTS: Eisig Silberschlag told *CA:* "Writing in general is an inner urge. I write, then, under some sort of compulsion. The process—a mixture of pleasure and pain—began at twelve and continued throughout life. The pleasure comes from the approximation to the primary vision of a poem, a play or even an essay. The pain comes from a failure of approximation. The closer the approximation to the truth of the vision, the greater the impact on the reader. Each artifact in prose or poetry is a beginning that leads to another beginning—hopefully in vertical procession. The honor—or recognition—accorded to a writer is a self-congratulatory satisfaction on the part of the honorer."

BIOGRAPHICAL/CRITICAL SOURCES:

PERIODICALS

Barkai, December 16, 1963.
Bulletin of the School of Oriental and African Studies (London), Volume XXIII, part 1, 1960.
Maariv Literary Supplement, March 10, 1965.
South African Jewish Times, July 19, 1963.

* * *

SILET, Charles L(oring) P(rovine) 1942-

PERSONAL: Born April 25, 1942, in Chicago, Ill.; son of Charles Leonard (a mechanical engineer) and Elizabeth (an artist; maiden name, Provine) Silet; married Kay Zickefoose (an editor), February 21, 1976; children: Kristin, Scott, Karin, Emily. *Education:* Attended University of Illinois, 1960-62, and University of Vienna, 1963-64; Butler University, B.A., 1966; Indiana University, M.A., 1968, Ph.D., 1973; Jesus College, Cambridge, graduate study, 1970-71.

ADDRESSES: Home—2400 Timberland Rd., Ames, Iowa 50010. *Office*—Department of English, Iowa State University, Ames, Iowa 50011.

CAREER: Indiana University at Bloomington, associate instructor in English, 1969-70, 1971-73; Iowa State University, Ames, instructor, 1973-74, assistant professor, 1974-79, associate professor of English, 1979—.

MEMBER: Modern Language Association of America, American Studies Association, Society for the Study of the Multi-Ethnic Literature of the United States, Midcontinent American Studies Association.

AWARDS, HONORS: National Endowment for the Humanities fellowship, summer, 1978.

WRITINGS:

(With Ronald Gottesmann) *Literary Manuscripts of Upton Sinclair*, Ohio State University Press, 1972.

Henry Blake Fuller and Hamlin Garland: A Reference Guide, G. K. Hall, 1977.

(With Gretchen Bataille and David Gradwohl) *The Worlds between Two Rivers: Perspectives on American Indians in Iowa*, Iowa State University Press, 1978.

(Editor with David Cummings, Will C. Jumper, and Zora Devrnja Zimmerman) *The Arc from Now: Poems, 1959-1977, by Richard Gustafson*, Iowa State University Press, 1978.

Lindsay Anderson: A Guide to References and Resources, G. K. Hall, 1979.

Transition: An Author Index, Whitston, 1979.

The Writings of Paul Rosenfeld: An Annotated Bibliography, Garland Publishing, 1979.

(With Bataille) *The Pretend Indians: Images of the Native Americans in the Film*, Iowa State University Press, 1980.

(With Bataille) *Images of American Indians on Film: An Annotated Bibliography*, Garland Publishing, 1985.

(With Robert E. Welch and Richard Boudreau) *The Critical Reception of Hamlin Garland, 1891-1978*, Whitston, 1985.

The Bibliographic Writings of A. N. Munby, Scarecrow, 1986.

CONTRIBUTOR

Randall M. Miller, editor, *The Kaleidoscopic Lens: How Hollywood Views Ethnic Groups*, Jerome Ozer, 1980.

Gerald Nemanic, general editor, *A Bibliographical Guide to Western Literature*, University of Iowa Press, 1981.

Frank N. Magill, editor, *Critical Survey of Long Fiction*, Salem Press, 1983.

Christopher Lyon and Susan Doll, editors, *The International Dictionary of Films and Filmmakers: Films, Directors and Actors*, Volumes I-III, St. James Press, 1984.

Alvin Sullivan, editor-in-chief, *British Literary Magazines: The Edwardian and Victorian Ages* [and] *The Modern Age*, Greenwood Press, 1985.

Magill, editor, *Critical Survey of Drama*, Salem Press, 1985.

Walton Beacham, editor, *Research Guide to Biography and Criticism*, Research Publishing, 1985.

Marshall Deutelbaum and Lealand Pogue, editors, *A Hitchcock Reader*, Iowa State University Press, 1986.

Contributing editor, *Poet and Critic*.

WORK IN PROGRESS: A critical study of John Reed; a collection of the film writing of Lindsay Anderson.

SIDELIGHTS: Charles L. P. Silet told *CA:* "The book on John Reed will be, I think, the first of perhaps three. The next will cover the radical climate of American intellectuals during the hectic months surrounding America's entrance into World War I, and it will center on the little magazine *The Seven Arts.* The third volume will deal with my interest in the attraction the Bolshevik Revolution had on American writers from its beginning through the nineteen twenties, until the Stalin purges of the early thirties began a process of disillusionment with Russian communism, which culminated in the Soviet-Nazi pact. I do not necessarily see these three works as part of a series except that they all treat American intellectual radicalism. It is a topic which has interested me for some time.

"I also have a growing fascination with the films of both Charlie Chaplin and Alfred Hitchcock and have been writing on both filmmakers over the past few years. Hopefully this will eventually evolve into a longer study on either one or both of these directors."

*   *   *

SILVERMAN, Kenneth   1936-

PERSONAL: Born February 5, 1936, in New York, N.Y.; son of Gustave (a builder) and Bessie (Goldberg) Silverman; married Sharon Medjuck, September 8, 1957 (divorced, 1976); children: Willa, Ethan. *Education:* Columbia University, B.A., 1956, M.A., 1958, Ph.D., 1964.

ADDRESSES: Home—7-13 Washington Square N., New York, N.Y. 10003. *Office*—Department of English, New York University, 19 University Place, New York, N.Y. 10003.

CAREER: University of Wyoming, Laramie, instructor in English, 1958-59; New York University, New York, N.Y., 1964—, began as instructor, currently professor of English and co-director of program in American civilization. Executive council member, Institute of Early American History and Culture.

MEMBER: Modern Language Association of America (chairman of bicentennial committee, 1973-76), P.E.N. American Center, American Antiquarian Society (elected member), Society of American Historians (honorary member), Phi Beta Kappa.

AWARDS, HONORS: Danforth associate, 1968-71; Bicentennial grant from National Endowment for the Humanities, 1973-76, for *A Cultural History of the American Revolution;* Pulitzer Prize in biography and Bancroft Prize in American history, both 1985, both for *The Life and Times of Cotton Mather.*

WRITINGS:

(Editor) *Colonial American Poetry*, Hafner, 1968.

Timothy Dwight, Twayne, 1969.

(Editor) *Literature in America: The Founding of a Nation*, Free Press, 1971.

(Editor) *Selected Letters of Cotton Mather*, Louisiana State University Press, 1971.

A Cultural History of the American Revolution: Painting, Music, Literature and the Theatre in the Colonies and the United States from the Treaty of Paris to the Inauguration of George Washington, 1763-1789, Crowell, 1976.

The Life and Times of Cotton Mather, Harper, 1984.

Contributor to scholarly periodicals in his field. Member of editorial board, *Early American Literature*, 1971-73, 1977-80, and *William and Mary Quarterly*, 1985—.

WORK IN PROGRESS: A biography of Edgar Alan Poe.

SIDELIGHTS: Kenneth Silverman specializes in American literature of the colonial period. His book *A Cultural History of the American Revolution*, published during the nation's bicentennial year, has won considerable critical acclaim for its appraisal of the music, poetry, and painting of the North American colonies. Silverman's study follows the progress of American arts from the time of the French and Indian War through the inauguration of George Washington. In the *Washington Post Book World*, John Seelye suggests that few readers "will finish Silverman's book without an overwhelming impression of the richness and variety . . . of the culture generated by the events leading up to, including and immediately following the Revolution." Alden Whitman, a *New York Times* reviewer, calls the book "one of the best of the Bicentennial books for the searching light it throws on the beginnings of the arts in this country." "Silverman's research is awesome," Whitman continues. "If at the conclusion of the period covered by his book a distinct American culture is visible, the facts underlying it can be found in one place. That is no small feat, so one should 'rally round the flag, boys,' for Professor Silverman."

Even more renowned than *A Cultural History of the American Revolution* is Silverman's *The Life and Times of Cotton Mather,* a Pulitzer Prize-winning biography of the famous Puritan minister who was undeniably the most prolific writer of colonial America. "Silverman has almost literally moved heaven and earth to do justice to the most learned minister . . . of the early American church," writes Anatole Broyard in the *New York Times.* The author performed exhaustive research for *The Life and Times of Cotton Mather,* even finding pertinent records at a country auction in Amherst, Massachusetts, and in the basement of a Veterans Administration hospital in Grafton, Massachusetts. He also visited a dozen archives in the United States and Great Britain, including one in Boston that contained the Supreme Judicial Court records from Mather's time. The thoroughness of Silverman's investigation led Broyard to speculate, "He appears to have read all 388 of Mather's published works, which range from church history to a summary of seventeenth-century medical practice."

Mather, a third-generation member of Boston's well-known Puritan family, followed in the footsteps of his father and grandfathers and pursued a career in the ministry. With his father, he presided over the largest religious congregation in Boston from 1689, when he was only twenty-six, until shortly before he died in 1728. Central to Silverman's treatment of Mather is a psychological study based partly on Mather's relationships with his Puritan forebears, partly on his ambivalent and varying reactions to life in colonial Boston, and partly on the restraints imposed upon his personality by the Puritan faith. Edmund S. Morgan of the *New York Review of Books* feels that although Cotton Mather has been "miscast in the popular mind as the typical Puritan," Silverman's work "gives us an inside view . . . of what it meant to be an American Puritan." John Demos, in an article for *New Republic,* similarly claims: "The author seems virtually to have taken up residence inside Mather's head and heart; and the reader is repeatedly invited to see the world as Mather himself would have done—looking out."

Controversial in his own time for his reluctant support of the Salem witch trials, his political maneuverings, and his advocacy of the smallpox vaccine, Mather has been reviled by authors as famous as Nathaniel Hawthorne, William Carlos Williams, and Robert Lowell. Indeed, some modern writers have tended to portray Mather as, in the words of *Newsweek* reviewer David Gates, "the prototype of Calvinist self-loathing transmuted into self-righteous malice." David Levin, reviewing *The Life and Times of Cotton Mather* in the *Washington Post Book World,* says Silverman skillfully conveys a sense of why Mather has been the object of such derision. But the critic maintains that Silverman's portrait is unjustifiably harsh because "the narrative too often stumbles over Mather's difficult personality, which Silverman finds repellent. Perhaps such pejorative judgment helps to tilt the narrative against a favorable interpretation of Mather's behavior on several important issues," including the Salem witchcraft trials.

Many reviewers, however, believe as Demos does, that Silverman's biography presents Mather as "a figure of depth,

complexity, and surpassing interest—someone who still surprises and confounds us, even as we recognize his all-too-human strengths and weaknesses." *The Life and Times of Cotton Mather* is, according to Demos, "large in meaning and significance. For what Silverman achieves can well stand as a model for biographers and historians in general. . . . If it were nothing else [it] would surely be the most beautifully-composed biography of the year." The Puritan minister who has been maligned through nearly three centuries has finally found judicious treatment, in the view of Anatole Broyard. "Few men," Broyard writes, "have been so handsomely rewarded by posterity as Cotton Mather is in Mr. Silverman's book. It is a splendid day of judgment, in which Cotton Mather stands radiant in all his virtues and failings."

BIOGRAPHICAL/CRITICAL SOURCES:

PERIODICALS

Atlantic, April, 1984.
Commentary, August, 1984.
New Republic, August 13, 1984.
Newsweek, April 2, 1984.
New Yorker, August 30, 1976, April 23, 1984.
New York Review of Books, July 15, 1976, May 31, 1984.
New York Times, August 14, 1976, March 17, 1984.
New York Times Book Review, March 25, 1984.
Saturday Review, June 26, 1976.
Washington Post Book World, July 4, 1976, December 12, 1976, April 29, 1984.

—*Sketch by Anne Janette Johnson*

*   *   *

SIMON, George T(homas)   1912-

PERSONAL: Born May 9, 1912, in New York, N.Y.; son of Leo L. (a milliner) and Anna (Mayer) Simon; married Beverly Jean Alt, November 6, 1947; children: Julie Ann, Thomas George. *Education:* Harvard University, A.B., 1934.

ADDRESSES: Home—21 West 58th St., New York, N.Y. 10019. *Office*—157 West 57th St., New York, N.Y. 10019.

CAREER: Metronome (magazine), New York City, associate editor, 1935-39, editor, 1939-55; Jazztone Society (record mail-order club), New York City, program director, 1957-59; Bouree Productions (record producers), New York City, president, 1959-61; National Academy of Recording Arts and Sciences, New York City, executive director, 1961-73, special consultant, 1973—. Writer, producer, and consultant for numerous television programs relating to music, including "America's Greatest Bands," 1955-56, "Timex All Star Jazz" shows, 1958-59, "The Swinging Years" and "The Singing, Swinging Years," 1960, "Play Your Hunch," 1962, and "The Best on Record," 1963-67, ABC-TV music documentaries, 1965-67, "Timex All-Star Swing Session," 1973, "America's Greatest Tunes," 1982, and "Juke Box Saturday Night," 1983; producer of jazz record albums for Golden Records, Capitol, Warner Brothers, Columbia, RCA Victor, and others. Consultant for Time-Life Records, 1970-72, 1981, and Franklin Mint Record Society, 1981—. *Military service:* U.S. Army, 1943-45; member of Glenn Miller Band and later recording chief for V Discs.

MEMBER: American Society of Composers, Authors and Publishers, Writers Guild of America (East), National Academy of Recording Arts and Sciences.

AWARDS, HONORS: ASCAP-Deems Taylor award (first prize), 1969, for *The Big Bands;* Grammy Award, National Academy of Recording Arts and Sciences, 1977, for "Bing Crosby, 'A Legendary Performer.'"

WRITINGS:

Don Watson Starts His Band, Dodd, 1940.
(Self-illustrated with photographs) *The Bandleader,* Hendler & Woods, 1953.
The Feeling of Jazz, Simon & Schuster, 1961.
The Sinatra Report, Billboard Books, 1965.
The Big Bands, foreword by Frank Sinatra, Macmillan, 1967, 4th revised and enlarged edition, 1981.
Simon Says: The Sights and Sounds of the Swing Era, Arlington House, 1971.
Glenn Miller and His Orchestra, Crowell, 1974.
The Big Bands Song Book, Crowell, 1975.
(Editor) *Esquire's World of Jazz,* Crowell, 1975.
(With others) *The Best of the Music Makers,* Doubleday, 1979.
The Big Bands Trivia Quiz Book, Barnes & Noble, 1985.

Also author of program notes and booklet for recording "Bing Crosby, 'A Legendary Performer.'" Record critic, *New York Sun,* 1946-48; jazz commentator, *New York Herald Tribune,* 1961-63, and *New York Post,* 1981-82. Contributor of articles on jazz to *Esquire, Downbeat, Mademoiselle, Cosmopolitan,* and other magazines and newspapers.

SIDELIGHTS: The Best of the Music Makers, written by George T. Simon and some of his friends and associates, is described by Robert Palmer in the *New York Times Book Review* as "a collection of almost 300 brief, snappy profiles of jazz, folk, country, rock and pop musicians and singers, living and dead." His book *The Big Bands* is equally comprehensive. Russell Davies states in the *Times Literary Supplement* that, "as fat as a telephone directory and not unlike one in content sometimes, Mr. Simon's book is, of course, a riot of nomenclature, from Irving Aaronson and Trigger Alpert to Joe Yukl and Zeke Zarchy."

BIOGRAPHICAL/CRITICAL SOURCES:

PERIODICALS

National Review, December 17, 1971.
New York Times, December 18, 1971.
New York Times Book Review, November 11, 1979.
Times Literary Supplement, June 6, 1975.

*   *   *

SINGER, Jane Sherrod   1917-1985
(Jane Sherrod)

PERSONAL: Born May 26, 1917, in Wichita Falls, Tex.; died January 26, 1985, in Fullerton, Calif.; daughter of St. Clair and Nina (Bean) Sherrod; married Kurt D. Singer (author, lecturer, and director of B. P. Singer Features), January 21, 1955; children: Marian B., Kenneth W. *Education:* Fullerton Junior College, A.A., 1936; University of California, Los Angeles, B.E., 1938; University of California, Berkeley, M.A., 1954.

ADDRESSES: Office—B. P. Singer Features, 3164 West Tyler Ave., Anaheim, Calif. 92801.

CAREER: University of California, Berkeley, master teacher in elementary education, 1940-45; supervisor of elementary education in Piedmont, Calif., 1942-45; instructor in elementary education at San Francisco State College (now University), San Francisco, Calif., 1946-49, and Whittier College, Whittier, Calif., 1951; B. P. Singer Features, Anaheim, Calif., managing editor and vice-president, 1955-85. Educational consultant, John C. Winston Co., 1946-54.

WRITINGS:

(Editor) *Cooking with the Stars,* A. S. Barnes, 1969.
What You Should Know about Yourself, Volume I, Meredith Corp., 1969, Volume II, Peacock Press, 1972.
Zane Grey Western Cookbook, Prentice-Hall, 1969.
Positive: Self Analysis, Ace Books, 1975.
Quiz Book I, Meredith Corp., 1975.
Quiz Book II, Ace Books, 1975.

UNDER NAME JANE SHERROD; JUVENILES

(With husband, Kurt Singer) *Spies for Democracy,* Denison, 1960.
(With K. Singer) *Great Adventures in Crime,* Denison, 1962.
(With K. Singer) *Great Adventures of the Sea,* Denison, 1962.
(With Zel Thayer) *Ho-i-man and His Friends,* Denison, 1962, 2nd edition published as *Folk Tales of the South Pacific,* 1966.
(With K. Singer) *Ernest Hemingway, Man of Courage,* Denison, 1963.
(With K. Singer) *Dr. Albert Schweitzer, Medical Missionary,* Denison, 1963.
(Editor with K. Singer) *Ghost Book: The World's Greatest Stories of the Known Unknown,* W. H. Allen, 1963.
(With K. Singer) *Lyndon Baines Johnson, Man of Reason,* Denison, 1964.
(With K. Singer) *Folktales from Mexico,* Denison, 1969.

OTHER

Also author of column, "Pathways to Success," syndicated to about fifty newspapers, and column, "Test Yourself," syndicated to about thirty newspapers and magazines, including *Star, National Enquirer,* and *Redbook.*

SIDELIGHTS: The Singers traveled worldwide, "latitudinally and longitudinally from Micronesia to Africa, from Australia to Greenland." Jane Sherrod Singer's works have been translated into German, Dutch, and Spanish.

OBITUARIES:

PERIODICALS

Editor and Publisher Weekly, March 30, 1985.

[Sketch verified by husband, Kurt Singer]

*   *   *

SLAVUTYCH, Yar   1918-

PERSONAL: Surname legally changed in 1954; born January 11, 1918, in Blahodatne, Ukraine (now Ukrainian Soviet Socialist Republic); naturalized U.S. citizen in 1954; son of Mykhajlo and Tetiana (Bratunenko) Zhuchenko; married Elwira Cybar, November 10, 1948; children: Bohdan, Oksana. *Education:* Pedagogic Institute of Zaporizzia, diploma, 1940; Ukrainian Free University, Munich, Germany, graduate study, 1945-46; University of Pennsylvania, A.M., 1954, Ph.D., 1955.

ADDRESSES: Home—72 Westbrook Dr., Edmonton, Alberta, Canada T6J 2E1. *Office*—Department of Slavic Languages, University of Alberta, Edmonton, Alberta, Canada.

CAREER: High school teacher in Zaporizzia, Ukraine, 1940-41, Augsburg, Germany, 1945-49, and Philadelphia, Pa., 1950-55; U.S. Army Language School, Monterey, Calif., senior instructor in Slavic languages, 1955-60; University of Alberta, Edmonton, assistant professor, 1960-65, associate professor, 1966-79, professor of Slavic languages, 1980—.

MEMBER: Modern Language Association of America, Comparative Literature Association, American Name Society (member of board of directors, 1968-70; member of editorial board, 1971-80), American Association of Teachers of Slavic and East European Languages, American Association for the Advancement of Slavic Studies, Canadian Association of Slavists, Canadian Institute of Onomastic Sciences (secretary, 1966-73; vice-president, 1973-76; president, 1976-79), Ukrainian Shakespeare Society (president, 1979—), Ukrainian Free Academy of Sciences, Shevchenko Scientific Society (president of western Canadian branch, 1970-75), Ukrainian Literary and Art Club (president, 1961-65).

AWARDS, HONORS: Literary award from America Press, 1951; Canada Council Award, 1968-69; first prize for poetry from Ivan Franko Foundation, 1969, 1973, and 1981; Shevchenko Gold Medal, 1974; Poet Laureate, Ukrainian Mohylo-Mazepian Academy of Sciences, 1982.

WRITINGS:

Moderna ukrajins'ka poezija, 1900-1950, America Press, 1950.
The Muse in Prison, Svoboda, 1956.
Vybrani poeziji (translation of poems by John Keats), Ukrainian Publishers, 1958.
Oasis (poems; translated into English), Vantage, 1959.
Conversational Ukrainian, Gateway Publishers, 1959, 4th edition, 1973.
Trofeji, 1938-1963 (poems), Slavuta, 1963.
(Editor) *Pivnichne siajvo,* five volumes, Slavuta, 1964-71.
Zavojovnyky prerij (poems), Slavuta, 1968.
Mudroshchi mandriw (poems), Slavuta, 1972.
(Editor) *Zakhidnokanads'kyj zbirnyk,* Shevchenko Scientific Society, Volume I, 1973, Volume II, 1975.
The Conquerors of the Prairies (poems; contains original Ukrainian versions and translations), translation by R. H. Morrison, Slavuta, 1974.
Ukrainian Poetry in Canada: A Historical Account, Ukrainian Pioneers' Association of Alberta, 1975.
(Editor) *Antolohija ukrajins'koji poeziji v Kanadi, 1898-1973,* Ukrainian Writers' Association, 1975.
Ukrajins'ka poezija v Kanadi, Slavuta, 1976.
L'Oiseau de feu (poems), compiled and translated into French by Rene Coulet de Gard, Editions des Deux Mondes, 1976.
Zibrani tvory, Slavuta, 1978.
Zhyvi smoloskypy (poems), Slavuta, 1983.
Valogatott versek (poems), translation by Domokos Sandor, Hungarian Cultural Society of Edmonton, 1983.
An Annotated Bibliography of Ukrainian Literature in Canada, 1908-1983, Slavuta, 1984.
Mistsiamy zaporoz'kymy (memoirs), Slavuta, 1985.

Contributor to *Ukrainian Quarterly, Ukrainian Review, Canadian Slavonic Papers, Slavs in Canada, Names, Slavic and East European Journal, Slavic Review, Suchasnist', Vyzvol'nyj shliakh, Books Abroad,* and *Jahrbuch der Ukrainekunde.* Editor of *Kanads'ka Ukrajina,* 1976-78.

WORK IN PROGRESS: Research on Ukrainian literature in Canada and the United States.

BIOGRAPHICAL/CRITICAL SOURCES:

BOOKS

Andrusyshen, C. H., and Watson Kirkconnell, *The Ukrainian Poets, 1189-1962,* University of Toronto Press, 1963.
Jaremenko, S., compiler, *Vokal'ni tvory na slova Jara Slavutycha,* Slavuta, 1978.
Mandryka, M. I., *History of Ukrainian Literature in Canada,* Ukrainian Free Academy of Sciences, 1968.
Shcherbak, Mykola, and W. T. Zyla, *Polumjane slovo,* Ukrainian Publishers, 1969.
Slavutych, Vira, compiler, *Bibliohrafija pysan' pro Jara Slavutycha (1978-1985),* Slavuta, 1985.
Zyla, compiler, *Tvorchist' Jara Slavutycha: A Symposium,* Edmonton Jubilee Committee, 1978.

*   *   *

SMITH, Bernard (William) 1916-

PERSONAL: Born October 3, 1916, in Sydney, New South Wales, Australia; son of Charles and Rose (Tierney) Smith; married Kate Beatrice Hartley Challis, 1941; children: Elizabeth, John. *Education:* Attended Warburg Institute, London, England, 1949-50; University of Sydney, B.A., 1952; Australian National University, Ph.D., 1957.

ADDRESSES: Office—Australian Academy of the Humanities, 168 Nicholson St., Fitzroy, Victoria, Australia.

CAREER: National Art Gallery of New South Wales, Sydney, Australia, education officer, 1945-48, 1951-52; University of Melbourne, Melbourne, Australia, senior lecturer in department of fine arts, 1957-63, reader, 1964-66; University of Sydney, Sydney, professor of contemporary art, 1967-77; Australian Academy of the Humanities, Canberra, president, 1977—.

MEMBER: Society of Antiquaries of London (fellow), Hakluyt Society (London).

WRITINGS:

Place, Taste and Tradition: A Study of Australian Art since 1788, Ure Smith, 1945.
A Catalogue of Australian Oil Paintings in the National Gallery of New South Wales, National Gallery of New South Wales, 1953.
(Editor) *Education through Art in Australia,* Melbourne University Press, 1958.
European Vision and the South Pacific, 1768-1850, Oxford University Press, 1960, 2nd edition, Yale University Press, 1985.
Australian Painting, 1788 to 1960, Oxford University Press, 1962, 2nd edition published as *Australian Painting, 1788-1970,* 1972.
(With wife, Kate Smith) *The Architectural Character of Glebe, Sydney,* University Co-operative Bookshop (Sydney), 1973.
(Editor) *Concerning Contemporary Art: The Power Lectures, 1968-1973,* Clarendon Press, 1975.
(Editor) *Documents on Art and Taste in Australia: The Colonial Period, 1770-1914,* Oxford University Press, 1975.
The Antipodean Manifesto: Essays in Art and History, Oxford University Press, 1976.
The Spectre of Truganini, Australian Broadcasting Commission, 1980.
(Editor) *Culture and History Essays Presented to Jack Lindsay,* Hale & Iremonger, 1984.

The Boy Adeodatus: The Portrait of a Lucky Young Bastard
(autobiography), Penguin, 1984.
(With Rudiger Joppien) *The Art of Captain Cook's Voyages*
(three volumes), Oxford University Press, 1985.

Contributor to professional journals.

* * *

SMITH, Jessie Carney   1930-

PERSONAL: Born September 24, 1930, in Greensboro, N.C.;
daughter of James and Vesona (Bigelow) Carney; married
Frederick Douglas Smith, December 2, 1950 (divorced); children: Frederick Douglas, Jr. *Education:* North Carolina Agricultural and Technical State University, B.S., 1950; attended
Cornell University, 1950; Michigan State University, M.A.,
1956; George Peabody College for Teachers (now George Peabody College for Teachers of Vanderbilt University), M.A.L.S.,
1957; University of Illinois, Ph.D., 1964. *Politics:* Democrat.
Religion: Methodist.

ADDRESSES: Home—5039 Hillsboro Rd., No. 146, Nashville, Tenn. 37215. *Office*—University Library, Fisk University, 17th Ave. N., Nashville, Tenn. 37203.

CAREER: Tennessee State University, Nashville, instructor
and head cataloger at library, 1957-60, assistant professor of
library science and coordinator of library service, 1963-65;
Fisk University, Nashville, professor of library science and
university librarian, 1965—, director of library training institutes, 1970-75, 1978. Lecturer at George Peabody College for
Teachers of Vanderbilt University, 1969—, Alabama A&M
University, 1971-73, and University of Tennessee, 1973-74.

Guest lecturer at many colleges and universities, including
Cornell University, Howard University, University of Illinois,
and Bennett College. Director of numerous institutes, research
programs, and internships in black and ethnic studies librarianship, all at Fisk University, all supported by U.S. Office of
Education; also director of other publicly funded Fisk University programs related to black American literature. Member of
numerous professional committees on libraries, including Reference and Subscription Books Review, 1969-71, 1971-73,
Biomedical Library Review, 1972-76, and American Library
Association Committee on Accreditation, 1974—. Also member of various task forces and advisory councils, including
Tennessee Advisory Council on Libraries, 1971-75, Task Force
on Cultural Minorities, 1980-82, and Institute for Research in
Black Music, 1980—. Evaluator for Tennessee Committee for
the Humanities, Inc., on projects for Scarritt College, 1979,
Nashville Panel, 1980, and Tennessee State Museum, 1981-
82. Consultant to Southern Association of Colleges and Schools,
1968—, Oak Ridge National Laboratory, 1976, U.S. Office
for Civil Rights, 1979-80, and Association of College and
Research Libraries/National Endowment for the Humanities
workshops, 1983. Has appeared on local radio and television
shows.

MEMBER: American Library Association (member of council,
1969-71, 1971-74), Medical Library Association, Association
of College and Research Libraries, American Association of
University Professors, National Association for the Advancement of Colored People, African Studies Association, Links,
Inc. (president of Hendersonville area chapter, 1983-85),
Southeastern Library Association (member of nominating
committee, 1965-66), Tennessee Library Association (vice-
chairperson, 1968-69; chairperson of college and university

section, 1969-70), Beta Phi Mu (vice-president, 1976; president, 1976-77), Pi Gamma Mu, Alpha Kappa Alpha.

AWARDS, HONORS: National Urban League fellow, 1968,
1976; Council on Library Resources fellow, 1969; certificate
of achievement from Alpha Kappa Alpha, 1976, for outstanding work in the community and in the library profession; Martin Luther King, Jr., Black Author's Award, 1982.

WRITINGS:

(Author of introduction) *Special Collections in the Erastus
Milo Cravath Library*, Fisk University Library, 1966.
Bibliography for Black Studies Programs, Fisk University, 1969.
A Handbook for the Study of Black Bibliography, Fisk Uni-
versity Library, 1971.
Minorities in the United States: Guide to Resources, School
of Library Science, George Peabody College for Teach-
ers, 1973.
(Author of introduction) *Dictionary Catalog of the Negro Col-
lection of the Fisk University Library*, G. K. Hall, 1974.
*Black Academic Libraries and Research Collections: An His-
torical Survey*, Greenwood Press, 1977.
(Author of foreword) Dominique-Rene de Lerma, *Bibliog-
raphy of Black Music*, Volume I: *Reference Materials*,
Greenwood Press, 1981.
(Editor) *Ethnic Genealogy: A Research Guide*, Greenwood
Press, 1983.

CONTRIBUTOR

E. J. Josey, editor, *The Black Librarian in America*, Scarecrow, 1970.
Library and Information Services for Special Groups, American Society for Information Science in cooperation with
Science Associates/International, 1973.
Dictionary of American Library Biography, Libraries Unlimited, 1978.
Mark Tucker and Edwin S. Gleaves, editors, *Reference Services and Library Education*, Lexington Books, 1982.

Contributor to *Bibliographical Control of Afro-American Lit-
erature*. Also contributor to *Proceedings of the Workshop on
Social Science Approaches to the Study of Negro Culture*, Fisk
University, 1968, *Proceedings of the Workshop on Afro-Amer-
ican Culture*, University of Iowa, 1969, *Proceedings of the
Workshop on Negro Life and Culture in the Liberal Arts Cur-
riculum*, Fisk University, 1969, *Proceedings of the Black Cau-
cus of the American Library Association and Alabama State
University, Institute for Training Librarians for Special Black
Collections and Archives*, 1974, and *ALA Yearbook*, 1977-84.

OTHER

Contributor to professional journals, including *College and
Research Libraries, Southeastern Librarian, Black Information Index, Black World*, and *South Carolina Librarian*. Member of editorial board of *Choice*, 1969-72, 1972-75.

*WORK IN PROGRESS: Images of Blacks in American Cul-
ture: A Reference Guide to Information Sources*, for Greenwood Press; a directory of minority women in America.

SIDELIGHTS: Jessie Carney Smith writes: "Librarianship offers tremendous opportunities for research and publication,
particularly when the resources needed for such activities are
found in the library where the researcher is employed. Fisk
University Library and its notable special collections on black
themes have been among the various motivating factors that
influenced my writing, my consultant work, and my involve-

ment in professional activities for librarians who needed to develop or to enhance their expertise on black and ethnic themes.

"I have difficulty assuming full credit for any of my publications, for I attribute each piece of work to the stimulation of various people who, without realizing it, influenced my development and my writing. I attribute my addiction to work to my father, who considered every moment too precious to waste in unproductivity. I learned from [my] mother and from my maternal grandparents that one must share resources with others, that helpfulness is a gift to be passed along. Educators who shaped my early life in a four-room school, and who taught me to speak correctly and to write clearly in elementary school, high school, and college, mean much more to me in retrospect than I realized as they prepared me for a career. My graduate schools helped to cultivate my self-confidence as one who could write professionally, and there, for the first time, I knew that I would soon publish, thus bringing to the forefront the inspiration from everyone who had helped to shape my life.

"I write almost exclusively on black themes because of my experiences, my·surroundings, my vision of the need for published information in these areas, and my love for the subjects. I have a similar love for ethnic themes; thus some of my works reflect this interest. Because I am a perfectionist, I work arduously to produce works that reflect high standards. Whether I have been as successful as I wish is very much left to the judgement of my critics and my reviewers.

"Works which hold special meaning for me are *Ethnic Genealogy, Images of Blacks in American Culture*, and *Minority American Women*. The latter work haunts me, for it has been in preparation for a number of years, but my yearning for perfection keeps it from being available for public consumption.

"Writing, then, is a rewarding part of my life, and it provides a balance between professional responsibilities and personal gratification so necessary in the complexities of contemporary society."

BIOGRAPHICAL/CRITICAL SOURCES:

PERIODICALS

College and Research Libraries, summer, 1965.
Ebony, June, 1967.

*   *   *

SOLO, Robert A(lexander) 1916-

PERSONAL: Born August 2, 1916, in Philadelphia, Pa.; son of Louis (a merchant) and Rebecca (Muchnick) Solo; married Carolyn Shaw Bell, June, 1942 (divorced, 1949); married Roselyn Starr (a university teacher), August, 1958; children: (first marriage) Tova. *Education:* Harvard University, B.S. (magna cum laude), 1938; American University, M.A., 1941; Cornell University, Ph.D., 1953; also attended London School of Economics and Political Science. *Politics:* "Democratic Left." *Religion:* Jewish.

ADDRESSES: Office—Department of Economics, Michigan State University, East Lansing, Mich. 48823.

CAREER: Economist in U.S. Government agencies, Washington, D.C., 1939-41; WCAU-Television (Columbia Broadcasting System affiliate), Philadelphia, Pa., writer and script chief, 1948-49; Rutgers University, New Brunswick, N.J.,

instructor, 1952-54, assistant professor of economics, 1954-55; McGill University, Montreal, Quebec, visiting lecturer in economics, 1955-56; City College (now City College of the City University of New York), New York, N.Y., assistant professor of economics, 1956-59; Economic Development Administration of Commonwealth of Puerto Rico, San Juan, consultant, 1959-61; National Planning Association, Washington, D.C., project director, 1961-63; Organization for Economic Cooperation and Development, Paris, France, consultant to directorate of scientific affairs, 1963-64; Sorbonne, University of Paris, Paris, France, lecturer in economics, 1964-65; National Academy of Sciences and National Research Council, Washington, D.C., special associate to foreign secretary, 1965; Princeton University, Princeton, N.J., senior research economist, 1965-66; Michigan State University, East Lansing, professor of economics and management, 1966—, director of Institute of International Business and Economic Development Studies, 1966-68.

Visiting lecturer, University of Michigan, summer, 1955; professeur associe, University of Paris, 1971; Fulbright lecturer, University of Grenoble, 1972-73. Consultant to U.S. Senate subcommittee on patents, trademarks, and copyrights, 1956-58, to National Aeronautics and Space Administration (NASA), 1965-67, and to National Conference Board, 1970-72. *Military service:* U.S. Navy, 1941-46.

WRITINGS:

Industrial Capacity in the United States, Office of Price Administration and Civilian Supply, 1941.
(With Georges Agadjanian) *La Vallee des ombres* (novel), Editions de la Maison Francaise, 1941.
(Editor and contributor) *Economics and the Public Interest*, Rutgers University Press, 1955.
Synthetic Rubber: A Case Study in Technological Development under Government Direction, U.S. Government Printing Office (for U.S. Senate Committee on the Judiciary), 1959.
Essai sur l'Amerique, Editions de la Diaspora Francaise, 1960.
Journal, Editions de la Diaspora Francaise, 1961.
Economic Organizations and Social Systems, Bobbs-Merrill, 1967.
(Editor with Everett Rogers and contributor) *Inducing Technological Advance in Economic Growth and Development*, Michigan State University Press, 1973.
Organizing Science for Technology Transfer in Economic Development, Michigan State University Press, 1975.
Across the High Technology Threshold: The Case of Synthetic Rubber, Norwood Editions, 1980.
(Editor with Charles Anderson and contributor) *Value Judgements and Income Distribution*, Praeger, 1981.
The Positive State, South-Western, 1982.

CONTRIBUTOR

Nathan Rosenberg, editor, *The Economics of Technological Change*, Penguin, 1971.
Does Economics Ignore You?, Committee on Economic Development, 1972.
Martin Pfaff, editor, *Frontiers of Social Thought*, North-Holland Publishing, 1975.
Lindberg, Alford, Crouch, and Offe, editors, *Stress and Contradiction in Modern Capitalism*, Lexington Books, 1976.
Pfaff, editor, *Grants and Exchange*, North-Holland Publishing, 1976.
Warren Samuels, editor, *The Chicago School of Political Economy*, Michigan State University Press, 1976.

Samuels, editor, *The Economy as a System of Power*, Transaction Books, 1979.

Pfaff, editor, *Public Transfers and Some Private Alternatives during Recession*, Duncker & Humblot (Berlin), 1982.

Spiegel and Samuels, editors, *Contemporary Economists in Perspective*, JAI Press, 1984.

Tool, editor, *An Institutionalist Guide to Economics and Public Policy*, Sharpe, 1984.

Alperovitz and Skurski, editors, *American Economic Policy*, University of Notre Dame Press, 1984.

Also contributor to *America's World Role for the Next Twenty-five Years*, proceedings of a professional conference in Taiwan, 1976.

OTHER

Contributor of about eighty articles and reviews to economics journals and other publications, including *Saturday Review, Technology and Culture, Current, Looking Ahead, Challenge, Canadian Bar Review, Journal of Philosophy*, and *Social Science*.

SIDELIGHTS: In a *Science* review, Kenneth E. Boulding calls *Economic Organizations and Social Systems* "an important work, a milestone on the long and difficult road toward the development of an adequate theory of the dynamics of the world social system." He notes that although the book is somewhat uneven in style "with some long, textbookish passages of rather dull though usually accurate and insightful analysis of social systems," these are interspersed with "passages that are on fire with intellectual and humane passion, and historical vignettes which are masterpieces of condensation and insight with not a word wasted." Boulding concludes that "if this is a work of insight rather than of science it is because of the absence of an adequate system of social instrumentation. . . . The cognitive theory of social change, which Solo is propounding, will remain in the realm of insight until we develop an adequate information system for what might be called a mass cognitive structure. This we do not now have, and in its absence we have to rely on illustration rather than demonstration."

Robert A. Solo told *CA:* "I sometimes wonder why many who are so beautifully articulate verbally cannot write effectively. I think it has something to do with the need for an audience. Writing is a kind of talking to yourself, listening to yourself, evaluating yourself by yourself, a solitary business in a way, not for the one geared into and needing the active interplay of conversation and the immediacy of discourse. Before the writer is the dreamer, and for both there is a closed world, a space of rich solitude, for them a haven and the vital source."

BIOGRAPHICAL/CRITICAL SOURCES:

PERIODICALS

Science, September, 1967.

*   *   *

SOLOMON, Ezra 1920-

PERSONAL: Born March 20, 1920, in Rangoon, Burma; came to United States in 1947, naturalized citizen in 1951; son of Ezra and Emily (Rose) Solomon; married Janet Lorraine Cameron, May 7, 1949; children: Catherine Shan, Janet Ming, Lorna Cameron. *Education:* University of Rangoon, A.B. (with honors), 1940; University of Chicago, Ph.D., 1950.

ADDRESSES: Home—775 Santa Ynez, Stanford, Calif. 94305. *Office*—Graduate School of Business, Stanford University, Stanford, Calif. 94305.

CAREER: University of Chicago, Chicago, Ill., instructor, 1948-51, assistant professor, 1951-55, associate professor, 1955-57, professor of finance, 1957-60; Stanford University, Graduate School of Business, Stanford, Calif., professor of finance and director of International Center for the Advancement of Management Education, 1961-64, Dean Witter Professor of Finance, 1965—. Visiting professor at Massachusetts Institute of Technology, University of North Carolina, Istituto Superiore per Impreditorie Dirigenti D'Azienda, Palermo, Italy, Universidad del Valle, Cali, Colombia, and Instituto para el Desarrollo de Empresarios en la Argentina. Director of Kaiser Aluminum & Chemical Corp., Encyclopaedia Britannica, Inc., United Financial Corp., Capital Preservation Fund, and Foremost-McKesson, Inc. Member of Commission on Higher Education for Management, government of Australia, 1970—, and Presidential Commission on Financial Structure and Regulation, 1970-71; President's Council of Economic Advisors, consultant, 1970-71, member, 1971-73. Consulting editor in finance to Prentice-Hall, Inc., 1962—. Consultant to Federal Reserve System board of governors, 1970-71, and U.S. Secretary of the Treasury, 1973-75; consulting economist to government of Manitoba, U.S. Senate Committee on Banking and Currency, National Commission of Money and Credit, American Institute of Certified Public Accountants, and several private corporations. *Military service:* Royal Naval Volunteer Reserve, Burma Division, 1942-47; became lieutenant.

MEMBER: American Economic Association, American Finance Association.

WRITINGS:

(Editor) *The Management of Corporate Capital*, Free Press, 1959.

(With Zarko G. Bilbija) *Metropolitan Chicago: An Economic Analysis*, Free Press, 1960.

The Theory of Financial Management, Columbia University Press, 1963.

(With Eli Shapiro and William L. White) *Money and Banking*, 5th edition, Holt, 1968.

(With others) *Money and Banking in Canada*, Holt, 1970.

Wall Street in Transition, New York University Press, 1974.

The Anxious Economy, San Francisco Book, 1976.

(With John J. Pringle) *An Introduction to Financial Management*, 2nd edition (Solomon was not associated with earlier edition), Goodyear Publishing, 1980.

Beyond the Turning Point: The U.S. Economy in the 1980s, Stanford Alumni Association, 1981.

International Patterns of Inflation, Conference Board, 1984.

General editor of "Foundation of Finance" series, Prentice-Hall, 1964—. Editor of *Journal of Business*, 1953-57; member of editorial board of *Journal of Finance*, 1963-65, *Journal of Quantitative and Financial Analysis*, 1965-66, and *Journal of Business Finance*, 1968-73.

SIDELIGHTS: The Theory of Financial Management has been translated into Spanish, Portuguese, Turkish, French, Japanese, and Italian.

*   *   *

SONNICHSEN, C. L. 1901-

PERSONAL: Born September 20, 1901, in Fonda, Iowa; son

of Henry Matthew and Mary (Hults) Sonnichsen; married Augusta Jones, 1933 (divorced, 1950); married Carol Wade, 1956; children: Charles Philip, Mary Augusta, Nancy Leland. *Education:* University of Minnesota, B.A., 1924; Harvard University, M.A., 1927, Ph.D., 1931.

ADDRESSES: Home—884 West Safari Dr., Tucson, Ariz. 85704. *Office*—Arizona Historical Society, 949 East Second Ave., Tucson, Ariz. 85719.

CAREER: St. James School, Faribault, Minn., assistant master, 1924-26; Carnegie Institute of Technology (now Carnegie-Mellon University), Pittsburgh, Pa., instructor, 1927-29; University of Texas at El Paso, associate professor, 1931-33, professor of English and chairman of department, 1933-60, dean of graduate division, 1960-67, H. Y. Benedict Professor Emeritus, 1972—. Visiting professor, University of Texas, 1936, 1938. Lecturer on southwestern subjects.

MEMBER: Order of American Historians, Western Writers of America (president, 1977), Western History Association (president, 1984), Western American Literature Association (president, 1966), Southwestern American Literature Association, Arizona Historical Society, Texas State Historical Association (fellow), Texas Institute of Letters, Texas Folklore Society (president, 1935), New Mexico Folklore Society, El Paso County Historical Society, El Paso Westerners (sheriff, 1966), Tucson Westerners, English Westerners, Tucson Literary Club, Adobe Corral, Scabbard and Blade, Alpha Chi, Lambda Alpha Psi.

AWARDS, HONORS: Bowdoin Prize, Harvard University, 1931; Rockefeller fellowship, 1948; grant, Huntington Library, 1956; Friends of the Dallas Public Library Award, 1969; first annual faculty research award, University of Texas at El Paso, 1972; Standard Oil of Indiana Outstanding Teacher Award, 1972; Wrangler Award, Cowboy Hall of Fame, 1975; Western Writers of America, Spur Award, 1975, for *Colonel Greene and the Copper Skyrocket,* and 1977, and Golden Saddleman Award, 1980; Little Joe Award, Westerners International, 1975; Western Heritage Award, 1975, for *Colonel Greene and the Copper Skyrocket;* Western History Association award of merit, 1977; American Association for State and Local History award of merit, 1979.

WRITINGS:

Billy King's Tombstone, Caxton Printers, 1942, revised edition published as *Billy King's Tombstone: The Private Life of an Arizona Boom Town,* University of Arizona Press, 1972.
Roy Bean: Law West of the Pecos, Macmillan, 1943, reprinted, University of New Mexico Press, 1986.
Cowboys and Cattle Kings, University of Oklahoma Press, 1950, reprinted, Greenwood Press, 1980.
I'll Die before I'll Run, Harper, 1951, revised edition, Devin-Adair, 1961.
Alias Billy the Kid, University of New Mexico Press, 1955.
Ten Texas Feuds, University of New Mexico Press, 1957.
The Mescalero Apaches, University of Oklahoma Press, 1958.
Tularosa: Last of the Frontier West, Devin-Adair, 1960, revised edition, University of New Mexico Press, 1980.
The El Paso Salt War, Texas Western Press, 1961.
(Editor) *The Southwest in Life and Literature* (anthology), Devin-Adair, 1962.
Outlaw: Bill Mitchell, Alias Baldy Russell, Swallow Press, 1965, published as *Outlaw: On the Dodge with Baldy Russell,* Ohio University Press, 1984.

Pass of the North, Texas Western Press, 1968, revised and enlarged edition, 1980.
The State National Bank of El Paso, Texas Western Press, 1971.
(Editor) Morris B. White, *White Oaks: Life in a New Mexico Gold Camp,* University of Arizona Press, 1971.
Colonel Greene and the Copper Skyrocket, University of Arizona Press, 1974.
San Agustin: First Cathedral Church in Arizona, Arizona Historical Society, 1974.
From Hopalong to Hud: Thoughts on Western Fiction, Texas A&M University Press, 1978.
(Editor with Nancy Dickey) Clifford A. Perkins, *Border Patrol,* Texas Western Press, 1978.
The Grave of John Wesley Hardin, Texas A&M University Press, 1979.
The Ambidextrous Historian, University of Oklahoma Press, 1981.
Tucson: The Life and Times of an American City, University of Oklahoma Press, 1982.
Pioneer Heritage: The First Century of the Arizona Historical Society, Arizona Historical Society, 1984.
From Rattlesnakes to Road Agents: Rough Times on the Frio, Texas Christian University Press, 1985.

Senior editor, *Journal of Arizona History,* 1972—.

WORK IN PROGRESS: The Laughing West, an anthology.

SIDELIGHTS: C. L. Sonnichsen told *CA* that his work is "in a gray area between history and literature and has connections with folklore and popular culture." Sonnichsen collects and studies Western fiction, which he regards "as social history, watching for changes in the basic assumptions of consumers as well as producers of both superior and commercial novels." He notes that he has studied Texan and New Mexican feuds, "written biographies, city histories, and studies of popular literature, looking for reasons and noting the ironies and inconsistencies of life." He says that, never content with "how" and "when," he always asks, "why?"

BIOGRAPHICAL/CRITICAL SOURCES:

BOOKS

Roach, Joyce, *C. L. Sonnichsen,* Boise State University, 1979.
Walker, Dale, *C. L. Sonnichsen: Grassroots Historian,* Texas Western Press, 1972.

PERIODICALS

Book World, August 13, 1972.
Business History Review, autumn, 1977.
Journal of American History, September, 1969, December, 1975.
Pacific Historical Review, May, 1970, May, 1976.
Southwest Review, winter, 1975.

*   *   *

STACEY, Margaret 1922-

PERSONAL: Born March 27, 1922, in London, England; daughter of Conrad Eugene (a printer) and Grace Priscilla (Boyce) Petrie; married Frank Arthur Stacey (a university professor), May 20, 1945 (died, 1978); children: Patricia, Richard, Kate, Peter, Michael. *Education:* London School of Economics and Political Science, B.Sc. (Econ.), 1943. *Politics:* Labour. *Religion:* Agnostic.

ADDRESSES: Home—8 Landsdowne Circus, Leanington Spa, Warwickshire CV32 4SW, England. *Office*—Department of Sociology, University of Warwick, Coventry CV4 7AL, England.

CAREER: Royal Ordnance Factory, Glasglow, Scotland, labor officer, 1943-44; Oxford University, Oxford, England, tutor, 1944-51; University College of Swansea, Singleton Park, Swansea, Wales, research officer, 1961-62, research fellow, 1962-63, lecturer, 1963-70, senior lecturer in sociology, 1970-74; University of Warwick, Coventry, England, professor of sociology, 1974—, chairperson of department, 1974-79. Member, Welsh Hospital board, 1970-74, and General Medical Council, 1976-84.

MEMBER: British Sociological Association (honorary general secretary, 1968-70; vice-chairperson, 1975-76; chairperson, 1977-79; president, 1981-83).

AWARDS, HONORS: Fawcett Prize, 1982, for *Women, Power and Politics.*

WRITINGS:

Tradition and Change: A Study of Banbury, Oxford University Press, 1960.
(Contributor) K. J. Hilton, editor, *The Lower Swansea Valley Project*, Longmans, Green, 1967.
Methods of Social Research, Pergamon, 1969.
(Editor) *Comparability in Social Research*, Heinemann, 1969.
(Editor) *Hospitals, Children, and Their Families: The Report of a Pilot Study*, Routledge & Kegan Paul, 1970.
(With others) *Power, Persistence and Change: A Second Study of Banbury*, Routledge & Kegan Paul, 1975.
(Co-editor) *Health Care and Health Knowledge*, Croom Helm, 1977.
Health and the Division of Labour, Croom Helm, 1977.
(Editor with D. Hall) *Beyond Separation: Further Studies of Children in Hospital*, Routledge & Kegan Paul, 1979.
(With Marian Price) *Women, Power and Politics*, Tavistock Publications, 1981.

Also editor of *Sociology of the HS*, a sociological review monograph for the University of Keele.

SIDELIGHTS: Margaret Stacey told *CA:* "My main concern is with the individual and society; currently I am most interested in its specification to the patient in hospitals, but this interest also led to locality studies undertaken. My children are a main matter of life importance; my work and writing have been undertaken as possible within this consideration.

"In the past decade my work has moved increasingly into the area of women's studies and the importance of the gender order in the health care division of labor."

*   *   *

STALLINGS, Constance L(ee)   1932-

PERSONAL: Born March 7, 1932, in Springfield, Mass.; daughter of Udell Harrison (a teacher) and Marion (a realtor; maiden name, Beck) Stallings. *Education:* Oberlin College, A.B., 1954; attended Foreign Service Institute, Ankara, Turkey, 1962, New York University, 1966, and Columbia University, 1967.

ADDRESSES: Home—349 East 50th St., New York, N.Y. 10022.

CAREER: U.S. Department of State, Washington, D.C., on staff of American Embassy in London, England, 1959-61, and Ankara, Turkey, 1961-63; Time, Inc., New York City, on staff of News Service, 1965-68; Sierra Club Books, New York City, editor and staff writer, 1970-72; National Audubon Society, New York City, editor and staff writer, 1973-84. President and editor of East Woods Press, 1973—.

MEMBER: Vocal Record Collectors Society.

WRITINGS:

(With John G. Mitchell) *Ecotactics: The Sierra Club Handbook for Environment Activists*, Sierra Club Books, 1970.
(With Dick Murlless) *Hiker's Guide to the Smokies*, Sierra Club Books, 1973.
A People's Agenda for Open Space, Conservation Foundation, 1974.
(Editor) *John Muir's Longest Walk*, Doubleday, 1975.
(Editor) *The Professional Singer's Guide to New York*, AIMS, 1984.
Toward a Career in Europe, AIMS, 1985.

Contributor to popular magazines, including *Reader's Digest* and *Audubon*. Associate editor of *Open Space Action*, 1969, and *Backpacker*, 1973-79.

SIDELIGHTS: Constance L. Stallings commented to *CA:* "My major interest is in the conservation of resources and improving the environment. The miracle of the human singing voice is a happier subject."

*   *   *

STANLEY, George Edward   1942-

PERSONAL: Born July 15, 1942, in Memphis, Tex.; son of Joseph (a farmer) and Cellie (a nurse; maiden name, Lowe) Stanley; married Gwen Meshew (a Slavic specialist), June 29, 1974; children: James Edward, Charles Albert Andrew. *Education:* Texas Tech University, B.A., 1965, M.A., 1967; University of Port Elizabeth, D.Litt., 1974. *Religion:* Baptist.

ADDRESSES: Home—5527 Eisenhower Dr., Lawton, Okla. 73505. *Office*—Department of Languages and Communication, Cameron University, P.O. Box 16355, Lawton, Okla. 73505.

CAREER: East Texas State University, Commerce, instructor in English as a foreign language, 1967-69; University of Kansas, Lawrence, instructor in English as a foreign language, 1969-70; Cameron University, Lawton, Okla., instructor, 1970-73, assistant professor, 1973-76, associate professor, 1976-79, professor of French, Italian, and Romanian, 1979—, chairman of department of languages, 1984—, director of creative writing program. Fulbright lecturer at University of Chad, 1973.

MEMBER: Mystery Writers of America, Crime Writers Association of Great Britain, Society of Children's Book Writers, American Association of Teachers of Italian.

AWARDS, HONORS: Distinguished faculty award from Phi Kappa Phi, 1974; member of the year award from Society of Children's Book Writers, 1979.

WRITINGS:

JUVENILES

Mini-Mysteries, Saturday Evening Post Co., 1979.
The Crime Lab, Avon, 1985.

The Case of the Clever Marathon Cheat, Meadowbrook, 1985.
The Ukrainian Egg Mystery, Avon, 1986.

OTHER

Author of ''Mini-Mystery Series,'' a monthly short story in *Child Life Mystery and Science Fiction,* 1977—. Contributor of articles, stories, and reviews to scholarly journals and popular magazines for adults and children, including *Darling, Women's Choice,* and *Jack and Jill.*

WORK IN PROGRESS: *The Codebreaker Kids!; The Italian Spaghetti Mystery; The Mexican Tamale Mystery.*

SIDELIGHTS: George Edward Stanley told *CA:* ''I have to write. Most writers I know do. But I want to write to entertain. Solely. If there are some truths in what I write, so be it. But the main thing I want to do is make children laugh. Children don't laugh enough today. They grow up much too soon. I had a wonderful childhood. A slow childhood! My eight-year-old son knows things about life that I didn't know until I was out of college!''

*   *   *

STARR, S(tephen) Frederick 1940-
(S. Schwartz, A. B. Valeran)

PERSONAL: Born March 24, 1940, in New York, N.Y.; son of Stephen Z. (a historian) and Ivy-Jane (a sculptor; maiden name, Edmondson) Starr; married second wife, Christine Mentschel; children: (first marriage) Anna Edmondson, Elizabeth Hines. *Education:* Yale University, B.A., 1962; King's College, Cambridge, M.A., 1964; Princeton University, Ph.D., 1968.

ADDRESSES: *Home*—154 Forest St., Oberlin, Ohio 44074. *Office*—Cox Administration Bldg., Oberlin College, Oberlin, Ohio 44074.

CAREER: Princeton University, Princeton, N.J., instructor, 1968-69, assistant professor, 1969-74, associate professor of history, 1974-76; Kennan Institute for Advanced Russian Studies, Washington, D.C., secretary of institute and assistant director of Wilson International Center, 1974-79; Tulane University, New Orleans, La., vice-president for academic affairs, 1979-82, professor of history and adjunct professor of architecture, 1979-83; Oberlin College, Oberlin, Ohio, president, 1983—. Scholar in residence, The Historic New Orleans Collection, New Orleans, 1982. Member of selection board of International Research and Exchange Board, 1973-75; Yale University, member of Council Committee on Foreign Languages and Area Studies, 1978-81, member of Council Committee for the Concilium on International and Area Studies, 1979—; Harvard University, member of visiting committee, Russian Research Center, 1978—, member of visiting committee, department of Slavic languages and literature, 1978—; member of academic council, Institute of Modern Russian Culture, Austin, Tex., 1979—. Founding member of board of trustees and principal organizer of Greater New Orleans Regional Foundation, 1983—. Special consultant to President's Commission on Foreign Languages and International Studies, 1978-79; member of international advisory board, United Auto Workers, 1979—.

MEMBER: American Historical Association (member of committee on international conferences, 1971-73), American Association for the Advancement of Slavic Studies (member of executive committee, 1979—), National Council for Soviet

and East European Research (vice-chairman, 1978-80), Council on Learning (member of national advisory board, 1980-81), Institute of International Education (member of southern regional advisory board, 1980-83), American Association for the Advancement of the Humanities, Council on Foreign Relations, Southern Center for International Studies, Foreign Relations Association of New Orleans, New Orleans Museum of Art (member of board of directors, 1980-83).

AWARDS, HONORS: Ehrman studentship for King's College, Cambridge University, 1962-64; National Defense Education Act fellowship, 1965-66; Inter-University Committee on Travel grants, 1966-67; Fulbright-Hays grant, 1966-67; Foreign Area fellowship, 1967-68; fellow of International Research and Exchanges Board, 1971-72; National Book Award nomination, 1973, for *Studies on the Russian Interior;* National Endowment for the Humanities younger humanist fellow, 1973; Mellon fellow of Aspen Institute for Humanistic Studies, 1974-75; American Society of Composers, Authors, and Publishers award and International Studies Association award, both for *Red and Hot: The Fate of Jazz in the U.S.S.R.*

WRITINGS:

The Archaeology of Hamilton County, Ohio, Cincinnati Museum of Natural History, 1960, 2nd edition, 1967.
(Editor) *The Horizon Book of Russian Art,* Horizon Press, 1970.
(Editor of translation and author of biographical section) August von Haxthausen, *Studies on the Russian Interior,* translated from the German by Eleanore L. Schmidt, University of Chicago Press, 1972.
Decentralization and Self-Government in Russia, 1830-1870, Princeton University Press, 1972.
(With Cyril E. Black and others) *Modernization of Japan and Russia: A Comparative Study,* Free Press, 1975.
Konstantin Melnikov: Solo Architect in a Mass Society, Princeton University Press, 1978.
Il padiglione di Melnikov a Parigi, Officina Edizioni (Rome), 1979.
(With Hans von Herwarth) *Against Two Evils: Memoirs of a Diplomat-Soldier during the Third Reich,* Rawson, Wade, 1981.
(Editor with D. F. Trask and others) *The United States and Russia: The Beginning of Relations, 1765-1815,* U.S. Government Printing Office, 1980.
Red and Hot: The Fate of Jazz in the U.S.S.R., Oxford University Press, 1983.
New Orleans Unmasqued, Dedeaux Publishers, 1984.

CONTRIBUTOR

(Author of introductory essay) *The Avant-Garde in Russia,* Hutton-Hutchnecker Gallery, 1971.
Art and Architecture: U.S.S.R., 1917-1932, Wittenborn, 1971.
George Gibian, editor, *Russian Modernism: Culture and the Avant-Garde, 1900-1930,* Cornell University Press, 1974.
Michael Hamm, editor, *The City in Russian History,* University Press of Kentucky, 1975.
Sheila Fitzpatrick, editor, *The Cultural Revolution in Russia, 1928-1931,* Indiana University Press, 1977.
Jeremy Azrael, editor, *Soviet Nationality Policies and Practices,* Praeger, 1978.
Perceptions: Relations between the United States and the Soviet Union, U.S. Government Printing Office, 1979.
Barbara B. Burn, editor, *Expanding the International Dimensions of Higher Education,* Jossey-Bass, 1980.

(Author of biographical introduction) Angelica Rudenstine, editor, *The Russian Avant-Garde: The George Costakis Collection,* Abrams, 1981.

Wayne Vucinich, editor, *The Zemstvos: Russia's Democratic Experiment,* Cambridge University Press, 1982.

OTHER

Also author of *Ante-Bellum Suburbia: The Garden District of New Orleans,* 1985. Contributor, sometimes under pseudonyms S. Schwartz and A. B. Valeran, of more than forty articles and reviews to scholarly journals, popular magazines, including *Smithsonian,* and newspapers. Member of editorial board, *Wilson Quarterly,* 1976—.

SIDELIGHTS: Historian and international studies scholar S. Frederick Starr has conducted a variety of research missions abroad, including archaeological excavations in Turkey and resident studies in the Soviet Union, Austria, France, and England. Also a clarinetist who performed with the Louisiana Repertory Jazz Ensemble of New Orleans, Starr has combined his professional and avocational interests in writing *Red and Hot: The Fate of Jazz in the Soviet Union,* a work that Richard Freed of the *Washington Post Book World* calls "an illuminating, entertaining, and occasionally chilling chronicle" that has much "to interest, and indeed to fascinate, the general reader as well as the confirmed jazz buff." The book exposes, among other things, the uneven official Soviet policy towards jazz over the past sixty years. In the *Times Literary Supplement,* Eric Hobsbawm writes of Starr's work: "His excellent book is clearly a splendid contribution to Soviet history, and—for practically all of us—a very surprising one.... Starr's book shows what can be done by a serious historian who turns his attention and enthusiasm to the subject, and who knows what he is talking about."

BIOGRAPHICAL/CRITICAL SOURCES:

PERIODICALS

Newsweek, May 16, 1983.
Times Literary Supplement, August 12, 1983.
Washington Post Book World, July 3, 1983.

*   *   *

STARR, Stephen Z.   1909-1985

PERSONAL: Born November 1, 1909, in Budapest, Hungary; died January 19, 1985, in Cambridge, Vt.; son of Alexander and Regina Starr; married Ivy-Jane Edmondson, November 11, 1933; children: George Alexander, Ivy-Elizabeth Starr Minely, Stephen Frederick, Diana Jane Starr Cooper. *Education:* Western Reserve University (now Case Western Reserve University), B.A., 1930; New York University, J.D., 1941. *Politics:* "Mugwump—mostly conservative." *Religion:* Roman Catholic.

ADDRESSES: Home—R.D. 1, Box 640, Cambridge, Vt. 05444.

CAREER: Schenley Industries, New York, N.Y., executive, prior to 1953; Clopay Corp., Cincinnati, Ohio, secretary-treasurer, 1953-73; Cincinnati Historical Society, Cincinnati, director, 1973-78.

MEMBER: Cincinnati Historical Society, Literary Club (Cincinnati).

AWARDS, HONORS: Jules F. Landry Award, 1985, for *The Union Cavalry in the Civil War.*

WRITINGS:

Colonel Grenfell's Wars, Louisiana State University Press, 1971.
Jennison's Jayhawkers, Louisiana State University Press, 1973.
The Union Cavalry in the Civil War, Louisiana State University Press, Volume I: *From Fort Sumter to Gettysburg, 1861-1863,* 1979, Volume II: *The War in the East, from Gettysburg to Appomattox, 1863-1865,* 1981, Volume III: *The War in the West, 1861-1865,* 1985.

Contributor to history journals.

[Sketch verified by wife, Ivy E. Starr]

*   *   *

STEELE, Fred I(rving)   1938-
(Fritz Steele)

PERSONAL: Born November 1, 1938, in Kansas City, Mo.; son of Fred L. and Mildred (Stubbs) Steele; married; children: two. *Education:* Yale University, B.S., 1960; Massachusetts Institute of Technology, Ph.D., 1965.

ADDRESSES: Home and office—37 Winchester St., Boston, Mass. 02116.

CAREER: Yale University, New Haven, Conn., assistant professor of administrative sciences, 1964-69; free-lance consultant on organizational and environmental change, 1969—; Development Research Associates, Newton, Mass., partner, 1973-79; principal, Partners Consulting Group (PCG), 1980—. Lecturer, Harvard Graduate School of Education, 1976-77.

WRITINGS:

(With Warren Bennis, Edgar Schein, and David Berlew) *Interpersonal Dynamics,* Dorsey, 1964, 3rd edition, 1973.
Physical Settings and Organization Development, Addison-Wesley, 1973.

UNDER NAME FRITZ STEELE

The Open Organization, Addison-Wesley, 1975.
Consulting for Organizational Change, University of Massachusetts Press, 1975.
(With Steve Jenks) *The Feel of the Work Place,* Addison-Wesley, 1977.
The Sense of Place, Van Nostrand, 1981.
The Role of the Internal Consultant, Van Nostrand, 1982.
Making and Managing High-Quality Workplaces, Teachers College Press, Columbia University, 1985.

Contributor to *Journal of Applied Behavioral Science,* sometimes under name Fritz Steele.

WORK IN PROGRESS: Choosing Places, a mystery novel.

AVOCATIONAL INTERESTS: Travel, hiking, psychology of places, art.

*   *   *

STEELE, Fritz
See STEELE, Fred I(rving)

*   *   *

STEINBERG, Leo   1920-

PERSONAL: Born July 7, 1920, in Moscow, U.S.S.R.; son of Isaac N. and Nehama (Esselson) Steinberg. *Education:* Slade

School, London, fine arts diploma, 1940; New York University, B.S., 1954, Ph.D., 1960.

ADDRESSES: Home—New York, N.Y. *Office*—Department of Art History, University of Pennsylvania, G-29 Fine Arts Bldg., Philadelphia, Pa. 19174.

CAREER: Hunter College of the City University of New York, New York, N.Y., associate professor, 1962-67, professor of art history, 1967-75; University of Pennsylvania, Philadelphia, Benjamin Franklin Professor and University Professor of the History of Art, 1975—.

MEMBER: American Academy of Arts and Sciences (fellow).

AWARDS, HONORS: Award in literature, American Academy-Institute of Arts and Letters, 1983; award for criticism, National Book Critics Circle, 1984, for *The Sexuality of Christ in Renaissance Art and in Modern Oblivion.*

WRITINGS:

Jasper Johns, Wittenborn, 1963.
(Contributor) Theodore R. Bowie and Cornelia V. Christenson, editors, *Studies in Erotic Art,* Basic Books, 1970.
Other Criteria, Oxford University Press, 1972.
Michelangelo's Last Paintings, Oxford University Press, 1975.
Borromini's San Carlo alle Quattro Fontane: A Study in the Multiple Form and Architectural Symposium, Garland Publishing, 1977.
The Sexuality of Christ in Renaissance Art and in Modern Oblivion, Pantheon, 1984.

Columnist, *Arts,* 1955-56. Contributor to *Art Bulletin, Art News, Art Quarterly, Art in America, Critical Inquiry,* and *Daedalus.*

SIDELIGHTS: Leo Steinberg's *The Sexuality of Christ in Renaissance Art and in Modern Oblivion* is hailed by Michael Levey in the *Washington Post Book World* as a "remarkable, somewhat startling book" by a "notably original, clever scholar." In this volume, the author attempts to illustrate a potentially offensive, even sacreligious theory: that Renaissance paintings of Christ are strongly focused on his private parts. Renaissance artists were interested in anatomy and in realism, and art historians have traditionally dismissed the profusion of revealing images of Christ as nothing more than a reflection of those artistic concerns. Steinberg's "arguments are more sophisticated and aim to suggest a climate in which painters were responding to specific currents of religious thought," writes Levey. Steinberg reminds his readers that during the Renaissance, Christ's divinity was unquestioned; it was his incarnation into human form that was considered most miraculous and fascinating to contemplate. He suggests that Renaissance artists were consciously emphasizing Christ's humanity in male form by including his genitalia in their portrayals of him.

Both Levey and Richard Wollheim, *New York Times Book Review* contributor, express some concern over a book whose subject can be disturbing to some readers. "For advanced students, only . . . are Professor Steinberg's discussion of the hand of Christ—as child and as adult—on his own groin," notes Levey, even while praising the art historian's creative hypothesis. "He is fully aware that his views are likely to cause mild shock and incredulity (with possibly some mild ribaldry), but he is firm in the conviction that he is—one may say—on to something. . . . Even the most skeptical must admit that the author has assembled an impressive corpus of evidence." Though Levey points out that not "all that passes here as evidence can be accepted as such," he goes on to state

that "Steinberg illustrates certain images which are extraordinary and which retain a power to shock. He deserves credit for seeking some reason for the way they look." Wollheim concurs that not all of Steinberg's "proof" can be wholly accepted, and adds that for him, "the most disturbing aspect of this strange, haunting book, with its great boldness of conception, is the resolute silence it maintains on all alternative views." In spite of this shortcoming, concludes Wollheim, "one of the sharpest intellects working in art history . . . has gathered together a remarkable and fascinating corpus of pictorial material. . . . [Steinberg] has also provided us with an exotic feast for which we should be grateful. . . . This is a very clever book."

BIOGRAPHICAL/CRITICAL SOURCES:

PERIODICALS

New York Times Book Review, April 19, 1984.
Washington Post Book World, January 1, 1984.

*   *   *

STEYERMARK, Julian A(lfred)   1909-

PERSONAL: Born January 27, 1909, in St. Louis, Mo.; son of Leo L. (a merchant) and Mamie (Isaacs) Steyermark; married Cora Shoop, September 1, 1939. *Education:* Washington University, St. Louis, Mo., A.B., 1929, M.S., 1930, Ph.D., 1933; Harvard University, M.A., 1931.

ADDRESSES: Office—Missouri Botanical Garden, Box 299, St. Louis, Mo. 63166.

CAREER: Missouri Botanical Garden, St. Louis, research fellow, 1932-33, research assistant, 1934, member of expedition to Panama, 1934-35; University City Senior High School, University City, Mo., biology instructor, 1935-36; Chicago Natural History Museum, Chicago, Ill., assistant curator of herbarium, 1937-47, associate curator, 1947-49, curator, 1950-58; Venezuela Ministry of Agriculture, botanist at Instituto Botanico, Caracas, 1959-80, curator herbarium, 1975-80, assessor to the director, 1981-84, honorary assessor, 1984—; Missouri Botanical Garden, curator, 1984—. Taxonomist and ecologist, U.S. Forest Service, summers, 1936-37; visiting professor, Southern Illinois University, 1958. Leader or member of botanical expeditions to Guatemala, 1939-40, 1941-42, Panama, Ecuador, Venezuela, 1944-45, 1953, 1954-55, 1959, and other Latin American countries. Nature Conservancy, member of Missouri board of directors, 1955-56, chairman of Illinois committee for preservation of Volo and Wauconda Bogs, 1956-57; visiting curator, New York Botanical Gardens, 1961-65, 1968-69. Botanical consultant, Eli Lilly & Co.

MEMBER: International Association of Plant Taxonomists, American Association for the Advancement of Science (fellow), Botanical Society of America, American Society of Plant Taxonomists, Ecological Society of America, America Fern Society, Audubon Society of Venezuela (member of advisory board, 1976—), New England Botanical Society, Sociedad Venezolana de Ciencias Naturales (honorary), honorary member of naturalist societies in North, Central, and South America, Barrington Natural History Society (president, 1947-53), Torrey Botanical Club.

AWARDS, HONORS: Honorary research associate, Missouri Botanical Gardens, 1947-58; special plaque for botanical achievement, Washington University, St. Louis, Mo., 1954; National Science Foundation grant, 1958-59; Order of Quetzal

(Guatemala), 1961, for work on flora of Guatemala; Order Andres Bello (Venezuela); Amigos Venezuela, 1972; other distinguished service awards.

WRITINGS:

Spring Flora of Missouri, Missouri Botanical Garden, 1940, reprinted, Lucas Brothers, 1964.
(With P. C. Standley) *Flora of Guatemala,* Chicago Natural History Museum, 1946-59.
(Contributor) *Flora of Venezuela,* eight volumes, Chicago Natural History Museum, 1953-57.
Vegetational History of the Ozark Forest, University of Missouri Press, 1959.
Flora of Missouri, Iowa State University Press, 1963.
Rubiaceae of Venezuela, three volumes, Venezuela Ministry of Environment, 1974.
Flora of Avila, Venezuela Ministry of Environment, 1977.
Piperacece of Venezuela, Venezuela Ministry of Environment, 1984.
Flora of the Venezuelan Guayana, Missouri Botanical Garden, 1984.

Contributor of about three hundred articles on plant life discoveries to periodicals.

WORK IN PROGRESS: Articles on new species discovered in Venezuela, for botanical journals.

SIDELIGHTS: Julian A. Steyermark speaks and reads Spanish, reads Latin, German, and French.

AVOCATIONAL INTERESTS: Playing piano, all types of music, tennis, swimming, and hiking.

*   *   *

STICK, David   1919-

PERSONAL: Born December 21, 1919, in Interlaken, N.J.; son of Frank (an artist) and Maud H. (a model) Stick; children: Michael A., Gregory, Timothy B. *Education:* Attended University of North Carolina.

ADDRESSES: Home—P.O. Box 180, Kitty Hawk, N.C. 27949.

CAREER: Nags Head correspondent for *Elizabeth City Independent,* Elizabeth City, N.C.; manager of Dare County bureau for *Elizabeth City Daily Advance,* Elizabeth City, N.C.; state capital reporter for *Raleigh Times,* Raleigh, N.C.; newspaper reporter in Manteo, N.C.; radio reporter for MBS, Washington, D.C.; U.S. Marine Corps combat correspondent; free-lance writer, 1947—. Founder and current president of Outer Banks Community Foundation. Former mayor of Southern Shores, N.C. Licensed real estate broker, until 1976; contractor; bookshop operator. Past chairperson of Kill Devil Hills Zoning Board, Dare County Board of Commissioners, Dare County Erosion Control Board, Dare County Friends of the Lost Colony, Wright Memorial Museum Committee, Dare Coast Pirates Jamboree, North Carolina Legislative Commission to Study Library Support, and North Carolina Coastal Resources Commission; past president of Carolina Charter Corp., Outer Banks Chamber of Commerce, Carolina Charter Corporation, Dare County Tourist Bureau, and other organizations.

WRITINGS:

Fabulous Dare: The Story of Dare County, Past and Present, Dare Press, 1949.
Graveyard of the Atlantic: Shipwrecks of the North Carolina Coast, University of North Carolina Press, 1952.

The Outer Banks of North Carolina, 1584-1958, University of North Carolina Press, 1958.
(With Bruce Robert) *The Cape Hatteras Seashore,* Rand McNally, 1964, revised edition, 1973.
Dare County: A History, North Carolina Archives and History, 1970.
(Editor) *Aycock Brown's Outer Banks,* Donning, 1976.
North Carolina Lighthouses, North Carolina Archives and History, 1980.
(Editor) *An Artist's Catch: Watercolors by Frank Stick,* University of North Carolina Press, 1981.
Roanoke Island: The Beginnings of English America, University of North Carolina Press, 1983.
Bald Head: A History of Smith Island and Cape Fear, Broadfoot, 1985.

Associate editor of *American Legion Magazine.*

SIDELIGHTS: David Stick told *CA:* ''My primary efforts for more than 35 years have been directed toward writing factual books on the history of the North Carolina coastal area in a style that will hold the interest of the lay reader as well as the scholar. Making history both readable and factual is not an easy task, and though there have been days when I turned out several thousand words, there have been others when my production was limited to a single paragraph, or less. If I have succeeded in bringing history to life it has been because I write with the literate eighth-grader in mind, on the assumption that if the young reader can understand and enjoy it, then the scholar should be able to as well.''

AVOCATIONAL INTERESTS: Organizing a research library of North Caroliniana.

*   *   *

STINEMAN, Esther F.   1947-

PERSONAL: Born June 7, 1947. *Education:* University of Colorado at Boulder, M.A. (English); University of Chicago, M.A. (librarianship), 1976; Yale University, M.Phil., 1984.

ADDRESSES: Home—P.O. Box 494, Monument, Colo. 80132.

CAREER: University of Wisconsin—Madison, librarian-at-large for women's studies, 1977-79; Threshold Consulting, Colorado Springs, Colo., vice-president, 1981-85; University of Colorado at Colorado Springs, director of women's studies, 1986—. Former reference librarian and instructor in library science at University of Colorado at Colorado Springs and Colorado College.

AWARDS, HONORS: Women's Studies: A Recommended Core Bibliography was named an American Library Association best reference book, 1980, and a *Choice* outstanding academic book, 1981.

WRITINGS:

(With Catherine Loeb) *Women's Studies: A Recommended Core Bibliography,* Libraries Unlimited, 1979.
American Political Women: Contemporary and Historical Profiles, Libraries Unlimited, 1980.
(With Charles L. Hinkle) *Cases in Marketing Management: Issues for the 1980s,* Prentice-Hall, 1984.

Also author of *Mary Hunter Austin: An American Woman of Letters,* 1985.

Contributor to library and women's studies journals.

BIOGRAPHICAL/CRITICAL SOURCES:

PERIODICALS

College and Research Library News, January, 1978.

* * *

STODDARD, Ellwyn R(eed) 1927-

PERSONAL: Born February 16, 1927, in Garland, Utah; son of Roscoe and Mary (Redford) Stoddard; married Elaine Kirby; children: Ellwyn R., Jr., Michael V., Dawn D., Jared Evan, Sunday, Summer; stepchildren: Laura Jane Packham, George H. Packham, R. Kirby Packham. *Education:* Utah State University, B.S., 1952; Brigham Young University, M.S., 1955; Michigan State University, Ph.D., 1961. *Religion:* Church of Jesus Christ of Latter-day Saints (Mormon).

ADDRESSES: Home—747 Camino Real, El Paso, Tex. 79922. *Office*—University of Texas, El Paso, Tex. 79968.

CAREER: Drake University, Des Moines, Iowa, assistant professor, 1959-63, associate professor of sociology, 1963-65; University of Texas at El Paso, associate professor, 1965-70, professor of sociology and anthropology, 1970—. National Institute of Health Lecturer, College of Osteopathic Medicine and Surgery, 1963-64; New Mexico State University, National Endowment for the Humanities Lecturer, 1969-70, National Institute of Mental Health Lecturer, 1972. Sociological researcher, 1955—. Consultant to over seventy research and action projects involving civil defense, disaster relief, racial awareness, organizational functioning, health and social services delivery systems, and other subjects. Presenter and panelist at numerous professional conferences and workshops. *Military service:* U.S. Coast Guard, Amphibious Corps, 1944-46; served as radioman. U.S. Army, Artillery Corps, 1952-53; served as battalion communications officer.

MEMBER: International Rural Sociological Society, American Sociological Association, Association of Borderland Scholars (founder; past president), Inter-University Seminar on Armed Forces and Society, Rural Sociological Society, Pacific Sociological Association, Western Social Science Association, Southwestern Anthropological Association, Southwestern Social Science Association, Southwestern Sociological Association, Rocky Mountain Conference for Latin American Studies (member of executive council, 1970-73), Phi Kappa Phi, Alpha Kappa Delta, Delta Tau Kappa International Social Science Honor Society (life member).

AWARDS, HONORS: 1983 Southwest Book Award, Border Regional Library Association, 1984, for *Borderlands Sourcebook.*

WRITINGS:

Mexican Americans, Random House, 1973.
Each Man Must Climb His Own Mountain: An Autobiography, privately printed, 1980.
A Bibliographical Resource Guide: Ancient and Modern Cultures of Northern Mexico and the Greater Southwest, University of Texas at El Paso, 1981.
(Editor with Richard L. Nostrand and Jonathan P. West) *Borderlands Sourcebook,* University of Oklahoma Press, 1983.
Industrial and Military Organization: Readings, Niftee, 1983.
Border Immigration Policy: Readings, Niftee, 1984.

CONTRIBUTOR

Norman Johnston, Leonard Savitz, and Marvin E. Wolfgang, editors, *The Sociology of Punishment and Correction,* Wiley, 2nd edition (Stoddard was not associated with earlier edition), 1970.
Clifton D. Bryant, editor, *Social Problems Today,* Lippincott, 1971.
Bryant, editor, *The Social Dimensions of Work,* Prentice-Hall, 1972.
Arthur Shostak, editor, *Putting Sociology to Work,* McKay, 1974.
Jerome H. Skolnick and Thomas C. Gray, editors, *Police in America,* Little, Brown, 1974.
Bryant, editor, *Deviant Behavior: Occupational and Organizational Bases,* Rand McNally, 1974.
Lawrence W. Sherman, editor, *Police Corruption: A Sociological Perspective,* Doubleday, 1974.
(With C. Cabanillas) Nancy L. Goldman and David R. Segal, editors, *The Social Psychology of Military Service,* Sage Publications, 1976.
Edna J. Hunter and D. Stephen Nice, editors, *Military Families: Adaptation to Change,* Praeger, 1978.
Guy Poitras, editor, *Immigration and the Mexican National: Proceedings,* Trinity University Border Research Institute, 1978.
Academic American Encyclopedia, Arete Publishing, 1979.
Richard Lundman, editor, *Police Behavior: A Sociological Perspective,* Oxford University Press (New York), 1979.
Matt S. Meier and Feliciano Rivera, editors, *Dictionary of Mexican American History,* Greenwood Press, 1981.
Impact of Peso Devaluations on U.S. Small Business and Adequacy of SBA's Peso Pack Program, Government Printing Office, 1983.
Rosalie Cohen, Lynn Gregory, and Thomas D. Hall, editors, *Teaching Social Change: Course Designs, Syllabi, and Instructional Materials,* Teaching Resource Center, American Sociological Association, 1983.
(With Stephanie Shanks) Stephen C. Hey, Gary Kiger, and John Seidel, editors, *Social Aspects of Chronic Illness, Impairment and Disability,* Willamette University, 1984.
Paul Anaejionu, Nathan C. Goldman, and Philip J. Meeks, editors, *Space and Society: Challenges and Choices,* Univelt, 1984.

OTHER

Also author of numerous booklets and reports. Contributor of articles and reviews to numerous professional journals, including *International Migration Review, American Sociologist, Contemporary Sociology, Rocky Mountain Social Science Quarterly, Rural Sociology, Frontera,* and *New Scholar.* Manuscript evaluator for numerous journals, including *American Journal of Sociology, Hispanic American Historical Review, Journal of Political and Economic Sociology, Pacific Historical Review,* and *Social Problems.*

WORK IN PROGRESS: Multidisciplinary coordination of U.S.-Mexico border research, in comparison with African and Eastern European borders; *Contemporary Policy Issues in the U.S.-Mexico Borderlands: Institutional Adaptations in Historical Context.*

SIDELIGHTS: Ellwyn R. Stoddard told *CA:* "My professional research and writing converges a multidisciplinary/multicultural orientation with selected problems of human survival: institutional adaptation to national borders, human colonies in space, disaster behavior and relief efforts, and ethnic minorities. Although this creative experience emerging from the constant interfertilization of concepts born in more than a dozen academic disciplines is personally rewarding, it is a perilous risk for the neophyte scholar, and he should enter such a path forewarned and forearmed. Since our contemporary society lionizes the 'specialist' who is easily categorized and can be plugged into an existing system, the broadly-based generalist finds acceptance within narrow disciplinary confines somewhat less rewarding than those who remain as mainstream disciples.

"The professional strength required of scientific research pioneers is not gained from scientific truths but is a product of self-respect and ethical values, reinforced by security of hearth and home. One is then free from personal ego concerns and can explore the capacity of mankind to adapt and survive against terrifying odds with objectivity. Perhaps science progresses best in modest settings wherein grave contemporary problems create the furnace in which the stable traditions of future generations are forged. At least this is the way I have experienced it."

*   *   *

STOKESBURY, James L(awton)   1934-

PERSONAL: Born December 27, 1934, in Derby, Conn.; son of James E. (a civil servant) and Estelle (Little) Stokesbury; married Elizabeth D'Orsay Dickinson, August 29, 1961; children: Kevin, Brianna, Michael. Education: Acadia University, B.A., 1960; University of Western Ontario, M.A., 1962; Duke University, Ph.D., 1968. Politics: None. Religion: Congregationalist.

ADDRESSES: Home—R.R.1, Wolfville, Nova Scotia, Canada B0P 1X0. Office—Department of History, Acadia University, Wolfville, Nova Scotia, Canada B0P 1X0. Agent—Ann Elmo Agency, Inc., 60 East 42nd St., New York, N.Y. 10017.

CAREER: Acadia University, Wolfville, Nova Scotia, lecturer in history, 1960-61; University of Western Ontario, London, lecturer in history, 1962; Acadia University, assistant professor, 1964-68, associate professor, 1968-73, professor of history, 1973—. Sessional lecturer at University of Waterloo, 1968. Military service: U.S. Navy, 1953-57; became quartermaster first class.

WRITINGS:

(With Martin Blumenson) Masters of the Art of Command, Houghton, 1975.
A Short History of World War II, Morrow, 1979.
A Short History of World War I, Morrow, 1981.
Navy and Empire, Morrow, 1983.

Contributor of about forty articles to history journals.

WORK IN PROGRESS: Napoleon and Hitler; A Short History of Air Power.

SIDELIGHTS: James L. Stokesbury told CA: "My interests have always been in military and naval history, and by choice I would write about the Napoleonic period. However, by the accidents of the publishing business, most of my publications have been either in colonial American military history or World Wars I and II; hence the development of the theme of Masters of the Art of Command, and the more recent development of a general survey of World War II and of World War I. The treatment of Napoleon and Hitler is an obvious combination of my first love and my current direction of interest, and there are surprising parallels between the two, some accidental, some historical, some geographical.

"I have always wanted to write. I think the particular area in which I like to write lies in the gap between the scholar who writes only for his peers and does not reach any wider audience, and the popular writer who may reach the wider audience but is not up on the latest scholarly advances. There are some real problems in this, and it's rather like being a 'philosophe' instead of a philosopher, but it seems to me a useful thing; I'd be quite happy to have someone think I was a philosophe. Mostly, it's a lot of fun."

Stokesbury's A Short History of World War I has been called "an ideal work for the new student of the period" by John Yohalem, writing for the New York Times Book Review. Yohalem, impressed with the thoughtfulness of such a brief treatment of a complicated war, notes: "Remarkable enough that it could be done—astonishing that it is done well." In the Los Angeles Times, Robert Kirsch gives similar praise to A Short History of World War II, which he believes "fills a need for an overview narrative of the causes, events, and aftermath of the conflict." Kirsch further cites the book for the lessons its topic can teach current generations, commenting: "This is a volume that invites reflection on present-day foreign and strategic policy."

BIOGRAPHICAL/CRITICAL SOURCES:

PERIODICALS

Los Angeles Times, February 13, 1980.
New York Times Book Review, February 22, 1981.

*   *   *

STONE, Elaine Murray   1922-

PERSONAL: Born January 22, 1922, in New York, N.Y.; daughter of Herman (a banker and diplomat) and Catherine (Fairbanks) Murray-Jacoby; married Frederic Courtney Stone (an electrical engineer), May 30, 1944 (died February, 1985); children: Catherine (Mrs. Robert Rayburn), Pamela (Mrs. Don E. Webb), Victoria. Education: Attended Juilliard School of Music, 1939-41; New York College of Music, diploma, 1942; Trinity College of Music, licentiate, 1947. Politics: Independent. Religion: Episcopal.

ADDRESSES: Home—1945 Pineapple Ave., Melbourne, Fla. 32935. Office—Fountain Cove Condominiums, 3165 N. Atlantic Ave., Coco Beach, Fla. 32931. Agent—Theron Raines, 475 Fifth Ave., New York, N.Y. 10017.

CAREER: Musician, composer, television producer, and writer. Organist, choir director, and piano and organ teacher, 1940-70; accompanist with Strawbridge Ballet, 1944-45; Melbourne Times, Melbourne, Fla., feature writer 1965-67; Consolidated Cybertronics, Cocoa Beach, Fla., vice-president, 1968; Cass, Inc., Melbourne, editor-in-chief of educational tape cassettes, 1970-71; WTAI-Radio, Melbourne, director of continuity, 1971-74, host and producer of daily radio program "Good News," 1973-74; Engle Realty, Inc., Indialantic, Fla., realtor associate, 1975-78; KXTX-TV, Dallas, Tex., writer and producer of juvenile news program "Countdown," 1978-80; host and producer of weekly television show "Focus on History," TV6, Melbourne, 1982—. Part-time real estate agent, Fountain Cove Condominiums, 1985—. Diocese of Central Florida, producer of television program "Episcopal Digest," member of board of evangelism, 1984—. Member of board of promotion of Diocese of Southern Florida, 1960. Cape Kennedy correspondent, 1961-74; Religious News Service correspondent, beginning 1962; board member, Brevard Symphony, Melbourne, Fla.

MEMBER: American Society of Composers, Authors, and Publishers, National League of American Penwomen (former president, Cape Canaveral branch; president, Dallas branch, 1980), Women in Communications, Space Pioneers, Daughters of the American Revolution (state chairman of music in Florida, 1964; former vice-president, Abigail Chamberlain chapter; former organizing regent, Rufus Fairbanks chapter), Florida Press Women.

AWARDS, HONORS: Won South Carolina music contest, 1939; first prize in photojournalism contest in Florida, 1966, and first place book and short story in Dallas, 1979, both from National League of American Penwomen.

WRITINGS:

BOOKS

The Taming of the Tongue, Holy Cross Press, 1954.
Love One Another, Holy Cross Press, 1957.
Pedro Menendez de Aviles and the Founding of St. Augustine, Kenedy, 1969.
The Melbourne Bicentennial Book, Melbourne Bicentennial Commission, 1976.
Uganda: Fire and Blood, Logos, 1977.
Tekla and the Lion, Association Press, 1981.

AUDIO TAPE CASSETTES

Bedtime Bible Stories, Cass, Inc., 1970.
Improve Your Business Spelling, Cass, Inc., 1970.
Improve Your Spelling for Better Grades, Cass, Inc., 1970.
Sleepytime Tales, Cass, Inc., 1970.
Tranquility Tapes, Cass, Inc., 1970.
Travel Fun, Cass, Inc., 1970.

OTHER

"The Examination" (play), first produced in Melbourne, Fla., at Holy Trinity Episcopal Church, 1962.

Author of more than two hundred scripts for television series "Countdown," 1978—. Associate editor of *Goodtime Gazette,* 1978-79. Contributor to periodicals, including *Charleston News, Christian Life, Holy Cross, Indian River, New York Herald Tribune, Guideposts, LOGOS, Living Church,* and *Episcopal Churchnews.*

WORK IN PROGRESS: Saints and Martyrs of Today; The Judas Touch; Ten Thousand Tears; Paths to Peace.

SIDELIGHTS: Elaine Murray Stone told *CA:* "I spent the first half of my life on Fifth Avenue in New York as the child of a very successful banker and diplomat. My father was chairman of the board of North American Waterworks, in addition to being president of his own banking concern on Wall Street. He was appointed by Herbert Hoover to represent the United States at the coronation of Haile Selassie in 1930. My parents entertained many of the greats of this century at our home. I attended private schools and in 1939 won the South Carolina state music contest in piano. I then applied to enter the Juilliard School of Music, which I attended from 1939-41. Due to poor health, repeated pneumonia, etc., I changed to the New York College of Music, from which I graduated in 1942. I have composed music since I was nine and have had my works performed all over the United States. After leading such a social life the first half of my existence, my husband and daughters and I moved to Florida for my health in 1950 and

lived in the shadow of Cape Canaveral until 1978. We lived in Dallas from 1978-80, then returned to retire in Florida at our riverfront home in Melbourne.

"My interests are very broad. This is fortunate, because the television show I write and produce covers every subject imaginable. I adore research and enjoy tracking down impossible bits of information no one else can find.

"As the space correspondent for Religious News Service, I covered every manned space launch in U.S. history. I was also at the Kennedy Space Center for many other important launches all through the sixties and seventies and hobnobbed with the great newscasters and journalists from every country on earth. I was also in a documentary called 'In the Shadow of the Moon.' I have been interviewed on many television and radio stations about my book *Uganda: Fire and Blood.* I have a huge scrapbook just filled with ads, reviews, and other mementos about that book.

"I guess I've enjoyed being a television producer about as much as anything I've ever done in my life. I had no training in it and learned on the job after I was hired to write the scripts. 'Countdown' was aired thirty times per week on the entire CBN network. 'Countdown' was a sixty second news show broadcast during the cartooning periods to educate children. We went on location and had guests come to the studio, but mostly we used films and slides to illustrate the story.

"My father, the United States ambassador to Ethiopia, made many trips to Africa. This sparked my interest in the 'Dark Continent' at an early age. This resulted in a book on Uganda and one on Ethiopia. I have traveled extensively myself since I was a small child. I speak French and Spanish. I became unusually devout during my teens, which resulted in the reading of most of the great saints and mystics. Out of this grew over half of my books and all of my published articles. Even though all of my education was in music, I have yet to write on this subject!"

AVOCATIONAL INTERESTS: "My favorite occupations are travel, sailing, swimming, surfing, collecting autographs, composing and improvising music, television, Greek, reading, visiting my grandchildren, conversation, movies, theatre, attending concerts, eating; my favorite composer is Bach, my favorite writer is C. S. Lewis; I enjoy needlepoint and embroidery."

*　　　*　　　*

STONE, Merlin 1931-

PERSONAL: Born September 27, 1931, in New York, N.Y.

CAREER: Sculptor, 1958-67; university teacher of art and art history, formerly on the faculty of State University of New York at Buffalo and San Francisco Extension of the University of California, Berkeley; writer.

WRITINGS:

When God Was a Woman, Dial, 1976 (published in England as *The Paradise Papers: The Suppression of Women's Rites,* Quartet Books, 1976).
Ancient Mirrors of Womanhood: Our Goddess and Heroine Heritage, New Sibylline, 1979.
Three Thousand Years of Racism—Recurring Patterns in Racism (booklet), New Sibylline, 1981.

CONTRIBUTOR

Carol Christ and Judith Plaskow, editors, *Womanspirit Rising*, Harper, 1979.

Charlene Spretnak, editor, *Politics of Women's Spirituality*, Doubleday-Anchor, 1982.

Macmillan Encyclopedia of Religion, Macmillan, 1986.

WORK IN PROGRESS: Writing and directing a radio series for the Canadian Broadcasting Corporation, "Return of the Goddess."

*   *   *

STOOPS, Emery 1902-

PERSONAL: Born December 13, 1902, in Pratt, Kan.; son of Eli and Marry Elizabeth (Brubaker) Stoops; married Evelyn R. FitzSimmons, 1929 (died, 1937); married Maude F. FitzSimmons, 1937 (died, 1967); married Joyce B. King, 1968; children: Emelyn Ruth Jackson, Emerson F., Eileen C. Gardner. *Education:* University of Colorado, A.B., 1930; University of Southern California, M.A. in Ed., 1934, Ed.D., 1941. *Religion:* Christian.

ADDRESSES: Home—1634 Casale Rd., Pacific Palisades, Calif. 90272. *Office*—University of Southern California, Los Angeles, Calif. 90007.

CAREER: Superintendent of schools in Richfield, Kan., 1932-33; teacher and principal in Whittier, Beverly Hills, and Los Angeles, all Calif., 1934-45; Office of County Superintendent of Schools, Los Angeles, administrative assistant, 1945-53; University of Southern California, Los Angeles, professor, 1953-70, professor emeritus, 1970—; currently involved in estate planning, life insurance, and real estate investments.

MEMBER: American Educational Research Association, National Education Association, National Vocational Guidance Association, American Association of School Administrators, National Conference of Professors of Educational Administration, California Teachers Association, Phi Delta Kappa (international president, 1953-55), American Quill, Adelphi, Delta Epsilon, Kiwanis International.

WRITINGS:

Principles and Practices in Guidance, McGraw, 1958.
Guidance Service: Organization and Administration, McGraw, 1959.
Classroom Discipline, Economics Press, 1959.
Practices and Trends in School Administration, Ginn, 1961.
Classroom Personalities, Economics Press, 1961.
Home Discipline, Economics Press, 1962.
Just a Minute, Junior, Economics Press, 1964.
Problems with Parents, Economics Press, 1964.
Elementary School Supervision, Allyn & Bacon, 1965.
How Johnny Learns, Economics Press, 1966.
Elementary School Education, McGraw, 1969.
Handbook of Educational Supervision, Allyn & Bacon, 1971, revised edition, 1978.
Discipline or Disaster, Phi Delta Kappa, 1972.
Handbook of Educational Administration, Allyn & Bacon, 1975, revised edition, 1981.
Handbook for School Secretaries, Allyn & Bacon, 1982.
Psychology of Success, Mojave Books, 1982.
Prairie Pioneers (novel), Mojave Books, 1985.

Author of six educational monographs; also author of "Discipline Service" (bi-weekly letter), Economics Press, 1962—;

contributor of chapters to school surveys. Contributor of articles to professional journals.

AVOCATIONAL INTERESTS: Travel, agriculture, real estate.

*   *   *

STORR, Anthony 1920-

PERSONAL: Born May 18, 1920, in Bentley, England; son of Vernon Faithfull and Katherine Cecilia (Storr) Storr; married Catherine Cole, February 6, 1942 (divorced); married Catherine Peters (a writer and lecturer in English at Sommerville College, Oxford), October 9, 1970; children: Sophia, Polly, Emma. *Education:* Christ's College, Cambridge, Bachelor of Medicine and Bachelor of Surgery, 1944, diploma in psychological medicine, 1950.

ADDRESSES: Home—45 Chalfont Rd., Oxford OX2 6TJ, England. *Agent*—A. D. Peters & Co. Ltd., 10 Buckingham St., London WC2N 6BU, England.

CAREER: Private practice of psychiatry, 1944-74; Oxford Area Health Authority, Oxford, England, consultant psychotherapist, 1974-84; writer and lecturer, 1984—. Emeritus fellow of Green College, Oxford.

MEMBER: Royal College of Physicians (fellow), Royal College of Psychiatrists (fellow).

WRITINGS:

The Integrity of the Personality, Atheneum, 1961.
Sexual Deviation, Penguin, 1964.
Human Aggression, Atheneum, 1968.
Human Destructiveness, Basic Books, 1972.
C. G. Jung, Viking, 1973 (published in England as *Jung*, Fontana, 1973).
The Dynamics of Creation, Secker & Warburg, 1972, Atheneum, 1973.
The Art of Psychotherapy, Methuen, 1980.
(Editor and author of introduction) *The Essential Jung*, Princeton University Press, 1983.
(Contributor) *Paths and Labyrinths*, Institute of Germanic Studies, University of London, 1985.
(Contributor) *Freud and the Humanities*, Duckworth, 1985.
(Contributor) *William Golding*, Faber, in press.

Contributor to newspapers.

WORK IN PROGRESS: Book reviews.

SIDELIGHTS: Anthony Storr wrote: "In 1974 I gave up private practice to become a full-time employee of the National Health Service, in which my job was to teach postgraduate doctors who are becoming psychiatrists the elements of psychotherapy." Storr's book *The Art of Psychotherapy* is intended as a manual for would-be psychotherapists, but Howard Gardner, writing for the *New York Times Book Review*, feels that it "provides an accessible overview of psychotherapeutic practice. Seldom have 'outsiders' had the opportunity to peer over the therapist's shoulder and into his mind." The book suggests that psychotherapy is not a science, but rather an art, based as it is upon empathy, difficulty in formulating general theories, and interest in people. According to Gardner, Storr's goal for individuals involved in this type of therapy is simply "insight into . . . problems and how to cope with them." While Gardner disagrees with Storr's definition of psychotherapy as more art than science, he nevertheless states: "I expect I will not be alone among Dr. Storr's readers in concluding that he would be an excellent minister to my 'problems in living.'"

BIOGRAPHICAL/CRITICAL SOURCES:

PERIODICALS

Best Sellers, November 15, 1972.
New Republic, October 14, 1972.
New Statesman, September 22, 1972.
New York Review of Books, December 14, 1972, February 23, 1973.
New York Times, August 5, 1980.
New York Times Book Review, February 25, 1973, June 27, 1976, October 5, 1980, November 8, 1981.
Observer, January 10, 1971, September 3, 1972, November 5, 1972.
Times Literary Supplement, September 22, 1972, September 14, 1973, May 9, 1980.

*　　　*　　　*

STURROCK, Jeremy
See HEALEY, Ben (James)

*　　　*　　　*

SUFRIN, Sidney Charles 1910-

PERSONAL: Born March 4, 1910, in New York, N.Y.; son of Maurice N. and Sarah (Silverstein) Sufrin: married Grace R. deJong, 1937 (deceased); married Irene Berman, 1969; children: Erica M., James W., Jacoba J., Judith G., Patricia G. *Education:* University of Pennsylvania, B.A., 1931; University of Chicago, graduate study, 1931-33; Ohio State University, Ph.D., 1940.

ADDRESSES: Home—25 Hitching Post Rd., Amherst, Mass. 01002. *Office*—School of Business Administration, University of Massachusetts, Amherst, Mass. 01003.

CAREER: U.S. Government, Washington, D.C., with National Recovery Administration and other agencies, 1933-35; Ohio State University, Columbus, instructor in economics, 1935-40; U.S. Government, Department of Labor, Washington, D.C., with War Production Board, 1939-42, and U.S. Embassy, London, England, 1945-46; Syracuse University, Syracuse, N.Y., 1946-69, professor of economics and business administration, 1948-69; University of Massachusetts—Amherst, professor of business economics, 1969—. Member of staff, International Labor Office, Geneva, Switzerland, 1938-39. Chief of U.S. Economic Cooperation Administration mission to Spain, 1950-51. Business consultant; economic consultant to New York State. Member of Potential Committee, Syracuse Community Chest, 1959-69. *Military service:* U.S. Army, Army Service Forces, Industrial Personnel Division, 1942-45; became lieutenant colonel; received commendation.

MEMBER: American Economic Association, American Academy for the Advancement of Science (fellow, 1962), Philomathean Society, Pi Gamma Mu, Beta Gamma Sigma.

AWARDS, HONORS: Rockefeller fellow, 1939; Chancellor's commendation medal, University of Massachusetts—Amherst, 1979.

WRITINGS:

Labor Policy and the Business Cycle, American Council on Public Affairs, 1944.
(Contributor) *Great Issues,* Harper, 1949.
Union Wages and Labor's Earnings, Syracuse University Press, 1950.

(With R. C. Sedgwick) *Labor Law,* Crowell, 1952.
Labor Economics and Problems at Mid-Century, Knopf, 1954.
(With C. Wolf) *Capital Formation and Foreign Investment in Underdeveloped Areas,* Syracuse University Press, 1955.
(With E. E. Palmer) *New St. Lawrence Frontier,* Syracuse University Press, 1957.
(With Buck and Thompson) *Economic Status of Upstate New York,* Business Research Center, Syracuse University, 1960.
(With F. E. Wagner) *Annotated Bibliography of Labor in Emerging Society,* Maxwell Graduate School, Syracuse University, 1962.
Issues in Federal Aid to Education, Syracuse University Press, 1962.
Administration of National Defense Education Act, Syracuse University Press, 1963.
Abstracted Papers on Labor and Administration, Maxwell Graduate School, Syracuse University, 1963.
Unions in Emerging Societies, Syracuse University Press, 1964.
(With M. Buck) *What Price Progress,* Rand McNally, 1964.
Technical Assistance: Theory and Guide Lines, Syracuse University Press, 1966.
(With F. D. Levy) *Basic Economics,* Harper, 1973.
Management of Business Ethics, Kennikat, 1980.
(With T. Ashtow) *The Business and Politics of Economic Responsibilities,* Ajanta Books International (India), 1985.
Bhopal, Ajanta Books International, 1985.
The Decentralization of America: The Breakup of Washington, Devin-Adair, 1986.

Contributor to professional journals and magazines.

WORK IN PROGRESS: A study of business and social ethical considerations, tentatively entitled *Ethics, Markets, and Policy.*

*　　　*　　　*

SULKIN, Sidney 1918-

PERSONAL: Born February 2, 1918, in Boston, Mass.; son of Frank Samuel and Celia (Glazer) Sulkin; married Naomi Ann Levenson, October 4, 1950; children: Jonathan Leigh. *Education:* Harvard University, B.A., 1939. *Politics:* Democrat. *Religion:* Jewish.

ADDRESSES: Home—5012 Elsmere Pl., Bethesda, Md. 20814.

CAREER: Howell-Suskin Publishing Co., New York City, editorial assistant, 1940-41; U.S. Office of War Information, New York City, chief of English language radio programs, 1942-44; American Broadcasting Station in Europe, London, England, deputy chief editor, 1945; Supreme Headquarters, Allied Expeditionary Forces, The Hague, Netherlands, director of publications, 1945; U.S. International Book Association, Stockholm, Sweden, director for northern and eastern Europe, 1945-47; Columbia Broadcasting System, Stockholm, Sweden, and Minneapolis, Minn., special correspondent and commentator, 1945-47; Voice of America, Washington, D.C., chief of Washington bureau, 1949-53; National Issues Committee, Washington, D.C., editorial director, 1953-55; *Changing Times,* Washington, D.C., associate editor, 1955-71, managing editor, 1971-75, editor, 1975-81. Consultant to Office of Military Government, United States (OMGUS) in Germany, 1947. Member of board of directors, Kiplinger Washington Editors, Inc., 1975-81.

MEMBER: National Press Club, Authors Guild, P.E.N., Academy of American Poets, Authors League of America, Dramatists Guild, Poetry Society of America.

AWARDS, HONORS: School Bell Award, 1957, 1958, 1962, 1963, 1964, 1965, and 1966, for "distinguished service in interpretation of education"; Education Writers Association awards, 1962, 1963, and 1966, for "outstanding articles" on education; Quarterly Review of Literature prize, 1980, for verse play Gate of the Lions.

WRITINGS:

(Co-editor) For Your Freedom and Ours, Ungar, 1943.
(Co-translator and adaptor) Janusz Korczak, Matthew, the Young King, Roy, 1944.
(Contributor) Herschel Brickell, editor, O. Henry Prize Stories, Doubleday, 1948.
(Contributor) Martha Foley, editor, Best American Short Stories, Houghton, 1948.
(Contributor) Harold Ribalow, editor, This Land, These People, Beechurst Press, 1950.
The Family Man (novel), Robert B. Luce, Inc., 1962.
Complete Planning for College, McGraw, 1962, revised edition, Harper, 1968.
(Contributor) F. B. Lewis, editor, Modern Educational Developments: Another Look, Educational Records Bureau, 1966.
(Author of introduction) The Challenge of Curriculum Change, College Entrance Examination Board, 1968.
Gate of the Lions (verse play; first produced in Tucson, Ariz., by Invisible Theatre Co. at "Shakespeare under the Stars Classical Theatre Festival," 1982), Quarterly Review of Literature Poetry Series, 1980.
Secret Seed: Stories and Poems, Dryad, 1984.

Also author of play "The Other Side of Babylon," first produced in Washington, D.C., by Source Theatre Co., 1984. Contributor of articles, poems, and short stories to numerous magazines, including Kenyon Review, Michigan Quarterly Review, Sewanee Review, Harper's, New Republic, North American Review, Quarterly Review of Literature, Virginia Quarterly Review, Saturday Review, Arizona Quarterly, and Confrontation.

WORK IN PROGRESS: A novel.

SIDELIGHTS: Sidney Sulkin points to Samuel Johnson's admonition that "No man but a blockhead ever wrote except for money" and concludes: "Sam was wrong. Anyone who sets out to write in order to make money is a fool. You can do better at the race track, or on the commodity exchange, or as a fast food waiter for that other Johnson, Howard. You write because you have no choice. Perhaps the secret avarice is for immortality, but you are lucky if what you get is the pleasure that comes in small rushes—at the beginning when you know you have hold of an idea, during the writing when it goes well, at the finish when you feel it has worked, at the moment of acceptance when an editor you respect says yes we'll take it, and finally, most finally, on the day the printed thing arrives. That day is the end of it. Unless you are especially fortunate, no one will ever say another word to you about it. You've had about all the joy you are going to get; you'd better be on to something else.

"As for working habits, techniques, etc., your most useful quality, if you've got it, is bull-headedness, the kind of stub-bornness that pushes on, works and reworks. Deep in that compulsion lies the seed of the magic."

*   *   *

SUTTON-SMITH, Brian   1924-

PERSONAL: Born July 15, 1924, in New Zealand; son of Ernest James and Nita (Sutton) Sutton-Smith; married Shirley L. Hicks, January 6, 1953; children: Katherine, Mark, Leslie, Mary, Emily. Education: University of Wellington, B.A., 1946, M.A., 1948, Diploma of Education, 1952; University of New Zealand, Ph.D., 1954.

ADDRESSES: Home—612 Harwick Rd., Wayne, Pa. 19087. Office—Graduate School of Education, University of Pennsylvania, 3700 Walnut St., Philadelphia, Pa. 19104.

CAREER: Bowling Green State University, Bowling Green, Ohio, professor of psychology, 1956-67; Columbia University, Teachers College, New York, N.Y., professor of psychology and education, 1967-77; University of Pennsylvania, Graduate School of Education, Philadelphia, professor of education and folklore, and head of program in interdisciplinary studies in human development, 1977—. Visiting professor at Clark University, 1963-64; Fulbright professor at University of Belgrade, 1984.

MEMBER: American Psychological Association (president of Division 10, psychology and the arts, 1984-85), Association for the Anthropological Study of Play (president, 1983-84), Society for Research in Child Development, American Folklore Society, American Association for Health, Physical Education and Recreation.

AWARDS, HONORS: Fulbright scholar at University of California, Berkeley, 1952-53.

WRITINGS:

Our Street (juvenile), A. H. & A. W. Reed, 1952.
Smitty Does a Bunk (juvenile), Price-Milburn, 1959.
The Games of New Zealand Children, University of California Press, 1959.
(With B. G. Rosenberg) The Sibling, Holt, 1970.
(With E. M. Avedon) The Study of Games, Wiley, 1971.
(With R. E. Herron) Child's Play, Wiley, 1971.
(With Rosenberg) Sex and Identity, Holt, 1972.
The Folkgames of Children, University of Texas Press, 1972.
(With wife, Shirley Sutton-Smith) How to Play with Your Children, Hawthorn, 1974.
(Editor) Classics in Play and Games, Arno, 1976.
The Cobbers (juvenile), Price-Milburn, 1976.
Die Dialektik des Spiels, Verlag Karl Hoffman, 1978.
Play and Learning, Gardner, 1979.
The Folkstories of Children, University of Pennsylvania, 1981.
A History of Children's Play, University of Pennsylvania, 1981.
(With Michael Lamb) Sibling Relationships throughout the Life Span, Lawrence Erlbaum, 1982.
(With Diana Kelly-Byrne) The Masks of Play, Leisure Press, 1984.
Toys as Culture, Gardner Press, 1985.

WORK IN PROGRESS: The Handbook of Children's Folklore; a play for adults.

SIDELIGHTS: Brian Sutton-Smith told CA: "I have spent my life studying play and games and continue to find the subject both fascinating and unreachable. I hope it stays that way for me until the end."

BIOGRAPHICAL/CRITICAL SOURCES:

PERIODICALS

Contemporary Psychology, June, 1971.
Diner's Club Magazine, November 16, 1970.

*   *   *

SWAN, Gladys 1934-

PERSONAL: Born October 15, 1934, in New York, N.Y.; daughter of Robert J. (in business) and Sarah (Taub) Rubenstein; married Richard Borders Swan (a professor), September 9, 1955; children: Andrea, Leah. *Education:* Territorial Normal School (now Western New Mexico University), B.A., 1954; Claremont Graduate School, M.A., 1955.

ADDRESSES: Home—450 East Madison, Franklin, Ind. 46131.

CAREER: Junior high school English teacher at public schools in Raton, N.M., 1958-59; part-time lecturer and instructor, 1961-66; Franklin College, Franklin, Ind., assistant professor, 1968-78, associate professor of English, 1979-83; Norwich University, Vermont College Campus, Montpelier, member of faculty of masters in fine arts program in creative writing, 1981—. Distinguished visiting writer-in-residence, University of Texas at El Paso, 1984-85.

MEMBER: Associated Writing Programs.

AWARDS, HONORS: Lilly Endowment fellowship, 1975-76; distinguished service award for literature, Western New Mexico University, 1985.

WRITINGS:

On the Edge of the Desert (short fiction), University of Illinois Press, 1979.
Carnival for the Gods (novel), Random House, 1986.

WORK IN PROGRESS: Ghost Dance, a novel.

SIDELIGHTS: Gladys Swan wrote *CA:* "What I am trying to communicate through my fiction is a way of perceiving, a way of knowing and responding to experience that goes beyond the intellect or rational mind. What some people have been ready to call 'mood' in my stories is to my mind that area of sensibility evoked by image and which is the province of imagination, intuition, and feeling. My efforts in my stories have been to explore what seems to me a largely neglected area of the psyche, particularly in modern America.

"I have also been largely devoted to exploring the West, where I grew up, as the imaginative landscape in which various people existing outside the framework of society have conducted their individual search for meaning. Because the conventional structures no longer answer to their deepest needs and longings, the people I write about have the task of facing the chaos such a situation presents—its inherent threat and promise—and recognizing and responding to their condition. My stories deal with how they make that response or come to that recognition.

"The West has long served an important imaginative function in American life. As Paul Horgan says in his book *Great River: The Rio Grande,* Jefferson had, in his concept of democracy, 'opened up political frontiers in the thoughts of men that only the West, in its sheer space, could contain.' But the implications of the West have been far more than political or economic, though generated by these. For the imagination, the West has been the landscape in which the individual could achieve his fullest potentiality and to which he could venture in search of a new life. Nor, I believe, have these implications been lost under the pressures of modern society, fearful of the loss of individual freedom. What then are the territories to be discovered, the possibilities to be realized? Perhaps they lie within. This is the point at which my fiction begins."

Swan added: "My new novel, *Carnival for the Gods,* is a kind of comic fantasy, set in a mythical territory between Mexico and the United States, where the legendary Seven Cities of Cibola are located. It concerns the adventures of a small traveling carnival—a giant, a midget, a dancer, etc. It is quite different from my other work, and in some ways, the most outrageous thing I've ever written. Though I've always admired comedy and envied those who write it, I never expected to wander into the comic mode myself. I think that is one of the excitements of the whole creative process—discovering new potentialities, new forms. I'm continually surprised at how my work keeps changing, at the new elements that enter into the brew. It's what keeps me at the typewriter—I'm curious to find out what's going on.

"Recently I returned to the Southwest for a year, after a long absence. My new work, a number of stories and the novel I've begun, grew out of that experience. I left that part of the country many years ago, but imaginatively I keep returning. There, and to Greece. The study of Greek literature has had an important effect on my writing. Now that I've had a chance to travel in Greece, I have seen the resemblance between that landscape and the Southwest. Both are very powerful.

"Travel is of most importance to my work. Not only is it fruitful to see how other people respond to their surroundings and create a certain culture in relation to them, but traveling takes one out of the structures he is accustomed to and forces him to look with a different eye. Good literature should do the same."

AVOCATIONAL INTERESTS: Ethnic art, cinema, analytical psychology, travel.

BIOGRAPHICAL/CRITICAL SOURCES:

PERIODICALS

Washington Post Book World, March 30, 1980.

*   *   *

SZOEVERFFY, Joseph 1920-

PERSONAL: Born June 19, 1920, in Clausenbourgh, Transylvania (now part of Romania); came to the United States in 1962, naturalized U.S. citizen; son of Louis (a businessman) and Anna Ilona (von Simkovith) de Szoeverffy. *Education:* St. Emeric College, Budapest, Hungary, B.A., 1939; Budapest University, Ph.D., 1943; State Teachers College, Budapest, staatsexamen, 1944; University of Fribourg, Dr.Phil.Habil., 1950. *Religion:* Armenian Catholic.

ADDRESSES: Home—374 Canton St., Randolph, Mass. 02368.

CAREER: Budapest University, Budapest, Hungary, assistant professor of German philology, 1943-48; Hungarian General Credit Bank, Budapest, assistant to the vice-president, 1944-48; University of Fribourg, Fribourg, Switzerland, visiting lecturer in medieval studies, 1949-50; Glenstal College, County Limerick, Ireland, professor of modern languages, 1950-52; Irish Folklore Commission, University College, Dublin, Ireland, archivist and special research librarian, 1952-57; University of Ottawa, Ottawa, Ontario, lecturer in classics, 1957-58, assistant professor of classical and medieval Latin literature, 1958-59; University of Alberta, Edmonton, assistant professor, 1959-61, associate professor of Germanic philology and German literature, 1961-62; Yale University, New Haven, Conn., associate professor of medieval German literature and philology, 1962-65, fellow of Calhoun College, 1962-65; Boston College, Chestnut Hill, Mass., professor of German and medieval studies, 1965-70; State University of New York at Albany, professor of comparative and world literature and of German, 1970-77, chairman of department, 1972-75; Dumbarton Oaks Center for Byzantine Studies, Washington, D.C., visiting professor of Byzantine studies, 1977-78; Freie University, Berlin, Germany, Richard Merton Visiting Professor of Medieval Studies, 1980-83; University of Vienna, Vienna, Austria, visiting professor, 1984—.

Secretary-general, Foederatio Emericana in Budapest, 1943-46; member of board of directors, Institute for Early Christian Iberian Studies; visiting professor, University of Poitiers, 1961; Harvard University, James C. Loeb memorial lecturer, 1967, visiting professor, 1968, honorary research associate, 1975—; fellow, Center of Medieval and Renaissance Studies, 1973—, and Institute for Advanced Study, Berlin, 1982-83; lifetime faculty exchange scholar, State University of New York, 1974—; project director, Dumbarton Oaks Center for Byzantine Studies, 1984-87.

MEMBER: International Platform Association, Internationale Vereinigung der Germanisten, Comparative Literature Association, Modern Language Association of America, Mediaeval Academy of America, American Folklore Society, American Association of University Professors, American Association of Teachers of German, Canadian Linguistic Association, Northeast Modern Language Association (chairman of Renaissance and Baroque section, 1972-74), Connecticut Academy of Arts and Sciences.

AWARDS, HONORS: University of Chicago folklore prize, 1954; Canada Council lecture grant, 1960-61; American Council of Learned Societies grants, 1960-61, 1964, and 1967; Guggenheim fellowships, 1961 and 1969-70, grants, 1963, 1965, 1970, and 1975; American Philosophical Society fellowships, 1964-65 and 1973; Ella Lyman Cabot grant, 1965; Federal Republic of Germany grant, 1969; Government of Portugal grant, 1969; State University of New York Research Foundation fellowships, 1971 and 1972.

WRITINGS:

Der heilige Christophorus und sein Kult (title means "St. Christopher and His Cult"), Budapest University Press, 1943.

Irisches Erzaehlgut in Abendland (title means "Irish Literary Tradition in the Western World"), Erich Schmidt Verlag, 1957.

An Ungair (title means "Hungary"), FAS (Dublin), 1958.

Annalen der lateinischen Hymnendichtung (title means "Annals of Medieval Latin Hymnody"), Erich Schmidt Verlag, Volume I, 1965, Volume II, 1965.

A Mirror of Medieval Culture: Saint Peter Hymns of the Middle Ages, Connecticut Academy of Arts and Sciences, 1965.

Weltliche Dichtungen des lateinischen Mittelalters (title means "Secular Latin Lyrics of the Middle Ages"), Volume I, Erich Schmidt Verlag, 1970.

Iberian Hymnody: Survey and Problems, Classical Folia Editions, 1971.

(Author of Volume I and of notes to text in Volume II) Peter Abelard, *Hymnarius Paraclitensis,* E. J. Brill, 1975.

A Guide to Byzantine Hymnography, E. J. Brill, Volume I, 1979, Volume II, 1980.

Repertorium Novum Hymnorum Medii Aevi (four volumes), E. J. Brill, 1983.

Religious Lyrics of the Middle Ages, E. J. Brill, 1983.

A Concise History of Medieval Latin Hymnody, E. J. Brill, 1985.

Maeranische Motive der Hymen, E. J. Brill, 1985.

Editor of the series "Medieval Classics: Text and Studies" and "Baroque, Romanticism and the Modern Mind"; co-editor, *Mittellateinisches Jahrbuch,* 1970—. Contributor to *New Catholic Encyclopedia,* McGraw, 1967. Contributor of articles and reviews to sixty international scholarly journals. Member of editorial board, *Mediaevalia.*

WORK IN PROGRESS: Researching German folklore, the lyric poetry of the Middle Ages, literature and politics, language minorities abroad, and the cultural history of Transylvania.

SIDELIGHTS: Joseph Szoeverffy has traveled in twenty-eight countries abroad and has acquaintance with fourteen languages.

AVOCATIONAL INTERESTS: Higher education reform in the United States; photography; journalism and public opinion; public lecturing on East-Central European affairs, folklore, mythology, and modern culture.

T

TAPSCOTT, Stephen (J.) 1948-

PERSONAL: Born November 5, 1948, in Des Moines, Iowa; son of Leo J. (a farmer) and Mary Jean (a journalist; maiden name, Nesbitt) Tapscott. *Education:* University of Notre Dame, B.A., 1970; Cornell University, Ph.D., 1975.

ADDRESSES: Home—24 Concord Ave., Cambridge, Mass. 02138. *Office*—Department of Humanities, Massachusetts Institute of Technology, Cambridge, Mass. 02139.

CAREER: University of Kent at Canterbury, Canterbury, England, lecturer in English, 1976-77; Massachusetts Institute of Technology, Cambridge, assistant professor of English, 1977—. Member of faculty at Goddard College, 1976-82.

WRITINGS:

Mesopotamia (poems), Wesleyan University Press, 1975.
Penobscot: Nine Poems, Pym-Randall, 1983.
American Beauty: William Carlos Williams and the Tradition of the Modernist Whitman, Columbia University Press, 1984.
(Translator from the Spanish) Pablo Neruda, *100 Love Sonnets*, University of Texas, 1985.

*   *   *

TARGAN, Barry 1932-

PERSONAL: Born November 30, 1932, in Atlantic City, N.J.; son of Albert and Blanche (Simmons) Targan; married Arleen Shanken (an artist), March 9, 1958; children: Anthony, Eric. *Education:* Rutgers University, B.A., 1954; University of Chicago, M.A., 1955; Brandeis University, Ph.D., 1962.

ADDRESSES: Home—R.D. No. 2, Box 194-C, Mahaffey Rd., Greenwich, N.Y. 12834. *Office*—Department of English, State University of New York, Binghamton, N.Y. 13901.

CAREER: Syracuse University, Syracuse, N.Y., assistant professor of English, 1962-67; State University of New York College at Cortland, assistant professor of English, 1967-69; Skidmore College, Saratoga Springs, N.Y., assistant professor, 1969-72, associate professor of English, 1972-78, director of external degree program, 1975-78; State University of New York at Binghamton, associate professor, 1978—. *Military service:* U.S. Army, 1956-58.

AWARDS, HONORS: Short fiction award from University of Iowa, 1975, for *Harry Belten and the Mendelssohn Violin Concerto;* Associated Writing Programs Award, 1980, for *Kingdoms;* Saxifrage Award, 1981, for *Surviving Adverse Seasons;* National Endowment for the Arts grant, 1983.

WRITINGS:

Let the Wild Rumpus Start (poetry), Best Cellar, 1972.
Thoreau Stalks the Land Disguised as a Father (poetry), Greenfield Review Press, 1975.
Harry Belten and the Mendelssohn Violin Concerto (short stories), University of Iowa Press, 1975.
Surviving Adverse Seasons (short stories; also see below), University of Illinois Press, 1980.
Kingdoms (novel; expanded version of story of the same name in *Surviving Adverse Seasons*), State University of New York Press, 1981.

Contributor of short stories to periodicals, including *Virginia Quarterly Review, Carolina Quarterly, Sewanee Review,* and *Salmagundi.*

SIDELIGHTS: David Guy, writing for the *Washington Post Book World,* calls Barry Targan "a careful writer with a close eye for detail, a deep love of nature, a love of kinds of work and the details of methods of working." Of the novel *Kingdoms,* which grew out of a story by the same name in *Surviving Adverse Seasons,* Guy writes: "*Kingdoms* ultimately is a powerful novel of a moving relationship between a father and son, and of a courageous intellectual pilgrimage." Anatole Broyard also reviews the book favorably in the *New York Times:* "*Kingdoms* is an unusual love story, drawing a parallel between a man's dead wife and a dying way of life. . . . To see the countryside through [Targan's] 'quaint enamelled eyes' is quite a pleasure." David Evanier, in the *New York Times Book Review,* comments upon *Surviving Adverse Seasons:* "[Targan] needs to become less ponderous, more immediate, more responsive." "Nevertheless," Evanier concludes, "because of Mr. Targan's energy and clarity, the stories do prevail."

BIOGRAPHICAL/CRITICAL SOURCES:

PERIODICALS

New York Times, December 24, 1980.
New York Times Book Review, July 27, 1980.
Times Literary Supplement, March 13, 1981.

Washington Post Book World, March 30, 1980, April 5, 1981.

*　　*　　*

TAYLOR, Charles D(oonan) 1938-

PERSONAL: Born October 20, 1938, in Hartford, Conn.; son of Jack D. (a financier) and Ruth (a teacher; maiden name, Hunter) Taylor; married Georgeanne L. Laitala (a teacher), July 24, 1965; children: Jack M. T., Bennett Hunter. *Education:* Middlebury College, B.A., 1960.

ADDRESSES: Home—Manchester, Mass. 01944.

CAREER: Addison-Wesley Publishing Co., Reading, Mass., salesman and editor, 1965-71; Book Production Services, Inc., Danvers, Mass., president and treasurer, 1971-78; Books and Production East, Inc., Manchester, Mass., packager and agent, 1979-83; writer. *Military service:* U.S. Naval Reserve, 1961-64; became lieutenant junior grade.

MEMBER: U.S. Naval Institute.

WRITINGS:

Show of Force, St. Martin's, 1980.
The Sunset Patriots, Charter, 1982.
First Salvo, Charter, 1985.
Choke Point, Charter, 1986.

WORK IN PROGRESS: Transit of Imperator, "a novel of submarine underice warfare in the near future based on U.S./ U.S.S.R. recognition of how vital the Arctic really is to both nations."

SIDELIGHTS: Charles D. Taylor told *CA:* "Sales continue to improve with each new title and, while I would like to think that it is because the writing and stories improve, I hope that much of the interest in my books is because readers have recognized the very real international situations employed. While storytelling is the key to good fiction, the feedback I receive indicates a strong appreciation for the geopolitics involved. The latter becomes geostrategy which in turn invokes the geoaction of the fiction. Interested, attentive readers demand reality, substantiation of situations, and factual details before they can suspend believability to accept the actions of the characters. What a pleasure to be able to do that and make a living—but solid research is the key."

*　　*　　*

TAYLOR, George
See PARULSKI, George R(ichard), Jr.

*　　*　　*

TEICHMANN, Howard (Miles) 1916-

PERSONAL: Born January 22, 1916, in Chicago, Ill.; son of Jack (a businessman) and Roscoe (Berliner) Teichmann; married Evelyn Goldstein (a writer), April 2, 1939; children: Judith. *Education:* University of Wisconsin, B.A., 1938.

ADDRESSES: Home—863 Park Ave., New York, N.Y. 10021. *Agent*—Candida Donadio, 231 West 22nd St., New York, N.Y. 10011.

CAREER: "Orson Welles's Mercury Theatre of the Air," New York City, stage manager, 1938-40, writer of scripts, 1939-40, producer, 1940-41; Office of War Information, New York City, senior editor with overseas branch, 1942-43; expert con-

sultant in radio to Lieutenant General Brehon Somervell, Washington, D.C., 1943-45; Columbia University, Barnard College, New York City, lecturer, 1946, professor of English, beginning 1947. Cultural consultant and vice-president, Shubert Theatrical Enterprises, 1962-72; administrator, Sam S. Shubert Foundation, 1962-72.

MEMBER: Dramatists Guild, Authors League of America, Sigma Delta Chi, Zeta Beta Tau.

AWARDS, HONORS: Women's Overseas Press Club award, 1942; Peabody Award, 1953; Emmy Award, Academy of Television Arts and Sciences, 1954; University of Wisconsin Distinguished Service award, 1959.

WRITINGS:

PLAYS

(With George S. Kaufman) *The Solid Gold Cadillac* (two-act), Random House, 1954.
Miss Lonelyhearts (two-act), Dramatists Play Service, 1959.
The Girls in 509 (two-act), Samuel French, 1959.
Julia, Jake and Uncle Joe (two-act), Samuel French, 1961.
A Rainy Day in Newark (two-act), Samuel French, 1964.
"Smart Aleck: Alexander Woollcott at 8:40," first performed Off-Broadway at the American Place Theater, October 25, 1979.

NONFICTION

George S. Kaufman: An Intimate Portrait, Atheneum, 1972.
Smart Aleck: The Wit, World and Life of Alexander Woollcott, Morrow, 1976.
Alice: The Life and Times of Alice Roosevelt Longworth, Prentice-Hall, 1979.
Fonda: My Life; As Told to Howard Teichmann, New American Library, 1981.

OTHER

Also author of radio dramas produced on "Mercury Theatre of the Air," "Campbell Playhouse," "Helen Hayes Theatre," "Texaco Star Theatre," "CBS Workshop," "Cavalcade of America," "Gertrude Lawrence Review," "They Live Forever," "Ford Theatre of the Air," and others; author of television dramas for "Theatre USA," "Showtime USA," "USA Canteen," and others.

SIDELIGHTS: Howard Teichmann first became friends with the noted satirist George S. Kaufman in the early 1950s when they collaborated on a play called "The Solid Gold Cadillac," and the two remained close until the playwright's death in 1961. Despite their long association, Teichmann realized when he began to do research for a Kaufman biography that neither he nor anyone "really knew the private character of the public figure," to use *Variety*'s words. In his book, *George S. Kaufman: An Intimate Portrait,* Teichmann explores his subject's contradictions, showing how this complicated man was both generous and greedy, shy and outgoing, prudish and promiscuous, and unfailingly sharp with his wit. "I saw the play at a disadvantage. The curtain was up," Kaufman reported in one of his theatrical reviews. On another occasion, the caustic Kaufman—who worked as the *New York Times* drama critic before becoming a dramatist himself—reported being "underwhelmed" by Broadway's offerings. Teichmann's book abounds with Kaufman witticisms like these.

In organizing his material, Teichmann avoided the standard chronological recitation of events, choosing instead to open the book with their first meeting, flashing back to Kaufman's impoverished childhood and struggling beginnings as a writer, and ending with the triumphant Broadway opening of his last hit, "The Solid Gold Cadillac." According to *New York Times Book Review* contributor Clive Barnes, Teichmann's "method has obvious advantages, not the least in the way it enables the author to maintain a warmly personal tone, while at the same time examining the various, often contradictory aspects of the man. The entire book is written a little like a report card on a friend." A *Variety* reporter offers this assessment: "It is obviously written with affection, respect approaching idolization, extensive knowledge and considerable understanding. Although it doesn't ignore the subject's warts, it recognizes his unique qualities—his greatness. . . . [Tiechmann] has written an enthralling, entertaining and satisfying book."

BIOGRAPHICAL/CRITICAL SOURCES:

PERIODICALS

New York Times, May 16, 1976, October 22, 1979, October 27, 1979.
New York Times Book Review,. June 25, 1972, May 16, 1976.
Saturday Review, July 22, 1972, May 15, 1976.
Variety, June 21, 1972.
Washington Post Book World, September 9, 1979, October 28, 1981.

*   *   *

TEMKO, Florence

PERSONAL: Married second husband, Henry Petzal; children: (first marriage) Joan Temko, Ronald Temko, Stephen Temko. *Education:* Attended Wycombe Abbey, London School of Economics and Political Science, and New School for Social Research.

ADDRESSES: Home and office—1855 Diamond St., 5-324, San Diego, Calif. 92109.

CAREER: Berkshire Museum, Pittsfield, Mass., former assistant to the director.

MEMBER: American Society of Journalists and Authors, Authors League of America, Authors Guild, National League of American Pen Women, American Craftsman, Artist-Craftsmen of New York.

WRITINGS:

Kirigami: The Creative Art of Papercutting, Platt, 1962.
Party Fun with Origami, Platt, 1963.
Paperfolding to Begin With, Bobbs-Merrill, 1968.
Papercutting, Doubleday, 1973.
Feltcraft, Doubleday, 1974.
Paper: Folded, Cut, Sculpted, Macmillan, 1974.
Paper Capers, Scholastic Book Services, 1974.
Self-Stick Craft, Doubleday, 1975.
Decoupage Crafts, Doubleday, 1976.
Folk Crafts for World Friendship, Doubleday, 1976.
(Contributor) *The Golden Happy Birthday Book,* Golden Press, 1976.
The Big Felt Burger and 27 Other Craft Projects to Relish, Doubleday, 1977.
The Magic of Kirigami, Japan Publications, 1978.
Paperworks, Bobbs-Merrill, 1979.
Let's Take a Trip, Milton Bradley Co., 1982.
Chinese Papercuts, China Books, 1982.
Elementary Art Games and Puzzles, Prentice-Hall, 1983.
New Knitting, HP Publishing, 1984.

Also contributor to *National Camp Directors Guide,* 1974. Author of weekly column, "Things to Make," in *Berkshire Eagle* and other newspapers. Contributor to magazines and newspapers, including *Grade Teacher, New York Times,* and *Boston Globe.*

WORK IN PROGRESS: Paperfolding, for China Books.

SIDELIGHTS: Florence Temko told *CA:* "Crafting with paper is my specialty, and I love origami (paper folding) and kirigami (paper cutting) for the wonderful ways in which paper can be turned into holiday decorations or works of art. I felt that a book could spread my enthusiasm to a large number of people and was very surprised that not one of fifteen New York publishers ageed with me. Finally my first book did make it and once you are in print, it is easier to do again. But I never thought I would end up writing [so many] books. One of my editors discovered I could write clear instructions that readers could follow easily, a writing talent I did not know I possessed."

*   *   *

TEMPLE, Dan
See NEWTON, D(wight) B(ennett)

*   *   *

TEMPLE, Wayne C(alhoun)   1924-

PERSONAL: Born February 5, 1924, near Richwood, Ohio; son of Howard Milton and Ruby March (Calhoun) Temple; married Lois Marjorie Bridges, September 22, 1956 (died April 21, 1978); married Sunderine Wilson Mohn, April 9, 1979. *Education:* University of Illinois, A.B. (cum laude), 1949, A.M., 1951, Ph.D., 1956. *Religion:* Presbyterian.

ADDRESSES: Home—1121 South Fourth Ct., Springfield, Ill. 62703. *Office*—Illinois State Archives, Springfield, Ill. 62756.

CAREER: University of Illinois at Urbana-Champaign, research assistant, 1949-53, teaching assistant, 1953-54; Illinois State Museum, Springfield, curator of ethnohistory, 1954-58; Lincoln Memorial University, Harrogate, Tenn., associate professor of American history, 1958, John Wingate Weeks Professor of History and director of department of Lincolniana, 1958-64, chairman of department of history, 1959-62; Illinois State Archives, Springfield, archivist, 1964-77, deputy director, 1977—. Occasional lecturer, Lincoln Land Community College and U.S. Military Academy. President, Midwest Conference on Masonic Education, 1984-85; member of advisory council, U.S. Civil War Centennial Commission, 1960-65; secretary-treasurer, National Lincoln Civil War Council. Assistant district commissioner, Boy Scouts of America, 1958-60. Regent, Lincoln Academy of Illinois. Member of board of governors, Shriners Hospital for Crippled Children. *Military service:* U.S. Army, 1943-46; received two commmendations for action under fire in European Theater; lieutenant general in militia.

MEMBER: Royal Society of Arts (London; life fellow), Civil War Press Corps (major), Lincoln Group of District of Columbia (honorary), Phi Alpha, Sigma Tau Delta, Delta Sigma Rho, Phi Alpha Theta, Chi Gamma Iota, Tau Kappa Alpha, Alpha Psi Omega, Sigma Pi Beta (headmaster), Order of the Arrow.

AWARDS, HONORS: Lincoln Medallion of Lincoln Sesquicentennial Commission, 1960; Scouter's Award, Boy Scouts of America, 1960; Lincoln Diploma of Honor, Lincoln Memorial University, 1963; award of achievement, U.S. Civil War Centennial commission, 1965; distinguished service awards, Illinois State Historical Library, 1969 and 1977; honorary degree International Supreme Council for the Order of De Molay, 1972; Distinguished Service Award, Civil War Round Table (Chicago), 1983.

WRITINGS:

Indian Villages of the Illinois Country: Historic Tribes, Illinois State Museum, 1958, revised edition, 1977.
Lincoln the Railsplitter, Willow House, 1961.
(Editor) *Campaigning with Grant,* Indiana University Press, 1961.
(Editor) *The Civil War Letters of Henry C. Bear,* Lincoln Memorial University Press, 1961.
Lincoln as Seen by C. C. Brown, Crabgrass, 1963.
Abraham Lincoln and Others at the St. Nicholas, St. Nicholas Hotel, 1968.
Alexander Williamson: Tutor to the Lincoln Boys, Lincoln Fellowship of Wisconsin, 1971.
Indian Villages of the Illinois Country, Illinois State Museum, 1975.
First Steps to Victory: Grant's March to Naples, Seventh Cavalry, 1977.
Stephen A. Douglas: Freemason (selection of two book clubs), Masonic Book Club, 1982.
By Square and Compasses: The Building of Lincoln's Home and Its Saga (selection of two book clubs), Ashlar, 1984.

Also author of *Lincoln's Connections with the Illinois and Michigan Canal,* in press; also author of *Lincoln-Grant: Illinois Militiamen,* 1981; also co-author of play, "Abe Lincoln Takes a Wife." Also contributor to *A Civil War Cook Book, Mountain Life and Work,* and *Lincoln Day by Day;* also contributor to *World Book Encyclopedia.*

Editor of scripts for radio series, "A. Lincoln, 1809-1959," for Broadcast Music. Contributor to magazines. *Lincoln Herald,* editor-in-chief, 1958-73, associate editor, 1973—.

WORK IN PROGRESS: Mrs. Lincoln's Cookbook; writing about Lincoln and his father as farmers, and Lincoln in Sangamon County; a book on Lincoln as a lecturer.

SIDELIGHTS: Wayne C. Temple told *CA:* "Since 1949, I have been a professional Lincoln scholar. Only the unknown facets of Lincoln's life interest me. And I have been successful in finding new facts about the sixteenth president because I love primary research in manuscript sources. Even a blind hog finds acorns if he roots, and I have rooted through a forest of trees looking for the oaks which produce the new acorns. By sifting through the manuscripts in my own place of employment, I often discover unknown Lincoln documents which help answer important questions about Lincoln's history.

"In addition to careful and exhaustive research, an author must be inspired. Fortunately, I have always had a wife who encouraged me and took a deep interest in my literary work. We often travel to the places I write about; one cannot describe adequately a spot never seen in person. If a writer composes without visting the site, the end product will not sparkle and bubble. History writing does not have to be dull. When supported by cold facts, go ahead and compose the story in an interesting style and manner."

BIOGRAPHICAL/CRITICAL SOURCES:

PERIODICALS

Bloomington Pantagraph, February 10, 1985.
Journal of the Illinois State Historical Society, summer, 1958.
Knoxville Journal, February 12, 1962.
Louisville Courier-Journal, February 8, 1962.
Springfield State Journal Register, January 13, 1985.

*   *   *

TENAX
   See LEAN, Garth Dickinson

*   *   *

TENGBOM, Mildred   1921-

PERSONAL: Born June 6, 1921, in Center City, Minn.; daughter of Nels Oscar and Harriet (Brink) Hasselquist; married Luverne C. Tengbom (a professor), May 23, 1953; children: Daniel, Judy Tengbom Collins, Janet, David. *Education:* Attended Minneapolis Business College, University of Minnesota, University of Oklahoma, Lutheran Bible Institute, Cypress College, Biola University, and Fuller Theological Seminary. *Religion:* Lutheran.

ADDRESSES: Home—Singapore; Anaheim, Calif. (permanent). *Office*—1661 Carnelian St., Anaheim, Calif. 92802.

CAREER: Worked as secretary and bookkeeper, 1938-43; The Lutheran Book Store, LaCrosse, Wis., founder and manager, 1943; The Lutheran Book Store, Racine, Wis., founder, 1944, manager, 1944-45; World Mission Prayer League missionary in India, 1945-53; CKXL-Radio, Calgary, Alberta, host of children's program "Sunday Morning Children's Hour," 1953-56; Lutheran Church in America, missionary in Tanzania, 1957-67; writer, 1968—. Lutheran Church in America, member of board of management for the office of communication, 1979-82, member of board of management for the Division for World Mission and Ecumenism, 1982-85, missionary in Singapore, 1985—. Writer for Lutheran television, Missouri Synod. Instructor at writing conferences; speaker at conferences, seminars, and retreats.

WRITINGS:

Is Your God Big Enough?, Augsburg, 1973.
The Bonus Years, Augsburg, 1975.
Table Prayers, Augsburg, 1976.
A Life to Cherish, Revell, 1977.
Especially for Mother, Revell, 1977.
No Greater Love: The Story of Clara Maass, Concordia, 1978.
(With husband, Luverne C. Tengbom) *Fill My Cup, Lord: A Devotional Study of Key Greek Words,* Augsburg, 1979.
Sometimes I Hurt: Insights and Reflections from the Book of Job, Thomas Nelson, 1980.
(With L. C. Tengbom) *Family Bible Readings,* Augsburg, 1980.
Does Anyone Care How I Feel?, Bethany House, 1981.
Help for Bereaved Parents, Concordia, 1981.
Help for Families of the Terminally Ill, Concordia, 1982.
I Wish I Felt Good All the Time, Bethany House, 1982.
Devotions for New Mothers, Bethany House, 1982.
Does It Make Any Difference What I Do?, Bethany House, 1984.
Why Waste Your Illness?, Augsburg, 1984.
Mealtime Prayers, Augsburg, 1985.

Talking Together about Love and Sexuality, Bethany House, 1985.
September Morning, Brethren Press, 1985.
Bible Readings for Mothers, Augsburg, 1986.

Author of radio scripts. Columnist for *Western Canada Lutheran;* Pacific Southwest correspondent for *The Lutheran;* regular contributor to *Christian Ambassador;* contributor of articles and stories to more than fifty religious and secular periodicals.

WORK IN PROGRESS: Research on the seven churches of the first century mentioned in the book of Revelation, with special emphasis on the historical, cultural, and geographical background; devotional writings; a book on bereavement.

SIDELIGHTS: Mildred Tengbom told *CA:* "Seven years in India, almost ten in East Africa, three years in Canada, and now in Singapore have broadened my outlook and have helped me view American life from a different perspective. Much of what I see in our present day culture concerns me deeply. Extensive travel in Europe, Scandinavia, India, Pakistan, Turkey, Israel, Hong Kong, Japan, Nepal, Ghana, Liberia, Kenya, and Tanzania has opened more doors of understanding—and questioning. Learning to speak, read, and write Nepali and Swahili has enhanced my fascination with words and broadened my modes of expressing thought.

"In my writing I find myself returning again and again to the themes of family, relationships, wholeness (physical, mental, and spiritual), grief and bereavement, values, order, and our worldwide dependency on one another. Writing was a postponed dream for me. As a teenager I dreamed of being an overseas news reporter. That dream was finally fulfilled in a unique way when I was commissioned by our church in 1980 for an eighty-day trip to India, Nepal, Hong Kong, and Japan and again in 1982 for a forty-day trip to Liberia, Ghana, Kenya, and Tanzania to interview and write. My husband, who accompanied me, did the photography.

"I began studying writing and writing for publication in 1968. I set a goal of writing for periodicals for five years and then wanted to publish my first book. That dream was realized. Several more books have followed with more in the works. My articles on the POW/MIA issue have been filed in Congressional Records. *No Greater Love: The Story of Clara Maass* has been placed in military libraries.

"I love to write. It is sheer joy, and I never tire of it. I hope to continue to write as long as I have a sound mind. The reader response which I receive continually is rich reward for hours spent at my craft. And presently I also am enjoying studying under Asian professors. What a rare opportunity!"

*   *   *

TERRELL, Robert L(ouis)   1943-

PERSONAL: Born July 19, 1943; son of Jack (a laborer) and Bessie (Naylor) Terrell; married Venita L. Sharpe, March, 1967; children: Iman Makeba. *Education:* Morehouse College, B.A., 1969; University of California, Berkeley, M.A., 1973, Ph.D., 1978.

ADDRESSES: Office—Department of Journalism and Mass Communication, New York University, 1021 Main Bldg., New York, N.Y. 10003. *Agent*—Lois Wallace, William Morris Agency, 1350 Avenue of the Americas, New York, N.Y. 10019.

CAREER: New York Post, New York City, reporter, 1967-68; Southern Regional Council, Atlanta, Ga., researcher and writer, 1968-69; *San Francisco Chronicle,* San Francisco, Calif., copy editor, 1970; Golden Gate College (now University), San Francisco, instructor in writing and literature at School of Law, 1970-71; St. Mary's College, Moraga, Calif., assistant professor of social and psycholingual foundations of education, 1971-76; University of Missouri—Columbia, associate professor of journalism, 1976-84; New York University, New York City, associate professor of journalism and mass communication, 1985—.

Instructor at Negro College Newspaper Editor's Workshop, Clark College, Atlanta, 1969; lecturer at Institute of Labor and Industrial Relations, University of California, Berkeley, 1971; visiting professor at Stanford University, 1976 and 1981, and University of California, Berkeley, 1979. Stringer for *Newsweek,* 1968-69; copy editor, *Beijing Review,* Peking (Beijing), China, 1981-82. Member of board of directors, California Council on Teacher Education, 1972-75; member of advisory screening committee in communications, Council for the International Exchange of Scholars, 1980-83.

MEMBER: Association for Education in Journalism.

AWARDS, HONORS: Faculty research council grants, University of Missouri—Columbia, 1977 and 1979; Shell research grant, 1983; Fulbright fellowship, University of Nairobi, 1984-85.

WRITINGS:

(With Cleveland Sellers) *The River of No Return: The Autobiography of a Black Militant and the Life and Death of SNCC,* Morrow, 1973.
(Editor) *American Mass Media Experience,* Waveland, 1978.

Contributor to *A Handbook on the War in Asia.* Contributor of articles and poems to magazines and newspapers, including *Evergreen Review, Eye, Urban West, Negro Digest, Great Speckled Bird,* and *Guardian. California Journal of Teachers Education,* managing editor, 1972-73, editorial referee, 1973—.

WORK IN PROGRESS: Research for a book, tentatively entitled *Developing Nations and the Communications Explosion.*

SIDELIGHTS: Robert L. Terrell told *CA:* "I write because it provides me opportunities to contribute to the ongoing dialogue regarding the best ways to improve the quality of life for as many of the planet's inhabitants as possible. Although I frequently find the act of writing to be extremely arduous, I cannot deny that it is one of the most deeply satisfying activities in my life. For the most part, I concentrate on problems and issues which tend to be avoided by most other writers. This is particularly true regarding my writings about the poor and disenfranchised.

"Although I sometimes get discouraged because of editorial reluctance to present my point of view, I feel that the long range trend is in my favor. In that regard, I expect to be much more highly regarded as a writer, academic, intellectual and social critic in the future than I am at present."

*   *   *

THOMAS, D(onald) M(ichael)   1935-

PERSONAL: Born January 27, 1935, in Redruth, Cornwall, England; son of Harold Redvers (a builder) and Amy (a housewife; maiden name, Moyle) Thomas; children: Caitlin, Sean,

Ross. *Education:* New College, Oxford, B.A. (with first class honors), 1958, M.A., 1961.

ADDRESSES: Home—10 Greyfriars Ave., Hereford, England. *Agent*—John Johnson, Clerkenwell Green, London ECR 0HT, England.

CAREER: Grammar school English teacher in Teignmouth, Devonshire, England, 1960-64; Hereford College of Education, Hereford, England, lecturer, 1964-66, senior lecturer in English, 1966-79, head of department, 1977-79; writer, 1979—. Visiting lecturer in English, Hamline University, 1967; visiting professor of literature, American University, spring, 1982 (resigned). *Military service:* British Army, two years.

MEMBER: Bard of the Cornish Gorseth.

AWARDS, HONORS: Richard Hilary Award, 1960; Translators award from British Arts Council, 1975, for translations of works by Anna Akhmatova; Chomondeley Award, 1978, for poetry; *Guardian*-Gollancz Fantasy Novel Award, 1979, for *The Flute-Player;* Cheltenham Prize, *Los Angeles Times* Book Award, and Booker McConnell Prize nomination, all 1981, all for *The White Hotel.*

WRITINGS:

POETRY

Personal and Possessive, Outposts, 1964.
(With Peter Redgrove and D. M. Black) *Modern Poets 11,* Penguin, 1968.
Two Voices, Grossman, 1968.
Logan Stone, Grossman, 1971.
Lilith-Prints, Second Aeon Publications, 1974.
Love and Other Deaths, Merrimack Book Service, 1975.
The Honeymoon Voyage, Secker & Warburg, 1978.
Dreaming in Bronze, Secker & Warburg, 1981.
Selected Poems, Viking, 1983.

FICTION

The Devil and the Floral Dance (juvenile), Robson, 1978.
The Flute-Player (novel), Dutton, 1979.
Birthstone (novel), Gollancz, 1980.
The White Hotel (novel), Gollancz, 1980, Viking, 1981.
Ararat (first novel in trilogy), Viking, 1983.
Swallow (second novel in trilogy), Viking, 1984.

EDITOR

The Granite Kingdom: Poems of Cornwall, Barton, 1970.
Poetry in Crosslight (textbook), Longman, 1975.
Songs from the Earth: Selected Poems of John Harris, Cornish Miner 1820-84, Lodenek Press, 1977.

TRANSLATOR

Anna Akhmatova, *Requiem, and Poem without a Hero,* Ohio University Press, 1976.
Akhmatova, *Way of All the Earth,* Ohio University Press, 1979.
Yevgeny Yevtushenko, *Invisible Threads,* Macmillan, 1981.
Alexander Pushkin, *The Bronze Horseman,* Viking, 1982.
Yevtushenko, *A Dove in Santiago,* Viking, 1983.

OTHER

Work is represented in anthologies, including *Best SF: 1969,* edited by Harry Harrison and Brian W. Aldiss, Putnam, 1970, *Inside Outer Space,* edited by Robert Vas Dias, Anchor Books, 1970, and *Twenty-Three Modern British Poets,* edited by John Matthias, Swallow Press, 1971. Contributor to literary journals in England and the United States.

WORK IN PROGRESS: The third novel in the trilogy begun with *Ararat* and *Swallow,* tentatively entitled *Sphinx.*

SIDELIGHTS: In 1980, after spending nearly a year closeted in a small study at Oxford University, D. M. Thomas emerged with the manuscript for his third novel. Known until that time primarily as a poet and translator of Russian verse, Thomas had first branched out into adult fiction with the 1979 book *The Flute-Player,* a fantasy-like meditation on art and its struggle to endure and even flourish in a totalitarian regime. A second fantasy novel, *Birthstone,* followed soon after; it tells the story of a woman trying to create a single, stable identity out of the fragmented parts of her personality. Both works—especially *The Flute-Player,* which won a contest for best fantasy novel—received praise for their imaginative, poetic treatments of familiar themes. But neither work sold more than a few hundred copies.

Upon its publication in late 1980, Thomas's new novel, *The White Hotel,* seemed destined for the same fate. A complex blend of the real and the surreal, of the apparent dichotomy between the Freudian concepts of the pleasure instinct and the death instinct, the work generated relatively little interest among British critics and readers; what reaction there was, the author later recalled in a *New York Times Magazine* article, could best be summed up as "restrained approval." Within just a few months, however, it became clear that on the other side of the Atlantic, at least, that would not be the case. Appearing in the United States in the spring of 1981, *The White Hotel* met with what William Borders referred to in the *New York Times* as a "thunderclap of critical praise" that sparked sales and made Thomas an instant celebrity. Already into its second printing before the official publication date, *The White Hotel* eventually sold more than 95,000 copies in its hardcover edition and almost 1.5 million copies in the paperback reprint—making it without a doubt "the sleeper novel of the season," to quote a *Publishers Weekly* writer.

Less than two years before, Thomas had been at a crucial turning point in his life and career. When government budget cuts led to the closing of the Hereford College of Education, the forty-four-year-old head of the English department found himself suddenly jobless (but with a full year's severance pay to live on while he searched for a new position). Thomas's first thought was to return to Oxford University and pursue another degree, a move his former tutor advised against—unless he had some other compelling reason to be there. As it turned out, he did. "I was becoming dissatisfied at writing my ideas as poems," Thomas told *Publishers Weekly* interviewer Ion Trewin. "I wanted a larger form, and in our age I think you can only do that as a novel. But with the college closing down I wanted to be more involved in human lives, which I found I could be with a novel. And again, I think that by middle age you find you've gathered a lot of material that's waiting to be used, material that was no good for a poem."

Some of this material "waiting to be used" included parts of a poem that Thomas had been working on for quite some time. Based on an image of two young lovers on a train journey in 1912 (with Karl Jung and Sigmund Freud as fellow passengers), the verses he had composed never seemed quite finished to Thomas, and the image continued to haunt him. Then, while searching for a long book to read on a flight to the United States, he came across Anatoli Kuznetsov's *Babi Yar,* a description of the wartime massacre of Jews at Kiev in the Soviet Union. As Thomas explained to Trewin: "The account of the Holocaust suddenly connected to my poems. Everything fell into place. And I didn't go to the United States after all—I started to write the novel instead." He spent the next nine months at Oxford, expanding on the image of the train journey, Freud, and the Holocaust, weaving a tale that is part epistolary, part poetic, and part straight narrative.

Divided into seven distinct sections, *The White Hotel* begins with a prologue that consists of a series of letters to, from, or about Freud and several of his colleagues in which the doctor discusses the case of one of his female patients, "Frau Anna G.," who is suffering from a severe hysterical illness. Her psychic distress manifests itself physically as asthma, anorexia, pains in the left breast and ovary, and a general feeling of anxiety that conventional treatments have not alleviated. In his letters, Freud speculates that the case of "Frau Anna G." will substantiate his theory of a death instinct that coexists with the erotic one.

Following the prologue are two sections devoted to writings by the mysterious "Frau Anna G." herself. The first sample is a long poem in which "Anna" describes an erotic fantasy she has concerning an affair with Freud's son. The affair begins in a train compartment and continues at a lakeside "white hotel," where a series of explicit and unusual love scenes are played out against a backdrop of horrible death and destruction involving other guests at the hotel; none of the violence, however, interferes with or diminishes the lovers' passion and self-absorbed pursuit of physical pleasure. The second writing sample, ostensibly written at Freud's request, is an expanded prose version of "Anna's" fantasy, "a wild, lyrical, irrational embroidery upon her original," remarked Thomas Flanagan in the *Nation*. According to *Village Voice* critic Laurie Stone, it is this prose version that serves as "a key to [Anna's] fears, imaginative transformations, and clairvoyant projections."

The fourth section of *The White Hotel* is comprised of Freud's long analysis of the case of "Frau Anna G.," now revealed to be Lisa Erdman, an opera singer of Russian-Jewish descent. A pastiche of actual case histories written by Freud, the section connects Lisa's fantasies to events in her real life and concludes with the doctor's observation that "she was cured of everything but life, so to speak. . . . She took away with her a reasonable prospect of survival, in an existence that would doubtless never be less than difficult."

The fifth and sixth sections of the novel chronicle in detached prose the course of Lisa's life after she is treated and "cured" by Dr. Freud. The conventional narrative ends with a chilling account of her execution in 1941 at Babi Yar along with thousands of other Russian Jews; the reader then discovers what Lisa's fantasies have always meant in terms of her life and death and, in a broader sense, all of European history in the twentieth century.

The White Hotel's seventh and final section is a surreal epilogue in which Lisa, now in a purgatory-like land that is unmistakably Palestine, is reunited with people who had figured prominently in her life, including her mother and Freud. There, too, in this strange place are thousands of other souls awaiting forgiveness, love, and understanding; Lisa is last seen agreeing to help the latest wave of "immigrants" settle in: "No one could, or would, be turned away; for they had nowhere else to go."

The initial reaction to *The White Hotel* among British critics was "bafflingly contradictory," as Thomas himself reported in the *New York Times Magazine*. Among the few major periodicals that published reviews, the discussions often high-lighted the novel's "pornographic" content, especially the two chapters containing Lisa's poetic and prose versions of her fantasy. *Punch* reviewers Mary Anne Bonney and Susan Jeffreys, for example, dismissed the entire book as "humourlessly insubstantial" and singled out Lisa's poem in particular as "a sexual fantasy of some crudity and little literary worth." This view was shared by Brian Martin, who added in a *New Statesman* article that "no amount of fumbling with artistic devices and excuses makes it any different." Commenting in the *Times Literary Supplement*, Anne Duchene agreed that the early sections of the book "are not for the squeamish," but conceded that "they have to be undergone, by committed readers, as part of the raw material for the later, much more interesting sections."

Though *London Review of Books* critic Robert Taubman also found the sexual scenes "not real or erotic," with an "unconvincing look of pornography," he nevertheless went on to declare: "The analysis that follows sounds an authentic note. . . . At the same time, it provides the reader with an absorbing Chinese box narrative of hidden memories, reversals of meaning and deceptions uncovered." A reviewer for *Encounter* compared reading *The White Hotel* to watching an Ingmar Bergman film: "You are battered with symbolism, in perpetual pursuit of images, of references, of bizarre surrealist objects. . . . I'm not sure that I enjoyed it, but I am certainly respectful; this is a powerful piece of writing, highly complex, carefully structured. Its meanings and intention fall gradually into place; I suspect that it would improve still further on subsequent readings. . . . The novel either has to be accepted on its own terms or not at all. Either the reader enters into [the author's] psychological construction . . . or he doesn't."

In the months immediately following *The White Hotel*'s publication in Britain, it seemed that few people were willing to accept the novel on *any* terms. As Thomas put it in the *New York Times Magazine*, "Any serious novel needs a miracle to bring it to the public's attention, and that miracle did not happen in Britain. It happened, instead, in the United States." By and large, American critics lauded *The White Hotel* as an ambitious, brilliant, and gripping *tour de force*. According to Thomas, their reviews were "individual, lengthy, well-considered, and concentrated within a short period of time; in Britain [*The White Hotel*] generally appeared among a miscellaneous bundle of three or four novels. . . . The British reviews stressed the book's complexity; the American reviews stressed its readability. The Americans seemed more open to largeness of theme and inventiveness of form. Their lips weren't so pursed."

The Americans, for example, were far less inclined than the British to make an issue out of *The White Hotel*'s "pornographic" content. The few who even raised the possibility described Thomas's poem and its prose rendition as highly erotic rather than pornographic; several reviewers mentioned that the decision to use such a technique was an unusual and very effective way of revealing the soul of Lisa Erdman.

Though George Levine commented in the *New York Review of Books* that the author's language is occasionally "merely vulgar, or banal," he went on to note that it often achieves "a lush, romantic intensity, with a remarkable precision of imagery. [The] writing is full of dislocation and surprise; it is seductive, frightening, and beautifully alive. . . . Such language immediately establishes the mysterious 'Anna G.' as a powerful presence." Leslie Epstein expressed a similar opinion, declaring in the *New York Times Book Review* that "the poem seems to speak directly from the unconscious.'' In short, declared *Time*'s Paul Gray, *The White Hotel* ''easily transcends titillation. Those who come to [Thomas's] novel with prurient interests alone will quickly grow baffled and bored.''

While British reviewers by no means focused exclusively on the subject of eroticism in *The White Hotel,* they did devote less space than their American counterparts to discussions of the novel's other major features. Its structure in particular impressed a number of critics on this side of the Atlantic, most of whom praised it as an innovative mixture of traditional forms that results in ''what feels like entirely new fictional terrain,'' to use Stone's words.

Because she felt *The White Hotel* is much more than a novel, Elaine Kendall hesitated referring to it as such. Instead, she maintained in her *Los Angeles Times* review, it is ''a *belles lettres* revival in itself, encompassing not only the three traditional disciplines [of fiction, poetry and drama] but also history, myth, biography and science. D. M. Thomas has written a book that enlarges the usual notion of the novel, so radically that to classify it with a single noun diminishes the author's intent and achievement.''

Newsweek's Peter S. Prescott found the book ''in its conception and design a daring enterprise, brought off with dazzling virtuosity.... [Thomas] has made of his story a full-dress tragedy incorporating a variety of moods and narrative styles which reinforce each other to an astonishing degree. Each segment succeeds in its own way ... yet they are bound together by a repetition of symbol and event whose significance shifts slightly from one segment to the next, always adding to our understanding of the whole. By the end ... Thomas has achieved the kind of serenity we associate with Sophocles and Shakespeare.''

Writing in the *Nation,* Thomas Flanagan described *The White Hotel* as ''a book of extraordinary beauty, power and audacity—powerful and beautiful in its conception, audacious in its manner of execution. It is as stunning a work of fiction as has appeared in a long while.... [Thomas] is not one of those writers who, having been informed by the hum of the general culture that 'narrative' has fallen from favor, has looked about for more modish equivalents. His form issues directly from his vision, is compelled by his vision.... It becomes literally impossible to respond to the novel ... without disentangling the submerged narrative from the manner of its telling, the shifting viewpoints and chronologies, the rich and shifting imagery.''

Partisan Review critic Frank Conroy suggested that these contrasting modes and shifting viewpoints serve to link *The White Hotel*'s structure with Freudian methods and theories of psychotherapy, especially the idea of a life instinct-death instinct, a major thematic component of the novel. As Conroy explained, *The White Hotel*'s seven separate sections ''come at the story from different angles, creating the effect of the author circling in on his subject in a spiral,'' a method that ''echoes the process of psychoanalysis'' developed by Freud. The eminent doctor is, in fact, a major character in the novel, and Thomas's realistic portrayal garnered many compliments from American as well as British reviewers.

Freud and his life instinct-death instinct theory are first introduced via the letters that form *The White Hotel*'s prologue. In one of these letters, the doctor mentions to a colleague that the writings of a young female patient of his ''seem to lend support to my theory: an extreme of libidinous phantasy com-

bined with an extreme of morbidity.'' Several sections later, following the poetry and prose versions of Lisa's fantasy, Freud appears again as the author of the case history of ''Frau Anna G.'' According to *New Republic* reviewer Michele Slung, ''the Freud Thomas gives us, viewed through the lens of fiction, does not seem to be different from the Freud of contemporary witnesses: he is kind, diplomatic, tolerant, insightful, self-assured.'' Thomas's imitation of a case history, said Gray, ''is uncannily accurate and convincing. It has the same whodunit intensity of the originals, the same bristling of symbols, the same gentle prodding to make the patient reveal more than she wants to know.'' The *Spectator*'s Paul Ableman remarked that ''the document is so finely-attuned to the style of the founder of psychoanalysis that it seems merely fortuitous that 'Anna G.' never occupied the famous couch in the Berggasse.'' Thus, it is within this ''model of affectionate impersonation,'' to use Flanagan's words, that Lisa's fantasy ''is artfully joined to her painfully remembered past.''

As Thomas makes clear, however, the fictional Freud is aware that there remain images in Lisa's fantasies that cannot be readily explained in terms of her childhood and early life. During the course of the case history, it is revealed that Lisa has ''telepathic powers''—an ability to foresee the future without actually understanding it—a talent that Freud dismisses at first but eventually comes to accept. The reader's acceptance of Lisa's gift (or ''curse,'' to use her words) is crucial, for the entire second half of the novel builds on the premise that her physical pains and violent fantasies are related to *future* events, not past ones, and that her personal suffering prefigures and eventually becomes part of the horror of the Holocaust. In short, observed Flanagan, Thomas proposes that ''far more has been at stake [in *The White Hotel*] than Lisa Erdman's damaged psyche. The fate of our culture has been implied.''

Whether a reviewer was able to make the ''imaginative leap'' necessary at this point in the story usually determined how he or she ultimately felt about *The White Hotel.* For some, the leap was impossible, often because they believed that neither Lisa Erdman's character nor Freud's life instinct-death instinct theory was developed enough to sustain such a metaphor. For others, like the *New York Times*'s Christopher Lehmann-Haupt, the poetic transformation of Lisa's tragic personal history into a collective one was nothing less than ''heart-stunning.''

Susan Fromberg Schaeffer, for instance, stated in the *Chicago Tribune Book World* that ''the bones of a wonderful story are here [in *The White Hotel*], but Lisa Erdman and her world do not come alive.... [Thomas] clearly means to pay tribute to Freud's vision, and [he] does. In the process, however, [he] loses sight of the real Freud, who always refused easy comfort, either in religion or in mysticism. Worse still, Thomas loses sight of his own characters, his own obligation to breathe life and power into his fictional world.'' Epstein agreed, pointing out that Lisa ''seems to float through the various crises that afflict her,'' and she has ''no intellectual life'' despite the complex political, social, and cultural forces that swirl around her. She is, in essence, no more than a ''casualty at first of her psyche and then of history,'' in Taubman's opinion. In addition, Epstein contended, ''the notion of the death instinct is shaky enough in Freud's own theory, and the application of a 'struggle between the life instinct and the death instinct' to this poor patient strikes me as nothing more than a bald assertion, unsupported by the evidence.''

Though he described Thomas's "expansion of imagery and structure from the fate of an individual to the fate of the culture itself" as "a dazzling accomplishment," Flanagan nonetheless concluded that the author's decision to authenticate his case by making Lisa clairvoyant "has exacted a price. . . . The device remains a device, a willed literary artifice that demands, but cannot fully claim, our assent. And at the end we are left with a 'solution' more esthetically satisfying, perhaps, than that of the rational psychologist, but just as arbitrary. Thomas is no less imprisoned by the conditions of his art than was Freud by his. His deepest theme, the joined threads of desolation and joy, is communicable only through images that are mute save in their power and their beauty, [and] his 'explanation' [of them] imperils both of these qualities."

Among those who were of a different opinion was Daphne Merkin, who affirmed in the *New Leader* that "despite intricate schema of interlocking myths and recurring symbols, the novel manages to sustain a clear, pure intention, always presenting Lisa in terms of her own story. Her desires and the impediments to their fulfillment are never less than unique, yet within the remarkable context of their telling they acquire the weight of allegory."

New York magazine critic Edith Milton made a similar observation, declaring that Thomas's "interweaving of psychological symbols and cultural myth, of prophetic intuition and the dismal truths of twentieth-century history, did not seem to me merely the fabric of a convincing fiction, but the brilliant representation and clarification of some troubled and important mystery at the heart of my own world. . . . Lisa's dream of love and death is more than an exercise in clairvoyance. It is an apocalyptic vision of the eternal destruction and resurrection of the human spirit. And Freud's interpretation of it is the rational man's battle to make some sense of the senseless equilibrium between chaos and survival."

The White Hotel's epilogue requires readers to make yet another imaginative leap, one that most reviewers, including several of those who had criticized Lisa's clairvoyance as an implausible device, found possible and even somewhat exhilarating in light of what Levine called "Thomas's refusal to end his novel with the shocking finality of Babi Yar." Set in a dreamlike world beyond death that is almost, but not quite, paradise, the epilogue weaves together all the novel's symbols and images "into a somehow reassuring unity, reassuring even in the aftermath of the agony," observed Slung. More important, it underscores the author's belief that the forces on the side of life and love are more powerful than those on the side of death and hatred, transforming what has appeared to be a vision of despair into a vision of hope.

To Richard A. Blake of *America*, the ending of *The White Hotel* tells us that Lisa "can never really die, because she is the race itself, a victim of its own deep mysterious evil, yet resilient, responsive to love and ever hopeful. Lisa can, it seems, return one day to her 'white hotel,' the womb where she rests secure from her nightmares and her memory." Even Epstein, who was critical of Thomas's decision to propel the story forward by giving Lisa telepathic powers and a death instinct, felt that the ending overcame the weaknesses in the earlier section. "It is a remarkable and perhaps even necessary conclusion," the reviewer wrote. "It made me realize that I had, after all, read the story of a particular life, that it was one I could respect and for which I had come to feel real fondness."

"Thomas's conclusion is audacious, yet it seems exactly right for all that has gone before," declared Gray. "Given the many mysteries in Lisa's life, the last one is almost commonplace. . . . [The White Hotel] is a reminder that fiction can amaze as well as inform." As *Esquire*'s James Wolcott put it, "*The White Hotel* is so cleanly propelled by its obsessions that it slices through platitude and serves as a tribute to the silenced millions—to all those whose blood crimsoned the bayonet's edge. [It] is one of the rare novels written for grownups that aren't afraid to leap over the railing into passionate, lyrical excess."

For others, including a few who found the rest of *The White Hotel* moving, the ending was anticlimactic, a disappointment—somewhat of a "technicolour sunset with angelic choir," as Anne Duchene remarked in the *Times Literary Supplement*. Her British colleague Taubman voiced a similar opinion, maintaining that "it's more of a sentimental fantasy than that of the white hotel at the beginning, and too insubstantial for Lisa's final conviction—'we were made to be happy and to enjoy life'—to carry much weight." At least one of the American critics, Conroy, supported this contention that the ending is too weak to sustain the rest of the story. "The various sections of [The White Hotel] are like elaborate, highly decorated checks for vast amounts," he wrote, "and the end is like a trip to the bank, where one discovers, sadly, that they can't be cashed."

Levine, too, was not entirely satisfied with the ending, especially its pervasive sense of hope, which he believed was not entirely justified. Nevertheless, he defended *The White Hotel* as "a novel of immense ambition and virtuosity" based on a fictional world of "unmanageable, inexpressible reality." Continued the critic: "It is inevitable that a book taking so many risks, in a manner distinctly less English than continental, or even American, should be marked by some unevenness. Whatever one's doubts its strengths remain. The image of the 'white hotel' is an image of the womb, an image of peace, but the novel that takes this image for its title suggests that life can be seen neither as a matter of peace or of violence. . . . In his emotionally precise and inventive prose, Thomas suggests a reality at once vital and deadly, and more accessible than we—protected behind our documents and books—might care to know."

Paul Ableman, one of the few British reviewers who praised Thomas's novel virtually without qualification, agreed that "*The White Hotel* is a work of vast ambition and impressive achievement. It aspires to being little less than a comprehensive synthesis of the forces of life and death operating on this planet in the context of a civilisation that apparently obeys quite different laws but in which their influence is always present. If that sounds forbidding it should immediately be added that it is also a gripping human story." Echoing Levin's observation, Ableman concluded, "*The White Hotel* transcends the parochialism of most contemporary English novels and shows that fiction, when it escapes the dead conventions of the nineteenth century and, of course, when written by a major talent, is still full of vitality."

Since the success of *The White Hotel*, which made its author a very reluctant celebrity, Thomas has published two additional novels (part of a proposed trilogy), two poetry collections, and three translations. Despite the variety of his output, he considers himself primarily a poet who also happens to write novels. "It's a problem," he told *Publishers Weekly* interviewer Trewin. "Trying to be a juggler and keep two balls in the air is difficult enough, but to be a translator too. . . .'' What is most important for him to keep in mind regarding his work, Thomas believes, is to keep his distance from the critical and commercial "hype" and continue *writing.* "I can enjoy the bursts of travel, and the small vanities of success," he remarked in the *New York Times Magazine.* "Yet [I] know that the reality is where the blank sheet rests in the typewriter, where the new novel or poem is as great a struggle as ever. . . . I know [too that with each new book] the critics will be breathing down my neck . . . , but that doesn't worry me. I simply carry on writing the best way I know how, and enjoy it." As he further explained to Borders in a *New York Times* interview: "Serious work can come only from your psyche. You go along for years and then all of a sudden there comes a divine spark and it all works. All I can do now, as I write, is hope and pray that it will strike again."

AVOCATIONAL INTERESTS: "Besides sex and death, I am interested in Russian literature, music, most sport, and my Celtic homeland, Cornwall."

CA INTERVIEW

CA interviewed D. M. Thomas by telephone on October 12, 1984, at his home in Hereford, England.

CA: In your article "On Literary Celebrity" in the June 13, 1982, New York Times Magazine *you wrote about the burdens that can come with popular success, especially in America. Two novels and more than two years later, have you recovered from the tumultuous reception of* The White Hotel?

THOMAS: Oh yes, I think I have. There are various kinds of popular success, and I was perhaps in the less usual situation of being not by nature a best-selling author who happened to write a best-selling book. There could still be pressures on me in a way, more of the expectations of the public that you can somehow repeat *The White Hotel* as if to a formula, and of course you can't, whereas authors who strike a particular genre like thrillers more or less can guarantee that they will repeat it. I know that I can just do it a book at a time. The combination of themes in *The White Hotel* made it unusually popular, in a sense. So there is a certain psychological pressure on me, but I really have, I think, recovered from that state I was in then.

CA: In Hereford, are you treated much as everyone else?

THOMAS: Yes, totally ignored. They know of me, but they go about their business. It's a very down-to-earth farming community, and I just flit in and out, so there's no sort of celebrity status here, and I'm very relieved at that. I feel that it's good for me to live somewhere where there isn't that pressure. It would be unhealthy if I were in it all the time. I like to travel as I am doing. That's one of the great benefits of what happened with *The White Hotel,* that I get invited around a lot more. I enjoy the sort of recharging of batteries that gives me and a break from the solitude. It's a question of balancing the necessary solitude and then meeting people and having the wider experience.

CA: In the introduction to Poetry in Crosslight *you wrote: "A poem is able to catch at our breaths by leaping across huge gulfs of experience and making nothing of them." Do you think it's possible to do anything like that in the novel?*

THOMAS: I think it is. I suppose the novel is entirely different from poetry, but it's a spectrum really, although one expects greater logic in the novel and a more orderly progression. I set out to try in my own novels, particularly in *The White Hotel,* to make those leaps, because life is like that. It doesn't follow an orderly progression. It may seem to for a while, but then you get jolted into a new experience like falling in love, or bereavement, and you have to make those leaps. And since the novel is about life, then I don't see why it shouldn't do that. Joyce is the supreme example of someone who could leap from one style to another. I suppose one of the characteristics of my own writing is moving into different voices, so that it's possible to go from a lyrical poetic voice to a very realistic narrative. That provides the kind of leap that you get through metaphor in poetry.

CA: Do you still regard yourself primarily as a poet who sometimes writes novels?

THOMAS: Yes, except that I'm a poet who *mainly* writes novels now. I'm very uneasy about the distinction. If I'm introduced as a novelist, I think, help! That's not me. I don't know how to write a novel. And I really believe that is true in a way. And yet I also feel slightly guilty if I'm referred to as a poet, because I think, when was the last lyric poem I wrote? And it's quite a long time ago. I think of the poet, as I said in the introduction to my *Selected Poems,* in the original sense of a *maker.* That is what I'm doing. I'm not a novelist in the orthodox sense of writing a coherent narrative with a steady, careful creation of characters and motivation. I can't do that. I'm a poet in that when I'm writing a novel, it is all striking off my imagination instantly; I simply don't know what is going to happen. But of course I'm using prose. So it's a curious borderland I'm in, and I don't think there's quite a word to describe it. Maybe *improviser* is the only word, except that we don't really have it. That's why perhaps I've been writing about *improvisatori* recently—because I'm probably looking for a word that describes my kind of writing.

CA: In your New York Times Magazine *piece that I mentioned earlier, you said that* Ararat *had been much harder to write than* The White Hotel. *Did the difficulty have to do with the novel's complex structure?*

THOMAS: Probably, except that again the complex structure just happened to fall out that way. But I did have to work very hard at putting it together. I just think there are some books that do sort of leap at you and where you strike it lucky, and others you have to work much harder for. And that goes for any art form. *The White Hotel* in a way was easy because the form of it seemed to leap at me. But actually there were many years of searching for that and writing the initial poems, for example, and not knowing where it was going to lead. I was doing a lot of work without realizing it was work on the novel. But when I actually got the idea for the novel, the form fell into place, and the voices, so that what was left was mainly just the hard craftsmanship. What I'm really saying is that *The White Hotel* was a book which was in some way a summation of a lot of things I'd been writing or trying to write for several years. I kid myself that it only took me nine months to write, but of course it was actually a lot longer than that. Then I had to start in all over again with *Ararat;* that was the problem.

CA: Your interest in Freud's case histories, I know, had a lot to do with the idea for The White Hotel. *How did that interest begin?*

THOMAS: Simply reading Freud for pleasure, more as a storyteller, as a mythmaker, than as a scientist or an ideologist of the mind. I loved the detective-story aspect and the neurotic aspect of his stories. I enjoyed the subdued, very dry way in which he expressed his most explosive personal stories. And I thought his sense of form of a story was beautiful, very like the Greek myth of Oedipus, the same sort of structure, building up to a sudden revelation, that he himself was using as the basis of some of his theories. So it was an artistic fascination, and wanting for a long time to write a story which would be a kind of imitation of a Freudian case study. And of course one of those lucky things in *The White Hotel* was that I realized instantly that I could use it, I could do it, but simply as a central part of a larger work.

CA: You've described with some humor your early lack of proficiency in Russian, which you started learning as part of your compulsory national service. Did you have an extensive Russian vocabulary by the time you began your translations of Russian poets?

THOMAS: Well, I did two years in the army, and it was a fairly intensive course, so if I was any sort of linguist I would know it backwards. I have a reasonable vocabulary, but I am not now and I wasn't then an expert Russian speaker. I had to labor and consult the dictionary. It was sort of end-of-first-year university course, I suppose.

CA: Are there special difficulties in translating poetry from Russian to English, as opposed to translating from the French or German, say?

THOMAS: Certainly it's different from the French in that it's an inflected language, so the Russians have many more opportunities for melodic echoes simply because of case endings: you can have three or four genitive cases in one line which have more or less the same sound. You translate it into English and you've lost that sound effect. Since it's an inflected language, they can change the order of a sentence, and this again we lose, as in translating Greek or Latin poetry. We English are more or less stuck with one set order.

Also I think Russian has an even richer vocabulary than English. You can have innumerable prefixes or suffixes which slightly change the meaning of the word. Pushkin, for example, talks about a young woman's *nozhki*, which means her "little feet," and it's kind of an affectionate term. You try to say someone's "little foot" in English and it just sounds ridiculous. So you have to forget about the littleness or phrase it some other way. It is extremely rich, and our particular richness doesn't quite match it.

CA: The poet Anna Akhmatova, whose work you have translated, seems to be a continuing inspiration to you. How did you discover her, and what did you find in her writing that tugged at you in such a personal way?

THOMAS: I first discovered her in a review of *Requiem*, a lyrical sequence which came out around 1963 "without her permission or knowledge"—that was the publishers' way of exonerating her from its appearance in the West. There was a literal translation, in the review I read, of her foreword, which talked about her in the queue. A woman with blue lips recognized her and said, "Can you describe this?" and she said, "Yes, I can." I thought, this is marvelous. I think what I took to immediately was the mixture of exceptional majesty and

beauty of utterance with a kind of basic, down-to-earth simplicity, and the way she seemed to be very much a part of her people, what the Russians call the *narod*, the race. This is something that most English or English-speaking poets have lost, in a way. There's much more pressure to specialize and become detached from the rootedness of ordinary people. So I immediately got hold of *Requiem* in the Russian and thought it was even more marvelous, and later still thought, why not use my Russian to translate her?

I think I take to poets whose utterance is almost proselike in lucidity, or at least they are the poets whom I find most inspiring for my own work. I go for the poets who seem to walk on that borderline which I do—Pushkin is the same, and Pasternak; and of the English-language poets, Yeats, Robert Frost—or on the other hand, novelists who seem to stray into poetry, like James Joyce, Thomas Hardy, Tolstoy, Turgenev.

CA: Have you been to Russia yet?

THOMAS: Yes, I went about three years ago, just for a short holiday, to Moscow and Leningrad.

CA: How was it? You must have had some anxiety about going, that it might somehow let you down after all your work with the poets.

THOMAS: Yes, it was one of those curious things where I almost didn't want to go anymore because I'd written so much about it. But all I'd written was really about the mythic state of Russia, treating Russia almost as Dante treats Hell—as a land of the imagination. But I thought at last I had to see the reality. I suppose it more or less conformed to my expectations in that I found it appallingly drab; and the party slogans, which are everywhere in red, grated on my teeth. I couldn't imagine staying there. I even preferred American advertising rather than simple party advertising—one product. But on the other hand I had experiences which were inspiring, like going to a Russian church and feeling the power of the spirit still there, very much.

CA: Some of your work, including your first two adult novels, is classified as fantasy or science fiction, yet some of the elements that account for that labeling are also present in your other work. Do you see a clear division between fantasy and so-called mainstream fiction?

THOMAS: No. I don't think fantasy is a good label for my work. In fact, *The Flute-Player* was called a fantasy only because I happened to submit it for a fantasy competition, and they liked it enough to award it the prize. They couldn't decide if it was really fantasy, but they let me have it anyway. So *The Flute-Player* was stuck with the term *fantasy novel*. In all of my writing I like to marry fantasy and reality. I don't go for the Tolkien-type pure fantasy. Where there is fantasy in my novels, it can always be justified on realistic terms. For example, the sexual fantasy in *The White Hotel* is Lisa's fantasy; it comes out of a real human being who has a life of her own. In *Birthstone* again there's a lot of fantasy that comes out of a disturbed personality. I would prefer to use the term *poetry* rather than *fantasy*.

CA: You've said that you like a kind of distance between you and the subjects of your work. How do you achieve that—or is it something that already exists and requires only to be maintained?

THOMAS: There is often a stage where it does seem very close, and I think distance is achieved over a period of time. Gradually you fictionalize things which maybe originally are too close to you. It depends on the theme. I find that if I'm writing for a female persona it's probably easier to have that distance because the main character is obviously not me. If there's a man as the central character, as in *Ararat*, it's more difficult because I'm closer to a male's feelings. There it was harder to get that necessary distance.

CA: Do you still write in "imaginative leaps" rather than on a day-in, day-out schedule?

THOMAS: I do write every day if I'm here. But obviously at the end of the day I may scrap the whole of it. Occasionally one gets good ideas and they stick. There are more days when the ideas are rotten and they don't stick, but I have a regular schedule of getting to the typewriter and sitting, because I don't think ideas tend to come unless you positively court the muse by entering a room which you associate with writing. But there's also a lazy hour, every morning, when I just wander around the house daydreaming ideas and images.

CA: When you travel or get completely away from home, do you rest from the work or is it always somehow going on in your mind?

THOMAS: It goes wherever I go, but not physically. Usually, even though I may be looking forward to going somewhere, when the time comes I think, God, I'd rather be staying home and working. But I do find the trips important because they allow you to forget the sheet of paper and just think, or daydream, really (which is what much of creation is), about the work as a whole. And often good ideas come when I'm away having to do readings or some kind of promotion work. But I never completely leave it behind. I wish I could. It's something I regret. I cannot let go; I'm obsessional, I suppose. It has to go with me in some form or other.

CA: You've named Joyce as your favorite novelist. Are there current writers whose work you enjoy a great deal?

THOMAS: I'm still waiting for Solzhenitsyn's next novel. That may sound odd because he doesn't write in any sense like I do, and I obviously couldn't begin to write like him, but I do find that he has that sort of total magical realism which I like very much. There is a poet who possibly isn't well known in the new world, Charles Causley. He is a fellow Cornishman whose work I think is marvelous. But there are really very few that I would leap to the bookshelves for. I find, actually, that I'm not reading very much lately. I'm more concerned with writing. Or I read nonfiction which has to do with some sort of research. Maybe it's because I taught for a long time, and then I had to read books for my courses. In a way I think I'm still enjoying not having to read. I tend to read more or less at random and just happenstance.

CA: I know that music is an interest of yours and it figures in various ways in your stories. Does it have anything to do directly with your work? Do you listen to music while you're writing or thinking about writing?

THOMAS: Occasionally I do—it is useful in setting up the lyrical mood—but not very often. I find that sometimes my work takes on a kind of musical structure, as I see it later, although it's not intentional. Perhaps this is an aspect of the more poetic kind of writing. I could see *The White Hotel* more easily as some kind of symphonic structure, having symphonic movements, rather than a literary one. But this is something that only occurs to me later. Repetition of motif does occur often in my work. Images gather new meanings, and this is rather like repetition of motif in music.

CA: Would you consider a stint at a college or university as visiting professor or writer-in-residence under better circumstances than you faced at American University?

THOMAS: Yes, I always consider anything—or almost anything. I did have that unfortunate experience in Washington, and it slightly put me off from making long-term commitments. But I can well imagine needing—maybe financially, but more likely psychologically—to go back into teaching for a semester or a year. So it is possible. At the moment I enjoy doing short spells of teaching—where I only need to pack one suitcase!

CA: What's in the future that you'd like to talk about?

THOMAS: I'm continuing the theme of improvisation. *Swallow* has just come out, the second book in the sequence begun with *Ararat*, and I'm working on a third, which is provisionally called *Sphinx*. It's proving tough, like *Ararat;* I've been writing it for about a year and I don't know when I'll finish it. What I'm trying to do in these books is not only to write about the nature of inspiration and creation, but also to say something about the cold war, the contemporary world. As I saw it in *The White Hotel*, I was taking as my theme our world in the early part of the century. Then it seemed to me natural to go on to the contemporary world, the world of the H-bomb and of darkness and light, the division as both sides see it: each side thinks it's the light and the other side is darkness. I wanted to study that in relation to the individual, who also has two sides to the divided self in the modern world. This is the theme I'm struggling with.

BIOGRAPHICAL/CRITICAL SOURCES:

BOOKS

Contemporary Literary Criticism, Gale, Volume XIII, 1980, Volume XXII, 1982, Volume XXXI, 1985.
Dictionary of Literary Biography, Volume XL: *Poets of Great Britain and Ireland since 1960*, Gale, 1985.
Dictionary of Literary Biography Yearbook: 1982, Gale, 1983.
Thomas, D. M., *The White Hotel*, Gollancz, 1980, Viking, 1981.

PERIODICALS

America, October 17, 1981, April 16, 1983.
Atlantic, April, 1983.
Best Sellers, May, 1981.
Books and Bookmen, July, 1980, March, 1983.
Chicago Tribune Book World, March 22, 1981, June 12, 1983.
Commentary, August, 1981.
Commonweal, October 7, 1983.
Detroit News, March 22, 1981, November 17, 1982.
Encounter, August, 1981, July-August, 1983.
Esquire, April, 1981, November, 1982.
Globe and Mail (Toronto), March 10, 1984, July 21, 1984.
Hudson Review, autumn, 1983.
Listener, July 19, 1979, January 22, 1981, March 3, 1983.
London Review of Books, February 5, 1981, April 1, 1983.

London Times, January 15, 1981, June 9, 1983, March 10, 1984, June 28, 1984.
Lone Star Review, April, 1981.
Los Angeles Times, March 17, 1981.
Los Angeles Times Book Review, October 31, 1982, April 3, 1983, November 18, 1984.
Maclean's, April 11, 1983, June 25, 1984.
Nation, May 2, 1981, April 23, 1983.
New Leader, April 20, 1981, May 30, 1983.
New Republic, March 28, 1981, April 4, 1983.
New Statesman, June 22, 1979, March 21, 1980, January 16, 1981, March 4, 1983, June 29, 1984.
Newsweek, March 16, 1981, March 15, 1982, April 4, 1983.
New York, March 16, 1981.
New Yorker, March 30, 1981.
New York Review of Books, May 28, 1981, June 16, 1983, November 22, 1984.
New York Times, March 13, 1981, March 24, 1981, September 21, 1982, March 29, 1983, October 31, 1984.
New York Times Book Review, March 15, 1981, June 28, 1981, September 26, 1982, March 27, 1983.
New York Times Magazine, June 13, 1982.
Observer, June 24, 1979, February 27, 1983, July 1, 1984.
Partisan Review, January, 1982.
People, June 29, 1981.
Poetry, May, 1971.
Publishers Weekly, March 27, 1981, April 17, 1981, January 8, 1982.
Punch, October 14, 1981, March 2, 1983.
Saturday Review, March, 1981, July, 1981.
Spectator, July 7, 1979, January 17, 1981, March 19, 1983, June 30, 1984.
Time, March 16, 1981, April 25, 1983.
Times Literary Supplement, November 30, 1979, March 14, 1980, January 16, 1981, January 22, 1982, June 29, 1983, June 29, 1984.
Village Voice, March 18, 1981, April 26, 1983.
Virginia Quarterly Review, summer, 1981.
Voice Literary Supplement, October, 1982.
Washington Post, December 15, 1979, January 27, 1982.
Washington Post Book World, March 15, 1981, May 16, 1982, March 27, 1983, September 9, 1984.
West Coast Review of Books, May-June, 1983.

OTHER

Kessler, Jascha, "D. M. Thomas: *Selected Poems*" (radio broadcast), KUSC-FM, Los Angeles, Calif., May 18, 1983.†

—*Sketch by Deborah A. Straub*

—*Interview by Jean W. Ross*

*   *   *

THOMPSON, Jacqueline 1945-

PERSONAL: Born December 4, 1945, in Morristown, N.J.; daughter of Bernard Lee Thompson (an advertising executive) and Dorothy Bischoff Hussa. *Education:* Barnard College, B.A., 1969. *Religion:* Protestant.

ADDRESSES: Home and office—10 Bay St. Landing, 7K, St. George, Staten Island, N.Y. 10301. *Agent*—Barbara Lowenstein, 250 West 57th St., New York, N.Y. 10107.

CAREER: American Bureau of Shipping, New York City, editorial assistant, 1969-70; Peat, Marwick, Mitchell & Co., New York City, editor and writer, 1970-73; free-lance writer

and editor, 1973—. Part-time public relations consultant for Alan Towers Associates, 1976-82, and Carl Byoir Associates, 1983-84.

MEMBER: American Society of Journalists and Authors.

WRITINGS:

(Contributor) William Albrecht, *Economics* (textbook), Prentice-Hall, 1974.
(Contributor) Daniel T. Pollitoske, *Music* (textbook with study guide and workbook), Prentice-Hall, 1974.
(Contributor) Harold H. Frank, editor, *Women in the Organization,* University of Pennsylvania Press, 1977.
(Compiler and editor) *Directory of Personal Image Consultants,* Editorial Services, 1978-85.
(Contributor) *What to Do with the Rest of Your Life: The Catalyst Career Guide for Women in the '80s,* Simon & Schuster, 1980.
The Very Rich Book: America's Supermillionaires and Their Money—Where They Got It, How They Spend It, Morrow, 1981.
(Editor) *Image Impact: The Aspiring Woman's Personal Packaging Program* (anthology), A & W Publishers, 1981.
Upward Mobility: A Comprehensive Career Advancement Plan for Women Determined to Succeed in the Working World, Holt, 1982.
Future Rich: The People, Companies and Industries Creating America's Next Fortunes, Morrow, 1985.
(Ghostwriter) J. Nicholson and J. Lewis-Crum, *Color Magic: The Revolutionary Color 1 Wardrobe and Makeup Program,* Bantam, 1985.
(Editor) *Image Impact for Men: The Business and Professional Man's Personal Packaging Program* (anthology), Dodd, 1985.

Author of scripts for "Family Health TV News," WPIX-TV, 1976. Also author of promotional brochures. Contributor of more than seventy feature articles to magazines, including *Us, New York, Gentlemen's Quarterly, Ms., Parade, Working Woman,* and *Financial World.*

*   *   *

THORN, John 1947-
(Sanford W. Jones)

PERSONAL: Born April 17, 1947, in Stuttgart, Germany (now West Germany); brought to the United States in 1949, naturalized in 1963; son of Richard Berthold (a merchant) and Victoria (Gruber) Thorn; married Sharon McFarland, September 7, 1968 (divorced April 30, 1984); children: Jedediah McFarland, Isaac Turner. *Education:* Beloit College, B.A., 1968; graduate study at Washington University, St. Louis, Mo. *Religion:* Jewish.

ADDRESSES: Home and office—18 Virginia Ave., Saugerties, N.Y. 12477. *Agent*—David Reuther, 271 Central Park W., New York, N.Y. 10024.

CAREER: New Leader, New York City, editor, 1969-72; Hart Publishing Co., New York City, editor, 1972-76; writer, 1976—. Publications director, Society for American Baseball Research, 1985—.

MEMBER: Authors Guild, Authors League of America, Society for American Baseball Research, Professional Football Researchers' Association, New York Historical Society.

WRITINGS:

A Century of Baseball Lore, Hart Publishing, 1974, revised edition, 1976.
(Under pseudonym Sanford W. Jones) *Great Recitations* (poems), Hart Publishing, 1975.
The Relief Pitcher, Dutton, 1979.
Baseball's Ten Greatest Games, Four Winds, 1980.
Pro Football's Ten Greatest Games, Four Winds, 1981.
(Editor) *The Armchair Quarterback*, Scribner, 1982.
(Editor) *The Armchair Aviator*, Scribner, 1983.
(With Pete Palmer) *The Hidden Game of Baseball*, Doubleday, 1984.
(Editor with David Reuther) *The Armchair Mountaineer*, Scribner, 1984.
(Author of introduction) *Sphere and Ash*, Camden House, 1984.
The Armchair Book of Baseball, Scribner, 1985.
The Complete Book of the Pitcher, Macmillan, 1986.

Editor, *The National Pastime: A Review of Baseball History*, 1982—.

SIDELIGHTS: The Armchair Mountaineer, an anthology of mountaineering literature edited by John Thorn and David Reuther, manages "to be comprehensive while at the same time dredging up some novelties, like a climbing piece by Evelyn Waugh," Dennis Drabelle comments in the *Washington Post Book World*. And Thorn's *The Armchair Aviator* is described by Bart Everett in the *Los Angeles Times Book Review* as a compilation of "bits and pieces that just might include anything ever written about flying." Everett concludes that "here is a book of history, science, romance and humor—blessed with a most proper touch of whimsy."

BIOGRAPHICAL/CRITICAL SOURCES:

PERIODICALS

Los Angeles Times Book Review, January 15, 1984.
New York Times Book Review, May 6, 1979.
Washington Post Book World, January 28, 1985.

*   *   *

THORPE, James   1915-

PERSONAL: Born August 17, 1915, in Aiken, S.C.; son of J. Ernest (a merchant) and Ruby (Holloway) Thorpe; married Elizabeth Daniells, July 19, 1941; children: James III, John Daniells, Sarah Jans-Thorpe. *Education:* The Citadel, A.B., 1936; University of North Carolina, M.A., 1937; Harvard University, Ph.D., 1941. *Politics:* Democrat. *Religion:* Episcopalian.

ADDRESSES: Home—1199 Arden Rd., Pasadena, Calif. 91106. *Office*—Henry E. Huntington Library and Art Gallery, San Marino, Calif. 91108.

CAREER: Princeton University, Princeton, N.J., 1946-66, began as assistant professor, became professor of English, master of Graduate College, 1948-54, assistant dean of graduate school, 1948-58; Henry E. Huntington Library and Art Gallery, San Marino, Calif., director, 1966-83, senior research associate, 1966—. Member of board of trustees, Kent School, 1952-59; member of Fulbright selection advisory committee, 1964-66; member of Henry Francis DuPont Winterthur advisory committee, 1967-71; member of board of fellows, Claremont University Center. *Military service:* U.S. Army Air Forces, 1941-46; became colonel; received Bronze Star.

MEMBER: Modern Language Association of America (member of committee on research activities, 1950-73), American Antiquarian Society (fellow), American Academy of Arts and Sciences (fellow), American Philosophical Society, Milton Society.

AWARDS, HONORS: Guggenheim fellow, 1949-50, 1965-66; Litt.D., Occidental College, 1968; L.H.D., Claremont Graduate School, 1968; LL.D., The Citadel, 1971; H.H.D., University of Toledo, 1977.

WRITINGS:

A Bibliography of the Writings of George Lyman Kittredge, Harvard University Press, 1948.
(Editor) *Milton Criticism*, Rinehart, 1950, reprinted, Macmillan, 1969.
Rochester's Poems on Several Occasions, Princeton University Press, 1950.
(Editor) *The Poems of Sir George Etherege*, Princeton University Press, 1963.
(Editor) *The Aims and Methods of Scholarship*, Modern Language Association of America, 1963, 2nd edition, 1970.
Literary Scholarship, Houghton, 1964.
(Editor) *Relations of Literary Study*, Modern Language Association of America, 1967.
(With others) *Founding of the Henry E. Huntington Library and Art Gallery*, Huntington Library, 1969.
(Editor and author of introduction) John Bunyan, *The Pilgrim's Progress from This World to That Which Is to Come, and Grace Abounding to the Chief of Sinners*, Houghton, 1969.
Principles of Textual Criticism, Huntington Library, 1972, 2nd edition, 1979.
Use of Manuscripts in Literary Research, Modern Language Association of America, 1974, 2nd edition, 1979.
Gifts of Genius, Huntington Library, 1980.
Behind the Scenes, Huntington Library, 1980.
A Word to the Wise, Huntington Library, 1982.
John Milton: The Inner Life, Huntington Library, 1983.

Also editor of *Journal of Proceedings of Association of American Universities*, 1951-55.

WORK IN PROGRESS: The Sense of Style: The Structure of English Prose.

BIOGRAPHICAL/CRITICAL SOURCES:

PERIODICALS

Los Angeles Times Book Review, January 23, 1983.
Sewanee Review, spring, 1984.
Times Literary Supplement, November 25, 1983.

*   *   *

THURBER, James (Grover)   1894-1961

PERSONAL: Born December 8, 1894, in Columbus, Ohio; died November 2, 1961, in New York, N.Y., of pneumonia following a stroke; son of Charles Leander (name later changed to Lincoln; a politician) and Mary Agnes (Fisher) Thurber; married Althea Adams, May 20, 1922 (divorced, May 24, 1935); married Helen Wismer, June 25, 1935; children: (first marriage) Rosemary. *Education:* Attended Ohio State University, 1913-1918.

CAREER: Columbus Dispatch, Columbus, Ohio, reporter, 1921-24; *Chicago Tribune*, Chicago, Ill., reporter for Paris edition,

1925-26; *New York Evening Post*, New York City, reporter, 1926; *New Yorker*, New York City, managing editor, 1927, staff writer, chiefly for "Talk of the Town" column, 1927-33, regular contributor, 1933-61. Artwork was exhibited in several one-man shows, including shows at the Valentine Gallery, New York City, 1933, and the Storran Gallery, London, England, 1937. *Wartime service:* Code clerk at the Department of State, Washington, D.C., and at the American Embassy, Paris, France, 1918-20.

MEMBER: Authors League of America, Dramatists Guild, Phi Kappa Psi, Sigma Delta Chi.

AWARDS, HONORS: Ohioana Book Award, Martha Kinney Cooper Ohioana Library Association, 1946, for *The White Deer;* Laughing Lions of Columbia University Award, 1949; Litt.D., Kenyon College, 1950, and Yale University, 1953; L.H.D., Williams College, 1951; Sesquicentennial Career Medal, Martha Kinney Cooper Ohioana Library Association, 1953; T-Square Award, American Cartoonists Society, 1956; Library and Justice Award, American Library Association, 1957, for *Further Fables for Our Time;* Antoinette Perry ("Tony") Special Award, 1960, for *A Thurber Carnival;* Certificate of Award from Ohio State University Class of 1916 for "Meritorious Service to Humanity and to Our Alma Mater," 1961.

WRITINGS:

(With E. B. White) *Is Sex Necessary?; or, Why You Feel the Way You Do*, Harper, 1929, reprinted, 1984.
The Owl in the Attic and Other Perplexities, Harper, 1931, reprinted, 1965.
The Seal in the Bedroom and Other Predicaments, Harper, 1932, reprinted, 1950.
My Life and Hard Times, Harper, 1933, reprinted, 1973.
The Middle-Aged Man on the Flying Trapeze: A Collection of Short Pieces, Harper, 1935, reprinted, Queens House, 1977.
Let Your Mind Alone!, and Other More or Less Inspirational Pieces, Harper, 1937, reprinted, Queens House, 1977.
The Last Flower: A Parable in Pictures, Harper, 1939, reprinted, Queens House, 1977.
Cream of Thurber, Hamish Hamilton, 1939.
Fables for Our Time and Famous Poems Illustrated, Harper, 1940, reprinted, 1983.
My World—and Welcome to It, Harcourt, 1942, reprinted, 1983.
Thurber's Men, Women, and Dogs, Harcourt, 1943, reprinted, Dodd, 1975.
The Thurber Carnival, Harper, 1945, reprinted, 1975, abridged editon published as *Selected Humorous Stories from "The Thurber Carnival,"* edited by Karl Botzenmayer, F. Shoeningh, 1958.
The Beast in Me and Other Animals, Harcourt, 1948, reprinted, 1973.
The Thurber Album: A New Collection of Pieces about People, Simon & Schuster, 1952, reprinted, 1965.
Thurber Country: A New Collection of Pieces about Males and Females, Simon & Schuster, 1953, reprinted, 1982.
Thurber's Dogs: A Collection of the Master's Dogs, Simon & Schuster, 1955.
A Thurber Garland, Hamish Hamilton, 1955.
Further Fables for Our Time, Simon & Schuster, 1956, reprinted, Penguin, 1962.
Alarms and Diversions, Harper, 1957, reprinted, 1981.
The Years with Ross (Book-of-the-Month Club selection), Little, Brown, 1959, reprinted, Penguin, 1984.
Lanterns and Lances, Harper, 1961.

Credos and Curios, Harper, 1962, reprinted, 1983.
Vintage Thurber, two volumes, Hamish Hamilton, 1963.
Thurber & Company, Harper, 1966.
Snapshot of a Dog, Associated Educational Services, 1966.
The Secret Life of Walter Mitty, Associated Educational Services, 1967, reprinted, Creative Education, Inc., 1983.
The Catbird Seat, Associated Educational Services, 1967.
Selected Letters of James Thurber, edited by his wife, Helen Thurber, and Edward Weeks, Little, Brown, 1981.
The Night the Ghosts Got In, Creative Education, Inc., 1983.

PLAYS

(With Elliott Nugent) *The Male Animal* (three-act; first produced on Broadway at the Cort Theatre, January 9, 1940), Random House, 1940.
"Many Moons" (also see below), produced in New York, 1947.
A Thurber Carnival (produced in Columbus, Ohio, at the Hartman Theatre, January 7, 1960; first produced on Broadway at the ANTA Theatre, February 26, 1960), Samuel French, 1962.

Also author of librettos for "Oh My, Omar" and other musicals produced by the Scarlet Mask Club, Columbus, Ohio, and of the play, "Nightingale" (two-act musical).

JUVENILES

Many Moons, illustrations by Louis Slobodkin, Harcourt, 1943, reprinted, 1973.
The Great Quillow, illustrations by Doris Lee, Harcourt, 1944, reprinted, Peter Smith, 1984.
The White Deer, illustrations by Thurber and Don Freeman, Harcourt, 1945, reprinted, 1968.
The 13 Clocks (also see below), illustrations by Marc Simont, Simon & Schuster, 1950, reprinted, 1977.
The Wonderful O (also see below), illustrations by Simont, Simon & Schuster, 1957, reprinted, 1976.
The 13 Clocks [and] *The Wonderful O*, illustrations by Ronald Searle, Penguin, 1962.

ILLUSTRATOR

Margaret Samuels Ernst, *The Executive's in a Word Book*, Knopf, 1939, reprinted, Belmont Books, 1963.
Elizabeth Howes, *Men Can Take It*, Random House, 1939.
James R. Kinney, *How to Raise a Dog*, Simon & Schuster, 1953 (published in England as *The Town Dog*, Harvill, 1954, reprinted, 1966).

SIDELIGHTS: Called "one of the world's greatest humorists" by Alistair Cooke in the *Atlantic*, James Thurber was one of the mainstays of the *New Yorker* magazine, where his short stories, essays, and numerous cartoons were published for over thirty years. "Comedy is his chosen field," Malcolm Cowley wrote in *Thurber: A Collection of Critical Essays*, "and his range of effects is deliberately limited, but within that range there is nobody who writes better than Thurber, that is, more clearly and flexibly, with a deeper feeling for the genius of the language and the value of words." After losing an eye in a childhood accident—playing William Tell with his brother—Thurber later developed a progressive condition in his remaining eye that eventually robbed him of all sight. Despite his handicap, Thurber continued to work as a popular cartoonist and illustrator and to write some of the best humor of his time. Alan Coren of the *Times Literary Supplement* emphasized "the magnitude of the tragedy which Thurber overcame in order to produce the dazzling magnitude of his comedy."

"I'm always astounded when my humor is described as gentle," Thurber is quoted as saying in Burton Bernstein's *Thurber*. "It's anything but that." An underlying tension, a desperation, is present in Thurber's work. Richard C. Tobias, writing in his *The Art of James Thurber*, pointed out that he made "laughter possible for us by deliberately choosing subjects that will create nervous, unsettling and unbearable tensions." Charles S. Holmes, in his *Thurber: A Collection of Critical Essays*, also noted "the pessimism and the sense of disaster which give Thurber's world its special atmosphere." Speaking of himself and other "writers of light pieces" in his foreword to *My Life and Hard Times*, Thurber wrote: "The notion that such persons are gay of heart and carefree is curiously untrue.... To call such persons 'humorists,' a loose-fitting and ugly word, is to miss the nature of their dilemma and the dilemma of their nature. The little wheels of their invention are set in motion by the damp hand of melancholy." "Thurber's genius," John Updike wrote in *Thurber: A Collection of Critical Essays*, "was to make of our despair a humorous fable."

Although Thurber's writings cover a wide range of genres, including essays, short stories, fables, and children's books, it is his stories concerned with middle-class domestic situations, often based on actual events in Thurber's own life, that made his reputation. In these stories, timid and befuddled men are overwhelmed by capable and resourceful women or by the mechanical contraptions of modern life. The conflict between the sexes—inspired in part by Thurber's troubled first marriage—and the dangerously precarious nature of everyday life are the recurring subjects in all of Thurber's work.

Thurber's career began after a stint as a code clerk in Paris during World War I. Unable to join the Army because of his bad eyesight, Thurber instead worked for the Department of State. When the war ended, Thurber returned to his native Columbus, Ohio, where he worked as a newspaper reporter for the *Columbus Dispatch*. For a time he wrote a weekly column for the paper entitled "Credos and Curios" in which he covered current books, films, and plays. After marrying in 1922, Thurber and his wife left for Paris. Thurber was attracted to Paris by the budding literary scene of American exiles there. He found work with the Paris edition of the *Chicago Tribune*. Although, as Judith S. Baughman wrote in the *Dictionary of Literary Biography*, "France does not figure prominently as a subject in James Thurber's works," the country was a favorite of Thurber's; he lived there for three extended periods during the 1920s and 1930s. These European visits, Baughman related, "provided Thurber with norms against which to measure the American attitudes and manners examined in his best essays, stories, and drawings."

It was not until 1927, when he joined the staff of the *New Yorker* magazine, that Thurber's career blossomed. Thurber had met E. B. White at a Greenwich Village party in February of that year. White, already working for the *New Yorker*, thought Thurber might make a fine addition to the staff. He introduced him to Harold Ross, editor of the magazine, and Thurber was hired as managing editor. "I found out that I was managing editor three weeks later," Thurber wrote in *The Years with Ross*, "when I asked my secretary why I had to sign the payroll each week, approve the items in Goings On [the *New Yorker* calendar of events], and confer with other editors on technical matters." Thurber did not last long as managing editor. "An editor and organizer Thurber was not," Peter A. Scholl admitted in the *Dictionary of Literary Biography*, "but he could not convince Ross that he would be happier and more effective as a staff writer. Ross was finally convinced when Thurber returned two days late from a visit to Columbus, having overstayed his leave to look for his lost dog." In *The Years with Ross*, Thurber remembered Ross's reaction to this incident: "I thought you were an editor, goddam it," Ross said, "but I guess you're a writer, so write."

Thurber wrote for the *New Yorker* full time until 1933 and was a regular contributor to the magazine until his death in 1961. "Between 1927 and 1935," Baughman wrote, "Thurber became one of the most prolific and best known of the *New Yorker* writers." He always credited White with having helped him fine tune his writing style for the magazine. "I came to the *New Yorker*," Scholl quoted Thurber explaining, "a writer of journalese and it was my study of White's writing, I think, that helped me to straighten out my prose so that people could see what I meant." This style, described by Thurber as "played-down," was economical, lean, and conversational. Because many of his humorous subjects bordered on the bizarre, Thurber deliberately chose a writing style that was calm and precise. Thurber understood, Scholl argues, "that the comedy is heightened by the contrast between the unexcitable delivery and the frenetic events described." Michael Burnett, in his contribution to *Thurber: A Collection of Critical Essays*, also noted the unobtrusive nature of Thurber's style. "It is a style," Burnett wrote, "which does its best not to call attention to itself through any deviations from the norm." Louis Hasley, writing in the *South Atlantic Quarterly*, found that Thurber "was, it must be conceded, a fastidious stylist with psychological depth, subtlety and complexity; with a keen sense of pace, tone, ease, and climax; and with imagination that often wandered into surrealism."

White was also instrumental in bringing Thurber's drawings to public attention. Thurber often doodled cartoons while working at the office, absently filling pads of notepaper with pencil drawings. As Brendan Gill recounted in his *Here at the New Yorker*, he even drew upon the walls of the *New Yorker* offices: "There were Thurber drawings of men marching up endless flights of stairs, of dogs romping or fighting . . . , and of men and women engaged in contests wholly mysterious to us, thanks to Thurber's having failed to provide any captions for the drawings." White urged Thurber to submit his drawings to the magazine's art department, but he refused. One day White, who shared an office with Thurber, retrieved some of the discarded drawings from Thurber's wastebasket, inked them in, and took them to the *New Yorker* art editor. To everyone's surprise, the drawings were accepted.

Because he had no formal art training, Thurber's cartoons were simple and rudimentary. Dorothy Parker, in her foreword to *The Seal in the Bedroom and Other Predicaments*, fondly remarked that all of Thurber's characters "have the outer semblance of unbaked cookies." Thurber told Cooke that "somebody once asked Marc Connelly how you could tell a Thurber man from a Thurber woman. He said, 'The Thurber women have what appears to be hair on their heads.'" Thurber noted in his preface to *The Thurber Carnival* that his drawings "sometimes seemed to have reached completion by some other route than the common one of intent." One famous Thurber cartoon was indeed unintentional. Attempting to draw a crouching woman at the top of a staircase, Thurber got the perspective wrong and the woman was instead perched on the top of a bookcase. Unperturbed, Thurber drew in three other characters, two men and a woman, standing on the floor. One of the men is speaking: "That's my first wife up there, and this is the *present* Mrs. Harris." "My husband," Helen Thurber wrote in her introduction to *Thurber & Company,* "never cared much for the label of cartoonist, but he was equally reluctant about being called an artist. He had so much fun drawing pictures that he never really took them seriously."

Thurber's writing career, Tobias noted, falls into three loosely-defined periods. The first, from 1929 until about 1937, "develops the comedy of the little man menaced by civilization." The second period is a time of exploration for Thurber, when he published fables like *The Last Flower: A Parable in Pictures* and *Fables for Our Time and Famous Poems Illustrated,* had his play *The Male Animal* successfully produced, and wrote the first of his children's books. The last period, the 1950s, saw Thurber return to the subject matter of his early work but with a deeper understanding. The books of Thurber's first period, collections of short pieces and drawings first published in the *New Yorker,* are generally considered to contain most of his best work. Many later titles reprint pieces from these books, sometimes including other Thurber material not previously reprinted from the *New Yorker.*

In 1929 Thurber teamed with White to produce a spoof of the sex manual genre. Their effort, entitled *Is Sex Necessary?; or, Why You Feel the Way You Do,* covered such topics as "Osculatory Justification," "Schmalhausen Trouble" (when couples live in small apartments), and "The Nature of the American Male: A Study of Pedestalism." As Edward C. Simpson of the *Dictionary of Literary Biography* reported, the two authors "parody the serious writers on the subject, making light of complexities, taking a mock-serious attitude toward the obvious, delighting in reducing the case-history technique to an absurdity, and making fun of those writers who proceeded by definition." The two men wrote alternate chapters of the manual, while Thurber provided the illustrations. The artwork—some forty drawings—took Thurber only one night to produce. "The next morning," Thurber told Cooke, "we took them down to the publishers, and when we got there, we put them down on the floor. Three bewildered and frightened publishers looked at them, and one man, the head publisher, said, 'These I suppose are rough sketches for the guidance of some professional artist who is going to do the illustrations?' and Andy [E. B. White] said, 'Those are the actual drawings that go in the book.'" The drawings were included. In his foreword to the manual, White found in Thurber's artwork "a strong undercurrent of grief" and described Thurber's men as "frustrated, fugitive beings." White went on to speak of "the fierce sweep, the economy, and the magnificent obscurity of Thurber's work.... All I, all anybody, can do is to hint at the uncanny faithfulness with which he has caught—caught and thrown to the floor—the daily, indeed the almost momently, severity of life's mystery, as well as the charming doubtfulness of its purpose." *Is Sex Necessary?* has gone through over twenty-five printings since its initial publication.

The Owl in the Attic and Other Perplexities, Thurber's second book and first collection of *New Yorker* pieces, includes eight stories, a section of drawings and short writings about pets, and the "Ladies' and Gentlemen's Guide to Modern English." Most of the stories are taken from Thurber's own life and feature the character John Monroe in domestic battles with his wife and with uncooperative household products. Some of the marital battles are based on Thurber's stormy first marriage. The Monroe stories, Tobias believed, combine the comic with the tragic. John Monroe "has more potential for pathos than comedy," Tobias wrote, "but his frightening and agonizing situations are more extreme than that and thus comic. Further, the situations also suggest that behind the comic mask is a raw

human experience which the writer, by his craft, has subdued for our pleasure. What is painful in life is transformed into a finer tone by the comic vision." Scholl reported that with the publication of *The Owl in the Attic* "Thurber's reputation as a writer and an artist was firmly established." Tobias found *Is Sex Necessary?* and *The Owl in the Attic* to be "astonishing performances for the beginning of a career."

The Seal in the Bedroom and Other Predicaments, a collection of Thurber's drawings, takes its title from one of his most famous cartoons. Like other of his works, this cartoon evolved by accident. The original cartoon—drawn in pencil while doodling at the office—showed a seal on a rock in the arctic waste. In the distance are two specks. "Hmmm, explorers," says the seal. The published version of the cartoon is quite different. After drawing the seal on the rock, this time in ink, Thurber decided that his rock looked less like a rock and more like a headboard for a bed. So he added a couple laying in the bed. The wife is saying, "All right, have it your way—you heard a seal bark!"

Perhaps the most important of Thurber's early books is the story collection *My Life and Hard Times,* which recounts some outlandish events and disastrous misunderstandings from Thurber's childhood. Included here are "The Night the Bed Fell," "The Night the Ghost Got In," and "The Day the Dam Broke." Charles S. Holmes, writing in *The Clocks of Columbus: The Literary Career of James Thurber,* called *My Life and Hard Times* "the peak achievement of Thurber's early career.... For many readers it is his one unquestioned masterpiece." One of the chief virtues of the collection is the distance that Thurber maintained between himself and his past experiences, allowing him to use his own life to comic effect. As he wrote in "A Note at the End," the afterword to the collection, "the confusions and the panics of last year and the year before are too close for contentment. Until a man can quit talking loudly to himself in order to shout down the memories of blunderings and gropings, he is in no shape for the painstaking examination of distress and the careful ordering of event so necessary to a calm and balanced exposition of what, exactly, was the matter."

My Life and Hard Times, Scholl stated, "is Thurber's best single collection of integrated stories, a series that can be read as a well-wrought and unified work of art." Hasley wrote that, "despite its autobiographical basis, [*My Life and Hard Times*] is the most consistently creative and humorous of all his books." Hasley found, too, that it displayed "Thurber's eminence in the portrayal of actual people." Holmes analyzed the stories in this collection and believed that throughout the book Thurber had celebrated "what might be called the Principle of Confusion.... Nearly every episode shows the disruption of the orderly pattern of everyday life by the idiosyncratic, the bizarre, the irrational." With *My Life and Hard Times,* Holmes concluded, Thurber "arrived at full artistic maturity."

In *The Middle-Aged Man on the Flying Trapeze,* a book described by Baughman as a "generally darker-toned miscellany," there is one curiously unfunny piece that sheds light on Thurber's personal life. The story "One Is a Wanderer" portrays a lonely middle-aged man in New York City who lives alone, drinks too much, and has alienated most of his friends. Taken from Thurber's situation during his first marriage, when he lived alone in New York while his wife and daughter lived in the country, the story ends with the revelation that "Two is company, four is a party, three is a quarrel. One is a wanderer." In the humorous stories, too, there are depictions of Thurber's troubled life. "The quarrels, the fights, the infidelities, and the loneliness of these years are animated in the humorous pieces," Scholl commented. In "Mr. Preble Gets Rid of His Wife," for example, Thurber successfully blends the absurdly comic with the tragic. Mr. Preble wants his wife to go in the cellar with him. She knows he wants to kill her there. But, because she is tired of arguing about it and because she is as dissatisfied with their marriage as he is, Mrs. Preble accompanies him. Another argument develops in the cellar over Mr. Preble's choice of murder weapon. Mrs. Preble does not wish to be hit on the head with a shovel. The story ends with the husband leaving for the store to buy a more suitable weapon. His wife waits patiently in the cellar for his return.

In *Let Your Mind Alone!* Thurber returned to the satirical mode of *Is Sex Necessary?*, this time writing a self-help psychology book. It is, Kenneth Burke remarked in *The Critic as Artist: Essays on Books, 1920-1970,* "a very amusing burlesque of psychoanalysis." Thurber proposed in the book that "the undisciplined mind . . . is far better adapted to the confused world in which we live today than the streamlined mind." He then gives examples of real-life cases where this idea is proven to be true. E. L. Tinker of the *New York Times* judged it to be "intelligent humor of a particularly refreshing brand which is very rare today. It appeals to the adult and sophisticated mind." The *Canadian Forum* reviewer thought popular psychology had been handled in "a brilliantly amusing fashion."

In his second period Thurber explored new types of writing, although he also continued to write the essays and short stories that had made his reputation. During the 1940s he wrote fables, a play, and children's books in addition to several collections of *New Yorker* pieces. In *The Last Flower,* published in 1940, Thurber created a picture book fable for adults that tells the story of World War XII and what survived: a man, a woman, and a single flower. From these three items, love emerges in the waste land. But love leads to family, to tribe, to civilization, and, inevitably and sadly, to another war. The book was inspired by the Spanish Civil War of the 1930s and the joint Soviet and Nazi invasion of Poland in 1939. It was published shortly before America's entry into World War II. The book "is not funny," the *Boston Transcript* reviewer wrote. "It isn't meant to be funny. 'The Last Flower' is magnificent satire." "The message of the work," E. Charles Vousden stated in the *Dictionary of Literary Biography,* ". . . is . . . one of despair—humanity will never learn to avoid war."

Thurber returned to the allegorical fable in his *Fables for Our Time,* a collection of Aesop parodies that Fred Schwed, Jr., of the *Saturday Review of Literature* thought showed "rather conclusively, I'm afraid, that at its worst the human race is viciously silly, while at its best it is just silly." Containing what Vousden called "astute observations on the human condition," *Fables for Our Time* commented on such contemporary figures as Adolf Hitler and had fun with some of the more familiar fairy tale situations. Thurber's version of "Little Red Riding Hood," for instance, ended with Little Red shooting the wolf with a pistol. "You can read as much or as little as you please into these light and perfectly written little tales," G. W. Stonier wrote in the *New Statesman and Nation.*

The Male Animal, Thurber's first produced play, was written with his old friend Elliott Nugent and staged in 1940. It is set at a midwestern college where an English professor finds himself at odds with a university trustee who is more interested in football and alumni support than with academic values.

"For the first time," Tobias remarked, "the tart, astringent Thurber dialogue gets a larger framework." Thurber learned some important things concerning the differences between writing a play and having it produced. He told *New Yorker* colleague Wolcott Gibbs: "During rehearsal you discover that your prettiest lines do not cross the footlights, because they are too pretty, or an actor can't say them, or an actress doesn't know what they mean. . . . On the thirteenth day of rehearsal, the play suddenly makes no sense to you and does not seem to be written in English." *The Male Animal* was a huge sucess for Thurber, running for 243 performances in New York and being adapted as a film starring Henry Fonda.

"The Secret Life of Walter Mitty," one of Thurber's most famous short stories, is included in the collection *My World—and Welcome to It.* The story concerns a man who daydreams heroic adventures to escape from a domineering wife and a boring job. "The story is a masterpiece of associational psychology," Hasley wrote, "in its shuttling between the petty, humiliating details of his outer life and the flaming heroism of his self-glorifying reveries." In this story, Carl M. Lindner stated in the *Georgia Review,* Thurber "touched upon one of the major themes in American literature—the conflict between individual and society."

It was during this second period, too, that Thurber began to write books for children, publishing *Many Moons, The Great Quillow,* and *The White Deer.* All of these books are fairy tales subtly modernized by Thurber's perspective. *The White Deer,* the story of an enchanted princess and the three princes who must do an impossible labor to free her, was called "a serene and beautiful fantasy" by Isabelle Mallet of the *New York Times.* Edmund Wilson, in his review for the *New Yorker,* compared Thurber's children's books to the works of Frank Stockton. Like Stockton, Wilson maintained, Thurber took traditional fairy tale situations and made "them produce unexpected results."

Thurber's later children's books, *The 13 Clocks* and *The Wonderful O,* are also fairy tales. The evil duke of *The 13 Clocks* is so bad that time itself has stopped because of him. When he holds his niece captive in a castle, the hero of the story must save her and in so doing restore time to the kingdom. Irwin Edman of the *New York Herald Tribune Book Review* called the book "a fairy tale, a comment on human cruelty and human sweetness or a spell, an incantation, compounded of poetry and logic and wit." While noting that Thurber had employed traditional fairy tale elements in *The 13 Clocks,* the *New Yorker* critic thought the story to be essentially an "ingenius satire on that form, written in a many-tiered, poetic prose style."

Perhaps Thurber's most important book of the 1950s is *The Years with Ross.* An informal biography of Harold Ross, founder and editor of the *New Yorker,* the book is also a history of the magazine and a recounting of Thurber's friendship with Ross. Told in a rambling and anecdotal style, the book is divided into sections dealing with various aspects of Ross's life and career, treating each one "as an entity in itself," as Thurber explained in the book's foreword. "The unity I have striven for . . . ," Thurber wrote, "is one of effect." Thurber relied on his own memories of Ross, the memories of other *New Yorker* staff members, and on letters and published articles to trace Ross's career. The book fared well with the critics, although several reviews found Thurber's portrait of Ross a bit unclear. Gerald Weales of *Commonweal,* for example, said that he "came out with the feeling that Thurber must still know something that he has failed to tell me." But Peter Salmon of the *New Republic* called *The Years with Ross* "a great book," while Weales concluded that it is "often fascinating." "This is a book to savor," Mark Schorer wrote in the *San Francisco Chronicle,* "and to treasure. It has two heroes: The first, obviously, is Harold Ross himself, a flashing and fascinating man; the second is James Thurber, a retiring and a great one." The criticism that especially hurt Thurber came from his friends. E. B. White and his wife Katharine, friends of both Thurber and Ross for many years, did not like the book. Scholl noted, however, that *The Years with Ross* "has a lasting power to entertain and move the reader."

Thurber's last major work, "A Thurber Carnival," is a series of skits, some of which are adapted from earlier stories and some of which are new material. In one skit a woman reads from *The Last Flower* and displays the book's illustrations on an easel. Some of Thurber's cartoons were enlarged and used as backdrops for the New York production of the play. "A Thurber Carnival," Kenneth Hurren wrote in *Spectator,* "managed to turn a lot of the stories and observations of the minutiae of American living into engaging sketches." After premiering in Thurber's hometown of Columbus, the play opened on Broadway on February 26, 1960. There was also a national road tour. When ticket sales for the Broadway production slowed, Thurber himself joined the cast, playing himself in one of the skits for some 88 performances. Ticket sales increased. A critical and popular success, "A Thurber Carnival" won a special Tony Award in 1960.

On October 3, 1961, Thurber suffered a stroke at his home in New York City. While in the hospital he developed pneumonia and on November 2, 1961, Thurber passed away. Towards the end of his life it seemed to many observers that Thurber's work had become pessimistic. "During the last ten years of his life," Hasley noted, "Thurber turned more and more to serious treatments of literary subjects and people.... While he never yielded wholly to despair, the note of gloom is unmistakable." Holmes, too, found this bleak outlook. "The theme of all of Thurber's late work is decline—of form, style, good sense, 'human stature, hope, humor,'" he wrote. This outlook is reflected in his personal life, too. Scholl quoted Thurber as saying to Elliott Nugent shortly before his death, "I can't hide anymore behind the mask of comedy.... People are not funny; they are vicious and horrible—and so is life!"

But much of this pessimism has been attributed to Thurber's developing illness. "In his old age, racked by disease and incapacitated by blindness," John Seelye wrote in *Thurber: A Collection of Critical Essays,* "Thurber became a sort of resident western curmudgeon, snarling at a changing world he could not comprehend." Jesse Bier argued in *The Rise and Fall of American Humor* that "Thurber's last stage represents a retreat from humor. And his irritabilities, his explicitness, his animus, his borderline perversities and grotesqueries, his final hopelessness, and his ingrownness are indices to the whole contemporary epoch, not only to his own career."

Holmes defines two ways of approaching Thurber's body of work: "The humanistic view sees Thurber as the defender of the individual in an age of mass culture, the champion of imagination over the logic-and-formula-ridden mind, the enemy of political fanaticism.... The darker view focuses on Thurber as a man writing to exorcise a deep inner uncertainty, to come to terms with fears and resentments which threatened his psychic balance." In *Thurber: A Collection of Critical Essays,* Robert H. Elias examined Thurber's place in Ameri-

can literature and found that many Thurber stories are "as well shaped as the most finely wrought pieces of Henry James, James Joyce and Ernest Hemingway, as sensitively worded as the most discriminatingly written prose of H. L. Mencken, Westbrook Pegler and J. D. Salinger, and as penetrating ... as the most pointed insights of those two large poets of our century, E. A. Robinson and Robert Frost." Jonathan Yardley, writing in the *Washington Post Book World,* judged Thurber's contribution to letters to be of lasting value. "Thurber's humor...," Yardley wrote, "has a timeless quality that should guarantee him a readership far into the future."

MEDIA ADAPTATIONS:

My Life and Hard Times was filmed as "Rise and Shine," Twentieth Century-Fox, 1941; *The Male Animal* was filmed by Warner Bros., 1942, and as "She's Working Her Way Through College," Warner Bros., 1952; "The Secret Life of Walter Mitty" was filmed by RKO, 1949; "A Unicorn in the Garden" was adapted as an animated film by Learning Corp. of America, 1952; *The 13 Clocks* was adapted as an opera and as a television special in 1954; several of Thurber's stories were adapted as the play "Three by Thurber," written by Paul Ellwood and St. John Terrell, first produced in New York at the Theatre de Lys, 1955; some of Thurber's work was adapted for the film "Fireside Book of Dog Stories," State University of Iowa, 1957; *The Last Flower* was adapted as a dance by a French ballet company, 1959; "The Catbird Seat" was filmed as "The Battle of the Sexes," Continental Distributing, 1960; *Many Moons* was filmed by Rembrandt Films, c. 1960, was adapted as a filmstrip by H. M. Stone Productions, 1972, and adapted as an animated film by Contemporary Films/McGraw, 1975; *My World—and Welcome to It* was adapted as a television series in 1969; several of Thurber's stories were adapted as "The War between Men and Women," National General Pictures Corp., 1972.

RECORDINGS

"A Thurber Carnival," Columbia Records, 1960.
"The Great Quillow," Caedmon Records, 1972.
"The Grizzly and the Gadgets, and Further Fables for Our Time," Caedmon Records, 1972.
"The Unicorn in the Garden, and Other Fables for Our Time," Caedmon Records, 1972.
"Many Moons," Caedmon Records, 1973.
"The World of James Thurber," Miller-Brody Productions.

BIOGRAPHICAL/CRITICAL SOURCES:

BOOKS

Atteberry, Brian, *The Fantasy Tradition in American Literature,* Indiana University Press, 1980.
Bernstein, Burton, *Thurber,* Dodd, 1975, published as *Thurber: A Biography,* Ballantine, 1976.
Bier, Jesse, *The Rise and Fall of American Humor,* Holt, 1968.
Black, Stephen Ames, *James Thurber: His Masquerades,* Mouton, 1970.
Blair, Walter and Hamlin Hill, *America's Humor: From Poor Richard to Doonesbury,* Oxford University Press, 1978.
Bowden, Edwin T., *James Thurber: A Bibliography,* Ohio State University Press, 1968.
Contemporary Literary Criticism, Gale, Volume V, 1976, Volume XI, 1979, Volume XXV, 1983.
Cowley, Malcolm, *Writers at Work: The Paris Review Interviews,* Viking, 1959.

Dictionary of Literary Biography, Gale, Volume IV: *American Writers in Paris, 1920-1939*, 1980, Volume XI: *American Humorists, 1800-1950*, 1982, Volume XXII: *Americn Writers for Children, 1900-1960*, 1983.
Eastman, Max, *The Enjoyment of Laughter*, Simon & Schuster, 1936.
Gill, Brendan, *Here at the New Yorker*, Random House, 1975.
Holmes, Charles S., *The Clocks of Columbus: The Literary Career of James Thurber*, Atheneum, 1972.
Holmes, Charles S., editor, *Thurber: A Collection of Critical Essays*, Prentice-Hall, 1974.
Kramer, Dale, *Ross and the "New Yorker"*, Doubleday, 1951.
Morseberger, Robert E., *James Thurber*, Twayne, 1964.
Sheed, Wilfrid, *The Good Word and Other Words*, Dutton, 1978.
Shirer, William L., *Twentieth Century Journey, a Memoir of a Life and the Times: The Start, 1904-1930*, Simon & Schuster, 1976.
Thurber, James and E. B. White, *Is Sex Necessary?; or, Why You Feel the Way You Do*, Harper, 1929, reprinted, 1984.
Thurber, James, *The Seal in the Bedroom and Other Predicaments*, Harper, 1932, reprinted, 1950.
Thurber, James, *My Life and Hard Times*, Harper, 1933, reprinted, 1973.
Thurber, James, *The Middle-Aged Man on the Flying Trapeze: A Collection of Short Pieces*, Harper, 1935, reprinted, Queens House, 1977.
Thurber, James, *Let Your Mind Alone!, and Other More or Less Inspirational Pieces*, Harper, 1937, reprinted, Queens House, 1977.
Thurber, James, *The Thurber Carnival*, Harper, 1945, reprinted, 1975.
Thurber, James, *The Years with Ross*, Little, Brown, 1959, reprinted, Penguin, 1984.
Thurber, James, *Thurber & Company*, Harper, 1966.
Tobias, Richard C., *The Art of James Thurber*, Ohio State University Press, 1969.
Yates, Norris W., *The American Humorist: Conscience of the Twentieth Century*, Iowa State University Press, 1964.

PERIODICALS

Atlantic, August, 1956.
Books, November 24, 1935, November 1, 1942.
Boston Transcript, December 9, 1939.
Christian Science Monitor, May 28, 1959, December 14, 1981.
Commonweal, July 17, 1959.
Economist, February 13, 1982.
Esquire, August, 1975.
Georgia Review, summer, 1974.
Listener, January 28, 1982.
Lost Generation Journal, winter, 1975.
Maclean's, January 18, 1982.
Nation, June 13, 1959, November 21, 1981.
National Review, April 2, 1982.
New Republic, September 20, 1940, June 29, 1959.
New Statesman, December 14, 1962.
New Statesman and Nation, December 23, 1939, December 14, 1940, December 19, 1942.
Newsweek, March 24, 1975.
New Yorker, October 27, 1945, December 9, 1950, November 11, 1961, June 23, 1975.
New York Herald Tribune Book Review, December 3, 1950.
New York Times, February 22, 1931, September 12, 1937, February 4, 1945, September 30, 1945, May 31, 1959.
New York Times Book Review, March 25, 1973, November 8, 1981.
New York Times Magazine, December 4, 1949.
Reader's Digest, September, 1972.
Saturday Review, November 17, 1956, March 22, 1975.
Saturday Review of Literature, December 2, 1939, November 23, 1940, February 3, 1945.
Smithsonian, January, 1977.
South Atlantic Quarterly, autumn, 1974.
Spectator, July 5, 1975.
Time, July 9, 1951, March 31, 1975.
Times Literary Supplement, January 29, 1982.
Washington Post Book World, November 8, 1981.
Yale Review, autumn, 1965.

OBITUARIES:

Illustrated London News, November 11, 1961.
Newsweek, November 13, 1961.
New York Times, November 9, 1961.
Publishers Weekly, November 13, 1961.
Time, November 10, 1961.†

—*Sketch by Thomas Wiloch*

*   *   *

TIMPERLEY, Rosemary Kenyon   1920-

PERSONAL: Born March 20, 1920, in London, England; daughter of George Kenyon (an architect) and Emily Mary (a teacher; maiden name, Lethem) Timperley; married James McInnes Cameron, March, 1952 (died, 1968). *Education:* King's College, London, B.A., 1941. *Politics:* Socialist. *Religion:* Taoist.

ADDRESSES: Home and office—21 Ellerker Gardens, Richmond, Surrey TW10 6AA, England. *Agent*—Harvey Unna & Stephen Durbridge Ltd., 24 Pottery Lane, London W11 4LZ, England.

CAREER: Teacher at technical school in Essex County, England, 1941-49; *Reveille*, London, England, staff writer, 1950-59; free-lance writer, 1959—.

MEMBER: Society of Authors.

WRITINGS:

NOVELS

Child in the Dark, Crowell, 1956 (published in England as *The Listening Child*, James Barrie, 1956).
Doctor Z, R. Hale, 1969.
The Mask Shop, R. Hale, 1970.
House of Secrets, R. Hale, 1970.
Walk to San Michele, R. Hale, 1971.
The Summer Visitors, R. Hale, 1971.
The Long Black Dress, R. Hale, 1972.
The Passionate Marriage, R. Hale, 1972.
Shadows in the Park, R. Hale, 1973.
The Echo-Game, R. Hale, 1973.
Journey with Doctor Godley, R. Hale, 1973.
Juliet, R. Hale, 1974.
The White Zig-Zag Path, R. Hale, 1974.
Ali and Little Camel, R. Hale, 1975.
The Private Prisoners, R. Hale, 1975.
The Egyptian Woman, R. Hale, 1976.
The Stranger, R. Hale, 1976.
The Devil of the Lake, R. Hale, 1976.

The Man with the Beard, R. Hale, 1977.
The Nameless One, R. Hale, 1977.
The Phantom Husband, R. Hale, 1977.
Syrilla Black, R. Hale, 1978.
Suspicion, R. Hale, 1978.
Miss X, R. Hale, 1979.
The Secretary, R. Hale, 1979.
Justin and the Witch, R. Hale, 1979.
The House of Mad Children, R. Hale, 1980.
Homeward Bound, R. Hale, 1980.
That Year at the Office, R. Hale, 1981.
Chidori's Room, R. Hale, 1983.
The Office Party and After, R. Hale, 1984.
Love and Death, R. Hale, 1985.
Tunnel of Shadows, R. Hale, in press.

EDITOR

The Fifth Ghost Book, Barrie & Rockliff, 1969.
The Sixth Ghost Book, Barrie & Rockliff, 1970, abridged edition published as *The Sixth Ghost Book*, Volume I: *The Blood Goes Round and Other Stories*, Volume II: *The Judas Joke and Other Stories*, Pan Books, 1972.
The Seventh Ghost Book, Barrie & Jenkins, 1971.
The Eighth Ghost Book, Barrie & Jenkins, 1972.
The Ninth Ghost Book, Barrie & Jenkins, 1973.

SIDELIGHTS: Rosemary Kenyon Timperley told *CA*: "My novels *The Nameless One*, *The Man with the Beard*, and *Miss X* deal particularly with different sorts of mental unbalance—hallucination and all that. *The House of Mad Children* is about a household of mentally disturbed young people. I've read Bettelheim on schizophrenia in children.

"Some of my novels have foreign backgrounds, as I've visited Russia, Italy, Greece, Morocco, and Belgium. My languages include a smattering of Russian and Chinese. I enjoy the latter mainly because of the enchanting ideograms—it's nicer to write than to speak.

"I'm devoted to the *I Ching*, which has become a sort of Bible to me, not in a fortune-telling sense, but as general advice on how to behave in this arduous and complicated life we all lead, and I get a lot out of Lao Tzu, whose work is packed with wisdom, simple and yet mysterious.

"Now that I'm old I lead rather a recluse-like life. Although I've written a lot, I've never had a best-seller or 'hit the headlines,' which is probably a good thing, as I don't think I could have stood up to any sort of notoriety—what the shrinks call 'inadequate personality.' I live very much in my own mind and in the fictional world of my rather unsuccessful little novels. I regard myself as lucky in being able to scrape a living out of doing something I enjoy doing, when so many people are tied to jobs they don't like."

*   *   *

TIPPETTE, Giles   1934-

PERSONAL: Born August 25, 1934, in Texas; son of O. B. and Mary Grace (Harpster) Tippette; married Mildred Ann Mebane, 1956 (divorced, 1975); married Betsyanne Wright Pool, 1981; children: (first marriage) Shanna, Lisa. *Education:* Sam Houston University, B.S., 1959. *Politics:* "Distrust all politics and politicians." *Religion:* No formal.

ADDRESSES: *Home*—P.O. Box 2269, Brenham, Tex. 77833. *Agent*—Owen Laster, William Morris Agency, 1350 Avenue of the Americas, New York, N.Y. 10019.

CAREER: Held a variety of jobs, including rodeo contestant, diamond courier, and gold miner in Mexico; now a writer.

MEMBER: Authors Guild, Authors League of America.

WRITINGS:

The Bank Robber (novel), Macmillan, 1970, published as *The Spikes Gang*, Pocket Books, 1971.
The Trojan Cow (novel), Macmillan, 1971.
The Brave Man (nonfiction), Macmillan, 1972.
Saturday's Children (nonfiction), Macmillan, 1973.
The Survivalist (novel), Macmillan, 1975.
Austin Davis (novel), Dell, 1975.
The Sunshine Killers (novel), Dell, 1975.
The Mercenaries, Delacorte, 1976.
Wilson's Gold, Dell, 1980.
Wilson's Luck, Dell, 1980.
Wilson's Revenge, Dell, 1981.
Wilson's Woman, Dell, 1982.
The Texas Bank Robbing Company, Dell, 1982.
Hard Luck Money, Dell, 1982.
Wilson Young on the Run, Dell, 1983.
China Blue, Dell, 1984.

Also author of manuscript, "Man of Ice." Contributor to magazines, including *Time*, *Sports Illustrated*, *Texas Monthly*, *Esquire*, *Newsweek*, and *Argosy*.

WORK IN PROGRESS: *Our Blue Heaven*.

MEDIA ADAPTATIONS: Two of Giles Tippette's novels, *Austin Davis* and *The Bank Robber*, have been made into movies. His manuscript "Man of Ice" was adapted for a television movie, "Target Risk."

*   *   *

TOLZMANN, Don Heinrich   1945-

PERSONAL: Born August 12, 1945, in Granite Falls, Minn.; son of Eckhart Heinrich and Pearl (Lundeberg) Tolzmann; married Patricia Ann Himebaugh, March 20, 1971; children: Anna Maria Patricia. *Education:* University of Minnesota, B.A., 1968; Northwestern Lutheran Theological Seminary, graduate study, 1968-71; United Theological Seminary, M.Div., 1972; University of Kentucky, M.A., 1973; University of Cincinnati, Ph.D., 1983. *Religion:* Lutheran.

ADDRESSES: *Home*—3418 Boudinot Ave., Cincinnati, Ohio 45211. *Office*—Blegen Library M.L. 113, University of Cincinnati, Cincinnati, Ohio 45221.

CAREER: University of Cincinnati, Central Library, Cincinnati, Ohio, 1974—, began as reference librarian and bibliographer, currently senior librarian in German and philosophy. Delegate, White House Conference on Ethnicity and the 1980 Census, 1976.

MEMBER: Society for German-American Studies, American Library Association, Immigration History Society.

AWARDS, HONORS: Citation of honor, State of Minnesota, 1972; citation of appreciation, President of the United States, 1972; certificate of merit from Society for German-American Studies, 1973; Tricentennial Medal, Goethe House New York at the University of Cincinnati, 1983.

WRITINGS:

German-Americana: A Bibliography, Scarecrow, 1975.

America's German Heritage: Bicentennial Minutes, German-American National Congress, 1976.
German-American Literature, Scarecrow, 1977.
Festschrift for the German-American Tricentennial Jubilee: Cincinnati 1983, Cincinnati Historical Society, 1982.
The Cincinnati Germans after the Great War, Verlag Peter Lang, 1986.

Editor of "German American Poetry" series. Associate editor of *Journal of German-American Studies*, 1974-80, and *German-American Genealogist*, 1975-76; editor of *Zeitschrift fuer deutschamerikanische literatur*, 1974-78, and *Bulletin of the Society for German-American Studies*, 1977-79.

WORK IN PROGRESS: The German-Americana Collection Catalog; A Catalog of Materials in the University of Cincinnati Blegen Library.

SIDELIGHTS: Don Heinrich Tolzmann told *CA:* "The German-Americana Collection at the University of Cincinnati Blegen Library was established in 1974 and is one of the nation's largest such collections. It consists of books, pamphlets, documents, journals, and manuscripts of special value to students, scholars, researchers, and the general public interested in the history, literature, and culture of the German-American element. Mail and telephone inquiries and questions regarding the collection are welcome before one comes to the Blegen Library to use the collection. The catalog I am currently preparing will provide access to one of the richest and strongest collections of German-Americana in the United States."

*　　*　　*

TOMPKINS, Jane P(arry)　1940-

PERSONAL: Born January 18, 1940, in New York, N.Y.; daughter of Henry T. and Lucille (Reilly) Parry; married Daniel P. Tompkins, September 7, 1963 (divorced); married E. Daniel Larkin, November, 1975 (divorced); married Stanley Fish, August, 1982. *Education:* Bryn Mawr College, B.A., 1961; Yale University, M.A., 1962, Ph.D., 1966.

ADDRESSES: Home—201 Southway, Baltimore, Md. 21218. *Office*—Department of English, Duke University, Durham, N.C.

CAREER: Connecticut College, New London, instructor, 1966-67, assistant professor of English, 1967-68; Greater Hartford Community College, Hartford, Conn., assistant professor of English, 1969-70; Temple University, Philadelphia, Pa., visiting assistant professor, 1970-76, associate professor, 1976-82, professor of English, 1982-83; Columbia University, New York City, visiting professor, 1983-84; Graduate School and University Center of the City University of New York, New York City, visiting professor, 1984-85; Duke University, Durham, N.C., professor of English, 1985—. Visiting professor, University of Southern California, summer, 1981; lecturer, School of Criticism and Theory, summer, 1985.

WRITINGS:

(Editor) *Twentieth Century Interpretations of "The Turn of the Screw" and Other Tales*, Prentice-Hall, 1970.
(Editor and contributor) *Reader-Response Criticism: From Formalism to Post-Structuralism*, John Hopkins University Press, 1980.
(Contributor) Sacvan Bercovitch and Myra Jehlen, editors, *Ideology and American Literature*, Cambridge University Press, 1984.

Sensational Designs: The Cultural Work of American Fiction, 1790-1860, Oxford University Press, 1985.
(Contributor) *American Renaissance Reconsidered: Selected Papers from the English Institute, 1982-83*, Johns Hopkins University Press, 1985.

Contributor to academic journals.

WORK IN PROGRESS: Escape into Reality, a study of popular American fiction.

*　　*　　*

TOTMAN, Conrad　1934-

PERSONAL: Born January 5, 1934, in Conway, Mass.; son of Raymond S. (a farmer) and Mildred (Kingsbury) Totman; married Michiko Ikegami (a bilingual teacher), February 10, 1958; children: Kathleen, Christopher. *Education:* University of Massachusetts, B.A., 1958; Harvard University, M.A., 1960, Ph.D., 1964.

ADDRESSES: Home—Hamden, Conn. *Office*—Department of History, Yale University, New Haven, Conn. 06520.

CAREER: University of California, Santa Barbara, assistant professor of history, 1964-66; Northwestern University, Evanston, Ill., assistant professor, 1966-68, associate professor, 1968-72, professor of history, 1972-84, chairman of department, 1977-80; Yale University, New Haven, Conn., professor of history, 1984—. Chairman of Council for East Asian Studies, 1985—. *Military service:* U.S. Army, 1953-56.

MEMBER: Association for Asian Studies (chairman of Northeast Asia Council; member of executive committee, 1978-80), Forest History Society.

AWARDS, HONORS: Fulbright grant; National Endowment for the Humanities senior fellow; Japan Foundation fellow.

WRITINGS:

Politics in the Tokugawa Bakufu, 1600-1843, Harvard University Press, 1968.
The Collapse of the Tokugawa Bakufu, 1862-1868, University Press of Hawaii, 1980.
Japan before Perry, University of California Press, 1981.
Tokugawa Ieyasu: Shogun, Heian International, 1983.
The Origins of Japan's Modern Forests, University of Hawaii Press, 1985.

Contributor to Asian studies journals.

WORK IN PROGRESS: A continuing study of forest management during Japan's Tokugawa period.

*　　*　　*

TOULSON, Shirley　1924-

PERSONAL: Born May 20, 1924, in Henley-on-Thames, England; daughter of Douglas Horsfall Dixon (a writer) and Marjorie Brown; married Alan Brownjohn, February 6, 1960 (divorced, March, 1969); children: Janet Sayers, Ian Toulson, Steven Brownjohn. *Education:* Birkbeck College, London, B.A., 1953.

ADDRESSES: Home—16 Priest Row Wells, Somerset, England. *Agent*—Bruce Hunter, David Higham Associates, 5-8 Lower John St., Golden Sq., London W1R 4HA, England.

CAREER: Writer. Features editor of *Teacher* (journal of National Union of Teachers), 1967-70; editor of *Child Education*, 1970-74. Teacher of creative writing for adults.

WRITINGS:

Shadows in an Orchard (poems), Scorpion Press, 1960.
Circumcision's Not Such a Bad Thing After All and Other Poems, Keepsake Press, 1970.
All Right, Auden, I Know You're There: A Quick Thought (poems), Offcut Press, 1970.
For a Double Time (poems), Sceptre Press, 1970.
The Fault, Dear Brutus: A Zodiac of Sonnets, Keepsake Press, 1972.
Education in Britain, M. Evans, 1974.
Farm Museums and Farm Parks, Shire, 1977.
(With Fay Godwin) *Drovers' Roads of Wales*, Wildwood House, 1977.
(With John Loveday) *Bones and Angels* (poems), Mid-Day Publications, 1978.
East Anglia: Walking the Leylines and Ancient Tracks, Wildwood House, 1979.
The Drovers, Shire Publications, 1980.
Derbyshire: Exploring the Ancient Tracks and Mysteries of Mercia, Wildwood House, 1980.
The Winter Solstice, Jill Norman & Hobhouse, 1981.
The Moors of the Southwest, Hutchinson, Volume I, 1983, Volume II, 1984.
The Mendip Hills: A Threatened Landscape, Gollancz, 1984.
Celtic Journeys, Scotland and the North of England, Hutchinson, 1985.

EDITOR

The Remind-Me Hat and Other Stories (juvenile), M. Evans, 1973.
Dickens, S. Low, 1977.
Kipling, S. Low, 1977.
Milton, S. Low, 1977.
Shakespeare, S. Low, 1977.

OTHER

Contributor to *Reader's Digest, The Past around Us,* and *Mysteries of the World.* Regular reviewer for British Council's *British Book News.*

WORK IN PROGRESS: A book about the Celtic church in Britain from the third to the eighth centuries.

SIDELIGHTS: Shirley Toulson told *CA:* "Apart from the social history of the British countryside, my main interest is in contemporary English and American verse. I have recently started working on the interpretation of folklore, and am particularly interested in comparing the traditions of the American Indians with what is being discovered about pre-Celtic rituals in Britain."

*   *   *

TRACZ, Richard Francis 1944-

PERSONAL: Surname is pronounced *tray*-see; born January 14, 1944; son of Boley John (a businessman) and Frances Delores (Yoda) Tracz. *Education:* Rockhurst College, Cl.A.B. (with honors), 1965; University of Kansas, M.A., 1967. *Politics:* Independent. *Religion:* Catholic.

ADDRESSES: Home—1400 North State Pkwy., Chicago, Ill. 60610. *Office*—Oakton Community College, Des Plaines, Ill. 60016.

CAREER: University of Kansas, Lawrence, assistant instructor, 1966-67; Tarrant County Junior College, Fort Worth, Tex., instructor in English, 1967-69; Southern Methodist University, Dallas, Tex., instructor in discourse and literature, 1969-75; Richland College, Dallas, instructor in writing, 1975-78; Oakton Community College, Des Plaines, Ill., associate professor of English, 1978—.

MEMBER: National Council of Teachers of English, Modern Language Association, College English Association, Conference of College Teachers of English, Conference on College Composition and Communication, South Central Modern Language Association.

WRITINGS:

(Compiler with C. Jeriel Howard) *The Responsible Man: Essays, Short Stories and Poems*, Canfield Press, 1970, 2nd edition, 1975.
(With Howard) *TEMPO: A Thematic Approach to Sentence/Paragraph Writing*, Canfield Press, 1971.
--30--A Journalistic Approach to Freshman Composition, Goodyear Publishing, 1973.
CONTACT: A Textbook in Applied Communications, Prentice-Hall, 1974, 4th edition, 1984.
Writing Effective Paragraphs, Winthrop Publishing, 1976.
(With Howard) *The Paragraph Book*, Little, Brown, 1982.
The Essential English Handbook and Rhetoric, Bobbs-Merrill, 1985.

Contributor to *Montana English Journal.*

*   *   *

TRAHEY, Jane 1923-
(Baba Erlanger)

PERSONAL: Born November 19, 1923, in Chicago, Ill.; daughter of David and Margaret (Hennessey) Trahey. *Education:* Mundelein College, B.A., 1943; University of Wisconsin, graduate study, 1945; Columbia University, M.A., 1975.

ADDRESSES: Home—3500 North Lake Shore Dr., Chicago, Ill. 60657. *Office*—Trahey Advertising, Inc., 1 Lincoln Plaza, New York, N.Y. 10023.

CAREER: Carson, Pirie, Scott & Co. (department store), Chicago, Ill., copywriter, 1945-47; Neiman-Marcus (specialty store), Dallas, Tex., copywriter, advertising manager, and sales promotion director, 1947-58; Kayser-Roth (apparel manufacturer), New York, N.Y., director of advertising, 1955-57; Trahey Advertising, Inc., New York, N.Y., president, 1958—. Board member of Seligman & Latz, 1978—.

MEMBER: Fashion Group, Advertising Club, American Institute of Graphic Arts, Authors League of America, Writers Guild, Dramatists Guild.

AWARDS, HONORS: Good Housekeeping Award; named Advertising Woman of the Year by American Advertising Federation, 1969; D.H.L. from Mundelein College, 1975.

WRITINGS:

The Taste of Texas, Random House, 1955.
(With Daren Pierce, under pseudonym Baba Erlanger) *The Compleat Martini Cookbook*, Random Thoughts, 1957.
Gin and Butter Diet, Random Thoughts, 1960.
1000 Names and Where to Drop Them, Random Thoughts, 1960.

The Magic Yarn, Random Thoughts, 1961.
Life with Mother Superior, Farrar, Straus, 1962.
(Editor) *Harper's Bazaar: 100 Years of the American Female,* Random House, 1967.
(With Pierce) *Son of the Martini Cookbook,* illustrations by Edward Gorey, Clovis Press, 1967.
Ring round the Bathtub (three-act play; first produced in Houston at the Alley Theater, 1970, produced on Broadway at Martin Beck Theatre, April 29, 1972), Samuel French, 1968.
Pecked to Death by Goslings, Prentice-Hall, 1969.
Jane Trahey on Women and Power: Who's Got It? How to Get It?, Rawson Associates, 1977.
Thursdays 'til 9, Harcourt, 1980.
The Clovis Caper, Avon, 1983.

MEDIA ADAPTATIONS: Life with Mother Superior was made into the film, "The Trouble with Angels," Columbia Pictures Industries, 1966, and "Where Angels Go Trouble Follows" (based on Trahey's characters) was filmed by Columbia Pictures, 1968. *Thursdays 'til 9* and *The Clovis Caper* have been optioned for movie productions by Walt Disney. *Pecked to Death by Goslings* has been optioned for independent production.

BIOGRAPHICAL/CRITICAL SOURCES:

PERIODICALS

New York Times Book Review, June 15, 1980.

* * *

TRASK, David F(rederic) 1929-

PERSONAL: Born May 15, 1929, in Erie, Pa.; son of Hugh Archie and Ruth (Miller) Trask; married Roberta Kirsch, 1959 (divorced, July, 1964); married Elizabeth Marie Brooks, February 6, 1965; children: (first marriage) Noel Hugh, Amanda Ruth. *Education:* Wesleyan University, B.A., 1951; Harvard University, A.M., 1952, Ph.D., 1958.

ADDRESSES: Home—3223 B Sutton Place N.W., Washington, D.C. 20016. *Office*—U.S. Army Center of Military History, 20 Massachusetts Ave. N.W., Washington, D.C. 20314.

CAREER: Boston University, Boston, Mass., instructor in political economy, 1955-58; Wesleyan University, Middletown, Conn., 1958-62, began as instructor, became assistant professor of history; University of Nebraska, Lincoln, assistant professor, 1962-63, associate professor of history, 1963-66; State University of New York at Stony Brook, Long Island, N.Y., 1966-76, began as associate professor, became professor of history, chairman of department, 1969-74; U.S. State Department, Office of the Historian, Washington, D.C., director, 1976-81; U.S. Army Center of Military History, Washington, D.C., chief historian, 1981—. Visiting professor, Naval War College, 1974-75. Member, National Historic Publications and Records Commission, 1976-81. *Military service:* U.S. Army, Infantry, 1952-54; became lieutenant.

MEMBER: American Historical Association, Organization of American Historians, Society of Historians of American Foreign Relations (member of board of directors, 1973-75), Society for History in the Federal Government (president, 1981-83), National Association for the Advancement of Colored People (president, Portland-Middletown branch, 1960-61), United Nations Association of the United States of America (president, Lincoln, Neb., branch, 1965), Phi Beta Kappa, Phi Alpha Theta.

AWARDS, HONORS: Ford Foundation grant; Danforth Foundation faculty research grant; University of Nebraska faculty summer grant.

WRITINGS:

(Compiler with John C. Rule and others) *A Select Bibliography for Students of History,* [Cambridge], 1958.
The United States in the Supreme War Council: American War Aims and Inter-Allied Strategy, 1917-1918, Wesleyan University Press, 1961, reprinted, Greenwood Press, 1978.
General Tasker Howard Bliss and the "Sessions of the World," 1919, American Philosophical Society, 1966.
(Compiler with Michael C. Meyer and Roger R. Trask) *A Bibliography of United States-Latin American Relations since 1810,* University of Nebraska Press, 1968.
Victory without Peace: American Foreign Relations in the Twentieth Century, Wiley, 1968.
(Editor) *World War I at Home: Readings on American Life, 1914-1920,* Wiley, 1969.
Captains and Cabinets: Anglo-American Naval Relations, 1917-1918, University of Missouri Press, 1972.
(With Samuel F. Wells, Jr., and Robert H. Ferrell) *The Ordeal of World Power: American Diplomacy since 1909,* Little, Brown, 1975.
The War with Spain in 1898, Macmillan, 1981.
(Compiler with Robert C. Pomeroy III) *The Craft of Public History,* Greenwood Press, 1983.
(Editor) William S. Sims, *The Victory at Sea,* Naval Institute Press, 1984.

Also author of "American History, 1900-1961," in *Collier's Encyclopedia,* 1962; contributor to *Encyclopaedia Britannica* and professional journals. Member of editorial board, *Journal of American History,* 1973-76, and *The Public Historian,* 1983—.

* * *

TRUE, Michael 1933-

PERSONAL: Born November 8, 1933, in Oklahoma City, Okla.; son of Guy Herbert and Agnes (Murphy) True; married Mary Patricia Delaney, April 20, 1958; children: Mary, Michael, John, Christopher, Elizabeth, Anne. *Education:* University of Oklahoma, B.A., 1955; University of Minnesota, M.A., 1957; Duke University, Ph.D., 1964; postdoctoral study at Harvard University, 1967-68. *Religion:* Roman Catholic.

ADDRESSES: Home—4 Westland St., Worcester, Mass. 01602. *Office*—Department of English, Assumption College, Worcester, Mass. 01609.

CAREER: Remington Rand Univac, St. Paul, Minn., technical writer, 1958-59; Duke University, Durham, N.C., lecturer in English, 1960-61; North Carolina College at Durham (now North Carolina Central University), lecturer in English, 1961; Indiana State University, Terre Haute, assistant professor of English, 1961-65; Assumption College, Worcester, Mass., assistant professor, 1965-67, associate professor, 1967-74, professor of English, 1974—, chairman of department, 1974-76. Visiting professor of education and English, Clark University, 1967-80, and Nanjing University, People's Republic of China, 1984-85. Consultant in nonfiction writing, Upper Midwest Writer's Conference, 1973, 1975, 1977-78, 1979-80, 1982; consultant to University of Central Arkansas Writers Conference, 1976-77; consultant to European Council of International Schools in London, 1979, in Brussels, 1980, in The Hague,

1981, and in Geneva, 1982. Member, National Humanities Faculty, 1977—. *Military service:* U.S. Army, 1957-58.

MEMBER: American Studies Association, National Council of Teachers of English (director, 1973-78), Modern Language Association of America, New England College English Association (director, 1965-69, 1975-79; president, 1980-81).

AWARDS, HONORS: National Endowment for the Humanities fellow at Columbia University, 1976-77; F. Andre Favat Award from Massachusetts Council of Teachers of English, 1980.

WRITINGS:

Should the Catholic College Survive? and Other Impertinent Questions, Assumption Student Press, 1971.
Worcester Poets, with Notes toward a Literary History, Worcester County Poetry Association, 1972.
(Contributor of critical essays) James Vinson, editor, *Contemporary Poets,* St. Martin's, 1975, 4th edition, 1985.
(Contributor) *Three Mountains Press Poetry Anthology, 1975,* edited by Denis Carbonneau, Three Mountains Press, 1976.
Poets in the Schools: A Handbook, National Council of Teachers of English, 1976.
(Contributor) *American Writers,* Scribner, 1979, 1982.
(Contributor) *War or Peace? The Search for New Answers,* Orbis Books, 1981.
Homemade Social Justice, Fides/Claretian, 1982.
Justice-Seekers, Peacemakers: Thirty-two Portraits in Courage, XXIII Publications, 1985.

Also contributor to numerous periodicals, including *Commonweal, Progressive, New Republic, Cross-Currents, Bulletin of the New York Public Library,* and *Ms.*

WORK IN PROGRESS: A study of postmodernist literature in America from 1945 to the present, with essays on Flannery O'Connor, Allen Ginsberg, Bernard Malamud, Robert Bly, Stanley Kunitz, and Denise Levertov; a reader, with essays and poems on the theme of social justice.

SIDELIGHTS: Michael True wrote *CA:* "I want to write good, clear prose, like George Orwell's, about literature and survival. I am deeply concerned about various threats to the moral imagination posed by injustice and nuclear armaments in our time; and especially after teaching in China for a year, I am convinced that twentieth-century art and literature in America speak directly to these issues."

TURNER, Alberta Tucker   1919-

PERSONAL: Born October 22, 1919, in New York, N.Y.; daughter of Albert Chester (a financier) and Marion (Fellows) Tucker; married William Arthur Turner (a college professor), April 9, 1943; children: Prudence Mab (Mrs. Peter Richards), Arthur Brenton. *Education:* Hunter College (now Hunter College of the City University of New York), B.A., 1940; Wellesley College, M.A., 1941; Ohio State University, Ph.D., 1946. *Politics:* None. *Religion:* Protestant.

ADDRESSES: Home—482 Caskey Ct., Oberlin, Ohio 44074. *Office*—Department of English, Cleveland State University, Euclid at 24th St., Cleveland, Ohio 44115.

CAREER: Oberlin College, Oberlin, Ohio, lecturer in English literature, 1947-50, 1951-69; Cleveland State University, Cleveland, Ohio, lecturer, 1964-69, assistant professor, 1969-73, associate professor, 1973-78, professor of English literature, 1978—, director of Poetry Center, 1964—.

MEMBER: Milton Society of America, P.E.N., Midwest Modern Language Association.

WRITINGS:

North (poems), Triskelion Press, 1970.
Need (poems), Ashland Poetry Press, 1971.
Learning to Count (poems), University of Pittsburgh Press, 1974.
Lid and Spoon (poems), University of Pittsburgh Press, 1977.
(Editor) *Fifty Contemporary Poets: The Creative Process,* McKay, 1977.
(Editor) *Poets Teaching: The Creative Process,* Longman, 1980.
To Make a Poem, Longman, 1982.
A Belfry of Knees (poems), University of Alabama Press, 1983.
(Editor) *Forty-five Contemporary Poems: The Creative Process,* Longman, 1985.

Associate editor, *Field: Contemporary Poetry and Poetics,* 1969—.

WORK IN PROGRESS: Criticism of contemporary poetry and poetics; poems.

AVOCATIONAL INTERESTS: Collecting islands.

U

UNSWORTH, Walt(er) 1928-

PERSONAL: Born December 16, 1928, in Littleborough, Lancashire, England; married Dorothy Winstanley, 1952; children: Gail, Timothy Duncan. *Education:* Attended Wigan Technical College, 1942-47, and Chester College, 1949-51; Licentiate of the College of Preceptors (L.C.P.), 1956.

ADDRESSES: Home—Harmony Hall, Milnthorpe, Cumbria, England.

CAREER: Teacher in Wednesfield, Staffordshire, and in Horwich, Lancashire, England; Worsley Walkden Secondary School, Worsley, Lancashire, England, head of physics department, 1957-73; editor, *Climber & Rambler* (magazine), 1974—. Managing editor and partner, Cicerone Press (publishers of specialist mountaineering booklets); has worked as a professional mountain-climbing instructor during summer months. *Military service:* British Army, Royal Artillery, 1947-49; served in Malta and Libya.

MEMBER: Alpine Club, Society of Authors, Wayfarer's Club, Lancashire Teachers Mountaineering Club (honorary vice-president).

WRITINGS:

The Young Mountaineer, Hutchinson, 1959.
A Climber's Guide to Pontesford Rocks, Wilding & Son, 1962.
The English Outcrops, Gollancz, 1964.
Matterhorn Man: The Life of Edward Whymper, Gollancz, 1965.
(Contributor) *The Mountaineer's Companion,* Eyre & Spottiswoode, 1966.
(Contributor) *Miscellany Four,* Oxford University Press, 1967.
Tiger in the Snow: The Life and Adventures of A. F. Mummery, Gollancz, 1967.
Because It Is There: Famous Mountaineers 1840-1940, Gollancz, 1968.
The Devil's Mill (juvenile novel), Gollancz, 1968.
The Book of Rock-Climbing, Arthur Barker, 1968.
(Compiler) *Otztal Alps: A Selection of Climbs* (climbing guide), West Col Productions, 1969.
North Face: The Second Conquest of the Alps, Hutchinson, 1969.
Whistling Clough (juvenile novel), Gollancz, 1970.

(With R. B. Evans) *The Southern Lakes* (climbing guide), Cicerone Press, 1971.
Portrait of the River Derwent, R. Hale, 1971.
The High Fells of Lakeland, R. Hale, 1972.
Colour Book of the Lake District, Batsford, 1974.
Colour Book of the Peak District, Batsford, 1974.
Grimsdyke (juvenile novel), Gollancz, 1974.
Encyclopaedia of Mountaineering, R. Hale, 1975.
Walking and Climbing, (juvenile), Routledge & Kegan Paul, 1977.
Everest: A Mountaineering History, Houghton, 1981.
(Compiler and author of introduction) *Peaks, Passes, and Glaciers: Selections from the Alpine Journal,* Mountaineers-Books, 1981.
The Pennine Playground, Penguin Books, 1984.
This Climbing Game, Viking, 1984.
Classic Walks of the World, Oxford Illustrated Press, 1985.

Also author of *Everest 72,* the official booklet of the British Mount Everest Expedition, 1972. Contributor of articles and reviews to magazines, mountaineering journals, and newspapers in Great Britain, the United States, and Australia.

WORK IN PROGRESS: World History of Mountaineering, for Hodder & Stoughton; *Savage Snows,* for Hodder & Stoughton.

SIDELIGHTS: Walt Unsworth's book *Everest: A Mountaineering History* tells the story of "the men and the few women who climbed—or didn't succeed in climbing—the mountain, and it shows them to be fully human and often flawed characters," writes Jeremy Bernstein in the *New Yorker.* Unsworth's account of the climbing history of the mountain is based on numerous books written by climbers, the private papers of the British Alpine Club and the Royal Geographical Society, and interviews and letters from those pioneering climbers still living. "By a careful sifting of the records Unsworth has filled in some of the gaps in the Everest story, although he has sometimes been obliged to resort to intelligent guesswork," comments Ronald Faux in the *Times Literary Supplement.* In *Everest,* Unsworth details forty-five expeditions, from the first British expedition in 1921 to the first successful climb without oxygen in 1978. The author offers much new information about George Leigh Mallory and his ill-fated climb in 1924; Unsworth also provides an in-depth look at the events that led to the first successful climb and return from the summit by the Englishman Edmund Hillary and the Sherpa Tenzing Norgay in 1953.

Of Walt Unsworth, Jan Morris writes in the London *Times,* "No chronicler was ever fairer, more sympathetic or more encyclopedically knowledgeable, but still the sorry conclusion to be drawn from his book is that all in all, with exceptions, the protracted confrontation between mankind and Mount Everest has not been very edifying." Morris adds that the "attempts have been obfuscated by bureaucracy, degraded by chauvinism, soured by private rivalry, cheapened by snobbery of one sort and another or made ridiculous by self importance. Mr. Unsworth dispassionately records it all, motives and manners alike, in a dry, spare and lucid style." Jeremy Bernstein concludes that *Everest* "is a serious historical study, done in high style, of a world that most of us will never know but that many of us dream about."

AVOCATIONAL INTERESTS: Mountain climbing, photography, industrial archaeology.

BIOGRAPHICAL/CRITICAL SOURCES:

PERIODICALS

Listener, November 14, 1968.
New Statesman, November, 1968.
New Yorker, June 7, 1982.
Times (London), September 24, 1981.
Times Literary Supplement, October 16, 1969, October 30, 1970, January 1, 1982.

*   *   *

URDANG, Laurence   1927-

PERSONAL: Born March 21, 1927, in New York, N.Y.; son of Harry (a teacher) and Annabel (a teacher; maiden name, Schafran) Urdang; married Irena Ehrlich vel Sluszny (an antiques dealer), May 23, 1952 (divorced); children: Nicole Severyna, Alexandra Stefanie. *Education:* Columbia University, B.S., 1954.

ADDRESSES: Home—Essex, Conn. *Office*—Laurence Urdang, Inc., P.O. Box 668, Essex, Conn. 06426.

CAREER: Funk & Wagnalls Co., New York City, editor, 1955-57; Random House, Inc., New York City, director of reference department, 1957-69; Laurence Urdang, Inc. (preparer of reference books), Essex, Conn., president, 1969—. Head of Laurence Urdang Associates Ltd., Aylesbury, England, 1970—. *Military service:* U.S. Naval Reserve, active duty, 1944-45.

MEMBER: Dictionary Society of North America, American Dialectic Society, American Name Society, Association for Computational Linguistics, Association for Computing Machinery, Association for Literary and Linguistic Computing, Linguistic Society of America, Popular Culture Association, American Association for Applied Linguistics, American Society of Indexers, Name Society (England), British Association for Applied Linguistics, New York Academy of Sciences, Naval Club (London), Athenaeum (London).

WRITINGS:

EDITOR

The Random House Vest Pocket Dictionary of Synonyms and Antonyms, Random House, 1960.

The Random House Dictionary of the English Language, college edition, Random House, 1968.
The Random House College Dictionary, Random House, 1968.
The New York Times Everyday Reader's Dictionary of Misunderstood, Misused, Mispronounced Words, Quadrangle, 1972 (published in England as *A Dictionary of Misunderstood, Misused, Mispronounced Words,* Thomas Nelson, 1972).
Dictionary of Advertising Terms, Tatham-Laird & Kudner, 1977.
Verbatim: Volumes I and II, Verbatim, 1978.
Roget's Thesaurus, Dale Books, 1978.
Webster's Dictionary, Dale Books, 1978.
The Basic Book of Synonyms and Antonyms, New American Library, 1978 (published in England as *A Basic Dictionary of Synonyms and Antonyms,* Thomas Nelson, 1979).
Synonym Finder, Rodale Press, 1978.
Nelson's Children's Encyclopedia, Thomas Nelson, 1978.
Word for Word, Verbatim, 1979.
Twentieth Century American Nicknames, H. W. Wilson, 1979.
British English: A to Zed, Verbatim, 1979.
Dictionary of Allusions, Gale, 1980.
Dictionary of Suffixes in English, Gale, 1980.
Treasury of Picturesque Expressions, Gale, 1980.
Timetables of American History, Simon & Schuster, 1981.
World Almanac Dictionary of Dates, World Almanac, 1982.
Modifiers, Gale, 1982.
Literary, Rhetorical, and Linguistics Terms Index, Gale, 1983.
Loanwords Index, Gale, 1983.
Mosby's Medical and Nursing Dictionary, Mosby, 1983.
Fine and Applied Arts Terms Index, Gale, 1983.
Idioms and Phrases Index, Gale, 1983.
Prefixes, Gale, 1984.
Slogans, Gale, 1984.
(Editorial director) *Holidays and Anniversaries of the World,* Gale, 1985.

OTHER

Editor and publisher of *Verbatim: Language Quarterly,* 1974—.

*   *   *

URY, Zalman F.   1924-

PERSONAL: Surname originally Fajwusowicz; name legally changed, 1955; born December 17, 1924, in Stolpce, Poland; came to United States in 1947, naturalized citizen, 1954; son of Abraham (a merchant) and Cypa (a housewife; maiden name, Borishanski) Fajwusowicz; married Eva Perl (a hospital administrator), August 30, 1945; children: Celia (Mrs. Hosea Rabinowitz), Natalie (Mrs. Moshe Amster), Ramma (Mrs. Robert Hoffnung), Israel. *Education:* Washington University, B.Sc., 1955; Loyola University, Los Angeles, Calif., M.A., 1962; University of California at Los Angeles, D.Ed. (with honors), 1966. *Politics:* "Apolitical." *Religion:* Jewish Orthodox.

ADDRESSES: Home—465 South Wetherly Dr., Beverly Hills, Calif. 90211. *Office*—Bureau of Jewish Education, 6505 Wilshire Blvd., Los Angeles, Calif. 90048.

CAREER: Received rabbinical ordination, 1948. Teacher of Jewish subjects in Russia, 1941-45; elementary and high school teacher, principal, superintendent, and educational director in parochial schools in St. Louis, Mo., 1948-59; Epstein Academy, St. Louis, principal, 1952-57; Hillel Hebrew Academy,

Beverly Hills, Calif., principal, 1957-59; Jewish Federation-Council of Greater Los Angeles, Bureau of Jewish Education, Los Angeles, Calif., supervisor, 1959-65, head consultant for orthodox schools, 1965—. Part-time parochial high school teacher of Judaica in Los Angeles, 1959-65; part-time instructor in education, West Coast Teachers College of Yeshiva University, Los Angeles, 1962—. Rabbi, part-time, Young Israel of Beverly Hills, 1968—.

MEMBER: National Council for Jewish Education, National Conference of Yeshiva Principals, Educators Council of America (West Coast vice-president, 1974—), National Council of Young Israel Rabbis, Association of Orthodox Jewish Scientists, Torah Umesorah, Doctor of Education Association (U.C.L.A.).

WRITINGS:

(Editor) *Torat Elhanan* (title means ''Teachings of Elhanan''), Twersky, 1954.

(Contributor) Norman Paris, editor, *Brakha LiMenahem* (a salute to Rabbi Menahem Eichenstein), Twersky, 1955.
Remember What Germany Did to You, Hillel Hebrew Academy, 1958.
The Musar Movement: A Quest for Excellence in Character Education, Yeshiva University Press, 1970.
The Story of Rabbi Yisroel Salanter (juvenile), Torah Umesorah, 1971.
(Contributor) Menaham Zohorietal, editor, *Hagut Ivrit Be-America* (studies on Jewish themes by contemporary American scholars), Volume II, Yavneh Publishers, 1973.
(Contributor) Kaminetsky and Friedman, editors, *Building Jewish Ethical Character,* Fryer Foundation of Torah Umesorah, 1975.

Also author of teachers' guides and pedagogic syllabi in history, bible, ethics, and curricula. Contributor to numerous periodicals, including *Jewish Parent, Educational Forum, Jewish Life, Tradition,* and *Sheviley Hahinuch.*†

V

VALE, Lewis
   See OGLESBY, Joseph

*   *   *

VALERAN, A. B.
   See STARR, S(tephen) Frederick

*   *   *

VANCE, Jack
   See VANCE, John Holbrook

*   *   *

VANCE, John Holbrook   1916-
   (Jack Vance; pseudonyms: Peter Held, Alan Wade)

PERSONAL: Born August 28, 1916, in San Francisco, Calif.; son of Charles Albert (a rancher) and Edith (Hoefler) Vance; married Norma Ingold, August 24, 1946; children: John Holbrook II. *Education:* University of California, Berkeley, B.A., 1942. *Politics:* "Above and between Left and Right." *Religion:* None.

ADDRESSES: Home—6383 Valley View Rd., Oakland, Calif. 94611. *Agent*—Kirby McCauley, 432 Park Ave. S., Suite 1509, New York, N.Y. 10016.

CAREER: Writer. Worked briefly at one point for Twentieth Century-Fox.

AWARDS, HONORS: Edgar Allan Poe Award, Mystery Writers of America, 1961, for *The Man in the Cage;* Hugo Award, World Science Fiction Convention, 1964, for *The Dragon Masters,* and 1967, for *The Last Castle;* Nebula Award, Science Fiction Writers of America, 1966, for *The Last Castle;* Jupiter Award for best novelette, 1975, for "The Seventeen Virgins"; nominated for Gandalf Life Award, 1979; World Fantasy Life Achievement Award, 1984.

WRITINGS:

The Man in the Cage, Random House, 1960.

The Fox Valley Murders, Bobbs-Merrill, 1966.
The Pleasant Grove Murders, Bobbs-Merrill, 1967.
The Deadly Isles, Bobbs-Merrill, 1969.
Bad Ronald, Ballantine, 1973.
The View from Chickweed's Window, Underwood-Miller, 1978.
The House on Lily Street, Underwood-Miller, 1979.
The Dark Ocean, Underwood-Miller, 1985.
Strange Notions, Underwood-Miller, 1985.

UNDER NAME JACK VANCE

Vandals of the Void, Winston, 1953.
The Space Pirate, Toby Press, 1953, published as *The Five Gold Bands,* Ace Books, 1962 (bound with *The Dragon Masters,* Ace Books, 1962, Berkley, 1985).
To Live Forever, Ballantine, 1956.
Big Planet, Ace Books, 1957.
Slaves of the Klau, Ace Books, 1958.
The Languages of Pao, Avalon, 1958.
The Houses of Iszm [and] *Son of the Tree* (also see below), Ace Books, 1964.
Future Tense, Ballantine, 1964.
Space Opera, Pyramid Publications, 1965, reprinted Underwood-Miller, 1984.
Monsters in Orbit [and] *The World Between and Other Stories,* Ace Books, 1965.
The Brains of Earth [and] *The Many Worlds of Magnus Ridolph,* Ace Books, 1966.
The Blue World, Ballantine, 1966.
The Last Castle (bound with *World of the Sleeper,* by Tony R. Wayman), Ace Books, 1967.
Eight Fantasms and Magics: A Science Fiction Adventure, Macmillan, 1969 (published in England as *Fantasms and Magics,* Mayflower, 1978).
Emphyrio, Doubleday, 1969.
The Worlds of Jack Vance, Ace Books, 1973.
(Contributor) *Three Trips in Time and Space: Original Novellas of Science Fiction,* Hawthorn Books, 1973.
The Gray Prince, Bobbs-Merrill, 1974.
Showboat World, Pyramid Publications, 1975.
The Best of Jack Vance, Pocket Books, 1976.
Maske: Thaery, Berkley Publications, 1976.
Nopalgarth (includes *The Houses of Iszm* and *Son of the Tree*), DAW Books, 1980.

464

Galactic Effectuator, Underwood-Miller, 1980.
The Complete Magnus Ridolph, Underwood-Miller, 1984.

UNDER NAME JACK VANCE; "DYING EARTH" SERIES

The Dying Earth, Hillman, 1950.
The Eyes of the Overworld, Ace Books, 1966.
Cugel's Saga, Pocket Books, 1983.
Rhialto the Marvellous, Baen Books, 1984.

UNDER NAME JACK VANCE; "DEMON PRINCE" SERIES

The Star King, Berkley Publishing, 1964.
The Killing Machine, Berkley Publishing, 1964.
The Palace of Love, Berkley Publishing, 1967.
The Face, DAW Books, 1979.
The Book of Dreams, DAW Books, 1981.

UNDER NAME JACK VANCE; "PLANET OF ADVENTURE" SERIES

City of the Chasch, Ace Books, 1968, reprinted, Bluejay Books, 1985.
Servants of the Wankh, Ace Books, 1969.
The Dirdir, Ace Books, 1969.
The Pnume, Ace Books, 1970.

UNDER NAME JACK VANCE; "DURDANE" SERIES

The Anome, Dell, 1973.
The Brave Free Men, Dell, 1973.
The Asutra, Dell, 1974.

UNDER NAME JACK VANCE; "ALASTOR" SERIES

Trullion: Alastor 2262, Ballantine, 1973, reprinted Underwood-Miller, 1984.
Maruen: Alastor 933, Ballantine, 1975.
Wyst: Alastor 1716, DAW Books, 1978.

UNDER NAME JACK VANCE; "LYONESSE" SERIES

Lyonesse I: Suldrun's Garden, Underwood-Miller, 1983.
Lyonesse II: The Green Pearl, Underwood-Miller, 1985.

UNDER PSEUDONYM PETER HELD

Take My Face, Mystery House, 1957.

UNDER PSEUDONYM ALAN WADE

Isle of Peril, Mystery House, 1957.

OTHER

Also author of television scripts for "Captain Video." Contributor of fiction to periodicals.

WORK IN PROGRESS: Madouc, the final book in the "Lyonesse" series.

SIDELIGHTS: A prolific author who has published more than sixty books, John Holbrook Vance, known to most readers as Jack Vance, started off writing short stories for magazines and eventually progressed to novels, many of which have evolved into series. "I'm not one of these chaps who was an instant success," he told Charles Platt in a rare interview for *Dream Makers,* Volume II: *The Uncommon Men and Women Who Write Science Fiction.* "There was a long period in which I wrote a lot of junk, as an apprentice, learning my trade. I found out I was no good at gadget stories, or at least they were very boring to me, and I found out that I didn't enjoy writing whimsy, and I finally blundered into this thing which

I keep on doing, which is essentially a history of the human future." *Washington Post* reviewer Michael Dirda believes that whether Vance is writing "science fiction, high fantasy, or mysteries . . . his delicious sentences linger as the chief pleasure of his inventive books." *Village Voice* contributor Baird Searles calls him "science fiction's most elegant stylist."

Vance's "sensuous, elevated style, at times reminiscent of the art-prose of Ruskin or Huysmans, can easily cloy or become mere bejeweled description, gaudy but insubstantial," according to a *Washington Post Book World* reviewer. "Vance skirts this danger by fixing on traditional adventure plots: the revenge saga, the picaresque journey or marvel-filled odyssey, the murder mystery, the novel of education (his most common form), sword-and-laser battle epics. . . . All these strong story lines prevent the novels from bogging down in the merely evocative."

Many of these elements are present in Vance's first book, *The Dying Earth,* a collection of stories in which different characters inhabit the same futuristic setting. These characers "seek power or knowledge, and they compete fiercely for it," according to Russell Letson in the *Dictionary of Literary Biography,* Volume VIII: *Twentieth-Century Science Fiction Writers.* He believes that here, "as in much of Vance's work, it is less the characters or actions than the settings, atmosphere, and above all the language that make these stories in *The Dying Earth* memorable."

In the sixties, Vance began to specialize in science fiction series, and he returned to the milieu of *The Dying Earth* in 1966 with *The Eyes of the Overworld.* Cugel the Clever, a picaresque rogue and Vance's favorite character, dominates this tale, and his journey across the treacherous planet to retrieve a magic cusp forms the heart of the novel. Letson believes that while "the characters are no less amoral and self interested and the world no less savage and dangerous," this story is "less elegiac than the earlier ones, and the atmosphere is lightened by picaresque escapades and by the avoidance of the serious themes of love and loyalty." *The Eyes of the Overworld* ends with Cugel, who has acquired the magic cusp and completed his hazardous journey, outwitting himself at the last moment and being thrust back to where he began.

In *Cugel's Saga,* the next installment, Cugel must again complete the journey, by a different but equally dangerous route. In his *Washington Post* review of the book, Michael Dirda says, "any reader who has ever enjoyed the voyages of Sinbad, the club stories of Mr. Joseph Jorkens or the tales of Tarzan will hardly find a more diverting literary entertainment . . . than 'Cugel's Saga.' Mellower, softer, less rich in texture and invention than 'The Eyes of the Overworld,' it nonetheless possesses that distinctive winey tang that is Vance's alone."

BIOGRAPHICAL/CRITICAL SOURCES:

Contemporary Literary Criticism, Volume XXXV, Gale, 1985.
Dictionary of Literary Biography, Volume VIII: *Twentieth-Century American Science Fiction Writers,* Gale, 1981.
Platt, Charles, *Dream Makers,* Volume II: *The Uncommon Men and Women Who Write Science Fiction,* Berkley Books, 1983.

Village Voice, July 7, 1975.
Washington Post, December 13, 1983, October 27, 1985.

Washington Post Book World, April 26, 1981, April 24, 1983, January 27, 1985.

*   *   *

van LHIN, Erik

See del REY, Lester

*   *   *

VINCENT, William R.

See HEITZMANN, William Ray

*   *   *

von DAENIKEN, Erich 1935-

PERSONAL: Born April 14, 1935, in Zofingen, Switzerland; son of Otto (a clothing manufacturer) and Lena (Weiss) von Daeniken; married Elisabeth Skaja, July 20, 1960; children: Cornelia. *Education:* Attended College St. Michel, Fribourg, Switzerland, 1949-54.

ADDRESSES: Baselstrasse 10, 4532 Feldbrunnen, Switzerland.

CAREER: Hotel-keeper and writer.

WRITINGS:

Erinnerungen an die Zukunft, Econ-Verlag, 1968, translation by Michael Heron published as *Chariots of the Gods?: Unsolved Mysteries of the Past,* Putnam, 1969.
Zurueck zu den Sternen: Argumente fuer das Unmoegliche, Econ-Verlag, 1969, translation by Heron published as *Gods Return to the Stars: Evidence for the Impossible,* Putnam, 1971.
Aussaat und Kosmos: Spuren und Plaene ausserirdischer Intelligenzen, Econ-Verlag, 1972, translation by Heron published as *The Gold of the Gods,* Putnam, 1973.
Erscheinunen: Phaenomene, die d. Welt erregen, Econ-Verlag, 1974, translation by Heron published as *Miracles of the Gods: A Hard Look at the Supernatural,* Delacorte, 1975.
In Search of Ancient Gods: My Pictorial Evidence for the Impossible, Delacorte, 1976.
According to the Evidence, Souvenir, 1977.
Erich von Daeniken's Proof, Bantam, 1978.
Signs of the Gods, Putnam, 1980.
Pathways to the Gods, Putnam, 1982.
The Gods and Their Grand Design, Putnam, 1984.

Also author of *Der Tag an dem die Goetter kamen,* Bertelsmann, published in English translation, Putnam, 1985.

SIDELIGHTS: Erich von Daeniken theorizes that *Homo sapiens* was created by advanced, extra-terrestrial beings who visited earth millenia ago and mated with our ancestors. It is on this premise that von Daeniken's books are based, and he spends much of his time traveling around the world seeking information in support of his theory.

"It is my very Catholic background which started it all," von Daeniken told *Washington Post* reviewer Adam Shaw. In answer to his questions concerning religion, von Daeniken's high school teachers suggested he read the Old Testament. He followed their advice and became especially interested in certain verses of Genesis which to him suggested many gods, rather than one. From then on he felt compelled to study works of other religions and to travel to "South America, Russia, Egypt to see with my own eyes the inscriptions, the monuments, the traces left behind by the 'gods' to let us know they were here," he explained to Shaw. He discovered in many of the religions and legends the following recurring theme: "The gods have come down from the sky, often with a loud noise and in fiery vehicles. They 'created' man, went back into the sky, and promised to return."

Throughout his travels, von Daeniken has accumulated such supporting evidence as "the illustrations of [ancient people from outer space] in the thousands-of-years-old rock formations, whether in South America, Alaska, Easter Island, Africa, or Asia which all show headgear that . . . can be likened to the headgear of astronauts, and what was at first supposed to be horns are really antennae," as reviewer Sister M. Marguerite writes in *Best Sellers.* "Also, there is in the Palpa Valley a strip of level ground some thirty-seven miles long. From the air, one can make out gigantic lines, laid out geometrically, which look marvelously like a modern landing space for airships. The archaeologists say they are Inca roads; but von Daeniken questions: of what use to the Incas were roads that ran parallel and came to a sudden end?" And in the instance of Elephant Island, the island resembles an elephant only when viewed from great height; how could primitive inhabitants who supposedly named the island have known this?

S. K. Oberbeck, reviewing *The Gold of the Gods* in *Newsweek,* calls the author's style a mixture of "Carlos Castaneda, Ripley's 'Believe It or Not,' and 'Star Trek.'" A *Choice* reviewer writes of *Chariots of the Gods,* "The book undoubtedly deserves a place of honor beside J. Churchward's *The Lost Continent of Mu* and related texts on the lost continent of Atlantis, but it cannot be recommended, in all conscience, for an academic library."

Prominent scientists and proponents of orthodox religion are also skeptical of von Daeniken's theories. But he predicts that his interpretations of ancient enigmas, now considered unusual, will, in another generation, be taught in college classrooms.

Oscar Dystel, president of Bantam Books, Inc., responded with a "yes" when asked in a 1973 interview for *New York* if he felt the von Daeniken following was an offshoot of the interest in UFOs (Unidentified Flying Objects) that flourished during the 1950s and 1960s. In reference to this following, and to *Chariots of the Gods* in particular, he is quoted as saying: "We can't find any pattern of sales. Hippies are buying it, college students, Middle America, your uncle and aunt, the sophisticated and the unsophisticated. People seem to be looking for something, and these books provide that something."

MEDIA ADAPTATIONS: A color documentary, "Erinnerungen an die Zukunft," based on von Daeniken's first two books and produced by Terra Filmkunst, was released in Berlin, Germany, in April, 1970. Harald Reinl wrote and directed the film, which had its first showing in England as "Memories of the Future" in December, 1970. The National Broadcasting Company (NBC-TV) aired a special based on von Daeniken's theories on January 5, 1973. Produced by Alan Landsburg Productions for Tomorrow Entertainment, a General Electric subsidiary, the special resulted in a sales boom of *Chariots of the Gods.*

BIOGRAPHICAL/CRITICAL SOURCES:

BOOKS

Authors in the News, Volume I, Gale, 1976.

PERIODICALS

Atlantic, March, 1970.
Best Sellers, February 1, 1970.
Book World, February 22, 1970.
Choice, May, 1970, December, 1971.
Christian Century, February 25, 1970.
Cincinnati Enquirer, November 3, 1974.
Guardian, May 30, 1973.
Macon Telegraph and News, October 20, 1974.
Milwaukee Journal, November 3, 1974.
National Review, February 24, 1970.
Newsweek, October 8, 1973.
New York, May 7, 1973.
New York Post, December 19, 1973.
New York Times Book Review, March 31, 1974.
Playboy, August, 1974.
Washington Post, December 2, 1973.

W

WADE, Alan
See VANCE, John Holbrook

*   *   *

WAKIN, Edward 1927-

PERSONAL: Born December 13, 1927, in Brooklyn, N.Y.; son of Thomas Najem and Josephine (Aziz) Wakin; married, November 11, 1952; married second wife, Eleanor Kestor, December 3, 1967; children: Daniel. *Education:* Fordham University, B.A., 1948, Ph.D., 1973; Northwestern University, M.S.J., 1950; Columbia University, M.A., 1962.

ADDRESSES: Home—45 Wellington Ave., New Rochelle, N.Y. 10408. *Office*—Fordham University, Bronx, N.Y. 10458.

CAREER: Buffalo Evening News, Buffalo, N.Y., assistant city editor, 1950-52; *New York World-Telegram*, New York, N.Y., variously night city editor, feature editor, and Brooklyn city editor, 1952-59; Fordham University, Bronx, N.Y., 1960—, began as assistant professor, currently professor in communications department and director of graduate program. United States Information Service lecturer in Africa, the Middle East, and the Far East, 1971 and 1973. Consulting education editor, WCBS-TV, 1966-69; consultant to numerous corporations and government agencies.

AWARDS, HONORS: George Polk Memorial Award for Journalism, 1957; mass media fellowship, Fund for Adult Education, 1959-60.

WRITINGS:

A Lonely Minority: The Modern Story of Egypt's Copts, Morrow, 1963.
The Catholic Campus, Macmillan, 1963.
At the Edge of Harlem: Portrait of a Middle-Class Negro Family, Morrow, 1965.
(With J. F. Scheuer) *The De-Romanization of the American Catholic Church,* Macmillan, 1966.
Controversial Conversations with Catholics, Pflaum Press, 1969.
(With Christiane Brusselmans) *A Parents' Guide: Religion for Little Children,* Our Sunday Visitor, 1970, revised edition, 1977.
Black Fighting Men in U.S. History, Lothrop, 1971.

(With James DiGiacomo) *We Were Never Their Age,* Holt, 1971.
The Battle for Childhood, Abbey Press, 1973.
Careers in Communication, Lothrop, 1974.
Children without Justice, NCJW Books, 1975.
Enter the Irish-American, Crowell, 1976.
The Immigrant Experience, OSV Books, 1977.
Communications: An Introduction to Media, American Book Co., 1978.
(With Richard Armstrong) *You Can Still Change the World,* Harper, 1978.
(With Frank J. McNutly) *Should You Ever Feel Guilty?,* Paulist/Newman, 1978.
Monday Morality: Right and Wrong in Daily Life, Paulist/Newman, 1980.
(With DiGiacomo) *Understanding Teenagers,* Argus, 1983.
(With Charles Fahey) *A Catholic Guide to the Mature Years,* Our Sunday Visitor, 1984.
(With Sean K. Cooney) *Beyond Loneliness,* Twenty-Third, 1985.
Trevor's Place: The Story of the Boy Who Brings Hope to the Homeless, Harper, 1985.

Contributor of more than two hundred articles to magazines, including *Saturday Review, Harper's, Nation, Science Digest,* and *Commonweal.* Contributing editor, *50 Plus* and *Today's Office.*

*   *   *

WALDER, (Alan) David 1928-1978

PERSONAL: Born November 13, 1928, in London, England; died October 26, 1978, in London, England; son of James (a civil servant) and Helen (McColville) Walder; married Elspeth Margaret Milligan (an economist), July 28, 1956; children: Robert, Isobel, Catherine, Alexandra. *Education:* Christ Church, Oxford, B.A., 1952, M.A., 1954.

ADDRESSES: Home—White House, Grimsargh near Preston, Lancashire PR2 5JR, England; 45 Courtenay St., London SE11 5PH, England.

CAREER: British Army, 1948-65, member of Fourth Queen's Own Hussars in Malaya, Germany, Aden, and Borneo, 1949-58, and Emergency Reserve, Queen's Royal Irish Hussars, 1958-65, leaving service as a major; called to the bar, Inner

Temple, 1956; practiced as a barrister, 1956-66; Conservative member of Parliament from High Peak, Derbyshire, 1961-66; Conservative member of Parliament from Clitheroe, 1970-78. Parliamentary private secretary to Joint Under-Secretaries of State, Scottish Office, 1963-64, and to Minister for Trade, 1970-72; member of United Kingdom Parliamentary Delegation to the Republic of China, 1972, and to the Council of Europe and Assembly of Western European Union, 1972, 1973; vice-chairman of Conservative Home Affairs Committee, 1972; assistant government whip, 1973-74; vice-chairman of Conservative Defence Committee, 1974. Member of court of University of Lancaster. Consultant, Lexington International Public Relations Ltd., London, 1977-78.

MEMBER: Institute for Strategic Studies, National Book League (executive, 1976-78), Royal United Services Institute, Anglo-Omani Society, Wembley South Conservative Association (chairman, 1959), Cavalry and Guards Club, 1922 Committee (former executive member).

AWARDS, HONORS: Forster-Boulton Prize and Paul Methven scholarship from the Inner Temple, both 1956; Emergency Reserve decoration, 1965.

WRITINGS:

Bags of Swank (novel), Hutchinson, 1963.
The Short List (novel), Hutchinson, 1964.
The Gift Bearers (novel), Coward, 1966.
The House Party (novel), Hutchinson, 1966.
The Fair Ladies of Salamanca (novel), Hutchinson, 1967.
The Chanak Affair (nonfiction), Macmillan, 1969.
The Short Victorious War: The Russo-Japanese Conflict, 1904-1905, Hutchinson, 1973, Harper, 1974.
Nelson (biography), Dial/J. Wade, 1978.

Also author with Julian Critchley, *Stability and Survival*, 1961. Contributor to *Purnell's History of the First World War*.

SIDELIGHTS: Although several biographies of the British naval hero Horatio Nelson have been written, "a new and objective biography was needed," writes Byron Farwell in the *Washington Post Book World*. With his book, *Nelson*, "David Walder has supplied the need and his efforts have surpassed all others."

Nelson has frequently inspired biographies because of his many-faceted life. He separated from his wife after fourteen years of marriage to pursue a public affair with Emma Hamilton, the wife of a British ambassador. As a naval officer, Nelson "had extreme professional skill, compassion, and a nice respect for insubordination; he had a sense of mission and occasion," observes Joanna Richardson in *Books and Bookmen*. He was also a charismatic leader, and Richardson notes that "it is one of Mr. Walder's merits that he conveys a sense of Nelson's charisma." Yet more than anything, Nelson was a fearless and brilliant sea captain. He lost the sight of his right eye in a battle off Corsica; later he lost his right arm below the elbow in a battle at Teneriffe. He continued to command, however, and led the British to victory in three major sea battles. During the battle of Trafalgar in 1805, while orchestrating the complete destruction of the combined French and Spanish fleet, he was shot to death. Farwell finds that Walder's "descriptions of battles, accompanied by simple, clear illustrations, are superb."

Walder "is properly critical of Nelson's defects as he is generous in his praise of his achievements," remarks Christopher Lloyd in the *Times Literary Supplement*. As Richardson indicates in her review, Walder bases his conclusions on "an historian's knowledge of the general background," "a sound understanding of naval tactics and strategy," and "a sensitive appreciation of character." "His biography is a masterpiece," claims Byron Farwell, "the most brilliant appraisal of Nelson yet written."

AVOCATIONAL INTERESTS: Shooting, ornithology, opera.

BIOGRAPHICAL/CRITICAL SOURCES:

PERIODICALS

Books and Bookmen, September, 1978.
New Statesman, June 9, 1978.
Times Literary Supplement, October 20, 1978.
Washington Post Book World, April 16, 1978.

OBITUARIES:

PERIODICALS

Publishers Weekly, December 11, 1978.

*   *   *

WALLIS, Roy   1945-

PERSONAL: Born February 25, 1945, in London, England; son of John (a bricklayer) and Constance (Inkpen) Wallis; married Veronica Abel; children: Imogen, Jacob, Samuel. *Education:* University of Essex, B.A. (with honors), 1970; Oxford University, D.Phil., 1974. *Politics:* "Wishy-washy liberal." *Religion:* None.

ADDRESSES: Home—47 Marlborough Park Central, Belfast, Northern Ireland. *Office*—Department of Social Studies, Queen's University, Belfast, Northern Ireland.

CAREER: University of Stirling, Stirling, Scotland, lecturer in sociology, 1972-77; Queen's University, Belfast, Northern Ireland, professor of sociology, 1977—.

WRITINGS:

(Editor) *Sectarianism: Analyses of Religious and Non-Religious Sects*, P. Owen, 1975.
The Road to Total Freedom, Heinemann, 1976, Columbia University Press, 1977.
(Editor with Peter Morley) *Marginal Medicine*, Free Press, 1976.
(Editor with Morley) *Culture and Curing*, University of Pittsburgh Press, 1978.
Salvation and Protest, St. Martin's, 1979.
(Editor) *On the Margins of Science*, Sociological Review Monographs, 1979.
(Editor) *Millennialism and Charisma*, Queen's University of Belfast, 1982.
The Elementary Forms of the New Religious Life, Routledge & Kegan Paul, 1984.
(With Steve Bruce) *Sociological Theory, Religion and Collective Action*, Queen's University of Belfast, 1985.

WORK IN PROGRESS: God's New Nation, a sociological study of the Children of God; *The Soul of a Stranger*, reflective essays.

BIOGRAPHICAL/CRITICAL SOURCES:

PERIODICALS

Times Literary Supplement, June 1, 1984.

WALSTER, Elaine
See HATFIELD, Elaine (Catherine)

* * *

WALSTER, Elaine Hatfield
See HATFIELD, Elaine (Catherine)

* * *

WALTER, Elizabeth

PERSONAL: Born in England.

ADDRESSES: Office—William Collins Sons & Co., 8 Grafton St., London W1X 3LA, England.

CAREER: William Collins Sons & Co., London, England, 1961—, currently senior editor and editor of Collins Crime Club.

AWARDS, HONORS: Received Scott Moncrieff Translation Prize for *A Scent of Lilies.*

WRITINGS:

The More Deceived, J. Cape, 1960.
The Nearest and Dearest, Harvill, 1962.
Snowfall, and Other Chilling Events, Stein & Day, 1965.
The Sin-Eater, and Other Scientific Impossibilities, Stein & Day, 1967.
Davy Jones's Tale, and Other Supernatural Stories, Harvill, 1971.
Come and Get Me, and Other Uncanny Invitations, Harvill, 1973.
Dead Woman, and Other Haunting Experiences, Harvill, 1975, St. Martin's, 1976.
In the Mist, and Other Uncanny Encounters, Arkham, 1979.
A Christmas Scrapbook (nonfiction), Collins, 1979.
Season's Greetings, Collins, 1980.
A Wedding Bouquet, Collins, 1981.

TRANSLATOR

Claire Gallois, *A Scent of Lilies,* Stein & Day, 1971.
Bernard Claved, *Lord of the River,* Little, Brown, 1973.
Janine Boissard, *A Matter of Feeling,* Little, Brown, 1979.

* * *

WALVIN, James   1942-

PERSONAL: Born February 1, 1942, in Manchester, England; son of James (an engineer) and Emma (Wood) Walvin. *Education:* University of Keele, B.A. (with first-class honors), 1964; McMaster University, M.A. (with first-class honors), 1965; University of York, Ph.D., 1970.

ADDRESSES: Office—Department of History, University of York, York, England.

CAREER: University of York, York, England, currently member of faculty in department of history.

AWARDS, HONORS: Martin Luther King Memorial Prize, 1974, for *Black and White: The Negro and English Society, 1555-1945.*

WRITINGS:

(With M. J. Craton) *A Jamaican Plantation,* University of Toronto Press, 1970.

The Black Presence: A Documentary of the Negro in Britain, Orbach & Chambers, 1971, Schocken, 1972.
Black and White: The Negro and English Society, 1555-1945, Allen Lane, 1972.
The People's Game: A Social History of British Football, Allen Lane, 1975.
(Editor with Craton) *Slavery, Abolition and Emancipation,* Longman, 1976.
Beside the Seaside: A Social History of the Popular Seaside Holiday, Allen Lane, 1978.
Leisure and Society, 1830-1950, Longman, 1978.
(Editor with Eltis) *Abolition of the Atlantic Slave Trade,* University of Wisconsin Press, 1981.
A Child's World: A Social History of English Childhood, 1800-1914, Penguin Books, 1982.
(Editor) *Slavery and British Society, 1776-1848,* Macmillan, 1982.
(With E. Royle) *English Radicals and Reformers, 1760-1848,* University of Kentucky Press, 1982.
Slavery and Slave Trade: An Illustrated History, University of Mississippi, 1983.
Black Personalities: Africans in Britain in the Era of Slavery, Louisiana State University Press, 1983.
(Editor with John Walton) *Leisure in Britain since 1800,* Manchester University Press, 1983.
Passage to Britain: Immigration in History and Politics, Penguin Books, 1984.
English Urban Life, 1776-1851, Hutchinson, 1984.

SIDELIGHTS: A history of the rise and fall of British radicalism, *English Radicals and Reformers, 1760-1848,* which James Walvin co-authored with Edward Royle, closely examines the tendencies of this political movement, its promotion of a free and widespread press, and the accompanying attitude that government required constant monitoring in order to minimize its abuses. I. J. Prothero finds in the *Times Literary Supplement* that the book's "value is as a very serviceable and succinct survey of recent historical scholarship, commented on and used in a common-sense way from the vantage-point of broad familiarity with the politics of the period."

BIOGRAPHICAL/CRITICAL SOURCES:

PERIODICALS

Times Literary Supplement, January 23, 1983.

* * *

WARBLER, J. M.
See COCAGNAC, Augustin Maurice(-Jean)

* * *

WARNER, Sam Bass, Jr.   1928-

PERSONAL: Born April 6, 1928, in Boston, Mass.; son of Sam Bass (a publisher) and Helen (Wilson) Warner; married Lyle Lobel, June 21, 1952; children: Rebecca Helen, William Eaton, Kate Sidney, Alice Louise. *Education:* Harvard University, A.B., 1950, Ph.D., 1959; Yale University, law studies, 1950-51; Boston University, M.S. in Journalism, 1952. *Politics:* Democrat.

ADDRESSES: Home—24 West Cedar St., Boston, Mass. *Office*—Department of History, Boston University, Boston, Mass. 02215.

CAREER: Watertown Sun, Watertown, Mass., editor and publisher, 1951-52; Massachusetts Institute of Technology-Harvard University Joint Center for Urban Studies, Cambridge, Mass., research associate, 1959-63; Harvard University, Cambridge, Mass., instructor, 1960-63; Washington University, St. Louis, Mo., associate professor of history and architecture and research associate at Institute for Urban and Regional Studies, 1963-67; University of Michigan, Ann Arbor, professor of history, 1967-72; Boston University, Boston, Mass., William Edwards Huntington Professor of History, 1973—. Visiting professor of architecture, Massachusetts Institute of Technology, 1977. Member of advisory council, United States National Archives, 1969-72; director, National Committee for Educational Change, 1974-75; member of advisory board, Center for Urban Studies, Harvard University, 1975-76; member of national research council, Committee on Basic Research in the Behavioral and Social Sciences, 1980—. Consultant, National Endowment for the Humanities, 1979-80.

MEMBER: American Historical Association (member of research committee, 1973-74), Society of Architectural Historians, Organization of American Historians (member of executive committee, 1980—).

AWARDS, HONORS: Ford Foundation fellow in metropolitan studies, 1957-58; Albert J. Beveridge Award, American Historical Association, 1969, for *The Private City: Philadelphia in Three Periods of Its Growth;* Charles Warren Center for Studies in American History fellow, 1974; Guggenheim Foundation fellow, 1976; Rockefeller Foundation fellow, 1977; National Endowment for the Humanities research fellow, 1981-82.

WRITINGS:

Streetcar Suburbs: The Process of Growth in Boston, 1870-1900, Harvard University Press, 1962.
(Editor) Albert J. Kennedy and Robert A. Woods, *The Zone of Emergence,* Harvard University Press, 1962, 2nd edition, 1969.
(Contributor) J. E. Burchard and O. Handlin, editors, *The Historian and the City,* Massachusetts Institute of Technology, 1963.
(Editor) *Planning for a Nation of Cities,* MIT Press, 1966.
The Private City: Philadelphia in Three Periods of Its Growth, University of Pennsylvania Press, 1968.
(Editor) Jacob Riis, *How the Other Half Lives,* Dover, 1970.
The Urban Wilderness: A History of the American City, Harper, 1972.
(Editor) *The American Experiment: Perspectives on Two Hundred Years,* Houghton, 1976.
(With Sylvia Fleisch) *Measurements for Social History: Metropolitan America, 1860-1960,* Sage Publishing, 1977.
The Way We Really Live: Social Change in Metropolitan Boston since 1920, Boston Public Library, 1978.
(Contributor) Thomas Hall and Ingrid Hammerstroem, editors, *Growth and Transformation of the Modern City,* Almqvist & Wiksell, 1979.
(Contributor) Paula Dubeck and Zane L. Miller, editors, *Urban Professionals and the Future of the Metropolis,* Kennikat, 1980.
(Contributor) Derek Fraser and Anthony Sutcliffe, editors, *The Pursuit of Urban History,* Edward Arnold, 1983.
Province of Reason: American Lives in a New Age of Science, Harvard University Press, 1984.

Also contributor of articles to numerous journals.

WORK IN PROGRESS: A history of social science and the city from the seventeenth century to the present.

SIDELIGHTS: In *Province of Reason: American Lives in a New Age of Science,* Sam Bass Warner, Jr., examines the changes to society between 1850 and 1980 "through the eyes of particular people in one particular region of the United States in order to understand the vastness, the barbarism, and the unimaginable that are the central experiences of recent history," as he explains. Warner offers biographical essays of fourteen people who lived in and around Boston, Massachusetts. "All found themselves bewildered about how to adapt to a rapidly changing world," writes Nancy Ramsey in the *New York Times Book Review.* Some adapted to the changes in social climate; others failed. "Warner's enthusiasms go to those who sacrifice upward momentum for social and cultural inclusiveness," comments Richard Eder in the *Los Angeles Times Book Review.* Warner presents Mary Antin, a campaigner for the rights of immigrants, and Nobel Peace Prize winner Emily Greene Balch as examples of positive responses to social turmoil. Yet, Eder believes that in the end, this book "is not so much the example of those who overcame the limitations of their province, as the notion that all real virtues are provincial and that being provincial, they will pass." Nancy Ramsey concludes, "'Province of Reason' is a quiet but impassioned plea for man to consider the consequences of his actions."

BIOGRAPHICAL/CRITICAL SOURCES:

PERIODICALS

Los Angeles Times Book Review, October 7, 1984.
New York Times Book Review, November 4, 1984.

*   *   *

WATKINS, John G(oodrich)   1913-

PERSONAL: Born March 17, 1913, in Salmon, Idaho; son of John Thomas and Ethel (Goodrich) Watkins; married Helen Huth, 1971; children: (previous marriage) John Dean, Jonette Alison, Richard Douglas, Gregory Keith, Rodney Phillip; (present marriage) Marvin Huth, Karen Eiblmayr. *Education:* Attended College of Idaho, 1929-30, 1931-32; University of Idaho, B.S., 1932, M.S., 1936; Columbia University, Ph.D., 1941. *Politics:* Democrat. *Religion:* Unitarian Universalist.

ADDRESSES: Home—413 Evans St., Missoula, Mont. *Office*—Department of Psychology, University of Montana, Missoula, Mont. 59801.

CAREER: High school teacher in Homedale, Rupert, and Mountain Home (all Idaho), 1933-39; Columbia University, New York, N.Y., assistant, 1940; Ithaca College, Ithaca, N.Y., assistant professor, 1940-41; Alabama Polytechnic Institute (now Auburn University), Auburn, professor, 1941-43; Washington State College (now University), Pullman, associate professor, 1946-49; Veterans Administration Hospital, American Lake, Wash., clinical psychologist, 1949-50; Veterans Administration Mental Hygiene Clinic, Chicago, Ill., chief clinical psychologist, 1950-53; Veterans Administration Hospital, Portland, Ore., chief clinical psychologist, 1953-64; University of Montana, Missoula, professor of psychology and director of clinical training, 1964-84, professor emeritus, 1984—.

Lecturer, University of Washington, University of Portland, Northwestern University, Portland State College (now University), and Florida Institute of Technology; visiting professor, University of California, Los Angeles, and State University of New York at Binghamton; lectures and presents workshops in Europe, South America, and Asia and at numerous institutions throughout the United States; director of planning and development, International Graduate University, Switzerland, 1974-77. Diplomate in clinical psychology, American Board of Examiners in Professional Psychology; part-time practice in psychotherapy and psychological consultation. Acting chief of training in clinical psychology for Illinois Region of Veterans Administration, 1950-51; president, American Board of Examiners in Psychological Hypnosis, 1959-62. Consulting psychologist, Dammasch State Hospital, Oregon, 1961-64, and V.A. Hospitals and Montana State Prison, 1965—. *Military service:* U.S. Army, Quartermaster Corps, 1943-46; served as chief clinical psychologist at Welch Convalescent Hospital, Daytona Beach, Fla.; became first lieutenant.

MEMBER: International Society for Clinical and Experimental Hypnosis (executive secretary, 1958-62; president-elect, 1962-64; president, 1965-67), American Psychological Association (president of Division 30, 1975-76), Society for Clinical and Experimental Hypnosis (president, 1969-71), Montana Psychological Association, Phi Delta Kappa, Kappa Delta Pi, Phi Mu Alpha.

WRITINGS:

Objective Measurement of Instrumental Performance, Columbia University Press, 1942.
Hypnotherapy of War Neuroses, Ronald, 1949.
General Psychotherapy, C. C Thomas, 1960.
The Therapeutic Self, Human Sciences Press, 1978.
(With R. J. Johnson) *We, the Divided Self,* Irvington, 1984.

CONTRIBUTOR

B. B. Wolman, editor, *Handbook of Clinical Psychology,* McGraw, 1965.
I. A. Berg and L. A. Pennington, editors, *Introduction to Clinical Psychology,* Ronald, 1966.
H. L. Collier, editor, *What's Psychotherapy and Who Needs It?,* O'Sullivan Woodside, 1976.
R. Corsini, editor, *Handbook of Innovative Psychotherapies,* Wiley, 1982.
L. E. Abt and I. R. Stuart, editors, *The Newer Therapies: A Sourcebook,* Van Nostrand, 1982.
C. E. Walker, editor, *The Handbook of Clinical Psychology,* Dow Jones-Irwin, 1983.
Corsini, editor, *Encyclopedia of Psychology,* Wiley, 1984.

Also contributor of chapters to several other books, including *Medical Hypnosis,* edited by Jerome Schneck, *Hypnosis throughout the World,* edited by Fred Marcuse, *Taboo Topics,* edited by Norman L. Farberow, *Short Term Approaches to Psychotherapy,* edited by H. Grayson, and *Therapy in Psychosomatic Medicine,* edited by F. Antonelli.

OTHER

Contributor of over 110 articles and reviews to professional journals. Member of editorial boards of four journals.

WORK IN PROGRESS: Working in areas of hypnoanalysis, psychosomatic medicine, psychological theory, and psychotherapy; novels, short stories.

SIDELIGHTS: John G. Watkins told *CA:* "As a psychologist I am continually trying to understand human behavior, both in myself and others. As a writer I transmit the results of this search with the hope of promoting the betterment of mankind. I am conceited enough to think that my writings do make a contribution, and trust that when it seems to be otherwise I will have the good sense to stop writing. I read voraciously

and am willing to borrow or steal from any source which might improve my contributions—but expect to give proper credit to those whose ideas I have purloined.

"I am also lazy, with islands of intense productivity occasionally looming out of an ocean of non-creative hours. When the time, the place, and the feelings bloom simultaneously inspirations spring forth, alive with near-ripened fruit. When not, the land is a desert. The hardest job is to sit down and start writing; after that it's easy."

AVOCATIONAL INTERESTS: Music, boating, public speaking.

*   *   *

WATSON, (John Hugh) Adam 1914- (Scipio)

PERSONAL: Born August 10, 1914, in Leicester, England; son of Joseph Charlton (a company director) and Alice (Tate) Watson; married Katharine Anne Campbell, September 9, 1950; children: Douglas, Katharine, Alaric. *Education:* King's College, Cambridge, B.A., 1936, M.A., 1939; additional study at University of Munich, University of Madrid, and University of Marburg. *Religion:* Church of England.

ADDRESSES: Home—Polly's Cottage, Sharnden Old Manor, Mayfield, East Sussex, England; and 1871 Field Rd., Charlottesville, Va.

CAREER: British Diplomatic Service, 1937-68, serving in five ambassadorships and finally as under-secretary in Foreign Office. First overseas post was in Bucharest, Romania, 1939-40, followed by Cairo, Egypt (liaison with Free French), 1940-44, and Moscow, U.S.S.R., 1944-47, assigned to Foreign Office, London, England, 1947-50, and British Embassy, Washington, D.C., 1950-56, head of African Department, Foreign Office, London, 1956-59, minister and consul-general to French West Africa, 1959-60, British Ambassador to Federation of Malaysia, 1960-61, to Senegal, Togo, and Mauritania, 1960-62, and to Cuba, 1963-66, under-secretary in Foreign Office, London, 1966-68; British Leyland Motor Corp., London, diplomatic advisor, 1968-73; International Association for Cultural Freedom, Paris, France, director-general, 1974-79; University of Virginia, Charlottesville, visiting professor in department of government and international relations, 1978—, research scholar at Center for Advanced Studies, 1980—. Board member, Fondation pour une Entraide Intellectuelle Europeenne, Paris, 1974—.

MEMBER: National Book League, Brooke's Club, Buckstone Theatre Club.

AWARDS, HONORS: Commander of Order of St. Michael and St. George, 1958; M.A. from Oxford University, 1962; Gwilym Gibbon fellow at Nuffield College, Oxford University, 1962-63.

WRITINGS:

The War of the Goldsmith's Daughter, Chatto & Windus, 1963.
(Under pseudonym Scipio) *Emergent Africa,* Chatto & Windus, 1965, revised edition, Simon & Schuster, 1967.
The Nature and Problems of the Third World, Claremont Colleges Press, 1968.
Toleration in Religion and Politics, Council on Religion and International Affairs, 1980.
(Editor and author of introduction) Herbert Butterfield, *The Origins of History,* Methuen, 1981.

Diplomacy: The Dialogue between States, Methuen, 1982, McGraw, 1983.
(With Hedley Bull) *The Expansion of International Society,* Oxford University Press, 1984.

Also author, adaptor, and translator from the French, German, and Spanish of several plays which have been produced by British Broadcasting Corp. and other organizations. Contributor of several articles to various festschrifts and periodicals.

WORK IN PROGRESS: The Evolution of the Present International System, an investigation from the earliest locally-based manifestations with an examination of the options now available; *God, Government and Science,* a study of the relation between religion, government and science in Western civilizations from ancient times to the present; a biographical study of Catherine I of Russia; an anthology of dramatic verse, with R. D. Smith.

SIDELIGHTS: Adam Watson writes *CA:* "It seems to me that the historian, the playwright, the novelist and the poet are all trying to communicate a clearer, more vivid awareness of some aspect of human experience. Although the medium is slightly different, the purpose is the same. History remains *una storia* in spite of the efforts of some statisticians of the past to eliminate narrative; and the same is true of the novel. History and the drama share a dramatic quality. I feel most at home in history and the theater, but I am an eager consumer of novels and poetry also."

Watson's *Diplomacy: The Dialogue between States* is described by David Hunt in a 1982 London *Times* review as "the first major study of its subject for some forty years." According to Hedley Bull in the *Times Literary Supplement,* who calls it a "penetrating" study, Watson's "admirable book provides a defence in depth of the role which diplomacy, in the broad sense of 'the dialogue between states,' has played and can still play in relation to international order." It is among Watson's "principal arguments that the recent era—marked by military stalemate between the superpowers, the proliferation of new states, the centralization of power, and economic interdependence—calls for new wrinkles in diplomatic method," says Edwin M. Yoder, Jr., in the *Washington Post Book World.* And in Hunt's opinion, "when he expresses his feelings on world peace and the duty of diplomats to ensure it Adam Watson can achieve a sensible elevation of tone."

AVOCATIONAL INTERESTS: History, theater, international affairs.

BIOGRAPHICAL/CRITICAL SOURCES:

BOOKS

Watson, Adam, *Diplomacy: The Dialogue between States,* Methuen, 1982, McGraw, 1983.

PERIODICALS

New York Times Book Review, January 6, 1985.
Times (London), April 15, 1982.
Times Literary Supplement, June 11, 1982, February 1, 1985.
Washington Post Book World, March 20, 1983.

*   *   *

WEBBER, Bert
    See WEBBER, Ebbert T(rue)

WEBBER, Ebbert T(rue)   1921-
    (Bert Webber)

PERSONAL: Born October 22, 1921, in Edgewood Arsenal, Md.; son of Matthew Ebbert and Mary (True) Webber; married Marjorie Jean Renfroe (a registered nurse), July 9, 1944; children: Richard, Mary Merle (Mrs. Richard F. Greenlaw), Dale Brien, Lauren Thomas. *Education:* Attended University of Nevada, 1943; Sperry-Rand Corp. National Sales Training Institute, certificate, 1956; Whitworth College, B.A., 1965; Portland State University, graduate study, 1968; University of Portland, M.L.S., 1968. *Politics:* Independent. *Religion:* Protestant.

ADDRESSES: Home—Box 314, Medford, Ore. 97501.

CAREER: Owner of commercial photography studio and camera supply company in Sedro-Woolley, Wash., 1945-55; Sperry-Rand Corp., Office Machines Division, Seattle and Spokane, Wash., sales representative, 1955-59, Lewiston, Idaho, resident manager, 1959-61; Whitworth College, Spokane, Wash., chief of photo services, 1962-65; Waluga Junior High School, Lake Oswego, Ore., head librarian, 1965-69; Medford Senior High School, Medford, Ore., director of Library and Media Services, 1969-70; free-lance photojournalist based in Medford, Ore., 1970—. *Military service:* U.S. Army, Signal Corps cameraman, 1940-45; served in European Theater and Aleutian Islands.

MEMBER: Pacific Northwest Writers Conference, Oregon Library Association, Oregon Association of School Librarians (member of board of directors, 1969-70), Southern Oregon Writers Conference, Clackamas County Historical Society (member of board of directors, 1967-69), Curry County Historical Society (life member), Jackson County Historical Society.

AWARDS, HONORS: Oregon Library Association award and certificate, both 1979; Washington (state) Library Association award and certificate, both 1984; Helen Krebs Smith Sociological History Book Award, 1984, for *Silent Siege: Japanese Attacks against North America in World War II.*

WRITINGS:

The Pacific Northwest in Books, Lanson's, Inc., 1967, revised edition, 1969.

UNDER NAME BERT WEBBER

Photoengraving: Impact on Visual Communication, Clackamas County School Board, 1967.
Beachcombing for Driftwood, for Glass Floats, for Agates, for Fun, Ye Galleon, 1973, revised edition, 1975.
What Happened at Bayocean—Is Salishan Next?, Ye Galleon, 1973.
Oregon's Great Train Holdup, Ye Galleon, 1973, revised edition, 1974.
Hero of Battle Rock, Ye Galleon, 1973.
Retaliation: Japanese Attacks and Allied Countermeasures on the Pacific Coast in World War II, Oregon State University Press, 1975.
Swivel-Chair Logger: The Life and Work of Anton A. Lausmann, Ye Galleon, 1976.
Imperial Dragon Fish, Webb Research Group, 1980.
(Author of introduction) Caroline Leighton, *Life at Puget Sound,* Ye Galleon, 1980.
(Author of introduction) John Beeson, *A Plea for the Indians,* Ye Galleon, 1981.

(With wife, Marjorie R. Webber) *Jacksonville, Oregon: The Making of a National Historic Landmark*, Ye Galleon, 1983.

(With M. R. Webber) *Maimed by the Sea: Erosion along the Coasts of Oregon and Washington—Documentary*, Ye Galleon, 1983.

Wrecked Japanese Junks Adrift in the North Pacific Ocean, Ye Galleon, 1984.

Silent Siege: Japanese Attacks against North America in World War II, Ye Galleon, 1984.

The Oregon Trail Memorial Half-Dollar, Smith, Smith & Smith, 1985.

(With M. R. Webber) *Railroading in Southern Oregon and the Founding of Medford*, Ye Galleon, 1985.

(Author of introduction and contributor of photographs) Lulu Downen, *Covered Wagon Days in the Palouse Country*, Ye Galleon, 1985.

CONTRIBUTOR OF PHOTOGRAPHS

Miles Cannon, *Waillatpu, Its Rise and Fall*, Ye Galleon, 1969.
Mary Saunders, *The Whitman Massacre*, Ye Galleon, 1978.
James P. Dowd, *Custer Lives!*, Ye Galleon, 1982.
Francis Xavier Blanchet, *Ten Years on the Pacific Coast*, Ye Galleon, 1982.

OTHER

Also co-author with M. R. Webber of *Beachcombing and Camping along the Northwest Coast*, 1978. Author of several booklets published by Webb Research Group. Contributor to *Sea Frontiers, Oregon Journal, Seattle Post-Intelligencer*, and other publications. Editorial consultant, *Oregon School Librarian and Media Specialist*, 1964-72; editor, *Laubach Literary of Southern Oregon Newsletter*, 1971-72; assistant book review editor, *Interchange*, 1972-76.

WORK IN PROGRESS: Aleutian Headache, a book about World War II battles in the Aleutian Islands; *I Shoot the News*, a biography of Will E. Hudson, first newsreel cameraman in the Pacific Northwest; *Postal History of Jackson and Josephine Counties, Oregon*; a series of three volumes on the postal history of ten Washington (state) counties.

SIDELIGHTS: Ebbert T. Webber told *CA:* "I write when the spirit moves me to write, but the search for data on potential subjects is never-ending because details that have escaped other writers are meat for my typewriter. When the research data is ready, I can write at any time of the day or night, but I require at least eight hours of sound sleep, preferably at night with my wife." Because of his knowledge of Japanese submarines, Webber was a technical advisor for the Columbia Pictures film "1941."

Wrecked Japanese Junks Adrift in the North Pacific Ocean has been translated into Japanese.

AVOCATIONAL INTERESTS: Travel, beachcombing, camping, photography, substitute teaching, stamp collecting, writing about forest fires, postal history, airplanes, World War II, music.

*　　*　　*

WELBURN, Ron(ald Garfield) 1944-

PERSONAL: Born April 30, 1944, in Berwyn, Pa.; stepson of Howard (a welder) and Jessie W. Watson; married Eileen D. Millett, August 21, 1971. *Education:* Lincoln University, Lincoln University, Pa. B.A., 1968; University of Arizona, M.A., 1970; New York University, Ph.D., 1983.

ADDRESSES: Home—Box 692, Guilderland, N.Y. 12084. *Office*—Poets & Writers, New York, N.Y.; and Institute of Jazz Studies, Rutgers University, Newark, N.J. 08903.

CAREER: File clerk in New York, N.Y., and Philadelphia, Pa., 1962-64; Lincoln University, Lincoln University, Pa., instructor in humanities, summer, 1968; Syracuse University, Syracuse, N.Y., assistant professor of Afro-American studies, 1970-75; Rutgers University, New Brunswick, N.J., formerly affiliated with Institute for Jazz Studies, assistant professor of English, fall, 1983. Adjunct teacher at Onondaga Community College, 1972-73, State University College at Oneonta, fall, 1973, City College of the City University of New York, summers, 1977-79, LaGuardia Community College, 1978, Hofstra University, 1978, Center for Labor Studies, 1978-79, Rutgers University, 1978-80, Bloomfield College, 1982-83, and Russell Sage-Junior College at Albany, 1984-85; visiting lecturer, Auburn Correctional Facility, 1972. Writer-in-residence at Lincoln University, 1973-74, Hartley House, 1982, and Schenectady County Public Library, 1985.

AWARDS, HONORS: Silvera Award for poetry from Lincoln University, 1967, 1968; fellow, Smithsonian Institute and Music Critics Association, 1975; Langston Hughes Legacy Certificate, Lincoln University, 1981.

WRITINGS:

Peripheries: Selected Poems, 1966-1968, Greenfield Review Press, 1972.

Brownup: Selected Poems, Greenfield Review Press, 1977.

The Look in the Night Sky, Poems, BkMk Press, 1978.

Heartland, Selected Poems, Lotus Press, 1981.

Contributor of poetry, fiction, book reviews, and music reviews to *Giant Talk, Groundswell, Abraxas, Nickel Review, Coda, Jazz Times, Down Beat, Black World, Black Fire, Greenfield Review, Intro*, and other periodicals. Co-founding editor, *Grackle*, 1976.

WORK IN PROGRESS: Stories of the Indian-Black color line; several poetry and short fiction manuscripts.

SIDELIGHTS: Ron Welburn told *CA:* "Important to my career and development are a Pennsylvania oral tradition of several generations, a semi-rural sensibility and love of nature, a love of music, and a love-hate regard for urban life. I began writing as an undergraduate in the midst of an Afro-American sense of being; however, I believe my writing has always been subtly informed and shaped by a strong childhood awareness of an American Indian heritage and therefore a mixed-blood sense of self. Since the mid-1970s my creative writings increasingly probe the facets of life on the Indian-Black color line. And while I wear glasses, I am proud of my ability to see long distances. Most prominent influences have been Twain, Cicero, Levertov, the *Anthology of Negro Poets* on Folkways, Aiken, Eliot, William Carlos Williams's school, U'Tamsi, Faulkner. I am not very political. The current literary scene has some fine people as well as various levels of sharecroppers, brokers, martyrs, henchmen and women, hit men and women, left- and right-wing secret societies, and meetings and cliques. Small presses continue to salvage the works of this country's better writers. I'm partial to the *Greenfield Review*.

"I write to confront questions of the inner self and the world at large. Perversely I enjoy the special selfishness of artistic creation; I hope someone will gain insights about the self and the world in what I do. Everywhere I've traveled, in this country and abroad, I've met someone who's expressed appreciation for something of mine they've read. That's something to show for an 'obscure' career, something that money can't buy.''

AVOCATIONAL INTERESTS: Musical composition, chess, bird watching, squash, hiking.

* * *

WESTERHOFF, John H(enry) III 1933-

PERSONAL: Born June 28, 1933, in Paterson, N.J.; son of John Henry, Jr., and Nona C. Westerhoff; married Alberta Barnhart, December 27, 1955; children: Jill, Jack, Beth. *Education:* Ursinus College, B.S., 1955; Harvard University, M.Div., 1958; Columbia University, Ed.D., 1959.

ADDRESSES: Home—3510 Racine St., Durham, N.C. 27707. *Office*—Divinity School, Duke University, Durham, N.C. 27706.

CAREER: Ordained minister of United Church of Christ, 1958; minister in Presque Isle, Me., 1958-60, Needham, Mass., 1960-64, and Williamstown, Mass., 1964-66; United Church Board for Homeland Ministries, Philadelphia, Pa., staff member in Division of Christian Education, 1966-74; Duke University, Divinity School, Durham, N.C., associate professor, 1974-76, professor of religion and education, 1976—; ordained priest of Episcopal Church, 1978. Visiting lecturer at Union Theological Seminary, 1970-71, Harvard Divinity School, 1972-73, Andover Newton Theological Seminary, 1972-73, University of Toronto, summer, 1973, and Fordham University, summer, 1973. Reporter for Religious News Service, 1969-70; associate with T.D.R. Associates (educational consultant firm), Newton, Mass., 1970-73; director of United Ministries in Public Education, Washington, D.C., 1970-73.

MEMBER: Association of Supervision and Curriculum Development, National Education Association, Council on Education and Anthropology, Religious Education Association, Society for the Scientific Study of Religion, Association of Professors and Researchers in Religious Education, Associated Church Press, Harvard Divinity School Alumni Association.

WRITINGS:

Values for Tomorrow's Children, Pilgrim Press, 1970.
(Contributor) George Devone, editor, *Theology in Revolution,* Alba, 1970.
(Contributor) Gerson Meyer, editor, *Encuentro,* World Council of Churches, 1971.
Liberation Letters, United Church Press, 1972.
(With Joseph Williamson) *Learning to Be Free,* United Church Press, 1972.
(Editor) *A Colloquy on Christian Education,* Pilgrim Press, 1972.
(With Gwen K. Neville) *Generation to Generation,* Pilgrim Press, 1974.
Tomorrow's Church: A Community of Change, Word Books, 1976.
Will Our Children Have Faith?, Seabury, 1976.
Who Are We? The Quest for a Religious Education, Religious Education Press, 1978.
McGuffey and His Readers: Piety, Morality and Education in Nineteenth-Century America, Abingdon, 1978.
(With Neville) *Learning through Liturgy,* Seabury, 1978.
Inner Growth-Outer Change: An Educational Guide to Church Renewal, Seabury, 1979.

(With Urban T. Holms) *Christian Believing,* Seabury, 1979.
Bringing up Children in Christian Faith, Winston Press, 1980.
(With William Williams) *Liturgy and Learning through the Life Cycle,* Seabury, 1980.
(With O. C. Edwards) *A Faithful Church: Issues in the History of Catechetics,* Morehouse, 1981.
(With John Eusden) *The Spiritual Life: Learning East and West,* Seabury, 1982.
Building God's People, Seabury, 1983.
A Pilgrim People, Winston Press, 1984.
Living a Faith Community, Winston Press, 1985.
(With Caroline Hughes) *Images: On the Threshold of God's Future,* Winston Press, 1986.

Also author of several booklets. Contributor to journals, including *AAUW Journal, Catechist, New Jersey Law Review, Perspectives on Education, Religious Education,* and *Andover Newton Quarterly.* Editor, *Colloquy,* 1966-74.

* * *

WESTING, Arthur H(erbert) 1928-

PERSONAL: Born July 18, 1928, in New York, N.Y.; son of S. W. (a physician) and Paula (Riesenfeld) Westing; married Carol A. Eck (a teacher), June 5, 1956; children: Jeanne K., Stephen H. *Education:* Columbia University, A.B., 1950; Yale University, M.F., 1954, Ph.D., 1959.

ADDRESSES: Home—Djursholm, Sweden. *Office*—Stockholm International Peace Research Institute, S-171 73 Solna, Sweden.

CAREER: U.S. Forest Service, Lansing, Mich., research forester, 1954-55; Purdue University, Lafayette, Ind., assistant professor of forestry, 1959-64; University of Massachusetts—Amherst, associate professor of tree physiology, 1964-65; Middlebury College, Middlebury, Vt., associate professor of biology, 1965-66; Windham College, Putney, Vt., associate professor, 1966-71, professor of botany, 1971-76, chairman of department of biology, 1966-75; Stockholm International Peace Research Institute, Solna, Sweden, senior research fellow, 1976-78; Hampshire College, Amherst, professor of ecology and dean of School of Natural Science, 1978-83; Stockholm International Peace Research Institute, senior research fellow, 1983—. Fellow in forest biology, North Carolina State College of Agriculture and Mechanical Arts (now North Carolina State University at Raleigh), 1960; Charles Bullard fellow, Harvard University, 1963-64. Trustee, Vermont Wild Land Foundation, 1966-75; planning commissioner, Town of Westminster, Vt., 1968-72. *Military service:* U.S. Marine Corps, 1950-52, 1954; became captain.

MEMBER: International Peace Research Association, World Federation of Scientific Workers, International Primate Protection League (scientific advisor), Rachel Carson Council (trustee), Fauna and Flora Preservation Society, American Association for the Advancement of Science (fellow; director of herbicide commission, 1970-71), Scientists' Institute of Public Information (fellow), Vermont Academy of Arts and Sciences (trustee, 1967-71), Sigma Xi, Xi Sigma Pi.

WRITINGS:

(With J. B. Neilands) *Harvest of Death,* Free Press, 1972.
Ecological Consequences of the Second Indochina War, Almqvist & Wiksell, 1976.
Weapons of Mass Destruction and the Environment, Taylor & Francis, 1978.

Warfare in a Fragile World, Taylor & Francis, 1980.
Environmental Warfare, Taylor & Francis, 1984.
Herbicides in War, Taylor & Francis, 1984.
Explosive Remnants of War, Taylor & Francis, 1985.

CONTRIBUTOR

Research Problems in Biology, Doubleday, 1965, 2nd edition, Oxford University Press, 1976.
Barry Weisberg, *Ecocide in Indochina: The Ecology of War,* Canfield Press, 1970.
Thomas Whiteside, *The Withering Rain: America's Herbicidal Folly,* Dutton, 1971.
Gravity and the Organism, University of Chicago Press, 1971.
Understanding Environmental Pollution, Mosby, 1971.
The Wasted Nations, Harper, 1972.
Jules Janick, *Horticultural Science,* 2nd edition, W. H. Freeman, 1972.
Essays Today, Harcourt, 1972.
Marek Thee, *Armaments and Disarmament in the Nuclear Age,* Almqvist & Wiksell, 1977.
F. H. Perring, *Ecological Effects of Pesticides,* Academic Press, 1978.
F. Barnaby, *Future War,* M. Joseph, 1984.

Contributor to *World Book Encyclopedia,* 1983.

OTHER

Contributor of over one hundred articles to scientific journals.

*   *   *

WHEELER, (John) Harvey   1918-

PERSONAL: Born October 17, 1918, in Waco, Tex.; married second wife, Norene Burleigh (a psychiatric counselor and professor of psychology), March 26, 1971; children: (first marriage) David Carroll, John Harvey III; (second marriage) Mark Jefferson. *Education:* Attended Wabash College; Indiana University, B.A., 1946, M.A., 1947; Harvard University, Ph.D., 1950.

ADDRESSES: Home—7200 Casitas Pass Rd., Carpinteria, Calif. 93013. *Agent*—Zeigler, Diskant, Inc., 9255 Sunset Blvd., Suite 1122, Hollywood, Calif. 90069. *Office*—Institute for Higher Studies, Box 704, Carpinteria, Calif. 93013.

CAREER: Johns Hopkins University, Baltimore, Md., assistant professor of political science, 1950-54; Washington and Lee University, Lexington, Va., associate professor, 1954-56, professor of political science, 1956-60; Center for the Study of Democratic Institutions, Santa Barbara, Calif., senior fellow-in-residence, 1960-75, visiting scholar, 1961-63, program director, 1969-72 and 1974-75; Institute for Higher Studies, Carpinteria, Calif., founder and president, 1975—. Consultant, Fund for the Republic (which established Center for the Study of Democratic Institutions), 1958—. *Military service:* U.S. Army, 1941-46.

MEMBER: American Political Science Association, Pi Sigma Alpha.

WRITINGS:

(Editor with George Boas) *Lattimore: The Scholar,* [Baltimore], 1950.
The Conservative Crisis, Public Affairs Press, 1956.
(With Eugene Burdick) *Fail-Safe,* McGraw, 1962, new edition, edited by Virginia P. Allen, Falcon Books, 1967.

(With others) *Natural Law and Modern Society,* World Publishing, for Center for the Study of Democratic Institutions, 1963.
Democracy in a Revolutionary Era, Praeger, 1968.
Politics of Revolution, Glendessary, 1971.
(Editor) *Beyond the Punitive Society: Operant Conditioning, Social and Political Aspects,* W. H. Freeman, 1973.
(Co-editor) *Goethe's Science,* Reidel, 1985.
Science out of Law, State University of New York Press, 1985.
(Editor and contributor) *Structure of Ancient Wisdom,* State University of New York Press, in press.

CONTRIBUTOR

Larry Ng, editor, *Alternative to Violence,* Time-Life, 1968.
Anti-Ballistic Missile: Yes or No?, Hill & Wang, for Center for the Study of Democratic Institutions, 1968.
Nigel Calder, editor, *Unless Peace Comes,* Viking, 1968.
Asian Dilemma: United States, Japan and China, Valley Publishing, for the Center for the Study of Democratic Institutions, 1969.

OTHER

Contributor to other symposia published by Center for the Study of Democratic Institutions and author of a number of the Center's "Occasional Papers." Contributor of over 200 articles to *American Historical Review, Comparative Politics, Saturday Review, Nation, Center Magazine, Astronautics and Aeronautics, Conflict Resolution, Reporter,* and other journals. Co-founder and chief editor, *Journal of Social and Biological Structures.*

WORK IN PROGRESS: Rise of the Elders, Romandala Process of Creative Writing, and *Constitutionalism.*

SIDELIGHTS: Harvey Wheeler wrote *CA:* "Since I was a kid I've been interested in model societies the way most kids are interested in model airplanes or race cars. World War II and the bomb gave me a presentiment of impending catastrophe; I studied political science out of both influences: to try to understand why everything went wrong and what might be done to make things better. . . . My fiction has been a spin-off from my academic work. When I thought I had run into something important that people in general ought to know about, I chose fiction as the medium for communicating that message. Some people go into politics; I went into novels."

MEDIA ADAPTATIONS: Fail-Safe was made into a movie by Columbia in 1964.

BIOGRAPHICAL/CRITICAL SOURCES:

PERIODICALS

Saturday Review, October 20, 1962.

*   *   *

WHITE, Phyllis Dorothy James   1920-
(P. D. James)

PERSONAL: Born August 3, 1920, in Oxford, England; daughter of Sidney Victor (a tax officer) and Dorothy May (Hone) James; married Ernest Conner Bantry White (a medical practitioner), August 8, 1941 (died, 1964); children: Claire, Jane. *Politics:* "I belong to no political party." *Religion:* Church of England.

ADDRESSES: Agent—Elaine Greene Ltd., 31 Newington Green, Islington, London N16 9PU, England.

CAREER: Former assistant state manager, Festival Theatre, Cambridge, England; worked as a Red Cross nurse and at the Ministry of Food during World War II; North West Regional Hospital Board, London, England, administrative assistant, 1949-68; Department of Home Affairs, London, civil servant, 1968-72, senior civil servant in crime department, 1972-79; full-time writer, 1979—.

MEMBER: Institute of Hospital Administration (fellow).

AWARDS, HONORS: Crime Writers Association prize, 1967.

WRITINGS—Under name P. D. James:

MYSTERY NOVELS

Cover Her Face, Faber, 1962, Scribner, 1966.
A Mind to Murder, Faber, 1963, Scribner, 1967.
Unnatural Causes, Scribner, 1967.
Shroud for a Nightingale, Scribner, 1971.
An Unsuitable Job for a Woman, Faber, 1972, Scribner, 1973.
The Black Tower, Scribner, 1975.
Death of an Expert Witness, Scribner, 1977.
Innocent Blood (Book of the Month Club selection), Scribner, 1980.
The Skull beneath the Skin, Scribner, 1982.

OMNIBUS VOLUMES

Crime Times Three, Scribner, 1979.
Murder in Triplicate, Scribner, 1982.
Trilogy of Death, Scribner, 1984.

Also author of *A Case of Classic Whodunits,* Warner Books.

CONTRIBUTOR

Ellery Queen's Murder Menu, World Publishing, 1969.
Winter's Crimes #5, Macmillan (London), 1973.
Ellery Queen's Masters of Mystery, Davis Publications, 1975.
Winter's Crimes #8, Macmillan (London), 1976.
Dilys Wynn, editor, *Murder Ink: The Mystery Reader's Companion,* Workman Publishing, 1977.
Crime Writers, BBC Publications, 1978.

OTHER

(With Thomas A. Critchley) *The Maul and the Pear Tree: The Ratcliffe Highway Murders, 1811,* Constable, 1971.
"A Private Treason," first produced on the West End at the Palace Theatre, March 12, 1985.

SIDELIGHTS: As P. D. James, a name she chose because it is short and sexually neutral, Phyllis Dorothy James White has established herself as one of England's most prominent mystery writers. Often ranked with such masters of the genre as Agatha Christie, Dorothy L. Sayers, and Margery Allingham, James is critically acclaimed for her ability to combine complex and puzzling plots with psychologically believable characters, particularly in her novels featuring Commander Adam Dalgleish of Scotland Yard. Her "keen, cunning mind and a positively bloody imagination" make her "one of the finest and most successful mystery writers in the world," Peter Gorner writes in the *Chicago Tribune*.

When her husband returned from World War II suffering from severe schizophrenia, James needed to support her family on her own. For nineteen years she worked as a hospital administrator and then, following her husband's death, entered the British Department of Home Affairs as a civil servant in the criminal department. Her work there brought her into daily contact with police officials, judges, and magistrates. In her mystery novels, James draws upon these experiences, setting her stories in such places as a police forensic laboratory, a nurses' training school, and a home for the disabled.

Although she had wanted to write for many years, James was not able to devote time to this pursuit until the late 1950s. At that time, while working in a hospital, she began her first novel, *Cover Her Face*. Over a three-year period James wrote for two hours every morning before going to work, composing her story in longhand on notepaper, a method she still prefers. Once completed, the novel was accepted by the first publisher to whom it was sent and James's career as a mystery writer was launched. Since then she has published seven more novels. She has been a full-time writer since her retirement from government service in 1979.

There is an old-fashioned quality to James's novels that puts them squarely in the tradition of classic English detective fiction as practiced by Agatha Christie and similar writers. The character of Adam Dalgleish, Scotland Yard detective and published poet, for example, follows the familiar pattern of the gentleman detective popularized by such earlier writers as Dorothy L. Sayers and Ngaio Marsh. James's plots are puzzles which, she tells Wayne Warga of the *Los Angeles Times,* follow the traditional formula. "You have a murder, which is a mystery," she explains. "There is a closed circle of suspects. . . . You have, in my case, a professional detective. He finds clues and information which, as he discovers them, are also available to the reader. And at the end of the story there is a credible and satisfactory resolution that the reader could have arrived at as well." James's style, too, writes Thomas Lask in the *New York Times,* "is what we think of as typically British. Her writing is ample, leisurely, and full of loving description of house and countryside." And in common with a number of other writers of mysteries, Norma Siebenheller states in her study *P. D. James,* James's "work is literate, tightly constructed, and civilized. Her people are genteel and polite."

Yet, while conforming to many of the expectations of the genre, James goes beyond its limitations. For instance, where other writers have concentrated almost entirely on the puzzles in their books to the detriment of such things as characterization, James has not. Although she creates a puzzle for her readers, she focuses her attention on writing realistic mysteries with fully-rounded characters. "The classic English mystery, as practiced by many of its female creators," Siebenheller explains, "is basically a puzzle-solving exercise. . . . One never gets over the feeling, when reading these books, that they are all make-believe. . . . James departs from that tradition. . . . The worlds she creates are peopled with varied and interesting characters whose actions spring from believable motivations and whose reactions are true to their complex personalities." As James tells Carla Heffner in the *Washington Post,* her frequent comparison to Agatha Christie "amazes me. . . . Hers are the stereotype English crime novel which is set in the small English village where everyone knows their place. . . . I don't set my novels in that never-never land."

James's concern for realism is reflected in her creation of Adam Dalgleish, a complex character who is, Siebenheller believes, "a far cry from the almost comical characters who served Christie and Sayers as sleuths." Dalgleish is an introspective, serious figure—intensely devoted to solving the case at hand—who suppresses his personal feelings. His personality was shaped by one tragic event many years before: the death of his wife and son during childbirth. It is this painful memory, and the essential chaos it implies, that has formed Dalgleish's "vision of the world," as Erlene Hubly states in *Clues: A Journal of Detection*. Because of this memory, Dalgleish is a "Byronic hero," Hubly argues, unable "to adjust to or accept society." Yet, because of his fear of chaos and death, he enforces the rules of society, convinced that they are all humanity has with which to create order. Dalgleish tries, writes Hubly, "to bring order out of chaos: if he cannot stop death he can at least catch and punish those who inflict it on others."

While Dalgleish is her most popular character, James's secondary characters are equally realistic. All of her books, Julian Symons notes in the *New York Times Book Review*, "are marked by powerful and sympathetic characterizations." Perhaps her most fully-realized character after Dalgleish is Cordelia Gray, a female private detective who appears in *An Unsuitable Job for a Woman* and *The Skull beneath the Skin*. As James relates in the first of these two novels, Gray was raised in a series of foster homes she found "very interesting." Despite her past misfortunes, Gray is "a totally positive person," Siebenheller relates. "Not only is she optimistic, capable, and clever, she is good-natured as well. . . . This is not to say Cordelia is a Pollyanna. She fully acknowledges the rougher edges of life." She and Dalgleish enjoy a cordial rivalry whenever they meet on a murder case.

Many of James's other characters are from the respectable English middle class—educated and humanistic, they find themselves "consumed by jealousy, hatred, lust, sexual fears, and ambition," Gorner states. James explores her characters' labyrinthine emotional and psychological states with a penetrating and compassionate eye. Heffner, for example, sees James as someone "passionately curious about people and their peculiarities." Lask believes that James's work, despite its veneer of traditional English fiction, "is modern in the ambiguous makeup of her characters, their complex motives and the shrewd psychological touches of the relationship between the police and the criminals they pursue."

Moved by a deep moral concern, James sees mystery writing as an important expression of basic human values. Mystery novels, she tells Heffner, "are like 20th-century morality plays; the values are basic and unambiguous. Murder is wrong. In an age in which gratuitous violence and arbitrary death have become common, these values need no apology." The "corrosive, destructive aspect of crime," Siebenheller maintains, is one of James's major themes. She traces the effects of crime not only on the victim and criminal, but on their family and friends as well. James's concern is obvious, too, in the values she gives her characters. Comparing Adam Dalgleish with James, Warga describes him as "a man who is a realistic moralist much like his creator."

The success of James's novels can be attributed to their popularity among two different audiences, Heffner argues, "the lovers of a good 'whodunit' who read her novels for their action and intricate plots; and the literary world that admires the books for their character and motivation." In the words of Christopher Lehmann-Haupt, this wide acceptance has made James "one of the most esteemed practitioners of the [mystery] genre in the English-speaking world."

BIOGRAPHICAL/CRITICAL SOURCES:

BOOKS

Contemporary Literary Criticism, Volume XVIII, Gale, 1981.
James, P. D., *An Unsuitable Job for a Woman*, Faber, 1972, Scribner, 1973.

Siebenheller, Norma, *P. D. James*, Ungar, 1981.
Wynn, Dilys, editor, *Murder Ink*, Workman Publishing, 1977.
Wynn, Dilys, editor, *Murderess Ink*, Workman Publishing, 1977.

PERIODICALS

Atlantic, June, 1980.
Chicago Tribune, June 10, 1980.
Chicago Tribune Book World, May 18, 1980, September 19, 1982.
Christian Science Monitor, June 25, 1980.
Clues: A Journal of Detection, fall/winter, 1982, spring/summer, 1985.
Listener, June 5, 1975.
Los Angeles Times, June 6, 1980.
Los Angeles Times Book Review, June 22, 1980.
Maclean's, June 30, 1980.
Ms., April, 1974, August, 1979.
New Republic, July 31, 1976, November 26, 1977.
Newsweek, January 23, 1978, May 12, 1980, September 13, 1982.
New Yorker, March 11, 1976, March 6, 1978, June 23, 1980.
New York Review of Books, July 17, 1980.
New York Times, December 11, 1977, July 18, 1979, February 8, 1980, May 7, 1980.
New York Times Book Review, July 24, 1966, January 16, 1972, April 22, 1973, November 23, 1975, April 27, 1980, September 12, 1982.
Publishers Weekly, January 5, 1976.
Spectator, December 23, 1972, June 12, 1976.
Time, April 17, 1978, May 26, 1980.
Times (London), March 27, 1980, May 14, 1982, March 9, 1985, March 22, 1985.
Times Literary Supplement, October 22, 1971, December 13, 1974, March 21, 1980, October 29, 1982.
Village Voice, December 15, 1975, December 18, 1978.
Voice Literary Supplement, October, 1982.
Washington Post, April 30, 1980.
Washington Post Book World, April 15, 1977, April 27, 1980, September 19, 1982.

                            —Sketch by Thomas Wiloch

*   *   *

WILHELM, Kate
See WILHELM, Katie Gertrude

*   *   *

WILHELM, Katie Gertrude   1928-
(Kate Wilhelm)

PERSONAL: Born June 8, 1928, in Toledo, Ohio; daughter of Jesse Thomas and Ann (McDowell) Meredith; married Joseph B. Wilhelm, May 24, 1947 (divorced, 1962); married Damon Knight (a writer and editor), February 23, 1963; children: (first marriage) Douglas, Richard; (second marriage) Jonathan. *Education:* Attended high school in Louisville, Ky.

ADDRESSES: Home—1645 Horn Lane, Eugene, Ore. 97404. *Agent*—Brandt & Brandt, 101 Park Ave., New York, N.Y. 10017.

CAREER: Employed as a model, telephone operator, sales clerk, switchboard operator, and insurance company underwriter; full-time writer, 1956—. Co-director, Milford Science

Fiction Writers Conference, 1963-76; lecturer at Clarion Fantasy Workshop, Michigan State University, beginning 1968.

MEMBER: Science Fiction Writers of America, Authors Guild, Authors League of America, P.E.N.

AWARDS, HONORS: Nebula Award of Science Fiction Writers of America, 1968, for best short story, "The Planners"; Hugo Award of World Science Fiction Convention, 1977, Jupiter Award, 1977, and second place for the John W. Campbell Memorial Award, 1977, all for *Where Late the Sweet Birds Sang;* American Book Award nomination, 1980, for *Juniper Time: A Novel.*

WRITINGS—Under name Kate Wilhelm:

More Bitter Than Death, Simon & Schuster, 1962.
The Mile-Long Spaceship (short stories), Berkley Publishing, 1963 (published in England as *Andover and the Android,* Dobson, 1966).
(With Theodore L. Thomas) *The Clone,* Berkley, 1965.
The Nevermore Affair, Doubleday, 1966.
The Killer Thing, Doubleday, 1967 (published in England as *The Killing Thing,* Jenkins, 1967).
The Downstairs Room, and Other Speculative Fiction (short stories), Doubleday, 1968.
Let the Fire Fall, Doubleday, 1969.
(With Thomas) *The Year of the Cloud,* Doubleday, 1970.
Abyss: Two Novellas, Doubleday, 1971.
Margaret and I, Little, Brown, 1971.
City of Cain, Little, Brown, 1973.
(Editor) *Nebula Award Stories,* Number 9, Gollancz, 1974, Harper, 1975.
The Clewiston Test, Farrar, Straus, 1976.
Where Late the Sweet Birds Sang, Harper, 1976.
The Infinity Box: A Collection of Speculative Fiction (short stories), Harper, 1976.
Fault Lines: A Novel, Harper, 1976.
(Editor) *Clarion SF,* Berkley Publishing, 1976.
Somerset Dreams and Other Fictions, Harper, 1978.
"Axoltl" (multimedia science fantasy), first produced in Eugene, Ore., at University of Oregon Art Museum, April 6, 1979.
Juniper Time: A Novel, Harper, 1979.
(With husband, Damon Knight) *Better Than One,* New England Science Fiction Association, 1980.
A Sense of Shadow, Houghton, 1981.
Listen, Listen, Houghton, 1981.
Oh, Susannah!: A Novel, Houghton, 1982.
Welcome Chaos, Houghton, 1983.
"The Hindenberg Effect" (radio play), first broadcast by KSOR (Ashland, Ore.), 1985.

CONTRIBUTOR

Samuel R. Delany and Marilyn Hacker, editors, *Quark No. 3,* Popular Library, 1971.
Harlan Ellison, editor, *Again, Dangerous Visions: 46 Original Stories,* Doubleday, 1972.
Thomas M. Disch, editor, *Bad Moon Rising: An Anthology of Political Foreboding,* Harper, 1973.
Knight, editor, *A Shocking Thing,* Pocket Books, 1974.
Roger Elwood and Robert Silverberg, editors, *Epoch,* Berkley Publishing, 1975.
Femmes au futur: Anthologie de nouvelles de science-fiction feminine (short stories), Marabout, 1976.

CONTRIBUTOR TO "ORBIT" ANTHOLOGY SERIES; EDITED BY KNIGHT

Orbit 1, Putnam, 1966.
Orbit 2, Putnam, 1967.
Orbit 3, Putnam, 1968.
Orbit 4, Putnam, 1968.
Orbit 5, Putnam, 1969.
Orbit 6, Putnam, 1970.
Orbit 7, Putnam, 1970.
Orbit 8, Putnam, 1970.
Orbit 9, Putnam, 1971.
Orbit 10, Putnam, 1972.
Orbit 11, Putnam, 1972.
Orbit 12, Putnam, 1973.
Orbit 13, Putnam, 1974.
Orbit 14, Harper, 1974.
Orbit 15, Harper, 1974.
Orbit 18, Harper, 1976.
Orbit 19, Harper, 1977.
Orbit 20, Harper, 1978.

OTHER

Contributor to periodicals, including *Fantastic, Future, Magazine of Fantasy and Science Fiction, Amazing, Cosmopolitan,* and *Strange Fantasy.*

SIDELIGHTS: A versatile author praised for the psychic reality in her fiction, Katie Gertrude Wilhelm—better known as Kate Wilhelm—has been called a "serene and powerful talent" by Michael Bishop in the *Magazine of Fantasy and Science Fiction.* Wilhelm feels strongly about the political and social forces shaping the modern world and examines them in her novels, writing about such issues as women's roles in society and the threat of environmental collapse. Commenting on the combination of her writing goals and social concerns in a letter to *CA,* Wilhelm writes: "If I could sum up my philosophies and compulsions in a few paragraphs, there would be no need to write books, and there is a need. I believe we are living in an age of cataclysmic changes; we are living in an age that is the end of an era. My work is my attempt to understand how we got here, why we stay, and what lies ahead if anything does."

Wilhelm's Hugo and Jupiter award-winning novel, *Where Late the Sweet Birds Sang,* explores cloning and its consequences for humanity. In this book, the Sumner family survives a nuclear disaster on earth. With scientific equipment, they produce clones intended to eventually breed in a natural way. But the clones, born with telepathic powers, believe they are superior and plot to transform the earth into a clone utopia. Human individuality eventually triumphs; the clones are too dependent on each other to take chances necessary for survival, and in the end, a human escapes the colony to form a new society.

New York Times Book Review contributor Gerald Jonas praises Wilhelm for her technique in this novel. While noting that "at times, her prose strains for 'poetic effects,'" he maintains that for the most part, her writing is powerful and effective: "Her cautionary message comes through loud and clear: giving up our humanity to save our skins is a bad bargain no matter how you look at it." Anne Hudson Jones adds in the *Dictionary of Literary Biography* that the novel "offers a poignant reminder that human strengths and weaknesses are inextricably bound together. It also serves as a timely warning that altering human reproduction may alter the species itself."

Wilhelm focuses on the issues of environmental disaster and alien contact in *Juniper Time*. During a prolonged drought in the United States, an alien message is discovered in space that many believe will contain information to end the drought. Jean Brighton, a young linguist, is the only one capable of decoding it. But instead of relying on the cryptic sign, Jean turns to members of an American Indian tribe who show her how to survive by utilizing the environment carefully. In another *New York Times Book Review* article, Jonas says Wilhelm draws a parallel between *Juniper Time*'s plot and similar events in history where contact between cultures totally ignorant of each other has caused the decimation of one of them. ''As Montezuma and the Incas learned,'' he observes, ''gods in machines can kill as well as succor. If this fine novel has a moral, it is a cautionary one, not often found in science fiction: Choose your myths with care; the culture you save may be your own.''

Wilhelm writes this novel in a style that is muted and evocative, notes Bishop, who claims that many science fiction novels are written with ''clumsy prose, threadbare plotting, comic-book characterization, . . . and out-and-out dumbness in the service of high and honorable ideals.'' But strong characterization and plot are Wilhelm's tools, according to Bishop. He believes that *Juniper Time* is written by ''completely overstepping the most tenacious and annoying bugaboos of [the science fiction] genre.''

In *The Clewiston Test* Wilhelm departs from conventional science fiction to explore a woman's alienation from her husband. Anne Clewiston Symons is a brilliant scientist, married to a scientist of lesser ability who underestimates her personally as well as professionally. Anne has isolated a serum in blood that stifles all pain but also causes personality disorders in test chimpanzees, who become violent and then withdrawn. After Anne is in a car accident, she begins to withdraw emotionally from her husband, Clark. Suspecting that she has taken the serum, Clark takes over her research in the lab. As tensions in their relationship mount, it is unclear whether Anne's problems are caused by her marriage or by taking the serum. Anne eventually leaves her husband in order to feel complete as a person.

Several critics praise *The Clewiston Test* for its powerful theme and strong technique. Jones calls the book a ''compelling feminist'' novel, and Christopher Lehmann-Haupt commends Wilhelm's portrayal of the sexual dynamics of a relationship, observing in the *New York Times* that ''whatever is bothering Anne serves as a nice little litmus test for the chauvinism of the male ego.'' In the *New York Times Book Review*, Jerome Charyn points out that Wilhelm's craftsmanship in this piece of mainstream fiction is as solid as that of her science-fiction works. ''Written in a style that never calls attention to itself,'' Charyn continues, '' 'The Clewiston Test' is a horror story that avoids the usual trappings of its genre. Kate Wilhelm isn't interested in futuristic nightmares.''

In discussing the variety in Wilhelm's writing, Jones concludes that ''whatever the external settings of [Wilhelm's] works, the psychic landscapes in them are very real.'' Furthermore, she states, ''the body of Wilhelm's fiction shows a steady progression in technical control and thematic complexity, and her reputation as a writer has risen with each new work. . . . As Wilhelm continues to develop, her readers have much to look forward to in the future.''

CA INTERVIEW

CA interviewed Kate Wilhelm by telephone on January 7, 1985, at her home in Eugene, Oregon.

CA: You were married and had two children before you began to write fiction. Was writing a long-time ambition?

WILHELM: Not really. I had written in high school, as most of us do. Then I got married right out of high school and didn't really do much of anything. After a few years went by, when my younger child was about two, I started to write. I read an anthology, actually, and some of the stories were so incredibly bad, I thought, gee, I could do that. And I could— I could write bad stories, like anyone else!

CA: In the introduction to The Infinity Box *you wrote about your wide-ranging reading tastes as a youngster. When you started writing, what attracted you heavily to science fiction?*

WILHELM: There were two things. One was that I was just intrigued by the use of philosophical ideas in fiction. That struck me as something I had never considered, and I had read a lot of philosophy. So I was really attracted to that. The other was that all of my life I had ideas that didn't seem to fit into the scheme of reality of most people. I thought, well, here's a place where they wouldn't look at me as if I had gone suddenly stark raving mad.

CA: Since your first novel was published in 1962, you've managed to average roughly a book a year, including novels and collections of shorter fiction. What kind of writing schedule do you work on?

WILHELM: It has varied a whole lot over the years. When my children were small, I worked exclusively at nighttime— but I worked almost every night. Then after they were all up in school and out of the house through the day, I went to a daytime schedule, and I worked every day from roughly ten or eleven in the morning until two or three in the afternoon. I have found over the last few years—now the children are all pretty much grown—that I've gone back to the night schedule, and this time out of preference. It suits me fine, and most of the time, while I'm actively writing on something, I work almost every night. I'll start at nine or ten and work until maybe two in the morning.

CA: Do you do a lot of revising?

WILHELM: Not a lot, no. I hate rewriting. I'm such a terrible typist, and I early on thought, if I have to retype everything ten times, I just won't do it. So I try not to put anything on paper until I'm fairly certain that it's what I want. I do a lot of revising mentally.

CA: Your husband, Damon Knight, is known for his award-winning criticism in the field of science fiction, among other accomplishments. Is he also your first critic?

WILHELM: Yes. In fact, we're both each other's first and best critics, I think. We don't show each other unfinished work, but as soon as it's finished in any kind of form that can be read, each of us reads the other's work.

CA: That sounds like a very nice arrangement.

WILHELM: It's very nice in many ways. For one thing, we can trust each other. Neither of us will soft-soap criticism for the other, and we know that. And we've both had a lot of training now as critics and as teachers, so I think we give each other pretty honest evaluations. On the other hand, we're both each other's best fans. And that's really good.

CA : Are you doing any teaching or lecturing now?

WILHELM: I do workshops. I've been associated with the Clarion Workshop at Michigan State for eighteen years now, and I do local workshops now and again.

CA: How do you find you're able to help people most in workshop situations?

WILHELM: Well, of course we can't give people ideas or inspiration, and we tell them that right up front. But if they have the ideas, and if they have the desire and the will, we can tell them a lot of technical things. There is a lot to be learned about technical things, and these things can be taught. Whether the student can *apply* them is something else, but they can be taught.

CA: Do you find that workshops tend to get aspiring writers really writing?

WILHELM: Generally the kinds of workshops I do are for people who really want to write and have been doing some writing. They need direction; they need to know why their stories aren't working. I have never taken a class of just average students who need the credit, for example. Our students all come out of the workshop writing furiously. Most of them from Clarion—at least half of them, and we think it's probably higher, maybe sixty percent—end up as professional writers. I don't think any other workshop has anything like that kind of success ratio.

CA: Actual scientific elements sometimes play an important part in your fiction. Do you have some background in the sciences, or do you do specific research for whatever you need at a given time?

WILHELM: I don't have the background, the education, but I've always liked to read science. It works both ways. I read science books or magazines or whatever and something lodges in my mind. Then maybe years later when I'm writing something, I'll remember that I read something about the scientific aspect of it, and I can go and research it. So it seeds both ways. I think it's a feedback mechanism at work there. I can't wait until I need the specific scientific idea; I have to have something working that I need to know more about. But if I didn't know a little about it to begin with, I doubt that it would work.

CA: How did your collaborations with Theodore L. Thomas come about?

WILHELM: The first one was very strange. He is a patent attorney, and he was a good friend of ours for many years. He had written a very short story that had absolutely no human character in it, about this organic compound that begins to multiply. It was a delightful story, and people kept asking him to please expand it and make a novel. However, he was very busy. We saw him one summer and I asked him if he was ever going to have time to work on the story, and he said, "Why don't you collaborate on it with me?" and we did it. We had a lot of fun doing it; we really enjoyed it. The second one wasn't so successful.

CA: You have described the process by which, for you, a scrap of an idea or a bit of information evolves slowly, sometimes subconsciously, into fiction. Do you usually know early in the writing whether an idea is going to become a novel or a shorter piece?

WILHELM: I know fairly early. I think all creation is a mysterious process, but there are signals that I imagine I am receiving, and I know fairly early. And I can pretty much predict the length. I know if it's a 70,000-word novel or a 100,000-word one; I know if it's a 5000-word story or 12,000. I'm pretty good at predicting exactly the length.

CA: Do you prefer one length to another, as far as the actual writing goes?

WILHELM: No. When I'm doing a lot of short fiction, I think that is the only form; and when I'm doing a novel, I wonder why I bother with the short stuff.

CA: Many of your works have strongly developed female characters, and some have themes or elements that might be called feminist. Do you consider yourself a feminist?

WILHELM: I don't see how I can *not*. I do observe my world pretty closely, and I don't see how any thinking woman can not be a feminist. I know many who aren't, and I don't understand it.

CA: You won both the Hugo and Jupiter awards for Where Late the Sweet Birds Sang *(1976), and it is surely one of your most popular books. Does it express your own concerns for our society?*

WILHELM: Absolutely. I think we are on a disaster course. It's hard to predict in what area the disaster might take place, there are so many that are threatening—not just the nuclear war, which is the primary one, but there's also such disparity between wealth and poverty. I think this leads to disastrous conditions. The whole attitude that was expressed some years ago that "if it's good for General Motors, it's good for the country" is not being expressed just that way today, but it's being lived: if it's good for industry, it's good for everybody. This led to the tragedy in Bhopal, where thousands of people died as a result of that attitude. And that kind of disaster is in the making in numerous places on earth, from industry that has not been regulated, that has not been overseen, that just goes its own way. Then there's the resource depletion. Now people are talking about the end of fresh-water supplies in so many places. I wrote a story about that in '69 or '70; it isn't something that developed last Tuesday. The depletion of resources, overpopulation, the great spread between the very wealthy and the very poor, within countries and worldwide, within cities, within small communities—any one of these could lead to an explosive situation. And of course, foremost is the real threat of nuclear war.

CA: Are you actively involved in working against nuclear weapons?

WILHELM: No, and I sometimes feel very guilty because I'm not. But some years ago I had to make a choice. I was fairly involved during the Vietnam War. One does have to make a choice: are you going to do this, or are you going to do what you're doing, which may be important in its own right. It's a toss-up. Sometimes I feel guilty; I feel I should be out there doing that. And then I think, no, I should be writing about my fears. It's hard to know.

CA: And it's hard to do both things well.

WILHELM: I couldn't. When I was active against the Vietnam War, that's all I did.

CA: Your concern about the disparity between rich and poor was important in Juniper Time *(1979), in which the poor lived in their squalid Newtowns. That was a frightening projection of what really might happen with a larger poor population.*

WILHELM: I've read quite a bit of history, and so often this is the last step before tremendous internal conflicts, where this spread between rich and poor is so wide and the people at the bottom are filled with so much resentment or apathy—one or the other, and either one can be very dangerous. I think it's criminal, personally, to have that kind of spread when it's the earth that's providing the resources that provide the wealth. I feel very strongly that the earth does not belong to GM or DuPont.

CA: What about the clone society in Where Late the Sweet Birds Sang? *Do you feel we have something of a clone society already, or is it merely a threat at this point?*

WILHELM: I think it's encroaching. This whole tendency toward what is called normalization, standardization—all of this to fit people into their little economic groups or their geographic groups or geopolitical groups or whatever—is very much a part of modern society.

CA: Are the fanzines as important today as they were in the earlier days of science fiction?

WILHELM: I don't really know much about them, because I never did anything with them. I didn't enter science fiction through fandom. I knew nothing about fanzines until I'd been writing for a number of years, and they've never been very important to me personally. So I pay very little attention to them. Some come through the house, and sometimes I look at them and sometimes I don't.

CA: Not all of your work is science fiction, yet you are largely thought of as a science fiction writer—that kind of labeling of work that you have written and spoken out against. Do you think it has limited your readership in any way?

WILHELM: I think definitely it has. I think that's almost the kiss of death for acceptance with a lot of people. I've been very vocal about the whole thing of labeling; I don't like being labeled anything—just a writer. I would live with that very happily.

CA: Do you think anything can be done to change that? Could publishers find a better way to promote the work of their writers?

WILHELM: No, I think this is established, and I think it's going to stay. And the categorization, in fact, is increasing. Now you're a science fiction writer of fantasy or heroic fantasy or what-not, but it's all under science fiction. They like to keep people in their little slots because it makes marketing easier. I don't think that will change. It's going to get worse.

CA: It certainly shows up in the libraries, as you have pointed out.

WILHELM: Yes. It wasn't like that when I was a teenager. I just browsed those aisles so happily, being surprised again and again. That was much nicer.

CA: You did the script for "Axolotl," a multimedia science fantasy produced at the University of Oregon Art Museum in 1979. Are there are other plays, or movie or television scripts, in the works?

WILHELM: I have done a radio play that hasn't been produced yet. It's for local public radio, and I think they ran into funding problems. Someday it's going to be produced, I hope.

CA: What would you like to try that you haven't done?

WILHELM: I haven't thought of that! I did a comic novel in 1982, *Oh, Susannah!* I had never done a comic novel before, and that was fun. If I think of something I haven't done that really intrigues me, I'll just go ahead and do it. It may be a dismal flop, of course—you never know. But sometimes it can be very intriguing just to think of doing something you've never tried.

CA: Especially after you've become established—if any writer can ever feel really established. A flop wouldn't be so devastating then as it would be early in one's career.

WILHELM: That's true. If you've had any success at all, you can gamble more—although every piece of writing is a gamble.

CA: Is there any advice you'd give to people who want to write, who are struggling to get started?

WILHELM: Yes. In fact, I am asked this often, and I've really given it a lot of thought. I used to address it mostly to women, but now I think it's for men and women, maybe with a little emphasis on women. You have to be really fierce about your time. A new writer has so many pressures—we all do, of course, but a new writer feels them so much more desperately—to produce something that will make money, to show immediate gain or predictable gain. With writing, with any art form, you can't do that. People must just realize that they have to guard their time so jealously, to set aside the time that they are going to devote to writing and not let the world have it. It is very hard, because the people you love and the people who love you are the ones who want your time; those are the hardest ones on earth to say no to, and you have to.

BIOGRAPHICAL/CRITICAL SOURCES:

BOOKS

Contemporary Literary Criticism, Volume VII, Gale, 1977.
Dictionary of Literary Biography, Volume VIII: *Twentieth-Century American Science Fiction Writers*, Gale, 1981.
Platt, Charles, *Dream Makers: The Uncommon People Who Write Science Fiction*, Volume I, Berkley Publishing, 1980.

PERIODICALS

Los Angeles Times, May 8, 1981, November 15, 1983.
Los Angeles Times Book Review, December 19, 1982.
Magazine of Fantasy and Science Fiction, November, 1971, April, 1979, January, 1980.
Newsweek, November 29, 1971, February 9, 1976.

New York Times, May 13, 1976.
New York Times Book Review, March 10, 1974, January 18, 1976, February 22, 1976, August 26, 1979.
Psychology Today, October, 1975.
Saturday Review, April 30, 1977.
Washington Post, September 21, 1982.

—Sketch by Nancy E. Rampson
—Interview by Jean W. Ross

*   *   *

WILKES, Glenn Newton   1928-

PERSONAL: Born November 28, 1928, in Mansfield, Ga.; son of Homer Thomas and Frances (Blasingame) Wilkes; married, 1957; wife's name Jan; children: Glenn, Scott, Tom, Robert, Angela. *Education:* Mercer University, A.B., 1950; Peabody College, M.A., 1956, Ed.D., 1965. *Religion:* Baptist.

ADDRESSES: Office—Stetson University, DeLand, Fla. 32720.

CAREER: Brewton-Parker College, Mt. Vernon, Ga., coach, 1950-51; Baker County High School, Newton, Ga., coach, 1953; Brewton-Parker College, coach, 1953-57; Stetson University, DeLand, Fla., coach, 1957—. *Military service:* U.S. Army, 1951-53; became sergeant.

MEMBER: National Association of Basketball Coaches, Florida Association for Health and Physical Education.

WRITINGS:

Winning Basketball Strategy, Prentice-Hall, 1959.
Basketball Coach's Complete Handbook, Prentice-Hall, 1962.
Men's Basketball, W. C. Brown, 1969, 3rd edition published as *Basketball for Men,* 1977, 4th edition published as *Basketball,* 1982, 5th edition, 1984.
Fundamentals of Coaching Basketball, W. C. Brown, 1982.

*   *   *

WILKINSON, Rosemary C(halloner)   1924-

PERSONAL: Born February 21, 1924, in New Orleans, La.; daughter of William Lindsay (in wholesale jewelry materials) and Julia (Sellen) Challoner; married Henry Bertram Wilkinson, 1949; children: Denis, Marian, Paul, Richard. *Education:* Attended College of San Mateo, 1964-66; University of Minnesota, student by correspondence, 1967; attended Canada College for training in television communications. *Politics:* Democrat. *Religion:* Catholic.

ADDRESSES: Home—1239 Bernal Ave., Burlingame, Calif. 94010.

CAREER: Bookkeeper at hospitals in Lafayette and New Albany, Ind., 1939-44; St. James Hospital, Chicago Heights, Ill., administrative supervisor, 1944-47; St. Joseph Hospital, Phoenix, Ariz., administrative supervisor, 1947-48; West Disinfecting Co., San Francisco, Calif., bookkeeper, 1948-51; Peninsula Hospital, Burlingame, Calif., billing officer, 1961-62; full-time writer, 1964—. Advisor to Third World Congress of Poets, 1976, member of board, Fourth World Congress of Poets, and chairman of organizing committee and president, Fifth World Congress of Poets, 1981. Vice-president, Poetry in Media, charter 1981; founder, San Mateo County Fair Poetry Competition. Coordinator of California's second chapter of Hospital Audiences, Inc., 1972. Has given poetry readings to schools and hospitals and has been interviewed on radio and television about poetry.

MEMBER: International Academy of Poets (England; co-founder, 1977), World Academy of Arts and Culture (Republic of China; vice-president and member of board of trustees), World Poetry Society Intercontinental (India; vice-president, 1983), Soroptomist International, International Order of Volunteers for Peace (Italy), International League of Contemporary Bards (Australia), Accademia Internationale Leonardo da Vinci (Italy), Accademia Internazionale di Lettere, Scienze, Arti (Italy), International Union of Women Writers (Belgium), Union International de Escritoras (Mexico), Academie Universelle de Lausanne (Switzerland), Research into Lost Knowledge Organization (England), Authors Guild, Authors League of America, National League of American Pen Women (fifth vice-president, 1984-86), National Federation of State Poetry Societies-Federal Poets, Poetry Society of England, Cinque Ports Poets Society (England), St. David's Society of the State of New York (Wales), Consejo Comunero-Burgos (Spain), American-Romanian Academy of Arts and Letters, Tagore Institute of Creative Writing (India), Cosmosynthesis League (Australia), California Federation of Chaparral Poets (president of Toyon chapter, 1973-74), Ina Coolbrith Circle (San Francisco; member of board), New York Poetry Forum (life membership), and numerous civic organizations.

AWARDS, HONORS: Plaque and medal, Second World Congress of Poets (Republic of China), 1973; Certificate of Merit from American Poets Fellowship Society, Charleston, Ill., 1973; named International Woman of 1975 with laureate honors (Philippines); Knight Grand Dame of Merit (Grace), Knights of Malta, Europe, 1981. Honorary diplomas from Universita Delle Arti, Accademia Internationale Leonardo da Vinci, and Accademia Internazionale di Lettere, Scienze, Arti, all in Italy; honorable special mention for an essay on Waka/Tanka, Poetry Society of Japan; California Teaching Credential in Poetry for life, San Francisco State University, 1978; honorary doctorates from Libre University (Pakistan), 1975, and World Academy of Arts and Culture (Republic of China), 1982.

WRITINGS:

POETRY

A Girl's Will, Prairie Press, 1973.
An Historical Epic, New Literature (Republic of China), 1975.
California Poet, Burlingame Press, 1976.
Earth's Compromise, Burlingame Press, 1977.
It Happened to Me, Burlingame Press, 1978.
I Am Earth Woman, Burlingame Press, 1979.
The Poet and the Painter, Burlingame Press, 1981.
Poetry and Arte, Farris Press, 1982.
Gems Within, Farris Press, 1984.
Nature's Guest, Farris Press, 1984.
In the Pines, Sayeeda-India, 1985.

Also author of *Epic of the Ship's Captain/Artist* (biographical poem), 1978, and *Poet: Uplift Mankind* (autobiographical poem).

Contributor to numerous poetry anthologies, including *Toyon Poems, Anthology of New American Verse, Poetic Village,* and *Crow's Nest* (all in the United States), *The Album of International Poets* (India), *Anthology of World Brotherhood and Peace* (Philippines), 1982, and *World Poetry* (Korea), 1983.

OTHER

Author of music and lyrics to songs "Alabama March of 1965," "200 Years U.S.A.," "Something's Happening," and "Birthday Sonnet to Dr. Yuzon." Contributor of articles, poems and reviews to numerous periodicals, including *Transnational Perspectives* (Switzerland), *Pen Woman Magazine,* and *New Hye Armenian Weekly* (Spain).

WORK IN PROGRESS: Poetry books *Sacred in Nature, Earth's Children, New Seed, Poet: Purify the Earth,* and *Poems from Welsh Ancestors and Me.*

SIDELIGHTS: Rosemary C. Wilkinson writes: "I wrote my first poem at age fourteen and my second at age forty, when President Kennedy was shot. From then on I could not stop the poetry from erupting. I study from seven in the morning until noon, writing three of those hours. My poems just come at any time, but I work at my prose. I have had the first epic published in the Republic of China, about World War II here in the United States. The epic-biography of the artist/ship's captain is the life of an unknown nineteenth-century painter, and the third epic is my own autobiography, having served as a hospital administrator, a mother of four, and a writer and internationally known poet since 1963.

"I read the classical poets and teach classical forms. I would like to see more historical documentaries on television, for they enhance our culture. Poetry is my soul's sustenance. The work of the poet serves to uplift all mankind."

Rosemary Wilkinson's work has been translated into seventeen foreign languages, including Chinese, Korean, Romanian, Armenian, Hindi, Russian, Sanskrit, Greek, German, and French. She has traced her ancestry to an ancient Welsh tribe of poets and clerics. As president of the Fifth World Congress of Poets, she gathered representatives of forty-two nations for meetings in San Francisco, California.

*   *   *

WILLIAMS, Barbara   1925-

PERSONAL: Born January 1, 1925, in Salt Lake City, Utah; daughter of Walter (a lawyer) and Emily (Jeremy) Wright; married J. D. Williams (a professor of political science), July 5, 1946; children: Kirk, Gil, Taylor, Kimberly. *Education:* Attended Banff School of Fine Arts, 1945; University of Utah, B.A., 1946, M.A., 1972; Boston University, additional study, 1949-50. *Politics:* Democrat.

ADDRESSES: Home—3399 East Loren Von Dr., Salt Lake City, Utah 84124. *Agent*—Amy Berkower, Writers House, 21 West 26th St., New York, N.Y. 10010.

CAREER: Deseret News, Salt Lake City, Utah, occasional society reporter and columnist, 1944-50; Library of Congress, Washington, D.C., secretary, 1946-48, 1951; University of Utah, Salt Lake City, remedial English teacher, 1960-71; teacher of classes in writing for children and teenagers, 1974—.

MEMBER: Authors Guild, Authors League of America, Mortar Board, Phi Beta Kappa, Phi Kappa Phi.

AWARDS, HONORS: First place winner in Utah Fine Arts Writing Contest, 1965, for *William H. McGuffey: Boy Reading Genius,* 1971, for *The Secret Name,* 1975, for *Desert Hunter and Other Stories,* and 1978, for *Where Are You, Angela von Hauptmann, Now That I Need You?; Albert's Toothache* was a Children's Book Showcase title, 1975, was listed as one of American Institute of Graphic Arts 50 Books of the Year, and was selected by American Library Association as a Notable Book; awarded bronze medallion from the Christophers, 1979, for *Chester Chipmunk's Thanksgiving.*

WRITINGS:

JUVENILES

Let's Go to an Indian Cliff Dwelling, Putnam, 1965.
I Know a Policeman, Putnam, 1966.
I Know a Fireman, Putnam, 1967.
I Know a Mayor, Putnam, 1967.
I Know a Garageman, Putnam, 1968.
William H. McGuffey: Boy Reading Genius, Bobbs-Merrill, 1968.
I Know a Bank Teller, Putnam, 1968.
Boston: Seat of American History, McGraw, 1969.
I Know a Weatherman, Putnam, 1970.
The Secret Name, Harcourt, 1972.
Gary and the Very Terrible Monster, Children's Press, 1973.
We Can Jump, Children's Press, 1973.
Albert's Toothache (Junior Literary Guild selection), Dutton, 1974.
Kevin's Grandma, Dutton, 1975.
Desert Hunter and Other Stories, Harvey House, 1975.
Someday, Said Mitchell (Junior Literary Guild selection), Dutton, 1976.
Cornzapoppin'! (Junior Literary Guild selection), Holt, 1976.
If He's My Brother, Harvey House, 1976.
Never Hit a Porcupine, Dutton, 1977.
Pins, Picks and Popsicle Sticks, Holt, 1977.
Seven True Elephant Stories, Hastings House, 1978.
Chester Chipmunk's Thanksgiving, Dutton, 1978.
Guess Who's Coming to My Tea Party, Holt, 1978.
Brigham Young and Me, Clarissa, Doubleday, 1978.
I Know a Salesperson, Putnam, 1978.
Jeremy Isn't Hungry (Junior Literary Guild selection), Dutton, 1978.
Whatever Happened to Beverly Bigler's Birthday?, Harcourt, 1978.
Hello, Dandelions!, Holt, 1979.
Breakthrough: Women in Politics, Walker & Co., 1979.
Where Are You, Angela von Hauptmann, Now That I Need You?, Holt, 1979.
A Valentine for Cousin Archie, Dutton, 1980.
So What If I'm a Sore Loser?, Harcourt, 1981.
Tell the Truth, Marly Dee, Dutton, 1982.
Mitzi and the Terrible Tyrannosaurus Rex (My Weekly Reader Book Club selection), Dutton, 1982.
Mitzi's Honeymoon with Nana Potts, Dutton, 1983.

Also author of *Mitzi and Frederick the Great.*

PLAYS

Eternally Peggy (three-act), Deseret News Press, 1957.
The Ghost of Black Jack (one-act), Samuel French, 1961.
Just the Two of Us (one-act), Utah Printing, 1965.

OTHER

Twelve Steps to Better Exposition (textbook), C. E. Merrill, 1968.
The Well-Structured Paragraph (textbook), C. E. Merrill, 1970.
Twenty-Six Lively Letters (adult book), Taplinger, 1977.

Also author of *Cookie Craft,* Holt. Children's book reviewer, *Marriage,* 1974-76.

WORK IN PROGRESS: A novel for children in the middle grades.

SIDELIGHTS: Barbara Williams told *CA:* "As I look back upon it, I feel sure I must have turned to pencils and typewriters in self-defense. The only non-athlete in the neighborhood (I failed courses in beginning swimming seven times, among other things), no captain ever chose me for his team; and I had to find something to do while all the other kids were playing football and baseball. As a result, I spent a good part of my childhood living in the realm of my imagination and setting down my ideas on an antique typewriter which I attacked with one finger.

"Like many other writers for children, I didn't turn to this genre until I had children of my own to read to and realized how interesting and how satisfying children's books could be. Although my college textbooks (which I wrote while I was teaching at the University of Utah) earn far more money than my children's books do, no reader of one of those books has ever sent me a 'thank you' letter. Children are the most appreciative readers in the world!"

BIOGRAPHICAL/CRITICAL SOURCES:

PERIODICALS

Language Arts, April, 1983.
Mountain West, December, 1979.
New York Times, February 17, 1980.
New York Times Book Review, May 4, 1975, February 24, 1980.

*   *   *

WILLIAMS, Denis (Joseph Ivan) 1923-

PERSONAL: Born February 1, 1923, in Georgetown, Guyana; son of Joseph Alexander (a merchant) and Isabel (Adonis) Williams; married Catherine Hughes, 1949 (divorced, 1974); married Toni Dixon (a poultry farmer), August 21, 1975; children (first marriage) Janice, Evelyn, Isabel, Charlotte, Beatrice; (second marriage) Miles, Morag, Everard, Rachael, Denis. *Education:* Attended Camberwell School of Art, 1946-48; University of Guyana, M.A., 1979. *Politics:* None. *Religion:* Christian.

ADDRESSES: Home—18-D Thorn's Dr., D'Urban Backlands, Botanic Gardens, Georgetown, Guyana. *Office*—Department of Culture, Ministry of Education, 15 Carifesta Ave., Georgetown, Guyana. *Agent*—John Wolfers, 42 Russel Sq., London W.C. 1, England.

CAREER: Central School of Art, London, England, lecturer in art, 1950-57; Khartoum School of Art, Khartoum, Sudan, lecturer in art, 1957-62; University of Ife, Ife, Nigeria, lecturer in African studies, 1962-66; University of Lagos, Lagos, Nigeria, lecturer in African studies, 1966-68; National History and Arts Council, Georgetown, Guyana, art consultant, 1968-74; Ministry of Education, Georgetown, director of art and department of culture, 1974—. Director of Walter Roth Museum. Visiting tutor at Slade School of Fine Art, London, 1950-52; visiting professor at Makerere University, 1966. Chairman of National Trust, Georgetown, 1978—.

MEMBER: National Commissions for the Acquisition, Preservation, and Republication of Research Materials on Guyana.

AWARDS, HONORS: Second prize from *London Daily Express* "Artists under Thirty-five" competition, 1955; national honor from government of Guyana, 1973, for "The Golden Arrow of Achievement"; first prize in National Theatre's mural competition, 1976.

WRITINGS:

Other Leopards (novel), Hutchinson, 1963.
(Contributor) Joseph C. Anene and Godfrey N. Brown, editors, *Africa in the Nineteenth and Twentieth Centuries,* Thomas Nelson, 1966.
The Third Temptation (novel), Calder & Boyars, 1968.
(Contributor) John Ferguson and L. A. Thompson, editors, *Africa in Classical Antiquity,* Ibadan University Press, 1969.
(Contributor) *Island Voices* (anthology), Liveright, 1970.
Giglioli in Guyana, 1922-1972 (biography), National History and Arts Council (Georgetown, Guyana), 1970.
Image and Idea in the Arts of the Caribbean, National History and Arts Council, 1970.
(Contributor) *New Writings in the Caribbean* (anthology) National History and Arts Council, 1972.
(Contributor) S. O. Biobaku, editor, *Sources of Yoruba History,* Clarendon Press, 1973.
Icon and Image: A Study of Sacred and Secular Forms of African Classical Art, New York University Press, 1974.
The Amerindian Heritage, Walter Roth Museum (Georgetown, Guyana), 1984.
Habitat and Culture in Ancient Guyana, Edgar Mittelholzer Memorial Lectures, ninth series, 1984.
(Contributor) *Advances in World Archaeology,* Volume IV, Academic Press, 1985.

Contributor of numerous articles to African studies and anthropology journals. Editor of *Odu,* 1964, *Lagos Notes and Records,* 1967, and *Archaeology and Anthropology,* 1978—.

WORK IN PROGRESS: Ancient Guiana; Amazonian Petroglyphs.

SIDELIGHTS: Denis Williams told *CA:* "A Colonial artist or writer who has received his professional education in Britain and made his first home there is not likely easily to forget that experience. I find that in my own case the experience has proven not only formative, but to a degree even determinative. It seems to have shaped the entire course of my subsequent development. Thus, to me, it is impossible to imagine a career built other than upon the solid foundation of early recognition and acceptance which was accorded to me during the first half of the fifties in London. Paradoxically, however, as Fanon has so perceptively shown, given the circumstances and the day, acceptance on this level was in fact far the most unacceptable, indeed probably the most humiliating, of choices open to the Colonial artist.

"This may explain the rapid and apparently permanent darkness which followed the explosion of Caribbean writing in Britain during the time I was there. Colonial territories were all becoming independent, which was quickly to render the Colonial artist or writer obsolete; for just as national independence seems to have pulled the rug from under the feet of the Colonial writer, new national writers were arising in English- and French-speaking West Africa and in the Caribbean.

"By this time I was myself in Africa writing *Other Leopards,* or trying to resolve some of the problems of identity which provided the theme for that novel. By the time of its completion it was becoming evident that even though the new African literature was being written all around me, and by familiar hands, Africa did not represent the uttermost swing of the pendulum in my reaction from an unwilling acceptance in Europe. Indeed, the African experience tended to reveal to me deeply ingrained attitudes to various aspects of European art, life, and literature that had remained so far undetected. Odd as it may seem, it was very easy for me to write *The Third Temptation* (in an experimental French idiom) simultaneously with my study of African classical art, which in itself represented an intellectual search for African roots.

"I have since returned to Guyana, and see clearly that such a thing could never take place against my rediscovered background. However, if this means that the pendulum has at last reached its ultimate distance of travel, it is no comfort to realize that my first true Caribbean novel, *The Sperm of God,* has remained unfinished now for over thirteen years."

BIOGRAPHICAL/CRITICAL SOURCES:

BOOKS

Dathorne, O. R., *The Black Mind: A History of African Literature,* University of Minnesota Press, 1974.
Fox, C. J. and Walter Michel, *Wyndham Lewis on Art: Collected Writings, 1913-1956,* Thames & Hudson, 1969.
Moore, Gerald, *The Chosen Tongue,* Longman, 1969.
Ramchand, Kenneth, *The West Indian Novel and Its Background,* Faber, 1974.

PERIODICALS

Daily Express, April 28, 1955.
Geo, May, 1981.
Listener, July 14, 1949, December 14, 1950.
Science Digest, November, 1981.
Time, December, 1950.
Times British Colonies Review, spring, 1955.

*   *   *

WILLIS, Roy (Geoffrey) 1927-

PERSONAL: Born September 15, 1927, in London, England; son of Edward Ernest (a businessman) and Doris (Connel) Willis; married Audrey Grant, June 7, 1968 (divorced); married Mary Taylor Smith, September 25, 1984; children (first marriage) Joseph, Maryam. *Education:* Attended school in Brentwood, England. *Politics:* Independent. *Religion:* "Neo-pagan."

ADDRESSES: Home—Firview Cottage, Loan, Linlithgow, Scotland. *Office*—Department of Social Anthropology, University of Edinburgh, Edinburgh, Scotland.

CAREER: Romford Recorder, Romford, England, apprentice reporter, 1944-45; Betterwear Products Ltd., Romford, business trainee, 1946-51; reporter for *The Grocer,* 1951-53; *Northern News,* Zambia, Rhodesia, reporter, 1953-55; *Uganda Argus,* Kampala, Uganda, sub-editor, 1955-58; Reuters News Agency, London, England, sub-editor, 1958-60; Oxford University, Oxford, England, lecturer in social anthropology, 1960-65; University of London, University College, London, lecturer in social anthropology, 1965-67; University of Edinburgh, Edinburgh, Scotland, lecturer and reader, 1967-80, research fellow in social anthropology, 1981—. Participated in anthropological research in Tanzania, 1962-64, 1966, and 1967. *Military service:* British Army, Royal Artillery, 1945-46.

MEMBER: Association of Social Anthropologists, American Anthropological Association, African Studies Association (U.S.), New York Academy of Sciences, Mensa.

WRITINGS:

Man and Beast, Hart-Davis, 1974.

There Was a Certain Man (on the spoken art of the Fipa of southwest Tanzania), Oxford University Press, 1978.
A State in the Making, Indiana University Press, 1981.
The Drunken King, Indiana University Press, 1982.

WORK IN PROGRESS: Accounts Rendered, a translation of *Paroles Donnees,* by Claude Levi-Strauss; *Through the Looking Glass,* a book on social science and "magic"; *Anthropology of War and Peace; Cosmology and History in Himalayan India.*

SIDELIGHTS: Roy Willis writes: "My major and developing interests include social and cultural anthropology, cosmology, parapsychology, humanistic psychology, and philosophy. Writing, for me, is both self-discovery and discovery of the world and ultimately these are the same. The enormous advantage of getting older is that the material of one's own experience becomes so much more abundant, complex, and meaningful. This means that the world is expanding in a way which I find both disturbing and delightful."

*   *   *

WILLOUGHBY, Lee Davis
See BRANDNER, Gary

*   *   *

WILSON, Jacqueline 1945-

PERSONAL: Born December 17, 1945, in Bath, England; daughter of Harry Albert (a civil servant) and Margaret (Clibbens) Aitken; married William Millar Wilson (a police chief inspector), August 28, 1965; children: Emma Fiona. *Education:* Attended Carshalton Technical College. *Politics:* None. *Religion:* None.

ADDRESSES: Home—1B Beaufort Rd., Kingston-on-Thames, Surrey, England. *Agent*—Gina and Murray Pollinger, 4 Garrick St., London WCZE 9BH, England.

CAREER: Journalist, free-lance magazine writer, and author of books and radio plays. Employed by D. C. Thomsons, Dundee, Scotland, 1963-65.

WRITINGS:

SUSPENSE NOVELS

Hide and Seek, Macmillan (London), 1972, Doubleday, 1973.
Truth or Dare, Doubleday, 1973.
(Contributor) Virginia Whitaker, editor, *Winter's Crimes,* Macmillan (London), 1973.
Snap, Macmillan (London), 1974.
Let's Pretend, Macmillan (London), 1976.
Making Hate, Macmillan (London), 1977, St. Martin's, 1978.

CHILDREN'S BOOKS

Nobody's Perfect, Oxford University Press, 1982.
Waiting for the Sky to Fall, Oxford University Press, 1983.
The Other Side, Oxford University Press, 1984.
The School Trip, Hamilton, 1984.
The Killer Tadpole, Hamilton, 1984.
How to Survive Summer Camp, Oxford University Press, 1985.

OTHER

Also author of radio plays "Are You Listening," "It's Disgusting at Your Age," and "Ask a Silly Question," broadcast on British Broadcasting Corp. (BBC), 1982-84.

BIOGRAPHICAL/CRITICAL SOURCES:

PERIODICALS

Times Literary Supplement, July 23, 1982.

*   *   *

WILSON, Raymond 1925-

PERSONAL: Born December 20, 1925, in Gateshead, England; son of John William and Edith (Walker) Wilson; married Gertrude Mary Russell (a teacher), July 29, 1950; children: John Russell, Moira Christine, Mark Robert. *Education:* University of London, B.A. (with first class honors), 1954.

ADDRESSES: Home—Roselawn, Station Rd., Shiplake, Henley-on-Thames, England. *Office*—School of Education, University of Reading, Reading, Berkshire RG6 2AH, England.

CAREER: Schoolmaster in Birmingham, Gateshead, and Blyth, England, 1950-57; Dulwich College, London, England, chief English master, 1957-65; University of Southampton, Southampton, England, lecturer in education, 1965-68; University of Reading, Reading, England, professor of education, 1968—. *Military service:* Royal Navy, 1943-46.

WRITINGS:

Pride and Prejudice (critical guidebook), Macmillan, 1985.

EDITOR

A Coleridge Selection, Macmillan, 1963.
(With James Gibson) *Rhyme and Rhythm,* Macmillan, 1965.
Poems to Compare, Macmillan, 1965.
Time's Delights: Poems for All Seasons (juvenile), Hamlyn, 1977.
Junkets and Jumbles, Hamlyn, 1977.
Beaver Book of Funny Verse, Hamlyn, 1978.
Beaver Book of Animal Verse, Hamlyn, 1981.
Suspense (short stories), John Murray, 1981.
Beaver Book of Adventure Stories, Hamlyn, 1982.
Jane Austen, *Pride and Prejudice,* Macmillan, 1982.
Austen, *Northanger Abbey,* Macmillan, 1983.
Austen, *Sense and Sensibility,* Macmillan, 1984.
Nine O'Clock Bell: Poems about School, Penguin Books, 1985.

OTHER

Also contributor of poetry to anthologies. Contributor to language, literature, and philosophy journals. Review editor of *British Journal of Educational Studies,* 1975—.

WORK IN PROGRESS: Research on language and philosophy.

SIDELIGHTS: Raymond Wilson told *CA:* "I am opposed to Anglo-Saxon philosophy, and in particular to the raptureless philosophy of education that is dominant in Britain and America, basically because of its over-valuation of rationality and its Faustian preoccupation with knowledge *unrelated* to value. My belief is that education has never stood in greater need of the arts and literature than it does now."

AVOCATIONAL INTERESTS: Walking, talking.

*   *   *

WINTHER, Barbara 1926-

PERSONAL: Born October 25, 1926, in Washington, D.C.; daughter of Daniel Orren (an engineer) and Virginia (in social services; maiden name, Tracy) Hunter; married John E. Johnson, April 2, 1948 (divorced, 1961); married Grant Anton Winther (an attorney), December 24, 1963; children: (first marriage) Mikael, David. *Education:* University of California, Los Angeles, B.A., 1948; University of California, Santa Barbara, teaching credential, 1957; also attended Golden Gate Law School, 1962-63, and California Academy of Sciences, 1977-78.

ADDRESSES: Home—California; and Bainbridge Island, Washington.

CAREER: Writer. School teacher in Goleta, Calif., 1957-59, Sausalito, Calif., 1961-62, and Palo Alto. Calif. (also play director), 1963-69; instructor of yearly seminars on American Indian Art at University of California Extension, 1980—. Host of interview show on station KDB in Santa Barbara, Calif., 1968-69. Member of board of directors, Center for Cross-Cultural Communications, 1975-79; also member of Smithsonian, Southwest Museum, and Museum of Northern Arizona; M. H. de Young Museum, member and training chairman for Africa, Oceania, and the Americas. Actress at Santa Barbara Repertory Theatre and Alhecama Players, 1952-60. Consultant to California Academy of Sciences.

MEMBER: American Theatre Association, American Folklore Society, Native American Art Studies Association, Western History Association, Western Writers of America, California Academy of Sciences, University of California Alumni Association.

AWARDS, HONORS: New Names Award from California State College (now University), Los Angeles, 1955.

WRITINGS:

Addison-Wesley Early Reading Program: Teachers' Manual, Addison-Wesley, 1973.
Hi-Ho, Hortense (juvenile), Addison-Wesley, 1973.
Oh, No! Cornelia! (juvenile), Addison-Wesley, 1973.
Plays from Folktales of Africa and Asia (juvenile), Plays, 1976.
Where Has Christmas Gone? (play), Contemporary Drama Service, 1976.
The Samurai (juvenile booklet), Educational Development Corp., 1976.
The Story of Jane Addams (juvenile booklet), Educational Development Corp., 1976.
African Trickster Tales (juvenile booklet), Educational Development Corp., 1976.
Hani (juvenile booklet), Educational Development Corp., 1977.
Race to the Top of the World (juvenile booklet), Educational Development Corp., 1977.
How We Nearly Lost the Lighthouse (play), Houghton, 1981.
Jean Lafitte, Privateer (play), Houghton, 1981.
Trickster Hare (play), Houghton, 1981.
Hopitu, Jesse Peter Museum, 1985.

CONTRIBUTOR TO ANTHOLOGIES

Richard G. Smith and Robert Tierney, editors, *Fens and Tales,* Scott, Foresman, 1978.
Sylvia Kamerman, editor, *On Stage for Christmas,* Plays, 1978.
Ring around the World, Harcourt, 1980.

Also contributor to other anthologies.

OTHER

Contributor of numerous plays for children to *Plays: The Drama Magazine for Young People* and *Instuctor.*

Contributor to *American Indian Art.*

WORK IN PROGRESS: *Winnebago Legends; The Leopard Sings* (an African-based novel); "moving towards writing adult fiction and articles on American Indian art and away from plays and juvenile stories."

SIDELIGHTS: Barbara Winther wrote: "My childhood was spent on an island in Maine and in a little town in California. Creating plays, first with my dolls and then with other children, was an important part of my world of fun. Even as early as five, I remember putting on a play for my grandmother, my uncle and two aunts, plus a stray cat and an inquisitive muskrat which came near my wharf stage.

"My interest in folklore started when I was teaching school. I realized that one of the best ways to begin an understanding of a culture was to examine its folklore, since the dreams, needs, and beliefs of a people are reflected there. Further, through folklore plays, children could identify more easily with other people, acting out, feeling the problems and the joys. And through this medium children could come to the conclusions that all peoples have the same basic needs and desires and that the different mores, art forms, and material cultures are created by environments and degrees of isolation. Since I could find few folktale plays, I began to write them, traveling all over the world to find materials and stories to adapt.

"The years I spent as an actress have been invaluable to me in writing. In my little typing room I play the various roles and visualize the stage as I work our my scripts. It is lucky I have an understanding husband, for often when I am having a problem with a scene he is called upon to assume a character, and even my friends may be hauled in for a taped session.

"Studying and collecting American Indian Art from 1967-84 led me to my present interest in teaching and writing in that field. Writing adult fiction, especially humorous, allows me a complete change and relaxation from the rigors of research and the preciseness needed in my technical writing on Indian art."

BIOGRAPHICAL/CRITICAL SOURCES:

PERIODICALS

International Folk Theatre Olympiad '79, July, 1979.

*   *   *

WITT, Harold (Vernon) 1923-

PERSONAL: Born February 6, 1923, in Santa Ana, Calif.; son of Oscar Solomon (an orange rancher) and Blanche (Talcott) Witt; married Beth Hewitt, September 8, 1948; children: Emily, Eric, Jessamyn. *Education:* University of California, Berkeley, B.A., 1943, B.L.S., 1953; University of Michigan, M.A., 1947.

ADDRESSES: *Home*—39 Claremont Ave., Orinda, Calif. 94563.

CAREER: Washoe County Library, Reno, Nev., reference librarian, 1953-55; San Jose State College (now University), San Jose, Calif., reference librarian, 1956-59; free-lance writer, 1949—. Has displayed collages accompanied by poems at several exhibitions, including a one-man show at Trinity Gallery, Berkeley, 1977.

MEMBER: Poetry Society of America, Phi Beta Kappa, Alpha Mu Gamma.

AWARDS, HONORS: Hopwood Award for poetry, 1947; Phelan Award for narrative poetry, 1960; first prize, San Francisco

Poetry Center poetic drama competition, 1963, for "Eros on the Shield"; Poetry Society of America, Emily Dickinson Award, 1972; World Order of Narrative Poets Awards, 1982, 1983, 1984.

WRITINGS:

POETRY

Family in the Forest, Porpoise Bookshop, 1956.
Superman Unbound, New Orleans Poetry Journal, 1956.
The Death of Venus (Book Club for Poetry selection), Golden Quill, 1958.
Beasts in Clothes, Macmillan, 1961.
Winesburg by the Sea: A Preview, Hearse Press, 1970.
Population by 1940: 40,000, Best Cellar Press, 1971.
Now, Swim, Ashland Poetry Press, 1974.
Surprised by Others at Fort Cronkhite, Sparrow, 1975.
Winesburg by the Sea: Poems, Thorp Springs Press, 1979.
(Self-illustrated) *The Snow Prince: Poems and Collages,* Blue Unicorn, 1982.

CONTRIBUTOR; ANTHOLOGIES

Eight American Poets, Villiers, 1952.
A Western Sampler: Nine Contemporary Poets, Talisman Press, 1963.
William Cole, editor, *Erotic Poetry,* Random House, 1963.
The New Yorker Book of Poems, Viking, 1969.
S. Dunning and others, editors, *Some Haystacks Don't Even Have Any Needle,* Scott, Foresman, 1969.
Thomas Lask, editor, *The New York Times Book of Verse,* Macmillan, 1970.
Jean Burden, editor, *A Celebration of Cuts,* Eriksson, 1974.
Lawrence P. Spingarn, editor, *Poets West,* Perivale, 1975.
David Kherdian, editor, *Traveling America with Today's Poets,* Macmillan, 1977.
David Ray, editor, *From A to Z: Two Hundred Contemporary American Poets,* Swallow Press, 1981.
Harry Thomas and Steven Lavnie, editors, *The Hopwood Anthology: Five Decades of American Poetry,* University of Michigan Press, 1981.

OTHER

Also author of a play, "Eros on the Shield," and a novel, *Handled with a Chain.* Contributor of poetry to *Atlantic, New Yorker, Saturday Review, Nation, New Republic, Hudson Review, Poetry, Kenyon Review, Poetry Northwest, Harper's* and other magazines and journals. Co-editor, *California State Poetry Quarterly,* 1976, and *Blue Unicorn,* 1977—; consulting editor, *Poet Lore,* 1976—.

WORK IN PROGRESS: *Over Fifty* and *Over Sixty,* two collections of sonnets on the subject of aging; *Flashbacks and Reruns* and *Among the Cloverleaves,* sequels to *Winesburg by the Sea; Light Traveler: Selected and New Poems; The Many Masks of Mrs. Asgrith,* a novel.

SIDELIGHTS: Harold Witt told *CA:* "I am not a believer in throwing away the past, and I have built my poetry on what has gone before, preferring a memorable music and meaning to disposable lines. I have used old forms for new purposes and have particularly varied the sonnet to make it my own, discovering its confinement of fourteen lines, if not slavishly rhymed, can be almost limitless.

"In *Winesburg by the Sea* I have written a book about growing up in a pre-World War II southern California town, which might be everywhere U.S.A., and its people, sometimes looked back on from the present, sometimes then and there as told by the voices of citizens. It is not only nostalgia but an attempted insight into where we have come from and why we stay the same in spite of changes. If that weren't true the literature of the past would be incomprehensible today, and no one would find Shakespeare or the Greek dramatists as modern as ever. I am continuing to write of the changes and samenesses in a second and third volume, in which some of the characters age and new ones appear, confronted by today's technology, discoveries and morality, and usually no happier or wiser. The tragedy and comedy remain even if the setting has become more urban than rural and, as advertisers like to boast, the products are 'new and improved.'

"In the past few years I have also become interested in another artform—collage. I have produced many collages which accompany poems, some of which have been published in magazines, some of which have been in shows, and some of which have been illustrations for *The Snow Prince*."

*   *   *

WOLFF, Kurt H(einrich)   1912-

PERSONAL: Born May 20, 1912, in Darmstadt, Germany; came to United States in 1939, naturalized in 1945; son of Oscar Louis and Ida Bertha (Kohn) Wolff; married Carla Elisabeth Bruck, June 11, 1936; children: Carlo Thomas. *Education:* Attended University of Frankfurt, 1930-31 and 1932-33, and University of Munich, 1931-32; University of Florence, laurea (doctorate), 1935; postdoctoral study, University of Chicago, 1943-44, and Harvard University, 1955-56.

ADDRESSES: Home—58 Lombard St., Newton, Mass. 02158. *Office*—Department of Sociology, Brandeis University, Waltham, Mass. 02254.

CAREER: Teacher, Schule am Mittelmeer, Recco, Italy, 1934-36, and Istituti Mare-Monti, Ruta, Italy, 1936-38; Southern Methodist University, Dallas, Tex., research assistant in sociology, 1939-43; Earlham College, Richmond, Ind., assistant professor of sociology, 1944-45; Ohio State University, Columbus, assistant professor, 1945-52, associate professor of sociology, 1952-59; Brandeis University, Waltham, Mass., professor of sociology, 1959-69, Yellen Professor of Social Relations, 1969-82, professor emeritus, 1982—, chairman of department of sociology, 1959-62.

Visiting professor, College of the Pacific, summer, 1948, New School for Social Research, summer, 1950, Institute of Social Research (Oslo, Norway), 1959, Sir George Williams University, 1965, University of Freiburg, summer, 1966, University of Frankfurt, 1966-67, University of Paris-Nanterre, spring, 1967, York University, 1971, Memorial University of Newfoundland, fall, 1982, and University of Rome, 1983. Senior Fulbright Lecturer, University of Rome, 1963-64; Simon Visiting Professor, University of Manchester, May, 1980. Member of Social Science Research Council summer seminar, Northwestern University, 1952; U.S. Department of State specialist, Frankfurt Institute of Social Research, 1952 and 1953.

MEMBER: International Sociological Association (chairman of research committee on the sociology of knowledge, 1966-72), International Society for the Sociology of Knowledge (president, 1972—), American Sociological Association (fellow), American Association of University Professors, American Civil Liberties Union.

AWARDS, HONORS: Social Science Research Council fellowship, 1943-44, grant, 1966-67; Viking Fund (now Wenner-Gren Foundation for Anthropological Research) grant, 1947 and 1949; Fund for Advancement of Education faculty fellow, Harvard University, 1955-56; senior Fulbright scholar, La Trobe University, University of New South Wales, and Australian National University, all 1980.

WRITINGS:

(Editor and translator) Georg Simmel, *The Sociology of Georg Simmel*, Free Press of Glencoe, 1950.
(Translator with Reinhold Bendix) Simmel, *Conflict and the Web of Group Affiliations*, Free Press of Glencoe, 1955.
(Editor, contributor, and translator) *Georg Simmel, 1858-1918*, Ohio State University Press, 1959, published as *Essays on Sociology, Philosophy and Aesthetics*, Harper, 1965.
(Editor, contributor, and translator) *Emile Durkheim, 1858-1917*, Ohio State University Press, 1960, published as *Essays on Sociology and Philosophy*, Harper, 1964.
(Editor and contributor) *Transactions of the Fourth World Congress of Sociology*, Volume 4, International Sociological Association, 1961.
(Editor and author of introduction) Karl Mannheim, *Wissenssoziologie*, Luchterhand, 1964.
(Editor with Barrington Moore, Jr., and contributor) *The Critical Spirit: Essays in Honor of Herbert Marcuse*, Beacon Press, 1967.
The Sociology of Knowledge in the United States of America, Mouton, 1967.
Versuch zu einer Wissenssoziologie, Luchterhand, 1968.
Hingeburg und Begriff, Luchterhand, 1968.
(Editor, translator, and author of introduction) Mannheim, *From Karl Mannheim*, Oxford University Press, 1971.
From Einhorn zu Einhorn, Erato Press, 1972.
Trying Sociology, Wiley, 1974.
Surrender and Catch: Experience and Inquiry Today, D. Reidel, 1976.
Vorgang und immerwaehrende Revolution, Heymann, 1978.
Beyond the Sociology of Knowledge: An Introduction and a Development, University Press of America, 1983.
(Editor and contributor) *Alfred Schutz: Appraisals and Developments*, Nijhoff, 1984.

Contributor to symposia and to professional journals. Member of board of directors, *Sociological Abstracts*, 1963—; member of editorial advisory board, *Praxis*, 1966-73, *International Journal of Contemporary Sociology*, 1971—, *Phenomenology and Social Science*, 1973—, and *Phenomenological Sociology Newsletter*, 1976-77; member of editorial board, *Sociological Focus*, 1972—, and *Philosophy and Social Criticism*, 1978—. Associate editor, *Human Studies*, 1977—.

WORK IN PROGRESS: A book on "Loma."

AVOCATIONAL INTERESTS: Drawing and painting.

BIOGRAPHICAL/CRITICAL SOURCES:

PERIODICALS

Human Studies, October-December, 1981.
La critica sociologica, summer, 1978.
Phenomenological Sociology Newsletter, March, 1978.
Philosophical Forum, fall, 1980.
Philosophy and Social Criticism, spring, 1979.
Philosophy of the Social Sciences, June, 1982.
Salmagundi, winter, 1978.
Society, January-February, 1978.

WOLSELEY, Roland E. 1904-

PERSONAL: Born March 9, 1904, in New York, N.Y.; son of Enrique de G. and Erminie (Rath) Wolseley; married Bernice Mather Browne, November 28, 1928 (died, 1980); married Isabel C. Champ, January 16, 1982. *Education:* Attended Schuylkill College (now Albright College), 1923-24; Northwestern University, B.S., 1928, M.S., 1934. *Politics:* Independent. *Religion:* United Methodist.

ADDRESSES: Home—1307 Westmoreland Ave., Syracuse, N.Y. 13210. *Office*—School of Public Communications, Syracuse University, Syracuse, N.Y. 13210.

CAREER: Herald-Telegram, Reading, Pa., reporter, 1922-23; *News-Times*, Reading, reporter, 1923-24; *Tribune*, Reading, reporter, 1924; *Daily News-Index*, Evanston, Ill., copy editor, 1927; *Pennsylvania Railroad-News*, Chicago, Ill., 1928-31, began as editorial assistant, became managing editor; *Daily News-Index*, 1934-37, began as reporter and copyreader, became managing editor; Northwestern University, Evanston, 1938-46, began as instructor, became assistant professor; Syracuse University, Syracuse, N.Y., associate professor, 1946-47, professor of journalism, 1947-72, professor emeritus, 1972—, chairman of magazine department, 1947-69. Fulbright lecturer, Nagpur University, Nagpur, India, 1952-53.

MEMBER: Association for Education in Journalism (president, 1948-49), American Association of University Professors, Religion Newswriters Association, Society of Professional Journalists, Sigma Delta Chi.

AWARDS, HONORS: D. Litt., Albright College, 1955; Kappa Tau Alpha citation, 1972, for *The Black Press, U.S.A.;* Associated Church Press citation, 1984, for contribution to field of religion journalism; award from Association for Education in Journalism and Mass Communication, Magazine Division, 1985, for "distinguished service as an educator."

WRITINGS:

(With Bastian and Case) *Around the Copydesk*, Macmillan, 1933.
(With H. F. Harrington) *The Copyreader's Workshop*, Heath, 1934.
(Compiler) *The Journalist's Bookshelf*, Burgess, 1939, 8th edition, R. J. Berg, 1985.
(With L. R. Campbell) *Exploring Journalism*, Prentice-Hall, 1943, 3rd edition, 1957.
(With others) *New Survey of Journalism*, Barnes & Noble, 1947, 4th edition, 1959.
(With Campbell) *Newsmen at Work*, Houghton, 1949.
The Magazine World, Prentice-Hall, 1951.
Interpreting the Church through Press and Radio, Muhlenberg, 1951.
(Co-author and editor) *Journalism in Modern India*, Asia Publishing House, 1954, 2nd edition, 1964.
Face to Face with India, Friendship, 1954.
Careers in Religious Journalism, Association Press, 1955, 3rd edition, Herald Press, 1977.
(Co-author and editor) *Writing for the Religious Market*, Association Press, 1956.
Critical Writing for the Journalist, Chilton, 1959.
(With Campbell) *How to Report and Write the News*, Prentice-Hall, 1961.
Understanding Magazines, Iowa State University Press, 1965, 2nd edition, 1969.

(With P. D. Tandon) *Gandhi*, National Book Trust, 1969.
The Low Countries, Thomas Nelson, 1969.
The Black Press, U.S.A., Iowa State University Press, 1971.
(Co-author) *The Reluctant Revolution*, Iowa State University Press, 1971.
The Changing Magazine, Hastings House, 1973.
(Co-author) *Perspectives of the Black Press*, Mercer House, 1974.
(With Tandon) *Three Women to Remember*, St. Paul Press, 1975.
(Co-author) *The New Languages*, Prentice-Hall, 1977.
(Co-author) *Mass Media and Communication*, 2nd edition (original edition published in Spanish in 1966), Hastings House, 1977.
(With Tandon) *Four Flames of Lamps* (in Hindi), Raipal & Sons, 1982.
(Co-author) *Writing to Inspire*, Writers Digest, 1982.
Still in Print, David Cook, 1985.

Also contributor to *Encyclopedia Americana, Academic American Encyclopedia*, and others. Contributor of articles to 250 newspapers and magazines in the United States, England, Sweden, and India, including *Christian Science Monitor, Economic Times, Cleveland Plain Dealer, Washington Post, Dallas News, Interlit*, and *World Traveling*.

Contributing editor, *Freelancer's Newsletter*, 1981—; book section editor, *Quill and Scroll*, 1934.

WORK IN PROGRESS: Nansen; new edition of *The Black Press, U.S.A.*

SIDELIGHTS: Roland E. Wolseley told *CA:* "One of my strongest motivations for writing is my belief that teachers of journalism and other types of writing are more effective if they can do well what they teach. It does not follow that only those who can do what they teach can be able as teachers, for there are excellent teachers who, nevertheless, are not as competent technically as some of their students. But the teacher-cum-writer is less likely than the unproductive teacher to lose sight of the problems involved in modern writing and therefore is both more practical in teaching and better understands student writers. . . . Another strong motivation is attempting to fill needs for books on communications. Five of my books were the first in their fields, largely because when I searched for a text for some new course I found there was none. So I wrote it. Or joined with others to provide it. These materials were tested for a few years in the classroom before being shaped into books."

BIOGRAPHICAL/CRITICAL SOURCES:

PERIODICALS

Hindi Udyama, July, 1953.
Journal of Education, January, 1952.
Lutheran Magazine, September 14, 1955.
Quill and Scroll, December, 1951, January, 1952, April/May, 1969.

*   *   *

WOOD, Allen W(illiam) 1942-

PERSONAL: Born October 26, 1942, in Seattle, Wash.; son of Forrest Elmer (a supervisor at Boeing Aircraft Co.) and Alleen (Blumberg) Wood; married Rega Clark, June 20, 1965; children: Henry Engelsberg, Stephen Frederick. *Education:* Reed College, B.A., 1964; Yale University, M.A., 1966, Ph.D., 1968.

ADDRESSES: *Home*—206 University Ave., Ithaca, N.Y. 14850. *Office*—Department of Philosophy, 218 Goldwin Smith Hall, Cornell University, Ithaca, N.Y. 14853.

CAREER: Cornell University, Ithaca, N.Y., assistant professor, 1968-73, associate professor, 1973-80, professor of philosophy, 1980—. Visiting assistant professor, University of Michigan, 1973.

AWARDS, HONORS: Cornell Society for Humanities summer fellowship, 1970; Guggenheim fellowship, 1983, for *Hegel's Moral Philosophy*.

WRITINGS:

Kant's Moral Religion, Cornell University Press, 1970.
Kant's Rational Theology, Cornell University Press, 1978.
(Translator with Gertrude M. Clark) Immanuel Kant, *Lectures on Philosophical Theology*, Cornell University Press, 1978.
Karl Marx, Routledge & Kegan Paul, 1981.
(Editor) *Self and Nature in Kant's Philosophy*, Cornell University Press, 1984.

WORK IN PROGRESS: *Hegel's Moral Philosophy*.

*   *   *

WOODBURY, Marda   1925-

PERSONAL: Born September 20, 1925, in New York, N.Y.; daughter of Walter W. (a newspaper journalist) and Edith (a journalist; maiden name, Fleischer) Liggett; married Philip J. Evans, 1948 (divorced, 1950); married Mark Lee Woodbury, 1956 (divorced, 1969); children: (first marriage) Mark; (second marriage) Brian, Heather. *Education:* Bard College, B.A., 1946; Columbia University, B.S., 1948; also attended University of California, Berkeley, 1955-56, 1960-61.

ADDRESSES: *Home and office*—3050 College Ave., Berkeley, Calif. 94705.

CAREER: Worked in special, medical, and public libraries, 1946-60; high school librarian in Mt. Diablo, Calif., 1962-67; elementary school librarian in Oakland and Berkeley, Calif., 1967-69; Far West Laboratory for Educational Research and Development, organizer of research library, 1969-73; Gifted Resource Center of San Mateo County, Calif., librarian, editor, and resource consultant, 1974-75; Research Ventures (library consultants and information specialists), Berkeley, Calif., coordinator, 1975—; library director, Life Chiropractic College-West, 1980—. Member of extension faculty at University of California, Berkeley, and evening faculty at Holy Names College.

MEMBER: National Association for the Education of Young Children, Medical Library Association.

WRITINGS:

A Guide to Sources of Educational Information, Information Resources Press, 1976, 2nd edition, 1982.
Selecting Instructional Materials, Phi Delta Kappa, 1978.
Selecting Materials for Instruction, Libraries Unlimited, Volume I: *Issues and Policies*, 1979, Volume II: *Media and the Curriculum*, 1980, Volume III: *Subject Areas and Implementation*, 1980.
Childhood Information Resources, Information Resources Press, 1985.

Also author of *A Guide to Educational Resources*. Author of resource series, "Curriculum Catalysts," D.O.K. Publishers,

1977-78, and "Distinguished Women Poster Series," Celestial Arts, 1976. Also author of pamphlets, booklets, teaching guides, and short stories. Correspondent for *Santa Rosa Press-Democrat*, 1973-74. Contributor of articles and reviews to library publications and professional journals. Member of editorial board, *Reference Librarian*.

WORK IN PROGRESS: *Youth Information Resources*.

SIDELIGHTS: Marda Woodbury told *CA*: "Though I come from a family of writers (on both sides), I did not become a serious writer until I lost my library position at Far West Laboratory for Educational Research as the result of a cut in federal funding. Since library positions were difficult to find, I decided I was obviously the best person to put together a basic reference work on educational sources. I wrote this first book while working part-time as a newspaper correspondent. Since I'd been a reference librarian in an educational setting, I knew just how to organize a reference book and had strong ideas on what to include. Beyond that, I had lots of on-the-job training. Working for a newspaper and rewriting educational handouts for clarity helped me with speed and expository prose.

"My reference books have been well-reviewed and much copied (though not always acknowledged). Though the economic rewards are modest, I think my books have definitely improved the dispersal of educational information as well as the design of federal structures intended to disseminate information.

"My current series, *Childhood Information Resources* and *Youth Information Resources*, are multidisciplinary guides to help all those working with children or youths (in whatever discipline) locate the information they need.

"I have always considered the role of librarian to be an interface between people and ideas in print. In my written works, I like to function as a resource person and go-between, to help people establish meaningful relations with ideas, information, resources that will prove interesting or valuable to them. In my reference works and educational works, I try to see things steady and see them whole. I cast a wide net. I hope to expand the horizons of my readers.

"Life, in my mostly unpublished short stories, is illuminated differently. These are mostly vignettes or scenes, glimpsed as it were by a campfire or flashlight on a windy night. I leave a lot to my readers' imaginations. The elliptical quality of my short stories balances out—at least to my satisfaction—the plodding, conscientious thoroughness of my expository reference works."

*   *   *

WOODSON, Jeff
See OGLESBY, Joseph

*   *   *

WOODWARD, C(omer) Vann   1908-

PERSONAL: Born November 13, 1908, in Vanndale, Ark.; son of Hugh Alison and Bess (Vann) Woodward; married Glenn Boyd MacLeod, December 21, 1937 (died, 1982); children: Peter V. (deceased). *Education:* Emory University, A.B., 1930; Columbia University, M.A., 1932; University of North Carolina, Ph.D., 1937.

ADDRESSES: Home—83 Rogers Rd., Hamden, Conn. 06514. *Office*—Department of History, Yale University, New Haven, Conn.

CAREER: Georgia School of Technology (now Georgia Institute of Technology), Atlanta, instructor in English, 1930-31, 1932-33; worked for Works Progress Administration, 1933-34; University of Florida, Gainesville, assistant professor of history, 1937-39; Scripps College, Claremont, Calif., associate professor of history, 1940-43; Johns Hopkins University, Baltimore, Md., professor of history, 1946-61; Yale University, New Haven, Conn., Sterling Professor of History, 1961-77, professor emeritus, 1977—. University of Virginia, visiting assistant professor of history, 1939, James W. Richard Lecturer in History, 1954; Commonwealth Lecturer, University of London, 1954; Harmsworth Professor of American History, Oxford University, 1954-55; Jefferson Lecturer in Humanities, 1978. *Military service:* U.S. Naval Reserve, 1943-46; became lieutenant.

MEMBER: American Philosophical Society, American Historical Association (president, 1969), Organization of American Historians (president, 1968-69), American Academy and Institute of Arts and Sciences, American Academy of Arts and Sciences, Royal Historical Society, British Academy, Southern Historical Association (president, 1952).

AWARDS, HONORS: Bancroft Prize for one of year's two best works in American history, 1952, for *Origins of the New South: 1877-1913;* National Institute of Arts and Letters award in literature, 1954; annual award of American Council of Learned Societies, 1962; LL.D. from University of Arkansas, University of North Carolina, and University of Michigan, 1971; Litt.D. from Princeton University, 1971, and Cambridge University, 1975; L.H.D. from Columbia University, 1972, and Northwestern University, 1977; Brandeis University Creative Arts Award, 1982; American Book Award nomination and Pulitzer Prize in history, both 1982, both for *Mary Chesnut's Civil War.*

WRITINGS:

Tom Watson: Agrarian Rebel, Macmillan, 1938, reprinted with new introduction, 1955, reprinted, Oxford University Press, 1975.

The Battle for Leyte Gulf, Macmillan, 1947.

Reunion and Reaction: The Compromise of 1877 and the End of Reconstruction (also see below), Little, Brown, 1951, 2nd revised edition, Doubleday, 1956.

Origins of the New South: 1877-1913 (contains condensed version of *Reunion and Reaction*), Louisiana State University Press, 1951, revised edition, 1971.

The Strange Career of Jim Crow (James W. Richard lectures), Oxford University Press, 1955, 3rd revised edition, 1974.

The Burden of Southern History, Louisiana State University Press, 1960, revised edition, 1968.

(Editor) George Fitzhugh, *Cannibals All!,* Harvard University Press, 1960.

(Contributor) John A. Garraty, editor, *Quarrels That Have Shaped the Constitution,* Harper, 1962.

(With others) *The National Experience,* Harcourt, 1963.

(Editor) Lewis H. Blair, *A Southern Prophecy,* Little, Brown, 1964.

(Contributor) Willie Morris, editor, *The South Today: One Hundred Years after Appomattox,* Harper, 1965.

(Editor) Whitelaw Reid, *After the War: A Tour of the Southern States, 1865-1866,* Harper, 1965.

(Editor) *The Comparative Approach to American History,* Basic Books, 1968.

American Counterpoint: Slavery and Racism in the North-South Dialogue, Little, Brown, 1971.

Responses of the Presidents to Charges of Misconduct, Delacorte, 1974.

(Contributor) Charles F. Delzell, editor, *The Future of History: Essays in the Vanderbilt University Centennial Symposium,* Vanderbilt University Press, 1977.

(Editor) *Mary Chesnut's Civil War,* Yale University Press, 1981.

(General editor) *Oxford History of the United States,* eleven volumes, Oxford University Press, 1982—.

(Author of preface) Robert Middlekauff, *The Glorious Cause: The American Revolution, 1763-1789,* Oxford University Press, 1982.

(Editor with Elisabeth Muhlenfeld) *The Private Mary Chesnut: The Unpublished Civil War Diaries,* Yale University Press, 1984.

Thinking Back: The Perils of Writing History, Louisiana State University Press, 1986.

Former editor, "Forum Lectures on American History" series, Voice of America. Contributor to numerous scholarly journals. Contributor of essays and reviews to periodicals, including *Commentary, Harper's,* and *New York Review of Books.*

WORK IN PROGRESS: Editing additional volumes of *Oxford History of the United States.*

SIDELIGHTS: C. Vann Woodward, an historian of the American South, is considered one of the twentieth century's preeminent scholars in his field. Elisabeth Muhlenfeld, writing in the *Dictionary of Literary Biography,* describes Woodward as "the one historian whose works must be mastered and reckoned with by serious students of Southern history." Muhlenfeld further states that Woodward is "a significant figure in what has sometimes been called the second generation of the Southern Renaissance: its historian, one of its finest essayists, and even to some degree its philosopher." Woodward's career, which now spans more than forty-five years, has been devoted primarily to studies of race relations in America and the American South since the Civil War. He received the Pulitzer Prize in history in 1982 for editing *Mary Chesnut's Civil War,* but Muhlenfeld feels that the prize in this case, "by implication, took notice of the consistently high quality of the whole body of Woodward's work."

Woodward established a considerable reputation as an historian by virtue of his books *Tom Watson: Agrarian Rebel* and *Origins of the New South: 1877-1913.* These publications, according to Muhlenfeld, recast postbellum Southern history and "made a major departure from prevailing interpretations," including the well-entrenched notion that postwar political struggles in the South raged between the agrarian landowners of the "Old South" and the industrial, capitalistic forces from the North, known most commonly as "carpetbaggers." Woodward saw the struggle as an internal conflict within the South, fueled by Southern industrialists, rather than a regional fight pitting North against South. From this revolutionary discovery, Woodward went on to demonstrate that economic recovery never really occurred in the "New South" of the post-Reconstruction era. Muhlenfeld states: "He painted a picture of a region mired in a poverty so deep and so far-reaching that it infected every dimension of Southern life." Woodward's thorough research and startling conclusions, in Muhlenfeld's view, "in effect defined a whole new area of historical study waiting to be done.'' In the thirty years following publication of *Origins of the New South*, ''Southern historiography . . . has built on Woodward's work, . . . not as yet offering a successful challenge to [his] larger outline.''

Within *Origins of the New South*, Woodward began an exposure of the beginnings of Southern segregationist practices. In 1955, he expanded upon this aspect of his research with publication of the popularly-acclaimed *The Strange Career of Jim Crow*. Based on the premise that, according to Woodward, ''the policies of proscription, segregation, and disfranchisement that are often described as the immutable 'folkways' of the South . . . are of a more recent origin [than Reconstruction],'' the book contributed a powerful idea to the growing civil rights movement. Woodward demonstrated that post-Reconstruction Southern blacks and whites mingled more freely before 1890 than they were able to after that date, when segregational ''Jim Crow'' laws began to be enacted. In the course of proving that these laws did not spring from necessity during Reconstruction, and that they were not unchangeable through a long course of history, Woodward showed with finality that legal racial discrimination was a twentieth-century phenomenon and therefore was far easier to change than established opinion supposed. The work was challenged by critics on the grounds that Woodward concentrated on legal aspects of segregation while neglecting the emotions underlying racial tension, emotions that they argued were indeed ''folkways'' of the South. This problem with the first edition of *The Strange Career of Jim Crow* caused Woodward ''some embarrassment,'' according to Muhlenfeld. It prompted him to reply in a revised edition of the work: ''Acts of intolerance, discourtesy, and inhumanity, acts of segregation acquire a new significance when they are endowed with . . . the majesty of law.'' The difficulties Woodward encountered with his first popularly successful work, in Muhlenfeld's words, ''in no way diminished his commitment to history as an important tool for the present.''

Shortly after his retirement from the faculty of Yale University in 1977, Woodward began to edit the work of Civil War diarist Mary Chesnut. Chesnut, the wife of a United States senator who became an aide to Jefferson Davis, was in a unique position to observe events during the Civil War, as she moved within the highest circles of the Confederate government, attended numerous political functions, and even observed battles and their aftermath. She kept her diary only intermittently through the war years, but almost twenty years after the war ended, at the end of her own life, she revised the diary extensively, hoping for publication. The rewritten version, broadly expanded from its original length and quality, came eventually to be mistaken for a veritable wartime work. Portions of it were published in 1905 and 1949 without any indication that it had undergone extensive revision twenty years after the fact.

With both the original and the revised version at his disposal, Woodward chose to publish a full-length edition of the latter first. The resulting *Mary Chesnut's Civil War* won the Pulitzer Prize and has been described by Walter Clemons of *Newsweek* as ''one of the two best firsthand records of the Confederate experience.''

A division of critical opinion, however, has led Woodward to defend his concentration on the 1880s rewrite, even though he has been careful to describe Chesnut's method of operation. Woodward supports the revision because he feels that the later version has the integrity of a literary work and avoids Reconstruction-era biases which might have crept into it during Chesnut's decline. ''His claim for Mrs. Chesnut is not on the grounds of the specific information she provides, but the vivid and life-like picture which she paints of a society in the throes of its life-and-death struggle,'' writes P. J. Parish in the *Times Literary Supplement*. Parish feels that in the absence of the original diaries ''it is impossible to be certain about any specific point'' among Mary Chesnut's judgements and opinions. Kenneth Lynn, writing for the *New York Times Book Review*, states: ''The 1880's diary . . . reads more like a product of the dishonest time in which it was written than like a replication of the more honest document written 20 years earlier.'' Muhlenfeld, Chesnut's biographer, nonetheless supports Woodward's decision. ''*Mary Chesnut's Civil War* . . . [is] an impressive achievement,'' declares Muhlenberg in the *Dictionary of Literary Biography*. ''With its introductory material detailing the nature of the text and with its copious and yet admirably brief annotations, the work [makes] clear Mary Boykin Chesnut's own achievement.''

Despite the controversy surrounding Chesnut's ''diary'' and Woodward's approach to it, historians and general readers alike have welcomed Woodward's comprehensive edition. Parish claims, ''Now, at last, we have the full, scholarly edition which has been so much needed. It has been well worth waiting for.'' Indeed, Woodward's editorial decision on the work has been supported by the confusing text of the original Civil War era diary, edited by Woodward and Muhlenfeld and subsequently published as *The Private Mary Chesnut: The Unpublished Civil War Diaries*. Reading the original, says Thomas Mallon in the *Los Angeles Times Book Review*, ''is like watching a television with a broken vertical hold [because the reader must constantly consult footnotes]. The fuller 'Mary Chesnut's Civil War' makes for more pleasurable reading.''

In 1977, upon his retirement as Sterling Professor of History at Yale University, Woodward said: ''Finishing something is in some cases a cause for celebration, like finishing a book. It's sometimes a cause of pain and tribulation, like finishing a love affair—and teaching is sort of in between.'' His professorial duties concluded, Woodward has been concentrating on numerous projects, including the Chesnut diaries, an eleven-volume *Oxford History of the United States* that he is editing, and a volume of essays on his experiences as an historian. With nearly a half century of scholarly work to his credit, he remains, in the words of *Newsweek*, ''one of this country's most eminent living historians,'' and in the words of Elisabeth Muhlenfeld, ''a humane voice in a troubled world.''

BIOGRAPHICAL/CRITICAL SOURCES:

BOOKS

Cunliffe, Marcus, and Robin W. Winks, editors, *Pastmasters: Some Essays on American Historians*, Harper, 1969.
Dictionary of Literary Biography, Volume XVII: *Twentieth-Century American Historians*, Gale, 1983.
Garraty, John A., *Interpreting American History: Conversations with Historians*, Macmillan, 1978.
Genovese, Eugene D., *In Red and Black*, Pantheon, 1968.
Kausser, J. Morgan and James M. McPherson, *Region, Race, and Reconstruction: Essays in Honor of C. Vann Woodward*, Oxford University Press, 1982.
King, Richard H., *A Southern Renaissance: The Cultural Awakening of the American South, 1930-1955*, Oxford University Press, 1980.
Woodward, C. Vann, *The Strange Career of Jim Crow*, Oxford University Press, 1974.

PERIODICALS

American Historical Review, July, 1952, February, 1969, April, 1973, June, 1973.
American Sociological Review, October, 1955.
Books, April 17, 1938.
Christian Century, August 17, 1938, February 6, 1952, August 10, 1955.
Chicago Tribune Book World, July 26, 1981.
Georgia Historical Quarterly, spring, 1980.
Georgia Review, fall, 1974.
Humanities, April, 1978.
Journal of American History, September, 1973.
Journal of Southern History, May, 1972.
Los Angeles Times Book Review, December 23, 1984.
Nation, May 17, 1952, December 3, 1955.
New Republic, April 20, 1938.
Newsweek, April 13, 1981.
New Yorker, April 15, 1972.
New York Herald Tribune Book Review, December 23, 1951, May 29, 1955.
New York Review of Books, September 11, 1967.
New York Times, April 3, 1938.
New York Times Book Review, April 26, 1981.
Saturday Review, February 23, 1952, June 11, 1955.
Saturday Review of Literature, April 9, 1938.
South Atlantic Quarterly, winter, 1978.
Springfield Republican, March 27, 1938.
Times Literary Supplement, November 6, 1981.
Washington Post Book World, September 22, 1974, December 15, 1974, April 12, 1981.
Yale Review, autumn, 1955.

—*Sketch by Anne Janette Johnson*

*   *   *

WRIGHT, Kenneth
See del REY, Lester

*   *   *

WYNAND, Derk   1944-

PERSONAL: Born June 12, 1944, in Bad Suderode, Germany; son of Jan W. (an engineer) and Odette E. (Bergamy) Wynand; married W. Eva Kortemme, May 8, 1971. *Education:* University of British Columbia, B.A., 1966, M.A., 1969.

ADDRESSES: Home—70 Moss St., Victoria, British Columbia, Canada V8V 4L8. *Office*—Department of Creative Writing, University of Victoria, Victoria, British Columbia, Canada.

CAREER: University of Victoria, Victoria, British Columbia, visiting lecturer, 1969-71, lecturer in English, 1971-73, assistant professor, 1973-81, associate professor of creative writing, 1981—.

MEMBER: American Literary Translators Association.

AWARDS, HONORS: French Government Book Award, 1963, for proficiency in French; Canada Council grants, 1969, 1976, and 1983.

WRITINGS:

Locus, Fiddlehead Poetry Books, 1971.
Snowscapes (poems and prose poems), Sono Nis Press, 1974.
"Cyanide" (radio play), Canadian Broadcasting Corp., 1975.
Pointwise, Fiddlehead Poetry Books, 1979.
One Cook, Once Dreaming (fiction), Sono Nis Press, 1980.
Second Person (poems), Sono Nis Press, 1983.
Fetishistic (poems), Porcupine's Quill, 1984.

Adaptor and translator from the German of plays broadcast on Canadian Broadcasting Corp. radio. Contributor of more than a hundred poems and translations to literary journals, including *Fiddlehead, Expression,* and *Chicago Review.* Guest editor of *Malahat Review,* 1976.

WORK IN PROGRESS: Dead Man's Float, a work of fiction; *Heat Waves,* a book of poetry.

SIDELIGHTS: Derk Wynand writes: "Though I write mostly poetry and prose pieces, I am intrigued by the possibilities of the 'new radio play' written in Germany and Austria. The Canadian Broadcasting Corporation has broadcast my translations of such plays by Dieter Wellershoff, Juergen Becker, Helmut Heissenbuettel, Wolf Wondratschek, Ernst Jandl, and Friederike Mayroecker. The rapidly aging 'new radio play,' influenced by Mallarme, Bense, Gage, and others, is less concerned than are most North American radio plays with verisimilitude (linear plots and 'realistic' interior monologues, etc.), but more with words and sounds as a semiotic system, with concrete music. This is not new to North American artists, of course, though it may well be to most of our producers."

Y

YANKOWITZ, Susan 1941-

PERSONAL: Born February 20, 1941, in Newark, N.J.; daughter of Irving N. and Ruth (Katz) Yankowitz; married Herbert Leibowitz, 1978; children: Gabriel. *Education:* Sarah Lawrence College, B.A., 1963; Yale University, M.F.A., 1968.

ADDRESSES: Home—205 West 89th St., New York, N.Y. 10024. *Agent*—Gloria Loomis, A. Watkins, Inc., 150 W. 35th St., New York, N.Y.

CAREER: Writer. Playwright-in-residence at the Academy Theatre, Atlanta, Ga., the Provisional Theatre, Los Angeles, Calif., and the Magic Theatre, Omaha, Neb. Teacher of playwriting and dramatic literature at Quinnipiac College, Southern Connecticut State College, Harvard University, and Bronx Community College.

AWARDS, HONORS: Joseph E. Levine fellowship in screenwriting, 1968-69; Vernon Rice Drama Desk Award for most promising playwright, 1969; MacDowell Colony fellowship, 1971; National Endowment for the Arts creative writing fellowship grant, 1972-73, 1979; Rockefeller Foundation grant in playwriting, 1973-74; CAPS Award in playwriting, 1974; Guggenheim fellowship, 1975; National Endowment for the Arts U.S./Japan grant, 1985.

WRITINGS:

PLAYS

"The Cage" (one-act), first produced in New York, N.Y., at Omar Khayyam Cafe, 1965.

"Nightmare" (one-act), first produced in New Haven, Conn., at Yale University Theatre, 1967.

"That Old Rock-A-Bye" (one-act), first produced Off-Off-Broadway at Cooper Square Arts Theatre, 1968.

"Terminal" (full-length; published in *Scripts,* October, 1971), first produced Off-Broadway at American Place Theatre, 1969.

"The Ha-Ha Play" (one-act; published in *Scripts,* October, 1972), first produced Off-Off-Broadway at Cubiculo Theatre, 1970.

"The Lamb" (one-act), first produced Off-Off-Broadway at Cubiculo Theatre, 1970.

"Transplant" (full-length), first produced in Omaha, Neb., at Magic Theatre, 1971.

"Slaughterhouse Play" (full-length; published in *Yale/Theatre,* summer, 1969), first produced Off-Broadway at Public Theatre, 1971.

"Positions" (one-act), first produced in New York, N.Y., at Westbeth Cabaret, 1972.

"Boxes" (full-length), first produced in Berkeley, Calif., at Magic Theatre, 1972.

"Acts of Love" (full-length), first produced in Atlanta, Ga., at Academy Theatre, 1973.

"Wooden Nickels" (full-length), first produced in New York, N.Y., at Theatre for the New City, 1973.

"Still Life" (full-length), first produced in New York, N.Y., at Interart Theatre, 1976.

"True Romances" (full-length), first produced in Los Angeles, Calif., at Mark Taper Lab, 1978.

"Qui est Anna Marks" (full-length), first produced in Paris, France, 1979.

"A Knife in the Heart," first produced at the O'Neill Theatre Conference, 1982.

"Baby," first produced on Broadway, 1984.

Also author of "Basics," in *Tabula Rasa,* first produced at Brooklyn Academy of Music, and "Sideshow," produced on tour by National Theatre of the Deaf.

OTHER

"Rats' Alley" (radio play), WGBH, 1969.

(Contributor) William H. Hoffman, editor, *New American Plays,* Volume IV, Hill & Wang, 1971.

(Contributor) Arthur H. Ballet, *Playwrights for Tomorrow,* University of Minnesota Press, 1973.

Silent Witness (novel; also see below), Knopf, 1976.

"The Prison Game" (teleplay), produced on "Visions" series, KCET-TV (Los Angeles), 1976.

"Milk and Honey" (musical teleplay), produced on "Visions" series, KCET-TV, 1977.

"Sylvia Plath" (documentary), Public Broadcasting Systems, 1986.

Also author of teleplay "The Forerunner: Charlotte Perkins Gilman," Public Broadcasting Systems, screenplays "Silent Witness" and "Danny Awol," 1969, and a series of monologues in "The Wicked Women Revue," 1973. Also contributor to *Three Works by the Open Theatre,* Drama Book Specialists.

WORK IN PROGRESS: A play with puppets, for Interart Theatre; three other plays, including "Cassandra," for Monstrous Regiment, "Monk's Revenge," and "True Romances"; a musical for Goodspeed Theatre.

*   *   *

YARMEY, A(lexander) Daniel 1938-

PERSONAL: Born December 17, 1938, in Toronto, Ontario, Canada; son of William Jerry (a physician) and Helen (Keller) Frey; married Judith Sutherland (a registered nurse), September 7, 1963; children: Craig, Linda, Meagan. *Education:* Attended Wilfrid Laurier University, 1958-60; University of Western Ontario, B.A., 1962, M.A., 1963, Ph.D., 1965.

ADDRESSES: Home—37 Sherwood Dr., Guelph, Ontario, Canada N1E 6E6. *Office*—Department of Psychology, University of Guelph, Guelph, Ontario, Canada N1G 2W1.

CAREER: Wilfrid Laurier University, Waterloo, Ontario, assistant professor of psychology, 1965-67; University of Guelph, Guelph, Ontario, assistant professor, 1967-70, associate professor, 1970-80, professor of psychology, 1980—. Visiting professor at University of Tennessee, 1975-76. Consultant to Guelph Department of Corrections.

MEMBER: Canadian Psychological Association (fellow), Psychonomic Society.

WRITINGS:

Human Behavior (staff training manual), Ontario Department of Corrections, 1975.
The Psychology of Eyewitness Testimony, Free Press, 1979.

CONTRIBUTOR

A. Trankell, editor, *Reconstructing the Past: The Role of Psychologists in Criminal Trials,* Kluwer (Deventer, Netherlands), 1982.
J. C. Yuille, editor, *Imagery, Memory and Cognition: Essays in Honour of Allan Paivio,* Lawrence Erlbaum, 1983.
(With H.P.T. Jones) S. Lloyd Bostock and B. R. Clifford, editors, *Evaluating Witness Evidence: Recent Psychological Research and New Perspectives,* Wiley, 1983.
S. H. Kadish, editor, *Encyclopedia of Crime and Justice,* Free Press, 1983.
G. L. Wells and E. F. Loftus, editors, *Eyewitness Testimony: Psychological Perspectives,* Cambridge University Press, 1984.
A. A. Sheikh, editor, *International Review of Mental Imagery,* Volume I, Human Sciences, 1984.

(With Jones and S. Rashid) D. J. Muller, D. E. Blackman, and A. J. Chapman, editors, *Psychology and Law,* Wiley, 1984.

OTHER

Contributor to journals in the behavioral sciences. Member of editorial board of *International Review of Mental Imagery.*

WORK IN PROGRESS: Social Psychology of Law, for police officers; research on eyewitness identification; research on missing children.

SIDELIGHTS: A. Daniel Yarmey wrote to *CA:* "I am one of the fortunate people who like their work. My teaching and research are complementary, and both give me a sense of accomplishment. I believe that scientists should be interested in the practical application of their work, and that motivated me to turn from the traditional study of human memory to the psychology of law."

BIOGRAPHICAL/CRITICAL SOURCES:

PERIODICALS

Psychology Today, March, 1980.
Victimology, May, 1980.

*   *   *

YOUNG, Robert Doran 1928-

PERSONAL: Born March 12, 1928, in Philadelphia, Pa.; son of Earl Melroy (a certified public accountant) and Emma (Doran) Young; married Louisa Anna Grace, June 28, 1952; children: Linda L., David E., Carol S. *Education:* Eastern Baptist College and Seminary, B.A. and B.D., 1953; University of Pennsylvania, M.A., 1953; Temple University, Ph.D., 1968. *Politics:* Republican.

ADDRESSES: Home—803 Spruce Ave., West Chester, Pa. 19382.

CAREER: Westminster Presbyterian Church, West Chester, Pa., minister, 1966-76; Eastern Baptist College, St. David's, Pa., instructor in Hinduism and Buddhism, 1976-80; Westminster Presbyterian Church, minister, 1980—. Part-time instructor in homiletics, Princeton Theological Seminary, 1980-84.

WRITINGS:

Encounter with World Religions, Westminster, 1970.
Religious Imagination: God's Gift to Prophets and Preachers, Westminster, 1979.
Be Brief about It, Westminster, 1980.

Z

ZIM, Herbert S(pencer)   1909-

PERSONAL: Born July 12, 1909, in New York, N.Y.; son of Marco (a painter and sculptor) and Minnie (Orlo) Zim; married Sonia Elizabeth Bleeker (an author), January 16, 1934 (died, 1971); married Grace K. Showe, June 4, 1978; children: (first marriage) Aldwin H., Roger S. *Education:* Attended City College (now City College of the City University of New York), 1927-29; Columbia University, B.S., 1933, M.A., 1934, Ph.D., 1940. *Religion:* Society of Friends.

ADDRESSES: Home—Plantation Key, 88835 Old Highway, Tavernier, Fla. 33070.

CAREER: Ethical Culture Schools, New York, N.Y., instructor in science, 1932-50, developed first elementary science laboratories, 1934-36, head of science department, 1937-45; University of Illinois at Urbana-Champaign, associate professor, 1950-54, professor of education (science), 1954-57; full-time writer and editor on science subjects and consultant, 1957—. Conductor of study of science interests of adolescents, 1934-37; Columbia University, instructor, summers, 1935, 1936, and conductor of summer field trips through North America, 1937-41. Educational director, Artists and Writers Press, 1957-69; adjunct professor of education, University of Miami, Miami, Fla., 1968—. Member of steering committee for Biological Sciences Curriculum Study and participant in Elementary Science Study. Educational consultant, U.S. Fish and Wildlife Service, 1947-51, Western Publishing Co., 1967-70, and American Friends Service Committee, 1968-75; editorial consultant for Physical Science Study Program. *Wartime service:* Conscientious objector working on Pre-induction Training Program, U.S. War Department, 1942-43, and in Civilian Public Service, 1943-45.

MEMBER: International Union for the Conservation of Nature, American Institute of Biological Sciences, American Association for the Advancement of Science (fellow), American Nature Study Society (director, 1968-70), National Science Teachers Association, National Association for Research in Science Teaching, National Association of Biology Teachers, Union of Concerned Scientists, Authors Guild, Authors League of America, Audubon Society, Association for Supervision and Curriculum Development, Nature Conservancy, Isaac Walton League, Western Society of Naturalists, Pacific Science Association, Everglades Natural History Association, Sierra Club.

AWARDS, HONORS: D.Sc. from Beloit College, 1967, and from Florida State University, 1977.

WRITINGS:

Science Interests and Activities of Adolescents, Ethical Culture Schools, 1940.
Mice, Men and Elephants, Harcourt, 1942.
Submarines, Harcourt, 1942.
Parachutes, Harcourt, 1942.
Air Navigation, Harcourt, 1943.
Man in the Air, Harcourt, 1943.
(With E. K. Cooper) *Minerals,* Harcourt, 1943.
Rockets and Jets, Harcourt, 1945, Armed Forces edition, 1945.
Elephants, Morrow, 1946.
Goldfish, Morrow, 1947.
Plants, Harcourt, 1947.
Rabbits, Morrow, 1948.
(With R. W. Burnett and B. Jaffe) *New World of Science,* Silver Burdett, 1948, 2nd edition, 1953.
Codes and Secret Writing, Morrow, 1948.
Homing Pigeons, Morrow, 1949.
(With A. C. Martin and I. N. Gabrielson) *American Birds and Wildflowers,* Simon & Schuster, 1949.
Snakes, Morrow, 1949.
(With Gabrielson) *Birds,* Golden Press, 1949, revised edition, 1956.
(With Martin) *Flowers,* Golden Press, 1950.
Frogs and Toads, Morrow, 1950.
Owls, Morrow, 1950, revised edition, 1977.
The Great Whales, Morrow, 1951.
Golden Hamsters, Morrow, 1951.
(With C. Cottam) *Insects,* Golden Press, 1951, revised edition, 1964.
(With Martin and A. Nelson) *American Wildlife and Plants,* McGraw, 1951.
(With R. H. Baker) *Stars,* Golden Press, 1951, revised edition, 1956.
Lightning and Thunder, Morrow, 1952.
(With Martin) *Trees,* Golden Press, 1952, revised edition, 1956.
Alligators and Crocodiles, Morrow, 1952, revised edition, 1978.
What's Inside of Me?, Morrow, 1952.
What's Inside of Plants?, Morrow, 1952.

The Sun, Morrow, 1953, revised edition, 1975.
What's Inside of Engines?, Morrow, 1953.
What's Inside of Animals?, Morrow, 1953.
Science for Children and Teachers, Association for Childhood Education, 1953.
What's Inside the Earth?, Morrow, 1953.
Parakeets, Morrow, 1953.
(With H. M. Smith) *Reptiles and Amphibians*, Golden Press, 1953, revised edition, 1956.
Dinosaurs, Morrow, 1954.
Things around the House, Morrow, 1954.
Monkeys, Morrow, 1955.
(With N. Dodge) *The Southwest*, Golden Press, 1955.
(With D. F. Hoffmeister) *Mammals*, Golden Press, 1955.
(With L. Ingle) *Seashores*, Golden Press, 1955.
The Big Cats, Morrow, 1955, revised edition, 1976.
(With Ira N. Gabrielson) *Birds*, Golden Press, 1956.
Our Senses, Morrow, 1956.
(With Burnett) *Photography*, Golden Press, 1956, revised edition (with Burnett and W. B. Brummitt), 1964.
(With H. H. Shoemaker) *Fishes*, Golden Press, 1956.
(With Burnett and P. E. Lehr) *Weather*, Golden Press, 1957.
Comets, Morrow, 1957.
Your Food and You, Morrow, 1957.
(With P. R. Schaffer) *Rocks and Minerals*, Golden Press, 1957.
Ostriches, Morrow, 1958.
Shooting Stars, Morrow, 1958.
(With Burnett and H. I. Fisher) *Zoology*, Golden Press, 1958.
Diamonds, Morrow, 1959.
The Southeast, Golden Press, 1959.
Giant Little Golden Book of Fish, Golden Press, 1959.
(With N. N. Dodge) *The Pacific Northwest*, Golden Press, 1959.
Your Heart and How It Works, Morrow, 1959.
Guide to Everglades National Park and Nearby Florida Keys, Golden Press, 1960.
How Things Grow, Morrow, 1960.
The Universe, Morrow, 1961, revised edition, 1973.
Rocks and How They Were Formed, Golden Press, 1961.
(With A. Sprunt IV) *Gamebirds*, Golden Press, 1961.
(With F.H.T. Rhodes and P. R. Shaffer) *Fossils*, Golden Press, 1962.
The Rocky Mountains, Golden Press, 1964.
(With R. T. Mitchell) *Butterflies and Moths*, Golden Press, 1964.
Sharks, Morrow, 1966.
Corals, Morrow, 1966.
(With Chandler Robbins) *Birds of North America*, Golden Press, 1966.
Waves, Morrow, 1967.
(With Floyd Shuttleworth) *Non-Flowering Plants*, Golden Press, 1967.
Blood, Morrow, 1968.
(With Sonia Bleeker Zim) *Mexico*, Golden Press, 1969.
Bones, Morrow, 1969.
(With James Skelly) *Hoists, Cranes, and Derricks*, Morrow, 1969.
(With Skelly) *Machine Tools*, Morrow, 1969.
(With Shuttleworth) *Orchids*, Golden Press, 1970.
(With Skelly) *Trucks*, Morrow, 1970.
(With S. B. Zim) *Life and Death*, Morrow, 1970.
(With Taylor Alexander) *Botany*, Golden Press, 1970.
(With Skelly) *Cargo Ships*, Morrow, 1970.
Armored Animals, Morrow, 1971.
(With Skelly) *Telephone Systems*, Morrow, 1971.

Your Brain and How It Works, Morrow, 1972.
(With Skelly) *Tractors*, Morrow, 1972.
Your Stomach and Digestive Tract, Morrow, 1973.
(With Lucretia Krantz) *Commercial Fishing*, Morrow, 1973.
(With Krantz) *Crabs*, Morrow, 1974.
(With Skelly) *Pipes and Plumbing Systems*, Morrow, 1974.
Medicine, Morrow, 1974.
(WIth Skelly) *Metric Measure*, Morrow, 1974.
(With Skelly) *Eating Places*, Morrow, 1975.
(With Krantz) *Snails*, Morrow, 1975.
(With Krantz) *Sea Stars*, Morrow, 1976.
Caves and Life, Morrow, 1978.
Little Cats, Morrow, 1978.
Your Skin, Morrow, 1979.
The New Moon, Morrow, 1980.
Quartz, Morrow, 1981.

EDITOR; PUBLISHED BY GOLDEN PRESS

(With O. L. Austin, Jr., and A. Singer) *Birds of the World*, 1961.
R. T. Abbott, *Sea Shells of the World*, 1962.
J.F.G. Clarke, *Butterflies*, 1963.
R. E. Smallman, *Washington*, 1964.
H. Gasser, *Painting*, 1964.
Austin, *Song Birds of the World*, 1967.
Abbott, *Sea Shells of North America*, 1968.
G. W. Sharpe, *A Guide to Arcadia National Park and the Nearby Coast of Maine*, 1968.
C. Frank Brokman, *Trees of North America*, 1968.
Austin, *Families of Birds*, 1971.
Kai Curry-Kindahl and Jean-Paul Harvey, *National Parks of the World*, two volumes, 1972.
Charles Sorell, *Minerals of the World*, 1973.

Also editor of the Junior Golden Guides "Quiz Me" series, fourteen books, 1963-65.

EDITOR-IN-CHIEF

Our Wonderful World, eighteen volumes, Spencer Press (Chicago), 1955-60.
What Is Happening in Our Wonderful World, Spencer Press, 1958, 1960, 1961.
The Golden Book Encyclopedia of Natural Science, sixteen volumes, Golden Press, 1962.

Also editor-in-chief of the "Golden Guide" series, Golden Press, 1947-70, the "Fact and Fiction" series, three books, Spencer Press, 1958-61, and the "Golden Bookshelf of Natural History," three books, Golden Press, 1963-64.

CONTRIBUTOR

(Compiler of science sections) *Bibliography of Books for Children*, Association for Childhood Education, 1942, 1945, 1946, 1948, 1950, 1952.
Collecting Science Literature for General Reading, Graduate School of Library Science, University of Illinois, 1961.
Man/Problem Solver, International Design Conference, 1961.

OTHER

Contributor of articles and reviews on science and natural history subjects to magazines and professional journals.

SIDELIGHTS: Herbert S. Zim has established what a writer for *Virginia Kirkus' Service* calls "a standard of clarity and factual generosity" for science and nature books aimed at young readers. As a child, Zim was keenly interested in natural science; before the age of twelve, he had begun collecting plants, flowers, minerals, toads, snakes, and salamanders. While still a high school student, he taught his first nature study course in New York City's summer play schools. It was while working on his Ph.D. at Columbia University that Zim, sponsored by the Progressive Education Association, began a five-year study on the scientific interests of adolescents. It demonstrated that young people actually enjoy reading scientific material as long as it is brief and to the point. Zim's research also revealed that children are most curious about themselves and about other living creatures.

These findings convinced Zim of the need for truly informative children's books. Few existed at the time, and Zim was determined to create them. His aim was to present essential facts, without oversimplification, in an interesting, easy-to-understand style. His first attempt, entitled *Mice, Men and Elephants,* was based on experimental work that he had done involving sex education for fifth graders. It "essentially deals with the fundamental characteristics of mammals," explains Zim in Lee Bennett Hopkin's *Books Are by People.* "These characteristics include factors of intelligence and reproduction, two areas in which young adolescents are specifically interested." By comparing man to the other members of the animal kingdom, *Mice, Men and Elephants* satisfied children's curiosity about their own bodies as well as their curiosity about other animals. A *Books* reviewer called this volume an "alluring, rewarding book," and a writer for the *Scientific Book Club Review* praised the author's "chatty, informal" style as a very effective method for "imparting knowledge to eager young minds."

Continuing research showed Zim that even the youngest children need and want factual information about themselves and their world. Accordingly, he designed a series of books for beginning readers, as well as a series for the nine-to-twelve age group. Submarines, hamsters, rockets, and rabbits are only a few of the subjects that Zim has treated in his unique style. The author emphasizes that his books are not written to fit any formula; each subject is treated individually. However, they do share some common characteristics. Describing a typical Zim book, a *Publishers Weekly* writer says: "[He] tries to make his book brief but packed with facts, and the pictures and captions are carefully planned to give information not repeated in the text." The result is so entertaining and informative that it is valuable to adults as well. "Often the adult reader is curious about a subject, but not sufficiently interested to make a thorough study of it," notes *Publishers Weekly.* "Dr. Zim's juveniles give him just about as much information as he really wants."

The appeal and usefulness that Zim's books hold for readers of all ages is further described in a *Science Books* review of *Crabs:* "This is a curious little book. The large font and simple, crisp illustrations suggest to the casual examiner that *Crabs* is a superficial story written for preschool children. Actually the information content is quite advanced. The crabs' relatives, structure and many aspects of their biology are discussed in a remarkably informative fashion.... If only half the knowledge gleaned is remembered, the reader will know as much or more about crabs as does the average college student taking an introductory course in zoology."

Zim's books reflect his faith in the ability of children to learn. According to *Publishers Weekly,* he believes that "adults tend to underestimate the intelligence of children. When a child is really interested in something, he can generally absorb a lot of information." The key to catching a child's interest, says

Zim, is to appeal to his natural inquisitiveness. "Every child," he is quoted as saying, "is a scientist. He is interested in everything. Adults are blase and bored. As children grow up, their lives become a series of 'don'ts'. We wring their curiosity out of them. We *can* hold on to some of it." Summarizes Henry W. Hubbard in the *New York Times Book Review:* "[Zim treats] young minds in his audience with respect, with no condescending tone and no compromised facts."

Many of Zim's books are still in print, with sales exceeding one hundred million copies. They have appeared as translations or adaptations in eighteen countries in Europe, Asia, and Central and South America.

AVOCATIONAL INTERESTS: Fishing, gardening, and travel.

BIOGRAPHICAL/CRITICAL SOURCES:

BOOKS

Children's Literature Review, Gale, 1976.
Hopkins, Lee Bennett, *Books Are by People,* Citation Press, 1969.

PERIODICALS

Books, May 10, 1942.
New York Times Book Review, May 21, 1961.
Publishers Weekly, July 26, 1952.
Science Books, December, 1974.
Scientific Book Club Review, August, 1942.
Virginia Kirkus' Service, August 15, 1959.

* * *

ZIMMERMAN, Joseph Francis 1928-

PERSONAL: Born June 29, 1928, in Keene, N.H.; son of John Joseph (a sporting goods dealer) and May (Gallagher) Zimmerman; married Margaret B. Brennan, August 2, 1958; children: Deirdre Ann. *Education:* University of New Hampshire, B.A., 1950; Syracuse University, M.A., 1951, Ph.D., 1954. *Politics:* Independent. *Religion:* Roman Catholic.

ADDRESSES: Home—82 Greenock Rd., Delmar, N.Y. 12054. *Office*—Graduate School of Public Affairs, State University of New York, Albany, N.Y. 12222.

CAREER: Worcester Polytechnic Institute, Worcester, Mass., instructor, 1954-55, assistant professor, 1955-57, associate professor, 1957-62, professor of government, 1962-65; State University of New York at Albany, Graduate School of Public Affairs, professor of political science, 1965—, chairman of department of political science, 1973-74, director of Local Government Studies Center, 1965-68. Lecturer in government, Clark University, Worcester, Mass., 1956-65. Staff director, New York State Joint Legislative Committee on Mass Transportation, 1967-68; research director, New York State Joint Legislative Committee on Transportation, 1968-73, New York State Select Legislative Committee on Transportation, 1974-76, New York State Senate Committee on Transportation, 1976-82, and Legislative Commission on Critical Transportation Problems, 1982—. Corporator, Visiting Nurse Association, 1960-65; director, Lincoln Neighborhood Center, 1960-65; chairman, Albany County Citizens Charter Commission, 1976-78. Consultant, Massachusetts Department of Commerce, Massachusetts Commission on Atomic Energy, United States Railway Association, city of Houston, New York State Association of Towns, and others. *Military service:* U.S. Air Force, 1951-53; became first lieutenant.

MEMBER: American Political Science Association, Academy of Political Science, National Municipal League, American Academy of Political and Social Science, American Society for Public Administration, Public Personnel Association, American Planning and Civic Association, New England Political Science Association, Worcester Association of Historians and Political Scientists.

AWARDS, HONORS: Choice award, American Association of Research and University Libraries, 1984, for State-Local Relations: A Partnership Approach.

WRITINGS:

State and Local Government, Barnes & Noble, 1962, 3rd edition, 1978.
Readings in State and Local Government, Holt, 1964.
(Contributing editor) Dictionary of Political Science, Philosophical Library, 1964.
The Massachusetts Town Meeting: A Tenacious Institution, State University of New York at Albany, 1967.
(Editor) Government of the Metropolis, Holt, 1968.
Subnational Politics, Holt, 1970.

The Federated City: Community Control in Large Cities, St. Martin's, 1972.
Pragmatic Federalism: The Reassignment of Functional Responsibility, U.S. Advisory Commission on Intergovernmental Relations, 1976.
(With Frank W. Prescott) The Politics of the Veto of Legislation in New York, University Press of America, 1980.
The Government and Politics of New York State, New York University Press, 1981.
Measuring Local Discretionary Authority, Advisory Commission on Intergovernmental Relations, 1981.
(With daughter, Deirdre A. Zimmerman) The Politics of Subnational Governance, University Press of America, 1983.
State-Local Relations: A Partnership Approach, Praeger, 1983.

Contributor to Encyclopaedia Britannica; also contributor of articles to educational, civic, and finance journals and to Worcester Telegram. Editor, Metropolitan Area Annual, Metropolitan Area Digest, Metropolitan Surveys, and Metropolitan Viewpoints, 1965-68.

WORK IN PROGRESS: Participatory Democracy: Populism Revived; Preemptive Federalism.